MW00463016

HOCKEY GUIDE

2003-2004 EDITION

Editors/Hockey Guide
JOE HOPPEL
STEVE MEYERHOFF
TONY NISTLER

CONTENTS

2003-2004 NHL Season...................................**3**
National Hockey League directory 4
Individual teams section
    (schedules, directories, rosters, etc.).....................5
Mighty Ducks of Anaheim.....................................5
Atlanta Thrashers..8
Boston Bruins 11
Buffalo Sabres 14
Calgary Flames 17
Carolina Hurricanes 20
Chicago Blackhawks 23
Colorado Avalanche 26
Columbus Blue Jackets..29
Dallas Stars..32
Detroit Red Wings 35
Edmonton Oilers..38
Florida Panthers..41
Los Angeles Kings 44
Minnesota Wild..47
Montreal Canadiens 50
Nashville Predators 53
New Jersey Devils..56
New York Islanders 59
New York Rangers 62
Ottawa Senators..65
Philadelphia Flyers 68
Phoenix Coyotes 71
Pittsburgh Penguins 74
St. Louis Blues..77
San Jose Sharks...80
Tampa Bay Lightning 83
Toronto Maple Leafs 86
Vancouver Canucks 89
Washington Capitals 92
Schedule, day by day 95
2002-03 NHL Review...................................**103**
Regular season 104
Final standings..104
Individual leaders..104

Statistics of players with two or more teams 109
Miscellaneous 114
Stanley Cup playoffs 119
Results, round by round 119
Game summaries, Stanley Cup finals 120
Individual leaders...121
Individual statistics 122
Miscellaneous 130
All-Star Game...131
Awards...132
Player draft 133
NHL History..**139**
Stanley Cup champions 140
All-Star Games..141
Year-by-year standings 143
Records 161
Statistical leaders 164
Award winners 181
The Sporting News awards 192
Hall of Fame...196
Milestones 204
Team by team 212
Minor Leagues **261**
American Hockey League......................................262
East Coast Hockey League...................................286
Central Hockey League 305
United Hockey League 314
Other Leagues..**323**
Canadian Hockey League 324
Ontario Hockey League..324
Quebec Major Junior Hockey League 324
Western Hockey League 325
NCAA Division I 325
Central Collegiate Hockey Association 326
Eastern College Athletic Conference 326
Hockey East 326
Western Collegiate Hockey Association 327
Canadian Interuniversity Sport............................327
Canadian colleges 327

ON THE COVER: Top photo: Scott Stevens (photo by Bob Leverone/THE SPORTING NEWS.); bottom left to right: Peter Forsberg (Scott Rovak for THE SPORTING NEWS), Al MacInnis (Dilip Vishwanat/THE SPORTING NEWS), Mike Modano (Scott Rovak for THE SPORTING NEWS). Spine: Peter Forsberg (Scott Rovak for THE SPORTING NEWS).

NHL statistics compiled by STATS, Inc., a News Corporation company; 8130 Lehigh Avenue, Morton Grove, IL 60053. STATS is a trademark of Sports Team Analysis and Tracking Systems, Inc.

ISBN: 0-89204-710-0   10 9 8 7 6 5 4 3 2 1

2003-04 NHL SEASON

NHL directory

Team information

Schedule

NATIONAL HOCKEY LEAGUE
DIRECTORY

LEAGUE OFFICES

OFFICERS

Commissioner
Gary B. Bettman
Director, administration & executive assistant to the commissioner
Debbie Jordan
Exec. vice president & chief legal officer
William Daly
Exec. v.p. and dir. of hockey operations
Colin Campbell
Exec. v.p. and chief operating officer
Jon Litner
Exec. v.p. and chief financial officer
Craig Hartnett
Senior vice president, hockey operations
Jim Gregory (Toronto)
Senior vice president, general counsel
David Zimmerman
Senior vice president, finance
Joseph DeSousa

NHL ENTERPRISES

President, NHL Enterprises
Ed Horne
Sr. vice president & general counsel
Richard Zahnd
Group v.p., consumer products marketing
Brian Jennings
Group vice president & managing dir., NHL International
Ken Yaffe
Sr. v.p., television & media ventures
Doug Perlman
Pres., NHL ICE and Sr. v.p., new bus. dev.
Keith Ritter

NHL COMMUNICATIONS STAFF

Group vice president, communications
Bernadette Mansur
Vice president, media relations
Frank Brown

V.p., public relations & media services
Gary Meagher (Toronto)
Chief statistician
Benny Ercolani (Toronto)
Director, media relations
Amy Early
Director, communications
Jamey Horan
Director, news services
Greg Inglis
Manager, public relations
David Keon (Toronto)
Manager, news services
Adam Schwartz
Manager, p.r. & editorial services
Chris Tredree (Toronto)
Coordinator, public relations
Jennifer Perkinson
Associate, public relations
Julie Young (Toronto)
Assistant
Mary Kay Wright

CORPORATE COMMUNICATIONS

Director, community relations
Ken Martin
Manager, corporate communications & player publicity
Sandra Carreon
Manager, corporate communications
Brian Walker
Manager, diversity task force
Nirva Milord
Manager, community relations
Ann Marie Lynch
Assistant
Myrna Mollison
Assistant, diversity task force
Jessica Murray

NEW YORK OFFICE

Address
1251 Avenue of the Americas
47th Floor
New York, NY 10020
Phone
212-789-2000
FAX
212-789-2020

TAPPAN OFFICE (NHL PRODUCTIONS)

Address
183 Oak Tree Road
Tappan, NY 10983
Phone
845-365-6701
FAX
845-365-6010

TORONTO OFFICE

Address
50 Bay Street, 11th Floor
Toronto, Ont. M5J 2X8
Phone
416-981-2777
FAX
416-981-2779

MONTREAL OFFICE

Address
1800 McGill College Avenue
Suite 2600
Montreal, Que., Canada H3A 3J6
Phone
514-841-9220
FAX
514-841-1070

DIVISIONAL ALIGNMENT

EASTERN CONFERENCE

ATLANTIC DIVISION
New Jersey Devils
New York Islanders
New York Rangers
Philadelphia Flyers
Pittsburgh Penguins

NORTHEAST DIVISION
Boston Bruins
Buffalo Sabres
Montreal Canadiens
Ottawa Senators
Toronto Maple Leafs

SOUTHEAST DIVISION
Atlanta Thrashers
Carolina Hurricanes
Florida Panthers
Tampa Bay Lightning
Washington Capitals

WESTERN CONFERENCE

CENTRAL DIVISION
Chicago Blackhawks
Columbus Blue Jackets
Detroit Red Wings
Nashville Predators
St. Louis Blues

NORTHWEST DIVISION
Calgary Flames
Colorado Avalanche
Edmonton Oilers
Minnesota Wild
Vancouver Canucks

PACIFIC DIVISION
Mighty Ducks of Anaheim
Dallas Stars
Los Angeles Kings
Phoenix Coyotes
San Jose Sharks

MIGHTY DUCKS OF ANAHEIM
WESTERN CONFERENCE/PACIFIC DIVISION

Mighty Ducks' Schedule
Home games shaded; D=Day game; *Feb. 8 All-Star Game at St. Paul, Minn.

October

SUN	MON	TUE	WED	THU	FRI	SAT
5	6	7	8 DAL	9 NAS	10	11
12 PHO	13	14	15	16	17 OTT	18
19 BOS	20	21	22 PHI	23	24 BUF	25
26 CHI	27	28 NYR	29 WAS	30	31	

November

SUN	MON	TUE	WED	THU	FRI	SAT
						1 D NYI
2 CHI	3	4 STL	5	6	7	8 PHO
9 PHO	10	11	12 TOR	13	14	15
16 STL	17	18 COL	19 DAL	20	21 NAS	22
23	24	25	26 NJ	27	28 D CHI	29
30 MIN						

December

SUN	MON	TUE	WED	THU	FRI	SAT
	1	2 CBJ	3 DET	4	5 ATL	6
7 DAL	8	9	10 SJ	11	12	13 SJ
14 EDM	15	16	17	18	19 COL	20
21 SJ	22 SJ	23	24	25	26	27 FLA
28	29 TB	30	31 CAR			

January

SUN	MON	TUE	WED	THU	FRI	SAT
				1	2 BUF	3 DET
4	5 DAL	6	7 LA	8	9 VAN	10
11 CBJ	12	13 COL	14	15 EDM	16	17 VAN
18	19 CAL	20	21 DET	22	23 MIN	24 LA
25	26	27	28 LA	29	30 COL	31

February

SUN	MON	TUE	WED	THU	FRI	SAT
1 CAL	2 EDM	3	4 CAR	5	6	7
8*	9	10	11 PHO	12	13 CAL	14 VAN
15	16 DAL	17	18 CBJ	19	20 NAS	21
22 DAL	23 D PHO	24	25 EDM	26	27	28 D LA
29 D LA						

March

SUN	MON	TUE	WED	THU	FRI	SAT
	1	2	3 MIN	4	5 CHI	6 PIT
7	8 MON	9	10	11	12 NYI	13
14 D LA	15	16 PHO	17 STL	18	19 SJ	20
21 DET	22	23 NAS	24	25 STL	26 CBJ	27
28 D MIN	29	30	31 VAN			

April

SUN	MON	TUE	WED	THU	FRI	SAT
				1	2	3
4 D CAL	5	6	7	8	9	10

2003-04 SEASON
CLUB DIRECTORY

Governor
Jay Rasulo

Sr. vice president and general manager
Bryan Murray

Assistant general manager
David McNab

Director of scouting
Alain Chainey

Pro scout
Floyd Smith

Head coach
Mike Babcock

Assistant coaches
Lorne Henning
Paul MacLean

Mgr. of communications/team services
Alex Gilchrist

Media relations coordinator
Merit Tully

Media relations intern
Thomas LaRocca

Head athletic trainer
Chris Phillips

Strength and conditioning coordinator
Sean Skahan

Equipment manager
Mark O'Neill

Assistant equipment manager
John Allaway

DRAFT CHOICES

Rd.— Player	Overall	Pos.	Last team
1— Ryan Getzlaf	19	C	Calgary (WHL)
1— Corey Perry	28	RW	London (OHL)
3— Shane Hynes	86	RW	Cornell Univ. (ECAC)
3— Juha Alen	90	D	N. Michigan (CCHA)
4— Nathan Saunders	119	D	Moncton (QMJHL)
6— Andrew Miller	186	LW	River City (USHL)
7— Dirk Southern	218	C	N. Michigan (CCHA)
8— Shane O'Brien	250	D	Tor.-St.Michael's (OHL)
9— Ville Mantymaa	280	D	Tappara (Finland)

MISCELLANEOUS DATA

Home ice (capacity)
The Arrowhead Pond of Anaheim
(17,174)

Address
2695 E. Katella Avenue
P.O. Box 61077
Anaheim, CA 92803-6177

Business phone
714-940-2900

Ticket information
877-945-3946

Website
www.mightyducks.com

Training site
Anaheim

Club colors
Purple, jade, silver and white

Radio affiliation
830 AM KPLS

TV affiliation
KCAL (Channel 9), FOX Sports West 2
(Cable)

TRAINING CAMP ROSTER

No.	FORWARDS	Ht./Wt.	Place	Date	NHL exp.	2002-03 clubs
	Tim Brent (C)	6-0/175	Cambridge, Ont.	3-10-84	0	Toronto St. Michael's (OHL)
27	Mike Brown (LW)	6-4/225	Surrey, B.C.	4-27-79	3	Anaheim
21	Dan Bylsma (RW)	6-2/212	Grand Haven, Mich.	9-19-70	8	Anaheim
	Stanislav Chistov (LW)	5-9/169	Chelyabinsk, U.S.S.R.	4-17-83	1	Anaheim
32	Marc Chouinard (C)	6-5/204	Charlesbourg, Ont.	5-6-77	3	Anaheim
91	Sergei Fedorov (C)	6-2/200	Pskov, U.S.S.R.	12-13-69	13	Detroit
	Ben Guite (RW)	6-1/197		7-17-78	0	Cincinnati (AHL)
	J. Hedstrom (RW)	6-0/195	Skelleftea, Sweden	12-27-77	1	Cincinnati (AHL), Anaheim
	Mikael Holmqvist (C)	6-3/189	Stockholm, Sweden	6-8-79	0	
18	Patric Kjellberg (RW)	6-2/208	Trelleborg, Sweden	6-17-69	6	Anaheim
28	Jason Krog (C)	5-11/191	Fernie, B.C.	10-9-75	4	Cincinnati (AHL), Anaheim
37	Denny Lambert (RW)	5-10/215	Wawa, Ont.	1-7-70	8	Milwaukee (AHL)
12	Mike Leclerc (LW)	6-1/205	Winnipeg	11-10-76	7	Anaheim
	Joffrey Lupul (RW)	6-1/194	Edmonton	9-23-83	0	Medicine Hat (WHL)
19	Andy McDonald (C)	5-10/192	Strathroy, Ont.	8-25-77	3	Anaheim
44	Rob Niedermayer (C)	6-2/205	Cassiar, B.C.	12-28-74	10	Calgary, Anaheim
77	Adam Oates (C)	5-10/180	Weston, Ont.	8-27-62	18	Anaheim
26	Samuel Pahlsson (C)	5-11/190	Ornskoldsvik, Sweden	12-17-77	3	Cincinnati (AHL), Anaheim
	Pierre Parenteau (C/RW)	5-11/156	Hull, Que.	3-24-83	0	Sherbrooke (QMJHL)
29	Timo Parssinen (LW)	5-10/176	Lohja, Finland	1-19-77	1	HIFK Helsinki (Finland)
	Cory Pecker (C)	6-0/190	Montreal	3-20-81	0	Cincinnati (AHL)
	Joel Perreault (C)	6-2/165	Montreal	4-6-83	0	Baie-Comeau (QMJHL)
	Igor Pohanka (C)	6-3/185	Plestany, Czechoslovakia	7-5-83	0	Prince Albert (WHL)
	Vaclav Prospal (LW)	6-2/195	Ceske-Budejovice, Czech.	2-17-75	7	Tampa Bay
20	Steve Rucchin (C)	6-2/212	Thunder Bay, Ont.	7-4-71	9	Anaheim
25	Kevin Sawyer (LW)	6-2/205	Christina Lake, B.C.	2-21-74	6	Anaheim
	Cam Severson (LW)	6-1/215	Norquay, Sask.	1-15-78	1	Cincinnati (AHL), Anaheim
	Alexei Smirnov (LW)	6-3/211	Tver, U.S.S.R.	1-28-82	1	Cincinnati (AHL), Anaheim
	Jarrett Smith (C)	6-1/190	Edmonton	6-15-79	0	Cincinnati (AHL)
	Joel Stepp (C/LW)	6-1/185	Estevan, Sask.	2-11-83	0	Red Deer (WHL)
17	Petr Sykora (RW)	6-0/190	Plzen, Czechoslovakia	11-19-76	8	Anaheim
32	Steve Thomas (RW)	5-10/185	Stockport, England	7-15-63	19	Chicago, Anaheim
13	German Titov (C)	6-1/201	Moscow, U.S.S.R.	10-16-65	9	

No.	DEFENSEMEN	Ht./Wt.	Place	Date	NHL exp.	2002-03 clubs
	Chris Armstrong	6-0/205	Regina, Sask.	6-26-75	1	
3	Keith Carney	6-2/211	Providence, R.I.	2-3-70	12	Anaheim
28	Niclas Havelid	5-11/200	Stockholm, Sweden	4-12-73	4	Anaheim
4	Antti-Jussi Niemi	6-1/183	Vantaa, Finland	9-22-77	2	
19	Chris O'Sullivan	6-2/205	Dorchester, Mass.	5-15-74	5	Cincinnati (AHL), Anaheim
2	Fredrik Olausson	6-0/199	Dadsejo, Sweden	10-5-66	16	Anaheim
44	Sandis Ozolinsh	6-3/215	Riga, U.S.S.R.	8-3-72	11	Florida, Anaheim
	Peter Podhradsky	6-1/185	Bratislava, Czechoslovakia	12-10-79	0	Cincinnati (AHL)
	Mark Popovic	6-1/194	Stoney Creek, Ont.	10-11-82	0	Cincinnati (AHL)
28	Todd Reirden	6-5/220	Deerfield, Ill.	6-25-71	4	Cincinnati (AHL)
24	Ruslan Salei	6-1/206	Minsk, U.S.S.R.	11-2-74	7	Anaheim
	Kurt Sauer	6-3/220	St. Cloud, Minn.	1-16-81	1	Anaheim
5	Vitaly Vishnevski	6-2/190	Kharkov, U.S.S.R.	3-18-80	4	Anaheim
49	Lance Ward	6-3/220	Lloydminster, Alta.	2-6-78	3	Florida, Anaheim

No.	GOALTENDERS	Ht./Wt.	Place	Date	NHL exp.	2002-03 clubs
30	Ilja Bryzgalov	6-3/196	Togliatti, U.S.S.R.	6-22-80	1	Cincinnati (AHL)
	Martin Gerber	5-10/175	Burgdorf, Switzerland	9-3-74	1	Cincinnati (AHL), Anaheim
35	Jean-Sebastien Giguere	6-0/185	Montreal	5-16-77	6	Anaheim

2002-03 REVIEW

INDIVIDUAL STATISTICS

SCORING

	Games	G	A	Pts.	PIM	+/-	PPG	SHG	GWG	GTG	Sht.	Sht. Pct.	Faceoffs Won	Lost	Pct.	TOI
Paul Kariya	82	25	56	81	48	-3	11	1	2	1	257	9.7	12	27	30.8	20:17
Petr Sykora	82	34	25	59	24	-7	15	1	5	1	299	11.4	9	14	39.1	18:28
Steve Rucchin	82	20	38	58	12	-14	6	1	4	0	194	10.3	874	739	54.2	21:05
Adam Oates	67	9	36	45	16	-1	4	0	2	0	67	13.4	615	449	57.8	18:38
Niclas Havelid	82	11	22	33	30	5	4	0	5	0	169	6.5	0	3	0.0	22:29
Stanislav Chistov	79	12	18	30	54	4	3	0	2	0	114	10.5	0	3	0.0	13:35
Mike Leclerc	57	9	19	28	34	-8	1	0	4	0	122	7.4	5	12	29.4	16:56
Jason Krog	67	10	15	25	12	1	0	1	1	0	92	10.9	383	251	60.4	13:47

	Games	G	A	Pts.	PIM	+/-	PPG	SHG	GWG	GTG	Sht.	Sht. Pct.	Won	Lost	Pct.	TOI
Keith Carney	81	4	18	22	65	8	0	0	1	2	87	4.6	0	0	—	22:33
Andy McDonald	46	10	11	21	14	-1	3	0	1	0	92	10.9	338	266	56.0	18:30
Matt Cullen*	50	7	14	21	12	-4	1	0	1	0	77	9.1	137	134	50.6	14:18
Patric Kjellberg	76	8	11	19	16	-9	2	1	2	0	95	8.4	8	6	57.1	15:37
Sandis Ozolinsh*	31	5	13	18	16	10	1	0	1	0	54	9.3	0	0	—	22:08
Samuel Pahlsson	34	4	11	15	18	10	0	1	2	0	28	14.3	62	56	52.5	13:19
Steve Thomas*	12	10	3	13	2	10	1	0	3	0	27	37.0	1	4	20.0	13:41
Ruslan Salei	61	4	8	12	78	2	0	0	0	0	93	4.3	0	0	—	21:53
Pavel Trnka*	24	3	6	9	6	2	1	0	0	0	33	9.1	0	0	—	15:59
Fredrik Olausson	44	2	6	8	22	0	2	0	1	0	38	5.3	0	0	—	14:26
Vitaly Vishnevski	80	2	6	8	76	-8	0	1	0	0	65	3.1	0	0	—	14:10
Marc Chouinard	70	3	4	7	40	-9	0	1	0	0	52	5.8	361	301	54.5	9:24
Alexei Smirnov	44	3	2	5	18	-1	0	0	1	0	46	6.5	1	5	16.7	8:49
Dan Bylsma	39	1	4	5	12	-1	0	0	0	0	23	4.3	15	13	53.6	9:28
Rob Niedermayer*	12	2	2	4	15	3	1	0	0	0	21	9.5	6	8	42.9	15:20
Kevin Sawyer	31	2	1	3	115	-2	0	0	0	0	11	18.2	0	1	0.0	6:05
Kurt Sauer	80	1	2	3	74	-23	0	0	0	0	50	2.0	0	0	—	18:32
Mike Brown	16	1	1	2	44	0	0	0	1	0	8	12.5	0	0	—	4:58
Rob Valicevic	10	1	0	1	2	1	0	0	1	0	7	14.3	0	0	—	8:34
Chris O'Sullivan	2	0	1	1	0	0	0	0	0	0	3	0.0	0	0	—	12:45
Martin Gerber (g)	22	0	1	1	0	0	0	0	0	0	0	—	0	0	—	—
Lance Ward*	29	0	1	1	43	-2	0	0	0	0	18	0.0	0	0	—	7:08
Cam Severson	2	0	0	0	8	0	0	0	0	0	1	0.0	0	0	—	6:44
Jonathan Hedstrom	4	0	0	0	0	-1	0	0	0	0	3	0.0	0	1	0.0	7:50
J.-Sebastian Giguere (g)	65	0	0	0	8	0	0	0	0	0	—	0	0	—	—

GOALTENDING

	Games	GS	Min.	GA	SO	Avg.	W	L	T	EN	PPG Allow	SHG Allow	Shots	Save Pct.
Martin Gerber	22	18	1203	39	1	1.95	6	11	3	4	8	2	548	.929
Jean-Sebastien Giguere	65	64	3775	145	8	2.30	34	22	6	5	34	3	1820	.920

*Played with two or more NHL teams.

RESULTS

OCTOBER
10— At St. Louis ....W.....4-3
11— At Dallas ....L.....2-4
13— Detroit ....L.....2-4
16— Los Angeles ....L.....2-4
18— Vancouver ....T....*2-2
20— Colorado...........................W...*3-2
24— At Vancouver ....T....*2-2
26— At Edmonton ....L.....3-4
28— At Toronto ....L.....2-5
29— At Montreal....................T....*2-2
31— At Boston ....W.....4-1

NOVEMBER
3— San Jose..............................L.....3-4
6— Nashville.............................W.....2-1
8— At Colorado ....W...*3-2
10— Minnesota ....W.....1-0
12— At New Jersey ....OTL..*2-3
14— At Columbus ....W.....3-2
15— At Detroit..........................OTL..*1-2
17— At Atlanta ....W.....5-1
19— At N.Y. Rangers ....OTL..*2-3
22— Dallas..................................L.....0-4
24— Florida ....T....*4-4
27— Phoenix ....T....*2-2
29— Los Angeles....................T....*2-2

DECEMBER
1— Chicago ....W.....3-2
3— At Detroit.............................L.....1-2
4— At Buffalo.............................L.....0-4
6— At Chicago ....W.....4-3

8— Nashville..............................W.....3-0
11— Washington ....W.....3-0
15— Pittsburgh ....W.....5-0
18— St. Louis.............................W.....5-2
19— At Los Angeles ....L.....4-5
22— Phoenix ....W.....4-0
26— At San Jose.......................L.....1-4
28— At Vancouver ....L.....3-7
29— At Calgary ....L.....2-4
31— At Minnesota ....L.....1-4

JANUARY
3— Philadelphia ....L.....0-1
5— Dallas....................................T....*1-1
8— Edmonton ....L.....0-1
9— At Colorado ....W.....5-3
12— St. Louis.............................W.....2-1
15— At Columbus ....W.....4-3
16— At Ottawa ....L.....1-3
18— At Minnesota ....W.....1-0
20— Minnesota ....OTL..*1-2
22— Los Angeles......................W.....6-5
24— New Jersey ....L.....1-3
29— Ottawa ....W.....3-2
30— At San Jose.......................W.....4-3

FEBRUARY
4— At Calgary ....W.....3-2
5— At Edmonton ....L.....1-2
7— Phoenix ....W.....3-2
9— Carolina................................W.....2-1
12— Calgary...............................W...*4-3
14— At Dallas.............................W.....4-2

15— At Nashville ....L.....1-2
17— N.Y. Islanders ....T....*2-2
19— Columbus ....W.....2-0
21— N.Y. Rangers.....................L.....2-6
23— At Carolina ....W.....4-0
25— At Tampa Bay ....L.....0-2
26— At Florida ....W.....2-1
28— At Phoenix ....L.....1-3

MARCH
2— Atlanta ....L.....1-4
4— At Los Angeles ....W.....2-1
5— Montreal ....W.....3-1
7— Edmonton ....L.....1-4
9— Detroit ....W.....4-1
12— Chicago ....W.....5-2
13— San Jose ....W...*3-2
15— At Phoenix ....L.....2-4
16— Calgary ....T....*2-2
19— At Chicago ....W.....4-3
20— At St. Louis ....OTL..*2-3
22— At San Jose ....W...*3-2
24— Columbus ....W.....5-0
30— Vancouver ....W.....3-1

APRIL
1— At Nashville ....W...*2-1
2— At Dallas ....L.....1-2
4— Colorado ....OTL..*3-4
*Denotes overtime game.

ATLANTA THRASHERS
EASTERN CONFERENCE/SOUTHEAST DIVISION

ATLANTA THRASHERS

Thrashers' Schedule
Home games shaded; D=Day game; *Feb. 8 All-Star Game at St. Paul, Minn.

October
SUN	MON	TUE	WED	THU	FRI	SAT
5	6	7	8	9 CBJ	10	11 WAS
12	13	14 NYI	15	16 NYR	17	18 CHI
19	20	21 TB	22	23 NAS	24	25 FLA
26	27 TOR	28	29	30 MIN	31 WAS	

November
SUN	MON	TUE	WED	THU	FRI	SAT
						1
2 SJ	3	4	5 BUF	6	7 CBJ	8 NYI
9	10	11 OTT	12	13 CAR	14	15 PHI
16 FLA	17	18	19 BOS	20	21 FLA	22
23 D PHO	24	25 OTT	26	27 TOR	28	29 TB
30						

December
SUN	MON	TUE	WED	THU	FRI	SAT
	1 PIT	2	3 BOS	4	5 ANA	6 FLA
7	8	9	10 LA	11	12 PIT	13 NYI
14	15	16 WAS	17	18 NJ	19	20 PIT
21 PHI	22	23	24	25	26 TB	27
28 D OTT	29 MON	30	31 DET			

January
SUN	MON	TUE	WED	THU	FRI	SAT
				1	2	3 D MON
4	5	6	7	8 DAL	9	10 D SJ
11 PHO	12	13	14 MON	15	16 CAR	17
18 CAR	19	20 BUF	21	22 COL	23	24 NYI
25 NJ	26	27	28 STL	29	30 TOR	31 TB

February
SUN	MON	TUE	WED	THU	FRI	SAT
1	2	3 BOS	4	5 PHI	6	7
8*	9	10 CAL	11 EDM	12	13 VAN	14
15	16 D BUF	17 MON	18	19 OTT	20	21 D PHI
22	23	24	25 TB	26	27 NJ	28
29 D NYR						

March
SUN	MON	TUE	WED	THU	FRI	SAT
	1	2 NYR	3	4	5 CAR	6 BOS
7	8	9 NYR	10	11	12 CAR	13 WAS
14	15 CAR	16	17 BUF	18	19 FLA	20 WAS
21	22	23	24 WAS	25	26 NJ	27 FLA
28	29 TOR	30	31			

April
SUN	MON	TUE	WED	THU	FRI	SAT
				1	2 PIT	3 TB
4	5	6	7	8	9	10

2003-04 SEASON
CLUB DIRECTORY

President and governor
Stan Kasten
V.p. and g.m./alternate governor
Dave Waddell
Vice president of sales and marketing
Derek Schiller
Head coach
Bob Hartley
Assistant coaches
Brad McCrimmon
Steve Weeks
Director of player personnel
Jack Ferriera
Dir. of amateur scouting and player dev.
Dan Marr
Director of marketing
Jim Pfeifer
Director of media relations
Tom Hughes
Director of ticket sales
Dan Froehlich
Director of ticket operations
Wendell Byrne
Director of hockey administration
Larry Simmons
Director of team services
Michele Zarzaca
Senior manager of media relations
Rob Koch
Sr. mgr. of game pres. and spec. events
Peter Sorckoff

Sr. mgr. of publications and web site
Matt Musgrove
Senior manager of new account sales
Keith Brennan
Manager of marketing
Kimberly Hartley
Manager of community relations
Terry Hickman
Manager of special events
Connie Zaleski
Multimedia specialist
John Heid
Web site specialist
Kevin McCormack
Media relations assistant
Katie McLennan
Head trainer
Scott Green
Assistant trainer
Craig Brewer
Equipment manager
Bobby Stewart
Assistant equipment manager
Joe Guilmet
Strength and conditioning coach
Ray Bear
Massage therapist
Inar Treiguts

DRAFT CHOICES

Rd.— Player	Overall	Pos.	Last team
1— Braydon Coburn	8	D	Portland (WHL)
4— James Sharrow	110	D	Halifax (QMJHL)
4— Guillaume Desbiens	116	RW	Rouyn Noranda (QMJHL)
4— Michael Vannelli	136	D	Sioux Falls (USHL)
5— Brett Sterling	145	LW	Colorado Coll. (WCHA)
6— Mike Hamilton	175	F	Merritt (BCHL)
7— Denis Loginov	203	C	Kazan (Russia)
8— Tobias Enstrom	239	D	MoDo (Sweden)
9— Rylan Kaip	269	C	Notre Dame (SJHL)

MISCELLANEOUS DATA

Home ice (capacity)
Philips Arena (18,545)
Address
One Philips Drive
Atlanta, GA 30303
Business phone
404-827-5300
Ticket information
404-584-7825
Website
www.atlantathrashers.com

Training site
Ice Forum, Duluth, GA
Club colors
Navy, blue, copper, bronze and gold
Radio affiliation
WQXI (790 AM), WLKQ (102.3 FM)
TV affiliation
Turner South, WUPA/UPN (Channel 69)

TRAINING CAMP ROSTER

No.	FORWARDS	Ht./Wt.	Place	Date	NHL exp.	2002-03 clubs
18	Lubos Bartecko (LW)	6-1/195	Kezmarok, Czechoslovakia	7-14-76	5	Atlanta
	Zdenek Blatny (LW)	6-1/187	Brno, Czechoslovakia	1-14-81	1	Chicago (AHL), Atlanta
10	Yuri Butsayev (C)	6-1/183	Togliatti, U.S.S.R.	10-11-78	4	Chicago (AHL), Atlanta
16	Jeff Cowan (LW)	6-2/192	Scarborough, Ont.	9-27-76	4	Atlanta
	Jeff Farkas (C)	6-0/185	Amherst, Mass.	1-24-78	4	Atlanta, Manitoba (AHL), Chicago (AHL)
	Simon Gamache (LW) ...	5-10/185	Thetford Mines, Que.	1-3-81	1	Chicago (AHL), Atlanta
15	Dany Heatley (RW)	6-1/200	Freibourg, Germany	1-21-81	2	Atlanta
12	Tony Hrkac (C)	5-11/170	Thunder Bay, Ont.	7-7-66	13	Atlanta
24	Andreas Karlsson (C)	6-3/195	Ludvika, Sweden	8-19-75	3	Chicago (AHL)
17	Ilya Kovalchuk (LW).......	6-2/207	Tver, U.S.S.R.	4-15-83	2	Atlanta
	Slava Kozlov (LW)	5-10/195	Voskresensk, U.S.S.R.	5-3-72	12	Atlanta
23	Derek MacKenzie (C)	5-11/169	Sudbury, Ont.	6-11-81	1	Chicago (AHL)
	Shawn McEachern (LW)	5-11/193	Waltham, Mass.	2-28-69	12	Atlanta
20	Jeff Odgers (RW)	6-0/200	Spy Hill, Sask.	5-31-69	12	Atlanta
22	Kamil Piros (C).............	6-1/183	Most, Czechoslovakia	11-20-78	2	Chicago (AHL), Atlanta
27	Marc Savard (C)	5-10/188	Ottawa	7-17-77	6	Calgary, Atlanta
	Jim Slater (C)	6-0/190	Petoskey, Mich.	12-9-82	0	Michigan State (CCHA)
37	Dan Snyder (C)...........	6-0/185	Elmira, Ont.	2-23-78	3	Chicago (AHL), Atlanta
13	Patrik Stefan (LW)	6-3/200	Pribram, Czechoslovakia	9-16-80	4	Atlanta
39	Per Svartvadet (C)	6-1/190	Solleftea, Sweden	5-17-75	4	Chicago (AHL), Atlanta
19	Brad Tapper (RW).........	6-0/175	Scarborough, Ont.	4-28-77	3	Chicago (AHL), Atlanta
47	J.P. Vigier (RW)	6-0/200	Notre Dame de Lourdes, Man.	9-11-76	3	Chicago (AHL), Atlanta
	DEFENSEMEN					
	Jeff Dessner		Glenview, Ill.	4-16-77	0	Iserlohn (Germany)
	Joe DiPenta	6-2/220	Barrie, Ont.	2-25-79	1	Chicago (AHL), Atlanta
7	Dallas Eakins	6-1/198	Dade City, Fla.	2-27-67	10	Chicago (AHL)
	Garnet Exelby	6-1/210	Craik, Sask.	8-16-81	1	Chicago (AHL), Atlanta
	Kurtis Foster	6-5/205	Carp, Ont.	11-24-81	1	Chicago (AHL), Atlanta
8	Frantisek Kaberle	6-0/185	Kladno, Czechoslovakia	11-8-73	4	Atlanta
4	Uwe Krupp....................	6-6/233	Cologne, West Germany	6-24-65	17	Atlanta
6	Francis Lessard	6-2/184	Montreal	5-30-79	2	Chicago (AHL), Atlanta
29	Kirill Safronov................	6-2/196	Leningrad, U.S.S.R.	2-26-81	2	Chicago (AHL), Atlanta
40	Luke Sellars	6-1/195	Toronto	5-21-81	1	Greenville (ECHL), Chicago (AHL)
25	Andy Sutton..................	6-6/245	Kingston, Ont.	3-10-75	5	Atlanta
4	Chris Tamer	6-2/208	Dearborn, Mich.	11-17-70	10	Atlanta
36	Daniel Tjarnqvist............	6-2/180	Umea, Sweden	10-14-76	2	Atlanta
38	Yannick Tremblay	6-2/200	Pointe-aux-Trembles, Que.	11-15-75	7	Atlanta
	Libor Ustrnul	6-5/228	Olomouc, Czechoslovakia	2-20-82	0	Chicago (AHL)
43	Mike Weaver..................	5-9/185	Bramalea, Ont.	5-2-78	2	Chicago (AHL), Atlanta
	GOALTENDERS					
35	Frederic Cassivi	6-4/220	Sorel, Que.	6-12-75	2	Chicago (AHL), Atlanta
34	Byron Dafoe..................	5-11/190	Sussex, England	2-25-71	11	Atlanta
33	Milan Hnilicka	6-0/180	Kladno, Czechoslovakia	6-24-73	4	Chicago (AHL), Atlanta
	Kari Lehtonen	6-3/189	Helsinki, Finland	11-16-83	0	Jokerit Helsinki (Finland)
34	Norm Maracle...............	5-9/195	Belleville, Ont.	10-2-74	5	Chicago (AHL)
31	Pasi Nurminen...............	5-10/210	Lahti, Finland	12-17-75	2	Atlanta

2002-03 REVIEW

INDIVIDUAL STATISTICS

SCORING

	Games	G	A	Pts.	PIM	+/-	PPG	SHG	GWG	GTG	Sht.	Sht. Pct.	Faceoffs Won	Faceoffs Lost	Faceoffs Pct.	TOI
Dany Heatley	77	41	48	89	58	-8	19	1	6	0	252	16.3	18	31	36.7	21:57
Slava Kozlov..............	79	21	49	70	66	-10	9	1	2	0	185	11.4	23	44	34.3	20:00
Ilya Kovalchuk	81	38	29	67	57	-24	9	0	3	0	257	14.8	6	9	40.0	19:26
Marc Savard*	57	16	31	47	77	-11	6	0	4	0	127	12.6	635	612	50.9	19:49
Patrik Stefan..............	71	13	21	34	12	-10	3	0	2	1	96	13.5	514	611	45.7	16:49
Yannick Tremblay	75	8	22	30	32	-27	5	0	1	0	151	5.3	0	1	0.0	21:44
Shawn McEachern	46	10	16	26	28	-27	4	1	1	0	120	8.3	67	87	43.5	19:17
Tony Hrkac	80	9	17	26	14	-16	2	0	2	0	86	10.5	502	623	44.6	16:05
Frantisek Kaberle......	79	7	19	26	32	-19	3	1	2	0	105	6.7	0	0	—	21:56
Andy Sutton	53	3	18	21	114	-8	1	1	0	0	65	4.6	1	2	33.3	18:00
Lubos Bartecko	37	7	9	16	8	3	0	0	1	0	54	13.0	6	0	100.0	12:30
Daniel Tjarnqvist	75	3	12	15	26	-20	1	0	0	0	65	4.6	2	1	66.7	21:53
Brad Tapper..............	35	10	4	14	23	2	1	0	3	1	68	14.7	1	3	25.0	13:03
Dan Snyder	36	10	4	14	34	-4	0	1	1	1	41	24.4	148	208	41.6	10:53

	Games	G	A	Pts	PIM	+/-	PPG	SHG	GWG	GTG	Sht.	Sht. Pct.	Faceoffs Won	Lost	Pct.	TOI
Pascal Rheaume*......	56	4	9	13	24	-8	0	2	1	0	70	5.7	282	320	46.8	12:16
Richard Smehlik*......	43	2	9	11	16	-4	0	0	0	0	38	5.3	0	0	—	19:42
Chris Tamer.............	72	1	9	10	118	-10	0	0	0	0	53	1.9	0	0	—	15:40
Jeff Cowan	66	3	5	8	115	-15	0	0	0	0	52	5.8	3	7	30.0	8:23
Per Svartvadet..........	62	1	7	8	8	-11	0	0	0	0	47	2.1	14	22	38.9	11:46
Mark Hartigan	23	5	2	7	6	-8	1	0	0	0	25	20.0	104	116	47.3	10:51
Jeff Odgers..............	74	2	4	6	171	-13	0	0	1	0	48	4.2	1	3	25.0	7:47
Chris Herperger........	27	4	1	5	7	-11	0	0	0	0	26	15.4	83	104	44.4	12:30
Kamil Piros...............	3	3	2	5	2	4	0	0	1	0	8	37.5	19	28	40.4	17:05
Mike Weaver	40	0	5	5	20	-5	0	0	0	0	21	0.0	0	0	—	18:37
Kirill Safronov	32	2	2	4	14	-10	0	0	0	0	21	9.5	0	1	0.0	15:02
Pasi Nurminen (g).....	52	0	3	3	4	0	0	0	0	0	0	—	0	0	—	—
Yuri Butsayev	16	2	0	2	8	-5	0	0	0	0	21	9.5	8	18	30.8	12:04
Joey DiPenta	3	1	1	2	0	3	0	0	0	0	2	50.0	0	0	—	15:47
Tomi Kallio*	5	0	2	2	4	-2	0	0	0	0	3	0.0	0	0	—	12:46
Garnet Exelby	15	0	2	2	41	0	0	0	0	0	9	0.0	0	0	—	18:03
Francis Lessard	18	0	2	2	61	1	0	0	0	0	7	0.0	0	0	—	5:39
Ben Simon	10	0	1	1	9	0	0	0	0	0	7	0.0	17	37	31.5	9:24
Frederic Cassivi (g) ...	2	0	0	0	0	0	0	0	0	0	0	—	0	0	—	—
Kurtis Foster...........	2	0	0	0	0	-2	0	0	0	0	1	0.0	0	0	—	11:05
Simon Gamache.......	2	0	0	0	2	-1	0	0	0	0	3	0.0	0	0	—	12:37
Jeff Farkas..............	3	0	0	0	0	-1	0	0	0	0	5	0.0	1	1	50.0	13:32
Zdenek Blatny...........	4	0	0	0	0	-1	0	0	0	0	2	0.0	0	0	—	10:31
Uwe Krupp	4	0	0	0	10	-2	0	0	0	0	1	0.0	0	0	—	15:18
J.P. Vigier	13	0	0	0	4	-13	0	0	0	0	21	0.0	0	1	0.0	14:07
Byron Dafoe (g)	17	0	0	0	0	0	0	0	0	0	0	—	0	0	—	—
Milan Hnilicka (g)......	21	0	0	0	2	0	0	0	0	0	0	—	0	0	—	—

GOALTENDING

	Games	GS	Min.	GA	SO	Avg.	W	L	T	EN	PPG Allow	SHG Allow	Shots	Save Pct.
Pasi Nurminen	52	46	2856	137	2	2.88	21	19	5	6	38	7	1452	.906
Milan Hnilicka	21	17	1097	65	0	3.56	4	13	1	0	11	5	605	.893
Byron Dafoe	17	17	895	65	0	4.36	5	11	1	0	12	1	472	.862
Frederic Cassivi	2	2	123	11	0	5.37	1	1	0	0	4	1	58	.810

*Played with two or more NHL teams.

RESULTS

OCTOBER
11— At Carolina........................L.....3-5
12— Florida.......................OTL...*4-5
16— At Pittsburgh...................L.....2-3
18— At Tampa Bay ....L.....5-8
19— N.Y. Islanders.................L.....4-5
21— At Florida........................L.....2-3
23— New Jersey....................L.....1-2
26— At Boston........................L.....3-4
29— Los Angeles...................L.....0-4
31— At Toronto ....T....*3-3

NOVEMBER
2— At Florida........................W.....3-1
7— At Chicago......................L.....0-5
9— At Buffalo........................W.....6-4
11— Calgary..........................W.....2-1
13— San Jose.......................W...*3-2
15— Phoenix.........................L.....1-5
17— Anaheim........................L.....1-5
19— Florida............................W..*4-3
22— Pittsburgh......................L.....1-3
23— At Washington.................L.....3-6
26— At Montreal.....................L.....2-3
28— N.Y. Rangers ....W.....7-4

DECEMBER
1— Washington.....................W.....5-4
5— At Boston ....OTL...*3-4
6— At Washington ....OTL...*6-7
8— Edmonton.......................L.....0-3
11— At Phoenix......................L.....2-4

13— At Dallas ....L.....1-3
14— At St. Louis.....................L.....0-4
16— Toronto...........................W.....1-0
18— Philadelphia....................L.....1-3
20— Carolina......................OTL...*2-3
23— At Toronto ....L.....1-5
27— At Carolina ....W.....3-0
28— Boston............................L.....0-1
30— At Pittsburgh..................W...*3-2

JANUARY
2— At Ottawa........................L.....1-8
3— Pittsburgh.......................L.....1-4
5— Philadelphia....................L.....4-5
7— Carolina ....T...*3-3
9— At Tampa Bay ....W...*3-2
11— At N.Y. Islanders..............L.....3-7
13— At Philadelphia ....W.....7-4
15— Montreal.........................W.....1-0
17— Boston............................W.....3-1
19— N.Y. Islanders.................L.....1-4
21— St. Louis........................W.....8-4
23— Ottawa............................T...*3-3
25— At N.Y. Rangers ....W.....4-1
28— N.Y. Rangers ....W.....5-2
30— Toronto ....L.....2-5

FEBRUARY
4— At Montreal ....W.....4-3
7— At New Jersey ....W.....4-2
8— At Ottawa........................L.....1-3
12— Washington ....L.....1-5

14— Tampa Bay.......................T....*2-2
15— Detroit ....L.....2-6
17— Buffalo.............................W...*4-3
19— At Tampa Bay ....L.....0-2
23— At Edmonton ....T....*3-3
25— At Vancouver...................L.....0-8
27— At Colorado ....W...*4-3

MARCH
1— At Los Angeles ....L.....1-4
2— At Anaheim......................W.....4-1
6— At Washington ....T...*4-4
7— Florida ....L.....1-2
9— Minnesota........................L.....4-6
11— At New Jersey ....W.....3-2
13— Montreal ....L.....2-4
15— Buffalo.............................W.....5-3
17— Columbus ....W.....3-2
19— Dallas ....OTL...*4-5
21— Ottawa............................L.....1-5
22— At Columbus ....W.....3-2
24— At Philadelphia................L.....2-6
26— Carolina..........................W.....5-1
28— New Jersey ....T...*1-1
29— At Nashville ....W.....3-2
31— At N.Y. Rangers...............W...*4-3

APRIL
2— At Buffalo..........................L.....3-4
5— At N.Y. Islanders...............W.....3-2
6— Tampa Bay ....W.....6-2
*Denotes overtime game.

BOSTON BRUINS
EASTERN CONFERENCE/NORTHEAST DIVISION

BOSTON BRUINS

Bruins' Schedule
Home games shaded; D=Day game; *Feb. 8 All-Star Game at St. Paul, Minn.

October

SUN	MON	TUE	WED	THU	FRI	SAT
5	6	7	8 NJ	9	10 TB	11 FLA
12	13	14	15 DAL	16	17	18 LA
19 ANA	20	21 COL	22	23 CAR	24	25 NJ
26	27	28 MON	29	30 MON	31	

November

SUN	MON	TUE	WED	THU	FRI	SAT
						1 D PIT
2	3	4	5	6 SJ	7	8 DAL
9	10	11 EDM	12	13	14 CBJ	15 VAN
16	17	18	19 ATL	20 WAS	21	22 PHI
23	24	25 STL	26	27	28 D NAS	29
30 PHO						

December

SUN	MON	TUE	WED	THU	FRI	SAT
	1	2	3 ATL	4 TOR	5	6 PHI
7	8 OTT	9	10 FLA	11 WAS	12	13 OTT
14	15	16 MON	17	18 CAL	19	20 D CAR
21	22 NYR	23 TB	24	25	26	27 TB
28	29 WAS	30 OTT	31			

January

SUN	MON	TUE	WED	THU	FRI	SAT
				1 TOR	2	3 NYI
4	5	6	7 DET	8 PIT	9	10 D DET
11	12 BUF	13	14	15 BUF	16	17 OTT
18	19 D NYR	20 NYR	21	22 BUF	23	24 FLA
25	26	27 NYI	28	29 NYI	30	31 D MON

February

SUN	MON	TUE	WED	THU	FRI	SAT
1 D PIT	2	3 ATL	4	5 BUF	6	7
8*	9	10 PIT	11	12 OTT	13	14 D CHI
15	16	17 TOR	18	19 PHI	20	21 CAR
22	23 FLA	24 NYI	25	26 MON	27	28 D PHI
29						

March

SUN	MON	TUE	WED	THU	FRI	SAT
	1	2 TOR	3	4 NYR	5	6 ATL
7	8	9 NAS	10	11 BUF	12	13 D BUF
14	15	16 TOR	17	18 MIN	19	20 D TB
21	22	23 OTT	24	25 TOR	26	27 MON
28	29	30 CAR	31			

April

SUN	MON	TUE	WED	THU	FRI	SAT
				1 WAS	2	3 D NJ
4 NJ	5 D	6	7	8	9	10

2003-04 SEASON
CLUB DIRECTORY

Owner and governor
Jeremy M. Jacobs
Alternative governors
Charles Jacobs, Jeremy Jacobs Jr.
President and alternate governor
Harry Sinden
Senior assistant to the president
Nate Greenberg
V.p., g.m. and alternate governor
Mike O'Connell
Assistant general manager
Jeff Gorton
Executive vice presidents
Richard Krezwick, Charles Jacobs
Chief legal officer
Michael Wall
Chief financial officer
Jessica Rahuba
Director of administration
Dale Hamilton-Powers
Assistant to the president
Joe Curnane
Team travel coordinator/admin. asst.
Carol Gould
Coach
Mike Sullivan
Assistant coaches
Wayne Cashman
Norm Maciver

Director of pro scouting & player dev.
Sean Coady
Director of amateur scouting
Scott Bradley
Scouting staff
Nikolai Bobrov, Gerry Cheevers, Adam Creighton, Daniel Dore, Don Matheson, Mike McGraw, Tom McVie, Tom Songin, Svenake Svensson
Director of media relations
Heidi Holland
Media relations manager
Ryan Nadeau
Dir. of marketing and community rel.
Sue Byrne
Strength & conditioning coach
John Whitesides
Athletic trainer
Don Del Negro
Physical therapist
Scott Waugh
Equipment manager
Peter Henderson
Assistant equipment managers
Chris "Muggsy" Aldrich
Keith Robinson

DRAFT CHOICES

Rd.— Player	Overall	Pos.	Last team
1— Mark Stuart	21	D	Colo. College (WCHA)
2— Patrice Bergeron	45	C	Acadie-Bathurst (QMJHL)
2— Masi Marjamaki	66	LW	Red Deer (WHL)
4— Byron Bitz	107	RW	Nanaimo (BCHL)
4— Frank Rediker	118	D	Windsor (OHL)
4— Patrik Valcak	129	W	Ostrava Jr. (Czech Republic Jr.)
5— Mike Brown	153	G	Saginaw (OHL)
6— Nate Thompson	183	C	Seattle (WHL)
8— Benoit Mondou	247	C	Shawinigan (QMJHL)
9— Kevin Regan	277	G	St. Sebastian's HS

MISCELLANEOUS DATA

Home ice (capacity)
FleetCenter (17,565)
Address
One FleetCenter, Suite 250
Boston, MA 02114-1303
Business phone
617-624-1900
Ticket information
617-931-2222
Website
www.bostonbruins.com

Training site
Wilmington, MA
Club colors
Gold, black and white
Radio affiliation
WBZ (1030 AM) & Bruins Radio Network
TV affiliation
UPN38 (Channel 38) & NESN (New England Sports Network)

TRAINING CAMP ROSTER

No.	FORWARDS	Ht./Wt.	Place	Date	NHL exp.	2002-03 clubs
			——— BORN ———			
11	P.J. Axelsson (RW)	6-1/175	Kungalv, Sweden	2-26-75	6	Boston
	Carl Corazzini (LW)	5-9/170	Framingham, Mass.	4-21-79	0	Providence (AHL), Atlantic City (ECHL)
	Ted Donato (LW)	5-10/180	Boston	4-28-69	12	Hartford (AHL), New York Rangers
	Vladislav Evseev (LW)	6-2/196	Moscow, U.S.S.R.	9-10-84	0	Dynamo Moscow (CIS)
	Mike Gellard (LW)	6-1/193	Markham, Ont.	10-10-78	1	Providence (AHL)
37	Lee Goren (RW)	6-3/190	Winnipeg	12-26-77	2	Providence (AHL), Boston
17	Michal Grosek (LW)	6-2/216	Vyskov, Czechoslovakia	6-1-75	10	Boston
42	Matt Herr (LW)	6-1/205	Hackensack, N.J.	5-26-76	4	Providence (AHL), Boston
29	Andy Hilbert (C/LW)	5-11/190	Howell, Mich.	2-6-81	2	Providence (AHL), Boston
36	Ivan Huml (LW)	6-2/183	Kladno, Czechoslovakia	9-6-81	2	Providence (AHL), Boston
	Jiri Jakes (RW)	6-4/225	Prague, Czechoslovakia	10-4-82	0	Anchorage (WCHL), Vancouver (WHL)
56	Mattias Karlin (C)	5-11/183	Ornskoldsvik, Sweden	7-4-79	0	
26	Mike Knuble (LW)	6-3/222	Toronto	7-4-72	7	Boston
20	Martin Lapointe (RW)	5-11/215	Ville Ste.-Pierre, Que.	9-12-73	12	Augusta (ECHL), Boston
10	Marty McInnis (LW)	5-11/190	Weymouth, Mass.	6-2-70	12	Boston
27	Glen Murray (RW)	6-3/222	Halifax, Nova Scotia	11-1-72	12	Boston
	Brett Nowak (C/LW)	6-2/192	New Haven, Connecticut.	5-20-81	0	Harvard University (ECAC)
	Krzysztof Oliwa (LW)	6-5/235	Tychy, Poland	4-12-73	7	Hartford (AHL), New York Rangers, Boston
	Colton Orr (LW)	0-0/0	Winnipeg, Manitoba	12-30-99	0	Providence (AHL)
31	Jamie Rivers (C)	6-0/197	Ottawa	3-16-75	8	San Antonio (AHL), Florida
	Marcel Rodman (RW)	6-0/183	Jesenice, Slovenia	9-21-81	0	
12	Brian Rolston (C)	6-2/205	Flint, Mich.	2-21-73	9	Boston
14	Sergei Samsonov (LW)	5-8/184	Moscow, U.S.S.R.	10-27-78	6	Boston
	Martin Samuelsson (RW)	6-2/189	Upperlands Vasby, Sweden	1-25-82	1	Providence (AHL), Boston
42	P.J. Stock (RW)	5-10/190	Victoriaville, Que.	5-26-75	6	Boston
19	Joe Thornton (C)	6-4/225	London, Ont.	7-2-79	6	Boston
23	Darren Van Oene (LW)	6-3/207	Edmonton	1-18-78	0	Providence (AHL)
	Kris Vernarsky (C)	6-2/201	Warren, Mich.	4-5-82	1	Providence (AHL), Boston
17	Rob Zamuner (LW)	6-3/203	Oakville, Ont.	9-17-69	12	Boston
	Sergei Zinovjev (RW)	5-11/176	Prokopjeusk, U.S.S.R.	3-4-80	0	
	DEFENSEMEN					
34	Bryan Berard	6-1/190	Woonsocket, R.I.	3-5-77	7	Boston
44	Nick Boynton	6-2/210	Etobicoke, Ont.	1-14-79	4	Boston
12	Rich Brennan	6-2/205	Schenectady, N.Y.	11-26-72	6	Providence (AHL), Boston
23	Sean Brown	6-3/205	Oshawa, Ont.	11-5-76	7	Boston
25	Hal Gill	6-7/230	Concord, Mass.	4-6-75	6	Boston
55	Jonathan Girard	5-11/192	Joliette, Que.	5-27-80	5	Boston
5	Jeff Jillson	6-3/219	North Smithfield, R.I.	7-24-80	2	Cleveland (AHL), San Jose, Providence (AHL)
	Lars Jonsson	6-1/198	Borlange, Sweden	1-2-82	0	Leksand (Sweden Dv. 2)
	Milan Jurcina	6-4/198	Liptovsky Mikulas, Czech.	6-7-83	0	Halifax (QMJHL)
48	Chris Kelleher	6-1/210	Cambridge, Mass.	3-23-75	1	Providence (AHL)
64	Jarno Kultanen	6-2/198	Luumaki, Finland	1-8-73	3	Providence (AHL), Boston
39	Zdenek Kutlak	6-3/207	Budejovice, Czechoslovakia	2-13-80	2	Providence (AHL), Boston
	Tuukka Makela	6-3/202	Helsinki, Finland	5-24-82	0	HPK Hameenlinna (Finland)
3	Dan McGillis	6-2/225	Hawkesbury, Ont.	7-1-72	7	Philadelphia, Boston, San Jose
	Peter Metcalf	6-0/190	Colorado Springs, Colo.	2-25-79	0	Atlantic City (ECHL)
61	Jason Metcalfe	6-1/205	Toronto	3-15-78	0	Pee Dee (ECHL)
24	Ian Moran	6-0/206	Cleveland	8-24-72	9	Pittsburgh, Boston
	Shaone Morrisonn	6-3/182	Vancouver	12-23-82	1	Providence (AHL), Boston
21	Sean O'Donnell	6-3/230	Ottawa	10-13-71	9	Boston
	GOALTENDERS					
	Peter Hamerlik	6-1/187	Myjava, Czechoslovakia	1-2-82	0	Cincinnati (ECHL), Providence (AHL)
1	Andrew Raycroft	6-0/150	Belleville, Ont.	5-4-80	3	Providence (AHL), Boston
31	Steve Shields	6-3/215	Toronto	7-19-72	8	Boston
	Tim Thomas	5-11/182	Flint, Mich.	4-15-74	1	Providence (AHL), Boston
	Hannu Toivonen	6-2/191	Kalvola, Finland	5-18-84	0	

2002-03 REVIEW

INDIVIDUAL STATISTICS

SCORING

	Games	G	A	Pts.	PIM	+/-	PPG	SHG	GWG	GTG	Sht.	Sht. Pct.	Faceoffs Won	Faceoffs Lost	Faceoffs Pct.	TOI
Joe Thornton	77	36	65	101	109	12	12	2	4	1	196	18.4	874	892	49.5	22:32
Glen Murray	82	44	48	92	64	9	12	0	5	2	331	13.3	12	20	37.5	22:36
Mike Knuble	75	30	29	59	45	18	9	0	4	1	185	16.2	15	19	44.1	17:24
Brian Rolston	81	27	32	59	32	1	6	5	5	1	281	9.6	546	602	47.6	20:27
Jozef Stumpel	78	14	37	51	12	0	4	0	2	1	110	12.7	875	726	54.7	18:26
Bryan Berard	80	10	28	38	64	-4	4	0	1	0	205	4.9	0	0	—	21:21

	Games	G	A	Pts.	PIM	+/-	PPG	SHG	GWG	GTG	Sht.	Sht. Pct.	Faceoffs Won	Lost	Pct.	TOI
P.J. Axelsson	66	17	19	36	24	8	2	2	1	0	122	13.9	4	13	23.5	16:37
Nick Boynton	78	7	17	24	99	8	0	1	2	0	160	4.4	0	1	0.0	22:40
Jonathan Girard	73	6	16	22	21	4	2	0	2	0	123	4.9	0	0	—	20:49
Michal Grosek	63	2	18	20	71	2	0	0	1	0	74	2.7	41	54	43.2	10:43
Marty McInnis	77	9	10	19	38	-11	0	0	1	0	121	7.4	147	198	42.6	14:13
Martin Lapointe	59	8	10	18	87	-19	1	0	1	0	110	7.3	25	27	48.1	15:21
Ivan Huml	41	6	11	17	30	3	0	0	2	0	75	8.0	10	12	45.5	12:45
Hal Gill	76	4	13	17	56	21	0	0	0	0	114	3.5	0	0	—	20:41
Rob Zamuner	55	10	6	16	18	2	3	0	1	0	94	10.6	44	53	45.4	12:07
Sean O'Donnell	70	1	15	16	76	8	0	0	1	0	61	1.6	0	1	0.0	22:05
Sergei Samsonov	8	5	6	11	2	8	1	0	3	0	23	21.7	0	0	—	20:19
P.J. Stock	71	1	9	10	160	-5	1	0	0	0	38	2.6	83	102	44.9	6:13
Don Sweeney	67	3	5	8	24	-1	0	0	0	1	55	5.5	0	0	—	13:12
Sean Brown	69	1	5	6	117	-6	0	0	0	0	39	2.6	1	1	50.0	6:25
Lee Goren	14	2	1	3	7	-2	0	0	0	0	15	13.3	0	0	—	8:14
Andy Hilbert	14	0	3	3	7	-1	0	0	0	0	22	0.0	15	19	44.1	11:29
John Grahame (g)*	23	0	2	2	2	0	0	0	0	0	0	—	0	0	—	—
Zdenek Kutlak	4	1	0	1	0	0	0	0	0	0	1	100.0	0	0	—	5:15
Kris Vernarsky	14	1	0	1	2	-2	0	0	0	0	18	5.6	12	10	54.5	10:15
Rich Brennan	7	0	1	1	6	3	0	0	0	0	12	0.0	0	0	—	13:36
Ian Moran*	8	0	1	1	2	-1	0	0	0	0	11	0.0	1	0	100.0	16:22
Martin Samuelsson	8	0	1	1	2	-1	0	0	0	0	3	0.0	0	0	—	11:42
Dan McGillis*	10	0	1	1	10	2	0	0	0	0	18	0.0	0	0	—	21:15
Brantt Myhres	1	0	0	0	31	0	0	0	0	0	0	—	0	0	—	5:26
Jarno Kultanen	2	0	0	0	0	1	0	0	0	0	3	0.0	0	0	—	10:15
Matt Herr	3	0	0	0	0	0	0	0	0	0	1	0.0	4	4	50.0	8:17
Tim Thomas (g)	4	0	0	0	0	0	0	0	0	0	0	—	0	0	—	—
Andrew Raycroft (g)	5	0	0	0	0	0	0	0	0	0	0	—	0	0	—	—
Shaone Morrisonn	11	0	0	0	8	0	0	0	0	0	4	0.0	0	0	—	8:56
Jeff Hackett (g)*	18	0	0	0	2	0	0	0	0	0	0	—	0	0	—	—
Krzysztof Oliwa*	33	0	0	0	110	-4	0	0	0	0	11	0.0	0	1	0.0	3:55
Steve Shields (g)	36	0	0	0	8	0	0	0	0	0	0	—	0	0	—	—

GOALTENDING

	Games	GS	Min.	GA	SO	Avg.	W	L	T	EN	PPG Allow	SHG Allow	Shots	Save Pct.
Andrew Raycroft	5	5	300	12	0	2.40	2	3	0	0	4	0	146	.918
John Grahame*	23	23	1352	61	1	2.71	11	9	2	0	16	3	625	.902
Steve Shields	36	34	2112	97	0	2.76	12	13	9	2	31	3	930	.896
Tim Thomas	4	3	220	11	0	3.00	3	1	0	0	4	2	118	.907
Jeff Hackett*	18	17	991	53	1	3.21	8	9	0	1	10	3	500	.894

*Played with two or more NHL teams.

RESULTS

OCTOBER
11—At Minnesota .... L 1-5
14—At Colorado .... W 2-1
16—At Vancouver .... W 6-3
17—At Calgary .... T *3-3
19—At Edmonton .... W 4-3
21—At Toronto .... W 4-1
24—Ottawa .... T *2-2
26—Atlanta .... W 4-3
30—At Washington .... W 7-2
31—Anaheim .... L 1-4

NOVEMBER
2— N.Y. Rangers .... W 3-2
7— At Detroit .... OTL .. *1-2
9— Ottawa .... W 7-1
11—Edmonton .... W 6-1
12—At Buffalo .... W 4-3
14—N.Y. Islanders .... W 4-1
16—At Philadelphia .... T *2-2
19—At Toronto .... L 0-2
21—Carolina .... W 3-1
23—Buffalo .... W 4-1
26—Calgary .... W 7-2
29—Montreal .... W 4-2
30—At Pittsburgh .... W 3-2

DECEMBER
3— St. Louis .... L 0-4
5— Atlanta .... W *4-3
7— Tampa Bay .... W *3-2
8— At N.Y. Rangers .... W 4-1

10—Montreal .... L 2-4
12—Ottawa .... L 2-5
14—At Montreal .... L 2-4
18—At Buffalo .... L 2-4
19—At Washington .... L 3-5
21—Florida .... T *3-3
23—San Jose .... W 5-2
27—At Tampa Bay .... L 2-5
28—At Atlanta .... W 1-0
30—New Jersey .... L 0-1

JANUARY
3— At N.Y. Islanders .... L 4-8
4— Carolina .... L 2-4
7— At Toronto .... L 2-5
10—At Buffalo .... L 2-4
11—Toronto .... W 6-2
13—Pittsburgh .... L 1-2
15—At Florida .... L 0-3
17—At Atlanta .... L 1-3
18—Columbus .... W 7-2
20—Washington .... T *3-3
23—At Pittsburgh .... W 4-1
25—Philadelphia .... W *1-0
28—Nashville .... W 2-1
30—Chicago .... L 1-3

FEBRUARY
4— Colorado .... OTL .. *2-3
6— Montreal .... W 6-3
8— Pittsburgh .... L 2-5
11—At Montreal .... L 1-3

14—At Florida .... W *6-5
15—At Tampa Bay .... L 2-5
17—At Nashville .... L 1-5
19—At Carolina .... T *1-1
21—At New Jersey .... L 2-3
23—At N.Y. Islanders .... T *4-4
25—Dallas .... T *5-5
27—At N.Y. Rangers .... L 1-4

MARCH
1— Philadelphia .... OTL .. *2-3
3— Vancouver .... L 4-6
4— At Carolina .... W 4-2
6— N.Y. Islanders .... W 4-1
8— Washington .... W *5-4
9— At Chicago .... L 5-8
11—At Ottawa .... OTL .. *3-4
13—New Jersey .... W 4-3
15—Florida .... W 4-1
18—At Phoenix .... L 1-2
21—At San Jose .... L 2-3
22—At Los Angeles .... W *4-3
24—Toronto .... W 3-2
27—At Philadelphia .... T *2-2
29—N.Y. Rangers .... L 1-3
31—Tampa Bay .... T *2-2

APRIL
1— At Ottawa .... L 2-3
3— At New Jersey .... T *1-1
5— Buffalo .... W 8-5
*Denotes overtime game.

BUFFALO SABRES
EASTERN CONFERENCE/NORTHEAST DIVISION

Sabres' Schedule
Home games shaded; D=Day game; *Feb. 8 All-Star Game at St. Paul, Minn.

October

SUN	MON	TUE	WED	THU	FRI	SAT
5	6	7	8	9 PHI	10	11 NYI
12	13 D DAL	14	15	16 EDM	17	18 CAL
19	20 VAN	21	22	23 LA	24 ANA	25
26 COL	27	28 MIN	29	30 TOR	31	

November

SUN	MON	TUE	WED	THU	FRI	SAT
						1 OTT
2	3	4	5 ATL	6	7 MON	8 MON
9	10	11	12 NJ	13	14 PIT	15
16	17 OTT	18	19 NJ	20	21 CAR	22 TB
23	24 FLA	25	26 WAS	27	28 FLA	29 NAS
30						

December

SUN	MON	TUE	WED	THU	FRI	SAT
	1	2	3 CHI	4 PHO	5	6 TB
7	8	9	10 DET	11	12 NYR	13 MIN
14	15	16 PIT	17	18	19 NJ	20
21	22	23 OTT	24	25	26 CAR	27 WAS
28	29 CAR	30	31 WAS			

January

SUN	MON	TUE	WED	THU	FRI	SAT
				1	2 ANA	3 TOR
4	5	6 MON	7 PHI	8	9 OTT	10
11 BOS	12	13 PHI	14	15 BOS	16	17 NYI
18	19	20 ATL	21	22 BOS	23	24 D PHI
25 D CAR	26	27 MON	28	29	30 NYR	31 NYR

February

SUN	MON	TUE	WED	THU	FRI	SAT
1	2	3	4	5 BOS	6	7
8*	9	10 SJ	11	12	13 LA	14 TOR
15	16 D ATL	17	18 FLA	19	20 TB	21 NYI
22	23	24	25 NJ	26	27 NYI	28 OTT
29						

March

SUN	MON	TUE	WED	THU	FRI	SAT
	1	2	3 OTT	4	5	6 TOR
7 STL	8	9	10 WAS	11 BOS	12	13 D BOS
14	15 TOR	16	17 ATL	18 TB	19	20 FLA
21	22	23	24 MON	25	26 PIT	27 PIT
28	29 CBJ	30	31 NYR			

April

SUN	MON	TUE	WED	THU	FRI	SAT
				1	2 TOR	3 MON
4	5	6	7	8	9	10

2003-04 SEASON
CLUB DIRECTORY

Executive vice president/administration
Ron Bertovich
Exec. v.p./integrated marketing
John Cimperman
Senior v.p./corporate sales
Kerry Atkinson
Senior v.p./legal and business affairs
Kevin Billet
Senior vice president/marketing
Christye Peterson
Vice president/communications
Michael Gilbert
Vice president/corporate relations
Seymour H. Knox IV
V.p./ticket sales and operations
John Sinclair
General manager
Darcy Regier
Assistant to the general manager
Larry Carriere
Director of communications
Gregg Huller
Communications coordinator
Kevin Wiles
Director of player personnel
Don Luce
Professional scouts
Kevin Devine, Terry Martin

Scouting staff
Don Barrie, Jim Benning, Bo Berglund, Paul Merritt, Darryl Plandowski, Mike Racicot, Rudy Migay, David Volek
Head coach
Lindy Ruff
Assistant coaches
Scott Arneil
Brian McCutcheon
Strength and conditioning coach
Doug McKenney
Assistant strength coach
Dennis Cole
Goaltender coach
Jim Corsi
Administrative assistant coach
Jeff Holbrook
Head trainer/massage therapist
Jim Pizzutelli
Head equipment manager
Rip Simonick
Assistant equipment manager
George Babcock
On-site travel coordinator
Kim Christiano
Club doctor
Dr. John Marzo

DRAFT CHOICES

Rd.— Player	Overall	Pos.	Last team
1— Thomas Vanek	5	LW	Minnesota (WCHA)
2— Branislav Fabry	65	LW	Bratislava Jr. (Slovakia Jr.)
3— Clarke MacArthur	74	LW	Medicine Hat (WHL)
4— Jan Hejda	106	D	Slavia (Czech Republic)
4— Denis Ezhov	114	D	Togliatti (Russia)
5— Thomas Morrow	150	D	Des Moines (USHL)
6— Pavel Voroshnin	172	D	Mississauga (OHL)
7— Nathan Paetsch	202	D	Moose Jaw (WHL)
8— Jeff Weber	235	G	Plymouth (OHL)
9— Louis-Philippe Martin	266	RW	Baie Comeau (QMJHL)

MISCELLANEOUS DATA

Home ice (capacity)
HSBC Arena (18,690)
Address
HSBC Arena
One Seymour H. Knox III Plaza
Buffalo, NY 14203
Business phone
716-855-4100
Ticket information
888-223-6000
Website
www.sabres.com

Training site
Buffalo, NY
Club colors
Black, white, red, gray and silver
Radio affiliation
WNSA (107.7 FM)
TV affiliation
Empire Sports Network

BUFFALO SABRES

No.	FORWARDS	Ht./Wt.	Place	Date	NHL exp.	2002-03 clubs
	Jeremy Adduono (RW)..	6-0/182	Thunder Bay, Ont.	8-4-79	0	Bridgeport (AHL)
61	Maxim Afinogenov (RW)	5-11/176	Moscow, U.S.S.R.	9-4-79	4	Buffalo
	Milan Bartovic (LW).......	5-11/183	Trencin, Czechoslovakia	4-20-81	1	Rochester (AHL), Buffalo
26	Steve Begin (LW)..........	6-0/190	Trois-Rivieres, Que.	6-14-78	5	Calgary
28	Jason Botterill (LW).......	6-4/220	Edmonton	5-19-76	5	Rochester (AHL), Buffalo
26	Eric Boulton (LW)	6-0/201	Halifax, Nova Scotia	8-17-76	3	Buffalo
8	Daniel Briere (C)	5-10/181	Gatineau, Que.	10-6-77	6	Buffalo, Phoenix
37	Curtis Brown (C)...........	6-0/190	Unity, Sask.	2-12-76	9	Buffalo
18	Tim Connolly (C)	6-0/186	Syracuse, N.Y.	5-7-81	4	Buffalo
18	Chris Drury (LW)	5-10/180	Trumbull, Conn.	8-20-76	5	Calgary
17	J.P. Dumont (LW)	6-1/187	Montreal	4-1-78	5	Buffalo
	Paul Gaustad (C)	6-4/225	Fargo, N.D.	2-3-82	1	Rochester (AHL), Buffalo
	Jochen Hecht (LW).......	6-3/196	Mannheim, West Germany	6-21-77	5	Buffalo
	Jakub Klepis (C)	6-0/200	Prague, Czechoslovakia	6-5-84	0	Slavia Praha (Czech. Jrs.)
12	Ales Kotalik (RW)	6-1/198	Jindrichuv Hradec, Czech.	12-23-78	2	Rochester (AHL), Buffalo
	Jaroslav Kristek (RW) ...	6-0/183	Zlin, Czechoslovakia	3-16-80	1	Rochester (AHL), Buffalo
	Artem Kriukov (C).........	6-3/180	U.S.S.R.	3-5-82	1	
24	Adam Mair (C).............	6-2/194	Hamilton, Ont.	2-15-79	5	Buffalo
	Sean McMorrow (RW) ..	6-4/220	Vancouver, B.C.	1-19-82	1	Rochester (AHL), Buffalo
	Francois Methot (C).......	6-0/175	Montreal	4-26-78	0	Rochester (AHL)
19	Norm Milley (RW)	5-11/175	Toronto	2-14-80	2	Buffalo
	Jiri Novotny (C)	6-2/187	Pelhrimov, Czechoslovakia	8-12-83	0	Rochester (AHL)
	Dan Paille (LW).............	6-0/200	Welland, Ont.	4-15-84	0	Guelph (OHL)
	Andrew Peters (LW)	6-4/195	St. Catharines, Ont.	5-5-80	0	Rochester (AHL)
	Jason Pominville (RW)..	5-11/174	Repentigny, Que.	11-30-82	0	Rochester (AHL)
24	Taylor Pyatt (LW)	6-4/220	Thunder Bay, Ont.	8-19-81	3	Buffalo
	Derek Roy (C)..............	5-8/187	Ottawa	5-4-83	0	Kitchener (OHL)
	Mike Ryan (C)..............	6-1/170	Milton, Mass.	5-16-80	0	
81	Miroslav Satan (RW)	6-1/195	Topolcany, Czechoslovakia	10-22-74	8	Buffalo
16	Chris Taylor (C)	6-0/189	Stratford, Ont.	3-6-72	7	Rochester (AHL), Buffalo
	Michel Tessier (LW).......	6-2/180	Granby, Que.	8-14-84	0	
	Chris Thorburn (C)	6-2/190	Sault Ste. Marie, Ont.	5-3-83	0	Plymouth (OHL)
	DEFENSEMEN					
	John Adams	6-1/185	Orono, Maine	12-21-82	0	
	Keith Ballard	5-11/196	Baudette, Minn.	11-26-82	0	Univ. of Minnesota (WCHA)
18	Joel Bouchard..............	6-0/200	Montreal	1-23-74	9	Hartford (AHL), Pittsburgh, New York Rangers
51	Brian Campbell	5-11/185	Strathroy, Ont.	5-23-79	4	Buffalo
5	Andy Delmore...............	6-1/192	LaSalle, Ont.	12-26-76	5	Nashville
42	Rory Fitzpatrick	6-2/205	Rochester, N.Y.	1-11-75	6	Rochester (AHL), Buffalo
	Radoslav Hecl...............	6-3/202		10-11-74	1	Rochester (AHL), Buffalo
	Doug Janik	6-2/198	Agawam, Mass.	3-26-80	1	Rochester (AHL), Buffalo
45	Dmitri Kalinin................	6-2/198	Chelyabinsk, U.S.S.R.	7-22-80	4	Rochester (AHL), Buffalo
74	Jay McKee	6-3/205	Kingston, Ont.	9-8-77	8	Buffalo
3	James Patrick	6-2/200	Winnipeg	6-14-63	20	Buffalo
6	Peter Ratchuk	6-1/185	Buffalo	9-10-77	2	Rochester (AHL)
10	Henrik Tallinder.............	6-3/194	Stockholm, Sweden	1-10-79	2	Buffalo
44	Alexei Zhitnik	5-11/215	Kiev, U.S.S.R.	10-10-72	11	Buffalo
	GOALTENDERS					
	Tom Askey	6-2/185	Kenmore, N.Y.	10-4-74	2	Rochester (AHL)
43	Martin Biron	6-3/163	Lac St. Charles, Que.	8-15-77	6	Buffalo
	Ryan Miller	6-1/150	East Lansing, Mich.	7-17-80	1	Rochester (AHL), Buffalo
35	Mika Noronen...............	6-1/191	Tampere, Finland	6-17-79	3	Rochester (AHL), Buffalo

2002-03 REVIEW
INDIVIDUAL STATISTICS

SCORING

	Games	G	A	Pts.	PIM	+/-	PPG	SHG	GWG	GTG	Sht.	Sht. Pct.	Faceoffs Won	Faceoffs Lost	Faceoffs Pct.	TOI
Miroslav Satan	79	26	49	75	20	-3	11	1	3	1	240	10.8	2	8	20.0	21:23
Chris Gratton*..........	66	15	29	44	86	-5	4	0	2	1	187	8.0	647	452	58.9	16:25
Ales Kotalik..............	68	21	14	35	30	-2	4	0	2	2	138	15.2	19	18	51.4	15:15
J.P. Dumont..............	76	14	21	35	44	-14	2	0	2	0	135	10.4	3	12	20.0	15:03
Stu Barnes*	68	11	21	32	20	-13	2	1	2	0	124	8.9	452	471	49.0	18:29
Curtis Brown	74	15	16	31	40	4	3	4	4	0	144	10.4	687	700	49.5	16:52
Taylor Pyatt	78	14	14	28	38	-8	2	0	0	0	110	12.7	2	6	25.0	14:05
Jochen Hecht	49	10	16	26	30	4	2	0	2	0	145	6.9	10	23	30.3	17:54

	Games	G	A	Pts.	PIM	+/-	PPG	SHG	GWG	GTG	Sht.	Sht. Pct.	Won	Lost	Pct.	TOI
Tim Connolly	80	12	13	25	32	-28	6	0	2	0	159	7.5	362	483	42.8	15:59
Dmitri Kalinin	65	8	13	21	57	-7	3	1	0	1	83	9.6	0	0	—	21:40
Alexei Zhitnik	70	3	18	21	85	-5	0	0	1	0	138	2.2	0	1	0.0	26:32
Brian Campbell	65	2	17	19	20	-8	0	0	1	0	90	2.2	0	1	0.0	18:40
Adam Mair	79	6	11	17	146	-4	0	1	1	0	83	7.2	293	279	51.2	10:36
James Patrick	69	4	12	16	26	-3	2	0	1	0	63	6.3	2	0	100.0	18:54
Henrik Tallinder	46	3	10	13	28	-3	1	0	0	0	37	8.1	0	0	—	19:52
Daniel Briere*	14	7	5	12	12	1	5	0	1	0	39	17.9	103	103	50.0	17:48
Vaclav Varada*	44	7	4	11	23	-2	1	0	0	0	64	10.9	7	6	53.8	16:06
Maxim Afinogenov	35	5	6	11	21	-12	2	0	2	0	77	6.5	2	2	50.0	13:24
Rhett Warrener	50	0	9	9	63	1	0	0	0	0	47	0.0	0	0	—	18:14
Eric Boulton	58	1	5	6	178	1	0	0	0	0	33	3.0	2	4	33.3	6:34
Jason Botterill	17	1	4	5	14	1	1	0	0	0	20	5.0	2	3	40.0	10:48
Jay McKee	59	0	5	5	49	-16	0	0	0	0	44	0.0	0	0	—	18:45
Chris Taylor	11	1	3	4	2	-1	0	0	0	0	10	10.0	72	80	47.4	13:55
Rory Fitzpatrick	36	1	3	4	16	-7	0	0	0	0	29	3.4	0	0	—	17:01
Jason Woolley*	14	0	3	3	29	-1	0	0	0	0	29	0.0	0	0	—	15:58
Denis Hamel	25	2	0	2	17	-4	0	0	1	0	41	4.9	1	3	25.0	12:40
Norm Milley	8	0	2	2	6	-2	0	0	0	0	8	0.0	1	1	50.0	10:40
Milan Bartovic	3	1	0	1	0	0	0	0	0	0	5	20.0	1	0	100.0	9:52
Martin Biron (g)	54	0	1	1	12	0	0	0	0	0	0	—	0	0	—	—
Paul Gaustad	1	0	0	0	0	0	0	0	0	0	0	—	3	4	42.9	5:48
Doug Houda	1	0	0	0	2	-2	0	0	0	0	1	0.0	0	0	—	12:39
Sean McMorrow	1	0	0	0	0	0	0	0	0	0	0	—	0	0	—	1:27
Doug Janik	6	0	0	0	2	1	0	0	0	0	1	0.0	0	0	—	7:42
Jaroslav Kristek	6	0	0	0	0	-2	0	0	0	0	4	0.0	0	0	—	11:37
Radoslav Hecl	14	0	0	0	2	0	0	0	0	0	3	0.0	0	0	—	10:00
Ryan Miller (g)	15	0	0	0	0	0	0	0	0	0	0	—	0	0	—	—
Mika Noronen (g)	16	0	0	0	0	0	0	0	0	0	0	—	0	0	—	—
Rob Ray*	41	0	0	0	92	-5	0	0	0	0	14	0.0	1	2	33.3	4:23

GOALTENDING

	Games	GS	Min.	GA	SO	Avg.	W	L	T	EN	PPG Allow	SHG Allow	Shots	Save Pct.
Mika Noronen	16	14	891	36	1	2.42	4	9	3	2	6	0	411	.912
Martin Biron	54	53	3170	135	4	2.56	17	28	6	5	43	7	1468	.908
Ryan Miller	15	15	912	40	1	2.63	6	8	1	1	4	4	410	.902

*Played with two or more NHL teams.

RESULTS

OCTOBER
| | | | |
10— N.Y. Islanders ... W ... 5-1
12— At Montreal ... W ... 6-1
13— At Chicago ... L ... 0-3
17— N.Y. Rangers ... T ... *4-4
19— Phoenix ... L ... 2-3
22— Philadelphia ... W ... 2-1
25— New Jersey ... L ... 1-2
26— At Pittsburgh ... L ... 2-5
29— At Vancouver ... T ... *1-1
31— At Calgary ... L ... 0-3

NOVEMBER
1— At Edmonton ... T ... *1-1
3— At Columbus ... L ... 2-3
7— At Carolina ... L ... 0-2
9— Atlanta ... L ... 4-6
12— Boston ... L ... 3-4
15— Toronto ... L ... 2-3
16— At Ottawa ... L ... 1-4
19— At New Jersey ... OTL ... *3-4
22— Columbus ... W ... 5-4
23— At Boston ... L ... 1-4
27— Tampa Bay ... T ... *1-1
29— Pittsburgh ... L ... 1-4
30— At Toronto ... L ... 1-3

DECEMBER
4— Anaheim ... W ... 4-0
6— At N.Y. Rangers ... W ... 4-1
7— Washington ... W ... 4-3
10— Ottawa ... L ... 2-4

13— Chicago ... T ... *1-1
14— At Philadelphia ... L ... 0-2
18— Boston ... W ... 4-2
20— Florida ... L ... 0-3
21— At Montreal ... L ... 2-6
23— At Pittsburgh ... L ... 2-5
26— Ottawa ... L ... 2-3
28— Minnesota ... L ... 3-4
30— At Washington ... L ... 3-4
31— N.Y. Islanders ... OTL ... *0-1

JANUARY
3— Carolina ... W ... 6-3
4— At Ottawa ... W ... *2-1
7— At Philadelphia ... L ... 2-3
10— Boston ... W ... 4-2
11— At Montreal ... W ... 3-2
14— At Minnesota ... W ... 1-0
16— At San Jose ... T ... *2-2
18— At Phoenix ... W ... 1-0
21— Pittsburgh ... T ... *0-0
24— Toronto ... W ... 4-0
25— At Ottawa ... OTL ... *3-4
27— Nashville ... L ... 1-5
30— At St. Louis ... OTL ... *1-2

FEBRUARY
4— At New Jersey ... L ... 1-4
7— Vancouver ... L ... 2-4
8— At N.Y. Islanders ... L ... 1-3
11— St. Louis ... L ... 2-3
13— At Detroit ... L ... 2-4

15— N.Y. Rangers ... W ... 5-4
17— At Atlanta ... OTL ... *3-4
19— Montreal ... W ... *2-1
21— Los Angeles ... L ... 1-4
23— At Tampa Bay ... W ... 4-1
24— At Florida ... T ... *2-2
26— At Washington ... L ... 2-3
28— Dallas ... W ... 5-3

MARCH
1— At N.Y. Islanders ... OTL ... *1-2
4— Washington ... L ... 1-2
6— Toronto ... W ... 4-2
8— At Florida ... W ... 4-0
9— At Tampa Bay ... T ... *1-1
12— Carolina ... OTL ... *2-3
14— Tampa Bay ... L ... 2-4
15— At Atlanta ... L ... 3-5
18— Philadelphia ... W ... 5-2
19— At N.Y. Rangers ... L ... 0-3
22— At Toronto ... OTL ... *2-3
24— Colorado ... W ... *4-3
26— Florida ... W ... 2-1
28— Montreal ... W ... 4-1
29— At Carolina ... W ... 3-1
31— At Dallas ... L ... 0-3

APRIL
2— Atlanta ... W ... 4-3
5— At Boston ... L ... 5-8
6— New Jersey ... T ... *2-2
*Denotes overtime game.

CALGARY FLAMES
WESTERN CONFERENCE/NORTHWEST DIVISION

Flames' Schedule
Home games shaded; D=Day game; *Feb. 8 All-Star Game at St. Paul, Minn.

October

SUN	MON	TUE	WED	THU	FRI	SAT
5	6	7	8	9 VAN	10	11 SJ
12	13	14 EDM	15	16	17	18 BUF
19	20	21 MIN	22	23	24 STL	25 EDM
26	27	28 COL	29 DAL	30	31	

November

SUN	MON	TUE	WED	THU	FRI	SAT
						1 CBJ
2	3	4 DET	5	6	7 MIN	8
9 CBJ	10	11	12 CHI	13 NAS	14	15 EDM
16	17	18 TOR	19	20 MON	21	22 CHI
23	24	25	26	27 COL	28	29 VAN
30						

December

SUN	MON	TUE	WED	THU	FRI	SAT
	1	2 SJ	3	4 VAN	5 MIN	6
7 PIT	8	9 MIN	10	11 CAR	12	13 COL
14	15	16 PHI	17	18 BOS	19 CBJ	20
21	22	23 EDM	24	25	26 VAN	27
28 EDM	29 MIN	30	31 COL			

January

SUN	MON	TUE	WED	THU	FRI	SAT
				1	2	3 VAN
4	5 NYR	6 NYI	7	8 CHI	9	10 FLA
11	12	13 TOR	14 WAS	15	16	17 DAL
18 ANA	19	20 LA	21	22 NAS	23	24 TB
25	26	27 PHO	28 SJ	29	30 CHI	31

February

SUN	MON	TUE	WED	THU	FRI	SAT
1 ANA	2	3 LA	4	5 STL	6	7
8*	9	10 ATL	11 VAN	12	13 ANA	14
15 D MIN	16	17	18	19 MON	20	21 D OTT
22 NJ	23	24 COL	25	26 DET	27	28
29 PHO						

March

SUN	MON	TUE	WED	THU	FRI	SAT
	1	2 STL	3 DET	4	5 DAL	6
7 D COL	8	9 EDM	10	11 OTT	12	13 NAS
14 STL	15	16 DET	17	18 CBJ	19	20 NAS
21	22 DAL	23	24 PHO	25 SJ	26	27 D LA
28	29	30	31 PHO			

April

SUN	MON	TUE	WED	THU	FRI	SAT
				1	2 LA	3
4 D ANA	5	6	7	8	9	10

2003-04 SEASON
CLUB DIRECTORY

Co-owners
N. Murray Edwards, Harley N. Hotchkiss, Alvin G. Libin, Allan P. Markin, J.R. (Bud) McCaig, Byron J. Seaman, Daryl K. Seaman

President & chief executive officer
Ken King

General Manager/head coach
Darryl Sutter

Vice president, hockey administration
Michael Holditch

Vice president, building operations
Libby Raines

Vice president, business development
Jim Peplinski

Vice president, advertising/marketing
Jim Bagshaw

Vice president, sales
Rollie Cyr

Director, hockey administration
Mike Burke

Special assistant to the g.m.
Al MacNeil

Assistant coaches
Jim Playfair, Rich Preston, Rob Cookson

Development coach
Jamie Hislop

Goaltending coach
Wendell Young

Team services manager
Kelly Chesla

Director of scouting
Tod Button

Director of amateur scouting
Mike Sands

Pro scouts
Ron Sutter, Tom Webster

Scouts
Bob Atrill, Tomas Jelinek, Larry Johnston, Randy Hahn, Pertii Hasanen, Sergei Samoilov, Al Tuer

Athletic therapist
Morris Boyer

Assistant athletic therapist
Gerry Kurylowich

Strength & conditioning coach
Rich Hesketh

Equipment manager
Gus Thorson

Assistant equipment manager
Les Jarvis

Sports medicine physician
Dr. Kelly Brett

Team dentist
Dr. Bill Blair

Physicians
Dr. Rich Boorman, Dr. Jim Thorne

Director, communications
Peter Hanlon

Manager, media relations
Sean O'Brien

Admin. assistant, communications
Bernie Hargrave

Director, retail/FanAttic
Kip Reghenas

Director, advertising and publishing
Pat Halls

DRAFT CHOICES

Rd.— Player	Overall	Pos.	Last team
1— Dion Phaneuf	9	D	Red Deer (WHL)
2— Tim Ramholt	39	D	Zurich (Switzerland)
3— Ryan Donally	97	LW	Windsor (OHL)
4— Jamie Tardif	112	RW	Peterborough (OHL)
5— Greg Moore	143	RW	Maine (Hockey East)
6— Tyler Johnson	173	C	Moose Jaw (WHL)
7— Thomas Bellemare	206	D	Drummondville (QMJHL)
8— Cam Cunning	240	LW	Kamloops (WHL)
9— Kevin Harvey	270	LW	Georgetown (Ont. Prov. Jr. A)

MISCELLANEOUS DATA

Home ice (capacity)
Pengrowth Saddledome (17,448)

Address
P.O. Box 1540
Station M
Calgary, Alta. T2P 3B9

Business phone
403-777-2177

Ticket information
403-777-0000

Website
www.calgaryflames.com

Training site
Calgary

Club colors
Red, white, gold and black

Radio affiliation
The Team 960 (960 AM)

TV affiliation
Rogers Sportsnet, CBC, TSN

CALGARY FLAMES

No.	FORWARDS	Ht./Wt.	Place	Date	NHL exp.	2002-03 clubs
	Garrett Bembridge (RW)	6-0/164	Melfort, Sask.	7-6-81	0	Saint John (AHL)
15	Blair Betts (C)	6-3/200	Edmonton	2-16-80	2	Saint John (AHL), Calgary
17	Chris Clark (RW)	6-0/200	Manchester, Conn.	3-8-76	4	Calgary
22	Craig Conroy (C)	6-2/197	Potsdam, N.Y.	9-4-71	9	Calgary
59	Robert Dome (C/LW)	6-0/210	Skalica, Czechoslovakia	1-29-79	3	Saint John (AHL), Calgary
18	Shean Donovan (RW)	6-3/210	Timmins, Ont.	1-22-75	9	Pittsburgh, Calgary
	Martin Gelinas (LW)	5-11/195	Shawinigan, Que.	6-5-70	15	Calgary
	Josh Green (LW)	6-4/213	Camrose, Alta.	11-16-77	5	Edmonton, New York Rangers, Wash.
12	Jarome Iginla (RW)	6-1/207	Edmonton	7-1-77	8	Calgary
	Matthew Lombardi (C)	5-11/191	Montreal	3-18-82	0	Saint John (AHL)
10	Dave Lowry (LW)	6-1/195	Sudbury, Ont.	2-14-65	18	Saint John (AHL), Calgary
	Tomi Maki (RW)	5-11/172	Helsinki, Finland	8-19-83	0	Jokerit Helsinki (Finland)
37	Dean McAmmond (LW)	5-11/193	Grand Cache, Alta.	6-15-73	11	Colorado
	Brian McConnell (C)	6-2/190	Boston	2-1-83	0	Boston University (Hockey East)
52	Jason Morgan (C)	6-1/200	Kitchener, Ont.	10-9-76	2	Saint John (AHL)
	Eric Nystrom (LW)	6-1/195	Syosset, N.Y.	2-14-83	0	Univ. of Michigan (CCHA)
28	Steve Reinprecht (RW)	6-1/195	Edmonton	5-7-76	4	Colorado
19	Oleg Saprykin (LW)	6-0/187	Moscow, U.S.S.R.	2-12-81	4	Saint John (AHL), Calgary
	Egor Shastin (LW)	5-9/172	Kiev, U.S.S.R.	9-10-82	0	
24	Blake Sloan (RW)	5-10/196	Park Ridge, Ill.	7-27-75	5	Calgary
12	Martin Sonnenberg (LW)	6-0/184	Wetaskiwin, Alta.	1-23-78	2	Saint John (AHL)
26	Stephane Yelle (C)	6-1/190	Ottawa	5-9-74	8	Calgary
	DEFENSEMEN					
8	Petr Buzek	6-1/220	Jihlava, Czechoslovakia	4-26-77	6	Calgary
	Mike Commodore	6-4/225	Fort Saskatchewan, Alta.	11-7-79	3	Calgary, Cincinnati (AHL), Saint John (AHL)
7	Andrew Ference	5-10/190	Edmonton	3-17-79	4	Wilkes-Barre/Scranton (AHL), Pittsburgh, Calgary
3	Denis Gauthier	6-2/224	Montreal	10-1-76	6	Calgary
32	Toni Lydman	6-1/202	Lahti, Finland	9-25-77	3	Calgary
58	Steve Montador	6-0/210	Vancouver	12-21-79	2	Saint John (AHL), Calgary
	Mike Mottau	6-0/192	Quincy, Mass.	3-19-78	3	Calgary, Hartford (AHL), Saint John (AHL)
	Rick Mrozik	6-3/227	Duluth, Minn.	1-2-75	1	Saint John (AHL), Calgary
28	Robyn Regehr	6-3/226	Recife, Brazil	4-19-80	4	Calgary
	Rail Rozakov	6-1/198	Murmansk, U.S.S.R.	3-29-81	0	Cherepovets (Russian)
4	Rhett Warrener	6-1/210	Shaunavon, Sask.	1-27-76	8	Buffalo
	GOALTENDERS					
29	Jamie McLennan	6-0/190	Edmonton	6-30-71	8	Calgary
	Dany Sabourin	6-2/165	Val d'Or, Que.	9-2-80	0	Saint John (AHL)
1	Roman Turek	6-4/200	Pisek, Czechoslovakia	5-21-70	7	Calgary

2002-03 REVIEW

INDIVIDUAL STATISTICS

SCORING

	Games	G	A	Pts.	PIM	+/-	PPG	SHG	GWG	GTG	Sht.	Sht. Pct.	Faceoffs Won	Faceoffs Lost	Faceoffs Pct.	TOI
Jarome Iginla	75	35	32	67	49	-10	11	3	6	1	316	11.1	39	51	43.3	21:25
Craig Conroy	79	22	37	59	36	-4	5	0	2	0	143	15.4	900	679	57.0	19:47
Chris Drury	80	23	30	53	33	-9	5	1	5	2	224	10.3	507	435	53.8	18:32
Martin Gelinas	81	21	31	52	51	-3	6	0	3	1	152	13.8	49	47	51.0	16:33
Toni Lydman	81	6	20	26	28	-7	3	0	0	0	143	4.2	0	0	—	25:46
Stephane Yelle	82	10	15	25	50	-10	3	0	3	0	121	8.3	798	696	53.4	18:06
Oleg Saprykin	52	8	15	23	46	5	1	0	1	0	116	6.9	0	1	0.0	11:53
Chris Clark	81	10	12	22	126	-11	2	0	2	1	156	6.4	13	27	32.5	14:23
Dave Lowry	34	5	14	19	22	4	1	0	0	0	40	12.5	2	11	15.4	14:17
Rob Niedermayer*	54	8	10	18	42	-13	2	0	1	0	104	7.7	68	71	48.9	17:28
Bob Boughner	69	3	14	17	126	5	0	0	1	0	62	4.8	0	0	—	19:51
Jordan Leopold	58	4	10	14	12	-15	3	0	0	0	78	5.1	0	0	—	20:35
Denis Gauthier	72	1	11	12	99	5	0	0	1	0	50	2.0	0	0	—	19:52
Robyn Regehr	76	0	12	12	87	-9	0	0	0	0	109	0.0	1	0	100.0	22:45
Scott Nichol	68	5	5	10	149	-7	0	1	0	0	66	7.6	208	149	58.3	10:46
Blake Sloan	67	2	8	10	28	-5	0	0	0	0	56	3.6	4	27	12.9	12:23
Mathias Johansson*	46	4	5	9	12	-15	1	0	0	0	54	7.4	202	174	53.7	12:39

	Games	G	A	Pts.	PIM	+/-	PPG	SHG	GWG	GTG	Sht.	Sht. Pct.	Faceoffs Won	Lost	Pct.	TOI
Petr Buzek	44	3	5	8	14	-6	3	0	0	0	48	6.3	0	0	—	14:21
Chuck Kobasew	23	4	2	6	8	-3	1	0	1	0	29	13.8	0	5	0.0	11:48
Craig Berube	55	2	4	6	100	-6	0	0	1	0	21	9.5	8	19	29.6	5:15
Steve Begin	50	3	1	4	51	-7	0	0	1	0	59	5.1	30	20	60.0	9:13
Jamie Wright*	19	2	2	4	12	1	0	0	0	0	16	12.5	6	8	42.9	11:43
Blair Betts	9	1	3	4	0	3	0	0	0	1	16	6.3	38	33	53.5	11:33
Andrew Ference*	16	0	4	4	6	1	0	0	0	0	17	0.0	0	0	—	17:38
Roman Turek (g)	65	0	4	4	14	0	0	0	0	0	0	—	0	0	—	—
Marc Savard*	10	1	2	3	8	-3	0	0	0	0	21	4.8	47	42	52.8	14:40
Shean Donovan*	13	1	2	3	7	-2	0	0	1	0	22	4.5	2	1	66.7	15:39
Micki Dupont	16	1	2	3	4	-5	0	0	0	0	27	3.7	0	0	—	16:44
Steve Montador	50	1	1	2	114	-9	0	0	0	0	64	1.6	0	0	—	15:11
Ladislav Kohn	3	0	1	1	2	1	0	0	0	0	3	0.0	1	1	50.0	8:52
Mike Commodore	6	0	1	1	19	2	0	0	0	0	5	0.0	0	0	—	11:34
Robert Dome	1	0	0	0	0	0	0	0	0	0	1	0.0	0	0	—	8:16
Rick Mrozik	2	0	0	0	0	0	0	0	0	0	2	0.0	0	0	—	10:02
Mike Mottau	4	0	0	0	0	-1	0	0	0	0	0	—	0	0	—	9:49
Jamie McLennan (g)	22	0	0	0	14	0	0	0	0	0	0	—	0	0	—	—

GOALTENDING

	Games	GS	Min.	GA	SO	Avg.	W	L	T	EN	PPG Allow	SHG Allow	Shots	Save Pct.
Roman Turek	65	65	3822	164	4	2.57	27	29	9	4	50	5	1679	.902
Jamie McLennan	22	17	1165	58	0	2.99	2	11	4	2	15	5	537	.892

*Played with two or more NHL teams.

RESULTS

OCTOBER

10— Vancouver ....L 0-3
12— Philadelphia ....L 4-5
14— At Vancouver ....W 3-2
17— Boston ....T *3-3
19— At Chicago ....W 5-2
21— At Detroit ....L 0-4
22— At Minnesota ....OTL .*3-4
24— Dallas ....T *3-3
26— St. Louis ....OTL .*3-4
31— Buffalo ....W 3-0

NOVEMBER

2— Colorado ....T *4-4
4— At N.Y. Islanders ....W 4-2
5— At New Jersey ....W 3-2
7— At N.Y. Rangers ....OTL .*0-1
9— At Florida ....L 0-3
11— At Atlanta ....L 1-2
14— N.Y. Rangers ....L 1-2
16— St. Louis ....L 0-1
19— Detroit ....L 0-5
21— Edmonton ....L 1-3
23— Chicago ....W 3-1
26— At Boston ....L 2-7
27— At Washington ....L 2-4
29— At St. Louis ....L 2-7

DECEMBER

1— At Detroit ....L 2-4
3— At Colorado ....W 2-1
5— Minnesota ....T *1-1

JANUARY

2— Tampa Bay ....W 4-1
4— Minnesota ....W 3-2
7— At Colorado ....W 4-2
9— Ottawa ....L 0-1
11— Columbus ....L 2-7
13— At Montreal ....L 2-4
14— At Toronto ....L 2-3
16— Nashville ....T *2-2
18— Los Angeles ....W *2-1
20— Edmonton ....W 4-3
23— Phoenix ....L 1-7
25— Detroit ....W 4-1
28— At Phoenix ....L 3-4
29— At Dallas ....L 1-4

FEBRUARY

4— Anaheim ....L 2-3
6— Chicago ....T *2-2
7— At Edmonton ....W 4-3
9— At Colorado ....L 2-4

9— At Vancouver

9— At Vancouver ....W 2-1
12— Carolina ....L 3-4
14— Colorado ....L 1-3
15— At Vancouver ....T *3-3
17— At Nashville ....W 3-0
19— At Columbus ....L 0-3
21— At Pittsburgh ....L 0-2
23— At Minnesota ....W 3-2
27— Toronto ....L 3-4
29— Anaheim ....W 4-2
31— Montreal ....T *1-1

12— At Anaheim ....OTL .*3-4
13— At Los Angeles ....L 2-4
15— Vancouver ....T *2-2
17— At St. Louis ....L 3-5
19— At Dallas ....T *1-1
20— At Nashville ....L 1-4
23— At Phoenix ....W 4-2
24— At San Jose ....L 2-5

MARCH

1— San Jose ....W 4-3
5— New Jersey ....W *5-4
7— At Chicago ....W 2-0
8— At Columbus ....W *3-2
11— Edmonton ....L 2-5
13— Toronto ....W *4-3
15— At San Jose ....L 2-3
16— At Anaheim ....T *2-2
18— At Los Angeles ....W 4-1
20— Washington ....L 1-4
22— Nashville ....T *1-1
24— Phoenix ....W 2-0
27— Dallas ....W *2-1
29— Columbus ....L 4-6
31— At Minnesota ....L 0-3

APRIL

2— San Jose ....T *2-2
4— Los Angeles ....W *2-1
5— At Edmonton ....W 4-1
*Denotes overtime game.

CAROLINA HURRICANES

Hurricanes' Schedule
Home games shaded; D=Day game; *Feb. 8 All-Star Game at St. Paul, Minn.

October

SUN	MON	TUE	WED	THU	FRI	SAT
5	6	7	8	9 FLA	10	11 NJ
12	13 FLA	14	15	16	17	18 NYR
19	20	21	22 PIT	23 BOS	24	25 PHI
26	27	28 SJ	29	30 NYR	31	

November

SUN	MON	TUE	WED	THU	FRI	SAT
						1 TB
2 TOR	3	4	5	6 NYR	7	8 LA
9 TB	10	11	12 WAS	13 ATL	14	15 WAS
16	17 PHI	18	19	20 OTT	21 BUF	22
23 TB	24	25	26 NYI	27	28 D PHI	29 PIT
30						

December

SUN	MON	TUE	WED	THU	FRI	SAT
	1	2	3 NAS	4	5 MON	6 MON
7	8	9 EDM	10	11 CAL	12	13
14 VAN	15	16	17	18 PIT	19	20 D BOS
21	22 DAL	23	24	25	26 BUF	27 MON
28	29 BUF	30	31 ANA			

January

SUN	MON	TUE	WED	THU	FRI	SAT
				1	2 DET	3
4 D PHO	5	6 STL	7	8 NYR	9 WAS	10
11 OTT	12	13	14	15 TB	16 ATL	17
18 ATL	19	20 OTT	21 NJ	22	23 NYI	24
25 D BUF	26	27 TOR	28	29 WAS	30	31 DET

February

SUN	MON	TUE	WED	THU	FRI	SAT
1	2	3 COL	4 ANA	5	6	7
8*	9	10	11	12 WAS	13	14 D NJ
15	16 FLA	17	18	19 TOR	20	21 BOS
22	23 TOR	24	25 WAS	26	27	28 MON
29 MIN						

March

SUN	MON	TUE	WED	THU	FRI	SAT
	1	2 CBJ	3	4	5 ATL	6 NJ
7	8 CBJ	9	10 TB	11	12 ATL	13 TB
14	15 ATL	16	17 CHI	18	19 PIT	20 OTT
21	22	23 PHI	24	25 FLA	26	27 NYI
28	29 FLA	30 BOS	31			

April

SUN	MON	TUE	WED	THU	FRI	SAT
				1	2 NYI	3
4 FLA	5	6	7	8	9	10

2003-04 SEASON
CLUB DIRECTORY

Owner/governor
Peter Karmanos Jr.
General partner
Thomas Thewes
President/general manager
Jim Rutherford
Vice president/asst. general manager
Jason Karmanos
Chief financial officer
Mike Amendola
Head coach
Paul Maurice
Assistant coaches
Randy Ladouceur
Kevin McCarthy
Director of amateur scouting
Sheldon Ferguson
Amateur scouts
Willy Langer
Willy Lindstrom
Tony MacDonald
Bert Marshall
Terry E. McDonnell

Pro scout
Claude Larose
Video coordinator
Chris Huffine
Head athletic therapist/strength and conditioning coach
Peter Friesen
Assistant athletic therapist
Stu Lempke
Equipment managers
Skip Cunningham
Bob Gorman
Wally Tatomir
Executive assistants, hockey operations
Kelly Kirwin
Debbie Shannon
Director of media relations
Mike Sundheim
Manager of media relations
Kyle Hanlin

DRAFT CHOICES

Rd.— Player	Overall	Pos.	Last team
1— Eric Staal	2	C	Peterborough (OHL)
2— Danny Richmond	31	D	Michigan (CCHA)
4— Aaron Dawson	102	D	Peterborough (OHL)
4— Kevin Nastiuk	126	G	Medicine Hat (WHL)
4— Matej Trojovsky	130	D	Regina (WHL)
5— Tyson Strachan	137	D	Vernon (BCHL)
7— Shay Stevenson	198	LW	Red Deer (WHL)
8— Jamie Hoffmann	230	C	Des Moines (USHL)
9— Ryan Rorabeck	262	C	Toronto-St. Michael's (OHL)

MISCELLANEOUS DATA

Home ice (capacity)
RBC Center (18,730)
Address
1400 Edwards Mill Road
Raleigh, NC 27607
Business phone
919-467-7825
Ticket information
1-888-645-8491
Website
www.carolinahurricanes.com

Training site
Fort Myers, FL & Raleigh
Club colors
Red, black and silver
Radio affiliation
WKXU/WKIX (101.1/102.3 FM)
TV affiliation
FOX Sports Net (Cable), WRAZ FOX 50

TRAINING CAMP ROSTER

No.	FORWARDS	Ht./Wt.	Place	Date	NHL exp.	2002-03 clubs
			BORN			
27	Craig Adams (RW)	6-0/200	Calgary	4-26-77	3	Carolina
15	Kevyn Adams (C)	6-1/195	Washington, D.C.	10-8-74	6	Carolina
	Ryan Bayda (LW)	5-11/185	Saskatoon, Sask.	12-9-80	1	Lowell (AHL), Carolina
	Jesse Boulerice (C)	6-1/200	Plattsburgh, N.Y.	8-10-78	2	Carolina
55	Pavel Brendl (RW)	6-1/197	Opocno, Czechoslovakia	3-23-81	2	Philadelphia, Carolina
17	Rod Brind'Amour (C)	6-1/200	Ottawa	8-9-70	15	Carolina
26	Erik Cole (RW)	6-0/185	Oswego, N.Y.	11-6-78	2	Carolina
17	Jeff Daniels (LW)	6-1/200	Oshawa, Ont.	6-24-68	12	Carolina
39	Brad DeFauw (LW)	6-2/210	Edina, Minn.	11-10-77	1	Lowell (AHL), Carolina
10	Ron Francis (C)	6-3/200	Sault Ste. Marie, Ont.	3-1-63	22	Carolina
	Jeff Heerema (RW)	6-1/184	Thunder Bay, Ont.	1-17-80	1	Lowell (AHL), Carolina
17	Jan Hlavac (LW)	6-0/200	Prague, Czechoslovakia	9-20-76	4	Vancouver, Carolina
	Tomas Kurka (LW)	5-11/190	Litvinov, Czechoslovakia	12-14-81	1	Lowell (AHL), Carolina
	Brett Lysak (C)	6-0/190	Edmonton	12-30-80	0	Lowell (AHL)
	Craig MacDonald (C)	6-2/185	Antigonish, Nova Scotia	4-7-77	3	Lowell (AHL), Carolina
39	Marty Murray (C)	5-9/178	Deloraine, Man.	2-16-75	6	Philadelphia
92	Jeff O'Neill (LW)	6-0/195	Richmond Hill, Ont.	2-23-76	8	Carolina
	Damian Surma (C)	6-3/189	Lincoln Park, Mich.	3-17-79	1	Lowell (AHL), Carolina
62	Jaroslav Svoboda (RW)	6-1/174	Cervenka, Czechoslovakia	6-1-80	2	Lowell (AHL), Carolina
36	Joey Tetarenko (RW)	6-2/215	Prince Albert, Sask.	3-3-78	3	Ottawa, Florida, San Antonio (AHL), Binghamton (AHL)
63	Josef Vasicek (C)	6-4/196	Havlickuv Brod, Czech.	9-12-80	3	Carolina
17	Radim Vrbata (RW)	6-1/185	Mlada Boleslav, Czech.	6-13-81	2	Colorado, Carolina
12	Mike Watt (LW/C)	6-2/208	Seaforth, Ont.	3-31-76	5	Lowell (AHL), Carolina
16	Tommy Westlund (RW)	6-0/202	Fors, Sweden	12-29-74	4	Lowell (AHL), Carolina
	Mike Zigomanis (C)	6-0/183	North York, Ont.	1-17-81	1	Lowell (AHL), Carolina
	DEFENSEMEN					
49	Kaspars Astashenko	6-2/183	Riga, U.S.S.R.	2-17-75	2	Lowell (AHL)
	Bob Boughner	6-0/203	Windsor, Ont.	3-8-71	8	Calgary
	Sean Curry	6-4/230	Burnsville, Minn.	4-29-82	0	Lowell (AHL), Florida (ECHL)
	Brad Fast	6-0/185	Fort St. John, Sask.	2-21-80	0	Lowell (AHL)
	Shaun Fisher	5-11/185	Detroit	6-2-79	0	Florida (ECHL), Greenville (ECHL), Trenton (ECHL)
14	Steve Halko	6-1/190	Etobicoke, Ont.	3-8-74	6	Lowell (AHL), Carolina
6	Bret Hedican	6-2/205	St. Paul, Minn.	8-10-70	12	Carolina
22	Sean Hill	6-0/203	Duluth, Minn.	2-14-70	13	Carolina
	Tomas Malec	6-1/185	Skalica, Czechoslovakia	5-3-82	1	Lowell (AHL), Carolina
55	Danny Markov	6-1/190	Moscow, U.S.S.R.	7-11-76	6	Phoenix
	Jared Newman	6-2/201	Detroit	3-7-82	0	Florida (ECHL)
	Peter Reynolds	6-3/190	Waterloo, Ont.	4-27-81	0	Florida (ECHL)
42	Bruno St. Jacques	6-2/204	Montreal	8-22-80	2	Philadelphia, Carolina, Philadelphia (AHL), Lowell (AHL)
	Carter Trevesani	6-1/190	Carlisle, Ont.	6-6-82	0	
7	Niclas Wallin	6-2/207	Boden, Sweden	2-20-75	3	Carolina
4	Aaron Ward	6-2/225	Windsor, Ont.	1-17-73	9	Carolina
2	Glen Wesley	6-1/201	Red Deer, Alta.	10-2-68	16	Toronto, Carolina
	GOALTENDERS					
	Danny Boisclair	6-2/185	Sept-Iles, Que.	11-2-82	0	Florida (ECHL)
40	Patrick DesRochers	6-3/195	Penetang, Ont.	10-27-79	2	Phoenix, Carolina, Springfield (AHL), Lowell (AHL)
1	Arturs Irbe	5-8/190	Riga, U.S.S.R.	2-2-67	12	Lowell (AHL), Carolina
	Randy Petruk	5-10/185	Cranbrook, B.C.	4-23-78	0	Lowell (AHL), Florida (ECHL)
	Cam Ward	6-0/176	Sherwood Park, Alta.	2-29-84	0	Red Deer (WHL)
80	Kevin Weekes	6-0/195	Toronto	4-4-75	6	Carolina
	Rob Zepp	6-1/160	Scarborough, Ont.	9-7-81	0	Lowell (AHL), Florida (ECHL)

2002-03 REVIEW
INDIVIDUAL STATISTICS

SCORING

	Games	G	A	Pts.	PIM	+/-	PPG	SHG	GWG	GTG	Sht.	Sht. Pct.	Faceoffs Won	Faceoffs Lost	Pct.	TOI
Jeff O'Neill	82	30	31	61	38	-21	11	0	7	2	316	9.5	533	453	54.1	19:09
Ron Francis	82	22	35	57	30	-22	8	1	1	0	156	14.1	462	418	52.5	19:56
Rod Brind'Amour	48	14	23	37	37	-9	7	1	0	0	110	12.7	702	540	56.5	23:45
Sean Hill	82	5	24	29	141	4	1	0	0	0	188	2.7	0	1	0.0	24:20
Erik Cole	53	14	13	27	72	1	6	2	3	0	125	11.2	22	34	39.3	17:07
Jan Hlavac*	52	9	15	24	22	-9	6	0	1	1	116	7.8	8	13	38.1	17:10
Josef Vasicek	57	10	10	20	33	-19	4	0	1	0	87	11.5	323	329	49.5	15:57

	Games	G	A	Pts.	PIM	+/-	PPG	SHG	GWG	GTG	Sht.	Sht. Pct.	Faceoffs Won	Faceoffs Lost	Pct.	TOI
Bates Battaglia*	70	5	14	19	90	-17	0	1	1	0	96	5.2	4	12	25.0	18:38
Kevyn Adams	77	9	9	18	57	-8	0	0	0	0	169	5.3	540	478	53.0	14:38
Sami Kapanen*	43	6	12	18	12	-17	3	0	1	1	108	5.6	5	11	31.3	18:36
Craig Adams	81	6	12	18	71	-11	1	0	1	0	107	5.6	7	13	35.0	12:12
Bret Hedican	72	3	14	17	75	-24	1	0	1	0	113	2.7	0	0	—	23:01
Ryan Bayda	25	4	10	14	16	-5	0	0	1	0	49	8.2	2	0	100.0	17:14
Jaroslav Svoboda	48	3	11	14	32	-5	1	0	0	0	63	4.8	10	15	40.0	14:33
David Tanabe	68	3	10	13	24	-27	2	0	0	0	104	2.9	0	0	—	18:11
Niclas Wallin	77	2	8	10	71	-19	0	0	2	0	69	2.9	0	0	—	16:12
Aaron Ward	77	3	6	9	90	-23	0	0	1	0	66	4.5	0	0	—	18:43
Glen Wesley*	63	1	7	8	40	-5	1	0	0	0	72	1.4	0	0	—	21:24
Bruno St. Jacques*	18	2	5	7	12	-3	0	0	0	0	14	14.3	0	0	—	18:14
Radim Vrbata*	10	5	0	5	2	-7	3	0	0	0	44	11.4	7	8	46.7	19:00
Tomas Kurka	14	3	2	5	2	1	0	0	0	0	22	13.6	2	2	50.0	14:58
Craig MacDonald	35	1	3	4	20	-3	0	0	0	0	43	2.3	40	32	55.6	9:21
Jeff Daniels	59	0	4	4	8	-9	0	0	0	0	41	0.0	43	64	40.2	8:25
Brad DeFauw	9	3	0	3	2	-2	1	0	1	0	19	15.8	0	0	—	13:45
Jeff Heerema	10	3	0	3	2	-2	1	0	0	0	16	18.8	0	0	—	9:36
Mike Zigomanis	19	2	1	3	0	-4	1	1	0	0	19	10.5	87	60	59.2	9:43
Jesse Boulerice	48	2	1	3	108	-2	0	0	0	1	12	16.7	0	0	—	3:53
Marek Malik*	10	0	2	2	16	-3	0	0	0	0	9	0.0	0	0	—	17:01
Tomas Malec	41	0	2	2	43	-5	0	0	0	0	30	0.0	1	0	100.0	11:13
Damian Surma	1	1	0	1	0	0	0	0	0	0	1	100.0	0	0	—	7:15
Pavel Brendl*	8	0	1	1	2	-3	0	0	0	0	14	0.0	1	1	50.0	15:04
Harold Druken*	14	0	1	1	2	-1	0	0	0	0	5	0.0	19	20	48.7	4:02
P. DesRochers (g)*	2	0	0	0	0	0	0	0	0	0	0	—	0	0	—	—
Tommy Westlund	3	0	0	0	0	0	0	0	0	0	0	—	5	3	62.5	6:29
Mike Watt	5	0	0	0	0	-1	0	0	0	0	2	0.0	9	10	47.4	7:30
Steve Halko	6	0	0	0	0	1	0	0	0	0	5	0.0	0	0	—	10:14
Darren Langdon*	9	0	0	0	16	0	0	0	0	0	4	0.0	0	0	—	2:45
Arturs Irbe (g)	34	0	0	0	4	0	0	0	0	0	0	—	0	0	—	—
Kevin Weekes (g)	51	0	0	0	2	0	0	0	0	0	0	—	0	0	—	—

GOALTENDING

	Games	GS	Min.	GA	SO	Avg.	W	L	T	EN	PPG Allow	SHG Allow	Shots	Save Pct.
Kevin Weekes	51	49	2965	126	5	2.55	14	24	9	2	35	6	1438	.912
Arturs Irbe	34	31	1884	100	0	3.18	7	24	2	5	34	3	816	.877
Patrick DesRochers*	2	2	122	7	0	3.44	1	1	0	0	2	0	71	.901

*Played with two or more NHL teams.

RESULTS

OCTOBER
9— N.Y. Rangers .... L 1-4
11— Atlanta .... W 5-3
12— At Tampa Bay .... L 1-5
15— At St. Louis .... OTL ... *1-2
17— Washington .... L 1-2
19— New Jersey .... W 3-1
22— At N.Y. Islanders .... W 4-1
23— At Ottawa .... L 1-4
26— Chicago .... T *3-3
29— At New Jersey .... W 2-1
30— N.Y. Islanders .... W 4-2

NOVEMBER
1— Montreal .... T *2-2
5— Philadelphia .... OTL ... *1-2
7— Buffalo .... W 2-0
9— Pittsburgh .... W 3-2
12— Phoenix .... W 3-2
15— Philadelphia .... T *1-1
17— Tampa Bay .... OTL ... *1-2
19— Ottawa .... T *4-4
21— At Boston .... L 1-3
23— At Montreal .... W 7-3
25— At N.Y. Rangers .... L 1-3
27— Vancouver .... L 2-3
29— Detroit .... W 6-4
30— At Columbus .... W 4-2

DECEMBER
3— At Nashville .... W 2-1
4— At Florida .... L 2-4

6— Florida .... L 0-2
7— At Ottawa .... L 2-5
11— At Edmonton .... L 1-4
12— At Calgary .... W 4-3
15— At Minnesota .... L 1-2
18— Tampa Bay .... T *1-1
20— At Atlanta .... W *3-2
22— Dallas .... W 1-0
27— Atlanta .... L 3-5
28— At N.Y. Islanders .... L 0-3
31— N.Y. Rangers .... L 0-2

JANUARY
3— At Buffalo .... L 3-6
4— At Boston .... W 4-2
7— At Atlanta .... T *3-3
8— At N.Y. Rangers .... L 1-5
10— Washington .... L 1-4
12— Colorado .... OTL ... *2-3
15— Pittsburgh .... L 0-2
17— New Jersey .... L 1-2
18— At New Jersey .... L 2-5
20— St. Louis .... L 3-5
22— At Washington .... L 3-5
24— Florida .... W 3-1
25— At Florida .... OTL ... *2-3
29— Toronto .... L 2-3
30— At Tampa Bay .... L 1-3

FEBRUARY
5— At San Jose .... L 2-6
7— At Los Angeles .... L 2-8

9— At Anaheim .... L 1-2
11— At Dallas .... OTL ... *1-2
14— Washington .... W 3-1
15— At Philadelphia .... T *2-2
18— At Toronto .... L 3-4
19— Boston .... T *1-1
21— Tampa Bay .... T *2-2
23— Anaheim .... L 0-4
26— At Phoenix .... L 2-4

MARCH
1— At Toronto .... L 1-4
2— At Washington .... L 0-2
4— Boston .... L 2-4
6— At Pittsburgh .... W 4-0
7— Minnesota .... W 1-0
10— Columbus .... W 6-5
12— At Buffalo .... W *3-2
13— At Philadelphia .... L 3-5
15— Los Angeles .... T *0-0
18— Ottawa .... L 5-6
22— At Montreal .... L 3-5
25— Toronto .... T *3-3
26— At Atlanta .... L 1-5
29— Buffalo .... L 1-3
31— Montreal .... L 0-4

APRIL
2— At Pittsburgh .... L 2-3
4— At Florida .... L 1-4
6— N.Y. Islanders .... L 1-2

*Denotes overtime game.

CHICAGO BLACKHAWKS
WESTERN CONFERENCE/CENTRAL DIVISION

Blackhawks' Schedule
Home games shaded; D=Day game; *Feb. 8 All-Star Game at St. Paul, Minn.

October

SUN	MON	TUE	WED	THU	FRI	SAT
5	6	7	8 MIN	9	10 COL	11
12 LA	13	14	15	16 CBJ	17	18 ATL
19 NAS	20	21	22	23 SJ	24	25 LA
26 ANA	27	28 PHO	29	30 PIT	31	

November

SUN	MON	TUE	WED	THU	FRI	SAT
						1 STL
2 ANA	3	4	5	6	7 NAS	8
9 COL	10 DET	11	12 CAL	13	14 DET	15
16 NYR	17	18 EDM	19	20 VAN	21	22 CAL
23	24	25	26 SJ	27	28 D ANA	29 D LA
30						

December

SUN	MON	TUE	WED	THU	FRI	SAT
	1	2	3 BUF	4	5	6 NYI
7 PHO	8	9	10	11 DET	12 DAL	13
14 DAL	15	16	17	18 OTT	19 DET	20
21 NJ	22	23 STL	24	25	26 CBJ	27
28 DET	29 PIT	30	31 VAN			

January

SUN	MON	TUE	WED	THU	FRI	SAT
				1	2 SJ	3
4 EDM	5	6	7 MIN	8 CAL	9	10
11 COL	12 STL	13	14 DET	15	16	17
18 LA	19	20	21 MIN	22 CBJ	23	24 CBJ
25	26	27 VAN	28	29 EDM	30 CAL	31

February

SUN	MON	TUE	WED	THU	FRI	SAT
1 D MON	2	3 TOR	4	5	6	7
8*	9	10	11 NAS	12	13	14 D BOS
15 D WAS	16	17	18	19 SJ	20	21
22 D STL	23	24 PHI	25 CBJ	26	27 CBJ	28
29 D FLA						

March

SUN	MON	TUE	WED	THU	FRI	SAT
	1 NAS	2	3 TB	4	5 ANA	6
7 D EDM	8	9	10	11 NJ	12 WAS	13
14 D DAL	15	16	17 CAR	18	19 VAN	20
21 D PHO	22	23 COL	24	25 MIN	26	27 D STL
28 D STL	29	30 NAS	31			

April

SUN	MON	TUE	WED	THU	FRI	SAT
				1 NAS	2	3 D PHO
4 DAL	5 D	6	7	8	9	10

2003-04 SEASON
CLUB DIRECTORY

President
William W. Wirtz
Senior vice president
Robert J. Pulford
Vice president
Peter R. Wirtz
General manager
Mike Smith
Assistant general manager
Nick Beverley
Head coach
Brian Sutter
Assistant coaches
Al MacAdam
Denis Savard
Goaltending consultant
Vladislav Tretiak
Scouts
Ron Anderson, Michel Dumas, Bruce
Franklin, Tim Higgins, Sakari Pietela
Manager of team services
Matt Colleran
Head trainers
Michael Gapski

Equipment manager
Troy Parchman
Assistant equipment manager
Bill Stehle
Equipment assistant
Mark DePasquale
Massage therapist
Pawel Prylinski
Exec. director of communications
Jim De Maria
Dir. of community relations/p.r. asst.
Barbara Davidson
Manager of public relations
Tony Ommen
Exec. dir. of marketing/merchandising
Jim Sofranko
Manager, special events
Drew Stevenson
Manager, game operations
Mike Sullivan
Director of ticket operations
James K. Bare
Sales manager
Doug Ryan

DRAFT CHOICES

Rd.— Player	Overall	Pos.	Last team
1— Brent Seabrook	14	D	Lethbridge (WHL)
2— Corey Crawford	52	G	Moncton (QMJHL)
2— Michal Barinka	59	D	Budejovice (Czech Rep.)
5— Lasse Kukkonen	151	D	Karpat (Finland)
5— Alexei Ivanov	156	C	Yaroslavl Jr. (Russia Jr.)
6— Johan Andersson	181	C	Troja (Sweden)
7— Mike Brodeur	211	G	Camrose (AJHL)
8— Dustin Byfuglien	245	D	Prince George (WHL)
9— Michael Grenzy	275	D	Chicago (USHL)
9— Chris Porter	282	C	Lincoln (USHL)

MISCELLANEOUS DATA

Home ice (capacity)
United Center (20,500)
Address
1901 W. Madison Street
Chicago, IL 60612
Business phone
312-455-7000
Ticket information
312-943-7000
Website
www.chicagoblackhawks.com

Training site
Chicago
Club colors
Red, black and white
Radio affiliation
WSCR (670 AM)
TV affiliation
FOX Sports Chicago

CHICAGO BLACKHAWKS

No.	FORWARDS	Ht./Wt.	Place (BORN)	Date	NHL exp.	2002-03 clubs
39	Tyler Arnason (C)	5-11/185	Oklahoma City	3-16-79	2	Chicago
	Ajay Baines (C)	5-10/178	Kamloops. B.C.	3-25-78	0	Norfolk (AHL)
28	Mark Bell (LW)	6-3/198	St. Paul's, Ont.	8-5-80	3	Chicago
19	Kyle Calder (LW)...........	5-11/180	Mannville, Alta.	1-5-79	4	Chicago
55	Eric Daze (LW)..............	6-6/234	Montreal	7-2-75	9	Chicago
14	Theo Fleury (RW)	5-6/180	Oxbow, Sask.	6-29-68	15	Chicago
20	Casey Hankinson (LW) ..	6-1/187	Edina, Minn.	5-8-76	2	Norfolk (AHL)
16	Matt Henderson (RW) ...	6-1/205	White Bear Lake, Minn.	3-1-74	2	Norfolk (AHL)
22	Igor Korolev (C).............	6-1/190	Moscow, U.S.S.R.	9-6-70	11	Norfolk (AHL), Chicago
	Brett McLean (LW)	5-11/175	Comox, B.C.	8-14-78	1	Norfolk (AHL), Chicago
	Travis Moen (LW)	6-2/198	Swift Current, Sask.	4-6-82	0	Norfolk (AHL)
40	Scott Nichol (C).............	5-8/173	Edmonton	12-31-74	4	Calgary
17	Mike Peluso (RW)	6-1/208	Denver	9-2-74	1	Norfolk (AHL)
	Igor Radulov (LW)	6-0/176	Nizhny Tagil, U.S.S.R.	8-23-82	1	Norfolk (AHL), Chicago
	Tuomo Ruutu (C)..........	6-2/196	Vantaa, Finland	2-16-83	0	HIFK Helsinki (Finland)
17	Chris Simon (LW).........	6-4/234	Wawa, Ont.	1-30-72	11	Washington, Chicago
	Mike Souza (LW/C).......	6-1/190	Melrose, Mass.	1-28-78	0	Norfolk (AHL), Bridgeport (AHL)
26	Steve Sullivan (RW)	5-9/160	Timmins, Ont.	7-6-74	8	Chicago
	Shawn Thornton (RW) ..	6-2/210	Oshawa, Ont.	7-23-79	1	Norfolk (AHL), Chicago
14	R. VandenBussche (RW)	6-0/200	Simcoe, Ont.	2-28-73	7	Norfolk (AHL), Chicago
	Pavel Vorobiev (RW)	6-0/183	Karaganda, U.S.S.R.	5-5-82	0	Lokomotiv Yaroslavl (Russian)
	Mikhail Yakubov (C)	6-3/185	Bamaul, U.S.S.R.	2-16-82	0	Norfolk (AHL)
13	Alex Zhamnov (C)..........	6-1/200	Moscow, U.S.S.R.	10-1-70	11	Chicago
	DEFENSEMEN					
	Anton Babchuk	6-4/194	Kiev, U.S.S.R.	5-6-84	0	St. Petersburg (Russian Div. II)
	Nathan Dempsey	6-0/190	Spruce Grove, Alta.	7-14-74	5	Chicago
6	Sami Helenius	6-5/225	Helsinki, Finland	1-22-74	6	Utah (AHL), Chicago, Dallas
	Burke Henry.................	6-3/190	Ste. Rose, Man.	1-21-79	1	Norfolk (AHL), Chicago
	Kent Huskins	6-2/190	Ottawa	5-4-79	0	Norfolk (AHL)
25	Alexander Karpovtsev	6-3/215	Moscow, U.S.S.R.	4-7-70	10	Chicago
	Duncan Keith	6-0/168	Winnipeg	7-16-83	0	Kelowna (WHL), Univ. of Michigan (CCHA)
42	Jon Klemm	6-3/200	Cranbrook, B.C.	1-8-70	11	Chicago
5	Steve McCarthy	6-0/197	Trail, B.C.	2-3-81	4	Norfolk (AHL), Chicago
8	Steve Poapst.................	5-11/199	Cornwall, Ont.	1-3-69	5	Chicago
34	Jason Strudwick...........	6-3/220	Edmonton	7-17-75	7	Chicago
	Dmitri Tolkunov	6-2/191	Kiev, U.S.S.R.	5-5-79	0	Norfolk (AHL)
	GOALTENDERS					
	Mike Leighton................	6-2/175	Petrolia, Ont.	5-18-81	1	Norfolk (AHL), Chicago
29	Steve Passmore............	5-9/165	Thunder Bay, Ont.	1-29-73	5	Norfolk (AHL), Chicago
41	Jocelyn Thibault	5-11/170	Montreal	1-12-75	10	Chicago

2002-03 REVIEW
INDIVIDUAL STATISTICS

SCORING

	Games	G	A	Pts.	PIM	+/-	PPG	SHG	GWG	GTG	Sht.	Sht. Pct.	Faceoffs Won	Lost	Pct.	TOI
Steve Sullivan...........	82	26	35	61	42	15	4	2	3	0	190	13.7	176	206	46.1	19:15
Alexei Zhamnov.........	74	15	43	58	70	0	2	3	1	0	166	9.0	690	655	51.3	21:05
Eric Daze	54	22	22	44	14	10	3	0	5	0	170	12.9	1	3	25.0	16:16
Kyle Calder	82	15	27	42	40	-6	7	0	2	0	164	9.1	1	3	25.0	16:43
Tyler Arnason	82	19	20	39	20	7	3	0	6	0	178	10.7	252	374	40.3	14:30
Theo Fleury	54	12	21	33	77	-7	1	0	3	1	124	9.7	186	160	53.8	16:44
Sergei Berezin*	66	18	13	31	8	-3	5	0	0	0	171	10.5	7	8	46.7	16:18
Mark Bell..................	82	14	15	29	113	0	0	2	0	0	127	11.0	198	179	52.5	14:04
Phil Housley*	57	6	23	29	24	7	2	0	2	0	134	4.5	1	0	100.0	19:23
Nathan Dempsey.......	67	5	23	28	26	-7	1	0	2	0	124	4.0	0	0	—	20:54
Andrei Nikolishin.......	60	6	15	21	26	-3	0	1	0	0	73	8.2	536	411	56.6	17:01
Chris Simon*	61	12	6	18	125	-4	2	0	2	1	72	16.7	1	4	20.0	11:05
Steve Thomas*	69	4	13	17	51	0	0	0	1	0	91	4.4	7	12	36.8	12:44
Jon Klemm...............	70	2	14	16	44	-9	1	0	1	0	74	2.7	0	2	0.0	21:57
Alexander Karpovtsev	40	4	10	14	12	-8	3	0	1	0	36	11.1	0	0	—	21:40
Steve Poapst............	75	2	11	13	50	14	0	0	0	0	49	4.1	0	0	—	22:51
Mike Eastwood*	53	2	10	12	24	-6	0	0	0	0	32	6.3	380	333	53.3	12:54
Lyle Odelein*............	65	7	4	11	76	7	0	0	0	0	77	9.1	1	0	100.0	19:05

	Games	G	A	Pts.	PIM	+/-	PPG	SHG	GWG	GTG	Sht.	Sht. Pct.	Faceoffs Won	Lost	Pct.	TOI
Igor Korolev	48	4	5	9	30	-1	1	0	1	0	32	12.5	159	216	42.4	13:38
Igor Radulov	7	5	0	5	4	-3	3	0	0	0	14	35.7	0	0	—	15:06
Jason Strudwick	48	2	3	5	87	-4	0	0	0	0	19	10.5	0	3	0.0	8:31
Steve McCarthy	57	1	4	5	23	-1	0	0	0	0	55	1.8	0	0	—	16:24
Boris Mironov*	20	3	1	4	22	-1	1	0	0	1	14	21.4	0	0	—	19:12
Michael Nylander*	9	0	4	4	4	0	0	0	0	0	20	0.0	42	44	48.8	15:19
Shawn Thornton	13	1	1	2	31	-4	0	0	0	0	15	6.7	2	1	66.7	8:30
Burke Henry	16	0	2	2	9	-13	0	0	0	0	25	0.0	0	0	—	18:32
Todd Gill	5	0	1	1	0	3	0	0	0	0	9	0.0	0	0	—	19:31
Peter White	6	0	1	1	0	0	0	0	0	0	2	0.0	23	35	39.7	9:00
Sami Helenius*	10	0	1	1	28	3	0	0	0	0	5	0.0	0	0	—	11:15
Garry Valk	16	0	1	1	6	0	0	0	0	0	9	0.0	2	2	50.0	9:49
Brett McLean	2	0	0	0	0	-1	0	0	0	0	1	0.0	5	14	26.3	10:47
Louie DeBrusk	4	0	0	0	7	0	0	0	0	0	0	—	0	0	—	6:09
Craig Andersson (g)	6	0	0	0	0	0	0	0	0	0	0	—	0	0	—	—
Michael Leighton (g)	8	0	0	0	0	0	0	0	0	0	0	—	0	0	—	—
Steve Passmore (g)	11	0	0	0	4	0	0	0	0	0	0	—	0	0	—	—
Ryan VandenBussche	22	0	0	0	58	0	0	0	0	0	7	0.0	1	0	100.0	6:30
Jocelyn Thibault (g)	62	0	0	0	4	0	0	0	0	0	0	—	0	0	—	—

GOALTENDING

	Games	GS	Min.	GA	SO	Avg.	W	L	T	EN	PPG Allow	SHG Allow	Shots	Save Pct.
Jocelyn Thibault	62	62	3650	144	8	2.37	26	28	7	4	39	5	1690	.915
Michael Leighton	8	6	447	21	1	2.82	2	3	2	1	3	1	241	.913
Steve Passmore	11	9	617	38	0	3.70	2	5	2	0	8	2	284	.866
Craig Andersson	6	5	270	18	0	4.00	0	3	2	0	6	0	125	.856

RESULTS

OCTOBER
10— At Columbus .... L 1-2
13— Buffalo .... W 3-0
17— Florida .... W 4-1
19— Calgary .... L 2-5
24— Minnesota .... L 2-3
26— At Carolina .... T *3-3
27— San Jose .... W 3-2
29— Columbus .... W 3-2
31— Los Angeles .... W *2-1

NOVEMBER
2— At New Jersey .... L 1-5
3— Edmonton .... L 1-4
5— At Detroit .... W 2-0
7— Atlanta .... W 5-0
9— At Tampa Bay .... W *3-2
11— At Florida .... T *2-2
15— Washington .... T *2-2
17— Nashville .... W 4-2
19— At Edmonton .... L 1-3
20— At Vancouver .... L 3-5
23— At Calgary .... L 1-3
25— At Colorado .... L 0-1
28— At Phoenix .... W 4-2
30— At Los Angeles .... L 1-4

DECEMBER
1— At Anaheim .... L 2-3
4— Ottawa .... W 1-0
6— Anaheim .... L 3-4
8— Tampa Bay .... W 3-1

10— At N.Y. Islanders .... W 3-2
11— At N.Y. Rangers .... W 4-3
13— At Buffalo .... T *1-1
15— Dallas .... L 0-5
17— Vancouver .... W 3-2
20— Columbus .... W 3-1
22— Los Angeles .... W 3-1
26— Minnesota .... T *2-2
28— At San Jose .... T *3-3
30— At Los Angeles .... W 2-0

JANUARY
2— At St. Louis .... W 4-1
4— At Nashville .... T *3-3
5— Detroit .... OTL *3-4
8— Phoenix .... T *0-0
9— At Dallas .... OTL ... *3-4
12— Nashville .... W 2-0
13— At Detroit .... OTL *4-5
15— Detroit .... W 4-1
17— Vancouver .... L 2-4
18— At St. Louis .... L 2-4
20— At Columbus .... L 1-5
23— St. Louis .... T *3-3
25— At Pittsburgh .... L 3-5
26— At Montreal .... L 3-4
30— At Boston .... W 3-1

FEBRUARY
5— At Minnesota .... L 1-2
6— At Calgary .... T *2-2
8— At Edmonton .... W 3-0

10— At Vancouver .... L 1-2
12— Toronto .... L 1-3
14— San Jose .... L 2-4
15— At Columbus .... W 7-1
17— Colorado .... L 4-5
20— Phoenix .... L 1-2
23— Dallas .... L 0-3
25— Philadelphia .... L 0-2
27— At Philadelphia .... L 2-5

MARCH
1— At Nashville .... OTL ... *4-5
2— Colorado .... OTL ... *2-3
5— At Dallas .... L 4-7
7— Calgary .... L 0-2
9— Boston .... W 8-5
12— At Anaheim .... L 2-5
14— At Phoenix .... W 4-0
17— At San Jose .... W ... *3-2
19— Anaheim .... L 3-4
22— At Colorado .... L 1-8
23— Pittsburgh .... T ... *1-1
25— N.Y. Islanders .... L 2-9
27— Nashville .... W 4-1
28— At Minnesota .... OTL *3-4
30— Edmonton .... T ... *4-4

APRIL
3— At St. Louis .... W 6-4
4— St. Louis .... T ... *2-2
6— Detroit .... W ... *4-3
*Denotes overtime game.

COLORADO AVALANCHE
WESTERN CONFERENCE/NORTHWEST DIVISION

COLORADO AVALANCHE

Avalanche Schedule
Home games shaded; D=Day game; *Feb. 8 All-Star Game at St. Paul, Minn.

October

SUN	MON	TUE	WED	THU	FRI	SAT
5	6	7	8	9	10 CHI	11
12 STL	13	14	15	16 MIN	17	18 EDM
19	20	21 BOS	22	23 EDM	24	25 NAS
26 BUF	27	28 CAL	29	30	31	

November

SUN	MON	TUE	WED	THU	FRI	SAT
					1 NJ	D
2 NYR	3	4 MIN	5	6 PHO	7	8
9 CHI	10	11 SJ	12	13 PHO	14	15 DAL
16	17	18 ANA	19	20 NYR	21	22 LA
23	24 NAS	25	26	27 CAL	28 EDM	29
30 NJ						

December

SUN	MON	TUE	WED	THU	FRI	SAT
	1	2	3	4 SJ	5	6 CBJ
7	8 WAS	9	10	11 VAN	12	13 CAL
14	15	16	17 MIN	18	19 ANA	20 LA
21	22	23	24	25	26 STL	27 PHI
28	29 VAN	30	31 CAL			

January

SUN	MON	TUE	WED	THU	FRI	SAT
				1	2 VAN	3
4 MIN	5	6 CBJ	7	8 NAS	9	10 D DAL
11 CHI	12	13 ANA	14	15 DAL	16	17 SJ
18	19 TB	20	21 FLA	22 ATL	23	24 PIT
25	26	27 EDM	28	29 LA	30 ANA	31

February

SUN	MON	TUE	WED	THU	FRI	SAT
1	2	3 CAR	4	5 DET	6	7
8*	9	10 NYI	11	12 STL	13	14 D DET
15	16 VAN	17	18 EDM	19	20 DAL	21
22 MIN	23	24 CAL	25	26 STL	27	28 CBJ
29						

March

SUN	MON	TUE	WED	THU	FRI	SAT
	1 TB	2	3 VAN	4	5 SJ	6
7 D CAL	8 VAN	9	10 EDM	11	12 PHO	13
14 D PHO	15	16 MON	17	18 OTT	19	20 TOR
21	22	23 CHI	24	25 DET	26	27 D DET
28	29 LA	30	31 MIN			

April

SUN	MON	TUE	WED	THU	FRI	SAT
				1	2 CBJ	3
4 D NAS	5	6	7	8	9	10

2003-04 SEASON
CLUB DIRECTORY

Assistant to the general manager
Greg Sherman

Owner & governor
E. Stanley Kroenke

Alternate governor, president & general manager
Pierre Lacroix

Head coach
Tony Granato

Assistant coaches
Jacques Cloutier, Rick Tocchet

Goaltending consultant
Craig Billington

Vice president of player personnel
Michel Goulet

Assistant to the general manager
Greg Sherman

Director of hockey operations
Eric Lacroix

Director of hockey administration
Charlotte Grahame

Video coordinator
Jason Grahame

Team services assistant
Ronnie Jameson

Hockey administration assistant
Andrea Furness

Chief scout
Jim Hammett

Pro scouts
Brad Smith, Garth Joy

Scouts
Glen Cochrane, Yvon Gendron, Alan Hepple, Kirill Ladygin, Chris O'Sullivan, Don Paarup, Richard Pracey

European scout
Joni Lehto

Computer research consultant
John Donohue

Strength and conditioning coach
Paul Goldberg

Head athletic trainer
Pat Karns

Assistant athletic trainer
Matt Sokolowski

Massage therapist
Gregorio Pradera

Inventory manager
Wayne Flemming

Head equipment manager
Mark Miller

Assistant equipment managers
Terry Geer, Cliff Halstead

Vice president, communications & team services
Jean Martineau

Dir. of special projects/communications
Hayne Ellis

Assistant director of media relations
Damen Zier

DRAFT CHOICES

Rd.— Player	Overall	Pos.	Last team
2— David Liffiton	63	D	Plymouth (OHL)
4— David Svagrovsky	131	RW	Seattle (WHL)
5— Mark McCutcheon	146	C	New England (EJHL)
5— Brad Richardson	163	C	Owen Sound (OHL)
7— Linus Videll	204	LW	Sodertalje Jr. (Sweden Jr.)
7— Brett Hemingway	225	W	Coquitlam (BCHL)
8— Darryl Yacboski	257	D	Regina (WHL)
9— David Jones	288	RW	Coquitlam (BCHL)

MISCELLANEOUS DATA

Home ice (capacity)
Pepsi Center (18,007)

Address
1000 Chopper Cr.
Denver, CO 80204

Business phone
303-405-1100

Ticket information
303-405-1111

Website
www.coloradoavalanche.com

Training site
Denver

Club colors
Burgundy, silver, blue and black

Radio affiliation
KKFN (950 AM)

TV affiliation
FOX Sports Net Rocky Mountain, KTVD UPN-20

			——— BORN ———		NHL	
No.	FORWARDS	Ht./Wt.	Place	Date	exp.	2002-03 clubs
49	Serge Aubin (C)	6-0/190	Val d'Or, Que.	2-15-75	5	Colorado
13	Bates Battaglia (LW)	6-2/205	Chicago	12-13-75	6	Colorado, Carolina
	Eric Bertrand (LW)	6-1/205	St. Ephrem, Que.	4-16-75	2	Hershey (AHL)
	Danny Bois (RW)	6-0/192	Thunder Bay, Ont.	6-1-83	0	
	Travis Brigley (RW)	6-1/200	Coronation, Alta.	6-16-77	2	Cincinnati (AHL), Hershey (AHL)
	Steve Brule (RW)	6-0/200	Montreal	1-15-75	2	Hershey (AHL), Colorado
	Pierre-Luc Emond (C)	6-0/193	Valleyfield, Que.	10-10-82	0	Hershey (AHL)
20	Kelly Fairchild (C)	5-11/195	Hibbing, Minn.	4-9-73	5	
21	Peter Forsberg (C)	6-0/190	Ornskoldsvik, Sweden	7-20-73	9	Colorado
32	Riku Hahl (C)	6-0/190	Hameenlinna, Finland	11-1-80	2	Hershey (AHL), Colorado
23	Milan Hejduk (RW)	5-11/185	Usti-nad-Labem, Czech.	2-14-76	5	Colorado
13	Dan Hinote (RW)	6-0/190	Leesburg, Fla.	1-30-77	4	Colorado
	Jonas Johansson (RW)	6-1/180	Jonkoping, Sweden	3-18-84	0	Kamloops (WCHL)
	Paul Kariya (LW)	5-10/180	Vancouver	10-16-74	9	Anaheim
12	Mike Keane (RW)	6-0/185	Winnipeg	5-29-67	15	Colorado
37	Jordan Krestanovich (LW)	6-0/170	Langley, B.C.	6-14-81	1	Hershey (AHL)
	Mikhail Kuleshov (LW)	6-2/200	Perm, U.S.S.R.	1-7-81	0	Hershey (AHL)
9	Brad Larsen (LW)	6-0/210	Nakusp, B.C.	6-28-77	4	Hershey (AHL), Colorado
	Cail MacLean (RW)	5-11/202	Halifax, Nova Scotia	9-30-76	0	Hershey (AHL)
	Cody McCormick (C/RW)	6-2/200	London, Ont.	4-18-83	0	Belleville (OHL)
36	Steve Moore (C)	6-2/190	Windsor, Ont.	9-22-78	2	Hershey (AHL), Colorado
13	Andrei Nikolishin (C)	6-0/213	Vorkuta, U.S.S.R.	3-25-73	9	Chicago
19	Joe Sakic (C)	5-11/190	Burnaby, B.C.	7-7-69	15	Colorado
8	Teemu Selanne (RW)	6-0/200	Helsinki, Finland	7-3-70	11	San Jose
11	Jeff Shantz (C)	6-0/200	Duchess, Alta.	10-10-73	10	Colorado
	Charlie Stephens (C/RW)	6-4/225	Nilestown, Ont.	4-5-81	1	Hershey (AHL)
40	Alex Tanguay (LW)	6-0/190	Ste.-Justine, Que.	11-21-79	4	Colorado
50	Brian Willsie (RW)	6-0/190	London, Ont.	3-16-78	3	Hershey (AHL), Colorado
	Peter Worrell (LW)	6-6/235	Pierrefonds, Que.	8-18-77	6	Florida
	DEFENSEMEN					
4	Rob Blake	6-4/220	Simcoe, Ont.	12-10-69	14	Colorado
	Johnny Boychuk	6-2/209	Edmonton	1-19-84	0	Moose Jaw (WHL)
29	Brett Clark	6-1/185	Wapella, Sask.	12-23-76	5	Hershey (AHL)
	Dale Clarke	6-1/193	Belleville, Ont.	3-23-78	1	Hershey (AHL), Cincinnati (AHL)
52	Adam Foote	6-1/202	Toronto	7-10-71	12	Colorado
24	Chris McAllister	6-8/225	Saskatoon, Sask.	6-16-75	6	Philadelphia (AHL), Philadelphia, Colorado
53	Derek Morris	6-0/200	Edmonton	8-24-78	6	Colorado
2	Bryan Muir	6-4/220	Winnipeg	6-8-73	8	Colorado
	Jeff Paul	6-3/203	London, Ont.	3-1-78	1	Hershey (AHL), Colorado
41	Martin Skoula	6-3/218	Litomerice, Czechoslovakia	10-28-79	4	Colorado
3	Karlis Skrastins	6-1/205	Riga, U.S.S.R.	7-9-74	5	Nashville
	Tomas Slovak	6-1/191	Kosice, Czechoslovakia	4-5-83	0	Kelowna (WHL)
	D.J. Smith	6-2/205	Windsor, Ont.	5-13-77	3	Hershey (AHL), Colorado
22	Brent Thompson	6-2/205	Calgary	1-9-71	6	Hershey (AHL)
	GOALTENDERS					
1	David Aebischer	6-1/185	Fribourg, Switzerland	2-7-78	3	Colorado
	Peter Budaj	6-0/200	Banska Bystrica, Czech.	9-18-82	0	Quad City (UHL), Missouri (UHL)
	Philippe Sauve	6-0/175	Buffalo	2-27-80	0	Hershey (AHL)

2002-03 REVIEW
INDIVIDUAL STATISTICS

SCORING

	Games	G	A	Pts.	PIM	+/-	PPG	SHG	GWG	GTG	Sht.	Sht. Pct.	Faceoffs Won	Faceoffs Lost	Faceoffs Pct.	TOI
Peter Forsberg	75	29	77	106	70	52	8	0	2	0	166	17.5	333	376	47.0	19:19
Milan Hejduk	82	50	48	98	32	52	18	0	4	1	244	20.5	19	24	44.2	19:50
Alex Tanguay	82	26	41	67	36	34	3	0	5	2	142	18.3	48	75	39.0	17:48
Joe Sakic	58	26	32	58	24	4	8	0	1	0	190	13.7	690	669	50.8	21:12
Steve Reinprecht	77	18	33	51	18	-6	2	1	1	0	146	12.3	431	497	46.4	17:22
Derek Morris	75	11	37	48	68	16	9	0	7	0	191	5.8	0	0	—	23:49
Rob Blake	79	17	28	45	57	20	8	2	3	0	269	6.3	0	0	—	26:21
Greg de Vries	82	6	26	32	70	15	0	0	2	0	112	5.4	1	0	100.0	22:15
Adam Foote	78	11	20	31	88	30	3	0	2	0	106	10.4	0	0	—	25:42

	Games	G	A	Pts.	PIM	+/-	PPG	SHG	GWG	GTG	Sht.	Sht. Pct.	Faceoffs Won	Lost	Pct.	TOI
Radim Vrbata*	66	11	19	30	16	0	3	0	4	1	171	6.4	7	7	50.0	13:54
Martin Skoula	81	4	21	25	68	11	2	0	0	0	93	4.3	1	0	100.0	18:27
Dean McAmmond	41	10	8	18	10	1	2	0	2	0	72	13.9	5	4	55.6	14:24
Eric Messier	72	4	10	14	16	-2	0	1	1	0	52	7.7	3	14	17.6	12:20
Dan Hinote	60	6	4	10	49	4	0	0	3	0	65	9.2	102	116	46.8	10:36
Mike Keane	65	5	5	10	34	0	0	1	1	1	35	14.3	20	82	19.6	12:14
Serge Aubin	66	4	6	10	64	-2	0	0	1	0	62	6.5	308	305	50.2	11:57
Vaclav Nedorost	42	4	5	9	20	8	1	0	0	0	35	11.4	67	84	44.4	10:29
Jeff Shantz	74	3	6	9	35	-12	0	0	2	0	68	4.4	455	419	52.1	11:27
Riku Hahl	42	3	4	7	12	3	0	0	0	0	61	4.9	26	43	37.7	11:02
Bates Battaglia*	13	1	5	6	10	-2	1	0	1	0	27	3.7	0	3	0.0	15:19
Scott Parker	43	1	3	4	82	6	0	0	0	0	20	5.0	0	0	—	6:15
Brad Larsen	6	0	3	3	2	3	0	0	0	0	6	0.0	13	18	41.9	8:17
Bryan Marchment*	14	0	3	3	33	4	0	0	0	0	18	0.0	0	0	—	16:41
Bryan Muir	32	0	2	2	19	3	0	0	0	0	9	0.0	0	0	—	6:32
D.J. Smith	34	1	0	1	55	2	0	0	0	0	7	14.3	0	0	—	3:48
Brian Willsie	12	0	1	1	15	0	0	0	0	0	12	0.0	1	6	14.3	9:36
Chris McAllister*	14	0	1	1	26	6	0	0	0	0	4	0.0	0	0	—	8:02
Steve Brule	2	0	0	0	0	0	0	0	0	0	2	0.0	0	0	—	9:06
Jeff Paul	2	0	0	0	7	0	0	0	0	0	0	—	0	0	—	3:31
Charlie Stephens	2	0	0	0	0	0	0	0	0	0	1	0.0	0	0	—	5:19
Steve Moore	4	0	0	0	0	0	0	0	0	0	0	—	7	16	30.4	8:55
David Aebischer (g)	22	0	0	0	4	0	0	0	0	0	0	—	0	0	—	—
Patrick Roy (g)	63	0	0	0	20	0	0	0	0	0	0	—	0	0	—	—

GOALTENDING

	Games	GS	Min.	GA	SO	Avg.	W	L	T	EN	PPG Allow	SHG Allow	Shots	Save Pct.
Patrick Roy	63	63	3769	137	5	2.18	35	15	13	3	46	5	1723	.920
David Aebischer	22	19	1235	50	1	2.43	7	12	0	4	17	1	593	.916

*Played with two or more NHL teams.

RESULTS

OCTOBER

9— Dallas .... T *1-1
14— Boston .... L 1-2
17— At Los Angeles .... W 4-1
19— At San Jose .... W 3-1
20— At Anaheim .... OTL *2-3
22— Edmonton .... T *3-3
24— At Phoenix .... W 3-2
27— Minnesota .... T *3-3
29— At Minnesota .... OTL *2-3
31— At Vancouver .... W 5-1

NOVEMBER

2— At Calgary .... T *4-4
4— Vancouver .... L 2-4
6— Ottawa .... L 2-5
8— Anaheim .... OTL *2-3
10— Nashville .... L 3-4
12— Columbus .... W 5-4
14— At Nashville .... W 3-1
15— At Dallas .... L 2-4
17— At Phoenix .... T *4-4
21— Nashville .... T *1-1
23— At St. Louis .... W 3-1
25— Chicago .... W 1-0
27— St. Louis .... T *4-4
29— At Minnesota .... T *2-2
30— At Edmonton .... L 0-1

DECEMBER

3— Calgary .... L 1-2
6— Montreal .... W *7-6

11— At Vancouver .... L 1-3
13— At Edmonton .... OTL *3-4
14— At Calgary .... W 3-1
16— Washington .... T *2-2
19— Edmonton .... W 2-1
21— Minnesota .... W 4-2
23— Vancouver .... W 5-3
26— At St. Louis .... L 2-3
27— Philadelphia .... OTL *1-2
29— Los Angeles .... W 6-1

JANUARY

1— At Nashville .... W 7-3
2— Florida .... L 1-4
4— At San Jose .... W 6-1
7— Calgary .... L 2-4
9— Anaheim .... L 3-5
11— At Dallas .... L 3-6
12— At Carolina .... W *3-2
16— Detroit .... L 2-4
20— Dallas .... T *1-1
23— Columbus .... W 5-0
25— At Toronto .... W 3-0
28— At Columbus .... T *2-2
30— At N.Y. Rangers .... W *4-3

FEBRUARY

4— At Boston .... W *3-2
6— At Detroit .... W 1-0
8— Detroit .... W 5-3
9— Calgary .... W 4-2
11— New Jersey .... W 3-1

13— At Vancouver .... OTL *1-2
15— Minnesota .... W 3-2
17— At Chicago .... W 5-4
20— At Pittsburgh .... W 5-2
21— At N.Y. Islanders .... L 1-4
23— N.Y. Rangers .... W 4-1
25— Edmonton .... W 4-2
27— Atlanta .... OTL *3-4

MARCH

1— Pittsburgh .... W 4-1
2— At Chicago .... W *3-2
5— At Florida .... W 3-1
7— At Tampa Bay .... L 3-4
8— At Philadelphia .... W *2-1
10— Phoenix .... T *2-2
13— At Columbus .... W 5-1
15— At Detroit .... L 3-5
16— At Washington .... L 1-2
20— San Jose .... W 2-0
22— Chicago .... W 8-1
24— At Buffalo .... OTL *3-4
25— At Ottawa .... T *2-2
27— Los Angeles .... W 3-0
29— Phoenix .... W 6-1
31— San Jose .... W 3-1

APRIL

2— At Los Angeles .... L 3-5
4— At Anaheim .... W *4-3
6— St. Louis .... W 5-2
*Denotes overtime game.

COLUMBUS BLUE JACKETS
WESTERN CONFERENCE/CENTRAL DIVISION

Blue Jackets' Schedule
Home games shaded; D=Day game; *Feb. 8 All-Star Game at St. Paul, Minn.

October

SUN	MON	TUE	WED	THU	FRI	SAT
5	6	7	8	9 ATL	10	11 NYR
12	13 VAN	14	15	16 CHI	17	18 NAS
19	20	21	22 DET	23 TB	24	25 DAL
26	27	28 VAN	29	30 EDM	31	

November

SUN	MON	TUE	WED	THU	FRI	SAT
						1 CAL
2	3	4	5	6	7 ATL	8
9 CAL	10	11 MON	12	13 OTT	14 BOS	15
16 PHO	17	18	19 DET	20 DET	21	22 NYI
23	24	25 EDM	26 NAS	27	28	29 WAS
30						

December

SUN	MON	TUE	WED	THU	FRI	SAT
	1	2 ANA	3	4 NAS	5	6 COL
7	8	9	10 PHI	11	12 STL	13 PIT
14	15	16 STL	17	18	19 CAL	20 MIN
21	22	23 PHO	24	25	26 CHI	27 DAL
28	29 STL	30	31 SJ			

January

SUN	MON	TUE	WED	THU	FRI	SAT
				1	2 D TB	3 FLA
4	5	6 COL	7	8 SJ	9	10 LA
11 ANA	12	13	14	15 STL	16 LA	17
18 EDM	19	20	21 STL	22 CHI	23	24 CHI
25	26	27 NJ	28	29 NAS	30	31 MIN

February

SUN	MON	TUE	WED	THU	FRI	SAT
1	2 PHO	3	4 DAL	5	6	7
8*	9	10	11 LA	12 TOR	13	14 SJ
15	16 NAS	17	18 ANA	19	20 PHO	21 LA
22	23 SJ	24	25 CHI	26	27 CHI	28 COL
29						

March

SUN	MON	TUE	WED	THU	FRI	SAT
	1	2 CAR	3 DAL	4	5	6 VAN
7	8 CAR	9	10	11 DET	12	13 STL
14 MIN	15	16 EDM	17	18 CAL	19	20
21 VAN	22	23	24 MIN	25	26 ANA	27 NAS
28	29 BUF	30	31 DET			

April

SUN	MON	TUE	WED	THU	FRI	SAT
				1	2 COL	3 DET
4	5	6	7	8	9	10

2003-04 SEASON
CLUB DIRECTORY

Owner/governor
John H. McConnell
Alternate governor
John P. McConnell
G.m./head coach/alternate governor
Doug MacLean
Exec. v.p./assistant general manager
Jim Clark
Associate coach
Newell Brown
Assistant coach
Gord Murphy
Goaltending coach
Rick Wamsley
Director of amateur scouting
Don Boyd
Director of player development
Paul Castron

Director of pro scouting
Bob Strumm
Hockey operations manager
Chris MacFarland
Strength and conditioning coach
Mark Casterline
Athletic trainer
Chris Mizer
Equipment manager
Tim LeRoy
Assistant equipment manager
Jamie Healy
Director of communications
Todd Sharrock
Assistant director of communications
Jason Rothwell
Manager of multimedia
TBA

DRAFT CHOICES

Rd.— Player	Overall	Pos.	Last team
1— Nikolai Zherdev	4	RW	Russia
2— Dan Fritsche	46	C	Sarnia (OHL)
3— Dimitri Kosmachev	71	D	CSKA (Russia)
4— Kevin Jarman	103	LW	Stouffville (Ont. Prov. Jr. A)
4— Philippe Dupuis	104	C	Hull (QMJHL)
5— Arsi Piispanen	138	RW	Jokerit Jr. (Finland Jr.)
6— Marc Methot	168	D	London (OHL)
7— Alexander Guskov	200	D	Yaroslavl (Russia)
8— Mathieu Gravel	233	LW	Shawinigan (QMJHL)
9— Trevor Hendrikx	283	D	Peterborough (OHL)

MISCELLANEOUS DATA

Home ice (capacity)
Nationwide Arena (18,136)
Office address
Nationwide Arena
200 W. Nationwide Blvd.
Columbus, OH 43215
Business phone
614-246-4625
Ticket information
1-800-645-2657
Website
www.bluejackets.com

Training site
Columbus
Club colors
Red, white, blue, silver and electric
green
Radio affiliation
WBNS (1460 AM), WWCD (101.1 FM)
TV affiliation
Fox Sports Net Ohio

TRAINING CAMP ROSTER

COLUMBUS BLUE JACKETS

No.	FORWARDS	Ht./Wt.	BORN Place	Date	NHL exp.	2002-03 clubs
38	Blake Bellefeuille (C)	5-10/208	Framingham, Mass.	12-27-77	2	Syracuse (AHL), Columbus
25	Andrew Cassels (C)	6-1/185	Bramalea, Ont.	7-23-69	14	Columbus
19	Mathieu Darche (LW)	6-1/225	St. Laurent, Que.	11-26-76	3	Syracuse (AHL), Columbus
49	Matt Davidson (RW)	6-2/190	Flin Flon, Man.	8-9-77	3	Syracuse (AHL), Columbus
9	Mark Hartigan (C)	6-0/200	Fort St. John, B.C.	10-15-77	2	Chicago (AHL), Atlanta
	Hannes Hyvonen (RW)	6-2/200	Oulu, Finland	8-29-75	2	Columbus
	Tim Jackman (RW)	6-2/190	Minot, N.D.	11-14-81	0	Syracuse (AHL)
	Ben Knopp (LW)	6-0/185	Calgary	4-8-82	0	Dayton (ECHL), Syracuse (AHL)
21	Espen Knutsen (C)	5-11/180	Oslo, Norway	1-12-72	4	Columbus
18	Robert Kron (C)	5-11/182	Brno, Czechoslovakia	2-27-67	12	Lukko (Finland)
10	Trevor Letowski (RW)	5-10/180	Thunder Bay, Ont.	4-5-77	5	Vancouver
	Joakim Lindstrom (LW)	6-0/187	Skelleftea, Sweden	12-5-83	0	MoDo Ornskoldsvik (Sweden)
	David Ling (RW)	5-9/185	Halifax, Nova Scotia	1-9-75	4	Syracuse (AHL), Columbus
33	Don MacLean (C)	6-2/199	Sydney, Nova Scotia	1-14-77	3	Syracuse (AHL)
26	Todd Marchant (C)	5-10/178	Buffalo	8-12-73	10	Edmonton
	Kent McDonnell (RW)	6-2/198	Cornwall, Ont.	3-1-79	1	Syracuse (AHL), Columbus
40	Brad Moran (C)	5-11/180	Abbotsford, B.C.	3-20-79	1	Syracuse (AHL)
	Rick Nash (LW)	6-3/188	Brampton, Ont.	6-16-84	1	Columbus
26	Andrej Nedorost (C)	6-1/198	Trencin, Czechoslovakia	4-30-80	2	Syracuse (AHL), Columbus
	Mike Pandolfo (LW)	6-3/226	Winchester, Mass.	9-15-79	0	Syracuse (AHL)
	Martin Paroulek (LW)	5-11/187	Uherske Hradisti, Czech.	11-4-79	0	Syracuse (AHL)
	Lasse Pirjeta (C)	6-3/222	Oulu, Finland	4-4-74	1	Columbus
12	Sean Pronger (C)	6-3/210	Dryden, Ont.	11-30-72	7	Columbus
	Jeremy Reich (LW)	6-1/190	Craik, Sask.	2-11-79	0	Syracuse (AHL)
8	Geoff Sanderson (LW)	6-0/190	Hay River, NW Territories	2-1-72	13	Columbus
	Jonathan Schill (LW)	6-1/201	Kitchener, Ont.	6-28-79	0	Dayton (ECHL), Syracuse (AHL)
45	Jody Shelley (LW)	6-3/230	Yarmouth, Nova Scotia	2-7-76	3	Columbus
	Martin Spanhel (LW)	6-2/202	Zlin, Czechoslovakia	7-1-77	2	Sparta Praha (Czech Republic)
15	Petr Tenkrat (RW)	6-1/185	Kladno, Czechoslovakia	5-31-77	2	Karpat Oulu (Finland)
9	David Vyborny (RW)	5-10/183	Jihlava, Czechoslovakia	6-2-75	3	Columbus
14	Ray Whitney (LW)	5-10/175	Fort Saskatchewan, Alta.	5-8-72	12	Columbus
28	Tyler Wright (C)	5-11/187	Canora, Sask.	4-6-73	11	Columbus
	DEFENSEMEN					
33	Jamie Allison	6-1/195	Lindsay, Ont.	5-13-75	8	Columbus
32	Radim Bicanek	6-1/195	Uherske Hradiste, Czech.	1-18-75	7	Syracuse (AHL), Binghamton (AHL)
34	Jean-Luc Grand-Pierre	6-3/207	Montreal	2-2-77	5	Columbus
	Scott Heffernan	6-5/187	Montreal	3-9-82	0	Dayton (ECHL)
	Aaron Johnson	6-0/186	Point Hawksbury, N.S.	4-30-83	1	Rimouski (QMJHL),
44	Rostislav Klesla	6-3/206	Novy Jicin, Czechoslovakia	3-21-82	3	Columbus
	Scott Lachance	6-1/212	Charlottesville, Va.	10-22-72	12	Columbus
	Paul Manning	6-4/193	Red Deer, Alta.	4-15-79	1	Syracuse (AHL), Columbus
22	Luke Richardson	6-3/210	Ottawa	3-26-69	16	Columbus
	Darrel Scoville	6-3/215	Regina, Sask.	10-13-75	2	Syracuse (AHL), Columbus
	Tyler Sloan	6-4/190	Calgary	3-15-81	0	Dayton (ECHL), Syracuse (AHL)
3	Jaroslav Spacek	5-11/198	Rokycany, Czechoslovakia	2-11-74	5	Columbus
5	Darryl Sydor	6-1/205	Edmonton	5-13-72	12	Dallas
20	Darren Van Impe	6-1/205	Saskatoon, Sask.	5-18-73	9	Syracuse (AHL), Columbus
23	Derrick Walser	5-10/190	New Glasgow, Nova Scotia	5-12-78	2	Syracuse (AHL), Columbus
	Dan Watson	6-2/221	Glencoe, Ont.	10-5-79	0	Syracuse (AHL), Cleveland (AHL)
40	Duvie Westcott	5-11/180	Winnipeg	10-30-77	2	Syracuse (AHL), Columbus
	GOALTENDERS					
	Shane Bendera	5-10/170	St. Albert, Alta.	7-13-82	0	Dayton (ECHL)
40	Fred Brathwaite	5-7/175	Ottawa	11-24-72	8	St. Louis
30	Marc Denis	6-0/190	Montreal	8-1-77	6	Columbus
	Karl Goehring	5-8/160	Apple Valley, Minn.	8-23-78	0	Syracuse (AHL)
1	Jean-Francois Labbe	5-10/172	Sherbrooke, Que.	6-15-72	3	Syracuse (AHL)
	Pascal Leclaire	6-1/185	Repentigny, Que.	11-7-82	0	Syracuse (AHL)

2002-03 REVIEW
INDIVIDUAL STATISTICS

SCORING

	Games	G	A	Pts.	PIM	+/-	PPG	SHG	GWG	GTG	Sht.	Sht. Pct.	Faceoffs Won	Lost	Pct.	TOI
Ray Whitney	81	24	52	76	22	-26	8	2	2	1	235	10.2	13	16	44.8	21:00
Andrew Cassels	79	20	48	68	30	-4	9	1	5	0	113	17.7	804	845	48.8	19:51
Geoff Sanderson	82	34	33	67	34	-4	15	2	2	0	286	11.9	40	56	41.7	18:43
David Vyborny	79	20	26	46	16	12	4	1	4	0	125	16.0	15	31	32.6	16:20

	Games	G	A	Pts.	PIM	+/-	PPG	SHG	GWG	GTG	Sht.	Sht. Pct.	Faceoffs Won	Lost	Pct.	TOI
Jaroslav Spacek	81	9	36	45	70	-23	5	0	1	0	166	5.4	0	0	—	24:47
Mike Sillinger	75	18	25	43	52	-21	9	3	3	0	128	14.1	842	648	56.5	19:08
Rick Nash	74	17	22	39	78	-27	6	0	2	0	154	11.0	5	9	35.7	13:56
Tyler Wright	70	19	11	30	113	-25	3	2	3	0	108	17.6	314	446	41.3	16:07
Grant Marshall*	66	8	20	28	71	-8	3	0	2	0	96	8.3	12	14	46.2	13:56
Lasse Pirjeta.............	51	11	10	21	12	-4	2	0	2	0	80	13.8	141	186	43.1	11:28
Derrick Walser...........	53	4	13	17	34	-9	3	0	2	0	86	4.7	1	0	100.0	14:51
Rostislav Klesla........	72	2	14	16	71	-22	0	0	0	0	89	2.2	0	0	—	18:45
Sean Pronger	78	7	6	13	72	-26	1	0	0	0	67	10.4	324	331	49.5	11:31
Luke Richardson	82	0	13	13	73	-16	0	0	0	0	56	0.0	1	1	50.0	23:31
Espen Knutsen	31	5	4	9	20	-15	3	0	1	0	28	17.9	128	197	39.4	16:44
Matt Davidson	34	4	5	9	18	-12	0	0	0	0	28	14.3	2	5	28.6	11:48
Hannes Hyvonen	36	4	5	9	22	-11	0	0	0	0	48	8.3	2	6	25.0	10:02
Duvie Westcott.........	39	0	7	7	77	-3	0	0	0	0	27	0.0	0	0	—	18:40
David Ling	35	3	2	5	86	-6	0	0	0	0	37	8.1	6	9	40.0	7:56
Jody Shelley	68	1	4	5	249	-5	0	0	0	0	39	2.6	0	1	0.0	6:07
Tomi Kallio*	12	1	2	3	8	-7	0	0	0	0	20	5.0	1	1	50.0	14:52
Darren Van Impe	14	1	1	2	10	-6	0	1	0	1	11	9.1	0	0	—	18:28
Jean-Luc Grand-Pierre	41	1	0	1	64	-6	0	0	0	0	32	3.1	0	0	—	13:38
Andrej Nedorost	12	0	1	1	4	-6	0	0	0	0	10	0.0	11	19	36.7	9:15
Jamie Allison.............	48	0	1	1	99	-15	0	0	0	0	23	0.0	1	0	100.0	11:56
Scott Lachance.........	61	0	1	1	46	-20	0	0	0	0	35	0.0	0	0	—	20:00
Mathieu Darche.........	1	0	0	0	0	-1	0	0	0	0	0	—	0	0	—	6:57
Darrel Scoville	2	0	0	0	4	0	0	0	0	0	1	0.0	0	0	—	14:30
Blake Bellefeuille	3	0	0	0	0	0	0	0	0	0	0	—	11	6	64.7	7:00
Kent McDonnell.........	3	0	0	0	0	-1	0	0	0	0	4	0.0	0	0	—	8:40
Kevin Dineen	4	0	0	0	12	0	0	0	0	0	7	0.0	2	2	50.0	10:40
Paul Manning	8	0	0	0	2	0	0	0	0	0	4	0.0	0	0	—	13:02
J.-Francois Labbe (g) .	11	0	0	0	2	0	0	0	0	0	—	—	0	0	—	—
Marc Denis (g)	77	0	0	0	6	0	0	0	0	0	—	—	0	0	—	—

GOALTENDING

	Games	GS	Min.	GA	SO	Avg.	W	L	T	EN	PPG Allow	SHG Allow	Shots	Save Pct.
Marc Denis	77	77	4511	232	5	3.09	27	41	8	3	52	6	2404	.903
Jean-Francois Labbe.................	11	5	451	27	0	3.59	2	4	0	1	8	3	233	.884

*Played with two or more NHL teams.

RESULTS

OCTOBER
10— Chicago ....W.....2-1
12— At New Jersey ....L.....2-3
14— Phoenix ....L.....2-4
17— At St. Louis......................L.....1-7
19— Florida ....W.....4-1
23— Tampa Bay........................T....*2-2
25— San Jose ....L.....4-5
27— Los Angeles ....W.....5-1
29— At Chicago ....L.....2-3

NOVEMBER
1— Dallas ....W.....4-2
3— Buffalo ....W.....3-2
5— Washington ....OTL..*3-4
7— At St. Louis........................W.....5-2
9— N.Y. Rangers ....W.....6-3
12— At Colorado ....L.....4-5
14— Anaheim ....L.....2-3
16— At Nashville ....T...*1-1
17— At Dallas.......................OTL..*2-3
20— St. Louis ....W.....3-2
22— At Buffalo ....L.....4-5
23— At Ottawa ....L.....2-5
27— Edmonton ....L.....1-3
29— At N.Y. Islanders ....W.....4-2
30— Carolina ....L.....2-4

DECEMBER
3— At N.Y. Rangers ....L.....3-5
6— At San Jose ....L.....2-3
7— At Los Angeles ....W.....4-2

9— At Phoenix ....T....*3-3
12— New Jersey ....W.....4-2
14— At Detroit ....L.....4-6
19— At Calgary ....W.....3-0
20— At Chicago ....L.....1-3
23— Detroit ....L.....0-1
26— At Detroit ....L.....2-4
28— St. Louis ....L.....1-6
29— At St. Louis ....L.....2-5
31— Pittsburgh ....W.....5-2

JANUARY
3— At Washington ....T....*2-2
4— Phoenix ....W.....2-0
6— Nashville ....L.....1-5
8— At Minnesota ....W.....2-1
10— At Vancouver ....L.....3-2
11— At Calgary ....W.....7-2
13— At Edmonton ....L.....5-8
15— Anaheim ....L.....3-4
18— At Boston ....L.....2-7
20— Chicago ....W.....5-1
22— At Dallas ....L.....2-4
23— At Colorado ....L.....0-5
25— N.Y. Islanders ....W.....4-1
28— Colorado...............................T....*2-2
30— Nashville...............................W.....2-1

FEBRUARY
5— Vancouver ....T....*4-4
8— At Nashville ....L.....2-3
12— San Jose ....W.....1-0

13— At Montreal ....W....*2-1
15— Chicago ....L.....1-7
18— At Phoenix ....L.....2-5
19— At Anaheim ....L.....0-2
21— At San Jose ....L.....0-6
23— At Vancouver ....L.....2-7
25— At Nashville ....L.....0-5
27— Los Angeles ....W.....3-1

MARCH
1— Edmonton..........................T....*3-3
3— Detroit ....L.....2-3
6— Vancouver ....W....*5-4
8— Calgary ....OTL..*2-3
10— At Carolina ....L.....5-6
11— Dallas ....L.....0-2
13— Colorado ....L.....1-5
15— Minnesota ....W.....5-0
17— At Atlanta ....L.....2-3
20— Toronto ....W....*4-3
22— Atlanta ....L.....2-3
24— At Anaheim ....L.....0-5
25— At Los Angeles ....W....*2-1
28— At Edmonton ....L.....0-4
29— At Calgary ....W.....6-4

APRIL
1— At Philadelphia....................L.....0-4
2— Minnesota ....W.....3-0
4— Detroit ....T....*5-5
6— At Minnesota ....L.....3-4
*Denotes overtime game.

DALLAS STARS
WESTERN CONFERENCE/PACIFIC DIVISION

Stars' Schedule
Home games shaded; D=Day game; *Feb. 8 All-Star Game at St. Paul, Minn.

October
SUN	MON	TUE	WED	THU	FRI	SAT
5	6	7	8 ANA	9	10	11 NAS
12	13 D BUF	14	15 BOS	16	17 WAS	18
19 MIN	20	21	22 TOR	23	24 DET	25 CBJ
26	27	28	29 CAL	30	31	

November
SUN	MON	TUE	WED	THU	FRI	SAT
						1 NAS
2 NAS	3	4	5 NYR	6	7 NYI	8 BOS
9	10	11	12 DET	13	14 PHO	15 COL
16	17	18	19 ANA	20	21 LA	22 STL
23 PHO	24	25	26 MIN	27	28 NJ	29
30 LA						

December
SUN	MON	TUE	WED	THU	FRI	SAT
	1	2	3	4 LA	5	6 SJ
7 ANA	8	9	10 PHO	11	12 CHI	13
14 CHI	15	16	17 VAN	18	19 FLA	20 TB
21 CAR	22	23	24	25	26 NAS	27 CBJ
28	29 PHI	30	31 MON			

January
SUN	MON	TUE	WED	THU	FRI	SAT
				1	2 PHO	3 LA
4	5 ANA	6	7	8 ATL	9	10 D COL
11	12	13 SJ	14	15 COL	16	17 CAL
18	19 VAN	20 EDM	21	22	23 STL	24 STL
25	26 DET	27	28 OTT	29	30 SJ	31 PHO

February
SUN	MON	TUE	WED	THU	FRI	SAT
1	2	3	4 CBJ	5	6	7
8*	9	10	11 NYI	12	13	14 PHO
15	16 ANA	17	18 LA	19	20 COL	21
22 D ANA	23	24	25 LA	26	27 MIN	28
29 D EDM						

March
SUN	MON	TUE	WED	THU	FRI	SAT
	1	2	3 CBJ	4	5 CAL	6
7 D SJ	8	9 PIT	10	11 PHI	12	13 D DET
14 D CHI	15	16 SJ	17	18 VAN	19	20 D STL
21	22 CAL	23	24 EDM	25	26	27 VAN
28 SJ	29	30	31 EDM			

April
SUN	MON	TUE	WED	THU	FRI	SAT
				1	2 MIN	3
4 D CHI	5	6	7	8	9	10

2003-04 SEASON

CLUB DIRECTORY

Chairman of the board and owner
Thomas O. Hicks
President
Jim Lites
General manager
Doug Armstrong
Assistant general manager
Francois Giguere
Special assistant to the g.m.
Guy Carbonneau
Director of hockey operations
Les Jackson
Head coach
Dave Tippett
Associate coach
Rick Wilson
Assistant coach
Mark Lamb

Assistant coach/goaltending coach
Andy Moog
Sr. dir. of hockey communications
Rob Scichili
Director of media relations
Mark Janko
Mgr. of publications & media relations
Jason Rademan
Head athletic trainer
Dave Surprenant
Head equipment manager
Dave Smith
Equipment manager
Steve Sumner
Strength and conditioning coach
J.J. McQueen
Assistant athletic trainer
Craig Lowry

DRAFT CHOICES

Rd.— Player	Overall	Pos.	Last team
2— Loui Eriksson	33	LW	Frolunda Jr. (Sweden Jr.)
2— Vojtech Polak	36	W	Karlovy Vary (Czech Republic)
2— Brandon Crombeen	54	RW	Barrie (OHL)
3— Matt Nickerson	99	D	Texas (NAHL)
4— Alexander Naurov	134	W	Yaroslavl Jr. (Russia Jr.)
5— Eero Kilpelainen	144	G	Kalpa Jr. (Finland Jr.)
5— Gino Guyer	165	C	Minnesota (WCHA)
6— Francis Wathier	185	LW	Hull (QMJHL)
6— Drew Bagnall	195	D	Battlefords (SJHL)
6— Elias Granath	196	D	Leksand Jr. (Sweden Jr.)
8— Niko Vainio	259	D	Jokerit Jr. (Finland Jr.)

MISCELLANEOUS DATA

Home ice (capacity)
American Airlines Center (18,532)
Address
2601 Avenue of the Stars
Frisco, TX 75034
Business phone
972-831-2401
Ticket information
214-467-8277
Website
www.dallasstars.com

Training site
Frisco and Dallas, TX
Club colors
Green, black, gold and white
Radio affiliation
WBAP (820 AM)
TV affiliation
FOX Sports Southwest (Cable), KDFI
(Channel 27)

DALLAS STARS

No.	FORWARDS	Ht./Wt.	Place	BORN Date	NHL exp.	2002-03 clubs
44	Jason Arnott (C)	6-4/225	Collingwood, Ont.	10-11-74	10	Dallas
41	Stu Barnes (C)	5-11/186	Spruce Grove, Alta.	12-25-70	12	Buffalo, Dallas
	Jeff Bateman (C)	5-11/165	Belleville, Ont.	8-29-81	0	Utah (AHL), Lexington (ECHL)
	Garrett Burnett (LW)	6-3/230	Coquitlim, B.C.	9-23-75	0	Hartford (AHL)
	Justin Cox (RW)	6-0/160	Merritt, B.C.	3-13-81	0	Utah (AHL)
10	Ulf Dahlen (RW)	6-3/204	Ostersund, Sweden	1-12-67	14	Dallas
18	Rob DiMaio (RW)	5-10/190	Calgary	2-19-68	15	Dallas
	Aaron Downey (RW)	6-0/210	Shelburne, Ontario	8-27-74	4	Dallas
	Steve Gainey (LW)	6-0/180	Montreal	1-26-79	2	Utah (AHL)
13	Bill Guerin (RW)	6-2/210	Wilbraham, Mass.	11-9-70	12	Dallas
	Barrett Heisten (LW)	6-1/189	Anchorage, Alaska.	3-19-80	1	Utah (AHL)
	Marius Holtet (C/RW)	6-0/183	Hamar, Norway	8-31-84	0	
	Niko Kapanen (C)	5-9/180	Hameenlinna, Finland	4-29-78	2	Dallas
	Marcus Kristofferson (RW)	6-3/200	Ostersund, Sweden	1-22-79	0	Utah (AHL)
26	Jere Lehtinen (LW)	6-0/192	Espoo, Finland	6-24-73	8	Dallas
22	Claude Lemieux (RW)....	6-1/215	Buckingham, Que.	7-16-65	20	Dallas, Phoenix
27	Joel Lundqvist (C)	6-0/183	Are, Sweden	3-2-82	0	Vastra Frolunda (Sweden)
27	Manny Malhotra (C)	6-2/210	Mississauga, Ont.	5-18-80	5	Dallas
	Antti Miettinen (RW)......	5-11/176	Hameenlinna, Finland	7-3-80	0	
9	Mike Modano (C)..........	6-3/205	Livonia, Mich.	6-7-70	15	Dallas
19	Brenden Morrow (RW)..	5-11/200	Carlyle, Sask.	1-16-79	4	Dallas
22	Kirk Muller (C)	6-0/205	Kingston, Ont.	2-8-66	19	Dallas
	David Oliver (RW)	5-11/190	Sechelt, B.C.	4-17-71	7	Pensacola (ECHL), Utah (AHL), Bossier-Shreveport (CHL), Dallas
	Steve Ott (C/LW)	5-11/160	Stoney Point, Ont.	8-19-82	1	Utah (AHL), Dallas
	Mathias Tjarnqvist (C) ...	6-1/183	Umea, Sweden	4-15-79	0	Djurgarden Stockholm (Sweden)
77	Pierre Turgeon (C)	6-1/199	Rouyn, Que.	8-28-69	16	Dallas
	Janos Vas (LW)	6-1/183	Dunaferr, Hungary	1-29-84	0	Malmo (Sweden Jr.)
48	Scott Young (RW)	6-1/200	Clinton, Mass.	10-1-67	15	Dallas

DEFENSEMEN

No.		Ht./Wt.	Place	Date	exp.	2002-03 clubs
26	Bubba Berenzweig	6-2/218	Arlington Heights, Ill.	8-8-77	4	Nashville, Milwaukee (AHL), Utah (AHL)
43	Philippe Boucher	6-3/221	St. Apollinaire, Que.	3-24-73	11	Dallas
	Trevor Daley	5-10/207	Toronto	10-9-83	0	Sault Ste. Marie (OHL)
2	John Erskine.................	6-4/197	Kingston, Ont.	6-26-80	2	Utah (AHL), Dallas
4	Greg Hawgood	5-10/190	Edmonton	8-10-68	12	Utah (AHL)
	Dan Jancevski...............	6-3/208	Windsor, Ont.	6-15-81	0	Utah (AHL)
	Jeff MacMillan	6-3/202	Durham, Ontario	3-30-79	0	Utah (AHL)
24	Richard Matvichuk........	6-2/215	Edmonton	2-5-73	11	Dallas
	Teppo Numminen	6-2/199	Tampere, Finland	7-3-68	15	Phoenix
7	Lyle Odelein	6-0/210	Quill Lake, Sask.	7-21-68	14	Chicago, Dallas
56	Stephane Robidas.........	5-11/180	Sherbrooke, Que.	3-3-77	4	Dallas
32	Don Sweeney................	5-10/184	St. Stephen, N.B.	8-17-66	15	Boston
	Martin Vagner	6-1/214	Jaromer, Czechoslovakia	3-16-84	0	Hull (QMJHL)
4	Mark Wotton.................	6-1/195	Foxwarren, Man.	11-16-73	4	Utah (AHL)
56	Sergei Zubov	6-1/200	Moscow, U.S.S.R.	7-22-70	11	Dallas

GOALTENDERS

No.		Ht./Wt.	Place	Date	exp.	2002-03 clubs
	Chad Alban	5-9/165	Kalamazoo, Mich.	4-27-76	0	Grand Rapids (AHL), Kalamazoo (UHL)
	Jason Bacashihua..........	5-11/167	Garden City, Mich.	9-20-82	0	Utah (AHL)
	Dan Ellis	6-0/180	Saskatoon, Sask.	6-19-80	0	University of Nebraska-Omaha (NCAA)
31	Corey Hirsch.................	5-10/168	Medicine Hat, Alta.	7-1-72	7	Utah (AHL), Dallas
	Mike Smith	6-3/189	Kingston, Ont.	3-22-82	0	Utah (AHL)
	Tobias Stephan	6-3/178	Zurich, Switzerland	1-21-84	0	Kloten (Switzerland)
31	Ron Tugnutt..................	5-11/160	Scarborough, Ont.	10-22-67	15	Dallas
35	Marty Turco	5-11/183	Sault Ste. Marie, Ont.	8-13-75	3	Dallas

2002-03 REVIEW
INDIVIDUAL STATISTICS

SCORING

	Games	G	A	Pts.	PIM	+/-	PPG	SHG	GWG	GTG	Sht.	Sht. Pct.	Faceoffs Won	Faceoffs Lost	Faceoffs Pct.	TOI
Mike Modano	79	28	57	85	30	34	5	2	6	0	193	14.5	929	879	51.4	20:52
Sergei Zubov.............	82	11	44	55	26	21	8	0	2	0	158	7.0	0	0	—	25:50
Bill Guerin	64	25	25	50	113	5	11	0	2	1	229	10.9	5	15	25.0	18:33
Jere Lehtinen	80	31	17	48	20	39	5	0	3	2	238	13.0	8	28	22.2	18:47
Jason Arnott.............	72	23	24	47	51	9	7	0	6	1	169	13.6	602	528	53.3	16:11
Brenden Morrow	71	21	22	43	134	20	2	3	4	2	105	20.0	8	21	27.6	15:42

	Games	G	A	Pts.	PIM	+/-	PPG	SHG	GWG	GTG	Sht.	Sht. Pct.	Faceoffs Won	Lost	Pct.	TOI
Scott Young	79	23	19	42	30	24	5	1	4	1	237	9.7	3	5	37.5	16:08
Pierre Turgeon	65	12	30	42	18	4	3	0	5	1	76	15.8	156	134	53.8	14:37
Ulf Dahlen	63	17	20	37	14	11	9	0	1	0	100	17.0	9	9	50.0	13:49
Darryl Sydor	81	5	31	36	40	22	2	0	1	0	132	3.8	0	0	—	18:19
Niko Kapanen	82	5	29	34	44	25	0	1	1	0	80	6.3	528	583	47.5	14:39
Derian Hatcher	82	8	22	30	106	37	1	1	2	0	159	5.0	0	0	—	25:51
Philippe Boucher	80	7	20	27	94	28	1	1	3	1	137	5.1	0	1	0.0	20:29
Rob DiMaio	69	10	9	19	76	18	0	0	2	0	81	12.3	22	27	44.9	12:57
Manny Malhotra	59	3	7	10	42	-2	0	0	1	0	62	4.8	210	237	47.0	9:21
Stephane Robidas	76	3	7	10	35	15	0	0	1	0	47	6.4	1	0	100.0	12:53
Steve Ott	26	3	4	7	31	6	0	0	0	0	25	12.0	2	2	50.0	8:46
Stu Barnes*	13	2	5	7	8	2	2	0	1	0	25	8.0	34	42	44.7	17:23
Claude Lemieux*	32	2	4	6	14	-9	0	0	0	0	45	4.4	17	18	48.6	13:13
Kirk Muller	55	1	5	6	18	-6	0	0	0	0	48	2.1	113	88	56.2	9:28
Richard Matvichuk	68	1	5	6	58	1	0	0	1	0	59	1.7	0	3	0.0	19:23
Scott Pellerin*	20	1	3	4	8	-3	1	0	0	0	20	5.0	1	4	20.0	10:42
David Oliver	6	0	3	3	2	1	0	0	0	0	5	0.0	0	0	—	9:13
Marty Turco (g)	55	0	3	3	16	0	0	0	0	0	0	—	0	0	—	—
John Erskine	16	2	0	2	29	1	0	0	0	0	12	16.7	0	0	—	10:44
Aaron Downey	43	1	1	2	69	1	0	0	0	0	14	7.1	0	0	—	4:46
Jim Montgomery	1	0	0	0	0	0	0	0	0	0	0	—	1	1	50.0	6:41
Corey Hirsch (g)	2	0	0	0	0	0	0	0	0	0	0	—	0	0	—	—
Lyle Odelein*	3	0	0	0	6	0	0	0	0	0	1	0.0	0	0	—	17:48
Jon Sim*	4	0	0	0	0	-1	0	0	0	0	7	0.0	1	1	50.0	9:10
Sami Helenius*	5	0	0	0	6	1	0	0	0	0	2	0.0	0	0	—	9:48
Ron Tugnutt (g)	31	0	0	0	0	0	0	0	0	0	0	—	0	0	—	—

GOALTENDING

	Games	GS	Min.	GA	SO	Avg.	W	L	T	EN	PPG Allow	SHG Allow	Shots	Save Pct.
Marty Turco	55	52	3203	92	7	1.72	31	10	10	3	27	2	1359	.932
Ron Tugnutt	31	29	1701	70	4	2.47	15	10	5	0	23	4	672	.896
Corey Hirsch	2	1	97	4	0	2.47	0	1	0	0	0	0	39	.897

*Played with two or more NHL teams.

RESULTS

OCTOBER
9— At Colorado ....T....*1-1
11—Anaheim ....W....4-2
12—At Phoenix.......................W....5-2
15—Edmonton.........................W....3-0
17—At Minnesota ....L....1-3
19—At St. Louis ....L....3-5
20—Washington ....W....5-2
24—At Calgary ....T....*3-3
26—At Vancouver...................W....4-1
28—At Edmonton ....W....*4-3
30—Florida ....OTL...*2-3

NOVEMBER
1— At Columbus......................L....2-4
3— At Detroit..........................T....*3-3
6— Vancouver.........................W....4-0
8—Toronto.............................W....2-1
10—At N.Y. Islanders ....L....2-3
12—At Montreal ....W....4-2
13—At Washington ....W....6-1
15—Colorado..........................W....4-2
17—Columbus.........................W....*3-2
20—At Phoenix.......................T....*2-2
22—At Anaheim......................W....4-0
23—At Los Angeles ....L....0-2
25—Phoenix............................W....5-1
27—Minnesota ....W....5-0
29—N.Y. Rangers....................T....*3-3
30—At Nashville ....L....2-5

DECEMBER
4— Montreal...........................W....5-1

6— Detroit ....T....*3-3
11—Los Angeles ....L....0-3
13—Atlanta.............................W....3-1
15—At Chicago.......................W....5-0
17—At Philadelphia.................T....*2-2
19—At Detroit.........................T....*1-1
21—At New Jersey ....L....3-5
22—At Carolina.......................L....0-1
26—At Nashville ....L....1-3
27—At Florida ....W....4-0
29—Detroit ....T....*2-2
31—Edmonton........................W....4-1

JANUARY
2— At San Jose.......................W....3-1
4— At Los Angeles ....W....3-2
5— At Anaheim.......................T....*1-1
7— Los Angeles ....W....7-4
9—Chicago.............................W....*4-3
11—Colorado..........................W....6-3
18—At San Jose......................W....3-1
20—At Colorado ....T....*1-1
22—Columbus.........................W....4-2
24—Tampa Bay.......................L....1-4
25—At St. Louis ....W....4-2
27—Ottawa.............................W....5-3
29—Calgary ....W....4-1

FEBRUARY
5— St. Louis ....T....*2-2
8— At Phoenix........................W....3-1
9— Los Angeles ....W....3-1
11—Carolina...........................W....*2-1

14—Anaheim ....L....2-4
16—San Jose ....W....3-1
19—Calgary ....T....*1-1
21—Phoenix............................T....*2-2
23—At Chicago.......................W....3-0
25—At Boston..........................T....*5-5
27—At Ottawa.........................OTL...*2-3
28—At Buffalo..........................L....3-5

MARCH
2— Pittsburgh ....W....3-1
5—Chicago.............................W....7-4
7—Nashville ....L....1-2
9—San Jose ....W....3-0
11—At Columbus ....W....2-0
12—At Minnesota ....L....2-4
15—At Edmonton ....L....3-4
17—Vancouver........................L....2-4
19—At Atlanta.........................W....*5-4
21—Minnesota ....OTL...*2-3
23—St. Louis ....W....3-1
25—At Vancouver....................W....4-3
27—At Calgary ....OTL...*1-2
29—At San Jose.......................W....4-3
31—Buffalo.............................W....3-0

APRIL
2— Anaheim............................W....2-1
6— Nashville ....W....2-0
*Denotes overtime game.

DETROIT RED WINGS
WESTERN CONFERENCE/CENTRAL DIVISION

DETROIT RED WINGS

Red Wings' Schedule
Home games shaded; D=Day game; *Feb. 8 All-Star Game at St. Paul, Minn.

October

SUN	MON	TUE	WED	THU	FRI	SAT
5	6	7	8	9 LA	10	11 OTT
12	13	14	15	16 VAN	17	18 PIT
19	20 MON	21	22 CBJ	23	24 DAL	25 NYR
26	27	28	29 STL	30 NAS	31	

November

SUN	MON	TUE	WED	THU	FRI	SAT
						1 EDM
2	3 VAN	4 CAL	5	6	7	8 NAS
9 CHI	10	11	12 DAL	13	14 CHI	15 MIN
16	17	18	19 CBJ	20 CBJ	21	22 MIN
23 WAS	24	25	26 EDM	27	28 NYI	29 STL
30						

December

SUN	MON	TUE	WED	THU	FRI	SAT
	1	2	3 ANA	4 STL	5	6 TOR
7 LA	8	9	10 BUF	11 CHI	12	13 WAS
14	15 FLA	16	17 SJ	18	19 CHI	20 NAS
21 STL	22	23	24	25	26 MIN	27
28 CHI	29	30	31 ATL			

January

SUN	MON	TUE	WED	THU	FRI	SAT
				1	2 CAR	3 ANA
4 NAS	5	6	7 BOS	8	9	10 D BOS
11	12	13	14 CHI	15	16 PHO	17
18 SJ	19	20	21 ANA	22 LA	23	24 PHO
25 DAL	26	27	28	29 NJ	30	31 CAR

February

SUN	MON	TUE	WED	THU	FRI	SAT
1	2	3 NAS	4	5 COL	6	7
8*	9	10	11 SJ	12	13	14 D COL
15	16 EDM	17	18 PHO	19	20 STL	21
22	23 EDM	24 VAN	25	26 CAL	27	28
29 PHI						

March

SUN	MON	TUE	WED	THU	FRI	SAT
	1	2	3 CAL	4	5 VAN	6
7 TB	8	9	10	11 CBJ	12	13 D DAL
14 NAS	15	16 CAL	17	18 PHO	19	20 LA
21 ANA	22	23 SJ	24	25 COL	26	27 D COL
28	29 MIN	30	31 CBJ			

April

SUN	MON	TUE	WED	THU	FRI	SAT
				1 STL	2	3 CBJ
4	5	6	7	8	9	10

2003-04 SEASON
CLUB DIRECTORY

Owner/governor
Mike Ilitch

Owner/secretary-treasurer
Marian Ilitch

President, Ilitch Holdings/alt. governor
Christopher Ilitch

President, Ilitch Holdings/alt. governor
Denise Ilitch

Sr. vice president/alternate governor
Jim Devellano

General manager
Ken Holland

Assistant general manager
Jim Nill

Head coach
Dave Lewis

Associate coach
Barry Smith

Assistant coach
Joe Kocur

Goaltending consultant
Jim Bedard

NHL scout
Dan Belisle, Mark Howe,
Bob McCammon

Scouts
Hakan Andersson, Evgeni Erfilov, Bruce
Haralson, Vladimir Havluj, Mark
Leach, Joe McDonnell, Glenn
Merkosky, Marty Stein

Athletic trainer
Piet VanZant

Equipment manager
Paul Boyer

Assistant equipment manager
Tim Abbott

Assistant athletic trainer
Russ Baumann

Masseur
Sergei Tchekmarev

Team physicians
David Collon, M.D.
Anthony Colucci, M.D.

Team dentist
C.J. Regula, D.M.D.

Senior director of communications
John Hahn

Media relations manager
Mike Kuta

DRAFT CHOICES

Rd.— Player	Overall	Pos.	Last team
2— James Howard	64	G	Maine (Hockey East)
4— Kyle Quincey	132	D	London (OHL)
5— Ryan Oulahen	164	C	Brampton (OHL)
6— Andreas Sundin	170	LW	Linkoping (Sweden)
6— Stefan Blom	194	D	Hammarby Jr. (Sweden Jr.)
7— Tomas Kollar	226	LW	Hammarby (Sweden)
8— Vladimir Kutny	258	LW	Quebec (QMJHL)
9— Mikael Johansson	289	C	Arvika (Sweden)

MISCELLANEOUS DATA

Home ice (capacity)
Joe Louis Arena (20,058)

Address
600 Civic Center Drive
Detroit, MI 48226

Business phone
313-396-7544

Ticket information
313-396-7575

Website
www.detroitredwings.com

Training site
Center I.C.E., Traverse City, Mich.

Club colors
Red and white

Radio affiliation
Team 1270 WXYT (AM)

TV affiliation
FOX Sports Net Detroit (Cable)

DETROIT RED WINGS

No. FORWARDS	Ht./Wt.	Place	BORN Date	NHL exp.	2002-03 clubs
Bryan Adams (LW)	6-0/185	Fort St. James, B.C.	3-20-77	2	Grand Rapids (AHL)
Per Backer (RW/LW)	6-1/161	Grums, Sweden	1-4-82	0	
Ryan Barnes (LW)	6-1/201	Dunnville, Ont.	1-30-80	0	Grand Rapids (AHL)
Nicholas Beaulieu (LW) .	6-1/200	Rimouski, Que.	8-19-68	0	
13 Pavel Datsyuk (C)	5-11/180	Sverdlovsk, U.S.S.R.	7-20-78	2	Detroit
21 Boyd Devereaux (LW)....	6-2/195	Seaforth, Ont.	4-16-78	6	Detroit
33 Kris Draper (C)	5-10/190	Toronto	5-24-71	13	Detroit
Valtteri Filppula (C)........	5-11/174	Vantaa, Finland	3-20-84	0	
T. Fleischmann (LW)......	6-1/172	Koprivnice, Czechoslovakia	5-16-84	0	Moose Jaw (WHL)
Igor Grigorenko (LW)	5-11/183	Samara, U.S.S.R.	4-9-83	0	Lada Togliatti (Russian)
96 Tomas Holmstrom (RW)	6-0/198	Pieta, Sweden	1-23-73	7	Detroit
Jiri Hudler (C)...............	5-9/176	Olomouc, Czechoslovakia	1-4-84	0	Kazan (Russian Div. III)
17 Brett Hull (RW)	5-11/203	Belleville, Ont.	8-9-64	18	Detroit
Andreas Jamtin (RW)....	5-11/185	Stockholm, Sweden	5-4-83	0	
Mikael Johansson (C)....	5-10/185	Stockholm, Sweden	12-6-66	0	Djurgarden Stockholm (Sweden)
7 Derek King (LW)	5-11/212	Hamilton, Ont.	2-11-67	14	Grand Rapids (AHL)
Tomas Kopecky (C)	6-3/187	Ilava, Czechoslovakia	2-2-82	0	Grand Rapids (AHL)
8 Igor Larionov (C)	5-10/170	Voskresensk, U.S.S.R.	12-3-60	13	Detroit
18 Kirk Maltby (LW)	6-0/190	Guelph, Ont.	12-22-72	10	Detroit
25 Darren McCarty (RW)....	6-1/215	Burnaby, B.C.	4-1-72	10	Detroit
18 Mark Mowers (C)	5-11/184	Whitesboro, N.Y.	2-16-74	3	Grand Rapids (AHL)
34 Michel Picard (LW)	5-11/202	Beauport, Que.	11-7-69	9	Grand Rapids (AHL)
20 Luc Robitaille (LW)........	6-1/205	Montreal	2-17-66	17	Detroit
39 Stacy Roest (C)	5-9/185	Lethbridge, Alta.	3-15-74	5	Grand Rapids (AHL), Detroit
14 Brendan Shanahan (LW)	6-3/215	Mimico, Ont.	1-23-69	16	Detroit
29 Jason Williams (C)	5-11/185	London, Ont.	8-11-80	3	Grand Rapids (AHL), Detroit
19 Steve Yzerman (C)........	5-10/185	Cranbrook, B.C.	5-9-65	20	Detroit
Henrik Zetterberg (C).....	5-11/180	Njurunda, Sweden	10-9-80	1	Detroit
DEFENSEMEN					
Paul Ballantyne	6-3/200	Waterloo, Ont.	7-16-82	0	Toledo (ECHL), Grand Rapids (AHL)
Johan Berggen	6-3/176	Vastra Amtevik, Sweden	5-18-84	0	
39 Patrick Boileau	6-0/200	Montreal	2-22-75	4	Grand Rapids (AHL), Detroit
Dmitri Bykov	6-0/181	Izhevsk, U.S.S.R.		1	Detroit
Ed Campbell	6-2/200	Worcester, Mass.	11-26-74	0	Grand Rapids (AHL)
24 Chris Chelios	6-1/190	Chicago	1-25-62	20	Detroit
11 Mathieu Dandenault......	6-1/196	Sherbrooke, Que.	2-3-76	8	Detroit
2 Jiri Fischer....................	6-5/210	Horovice, Czechoslovakia	7-31-80	4	Detroit
2 Derian Hatcher..............	6-5/230	Sterling Heights, Mich.	6-4-72	12	Dallas
Niklas Kronwall.............	5-11/165	Stockholm, Sweden	1-12-81	0	Djurgarden Stockholm (Sweden)
5 Nicklas Lidstrom	6-2/190	Vasteras, Sweden	4-28-70	12	Detroit
10 Mathieu Schneider........	5-10/192	New York	6-12-69	15	Detroit, Los Angeles
3 Jesse Wallin	6-2/190	Saskatoon, Sask.	3-10-78	4	Detroit
John Wikstrom	6-3/200	Lulea, Sweden	1-30-79	0	
5 Jason Woolley	6-1/207	Toronto	7-27-69	12	Buffalo, Detroit
GOALTENDERS					
Jason Elliott....................	6-2/183	Chapman, Australia	10-11-75	0	TPS Turku (Finland)
39 Dominik Hasek	5-11/168	Pardubice, Czechoslovakia	1-29-65	12	
31 Curtis Joseph	5-11/190	Keswick, Ont.	4-29-67	14	Detroit
45 Marc Lamothe	6-2/210	New Liskeard, Ont.	2-27-74	1	Grand Rapids (AHL)
34 Manny Legace	5-9/165	Toronto	2-4-73	5	Detroit
Stefan Liv	6-0/172	Sweden	12-21-80	0	HV 71 Jonkoping (Sweden)
Nick Pannoni	6-0/170	Cardston, Alta.	4-5-83	0	Moose Jaw (WHL)

2002-03 REVIEW
INDIVIDUAL STATISTICS

SCORING

	Games	G	A	Pts.	PIM	+/-	PPG	SHG	GWG	GTG	Sht.	Sht. Pct.	Faceoffs Won	Lost	Pct.	TOI
Sergei Fedorov	80	36	47	83	52	15	10	2	11	0	281	12.8	843	737	53.4	21:10
Brett Hull	82	37	39	76	22	11	12	1	4	1	262	14.1	7	11	38.9	18:07
Brendan Shanahan	78	30	38	68	103	5	13	0	6	0	260	11.5	17	11	60.7	18:38
Nicklas Lidstrom	82	18	44	62	38	40	8	1	4	0	175	10.3	0	0	—	29:20
Pavel Datsyuk	64	12	39	51	16	20	1	0	1	1	82	14.6	375	403	48.2	15:27
Henrik Zetterberg	79	22	22	44	8	6	5	1	4	0	135	16.3	185	216	46.1	16:18

	Games	G	A	Pts.	PIM	+/-	PPG	SHG	GWG	GTG	Sht.	Sht. Pct.	Faceoffs Won	Lost	Pct.	TOI
Igor Larionov	74	10	33	43	48	-7	5	0	3	0	50	20.0	195	259	43.0	13:54
Tomas Holmstrom	74	20	20	40	62	11	12	0	2	0	109	18.3	0	2	0.0	12:27
Kirk Maltby	82	14	23	37	91	17	0	4	1	0	116	12.1	16	27	37.2	16:10
Kris Draper	82	14	21	35	82	6	0	1	2	0	142	9.9	603	456	56.9	16:11
Luc Robitaille	81	11	20	31	50	4	3	0	0	1	148	7.4	9	9	50.0	12:48
Jason Woolley*	62	6	17	23	22	12	1	0	2	0	52	11.5	0	0	—	16:58
Darren McCarty	73	13	9	22	138	10	1	0	2	0	129	10.1	185	135	57.8	13:17
Mathieu Dandenault	74	4	15	19	64	25	1	0	0	0	74	5.4	0	0	—	19:07
Chris Chelios	66	2	17	19	78	4	0	1	1	0	92	2.2	0	0	—	24:14
Boyd Devereaux	61	3	9	12	16	4	0	1	0	0	72	4.2	3	4	42.9	9:25
Dmitri Bykov	71	2	10	12	43	1	1	0	0	0	58	3.4	2	0	100.0	18:21
Sean Avery*	39	5	6	11	120	7	0	0	2	0	40	12.5	130	94	58.0	7:03
Steve Yzerman	16	2	6	8	8	6	1	0	1	0	13	15.4	75	59	56.0	15:35
Patrick Boileau	25	2	6	8	14	8	0	0	1	0	18	11.1	0	0	—	13:57
Mathieu Schneider*	13	2	5	7	16	2	1	0	0	0	37	5.4	0	0	—	22:42
Jason Williams	16	3	3	6	2	3	1	0	0	1	20	15.0	40	38	51.3	10:42
Jiri Fischer	15	1	5	6	16	0	0	0	0	0	19	5.3	0	0	—	21:23
Maxim Kuznetsov*	53	0	3	3	54	0	0	0	0	0	32	0.0	1	0	100.0	13:10
Manny Legace (g)	25	0	1	1	2	0	0	0	0	0	0	—	0	0	—	—
Jesse Wallin	32	0	1	1	19	-2	0	0	0	0	23	0.0	0	0	—	13:16
Stacy Roest	2	0	0	0	0	0	0	0	0	0	2	0.0	12	7	63.2	7:19
Curtis Joseph (g)	61	0	0	0	4	0	0	0	0	0	0	—	0	0	—	—

GOALTENDING

	Games	GS	Min.	GA	SO	Avg.	W	L	T	EN	PPG Allow	SHG Allow	Shots	Save Pct.
Manny Legace	25	22	1406	51	0	2.18	14	5	4	1	12	1	681	.925
Curtis Joseph	61	60	3566	148	5	2.49	34	19	6	3	43	3	1676	.912

*Played with two or more NHL teams.

RESULTS

OCTOBER

10—At San Jose ....W......6-3
12—At Los Angeles ....L......2-3
13—At Anaheim....................W......4-2
17—Montreal.......................L......2-3
19—At Minnesota..................W......5-3
21—Calgary........................W......4-0
23—Los Angeles..................T....*3-3
25—Pittsburgh.....................W......7-3
26—At Nashville ....L......1-3
29—San Jose ....W......3-2

NOVEMBER

2—At Ottawa.......................L......2-5
3—Dallas...........................T....*3-3
5—Chicago ....L......0-2
7—Boston ....W....*2-1
12—Nashville.......................W......4-1
15—Anaheim.......................W....*2-1
16—At Toronto.....................W......2-1
19—At Calgary.....................W......5-0
22—At Vancouver..................L......1-4
23—At Edmonton ....T....*1-1
25—Edmonton ....OTL....*4-5
27—New Jersey....................W....*3-2
29—At Carolina.....................L......4-6

DECEMBER

1—Calgary ....W......4-2
3—Anaheim........................W......2-1
5—At Phoenix.....................W......5-3
6—At Dallas........................T....*3-3

8—St. Louis........................W....*4-3
12—Minnesota.....................L......2-3
14—Columbus.....................W......6-4
17—At N.Y. Islanders ....T....*2-2
19—Dallas...........................T....*1-1
21—N.Y. Rangers ....W......3-2
23—At Columbus ....W......1-0
26—Columbus.....................W......4-2
28—At Nashville ....W......4-2
29—At Dallas.......................T....*2-2
31—St. Louis.......................W......5-1

JANUARY

3—Phoenix ....L......1-4
5—At Chicago ....W....*4-3
7—At Tampa Bay ....L......0-1
8—At Florida ....W....*2-1
11—At Philadelphia ....L......2-3
13—Chicago ....W....*5-4
15—At Chicago.....................L......1-4
16—At Colorado ....W......4-2
19—Vancouver.....................L......1-4
22—At Edmonton ....OTL..*3-4
24—At Vancouver..................W......5-2
25—At Calgary.....................L......1-4
28—At New Jersey.................L......0-1
30—Florida ....T....*2-2

FEBRUARY

4—Nashville........................T....*5-5
6—Colorado ....L......0-1
8—At Colorado ....L......3-5

10—San Jose ....W......5-4
13—Buffalo..........................W......4-2
15—At Atlanta.......................W......6-2
18—Vancouver....................OTL..*3-4
20—Edmonton......................W......6-2
22—At Washington ....W......5-1
24—Los Angeles...................W......5-4
27—Toronto.........................W......7-2

MARCH

2—Phoenix ....W......5-2
3—At Columbus...................W......3-2
5—Tampa Bay ....W......3-2
7—St. Louis.........................W......7-2
9—At Anaheim.....................L......1-4
10—At Los Angeles ....W......3-2
12—At Phoenix.....................W......3-2
15—Colorado.......................W......5-3
16—Ottawa..........................W......6-2
18—At Pittsburgh..................W......5-1
22—At St. Louis....................W......4-2
23—At Minnesota ....L......0-4
25—Minnesota.....................W......4-0
27—At San Jose....................L......0-3
29—At St. Louis....................W......6-2
31—Nashville.......................W......3-0

APRIL

3—N.Y. Islanders..................W......5-2
4—At Columbus....................T....*5-5
6—At Chicago.....................OTL..*3-4
*Denotes overtime game.

EDMONTON OILERS
WESTERN CONFERENCE/NORTHWEST DIVISION

Oilers' Schedule
Home games shaded; D=Day game; *Feb. 8 All-Star Game at St. Paul, Minn.

October
SUN	MON	TUE	WED	THU	FRI	SAT
5	6	7	8	9 SJ	10	11 VAN
12	13	14 CAL	15	16 BUF	17	18 COL
19	20	21 STL	22	23 COL	24	25 CAL
26	27	28	29	30 CBJ	31	

November
SUN	MON	TUE	WED	THU	FRI	SAT
						1 DET
2	3	4 MON	5	6 OTT	7	8 TOR
9	10 NYR	11 BOS	12	13 MIN	14	15 CAL
16	17	18 CHI	19	20 TOR	21	22 MON
23	24	25 CBJ	26 DET	27	28 COL	29
30 D SJ						

December
SUN	MON	TUE	WED	THU	FRI	SAT
	1	2	3 MIN	4	5	6 PIT
7	8	9 CAR	10	11 SJ	12 PHO	13
14 ANA	15	16 LA	17	18 MIN	19	20 VAN
21	22	23 CAL	24	25	26 VAN	27 VAN
28 CAL	29	30 MIN	31			

January
SUN	MON	TUE	WED	THU	FRI	SAT
				1	2 MIN	3
4 CHI	5 NJ	6	7	8 NYI	9	10 PHI
11 WAS	12	13 FLA	14	15 ANA	16	17 NAS
18 CBJ	19	20 DAL	21	22 TB	23	24 NAS
25	26	27 COL	28	29 CHI	30	31 LA

February
SUN	MON	TUE	WED	THU	FRI	SAT
1	2 ANA	3	4 STL	5	6	7
8*	9	10	11 ATL	12	13 MIN	14
15 D NAS	16 DET	17	18 COL	19	20	21 VAN
22	23 DET	24	25 ANA	26	27 PHO	28
29 D DAL						

March
SUN	MON	TUE	WED	THU	FRI	SAT
	1	2 PHO	3	4 STL	5	6
7 CHI	8 D	9	10 CAL	11 COL	12 VAN	13
14 OTT	15	16 CBJ	17	18	19 NAS	20
21 SJ	22 LA	23	24 DAL	25	26 LA	27
28 PHO	29	30 STL	31 DAL			

April
SUN	MON	TUE	WED	THU	FRI	SAT
				1	2	3 VAN
4	5	6	7	8	9	10

2003-04 SEASON
CLUB DIRECTORY

Owner
Edmonton Investors Group, Ltd.
Governor
Cal Nichols
Alternate governors
Bill Butler, Kevin Lowe
President & chief executive officer
Patrick LaForge
General manager
Kevin Lowe
Assistant general manager
Scott Howson
V.p. of player personnel/hockey ops.
Kevin Prendergast
Head coach
Craig MacTavish
Assistant coaches
Charlie Huddy, Bill Moores
Video coach
Brian Ross
Goaltending Coach
Pete Peeters
Scouting staff
Bob Brown, Bill Dandy, Brad Davis,
Lorne Davis, Morey Gare, Stu
MacGregor, Bob Mancini, Chris
McCarthy, Frank Musil, Kent Nilsson,
Gord Pell, Dave Semenko

Head medical trainer
Ken Lowe
Head equipment manager
Barrie Stafford
Equipment managers
Lyle Kulchisky, Jeff Lang
Massage therapist
Stewart Poirier
Team physician
Dr. David C. Reid
Vice president, public relations
Bill Tuele
Information coordinator
Steve Knowles
Public relations coordinator
J.J. Hebert
Vice president, finance
Darryl Boessenkool
V.p., sponsorships, sales & services
Allan Watt
Director of sales
Eric Upton
Director of ticketing
John Yeomans
Director of broadcast
Don Metz

DRAFT CHOICES

Rd.— Player	Overall	Pos.	Last team
1— Marc-Antoine Pouliot...	22	C	Rimouski (QMJHL)
2— Colin McDonald	51	RW	New England (EJHL)
2— Jean-Francois Jacques	68	LW	Baie Comeau (QMJHL)
3— Mishail Joukov............	72	LW	Arboga (Sweden)
3— Zachery Stortini	94	RW	Sudbury (OHL)
5— Kalle Olsson................	147	W	Frolunda Jr. (Sweden Jr.)
5— David Rohlfs	154	RW	Compuware (NAHL)
6— Dragan Umicevic.........	184	LW	Sodertalje (Sweden)
7— Kyle Brodziak	214	C	Moose Jaw (WHL)
7— Mathieu Roy	215	D	Val D'Or (QMJHL)
8— Josef Hrabal...............	248	D	Vsetin Jr. (Czech Republic Jr.)
9— Troy Bodie..................	278	RW	Kelowna (WHL)

MISCELLANEOUS DATA

Home ice (capacity)
Skyreach Centre (16,839)
Address
11230 110 Street
Edmonton, Alta. T5G 3H7
Business phone
780-414-4000
Ticket information
780-414-4625
Website
www.edmontonoilers.com

Training site
To be announced
Club colors
White, midnight blue, metallic copper
and red
Radio affiliation
CHED (630 AM)
TV affiliation
SportsNet & CBXT-TV

EDMONTON OILERS

No.	FORWARDS	Ht./Wt.	Place	BORN Date	NHL exp.	2002-03 clubs
28	Jason Chimera (C/LW) ..	6-0/180	Edmonton	5-2-79	3	Edmonton
89	Mike Comrie (C)	5-9/172	Edmonton	9-11-80	3	Edmonton
20	Radek Dvorak (RW).......	6-1/194	Tabor, Czechoslovakia	3-9-77	8	Edmonton, New York Rangers
	Ales Hemsky (RW)	6-0/170	Pardubice, Czechoslovakia	8-13-83	1	Edmonton
	Michael Henrich (RW) ...	6-2/206	Thornhill, Ont.	3-3-80	0	Hershey (AHL), Hamilton (AHL)
	Chad Hinz (RW).............	5-10/190	Saskatoon, Sask.	3-21-79	0	Hamilton (AHL)
10	Shawn Horcoff (LW/C)...	6-1/194	Trail, B.C.	9-17-78	3	Edmonton
15	Brad Isbister (LW)	6-4/230	Edmonton	5-7-77	6	Edmonton, New York Islanders
27	Georges Laraque (RW)..	6-3/240	Montreal	12-7-76	6	Edmonton
18	Ethan Moreau (LW)	6-2/205	Huntsville, Ont.	9-22-75	8	Edmonton
	Jesse Niinimaki (C)........	6-2/183	Tampere, Finland	8-19-83	0	Ilves Tampere (Finland)
	Fernando Pisani (LW)	6-1/185	Edmonton	12-27-76	1	Hamilton (AHL), Edmonton
15	Marty Reasoner (C)	6-0/203	Rochester, N.Y.	2-26-77	5	Hamilton (AHL), Edmonton
46	Jani Rita (LW)...............	6-1/206	Helsinki, Finland	7-25-81	2	Hamilton (AHL), Edmonton
	Tony Salmelainen (LW)..	5-9/176	Espoo, Finland	8-8-81	0	Hamilton (AHL)
	Peter Sarno (C).............	5-11/185	Toronto	7-26-79	0	Blues Espoo (Finland)
94	Ryan Smyth (LW)	6-1/195	Banff, Alta.	2-21-76	9	Edmonton
	Jarrett Stoll (C).............	6-1/199	Melville, Sask.	6-24-82	1	Edmonton
37	Brian Swanson (C)	5-10/185	Eagle River, Alaska	3-24-76	3	Edmonton
16	Raffi Torres (LW)	6-0/207	Toronto	10-8-81	2	New York Islanders
	Brad Winchester (LW) ...	6-5/208	Madison, Wis.	3-1-81	0	Univ. of Wisconsin (WCHA)
16	Mike York (LW).............	5-10/185	Waterford, Mich.	1-3-78	4	Edmonton

DEFENSEMEN

No.		Ht./Wt.	Place	Date	exp.	2002-03 clubs
	Bobby Allen	6-1/198	Braintree, Mass.	11-14-78	1	Hamilton (AHL), Edmonton
	Marc-Andre Bergeron	5-9/185	St-Louis-de-France, Que.	10-13-80	1	Hamilton (AHL), Edmonton
2	Eric Brewer...................	6-3/220	Vernon, B.C.	4-17-79	5	Edmonton
4	Cory Cross...................	6-5/219	Lloydminster, Alta.	1-3-71	10	Hartford (AHL), Edmonton, New York Rangers
32	Scott Ferguson	6-1/202	Camrose, Alta.	1-6-73	5	Edmonton
	Matt Greene..................	6-2/210	Grand Ledge. Mich.	5-13-83	0	Univ. of North Dakota (WCHA)
	Kari Haakana................	6-1/222	Outokumpu, Finland	11-8-73	1	Hamilton (AHL), Edmonton
	Jan Horacek.................	6-4/206	Benesov, Czechoslovakia	5-22-79	0	Havirov (Czech Republic)
	Alexander Ljubimov.......	6-3/196	Togliatti, U.S.S.R.	2-15-80	0	
	Doug Lynch	6-3/205	North Vancouver	4-4-83	0	Spokane (WHL)
	Alexei Semenov	6-6/210	Murmansk, U.S.S.R.	4-10-81	1	Hamilton (AHL), Edmonton
21	Jason Smith	6-3/208	Calgary	11-2-73	10	Edmonton
24	Steve Staios.................	6-1/200	Hamilton, Ont.	7-28-73	8	Edmonton

GOALTENDERS

No.		Ht./Wt.	Place	Date	exp.	2002-03 clubs
	Kristian Antila	6-3/207	Vammala, Finland	1-10-80	0	Wichita (CHL), Hamilton (AHL)
1	Ty Conklin	6-0/180	Anchorage, Alaska	3-30-76	1	Hamilton (AHL)
	Jeff Deslauriers.............	6-3/176	St-Jean-Richelieu, Que.	5-15-84	0	
35	Tommy Salo	5-11/173	Surahammar, Sweden	2-1-71	9	Edmonton

2002-03 REVIEW
INDIVIDUAL STATISTICS

SCORING

	Games	G	A	Pts.	PIM	+/-	PPG	SHG	GWG	GTG	Sht.	Sht. Pct.	Faceoffs Won	Lost	Pct.	TOI
Ryan Smyth	66	27	34	61	67	5	10	0	3	1	199	13.6	18	24	42.9	19:21
Todd Marchant	77	20	40	60	48	13	7	1	3	1	146	13.7	775	561	58.0	19:53
Anson Carter*	68	25	30	55	20	-11	10	0	1	1	176	14.2	95	122	43.8	19:38
Mike York	71	22	29	51	10	-8	7	2	4	0	177	12.4	171	219	43.8	19:04
Mike Comrie..............	69	20	31	51	90	-18	8	0	6	0	170	11.8	503	566	47.1	17:51
Shawn Horcoff	78	12	21	33	55	10	2	0	3	0	98	12.2	129	172	42.9	13:29
Ethan Moreau...........	78	14	17	31	112	-7	2	3	2	1	137	10.2	3	22	12.0	13:30
Marty Reasoner........	70	11	20	31	28	19	2	2	0	0	102	10.8	518	450	53.5	14:49
Ales Hemsky	59	6	24	30	14	5	0	0	1	0	50	12.0	1	2	33.3	12:04
Eric Brewer..............	80	8	21	29	45	-11	1	0	1	0	147	5.4	1	0	100.0	24:55
Janne Niinimaa*........	63	4	24	28	66	-7	2	0	0	0	90	4.4	0	1	0.0	26:47
Steve Staios	76	5	21	26	96	13	1	3	0	0	126	4.0	0	1	0.0	22:17
Jason Chimera	66	14	9	23	36	-2	0	1	4	1	90	15.6	6	5	54.5	10:45
Dan Cleary...............	57	4	13	17	31	5	0	0	1	0	89	4.5	2	3	40.0	11:57
Fernando Pisani	35	8	5	13	10	9	0	1	0	0	32	25.0	1	0	100.0	10:43
Georges Laraque.......	64	6	7	13	110	-4	0	0	2	0	46	13.0	0	0	—	9:14
Jason Smith..............	68	4	8	12	64	5	0	0	1	0	93	4.3	0	0	—	21:46

	Games	G	A	Pts.	PIM	+/-	PPG	SHG	GWG	GTG	Sht.	Sht. Pct.	Faceoffs Won	Lost	Pct.	TOI
Brian Swanson	44	2	10	12	10	-7	1	0	1	0	67	3.0	212	193	52.3	11:55
Radek Dvorak*	12	4	4	8	14	-3	1	0	0	1	32	12.5	0	1	0.0	16:07
Scott Ferguson	78	3	5	8	120	11	0	0	0	0	45	6.7	1	0	100.0	12:17
Alexei Semenov	46	1	6	7	58	-7	0	0	0	0	33	3.0	0	0	—	19:41
Jiri Dopita	21	1	5	6	11	-4	0	0	1	0	23	4.3	167	149	52.8	13:49
Brad Isbister*	13	3	2	5	9	0	0	0	1	0	29	10.3	5	5	50.0	13:14
Cory Cross*	11	2	3	5	8	3	1	0	1	0	11	18.2	0	0	—	17:50
Jani Rita	12	3	1	4	0	2	0	0	0	0	18	16.7	0	1	0.0	9:32
Ales Pisa*	48	1	3	4	24	11	1	0	0	0	34	2.9	0	0	—	12:56
Marc-Andre Bergeron	5	1	1	2	9	2	0	0	0	0	5	20.0	0	0	—	16:30
Josh Green*	20	0	2	2	12	-3	0	0	0	0	20	0.0	0	5	0.0	10:22
Jarret Stoll	4	0	1	1	0	-3	0	0	0	0	5	0.0	19	11	63.3	7:44
Jussi Markkanen (g)	22	0	1	1	2	0	0	0	0	0	0	—	0	0	—	—
Bobby Allen	1	0	0	0	0	0	0	0	0	0	0	—	0	0	—	2:53
Alex Henry*	3	0	0	0	0	-1	0	0	0	0	0	—	0	0	—	7:01
Kari Haakana	13	0	0	0	4	-2	0	0	0	0	2	0.0	0	0	—	7:55
Tommy Salo (g)	65	0	0	0	4	0	0	0	0	0	1	0.0	0	0	—	—

GOALTENDING

	Games	GS	Min.	GA	SO	Avg.	W	L	T	EN	PPG Allow	SHG Allow	Shots	Save Pct.
Jussi Markkanen	22	17	1180	51	3	2.59	7	8	3	3	12	1	533	.904
Tommy Salo	65	65	3814	172	4	2.71	29	27	8	4	49	7	1708	.899

*Played with two or more NHL teams.

RESULTS

OCTOBER

10— Philadelphia ....T....*2-2
12— At Nashville ....W.....3-2
15— At Dallas ....L.....0-3
17— At San Jose ....L.....3-4
19— Boston ....L.....3-4
22— At Colorado ....T....*3-3
24— St. Louis ....L.....1-2
26— Anaheim ....W.....4-3
28— Dallas ....OTL...*3-4

NOVEMBER

1— Buffalo ....T....*1-1
3— At Chicago......................W.....4-1
5— At N.Y. Rangers ....L.....2-5
8— At N.Y. Islanders ....L.....2-4
9— At New Jersey ....W.....6-3
11— At Boston.......................L.....1-6
12— At Minnesota ....W.....3-2
15— St. Louis........................W.....5-0
16— Los Angeles...................L.....1-4
19— Chicago ....W.....3-1
21— At Calgary ....W.....3-1
23— Detroit ....T....*1-1
25— At Detroit........................W...*5-4
27— At Columbus ....W.....3-1
30— Colorado........................W.....1-0

DECEMBER

3— Minnesota ....W...*2-1
5— At Tampa Bay ....L.....2-3
7— At Florida.........................W.....4-0

8— At Atlanta ....W.....3-0
11— Carolina.........................W.....4-1
13— Colorado.......................W...*4-3
14— Vancouver ....L.....3-6
17— At Minnesota ....OTL...*3-4
19— At Colorado ....L.....1-2
21— At Vancouver................OTL...*3-4
26— Vancouver ....L.....2-4
28— Toronto ....W...*3-2
30— At Phoenix....................OTL...*3-4
31— At Dallas ....L.....1-4

JANUARY

2— Minnesota ....OTL...*1-2
4— Montreal ....W...*5-4
6— At San Jose ....T....*5-5
8— At Anaheim ....W.....1-0
9— At Los Angeles ....W.....5-4
11— Ottawa ....L.....0-2
13— Columbus ....W.....8-5
16— Los Angeles ....W.....2-0
18— Nashville ....OTL...*2-3
20— At Calgary ....L.....3-4
22— Detroit ....W...*4-3
24— Phoenix ....L.....1-5
29— Minnesota ....W.....5-1
30— At Vancouver ....T....*3-3

FEBRUARY

5— Anaheim ....W.....2-1
7— Calgary ....L.....3-4
8— Chicago ....L.....0-3

11— At Toronto ....W......5-4
13— At Ottawa ....L.....0-2
15— At Montreal ....L.....2-3
18— At Pittsburgh.................OTL...*3-4
20— At Detroit.........................L.....2-6
22— Vancouver ....OTL...*2-3
23— Atlanta ....T....*3-3
25— At Colorado ....L.....2-4
27— At St. Louis.....................L.....1-4

MARCH

1— At Columbus....................T....*3-3
4— San Jose ....W.....2-1
6— At Los Angeles ....W.....2-1
7— At Anaheim ....W.....4-1
10— Toronto ....L.....2-3
11— At Calgary ....W.....5-2
13— N.Y. Islanders ....L.....2-5
15— Dallas ....W.....4-3
17— At Nashville ....W.....5-3
20— At Phoenix....................OTL...*2-3
22— Washington ....W.....5-3
23— Nashville.........................W...*3-2
26— Phoenix ....W.....4-3
28— Columbus ....W.....4-0
30— At Chicago ....T....*4-4
31— At St. Louis......................T....*5-5

APRIL

3— San Jose.........................T....*3-3
5— Calgary ....L.....1-4
*Denotes overtime game.

FLORIDA PANTHERS
EASTERN CONFERENCE/SOUTHEAST DIVISION

Panthers' Schedule
Home games shaded; D=Day game; *Feb. 8 All-Star Game at St. Paul, Minn.

October

SUN	MON	TUE	WED	THU	FRI	SAT
5	6	7	8	9 CAR	10	11 BOS
12	13 CAR	14	15 PHO	16	17	18 NYI
19	20 NYR	21	22 NJ	23	24 MIN	25 ATL
26	27	28	29 PHI	30 OTT	31	

November

SUN	MON	TUE	WED	THU	FRI	SAT
						1 SJ
2	3	4	5 LA	6	7 PIT	8 STL
9	10	11 TB	12	13 NJ	14	15 PIT
16 ATL	17	18	19 NYI	20	21 ATL	22 WAS
23	24 BUF	25	26 NYR	27	28 BUF	29 MON
30						

December

SUN	MON	TUE	WED	THU	FRI	SAT
	1	2	3 OTT	4	5	6 ATL
7	8	9	10 BOS	11	12 MON	13 NAS
14	15 DET	16	17 WAS	18	19 DAL	20
21	22 OTT	23 TOR	24	25	26	27 ANA
28	29 TOR	30	31 D TB			

January

SUN	MON	TUE	WED	THU	FRI	SAT
				1	2 PHI	3 CBJ
4	5	6	7	8 PHI	9	10 CAL
11 VAN	12	13 EDM	14	15	16	17 TB
18	19 STL	20	21 COL	22	23 WAS	24 BOS
25	26 NYR	27	28 PHI	29	30	31 NYI

February

SUN	MON	TUE	WED	THU	FRI	SAT
1	2	3 SJ	4 PHO	5	6	7
8*	9	10 MON	11	12 PIT	13	14 TB
15	16 CAR	17	18 BUF	19	20 PIT	21 WAS
22	23 BOS	24	25 TOR	26	27 WAS	28
29 D CHI						

March

SUN	MON	TUE	WED	THU	FRI	SAT
	1	2 WAS	3 NJ	4	5	6 TB
7	8	9 TOR	10	11 MON	12	13 NYR
14	15	16	17 NYI	18	19 ATL	20 BUF
21	22	23 NJ	24	25 CAR	26	27 ATL
28	29 CAR	30	31 OTT			

April

SUN	MON	TUE	WED	THU	FRI	SAT
				1 TB	2	3
4 CAR	D 5	6	7	8	9	10

2003-04 SEASON
CLUB DIRECTORY

General partner and chairman of the board/CEO/governor
Alan Cohen

Partner/president, Panthers Hockey LLLP & alternate governor
Jordan Zimmerman

Partners
Steve Cohen, David Epstein, Dr. Elliott Hahn, H. Wayne Huizenga, Bernie Kosar, Richard C. Lehman, M.D., Al Maroone, Michael Maroone

Alternate governor
William A. Torrey

Chief operating officer & alt. gov.
Jeff Cogen

Chief financial officer
Bill Duffy

Chief marketing officer & exec. v.p., business operations
Chris Overholt

Senior vice president, arena operations
Steve Dangerfield

General manager
Rick Dudley

Head coach
Mike Keenan

Assistant coach
John Torchetti

Director of hockey operations
Grant Sonier

Goaltending coach
Clint Malarchuk

Director of player development
Duane Sutter

Skating & skills instructor and scout
Paul Vincent

Director of amateur scouting
Scott Luce

Head amateur scout
Darwin Bennett

Amateur scouts
Erin Ginnell, Ron Harris

Pro scouts
Michael Abbamont, Billy Dea

European scouts
Niklas Blomgren, Jari Kekalainen

Part-time European scout
Vadim Podrezov

Head medical trainer
Dave Boyer

Strength & conditioning coach
Chris Reichart

Head equipment manager
Mark Brennan

Director of media relations
Randy Sieminski

Publications coordinator and historian
Michael Citro

Director of finance/controller
Evelyn Lopez

DRAFT CHOICES

Rd.— Player	Overall	Pos.	Last team
1— Nathan Horton	3	C	Oshawa (OHL)
1— Anthony Stewart	25	C	Kingston (OHL)
2— Kamil Kreps	38	C	Brampton (OHL)
2— Stefan Meyer	55	LW	Medicine Hat (WHL)
4— Martin Lojek	105	D	Brampton (OHL)
4— James Pemberton	124	D	Providence (Hockey East)
5— Dan Travis	141	RW	Deerfield HS
5— Martin Tuma	162	D	Litvinov Jr. (Czech Republic Jr.)
6— Denis Stasyuk	171	C	Novokuznetsk (Russia)
7— Dany Roussin	223	C	Rimouski (QMJHL)
8— Petr Kadlec	234	D	Slavia (Czech Rep.)
9— John Hecimovic	264	RW	Sarnia (OHL)
9— Tanner Glass	265	F	Nanaimo (BCHL)

MISCELLANEOUS DATA

Home ice (capacity)
Office Depot Center (19,250)

Address
One Panther Parkway
Sunrise, FL 33323

Business phone
954-835-7000

Ticket information
954-835-7825

Website
www.floridapanthers.com

Training site
Sunrise, FL

Club colors
Red, navy blue, yellow and gold

Radio affiliation
WQAM (560 AM)

TV affiliation
FOX SportsNet

FLORIDA PANTHERS

No.	FORWARDS	Ht./Wt.	Place	BORN Date	NHL exp.	2002-03 clubs
38	Eric Beaudoin (LW)	6-5/210	Ottawa	5-3-80	2	San Antonio (AHL), Florida
27	Jaroslav Bednar (RW)	5-11/198	Prague, Czechoslovakia	11-9-76	2	Los Angeles, Florida
20	Valeri Bure (RW)	5-10/185	Moscow, U.S.S.R.	6-13-74	9	St. Louis, Florida
	Gregory Campbell (C)	5-11/167	Tillsonburg, Ont.	12-17-83	0	Kitchener (OHL)
10	Jim Campbell (RW)	6-2/205	Worcester, Mass.	4-3-73	8	San Antonio (AHL), Florida
17	Matt Cullen (C)	6-0/195	Virginia, Minn.	11-2-76	6	Florida, Anaheim
26	Pierre Dagenais (RW)	6-5/215	Blainville, Que.	3-4-78	3	San Antonio (AHL), Florida
14	Niklas Hagman (LW)	6-0/200	Espoo, Finland	12-5-79	2	Florida
24	Darcy Hordichuk (LW)	6-1/200	Kamsack, Sask.	8-10-80	3	Springfield (AHL), Florida, Phoenix
22	Kristian Huselius (LW)	6-1/190	Stockholm, Sweden	11-10-78	2	Florida
32	Ryan Jardine (LW)	6-0/210	Ottawa	3-15-80	1	San Antonio (AHL)
12	Olli Jokinen (C)	6-3/205	Kuopio, Finland	12-5-78	6	Florida
25	Juraj Kolnik (RW)	5-10/182	Nitra, Czechoslovakia	11-13-80	3	San Antonio (AHL), Florida
25	Viktor Kozlov (C)	6-5/225	Togliatti, U.S.S.R.	2-14-75	9	Florida
	Andy Lundbohm (C)	6-3/225	Roseau, Minn.	3-24-77	0	San Antonio (AHL), Laredo (CHL)
37	Stephane Matteau (LW)	6-4/220	Rouyn-Noranda, Que.	9-2-69	13	San Antonio (AHL), Florida
	Eric Messier (LW)	6-2/200	Drummondville, Que.	10-29-73	7	Colorado
	David Morisset (RW)	6-2/195	Langley, B.C.	4-6-81	1	San Antonio (AHL)
	Vaclav Nedorost (C)	6-1/187	Budejovice, Czechoslovakia	3-16-82	2	Hershey (AHL), Colorado
18	Marcus Nilson (LW)	6-2/200	Balsta, Sweden	3-1-78	5	Florida
39	Ivan Novoseltsev (RW)	6-1/210	Golitsino, U.S.S.R.	1-23-79	4	Florida
	Sean O'Connor (RW)	6-2/211	Victoria, B.C.	10-19-81	0	Jackson (ECHL), San Antonio (AHL)
	Josh Olson (LW)	6-5/220	Grand Forks, N.D.	7-13-81	0	Jackson (ECHL), San Antonio (AHL)
	Serge Payer (C)	5-11/175	Rockland, Ont.	5-7-79	1	San Antonio (AHL)
43	Byron Ritchie (C)	5-10/195	Burnaby, B.C.	4-24-77	4	San Antonio (AHL), Florida
37	M. Samuelsson (RW)	6-1/195	Mariefred, Sweden	12-23-76	3	Pittsburgh, New York Rangers
21	Denis Shvidki (RW)	6-2/215	Kharkov, U.S.S.R.	11-21-80	3	San Antonio (AHL), Florida
	Janis Sprukts (C)	6-3/224	Aiga, U.S.S.R.	1-31-82	0	
	Petr Taticek (C)	6-2/188	Rakovnik, Czechoslovakia	9-22-83	0	
23	Rocky Thompson (RW)	6-2/205	Calgary	8-8-77	4	San Antonio (AHL)
21	Jeff Toms (LW)	6-5/213	Swift Current, Sask.	6-4-74	8	San Antonio (AHL), Florida
19	Stephen Weiss (C)	6-0/185	Toronto	4-3-83	2	Florida
	DEFENSEMEN					
43	Mathieu Biron	6-6/212	Lac St. Charles, Que.	4-29-80	4	San Antonio (AHL), Florida
	Jay Bouwmeester	6-3/206	Edmonton	9-27-83	1	Florida
	Paul Elliott	6-0/202	White Rock, B.C.	6-2-80	0	San Antonio (AHL)
29	Lukas Krajicek	6-2/185	Prostejov, Czechoslovakia	3-11-83	1	San Antonio (AHL)
25	Igor Kravchuk	6-1/218	Ufa, U.S.S.R.	9-13-66	12	Florida
3	Paul Laus	6-1/215	Beamsville, Ont.	9-26-70	9	
6	Andreas Lilja	6-3/220	Landskrona, Sweden	7-13-75	3	Los Angeles, Florida
	Ivan Majesky	6-5/225	Bystrica, Czech.	9-2-76	1	Florida
	Branislav Mezei	6-5/221	Nitra, Czechoslovakia	10-8-80	3	San Antonio (AHL), Florida
	Filip Novak	6-0/174	Ceske Budejovice, Czech.	5-7-82	0	San Antonio (AHL)
	Kyle Rossiter	6-3/218	Edmonton	6-9-80	2	San Antonio (AHL), Florida
	Vladimir Sapozhnikov	6-3/205	Seversk, U.S.S.R.	8-2-82	0	San Antonio (AHL)
7	Pavel Trnka	6-3/200	Plzen, Czechoslovakia	7-27-76	6	Florida, Anaheim
55	Igor Ulanov	6-3/220	Krasnokamsk, U.S.S.R.	10-1-69	12	San Antonio (AHL), Florida
43	Mike Van Ryn	6-1/190	London, Ont.	5-14-79	3	Worcester (AHL), St. Louis, San Antonio (AHL)
	GOALTENDERS					
35	Jani Hurme	6-0/187	Turku, Finland	1-7-75	4	Florida
	Denis Khlopotnov	6-4/198	Moscow, U.S.S.R.	1-27-78	0	
1	Roberto Luongo	6-3/205	Montreal	4-4-79	4	Florida

2002-03 REVIEW
INDIVIDUAL STATISTICS
SCORING

	Games	G	A	Pts.	PIM	+/-	PPG	SHG	GWG	GTG	Sht.	Sht. Pct.	Faceoffs Won	Lost	Pct.	TOI
Olli Jokinen	81	36	29	65	79	-17	13	3	6	0	240	15.0	898	1027	46.6	22:01
Viktor Kozlov	74	22	34	56	18	-8	7	1	1	1	232	9.5	173	231	42.8	22:35
Kristian Huselius	78	20	23	43	20	-6	3	0	3	3	187	10.7	2	4	33.3	17:20
Marcus Nilson	82	15	19	34	31	2	7	1	0	0	187	8.0	219	250	46.7	15:31
Ivan Novoseltsev	78	10	17	27	30	-16	1	0	0	1	115	8.7	12	27	30.8	15:01
Sandis Ozolinsh*	51	7	19	26	40	-16	5	0	2	0	83	8.4	0	0	—	28:22
Valeri Bure*	46	5	21	26	10	-11	3	0	2	0	150	3.3	6	13	31.6	18:37
Niklas Hagman	80	8	15	23	20	-8	2	0	0	0	132	6.1	2	15	11.8	13:30

	Games	G	A	Pts.	PIM	+/-	PPG	SHG	GWG	GTG	Sht.	Sht. Pct.	Faceoffs Won	Lost	Pct.	TOI
Stephen Weiss	77	6	15	21	17	-13	0	0	2	0	87	6.9	493	572	46.3	14:17
Jaroslav Bednar*	52	5	13	18	14	-2	2	0	1	2	66	7.6	18	24	42.9	14:09
Jay Bouwmeester	82	4	12	16	14	-29	2	0	0	2	110	3.6	0	0	—	20:08
Matt Cullen*	30	6	6	12	22	-4	2	1	1	0	54	11.1	200	223	47.3	14:43
Andreas Lilja*	56	4	8	12	56	8	0	0	0	0	59	6.8	0	0	—	19:10
Ivan Majesky	82	4	8	12	92	-18	0	0	2	0	52	7.7	0	0	—	20:53
Mathieu Biron	34	1	8	9	14	-18	0	1	0	0	52	1.9	0	0	—	21:08
Stephane Matteau	52	4	4	8	27	-9	0	0	0	0	47	8.5	7	12	36.8	10:45
Brad Ference*	60	2	6	8	118	2	0	0	0	0	41	4.9	0	0	—	15:57
Ryan Johnson*	58	2	5	7	26	-13	0	0	0	0	54	3.7	331	358	48.0	10:39
Dmitry Yushkevich*	23	1	6	7	14	-12	0	0	0	0	23	4.3	1	2	33.3	23:40
Denis Shvidki	23	4	2	6	12	-7	2	0	1	0	29	13.8	3	2	60.0	14:14
Peter Worrell	63	2	3	5	193	-14	0	0	0	0	52	3.8	2	11	15.4	9:15
Lance Ward*	36	3	1	4	78	-4	0	0	1	0	34	8.8	0	0	—	9:07
Jeff Toms	8	2	2	4	4	2	0	0	0	0	12	16.7	44	39	53.0	11:36
Pavel Trnka*	22	0	3	3	24	-1	0	0	0	0	25	0.0	0	0	—	17:24
Byron Ritchie	30	0	3	3	19	-4	0	0	0	0	29	0.0	121	130	48.2	9:17
Branislav Mezei	11	2	0	2	10	-2	0	0	1	0	10	20.0	0	0	—	18:22
Igor Ulanov	56	1	1	2	39	7	0	0	0	0	20	5.0	0	0	—	16:42
Igor Kravchuk	7	0	1	1	4	-3	0	0	0	0	8	0.0	0	0	—	18:46
Juraj Kolnik	10	0	1	1	0	1	0	0	0	0	14	0.0	0	1	0.0	10:33
Eric Beaudoin	15	0	1	1	25	-7	0	0	0	0	11	0.0	8	19	29.6	9:51
Wade Flaherty (g)*	0	0	0	0	0	0	0	0	0	0	0	—	0	0	—	—
Jim Campbell	1	0	0	0	0	0	0	0	0	0	3	0.0	0	1	0.0	8:56
Jamie Rivers	1	0	0	0	2	-2	0	0	0	0	2	0.0	0	0	—	18:27
Joey Tetarenko*	2	0	0	0	4	-1	0	0	0	0	2	0.0	0	0	—	6:18
Darcy Hordichuk*	3	0	0	0	15	-1	0	0	0	0	2	0.0	0	0	—	9:45
Kyle Rossiter	3	0	0	0	0	0	0	0	0	0	0	—	0	0	—	10:09
Pierre Dagenais	9	0	0	0	4	-1	0	0	0	0	5	0.0	0	0	—	6:00
Jani Hurme (g)	28	0	0	0	2	0	0	0	0	0	0	—	0	0	—	—
Roberto Luongo (g)	65	0	0	0	4	0	0	0	0	0	0	—	0	0	—	—

GOALTENDING

	Games	GS	Min.	GA	SO	Avg.	W	L	T	EN	PPG Allow	SHG Allow	Shots	Save Pct.
Roberto Luongo	65	62	3627	164	6	2.71	20	34	7	7	46	6	2011	.918
Jani Hurme	28	20	1376	66	1	2.88	4	11	6	0	20	3	707	.907

*Played with two or more NHL teams.

RESULTS

OCTOBER

10— Tampa Bay ....OTL... *3-4
12— At Atlanta ....W... *5-4
15— At Minnesota ....L......1-4
17— At Chicago ....L......1-4
19— At Columbus ....L......1-4
21— Atlanta..........................W......3-2
23— At Toronto ....W......4-1
24— At N.Y. Islanders ....L......3-5
26— Washington ....T... *1-1
28— Tampa Bay ....L......1-6
30— At Dallas ....W... *3-2

NOVEMBER

2— Atlanta...........................L......1-3
6— Pittsburgh ....W... *4-3
7— At Washington ....OTL... *1-2
9— Calgary ....W......3-0
11— Chicago ....T... *2-2
13— At Philadelphia...............T... *1-1
14— At Ottawa ....OTL... *2-3
16— San Jose ....L......3-7
19— At Atlanta ....OTL... *3-4
20— N.Y. Islanders ....T... *3-3
22— At Phoenix ....T... *3-3
24— At Anaheim ....T... *4-4
27— At Los Angeles ....W......5-2
30— Vancouver ....L......2-5

DECEMBER

4— Carolina ....W......4-2
6— At Carolina ....W......2-0

7— Edmonton.........................L......0-4
10— Philadelphia....................L......2-5
13— N.Y. Islanders ....T... *3-3
18— Toronto...........................T... *2-2
20— At Buffalo ....W......3-0
21— At Boston ....T... *3-3
23— Nashville ....OTL... *2-3
27— Dallas.............................L......0-4
28— N.Y. Rangers ....OTL... *1-2
30— At N.Y. Islanders ....OTL... *1-2

JANUARY

1— At New Jersey ....W......2-1
2— At Colorado ....W......4-1
4— At Vancouver ....L......2-3
8— Detroit ....OTL... *1-2
10— New Jersey ....L......1-2
11— At Washington ....L......2-12
13— At New Jersey ....L......2-6
15— Boston ....W......3-0
18— Pittsburgh ....W......3-0
20— Montreal ....L......2-3
22— Ottawa ....L......1-2
24— At Carolina ....L......1-3
25— Carolina ....W... *3-2
28— At Montreal ....L......3-6
30— At Detroit ....T... *2-2

FEBRUARY

5— Toronto............................L......0-6
6— At Pittsburgh ....W......6-0
8— Tampa Bay ....T... *4-4

12— N.Y. Rangers ....L......1-3
14— Boston.........................OTL... *5-6
15— Washington ....L......1-2
18— At Montreal ....W......3-0
20— At Ottawa ....W......4-3
22— At Philadelphia ....W......4-2
24— Buffalo ....T... *2-2
26— Anaheim ....L......1-2
27— At Tampa Bay ....L......1-3

MARCH

1— At N.Y. Rangers ....L......2-5
3— At Toronto ....W......2-1
5— Colorado ....L......1-3
7— At Atlanta ....W......2-1
8— Buffalo ....L......0-4
10— At N.Y. Rangers ....L......1-2
12— Montreal ....L......0-4
15— At Boston ....L......1-4
16— At Pittsburgh ....W......4-2
19— Minnesota ....L......1-3
22— Ottawa ....L......1-3
24— New Jersey ....L......1-4
26— At Buffalo ....L......1-2
27— At St. Louis ....L......1-2
29— At Tampa Bay ....T... *1-1

APRIL

1— At Washington ....L......0-3
4— Carolina ....W......4-1
6— Philadelphia.....................L......2-6
*Denotes overtime game.

LOS ANGELES KINGS
WESTERN CONFERENCE/PACIFIC DIVISION

Kings' Schedule
Home games shaded; D=Day game; *Feb. 8 All-Star Game at St. Paul, Minn.

October
SUN	MON	TUE	WED	THU	FRI	SAT
5	6	7	8	9 DET	10 PIT	11
12 CHI	13	14	15 OTT	16	17	18 BOS
19	20	21 PHI	22	23 BUF	24	25 CHI
26	27	28	29	30 VAN	31	

November
SUN	MON	TUE	WED	THU	FRI	SAT
						1 PHO
2	3	4	5 FLA	6 TB	7	8 CAR
9 WAS	10	11	12	13 TOR	14	15 D STL
16	17	18	19 NAS	20	21 DAL	22 COL
23	24	25 NJ	26	27 PHO	28	29 D CHI
30 DAL						

December
SUN	MON	TUE	WED	THU	FRI	SAT
	1	2 STL	3	4 DAL	5	6 WAS
7	8 DET	9	10 ATL	11 NAS	12	13 STL
14	15	16 EDM	17	18 PHO	19	20 COL
21	22 VAN	23	24	25	26 SJ	27 SJ
28	29	30 NYR	31 PHO			

January
SUN	MON	TUE	WED	THU	FRI	SAT
				1	2	3 DAL
4	5	6	7 ANA	8 VAN	9	10 CBJ
11	12	13 NAS	14 MIN	15	16 CBJ	17
18 CHI	19	20 MIN	21	22 DET	23	24 ANA
25	26 MIN	27	28 ANA	29 COL	30	31 EDM

February
SUN	MON	TUE	WED	THU	FRI	SAT
1	2	3 CAL	4	5	6	7
8*	9	10 MIN	11 CBJ	12	13 BUF	14
15 D NJ	16 D NYI	17	18 DAL	19	20	21 CBJ
22	23 NAS	24	25 DAL	26	27	28 D ANA
29 D ANA						

March
SUN	MON	TUE	WED	THU	FRI	SAT
	1	2	3	4 MIN	5	6 MON
7	8	9 PHO	10 PHO	11	12	13 D SJ
14 D ANA	15	16 STL	17	18 SJ	19	20 DET
21	22 EDM	23	24 VAN	25	26 EDM	27 D CAL
28	29 COL	30	31 SJ			

April
SUN	MON	TUE	WED	THU	FRI	SAT
				1	2 CAL	3
4 D SJ	5	6	7	8	9	10

2003-04 SEASON
CLUB DIRECTORY

Owners
Philip F. Anschutz
Edward P. Roski, Jr.
President/CEO
Tim Leiweke
Sr. vice president, general manager
Dave Taylor
Coach
Andy Murray
Assistant coaches
Mark Hardy
Ray Bennett
John Van Boxmeer
Goaltending consultant
Andy Nowicki
V.p. of hockey operations, asst. g.m.
Kevin Gilmore
Director of player personnel
Bill O'Flaherty
Assistant to general manager
John Wolf
Director of amateur scouting
Al Murray
Pro scout—dir. of European evaluation
Rob Laird

Scouting staff
Vaclav Nedomansky, Brian Putnam,
Parry Shockey, John Stanton, Jan
Vopat, Ari Vuori, Glen Williamson,
Michel Boucher, Jim Cassidy, Mike
Donnelly, Viacheslav Golovin, Gary
Harker, Jerry Sodomlak, Victor
Tjumenev, Janne Jarlefelt, Dan
Flynn, Barry Martinelli
Vice president of sales and marketing
Kurt Schwartzkopf
Dir., media relations and team services
Mike Altieri
Mgr., media relations and team services
Jeff Moeller
Asst. mgr., media relations/team services
Lee Callans
Trainers
Peter Demers, Peter Millar, Rick Burrill,
Rick Garcia, Robert Zolg, Dan Del
Vecchio, Mike Kadar, Marco
Yrjovuori

DRAFT CHOICES

Rd.— Player	Overall	Pos.	Last team
1— Dustin Brown	13	RW	Guelph (OHL)
1— Brian Boyle	26	C	St. Sebastian's (U.S. high school)
1— Jeff Tambellini	27	LW	Michigan (CCHA)
2— Konstantin Pushkaryov	44	W	Ust-Karpenogorsk (Russia)
3— Ryan Munce	82	G	Samia (QHL)
5— Brady Murray	152	C	Salmon Arm (BGHL)
6— Esa Pirnes	174	C	Tappora (Finland)
8— Matt Zaba	231	G	Vernon (BCHL)
8— Mike Sullivan	244	C	Stouffville (Ont. Prov. Jr. A)
9— Martin Guerin	274	RW	Des Moines (USHL)

MISCELLANEOUS DATA

Home ice (capacity)
STAPLES Center (18,118)
Address
STAPLES Center
1111 South Figueroa Street
Los Angeles, CA 90015
Business phone
213-742-7100
Ticket information
888-546-4752
Website
www.lakings.com

Training site
El Segundo, CA
Club colors
Purple, silver, black and white
Radio affiliation
KSPN (710 AM)
TV affiliation
FOX Sports Net

No.	FORWARDS	Ht./Wt.	Place	BORN Date	NHL exp.	2002-03 clubs
41	Jason Allison (C)	6-4/205	North York, Ont.	5-29-75	10	Los Angeles
	Sergei Anshakov (LW)	6-3/179	Moscow, U.S.S.R.	1-13-84	0	CSKA (CIS Jr.)
38	Derek Armstrong (C)	6-0/193	Ottawa	4-23-73	7	Manchester (AHL), Los Angeles
	Jared Aulin (C)	5-11/175	Calgary	3-15-82	1	Manchester (AHL), Los Angeles
42	Sean Avery (C)	5-10/188	North York, Ont.	4-10-80	2	Grand Rapids (AHL), Detroit, Los Angeles
	Scott Barney (C)	6-4/198	Oshawa, Ont.	3-27-79	1	Manchester (AHL), Los Angeles
	Derek Bekar (LW/C)	6-3/194	Burnaby, B.C.	9-15-75	2	Manchester (AHL), Los Angeles
25	Eric Belanger (C)	6-0/177	Sherbrooke, Que.	12-16-77	3	Los Angeles
12	Ken Belanger (LW)	6-4/225	Sault Ste. Marie, Ont.	5-14-74	9	Los Angeles
	Mike Cammalleri (C)	5-8/175	Richmond Hill, Ont.	6-8-82	1	Manchester (AHL), Los Angeles
29	Brad Chartrand (C)	5-11/191	Winnipeg	12-14-74	4	Los Angeles
28	Adam Deadmarsh (RW)	6-0/195	Trail, B.C.	5-10-75	9	Los Angeles
42	Mikko Eloranta (LW)	6-0/185	Turku, Finland	8-24-72	4	Los Angeles
	Ryan Flinn (LW)	6-4/210	Halifax, Nova Scotia	4-20-80	2	Manchester (AHL), Los Angeles
	Alexander Frolov (LW)	6-3/191	Moscow, U.S.S.R.	6-19-82	1	Los Angeles
57	Steve Heinze (RW)	5-11/193	Lawrence, Mass.	1-30-70	12	Manchester (AHL), Los Angeles
23	Craig Johnson (LW)	6-2/197	St. Paul, Minn.	3-8-72	9	Los Angeles
	Henrik Juntunen (RW)	6-2/185	Goteburg, Sweden	4-24-83	0	Karpat Oulu (Finland)
	Jens Karlsson (RW)	6-3/200	Goteburg, Sweden	11-7-82	0	Vastra Frolunda (Sweden)
11	Steve Kelly (C)	6-2/211	Vancouver	10-26-76	7	Manchester (AHL), Los Angeles
36	Greg Koehler (C)	6-2/195	Scarborough, Ont.	2-27-75	1	Milwaukee (AHL), Manchester (AHL)
22	Ian Laperriere (RW)	6-1/197	Montreal	1-19-74	10	Los Angeles
	Yanick Lehoux (C)	5-11/170	Montreal	4-8-82	0	
33	Ziggy Palffy (RW)	5-10/180	Skalica, Czechoslovakia	5-5-72	10	Los Angeles
9	Erik Rasmussen (LW)	6-2/205	Minneapolis	3-28-77	6	Los Angeles
	Chris Schmidt (LW)	6-3/212	Beaverlodge, Alta.	3-1-76	1	Manchester (AHL), Los Angeles
	Andrei Shefer (LW)	6-1/180	Sverdlovsk, U.S.S.R.	7-26-81	0	Cherepovets (Russian)
14	Jon Sim (LW)	5-10/184	New Glasgow, Nova Scotia	9-29-77	5	Utah (AHL), Los Angeles, Dallas, Nashville
	Jerred Smithson (C)	6-5/225	Meadow Lake, Sask.	2-4-79	1	Los Angeles, Manchester (AHL), Manchester (AHL), Los Angeles
	David Steckel (C)	6-5/200	Milwaukee	3-15-82	0	
16	Jozef Stumpel (C)	6-3/216	Nitra, Czechoslovakia	7-20-72	12	Boston
	DEFENSEMEN					
56	Joe Corvo	6-1/205	Oak Park, Ill.	6-20-77	2	Manchester (AHL), Los Angeles
	Tim Gleason	6-0/199	Southfield, Mich.	1-29-83	0	Windsor (OHL)
	Denis Grebeshkov	6-0/189	Yaroslavl, U.S.S.R.	10-11-83	0	Lokomotiv Yaroslavl (Russian)
53	Jason Holland	6-2/193	Morinville, Alta.	4-30-76	6	Manchester (AHL), Los Angeles
32	Maxim Kuznetsov	6-5/198	Pavlodar, U.S.S.R.	3-24-77	3	Detroit, Los Angeles
19	Chris McAlpine	6-0/210	Roseville, Minn.	12-1-71	8	Manchester (AHL), Los Angeles
3	Aaron Miller	6-3/205	Buffalo	8-11-71	10	Los Angeles
44	Jaroslav Modry	6-2/219	Ceske-Budejovice, Czech.	2-27-71	9	Los Angeles
14	Mattias Norstrom	6-2/201	Stockholm, Sweden	1-2-72	10	Los Angeles
42	Brad Norton	6-4/225	Cambridge, Mass.	2-13-75	2	Los Angeles
	Mike Pudlick	6-3/192	Fridley, Minn.	2-24-78	0	Manchester (AHL)
	Joe Rullier	6-3/198	Montreal	1-28-80	0	Manchester (AHL)
17	Lubomir Visnovsky	5-10/172	Topolcany, Czechoslovakia	8-11-76	3	Los Angeles
5	Tomas Zizka	6-1/198	Sternberk, Czechoslovakia	10-10-79	1	Manchester (AHL), Los Angeles
	GOALTENDERS					
32	Roman Cechmanek	6-3/187	Gottwaldov, Czechoslovakia	3-2-71	3	Philadelphia
34	Marcel Cousineau	5-9/180	Delson, Que.	4-30-73	4	Cherepovets (Russian)
	Cristobal Huet	6-0/194	St. Martin D'tteres, France	9-3-75	1	Los Angeles
39	Felix Potvin	6-1/190	Anjou, Que.	6-23-71	12	Los Angeles
45	Travis Scott	6-2/185	Kanata, Ont.	9-14-75	1	Manchester (AHL)
1	Jamie Storr	6-2/198	Brampton, Ont.	12-28-75	9	Los Angeles
	Alexei Volkov	6-1/185	Yekaterinburg, U.S.S.R.	3-15-80	0	Dynamo (Russian)

2002-03 REVIEW

INDIVIDUAL STATISTICS

SCORING

	Games	G	A	Pts.	PIM	+/-	PPG	SHG	GWG	GTG	Sht.	Sht. Pct.	Faceoffs Won	Lost	Pct.	TOI
Zigmund Palffy	76	37	48	85	47	22	10	2	5	0	277	13.4	3	7	30.0	22:26
Mathieu Schneider*	65	14	29	43	57	0	10	0	1	0	162	8.6	0	0	—	22:20
Bryan Smolinski*	58	18	20	38	18	-1	6	1	8	0	150	12.0	385	446	46.3	19:02
Jaroslav Modry	82	13	25	38	68	-13	8	0	1	0	205	6.3	0	1	0.0	22:38
Derek Armstrong	66	12	26	38	30	5	2	0	1	0	106	11.3	354	354	50.0	15:40
Eric Belanger	62	16	19	35	26	-5	0	3	1	0	114	14.0	592	551	51.8	17:42

	Games	G	A	Pts.	PIM	+/-	PPG	SHG	GWG	GTG	Sht.	Sht. Pct.	Faceoffs Won	Lost	Pct.	TOI
Alexander Frolov	79	14	17	31	34	12	1	0	3	0	141	9.9	2	7	22.2	14:23
Jason Allison	26	6	22	28	22	9	2	0	3	1	46	13.0	274	264	50.9	21:35
Lubomir Visnovsky	57	8	16	24	28	2	1	0	1	0	85	9.4	0	0	—	19:20
Ian Laperriere	73	7	12	19	122	-9	1	1	1	0	85	8.2	156	161	49.2	15:46
Adam Deadmarsh	20	13	4	17	21	2	4	0	1	0	55	23.6	12	14	46.2	19:18
Mikko Eloranta	75	5	12	17	56	-15	1	0	1	0	96	5.2	6	8	42.9	12:49
Erik Rasmussen	57	4	12	16	28	-1	0	0	1	0	75	5.3	124	154	44.6	13:39
Brad Chartrand	62	8	6	14	33	-10	0	1	2	0	64	12.5	320	303	51.4	12:14
Steve Heinze	27	5	7	12	12	-5	1	0	0	0	44	11.4	3	11	21.4	15:17
Joe Corvo	50	5	7	12	14	2	2	0	0	0	84	6.0	0	0	—	18:37
Craig Johnson	70	3	6	9	22	-13	0	0	0	0	87	3.4	9	19	32.1	14:04
Jaroslav Bednar*	15	0	9	9	4	3	0	0	0	0	29	0.0	4	3	57.1	13:59
Michael Cammalleri	28	5	3	8	22	-4	2	0	2	0	40	12.5	130	123	51.4	14:05
Brad Norton	53	3	3	6	97	1	0	0	0	0	19	15.8	0	2	0.0	6:04
Aaron Miller	49	1	5	6	24	-7	0	0	0	0	34	2.9	1	0	100.0	21:29
Mattias Norstrom	82	0	6	6	49	0	0	0	0	0	63	0.0	1	0	100.0	21:30
Steve Kelly	15	2	3	5	0	-6	0	0	1	0	14	14.3	57	76	42.9	12:29
Jared Aulin	17	2	2	4	0	-3	1	0	0	0	21	9.5	38	54	41.3	9:55
Sean Avery*	12	1	3	4	33	-0	0	0	0	0	19	5.3	23	26	46.9	13:50
Tomas Zizka	10	0	3	3	4	-4	0	0	0	0	12	0.0	0	0	—	15:23
Andreas Lilja*	17	0	3	3	14	5	0	0	0	0	13	0.0	0	0	—	20:03
Dmitry Yushkevich*	42	0	3	3	24	-4	0	0	0	0	36	0.0	0	2	0.0	19:56
Chris Schmidt	10	0	2	2	5	-1	0	0	0	0	10	0.0	2	0	100.0	10:01
Jon Sim*	14	0	2	2	19	-3	0	0	0	0	29	0.0	1	2	33.3	12:05
Chris McAlpine	21	0	2	2	24	-4	0	0	0	0	15	0.0	0	0	—	12:41
Jerred Smithson	22	0	2	2	21	-5	0	0	0	0	9	0.0	84	91	48.0	8:49
Ryan Flinn	19	1	0	1	28	1	0	0	0	0	13	7.7	0	0	—	5:27
Jason Holland	2	0	1	1	0	1	0	0	0	0	0	—	0	0	—	13:30
Jamie Storr (g)	39	0	1	1	8	0	0	0	0	0	0	—	0	0	—	
Pavel Rosa	2	0	0	0	0	-1	0	0	0	0	4	0.0	0	0	—	13:56
Maxim Kuznetsov*	3	0	0	0	0	1	0	0	0	0	1	0.0	0	0	—	16:37
Ken Belanger	4	0	0	0	17	0	0	0	0	0	0	—	0	0	—	4:03
Scott Barney	5	0	0	0	0	-1	0	0	0	0	5	0.0	0	0	—	9:04
Derek Bekar	6	0	0	0	4	-1	0	0	0	0	4	0.0	0	1	0.0	7:28
Cristobal Huet (g)	12	0	0	0	0	0	0	0	0	0	0	—	0	0	—	
Kip Brennan	19	0	0	0	57	0	0	0	0	0	6	0.0	0	2	0.0	4:52
Felix Potvin (g)	42	0	0	0	4	0	0	0	0	0	0	—	0	0	—	

GOALTENDING

	Games	GS	Min.	GA	SO	Avg.	W	L	T	EN	PPG Allow	SHG Allow	Shots	Save Pct.
Cristobal Huet	12	8	541	21	1	2.33	4	4	1	2	5	0	241	.913
Jamie Storr	39	33	2027	86	3	2.55	12	19	2	4	20	4	904	.905
Felix Potvin	42	41	2367	105	3	2.66	17	20	3	3	37	0	987	.894

*Played with two or more NHL teams.

RESULTS

OCTOBER

9— Phoenix ....W.....4-1
12—Detroit ....W.....3-2
16—At Anaheim.................W.....4-2
17—Colorado.....................L.....1-4
19—Vancouver ....T.....*2-2
23—At Detroit ....T.....*3-3
25—At N.Y. Rangers ....W.....6-2
27—At Columbus...............L.....1-5
29—At Atlanta ....W.....4-0
31—At Chicago..................OTL....*1-2

NOVEMBER

2— Nashville.....................W.....*6-5
4— Minnesota...................L.....2-5
5— At San Jose................L.....2-5
8— At Ottawa...................W.....3-2
9— At Montreal.................L.....1-3
12—At Toronto...................OTL...*3-4
14—At Vancouver..............L.....2-3
16—At Edmonton...............W.....4-1
19—At Minnesota..............T.....*2-2
21—At St. Louis.................OTL...*2-3
23—Dallas.........................W.....2-0
27—Florida........................L.....2-5
29—At Anaheim.................T.....*2-2
30—Chicago......................W.....4-1

DECEMBER

5— Nashville.....................L.....2-3
7— Columbus....................L.....2-4
10—At Nashville.................W.....3-0

JANUARY

11—At Dallas......................W.....3-0
14—Pittsburgh...................W....*3-2
15—At Phoenix..................L.....1-2
17—St. Louis.....................W.....6-2
19—Anaheim.....................W.....5-4
22—At Chicago..................L.....1-3
23—At St. Louis.................L.....0-5
26—Phoenix......................W....*4-3
29—At Colorado.................L.....1-6
30—Chicago......................L.....0-2

JANUARY

2— Philadelphia................L.....1-4
4— Dallas.........................L.....2-3
6— At Minnesota..............W.....3-2
7— At Dallas.....................L.....4-7
9— Edmonton...................L.....4-5
11—St. Louis.....................L.....1-2
13—San Jose....................W....*3-2
16—At Edmonton...............L.....0-2
18—At Calgary...................OTL...*1-2
22—At Anaheim.................L.....5-6
23—Minnesota...................L.....1-2
25—New Jersey.................W....*2-1
27—San Jose....................L.....0-3
28—At San Jose................L.....1-3
30—Ottawa.......................W.....3-0

FEBRUARY

5— Phoenix......................W.....4-3
7— Carolina......................W.....8-2
9— At Dallas.....................L.....1-3

MARCH

11—At Nashville.................W.....3-2
13—Calgary.......................W.....4-2
15—N.Y. Islanders.............L.....2-3
17—San Jose....................W.....3-2
20—At Philadelphia............L.....0-5
21—At Buffalo....................W.....4-1
24—At Detroit....................L.....4-5
25—At Pittsburgh...............W.....5-3
27—At Columbus...............L.....1-3

MARCH

1— Atlanta........................W.....4-1
4— Anaheim.....................L.....1-2
6— Edmonton...................L.....1-2
8— Montreal.....................W.....2-1
10—Detroit........................L.....2-3
12—At Tampa Bay.............L.....2-4
14—At Washington............W.....3-1
15—At Carolina..................T.....*0-0
18—Calgary.......................L.....1-4
20—Tampa Bay..................T.....*2-2
22—Boston........................OTL...*3-4
25—Columbus...................W.....*1-2
27—At Colorado.................L.....0-3
29—Vancouver..................L.....1-5
31—At Phoenix..................W.....*5-4

APRIL

2— Colorado.....................W.....5-3
4— At Calgary...................OTL...*1-2
6— At Vancouver..............W.....2-0
*Denotes overtime game.

MINNESOTA WILD
WESTERN CONFERENCE/NORTHWEST DIVISION

Wild Schedule
Home games shaded; D=Day game; *Feb. 8 All-Star Game at St. Paul, Minn.

October

SUN	MON	TUE	WED	THU	FRI	SAT
5	6	7	8 CHI	9	10 NYR	11
12 SJ	13	14	15	16 COL	17	18 VAN
19 DAL	20	21 CAL	22	23	24 FLA	25 TB
26	27	28 BUF	29	30 ATL	31	

November

SUN	MON	TUE	WED	THU	FRI	SAT
						1 WAS
2	3	4 COL	5	6	7 CAL	8 VAN
9	10	11 VAN	12	13 EDM	14	15 DET
16	17	18	19 PIT	20 PHI	21	22 DET
23	24	25	26 DAL	27	28 D SJ	29
30 ANA						

December

SUN	MON	TUE	WED	THU	FRI	SAT
	1	2	3 EDM	4	5 CAL	6 VAN
7	8	9 CAL	10	11 TOR	12	13 BUF
14	15 PHO	16	17 COL	18 EDM	19	20 CBJ
21	22	23 NAS	24	25	26 DET	27
28	29 CAL	30 EDM	31			

January

SUN	MON	TUE	WED	THU	FRI	SAT
				1	2 EDM	3
4 COL	5 STL	6	7 CHI	8	9 PHO	10
11 NAS	12 NAS	13	14 LA	15	16 PIT	17 STL
18 NAS	19 NAS	20	21 CHI	22	23 ANA	24 SJ
25 LA	26 LA	27	28	29 MON	30	31 CBJ

February

SUN	MON	TUE	WED	THU	FRI	SAT
1	2 STL	3	4 NYR	5	6	7
8*	9	10 LA	11	12	13 EDM	14
15 D CAL	16	17 NJ	18	19 VAN	20	21
22 COL	23	24	25	26 NAS	27 DAL	28
29 CAR						

March

SUN	MON	TUE	WED	THU	FRI	SAT
	1	2	3 ANA	4 LA	5	6
7 PHO	8	9 SJ	10 VAN	11	12	13
14 CBJ	15	16 OTT	17	18 BOS	19 NYI	20
21	22 PHO	23	24 CBJ	25 CHI	26	27
28 D ANA	29 DET	30	31 COL			

April

SUN	MON	TUE	WED	THU	FRI	SAT
				1	2 DAL	3
4 D STL	5	6	7	8	9	10

2003-04 SEASON
CLUB DIRECTORY

Chairman
Bob Naegele Jr.

Chief executive officer
Jac Sperling

President and chief operating officer
TBA

Exec. vice president/general manager
Doug Risebrough

Assistant general manager/player personnel
Tom Thompson

Head coach
Jacques Lemaire

Assistant coaches
Mike Ramsey
Mario Tremblay

Assistant general manager/hockey operations
Tom Lynn

V.p. of communications and broadcasting
Bill Robertson

Mgr. of media relations/team services
Brad Smith

Head athletic therapist
Don Fuller

DRAFT CHOICES

Rd.— Player	Overall	Pos.	Last team
1— Brent Burns	20	RW	Brampton (OHL)
2— Patrick O'Sullivan	56	C	Mississauga (OHL)
3— Danny Irmen	78	C	Lincoln (USHL)
5— Marcin Kolusz	157	F	Novy Targ (Poland)
6— Miroslav Kopriva	187	G	Kladno (Czech Republic)
7— Grigory Misharin	207	D	Yekaterinburg (Russia)
7— Adam Courchaine	219	C	Vancouver (WHL)
8— Mathieu Melanson	251	LW	Chicoutimi (QMJHL)
9— Jean-Michel Bolduc	281	D	Quebec (QMJHL)

MISCELLANEOUS DATA

Home ice (capacity)
Xcel Energy Center (18,064)

Office address
317 Washington Street
St. Paul, MN 55102

Business phone
651-602-6000

Ticket information
651-222-9453

Website
www.wild.com

Training site
Parade Ice Garden, Minneapolis

Club colors
Red, green, gold and wheat

Radio affiliation
WCCO (830 AM)

TV affiliation
FOX Sports Net (Cable), KMSP FOX (Channel 9)

TRAINING CAMP ROSTER

No.	FORWARDS	Ht./Wt.	Place (BORN)	Date	NHL exp.	2002-03 clubs
53	Chris Bala (LW)	6-1/180	Alexandria, Va.	9-24-78	1	Binghamton (AHL)
	Derek Boogaard (LW)	6-6/249	Saskatoon, Sask.	6-23-82	0	Louisiana (ECHL)
	P.-Marc Bouchard (C)	5-9/155	Sherbrooke, Que.	4-27-84	1	Minnesota
	Christoph Brandner (LW)	6-4/225	Bruck Mur, Austria	5-7-75	0	Krefeld Pinguine (Germany)
15	Andrew Brunette (LW)	6-1/210	Sudbury, Ont.	8-24-73	8	Minnesota
	Shawn Carter (LW)	6-2/210	Eagle River, Wis.	4-16-73	0	Augsburg (Germany)
	Dan Cavanaugh (C)	6-1/190	Springfield, Mass.	3-3-80	0	Houston (AHL)
	Marc Cavosie (C/LW)	6-0/180	Cohoes, N.Y.	8-6-81	0	Houston (AHL)
	Mark Cullen (C)	5-11/175	Moorhead, Minn.	10-28-78	0	Houston (AHL)
9	Hnat Domenichelli (LW)	6-0/194	Edmonton	2-17-76	7	Houston (AHL), Minnesota
34	Jim Dowd (C)	6-1/190	Brick, N.J.	12-25-68	12	Minnesota
11	Pascal Dupuis (LW)	6-0/196	Laval, Que.	4-7-79	3	Minnesota
	Mike Erickson (RW)	6-2/185	Eden Prairie, Minn.	4-12-83	0	
10	Marian Gaborik (RW)	6-1/183	Trencin, Czechoslovakia	2-14-82	3	Minnesota
38	Jay Henderson (LW)	5-11/188	Edmonton	9-17-78	4	Providence (AHL), Hartford (AHL), Houston (AHL)
14	Darby Hendrickson (C)	6-1/195	Richfield, Minn.	8-28-72	10	Minnesota
12	Matt Johnson (LW)	6-5/235	Welland, Ont.	11-23-75	9	Minnesota
	Mikko Koivu (C)	6-2/183	Turku, Finland	3-12-83	0	TPS Turku (Finland)
24	Antti Laaksonen (LW)	6-0/180	Tammela, Finland	10-3-73	5	Minnesota
	Bill Muckalt (RW)	6-1/200	Surrey, B.C.	7-15-74	5	Minnesota
18	Richard Park (RW)	5-11/190	Seoul, South Korea	5-27-76	7	Minnesota
7	Cliff Ronning (C)	5-8/165	Burnaby, B.C.	10-1-65	17	Minnesota
40	Jeremy Stevenson (LW)	6-2/217	San Bernardino, Calif.	7-28-74	7	Houston (AHL), Minnesota
	Jean-Guy Trudel (RW)	6-0/180	Cadillac, Que.	10-18-75	3	Houston (AHL), Minnesota
	Tony Tuzzolino (RW)	6-2/202	Buffalo	10-9-75	3	Louisiana (ECHL), Houston (AHL)
	Stephane Veilleux (LW)	6-1/187	Beaureville, Que.	11-16-81	1	Houston (AHL), Minnesota
18	Tony Virta (RW)	5-10/187	Hameenlinna, Finland	6-28-72	1	Houston (AHL)
	Rickard Wallin (C)	6-2/183	Stockholm, Sweden	4-9-80	1	Houston (AHL), Minnesota
37	Wes Walz (C)	5-10/185	Calgary	5-15-70	9	Minnesota
63	Kyle Wanvig (RW)	6-2/197	Calgary	1-29-81	1	Minnesota
33	Sergei Zholtok (C)	6-1/191	Riga, U.S.S.R.	12-2-72	9	Minnesota

No.	DEFENSEMEN	Ht./Wt.	Place (BORN)	Date	NHL exp.	2002-03 clubs
3	Ladislav Benysek	6-2/190	Olomouc, Czechoslovakia	3-24-75	4	Houston (AHL), Minnesota
5	Brad Bombardir	6-1/205	Powell River, B.C.	5-5-72	6	Minnesota
4	Brad Brown	6-4/218	Baie Verte, Nfld.	12-27-75	6	Minnesota
	Mike Crowley	5-11/190	Bloomington, Minn.	7-4-75	3	
	Chris Dyment	6-3/201	Stoneham, Mass.	10-24-79	0	Houston (AHL)
	Chris Heid	6-1/205	Langley, B.C.	3-14-83	0	Spokane (WHL)
17	Filip Kuba	6-3/205	Ostrava, Czechoslovakia	12-29-76	5	Minnesota
23	Jason Marshall	6-2/200	Cranbrook, B.C.	2-22-71	10	Minnesota
2	Willie Mitchell	6-3/205	Port McNeill, B.C.	4-23-77	4	Minnesota
	Eric Reitz	6-0/192	Detroit	8-29-82	0	Houston (AHL)
	Travis Roche	6-1/190	Whitecourt, Alta.	6-17-78	2	Houston (AHL)
55	Nick Schultz	6-0/187	Strasbourg, Sask.	8-25-82	2	Minnesota
77	Lubomir Sekeras	6-0//176	Trencin, Czechoslovakia	11-18-68	3	Minnesota
7	Andrei Zyuzin	6-1/210	Ufa, U.S.S.R.	1-21-78	6	New Jersey, Minnesota

No.	GOALTENDERS	Ht./Wt.	Place (BORN)	Date	NHL exp.	2002-03 clubs
	Frederic Cloutier	6-0/165	St. Honore, Que.	5-14-81	0	Louisiana (ECHL), Houston (AHL)
35	Manny Fernandez	6-0/185	Etobicoke, Ont.	8-27-74	8	Minnesota
31	Derek Gustafson	5-11/210	Gresham, Ore.	6-21-79	2	Louisiana (ECHL), Houston (AHL)
	Josh Harding	6-1/168	Regina, Sask.	6-18-84	0	Regina (WHL)
	Johan Holmqvist	6-1/200	Tolfta, Sweden	5-24-78	3	Charlotte (ECHL), New York Rangers, Hartford (AHL), Houston (AHL)
35	Dieter Kochan	6-1/165	Saskatoon, Sask.	11-5-74	4	Houston (AHL), Minnesota
30	Dwayne Roloson	6-1/190	Simcoe, Ont.	10-12-69	6	Minnesota

2002-03 REVIEW
INDIVIDUAL STATISTICS

SCORING

	Games	G	A	Pts.	PIM	+/-	PPG	SHG	GWG	GTG	Sht.	Sht. Pct.	Faceoffs Won	Faceoffs Lost	Faceoffs Pct.	TOI
Marian Gaborik	81	30	35	65	46	12	5	1	8	0	280	10.7	4	12	25.0	17:24
Pascal Dupuis	80	20	28	48	44	17	6	0	4	1	183	10.9	76	110	40.9	17:30
Cliff Ronning	80	17	31	48	24	-6	8	0	5	0	171	9.9	266	300	47.0	17:25
Andrew Brunette	82	18	28	46	30	-10	9	0	2	3	97	18.6	26	33	44.1	14:28
Sergei Zholtok	78	16	26	42	18	1	3	0	2	2	153	10.5	451	547	45.2	16:35
Wes Walz	80	13	19	32	63	11	0	0	4	0	115	11.3	759	746	50.4	15:56
Antti Laaksonen	82	15	16	31	26	4	1	2	4	2	106	14.2	15	36	29.4	15:54

	Games	G	A	Pts.	PIM	+/-	PPG	SHG	GWG	GTG	Sht.	Sht. Pct.	Won	Lost	Pct.	TOI
Filip Kuba	78	8	21	29	29	0	4	2	1	0	129	6.2	0	1	0.0	23:55
Jim Dowd	78	8	17	25	31	-1	3	1	2	0	78	10.3	445	485	47.8	13:02
Richard Park	81	14	10	24	16	-3	2	2	3	1	149	9.4	87	91	48.9	16:36
P.-Marc Bouchard......	50	7	13	20	18	1	5	0	1	0	53	13.2	193	281	40.7	13:16
Andrei Zyuzin*	66	4	12	16	34	-7	2	0	0	0	113	3.5	1	3	25.0	21:38
Brad Bombardir......	58	1	14	15	16	15	1	0	0	0	55	1.8	0	0	—	22:01
Willie Mitchell..........	69	2	12	14	84	13	0	1	1	0	67	3.0	0	0	—	21:28
Jeremy Stevenson.....	32	5	6	11	69	6	1	0	1	0	29	17.2	0	0	—	10:47
Lubomir Sekeras.......	60	2	9	11	30	-12	1	0	1	0	50	4.0	3	0	100.0	18:52
Nick Schultz	75	3	7	10	23	11	0	0	1	0	70	4.3	0	0	—	18:28
Bill Muckalt	8	5	3	8	6	5	0	0	0	0	13	38.5	3	3	50.0	13:00
Matt Johnson	60	3	5	8	201	-8	0	0	1	0	24	12.5	2	3	40.0	7:23
Darby Hendrickson....	28	1	5	6	8	-3	0	0	0	0	34	2.9	200	213	48.4	15:15
Jason Marshall.........	45	1	5	6	69	4	0	0	0	0	40	2.5	2	5	28.6	11:24
Stephane Veilleux......	38	3	2	5	23	-6	1	0	0	0	52	5.8	1	12	7.7	12:08
Rickard Wallin	4	1	0	1	0	1	0	0	1	0	1	100.0	15	13	53.6	7:43
Kyle Wanvig	7	1	0	1	13	0	0	0	0	0	5	20.0	1	0	100.0	9:14
Manny Fernandez (g)	35	0	1	1	6	0	0	0	0	0	0	—	0	0	—	—
Dwayne Roloson (g) .	50	0	1	1	4	0	0	0	0	0	0	—	0	0	—	—
Brad Brown	57	0	1	1	90	-1	0	0	0	0	10	0.0	0	0	—	9:13
Hnat Domenichelli.....	1	0	0	0	0	0	0	0	0	0	1	0.0	0	0	—	11:11
Dieter Kochan (g)......	1	0	0	0	0	0	0	0	0	0	0	—	0	0	—	—
Curtis Murphy	1	0	0	0	0	0	0	0	0	0	0	—	0	0	—	8:56
Jean-Guy Trudel	1	0	0	0	2	0	0	0	0	0	0	—	0	0	—	5:37
Sylvain Blouin*	2	0	0	0	4	0	0	0	0	0	1	0.0	0	1	0.0	7:37
Ladislav Benysek.......	14	0	0	0	8	-3	0	0	0	0	7	0.0	0	0	—	11:25

GOALTENDING

	Games	GS	Min.	GA	SO	Avg.	W	L	T	EN	PPG Allow	SHG Allow	Shots	Save Pct.
Dwayne Roloson......................	50	47	2945	98	4	2.00	23	16	8	1	19	3	1334	.927
Manny Fernandez	35	34	1979	74	2	2.24	19	13	2	0	24	2	972	.924
Dieter Kochan	1	1	60	5	0	5.00	0	1	0	0	0	0	28	.821

*Played with two or more NHL teams.

RESULTS

OCTOBER
11—Boston.............................W 5-1
12—At St. Louis...................T....*2-2
15—Florida............................W 4-1
17—Dallas ....W 3-1
19—Detroit ....L......3-5
22—Calgary...........................W....*4-3
24—At Chicago ....W 3-2
26—At Phoenix......................W 6-1
27—At Colorado ....T....*3-3
29—Colorado..........................W....*3-2
31—San Jose ....W *2-1

NOVEMBER
2— Vancouver ....L......2-4
4— At Los Angeles ....W 5-2
7— At Phoenix.......................L......1-4
9— At San Jose ....W 4-2
10—At Anaheim......................L......0-1
12—Edmonton........................L......2-3
14—Pittsburgh........................T....*1-1
16—Washington ....W 1-0
19—Los Angeles ....T....*2-2
21—At Washington ....W 4-3
23—Nashville..........................W 4-2
25—Vancouver ....L......1-2
27—At Dallas ....L......0-5
29—Colorado..........................T....*2-2

DECEMBER
3— At Edmonton ....OTL...*1-2
5— At Calgary........................T....*1-1

7— At Vancouver..................W 4-2
10—Tampa Bay ....W 5-3
12—At Detroit ....W 3-2
14—At Nashville......................L......1-3
15—Carolina...........................W 2-1
17—Edmonton.......................W *4-3
19—N.Y. Islanders..................L......2-4
21—At Colorado ....L......2-4
23—Calgary............................L......2-3
26—At Chicago ....T....*2-2
28—At Buffalo ....W 4-3
31—Anaheim...........................W 4-1

JANUARY
2— At Edmonton ....W *2-1
4— At Calgary........................L......2-3
6— Los Angeles ....L......2-3
8— Columbus ....L......1-2
10—Phoenix ....W 2-1
14—Buffalo ....L......0-1
16—Vancouver ....W 5-2
18—Anaheim...........................L......0-1
20—At Anaheim......................W....*2-1
23—At Los Angeles ....W 2-1
25—At San Jose ....L......1-4
28—At Vancouver ....T....*2-2
29—At Edmonton ....L......1-5

FEBRUARY
5— Chicago ....W 2-1
7— San Jose ....W 4-3
9— At New Jersey ....L......2-3

10—At Philadelphia ....W 1-0
12—Philadelphia......................W 2-0
14—Phoenix ....L......2-3
15—At Colorado ....L......2-3
19—N.Y. Rangers....................L......2-4
23—St. Louis ....W 3-1
25—At Ottawa ....W 3-0
27—At Montreal ....W 6-3

MARCH
1— At St. Louis.......................L......0-2
4— New Jersey.......................W 3-2
6— At Nashville ....T....*2-2
7— At Carolina........................L......0-1
9— At Atlanta ....W 6-4
12—Dallas ....W 4-2
14—Nashville...........................W 3-1
15—At Columbus ....L......0-5
17—At Tampa Bay ....T....*3-3
19—At Florida ....W 3-1
21—At Dallas ....W....*3-2
23—Detroit ....W 4-0
25—At Detroit ....L......0-4
26—St. Louis ....L......0-1
28—Chicago ....W *4-3
31—Calgary.............................W 3-0

APRIL
2— At Columbus......................L......0-3
3— At Toronto ....L......1-2
6— Columbus ....W 4-3
*Denotes overtime game.

MONTREAL CANADIENS
EASTERN CONFERENCE/NORTHEAST DIVISION

Canadiens' Schedule
Home games shaded; D=Day game; *Feb. 8 All-Star Game at St. Paul, Minn.

October
SUN	MON	TUE	WED	THU	FRI	SAT
5	6	7	8	9 OTT	10	11 TOR
12	13	14 WAS	15	16 PIT	17	18 TOR
19	20 DET	21	22	23 NYI	24	25 OTT
26	27 PHI	28 BOS	29	30 BOS	31	

November
SUN	MON	TUE	WED	THU	FRI	SAT
						1 NYR
2	3	4 EDM	5	6	7 BUF	8 BUF
9	10	11 CBJ	12	13 NYI	14	15 OTT
16	17	18 VAN	19	20 CAL	21	22 EDM
23	24	25 VAN	26	27	28 WAS	29 FLA
30						

December
SUN	MON	TUE	WED	THU	FRI	SAT
	1	2 TB	3	4	5 CAR	6 CAR
7	8 PHI	9	10 NYR	11	12 FLA	13 TB
14	15	16 BOS	17	18 NAS	19	20 TOR
21	22 PIT	23 WAS	24	25	26	27 CAR
28	29 ATL	30	31 DAL			

January
SUN	MON	TUE	WED	THU	FRI	SAT
				1	2	3 ATL D
4 WAS	5	6 BUF	7	8 TB	9	10 PIT D
11	12	13 STL	14 ATL	15	16	17 NYR
18	19	20 PHI	21	22	23 NJ	24 TOR
25	26	27 BUF	28	29 MIN	30	31 BOS D

February
SUN	MON	TUE	WED	THU	FRI	SAT
1 CHI	2 D	3 PIT	4	5 NYI	6	7
8*	9	10 FLA	11	12 TB	13	14 OTT
15	16	17 ATL	18	19 CAL	20	21 TOR
22 NYR	23	24 OTT	25	26 BOS	27	28 CAR
29						

March
SUN	MON	TUE	WED	THU	FRI	SAT
	1 NJ	2	3 SJ	4	5 PHO	6 LA
7 ANA	8	9	10	11 FLA	12	13 TOR
14	15	16 COL	17	18	19 NJ	20 NJ
21	22	23	24 BUF	25 OTT	26	27 BOS
28	29	30	31 NYI			

April
SUN	MON	TUE	WED	THU	FRI	SAT
				1 PHI	2	3 BUF
4	5	6	7	8	9	10

2003-04 SEASON
CLUB DIRECTORY

Chairman and governor
George N. Gillett Jr.
Vice-chairman
Jeff Joyce
President of club de hockey Canadien and the Bell Centre
Pierre Boivin
Assistant to the president
Foster Gillett
Executive v.p., hockey and g.m.
Bob Gainey
Chief financial officer
Fred Steer
Vice-president, marketing and sales
Ray Lalonde
V.p., comm. and community relations
Donald Beauchamp
Vice-president, operations, Bell Centre
Alain Gauthier
President, Gillett Entertainment Group
Aldo Giampaolo
Assistant general manager
André Savard
Director of legal affairs
Julien BriseBois
Director of player personnel
Trevor Timmins
Director of pro scouting
Pierre Gauthier
Head coach
Claude Julien

Assistant coaches
Roland Melanson, Rick Green, Guy Charron
Pro scout
Gordie Roberts
Amateur scouting coordinator
Pierre Dorion
Scouting staff
Elmer Benning, William A. Berglund, Hannu Laine, Dave Mayville, Trent McCleary, Antonin Routa, Nikolai Vakourov, Patrik Allvin
Equipment manager
Pierre Gervais
Assistants to the equipment manager
Robert Boulanger, Pierre Ouellette
Video supervisor
Mario Leblanc
Club physician and chief surgeon
Dr. David Mulder
Head athletic therapist
Graham Rynbend
Assistant to the athletic therapist
Jodi Van Rees
Strength & conditioning coordinator
Scott Livingston
Director of media relations
Dominick Saillant
Communications coordinator
Frédéric Daigle

DRAFT CHOICES

Rd.— Player	Overall	Pos.	Last team
1— Andrei Kastsitsyn	10	C-W	Belarus (Russia)
2— Cory Urquhart	40	C	Montreal (QMJHL)
2— Maxim Lapierre	61	C	Montreal (QMJHL)
3— Ryan O'Byrne	79	D	Nanaimo (BCHL)
4— Corey Locke	113	C	Ottawa (OHL)
4— Danny Stewart	123	LW	Rimouski (QMJHL)
6— C. Heino-Lindberg	177	G	Hammarby (Sweden)
6— Mark Flood	188	D	Peterborough (OHL)
7— Oskari Korpikari	217	D	Karpat (Finland)
8— Jimmy Bonneau	241	LW	Montreal (QMJHL)
9— Jaroslav Halak	271	G	Bratislava Jr. (Slovakia Jr.)

MISCELLANEOUS DATA

Home ice (capacity)
Molson Centre (21,273)
Address
1260 rue de la Gauchetiere Ouest
Montreal, Que. H3B 5E8
Business phone
514-932-2582
Ticket information
514-932-2582
Website
www.canadiens.com

Training site
Montreal
Club colors
Red, white and blue
Radio affiliation
CJAD (800 AM), CKAC (730 AM)
TV affiliation
CBFT (2), RDS (33), TSN (28)

TRAINING CAMP ROSTER

No.	FORWARDS	Ht./Wt.	Place (BORN)	Date (BORN)	NHL exp.	2002-03 clubs
82	Donald Audette (RW)	5-8/184	Laval, Que.	9-23-69	14	Hamilton (AHL), Montreal
	Jozef Balej (RW)	5-11/170	Ilava, Czechoslovakia	2-22-82	0	Hamilton (AHL)
	Maxime Blouin (C)	6-3/195	St. Henri, Que.	2-24-76	0	
36	Sylvain Blouin (LW)	6-2/222	Montreal	5-21-74	6	Hamilton (AHL), Montreal, Minnesota
38	Jan Bulis (C)	6-1/201	Pardubice, Czechoslovakia	3-18-78	6	Montreal
24	Andreas Dackell (RW) ...	5-10/195	Gavle, Sweden	12-29-72	7	Montreal
34	Gordie Dwyer (LW)	6-2/216	Dalhousie, N.B.	1-25-78	4	Hartford (AHL), Montreal, New York Rangers
	Benoit Gratton (LW)	5-11/194	Montreal	12-28-76	5	Hamilton (AHL)
	Chris Higgins (C)	5-11/192	Smithtown, N.Y.	6-2-83	0	Yale University (ECAC)
36	Marcel Hossa (LW)	6-1/200	Ilava, Czechoslovakia	10-12-81	2	Hamilton (AHL), Montreal
90	Joe Juneau (C)	6-0/199	Pont-Rouge, Que.	1-5-68	12	Montreal
25	Chad Kilger (LW)	6-4/215	Cornwall, Ont.	11-27-76	8	Montreal
11	Saku Koivu (C)	5-10/181	Turku, Finland	11-23-74	8	Montreal
26	Eric Landry (C)	5-11/185	Gatineau, Que.	1-20-75	4	Utah (AHL)
	Christian Larrivee (C)	6-2/185	Gaspe, Que.	8-25-82	0	Chicoutimi (QMJHL)
22	Bill Lindsay (LW)	6-0/195	Big Fork, Mont.	5-17-71	12	Hamilton (AHL), Montreal
	Randy McKay (RW)	6-2/210	Montreal	1-25-67	15	Montreal
	Duncan Milroy (RW)......	6-0/180	Edmonton	2-8-83	0	Kootenay (WHL)
29	Gino Odjick (LW)	6-3/227	Maniwaki, Que.	9-7-70	12	
	Alexander Perezhogin (C)	5-11/185	Ust-Kamenogorsk, U.S.S.R.	8-10-83	0	Avangard Omsk (Russian)
94	Yanic Perreault (C)	5-11/185	Sherbrooke, Que.	4-4-71	10	Montreal
	Tomas Plekanec (LW)	5-10/189	Kladno, Czechoslovakia	10-31-82	0	Hamilton (AHL)
37	Patrick Poulin (C)	6-1/216	Vanier, Que.	4-23-73	11	
71	Mike Ribeiro (C)	5-11/150	Montreal	2-10-80	4	Hamilton (AHL), Montreal
	Michael Ryder (C)	6-0/187	St. John's, Nfld.	3-31-80	0	Hamilton (AHL)
	Scott Selig (C/RW)	6-2/178	Philadelphia	3-2-81	0	Northeastern University (ECAC)
24	Niklas Sundstrom (LW) .	6-0/195	Ornskoldsvik, Sweden	6-6-75	8	Montreal, San Jose
61	Jason Ward (RW/C)	6-2/193	Chapleau, Ont.	1-16-79	3	Hamilton (AHL), Montreal
20	Richard Zednik (RW)	6-0/199	Bystrica, Czechoslovakia	1-6-76	8	Montreal
	DEFENSEMEN					
	Francois Beauchemin	5-11/190	Sorel, Que.	6-4-80	1	Hamilton (AHL), Montreal
51	Francis Bouillon	5-8/189	New York	10-17-75	4	Hamilton (AHL), Montreal, Nashville
43	Patrice Brisebois...........	6-1/203	Montreal	1-27-71	13	Montreal
	Mathieu Descoteaux	6-3/220	Pierreville, Que.	9-23-77	1	Utah (AHL)
28	Karl Dykhuis	6-3/214	Sept-Iles, Que.	7-8-72	11	Montreal
	Ron Hainsey	6-2/187	Bolton, Conn.	3-24-81	1	Hamilton (AHL), Montreal
59	Martti Jarventie	5-11/185	Tampere, Finland	4-4-76	1	Jokerit Helsinki (Finland)
	Mike Komisarek	6-4/225	Islip Terrace, N.Y.	1-19-82	1	Hamilton (AHL), Montreal
	Tomas Linhart	6-2/209	Pardubice, Czechoslovakia	2-16-84	0	London (OHL)
79	Andrei Markov	6-0/185	Voskresensk, U.S.S.R.	12-20-78	3	Montreal
	Matt O'Dette	6-4/205	East York, Ont.	11-9-75	0	Hamilton (AHL)
5	Stephane Quintal	6-3/234	Boucherville, Que.	10-22-68	15	Montreal
52	Craig Rivet	6-2/207	North Bay, Ont.	9-13-74	9	Montreal
	Matt Shasby	6-3/188	Sioux Falls, S.D.	7-2-80	0	Alaska-Anchorage (WCHA)
44	Sheldon Souray	6-4/230	Elk Point, Alta.	7-13-76	5	
54	Patrick Traverse	6-4/200	Montreal	3-14-74	6	Montreal
	GOALTENDERS					
	Luc Belanger................	5-10/172	Sherbrooke, Que.	6-25-75	0	
1	Eric Fichaud	5-11/171	Anjou, Que.	11-4-75	6	Hamilton (AHL)
30	Mathieu Garon	6-2/182	Chandler, Que.	1-9-78	3	Hamilton (AHL), Montreal
	Olivier Michaud.............	5-11/160	Beloeil, Que.	9-14-83	1	Baie-Comeau (QMJHL)
	Vadim Tarasov	5-11/158	Ust-Kamenogorsk, U.S.S.R.	12-31-76	0	Metallurg Novokuznetsk (Russian)
60	Jose Theodore	5-11/185	Laval, Que.	9-13-76	8	Montreal

2002-03 REVIEW

INDIVIDUAL STATISTICS

SCORING

	Games	G	A	Pts.	PIM	+/-	PPG	SHG	GWG	GTG	Sht.	Sht. Pct.	Faceoffs Won	Faceoffs Lost	Faceoffs Pct.	TOI
Saku Koivu	82	21	50	71	72	5	5	1	5	0	147	14.3	777	789	49.6	19:14
Richard Zednik	80	31	19	50	79	4	9	0	2	1	250	12.4	3	7	30.0	18:25
Yanic Perreault	73	24	22	46	30	-11	7	0	4	0	145	16.6	727	429	62.9	16:05
Jan Bulis	82	16	24	40	30	9	0	0	2	0	160	10.0	65	88	42.5	15:42
Andrei Markov...........	79	13	24	37	34	13	3	0	2	0	159	8.2	0	1	0.0	23:17
Doug Gilmour*	61	11	19	30	36	-6	3	0	0	0	85	12.9	180	181	49.9	16:45

MONTREAL CANADIENS

MONTREAL CANADIENS

	Games	G	A	Pts.	PIM	+/-	PPG	SHG	GWG	GTG	Sht.	Sht. Pct.	Faceoffs Won	Lost	Pct.	TOI
Patrice Brisebois	73	4	25	29	32	-14	1	0	1	0	105	3.8	0	0	—	23:23
Andreas Dackell	73	7	18	25	24	-5	0	0	1	0	74	9.5	5	13	27.8	14:53
Donald Audette	54	11	12	23	19	-7	4	0	4	1	118	9.3	2	4	33.3	15:29
Oleg Petrov*	53	7	16	23	16	-2	2	0	2	0	87	8.0	2	4	33.3	13:44
Craig Rivet	82	7	15	22	71	1	3	0	2	0	118	5.9	0	0	—	21:59
Joe Juneau	72	6	16	22	20	-10	0	0	2	0	88	6.8	647	588	52.4	16:46
Randy McKay	75	6	13	19	72	-14	2	0	0	1	52	11.5	4	13	23.5	11:02
Mike Ribeiro	52	5	12	17	6	-3	2	0	0	0	57	8.8	180	178	50.3	11:07
Chad Kilger	60	9	7	16	21	-4	0	0	1	0	60	15.0	97	111	46.6	10:42
Niklas Sundstrom*	33	5	9	14	8	3	0	0	1	0	35	14.3	4	6	40.0	14:25
Mariusz Czerkawski	43	5	9	14	16	-7	1	0	0	0	77	6.5	0	2	0.0	13:10
Marcel Hossa	34	6	7	13	14	3	2	0	1	0	51	11.8	2	2	50.0	13:58
Patrick Traverse	65	0	13	13	24	-9	0	0	0	0	63	0.0	0	0	—	20:11
Stephane Quintal	67	5	5	10	70	-4	0	0	0	0	73	6.8	0	0	—	18:38
Jason Ward	8	3	2	5	0	3	0	0	0	0	10	30.0	3	3	50.0	11:17
Karl Dykhuis	65	1	4	5	34	-5	0	0	0	0	24	4.2	0	1	0.0	14:59
Francis Bouillon*	20	3	1	4	2	-1	0	1	0	0	30	10.0	0	0	—	20:24
Bill Lindsay	19	0	2	2	23	-1	0	0	0	0	7	0.0	9	12	42.9	5:20
Jose Theodore (g)	57	0	2	2	6	0	0	0	0	0	0	—	0	0	—	—
Mike Komisarek	21	0	1	1	28	-6	0	0	0	0	26	0.0	0	0	—	16:41
Francois Beauchemin	1	0	0	0	0	-1	0	0	0	0	1	0.0	0	0	—	17:11
Mathieu Garon (g)	8	0	0	0	0	0	0	0	0	0	0	—	0	0	—	—
Gordie Dwyer*	11	0	0	0	46	-2	0	0	0	0	2	0.0	1	1	50.0	7:33
Sylvain Blouin*	17	0	0	0	43	-3	0	0	0	0	3	0.0	0	0	—	3:36
Jeff Hackett (g)*	18	0	0	0	0	0	0	0	0	0	0	—	0	0	—	—
Ron Hainsey	21	0	0	2	2	-1	0	0	0	0	12	0.0	0	0	—	12:24

GOALTENDING

	Games	GS	Min.	GA	SO	Avg.	W	L	T	EN	PPG Allow	SHG Allow	Shots	Save Pct.
Mathieu Garon	8	8	482	16	2	1.99	3	5	0	1	3	0	267	.940
Jeff Hackett*	18	17	1063	45	0	2.54	7	8	2	1	23	5	606	.926
Jose Theodore	57	57	3419	165	2	2.90	20	31	6	6	42	4	1797	.908

*Played with two or more NHL teams.

RESULTS

OCTOBER
11— At N.Y. Rangers .... W 4-1
12— Buffalo .... L 1-6
15— Philadelphia .... L 2-6
17— At Detroit .... W 3-2
19— Toronto .... T *2-2
22— Pittsburgh .... T *3-3
24— At Philadelphia .... L 2-6
26— Ottawa .... W 5-3
29— Anaheim .... T *2-2

NOVEMBER
1— At Carolina .... T *2-2
2— At Toronto .... W 5-2
5— St. Louis .... L 2-5
7— N.Y. Islanders .... W 3-0
9— Los Angeles .... W 3-1
12— Dallas .... L 2-4
15— At New Jersey .... L 1-5
16— New Jersey .... W 3-1
18— Pittsburgh .... W *5-4
20— At Pittsburgh .... W *3-2
21— At Ottawa .... L 2-3
23— Carolina .... L 3-7
26— Atlanta .... W 3-2
29— At Boston .... L 2-4
30— Philadelphia .... OTL *1-2

DECEMBER
4— At Dallas .... L 1-5
6— At Colorado .... OTL *6-7
7— At Phoenix .... W 4-2

10— At Boston .... W 4-2
12— Tampa Bay .... L 2-3
14— Boston .... W 4-2
16— At Ottawa .... W 3-2
17— San Jose .... L 1-3
19— At N.Y. Rangers .... W 3-1
21— Buffalo .... W 6-2
23— At N.Y. Islanders .... L 1-3
27— At Ottawa .... OTL *2-3
28— At Pittsburgh .... L 2-3
31— At Calgary .... T *1-1

JANUARY
2— At Vancouver .... L 2-3
4— At Edmonton .... OTL *4-5
7— At New Jersey .... L 2-3
9— N.Y. Rangers .... W 3-2
11— Buffalo .... L 2-3
13— Calgary .... W 4-2
15— At Atlanta .... L 0-1
16— At Philadelphia .... L 1-4
18— Toronto .... OTL *2-3
20— At Florida .... W 3-2
22— At Tampa Bay .... T *2-2
25— Washington .... T *1-1
26— Chicago .... W 4-3
28— Florida .... W 6-3
30— At N.Y. Islanders .... L 1-3

FEBRUARY
4— Atlanta .... L 3-4
6— At Boston .... L 3-6

8— At Toronto .... L 1-3
9— At Washington .... W 2-0
11— Boston .... W 3-1
13— Columbus .... OTL *1-2
15— Edmonton .... W 3-2
18— Florida .... L 0-3
19— At Buffalo .... OTL *1-2
22— Toronto .... L 3-5
24— At Washington .... L 1-4
27— Minnesota .... L 3-6

MARCH
1— Vancouver .... T *1-1
5— At Anaheim .... L 1-3
6— At San Jose .... OTL *3-4
8— At Los Angeles .... L 1-2
10— At Nashville .... W 3-1
12— At Florida .... W 4-0
13— At Atlanta .... W 4-2
15— Tampa Bay .... L 1-2
18— New Jersey .... L 0-1
20— N.Y. Islanders .... L 3-6
22— Carolina .... W 5-3
25— Washington .... OTL *3-4
28— At Buffalo .... L 1-4
29— Ottawa .... L 1-3
31— At Carolina .... W 4-0

APRIL
2— At Tampa Bay .... L 1-2
5— N.Y. Rangers .... W 5-4
*Denotes overtime game.

NASHVILLE PREDATORS
WESTERN CONFERENCE/CENTRAL DIVISION

Predators' Schedule
Home games shaded; D=Day game; *Feb. 8 All-Star Game at St. Paul, Minn.

October
SUN	MON	TUE	WED	THU	FRI	SAT
5	6	7	8	9 ANA	10	11 DAL
12	13	14	15	16 STL	17	18 CBJ
19 CHI	20	21	22	23 ATL	24	25 COL
26	27	28 STL	29	30 DET	31	

November
SUN	MON	TUE	WED	THU	FRI	SAT
						1 DAL
2 DAL	3	4	5 VAN	6	7 CHI	8 DET
9	10	11	12	13 CAL	14	15 NYI
16	17	18	19 LA	20	21 ANA	22 SJ
23	24 COL	25	26 CBJ	27	28 D BOS	29 BUF
30						

December
SUN	MON	TUE	WED	THU	FRI	SAT
	1	2	3 CAR	4 CBJ	5	6 STL
7	8	9	10	11 LA	12	13 FLA
14	15	16 VAN	17	18 MON	19	20 DET
21 PHO	22	23 MIN	24	25	26 DAL	27 PHO
28	29 SJ	30	31			

January
SUN	MON	TUE	WED	THU	FRI	SAT
				1 D	2	3 NJ
4	5 DET	6 TOR	7	8 COL	9	10 STL
11	12 MIN	13 LA	14	15 PHO	16	17 EDM
18 MIN	19	20	21	22 CAL	23	24 EDM
25 VAN	26	27	28	29 CBJ	30	31 SJ

February
SUN	MON	TUE	WED	THU	FRI	SAT
1	2	3 DET	4	5 TB	6	7
8*	9	10	11 CHI	12	13 WAS	14
15 D EDM	16 CBJ	17	18 SJ	19	20 ANA	21 PHO
22	23 LA	24	25	26 MIN	27	28 D NYR
29						

March
SUN	MON	TUE	WED	THU	FRI	SAT
	1 CHI	2	3 PHI	4 PIT	5	6 OTT
7	8	9 BOS	10	11 STL	12	13 CAL
14 DET	15	16 VAN	17	18	19 EDM	20 CAL
21	22	23 ANA	24	25 NYR	26	27 CBJ
28	29	30 CHI	31			

April
SUN	MON	TUE	WED	THU	FRI	SAT
				1 CHI	2	3 D STL
4 D COL	5	6	7	8	9	10

2003-04 SEASON
CLUB DIRECTORY

Owner, chairman and governor
Craig Leipold
President, COO and alternate governor
Jack Diller
Exec. v.p./g.m. and alternate governor
David Poile
Assistant general manager
Ray Shero
Director of communications
Ken Anderson
Communications coordinator
Tim Darling
Director of team services
Gregory Harvey
Head coach
Barry Trotz
Assistant coaches
Brent Peterson
Peter Horachek

Director of player personnel
Paul Fenton
Strength and conditioning coach
Mark Nemish
Goaltending coach
Mitch Korn
Head athletic trainer
Dan Redmond
Equipment manager
Pete Rogers
Assistant equipment manager
Chris Scoppetto
Massage therapist
Anthony Garrett
Video coach
Robert Bouchard

DRAFT CHOICES

Rd.— Player	Overall	Pos.	Last team
1— Ryan Suter	7	D	U.S. National under-18 (NTDP)
2— Konstantin Glazachev	35	LW	Yaroslavl (Russia)
2— Kevin Klein	37	D	Toronto-St. Michael's (OHL)
2— Shea Weber	49	D	Kelowna (WHL)
3— Richard Stehlik	76	D	Sherbrooke (QMJHL)
3— Paul Brown	89	RW	Kamloops (WHL)
3— Alexander Sulzer	92	D	Hamburg (Germany)
3— Grigory Shafigulin	98	C	Yaroslavl (Russia)
4— Teemu Lassila	117	G	TPS (Finland)
4— Rustam Sidikov	133	G	CSKA (Russia)
7— Andrei Mukhachev	210	D	CSKA (Russia)
7— Miroslav Hanuljak	213	G	Litvinov Jr. (Czech Republic Jr.)
9— Lauris Darzins	268	F	Lukko Jr. (Finland Jr.)

MISCELLANEOUS DATA

Home ice (capacity)
Gaylord Entertainment Center (17,113)
Address
501 Broadway
Nashville, TN 37203
Business phone
615-770-2300
Ticket information
615-770-7825
Website
www.nashvillepredators.com

Training site
Centennial Sportsplex, Nashville
Club colors
Blue, gold, silver, steel and orange
Radio affiliation
WTN (99.7 FM)
TV affiliation
FOX Sports Net

TRAINING CAMP ROSTER

No.	FORWARDS	Ht./Wt.	Place	BORN Date	NHL exp.	2002-03 clubs
48	Jonas Andersson (RW) .	6-2/189	Lidingo, Sweden	2-24-81	1	Milwaukee (AHL)
25	Denis Arkhipov (C)	6-3/195	Kazan, U.S.S.R.	5-19-79	3	Nashville
39	Marian Cisar (RW)	6-0/192	Bratislava, Czechoslovakia	2-25-78	4	, Lukko Rauma (Finland)
9	Greg Classen (C)	6-1/194	Aylsham, Sask.	8-24-77	3	Milwaukee (AHL), Nashville
19	Martin Erat (LW)	6-0/197	Trebic, Czechoslovakia	8-28-81	2	Milwaukee (AHL), Nashville
46	Mike Farrell (LW)	6-1/205	Edina, Minn.	10-20-78	2	Portland (AHL), Washington
	Vernon Fiddler (LW)	5-11/195	Edmonton, Alb.	5-9-80	1	Milwaukee (AHL), Nashville
41	Brent Gilchrist (LW)	5-11/180	Moose Jaw, Sask.	4-3-67	15	Nashville
8	Stu Grimson (LW)	6-5/239	Kamloops, B.C.	5-20-65	14	
34	Adam Hall (RW)	6-3/200	Kalamazoo, Mich.	8-14-80	2	Milwaukee (AHL), Nashville
17	Scott Hartnell (RW)	6-2/192	Regina, Sask.	4-18-82	3	Nashville
	Darren Haydar (RW)	5-9/163	Milton, Ont.	10-22-79	1	Milwaukee (AHL), Nashville
	Matt Hendricks (C)	5-11/190	Blaine, Minnesota	6-19-81	0	St. Cloud State (WCHA)
27	Jukka Hentunen (LW)	5-10/187	Joroinen, Finland	5-3-74	1	Jokerit Helsinki (Finland)
	Petr Hubacek (C)	6-2/183	Brno, Czechoslovakia	9-2-79	1	Vitkovice (Czech Republic)
21	Andreas Johansson (C) .	6-2/202	Hofors, Sweden	5-19-73	7	Nashville
22	Greg Johnson (C)	5-10/202	Thunder Bay, Ont.	3-16-71	10	Nashville
11	David Legwand (C)	6-2/185	Detroit	8-17-80	5	Nashville
	Cameron Mann (RW)	6-0/194	Thompson, Man.	4-20-77	5	Milwaukee (AHL), Nashville
	Jim McKenzie (LW)	6-4/227	Gull Lake, Sask.	11-3-69	14	New Jersey
17	Rem Murray (LW)	6-2/195	Stratford, Ont.	10-9-72	7	New York Rangers, Nashville
33	Vladimir Orszagh (RW)..	5-11/173	Banska Bystrica, Czech.	5-24-77	5	Nashville
20	Denis Pederson (C)	6-2/205	Prince Albert, Sask.	9-10-75	8	Nashville
14	Oleg Petrov (RW)	5-8/175	Moscow, U.S.S.R.	4-18-71	8	Montreal, Nashville
	Libor Pivko (LW)	6-3/192	Novy Vicin, Czechoslovakia	3-29-80	0	HC Continental Zlin (Czech Republic)
	Denis Platonov (C/LW) ..	6-1/194	Saratov, U.S.S.R.	11-6-81	0	Kazan (Russian Div. III)
	Oliver Setzinger (C)	6-0/180	Horn, Austria	7-11-83	0	Pelicans Lahti (Finland Div. 2)
45	Ben Simon (C)	5-11/178	Cleveland	6-14-78	2	Chicago (AHL), Atlanta
24	Reid Simpson (LW)	6-2/220	Flin Flon, Man.	5-21-69	11	Milwaukee (AHL), Nashville
	Wyatt Smith (C)	5-11/200	Thief River Falls, Minn.	2-13-77	4	Milwaukee (AHL), Nashville
	Sergei Soin (C/LW)	6-0/176	Moscow, U.S.S.R.	3-31-82	0	Kryla Sov. Moscow (Russian)
	Scottie Upshall (RW)	5-11/176	Fort McMurray, Alta.	10-7-83	1	Milwaukee (AHL), Nashville, Kamloops (WHL)
24	Scott Walker (RW)	5-10/190	Cambridge, Ont.	7-19-73	9	Nashville
21	Todd Warriner (LW)	6-2/205	Blenheim, Ont.	1-3-74	9	Philadelphia, Vancouver, Nashville
	Daniel Widing (RW)	6-0/185	Gavle, Sweden	4-13-82	0	Leksand (Sweden Dv. 2)
23	Clarke Wilm (C)	6-0/202	Central Butte, Sask.	10-24-76	5	Nashville
43	Vitali Yachmenev (RW)..	5-9/190	Chelyabinsk, U.S.S.R.	1-8-75	8	Nashville
DEFENSEMEN						
4	Mark Eaton	6-2/205	Wilmington, Del.	5-6-77	4	Milwaukee (AHL), Nashville
60	Dan Hamhuis	6-0/195	Smithers, B.C.	12-13-82	0	Milwaukee (AHL)
14	Brett Hauer	6-2/180	Richfield, Minn.	7-11-71	4	
	Timo Helbling	6-2/183	Basel, Switzerland	7-21-81	0	Toledo (ECHL), Milwaukee (AHL)
23	Bill Houlder	6-2/211	Thunder Bay, Ont.	3-11-67	16	Nashville
32	Cale Hulse	6-3/215	Edmonton	11-10-73	8	Nashville
51	Andrew Hutchinson	6-2/186	Evanston, Ill.	3-24-80	0	Toledo (ECHL), Milwaukee (AHL)
13	Jere Karalahti	6-2/210	Helsinki, Finland	3-25-75	3	
22	Tomas Kloucek	6-3/203	Prague, Czechoslovakia	3-7-80	3	Nashville, Hartford (AHL), Milw. (AHL)
	Curtis Murphy	5-8/185		12-3-75	1	Houston (AHL), Minnesota
	Robert Schnabel	6-6/216	Prague, Czechoslovakia	11-10-78	2	Milwaukee (AHL), Nashville
39	Ray Schultz	6-2/200	Red Deer, Alta.	11-14-76	6	Bridgeport (AHL), New York Islanders
	Pavel Skrbek	6-3/213	Kladno, Czechoslovakia	8-9-78	3	Lulea (Sweden)
44	Kimmo Timonen	5-10/196	Kuopio, Finland	3-18-75	5	Nashville
33	Jason York	6-1/200	Nepean, Ont.	5-20-70	11	Cincinnati (AHL), Nashville
GOALTENDERS						
31	Brian Finley	6-2/180	Sault Ste. Marie, Ont.	7-3-81	1	Toledo (ECHL), Milwaukee (AHL), Nashville
30	Wade Flaherty	6-0/187	Terrace, B.C.	1-11-68	11	San Antonio (AHL), Florida, Nashville
35	Jan Lasak	6-0/204	Zvolen, Czechoslovakia	4-10-79	2	Milwaukee (AHL), Nashville
29	Tomas Vokoun	6-3/183	Karlovy Vary, Czechoslovakia	7-2-76	6	Nashville

2002-03 REVIEW
INDIVIDUAL STATISTICS

SCORING

	Games	G	A	Pts.	PIM	+/-	PPG	SHG	GWG	GTG	Sht.	Sht. Pct.	Faceoffs Won	Lost	Pct.	TOI
David Legwand	64	17	31	48	34	-2	3	1	4	1	167	10.2	510	585	46.6	19:14
Kimmo Timonen	72	6	34	40	46	-3	4	0	0	0	144	4.2	0	0	—	22:24
Andreas Johansson...	56	20	17	37	22	-4	10	0	0	1	124	16.1	0	0	50.0	16:45
Denis Arkhipov	79	11	24	35	32	-18	3	0	1	1	148	7.4	499	570	46.7	15:08
Andy Delmore	71	18	16	34	28	-17	14	0	6	0	149	12.1	0	0	—	17:04
Scott Hartnell	82	12	22	34	101	-3	2	0	2	0	221	5.4	7	16	30.4	15:17
Scott Walker	60	15	18	33	58	2	7	0	5	0	124	12.1	165	171	49.1	19:49
Vladimir Orszagh	78	16	16	32	38	-1	3	0	3	0	152	10.5	5	12	29.4	17:34

	Games	G	A	Pts.	PIM	+/-	PPG	SHG	GWG	GTG	Sht.	Sht. Pct.	Faceoffs Won	Lost	Pct.	TOI
Adam Hall	79	16	12	28	31	-8	8	0	2	0	146	11.0	9	8	52.9	14:08
Vitali Yachmenev	62	5	15	20	12	7	0	0	1	0	68	7.4	5	19	20.8	16:38
Rem Murray*	53	6	13	19	18	1	1	0	0	0	81	7.4	354	366	49.2	17:16
Jason York	74	4	15	19	52	13	2	0	0	1	107	3.7	0	0	—	19:57
Greg Johnson	38	8	9	17	22	7	0	0	0	0	55	14.5	392	361	52.1	17:11
Clarke Wilm	82	5	11	16	36	-11	0	0	0	0	108	4.6	171	168	50.4	11:57
Karlis Skrastins	82	3	10	13	44	-18	0	1	0	0	86	3.5	0	0	—	20:17
Denis Pederson	43	4	6	10	39	2	0	0	0	1	64	6.3	221	219	50.2	12:48
Mark Eaton	50	2	7	9	22	1	0	0	0	1	52	3.8	0	0	—	15:45
Cale Hulse	80	2	6	8	121	-11	0	0	1	0	82	2.4	0	0	—	19:05
Martin Erat	27	1	7	8	14	-9	1	0	0	0	39	2.6	0	1	0.0	12:47
Vernon Fiddler	19	4	2	6	14	2	0	0	1	0	20	20.0	92	79	53.8	9:40
Bill Houlder	82	2	4	6	46	-2	0	0	1	0	51	3.9	0	2	0.0	19:06
Oleg Petrov*	17	2	2	4	2	-4	0	0	0	0	37	5.4	1	0	100.0	16:19
Brent Gilchrist	41	1	2	3	14	-11	0	0	0	0	41	2.4	8	17	32.0	10:45
Jon Sim*	4	1	0	1	0	0	0	0	0	0	3	33.3	5	9	35.7	9:18
Scottie Upshall	8	1	0	1	0	2	0	0	0	1	6	16.7	0	2	0.0	8:42
Wyatt Smith	11	1	0	1	0	-1	0	0	0	0	8	12.5	61	62	49.6	11:56
Wade Flaherty (g)*	1	0	1	1	0	0	0	0	0	0	—	—	0	0	—	—
Todd Warriner*	6	0	1	1	4	-1	0	0	0	0	6	0.0	3	2	60.0	11:15
Reid Simpson	26	0	1	1	56	-4	0	0	0	0	11	0.0	0	1	0.0	5:04
Tomas Vokoun (g)	69	0	1	1	28	0	0	0	0	0	0	—	0	0	—	—
Brian Finley (g)	1	0	0	0	0	0	0	0	0	0	0	—	0	0	—	—
Nathan Perrott	1	0	0	0	5	0	0	0	0	0	0	—	0	0	—	4:13
Robert Schnabel	1	0	0	0	0	0	0	0	0	0	0	—	0	0	—	4:28
Pascal Trepanier	1	0	0	0	0	0	0	0	0	0	1	0.0	0	0	—	9:55
Darren Haydar	2	0	0	0	0	-1	0	0	0	0	1	0.0	0	0	—	8:54
Domenic Pittis	2	0	0	0	2	0	0	0	0	0	1	0.0	1	5	16.7	4:59
Tomas Kloucek	3	0	0	0	2	1	0	0	0	0	1	0.0	0	0	—	9:44
Jan Lasak (g)	3	0	0	0	0	0	0	0	0	0	0	—	0	0	—	—
Bubba Berenzweig	4	0	0	0	0	0	0	0	0	0	5	0.0	0	0	—	17:47
Francis Bouillon*	4	0	0	0	2	-1	0	0	0	0	0	—	0	0	—	12:51
Cameron Mann	4	0	0	0	0	-2	0	0	0	0	5	0.0	0	0	—	5:53
Greg Classen	8	0	0	0	4	-3	0	0	0	0	2	0.0	34	31	52.3	10:02
Mike Dunham (g)*	15	0	0	0	0	0	0	0	0	0	0	—	0	0	—	—

GOALTENDING

	Games	GS	Min.	GA	SO	Avg.	W	L	T	EN	PPG Allow	SHG Allow	Shots	Save Pct.
Tomas Vokoun	69	68	3974	146	3	2.20	25	31	11	5	42	6	1771	.918
Mike Dunham*	15	13	819	43	0	3.15	2	9	2	0	15	2	397	.892
Jan Lasak	3	1	90	5	0	3.33	0	1	0	0	2	0	39	.872
Brian Finley	1	0	47	3	0	3.83	0	0	0	0	1	0	13	.769
Wade Flaherty	1	0	51	4	0	4.71	0	1	0	0	1	0	27	.852

*Played with two or more NHL teams.

RESULTS

OCTOBER
11— At Washington .... L 4-5
12— Edmonton .... L 2-3
15— At N.Y. Islanders .... OTL ... *3-4
18— At New Jersey .... OTL ... *2-3
19— At N.Y. Rangers .... T *2-2
22— Phoenix .... L 1-2
24— San Jose .... L 1-2
26— Detroit .... W 3-1
30— At St. Louis .... L 0-7

NOVEMBER
2— At Los Angeles .... OTL ... *5-6
3— At Phoenix .... OTL ... *1-2
6— At Anaheim .... L 1-2
7— At San Jose .... T *2-2
10— At Colorado .... W 4-3
12— At Detroit .... L 1-4
14— Colorado .... L 1-3
16— Columbus .... T *1-1
17— At Chicago .... L 2-4
21— At Colorado .... T *1-1
23— At Minnesota .... L 2-4
27— San Jose .... W 4-2
29— New Jersey .... L 1-2
30— Dallas .... W 5-2

DECEMBER
3— Carolina .... L 1-2
5— At Los Angeles .... W 3-2
7— At San Jose .... W 4-2
8— At Anaheim .... L 0-3

10— Los Angeles .... L 0-3
12— St. Louis .... T *2-2
14— Minnesota .... W 3-1
17— Calgary .... L 0-3
19— Vancouver .... L 1-3
21— At Tampa Bay .... T *2-2
23— At Florida .... W 3-2
26— Dallas .... W 3-1
28— Detroit .... L 2-4
30— Ottawa .... W 3-2

JANUARY
1— Colorado .... L 3-7
4— Chicago .... T *3-3
6— At Columbus .... W 5-1
7— St. Louis .... W *2-1
11— Phoenix .... W *4-3
12— At Chicago .... L 0-2
14— At Vancouver .... L 3-4
16— At Calgary .... T *2-2
18— At Edmonton .... W *3-2
21— Vancouver .... W 3-2
23— N.Y. Rangers .... L 2-4
25— Tampa Bay .... W 3-2
27— At Buffalo .... W 5-1
28— At Boston .... L 1-2
30— At Columbus .... L 1-2

FEBRUARY
4— At Detroit .... T *5-5
8— Columbus .... W 3-2
11— Los Angeles .... L 2-3

13— N.Y. Islanders .... W 2-0
15— Anaheim .... W 2-1
17— Boston .... W 5-1
20— Calgary .... W 4-1
22— At Ottawa .... L 0-4
23— At Toronto .... W 5-2
25— Columbus .... W 5-0
27— Pittsburgh .... W 6-0

MARCH
1— Chicago .... W *5-4
4— At St. Louis .... OTL ... *1-2
6— Minnesota .... T *2-2
7— At Dallas .... W 2-1
10— Montreal .... L 1-3
12— At Pittsburgh .... T *2-2
14— At Minnesota .... L 1-3
15— St. Louis .... L 0-1
17— Edmonton .... L 3-5
20— At Vancouver .... L 3-7
22— At Calgary .... T *1-1
23— At Edmonton .... OTL ... *2-3
25— Philadelphia .... T *1-1
27— At Chicago .... L 1-4
29— Atlanta .... L 2-3
31— At Detroit .... L 0-3

APRIL
1— Anaheim .... OTL ... *1-2
4— At Phoenix .... L 0-1
6— At Dallas .... L 0-2
*Denotes overtime game.

NEW JERSEY DEVILS
EASTERN CONFERENCE/ATLANTIC DIVISION

Devils' Schedule
Home games shaded; D=Day game; *Feb. 8 All-Star Game at St. Paul, Minn.

October

SUN	MON	TUE	WED	THU	FRI	SAT
5	6	7	8 BOS	9	10	11 CAR
12	13	14	15	16 TOR	17	18 TB
19	20	21	22 FLA	23	24 PIT	25 BOS
26	27	28 NYI	29	30 PHI	31	

November

SUN	MON	TUE	WED	THU	FRI	SAT
						1 D COL
2	3	4	5 SJ	6	7 TOR	8 OTT
9	10	11	12 BUF	13 FLA	14	15 D NYR
16	17	18	19 BUF	20	21 PIT	22
23	24	25 LA	26 ANA	27	28 DAL	29
30 COL						

December

SUN	MON	TUE	WED	THU	FRI	SAT
	1	2 PHO	3	4 WAS	5	6 OTT
7	8	9	10 NYI	11	12 PHI	13 PHI
14	15	16 NYI	17	18 ATL	19 BUF	20
21 CHI	22	23	24	25	26 NYI	27 PIT
28	29 NYI	30	31			

January

SUN	MON	TUE	WED	THU	FRI	SAT
				1 WAS	2	3 NAS
4	5 EDM	6	7 PIT	8	9 TB	10 TOR
11	12	13 OTT	14	15 NYR	16	17 D WAS
18	19	20 PIT	21 CAR	22	23 MON	24
25 ATL	26	27 CBJ	28	29 DET	30	31 STL

February

SUN	MON	TUE	WED	THU	FRI	SAT
1	2	3 OTT	4	5 VAN	6	7
8*	9	10 PHI	11 NYR	12	13	14 D CAR
15 D LA	16	17 MIN	18	19 WAS	20	21 D NYR
22 D CAL	23	24	25 BUF	26	27 ATL	28 TOR
29						

March

SUN	MON	TUE	WED	THU	FRI	SAT
	1 MON	2	3 FLA	4	5 TB	6 CAR
7	8	9 PHI	10	11 CHI	12	13 D PHI
14	15 NYR	16	17 PIT	18	19 MON	20 MON
21	22	23 FLA	24	25 TB	26 ATL	27
28 NYI	29	30 NYR	31			

April

SUN	MON	TUE	WED	THU	FRI	SAT
				1	2	3 D BOS
4 D BOS	5	6	7	8	9	10

2003-04 SEASON
CLUB DIRECTORY

CEO/president and general manager
Louis A. Lamoriello
Head coach
Pat Burns
Assistant coaches
Bob Carpenter
John MacLean
Goaltending coach
Jacques Caron
Medical trainer
Bill Murray

Strength & conditioning coordinator
Michael Vasalani
Equipment manager
Rich Matthews
Assistant equipment manager
Alex Abasto
Director, public relations
Jeff Altstadter
Director, information & publications
Mike Levine

DRAFT CHOICES

Rd.— Player	Overall	Pos.	Last team
1— Zach Parise	17	C	North Dakota (WCHA)
2— Petr Vrana	42	LW	Halifax (QMJHL)
3— Ivan Khomutov	93	C.W	Elektrostal (Russia)
5— Zach Tarkir	167	D	Chilliwack (BCHL)
6— Jason Smith	197	G	Lennoxville (Que. Jr.)
8— Joey Tenute	261	C	Sarnia (OHL)
9— Arseny Bonarev	292	LW	Yaroslavl (Russia)

MISCELLANEOUS DATA

Home ice (capacity)
Continental Airlines Arena (19,040)
Address
P.O. Box 504
50 Route 120 North
East Rutherford, N.J. 07073
Business phone
201-935-6050
Ticket information
201-935-3900
Website
www.newjerseydevils.com

Training site
West Orange, NJ
Club colors
Red, black and white
Radio affiliation
WABC (770 AM)
TV affiliation
FOX Sports Net New York

TRAINING CAMP ROSTER

No.	FORWARDS	Ht./Wt.	BORN Place	Date	NHL exp.	2002-03 clubs
10	Christian Berglund (C)...	5-11/185	Orebro, Sweden	3-12-80	2	Albany (AHL), New Jersey
9	Jiri Bicek (LW)	5-10/195	Kosice, Czechoslovakia	12-3-78	3	Albany (AHL), New Jersey
	Max Birbraer (LW)	6-2/185	Ust-Kamenogorsk, U.S.S.R.	12-15-80	0	Albany (AHL)
18	Sergei Brylin (LW)	5-10/190	Moscow, U.S.S.R.	1-13-74	9	New Jersey
	Scott Cameron (LW)	6-0/180	Sudbury, Ont.	4-11-81	0	Albany (AHL)
	Brett Clouthier (LW)	6-4/220	Ottawa	6-9-81	0	Albany (AHL)
	Mike Danton (C)			10-21-80	1	New Jersey
63	Craig Darby (C)	6-3/200	Oneida, N.Y.	9-26-72	8	Albany (AHL), New Jersey
26	Patrik Elias (LW)	6-1/200	Trebic, Czechoslovakia	4-13-76	8	New Jersey
	Adrian Foster (LW)	6-1/200	Lethbridge, Alta.	1-15-82	0	Albany (AHL)
39	Jeff Friesen (LW)	6-0/205	Meadow Lake, Sask.	8-5-76	9	New Jersey
14	Brian Gionta (RW)	5-7/160	Rochester, N.Y.	1-18-79	2	New Jersey
23	Scott Gomez (C)	5-11/200	Anchorage, Alaska	12-23-79	4	New Jersey
	Stanislav Gron (C)	6-2/210	Bratislava, Czechoslovakia	10-28-78	1	HC Vitkovice (Czech.)
12	Steve Guolla (C)	6-0/191	Scarborough, Ont.	3-15-73	6	Albany (AHL), New Jersey
48	Joe Hulbig (LW)	6-3/215	Norwood, Mass.	9-29-73	5	Albany (AHL)
18	Steve Kariya (LW)	5-7/170	Vancouver	12-22-77	3	Manitoba (AHL), Albany (AHL)
	Teemu Laine (RW)	6-0/194	Helsinki, Finland	8-9-82	0	Jokerit Helsinki (Finland)
15	J. Langenbrunner (RW).	6-1/200	Duluth, Minn.	7-24-75	9	New Jersey
11	John Madden (C)	5-11/195	Barrie, Ont.	5-4-75	5	New Jersey
29	Grant Marshall (RW)	6-1/193	Mississauga, Ont.	6-9-73	9	New Jersey, Columbus
25	Joe Nieuwendyk (C)	6-1/205	Oshawa, Ont.	9-10-66	17	New Jersey
20	Jay Pandolfo (LW)	6-1/190	Winchester, Mass.	12-27-74	7	New Jersey
	Thomas Pihlman (LW)...	6-2/205	Espoo, Finland	11-13-82	0	Jyraskyla (Finland)
	Andrei Posnov (C)	6-2/185	Moscow, U.S.S.R.	11-19-81	0	Spartak Moscow (Russian)
26	Pascal Rheaume (C)	6-1/209	Quebec City	6-21-73	7	New Jersey, Atlanta
25	Dave Roche (LW)	6-4/230	Lindsay, Ont.	6-13-75	5	Albany (AHL)
	Mike Rucinski (C)	5-11/188	Trenton, Mich.	3-30-75	3	
	Michael Rupp (LW)	6-5/228	Cleveland	1-13-80	1	Albany (AHL), New Jersey
	Rob Skrlac (LW)	6-5/240	Campbell, B.C.	6-10-76	0	Albany (AHL)
24	Turner Stevenson (RW).	6-3/226	Prince George, B.C.	5-18-72	11	New Jersey
	A. Suglobov (RW/LW) ...	6-0/176	Elektrostal, U.S.S.R.	1-15-82	0	Yaroslavl (Russia)
	Barry Tallackson (RW)...	6-4/196	Grafton, N.D.	4-14-83	0	Univ. of Minnesota (WCHA)
DEFENSEMEN						
6	Tommy Albelin	6-1/194	Stockholm, Sweden	5-21-64	16	Albany (AHL), New Jersey
	Matt DeMarchi	6-3/180	Bemidji, Minn.	5-4-81	0	Univ. of Minnesota (WCHA)
41	Ray Giroux	5-11/185	North Bay, Ont.	7-20-76	3	Albany (AHL), New Jersey
	David Hale	6-2/204	Colorado Springs, Colo.	6-18-81	0	Univ. of North Dakota (WCHA)
	Anton Kadeykin	6-2/180	Elektrostal, U.S.S.R.	4-17-84	0	Sarnia (OHL)
	Teemu Kesa	6-0/185	Nurmijarvi, Finland	6-7-81	0	Lukko Rauma (Finland)
	Paul Martin	6-1/170	Minneapolis	3-5-81	0	Univ. of Minnesota (WCHA)
	Mike Matteucci	6-3/225	Trail, B.C.	12-12-71	2	Albany (AHL)
27	Scott Niedermayer	6-1/200	Edmonton	8-31-73	12	New Jersey
28	Brian Rafalski	5-9/200	Dearborn, Mich.	9-28-73	4	New Jersey
42	Richard Smehlik	6-3/222	Ostrava, Czechoslovakia	1-23-70	11	New Jersey, Atlanta
4	Scott Stevens	6-1/215	Kitchener, Ont.	4-1-64	21	New Jersey
6	Ken Sutton	6-1/205	Edmonton	11-5-69	11	Albany (AHL)
10	Oleg Tverdovsky	6-0/200	Donetsk, U.S.S.R.	5-18-76	9	New Jersey
	Victor Uchevatov	6-4/205	Angarsk, U.S.S.R.	2-10-83	0	Albany (AHL)
5	Colin White	6-4/210	New Glasgow, Nova Scotia	12-12-77	4	New Jersey
GOALTENDERS						
	Ari Ahonen	6-2/170	Jyvaskyla, Finland	2-6-81	0	Albany (AHL)
30	Martin Brodeur	6-2/205	Montreal	5-6-72	11	New Jersey
40	Scott Clemmensen	6-2/185	Des Moines, Iowa	7-23-77	1	Albany (AHL)
32	Corey Schwab	6-0/180	North Battleford, Sask.	11-4-70	7	New Jersey

2002-03 REVIEW
INDIVIDUAL STATISTICS

SCORING

	Games	G	A	Pts.	PIM	+/-	PPG	SHG	GWG	GTG	Sht.	Sht. Pct.	Faceoffs Won	Lost	Pct.	TOI
Patrik Elias	81	28	29	57	22	17	6	0	4	1	255	11.0	187	240	43.8	18:05
Jamie Langenbrunner	78	22	33	55	65	17	5	1	5	0	197	11.2	34	38	47.2	17:47
Scott Gomez	80	13	42	55	48	17	2	0	4	1	205	6.3	410	454	47.5	16:00
Jeff Friesen	81	23	28	51	26	23	3	0	4	1	179	12.8	5	6	45.5	15:32

	Games	G	A	Pts.	PIM	+/-	PPG	SHG	GWG	GTG	Sht.	Sht. Pct.	Faceoffs Won	Lost	Pct.	TOI
Joe Nieuwendyk	80	17	28	45	56	10	3	0	4	0	201	8.5	809	574	58.5	16:45
John Madden	80	19	22	41	26	13	2	2	3	0	207	9.2	765	737	50.9	18:18
Brian Rafalski	79	3	37	40	14	18	2	0	0	0	178	1.7	0	1	0.0	23:08
Scott Niedermayer	81	11	28	39	62	23	3	0	3	0	164	6.7	0	1	0.0	24:29
Brian Gionta	58	12	13	25	23	5	2	0	3	0	129	9.3	8	6	57.1	14:47
Turner Stevenson	77	7	13	20	115	7	0	0	0	0	85	8.2	5	7	41.7	11:53
Scott Stevens	81	4	16	20	41	18	0	0	2	0	113	3.5	0	0	—	23:04
Sergei Brylin	52	11	8	19	16	-2	3	1	1	0	86	12.8	29	61	32.2	16:10
Jay Pandolfo	68	6	11	17	23	12	0	1	4	0	92	6.5	3	10	23.1	16:07
Oleg Tverdovsky	50	5	8	13	22	2	2	0	1	0	76	6.6	0	0	—	16:47
Colin White	72	5	8	13	98	19	0	0	1	0	81	6.2	0	0	—	19:40
Jim McKenzie	76	4	8	12	88	3	0	0	2	0	42	9.5	3	2	60.0	7:41
Jiri Bicek	44	5	6	11	25	7	1	0	1	0	63	7.9	0	3	0.0	11:48
Christian Berglund	38	4	5	9	20	3	0	0	0	0	50	8.0	1	10	9.1	10:10
Ken Daneyko	69	2	7	9	33	6	0	0	0	0	38	5.3	1	0	100.0	15:36
Michael Rupp	26	5	3	8	21	0	2	0	3	0	34	14.7	67	83	44.7	11:39
Tommy Albelin	37	1	6	7	6	10	0	1	0	0	30	3.3	0	0	—	15:13
Pascal Rheaume*	21	4	1	5	8	3	0	1	1	0	23	17.4	128	120	51.6	11:49
Grant Marshall*	10	1	3	4	7	-3	0	0	0	0	17	5.9	1	0	100.0	11:38
Stephen Guolla	12	2	0	2	2	1	0	0	0	0	6	33.3	25	36	41.0	7:59
Mike Danton	17	2	0	2	35	0	0	0	0	0	18	11.1	44	67	39.6	8:58
Richard Smehlik*	12	0	2	2	0	-1	0	0	0	0	11	0.0	0	0	—	17:20
Andrei Zyuzin*	1	0	1	1	2	-1	0	0	0	0	0	—	0	0	—	20:03
Craig Darby	3	0	1	1	0	-1	0	0	0	0	1	0.0	10	11	47.6	10:35
Ray Giroux	11	0	1	1	6	-2	0	0	0	0	20	0.0	0	0	—	18:18
Corey Schwab (g)	11	0	0	0	0	0	0	0	0	0	0	—	0	0	—	—
Martin Brodeur (g)	73	0	0	0	10	0	0	0	0	0	0	—	0	0	—	—

GOALTENDING

	Games	GS	Min.	GA	SO	Avg.	W	L	T	EN	PPG Allow	SHG Allow	Shots	Save Pct.
Corey Schwab	11	9	614	15	1	1.47	5	3	1	0	1	0	223	.933
Martin Brodeur	73	73	4374	147	9	2.02	41	23	9	4	31	4	1706	.914

*Played with two or more NHL teams.

RESULTS

OCTOBER
10—At Ottawa ....W....2-1
12—Columbus..........................W....3-2
18—Nashville...........................W... *3-2
19—At Carolina.........................L.....1-3
23—At Atlanta ....W....2-1
25—At Buffalo ....W....2-1
26—Tampa Bay ....W....5-1
29—Carolina ....L.....1-2

NOVEMBER
2—Chicago ....W....5-1
5—Calgary ....L.....2-3
7—At Philadelphia ....W....1-0
9—Edmonton ....L.....3-6
12—Anaheim ....W... *3-2
15—Montreal ....W....5-1
16—At Montreal ....L.....1-3
19—Buffalo ....W... *4-3
21—N.Y. Rangers ....T.... *4-4
23—Tampa Bay ....L.....1-3
27—At Detroit...........................OTL... *2-3
29—At Nashville ....W....2-1
30—At St. Louis ....W... *5-4

DECEMBER
2—At Philadelphia ....W... *1-0
4—Vancouver ....OTL... *2-3
6—Pittsburgh ....W....3-1
7—At Toronto ....L.....0-1
10—St. Louis...........................W....2-0
12—At Columbus......................L.....2-4

14—At Ottawa ....OTL... *3-4
18—Ottawa ....L.....0-3
19—At Pittsburgh ....W....3-1
21—Dallas ....W....5-3
23—At N.Y. Rangers ....T.... *2-2
27—At Washington ....L.....2-3
28—Washington ....W... *2-1
30—At Boston ....W....1-0

JANUARY
1—Florida ....L.....1-2
3—Toronto.............................W....2-0
4—At Toronto ....L.....1-2
7—Montreal ....W....3-2
10—At Florida ....W....2-1
11—At Tampa Bay ....T.... *3-3
13—Florida ....W....6-2
15—N.Y. Islanders ....W....5-0
17—At Carolina.........................W....2-1
18—Carolina ....W....5-2
22—At San Jose ....W... *5-4
24—At Anaheim.........................W....3-1
25—At Los Angeles ....OTL... *1-2
28—Detroit ....W....1-0
30—Philadelphia ....W....5-1

FEBRUARY
4—Buffalo..............................W....4-1
5—At Washington ....W....4-1
7—Atlanta ....L.....2-4
9—Minnesota ....W....3-2
11—At Colorado ....L.....1-3

12—At Phoenix.........................W....3-0
15—Pittsburgh..........................L.....1-4
18—At Philadelphia ....T.... *2-2
19—Ottawa ....L.....3-5
21—Boston ....W....3-2
23—At Pittsburgh ....W....4-3
25—N.Y. Rangers ....T.... *3-3
27—At N.Y. Islanders ....T.... *3-3

MARCH
1—Washington ....W... *2-1
4—At Minnesota ....L.....2-3
5—At Calgary ....OTL... *4-5
8—At N.Y. Islanders ....W....4-2
11—Atlanta ....L.....2-3
13—At Boston ....L.....3-4
15—N.Y. Rangers ....W....3-1
17—Philadelphia ....L.....2-4
18—At Montreal ....W....1-0
21—Pittsburgh ....W....3-1
22—At N.Y. Islanders ....W....4-2
24—At Florida ....W....4-1
27—At Tampa Bay ....T.... *2-2
28—At Atlanta ....T.... *1-1
30—N.Y. Islanders ....W....6-0

APRIL
1—Toronto ....OTL... *2-3
3—Boston ....T.... *1-1
4—At N.Y. Rangers ....W....2-1
6—At Buffalo...........................T.... *2-2

*Denotes overtime game.

NEW YORK ISLANDERS
EASTERN CONFERENCE/ATLANTIC DIVISION

Islanders' Schedule
Home games shaded; D=Day game; *Feb. 8 All-Star Game at St. Paul, Minn.

October

SUN	MON	TUE	WED	THU	FRI	SAT
5	6	7	8	9 WAS	10	11 BUF
12	13	14 ATL	15	16	17	18 FLA
19	20 TOR	21	22	23 MON	24	25 PIT
26	27	28 NJ	29 PIT	30	31	

November

SUN	MON	TUE	WED	THU	FRI	SAT
						1 D ANA
2	3 OTT	4	5	6 DAL	7	8 ATL
9	10	11 PHI	12	13 MON	14	15 NAS
16	17	18	19 FLA	20 TB	21	22 CBJ
23	24	25	26 CAR	27	28 DET	29 PHI
30						

December

SUN	MON	TUE	WED	THU	FRI	SAT
	1	2 WAS	3	4 NYR	5	6 CHI
7	8	9 TB	10 NJ	11	12	13 ATL
14	15	16 NJ	17	18 NYR	19	20 D PHI
21 WAS	22	23 PHI	24	25	26 NJ	27 TOR
28	29 NJ	30	31 D PIT			

January

SUN	MON	TUE	WED	THU	FRI	SAT
				1 OTT	2	3 BOS
4	5	6 CAL	7	8 EDM	9	10 D NYR
11	12	13 NYR	14	15 OTT	16	17 BUF
18	19 D OTT	20 TOR	21	22	23 CAR	24 ATL
25	26	27 BOS	28	29 BOS	30	31 FLA

February

SUN	MON	TUE	WED	THU	FRI	SAT
1	2	3 VAN	4	5 MON	6	7
8*	9	10 COL	11 DAL	12	13 PHO	14
15	16 D LA	17	18 PIT	19 NYR	20	21 BUF
22	23	24 BOS	25	26 NYR	27 BUF	28
29 D PIT						

March

SUN	MON	TUE	WED	THU	FRI	SAT
	1	2 PIT	3	4 TOR	5	6 STL
7	8	9 STL	10	11 SJ	12 ANA	13
14	15	16 TB	17 FLA	18	19 MIN	20
21 D TB	22	23 WAS	24	25 PHI	26	27 CAR
28 NJ	29	30	31 MON			

April

SUN	MON	TUE	WED	THU	FRI	SAT
				1	2 CAR	3
4 D PHI	5	6	7	8	9	10

2003-04 SEASON

CLUB DIRECTORY

Owner and governor
Charles B. Wang
Owner and alternate governor
Sanjay Kumar
Sr. v.p. of operations and alt. governor
Michael J. Picker
Sr. v.p. of sales and marketing
Paul Lancey
Alternate governor and general counsel
Roy E. Reichbach
Alternate governor
William M. Skehan
General manager and alt. governor
Mike Milbury
Manager, hockey administration
Joanne Holewa
Head coach
Steve Stirling
Assistant coaches
TBA
Goaltending consultant
Bill Smith
Director of pro scouting
Ken Morrow
Asst. director of pro scouting
Kevin Maxwell
Head amateur scout
Tony Feltrin
Western scout
Earl Ingarfield
Ontario scout
Doug Gibson
Russian amatuer scout
Yuri Karmonov
Sweden/Finland amateur scout
Anders Kallur

US amateur scout
Jay Heinbuck
Czech Republic amateur scout
Karel Pavlik
Scouting staff
Jim Madigan, Mario Saraceno, Brian Hunter, Harri Rindell, Greg Morrow, Harkie Singh, Ryan Jankowski
Video coordinator
Bob Smith
Director of medical services
Dr. Elliot Pellman
Internist
Dr. Clifford Cooper
Team orthopedists
Dr. Elliott Hershman, Dr. Kenneth Montgomery, Dr. David Gazzaniga
Team dentists
Dr. Bruce Michnick, Dr. Jan Sherman
Head athletic trainer
Rich Campbell
Assistant athletic trainer
Andy Wetstein
Strength & conditioning coach
Sean Donellan
Equipment managers
Vinnie Ferraiuolo, Joe McMahon, Scott Moon
V.p. communications
Chris Botta
Manager of media relations
Jamie Fabos
Media relations coordinator
Howie Wirtheim

DRAFT CHOICES

Rd.— Player	Overall	Pos.	Last team
1— Robert Nilsson	15	C	Sweden
2— Dimitri Chernykh	48	RW	Chimik (Russia)
2— Evgeni Tunik	53	C	Elektrostal (Russia)
2— Jeremy Colliton	58	C	Prince Albert (WHL)
4— Stefan Blaho	120	RW	Trencin Jr. (Slovakia Jr.)
6— Bruno Gervais	182	D	Acadie-Bathurst (QMJHL)
7— Denis Rehak	212	D	Trencin Jr. (Slovakia Jr.)
8— Cody Blanshan	238	D	Neb.-Omaha (CCHA)
8— Igor Volkov	246	RW	UFA (Russia)

MISCELLANEOUS DATA

Home ice (capacity)
Nassau Veterans Memorial Coliseum (16,234)
Address
1535 Old Country Road
Plainview, NY 11803
Business phone
516-501-6700
Ticket information
1-800-882-4753

Website
www.newyorkislanders.com
Training site
Iceworks, Syosset, NY
Club colors
Blue and orange
Radio affiliation
WJWR (620 AM)
TV affiliation
FOX Sports New York

NEW YORK ISLANDERS

No.	FORWARDS	Ht./Wt.	Place	BORN Date	NHL exp.	2002-03 clubs
	Arron Asham (RW)	5-11/195	Portage-La-Prairie, Man.	4-13-78	5	New York Islanders
17	Shawn Bates (C)	6-0/205	Melrose, Mass.	4-3-75	6	New York Islanders
	Sean Bergenheim (RW)	5-11/194	Helsinki, Finland	2-8-81	0	Jokerit Helsinki (Finland)
55	Jason Blake (C)	5-10/180	Moorhead, Minn.	9-2-73	5	New York Islanders
	Mariusz Czerkawski (RW)	6-0/199	Radomsko, Poland	4-13-72	10	Hamilton (AHL), Montreal
	Eric Godard (RW)	6-4/215	Vernon, B.C.	3-7-80	1	Bridgeport (AHL), New York Islanders
	Jeff Hamilton (C)				0	Bridgeport (AHL)
46	Matt Higgins (C)	6-2/190	Calgary	10-29-77	4	Bridgeport (AHL)
43	Trent Hunter (RW)	6-3/194	Red Deer, Alta.	7-5-80	2	Bridgeport (AHL), New York Islanders
12	Oleg Kvasha (LW)	6-5/230	Moscow, U.S.S.R.	7-26-78	5	New York Islanders
	Eric Manlow (C)	6-0/190	Belleville, Ont.	4-7-75	3	Bridgeport (AHL), New York Islanders
	Justin Mapletoft (C)	6-1/180	Lloydminster, Sask.	6-11-81	1	Bridgeport (AHL), New York Islanders
	Kristofer Ottoson (RW)	5-10/187	Sweden	1-9-76	0	
	Justin Papineau (C)	5-10/160	Ottawa	1-15-80	2	Worcester (AHL), St. Louis, New York Islanders, Bridgeport (AHL)
37	Mark Parrish (RW)	5-11/200	Edina, Minn.	2-2-77	5	New York Islanders
27	Michael Peca (C)	5-11/183	Toronto	3-26-74	10	New York Islanders
22	Randy Robitaille (C)	5-11/198	Ottawa	10-12-75	7	Pittsburgh, New York Islanders
38	Dave Scatchard (C)	6-3/224	Hinton, Alta.	2-20-76	6	New York Islanders
20	Steve Webb (RW)	6-0/208	Peterborough, Ont.	4-30-75	7	New York Islanders
	Mattias Weinhandl (LW)	6-0/183	Ljungby, Sweden	6-1-80	1	Bridgeport (AHL), New York Islanders
28	Jason Wiemer (C)	6-1/225	Kimberley, B.C.	4-14-76	9	New York Islanders
79	Alexei Yashin (C)	6-3/218	Sverdlovsk, U.S.S.R.	11-5-73	10	New York Islanders
	DEFENSEMEN					
3	Adrian Aucoin	6-2/214	Ottawa	7-3-73	9	New York Islanders
22	Sven Butenschon	6-4/215	Itzehoe, West Germany	3-22-76	6	Bridgeport (AHL), New York Islanders
33	Eric Cairns	6-6/230	Oakville, Ont.	6-27-74	7	New York Islanders
7	Kevin Haller	6-2/200	Trochu, Alta.	12-5-70	13	
4	Roman Hamrlik	6-2/207	Gottwaldov, Czechoslovakia	4-12-74	11	New York Islanders
29	Kenny Jonsson	6-3/217	Angelholm, Sweden	10-6-74	9	New York Islanders
	Alan Letang	6-0/205	Renfrew, Ont.	9-4-75	3	Bridgeport (AHL), New York Islanders
24	Radek Martinek	6-0/202	Havlicko Brod, Czech.	8-31-76	2	Bridgeport (AHL), New York Islanders
	Alain Nasreddine	6-1/203	Montreal	7-10-75	2	Bridgeport (AHL), New York Islanders
44	Janne Niinimaa	6-2/220	Raahe, Finland	5-22-75	7	Edmonton, New York Islanders
	Tomi Pettinen	6-3/211	Ylojarvi, Finland	6-17-77	1	Bridgeport (AHL), New York Islanders
36	Evgeny Skalde	6-1/214	Moscow, U.S.S.R.	7-24-78	3	Lokomotiv Yaroslavl (Russian)
53	Brandon Smith	6-1/196	Hazelton, B.C.	2-25-73	4	Bridgeport (AHL), New York Islanders
	Mattias Timander	6-3/215	Solleftea, Sweden	4-16-74	7	New York Islanders
	GOALTENDERS					
1	Rick DiPietro	6-0/185	Lewiston, Maine	9-19-81	2	Bridgeport (AHL), New York Islanders
30	Garth Snow	6-3/200	Wrentham, Mass.	7-28-69	10	New York Islanders

2002-03 REVIEW
INDIVIDUAL STATISTICS

SCORING

	Games	G	A	Pts.	PIM	+/-	PPG	SHG	GWG	GTG	Sht.	Sht. Pct.	Faceoffs Won	Lost	Pct.	TOI
Alexei Yashin	81	26	39	65	32	-12	14	0	7	1	274	9.5	507	567	47.2	18:32
Jason Blake	81	25	30	55	58	16	3	1	4	0	253	9.9	4	18	18.2	17:38
Mark Parrish	81	23	25	48	28	-11	9	0	5	0	147	15.6	4	5	44.4	16:11
Dave Scatchard	81	27	18	45	108	9	5	0	2	1	165	16.4	604	543	52.7	14:29
Michael Peca	66	13	29	42	43	-4	4	2	2	0	117	11.1	697	618	53.0	18:57
Shawn Bates	74	13	29	42	52	-9	1	6	1	1	126	10.3	227	171	57.0	18:25
Roman Hamrlik	73	9	32	41	87	21	3	0	2	0	151	6.0	0	0	—	26:34
Adrian Aucoin	73	8	27	35	70	-5	5	0	1	0	175	4.6	0	0	—	29:00
Arron Asham	78	15	19	34	57	1	4	0	1	0	114	13.2	7	10	41.2	12:12
Jason Wiemer	81	9	19	28	116	5	0	1	2	0	139	6.5	170	177	49.0	12:26
Oleg Kvasha	69	12	14	26	44	4	0	1	2	0	121	9.9	110	146	43.0	13:03
Kenny Jonsson	71	8	18	26	24	-8	3	1	0	1	108	7.4	3	3	50.0	23:11
Brad Isbister*	53	10	13	23	34	-9	2	0	2	1	90	11.1	6	7	46.2	13:54
Mattias Weinhandl	47	6	17	23	10	-2	1	0	0	0	66	9.1	3	2	60.0	13:52
Mattias Timander	80	3	13	16	24	-2	0	0	1	0	83	3.6	0	0	—	17:29
Radek Martinek	66	2	11	13	26	15	0	0	1	0	67	3.0	0	0	—	17:14
Claude Lapointe*	66	6	6	12	20	-3	0	0	1	0	67	9.0	377	309	55.0	12:15
Janne Niinimaa*	13	1	5	6	14	-2	1	0	0	0	11	9.1	0	0	—	23:02

	Games	G	A	Pts.	PIM	+/-	PPG	SHG	GWG	GTG	Sht.	Sht. Pct.	Faceoffs Won	Lost	Pct.	TOI
Eric Cairns.................	60	1	4	5	124	-7	0	0	0	0	31	3.2	0	0	—	11:50
Raffi Torres	17	0	5	5	10	0	0	0	0	0	12	0.0	1	3	25.0	7:40
Justin Mapletoft	11	2	2	4	2	-1	1	0	0	0	12	16.7	57	81	41.3	12:16
Trent Hunter	8	0	4	4	4	5	0	0	0	0	19	0.0	0	1	0.0	12:12
Sven Butenschon	37	0	4	4	26	-6	0	0	0	0	19	0.0	0	0	—	12:26
Eric Manlow	8	2	1	3	4	2	1	0	0	0	7	28.6	46	38	54.8	12:27
Justin Papineau*.......	5	1	2	3	4	1	0	0	1	0	8	12.5	8	7	53.3	14:50
Randy Robitaille*......	10	1	2	3	2	0	1	0	0	0	8	12.5	33	35	48.5	12:28
Steve Webb	49	1	0	1	75	-5	0	0	0	0	27	3.7	0	0	—	6:02
Tomi Pettinen	2	0	0	0	0	1	0	0	0	0	0	—	0	0	—	11:33
Alain Nasreddine	3	0	0	0	2	0	0	0	0	0	0	—	0	0	—	12:11
Brandon Smith	3	0	0	0	0	-2	0	0	0	0	1	0.0	0	0	—	9:59
Alan Letang	4	0	0	0	0	-1	0	0	0	0	2	0.0	0	0	—	13:27
Ray Schultz	4	0	0	0	28	-1	0	0	0	0	1	0.0	0	0	—	5:23
Rick DiPietro (g)	10	0	0	0	2	0	0	0	0	0	0	—	0	0	—	—
Eric Godard	19	0	0	0	48	-3	0	0	0	0	6	0.0	0	0	—	4:32
Chris Osgood (g)*	37	0	0	0	12	0	0	0	0	0	0	—	0	0	—	—
Garth Snow (g)	43	0	0	0	24	0	0	0	0	0	0	—	0	0	—	—

GOALTENDING

	Games	GS	Min.	GA	SO	Avg.	W	L	T	EN	PPG Allow	SHG Allow	Shots	Save Pct.
Garth Snow..............................	43	37	2390	92	1	2.31	16	17	5	8	30	3	1120	.918
Chris Osgood*.........................	37	36	1993	97	2	2.92	17	14	4	4	28	2	912	.894
Rick DiPietro............................	10	9	585	29	0	2.97	2	5	2	1	9	0	273	.894

*Played with two or more NHL teams.

RESULTS

OCTOBER
10— At Buffalo..........................L....1-5
12— Washington ....L....1-2
15— Nashville ....W...*4-3
17— At Philadelphia...................T....*3-3
19— At Atlanta ....W.....5-4
22— Carolina ....L.....1-4
24— Florida ....W.....5-3
26— Philadelphia ....L.....2-6
29— Phoenix ....L.....2-3
30— At Carolina ....L.....2-4

NOVEMBER
2— St. Louis.............................L.....1-6
4— Calgary ....L.....2-4
7— At Montreal ....L.....0-3
8— Edmonton ....W.....4-2
10— Dallas ....W.....3-2
12— Ottawa ....L.....3-5
14— At Boston ....L.....1-4
16— At Pittsburgh ....W.....3-2
20— At Florida ....T......*3-3
21— At Tampa Bay ....W.....7-2
23— At N.Y. Rangers ....W.....3-1
27— Ottawa ....T.....*2-2
29— Columbus ....L.....2-4
30— At Ottawa ....L.....2-4

DECEMBER
3— Vancouver ....W.....2-1
6— Toronto..............................W.....4-2
7— At Pittsburgh ....W.....6-3

10— Chicago ....L....2-3
13— At Florida ....T....*3-3
14— At Tampa Bay ....L.....3-4
17— Detroit ....T....*2-2
19— At Minnesota ....W.....4-2
21— Washington ....L.....1-3
23— Montreal ....W.....3-1
28— Carolina ....W.....3-0
30— Florida ....W...*2-1
31— At Buffalo ....W...*1-0

JANUARY
3— Boston................................W.....8-4
4— At Pittsburgh ....OTL...*2-3
7— Pittsburgh ....W.....6-3
9— Philadelphia ....L.....0-4
11— Atlanta ....W.....7-3
13— At Washington ....OTL...*3-4
15— At New Jersey ....L.....0-5
16— At St. Louis ....W...*3-2
19— At Atlanta ....W.....4-1
21— N.Y. Rangers ....L.....0-5
24— At Philadelphia ....W.....3-1
25— At Columbus ....L.....1-4
28— Pittsburgh ....W.....5-2
30— Montreal ....W.....3-1

FEBRUARY
4— Philadelphia ....L.....1-2
7— At Washington ....L.....0-3
8— Buffalo................................W....3-1
11— Tampa Bay ....W.....6-2

13— At Nashville ....L......0-2
15— At Los Angeles ....W.......3-2
17— At Anaheim ....T.....*2-2
19— At San Jose ....W.......3-0
21— Colorado.............................W.....4-1
23— Boston ....T.....*4-4
25— At Toronto ....L.....2-5
27— New Jersey ....T....*3-3

MARCH
1— Buffalo...............................W....*2-1
3— At N.Y. Rangers ....T....*1-1
4— Tampa Bay ....L.....1-3
6— At Boston ....L.....1-4
8— New Jersey ....L.....2-4
11— At Vancouver ....L.....3-4
13— At Edmonton ....W.....5-2
15— At Ottawa ....W.....5-2
17— At N.Y. Rangers ....L......0-1
18— At Toronto ....T....*3-3
20— At Montreal ....W.....6-3
22— New Jersey ....L.....2-4
25— At Chicago...........................W.....9-2
28— Toronto ....L.....2-5
30— At New Jersey ....L.....0-6

APRIL
1— N.Y. Rangers......................T...*2-2
3— At Detroit ....L.....2-5
5— Atlanta ....L.....2-3
6— At Carolina ....W.....2-1
*Denotes overtime game.

NEW YORK RANGERS
EASTERN CONFERENCE/ATLANTIC DIVISION

Rangers' Schedule
Home games shaded; D=Day game; *Feb. 8 All-Star Game at St. Paul, Minn.

October
SUN	MON	TUE	WED	THU	FRI	SAT
5	6	7	8	9	10 MIN	11 CBJ
12	13	14	15	16 ATL	17	18 CAR
19 FLA	20	21	22	23	24	25 DET
26	27	28 ANA	29	30 CAR	31	

November
SUN	MON	TUE	WED	THU	FRI	SAT
						1 MON
2 COL	3	4 DAL	5	6 CAR	7	8 PHI D
9	10 EDM	11	12 PIT	13	14	15 NJ D
16 CHI	17	18 SJ	19	20 COL	21	22
23 OTT	24	25 TB	26 FLA	27	28 PIT	29
30 TOR						

December
SUN	MON	TUE	WED	THU	FRI	SAT
	1	2 TOR	3	4 NYI	5	6
7 TB	8	9	10 MON	11	12 BUF	13 TOR
14	15	16	17	18 NYI	19	20 OTT
21	22 BOS	23	24	25	26 TOR	27
28	29 PHO	30 LA	31			

January
SUN	MON	TUE	WED	THU	FRI	SAT
				1 STL	2	3 PIT D
4	5 CAL	6	7	8 CAR	9	10 NYI D
11 TB	12	13 NYI	14	15 NJ	16	17 MON
18 BOS	19 D BOS	20	21	22 PHI	23	24 OTT
25 FLA	26	27	28 WAS	29	30 BUF	31 BUF

February
SUN	MON	TUE	WED	THU	FRI	SAT
1	2 VAN	3	4 MIN	5	6	7
8*	9	10	11 NJ	12 PHI	13	14 PHI D
15	16 D OTT	17	18	19 NYI	20	21 NJ D
22	23 MON	24	25	26 NYI	27	28 NAS D
29 ATL D						

March
SUN	MON	TUE	WED	THU	FRI	SAT
	1	2 ATL	3	4 BOS	5 WAS	6
7 PIT	8	9 ATL	10	11	12 TB	13 FLA
14	15 NJ	16	17	18 WAS	19	20 PHI D
21 D PIT	22	23 PIT	24	25 NAS	26	27 PHI D
28	29	30 NJ	31 BUF			

April
SUN	MON	TUE	WED	THU	FRI	SAT
				1	2	3 D WAS
4	5	6	7	8	9	10

2003-04 SEASON
CLUB DIRECTORY

Pres. and CEO, Cablevision Systems Corp.; Chairman, MSG; governor
James L. Dolan

Vice chairman, Cablevision Systems Corp.; Vice chairman, MSG
Robert S. Lemle

President and g.m., alternate governor
Glen Sather

President, sports team operations
Steve Mills

Exec. v.p. and general counsel/alt. gov.
Kenneth W. Munoz

V.p., player development and asst. g.m.
Don Maloney

Vice president, player development
Tom Renney

Dir., hockey administration and scouting
Peter Stephan

Head coach
Glen Sather

Assistant coaches
Ted Green
Terry O'Reilly
Tom Renney

Goaltending analyst
Sam St. Laurent

Amateur scouting staff
Ray Clearwater, Rich Brown, Andre Beaulieu, Bob Crocker, Jan Gajdosik, Ernie Gare, Martin Madden Jr., Christer Rockstom

Professional scouting staff
Dave Brown, Harry Howell, Gilles Leger

Scouting manager
Bill Short

Video analyst
Jerry Dineen

Vice president, operations
Mark Piazza

Vice president, public relations
John Rosasco

Director, public relations
Jason Vogel

Public relations coordinators
Jennifer Schoenfeld
Keith Soutar

Vice president, marketing
Jeanie Baumgartner

V.p., business and community dev.
Patricia Kerr

Medical trainer
Jim Ramsay

Equipment manager
Acacio Marques

Assistant equipment manager
James Johnson

Massage therapist
Bruce Lifrieri

Coaching staff assistant
Pat Boller

DRAFT CHOICES

Rd.— Player	Overall	Pos.	Last team
1— Hugh Jessiman	12	RW	Dartmouth (ECAC)
2— Ivan Baranka	50	D	Dubnica Jr. (Slovakia)
3— Ken Roche	75	C	St. Sebastian's HS
4— Corey Potter	122	D	Michigan State (CCHA)
5— Nigel Dawes	149	LW	Kootenay (WHL)
6— Ivan Dornic	176	C	Bratislava Jr. (Slov. Jr.)
6— Philippe Furrer	179	D	Bern (Switzerland)
6— Chris Holt	180	G	U.S. National under-18
7— Dylan Reese	209	C	Pittsburgh (NAHL)
8— Jan Marek	243	F	Trinec (Czech Rep.)

MISCELLANEOUS DATA

Home ice (capacity)
Madison Square Garden (18,200)

Address
2 Pennsylvania Plaza
New York, NY 10121

Business phone
212-465-6486

Ticket information
212-307-7171

Website
www.newyorkrangers.com

Training site
New York

Club colors
Blue, red and white

Radio affiliation
MSG Radio

TV affiliation
MSG Network

TRAINING CAMP ROSTER

No.	FORWARDS	Ht./Wt.	Place	BORN Date	NHL exp.	2002-03 clubs
36	Matthew Barnaby (LW)..	6-0/189	Ottawa	5-4-73	11	New York Rangers
9	Pavel Bure (RW)...........	5-10/189	Moscow, U.S.S.R.	3-31-71	12	New York Rangers
22	Anson Carter (RW).......	6-1/175	Toronto	6-6-74	7	Edmonton, New York Rangers
	Shawn Collymore (RW).	5-11/180	Lasalle, Que.	5-2-83	0	Val-d'Or (QMJHL), Quebec (QMJHL)
28	Nils Ekman (LW)...........	5-11/182	Stockholm, Sweden	3-11-76	2	Hartford (AHL)
	Lee Falardeau (C)	6-4/196	Midland, Mich.	7-22-83	0	Michigan State (CCHA)
	Ken Gernander (C/LW) ..	5-10/175	Grand Rapids, Minn.	6-30-69	2	Hartford (AHL)
16	Bobby Holik (C)	6-4/230	Jihlava, Czechoslovakia	1-1-71	13	New York Rangers
	Ryan Hollweg (C)	5-11/207	Langley, B.C.	4-23-83	0	
	David Inman (C)	6-1/205	New York	6-13-80	0	Charlotte (ECHL), Hartford (AHL)
27	Alexei Kovalev (RW)	6-1/215	Togliatti, U.S.S.R.	2-24-73	11	Pittsburgh, New York Rangers
33	Dan LaCouture (LW)......	6-1/201	Hyannis, Mass.	4-18-77	5	Pittsburgh, New York Rangers
	Cory Larose (C)	6-0/188	Campellton, N.B.	5-14-75	0	Houston (AHL), Hartford (AHL)
88	Eric Lindros (C)	6-4/236	London, Ont.	2-28-73	11	New York Rangers
16	Jamie Lundmark (C)......	6-0/174	Edmonton	1-16-81	1	Hartford (AHL), New York Rangers
29	Roman Lyashenko (C) ..	6-0/188	Murmansk, U.S.S.R.	5-2-79	4	Hartford (AHL), New York Rangers
10	Sandy McCarthy (RW)...	6-3/225	Toronto	6-15-72	10	New York Rangers
11	Mark Messier (C)...........	6-1/205	Edmonton	1-18-61	24	New York Rangers
	Dominic Moore (C)........	6-0/180	Thornhill, Ont.	8-3-80	0	Harvard University (ECAC)
	Garth Murray (LW)	6-1/205	Regina, Sask.	9-17-82	0	Hartford (AHL)
93	Petr Nedved (C)............	6-3/195	Liberec, Czechoslovakia	12-9-71	12	New York Rangers
36	Ronald Petrovicky (LW).	6-0/190	Zilina, Czechoslovakia	2-15-77	3	New York Rangers
28	Richard Scott (LW).......	6-2/195	Orillia, Ont.	8-1-78	1	Charlotte (ECHL), Hartford (AHL)
	Billy Tibbetts (RW)	6-2/215	Boston	10-14-74	7	Hartford (AHL), New York Rangers
	John Tripp (RW)	6-2/215	Kingston, Ont.	5-4-77	1	Hartford (AHL), New York Rangers

DEFENSEMEN

No.		Ht./Wt.	Place	Date	exp.	2002-03 clubs
	Pat Aufiero...................	6-2/186	Winchester, Mass.	7-1-80	0	Charlotte (ECHL), Hartford (AHL)
55	Vladimir Chebaturkin	6-2/212	Tyumen, U.S.S.R.	4-23-75	5	Hartford (AHL)
7	Greg de Vries...............	6-3/215	Sundridge, Ont.	1-4-73	8	Colorado
33	Dave Karpa	6-1/210	Regina, Sask.	5-7-71	12	Hartford (AHL), New York Rangers
	Darius Kasparaitis.........	5-11/212	Elektrenai, U.S.S.R.	10-16-72	11	New York Rangers
	Bryce Lampman	6-1/193	Rochester, Minn.	8-31-82	0	Hartford (AHL)
2	Brian Leetch	6-0/185	Corpus Christi, Texas	3-3-68	16	New York Rangers
24	Sylvain Lefebvre	6-3/205	Richmond, Que.	10-14-67	14	New York Rangers
23	Vladimir Malakhov.........	6-4/230	Ekaterinburg, U.S.S.R.	8-30-68	11	New York Rangers
2	Boris Mironov...............	6-3/223	Moscow, U.S.S.R.	3-21-72	10	New York Rangers, Chicago
	Lawrence Nycholat				0	Houston (AHL), Hartford (AHL)
45	Ales Pisa.....................	6-0/187	Pardubice, Czechoslovakia	1-2-77	2	Hamilton (AHL), Edmonton, New York Rangers
3	Tom Poti	6-3/215	Worcester, Mass.	3-22-77	5	New York Rangers
5	Dale Purinton................	6-3/214	Fort Wayne, Ind.	10-11-76	4	New York Rangers
	Fedor Tjutin	6-3/202	Izhevsk, U.S.S.R.	7-19-83	0	Kazan (Russian Div. III), SKA-2 St. Petersburg (Russian Div. III)
7	Mike Wilson..................	6-6/212	Brampton, Ont.	2-26-75	8	New York Rangers, Wilkes-Barre/Scranton (AHL), Hartford (AHL)

GOALTENDERS

No.		Ht./Wt.	Place	Date	exp.	2002-03 clubs
	Johan Asplund..............	6-1/180	Slutskar, Sweden	12-15-80	0	
31	Dan Blackburn	6-0/180	Montreal	5-20-83	2	New York Rangers
1	Mike Dunham	6-3/200	Johnson City, N.Y.	6-1-72	7	New York Rangers, Nashville
	Jason Labarbera...........	6-2/205	Burnaby, B.C.	1-18-80	1	Hartford (AHL)
30	Jussi Markkanen...........	5-11/183	Imatra, Finland	5-8-75	2	Edmonton
	Scott Meyer	6-0/190	White Bear Lake, Minn.	4-10-76	0	Charlotte (ECHL), Hartford (AHL)
35	Mike Richter	5-11/185	Abington, Pa.	9-22-66	15	New York Rangers

2002-03 REVIEW
INDIVIDUAL STATISTICS

SCORING

	Games	G	A	Pts.	PIM	+/-	PPG	SHG	GWG	GTG	Sht.	Sht. Pct.	Faceoffs Won	Lost	Pct.	TOI
Petr Nedved	78	27	31	58	64	-4	8	3	4	1	205	13.2	605	537	53.0	20:20
Eric Lindros..............	81	19	34	53	141	5	9	0	3	0	235	8.1	412	366	53.0	20:14
Tom Poti..................	80	11	37	48	60	-6	3	0	2	0	148	7.4	0	0	—	24:42
Mark Messier	78	18	22	40	30	-2	8	1	5	1	117	15.4	677	603	52.9	18:37
Matthew Barnaby	79	14	22	36	142	9	1	0	1	1	104	13.5	2	3	40.0	12:59
Bobby Holik.............	64	16	19	35	50	-1	3	0	2	0	213	7.5	809	581	58.2	18:06
Pavel Bure..............	39	19	11	30	16	4	5	1	3	1	136	14.0	0	3	0.0	18:56
Brian Leetch	51	12	18	30	24	-3	5	0	2	1	150	8.0	0	0	—	26:05
Radek Dvorak*	63	6	21	27	16	-3	2	0	0	0	134	4.5	4	5	44.4	15:42
Mikael Samuelsson* .	58	8	14	22	32	0	1	1	2	1	118	6.8	15	20	42.9	15:32
Jamie Lundmark	55	8	11	19	16	-3	0	0	0	0	78	10.3	27	35	43.5	12:03

	Games	G	A	Pts.	PIM	+/-	PPG	SHG	GWG	GTG	Sht.	Sht. Pct.	Faceoffs Won	Lost	Pct.	TOI
Vladimir Malakhov	71	3	14	17	52	-7	1	0	0	0	131	2.3	0	0	—	21:23
Sandy McCarthy........	82	6	9	15	81	-4	0	0	1	0	81	7.4	1	10	9.1	7:25
Ronald Petrovicky	66	5	9	14	77	-12	2	1	1	0	65	7.7	22	30	42.3	12:25
Darius Kasparaitis	80	3	11	14	85	5	0	0	1	0	84	3.6	0	0	—	18:53
Alexei Kovalev*	24	10	3	13	20	2	3	0	2	1	59	16.9	8	11	42.1	20:09
Rem Murray*	32	6	6	12	4	-3	1	1	1	0	62	9.7	63	55	53.4	15:39
Joel Bouchard*	27	5	7	12	14	6	1	0	2	0	41	12.2	0	0	—	20:06
Boris Mironov*	36	3	9	12	34	3	1	0	0	0	56	5.4	0	0	—	20:34
Dale Purinton	58	3	9	12	161	-2	0	0	0	0	50	6.0	0	0	—	15:02
Rico Fata*	36	2	4	6	6	-1	0	0	0	0	30	6.7	15	15	50.0	7:16
Anson Carter*	11	1	4	5	6	0	0	0	0	0	17	5.9	1	4	20.0	17:48
Dan LaCouture*	24	1	4	5	0	4	0	0	0	0	17	5.9	0	1	0.0	10:17
Cory Cross*	26	0	4	4	16	13	0	0	0	0	18	0.0	0	1	0.0	17:12
Ted Donato	49	2	1	3	6	-1	0	0	0	0	30	6.7	139	151	47.9	8:33
John Tripp	9	1	2	3	2	1	0	0	0	0	16	6.3	0	0	—	8:43
David Karpa	19	0	2	2	14	-1	0	0	0	0	13	0.0	0	1	0.0	14:34
Sylvain Lefebvre.......	35	0	2	2	10	-7	0	0	0	0	14	0.0	1	2	33.3	15:17
Richard Lintner*	10	1	0	1	0	-5	1	0	0	1	9	11.1	0	0	—	14:19
Gordie Dwyer*	17	0	1	1	50	-1	0	0	0	0	8	0.0	0	1	0.0	6:27
Mike Dunham (g)* ...	43	0	1	1	0	0	0	0	0	0	0	—	0	0	—	—
Johan Holmqvist (g) .	1	0	0	0	0	0	0	0	0	0	0	—	0	0	—	—
Mike Wilson	1	0	0	0	0	1	0	0	0	0	0	—	0	0	—	12:41
Roman Lyashenko.....	2	0	0	0	0	-2	0	0	0	0	4	0.0	6	5	54.5	11:46
Ales Pisa*	3	0	0	0	0	1	0	0	0	0	3	0.0	0	0	—	13:55
Josh Green*	4	0	0	0	2	-1	0	0	0	0	3	0.0	0	0	—	9:06
Dixon Ward	8	0	0	0	2	-2	0	0	0	0	7	0.0	6	5	54.5	8:44
Krzysztof Oliwa*	9	0	0	0	51	1	0	0	0	0	3	0.0	0	1	0.0	3:45
Billy Tibbetts	11	0	0	0	12	-2	0	0	0	0	6	0.0	31	44	41.3	9:58
Mike Richter (g)	13	0	0	0	0	0	0	0	0	0	0	—	0	0	—	—
Dan Blackburn (g)	32	0	0	0	2	0	0	0	0	0	0	—	0	0	—	—

GOALTENDING

	Games	GS	Min.	GA	SO	Avg.	W	L	T	EN	PPG Allow	SHG Allow	Shots	Save Pct.
Mike Dunham*	43	43	2467	94	5	2.29	19	17	5	3	50	6	1229	.924
Mike Richter	13	12	694	34	0	2.94	5	6	1	2	10	0	329	.897
Johan Holmqvist.......................	1	0	39	2	0	3.08	0	1	0	0	0	0	18	.889
Dan Blackburn	32	27	1762	93	1	3.17	8	16	4	3	28	4	842	.890

*Played with two or more NHL teams.

RESULTS

OCTOBER

9— At Carolina ....W......4-1
11—Montreal ....L......1-4
12— At Pittsburgh ....L......0-6
15—Toronto ....W......5-4
17—At Buffalo.......................T...*4-4
19—Nashville........................T...*2-2
21—Tampa Bay ....L......2-4
23—Washington ....L......1-2
25—Los Angeles ....L......2-6
26—At Toronto ....W......4-3
28—Phoenix ....W...*3-2
30—At Tampa Bay ....L......0-3

NOVEMBER

2— At Boston.........................L......2-3
3— St. Louis..........................L......2-3
5—Edmonton.........................W......5-2
7—Calgary............................W...*1-0
9—At Columbus......................L......3-6
11—At San Jose ....W......5-4
14—At Calgary ....W......2-1
16—At Vancouver ....L......1-3
19—Anaheim ....W...*3-2
21—At New Jersey ....T...*4-4
23—N.Y. Islanders ....L......1-3
25—Carolina ....W......3-1
28—At Atlanta ....L......4-7
29—At Dallas ....T...*3-3

DECEMBER

1— Tampa Bay ....W......4-3
3— Columbus ....W......5-3

5— At Philadelphia ....OTL....*2-3
6— Buffalo ....L......1-4
8— Boston ....L......1-4
11—Chicago ....L......3-4
14—At Toronto ....L......1-4
16—San Jose ....W...*2-1
19—Montreal ....L......1-3
21—At Detroit ....L......2-3
23—New Jersey ....T...*2-2
26—Pittsburgh.........................L......1-6
28—At Florida ....W...*2-1
29—At Tampa Bay ....L......3-5
31—At Carolina ....W......2-0

JANUARY

4— Washington ....T....*2-2
6— Ottawa ....L......2-5
8— Carolina ....W......5-1
9— At Montreal ....L......2-3
11—At Pittsburgh ....W......3-1
13—Toronto ....W......5-1
15—At Washington ....W...*2-1
19—Philadelphia ....L......2-4
21—At N.Y. Islanders ....W......5-0
23—At Nashville ....W......4-2
25—Atlanta ....L......1-4
26—At Washington ....L......2-7
28—At Atlanta ....L......2-5
30—Colorado ....OTL...*3-4

FEBRUARY

5— Ottawa ....L......3-5
6— At St. Louis........................T....*4-4

8— At Philadelphia...................L......1-2
12—At Florida ....W......3-1
14—Pittsburgh ....W......1-0
15—At Buffalo ....L......4-5
17—At Ottawa ....L......2-3
19—At Minnesota ....W......4-2
21—At Anaheim ....W......6-2
23—At Colorado ....L......1-4
25—At New Jersey ....T...*3-3
27—Boston ....W......4-1

MARCH

1— Florida ....W......5-2
3— N.Y. Islanders ....T...*1-1
7— Philadelphia ....W......5-1
10—Florida ....W......5-1
13—At Ottawa ....OTL...*2-3
15—At New Jersey ....L......1-3
17—N.Y. Islanders ....W......1-0
19—Buffalo ....W......3-0
22—At Philadelphia ....W......2-1
26—Pittsburgh.........................L......1-3
29—At Boston ....W......3-1
31—Atlanta ....OTL...*3-4

APRIL

1— At N.Y. Islanders................T....*2-2
4— New Jersey ....L......1-2
5— At Montreal ....L......4-5

*Denotes overtime game.

OTTAWA SENATORS
EASTERN CONFERENCE/NORTHEAST DIVISION

Senators' Schedule
Home games shaded; D=Day game; *Feb. 8 All-Star Game at St. Paul, Minn.

October

SUN	MON	TUE	WED	THU	FRI	SAT
5	6	7	8	9 MON	10	11 DET
12	13	14	15 LA	16	17 ANA	18 SJ
19	20	21	22	23 WAS	24	25 MON
26	27	28	29	30 FLA	31	

November

SUN	MON	TUE	WED	THU	FRI	SAT
						1 BUF
2	3 NYI	4	5	6 EDM	7	8 NJ
9	10	11 ATL	12	13 CBJ	14	15 MON
16	17 BUF	18	19	20 CAR	21	22 PIT
23 NYR	24	25 ATL	26	27 VAN	28	29 TOR
30						

December

SUN	MON	TUE	WED	THU	FRI	SAT
	1 PHI	2	3 FLA	4 TB	5	6 NJ
7	8 BOS	9	10	11 TB	12	13 BOS
14	15	16	17	18 CHI	19	20 NYR
21	22 FLA	23 BUF	24	25	26 PIT	27
28 D ATL	29	30 BOS	31			

January

SUN	MON	TUE	WED	THU	FRI	SAT
				1 NYI	2	3 WAS
4	5	6 TB	7	8 TOR	9 BUF	10
11 CAR	12	13 NJ	14	15 NYI	16	17 BOS
18 NYI	19 D	20 CAR	21	22 PIT	23	24 NYR
25	26	27	28 DAL	29 PHO	30	31 TOR

February

SUN	MON	TUE	WED	THU	FRI	SAT
1	2	3 NJ	4	5 TOR	6	7
8*	9	10 STL	11	12 BOS	13	14 MON
15 NYR	16 D WAS	17	18	19 ATL	20	21 D CAL
22 D PIT	23	24 MON	25	26 PHI	27	28 BUF
29						

March

SUN	MON	TUE	WED	THU	FRI	SAT
	1	2	3 BUF	4	5 PHI	6 NAS
7 WAS	8	9	10	11 CAL	12	13 VAN
14 EDM	15	16 MIN	17	18 COL	19	20 CAR
21	22	23 BOS	24	25 MON	26	27 TOR
28 TB	29	30	31 FLA			

April

SUN	MON	TUE	WED	THU	FRI	SAT
				1	2 PHI	3 TOR
4	5	6	7	8	9	10

2003-04 SEASON

CLUB DIRECTORY

Chairman, governor
TBA
President and CEO & alt. governor
Roy Mlakar
General manager
John Muckler
Chief operating officer
Cyril Leeder
Head coach
Jacques Martin
Assistant coaches
Don Jackson
Randy Lee
Perry Pearn
Director of legal relations
Peter Chiarelli
Director of player personnel
Anders Hedberg
Vice president, broadcast
Jim Steel
Vice president, communications
Phil Legault

Director, communications
Steve Keogh
Coordinator, communications
Tim Pattyson
Head equipment manager
John Gervais
Assistant equipment manager
Chris Cook
Head athletic trainer
Gerry Townend
Massage therapist
Brad Joyal
Team doctor
Don Chow
Scouts
Vaclav Burda, George Fargher, Bob Janecyk, Frank Jay, Lewis Mangelluzzo, Nick Polano, Patrick Savard, Boris Shagus, Ken Williamson

DRAFT CHOICES

Rd.— Player	Overall	Pos.	Last team
1— Patrick Eaves	29	RW	Boston College (Hockey East)
2— Igor Mirnov	67	C/W	Dynamo (Russia)
3— Philippe Seydoux	100	D	Kloten (Switzerland)
4— Mattias Karlsson	135	D	Brynas (Sweden)
5— Tim Cook	142	D	River City (USHL)
5— Sergei Gimayev	166	D	Cherepovets (Russia)
7— William Colbert	228	D	Ottawa (OHL)
8— Ossi Louhivaara	260	F	Kookoo (Finland)
9— Brian Elliott	291	G	Ajax (Ont. Prov. Jr. A)

MISCELLANEOUS DATA

Home ice (capacity)
Corel Centre (18,500)
Address
1000 Palladium Drive
Ottawa, Ont. K2VIA5
Business phone
613-599-0250
Ticket information
613-599-0103
Website
www.ottawasenators.com

Training site
Ottawa
Club colors
Black, red and white
Radio affiliation
Team 1200 (1200 AM), English
Radio 1150 CJRC (1150 AM), French
TV affiliation
New RO, Rogers Sportsnet

OTTAWA SENATORS

TRAINING CAMP ROSTER

No.	FORWARDS	Ht./Wt.	Place ——BORN——	Date	NHL exp.	2002-03 clubs
11	Daniel Alfredsson (RW).	5-11/195	Gothenburg, Sweden	12-11-72	8	Ottawa
20	Magnus Arvedson (LW).	6-2/198	Karlstad, Sweden	11-25-71	6	Ottawa
	Jan Bohac (C)	6-2/189	Tabor, Czechoslovakia	2-3-82	0	
14	Radek Bonk (C)	6-3/210	Krnov, Czechoslovakia	1-9-76	9	Ottawa
10	Toni Dahlman (RW)	5-11/194	Helsinki, Finland	9-3-79	2	Binghamton (AHL), Ottawa
12	Mike Fisher (C)	6-1/193	Peterborough, Ont.	6-5-80	4	Ottawa
	Alexandre Giroux (C)	6-2/165	Quebec	6-16-81	0	Binghamton (AHL)
55	Denis Hamel (C)	6-2/200	Lachute, Que.	5-10-77	4	Rochester (AHL), Buffalo
9	Martin Havlat (LW)	6-1/178	Mlada Boleslav, Czech.	4-19-81	3	Ottawa
18	Marian Hossa (LW)	6-1/199	Stara Lubovna, Czech.	1-12-79	6	Ottawa
11	Jody Hull (RW)	6-2/195	Cambridge, Ont.	2-2-69	15	Ottawa
	Dave Hymovitz (LW)	5-11/188	Boston	5-30-74	0	Binghamton (AHL)
	Alexei Kaigorodov (C)	6-1/183	Chelyabinsk, U.S.S.R.	7-29-83	0	
	Chris Kelly (LW)	6-0/179	Toronto	11-11-80	0	Binghamton (AHL)
39	Josh Langfeld (LW)	6-3/205	Fridley, Minn.	7-17-77	2	Binghamton (AHL), Ottawa
	Brian McGrattan (RW)	6-3/210	Hamilton, Ont.	9-2-81	0	Binghamton (AHL)
	Joe Murphy (LW)	6-0/194	Didsbury, Alta.	1-21-75	0	Binghamton (AHL)
25	Chris Neil (LW)	6-0/210	Markdale, Ont.	6-18-79	2	Ottawa
32	Rob Ray (RW)	6-0/215	Stirling, Ont.	6-8-68	14	Buffalo, Ottawa
72	Peter Schaefer (LW)	5-11/195	Yellow Grass, Sask.	7-12-77	4	Ottawa
19	Petr Schastlivy (LW)	6-1/204	Angarsk, U.S.S.R.	4-18-79	4	Ottawa
21	Bryan Smolinski (C)	6-1/208	Toledo, Ohio	12-27-71	11	Los Angeles, Ottawa
44	Jason Spezza (C)	6-2/214	Mississauga, Ont.	6-13-83	1	Binghamton (AHL), Ottawa
	Jeff Ulmer (LW)	5-11/190	Wilcox, Sask.	4-27-77	1	Binghamton (AHL)
27	Shaun Van Allen (C)	6-1/204	Calgary	8-29-67	12	Ottawa
25	Vaclav Varada (RW)	6-0/200	Vsetin, Czechoslovakia	4-26-76	8	Buffalo, Ottawa
	Antoine Vermette (C)	6-1/184	St-Agapit, Que.	7-20-82	0	Binghamton (AHL)
	Greg Watson (C)	6-1/177	Eastend, Sask.	3-2-83	0	Brandon (WHL)
28	Todd White (C)	5-10/180	Kanata, Ont.	5-21-75	6	Ottawa
	Bob Wren (C)	5-10/182	Preston, Ont.	9-16-74	3	St. John's (AHL), Milwaukee (AHL), Binghamton (AHL)

DEFENSEMEN

No.		Ht./Wt.	Place	Date	exp.	2002-03 clubs
16	Dennis Bonvie	5-11/205	Antigonish, Nova Scotia	7-23-73	8	Binghamton (AHL), Ottawa
	Wade Brookbank	6-4/219	Lanigan, Sask.	9-29-77	0	Binghamton (AHL)
	Derrick Byfuglien	6-1/202	Roseau, Minn.	12-23-80	0	Mississippi (ECHL), Greensboro (ECHL)
3	Zdeno Chara	6-9/246	Trencin, Czechoslovakia	3-18-77	6	Ottawa
	Ilja Demidov	6-2/185	Moscow, U.S.S.R.	4-14-79	0	
34	Shane Hnidy	6-1/200	Neepawa, Man.	11-8-75	3	Ottawa
	Neil Komadoski	6-1/212	St. Louis	2-10-82	0	Univ. of Notre Dame (CCHA)
29	Joel Kwiatkowski	6-2/201	Kindersley, Sask.	3-22-77	3	Binghamton (AHL), Wash., Ottawa
7	Curtis Leschyshyn	6-1/205	Thompson, Man.	9-21-69	15	Ottawa
57	Dean Melanson	5-11/196	Antigonish, Nova Scotia	11-19-73	2	Portland (AHL), Binghamton (AHL)
4	Chris Phillips	6-3/215	Fort McMurray, Alta.	3-9-78	6	Ottawa
	Brian Pothier	6-1/195	New Bedford, Mass.	4-15-77	3	Binghamton (AHL), Ottawa
23	Karel Rachunek	6-1/191	Gottwaldov, Czechoslovakia	8-27-79	4	Binghamton (AHL), Ottawa
6	Wade Redden	6-2/205	Lloydminster, Sask.	6-12-77	7	Ottawa
	Christoph Schubert	6-1/186	Germany	2-5-82	0	Binghamton (AHL)
	Peter Smrek	6-1/200	Martin, Czechoslovakia	2-16-79	2	Milwaukee (AHL)
	David Van Drunen	5-11/206	Sherwood Park, Alta.	1-31-76	1	Grand Rapids (AHL)
	Julien Vauclair	6-0/200	Delemont, Switzerland	10-2-79	0	Binghamton (AHL)
	Anton Volchenkov	6-0/209	Moscow, U.S.S.R.	2-25-82	1	Ottawa

GOALTENDERS

No.		Ht./Wt.	Place	Date	exp.	2002-03 clubs
	Mathieu Chouinard	6-1/209	Laval, Que.	4-11-80	0	Binghamton (AHL, Peoria (ECHL)
	Ray Emery	6-2/187	Hamilton, Ont.	9-28-82	1	Binghamton (AHL), Ottawa
	Simon Lajeunesse	6-0/170	Quebec City	1-22-81	1	Peoria (ECHL), Binghamton (AHL), San Antonio (AHL)
40	Patrick Lalime	6-3/185	St. Bonaventure, Que.	7-7-74	5	Ottawa
	Adam Munro	6-1/187	Burlington, Ont.	11-12-82	0	
31	Martin Prusek	6-0/176	Vitkovice, Czechoslovakia	12-11-75	2	Binghamton (AHL), Ottawa
	Billy Thompson	6-2/180	Saskatoon, Sask.	9-24-82	0	Binghamton (AHL)

2002-03 REVIEW
INDIVIDUAL STATISTICS

SCORING

	Games	G	A	Pts.	PIM	+/-	PPG	SHG	GWG	GTG	Sht.	Sht. Pct.	Faceoffs Won	Lost	Pct.	TOI
Marian Hossa	80	45	35	80	34	8	14	0	10	1	229	19.7	7	12	36.8	18:30
Daniel Alfredsson	78	27	51	78	42	15	9	0	6	0	240	11.3	16	24	40.0	19:31
Todd White	80	25	35	60	28	19	8	1	5	0	144	17.4	705	691	50.5	17:57
Martin Havlat	67	24	35	59	30	20	9	0	4	0	179	13.4	1	6	14.3	16:26

	Games	G	A	Pts.	PIM	+/-	PPG	SHG	GWG	GTG	Sht.	Sht. Pct.	Faceoffs Won	Lost	Pct.	TOI
Radek Bonk	70	22	32	54	36	6	11	0	4	2	146	15.1	563	655	46.2	17:32
Wade Redden	76	10	35	45	70	23	4	0	3	0	154	6.5	0	0	—	25:24
Zdeno Chara	74	9	30	39	116	29	3	0	2	0	168	5.4	0	0	—	24:57
Mike Fisher	74	18	20	38	54	13	5	1	3	0	142	12.7	518	559	48.1	15:59
Magnus Arvedson	80	16	21	37	48	13	2	0	4	0	138	11.6	11	19	36.7	17:54
Shaun Van Allen	78	12	20	32	66	17	2	2	3	0	53	22.6	377	461	45.0	12:29
Karel Rachunek	58	4	25	29	30	23	3	0	1	0	110	3.6	1	2	33.3	21:45
Peter Schaefer	75	6	17	23	32	11	0	0	1	0	93	6.5	9	35	20.5	14:58
Jason Spezza	33	7	14	21	8	-3	3	0	0	0	65	10.8	151	179	45.8	12:40
Petr Schastlivy	33	9	10	19	4	3	5	0	2	0	68	13.2	0	2	0.0	13:20
Chris Phillips	78	3	16	19	71	7	2	0	1	0	97	3.1	0	0	—	20:13
Anton Volchenkov	57	3	13	16	40	-4	0	0	0	0	75	4.0	0	0	—	15:30
Jody Hull	70	3	8	11	14	-3	0	0	1	0	42	7.1	10	28	26.3	10:31
Chris Neil	68	6	4	10	147	8	0	0	0	0	62	9.7	3	2	60.0	7:39
Bryan Smolinski*	10	3	5	8	2	1	0	0	0	0	26	11.5	59	68	46.5	15:41
Vaclav Varada*	11	2	6	8	8	3	1	0	0	0	17	11.8	0	8	0.0	14:57
Shane Hnidy	67	0	8	8	130	-1	0	0	0	0	58	0.0	0	1	0.0	13:54
Curtis Leschyshyn	54	1	6	7	18	11	0	0	0	0	30	3.3	0	0	—	15:13
Brian Pothier	14	2	4	6	6	11	0	0	1	0	23	8.7	0	0	—	15:23
Steve Martins*	14	2	3	5	10	3	0	0	0	0	13	15.4	62	49	55.9	9:44
Brad Smyth	12	3	1	4	15	-2	0	0	0	0	16	18.8	0	2	0.0	9:30
Joel Kwiatkowski*	20	0	2	2	6	2	0	0	0	0	28	0.0	0	2	0.0	12:12
Toni Dahlman	12	1	0	1	0	-1	0	0	1	0	5	20.0	1	0	100.0	6:09
Josh Langfeld	12	0	1	1	4	2	0	0	0	0	16	0.0	0	0	—	11:10
Patrick Lalime (g)	67	0	1	1	6	0	0	0	0	0	1	0.0	0	0	—	
Joey Tetarenko*	2	0	0	0	5	0	0	0	0	0	1	0.0	0	0	—	6:29
Ray Emery (g)	3	0	0	0	0	0	0	0	0	0	0	—	0	0	—	—
Rob Ray*	5	0	0	0	4	0	0	0	0	0	0	—	0	0	—	4:53
Dennis Bonvie	12	0	0	0	29	-1	0	0	0	0	3	0.0	0	0	—	3:04
Martin Prusek (g)	18	0	0	0	0	0	0	0	0	0	0		0	0	—	

GOALTENDING

	Games	GS	Min.	GA	SO	Avg.	W	L	T	EN	PPG Allow	SHG Allow	Shots	Save Pct.
Ray Emery	3	1	85	2	0	1.41	1	0	0	0	0	0	26	.923
Patrick Lalime	67	65	3943	142	8	2.16	39	20	7	1	40	8	1591	.911
Martin Prusek	18	16	935	37	0	2.37	12	2	1	0	10	0	415	.911

*Played with two or more NHL teams.

RESULTS

OCTOBER
10— New Jersey ....L....1-2
12— At Toronto ....W....2-1
15— Phoenix ....W....2-1
23— Carolina ....W....4-1
24— At Boston.....................T....*2-2
26— At Montreal.....................L....3-5
29— At Philadelphia.................L....1-2
30— Pittsburgh.......................L....1-4

NOVEMBER
2— Detroit ....W....5-2
6— At Colorado ....W....5-2
8— Los Angeles....................L....2-3
9— At Boston.......................L....1-7
12— At N.Y. Islanders.............W....5-3
14— Florida ....W...*3-2
16— Buffalo ....W....4-1
19— At Carolina ....T...*4-4
21— Montreal........................W....3-2
23— Columbus......................W....5-2
25— Toronto.........................W....2-0
27— At N.Y. Islanders.............T...*2-2
29— At Washington ....W....6-2
30— N.Y. Islanders.................W....4-2

DECEMBER
4— At Chicago ....L....0-1
5— At St. Louis.....................T...*2-2
7— Carolina ....W....5-2
10— At Buffalo ....W....4-2
12— At Boston ....W....5-2

14— New Jersey.....................W...*4-3
16— Montreal ....L....2-3
18— At New Jersey.................W....3-0
19— San Jose ....W....9-3
21— At Philadelphia................W....3-1
23— Philadelphia....................T...*2-2
26— At Buffalo ....W....3-2
27— Montreal ....W...*3-2
30— At Nashville.....................L....2-3
31— At Tampa Bay ....W....6-3

JANUARY
2— Atlanta............................W....8-1
4— Buffalo ....OTL...*1-2
6— At N.Y. Rangers...............W....5-2
8— At Vancouver ....L....4-6
9— At Calgary ....W....1-0
11— At Edmonton..................W....2-0
14— Tampa Bay.....................W....7-0
16— Anaheim ....W....3-1
18— Washington....................W....5-2
20— At Tampa Bay.................L....2-6
22— At Florida........................W....2-1
23— At Atlanta........................T...*3-3
25— Buffalo ....W...*4-3
27— At Dallas.........................L....3-5
29— At Anaheim.....................L....2-3
30— At Los Angeles................L....0-3

FEBRUARY
5— At N.Y. Rangers...............W....5-3
6— Philadelphia.....................T...*2-2

8— Atlanta............................W....3-1
12— At Pittsburgh...................W....3-0
13— Edmonton ....W....2-0
15— At Toronto ....L....1-2
17— N.Y. Rangers ....W....3-2
19— At New Jersey.................W....5-3
20— Florida............................L....3-4
22— Nashville.........................W....4-0
25— Minnesota.......................L....0-3
27— Dallas.............................W...*3-2

MARCH
1— Tampa Bay ....L....1-2
4— Toronto............................W....4-1
8— At Pittsburgh....................W....5-1
9— Pittsburgh ....W....4-2
11— Boston............................W...*4-3
13— N.Y. Rangers ....W...*3-2
15— N.Y. Islanders ....L....2-5
16— At Detroit.........................L....2-6
18— At Carolina ....W....6-5
21— At Atlanta.........................W....5-1
22— At Florida.........................W....3-1
25— Colorado.........................T...*2-2
28— Washington ....L....2-3
29— At Montreal ....W....3-1

APRIL
1— Boston.............................W....3-2
3— At Washington ....W....5-1
5— At Toronto ....W....3-1
*Denotes overtime game.

PHILADELPHIA FLYERS
EASTERN CONFERENCE/ATLANTIC DIVISION

Flyers' Schedule
Home games shaded; D=Day game; *Feb. 8 All-Star Game at St. Paul, Minn.

October

SUN	MON	TUE	WED	THU	FRI	SAT
5	6	7	8	9 BUF	10	11 PIT
12	13	14	15	16 SJ	17	18 PHO
19	20	21 LA	22 ANA	23	24	25 CAR
26	27 MON	28	29 FLA	30 NJ	31	

November

SUN	MON	TUE	WED	THU	FRI	SAT
						1 TOR
2	3	4	5	6 WAS	7	8 D NYR
9	10	11 NYI	12	13 VAN	14	15 ATL
16	17	18 CAR	19	20 MIN	21	22 BOS
23	24	25	26 PIT	27	28 D CAR	29 NYI
30						

December

SUN	MON	TUE	WED	THU	FRI	SAT
	1 OTT	2	3 PIT	4	5 PHO	6 BOS
7	8 MON	9	10 CBJ	11	12 NJ	13 NJ
14	15	16 CAL	17	18 TB	19	20 D NYI
21 ATL	22	23 NYI	24	25	26	27 COL
28 DAL	29 DAL	30 STL	31			

January

SUN	MON	TUE	WED	THU	FRI	SAT
				1	2 FLA	3 TB
4	5	6	7 BUF	8 FLA	9	10 EDM
11 PIT	12 BUF	13	14	15	16 TOR	17 TOR
18	19	20 MON	21	22 NYR	23	24 D BUF
25 WAS	26	27	28 FLA	29	30	31 D PIT

February

SUN	MON	TUE	WED	THU	FRI	SAT
1	2 TB	3	4 WAS	5 ATL	6	7
8*	9	10 NJ	11	12 NYR	13	14 D NYR
15	16 SJ	17 TB	18	19 BOS	20	21 D ATL
22	23	24 CHI	25	26 OTT	27	28 D BOS
29 DET						

March

SUN	MON	TUE	WED	THU	FRI	SAT
	1	2	3 NAS	4	5 OTT	6 WAS
7	8	9 NJ	10	11 DAL	12	13 D NJ
14 D PIT	15	16	17	18 TOR	19	20 D NYR
21	22	23 CAR	24	25 NYI	26	27 D NYR
28	29	30	31			

April

SUN	MON	TUE	WED	THU	FRI	SAT
				1 MON	2 OTT	3
4 D NYI	5	6	7	8	9	10

2003-04 SEASON
CLUB DIRECTORY

Chairman
Edward M. Snider
President
Ron Ryan
General manager
Bob Clarke
Executive vice president
Keith Allen
Exec. v.p. and chief operating officer
Ron Ryan
Assistant general manager
Paul Holmgren
Head coach
Ken Hitchcock
Assistant coaches
Wayne Fleming
Craig Hartsburg
Terry Murray
Goaltending coach
Rejean Lemelin
Director of pro hockey personnel
Ron Hextall
Pro scout
Al Hill
Chief scout
Dennis Patterson
Scouts
Serge Boudreault, John Chapman,
Inge Hammarstrom, Vaclav Slansky,
Simon Nolet, Chris Pryor, Evgeny
Zimin

Vice president of ticket operations
Cecilia Baker
Vice president, marketing
Joe O'Sullivan
Director of public relations
Zack Hill
Dir. of media services and publications
Joe Klueg
Assistant director, public relations
Jill Lipson
Director, fan services
Joe Kadlec
Public relations assistant
Katie Hammer
Athletic trainer/strength & conditioning coach
Jim McCrossin
Athletic trainer
John Worley
Head equipment manager
Jim Evers
Equipment managers
Harry Bricker
Anthony Oratorio
Orthopedic surgeon
Peter DeLuca

DRAFT CHOICES

Rd.— Player	Overall	Pos.	Last team
1— Jeff Carter	11	C	Sault Ste. Marie (OHL)
1— Mike Richards	24	C	Kitchener (OHL)
3— Colin Fraser	69	C	Red Deer (WHL)
3— Stefan Ruzicka	81	RW	Nitra (Slovakia)
3— Alexandre Picard	85	D	Halifax (QMJHL)
3— Ryan Potulny	87	C	Lincoln (USHL)
3— Rick Kozak	95	RW	Brandon (WHL)
4— Kevin Romy	108	W	Geneve (Switzerland)
5— David Tremblay	140	G	Hull (QMJHL)
6— Rejean Beauchemin	191	G	Prince Albert (WHL)
6— Ville Hostikka	193	G	Saipa (Finland)

MISCELLANEOUS DATA

Home ice (capacity)
First Union Center (19,523)
Address
First Union Center
3601 South Broad Street
Philadelphia, PA 19148
Business phone
215-465-4500
Ticket information
215-755-9700
Website
www.philadelphiaflyers.com

Training site
Sovereign Bank Flyers Skate Zone,
Voorhees, NJ
Club colors
Orange, white and black
Radio affiliation
WIP (610 AM)
TV affiliation
Comcast SportsNet (cable); UPN 57
WPSG-TV

TRAINING CAMP ROSTER

No.	FORWARDS	Ht./Wt.	Place	Born Date	NHL exp.	2002-03 clubs
10	Tony Amonte (RW)	6-0/190	Hingham, Mass.	8-2-70	13	Philadelphia, Phoenix
87	Donald Brashear (LW)	6-2/230	Bedford, Ind.	1-7-72	10	Philadelphia
	Eric Chouinard (C)	6-2/195	Atlanta	7-8-80	2	Utah (AHL), Philadelphia
	A. Drozdetsky (RW)	6-0/174	Moscow, U.S.S.R.	11-10-81	0	CSKA Moscow (Russian)
29	Todd Fedoruk (LW)	6-1/205	Redwater, Alta.	2-13-79	3	Philadelphia
11	Mark Freer (C)	5-10/180	Peterborough, Ont.	7-14-68	7	Hershey (AHL)
12	Simon Gagne (LW)	6-0/175	Ste. Foy, Que.	2-29-80	4	Philadelphia
	Mark Greig (RW)	5-11/190	High River, Alta.	1-25-70	9	Philadelphia (AHL), Philadelphia
	Michal Handzus (C)	6-5/210	Banska Bystrica, Czech.	3-11-77	5	Philadelphia
14	Tomi Kallio (RW)	6-1/180	Turku, Finland	1-27-77	3	Philadelphia, Atlanta, Columbus
29	Boyd Kane (LW)	6-2/218	Swift Current, Sask.	4-18-78	0	Springfield (AHL)
24	Sami Kapanen (RW)	5-10/175	Vantaa, Finland	6-14-73	8	Philadelphia, Carolina
13	Claude Lapointe (C)	5-9/188	Lachine, Que.	10-11-68	13	Philadelphia, New York Islanders
	Kirby Law (RW)	6-0/180	McCreary, Man.	3-11-77	2	Philadelphia (AHL), Philadelphia
10	John LeClair (LW)	6-3/226	St. Albans, Vt.	7-5-69	13	Philadelphia
	Mike Lephart (RW)	5-11/190	Niskayuna, N.Y.	4-3-77	0	Philadelphia (AHL)
	Ian MacNeil (C)	6-2/178	Halifax, Nova Scotia	4-27-77	1	Philadelphia (AHL), Philadelphia
25	Keith Primeau (C)	6-5/220	Toronto	11-24-71	13	Philadelphia
8	Mark Recchi (RW)	5-10/185	Kamloops, B.C.	2-1-68	15	Philadelphia
97	Jeremy Roenick (C)	6-0/207	Boston	1-17-70	15	Philadelphia
	K. Rudenko (LW)	5-10/163	Ust-Kamenogorsk, U.S.S.R.	7-23-81	0	Lokomotiv Yaroslavl (Russian)
14	Joe Sacco (RW)	6-1/190	Medford, Mass.	2-4-69	13	Philadelphia (AHL), Philadelphia
23	Yves Sarault (LW)	6-1/183	Valleyfield, Que.	12-23-72	8	Springfield (AHL)
28	Andre Savage (C)	6-0/195	Ottawa	5-27-75	4	Philadelphia (AHL), Philadelphia
	Patrick Sharp (C)	6-0/188	Thunder Bay, Ont.	12-27-81	1	Philadelphia (AHL), Philadelphia
	Colin Shields (RW)		Glasgow, Scotland	1-27-80	0	Univ. of Maine (Hockey East)
	Mike Siklenka (RW)	6-5/228	Meadow Lake, Sask.	12-18-79	1	Philadelphia (AHL), Philadelphia
8	Jarrod Skalde (C)	6-0/185	Niagara Falls, Ont.	2-26-71	9	Lausanne HC (Switzerland)
	Radovan Somik (LW)	6-2/194	Martin, Czechoslovakia	5-5-77	1	Philadelphia
11	Peter White (C)	5-11/200	Montreal	3-15-69	8	Chi., Philadelphia (AHL), Norfolk (AHL)
14	Justin Williams (RW)	6-1/176	Cobourg, Ont.	10-4-81	3	Philadelphia
18	Jamie Wright (LW)	6-0/194	Kitchener, Ont.	5-13-76	6	St. John (AHL), Phi., Calg., Phi. (AHL)
	DEFENSEMEN					
37	Eric Desjardins	6-1/205	Rouyn, Que.	6-14-69	15	Philadelphia
	Ian Forbes	6-6/180	Brampton, Ont.	8-2-80	0	Trenton (ECHL), Philadelphia (AHL)
	David Harlock	6-2/220	Toronto	3-16-71	8	Philadelphia (AHL)
5	Kim Johnsson	6-2/189	Malmo, Sweden	3-16-76	4	Philadelphia
	Marko Kauppinen	6-0/178	Mikkeli, Finland	3-23-79	0	TPS Turku (Finland)
	Dan Peters	5-10/185	St. Paul, Minn.	11-24-77	0	Philadelphia (AHL)
	Joni Pitkanen	6-3/202	Oulu, Finland	9-19-83	0	Karpat Oulu (Finland)
10	Marcus Ragnarsson	6-1/215	Ostervala, Sweden	8-13-71	8	Philadelphia, San Jose
	Dennis Seidenberg	6-0/181	Villingen, Germany	7-18-81	1	Philadelphia (AHL), Philadelphia
32	John Slaney	6-0/185	St. John's, Nfld.	2-7-72	8	Philadelphia (AHL)
6	Chris Therien	6-4/230	Ottawa	12-14-71	9	Philadelphia
	Jussi Timonen	6-0/200	Kuopio, Finland	6-29-83	0	TPS Turku (Finland)
	Jim Vandermeer	6-1/208	Carolina, Alta.	2-21-80	1	Philadelphia (AHL), Philadelphia
2	Eric Weinrich	6-1/213	Roanoke, Va.	12-19-66	15	Philadelphia
	Jeff Woywitka	6-2/197	Vermillion, Alta.	9-1-83	0	Red Deer (WHL)
36	Dmitry Yushkevich	5-11/208	Yaroslavl, U.S.S.R.	11-19-71	11	Philadelphia, Los Angeles, Florida
	GOALTENDERS					
	Berend Bruckler	6-1/180	Graz, Austria	9-26-81	0	
	Robert Esche	6-0/188	Utica, N.Y.	1-22-78	5	Philadelphia
31	Jeff Hackett	6-1/198	London, Ont.	6-1-68	14	Montreal, Boston
35	Neil Little	6-1/193	Medicine Hat, Alta.	12-18-71	1	Philadelphia (AHL)
	Roman Malek	5-11/161	Czechoslovakia	9-25-77	0	
	Antero Niittymaki	6-0/176	Turku, Finland	6-18-80	0	Philadelphia (AHL)

2002-03 REVIEW

INDIVIDUAL STATISTICS

SCORING

	Games	G	A	Pts.	PIM	+/-	PPG	SHG	GWG	GTG	Sht.	Sht. Pct.	Faceoffs Won	Lost	Pct.	TOI
Jeremy Roenick	79	27	32	59	75	20	8	1	6	2	197	13.7	577	511	53.0	18:47
Mark Recchi	79	20	32	52	35	0	8	1	3	1	171	11.7	88	80	52.4	18:50
Keith Primeau	80	19	27	46	93	4	6	0	4	1	171	11.1	829	784	51.4	19:16
Michal Handzus	82	23	21	44	46	13	1	1	9	0	133	17.3	706	644	52.3	17:32
Kim Johnsson	82	10	29	39	38	11	5	0	2	0	159	6.3	0	0	—	24:05
Eric Desjardins	79	8	24	32	35	30	1	0	2	0	197	4.1	0	0	—	22:54

PHILADELPHIA FLYERS

	Games	G	A	Pts.	PIM	+/-	PPG	SHG	GWG	GTG	Sht.	Sht. Pct.	Faceoffs Won	Lost	Pct.	TOI
John LeClair	35	18	10	28	16	10	8	0	4	1	99	18.2	2	1	66.7	16:09
Simon Gagne	46	9	18	27	16	20	1	1	3	1	115	7.8	30	40	42.9	17:23
Marty Murray	76	11	15	26	13	-1	1	1	0	0	105	10.5	260	212	55.1	12:22
Donald Brashear	80	8	17	25	161	5	0	0	1	0	99	8.1	9	18	33.3	13:22
Justin Williams	41	8	16	24	22	15	0	0	2	0	105	7.6	8	8	50.0	15:57
Eric Weinrich	81	2	18	20	40	16	1	1	0	0	103	1.9	0	1	0.0	21:23
Radovan Somik	60	8	10	18	10	9	0	1	2	0	95	8.4	7	13	35.0	15:48
Tony Amonte*	13	7	8	15	2	12	1	1	2	1	37	18.9	1	2	33.3	17:39
Sami Kapanen*	28	4	9	13	6	-1	2	0	1	0	81	4.9	2	3	40.0	19:21
Dennis Seidenberg	58	4	9	13	20	8	1	0	0	0	123	3.3	0	1	0.0	16:50
Pavel Brendl*	42	5	7	12	4	8	1	0	1	0	80	6.3	2	7	22.2	10:19
Eric Chouinard	28	4	4	8	8	2	1	0	0	0	45	8.9	4	8	33.3	9:37
Marcus Ragnarsson*	43	2	6	8	32	5	1	0	0	0	52	3.8	1	0	100.0	21:09
Chris Therien	67	1	6	7	36	10	0	0	0	0	93	1.1	0	0	—	17:23
Joe Sacco	34	1	5	6	20	0	0	0	1	0	48	2.1	0	3	0.0	12:27
Todd Fedoruk	63	1	5	6	105	1	0	0	0	0	33	3.0	0	1	0.0	6:29
Todd Warriner*	13	2	3	5	6	2	0	0	1	0	13	15.4	0	0	—	8:29
Claude Lapointe*	14	2	2	4	16	5	0	0	0	0	20	10.0	68	39	63.6	11:04
Dmitry Yushkevich*	18	2	2	4	8	7	0	0	0	0	16	12.5	0	0	—	18:05
Paul Ranheim*	28	0	4	4	6	-4	0	0	0	0	37	0.0	8	6	57.1	11:56
Andre Savage	16	2	1	3	4	2	0	0	1	0	13	15.4	41	33	55.4	7:49
Jim Vandermeer	24	2	1	3	27	9	0	0	0	0	22	9.1	0	0	—	13:42
Dan McGillis*	24	0	3	3	20	7	0	0	0	0	41	0.0	0	0	—	18:13
Tomi Kallio*	7	1	0	1	2	-1	0	0	0	0	5	20.0	0	0	—	9:29
Mark Greig	5	0	1	1	2	1	0	0	0	0	2	0.0	0	0	—	5:02
Mike Siklenka	1	0	0	0	0	0	0	0	0	0	1	0.0	0	0	—	4:26
Kirby Law	2	0	0	0	2	0	0	0	0	0	0	—	0	0	—	1:40
Ian MacNeil	2	0	0	0	0	1	0	0	0	0	2	0.0	0	0	—	10:08
Patrick Sharp	3	0	0	0	2	0	0	0	0	0	3	0.0	3	4	42.9	5:58
Jamie Wright*	4	0	0	0	4	-1	0	0	0	0	2	0.0	0	0	—	9:26
Bruno St. Jacques*	6	0	0	0	2	-1	0	0	0	0	5	0.0	0	0	—	14:34
Guillaume Lefebvre*	14	0	0	0	4	1	0	0	0	0	5	0.0	0	0	—	7:26
Chris McAllister*	19	0	0	0	21	-2	0	0	0	0	9	0.0	0	0	—	9:32
Robert Esche (g)	30	0	0	0	6	0	0	0	0	0	0	—	0	0	—	—
Roman Cechmanek (g)	58	0	0	0	8	0	0	0	0	0	0	—	0	0	—	—

GOALTENDING

	Games	GS	Min.	GA	SO	Avg.	W	L	T	EN	PPG Allow	SHG Allow	Shots	Save Pct.
Roman Cechmanek	58	57	3350	102	6	1.83	33	15	10	2	28	5	1368	.925
Robert Esche	30	25	1638	60	2	2.20	12	9	3	2	22	3	647	.907

*Played with two or more NHL teams.

RESULTS

OCTOBER
10—At Edmonton ....T....*2-2
12—At Calgary ....W....5-4
15—At Montreal ....W....6-2
17—N.Y. Islanders ....T....*3-3
19—Washington ....W....3-1
22—At Buffalo ....L.....1-2
24—Montreal ....W....6-2
26—At N.Y. Islanders ....W....6-2
29—Ottawa ....W....2-1
31—Phoenix ....W....6-2

NOVEMBER
2— Washington ....W....2-1
5—At Carolina ....W....*2-1
7— New Jersey ....L.....0-1
9—At Washington ....L.....1-4
13—Florida ....T....*1-1
15—At Carolina ....T....*1-1
16—Boston ....T....*2-2
19—At Tampa Bay ....W....3-2
21—San Jose ....T....*2-2
23—At Toronto ....L.....0-6
27—At Pittsburgh ....L.....2-7
29—Toronto ....L.....0-3
30—At Montreal ....W....*2-1

DECEMBER
2— New Jersey ....OTL...*0-1
5—N.Y. Rangers ....W....*3-2
7—St. Louis ....L.....1-3
10—At Florida ....W....5-2

12—Toronto ....W....2-1
14—Buffalo ....W....2-0
17—Dallas ....T....*2-2
18—At Atlanta ....W....3-1
21—Ottawa ....L.....1-3
23—At Ottawa ....T....*2-2
27—At Colorado ....W....*2-1
28—At Phoenix ....L.....0-4
30—At San Jose ....L.....1-2

JANUARY
2— At Los Angeles ....W....4-1
3—At Anaheim ....W....1-0
5—At Atlanta ....W....5-4
7—Buffalo ....W....3-2
9—At N.Y. Islanders ....W....4-0
11—Detroit ....W....3-2
13—Atlanta ....L.....4-7
16—Montreal ....W....4-1
18—Tampa Bay ....W....3-2
19—At N.Y. Rangers ....W....4-2
21—At Toronto ....W....3-1
24—N.Y. Islanders ....L.....1-3
25—At Boston ....OTL...*0-1
28—Tampa Bay ....L.....0-3
30—At New Jersey ....L.....1-5

FEBRUARY
4— At N.Y. Islanders...........W....2-1
6—At Ottawa ....T....*2-2
8—N.Y. Rangers ....W....2-1
10—Minnesota ....L.....0-1

12—At Minnesota ....L.....0-2
13—At St. Louis ....W....*4-3
15—Carolina ....T....*2-2
18—New Jersey ....T....*2-2
20—Los Angeles ....W....5-0
22—Florida ....L.....2-4
25—At Chicago ....W....2-0
27—Chicago ....W....5-2

MARCH
1— At Boston ....W....*3-2
4— Vancouver ....W....3-0
7— At N.Y. Rangers ....L.....1-5
8— Colorado ....OTL...*1-2
10—At Washington ....OTL...*1-2
13—Carolina ....W....5-3
15—At Pittsburgh ....W....4-1
17—At New Jersey ....W....4-2
18—At Buffalo ....L.....2-5
20—Pittsburgh ....W....4-2
22—N.Y. Rangers ....L.....1-2
24—Atlanta ....W....6-2
25—At Nashville ....T....*1-1
27—Boston ....T....*2-2
29—Pittsburgh ....W....3-0
31—At Pittsburgh ....W....6-1

APRIL
1— Columbus ....W....4-0
4— At Tampa Bay ....W....4-1
6— At Florida ....W....6-2
*Denotes overtime game.

PHOENIX COYOTES
WESTERN CONFERENCE/PACIFIC DIVISION

Coyotes' Schedule
Home games shaded; D=Day game; *Feb. 8 All-Star Game at St. Paul, Minn.

October
SUN	MON	TUE	WED	THU	FRI	SAT
5	6	7	8	9	10 STL	11
12 ANA	13	14	15 FLA	16 TB	17	18 PHI
19 ANA	20	21	22	23 TOR	24	25 SJ
26 VAN	27	28 CHI	29	30	31 VAN	

November
SUN	MON	TUE	WED	THU	FRI	SAT
						1 LA
2	3	4	5	6 COL	7	8 ANA
9 ANA	10	11	12	13 COL	14 DAL	15
16 CBJ	17	18	19 STL	20	21 SJ	22
23 ATL	24 DAL	25	26	27 LA	28	29
30 BOS						

December
SUN	MON	TUE	WED	THU	FRI	SAT
	1	2 NJ	3	4 BUF	5 PHI	6
7 CHI	8	9	10 DAL	11	12 EDM	13
14	15 MIN	16	17	18 LA	19	20 STL
21	22 NAS	23 CBJ	24	25	26	27 NAS
28	29 NYR	30	31 LA			

January
SUN	MON	TUE	WED	THU	FRI	SAT
				1	2 DAL	3
4 CAR	D 5	6	7 WAS	8	9 MIN	10
11 ATL	12	13 VAN	14	15 NAS	16 DET	17
18	19	20	21 SJ	22 SJ	23	24 DET
25	26	27 CAL	28	29 OTT	30	31 DAL

February
SUN	MON	TUE	WED	THU	FRI	SAT
1	2 CBJ	3	4 FLA	5 SJ	6	7
8*	9	10	11 ANA	12	13 NYI	14 DAL
15 STL	16	D 17	18 DET	19	20 CBJ	21 NAS
22	23 ANA	24	25 PIT	26	27 EDM	28
29 CAL						

March
SUN	MON	TUE	WED	THU	FRI	SAT
	1	2 EDM	3	4	5 MON	6
7 MIN	8	9 LA	10 LA	11	12 COL	13
14 COL	D 15	16 ANA	17	18 DET	19	20
21 CHI	D 22 MIN	23	24 CAL	25	26 SJ	27
28 EDM	D 29 VAN	30	31 CAL			

April
SUN	MON	TUE	WED	THU	FRI	SAT
				1	2	3 CHI D
4	5	6	7	8	9	10

2003-04 SEASON
CLUB DIRECTORY

Chairman and governor
Steve Ellman

Co-owner
Jerry Moyes

Managing partner
Wayne Gretzky

President and chief operating officer
Douglas Moss

Sr. executive v.p. of hockey operations
Cliff Fletcher

Executive v.p. and general manager
Michael Barnett

V.p. and asst. general nanager
Laurence Gilman

Head coach
Bob Francis

Assistant coaches
Rick Bowness
Pat Conacher

Goaltending coach
Benoit Allaire

Strength & conditioning coordinator
Stieg Theander

Video coordinator
Steve Peters

Head athletic therapist
Gord Hart

Massage therapist
Jukka Nieminen

Equipment managers
Stan Wilson
Tony Silva

Asst. equipment manager
Jason Rudee

V.p. of communications
Rich Nairn

Director of media relations
Rich Braunstein

Mgr. of pub. and media relations
Ryan Lichtenfels

DRAFT CHOICES

Rd.— Player	Overall	Pos.	Last team
2— Marc-Andre Bernier	60	RW	Halifax (QMJHL)
3— Tyler Redenbach	77	C/W	Swift Current (WHL)
3— Dimitri Pestunov	80	C/RW	Magnitogorsk (Russia)
4— Liam Lindstrom	115	C/RW	Mora (Sweden)
6— Ryan Gibbons	178	RW	Seattle (WHL)
7— Randall Gelech	208	C/RW	Kelowna (WHL)
8— Eduard Lewandowski	242	F	Koln (Germany)
9— Sean Sullivan	272	D	St. Sebastian's HS
9— Loic Burkhalter	290	F	Ambri (Switzerland)

MISCELLANEOUS DATA

Home ice (capacity)
America West Arena (16,210)

Address
Alltel Ice Den
9375 E. Bell Road
Scottsdale, AZ 85260

Business phone
480-473-5600

Ticket information
480-563-PUCK

Website
www.phoenixcoyotes.com

Training site
Scottsdale, AZ

Club colors
TBA

Radio affiliation
KDUS (1060 AM) and KDKB (93.3 FM)

TV affiliation
FOX Sports Arizona, WB 6/61, KTVK
(Channel 3)

PHOENIX COYOTES

No.	FORWARDS	Ht./Wt.	Place	BORN Date	NHL exp.	2002-03 clubs
	Kelly Buchberger (RW)..	6-2/210	Langenburg, Sask.	12-2-66	17	Phoenix
7	Dan Cleary (RW)	6-0/203	Carbonear, Nfld.	12-18-78	6	Edmonton
19	Shane Doan (RW).........	6-2/218	Halkirk, Alta.	10-10-76	8	Phoenix
	Ben Eager (LW)	6-2/210	Ottawa	1-22-84	0	Oshawa (OHL)
27	Chris Ferraro (C)...........	5-10/185	Port Jefferson, N.Y.	1-24-73	6	Portland (AHL)
28	Peter Ferraro (LW)........	5-9/180	Port Jefferson, N.Y.	1-24-73	6	Portland (AHL)
77	Chris Gratton (C)	6-4/219	Brantford, Ont.	7-5-75	10	Buffalo, Phoenix
38	Jan Hrdina (LW)	6-0/200	Hradec Kralove, Czech.	2-5-76	5	Pittsburgh, Phoenix
45	Jason Jaspers (C).........	6-0/185	Thunder Bay, Ont.	4-8-81	2	Springfield (AHL), Phoenix
12	Mike Johnson (RW)	6-2/200	Scarborough, Ont.	10-3-74	7	Phoenix
36	Krys Kolanos (C)	6-2/196	Calgary	7-27-81	2	Phoenix
	Jakub Koreis (C)...........	6-3/205	Plzen, Czechoslovakia	6-26-84	0	HC Keramika Plzen (Czech Republic)
11	Daymond Langkow (C)..	5-11/180	Edmonton	9-27-76	8	Phoenix
	Darren McLachlan (LW).	6-1/230	Penticton, B.C.	2-16-83	0	Seattle (WHL)
	Kiel McLeod (C)............	6-5/211	Fort Saskatchewan, Alta.	12-30-82	0	Kelowna (WHL)
17	Ladislav Nagy (LW)	5-11/183	Saca, Yugoslavia	6-1-79	4	Phoenix
9	Tyson Nash (LW)	5-11/195	Edmonton	3-11-75	5	St. Louis
44	Andrei Nazarov (LW)	6-5/234	Chelyabinsk, U.S.S.R.	4-22-74	10	Phoenix
33	Scott Pellerin (LW)	5-11/190	Shediac, N.B.	1-9-70	10	Dallas, Phoenix
	Martin Podlesak (C)......	6-6/200	Melnik, Czechoslovakia	9-26-82	0	Springfield (AHL)
29	Branko Radivojevic (RW)	6-1/185	Piestany, Czechoslovakia	11-24-80	2	Phoenix
19	Paul Ranheim (LW)	6-1/210	St. Louis	1-25-66	15	Philadelphia, Phoenix
49	Brian Savage (LW)........	6-2/192	Sudbury, Ont.	2-24-71	10	Phoenix
	Matthew Schutte (LW)...	6-2/200	Burlington, Ont.	7-28-79	0	
16	Mike Sillinger (C)..........	5-11/191	Regina, Sask.	6-29-71	13	Columbus
	Fredrik Sjostrom (RW) ..	6-0/194	Fargelanda, Sweden	5-6-83	0	Springfield (AHL)
	Jeff Taffe (C)	6-1/180	Hastings, Minn.	2-19-81	1	Springfield (AHL), Phoenix
	Erik Westrum (C)...........	5-11/186	Minneapolis	7-26-79	0	Springfield (AHL)
28	Landon Wilson (RW)	6-2/216	St. Louis	3-13-75	8	Phoenix
	DEFENSEMEN					
5	Drake Berehowsky........	6-2/212	Toronto	1-3-72	12	Springfield (AHL), Phoenix
	Goran Bezina	6-3/203	Split, Yugoslavia	3-21-80	0	Springfield (AHL)
45	Brad Ference...............	6-3/210	Calgary	4-2-79	4	Florida, Phoenix
38	Martin Grenier	6-5/230	Laval, Que.	11-2-80	2	Springfield (AHL), Phoenix
	Igor Knyazev................	6-0/183	Elektrosal, U.S.S.R.	1-27-83	0	Lowell (AHL)
23	Paul Mara	6-4/210	Ridgewood, N.J.	9-7-79	5	Phoenix
5	Deron Quint	6-2/209	Durham, N.H.	3-12-76	8	Springfield (AHL), Phoenix
2	Todd Simpson	6-3/215	North Vancouver	5-28-73	8	Phoenix
	Matthew Spiller.............	6-5/210	Daysland, Alta.	2-7-83	0	Seattle (WHL)
15	Radoslav Suchy............	6-1/191	Kezmarok, Czechoslovakia	4-7-76	4	Phoenix
45	David Tanabe	6-1/195	Minneapolis	7-19-80	4	Carolina
3	Nikos Tselios	6-4/187	Oak Park, Ill.	1-20-79	1	Lowell (AHL), Springfield (AHL)
4	Ossi Vaananen	6-3/200	Vantaa, Finland	8-18-80	3	Phoenix
	GOALTENDERS					
1	Zac Bierk......................	6-4/205	Peterborough, Ont.	9-17-76	5	Springfield (AHL), Phoenix
33	Brian Boucher...............	6-1/190	Woonsocket, R.I.	1-2-77	4	Phoenix
1	Sean Burke	6-4/210	Windsor, Ont.	1-29-67	15	Phoenix
	David Leneveu	6-1/170	Fernie, B.C.	5-23-83	0	
35	Jean-Marc Pelletier........	6-3/195	Atlanta	3-4-78	2	Phoenix, Lowell (AHL), Springfield (AHL)
	Colin Zulainello	6-1/189	Thunder Bay, Ont.	7-8-78	0	

2002-03 REVIEW
INDIVIDUAL STATISTICS

SCORING

	Games	G	A	Pts.	PIM	+/-	PPG	SHG	GWG	GTG	Sht.	Sht. Pct.	Faceoffs Won	Lost	Pct.	TOI
Mike Johnson............	82	23	40	63	47	9	8	0	3	1	178	12.9	17	17	50.0	19:38
Shane Doan............	82	21	37	58	86	3	7	0	2	0	225	9.3	248	375	39.8	18:47
Ladislav Nagy...........	80	22	35	57	92	17	8	0	6	0	209	10.5	14	27	34.1	17:27
Daymond Langkow ...	82	20	32	52	56	20	4	2	2	0	196	10.2	917	1055	46.5	20:59
Daniel Briere*..........	68	17	29	46	50	-21	4	0	3	1	142	12.0	582	526	52.5	17:01
Tony Amonte*..........	59	13	23	36	26	-12	6	0	3	0	170	7.6	19	34	35.8	19:27
Teppo Numminen.......	78	6	24	30	30	0	2	0	1	1	108	5.6	0	0	—	23:51
Branko Radivojevic....	79	12	15	27	63	-2	1	0	3	1	109	11.0	8	12	40.0	13:18
Paul Mara.................	73	10	15	25	78	-7	1	0	0	0	95	10.5	0	1	0.0	21:06
Danny Markov...........	64	4	16	20	36	2	2	0	0	1	105	3.8	0	0	—	23:16
Ramzi Abid*.............	30	10	8	18	30	1	4	0	3	0	52	19.2	1	0	100.0	12:30

	Games	G	A	Pts.	PIM	+/-	PPG	SHG	GWG	GTG	Sht.	Sht. Pct.	Faceoffs Won	Lost	Pct.	TOI
Deron Quint..............	51	7	10	17	20	-5	2	0	0	0	85	8.2	0	0	—	15:51
Brian Savage	43	6	10	16	22	-4	1	0	1	1	68	8.8	5	9	35.7	13:22
Landon Wilson	31	6	8	14	26	1	0	0	3	0	92	6.5	19	16	54.3	12:11
Claude Lemieux*......	36	6	8	14	30	-3	1	1	0	1	74	8.1	138	157	46.8	14:01
Kelly Buchberger.......	79	3	9	12	109	0	0	1	0	0	32	9.4	338	446	43.1	9:58
Todd Simpson	66	2	7	9	135	7	0	0	0	0	67	3.0	0	0	—	16:58
Ossi Vaananen..........	67	2	7	9	82	1	0	0	0	0	49	4.1	0	0	—	19:15
Radoslav Suchy	77	1	8	9	18	2	1	0	0	0	48	2.1	0	1	0.0	16:25
Brad May*................	20	3	4	7	32	3	0	0	0	0	24	12.5	0	0	—	9:56
Paul Ranheim*.........	40	3	4	7	10	-4	0	0	0	0	34	8.8	19	20	48.7	11:58
Jeff Taffe	20	3	1	4	4	-4	1	0	1	0	18	16.7	33	80	29.2	11:34
Jan Hrdina*..............	4	0	4	4	8	3	0	0	0	0	2	0.0	42	28	60.0	18:12
Andrei Nazarov.........	59	3	0	3	135	-9	2	0	0	0	35	8.6	2	4	33.3	6:33
Drake Berehowsky	7	1	2	3	27	0	0	0	0	0	8	12.5	0	0	—	10:51
Chris Gratton*..........	14	0	1	1	21	-11	0	0	0	0	28	0.0	132	99	57.1	17:12
Brad Ference*..........	15	0	1	1	28	-5	0	0	0	0	8	0.0	0	0	—	16:32
Scott Pellerin*.........	23	0	1	1	8	-5	0	0	0	0	17	0.0	7	5	58.3	9:31
Brian Boucher (g)......	45	0	1	1	0	0	0	0	0	0	0	—	0	0	—	—
Jason Jaspers	2	0	0	0	0	-1	0	0	0	0	0	—	8	6	57.1	7:16
Krystofer Kolanos......	2	0	0	0	0	0	0	0	0	0	8	0.0	5	11	31.3	14:06
J.-Marc Pelletier (g) ..	2	0	0	0	0	0	0	0	0	0	0	—	0	0	—	—
Martin Grenier..........	3	0	0	0	0	-1	0	0	0	0	0	—	0	0	—	6:11
P. DesRochers (g)* ..	4	0	0	0	0	0	0	0	0	0	0	—	0	0	—	—
Frank Banham	5	0	0	0	2	-1	0	0	0	0	5	0.0	0	1	0.0	7:51
Dan Focht*	10	0	0	0	10	-2	0	0	0	0	1	0.0	0	0	—	8:39
Zac Bierk (g)	16	0	0	0	2	0	0	0	0	0	0	—	0	0	—	—
Sean Burke (g)	22	0	0	0	4	0	0	0	0	0	0	—	0	0	—	—
Darcy Hordichuk*	25	0	0	0	82	-1	0	0	0	0	5	0.0	0	0	—	4:46

GOALTENDING

	Games	GS	Min.	GA	SO	Avg.	W	L	T	EN	PPG Allow	SHG Allow	Shots	Save Pct.
Sean Burke	22	22	1248	44	2	2.12	12	6	2	2	21	1	632	.930
Zac Bierk.................................	16	15	884	32	1	2.17	4	9	1	3	8	5	471	.932
Brian Boucher...........................	45	40	2544	128	0	3.02	15	20	8	4	42	5	1210	.894
Jean-Marc Pelletier....................	2	2	119	6	0	3.03	0	2	0	0	2	0	48	.875
Patrick DesRochers*..................	4	3	175	11	0	3.77	0	3	0	0	6	0	88	.875

*Played with two or more NHL teams.

RESULTS

OCTOBER

9— At Los Angeles ....L.....1-4
12—Dallas.............................L.....2-5
14—At Columbus...................W....4-2
15—At Ottawa.......................L.....1-2
17—At Toronto......................L.....3-5
19—At Buffalo ....W....3-2
22—At Nashville....................W....2-1
24—Colorado ....L.....2-3
26—Minnesota.......................L.....1-6
28—At N.Y. Rangers.............OTL....*2-3
29—At N.Y. Islanders............W....3-2
31—At Philadelphia...............L.....2-6

NOVEMBER

3— Nashville.........................W....*2-1
7— Minnesota.......................W....4-1
9— Vancouver ....L.....2-5
11—At Tampa Bay.................L.....2-4
12—At Carolina.....................L.....2-3
15—At Atlanta ....W....5-1
17—Colorado ....T.....*4-4
20—Dallas.............................T.....*2-2
22—Florida...........................T.....*3-3
25—At Dallas........................L.....1-5
27—At Anaheim.....................T.....*2-2
28—Chicago..........................L.....2-4
30—At San Jose....................W....3-2

DECEMBER

3— San Jose ....OTL....*2-3
5— Detroit ....L.....3-5

7— Montreal ....L.....2-4
9— Columbus ....T.....*3-3
11—Atlanta ....W....4-2
13—Washington ....L.....3-4
15—Los Angeles ....W....2-1
17—Pittsburgh ....W....5-2
20—St. Louis ....T.....*3-3
22—At Anaheim.....................L.....0-4
26—At Los Angeles ....OTL....*3-4
28—Philadelphia....................W....4-0
30—Edmonton.......................W....*4-3

JANUARY

1— At Washington ....W....*2-1
3— At Detroit........................W....4-1
4— At Columbus....................L.....0-2
8— At Chicago ....T.....*0-0
10—At Minnesota ....L.....1-2
11—At Nashville.....................OTL....*3-4
14—St. Louis ....L.....1-4
18—Buffalo ....L.....0-1
20—San Jose ....W....3-1
23—At Calgary ....W....7-1
24—At Edmonton...................W....5-1
26—At Vancouver ....L.....0-1
28—Calgary ....W....4-3

FEBRUARY

5— At Los Angeles ....L.....3-4
7— At Anaheim......................L.....2-3
8— Dallas..............................L.....1-3
12—New Jersey.....................L.....0-3

14—At Minnesota ....W....3-2
15—At St. Louis ....W....5-3
18—Columbus ....W....5-2
20—At Chicago ....W....2-1
21—At Dallas.........................T.....*2-2
23—Calgary ....L.....2-4
26—Carolina ....W....4-2
28—Anaheim.........................W....3-1

MARCH

2— At Detroit........................L.....2-5
4— At Pittsburgh ....W....4-1
6— At St. Louis......................L.....3-6
8— San Jose ....W....6-4
10—At Colorado ....T.....*2-2
12—Detroit ....L.....2-3
14—Chicago ....L.....0-4
15—Anaheim.........................W....4-2
18—Boston ....W....2-1
20—Edmonton.......................W....*3-2
22—Tampa Bay......................L.....0-4
24—At Calgary ....L.....0-2
26—At Edmonton...................L.....3-4
27—At Vancouver ....L.....1-5
29—At Colorado ....L.....1-6
31—Los Angeles ....OTL....*4-5

APRIL

2— Vancouver ....T.....*3-3
4— Nashville.........................W....1-0
6— At San Jose ....T.....*3-3
*Denotes overtime game.

PITTSBURGH PENGUINS
EASTERN CONFERENCE/ATLANTIC DIVISION

Penguins' Schedule
Home games shaded; D=Day game; *Feb. 8 All-Star Game at St. Paul, Minn.

October

SUN	MON	TUE	WED	THU	FRI	SAT
5	6	7	8	9	10 LA	11 PHI
12	13	14	15	16 MON	17	18 DET
19	20	21	22 CAR	23	24 NJ	25 NYI
26	27	28	29 NYI	30 CHI	31	

November

SUN	MON	TUE	WED	THU	FRI	SAT
						1 D BOS
2	3	4 TOR	5	6	7 FLA	8 TB
9	10	11	12 NYR	13	14 BUF	15 FLA
16	17	18	19 MIN	20	21 NJ	22 OTT
23	24	25	26 PHI	27	28 NYR	29 CAR
30						

December

SUN	MON	TUE	WED	THU	FRI	SAT
	1 ATL	2	3 PHI	4	5	6 EDM
7 CAL	8	9 VAN	10	11	12 ATL	13 CBJ
14	15	16 BUF	17	18 CAR	19	20 ATL
21	22 MON	23	24	25	26 OTT	27 NJ
28	29 CHI	30	31 D NYI			

January

SUN	MON	TUE	WED	THU	FRI	SAT
			1 D NAS	2	3 D NYR	
4	5 TOR	6	7 NJ	8 BOS	9	10 D MON
11	12 PHI	13 TB	14	15	16 MIN	17
18 D WAS	19	20 NJ	21	22 OTT	23	24 COL
25	26	27 TB	28	29 TB	30	31 D PHI

February

SUN	MON	TUE	WED	THU	FRI	SAT
1 D BOS	2	3 MON	4	5	6	7
8*	9	10 BOS	11	12 FLA	13	14 STL
15	16 TOR	17	18 NYI	19	20 FLA	21
22 D OTT	23	24	25 PHO	26	27 SJ	28
29 D NYI						

March

SUN	MON	TUE	WED	THU	FRI	SAT
	1	2 NYI	3	4 NAS	5	6 ANA
7 NYR	8	9 DAL	10	11 TOR	12	13
14 PHI	15	16 WAS	17 NJ	18	19 CAR	20
21 NYR	22	23 NYR	24	25	26 BUF	27 BUF
28	29	30 WAS	31			

April

SUN	MON	TUE	WED	THU	FRI	SAT
				1	2 ATL	3
4 D WAS	5	6	7	8	9	10

2003-04 SEASON
CLUB DIRECTORY

Chairman/CEO
Mario Lemieux
President and governor
Ken Sawyer
Executive v.p./general manager
Craig Patrick
Vice president & general counsel
Ted Black
Vice president & controller
Kevin Hart
V.p., communications/marketing
Tom McMillan
Vice president, sales
David Soltesz
General manager
Craig Patrick
Assistant general manager
Ed Johnston
Director of player development
Herb Brooks
Head coach
Eddie Olczyk
Assistant coaches
Randy Hillier, Lorne Molleken, Joe Mullen
Head scout
Greg Malone

Goaltending coach/scout
Gilles Meloche
Scouts
Wayne Daniels, Chuck Grillo, Charlie Hodge, Mark Kelley, Richard Rose, Neil Shea
Pro scout
Rick Kehoe
Strength & conditioning coach
John Welday
Equipment manager
Steve Latin
Team physician
Dr. Charles Burke
Head athletic trainer
Scott Johnson
Vice president & controller
Kevin Hart
Vice president, sales
David Soltesz
Senior director of ticketing
James Santilli
Vice president, sales
David Soltesz

DRAFT CHOICES

Rd.— Player	Overall	Pos.	Last team
1— Marc-Andre Fleury	1	G	Cape Breton (QMJHL)
2— Ryan Stone	32	C	Brandon (WHL)
3— Jonathan Filewich	70	RW	Prince George (WHL)
3— Daniel Carcillo	73	LW	Sarnia (OHL)
4— Paul Bissonnette	121	D	Saginaw (OHL)
5— Evgeni Isakov	161	LW	Cherepovets (Russia)
6— Lukas Bolf	169	D	Sparta JR (CzechRp.Jr.)
7— Andy Chiodo	199	G	Toronto-St) Michael's (OHL)
7— Stephen Dixon	229	C	Cape Breton (QMJHL)
8— Joe Jensen	232	C	St. Cloud State (WCHA)
9— Matt Moulson	263	LW	Cornell (ECAC)

MISCELLANEOUS DATA

Home ice (capacity)
Mellon Arena (16,958)
Address
Mellon Arena
66 Mario Lemieux Place
Pittsburgh, PA 15219
Business phone
412-642-1300
Ticket information
412-642-7367 and 1-800-642-7367
Website
www.pittsburghpenguins.com

Training site
Canonsburg, PA
Club colors
Black, gold and white
Radio affiliation
3WS (94.5FM), Fox Sports Radio 970AM
TV affiliation
Fox Sports Net Pittsburgh

TRAINING CAMP ROSTER

No.	FORWARDS	Ht./Wt.	Place	BORN Date	NHL exp.	2002-03 clubs
	Ramzi Abid (LW)	6-2/195	Montreal	3-24-80	1	Springfield (AHL), Pittsburgh, Phoenix
	Colby Armstrong (RW)..	6-1/180	Lloydminster, Sask.	11-23-82	0	Wilkes-Barre/Scranton (AHL)
16	Kris Beech (C)	6-2/178	Salmon Arm, B.C.	2-5-81	3	Wilkes-Barre/Scranton (AHL), Pittsburgh
28	Matt Bradley (RW)........	6-2/195	Stittsville, Ont.	6-13-78	3	San Jose
	Shane Endicott (C)	6-4/200	Saskatoon, Sask.	12-21-81	1	Wilkes-Barre/Scranton (AHL)
	Rico Fata (RW)	5-11/197	Sault Ste. Marie, Ont.	2-12-80	5	Hartford (AHL), Pit., N.Y. Rangers
9	Brian Holzinger (C)........	5-11/190	Parma, Ohio	10-10-72	9	Springfield (AHL), Pit., Tampa Bay
	Mathias Johansson (C)..	6-2/187	Oskarshamn, Sweden	2-22-74	1	Pittsburgh, Calgary
	Konstantin Koltsov (LW)	6-0/187	Minsk, U.S.S.R.	4-17-81	1	Wilkes-Barre/Scranton (AHL), Pit.
37	Tom Kostopoulos (RW) .	6-0/205	Mississauga, Ont.	1-24-79	2	Wilkes-Barre/Scranton (AHL), Pit.
14	Milan Kraft (C)	6-3/191	Plzen, Czechoslovakia	1-17-80	3	Wilkes-Barre/Scranton (AHL), Pit.
	Guillaume Lefebvre (LW)	6-1/200	Amos, Que.	5-7-81	2	Philadelphia, Pittsburgh, Philadelphia (AHL), Wilkes-Barre/Scranton (AHL)
66	Mario Lemieux (C).........	6-4/220	Montreal	10-5-65	19	Pittsburgh
	Ryan Malone (LW)........	6-3/190	Pittsburgh	12-1-79	0	Wilkes-Barre/Scranton (AHL)
26	Kent Manderville (C).....	6-3/200	Edmonton	4-12-71	12	Pittsburgh
7	Steve McKenna (LW)	6-8/255	Toronto	8-21-73	7	Pittsburgh
72	Eric Meloche (RW)	5-11/195	Montreal	5-1-76	2	Wilkes-Barre/Scranton (AHL), Pit.
95	Aleksey Morozov (RW)..	6-1/196	Moscow, U.S.S.R.	2-16-77	6	Pittsburgh
	Matt Murley (LW)	6-1/192	Troy, N.Y.	12-17-79	0	Wilkes-Barre/Scranton (AHL)
10	Ville Nieminen (LW).......	5-11/205	Tampere, Finland	4-6-77	4	Pittsburgh
	Michel Ouellet (RW)	6-1/182	Rimouski, Que.	3-5-82	0	Wheeling (ECHL), Wilkes-Barre/Scranton (AHL)
17	Toby Petersen (LW)	5-10/196	Minneapolis	10-27-78	2	Wilkes-Barre/Scranton (AHL)
	Michal Sivek (C)	6-3/209	Nachod, Czechoslovakia	1-21-81	1	Wilkes-Barre/Scranton (AHL), Pit.
82	Martin Straka (LW)	5-9/176	Plzen, Czechoslovakia	9-3-72	11	Pittsburgh
	Tomas Surovy (RW/LW)	6-0/191	Banska Bystrica, Czech.	9-24-81	1	Wilkes-Barre/Scranton (AHL), Pit.
	Alexander Zevakhin (RW)	6-0/187	Perm, U.S.S.R.	6-4-80	0	Wilkes-Barre/Scranton (AHL)
	DEFENSEMEN					
4	Marc Bergevin	6-1/214	Montreal	8-11-65	19	Pittsburgh, Tampa Bay
42	Micki Dupont	5-10/186	Calgary	4-15-80	2	Saint John (AHL), Calgary, Wilkes-Barre/Scranton (AHL)
	Drew Fata	6-1/211	Sault Ste. Marie, Ont.	7-28-83	0	Kingston (OHL)
37	Dan Focht	6-6/226	Regina, Sask.	12-31-77	2	Springfield (AHL), Pittsburgh, Phoenix
23	Shawn Heins.................	6-4/210	Eganville, Ont.	12-24-73	5	Pittsburgh, San Jose
8	Hans Jonsson...............	6-1/202	Jarved, Sweden	8-2-73	4	Pittsburgh
	David Koci	6-6/216	Prague, Czechoslovakia	5-12-81	0	Wheeling (ECHL), Wilkes-Barre/Scranton (AHL)
41	Richard Lintner.............	6-3/214	Trencin, Czechoslovakia	11-15-77	3	Pit., N.Y. Rangers, Hartford (AHL), Wilkes-Barre/Scranton (AHL)
	Ross Lupaschuk............	6-1/211	Edmonton	1-19-81	1	Wilkes-Barre/Scranton (AHL), Pit.
2	Josef Melichar	6-2/214	Ceske Budejovice, Czech.	1-20-79	3	Pittsburgh
	Ondrej Nemec...............	6-0/196	Tribec, Czechoslovakia	4-18-84	0	HC Vsetin (Czech Republic)
	Brooks Orpik.................	6-3/217	Amherst, N.Y.	9-26-80	1	Wilkes-Barre/Scranton (AHL), Pit.
3	Jamie Pushor	6-3/220	Lethbridge, Alta.	2-11-73	8	Pittsburgh
14	Bert Robertsson	6-3/210	Sodertalje, Sweden	6-30-74	4	Ilves Tampere (Finland)
	Darcy Robinson	6-3/229	Kamloops, B.C.	5-3-81	0	Wheeling (ECHL), Wilkes-Barre/Scranton (AHL)
	Alexandre Rouleau........	6-1/180	Mont-Laurier, Que.	7-29-83	0	Val-d'Or (QMJHL), Quebec (QMJHL)
28	Michal Rozsival	6-1/208	Vlasim, Czechoslovakia	9-3-78	4	Pittsburgh
	Robert Scuderi	6-1/194	Syosset, N.Y.	12-30-78	0	Wilkes-Barre/Scranton (AHL)
8	Dick Tarnstrom	6-0/206	Sundbyberg, Sweden	1-20-75	2	Pittsburgh
	Ryan Whitney	6-3/202	Boston	2-19-83	0	Boston University (Hockey East)
	GOALTENDERS					
30	Jean-Sebastien Aubin....	5-11/176	Montreal	7-17-77	5	Wilkes-Barre/Scranton (AHL), Pit.
	Sebastien Caron	6-1/150	Amqui, Que.	6-25-80	1	Wilkes-Barre/Scranton (AHL), Pit.
1	Johan Hedberg	5-11/185	Leksand, Sweden	5-5-73	3	Pittsburgh
	Joel Laing	5-10/185	Maryfield, Sask.		1	
35	Rob Tallas....................	6-0/163	Edmonton	3-20-73	6	Wilkes-Barre/Scranton (AHL)

2002-03 REVIEW
INDIVIDUAL STATISTICS
SCORING

	Games	G	A	Pts.	PIM	+/-	PPG	SHG	GWG	GTG	Sht.	Sht. Pct.	Faceoffs Won	Lost	Pct.	TOI
Mario Lemieux	67	28	63	91	43	-25	14	0	4	0	235	11.9	474	555	46.1	23:04
Alexei Kovalev*	54	27	37	64	50	-11	8	0	1	0	212	12.7	6	13	31.6	24:03
Martin Straka	60	18	28	46	12	-18	7	0	4	0	136	13.2	52	63	45.2	20:36
Dick Tarnstrom.........	61	7	34	41	50	-11	3	0	0	0	115	6.1	0	—		23:54
Jan Hrdina*	57	14	25	39	34	1	11	0	4	0	84	16.7	551	433	56.0	19:45

	Games	G	A	Pts.	PIM	+/-	PPG	SHG	GWG	GTG	Sht.	Sht. Pct.	Faceoffs Won	Lost	Pct.	TOI
Aleksey Morozov	27	9	16	25	16	-3	6	0	2	1	46	19.6	0	0	—	18:41
Ville Nieminen	75	9	12	21	93	-25	0	2	1	0	86	10.5	24	22	52.2	14:08
Randy Robitaille*	41	5	12	17	8	5	1	0	2	0	61	8.2	240	189	55.9	13:57
Wayne Primeau*	70	5	11	16	55	-30	1	0	0	0	101	5.0	625	615	50.4	16:16
Rico Fata*	27	5	8	13	10	-6	0	0	0	0	49	10.2	43	44	49.4	17:46
Milan Kraft	31	7	5	12	10	-8	0	0	1	0	50	14.0	169	223	43.1	13:55
Tomas Surovy	26	4	7	11	10	0	1	0	2	0	47	8.5	1	1	50.0	14:18
Steve McKenna	79	9	1	10	128	-18	5	0	3	0	59	15.3	0	1	0.0	7:45
Michal Rozsival	53	4	6	10	40	-5	1	0	0	0	61	6.6	0	0	—	20:25
Shean Donovan*	52	4	5	9	30	-6	0	1	0	0	66	6.1	9	28	24.3	13:00
Alexandre Daigle	33	4	3	7	8	-10	1	0	0	0	48	8.3	8	16	33.3	10:56
Marc Bergevin*	69	2	5	7	36	-9	0	0	0	0	27	7.4	0	0	—	18:45
Kent Manderville	82	2	5	7	46	-22	0	0	1	0	72	2.8	269	281	48.9	11:04
Janne Laukkanen*	17	1	6	7	8	-3	0	0	0	0	10	10.0	0	0	—	16:51
Ian Moran*	70	0	7	7	46	-17	0	0	0	0	85	0.0	3	1	75.0	18:37
Eric Meloche	13	5	1	6	4	-2	2	0	1	1	34	14.7	15	12	55.6	16:51
Michal Sivek	38	3	3	6	14	-5	1	0	0	0	45	6.7	14	18	43.8	13:04
Guillaume Lefebvre*	12	2	4	6	0	1	0	0	0	0	14	14.3	1	0	100.0	17:30
Mathias Johansson*	12	1	5	6	4	1	1	0	0	0	16	6.3	73	101	42.0	17:04
Richard Lintner*	19	3	2	5	10	-9	1	0	0	0	36	8.3	0	0	—	18:58
Hans Jonsson	63	1	4	5	36	-23	0	0	0	0	40	2.5	0	2	0.0	17:04
Jamie Pushor	76	3	1	4	76	-28	0	0	0	0	54	5.6	0	0	—	16:58
Dan LaCouture*	44	2	2	4	72	-8	0	0	0	0	30	6.7	4	1	80.0	9:12
Andrew Ference*	22	1	3	4	36	-16	1	0	0	0	22	4.5	1	0	100.0	19:33
Brian Holzinger*	9	1	2	3	6	-6	0	0	0	1	20	5.0	77	84	47.8	16:23
Dan Focht*	12	0	3	3	19	-7	0	0	0	0	11	0.0	0	1	0.0	18:13
Mikael Samuelsson*	22	2	0	2	8	-21	1	0	0	0	36	5.6	6	2	75.0	14:03
Shawn Heins*	27	1	1	2	33	-2	0	0	1	0	28	3.6	0	0	—	19:11
Johan Hedberg (g)	41	0	2	2	18	0	0	0	0	0	0	—	0	0	—	—
Vladimir Vujtek	5	0	1	1	0	-4	0	0	0	0	3	0.0	0	2	0.0	7:33
Joel Bouchard*	7	0	1	1	0	-6	0	0	0	0	6	0.0	0	0	—	21:49
Tom Kostopoulos	8	0	1	1	0	-4	0	0	0	0	6	0.0	0	2	0.0	4:33
Kris Beech	12	0	1	1	6	-3	0	0	0	0	6	0.0	41	55	42.7	10:34
J.-Sebastien Aubin (g)	21	0	1	1	2	0	0	0	0	0	0	—	0	0	—	—
Konstantin Koltsov	2	0	0	0	0	-2	0	0	0	0	4	0.0	0	0	—	13:06
Ramzi Abid*	3	0	0	0	2	-5	0	0	0	0	7	0.0	0	1	0.0	17:33
Ross Lupaschuk	3	0	0	0	4	-3	0	0	0	0	3	0.0	0	0	—	16:20
Brooks Orpik	6	0	0	0	2	-5	0	0	0	0	6	0.0	0	0	—	18:18
Josef Melichar	8	0	0	0	2	-2	0	0	0	0	6	0.0	0	0	—	15:18
Sebastien Caron (g)	24	0	0	0	6	0	0	0	0	0	0	—	0	0	—	—

GOALTENDING

	Games	GS	Min.	GA	SO	Avg.	W	L	T	EN	PPG Allow	SHG Allow	Shots	Save Pct.
Sebastien Caron	24	23	1408	62	2	2.64	7	14	2	1	12	3	741	.916
Jean-Sebastien Aubin	21	20	1132	59	1	3.13	6	13		3	10	2	589	.900
Johan Hedberg	41	39	2410	126	1	3.14	14	22	4	4	36	5	1197	.895

*Played with two or more NHL teams.

RESULTS

OCTOBER
10— Toronto ....L....0-6
12— N.Y. Rangers ....W....6-0
14— At Toronto ....W....5-4
16— Atlanta ....W....3-2
19— Tampa Bay ....T....*3-3
22— At Montreal ....T....*3-3
25— At Detroit ....L....3-7
26— Buffalo ....W....5-2
28— Washington ....W....3-2
30— At Ottawa ....W....4-1

NOVEMBER
2— Tampa Bay ....W....5-3
6— At Florida ....OTL...*3-4
8— At Tampa Bay ....L....1-4
9— At Carolina ....L....2-3
14— At Minnesota ....T....*1-1
16— N.Y. Islanders ....L....2-3
18— At Montreal ....OTL...*4-5
20— Montreal ....OTL...*2-3
22— At Atlanta ....W....3-1
23— San Jose ....W....4-1
27— Philadelphia ....W....7-2
29— At Buffalo ....W....4-1
30— Boston ....L....2-3

DECEMBER
3— Washington ....L....1-4
6— At New Jersey ....L....1-3
7— N.Y. Islanders ....L....3-6
10— At Toronto ....L....2-4

12— At San Jose ....L....2-5
14— At Los Angeles ....OTL...*2-3
15— At Anaheim ....L....0-5
17— At Phoenix ....L....2-5
19— New Jersey ....L....1-3
21— Calgary ....W....2-0
23— Buffalo ....W....5-2
26— At N.Y. Rangers ....W....6-1
28— Montreal ....W....3-2
30— Atlanta ....OTL...*2-3
31— At Columbus ....L....2-5

JANUARY
3— At Atlanta ....W....4-1
4— N.Y. Islanders ....W....*3-2
7— At N.Y. Islanders ....L....3-6
9— Toronto ....L....2-4
11— N.Y. Rangers ....L....1-3
13— At Boston ....W....2-1
15— At Carolina ....W....2-0
17— At Tampa Bay ....W....3-2
18— At Florida ....L....0-3
21— At Buffalo ....T....*0-0
23— Boston ....L....1-4
25— Chicago ....W....5-3
28— At N.Y. Islanders ....L....2-5
30— At Washington ....L....1-2

FEBRUARY
4— Vancouver ....L....2-3
6— Florida ....L....0-6
8— At Boston ....W....5-2

12— Ottawa ....L....0-3
14— At N.Y. Rangers ....L....0-1
15— At New Jersey ....W....4-1
18— Edmonton ....W....*4-3
20— Colorado ....L....2-5
22— St. Louis ....W....*2-1
23— New Jersey ....L....3-4
25— Los Angeles ....L....3-5
27— At Nashville ....L....0-6

MARCH
1— At Colorado ....L....1-4
2— At Dallas ....L....1-3
4— Phoenix ....L....1-4
6— Carolina ....L....0-4
8— Ottawa ....L....1-5
9— At Ottawa ....L....2-4
12— Nashville ....T....*2-2
15— Philadelphia ....L....2-4
16— Florida ....L....1-5
18— Detroit ....L....2-4
20— At Philadelphia ....L....2-4
21— At New Jersey ....L....1-3
23— At Chicago ....T....*1-1
26— At N.Y. Rangers ....W....3-1
29— At Philadelphia ....L....0-3
31— Philadelphia ....L....1-6

APRIL
2— Carolina ....W....3-2
5— At Washington ....L....3-5
*Denotes overtime game.

ST. LOUIS BLUES
WESTERN CONFERENCE/CENTRAL DIVISION

Blues' Schedule
Home games shaded; D=Day game; *Feb. 8 All-Star Game at St. Paul, Minn.

October

SUN	MON	TUE	WED	THU	FRI	SAT
5	6	7	8	9	10 PHO	11
12 COL	13	14	15	16 NAS	17	18 WAS
19	20	21 EDM	22 VAN	23	24 CAL	25
26	27	28 NAS	29 DET	30	31	

November

SUN	MON	TUE	WED	THU	FRI	SAT
						1 CHI
2	3	4 ANA	5	6 VAN	7	8 FLA
9	10	11	12	13 SJ	14	15 D LA
16 ANA	17	18	19 PHO	20	21	22 DAL
23	24	25 BOS	26	27	28 TB	29 DET
30						

December

SUN	MON	TUE	WED	THU	FRI	SAT
	1	2 LA	3	4 DET	5	6 NAS
7	8	9 TOR	10	11	12 CBJ	13 LA
14	15	16 CBJ	17	18 SJ	19	20 PHO
21 DET	22	23 CHI	24	25	26 COL	27
28	29 CBJ	30 PHI	31			

January

SUN	MON	TUE	WED	THU	FRI	SAT
				1 NYR	2	3 SJ
4	5 MIN	6 CAR	7	8	9	10 NAS
11 CHI	12 MON	13	14	15 CBJ	16	17 MIN
18 FLA	19	20	21 CBJ	22	23 DAL	24 DAL
25	26	27	28 ATL	29 VAN	30	31 NJ

February

SUN	MON	TUE	WED	THU	FRI	SAT
1	2 MIN	3	4 EDM	5 CAL	6	7
8*	9	10 OTT	11	12 COL	13	14 PIT
15	16 D PHO	17	18	19 TB	20 DET	21
22 D CHI	23	24	25	26 COL	27	28 VAN
29 SJ						

March

SUN	MON	TUE	WED	THU	FRI	SAT
	1	2 CAL	3	4 EDM	5	6 NYI
7 BUF	8	9 NYI	10	11 NAS	12	13 CBJ
14 CAL	15	16 LA	17 ANA	18	19	20 D DAL
21	22	23	24	25 ANA	26	27 D CHI
28 D CHI	29	30 EDM	31			

April

SUN	MON	TUE	WED	THU	FRI	SAT
				1 DET	2	3 D NAS
4 D MIN	5	6	7	8	9	10

2003-04 SEASON
CLUB DIRECTORY

Chairman of the board and owner
Bill Laurie
President & chief executive officer
Mark Sauer
Sr. vice president and general manager
Larry Pleau
Sr. v.p., marketing and communications
Jim Woodcock
V.p./director of hockey operations
John Ferguson Jr.
Head coach
Joel Quenneville
Assistant coaches
Mike Kitchen
Don Lever

Goaltending coach
Keith Allain
Athletic trainer
Ray Barile
Video coach
Jamie Kompon
Equipment manager
Bert Godin
Assistant equipment manager
Eric Bechtol
Director of communications
Frank Buonomo
Communications assistants
Scott Bonanni
Rich Jankowski

DRAFT CHOICES

Rd.— Player	Overall	Pos.	Last team
1— Shawn Belle	30	D	Tri-City (WHL)
2— David Backes	62	C/LW	Lincoln (USHL)
3— Konstantin Barulin	84	G	Tyumen (Russia)
3— Zach Fitzgerald	88	D	Seattle (WHL)
3— Konstantin Zakharov	101	F	Junost Minsk (Belarus)
4— Alexandre Bolduc	127	C	Rouyn Noranda (QMJHL)
5— Lee Stempniak	148	RW	Dartmouth (ECAC)
5— Chris Beckford-Tseu	159	G	Oshawa (OHL)
6— Jonathan Lehun	189	C	St. Cloud State (WCHA)
7— Evgeny Skachkov	221	LW	Kapitan Jr. (Russia)
8— Andrei Pervyshin	253	D	Yaroslavl Jr. (Russia Jr.)
9— Juha-Matti Aaltonen	284	W	Karpat Jr. (Finland Jr.)

MISCELLANEOUS DATA

Home ice (capacity)
Savvis Center (19,022)
Address
1401 Clark
St. Louis, MO 63103
Business phone
314-622-2500
Ticket information
314-241-1888
Website
www.stlouisblues.com

Training site
U.S. Ice, Chesterfield, MO
Club colors
Blue, gold, navy and white
Radio affiliation
KTRS (550 AM)
TV affiliation
KPLR (Channel 11) & FOX Sports
Midwest

TRAINING CAMP ROSTER

No.	FORWARDS	Ht./Wt.	Place	BORN Date	NHL exp.	2002-03 clubs
	Eric Boguniecki (LW)	5-8/192	New Haven, Conn.	5-6-75	4	St. Louis
	Marc Brown (LW)	6-1/200	Surrey, B.C.	3-10-79	0	Worcester (AHL)
	Petr Cajanek (C/LW)	5-11/194	Gottwaldov, Czech.	8-18-75	1	St. Louis
15	Daniel Corso (C)	5-10/184	Montreal	4-3-78	3	Worcester (AHL), St. Louis
10	Jason Dawe (LW)	5-10/190	North York, Ont.	5-29-73	8	Worcester (AHL)
38	Pavol Demitra (C)	6-0/190	Dubnica, Czechoslovakia	11-29-74	10	St. Louis
10	Dallas Drake (LW)	6-1/190	Trail, B.C.	2-4-69	11	St. Louis
18	Steve Dubinsky (RW)	6-0/190	Montreal	7-9-70	10	Worcester (AHL), St. Louis
	Colin Hemingway (RW)	6-0/170	Surrey, B.C.	8-12-80	0	
17	Ryan Johnson (C)	6-1/200	Thunder Bay, Ont.	6-14-76	6	St. Louis, Florida
34	Reed Low (RW)	6-5/228	Moose Jaw, Sask.	6-21-76	3	St. Louis
21	Steve Martins (C)	5-9/175	Gatineau, Que.	4-13-72	8	Binghamton (AHL), St. Louis, Ottawa
21	Jamal Mayers (RW)	6-2/212	Toronto	10-24-74	6	St. Louis
	Jay McClement (C)	6-1/193	Kingston, Ont.	3-2-83	0	Worcester (AHL)
19	Scott Mellanby (RW)	6-1/205	Montreal	6-11-66	18	St. Louis
	Andrei Mihknov (C/LW)	6-6/192	Kiev, U.S.S.R.	11-26-83	0	
21	Eric Nickulas (RW)	5-11/190	Hyannis, Mass.	3-25-75	4	Worcester (AHL), St. Louis
	Jeff Panzer (C)	5-10/160	Grand Forks, N.D.	4-7-78	0	Worcester (AHL)
25	Shjon Podein (RW)	6-2/200	Rochester, Minn.	3-5-68	11	St. Louis
	John Pohl (C)	6-1/186	Rochester, Minn.	6-1-79	0	Worcester (AHL)
	Jame Pollock (RW)	6-1/190	Quebec City	6-16-79	0	Worcester (AHL)
26	Martin Rucinsky (LW)	6-1/205	Most, Czechoslovakia	3-11-71	12	St. Louis
	Mark Rycroft (RW)	5-11/197	Nanaimo, B.C.	7-12-78	1	Worcester (AHL)
	Peter Sejna (LW)			10-5-79	1	St. Louis
	Alexei Shkotov (RW)	5-10/161	Elektrostal, U.S.S.R.	6-22-84	0	CSKA (CIS Jr.)
7	Keith Tkachuk (LW)	6-2/225	Melrose, Mass.	3-28-72	12	St. Louis
	Daniel Tkaczuk (C)	6-1/197	Toronto	6-10-79	1	Bridgeport (AHL)
	Igor Valeev (RW)	5-11/203	Chelyabinsk, U.S.S.R.	1-9-81	0	Worcester (AHL)
17	Sergei Varlamov (RW)	5-11/195	Kiev, U.S.S.R.	7-21-78	4	Worcester (AHL), St. Louis
	Tore Vikingstad (LW)	6-4/202	Oslo, Norway	10-8-75	0	DEG Metro Stars (Germany)
39	Doug Weight (C)	5-11/200	Warren, Mich.	1-21-71	13	St. Louis

DEFENSEMEN

No.	DEFENSEMEN	Ht./Wt.	Place	Date	exp.	2002-03 clubs
	Christian Backman	6-2/187	Alingsas, Sweden	4-28-80	1	Worcester (AHL), St. Louis
42	Steve Bancroft	6-1/214	Toronto	10-6-72	2	Worcester (AHL), Binghamton (AHL)
58	Aris Brimanis	6-3/195	Cleveland	3-14-72	6	Worcester (AHL)
	Trevor Byrne	6-3/200	Hingham, Mass.	5-7-80	0	Dartmouth College (ECAC)
37	Jeff Finley	6-2/205	Edmonton	4-14-67	14	St. Louis
5	Barret Jackman	6-1/190	Trail, B.C.	3-5-81	2	St. Louis
29	Alexander Khavanov	6-2/190	Dynamo, U.S.S.R.	1-30-72	3	St. Louis
	Tom Koivisto	5-10/194	Turku, Finland	6-4-74	1	Worcester (AHL), St. Louis
	Christian Laflamme	6-1/210	St. Charles, Que.	11-24-76	7	Worcester (AHL)
2	Al MacInnis	6-2/208	Inverness, Nova Scotia	7-11-63	22	St. Louis
47	Rich Pilon	6-2/220	Saskatoon, Sask.	4-30-68	14	
44	Chris Pronger	6-6/220	Dryden, Ont.	10-10-74	10	St. Louis
27	Bryce Salvador	6-1/194	Brandon, Man.	2-11-76	3	St. Louis
	Matt Walker	6-2/212	Beaverlodge, Alta.	4-7-80	1	Worcester (AHL), St. Louis

GOALTENDERS

No.	GOALTENDERS	Ht./Wt.	Place	Date	exp.	2002-03 clubs
	Reinhard Divis	5-11/200	Vienna, Austria	7-4-75	2	Worcester (AHL), St. Louis
35	Brent Johnson	6-2/200	Farmington, Mich.	3-12-77	4	Worcester (AHL), St. Louis
	Phil Osaer				0	Worcester (AHL), Trenton (ECHL), Louisiana (ECHL)
35	Chris Osgood	5-10/175	Peace River, Alta.	11-26-72	10	St. Louis, New York Islanders
	Cody Rudkowsky	6-1/200	Willingdon, Alta.	7-21-78	1	Worcester (AHL), Trenton (ECHL), St. Louis
1	Curtis Sanford	5-10/185	Owen Sound, Ontario	10-5-79	1	Worcester (AHL), St. Louis

2002-03 REVIEW
INDIVIDUAL STATISTICS

SCORING

	Games	G	A	Pts.	PIM	+/-	PPG	SHG	GWG	GTG	Sht.	Sht. Pct.	Faceoffs Won	Lost	Pct.	TOI
Pavol Demitra	78	36	57	93	32	0	11	0	4	1	205	17.6	578	675	46.1	19:47
Al MacInnis	80	16	52	68	61	22	9	1	2	0	299	5.4	2	0	100.0	26:54
Cory Stillman	79	24	43	67	56	12	6	0	4	0	157	15.3	111	155	41.7	18:19
Doug Weight	70	15	52	67	52	-6	7	0	3	0	182	8.2	528	520	50.4	20:22
Scott Mellanby	80	26	31	57	176	1	13	0	4	1	132	19.7	5	6	45.5	16:38
Keith Tkachuk	56	31	24	55	139	1	14	0	5	0	185	16.8	193	153	55.8	19:15
Eric Boguniecki	80	22	27	49	38	22	3	1	5	0	117	18.8	2	3	40.0	14:00
Petr Cajanek	51	9	29	38	20	16	2	2	1	0	90	10.0	384	409	48.4	15:55
Alexander Khavanov	81	8	25	33	48	-1	2	1	2	0	90	8.9	1	1	50.0	21:56
Dallas Drake	80	20	10	30	66	-7	4	1	2	1	113	17.7	22	34	39.3	14:48

	Games	G	A	Pts.	PIM	+/-	PPG	SHG	GWG	GTG	Sht.	Sht. Pct.	Won	Lost	Pct.	TOI
Martin Rucinsky	61	16	14	30	38	-1	4	4	3	1	135	11.9	11	8	57.9	16:54
Barret Jackman	82	3	16	19	190	23	0	0	0	0	66	4.5	0	0	—	20:02
Shjon Podein	68	4	6	10	28	7	1	0	0	0	52	7.7	88	102	46.3	10:53
Bryce Salvador	71	2	8	10	95	7	1	0	0	0	73	2.7	0	0	—	18:57
Tyson Nash	66	6	3	9	114	0	1	0	0	2	77	7.8	1	8	11.1	9:53
Christian Laflamme ...	47	0	9	9	45	1	0	0	0	0	44	0.0	0	0	—	15:09
Jamal Mayers	15	2	5	7	8	1	0	0	0	0	26	7.7	57	54	51.4	14:21
Steve Martins*	28	3	3	6	18	-8	0	1	0	0	25	12.0	202	167	54.7	13:37
Tomas Koivisto	22	2	4	6	10	1	0	0	1	0	26	7.7	0	0	—	16:44
Reed Low	79	2	4	6	234	3	0	0	0	1	48	4.2	10	4	71.4	6:19
Steve Dubinsky	28	0	6	6	4	3	0	0	0	0	23	0.0	152	116	56.7	10:44
Chris Pronger	5	1	3	4	10	-2	0	0	0	0	11	9.1	0	1	0.0	21:38
Mike Eastwood*	17	1	3	4	8	1	1	0	0	0	7	14.3	87	116	42.9	10:44
Jeff Finley	64	1	3	4	46	-2	0	0	0	0	30	3.3	0	0	—	15:37
Justin Papineau*	11	2	1	3	0	-1	0	0	1	0	15	13.3	44	55	44.4	10:59
Mike Van Ryn	20	0	3	3	8	3	0	0	0	0	21	0.0	0	0	—	15:03
Valeri Bure*	5	0	2	2	0	-2	0	0	0	0	11	0.0	0	0	—	15:11
Peter Sejna	1	1	0	1	0	0	1	0	0	0	3	33.3	0	0	—	15:22
Eric Nickulas	8	0	1	1	6	-2	0	0	0	0	3	0.0	0	0	—	9:31
Matt Walker	16	0	1	1	38	0	0	0	0	0	13	0.0	1	0	100.0	11:08
Brent Johnson (g)	38	0	1	1	2	0	0	0	0	0	0	—	0	0	—	—
Daniel Corso	1	0	0	0	0	-1	0	0	0	0	0	—	4	4	50.0	7:44
Cody Rudkowsky (g).	1	0	0	0	0	0	0	0	0	0	0	—	0	0	—	—
Reinhard Divis (g)	2	0	0	0	0	0	0	0	0	0	0	—	0	0	—	—
Sergei Varlamov	3	0	0	0	0	1	0	0	0	0	5	0.0	0	0	—	11:25
Christian Backman	4	0	0	0	0	-3	0	0	0	0	4	0.0	0	0	—	12:22
Tom Barrasso (g)	6	0	0	0	0	0	0	0	0	0	0	—	0	0	—	—
Curtis Sanford (g)	8	0	0	0	0	0	0	0	0	0	0	—	0	0	—	—
Chris Osgood (g)*	9	0	0	0	0	0	0	0	0	0	0	—	0	0	—	—
Ryan Johnson*	17	0	0	0	12	0	0	0	0	0	13	0.0	93	87	51.7	10:33
Fred Brathwaite (g) ...	30	0	0	0	0	0	0	0	0	0	0	—	0	0	—	—

GOALTENDING

	Games	GS	Min.	GA	SO	Avg.	W	L	T	EN	PPG Allow	SHG Allow	Shots	Save Pct.
Cody Rudkowsky	1	0	30	0	0	0.00	1	0	0	0	0	0	10	1.000
Reinhard Divis	2	2	83	1	0	0.72	2	0	0	0	1	0	34	.971
Curtis Sanford	8	7	397	13	1	1.96	5	1	0	0	6	1	148	.912
Brent Johnson	38	35	2042	84	2	2.47	16	13	5	2	25	3	844	.900
Fred Brathwaite	30	23	1615	74	2	2.75	12	9	4	4	26	3	631	.883
Chris Osgood*	9	9	532	27	2	3.05	4	3	2	1	34	2	241	.888
Tom Barrasso	6	6	293	16	1	3.28	1	4	0	0	7	0	132	.879

*Played with two or more NHL teams.

RESULTS

OCTOBER
10—Anaheim .... L 3-4
12—Minnesota .... T *2-2
15—Carolina .... W *2-1
17—Columbus .... W 7-1
19—Dallas .... W 5-3
24—At Edmonton .... W 2-1
26—At Calgary .... W *4-3
30—Nashville .... W 7-0

NOVEMBER
2— At N.Y. Islanders .... W 6-1
3— At N.Y. Rangers .... W 3-2
5— At Montreal .... W 5-2
7— Columbus .... L 2-5
9— Toronto .... W 6-3
12—At Vancouver .... L 3-6
15—At Edmonton .... L 0-5
16—At Calgary .... W 1-0
20—At Columbus .... L 2-3
21—Los Angeles .... W *3-2
23—Colorado .... L 1-3
25—San Jose .... L 1-4
27—At Colorado .... T *4-4
29—Calgary .... W 7-2
30—New Jersey .... OTL *4-5

DECEMBER
3— At Boston .... W 4-0
5— Ottawa .... T *2-2
7— At Philadelphia .... W 3-1
8— At Detroit .... OTL *3-4

10—At New Jersey .... L 0-2
12—At Nashville .... T *2-2
14—Atlanta .... W 4-0
17—At Los Angeles .... L 2-6
18—At Anaheim .... L 2-5
20—At Phoenix .... T *3-3
23—Los Angeles .... W 5-0
26—Colorado .... W 3-2
28—At Columbus .... W 6-1
29—Columbus .... W 5-2
31—At Detroit .... L 1-5

JANUARY
2— Chicago .... L 1-4
4— Tampa Bay .... W 5-1
7— At Nashville .... OTL *1-2
9— At San Jose .... W 4-1
11—At Los Angeles .... W 2-1
12—At Anaheim .... L 1-2
14—At Phoenix .... W 4-1
16—N.Y. Islanders .... OTL *2-3
18—Chicago .... W 4-2
20—At Carolina .... W 5-3
21—At Atlanta .... L 4-8
23—At Chicago .... T *3-3
25—Dallas .... L 2-4
28—At Washington .... W 5-3
30—Buffalo .... W *2-1

FEBRUARY
5— At Dallas .... T *2-2
6— N.Y. Rangers .... T *4-4

8— San Jose .... W 4-1
11—At Buffalo .... W 3-2
13—Philadelphia .... OTL *3-4
15—Phoenix .... L 3-5
17—Calgary .... W 5-3
20—Vancouver .... L 2-4
22—At Pittsburgh .... OTL *1-2
23—At Minnesota .... L 1-3
27—Edmonton .... W 4-1

MARCH
1— Minnesota .... W 2-0
4— Nashville .... W *2-1
6— Phoenix .... W 6-3
7— At Detroit .... L 2-7
11—At San Jose .... W 4-2
13—At Vancouver .... T *4-4
15—At Nashville .... W 1-0
18—Vancouver .... W 6-4
20—Anaheim .... W *3-2
22—Detroit .... L 2-4
23—At Dallas .... L 1-3
26—At Minnesota .... W 1-0
27—Florida .... W 2-1
29—Detroit .... L 2-6
31—Edmonton .... T *5-5

APRIL
3— Chicago .... L 4-6
4— At Chicago .... T *2-2
6— At Colorado .... L 2-5
*Denotes overtime game.

SAN JOSE SHARKS
WESTERN CONFERENCE/PACIFIC DIVISION

SAN JOSE SHARKS

Sharks' Schedule
Home games shaded; D=Day game; *Feb. 8 All-Star Game at St. Paul, Minn.

October

SUN	MON	TUE	WED	THU	FRI	SAT
5	6	7	8	9 EDM	10	11 CAL
12 MIN	13	14	15	16 PHI	17	18 OTT
19	20	21 ANA	22	23 CHI	24	25 PHO
26	27	28 CAR	29	30 TB	31	

November

SUN	MON	TUE	WED	THU	FRI	SAT
						1 FLA
2 ATL	3	4	5 NJ	6 BOS	7	8 WAS
9	10	11 COL	12	13 STL	14	15 TOR
16	17	18 NYR	19	20	21 PHO	22 NAS
23	24	25	26 CHI	27	28 D MIN	29
30 D EDM						

December

SUN	MON	TUE	WED	THU	FRI	SAT
	1	2 CAL	3	4 COL	5	6 DAL
7	8	9	10 ANA	11 EDM	12	13 ANA
14	15	16	17 DET	18 STL	19	20
21 ANA	22 ANA	23	24	25	26 LA	27 LA
28	29 NAS	30	31 CBJ			

January

SUN	MON	TUE	WED	THU	FRI	SAT
				1	2 CHI	3 STL
4	5 VAN	6	7	8 CBJ	9	10 D ATL
11	12	13 DAL	14	15 VAN	16	17 COL
18	19 DET	20	21 PHO	22 PHO	23	24 MIN
25	26	27	28 CAL	29	30 DAL	31 NAS

February

SUN	MON	TUE	WED	THU	FRI	SAT
1	2	3 FLA	4	5 PHO	6	7
8*	9	10 BUF	11 DET	12	13	14 CBJ
15	16 PHI	17	18 NAS	19 CHI	20	21
22	23 CBJ	24	25	26 VAN	27 PIT	28
29 STL						

March

SUN	MON	TUE	WED	THU	FRI	SAT
	1	2	3 MON	4	5 COL	6
7 D DAL	8	9 MIN	10	11 NYI	12	13 D LA
14	15	16 DAL	17	18 LA	19 ANA	20
21 EDM	22	23 DET	24	25 CAL	26 PHO	27
28 DAL	29	30	31 LA			

April

SUN	MON	TUE	WED	THU	FRI	SAT
				1	2 VAN	3
4 D LA	5	6	7	8	9	10

2003-04 SEASON
CLUB DIRECTORY

President, CEO and manager of the SJSEE Ownership Group
Greg Jamison

Exec. v.p. and general manager
Doug Wilson

Vice president & assistant g.m.
Wayne Thomas

Head coach
Ron Wilson

Assistant coaches
Tim Hunter
Rob Zettler

Goaltender coach
Warren Strelow

Strength & conditioning coordinator
Mac Read

Assistant to the general manager
Joe Will

Executive assistant
Cathy Hancock

Senior director of media relations & publishing
Ken Arnold

Media relations manager
Scott Emmert

Media relations coordinator
Ben Stephenson

Head trainer
Ray Tufts

Equipment manager
Mike Aldrich

Assistant equipment managers
Kurt Harvey
Roy Sneesby

Team physician
Dr. Arthur J. Ting

Director of advertising and publicity
Beth Brigino

DRAFT CHOICES

Rd.— Player	Overall	Pos.	Last team
1— Milan Michalek	6	RW	Czech Republic
1— Steve Bernier	16	RW	Moncton (QMJHL)
2— Josh Hennessy	43	C	Quebec (QMJHL)
2— Matthew Carle	47	D	River City (USHL)
5— Patrick Ehelechner	139	G	Hannover (Germany)
7— Jonathan Tremblay	201	RW	Acadie-Bathurst (QMJHL)
7— Joe Pavelski	205	C	Waterloo (USHL)
7— Kai Hospelt	216	F	Koln (Germany)
8— Alexander Hult	236	C	Tranas (Sweden)
9— Brian O'Hanley	267	D	Boston College (Hockey East)
9— Carter Lee	276	F	Canterbury HS

MISCELLANEOUS DATA

Home ice (capacity)
HP Pavilion at San Jose (17,496)

Address
525 West Santa Clara Street
San Jose, CA 95113

Business phone
408-287-7070

Ticket information
408-287-7070

Website
sjsharks.com

Training site
Logitech Ice at San Jose

Club colors
Deep pacific teal, gray, burnt orange and black

Radio affiliation
KFOX (98.5 FM)

TV affiliation
FOX Sports Net

TRAINING CAMP ROSTER

No.	FORWARDS	Ht./Wt.	Place	BORN Date	NHL exp.	2002-03 clubs
	Brad Boyes (C)	6-0/181	Mississauga, Ont.	4-17-82	0	St. John's (AHL), Cleveland (AHL)
	Jonathan Cheechoo (RW)	6-0/205	Moose Factory, Ont.	7-15-80	1	Cleveland (AHL), San Jose
25	Vincent Damphousse (C)	6-1/200	Montreal	12-17-67	17	San Jose
	Niko Dimitrakos (RW)	5-11/200	Somerville, Mass.	5-21-79	1	Cleveland (AHL), San Jose
	Jonas Fiedler (RW)	6-2/173	Jihlava, Czechoslovakia	5-29-84	0	Plymouth (OHL)
	Marcel Goc (C)	6-1/187	Calw, West Germany	8-24-83	0	Mannheim (Germany)
9	Adam Graves (LW)	6-0/200	Toronto	4-12-68	16	San Jose
13	Todd Harvey (RW)	6-0/205	Hamilton, Ont.	2-17-75	9	San Jose
15	Alex Korolyuk (RW)	5-9/195	Moscow, U.S.S.R.	1-15-76	5	Kazan (Russian Div. III)
	Ryan Kraft (C)	5-9/181	Bottineau, N.D.	11-7-75	1	Cleveland (AHL), San Jose
	Eric LaPlante (LW)	6-0/185	St. Maurice, Que.	12-1-79	0	Cleveland (AHL)
	Lynn Loyns (C)	5-11/200	Naicam, Sask.	2-22-81	1	San Jose
12	Patrick Marleau (C)	6-2/210	Aneroid, Sask.	9-15-79	6	San Jose
18	Alyn McCauley (C)	5-11/190	Brockville, Ont.	5-29-77	6	Toronto, San Jose
	Mike Morris (RW)	6-0/182	Dorchester, Mass.	7-14-83	0	Northeastern University (ECAC)
	Kris Newbury (C)	5-10/197	Brampton, Ont.	2-19-82	0	Sarnia (OHL)
27	Scott Parker (RW)	6-4/220	Hanford, Calif.	1-29-78	4	Colorado
	Tomas Plihal (LW/RW)	6-1/180	Frydlant, Czechoslovakia	3-28-83	0	Kootenay (WHL)
15	Wayne Primeau (C)	6-3/225	Scarborough, Ont.	6-4-76	9	Pittsburgh, San Jose
18	Mike Ricci (C)	6-0/190	Scarborough, Ont.	10-27-71	13	San Jose
16	Mark Smith (C)	5-10/200	Edmonton	10-24-77	3	San Jose
19	Marco Sturm (LW)	6-0/195	Dingolfing, West Germany	9-8-78	6	San Jose
17	Scott Thornton (LW)	6-3/216	London, Ont.	1-9-71	13	San Jose
	Chad Wiseman (LW)	6-0/190	Burlington, Ont.	3-25-81	1	San Jose
	Miroslav Zalesak (RW)	6-0/185	Skalica, Czechoslovakia	1-2-80	1	Cleveland (AHL), San Jose
	DEFENSEMEN					
	Matt Carkner	6-4/222	Winchester, Ont.	11-3-80	0	Cleveland (AHL)
	Tim Conboy	6-1/205	Farmington, Minn.	3-22-82	0	St. Cloud State (WCHA)
	Rob Davison	6-2/210	St. Catharines, Ont.	5-1-80	1	Cleveland (AHL), San Jose
	Christian Ehrhoff	6-2/183	Moers, West Germany	7-6-82	0	Krefeld Pinguine (Germany)
	Jim Fahey	6-0/215	Boston	5-11-79	1	Cleveland (AHL), San Jose
	Jesse Fibiger	6-3/205	Victoria, B.C.	4-4-78	1	Cleveland (AHL), San Jose
22	Scott Hannan	6-2/220	Richmond, B.C.	1-23-79	5	San Jose
	Michael Hutchins	6-0/185	Wolfeboro, N.H.	10-27-82	0	
15	John Jakopin	6-5/239	Toronto	5-16-75	6	Cleveland (AHL), San Jose
	Tero Maatta	6-1/205	Vantaa, Finland	1-2-82	0	Blues Espoo (Finland)
18	Kyle McLaren	6-4/219	Humboldt, Sask.	6-18-77	8	San Jose
40	Mike Rathje	6-5/235	Mannville, Alta.	5-11-74	10	San Jose
	Dan Spang	6-0/200	Winchester, Mass.	8-16-83	0	Boston University (ECAC)
7	Brad Stuart	6-2/210	Rocky Mountain House, Alta.	11-6-79	4	San Jose
	Tom Walsh	6-0/190	Arlington, Mass.	4-22-83	0	Harvard University (ECAC)
	GOALTENDERS					
37	Miikka Kiprusoff	6-2/190	Turku, Finland	10-26-76	3	San Jose
35	Evgeni Nabokov	6-0/200	Kamenogorsk, U.S.S.R.	7-25-75	4	San Jose
	Dimitri Patzold	6-0/183	Kamenogorsk, U.S.S.R.	2-3-83	0	
	Vesa Toskala	5-9/172	Tampere, Finland	5-20-77	2	Cleveland (AHL), San Jose

2002-03 REVIEW
INDIVIDUAL STATISTICS

SCORING

	Games	G	A	Pts.	PIM	+/-	PPG	SHG	GWG	GTG	Sht.	Pct.	Won	Lost	Pct.	TOI
Teemu Selanne	82	28	36	64	30	-6	7	0	5	1	253	11.1	45	62	42.1	19:13
Vincent Damphousse	82	23	38	61	66	-13	15	0	6	0	176	13.1	672	629	51.7	19:09
Patrick Marleau	82	28	29	57	33	-10	8	1	3	1	172	16.3	663	740	47.3	18:31
Marco Sturm	82	28	20	48	16	9	6	0	2	0	208	13.5	40	43	48.2	16:30
Owen Nolan*	61	22	20	42	91	-5	8	3	4	0	192	11.5	114	112	50.4	18:08
Mike Ricci	75	11	23	34	53	-12	5	1	2	0	101	10.9	594	558	51.6	16:30
Mike Rathje	82	7	22	29	48	-19	3	0	1	0	147	4.8	0	1	0.0	24:06
Scott Hannan	81	3	19	22	61	0	1	0	0	0	103	2.9	1	2	33.3	24:15
Scott Thornton	41	9	12	21	41	-7	4	0	1	0	64	14.1	3	3	50.0	13:52
Jim Fahey	43	1	19	20	33	-3	0	0	0	0	66	1.5	1	0	100.0	18:19
Todd Harvey	76	3	16	19	74	5	0	0	0	0	64	4.7	53	66	44.5	9:56
Adam Graves	82	9	9	18	32	-14	1	0	0	0	118	7.6	14	16	46.7	13:02
Jonathan Cheechoo	66	9	7	16	39	-5	0	0	3	1	94	9.6	3	5	37.5	10:42

	Games	G	A	Pts.	PIM	+/-	PPG	SHG	GWG	GTG	Sht.	Sht. Pct.	Won	Lost	Pct.	TOI
Dan McGillis*	37	3	13	16	30	-6	2	0	0	1	71	4.2	0	0	—	21:53
Mark Smith	75	4	11	15	64	1	0	0	0	0	68	5.9	360	272	57.0	9:20
Brad Stuart	36	4	10	14	46	-6	2	0	1	0	63	6.3	0	0	—	20:53
Niko Dimitrakos	21	6	7	13	8	-7	3	0	0	1	34	17.6	1	1	50.0	14:15
Niklas Sundstrom*	47	2	10	12	22	-4	0	0	0	0	36	5.6	0	1	0.0	14:09
Bryan Marchment*	67	2	9	11	108	-2	0	0	0	0	66	3.0	0	0	—	19:19
Alyn McCauley*	16	3	7	10	4	-2	3	0	0	0	29	10.3	41	40	50.6	17:29
Marcus Ragnarsson*	25	1	7	8	30	2	0	0	0	0	27	3.7	2	0	100.0	24:56
Kyle McLaren	33	0	8	8	30	-10	0	0	0	0	43	0.0	0	0	—	22:39
Jeff Jillson	26	0	6	6	9	-7	0	0	0	0	22	0.0	0	0	—	13:45
Matt Bradley	46	2	3	5	37	-1	0	0	0	0	21	9.5	0	1	0.0	7:53
Lynn Loyns	19	3	0	3	19	-4	0	0	0	0	12	25.0	0	1	0.0	7:50
Miroslav Zalesak	10	1	2	3	0	-2	0	0	0	0	8	12.5	0	1	0.0	9:27
Rob Davison	15	1	2	3	22	4	0	0	0	0	15	6.7	0	0	—	17:53
Wayne Primeau*	7	1	1	2	0	2	0	0	0	0	13	7.7	45	53	45.9	15:58
Ryan Kraft	7	0	1	1	0	2	0	0	0	0	1	0.0	14	27	34.1	8:32
Shawn Heins*	20	0	1	1	9	-2	0	0	0	0	10	0.0	0	0	—	8:31
Chad Wiseman	4	0	0	0	4	-2	0	0	0	0	1	0.0	0	0	—	9:18
Vesa Toskala (g)	11	0	0	0	0	0	0	0	0	0	0	—	0	0	—	—
John Jakopin	12	0	0	0	11	0	0	0	0	0	3	0.0	0	0	—	8:11
Jesse Fibiger	16	0	0	0	2	-5	0	0	0	0	2	0.0	0	0	—	6:04
Miikka Kiprusoff (g) ..	22	0	0	0	0	0	0	0	0	0	0	—	0	0	—	—
Evgeni Nabokov (g)...	55	0	0	0	10	0	0	0	0	0	0	—	0	0	—	—

GOALTENDING

	Games	GS	Min.	GA	SO	Avg.	W	L	T	EN	PPG Allow	SHG Allow	Shots	Save Pct.
Vesa Toskala	11	9	537	21	1	2.35	4	3	1	1	5	3	287	.927
Evgeni Nabokov	55	55	3227	146	3	2.71	19	28	8	5	48	4	1561	.906
Miikka Kiprusoff	22	18	1199	65	1	3.25	5	14	0	1	15	3	537	.879

*Played with two or more NHL teams.

RESULTS

OCTOBER

10— Detroit	L.....3-6
12— At Vancouver	L.....3-5
17— Edmonton	W.....4-3
19— Colorado	L.....1-3
21— Vancouver	L.....2-5
24— At Nashville	W.....2-1
25— At Columbus	W.....5-4
27— At Chicago	L.....2-3
29— At Detroit	L.....2-3
31— At Minnesota	OTL....*1-2

NOVEMBER

3— At Anaheim	W......4-3
5— Los Angeles	W.....5-2
7— Nashville	T....*2-2
9— Minnesota	L.....2-4
11— N.Y. Rangers	L.....4-5
13— At Atlanta	OTL....*2-3
15— At Tampa Bay	L.....2-4
16— At Florida	W.....7-3
19— At Washington	W.....3-2
21— At Philadelphia	T....*2-2
23— At Pittsburgh	L.....1-4
25— At St. Louis	W.....4-1
27— At Nashville	L.....2-4
30— Phoenix	L......2-3

DECEMBER

3— At Phoenix	W....*3-2
6— Columbus	W.....3-2
7— Nashville	L.....2-4

12— Pittsburgh	W.....5-2
14— Washington	W.....2-0
16— At N.Y. Rangers	OTL....*1-2
17— At Montreal	W.....3-1
19— At Ottawa	L.....3-9
21— At Toronto	T....*3-3
23— At Boston	L.....2-5
26— Anaheim	W.....4-1
28— Chicago	T....*3-3
30— Philadelphia	W.....2-1

JANUARY

2— Dallas	L.....1-3
4— Colorado	L.....1-6
6— Edmonton	T....*5-5
9— St. Louis	L.....1-4
11— Vancouver	W.....3-0
13— At Los Angeles	OTL....*2-3
16— Buffalo	T....*2-2
18— Dallas	L.....1-3
20— At Phoenix	L.....1-3
22— New Jersey	OTL....*4-5
25— Minnesota	W.....4-1
27— At Los Angeles	W.....3-0
28— Los Angeles	W.....3-1
30— Anaheim	L.....3-4

FEBRUARY

5— Carolina	W.....6-2
7— At Minnesota	L.....3-4
8— At St. Louis	L.....1-4
10— At Detroit	L.....4-5

12— At Columbus	L.....0-1
14— At Chicago	W.....4-2
16— At Dallas	L.....1-3
17— At Los Angeles	L.....2-3
19— N.Y. Islanders	L.....0-3
21— Columbus	W.....6-0
24— Calgary	W.....5-2
27— At Vancouver	W.....3-2

MARCH

1— At Calgary	L.....3-4
4— At Edmonton	L.....1-2
6— Montreal	W....*4-3
8— At Phoenix	L.....4-6
9— At Dallas	L.....0-3
11— St. Louis	L.....2-4
13— At Anaheim	OTL....*2-3
15— Calgary	W.....3-2
17— Chicago	OTL....*2-3
20— At Colorado	L.....0-2
21— Boston	W.....3-2
22— Anaheim	OTL....*2-3
24— Tampa Bay	L.....1-4
27— Detroit	W.....3-0
29— Dallas	L.....3-4
31— At Colorado	L.....1-3

APRIL

2— At Calgary	T....*2-2
3— At Edmonton	T....*3-3
6— Phoenix	T....*3-3

*Denotes overtime game.

TAMPA BAY LIGHTNING
EASTERN CONFERENCE/SOUTHEAST DIVISION

Lightning Schedule
Home games shaded; D=Day game; *Feb. 8 All-Star Game at St. Paul, Minn.

October

SUN	MON	TUE	WED	THU	FRI	SAT
5	6	7	8	9	10 BOS	11
12	13	14	15	16 PHO	17	18 NJ
19	20	21 ATL	22	23 CBJ	24	25 MIN
26	27	28	29	30 SJ	31	

November

SUN	MON	TUE	WED	THU	FRI	SAT
						1 CAR
2	3	4 WAS	5	6 LA	7	8 PIT
9 CAR	10	11 FLA	12	13	14 WAS	15
16	17	18	19	20 NYI	21	22 BUF
23 CAR	24	25 NYR	26	27	28 STL	29 ATL
30						

December

SUN	MON	TUE	WED	THU	FRI	SAT
	1	2 MON	3	4 OTT	5	6 BUF
7 NYR	8	9 NYI	10	11 OTT	12	13 MON
14	15	16 TOR	17	18 PHI	19	20 DAL
21	22	23 BOS	24	25	26 ATL	27 BOS
28	29 ANA	30	31 D FLA			

January

SUN	MON	TUE	WED	THU	FRI	SAT
				1	2 D CBJ	3 PHI
4	5	6 OTT	7	8 MON	9 NJ	10
11 NYR	12	13 PIT	14	15 CAR	16	17 FLA
18	19 COL	20	21 VAN	22 EDM	23	24 CAL
25	26	27 PIT	28	29 PIT	30	31 ATL

February

SUN	MON	TUE	WED	THU	FRI	SAT
1	2 PHI	3 WAS	4	5 NAS	6	7
8*	9	10 TOR	11	12 MON	13	14 FLA
15	16	17 PHI	18	19 STL	20 BUF	21
22 WAS	23	24	25 ATL	26 TOR	27	28 WAS
29						

March

SUN	MON	TUE	WED	THU	FRI	SAT
	1 COL	2	3 CHI	4	5 NJ	6 FLA
7	8 DET	9	10 CAR	11	12 NYR	13 CAR
14	15	16 NYI	17	18 BUF	19	20 D BOS
21 D NYI	22	23 TOR	24	25 NJ	26	27 WAS
28	29 OTT	30	31			

April

SUN	MON	TUE	WED	THU	FRI	SAT
				1 FLA	2	3 ATL
4	5	6	7	8	9	10

2003-04 SEASON
CLUB DIRECTORY

Chief executive officer & governor
Tom Wilson
President
Ron Campbell
General manager
Jay Feaster
Head coach
John Tortorella
Associate coach
Craig Ramsay

Goaltending coach
Jeff Reese
Vice president of public relations
Bill Wickett
Director of public relations
Jay Preble
Media relations manager
Jay Levin

DRAFT CHOICES

Rd.— Player	Overall	Pos.	Last team
2— Mike Egener	34	D	Calgary (WHL)
2— Matt Smaby	41	D	Shattuck-St. Mary's HS
3— Johnathan Boutin	96	G	Halifax (QMJHL)
6— Doug O'Brien	192	D	Hull (QMJHL)
7— Gerald Coleman	224	G	London (OHL)
7— Jay Rosehill	227	D	Olds (AJHL)
8— Raimonds Danilics	255	F	Stalkers (Latvia)
8— Brady Greco	256	D	Chicago (USHL)
9— Albert Vishnyakov	273	W	Kazan (Russia)
9— Zbynek Hrdel	286	C	Rimouski (QMJHL)
9— Nick TarnaskY	287	C	Lethbridge (WHL)

MISCELLANEOUS DATA

Home ice (capacity)
Ice Palace (19,758)
Address
401 Channelside Drive
Tampa, Fla. 33602
Business phone
813-301-6500
Ticket information
813-301-6600
Website
www.tampabaylightning.com

Training site
Brandon, FL
Club colors
Black, blue, silver and white
Radio affiliation
WDAE (620 AM)
TV affiliation
Sunshine Network (Cable)

TAMPA BAY LIGHTNING

No.	FORWARDS	Ht./Wt.	Place	Date	NHL exp.	2002-03 clubs
29	Dmitry Afanasenkov (LW)	6-2/200	Arkhangelsk, U.S.S.R.	5-12-80	2	Springfield (AHL)
15	Nikita Alexeev (RW)	6-5/215	Murmansk, U.S.S.R.	12-27-81	2	Springfield (AHL), Tampa Bay
25	Dave Andreychuk (LW) ..	6-4/220	Hamilton, Ont.	9-29-63	21	Tampa Bay
	Evgeni Artukhin (RW)	6-4/213	Moscow, U.S.S.R.	4-4-83	0	
	Dmitri Bezrukov (LW)	6-3/195	Tataria, U.S.S.R.	11-9-77	0	Spartak Moscow (Russian)
	Anton But (RW)	6-1/190	Kharkov, U.S.S.R.	7-3-80	0	Lokomotiv Yaroslavl (Russian)
46	Martin Cibak (C)	6-1/195	Liptovmikulas, Czech.	5-17-80	1	Springfield (AHL)
7	Ben Clymer (RW)	6-1/195	Edina, Minn.	4-11-78	4	Tampa Bay
11	Chris Dingman (LW)	6-4/245	Edmonton	7-6-76	6	Tampa Bay
	Matt Elich (RW)	6-3/196	Detroit	9-22-79	2	Pensacola (ECHL), Wheeling (ECHL)
	Ruslan Fedotenko (LW) .	6-2/190	Kiev, U.S.S.R.	1-18-79	3	Tampa Bay
	Adam Henrich (LW)	6-4/216	Toronto	1-19-84	0	Brampton (OHL)
28	Sheldon Keefe (RW)	5-11/185	Brampton, Ont.	9-17-80	3	Springfield (AHL), Tampa Bay
4	Vincent Lecavalier (C)....	6-4/205	Ile-Bizard, Que.	4-21-80	5	Tampa Bay
33	Fredrik Modin (LW)	6-4/220	Sundsvall, Sweden	10-8-74	7	Tampa Bay
41	Jimmie Olvestad (LW) ...	6-1/194	Stockholm, Sweden	2-16-80	2	Springfield (AHL), Tampa Bay
	Eric Perrin (C)	5-9/175	Laval, Que.	11-1-75	0	HPK Hameenlinna (Finland)
	Alexander Polushin (C)..	6-3/198	Kirov, U.S.S.R.	5-8-83	0	CSKA Moscow (Russian)
19	Brad Richards (C)........	6-1/187	Montague, P.E.I.	5-2-80	3	Tampa Bay
36	Andre Roy (RW)	6-4/213	Port Chester, N.Y.	2-8-75	6	Tampa Bay
	Eero Somervuori (RW) ...	5-10/167	Jarvenpaa, Finland	2-7-79	0	HPK Hameenlinna (Finland)
26	Martin St. Louis (RW) ...	5-9/185	Laval, Que.	6-18-75	5	Tampa Bay
61	Cory Stillman (RW)	6-0/194	Peterborough, Ont.	12-20-73	9	St. Louis
	Alexander Svitov (C)......	6-3/198	Omsk, U.S.S.R.	11-3-82	1	Springfield (AHL), Tampa Bay
27	Tim Taylor (C).............	6-1/188	Stratford, Ont.	2-6-69	10	Tampa Bay
	Ryan Tobler (LW)...........	6-3/192	Calgary	5-13-76	1	Springfield (AHL), Chicago (AHL)
24	Shane Willis (RW)	6-0/176	Edmonton	6-13-77	4	Springfield (AHL)
	DEFENSEMEN					
22	Dan Boyle	5-11/190	Ottawa	7-12-76	5	Tampa Bay
5	Jassen Cullimore	6-5/220	Simcoe, Ont.	12-4-72	9	Tampa Bay
	Gerard Dicaire...............	6-2/190	Faro, Yukon	9-14-82	0	Kootenay (WHL)
6	Sascha Goc...................	6-2/220	Calw, West Germany	4-17-79	3	
	Andreas Holmqvist	6-3/187	Stockholm, Sweden	7-23-81	0	Linkopings (Sweden)
	Mike Jones	6-4/195	Toledo, Ohio	5-18-76	0	Pensacola (ECHL)
13	Pavel Kubina	6-4/230	Celadna, Czechoslovakia	4-15-77	6	Tampa Bay
	Kristian Kudroc.............	6-6/229	Michalovce, Czechoslovakia	5-21-81	2	Springfield (AHL)
5	Janne Laukkanen	6-1/194	Lahti, Finland	3-19-70	9	Hartford (AHL), Pittsburgh, Tampa Bay
	Brad Lukowich...............	6-1/200	Cranbrook, B.C.	8-12-76	6	Tampa Bay
2	Stan Neckar	6-1/207	Ceske-Budejovice, Czech.	12-22-75	9	Tampa Bay
44	Nolan Pratt	6-2/208	Fort McMurray, Alta.	8-14-75	7	Tampa Bay
	Marek Priechodsky	6-2/194	Obranca, Slovakia.	10-24-79	0	Pensacola (ECHL)
21	Cory Sarich...................	6-3/193	Saskatoon, Sask.	8-16-78	5	Tampa Bay
3	Pascal Trepanier	6-0/210	Gaspe, Que.	4-9-73	6	Nashville, Milwaukee (AHL), San Antonio (AHL)
	Jeremy Van Hoof..........	6-3/200	Lindsay, Ont.	8-12-81	0	Pensacola (ECHL), Springfield (AHL)
	GOALTENDERS					
	Brian Eklund	6-4/200	Braintree, Mass.	5-24-80	0	Pensacola (ECHL), Springfield (AHL)
47	John Grahame	6-2/215	Denver	8-31-75	4	Boston, Tampa Bay
35	Nikolai Khabibulin..........	6-1/195	Sverdlovsk, U.S.S.R.	1-13-73	8	Tampa Bay
	Evgeny Konstantinov	6-0/167	Kazan, U.S.S.R.	3-29-81	2	Springfield (AHL), Tampa Bay
	Vasily Koshechkin.........	6-6/210	U.S.S.R.	3-27-83	0	
	Michal Lanicek..............	6-1/172	Benesov, Czechoslovakia	7-6-81	0	Muskegon (UHL)
	Fredrik Norrena.............	6-0/185	Pietasaari, Finland	11-29-74	0	
	Joseph Pearce	6-5/215	Mount Pleasant, N.J.	6-29-82	1	

2002-03 REVIEW
INDIVIDUAL STATISTICS

SCORING

	Games	G	A	Pts.	PIM	+/-	PPG	SHG	GWG	GTG	Sht.	Sht. Pct.	Faceoffs Won	Lost	Pct.	TOI
Vaclav Prospal..........	80	22	57	79	53	9	9	0	4	0	134	16.4	83	78	51.6	18:39
Vincent Lecavalier	80	33	45	78	39	0	11	2	3	1	274	12.0	527	673	43.9	19:32
Brad Richards	80	17	57	74	24	3	4	0	2	0	277	6.1	478	529	47.5	19:56
Martin St. Louis	82	33	37	70	32	10	12	3	5	3	201	16.4	14	23	37.8	19:42
Dan Boyle.................	77	13	40	53	44	9	8	0	1	1	136	9.6	0	2	0.0	24:30
Fredrik Modin...........	76	17	23	40	43	7	2	1	4	1	179	9.5	10	25	28.6	17:34

	Games	G	A	Pts.	PIM	+/-	PPG	SHG	GWG	GTG	Sht.	Sht. Pct.	Won	Lost	Pct.	TOI
Dave Andreychuk	72	20	14	34	34	-12	15	0	3	2	170	11.8	652	465	58.4	16:26
Ruslan Fedotenko	76	19	13	32	44	-7	6	0	6	0	114	16.7	44	46	48.9	16:00
Pavel Kubina	75	3	19	22	78	-7	0	0	0	0	139	2.2	0	1	0.0	21:24
Ben Clymer	65	6	12	18	57	-2	1	0	1	0	103	5.8	0	15	0.0	13:38
Andre Roy	62	10	7	17	119	0	0	0	2	0	85	11.8	4	3	57.1	10:45
Brad Lukowich	70	1	14	15	46	4	0	0	0	0	52	1.9	0	1	0.0	17:34
Cory Sarich	82	5	9	14	63	-3	0	0	2	0	79	6.3	0	3	0.0	19:35
Tim Taylor	82	4	8	12	38	-13	0	0	1	0	95	4.2	556	405	57.9	13:42
Alexander Svitov	63	4	4	8	58	-4	1	0	0	0	69	5.8	169	226	42.8	8:50
Nolan Pratt	67	1	7	8	35	-6	0	0	0	0	38	2.6	0	0	—	17:33
Sheldon Keefe	37	2	5	7	24	-1	0	0	0	0	51	3.9	14	18	43.8	10:14
Nikita Alexeev	37	4	2	6	8	-6	1	0	1	1	52	7.7	1	2	33.3	11:30
Stan Neckar	70	1	4	5	43	-6	0	0	1	0	38	2.6	0	0	—	18:41
Jassen Cullimore	28	1	3	4	31	3	0	0	0	0	23	4.3	0	0	—	18:25
Chris Dingman	51	2	1	3	91	-11	0	0	0	0	41	4.9	1	2	33.3	9:34
Jimmie Olvestad	37	0	3	3	16	-2	0	0	0	0	30	0.0	4	8	33.3	10:27
Nikolai Khabibulin (g)	65	0	3	3	8	0	0	0	0	0	0	—	0	0	—	—
Janne Laukkanen*	2	1	0	1	0	1	0	0	0	0	2	50.0	0	0	—	18:14
Brian Holzinger*	5	0	1	1	2	1	0	0	0	0	3	0.0	9	17	34.6	9:08
Marc Bergevin*	1	0	0	0	0	-2	0	0	0	0	0	—	0	0	—	18:26
E. Konstantinov (g)	1	0	0	0	2	0	0	0	0	0	0	—	0	0	—	—
Kevin Hodson (g)	7	0	0	0	2	0	0	0	0	0	0	—	0	0	—	—
John Grahame (g)*	17	0	0	0	9	0	0	0	0	0	0	—	0	0	—	—
Darren Rumble	19	0	0	0	6	-2	0	0	0	0	10	0.0	0	0	—	11:07

GOALTENDING

	Games	GS	Min.	GA	SO	Avg.	W	L	T	EN	PPG Allow	SHG Allow	Shots	Save Pct.
John Grahame*	17	15	914	34	2	2.23	6	5	4	1	24	3	424	.920
Nikolai Khabibulin	65	64	3787	156	4	2.47	30	22	11	5	45	4	1760	.911
Kevin Hodson	7	3	283	12	0	2.54	0	3	1	1	2	1	101	.881
Evgeny Konstantinov	1	0	20	1	0	3.00	0	0	0	0	0	0	6	.833

*Played with two or more NHL teams.

RESULTS

OCTOBER
10— At Florida ....W....*4-3
12— Carolina ....W.....5-1
18— Atlanta ....W.....8-5
19— At Pittsburgh ....T.....*3-3
21— At N.Y. Rangers ....W.....4-2
23— At Columbus ....T.....*2-2
25— Washington ....W.....3-2
26— At New Jersey ....L.....1-5
28— At Florida ....W.....6-1
30— N.Y. Rangers ....W.....3-0

NOVEMBER
1— At Washington ....L.....2-3
2— At Pittsburgh ....L.....3-5
5— At Toronto ....L.....3-4
8— Pittsburgh ....W.....4-1
9— Chicago ....OTL...*2-3
11— Phoenix ....W.....4-2
15— San Jose ....W.....4-2
17— At Carolina ....W...*2-1
19— Philadelphia ....L.....2-3
21— N.Y. Islanders ....L.....2-7
23— At New Jersey ....W.....3-1
27— At Buffalo ....T....*1-1
29— Vancouver ....L.....3-5

DECEMBER
1— At N.Y. Rangers ....L.....3-4
3— At Toronto ....OTL...*3-4
5— Edmonton ....W.....3-2
7— At Boston ....OTL...*2-3

JANUARY
8— At Chicago ....L.....1-3
10— At Minnesota ....L.....3-5
12— At Montreal ....W.....3-2
14— N.Y. Islanders ....W.....4-3
18— At Carolina ....T....*1-1
19— Toronto ....L.....1-2
21— Nashville ....T....*2-2
23— At Washington ....L.....0-3
27— Boston ....W.....5-2
29— N.Y. Rangers ....W.....5-3
31— Ottawa ....L.....3-6

JANUARY
2— At Calgary ....L.....1-4
4— At St. Louis ....L.....1-5
7— Detroit ....W.....1-0
9— Atlanta ....OTL...*2-3
11— New Jersey ....T....*3-3
14— At Ottawa ....L.....0-7
17— Pittsburgh ....L.....2-3
18— At Philadelphia ....L.....2-3
20— Ottawa ....W.....6-2
22— Montreal ....T....*2-2
24— At Dallas ....W.....4-1
25— At Nashville ....L.....2-3
28— At Philadelphia ....W.....3-0
30— Carolina ....W.....3-1

FEBRUARY
4— Washington ....L.....1-5
6— Toronto ....OTL...*2-3
8— At Florida ....T....*4-4

MARCH (column 3)
11— At N.Y. Islanders ....L.....2-6
14— At Atlanta ....T....*2-2
15— Boston ....W.....5-2
17— Washington ....W.....3-1
19— Atlanta ....W.....2-0
21— At Carolina ....T....*2-2
23— Buffalo ....L.....1-4
25— Anaheim ....W.....2-0
27— Florida ....W.....3-1

MARCH
1— At Ottawa ....W.....2-1
4— At N.Y. Islanders ....W.....3-1
5— At Detroit ....L.....2-3
7— Colorado ....W.....4-3
9— Buffalo ....T....*1-1
12— Los Angeles ....W.....4-2
14— At Buffalo ....W.....4-2
15— At Montreal ....W.....2-1
17— Minnesota ....T....*3-3
20— At Los Angeles ....T....*2-2
22— At Phoenix ....W.....4-0
24— At San Jose ....W.....4-1
27— New Jersey ....T....*2-2
29— Florida ....T....*1-1
31— At Boston ....T....*2-2

APRIL
2— Montreal ....W.....2-1
4— Philadelphia ....L.....1-4
6— At Atlanta ....L.....2-6
*Denotes overtime game.

TORONTO MAPLE LEAFS
EASTERN CONFERENCE/NORTHEAST DIVISION

TORONTO MAPLE LEAFS

Maple Leafs' Schedule
Home games shaded; D=Day game; *Feb. 8 All-Star Game at St. Paul, Minn.

October
SUN	MON	TUE	WED	THU	FRI	SAT
5	6	7	8	9	10	11 MON
12 13 WAS	14	15	16 NJ	17	18 MON	
19	20 NYI	21	22 DAL	23 PHO	24	25 WAS
26	27 ATL	28	29	30 BUF	31	

November
SUN	MON	TUE	WED	THU	FRI	SAT
						1 PHI
2 CAR	3	4 PIT	5	6	7 NJ	8 EDM
9	10	11	12 ANA	13 LA	14	15 SJ
16	17	18 CAL	19	20 EDM	21	22 VAN
23	24 VAN	25	26	27 ATL	28	29 OTT
30 NYR						

December
SUN	MON	TUE	WED	THU	FRI	SAT
	1	2 NYR	3	4 BOS	5	6 DET
7	8	9 STL	10	11 MIN	12	13 NYR
14	15	16 TB	17	18	19 WAS	20 MON
21	22	23 FLA	24	25	26 NYR	27 NYI
28	29 FLA	30	31			

January
SUN	MON	TUE	WED	THU	FRI	SAT
				1 BOS	2	3 BUF
4	5 PIT	6 NAS	7	8 OTT	9	10 NJ
11	12	13 CAL	14	15	16 PHI	17 PHI
18	19	20 NYI	21 WAS	22	23	24 MON
25	26	27 CAR	28	29	30 ATL	31 OTT

February
SUN	MON	TUE	WED	THU	FRI	SAT
1	2	3 CHI	4	5 OTT	6	7
8*	9	10 TB	11	12 CBJ	13	14 BUF
15	16 PIT	17 BOS	18	19 CAR	20	21 MON
22	23 CAR	24	25 FLA	26 TB	27	28 NJ
29						

March
SUN	MON	TUE	WED	THU	FRI	SAT
	1	2 BOS	3	4 NYI	5	6 BUF
7	8	9 FLA	10	11 PIT	12	13 MON
14	15 BUF	16 BOS	17	18 PHI	19	20 COL
21	22	23 TB	24	25 BOS	26	27 OTT
28	29 ATL	30	31			

April
SUN	MON	TUE	WED	THU	FRI	SAT
				1	2 BUF	3 OTT
4	5	6	7	8	9	10

2003-04 SEASON
CLUB DIRECTORY

Chairman of the board and governor
Larry Tananbaum
Alternate governor
Brian P. Bellmore
President, CEO and alt. governor
Richard Peddie
Vice chairman and alternate governor
Ken Dryden
Sr. v.p. and g.m., Air Canada Centre
Bob Hunter
Senior vice president, business, CMO
Tom Anselmi
Senior vice president, CFO
Ian Clarke
Vice president, sports communications & community development
John Lashway
Vice president, people
Mardi Walker
V.p. and gen. counsel
Robin Brudner
General manager and head coach
Pat Quinn
Assistant general manager
Mike Penny
Assistant coaches
Keith Acton, Rick Ley
Development coach
Paul Dennis
Community representatives
Wendel Clark, Darryl Sittler

Chief European scout
Thommie Bergman
Director, amateur scouting
Barry Trapp
Scouts
George Armstrong, Bob Johnson, Garth Malarchuk, Murray Oliver, Mike Palmateer, Mark Yannetti
European scouts
Leonid Vaysfeld, Jan Kovac
Director, team services
Casey Vanden Heuvel
Video coach
Reid Mitchell
Director, media relations
Pat Park
Director, community relations
Bev Deeth
Coordinators, community relations
Ryan Janzen, Paula dal Maso
Equipment manager
Brian Papineau
Team doctors
Dr. Michael Clarfield, Dr. Darrell Ogilvie-Harris, Dr. Leith Douglas, Dr. Rob Devenyi, Dr. Simon McGrail
Team dentist
Dr. Allan Hawryluk

DRAFT CHOICES

Rd.— Player	Overall	Pos.	Last team
2— John Doherty	57	D	Andover HS
3— Martin Sagat	91	LW	Trencin (Slovakia)
4— Konstantin Volkov	125	RW	Dynamo Jr. (Russ. Jr.)
5— John Mitchell	158	C	Plymouth (OHL)
7— Jeremy Williams	220	C	Swift Current (WHL)
8— Shaun Landolt	237	RW	Calgary (WHL)

MISCELLANEOUS DATA

Home ice (capacity)
Air Canada Centre (18,819)
Address
Air Canada Centre
40 Bay Street
Toronto, Ont. M5J 2X2
Business phone
416-815-5700
Ticket information
416-815-5700
Website
www.mapleleafs.com

Training site
Toronto
Club colors
Blue and white
Radio affiliation
Mojo Radio (640 AM)
TV affiliation
CBC, TSN, CTV Sportsnet

No.	FORWARDS	Ht./Wt.	Place	BORN Date	NHL exp.	2002-03 clubs
11	Nik Antropov (C)............	6-5/203	Vost, U.S.S.R.	2-18-80	4	Toronto
	Luca Cereda (C).............	6-2/203	Lugano, Switzerland	9-7-81	1	St. John's (AHL)
	Nicolas Corbeil (C)	5-10/177	Laval, Que.	3-30-83	0	Sherbrooke (QMJHL)
27	Shayne Corson (LW)	6-1/202	Barrie, Ont.	8-13-66	18	Toronto
45	Jeff Daw (C)	6-3/190	Carlisle, Ont.	2-28-72	1	Lowell (AHL), Springfield (AHL)
28	Tie Domi (RW)	5-10/200	Windsor, Ont.	11-1-69	14	Toronto
15	Harold Druken (C)	6-0/200	St. John's, Nfld.	1-26-79	4	St. John's (AHL), Vancouver, Toronto, Carolina, Lowell (AHL)
21	Tom Fitzgerald (RW)......	6-0/196	Billerica, Mass.	8-28-68	15	Toronto
44	Aaron Gavey (LW)	6-2/200	Sudbury, Ont.	2-22-74	8	St. John's (AHL), Toronto
93	Doug Gilmour (C)..........	5-11/185	Kingston, Ont.	6-25-63	20	Montreal, Toronto
39	Travis Green (C)............	6-2/200	Castlegar, B.C.	12-20-70	11	Toronto
26	Paul Healey (RW)	6-1/174	Edmonton	3-20-75	4	St. John's (AHL), Toronto
14	Jonas Hoglund (LW)......	6-3/218	Hammaro, Sweden	8-29-72	7	Toronto
	Josh Holden (C)	6-1/190	Calgary	1-18-78	5	St. John's (AHL), Toronto
	Bobby House (RW)........	6-1/210	Whitehorse, Yukon	1-7-73	1	
39	Craig Mills (RW)...........	6-0/195	Toronto	8-27-76	3	St. John's (AHL)
89	Alexander Mogilny (RW)	6-0/200	Khabarovsk, U.S.S.R.	2-18-69	14	Toronto
11	Owen Nolan (RW)..........	6-1/210	Belfast, Northern Ireland	2-12-72	13	Toronto, San Jose
20	Nathan Perrott (RW).......	6-0/215	Owen Sound, Ont.	12-8-76	2	Nashville, Milwaukee (AHL), St. John's (AHL)
22	A. Ponikarovsky (LW)....	6-4/196	Kiev, U.S.S.R.	4-9-80	3	St. John's (AHL), Toronto
21	Robert Reichel (C).........	5-10/186	Litvinov, Czechoslovakia	6-25-71	10	Toronto
19	Mikael Renberg (RW)	6-2/215	Pitea, Sweden	5-5-72	9	Toronto
7	Gary Roberts (LW)	6-1/190	North York, Ont.	5-23-66	17	Toronto
	Matthew Stajan (C)........	6-1/178	Mississauga, Ont.	12-19-83	1	St. John's (AHL), Toronto
	Alexander Steen (C).......	6-1/183	Winnipeg	3-1-84	0	Vastra Frolunda (Sweden)
13	Mats Sundin (C)	6-4/228	Bromma, Sweden	2-13-71	13	Toronto
16	Darcy Tucker (C)...........	5-11/182	Castor, Alta.	3-15-75	8	Toronto
	Kyle Wellwood (C)	5-9/190	Windsor, Ont.	5-16-83	0	Windsor (OHL)

No.	DEFENSEMEN	Ht./Wt.	Place	Date	exp.	2002-03 clubs
2	Wade Belak..................	6-4/225	Saskatoon, Sask.	3-7-76	7	Toronto
	Brendan Bell	6-1/198	Ottawa	3-31-83	0	Ottawa (OHL)
8	Aki Berg......................	6-3/202	Turku, Finland	7-28-77	7	Toronto
	Ryan Bonni	6-4/190	Winnipeg	2-18-79	1	St. John's (AHL)
	Christian Chartier..........	6-0/219	Russel, Man.	10-29-80	0	St. John's (AHL)
	Carlo Colaiacovo...........	6-1/184	Toronto	1-27-83	1	Toronto
44	Anders Eriksson	6-2/220	Bollnas, Sweden	1-9-75	8	St. John's (AHL), Toronto
	Jay Harrison	6-3/200	Oshawa, Ont.	11-3-82	0	St. John's (AHL)
6	Phil Housley	5-10/185	St. Paul, Minn.	3-9-64	21	Toronto, Chicago
	Richard Jackman..........	6-2/192	Toronto	6-28-78	4	St. John's (AHL), Toronto
15	Tomas Kaberle..............	6-2/200	Rakovnik, Czechoslovakia	3-2-78	5	Toronto
	Regan Kelly	6-2/185	Watrous, Sask.	3-9-81	0	St. John's (AHL)
25	Jyrki Lumme.................	6-1/210	Tampere, Finland	7-16-66	15	Toronto
	Bryan Marchment.........	6-1/185	Scarborough, Ont.	5-1-69	15	San Jose, Colorado
24	Bryan McCabe	6-1/204	St. Catharines, Ont.	6-8-75	8	Toronto
3	Marc Moro...................	6-1/220	Toronto	7-17-77	4	St. John's (AHL)
29	Karel Pilar...................	6-3/210	Prague, Czechoslovakia	12-23-77	2	St. John's (AHL), Toronto
	Allan Rourke................	6-2/210	Mississauga, Ont.	3-6-80	0	St. John's (AHL)
	Petr Svoboda................	6-2/200	Jihlava, Czechoslovakia	6-20-80	1	St. John's (AHL)

No.	GOALTENDERS	Ht./Wt.	Place	Date	exp.	2002-03 clubs
20	Ed Belfour....................	5-11/192	Carman, Man.	4-21-65	15	Toronto
30	Sebastien Centomo.......	6-1/193	Montreal	3-26-81	1	Greensboro (ECHL), St. John's (AHL)
	Jamie Hodson..............	6-2/192	Brandon, Man.	4-8-80	0	Greensboro (ECHL), St. John's (AHL)
37	Trevor Kidd	6-2/210	Dugald, Man.	3-29-72	11	Toronto
	Mikael Tellqvist.............	5-11/174	Sundbyberg, Sweden	9-19-79	1	St. John's (AHL), Toronto

2002-03 REVIEW
INDIVIDUAL STATISTICS

SCORING

	Games	G	A	Pts.	PIM	+/-	PPG	SHG	GWG	GTG	Sht.	Sht. Pct.	Faceoffs Won	Lost	Pct.	TOI
Alexander Mogilny	73	33	46	79	12	4	5	3	9	0	165	20.0	6	12	33.3	20:02
Mats Sundin..............	75	37	35	72	58	1	16	3	8	1	223	16.6	995	779	56.1	20:15
Tomas Kaberle...........	82	11	36	47	30	20	4	1	2	1	119	9.2	2	1	66.7	24:50
Nik Antropov	72	16	29	45	124	11	2	1	6	0	102	15.7	249	372	40.1	14:59
Robert Svehla............	82	7	38	45	46	13	2	0	1	0	110	6.4	0	0	—	23:44
Robert Reichel	81	12	30	42	26	7	1	1	1	0	111	10.8	586	537	52.2	14:32

	Games	G	A	Pts.	PIM	+/-	PPG	SHG	GWG	GTG	Sht.	Sht. Pct.	Faceoffs Won	Lost	Pct.	TOI
Darcy Tucker	77	10	26	36	119	-7	4	1	2	0	108	9.3	31	37	45.6	15:20
Mikael Renberg	67	14	21	35	36	5	7	0	1	0	137	10.2	3	6	33.3	13:32
Jonas Hoglund	79	13	19	32	12	2	2	0	3	0	157	8.3	1	2	33.3	12:46
Tie Domi	79	15	14	29	171	-1	4	0	0	0	91	16.5	4	17	19.0	10:56
Travis Green	75	12	12	24	67	2	2	1	3	0	86	14.0	429	373	53.5	12:57
Bryan McCabe	75	6	18	24	135	9	3	0	1	0	149	4.0	0	1	0.0	23:38
Jyrki Lumme	73	6	11	17	46	10	1	0	3	0	72	8.3	0	0	—	20:37
Tom Fitzgerald	66	4	13	17	57	10	0	0	0	0	89	4.5	45	45	50.0	12:06
Shayne Corson	46	7	8	15	49	-5	0	0	0	0	69	10.1	90	112	44.6	15:02
Alyn McCauley*	64	6	9	15	16	3	0	0	0	0	79	7.6	229	286	44.5	12:53
Owen Nolan*	14	7	5	12	16	2	5	0	1	0	29	24.1	27	29	48.2	16:59
Aki Berg	78	4	7	11	28	3	0	0	2	0	49	8.2	0	0	—	15:02
Paul Healey	44	3	7	10	16	8	1	0	0	0	43	7.0	5	8	38.5	12:00
Wade Belak	55	3	6	9	196	-2	0	0	0	0	33	9.1	0	0	—	10:50
Gary Roberts	14	5	3	8	10	-2	3	0	0	0	22	22.7	2	2	50.0	15:34
Karel Pilar	17	3	4	7	12	-7	1	0	1	0	22	13.6	0	0	—	18:29
Glen Wesley*	7	0	3	3	4	3	0	0	0	0	5	0.0	0	0	—	20:41
Alexei Ponikarovsky	13	0	3	3	11	4	0	0	0	0	13	0.0	1	3	25.0	10:43
Harold Druken*	5	0	2	2	2	1	0	0	0	0	8	0.0	11	14	44.0	12:50
Ric Jackman	42	0	2	2	41	-10	0	0	0	0	35	0.0	0	0	—	13:58
Ed Belfour (g)	62	0	2	2	24	0	0	0	0	0	0	—	0	0	—	—
Matt Stajan	1	1	0	1	0	1	0	0	0	0	1	100.0	4	8	33.3	11:00
Josh Holden	5	1	0	1	2	-2	0	0	0	0	6	16.7	0	0	—	8:05
Carlo Colaiacovo	2	0	1	1	0	0	0	0	0	0	1	0.0	0	0	—	13:42
Aaron Gavey	5	0	1	1	0	1	0	0	0	0	8	0.0	15	16	48.4	11:19
Doug Gilmour*	1	0	0	0	0	0	0	0	0	0	0	—	0	1	0.0	4:51
Phil Housley*	1	0	0	0	2	-1	0	0	0	0	3	0.0	0	0	—	16:04
Mikael Tellqvist (g)	3	0	0	0	0	0	0	0	0	0	0	—	0	0	—	—
Anders Eriksson	4	0	0	0	0	1	0	0	0	0	7	0.0	0	0	—	19:02
Trevor Kidd (g)	19	0	0	0	0	0	0	0	0	0	1	0.0	0	0	—	

GOALTENDING

	Games	GS	Min.	GA	SO	Avg.	W	L	T	EN	PPG Allow	SHG Allow	Shots	Save Pct.
Ed Belfour	62	62	3738	141	7	2.26	37	20	5	4	37	6	1816	.922
Mikael Tellqvist	3	1	86	4	0	2.79	1	1	0	0	0	0	38	.895
Trevor Kidd	19	19	1143	59	0	3.10	6	10	2	0	19	1	565	.896

*Played with two or more NHL teams.

RESULTS

OCTOBER
10—At Pittsburgh ....W.....6-0
12—Ottawa ....L......1-2
14—Pittsburgh.......................L......4-5
15—At N.Y. Rangers ....L......4-5
17—Phoenix ....W.....5-3
19—At Montreal......................T.....*2-2
21—Boston ....L......1-4
23—Florida ....L......1-4
26—N.Y. Rangers....................L......3-4
28—Anaheim ....W.....5-2
31—Atlanta ....T.....*3-3

NOVEMBER
2—Montreal ....L......2-5
5—Tampa Bay ....W.....4-3
8—At Dallas ....L......1-2
9—At St. Louis ....L......3-6
12—Los Angeles ....W....*4-3
15—At Buffalo ....W.....3-2
16—Detroit ....L......1-2
19—Boston ....W.....2-0
23—Philadelphia......................W.....6-0
25—At Ottawa ....L......0-2
26—Washington ....W.....5-4
29—At Philadelphia ....W.....3-0
30—Buffalo.............................W.....3-1

DECEMBER
3— Tampa Bay ....W....*4-3
6— At N.Y. Islanders................L......2-4
7— New Jersey.......................W.....1-0

10—Pittsburgh ....W.....4-2
12—At Philadelphia..................L......1-2
14—N.Y. Rangers ....W.....4-1
16—At Atlanta ....L......0-1
18—At Florida ....T.....*2-2
19—At Tampa Bay ....W.....2-1
21—San Jose..........................T.....*3-3
23—Atlanta ....W.....5-1
27—At Calgary ....W.....4-3
28—At Edmonton ....OTL...*2-3
31—At Vancouver....................W.....5-3

JANUARY
3— At New Jersey ....L......0-2
4— New Jersey.......................W.....2-1
7— Boston ....W.....5-2
9—At Pittsburgh ....W.....4-2
11—At Boston ....L......2-6
13—At N.Y. Rangers.................L......1-5
14—Calgary ....W.....3-2
17—At Washington ....W.....4-1
18—At Montreal ....W....*3-2
21—Philadelphia......................L......1-3
24—At Buffalo ....L......0-4
25—Colorado..........................L......0-3
29—At Carolina ....W.....3-2
30—At Atlanta ....W.....5-2

FEBRUARY
5— At Florida ....W.....6-0
6— At Tampa Bay ....W....*3-2
8— Montreal ....W.....3-1

11—Edmonton ....L......4-5
12—At Chicago ....W.....3-1
15—Ottawa ....W.....2-1
18—Carolina ....W.....4-3
20—At Washington ....W.....6-2
22—At Montreal ....W.....5-3
23—Nashville ....L......2-5
25—N.Y. Islanders....................W.....5-2
27—At Detroit ....L......2-7

MARCH
1—Carolina ....W.....4-1
3— Florida ....L......1-2
4—At Ottawa ....L......1-4
6—At Buffalo ....L......2-4
8—Vancouver ....T.....*3-3
10—At Edmonton ....W.....3-2
13—At Calgary ....OTL...*3-4
15—At Vancouver.....................W.....1-0
18—N.Y. Islanders....................T.....*3-3
20—At Columbus ....OTL...*3-4
22—Buffalo.............................W....*3-2
24—At Boston ....L......2-3
25—At Carolina ....T.....*3-3
28—At N.Y. Islanders................W.....5-2
29—Washington ....W....*4-3

APRIL
1— At New Jersey ....W....*3-2
3— Minnesota ....W.....2-1
5— Ottawa ....L......1-3
*Denotes overtime game.

VANCOUVER CANUCKS
WESTERN CONFERENCE/NORTHWEST DIVISION

VANCOUVER CANUCKS

Canucks' Schedule
Home games shaded; D=Day game; *Feb. 8 All-Star Game at St. Paul, Minn.

October

SUN	MON	TUE	WED	THU	FRI	SAT
5	6	7	8	9 CAL	10	11 EDM
12	13 CBJ	14	15	16 DET	17	18 MIN
19	20 BUF	21	22 STL	23	24	25
26 PHO	27	28 CBJ	29	30 LA	31 PHO	

November

SUN	MON	TUE	WED	THU	FRI	SAT
						1
2	3 DET	4	5 NAS	6 STL	7	8 MIN
9	10	11 MIN	12	13 PHI	14	15 BOS
16	17	18 MON	19	20 CHI	21	22 TOR
23	24 TOR	25 MON	26	27 OTT	28	29 CAL
30						

December

SUN	MON	TUE	WED	THU	FRI	SAT
	1	2	3	4 CAL	5	6 MIN
7	8	9 PIT	10	11 COL	12	13
14 CAR	15	16 NAS	17 DAL	18	19	20 EDM
21	22 LA	23	24	25	26 CAL	27 EDM
28	29 COL	30	31 CHI			

January

SUN	MON	TUE	WED	THU	FRI	SAT
				1	2 COL	3 CAL
4	5 SJ	6	7	8 LA	9 ANA	10
11 FLA	12	13 PHO	14	15 SJ	16	17 ANA
18	19 DAL	20	21 TB	22	23	24
25 NAS	26	27 CHI	28	29 STL	30	31 WAS

February

SUN	MON	TUE	WED	THU	FRI	SAT
1	2 NYR	3 NYI	4	5 NJ	6	7
8*	9	10	11 CAL	12	13 ATL	14 ANA
15	16 COL	17	18	19 MIN	20	21 EDM
22	23	24 DET	25	26 SJ	27	28 STL
29						

March

SUN	MON	TUE	WED	THU	FRI	SAT
	1	2	3 COL	4	5 DET	6 CBJ
7	8 COL	9	10 MIN	11	12 EDM	13 OTT
14	15	16 NAS	17	18 DAL	19 CHI	20
21 CBJ	22	23	24 LA	25	26	27 DAL
28	29 PHO	30	31 ANA			

April

SUN	MON	TUE	WED	THU	FRI	SAT
				1	2 SJ	3 EDM
4	5	6	7	8	9	10

2003-04 SEASON
CLUB DIRECTORY

Chairman & governor
John E. McCaw Jr.
President, chief executive officer
Stanley B. McCammon
President & general manager, alt. gov.
Brian P. Burke
Chief operating officer, alternate gov.
David Cobb
Senior v.p., sales and marketing
John Rizzardini
V.p. and g.m., arena operations
Harvey Jones
Vice president, finance & CFO
Victor de Bonis
V.p., broadcast and new media
Chris Hebb
Sr. v.p., director of hockey operations
David M. Nonis
Vice president, player personnel
Steve Tambellini
Head coach
Marc Crawford
Assistant coaches
Jack McIlhargey
Mike Johnston
Strength & conditioning coach
Peter Twist
Assistant coach, video
Barry Smith
Manager, media relations
Chris Brumwell
Director, community relations
Veronica Varhaug

Manager, game entertainment & special events
Karen Brydon
Mgr., community relations, foundation
Allanah Mooney
Professional scouts
Bob Murray, Shawn Dineen
European scouts
Thomas Gradin
Russian scouts
Sergei Chibisov
Chief amateur scout
Ron Delorme
Amateur scouts
Barry Dean, Jim Eagle, Tim Lenardon,
Mario Marois, Jack McCartan, Mike
McHugh, Dave Morrison, Ken Slater,
Daryl Stanley
Equipment manager
Pat O'Neill
Assistant equipment manager
Darren Granger
Assistant equipment trainer
Jamie Hendricks
Team doctors
Dr. Rui Avelar, Dr. Bill Regan
Team dentist
Dr. David Lawson
Team chiropractor
Dr. Sid Sheard
Team optometrist
Dr. Alan R. Boyco

DRAFT CHOICES

Rd.— Player	Overall	Pos.	Last team
1— Ryan Kesler	23	C/LW	Ohio State (CCHA)
4— Brandon Nolan	111	C	Oshawa (OHL)
4— Ty Morris	128	LW	St. Albert (AJHL)
5— Nicklas Danielsson	160	RW	Brynas (Sweden)
6— Chad Brownlee	190	D	Vernon (BCHL)
7— Francois-Pierre Guenette	222	C/RW	Halifax (QMJHL)
8— Sergei Topol	252	F	Omsk (Russia)
8— Nathan McIver	254	D	Toronto-St. Michael's (OHL)
9— Matthew Hansen	285	D	Seattle (WHL)

MISCELLANEOUS DATA

Home ice (capacity)
General Motors Place (18,422)
Address
800 Griffiths Way
Vancouver, B.C. V6B 6G1
Business phone
604-899-7400
Ticket information
604-280-4400
Website
www.canucks.com

Training site
Burnaby, B.C.
Club colors
Deep blue, sky blue, deep red, white and silver
Radio affiliation
CKNW (980 AM)
TV affiliation
Sportsnet (Cable)

TRAINING CAMP ROSTER

VANCOUVER CANUCKS

No.	FORWARDS	Ht./Wt.	Place	BORN — Date	NHL exp.	2002-03 clubs
44	Todd Bertuzzi (LW)	6-3/230	Sudbury, Ont.	2-2-75	8	Vancouver
	Tyler Bouck (RW)	6-0/185	Camrose, Alta.	1-13-80	2	Manitoba (AHL)
13	Artem Chubarov (C)	6-1/190	Gorky, U.S.S.R.	12-12-79	4	Vancouver
24	Matt Cooke (LW)	5-11/205	Belleville, Ont.	9-7-78	5	Vancouver
61	Fedor Fedorov (C)..........	6-3/187	Moscow, U.S.S.R.	6-11-81	1	Manitoba (AHL), Vancouver
	Chris Herperger (LW)	6-0/190	Esterhazy, Sask.	2-24-74	4	Atlanta, Chicago (AHL), Manitoba (AHL)
	Pat Kavanagh (RW)	6-3/192	Ottawa	3-14-79	2	Manitoba (AHL), Vancouver
	Jason King (RW)	6-1/195	Corner Brook, Nfld.	9-14-81	1	Manitoba (AHL), Vancouver
26	Trent Klatt (RW)	6-1/205	Robbinsdale, Minn.	1-30-71	12	Vancouver
20	Darren Langdon (LW)....	6-1/210	Deer Lake, Nfld.	1-8-71	9	Vancouver, Carolina
	Brad Leeb (LW)	5-11/180	Red Deer, Alta.	8-27-79	2	St. John's (AHL)
16	Trevor Linden (RW)	6-4/215	Medicine Hat, Alta.	4-11-70	15	Vancouver
10	Mats Lindgren (C)	6-2/202	Skelleftea, Sweden	10-1-74	7	Manitoba (AHL), Vancouver
32	Brad May (LW)	6-1/210	Toronto	11-29-71	12	Vancouver, Phoenix
7	Brendan Morrison (C)...	5-11/190	Pitt Meadows, B.C.	8-12-75	6	Vancouver
	Justin Morrison (RW)....	6-3/200	Los Angeles	8-10-79	0	Manitoba (AHL), Columbia (ECHL)
19	Markus Naslund (LW)....	6-0/195	Ornskoldsvik, Sweden	7-30-73	10	Vancouver
22	Chris Nielsen (RW)........	6-1/190	Moshi, Tanzania	2-16-80	2	Syracuse (AHL), Chicago (AHL), Manitoba (AHL)
	Ryan Ready (LW)..........	6-0/195	Peterborough, Ont.	11-7-78	0	Manitoba (AHL)
51	Brandon Reid (C)..........	5-9/170	Kirkland, Que.	3-9-81	1	Manitoba (AHL), Vancouver
37	Jarkko Ruutu (RW)........	6-2/195	Vantaa, Finland	8-23-75	4	Vancouver
22	Daniel Sedin (LW).........	6-1/200	Ornskoldsvik, Sweden	9-26-80	3	Vancouver
33	Henrik Sedin (C)...........	6-2/200	Ornskoldsvik, Sweden	9-26-80	3	Vancouver
	Jason Shmyr (LW)	6-4/221	Fairview, Ont.	7-27-75	0	Manitoba (AHL), Augusta (ECHL), Johnstown (ECHL)
	Nathan Smith (C)..........	6-1/192	Strathcona, Alta.	2-9-82	0	Manitoba (AHL)
	Tim Smith (C)...............	5-9/160	Rochfort Bridge, Alta.	7-21-81	0	Manitoba (AHL), Columbia (ECHL)
	R.J. Umberger (C)	6-2/200	Pittsburgh	5-3-82	0	Ohio State (CCHA)
29	Herbert Vasiljevs (C)......	5-11/180	Riga, U.S.S.R.	5-27-75	4	Manitoba (AHL)
	DEFENSEMEN					
7	Bryan Allen	6-4/220	Kingston, Ont.	8-21-80	3	Manitoba (AHL), Vancouver
23	Murray Baron	6-3/220	Prince George, B.C.	6-1-67	14	Vancouver
38	Nolan Baumgartner........	6-1/195	Calgary	3-23-76	6	Manitoba (AHL), Vancouver
62	Regan Darby	6-2/200	Estevan, Sask.	7-17-80	0	Manitoba (AHL), Columbia (ECHL)
	Denis Grot	6-1/180	Minsk, U.S.S.R.	1-6-84	0	
56	Darrell Hay	6-0/190	Kamloops, B.C.	4-2-80	0	Manitoba (AHL), Columbia (ECHL)
28	Bryan Helmer	6-1/210	Sault Ste. Marie, Ont.	7-15-72	5	Manitoba (AHL), Vancouver
	Mikko Jokela.................	6-1/215	Lappeenranta, Finland	3-4-80	1	Albany (AHL), Van., Manitoba (AHL)
55	Ed Jovanovski...............	6-2/210	Windsor, Ont.	6-26-76	8	Vancouver
	Kirill Koltsov	5-11/183	Chelyabinsk, U.S.S.R.	2-1-83	0	Avangard Omsk (Russian)
36	Zenith Komarniski..........	6-0/200	Edmonton	8-13-78	2	Manitoba (AHL), Vancouver
4	Justin Kurtz	6-0/200	Winnipeg	1-14-77	1	Manitoba (AHL)
5	Marek Malik..................	6-5/210	Ostrava, Czechoslovakia	6-24-75	8	Vancouver, Carolina
43	Jaroslav Obsut.............	6-1/185	Presov, Czechoslovakia	9-3-76	2	Manitoba (AHL)
2	Mattias Ohlund	6-3/220	Pitea, Sweden	9-9-76	6	Vancouver
5	Sami Salo	6-3/192	Turku, Finland	9-2-74	5	Vancouver
3	Brent Sopel..................	6-1/205	Calgary	1-7-77	5	Vancouver
	Rene Vydareny	6-1/198	Bratislava, Czechoslovakia	5-6-81	0	Manitoba (AHL)
	David Ytfeldt................	6-0/187	Ornskoldsvik, Sweden	9-29-79	0	
	GOALTENDERS					
	Alex Auld	6-4/196	Cold Lake, Alta.	1-7-81	2	Manitoba (AHL), Vancouver
39	Dan Cloutier.................	6-1/185	Mont-Laurier, Que.	4-22-76	6	Vancouver
	Lukas Mensator............	5-10/165	Sokolov, Czechoslovakia	8-18-84	0	Ottawa (OHA)
	Tyler Moss...................	6-0/185	Ottawa	6-29-75	4	Manitoba (AHL), Vancouver
1	Peter Skudra................	6-1/190	Riga, U.S.S.R.	4-24-73	6	Manitoba (AHL), Vancouver

2002-03 REVIEW
INDIVIDUAL STATISTICS

SCORING

	Games	G	A	Pts.	PIM	+/-	PPG	SHG	GWG	GTG	Sht.	Sht. Pct.	Faceoffs Won	Faceoffs Lost	Faceoffs Pct.	TOI
Markus Naslund	82	48	56	104	52	6	24	0	12	1	294	16.3	2	4	33.3	19:54
Todd Bertuzzi.............	82	46	51	97	144	2	25	0	7	1	243	18.9	98	110	47.1	20:34
Brendan Morrison	82	25	46	71	36	18	6	2	8	0	167	15.0	765	820	48.3	21:13
Ed Jovanovski	67	6	40	46	113	19	2	0	1	1	145	4.1	0	0	—	24:14
Matt Cooke...............	82	15	27	42	82	21	1	4	0	0	118	12.7	11	20	35.5	13:23
Trevor Linden	71	19	22	41	30	-1	4	1	1	0	116	16.4	309	259	54.4	15:51

	Games	G	A	Pts.	PIM	+/-	PPG	SHG	GWG	GTG	Sht.	Sht. Pct.	Faceoffs Won	Lost	Pct.	TOI
Henrik Sedin.............	78	8	31	39	38	9	4	1	1	1	81	9.9	480	515	48.2	13:57
Brent Sopel	81	7	30	37	23	-15	6	0	1	0	167	4.2	0	0	—	21:42
Daniel Sedin	79	14	17	31	34	8	4	0	2	0	134	10.4	11	13	45.8	12:26
Sami Salo.................	79	9	21	30	10	9	4	0	1	1	126	7.1	0	0	—	20:08
Trent Klatt................	82	16	13	29	8	10	3	0	2	0	127	12.6	19	28	40.4	12:25
Mattias Ohlund..........	59	2	27	29	42	1	0	0	0	0	100	2.0	0	0	—	25:23
Trevor Letowski........	78	11	14	25	36	8	1	1	1	0	136	8.1	29	41	41.4	12:26
Artem Chubarov........	62	7	13	20	6	4	1	0	1	0	78	9.0	438	424	50.8	14:20
Marek Malik*............	69	7	11	18	52	23	1	1	2	1	68	10.3	0	1	0.0	18:05
Mats Lindgren..........	54	5	9	14	18	-2	0	2	1	0	51	9.8	416	347	54.5	13:54
Todd Warriner*........	30	4	6	10	22	6	0	0	0	0	53	7.5	12	17	41.4	11:41
Bryan Allen..............	48	5	3	8	73	8	0	0	1	0	43	11.6	0	0	—	12:55
Murray Baron...........	78	2	4	6	62	13	0	0	0	0	34	5.9	0	0	—	17:01
Brandon Reid	7	2	3	5	0	4	0	0	0	0	15	13.3	38	31	55.1	9:47
Jarkko Ruutu............	36	2	2	4	66	-7	0	0	1	0	36	5.6	1	5	16.7	8:58
Nolan Baumgartner ...	8	1	2	3	4	4	1	0	0	0	7	14.3	0	0	—	11:35
Dan Cloutier (g)	57	0	3	3	24	0	0	0	0	0	0	—	0	0	—	—
Harold Druken*........	3	1	1	2	0	-1	0	0	0	0	3	33.3	10	11	47.6	8:48
Jan Hlavac*..............	9	1	1	2	6	-1	0	0	0	0	7	14.3	0	0	—	10:51
Jason King	8	0	2	2	0	0	0	0	0	0	12	0.0	0	0	—	11:16
Pat Kavanagh	3	1	0	1	2	2	0	0	1	0	4	25.0	10	17	37.0	10:22
Fedor Fedorov	7	0	1	1	4	0	0	0	0	0	2	0.0	12	14	46.2	9:09
Peter Skudra (g).......	23	0	1	1	0	0	0	0	0	0	0	—	0	0	—	—
Darren Langdon*	45	0	1	1	143	-2	0	0	0	0	15	0.0	0	1	0.0	5:25
Mikko Jokela	1	0	0	0	0	0	0	0	0	0	3	0.0	0	0	—	5:09
Zenith Komarniski	1	0	0	0	2	0	0	0	0	0	0	—	0	0	—	6:25
Tyler Moss (g)	1	0	0	0	0	0	0	0	0	0	0	—	0	0	—	—
Bryan Helmer	2	0	0	0	0	1	0	0	0	0	2	0.0	0	0	—	13:24
Brad May*..............	3	0	0	0	10	1	0	0	0	0	1	0.0	0	0	—	7:47
Alexander Auld (g)	7	0	0	0	0	0	0	0	0	0	0	—	0	0	—	—

GOALTENDING

	Games	GS	Min.	GA	SO	Avg.	W	L	T	EN	PPG Allow	SHG Allow	Shots	Save Pct.
Alexander Auld	7	5	382	10	1	1.57	3	3	0	0	4	0	165	.939
Dan Cloutier.............................	57	57	3376	136	2	2.42	33	16	7	6	35	8	1477	.908
Peter Skudra............................	23	20	1192	54	1	2.72	9	5	6	1	22	2	522	.897
Tyler Moss................................	1	0	22	1	0	2.73	0	0	0	0	1	0	14	.929

*Played with two or more NHL teams.

RESULTS

OCTOBER
10— At Calgary ....W.....3-0
12— San Jose ....W.....5-3
14— Calgary ....L.....2-3
16— Boston ....L.....3-6
18— At Anaheim ....T.....*2-2
19— At Los Angeles ....T.....*2-2
21— At San Jose ....W.....5-2
24— Anaheim ....T.....*2-2
26— Dallas ....L.....1-4
29— Buffalo ....T.....*1-1
31— Colorado ....L.....1-5

NOVEMBER
2— At Minnesota ....W.....4-2
4— At Colorado ....W.....4-2
6— At Dallas ....L.....0-4
9— At Phoenix ....W.....5-2
12— St. Louis ....W.....6-3
14— Los Angeles ....W.....3-2
16— N.Y. Rangers ....W.....3-1
20— Chicago ....W.....5-3
22— Detroit ....W.....4-1
25— At Minnesota ....W.....2-1
27— At Carolina ....W.....3-2
29— At Tampa Bay ....W.....5-3
30— At Florida ....W.....5-2

DECEMBER
3— At N.Y. Islanders................L.....1-2
4— At New Jersey ....W.....*3-2
7— Minnesota ....L.....2-4

JANUARY
2— Montreal............................W.....3-2
4— Florida ....W.....3-2
8— Ottawa ....W.....6-4
10— Columbus ....L.....2-3
11— At San Jose ....L.....0-3
14— Nashville ....W.....4-3
16— At Minnesota ....L.....2-5
17— At Chicago ....W.....4-2
19— At Detroit ....W.....4-1
21— At Nashville ....L.....2-3
24— Detroit ....L.....2-5
26— Phoenix ....W.....1-0
28— Minnesota ....T.....*2-2
30— Edmonton ....T.....*3-3

FEBRUARY
4— At Pittsburgh ....W.....3-2
5— At Columbus ....T.....*4-4
7— At Buffalo ....W.....4-2

9— Calgary ....L.....1-2
11— Colorado..........................W.....3-1
14— At Edmonton ....W.....6-3
15— Calgary ....T.....*3-3
17— At Chicago ....L.....2-3
19— At Nashville ....W.....3-1
21— Edmonton ....W.....*4-3
23— At Colorado ....L.....3-5
26— At Edmonton ....W.....4-2
28— Anaheim ....W.....7-3
31— Toronto ....L.....3-5

MARCH
1— At Montreal.......................T.....*1-1
3— At Boston ....W.....6-4
4— At Philadelphia..................L.....0-3
6— At Columbus ....OTL...*4-5
8— At Toronto ....T.....*3-3
11— N.Y. Islanders ....W.....4-3
13— St. Louis ....T.....*4-4
15— Toronto ....L.....0-1
17— At Dallas ....W.....4-2
18— At St. Louis ....L.....4-6
20— Nashville ....W.....7-3
23— Washington ....W.....6-0
25— Dallas ....L.....3-4
27— Phoenix ....W.....5-1
29— At Los Angeles ....W.....5-1
30— At Anaheim ....L.....1-3

10— Chicago ....W.....2-1
13— Colorado..........................W.....*2-1
15— At Calgary ....T.....*2-2
18— At Detroit ....W.....*4-3
20— At St. Louis ....W.....4-2
22— At Edmonton ....W.....*3-2
23— Columbus ....W.....7-2
25— Atlanta ....W.....8-0
27— San Jose ....L.....2-3

APRIL
2— At Phoenix ....T.....*3-3
6— Los Angeles ....L.....0-2
*Denotes overtime game.

WASHINGTON CAPITALS
EASTERN CONFERENCE/SOUTHEAST DIVISION

WASHINGTON CAPITALS

Capitals' Schedule
Home games shaded; D=Day game; *Feb. 8 All-Star Game at St. Paul, Minn.

October

SUN	MON	TUE	WED	THU	FRI	SAT
5	6	7	8	9 NYI	10	11 ATL
12	13 TOR	14 MON	15	16	17 DAL	18 STL
19	20	21	22	23 OTT	24	25 TOR
26	27	28	29 ANA	30	31 ATL	

November

SUN	MON	TUE	WED	THU	FRI	SAT
						1 MIN
2	3	4 TB	5	6 PHI	7	8 SJ
9	10 LA	11	12 CAR	13	14 TB	15 CAR
16	17	18	19	20 BOS	21	22 FLA
23	24 DET	25	26 BUF	27	28 MON	29 CBJ
30						

December

SUN	MON	TUE	WED	THU	FRI	SAT
	1	2 NYI	3	4 NJ	5	6 LA
7	8 COL	9	10	11 BOS	12	13 DET
14	15	16 ATL	17 FLA	18	19 TOR	20
21 NYI	22	23 MON	24	25	26	27 BUF
28	29 BOS	30	31 BUF			

January

SUN	MON	TUE	WED	THU	FRI	SAT
				1 NJ	2	3 OTT
4 MON	5	6	7 PHO	8	9 CAR	10
11 EDM	12	13	14 CAL	15	16	17 D NJ
18 D PIT	19	20	21 TOR	22	23 FLA	24
25 PHI	26	27	28 NYR	29 CAR	30	31 VAN

February

SUN	MON	TUE	WED	THU	FRI	SAT
1	2	3 TB	4 PHI	5	6	7
8*	9	10	11	12 CAR	13 NAS	14
15 D CHI	16	17 OTT	18	19 NJ	20	21 FLA
22	23 TB	24	25 CAR	26	27 FLA	28 TB
29						

March

SUN	MON	TUE	WED	THU	FRI	SAT
	1	2 FLA	3	4	5 NYR	6 PHI
7	8 OTT	9	10 BUF	11	12 CHI	13 ATL
14	15	16 PIT	17	18 NYR	19	20 ATL
21	22	23 NYI	24 ATL	25	26	27 TB
28	29	30 PIT	31			

April

SUN	MON	TUE	WED	THU	FRI	SAT
				1 BOS	2	3 NYR
4 D PIT	5	6	7	8	9	10

2003-04 SEASON
CLUB DIRECTORY

Owners
Ted Leonsis, Raul Fernandez, Dick Patrick, Jack Davies, Richard Fairbank, Rickard Kay, George Stamas, Jeong Kim

President and governor
Dick Patrick

Senior v.p. of business operations
Declan J. Bolger

Vice president/general manager
George McPhee

Director of hockey operations
Shawn Simpson

Assistant to the general manager
Frank Provenzano

Director of amateur scouting
Ross Mahoney

Head coach
Bruce Cassidy

Assistant coaches
Randy Carlyle
Glen Hanlon

Goaltending coach
Dave Prior

Team physician
Dr. Ben Shaffer

Trainer
Greg Smith

Assistant trainer
Tim Clark

Equipment manager
Doug Shearer

Assistant equipment manager
Craig Leydig

Equipment assistant
Brian Metzger

Strength and conditioning coach
Jim Fox

Massage therapist
Curt Millar

Senior director, communications
Kurt Kehl

Manager, media relations
Brian Potter

Manager, information
Kyle Hanlin

DRAFT CHOICES

Rd.— Player	Overall	Pos.	Last team
1— Eric Fehr	18	RW	Brandon (WHL)
3— Stephen Werner	83	RW	Massachusetts (Hockey East)
4— Andreas Valdix	109	LW	Malmo (Sweden)
5— Josh Robertson	155	C	Proctor HS
8— Andrew Joudrey	249	C	Notre Dame (SJHL)
9— Mark Olafson	279	RW	Kelowna (WHL)

MISCELLANEOUS DATA

Home ice (capacity)
MCI Center (18,277)

Address
MCI Center
401 9th Street, NW, Suite 750
Washington, DC 20004

Business phone
202-266-2200

Ticket information
202-266-2277

Website
www.washingtoncaps.com

Training site
Piney Orchard, MD

Club colors
Bronze, blue and black

Radio affiliation
WTEM (980 AM)

TV affiliation
NewsChannel 8

No.	FORWARDS	Ht./Wt.	Place	BORN Date	NHL exp.	2002-03 clubs
95	Sergei Berezin (LW)	5-10/200	Voskresensk, U.S.S.R.	11-5-71	7	Washington, Chicago
12	Peter Bondra (RW)	6-0/200	Luck, Ukraine	2-7-68	13	Washington
23	Ivan Ciernik (LW)	6-1/235	Levice, Czechoslovakia	10-30-77	4	Portland (AHL), Washington
48	Chris Corrinet (RW)	6-3/220	Derby, Conn.	10-29-78	1	Portland (AHL), Worcester (AHL), Philadelphia (AHL)
36	Colin Forbes (LW)	6-3/205	New Westminister, B.C.	2-16-76	7	Portland (AHL), Washington
	Owen Fussey (RW)	6-0/185	Winnipeg	4-2-83	0	Moose Jaw (WHL)
	Boyd Gordon (RW)	6-0/192	Unity, Sask.	10-19-83	0	Red Deer (WHL)
25	Mike Grier (RW)	6-1/227	Detroit	1-5-75	7	Washington
11	Jeff Halpern (C)	6-0/201	Potomac, Md.	5-3-76	4	Washington
68	Jaromir Jagr (RW)	6-2/232	Kladno, Czechoslovakia	2-15-72	13	Washington
22	S. Konowalchuk (LW)	6-2/208	Salt Lake City	11-11-72	12	Washington
	Robert Lang (C)	6-2/216	Teplice, Czechoslovakia	12-19-70	10	Washington
20	Glen Metropolit (C)	5-11/192	Toronto	6-25-74	4	Portland (AHL), Washington
	Kip Miller (C)	5-10/190	Lansing, Mich.	6-11-69	11	Washington
42	Mark Murphy (LW)	5-11/202	Stoughton, Mass.	8-6-76	0	Portland (AHL)
92	Michael Nylander (C)	6-1/195	Stockholm, Sweden	10-3-72	10	Washington, Chicago
51	Stephen Peat (RW)	6-2/218	Princeton, B.C.	3-10-80	2	Portland (AHL), Washington
18	Matt Pettinger (LW)	6-1/202	Edmonton	10-22-80	3	Portland (AHL), Washington
21	A. Salomonsson (LW)	6-1/185	Ornskoldsvik, Sweden	12-19-73	2	Portland (AHL), Washington
	Alexander Semin (LW)	6-0/174	Krasjonarsk, U.S.S.R.	3-3-84	1	
41	Brian Sutherby (C)	6-3/203	Edmonton	3-1-82	2	Portland (AHL), Washington
	Petr Sykora (C)	6-2/180	Pardubice, Czechoslovakia	12-21-78	1	HC Pardubice (Czech Republic)
	Roman Tvrdon (C/LW)	6-1/189	Trencin, Czechoslovakia	1-21-81	0	Portland (AHL)
23	Trent Whitfield (C)	5-11/199	Estevan, Sask.	6-17-77	4	Portland (AHL), Washington
9	Dainius Zubrus (LW)	6-4/231	Elektrenai, U.S.S.R.	6-16-78	7	Washington
	DEFENSEMEN					
6	Rick Berry	6-1/190	Brandon, Man.	11-4-78	3	Washington
	Josef Boumedienne	6-1/190	Stockholm, Sweden	1-12-78	2	Binghamton (AHL), Washington, Portland (AHL)
3	Sylvain Cote	5-11/201	Quebec City	1-19-66	19	Washington
34	Jakub Cutta	6-3/217	Jablonec nad Nisou, Czech.	12-29-81	2	Portland (AHL)
25	Jason Doig	6-3/228	Montreal	1-29-77	6	Portland (AHL), Washington
	Steve Eminger	6-1/196	Woodbridge, Ont.	10-31-83	1	Kitchener (OHL), Washington
58	Jean-Francois Fortin	6-2/205	Laval, Que.	3-15-79	2	Portland (AHL), Washington
55	Sergei Gonchar	6-2/208	Chelyabinsk, U.S.S.R.	4-13-74	9	Washington
	Chris Hajt	6-3/206	Saskatoon, Sask.	7-5-78	1	Portland (AHL)
	Alex Henry	6-5/220	Elliot Lake, Ont.	10-18-79	1	Portland (AHL), Edmonton, Wash.
6	Calle Johansson	5-11/203	Goteborg, Sweden	2-14-67	16	Washington
2	Ken Klee	6-0/210	Indianapolis	4-24-71	9	Washington
	Nathan Paetsch	6-0/195	Humboldt, Sask.	3-30-83	0	Moose Jaw (WHL)
	Alex Riazantsev	5-11/200	Moscow, U.S.S.R.	3-15-80	0	Hershey (AHL), Milwaukee (AHL)
38	Todd Rohloff	6-3/213	Grand Rapids, Minn.	1-16-74	1	Portland (AHL)
	Ryan Vanbuskirk	6-2/207	Sault Ste. Marie, Mich.	1-12-80	0	Richmond (ECHL), Portland (AHL)
19	Brendan Witt	6-2/229	Humboldt, Sask.	2-20-75	9	Washington
40	Nolan Yonkman	6-6/236	Punnichy, Sask.	4-1-81	1	Portland (AHL)
	GOALTENDERS					
1	Craig Billington	5-10/168	London, Ont.	9-11-66	15	Washington
35	Sebastien Charpentier	5-9/176	Drummondville, Que.	4-18-77	2	Portland (AHL), Washington
	Maxime Daigneault	6-1/194	St-Jacques-Le-Mineur, Que.	1-23-84	0	Val-d'Or (QMJHL)
37	Olaf Kolzig	6-3/225	Johannesburg, South Africa	4-9-70	12	Washington
	Maxime Ouellet	6-0/180	Beauport, Que.	6-17-81	1	Portland (AHL)
61	Rastislav Stana	6-2/160	Kosice, Czechoslovakia	1-10-80	0	Portland (AHL)

2002-03 REVIEW

INDIVIDUAL STATISTICS

SCORING

	Games	G	A	Pts.	PIM	+/-	PPG	SHG	GWG	GTG	Sht.	Sht. Pct.	Faceoffs Won	Lost	Pct.	TOI
Jaromir Jagr	75	36	41	77	38	5	13	2	9	0	290	12.4	1	4	20.0	21:18
Robert Lang	82	22	47	69	22	12	10	0	2	1	146	15.1	491	578	45.9	18:46
Sergei Gonchar	82	18	49	67	52	13	7	0	2	1	224	8.0	0	0	—	26:34
Peter Bondra	76	30	26	56	52	-3	9	2	4	0	256	11.7	4	9	30.8	18:53
Michael Nylander*	71	17	39	56	36	3	7	0	2	0	141	12.1	476	529	47.4	18:41
Kip Miller	72	12	38	50	18	-1	3	0	4	0	89	13.5	85	86	49.7	14:57

	Games	G	A	Pts.	PIM	+/-	PPG	SHG	GWG	GTG	Sht.	Sht. Pct.	Faceoffs Won	Lost	Pct.	TOI
Dainius Zubrus	63	13	22	35	43	15	2	0	0	0	104	12.5	284	281	50.3	16:25
Jeff Halpern	82	13	21	34	88	6	1	2	2	0	126	10.3	807	685	54.1	17:25
Mike Grier	82	15	17	32	36	-14	2	2	2	0	133	11.3	43	55	43.9	17:47
Steve Konowalchuk...	77	15	15	30	71	3	2	0	3	0	119	12.6	41	51	44.6	16:42
Ivan Ciernik	47	8	10	18	24	6	0	0	2	1	61	13.1	3	6	33.3	11:47
Ken Klee	70	1	16	17	89	22	0	0	0	0	67	1.5	0	0	—	21:48
Calle Johansson	82	3	12	15	22	9	1	0	0	0	77	3.9	0	1	0.0	21:45
Brendan Witt	69	2	9	11	106	12	0	0	0	0	80	2.5	0	0	—	20:55
Brian Sutherby	72	2	9	11	93	7	0	0	0	0	38	5.3	126	162	43.8	9:43
Sergei Berezin*	9	5	4	9	4	10	0	0	2	0	28	17.9	0	1	0.0	15:41
Jason Doig	55	3	5	8	108	-3	0	0	1	0	41	7.3	0	1	0.0	14:11
Glen Metropolit	23	2	3	5	6	4	0	0	1	0	22	9.1	49	50	49.5	10:07
Andreas Salomonsson	32	1	4	5	14	-1	0	0	0	1	20	5.0	11	18	37.9	8:49
Rick Berry	43	2	1	3	87	-3	0	0	1	0	40	5.0	0	0	—	12:57
Josh Green*	21	1	2	3	7	1	0	0	0	0	20	5.0	0	3	0.0	8:06
Joel Kwiatkowski*	34	0	3	3	12	1	0	0	0	0	28	0.0	0	2	0.0	15:32
Trent Whitfield	14	1	1	2	6	1	0	0	1	0	4	25.0	71	53	57.3	8:30
Chris Simon*	10	0	2	2	23	-3	0	0	0	0	16	0.0	0	0	—	8:52
Steve Eminger	17	0	2	2	24	-3	0	0	0	0	6	0.0	0	0	—	10:07
Josef Boumedienne...	6	1	0	1	0	-1	0	0	1	0	7	14.3	0	0	—	19:32
Stephen Peat	27	1	0	1	57	-3	0	0	0	0	7	14.3	0	0	—	4:09
Jean-Francois Fortin..	33	0	1	1	22	-3	0	0	0	0	20	0.0	0	0	—	15:14
Sylvain Cote	1	0	0	0	4	0	0	0	0	0	0	—	0	0	—	4:12
Matt Pettinger	1	0	0	0	0	0	0	0	0	0	0	—	0	1	0.0	3:30
Mike Farrell	4	0	0	2	1	0	0	0	0	0	2	0.0	0	0	—	2:48
Craig Billington (g)....	5	0	0	0	0	0	0	0	0	0	0	—	0	0	—	—
Colin Forbes	5	0	0	0	0	-2	0	0	0	0	3	0.0	6	6	50.0	9:38
S. Charpentier (g).......	17	0	0	0	0	0	0	0	0	0	0	—	0	0	—	—
Alex Henry*	38	0	0	0	80	-4	0	0	0	0	8	0.0	0	1	0.0	3:38
Olaf Kolzig (g)	66	0	0	0	0	0	0	0	0	0	0	—	0	0	—	—

GOALTENDING

	Games	GS	Min.	GA	SO	Avg.	W	L	T	EN	PPG Allow	SHG Allow	Shots	Save Pct.
Olaf Kolzig	66	65	3894	156	4	2.40	33	25	6	5	51	0	1925	.919
Sebastien Charpentier	17	12	859	40	0	2.79	5	7	1	2	16	2	426	.906
Craig Billington	5	5	217	17	0	4.70	1	3	1	0	5	2	96	.823

*Played with two or more NHL teams.

RESULTS

OCTOBER

11—Nashville..........................W.....5-4
12—At N.Y. Islanders.............W.....2-1
17—At Carolina.......................W.....2-1
19—At Philadelphia.................L.....1-3
20—At Dallas ....L.....2-5
23—At N.Y. Rangers...............W.....2-1
25—At Tampa Bay ....L.....2-3
26—At Florida.........................T.....*1-1
28—At Pittsburgh ....L.....2-3
30—Boston ....L.....2-7

NOVEMBER

1— Tampa Bay ....W.....3-2
2—At Philadelphia.................L.....1-2
5—At Columbus ....W.....*4-3
7—Florida ....W.....*2-1
9—Philadelphia......................W.....4-1
13—Dallas ....L.....1-6
15—At Chicago ....T.....*2-2
16—At Minnesota....................L.....0-1
19—San Jose..........................L.....2-3
21—Minnesota.........................L.....3-4
23—Atlanta ....W.....6-3
26—At Toronto ....L.....4-5
27—Calgary ....W.....4-2
29—Ottawa ....L.....2-6

DECEMBER

1— At Atlanta.........................L.....4-5
3— At Pittsburgh ....W.....4-1
6—Atlanta ....W.....*7-6

7—At Buffalo...........................L.....3-4
11—At Anaheim.......................L.....0-3
13—At Phoenix ....W.....4-3
14—At San Jose ....L.....0-2
16—At Colorado ....T.....*2-2
19—Boston ....W.....5-3
21—At N.Y. Islanders.............W.....3-1
23—Tampa Bay ....W.....3-0
27—New Jersey......................W.....3-2
28—At New Jersey ....OTL...*1-2
30—Buffalo ....W.....4-3

JANUARY

1—Phoenix ....OTL...*1-2
3—Columbus ....T.....*2-2
4—At N.Y. Rangers ....T.....*2-2
10—At Carolina.......................W.....4-1
11—Florida ....W.....12-2
13—N.Y. Islanders ....W.....*4-3
15—N.Y. Rangers ....OTL...*1-2
17—Toronto ....L.....1-4
18—At Ottawa ....L.....2-5
20—At Boston ....T.....*3-3
22—Carolina ....W.....5-3
25—At Montreal.......................T.....*1-1
26—N.Y. Rangers ....W.....7-2
28—St. Louis ....L.....3-5
30—Pittsburgh ....W.....2-1

FEBRUARY

4— At Tampa Bay ....W.....5-1
5— New Jersey.......................L.....1-4
7— N.Y. Islanders ....W.....3-0

9— Montreal ....L.....0-2
12—At Atlanta ....W.....5-1
14—At Carolina........................L.....1-3
15—At Florida..........................W.....2-1
17—At Tampa Bay ....L.....1-3
20—Toronto ....L.....2-6
22—Detroit ....L.....1-5
24—Montreal ....W.....4-1
26—Buffalo ....W.....3-2

MARCH

1— At New Jersey..................OTL...*1-2
2—Carolina ....W.....2-0
4—At Buffalo............................W.....2-1
6—Atlanta ....T.....*4-4
8—At Boston ....OTL...*4-5
10—Philadelphia.......................W.....*2-1
14—Los Angeles......................L.....1-3
16—Colorado ....W.....2-1
20—At Calgary ....W.....4-1
22—At Edmonton ....L.....3-5
23—At Vancouver ....L.....0-6
25—At Montreal ....W.....*4-3
28—At Ottawa ....W.....3-2
29—At Toronto ....OTL...*3-4

APRIL

1— Florida ....W.....3-0
3— Ottawa ....L.....1-5
5— Pittsburgh ....W.....5-3

*Denotes overtime game.

SCHEDULE

2003-04 NHL SEASON Schedule

* Denotes afternoon game.

WEDNESDAY, OCT. 8
New Jersey at Boston
Anaheim at Dallas
Minnesota at Chicago

THURSDAY, OCT. 9
Montreal at Ottawa
Buffalo at Philadelphia
N.Y. Islanders at Washington
Columbus at Atlanta
Carolina at Florida
Los Angeles at Detroit
Anaheim at Nashville
San Jose at Edmonton
Calgary at Vancouver

FRIDAY, OCT. 10
Los Angeles at Pittsburgh
Boston at Tampa Bay
N.Y. Rangers at Minnesota
Chicago at Colorado
St. Louis at Phoenix

SATURDAY, OCT. 11
N.Y. Islanders at Buffalo
Montreal at Toronto
Detroit at Ottawa
Pittsburgh at Philadelphia
Atlanta at Washington
New Jersey at Carolina
N.Y. Rangers at Columbus
Boston at Florida
Dallas at Nashville
San Jose at Calgary
Edmonton at Vancouver

SUNDAY, OCT. 12
Los Angeles at Chicago
San Jose at Minnesota
Phoenix at Anaheim
St. Louis at Colorado

MONDAY, OCT. 13
Dallas at Buffalo *
Florida at Carolina
Vancouver at Columbus
Washington at Toronto

TUESDAY, OCT. 14
Washington at Montreal
N.Y. Islanders at Atlanta
Edmonton at Calgary

WEDNESDAY, OCT. 15
Phoenix at Florida
Boston at Dallas
Ottawa at Los Angeles

THURSDAY, OCT. 16
Atlanta at N.Y. Rangers
Phoenix at Tampa Bay
Chicago at Columbus
Pittsburgh at Montreal
Toronto at New Jersey
Vancouver at Detroit
Colorado at Minnesota
St. Louis at Nashville
Buffalo at Edmonton
Philadelphia at San Jose

FRIDAY, OCT. 17
Washington at Dallas
Ottawa at Anaheim

SATURDAY, OCT. 18
Toronto at Montreal
Florida at N.Y. Islanders
Carolina at N.Y. Rangers
Chicago at Atlanta
Tampa Bay at New Jersey
Detroit at Pittsburgh
Washington at St. Louis
Columbus at Nashville
Vancouver at Minnesota
Buffalo at Calgary
Colorado at Edmonton
Philadelphia at Phoenix
Boston at Los Angeles
Ottawa at San Jose

SUNDAY, OCT. 19
Nashville at Chicago
Minnesota at Dallas
Boston at Anaheim

MONDAY, OCT. 20
Toronto at N.Y. Islanders
Florida at N.Y. Rangers
Detroit at Montreal
Buffalo at Vancouver

TUESDAY, OCT. 21
Atlanta at Tampa Bay
Calgary at Minnesota
Boston at Colorado
St. Louis at Edmonton
Philadelphia at Los Angeles
Anaheim at San Jose

WEDNESDAY, OCT. 22
Florida at New Jersey
Carolina at Pittsburgh
Columbus at Detroit
Toronto at Dallas
St. Louis at Vancouver
Philadelphia at Anaheim

THURSDAY, OCT. 23
Tampa Bay at Columbus
Carolina at Boston
N.Y. Islanders at Montreal
Washington at Ottawa
Nashville at Atlanta
Edmonton at Colorado
Toronto at Phoenix
Buffalo at Los Angeles
Chicago at San Jose

FRIDAY, OCT. 24
New Jersey at Pittsburgh
Minnesota at Florida
Dallas at Detroit
St. Louis at Calgary
Buffalo at Anaheim

SATURDAY, OCT. 25
Washington at Toronto
Ottawa at Montreal
Pittsburgh at N.Y. Islanders
Detroit at N.Y. Rangers
Carolina at Philadelphia

Florida at Atlanta
Dallas at Columbus
Boston at New Jersey
Minnesota at Tampa Bay
Colorado at Nashville
Calgary at Edmonton
Chicago at Los Angeles
Phoenix at San Jose

SUNDAY, OCT. 26
Chicago at Anaheim
Buffalo at Colorado
Phoenix at Vancouver

MONDAY, OCT. 27
Montreal at Philadelphia
Atlanta at Toronto

TUESDAY, OCT. 28
Minnesota at Buffalo
Boston at Montreal
New Jersey at N.Y. Islanders
San Jose at Carolina
Anaheim at N.Y. Rangers
Nashville at St. Louis
Chicago at Phoenix
Calgary at Colorado
Columbus at Vancouver

WEDNESDAY, OCT. 29
Florida at Philadelphia
Anaheim at Washington
N.Y. Islanders at Pittsburgh
St. Louis at Detroit
Calgary at Dallas

THURSDAY, OCT. 30
Montreal at Boston
Toronto at Buffalo
Carolina at N.Y. Rangers
San Jose at Tampa Bay
Florida at Ottawa
Philadelphia at New Jersey
Detroit at Nashville
Atlanta at Minnesota
Pittsburgh at Chicago
Columbus at Edmonton
Vancouver at Los Angeles

FRIDAY, OCT. 31
Atlanta at Washington
Vancouver at Phoenix

SATURDAY, NOV. 1
Colorado at New Jersey *
Anaheim at N.Y. Islanders *
Boston at Pittsburgh *
Philadelphia at Toronto
N.Y. Rangers at Montreal
Buffalo at Ottawa
Carolina at Tampa Bay
San Jose at Florida
Chicago at St. Louis
Dallas at Nashville
Washington at Minnesota
Columbus at Calgary
Detroit at Edmonton
Phoenix at Los Angeles

SUNDAY, NOV. 2
Colorado at N.Y. Rangers

– 95 –

Toronto at Carolina
San Jose at Atlanta
Anaheim at Chicago
Nashville at Dallas

MONDAY, NOV. 3
Ottawa at N.Y. Islanders
Detroit at Vancouver

TUESDAY, NOV. 4
Dallas at N.Y. Rangers
Washington at Tampa Bay
Pittsburgh at Toronto
Edmonton at Montreal
Anaheim at St. Louis
Minnesota at Colorado
Detroit at Calgary

WEDNESDAY, NOV. 5
Atlanta at Buffalo
San Jose at New Jersey
Los Angeles at Florida
Vancouver at Nashville

THURSDAY, NOV. 6
Dallas at N.Y. Islanders
Washington at Philadelphia
N.Y. Rangers at Carolina
Los Angeles at Tampa Bay
San Jose at Boston
Edmonton at Ottawa
Vancouver at St. Louis
Phoenix at Colorado

FRIDAY, NOV. 7
Atlanta at Columbus
Toronto at New Jersey
Pittsburgh at Florida
Montreal at Buffalo
Chicago at Nashville
Minnesota at Calgary

SATURDAY, NOV. 8
Philadelphia at N.Y. Rangers *
Dallas at Boston
Edmonton at Toronto
Buffalo at Montreal
New Jersey at Ottawa
Atlanta at N.Y. Islanders
San Jose at Washington
Los Angeles at Carolina
Pittsburgh at Tampa Bay
Nashville at Detroit
Florida at St. Louis
Anaheim at Phoenix
Minnesota at Vancouver

SUNDAY, NOV. 9
Calgary at Columbus *
Tampa Bay at Carolina
Colorado at Chicago
Phoenix at Anaheim

MONDAY, NOV. 10
Edmonton at N.Y. Rangers
Los Angeles at Washington
Chicago at Detroit

TUESDAY, NOV. 11
Edmonton at Boston
Columbus at Montreal
N.Y. Islanders at Philadelphia
Ottawa at Atlanta
Tampa Bay at Florida
Vancouver at Minnesota
Colorado at San Jose

WEDNESDAY, NOV. 12
New Jersey at Buffalo
Pittsburgh at N.Y. Rangers

Carolina at Washington
Calgary at Chicago
Detroit at Dallas
Toronto at Anaheim

THURSDAY, NOV. 13
Montreal at N.Y. Islanders
Vancouver at Philadelphia
Atlanta at Carolina
Columbus at Ottawa
Florida at New Jersey
Calgary at Nashville
Edmonton at Minnesota
Colorado at Phoenix
Toronto at Los Angeles
St. Louis at San Jose

FRIDAY, NOV. 14
Tampa Bay at Washington
Boston at Columbus
Pittsburgh at Buffalo
Detroit at Chicago
Phoenix at Dallas

SATURDAY, NOV. 15
N.Y. Rangers at New Jersey *
St. Louis at Los Angeles *
Vancouver at Boston
Montreal at Ottawa
Atlanta at Philadelphia
Washington at Carolina
Florida at Pittsburgh
N.Y. Islanders at Nashville
Detroit at Minnesota
Dallas at Colorado
Calgary at Edmonton
Toronto at San Jose

SUNDAY, NOV. 16
Florida at Atlanta
Phoenix at Columbus
N.Y. Rangers at Chicago
St. Louis at Anaheim

MONDAY, NOV. 17
Buffalo at Ottawa

TUESDAY, NOV. 18
Philadelphia at Carolina
Anaheim at Colorado
Toronto at Calgary
Chicago at Edmonton
Montreal at Vancouver
N.Y. Rangers at San Jose

WEDNESDAY, NOV. 19
Buffalo at New Jersey
Minnesota at Pittsburgh
Boston at Atlanta
N.Y. Islanders at Florida
Columbus at Detroit
Anaheim at Dallas
St. Louis at Phoenix
Nashville at Los Angeles

THURSDAY, NOV. 20
Washington at Boston
N.Y. Islanders at Tampa Bay
Carolina at Ottawa
Minnesota at Philadelphia
Detroit at Columbus
Montreal at Calgary
Toronto at Edmonton
N.Y. Rangers at Colorado
Chicago at Vancouver

FRIDAY, NOV. 21
Pittsburgh at New Jersey
Atlanta at Florida

Carolina at Buffalo
Los Angeles at Dallas
San Jose at Phoenix
Nashville at Anaheim

SATURDAY, NOV. 22
Boston at Philadelphia
Florida at Washington
N.Y. Islanders at Columbus
Montreal at Edmonton
Ottawa at Pittsburgh
Buffalo at Tampa Bay
Dallas at St. Louis
Detroit at Minnesota
Los Angeles at Colorado
Chicago at Calgary
Toronto at Vancouver
Nashville at San Jose

SUNDAY, NOV. 23
Phoenix at Atlanta *
Ottawa at N.Y. Rangers
Tampa Bay at Carolina

MONDAY, NOV. 24
Vancouver at Toronto
Buffalo at Florida
Washington at Detroit
Phoenix at Dallas
Nashville at Colorado

TUESDAY, NOV. 25
N.Y. Rangers at Tampa Bay
Edmonton at Columbus
Vancouver at Montreal
Ottawa at Atlanta
Boston at St. Louis
New Jersey at Los Angeles

WEDNESDAY, NOV. 26
Washington at Buffalo
Carolina at N.Y. Islanders
Philadelphia at Pittsburgh
N.Y. Rangers at Florida
Edmonton at Detroit
Columbus at Nashville
Dallas at Minnesota
New Jersey at Anaheim
Chicago at San Jose

THURSDAY, NOV. 27
Toronto at Atlanta
Vancouver at Ottawa
Colorado at Calgary
Los Angeles at Phoenix

FRIDAY, NOV. 28
Nashville at Boston *
Carolina at Philadelphia *
San Jose at Minnesota *
Chicago at Anaheim *
Montreal at Washington
N.Y. Rangers at Pittsburgh
St. Louis at Tampa Bay
N.Y. Islanders at Detroit
Florida at Buffalo
New Jersey at Dallas
Colorado at Edmonton

SATURDAY, NOV. 29
Chicago at Los Angeles *
Toronto at Ottawa
Florida at Montreal
Philadelphia at N.Y. Islanders
Pittsburgh at Carolina
Tampa Bay at Atlanta
Washington at Columbus
Detroit at St. Louis

Buffalo at Nashville
Vancouver at Calgary

SUNDAY, NOV. 30
San Jose at Edmonton *
Anaheim at Minnesota
Phoenix at Boston
Toronto at N.Y. Rangers
Los Angeles at Dallas
New Jersey at Colorado

MONDAY, DEC. 1
Philadelphia at Ottawa
Atlanta at Pittsburgh

TUESDAY, DEC. 2
Washington at N.Y. Islanders
Anaheim at Columbus
N.Y. Rangers at Toronto
Tampa Bay at Montreal
Phoenix at New Jersey
Los Angeles at St. Louis
San Jose at Calgary

WEDNESDAY, DEC. 3
Pittsburgh at Philadelphia
Nashville at Carolina
Boston at Atlanta
Ottawa at Florida
Anaheim at Detroit
Buffalo at Chicago
Minnesota at Edmonton

THURSDAY, DEC. 4
Toronto at Boston
Phoenix at Buffalo
N.Y. Rangers at N.Y. Islanders
Ottawa at Tampa Bay
Nashville at Columbus
Washington at New Jersey
Detroit at St. Louis
Calgary at Vancouver
Dallas at Los Angeles
Colorado at San Jose

FRIDAY, DEC. 5
Phoenix at Philadelphia
Montreal at Carolina
Anaheim at Atlanta
Minnesota at Calgary

SATURDAY, DEC. 6
Nashville at St. Louis *
Philadelphia at Boston
Tampa Bay at Buffalo
Detroit at Toronto
Carolina at Montreal
New Jersey at Ottawa
Chicago at N.Y. Islanders
Atlanta at Florida
Columbus at Colorado
Pittsburgh at Edmonton
Minnesota at Vancouver
Washington at Los Angeles
Dallas at San Jose

SUNDAY, DEC. 7
Tampa Bay at N.Y. Rangers
Phoenix at Chicago
Pittsburgh at Calgary
Dallas at Anaheim

MONDAY, DEC. 8
Ottawa at Boston
Philadelphia at Montreal
Los Angeles at Detroit
Washington at Colorado

TUESDAY, DEC. 9
Tampa Bay at N.Y. Islanders
St. Louis at Toronto
Calgary at Minnesota
Carolina at Edmonton
Pittsburgh at Vancouver

WEDNESDAY, DEC. 10
Montreal at N.Y. Rangers
Philadelphia at Columbus
N.Y. Islanders at New Jersey
Los Angeles at Atlanta
Boston at Florida
Detroit at Buffalo
Dallas at Phoenix
San Jose at Anaheim

THURSDAY, DEC. 11
Boston at Washington
Tampa Bay at Ottawa
Los Angeles at Nashville
Toronto at Minnesota
Detroit at Chicago
Carolina at Calgary
Colorado at Vancouver
Edmonton at San Jose

FRIDAY, DEC. 12
St. Louis at Columbus
Philadelphia at New Jersey
Pittsburgh at Atlanta
Montreal at Florida
N.Y. Rangers at Buffalo
Chicago at Dallas
Edmonton at Phoenix

SATURDAY, DEC. 13
N.Y. Rangers at Toronto
Boston at Ottawa
Atlanta at N.Y. Islanders
New Jersey at Philadelphia
Detroit at Washington
Columbus at Pittsburgh
Montreal at Tampa Bay
Los Angeles at St. Louis
Florida at Nashville
Buffalo at Minnesota
Colorado at Calgary
Anaheim at San Jose

SUNDAY, DEC. 14
Dallas at Chicago
Edmonton at Anaheim
Carolina at Vancouver

MONDAY, DEC. 15
Florida at Detroit
Minnesota at Phoenix

TUESDAY, DEC. 16
New Jersey at N.Y. Islanders
Calgary at Philadelphia
Tampa Bay at Toronto
Boston at Montreal
Buffalo at Pittsburgh
Washington at Atlanta
Columbus at St. Louis
Vancouver at Nashville
Edmonton at Los Angeles

WEDNESDAY, DEC. 17
Washington at Florida
San Jose at Detroit
Vancouver at Dallas
Minnesota at Colorado

THURSDAY, DEC. 18
Calgary at Boston
Tampa Bay at Philadelphia
Pittsburgh at Carolina
Nashville at Montreal
Chicago at Ottawa
New Jersey at Atlanta
N.Y. Islanders at N.Y. Rangers
San Jose at St. Louis
Minnesota at Edmonton
Phoenix at Los Angeles

FRIDAY, DEC. 19
Toronto at Washington
Calgary at Columbus
Dallas at Florida
Chicago at Detroit
New Jersey at Buffalo
Colorado at Anaheim

SATURDAY, DEC. 20
Carolina at Boston *
N.Y. Islanders at Philadelphia *
Montreal at Toronto
N.Y. Rangers at Ottawa
Atlanta at Pittsburgh
Dallas at Tampa Bay
Phoenix at St. Louis
Detroit at Nashville
Columbus at Minnesota
Vancouver at Edmonton
Colorado at Los Angeles

SUNDAY, DEC. 21
N.Y. Islanders at Washington
Philadelphia at Atlanta
New Jersey at Chicago
San Jose at Anaheim

MONDAY, DEC. 22
Boston at N.Y. Rangers
Dallas at Carolina
Pittsburgh at Montreal
Florida at Ottawa
St. Louis at Detroit
Phoenix at Nashville
Los Angeles at Vancouver
Anaheim at San Jose

TUESDAY, DEC. 23
Tampa Bay at Boston
Ottawa at Buffalo
Philadelphia at N.Y. Islanders
Montreal at Washington
Phoenix at Columbus
Florida at Toronto
Nashville at Minnesota
St. Louis at Chicago
Edmonton at Calgary

FRIDAY, DEC. 26
Toronto at N.Y. Rangers
Pittsburgh at Ottawa
N.Y. Islanders at New Jersey
Tampa Bay at Atlanta
Minnesota at Detroit
Carolina at Buffalo
Colorado at St. Louis
Columbus at Chicago
Nashville at Dallas
Vancouver at Calgary
Los Angeles at San Jose

SATURDAY, DEC. 27
Toronto at N.Y. Islanders
Buffalo at Washington

Montreal at Carolina
Dallas at Columbus
New Jersey at Pittsburgh
Boston at Tampa Bay
Anaheim at Florida
Philadelphia at Colorado
Nashville at Phoenix
Edmonton at Vancouver
San Jose at Los Angeles

SUNDAY, DEC. 28
Atlanta at Ottawa *
Detroit at Chicago
Calgary at Edmonton

MONDAY, DEC. 29
New Jersey at N.Y. Islanders
Boston at Washington
Buffalo at Carolina
Anaheim at Tampa Bay
St. Louis at Columbus
Chicago at Pittsburgh
Montreal at Atlanta
Toronto at Florida
Philadelphia at Dallas
Vancouver at Colorado
Minnesota at Calgary
N.Y. Rangers at Phoenix
Nashville at San Jose

TUESDAY, DEC. 30
Ottawa at Boston
Philadelphia at St. Louis
Minnesota at Edmonton
N.Y. Rangers at Los Angeles

WEDNESDAY, DEC. 31
N.Y. Islanders at Pittsburgh *
Florida at Tampa Bay *
Washington at Buffalo
Atlanta at Detroit
San Jose at Columbus
Anaheim at Carolina
Colorado at Calgary
Vancouver at Chicago
Montreal at Dallas
Los Angeles at Phoenix

THURSDAY, JAN. 1
Pittsburgh at Nashville *
New Jersey at Washington
Toronto at Boston
N.Y. Islanders at Ottawa
N.Y. Rangers at St. Louis

FRIDAY, JAN. 2
Columbus at Tampa Bay *
Philadelphia at Florida
Detroit at Carolina
Anaheim at Buffalo
Edmonton at Minnesota
Phoenix at Dallas
San Jose at Chicago
Colorado at Vancouver

SATURDAY, JAN. 3
N.Y. Rangers at Pittsburgh *
Atlanta at Montreal *
N.Y. Islanders at Boston
Buffalo at Toronto
Washington at Ottawa
Philadelphia at Tampa Bay
Columbus at Florida
Anaheim at Detroit
San Jose at St. Louis
New Jersey at Nashville
Vancouver at Calgary
Dallas at Los Angeles

SUNDAY, JAN. 4
Phoenix at Carolina *
Washington at Montreal
Edmonton at Chicago
Minnesota at Colorado

MONDAY, JAN. 5
Calgary at N.Y. Rangers
Edmonton at New Jersey
Toronto at Pittsburgh
Nashville at Detroit
Minnesota at St. Louis
San Jose at Vancouver
Dallas at Anaheim

TUESDAY, JAN. 6
Calgary at N.Y. Islanders
St. Louis at Carolina
Nashville at Toronto
Buffalo at Montreal
Tampa Bay at Ottawa
Columbus at Colorado

WEDNESDAY, JAN. 7
Philadelphia at Buffalo
Phoenix at Washington
Pittsburgh at New Jersey
Boston at Detroit
Chicago at Minnesota
Los Angeles at Anaheim

THURSDAY, JAN. 8
Pittsburgh at Boston
Edmonton at N.Y. Islanders
Ottawa at Toronto
Florida at Philadelphia
N.Y. Rangers at Carolina
Tampa Bay at Montreal
Colorado at Nashville
Calgary at Chicago
Atlanta at Dallas
Vancouver at Los Angeles
Columbus at San Jose

FRIDAY, JAN. 9
Carolina at Washington
Tampa Bay at New Jersey
Ottawa at Buffalo
Phoenix at Minnesota
Vancouver at Anaheim

SATURDAY, JAN. 10
Detroit at Boston *
N.Y. Rangers at N.Y. Islanders *
Montreal at Pittsburgh *
Colorado at Dallas *
Atlanta at San Jose *
New Jersey at Toronto
Edmonton at Philadelphia
St. Louis at Nashville
Florida at Calgary
Columbus at Los Angeles

SUNDAY, JAN. 11
Tampa Bay at N.Y. Rangers
Ottawa at Carolina
Edmonton at Washington
Atlanta at Phoenix
Colorado at Chicago
Columbus at Anaheim
Florida at Vancouver

MONDAY, JAN. 12
Buffalo at Boston
Pittsburgh at Philadelphia
Chicago at St. Louis
Nashville at Minnesota

TUESDAY, JAN. 13
Philadelphia at Buffalo
N.Y. Islanders at N.Y. Rangers
Calgary at Toronto
St. Louis at Montreal
Ottawa at New Jersey
Tampa Bay at Pittsburgh
Los Angeles at Nashville
Anaheim at Colorado
Florida at Edmonton
Vancouver at Phoenix
Dallas at San Jose

WEDNESDAY, JAN. 14
Calgary at Washington
Montreal at Atlanta
Chicago at Detroit
Los Angeles at Minnesota

THURSDAY, JAN. 15
Boston at Buffalo
New Jersey at N.Y. Rangers
Carolina at Tampa Bay
N.Y. Islanders at Ottawa
Columbus at St. Louis
Phoenix at Nashville
Dallas at Colorado
Anaheim at Edmonton
Vancouver at San Jose

FRIDAY, JAN. 16
Toronto at Philadelphia
Los Angeles at Columbus
Carolina at Atlanta
Phoenix at Detroit
Pittsburgh at Minnesota

SATURDAY, JAN. 17
Washington at New Jersey *
Philadelphia at Toronto
N.Y. Rangers at Montreal
Boston at Ottawa
Buffalo at N.Y. Islanders
Tampa Bay at Florida
Minnesota at St. Louis
Edmonton at Nashville
San Jose at Colorado
Dallas at Calgary
Anaheim at Vancouver

SUNDAY, JAN. 18
Pittsburgh at Washington *
Atlanta at Carolina
Edmonton at Columbus
Los Angeles at Chicago

MONDAY, JAN. 19
Ottawa at N.Y. Islanders *
N.Y. Rangers at Boston *
St. Louis at Florida
Colorado at Tampa Bay
Minnesota at Nashville
Calgary at Anaheim
Detroit at San Jose
Dallas at Vancouver

TUESDAY, JAN. 20
Boston at N.Y. Rangers
Montreal at Philadelphia
Ottawa at Carolina
N.Y. Islanders at Toronto
New Jersey at Pittsburgh
Buffalo at Atlanta
Dallas at Edmonton
Calgary at Los Angeles

WEDNESDAY, JAN. 21
Toronto at Washington
St. Louis at Columbus
Carolina at New Jersey
Colorado at Florida
Chicago at Minnesota
San Jose at Phoenix
Tampa Bay at Vancouver
Detroit at Anaheim

THURSDAY, JAN. 22
Buffalo at Boston
Pittsburgh at Ottawa
Colorado at Atlanta
Philadelphia at N.Y. Rangers
Columbus at Chicago
Nashville at Calgary
Tampa Bay at Edmonton
Detroit at Los Angeles
Phoenix at San Jose

FRIDAY, JAN. 23
N.Y. Islanders at Carolina
Montreal at New Jersey
Washington at Florida
St. Louis at Dallas
Minnesota at Anaheim

SATURDAY, JAN. 24
Buffalo at Philadelphia *
Florida at Boston
Toronto at Montreal
N.Y. Rangers at Ottawa
N.Y. Islanders at Atlanta
Chicago at Columbus
Colorado at Pittsburgh
Dallas at St. Louis
Detroit at Phoenix
Tampa Bay at Calgary
Nashville at Edmonton
Anaheim at Los Angeles
Minnesota at San Jose

SUNDAY, JAN. 25
Buffalo at Carolina *
Philadelphia at Washington
Atlanta at New Jersey
Nashville at Vancouver

MONDAY, JAN. 26
Florida at N.Y. Rangers
Detroit at Dallas
Minnesota at Los Angeles

TUESDAY, JAN. 27
Montreal at Buffalo
Boston at N.Y. Islanders
New Jersey at Columbus
Carolina at Toronto
Tampa Bay at Pittsburgh
Edmonton at Colorado
Calgary at Phoenix
Chicago at Vancouver

WEDNESDAY, JAN. 28
Washington at N.Y. Rangers
Philadelphia at Florida
St. Louis at Atlanta
Ottawa at Dallas
Los Angeles at Anaheim
Calgary at San Jose

THURSDAY, JAN. 29
Washington at Carolina
Pittsburgh at Tampa Bay
Nashville at Columbus
New Jersey at Detroit

N.Y. Islanders at Boston
Vancouver at St. Louis
Montreal at Minnesota
Chicago at Edmonton
Ottawa at Phoenix
Colorado at Los Angeles

FRIDAY, JAN. 30
Buffalo at N.Y. Rangers
Toronto at Atlanta
San Jose at Dallas
Chicago at Calgary
Colorado at Anaheim

SATURDAY, JAN. 31
Philadelphia at Pittsburgh *
Boston at Montreal *
N.Y. Rangers at Buffalo
Ottawa at Toronto
Florida at N.Y. Islanders
Vancouver at Washington
Carolina at Detroit
Minnesota at Columbus
Atlanta at Tampa Bay
New Jersey at St. Louis
San Jose at Nashville
Dallas at Phoenix
Los Angeles at Edmonton

SUNDAY, FEB. 1
Pittsburgh at Boston *
Chicago at Montreal *
Anaheim at Calgary

MONDAY, FEB. 2
Vancouver at N.Y. Rangers
Tampa Bay at Philadelphia
St. Louis at Minnesota
Anaheim at Edmonton
Columbus at Phoenix

TUESDAY, FEB. 3
Atlanta at Boston
Vancouver at N.Y. Islanders
Tampa Bay at Washington
Chicago at Toronto
Ottawa at New Jersey
Montreal at Pittsburgh
Detroit at Nashville
Carolina at Colorado
Los Angeles at Calgary
Florida at San Jose

WEDNESDAY, FEB. 4
Minnesota at N.Y. Rangers
Washington at Philadelphia
Columbus at Dallas
Florida at Phoenix
St. Louis at Edmonton
Carolina at Anaheim

THURSDAY, FEB. 5
Boston at Buffalo
N.Y. Islanders at Montreal
Toronto at Ottawa
Vancouver at New Jersey
Philadelphia at Atlanta
Tampa Bay at Nashville
St. Louis at Calgary
Detroit at Colorado
Phoenix at San Jose

SATURDAY, FEB. 7
NHL All-Star Saturday, Xcel Energy Center, St. Paul

SUNDAY, FEB. 8
NHL All-Star Game, Xcel Energy Center, St. Paul, Time TBD

TUESDAY, FEB. 10
San Jose at Buffalo
New Jersey at Philadelphia
Toronto at Tampa Bay
St. Louis at Ottawa
Boston at Pittsburgh
Montreal at Florida
Los Angeles at Minnesota
Atlanta at Calgary
N.Y. Islanders at Colorado

WEDNESDAY, FEB. 11
Los Angeles at Columbus
N.Y. Rangers at New Jersey
San Jose at Detroit
Nashville at Chicago
N.Y. Islanders at Dallas
Atlanta at Edmonton
Calgary at Vancouver
Phoenix at Anaheim

THURSDAY, FEB. 12
Philadelphia at N.Y. Rangers
Washington at Carolina
Montreal at Tampa Bay
Columbus at Toronto
Boston at Ottawa
Pittsburgh at Florida
Colorado at St. Louis

FRIDAY, FEB. 13
Los Angeles at Buffalo
Washington at Nashville
Edmonton at Minnesota
Anaheim at Calgary
N.Y. Islanders at Phoenix
Atlanta at Vancouver

SATURDAY, FEB. 14
Carolina at New Jersey *
N.Y. Rangers at Philadelphia *
Colorado at Detroit *
Boston at Chicago *
Buffalo at Toronto
Montreal at Ottawa
San Jose at Columbus
Florida at Tampa Bay
Pittsburgh at St. Louis
Dallas at Phoenix
Anaheim at Vancouver

SUNDAY, FEB. 15
Los Angeles at New Jersey *
Calgary at Minnesota *
Edmonton at Nashville *
Washington at Chicago *

MONDAY, FEB. 16
Los Angeles at N.Y. Islanders *
Ottawa at N.Y. Rangers *
Atlanta at Buffalo *
Phoenix at St. Louis *
Florida at Carolina
Nashville at Columbus
Toronto at Pittsburgh
Edmonton at Detroit
San Jose at Philadelphia
Dallas at Anaheim
Vancouver at Colorado

TUESDAY, FEB. 17
Ottawa at Washington
Philadelphia at Tampa Bay
Boston at Toronto
Atlanta at Montreal
Minnesota at New Jersey

WEDNESDAY, FEB. 18
Florida at Buffalo
Pittsburgh at N.Y. Islanders
Phoenix at Detroit
San Jose at Nashville
Edmonton at Colorado
Columbus at Anaheim
Dallas at Los Angeles

THURSDAY, FEB. 19
N.Y. Islanders at N.Y. Rangers
New Jersey at Washington
Toronto at Carolina
Calgary at Montreal
Atlanta at Ottawa
Boston at Philadelphia
San Jose at Chicago
Tampa Bay at St. Louis
Vancouver at Minnesota

FRIDAY, FEB. 20
Florida at Pittsburgh
St. Louis at Detroit
Tampa Bay at Buffalo
Colorado at Dallas
Columbus at Phoenix
Nashville at Anaheim

SATURDAY, FEB. 21
New Jersey at N.Y. Rangers *
Atlanta at Philadelphia *
Calgary at Ottawa *
Montreal at Toronto
Buffalo at N.Y. Islanders
Florida at Washington
Boston at Carolina
Nashville at Phoenix
Vancouver at Edmonton
Columbus at Los Angeles

SUNDAY, FEB. 22
Calgary at New Jersey *
Ottawa at Pittsburgh *
St. Louis at Chicago *
Anaheim at Dallas *
Colorado at Minnesota

MONDAY, FEB. 23
Florida at Boston
Montreal at N.Y. Rangers
Tampa Bay at Washington
Carolina at Toronto
Detroit at Edmonton
Anaheim at Phoenix
Nashville at Los Angeles
Columbus at San Jose

TUESDAY, FEB. 24
Ottawa at Montreal
Boston at N.Y. Islanders
Chicago at Philadelphia
Calgary at Colorado
Detroit at Vancouver

WEDNESDAY, FEB. 25
Carolina at Washington
Chicago at Columbus
Buffalo at New Jersey
Tampa Bay at Atlanta
Toronto at Florida
Los Angeles at Dallas
Pittsburgh at Phoenix
Edmonton at Anaheim

THURSDAY, FEB. 26
Montreal at Boston
N.Y. Rangers at N.Y. Islanders
Toronto at Tampa Bay

Philadelphia at Ottawa
Minnesota at Nashville
St. Louis at Colorado
Detroit at Calgary
San Jose at Vancouver

FRIDAY, FEB. 27
Atlanta at New Jersey
Washington at Florida
N.Y. Islanders at Buffalo
Columbus at Chicago
Minnesota at Dallas
Edmonton at Phoenix
Pittsburgh at San Jose

SATURDAY, FEB. 28
Philadelphia at Boston *
N.Y. Rangers at Nashville *
Anaheim at Los Angeles *
New Jersey at Toronto
Carolina at Montreal
Buffalo at Ottawa
Colorado at Columbus
Washington at Tampa Bay
St. Louis at Vancouver

SUNDAY, FEB. 29
N.Y. Rangers at Atlanta *
Florida at Chicago *
Edmonton at Dallas *
Pittsburgh at N.Y. Islanders *
Los Angeles at Anaheim *
Philadelphia at Detroit
Carolina at Minnesota
Phoenix at Calgary
St. Louis at San Jose

MONDAY, MARCH 1
New Jersey at Montreal
Chicago at Nashville
Tampa Bay at Colorado

TUESDAY, MARCH 2
Atlanta at N.Y. Rangers
Florida at Washington
Columbus at Carolina
Boston at Toronto
N.Y. Islanders at Pittsburgh
Calgary at St. Louis
Phoenix at Edmonton

WEDNESDAY, MARCH 3
Ottawa at Buffalo
Nashville at Philadelphia
New Jersey at Florida
Calgary at Detroit
Tampa Bay at Chicago
Columbus at Dallas
Vancouver at Colorado
Minnesota at Anaheim
Montreal at San Jose

THURSDAY, MARCH 4
N.Y. Islanders at Toronto
Nashville at Pittsburgh
N.Y. Rangers at Boston
Edmonton at St. Louis
Minnesota at Los Angeles

FRIDAY, MARCH 5
Washington at N.Y. Rangers
Ottawa at Philadelphia
Carolina at Atlanta
New Jersey at Tampa Bay
Vancouver at Detroit
Anaheim at Chicago
Calgary at Dallas
San Jose at Colorado
Montreal at Phoenix

SATURDAY, MARCH 6
Atlanta at Boston
Buffalo at Toronto
Nashville at Ottawa
St. Louis at N.Y. Islanders
New Jersey at Carolina
Vancouver at Columbus
Anaheim at Pittsburgh
Tampa Bay at Florida
Philadelphia at Washington
Montreal at Los Angeles

SUNDAY, MARCH 7
Edmonton at Chicago *
Calgary at Colorado *
San Jose at Dallas *
Pittsburgh at N.Y. Rangers
St. Louis at Buffalo
Minnesota at Phoenix

MONDAY, MARCH 8
Ottawa at Washington
Carolina at Columbus
Tampa Bay at Detroit
Colorado at Vancouver
Montreal at Anaheim

TUESDAY, MARCH 9
Florida at Toronto
Philadelphia at New Jersey
Dallas at Pittsburgh
N.Y. Rangers at Atlanta
N.Y. Islanders at St. Louis
Boston at Nashville
Edmonton at Calgary
Phoenix at Los Angeles
Minnesota at San Jose

WEDNESDAY, MARCH 10
Buffalo at Washington
Tampa Bay at Carolina
Colorado at Edmonton
Los Angeles at Phoenix
Minnesota at Vancouver

THURSDAY, MARCH 11
Boston at Buffalo
Dallas at Philadelphia
Detroit at Columbus
Pittsburgh at Toronto
Florida at Montreal
Chicago at New Jersey
Nashville at St. Louis
Ottawa at Calgary
N.Y. Islanders at San Jose

FRIDAY, MARCH 12
Chicago at Washington
Atlanta at Carolina
N.Y. Rangers at Tampa Bay
Vancouver at Edmonton
Colorado at Phoenix
N.Y. Islanders at Anaheim

SATURDAY, MARCH 13
Buffalo at Boston *
New Jersey at Philadelphia *
Dallas at Detroit *
Los Angeles at San Jose *
Toronto at Montreal
Washington at Atlanta
Carolina at Tampa Bay
N.Y. Rangers at Florida
Columbus at St. Louis
Calgary at Nashville
Ottawa at Vancouver

SUNDAY, MARCH 14
Philadelphia at Pittsburgh *
Dallas at Chicago *
Phoenix at Colorado *
Anaheim at Los Angeles *
Nashville at Detroit
Calgary at St. Louis
Columbus at Minnesota
Ottawa at Edmonton

MONDAY, MARCH 15
Toronto at Buffalo
New Jersey at N.Y. Rangers
Carolina at Atlanta

TUESDAY, MARCH 16
N.Y. Islanders at Tampa Bay
Boston at Toronto
Colorado at Montreal
Washington at Pittsburgh
Calgary at Detroit
Ottawa at Minnesota
San Jose at Dallas
Columbus at Edmonton
Anaheim at Phoenix
Nashville at Vancouver
St. Louis at Los Angeles

WEDNESDAY, MARCH 17
Pittsburgh at New Jersey
Buffalo at Atlanta
N.Y. Islanders at Florida
Carolina at Chicago
St. Louis at Anaheim

THURSDAY, MARCH 18
N.Y. Rangers at Washington
Buffalo at Tampa Bay
Colorado at Ottawa
Minnesota at Boston
Toronto at Philadelphia
Vancouver at Dallas
Columbus at Calgary
Detroit at Phoenix
San Jose at Los Angeles

FRIDAY, MARCH 19
Minnesota at N.Y. Islanders
Montreal at New Jersey
Carolina at Pittsburgh
Florida at Atlanta
Vancouver at Chicago
Nashville at Edmonton
San Jose at Anaheim

SATURDAY, MARCH 20
Tampa Bay at Boston *
N.Y. Rangers at Philadelphia *
St. Louis at Dallas *
Colorado at Toronto
New Jersey at Montreal
Carolina at Ottawa
Atlanta at Washington
Buffalo at Florida
Nashville at Calgary
Detroit at Los Angeles

SUNDAY, MARCH 21
Tampa Bay at N.Y. Islanders *

N.Y. Rangers at Pittsburgh *
Phoenix at Chicago *
Detroit at Anaheim
Edmonton at San Jose
Columbus at Vancouver

MONDAY, MARCH 22
Phoenix at Minnesota
Dallas at Calgary
Edmonton at Los Angeles

TUESDAY, MARCH 23
Ottawa at Boston
Washington at N.Y. Islanders
Philadelphia at Carolina
Tampa Bay at Toronto
Pittsburgh at N.Y. Rangers
New Jersey at Florida
Anaheim at Nashville
Chicago at Colorado
Detroit at San Jose

WEDNESDAY, MARCH 24
Minnesota at Columbus
Montreal at Buffalo
Washington at Atlanta
Calgary at Phoenix
Dallas at Edmonton
Los Angeles at Vancouver

THURSDAY, MARCH 25
Toronto at Boston
N.Y. Islanders at Philadelphia
Florida at Carolina
New Jersey at Tampa Bay
Ottawa at Montreal
Nashville at N.Y. Rangers
Anaheim at St. Louis
Detroit at Colorado
Minnesota at Chicago
Calgary at San Jose

FRIDAY, MARCH 26
Anaheim at Columbus
New Jersey at Atlanta
Pittsburgh at Buffalo
Los Angeles at Edmonton
San Jose at Phoenix

SATURDAY, MARCH 27
N.Y. Rangers at Philadelphia *
Colorado at Detroit *
Chicago at St. Louis
Los Angeles at Calgary
Montreal at Boston
Ottawa at Toronto
Carolina at N.Y. Islanders
Buffalo at Pittsburgh
Washington at Tampa Bay
Atlanta at Florida
Columbus at Nashville
Dallas at Vancouver

SUNDAY, MARCH 28
St. Louis at Chicago *
Anaheim at Minnesota *
Phoenix at Edmonton *
N.Y. Islanders at New Jersey
Dallas at San Jose

MONDAY, MARCH 29
Columbus at Buffalo
Ottawa at Tampa Bay
Minnesota at Detroit
Atlanta at Toronto
Carolina at Florida
Los Angeles at Colorado
Phoenix at Vancouver

TUESDAY, MARCH 30
Pittsburgh at Washington
Boston at Carolina
N.Y. Rangers at New Jersey
Edmonton at St. Louis
Chicago at Nashville

WEDNESDAY, MARCH 31
Montreal at N.Y. Islanders
Detroit at Columbus
Buffalo at N.Y. Rangers
Ottawa at Florida
Colorado at Minnesota
Edmonton at Dallas
Phoenix at Calgary
Vancouver at Anaheim
San Jose at Los Angeles

THURSDAY, APRIL 1
Florida at Tampa Bay
Washington at Boston
Philadelphia at Montreal
Detroit at St. Louis
Nashville at Chicago

FRIDAY, APRIL 2
Ottawa at Philadelphia
N.Y. Islanders at Carolina
Colorado at Columbus
Pittsburgh at Atlanta
Toronto at Buffalo
Dallas at Minnesota
Calgary at Los Angeles
Vancouver at San Jose

SATURDAY, APRIL 3
New Jersey at Boston *
N.Y. Rangers at Washington *
St. Louis at Nashville *
Chicago at Phoenix *
Buffalo at Montreal
Toronto at Ottawa
Atlanta at Tampa Bay
Columbus at Detroit
Edmonton at Vancouver

SUNDAY, APRIL 4
Boston at New Jersey *
Philadelphia at N.Y. Islanders *
Washington at Pittsburgh *
Carolina at Florida *
St. Louis at Minnesota *
Chicago at Dallas *
Nashville at Colorado *
Calgary at Anaheim *
Los Angeles at San Jose *

2002-03 NHL REVIEW

Regular season

Stanley Cup playoffs

All-Star Game

Awards

Player draft

REGULAR SEASON

FINAL STANDINGS

EASTERN CONFERENCE

ATLANTIC DIVISION

	G	W	L	T	OTL	Pts.	GF	GA	Home	Away	Div. Rec.
New Jersey Devils	82	46	20	10	6	108	216	166	25-11-3-2	21-9-7-4	13-2-5-0
Philadelphia Flyers	82	45	20	13	4	107	211	166	21-10-8-2	24-10-5-2	11-6-2-1
New York Islanders	82	35	34	11	2	83	224	231	18-18-5-0	17-16-6-2	6-9-4-1
New York Rangers	82	32	36	10	4	78	210	231	17-18-4-2	15-18-6-2	6-8-5-1
Pittsburgh Penguins	82	27	44	6	5	65	189	255	15-22-2-2	12-22-4-3	6-14-0-0

NORTHEAST DIVISION

	G	W	L	T	OTL	Pts.	GF	GA	Home	Away	Div. Rec.
Ottawa Senators	82	52	21	8	1	113	263	182	28-9-3-1	24-12-5-0	14-4-1-1
Toronto Maple Leafs	82	44	28	7	3	98	236	208	24-13-4-0	20-15-3-3	9-10-1-0
Boston Bruins	82	36	31	11	4	87	245	237	23-11-5-2	13-20-6-2	9-9-1-1
Montreal Canadiens	82	30	35	8	9	77	206	234	16-16-5-4	14-19-3-5	7-9-1-3
Buffalo Sabres	82	27	37	10	8	72	190	219	18-16-5-2	9-21-5-6	9-9-0-2

SOUTHEAST DIVISION

	G	W	L	T	OTL	Pts.	GF	GA	Home	Away	Div. Rec.
Tampa Bay Lightning	82	36	25	16	5	93	219	210	22-9-7-3	14-16-9-2	10-4-5-1
Washington Capitals	82	39	29	8	6	92	224	220	24-13-2-2	15-16-6-4	14-4-2-0
Atlanta Thrashers	82	31	39	7	5	74	226	284	15-19-4-3	16-20-3-2	7-7-3-3
Florida Panthers	82	24	36	13	9	70	176	237	8-21-7-5	16-15-6-4	7-7-3-3
Carolina Hurricanes	82	22	43	11	6	61	171	240	12-17-9-3	10-26-2-3	4-11-3-2

WESTERN CONFERENCE

CENTRAL DIVISION

	G	W	L	T	OTL	Pts.	GF	GA	Home	Away	Div. Rec.
Detroit Red Wings	82	48	20	10	4	110	269	203	28-6-5-2	20-14-5-2	14-3-2-1
St. Louis Blues	82	41	24	11	6	99	253	222	23-11-4-3	18-13-7-3	7-8-3-2
Chicago Blackhawks	82	30	33	13	6	79	207	226	17-15-7-2	13-18-6-4	11-3-3-3
Nashville Predators	82	27	35	13	7	74	183	206	18-17-5-1	9-18-8-6	6-9-4-1
Columbus Blue Jackets	82	29	42	8	3	69	213	263	20-14-5-2	9-28-3-1	5-13-2-0

NORTHWEST DIVISION

	G	W	L	T	OTL	Pts.	GF	GA	Home	Away	Div. Rec.
Colorado Avalanche	82	42	19	13	8	105	251	194	21-9-8-3	21-10-5-5	8-5-4-3
Vancouver Canucks	82	45	23	13	1	104	264	208	22-13-6-0	23-10-7-1	10-6-4-0
Minnesota Wild	82	42	29	10	1	95	198	178	25-13-3-0	17-16-7-1	7-8-4-1
Edmonton Oilers	82	36	26	11	9	92	231	230	20-12-5-4	16-14-6-5	7-7-2-4
Calgary Flames	82	29	36	13	4	75	186	228	14-16-10-1	15-20-3-3	9-6-4-1

PACIFIC DIVISION

	G	W	L	T	OTL	Pts.	GF	GA	Home	Away	Div. Rec.
Dallas Stars	82	46	17	15	4	111	245	169	28-5-6-2	18-12-9-2	14-3-3-0
Mighty Ducks of Anaheim	82	40	27	9	6	95	203	193	22-10-7-2	18-17-2-4	8-9-3-0
Los Angeles Kings	82	33	37	6	6	78	203	221	19-19-2-1	14-18-4-5	10-9-1-0
Phoenix Coyotes	82	31	35	11	5	78	204	230	17-16-6-2	14-19-5-3	6-7-4-3
San Jose Sharks	82	28	37	9	8	73	214	239	17-16-5-3	11-21-4-5	6-10-1-3

Note: OTL denotes overtime loss; teams receive two points for each victory, one for each tie and one for each overtime loss.

INDIVIDUAL LEADERS

SCORING

TOP SCORERS

	Games	G	A	Pts.	PIM	+/-	PPG	SHG	GWG	GTG	Sht.	Sht. Pct.	Faceoffs Won	Faceoffs Lost	Pct.	TOI
Peter Forsberg, Colo.	75	29	77	106	70	52	8	0	2	0	166	17.5	333	376	47.0	19:19
Markus Naslund, Van.	82	48	56	104	52	6	24	0	12	1	294	16.3	2	4	33.3	19:54
Joe Thornton, Boston	77	36	65	101	109	12	12	2	4	1	196	18.4	874	892	49.5	22:32
Milan Hejduk, Colo.	82	50	48	98	32	52	18	0	4	1	244	20.5	19	24	44.2	19:50
Todd Bertuzzi, Van.	82	46	51	97	144	2	25	0	7	1	243	18.9	98	110	47.1	20:34
Pavol Demitra, St.L.	78	36	57	93	32	0	11	0	4	1	205	17.6	578	675	46.1	19:47

	Games	G	A	Pts.	PIM	+/-	PPG	SHG	GWG	GTG	Sht.	Sht. Pct.	Faceoffs			TOI
													Won	Lost	Pct.	
Glen Murray, Boston.....	82	44	48	92	64	9	12	0	5	2	331	13.3	12	20	37.5	22:36
Mario Lemieux, Pit.	67	28	63	91	43	-25	14	0	4	0	235	11.9	474	555	46.1	23:04
Dany Heatley, Atlanta....	77	41	48	89	58	-8	19	1	6	0	252	16.3	18	31	36.7	21:57
Zigmund Palffy, L.A.	76	37	48	85	47	22	10	2	5	0	277	13.4	3	7	30.0	22:26
Mike Modano, Dallas....	79	28	57	85	30	34	5	2	6	0	193	14.5	929	879	51.4	20:52
Sergei Fedorov, Det.	80	36	47	83	52	15	10	2	11	0	281	12.8	843	737	53.4	21:10
Paul Kariya, Anaheim....	82	25	56	81	48	-3	11	1	2	1	257	9.7	12	27	30.8	20:17
Marian Hossa, Ott........	80	45	35	80	34	8	14	0	10	1	229	19.7	7	12	36.8	18:30
Alexander Mogilny, Tor.	73	33	46	79	12	4	5	3	9	0	165	20.0	6	12	33.3	20:02
Vaclav Prospal, T.B......	80	22	57	79	53	9	9	0	4	0	134	16.4	83	78	51.6	18:39
Vincent Lecavalier, T.B..	80	33	45	78	39	0	11	2	3	1	274	12.0	527	673	43.9	19:32
Daniel Alfredsson, Ott...	78	27	51	78	42	15	9	0	6	0	240	11.3	16	24	40.0	19:31
Alexei Kovalev, Pit.-N.Y.R.	78	37	40	77	70	-9	11	0	3	1	271	13.7	14	24	36.8	22:51
Jaromir Jagr, Wash.	75	36	41	77	38	5	13	2	9	0	290	12.4	1	4	20.0	21:18

LEADERS BY CATEGORY

Games played

Rem Murray, N.Y.R.-Nash. 85
Bates Battaglia, Car.-Colo................83
Dmitry Yushkevich, Fla.-L.A.-Phi. 83
70 tied with.......................................82

Goals

Milan Hejduk, Colorado 50
Markus Naslund, Vancouver................48
Todd Bertuzzi, Vancouver...................46
Marian Hossa, Ottawa........................45
Glen Murray, Boston..........................44
Dany Heatley, Atlanta 41
Ilya Kovalchuk, Atlanta.......................38
4 tied with...37

Goals by defensemen

Andy Delmore, Nashville.....................18
Sergei Gonchar, Washington 18
Nicklas Lidstrom, Detroit 18
Rob Blake, Colorado...........................17
Al MacInnis, St. Louis.........................16
Mathieu Schneider, L.A.-Det. 16
Dan Boyle, Tampa Bay........................13
Andrei Markov, Montreal 13
Jaroslav Modry, Los Angeles 13
Two tied with 12

Goals by rookies

Henrik Zetterberg, Detroit...................22
Ales Kotalik, Buffalo 21
Tyler Arnason, Chicago.......................19
Rick Nash, Columbus 17
Adam Hall, Nashville...........................16
Jason Chimera, Edmonton 14
Alexander Frolov, Los Angeles 14
Stanislav Chistov, Anaheim 12
Branko Radivojevic, Phoenix 12
Two tied with 10

Goals per game
(30 goals minimum)

Milan Hejduk, Colorado 0.61
Markus Naslund, Vancouver 0.59
Marian Hossa, Ottawa 0.56
Todd Bertuzzi, Vancouver..................0.56
Keith Tkachuk, St. Louis.....................0.55
Glen Murray, Boston 0.54
Dany Heatley, Atlanta........................0.53
Mats Sundin, Toronto 0.49
Zigmund Palffy, Los Angeles 0.49
Jaromir Jagr, Washington 0.48

Power-play goals

Todd Bertuzzi, Vancouver 25
Markus Naslund, Vancouver................24
Dany Heatley, Atlanta 19
Milan Hejduk, Colorado 18
Mats Sundin, Toronto 16
Dave Andreychuk, Tampa Bay.............15
Vincent Damphousse, San Jose 15
Geoff Sanderson, Columbus 15
Petr Sykora, Anaheim 15
Five tied with......................................14

Shorthanded goals

Shawn Bates, N.Y. Islanders 6
Brian Rolston, Boston...........................5
Curtis Brown, Buffalo 4
Matt Cooke, Vancouver.........................4
Kirk Maltby, Detroit...............................4
Martin Rucinsky, St. Louis 4
14 tied with...3

Even-strength goals

Milan Hejduk, Colorado 32
Glen Murray, Boston...........................32
Marian Hossa, Ottawa.........................31
Ilya Kovalchuk, Atlanta 29
Alexei Kovalev, Pit.-N.Y.R....................26
Jere Lehtinen, Dallas...........................26
Pavol Demitra, St. Louis 25
Alexander Mogilny, Toronto 25
Zigmund Palffy, Los Angeles 25
Four tied with 24

Unassisted goals

Zigmund Palffy, Los Angeles 6
Shawn Bates, N.Y. Islanders 5
Kirk Maltby, Detroit...............................5
Eight tied with......................................4

Game-winning goals

Markus Naslund, Vancouver................12
Sergei Fedorov, Detroit 11
Marian Hossa, Ottawa.........................10
Michal Handzus, Philadelphia 9
Jaromir Jagr, Washington.......................9
Alexander Mogilny, Toronto 9
Marian Gaborik, Minnesota...................8
Brendan Morrison, Vancouver...............8
Bryan Smolinski, L.A.-Ott. 8
Mats Sundin, Toronto 8

Game-tying goals

Andrew Brunette, Minnesota 3
Kristian Huselius, Florida 3
Martin St. Louis, Tampa Bay.................3
15 tied with...2

Empty-net goals

Mike Modano, Dallas 5
Eric Belanger, Los Angeles 4
11 tied with...3

Goal-scoring streaks
(consecutive games)

Geoff Sanderson, Columbus.................7
Milan Hejduk, Colorado 7
Patrick Marleau, San Jose 6
Markus Naslund, Vancouver 6
Owen Nolan, San Jose 6
Keith Tkachuk, St. Louis 6
Six tied with 5

Games with three or more goals

Marian Gaborik, Minnesota...................3
Marian Hossa, Ottawa...........................3
12 tied with...2

Assists

Peter Forsberg, Colorado 77
Joe Thornton, Boston...........................65
Mario Lemieux, Pittsburgh 63
Pavol Demitra, St. Louis 57
Mike Modano, Dallas 57
Vaclav Prospal, Tampa Bay.................57
Brad Richards, Tampa Bay...................57
Paul Kariya, Anaheim 56
Markus Naslund, Vancouver 56
Three tied with 52

Assists by defensemen

Al MacInnis, St. Louis..........................52
Sergei Gonchar, Washington 49
Nicklas Lidstrom, Detroit 44
Sergei Zubov, Dallas 44
Dan Boyle, Tampa Bay.........................40
Ed Jovanovski, Vancouver 40
Robert Svehla, Toronto 38
Derek Morris, Colorado 37
Tom Poti, N.Y. Rangers........................37
Brian Rafalski, New Jersey 37

Assists by rookies

Niko Kapanen, Dallas 29
Ales Hemsky, Edmonton.....................24
Jaroslav Bednar, L.A.-Fla. 22
Rick Nash, Columbus 22
Henrik Zetterberg, Detroit 22
Tyler Arnason, Chicago.......................20
Jim Fahey, San Jose 19
Stanislav Chistov, Anaheim...................18
Alexander Frolov, Los Angeles 17
Mattias Weinhandl, N.Y. Islanders 17

Assists per game
(41 assists minimum)

Peter Forsberg, Colorado.................1.03
Mario Lemieux, Pittsburgh 0.94
Joe Thornton, Boston 0.84
Doug Weight, St. Louis 0.74
Pavol Demitra, St. Louis 0.73
Mike Modano, Dallas 0.72
Vaclav Prospal, Tampa Bay 0.71
Brad Richards, Tampa Bay...............0.71
Paul Kariya, Anaheim......................0.68
Markus Naslund, Vancouver 0.68

Power-play assists

Brad Richards, Tampa Bay 34
Ray Whitney, Columbus 34
Mario Lemieux, Pittsburgh 31
Markus Naslund, Vancouver 30
Doug Weight, St. Louis 29
Al MacInnis, St. Louis.......................28
Mike Modano, Dallas 26
Andrew Cassels, Columbus 25
Pavol Demitra, St. Louis 25
Peter Forsberg, Colorado 25

Shorthanded assists

Ian Laperriere, Los Angeles 4
Todd Marchant, Edmonton 4
Sami Salo, Vancouver..........................4
Nine tied with 3

Even-strength assists

Peter Forsberg, Colorado 52
Joe Thornton, Boston 43
Vaclav Prospal, Tampa Bay 37
Todd Bertuzzi, Vancouver 34
Saku Koivu, Montreal 33
Pavol Demitra, St. Louis 32
Scott Gomez, New Jersey 32
Paul Kariya, Anaheim 32
Vincent Lecavalier, Tampa Bay 32
Mario Lemieux, Pittsburgh 32

Points by defensemen

Al MacInnis, St. Louis.........................68
Sergei Gonchar, Washington 67
Nicklas Lidstrom, Detroit 62
Sergei Zubov, Dallas..........................55
Dan Boyle, Tampa Bay 53
Mathieu Schneider, L.A.-Det. 50
Derek Morris, Colorado 48
Tom Poti, N.Y. Rangers.......................48
Tomas Kaberle, Toronto 47
Ed Jovanovski, Vancouver 46

Points by rookies

Henrik Zetterberg, Detroit 44
Tyler Arnason, Chicago 39
Rick Nash, Columbus 39
Ales Kotalik, Buffalo 35
Niko Kapanen, Dallas 34
Alexander Frolov, Los Angeles 31
Stanislav Chistov, Anaheim..................30
Ales Hemsky, Edmonton 30
Adam Hall, Nashville............................28
Two tied with 27

Points per game
(41 points minimum)

Peter Forsberg, Colorado.................1.41
Mario Lemieux, Pittsburgh 1.36
Joe Thornton, Boston 1.31
Markus Naslund, Vancouver 1.27
Milan Hejduk, Colorado 1.20
Pavol Demitra, St. Louis 1.19
Todd Bertuzzi, Vancouver.................1.18
Dany Heatley, Atlanta.....................1.16
Glen Murray, Boston 1.12
Zigmund Palffy, Los Angeles 1.12

Power-play points

Markus Naslund, Vancouver.................54
Mario Lemieux, Pittsburgh 45
Todd Bertuzzi, Vancouver...................42
Ray Whitney, Columbus 42
Dany Heatley, Atlanta 39
Brad Richards, Tampa Bay.................38
Al MacInnis, St. Louis........................37
Pavol Demitra, St. Louis....................36
Doug Weight, St. Louis.......................36
Two tied with 35

Shorthanded points

Brian Rolston, Boston............................7
Shawn Bates, N.Y. Islanders 6
Mike Sillinger, Columbus 6
Steve Staios, Edmonton 6
11 tied with...5

Even-strength points

Peter Forsberg, Colorado 73
Joe Thornton, Boston 65
Milan Hejduk, Colorado 63
Glen Murray, Boston 63
Pavol Demitra, St. Louis 57
Todd Bertuzzi, Vancouver 55
Zigmund Palffy, Los Angeles 55
Sergei Fedorov, Detroit 52
Vincent Lecavalier, Tampa Bay 52
Alex Tanguay, Colorado......................52

Point-scoring streaks
(consecutive games)

Alex Tanguay, Colorado.......................16
Marian Hossa, Ottawa..........................13
Milan Hejduk, Colorado 13
Milan Hejduk, Colorado 13
Todd Bertuzzi, Vancouver 12
Keith Tkachuk, St. Louis......................12
Jeff Friesen, New Jersey 12
Two tied with 11

Penalty minutes

Jody Shelley, Columbus 249
Reed Low, St. Louis...........................234

Matt Johnson, Minnesota 201
Wade Belak, Toronto..........................196
Peter Worrell, Florida 193
Barret Jackman, St. Louis..................190
Eric Boulton, Buffalo..........................178
Scott Mellanby, St. Louis 176
Tie Domi, Toronto 171
Jeff Odgers, Atlanta 171

Best plus/minus
(60 games minimum)

Peter Forsberg, Colorado 52
Milan Hejduk, Colorado 52
Nicklas Lidstrom, Detroit 40
Jere Lehtinen, Dallas 39
Derian Hatcher, Dallas........................37
Mike Modano, Dallas 34
Alex Tanguay, Colorado......................34
Eric Desjardins, Philadelphia 30
Adam Foote, Colorado 30
Zdeno Chara, Ottawa 29

Worst plus/minus
(60 games minimum)

Jay Bouwmeester, Florida ....-29
Wayne Primeau, Pit.-S.J......................-28
Jamie Pushor, Pittsburgh ....-28
Tim Connolly, Buffalo ....-28
Yannick Tremblay, Atlanta ....-27
David Tanabe, Carolina ....-27
Rick Nash, Columbus ....-27
Ray Whitney, Columbus ....-26
Sean Pronger, Columbus.....................-26
Mario Lemieux, Pittsburgh ....-25
Tyler Wright, Columbus.......................-25
Ville Nieminen, Pittsburgh..................-25

Shots

Glen Murray, Boston 331
Jarome Iginla, Calgary 316
Jeff O'Neill, Carolina 316
Al MacInnis, St. Louis........................299
Petr Sykora, Anaheim.........................299
Markus Naslund, Vancouver 294
Jaromir Jagr, Washington....................290
Geoff Sanderson, Columbus..............286
Sergei Fedorov, Detroit 281
Brian Rolston, Boston.........................281

Shooting percentage
(82 shots minimum)

Milan Hejduk, Colorado 20.5
Alexander Mogilny, Toronto 20.0
Brenden Morrow, Dallas 20.0
Scott Mellanby, St. Louis...................19.7
Marian Hossa, Ottawa 19.7
Todd Bertuzzi, Vancouver 18.9
Eric Boguniecki, St. Louis 18.8
Andrew Brunette, Minnesota 18.6
Joe Thornton, Boston 18.4
Tomas Holmstrom, Detroit 18.3

Faceoffs

Daymond Langkow, Phoenix 1,972
Olli Jokinen, Florida 1,925
Mike Modano, Dallas 1,808
Mats Sundin, Toronto 1,774
Joe Thornton, Boston 1,766

Andrew Cassels, Columbus	1,649
Keith Primeau, Philadelphia	1,613
Steve Rucchin, Anaheim	1,613
Jozef Stumpel, Boston	1,601
Brendan Morrison, Vancouver	1,585

Faceoffs won

Mats Sundin, Toronto	995
Mike Modano, Dallas	929
Daymond Langkow, Phoenix	917
Craig Conroy, Calgary	900
Olli Jokinen, Florida	898
Jozef Stumpel, Boston	875
Steve Rucchin, Anaheim	874
Joe Thornton, Boston	874
Sergei Fedorov, Detroit	843
Mike Sillinger, Columbus	842

Faceoff percentage
(200 faceoffs minimum)

Yanic Perreault, Montreal	.629
Jason Krog, Anaheim	.604
Chris Gratton, Buf.-Pho.	.586
Joe Nieuwendyk, New Jersey	.585

Dave Andreychuk, Tampa Bay	.584
Scott Nichol, Calgary	.583
Bobby Holik, N.Y. Rangers	.582
Todd Marchant, Edmonton	.580
Tim Taylor, Tampa Bay	.579
Darren McCarty, Detroit	.578

Minutes per game by forwards
(41 games minimum)

Rod Brind'Amour, Carolina	23:45
Mario Lemieux, Pittsburgh	23:04
Alexei Kovalev, Pit.-N.Y.R.	22:51
Glen Murray, Boston	22:36
Viktor Kozlov, Florida	22:35
Joe Thornton, Boston	22:32
Zigmund Palffy, Los Angeles	22:26
Olli Jokinen, Florida	22:01
Dany Heatley, Atlanta	21:57
Jarome Iginla, Calgary	21:25

Minutes per game by defensemen
(41 games minimum)

| Nicklas Lidstrom, Detroit | 29:20 |
| Adrian Aucoin, N.Y. Islanders | 29:00 |

Al MacInnis, St. Louis	26:54
Sergei Gonchar, Washington	26:34
Roman Hamrlik, N.Y. Islanders	26:34
Alexei Zhitnik, Buffalo	26:32
Rob Blake, Colorado	26:21
Janne Niinimaa, Edm.-N.Y.I.	26:09
Brian Leetch, N.Y. Rangers	26:05
Sandis Ozolinsh, Fla.-Ana.	26:01

Shifts per game
(60 games minimum)

Adam Foote, Colorado	35.4
Rob Blake, Colorado	34.8
Derek Morris, Colorado	34.1
Mattias Ohlund, Vancouver	33.2
Filip Kuba, Minnesota	32.6
Greg de Vries, Colorado	32.3
Toni Lydman, Calgary	32.0
Ed Jovanovski, Vancouver	31.7
Brad Bombardir, Minnesota	31.4
Steve Poapst, Chicago	30.8

GOALTENDING

TOP GOALTENDERS
(Based on goals-against average, minimum 27 games)

	Games	GS	Min.	GA	SO	Avg.	W	L	T	EN	PPG Allow	SHG Allow	Shots	Save Pct.
Marty Turco, Dallas	55	52	3203	92	7	1.72	31	10	10	3	27	2	1359	.932
Roman Cechmanek, Phi.	58	57	3350	102	6	1.83	33	15	10	2	28	5	1368	.925
Dwayne Roloson, Minnesota	50	47	2945	98	4	2.00	23	16	8	1	19	3	1334	.927
Martin Brodeur, New Jersey	73	73	4374	147	9	2.02	41	23	9	4	31	4	1706	.914
Patrick Lalime, Ottawa	67	65	3943	142	8	2.16	39	20	7	1	40	8	1591	.911
Patrick Roy, Colorado	63	63	3769	137	5	2.18	35	15	13	3	46	5	1723	.920
Tomas Vokoun, Nashville	69	68	3974	146	3	2.20	25	31	11	5	42	6	1771	.918
Robert Esche, Philadelphia	30	25	1638	60	2	2.20	12	9	3	2	22	3	647	.907
Manny Fernandez, Minnesota	35	34	1979	74	2	2.24	19	13	2	0	24	2	972	.924
Ed Belfour, Toronto	62	62	3738	141	7	2.26	37	20	5	4	37	6	1816	.922
Jean-Sebastien Giguere, Ana.	65	64	3775	145	8	2.30	34	22	6	5	34	3	1820	.920
Garth Snow, N.Y. Islanders	43	37	2390	92	1	2.31	16	17	5	8	30	3	1120	.918
Jocelyn Thibault, Chicago	62	62	3650	144	8	2.37	26	28	7	4	39	5	1690	.915
Olaf Kolzig, Washington	66	65	3894	156	4	2.40	33	25	6	5	51	0	1925	.919
Dan Cloutier, Vancouver	57	57	3376	136	2	2.42	33	16	7	6	35	8	1477	.908
Ron Tugnutt, Dallas	31	29	1701	70	4	2.47	15	10	5	0	23	4	672	.896
Nikolai Khabibulin, Tampa Bay	65	64	3787	156	4	2.47	30	22	11	5	45	4	1760	.911
Brent Johnson, St. Louis	38	35	2042	84	2	2.47	16	13	5	2	25	3	844	.900
Curtis Joseph, Detroit	61	60	3566	148	5	2.49	34	19	6	3	43	3	1676	.912
Mike Dunham, Nash.-N.Y.R.	58	56	3286	137	5	2.50	21	26	7	3	51	7	1626	.916

LEADERS BY CATEGORY

Games played

Marc Denis, Columbus	77
Martin Brodeur, New Jersey	73
Tomas Vokoun, Nashville	69
Patrick Lalime, Ottawa	67
Olaf Kolzig, Washington	66
Jean-Sebastien Giguere, Anaheim	65
Nikolai Khabibulin, Tampa Bay	65
Roberto Luongo, Florida	65
Tommy Salo, Edmonton	65
Roman Turek, Calgary	65

Minutes played

Marc Denis, Columbus	4,511
Martin Brodeur, New Jersey	4,374
Tomas Vokoun, Nashville	3,974
Patrick Lalime, Ottawa	3,943
Olaf Kolzig, Washington	3,894
Roman Turek, Calgary	3,822
Tommy Salo, Edmonton	3,814
Nikolai Khabibulin, Tampa Bay	3,787
Jean-Sebastien Giguere, Anaheim	3,775
Patrick Roy, Colorado	3,769

Goals allowed

Marc Denis, Columbus	232
Tommy Salo, Edmonton	172
Jose Theodore, Montreal	165
Roberto Luongo, Florida	164
Roman Turek, Calgary	164
Nikolai Khabibulin, Tampa Bay	156
Olaf Kolzig, Washington	156
Curtis Joseph, Detroit	148
Martin Brodeur, New Jersey	147
Two tied with	146

Shutouts

Martin Brodeur, New Jersey 9
Jean-Sebastien Giguere, Anaheim 8
Patrick Lalime, Ottawa 8
Jocelyn Thibault, Chicago.....................8
Ed Belfour, Toronto 7
Marty Turco, Dallas...............................7
Roman Cechmanek, Philadelphia 6
Roberto Luongo, Florida 6
Five tied with..5

Worst goals-against average
(27 games minimum)

Arturs Irbe, Carolina 3.18
Dan Blackburn, N.Y. Rangers............3.17
Johan Hedberg, Pittsburgh 3.14
Marc Denis, Columbus 3.09
Brian Boucher, Phoenix 3.02
Chris Osgood, N.Y.I.-St.L. 2.95
Jose Theodore, Montreal....................2.90
Pasi Nurminen, Atlanta 2.88
Jani Hurme, Florida 2.88
Jeff Hackett, Mon.-Bos. 2.86

Best winning percentage
(27 games minimum)

Marty Turco, Dallas .... .706
Patrick Roy, Colorado .... .659
Roman Cechmanek, Philadelphia .. .655
Dan Cloutier, Vancouver .... .652
Patrick Lalime, Ottawa.................... .644
Ed Belfour, Toronto .... .637
Curtis Joseph, Detroit .... .627
Martin Brodeur, New Jersey .... .623
Jean-Sebastien Giguere, Anaheim .. .597
Manny Fernandez, Minnesota .... .588

Worst winning percentage
(27 games minimum)

Arturs Irbe, Carolina .... .242
Jani Hurme, Florida .... .333
Dan Blackburn, N.Y. Rangers......... .357
Roberto Luongo, Florida .... .385
Martin Biron, Buffalo .... .392
Kevin Weekes, Carolina .... .394
Jamie Storr, Los Angeles................ .394
Johan Hedberg, Pittsburgh .... .400
Jose Theodore, Montreal................. .404
Marc Denis, Columbus .... .408

Wins

Martin Brodeur, New Jersey 41
Patrick Lalime, Ottawa 39
Ed Belfour, Toronto 37
Patrick Roy, Colorado 35
Jean-Sebastien Giguere, Anaheim 34
Curtis Joseph, Detroit..........................34
Roman Cechmanek, Philadelphia 33
Dan Cloutier, Vancouver 33

Olaf Kolzig, Washington 33
Marty Turco, Dallas.............................31

Consecutive games won

Dan Cloutier, Vancouver 9
Martin Prusek, Ottawa 9
Chris Osgood, N.Y. Islanders 7
Many Fernandez, Minnesota 6
John Grahame, Boston 6
Ed Belfour, Toronto 6
Curtis Joseph, Detroit...........................6
10 tied with 5

Longest undefeated streaks
(wins-losses-ties listed)

Marty Turco, Dallas 12-0-4
Nikolai Khabibulin, Tampa Bay 12-0-4
Dan Cloutier, Vancouver..................7-0-3
Dan Cloutier, Vancouver..................9-0-0
Martin Prusek, Ottawa 9-0-0
John Grahame, Boston 8-0-1
Roman Cechmanek, Philadelphia....7-0-2
Nikolai Khabibulin, Tampa Bay 7-0-2
Chris Osgood, N.Y. Islanders 7-0-2

Losses

Marc Denis, Columbus 41
Roberto Luongo, Florida......................34
Jose Theodore, Montreal 31
Tomas Vokoun, Nashville 31
Roman Turek, Calgary 29
Martin Biron, Buffalo 28
Evgeni Nabokov, San Jose 28
Jocelyn Thibault, Chicago...................28
Tommy Salo, Edmonton 27
Mike Dunham, Nash.-N.Y.R. 26

Longest winless streaks
(wins-losses-ties listed)

Tomas Vokoun, Nashville 0-11-3
Jamia McLennan, Calgary 0-10-3
Kevin Weekes, Carolina 0-11-0
Johan Hedberg, Pittsburgh 0-10-1
Martin Biron, Buffalo 0-9-2
Arturs Irbe, Carolina.....................0-10-0
Jocelyn Thibault, Chicago 0-10-0
Martin Gerber, Anaheim 0-7-3

Shots faced

Marc Denis, Columbus 2,404
Roberto Luongo, Florida 2,011
Olaf Kolzig, Washington.................1,925
Jean-Sebastien Giguere, Anaheim ..1,820
Ed Belfour, Toronto 1,816
Jose Theodore, Montreal 1,797
Tomas Vokoun, Nashville...............1,771
Nikolai Khabibulin, Tampa Bay.......1,760
Patrick Roy, Colorado 1,723
Tommy Salo, Edmonton 1,708

Saves

Marc Denis, Columbus 2,172
Roberto Luongo, Florida 1,847
Olaf Kolzig, Washington..................1,769
Ed Belfour, Toronto 1,675
Jean-Sebastien Giguere, Anaheim ..1,675
Jose Theodore, Montreal................1,632
Tomas Vokoun, Nashville 1,625
Nikolai Khabibulin, Tampa Bay........1,604
Patrick Roy, Colorado 1,586
Martin Brodeur, New Jersey 1,559

Best save percentage
(27 games minimum)

Marty Turco, Dallas .... .932
Dwayne Roloson, Minnesota .... .927
Roman Cechmanek, Philadelphia .. .925
Manny Fernandez, Minnesota .... .924
Ed Belfour, Toronto .... .922
Patrick Roy, Colorado .... .920
Jean-Sebastien Giguere, Anaheim .. .920
Olaf Kolzig, Washington .... .919
Roberto Luongo, Florida .... .918
Garth Snow, N.Y. Islanders .... .918

Worst save percentage
(27 games minimum)

Arturs Irbe, Carolina .... .877
Fred Brathwaite, St. Louis .... .883
Dan Blackburn, N.Y. Rangers.......... .890
Chris Osgood, N.Y.I.-St.L. .... .892
Felix Potvin, Los Angeles............... .894
Brian Boucher, Phoenix .... .894
Johan Hedberg, Pittsburgh .... .895
Steve Shields, Boston .... .896
Ron Tugnutt, Dallas........................ .896
Tommy Salo, Edmonton .... .899

Times pulled

Roberto Luongo, Florida........................9
Nikolai Khabibulin, Tampa Bay 7
Chris Osgood, N.Y.I.-St.L......................7
Marc Denis, Columbus 6
Felix Potvin, Los Angeles 6
Tomas Vokoun, Nashville 6
Eight tied with.......................................5

Penalty minutes

Tomas Vokoun, Nashville 28
Ed Belfour, Toronto 24
Dan Cloutier, Vancouver 24
Garth Snow, N.Y. Islanders 24
Patrick Roy, Colorado 20
Johan Hedberg, Pittsburgh 18
Marty Turco, Dallas 16
Jamie McLennan, Calgary....................14
Roman Turek, Calgary 14
Two tied with 12

SCORING

	Games	G	A	Pts.	PIM	+/-	PPG	SHG	GWG	GTG	Sht.	Sht. Pct.	Won	Lost	Pct.	TOI
Ramzi Abid, Phoenix	30	10	8	18	30	1	4	0	3	0	52	19.2	1	0	100.0	12:30
Ramzi Abid, Pit.	3	0	0	0	2	-5	0	0	0	0	7	0.0	0	1	0.0	17:33
Totals	33	10	8	18	32	-4	4	0	3	0	59	16.9	1	1	50.0	12:57
Tony Amonte, Phoenix..	59	13	23	36	26	-12	6	0	3	0	170	7.6	19	34	35.8	19:27
Tony Amonte, Phi.	13	7	8	15	2	12	1	1	2	1	37	18.9	1	2	33.3	17:39
Totals	72	20	31	51	28	0	7	1	5	1	207	9.7	20	36	35.7	19:07
Sean Avery, Detroit.......	39	5	6	11	120	7	0	0	2	0	40	12.5	130	94	58.0	7:03
Sean Avery, L.A.	12	1	3	4	33	0	0	0	0	0	19	5.3	23	26	46.9	13:50
Totals	51	6	9	15	153	7	0	0	2	0	59	10.2	153	120	56.0	8:39
Stu Barnes, Buffalo.......	68	11	21	32	20	-13	2	1	2	0	124	8.9	452	471	49.0	18:29
Stu Barnes, Dallas	13	2	5	7	8	2	2	0	1	0	25	8.0	34	42	44.7	17:23
Totals	81	13	26	39	28	-11	4	1	3	0	149	8.7	486	513	48.6	18:18
Bates Battaglia, Car......	70	5	14	19	90	-17	0	1	1	0	96	5.2	4	12	25.0	18:38
Bates Battaglia, Colo.....	13	1	5	6	10	-2	1	0	1	0	27	3.7	0	3	0.0	15:19
Totals	83	6	19	25	100	-19	1	1	2	0	123	4.9	4	15	21.1	18:18
Jaroslav Bednar, L.A. ...	15	0	9	9	4	3	0	0	0	0	29	0.0	4	3	57.1	13:59
Jaroslav Bednar, Fla.....	52	5	13	18	14	-2	2	0	1	2	66	7.6	18	24	42.9	14:09
Totals	67	5	22	27	18	1	2	0	1	2	95	5.3	22	27	44.9	14:07
Sergei Berezin, Chi.	66	18	13	31	8	-3	5	0	0	0	171	10.5	7	8	46.7	16:18
Sergei Berezin, Wash....	9	5	4	9	4	10	0	0	2	0	28	17.9	0	1	0.0	15:41
Totals	75	23	17	40	12	7	5	0	2	0	199	11.6	7	9	43.8	16:13
Marc Bergevin, Pit.	69	2	5	7	36	-9	0	0	0	0	27	7.4	0	0	–	18:45
Marc Bergevin, T.B.	1	0	0	0	0	-2	0	0	0	0	0		0	0	–	18:26
Totals	70	2	5	7	36	-11	0	0	0	0	27	7.4	0	0	–	18:45
Sylvain Blouin, Min.......	2	0	0	0	4	0	0	0	0	0	1	0.0	0	1	0.0	7:37
Sylvain Blouin, Mon......	17	0	0	0	43	-3	0	0	0	0	3	0.0	0	0	–	3:36
Totals	19	0	0	0	47	-3	0	0	0	0	4	0.0	0	1	0.0	4:01
Joel Bouchard, N.Y.R.....	27	5	7	12	14	6	1	0	2	0	41	12.2	0	0	–	20:06
Joel Bouchard, Pit.	7	0	1	1	0	-6	0	0	0	0	6	0.0	0	0	–	21:49
Totals	34	5	8	13	14	0	1	0	2	0	47	10.6	0	0	–	20:27
Francis Bouillon, Nash..	4	0	0	0	2	-1	0	0	0	0	0	–	0	0	–	12:51
Francis Bouillon, Mon...	20	3	1	4	2	-1	0	1	0	0	30	10.0	0	0	–	20:24
Totals	24	3	1	4	4	-2	0	1	0	0	30	10.0	0	0	–	19:08
Pavel Brendl, Phi.	42	5	7	12	4	8	1	0	1	0	80	6.3	2	7	22.2	10:19
Pavel Brendl, Carolina ..	8	0	1	1	2	-3	0	0	0	0	14	0.0	1	1	50.0	15:04
Totals	50	5	8	13	6	5	1	0	1	0	94	5.3	3	8	27.3	11:05
Daniel Briere, Phoenix ..	68	17	29	46	50	-21	4	0	3	1	142	12.0	582	526	52.5	17:01
Daniel Briere, Buffalo....	14	7	5	12	12	1	5	0	1	0	39	17.9	103	103	50.0	17:48
Totals	82	24	34	58	62	-20	9	0	4	1	181	13.3	685	629	52.1	17:09
Valeri Bure, Florida	46	5	21	26	10	-11	3	0	2	0	150	3.3	6	13	31.6	18:37
Valeri Bure, St. Louis....	5	0	2	2	0	-2	0	0	0	0	11	0.0	0	0		15:11
Totals	51	5	23	28	10	-13	3	0	2	0	161	3.1	6	13	31.6	18:17
Anson Carter, Edm........	68	25	30	55	20	-11	10	0	1	1	176	14.2	95	122	43.8	19:38
Anson Carter, N.Y.R.	11	1	4	5	6	0	0	0	0	0	17	5.9	1	4	20.0	17:48
Totals	79	26	34	60	26	-11	10	0	1	1	193	13.5	96	126	43.2	19:23
Cory Cross, N.Y.R.	26	0	4	4	16	13	0	0	0	0	18	0.0	0	1	0.0	17:12
Cory Cross, Edm.	11	2	3	5	8	3	1	0	1	0	11	18.2	0	0	–	17:50
Totals	37	2	7	9	24	16	1	0	1	0	29	6.9	0	1	0.0	17:23
Matt Cullen, Anaheim ...	50	7	14	21	12	-4	1	0	1	0	77	9.1	137	134	50.6	14:18
Matt Cullen, Florida	30	6	6	12	22	-4	2	1	1	0	54	11.1	200	223	47.3	14:43
Totals	80	13	20	33	34	-8	3	1	2	0	131	9.9	337	357	48.6	14:27
P. DesRochers, Pho......	4	0	0	0	0	0	0	0	0	0	0	–	0	0	–	–
P. DesRochers, Car.	2	0	0	0	0	0	0	0	0	0	0	–	0	0	–	–
Totals	6	0	0	0	0	0	0	0	0	0	0	–	0	0	–	–
Shean Donovan, Pit.	52	4	5	9	30	-6	0	1	0	0	66	6.1	9	28	24.3	13:00
Shean Donovan, Cal......	13	1	2	3	7	-2	0	0	1	0	22	4.5	2	1	66.7	15:39
Totals	65	5	7	12	37	-8	0	1	1	0	88	5.7	11	29	27.5	13:32
Harold Druken, Van.......	3	1	1	2	0	-1	0	0	0	0	3	33.3	10	11	47.6	8:48
Harold Druken, Car.	14	0	1	1	2	-1	0	0	0	0	5	0.0	19	20	48.7	3:59
Harold Druken, Tor........	5	0	2	2	2	1	0	0	0	0	8	0.0	11	14	44.0	12:50
Totals	22	1	4	5	4	-1	0	0	0	0	16	6.3	40	45	47.1	6:39
Mike Dunham, Nash.	15	0	0	0	0	0	0	0	0	0	0	–	0	0	–	–
Mike Dunham, N.Y.R.	43	0	1	1	0	0	0	0	0	0	0	–	0	0	–	–
Totals	58	0	1	1	0	0	0	0	0	0	0	–	0	0	–	–
Radek Dvorak, N.Y.R. ...	63	6	21	27	16	-3	2	0	0	0	134	4.5	4	5	44.4	15:42
Radek Dvorak, Edm.	12	4	4	8	14	-3	1	0	0	1	32	12.5	0	1	0.0	16:07
Totals	75	10	25	35	30	-6	3	0	0	1	166	6.0	4	6	40.0	15:46

	Games	G	A	Pts.	PIM	+/-	PPG	SHG	GWG	GTG	Sht.	Sht. Pct.	Won	Lost	Pct.	TOI
Gordie Dwyer, N.Y.R.	17	0	1	1	50	-1	0	0	0	0	8	0.0	0	1	0.0	6:27
Gordie Dwyer, Mon.......	11	0	0	0	46	-2	0	0	0	0	2	0.0	1	1	50.0	7:33
Totals........................	28	0	1	1	96	-3	0	0	0	0	10	0.0	1	2	33.3	6:53
Mike Eastwood, St.L.....	17	1	3	4	8	1	1	0	0	0	7	14.3	87	116	42.9	10:44
Mike Eastwood, Chi.	53	2	10	12	24	-6	0	0	0	0	32	6.3	380	333	53.3	12:54
Totals........................	70	3	13	16	32	-5	1	0	0	0	39	7.7	467	449	51.0	12:22
Rico Fata, N.Y.R.	36	2	4	6	6	-1	0	0	0	0	30	6.7	15	15	50.0	7:16
Rico Fata, Pittsburgh	27	5	8	13	10	-6	0	0	0	0	49	10.2	43	44	49.4	17:46
Totals........................	63	7	12	19	16	-7	0	0	0	0	79	8.9	58	59	49.6	11:46
Andrew Ference, Pit......	22	1	3	4	36	-16	1	0	0	0	22	4.5	1	0	100.0	19:33
Andrew Ference, Cal. ...	16	0	4	4	6	1	0	0	0	0	17	0.0	0	0	_	17:38
Totals........................	38	1	7	8	42	-15	1	0	0	0	39	2.6	1	0	100.0	18:44
Brad Ference, Florida....	60	2	6	8	118	2	0	0	0	0	41	4.9	0	0	_	15:57
Brad Ference, Phoenix..	15	0	1	1	28	-5	0	0	0	0	8	0.0	0	0	_	16:32
Totals........................	75	2	7	9	146	-3	0	0	0	0	49	4.1	0	0	_	16:04
Wade Flaherty, Florida ..	0	0	0	0	0	0	0	0	0	0	0	_	0	0	_	_
Wade Flaherty, Nash.....	1	0	1	1	0	0	0	0	0	0	0	0.0	0	0	_	_
Totals........................	1	0	1	1	0	0	0	0	0	0	0	_	0	0	_	_
Dan Focht, Phoenix	10	0	0	0	10	-2	0	0	0	0	1	0.0	0	0	_	8:39
Dan Focht, Pittsburgh...	12	0	3	3	19	-7	0	0	0	0	11	0.0	0	1	0.0	18:13
Totals........................	22	0	3	3	29	-9	0	0	0	0	12	0.0	0	1	0.0	13:52
Doug Gilmour, Mon.......	61	11	19	30	36	-6	3	0	0	0	85	12.9	180	181	49.9	16:45
Doug Gilmour, Tor.	1	0	0	0	0	0	0	0	0	0	0	_	0	1	0.0	4:51
Totals........................	62	11	19	30	36	-6	3	0	0	0	85	12.9	180	182	49.7	16:33
John Grahame, Bos.	23	0	2	2	2	0	0	0	0	0	0	_	0	0	_	_
John Grahame, T.B.	17	0	0	0	9	0	0	0	0	0	0	_	0	0	_	_
Totals........................	40	0	2	2	11	0	0	0	0	0	0	_	0	0	_	_
Chris Gratton, Buffalo...	66	15	29	44	86	-5	4	0	2	1	187	8.0	647	452	58.9	16:25
Chris Gratton, Pho........	14	0	1	1	21	-11	0	0	0	0	28	0.0	132	99	57.1	17:12
Totals........................	80	15	30	45	107	-16	4	0	2	1	215	7.0	779	551	58.6	16:33
Josh Green, Edm.	20	0	2	2	12	-3	0	0	0	0	20	0.0	0	5	0.0	10:22
Josh Green, N.Y.R.	4	0	0	0	2	-1	0	0	0	0	3	0.0	0	0	_	9:06
Josh Green, Wash.	21	1	2	3	7	1	0	0	0	0	20	5.0	0	3	0.0	8:06
Totals........................	45	1	4	5	21	-3	0	0	0	0	43	2.3	0	8	0.0	9:12
Jeff Hackett, Montreal ..	18	0	0	0	0	0	0	0	0	0	0	_	0	0	_	_
Jeff Hackett, Boston	18	0	0	0	2	0	0	0	0	0	0	_	0	0	_	_
Totals........................	36	0	0	0	2	0	0	0	0	0	0	_	0	0	_	_
Shawn Heins, S.J.	20	0	1	1	9	-2	0	0	0	0	10	0.0	0	0	_	8:31
Shawn Heins, Pit.	27	1	1	2	33	-2	0	0	1	0	28	3.6	0	0	_	19:11
Totals........................	47	1	2	3	42	-4	0	0	1	0	38	2.6	0	0	_	14:39
Sami Helenius, Dallas ..	5	0	0	0	6	1	0	0	0	0	2	0.0	0	0	_	9:48
Sami Helenius, Chi.	10	0	1	1	28	3	0	0	0	0	5	0.0	0	0	_	11:15
Totals........................	15	0	1	1	34	4	0	0	0	0	7	0.0	0	0	_	10:46
Alex Henry, Edmonton..	3	0	0	0	0	-1	0	0	0	0	0	_	0	0	_	7:01
Alex Henry, Wash.	38	0	0	0	80	-4	0	0	0	0	8	0.0	0	1	0.0	3:38
Totals........................	41	0	0	0	80	-5	0	0	0	0	8	0.0	0	1	0.0	3:53
Jan Hlavac, Vanc.	9	1	1	2	6	-1	0	0	0	0	7	14.3	0	0	_	10:51
Jan Hlavac, Carolina	52	9	15	24	22	-9	6	0	1	1	116	7.8	8	13	38.1	17:10
Totals........................	61	10	16	26	28	-10	6	0	1	1	123	8.1	8	13	38.1	16:14
Brian Holzinger, T.B.	5	0	1	1	2	1	0	0	0	0	3	0.0	9	17	34.6	9:08
Brian Holzinger, Pit.	9	1	2	3	6	-6	0	0	0	1	20	5.0	77	84	47.8	16:23
Totals........................	14	1	3	4	8	-5	0	0	0	1	23	4.3	86	101	46.0	13:48
Darcy Hordichuk, Pho...	25	0	0	0	82	-1	0	0	0	0	5	0.0	0	0	_	4:46
Darcy Hordichuk, Fla. ...	3	0	0	0	15	-1	0	0	0	0	2	0.0	0	0	_	9:45
Totals........................	28	0	0	0	97	-2	0	0	0	0	7	0.0	0	0	_	5:18
Phil Housley, Chicago...	57	6	23	29	24	7	2	0	2	0	134	4.5	1	0	100.0	19:23
Phil Housley, Toronto ...	1	0	0	0	2	-1	0	0	0	0	3	0.0	0	0	_	16:04
Totals........................	58	6	23	29	26	6	2	0	2	0	137	4.4	1	0	100.0	19:19
Jan Hrdina, Pittsburgh..	57	14	25	39	34	1	11	0	4	0	84	16.7	551	433	56.0	19:45
Jan Hrdina, Phoenix	4	0	4	4	8	3	0	0	0	0	2	0.0	42	28	60.0	18:12
Totals........................	61	14	29	43	42	4	11	0	4	0	86	16.3	593	461	56.3	19:39
Brad Isbister, N.Y.I.	53	10	13	23	34	-9	2	0	2	1	90	11.1	6	7	46.2	13:54
Brad Isbister, Edm.	13	3	2	5	9	0	0	0	1	0	29	10.3	5	5	50.0	13:14
Totals........................	66	13	15	28	43	-9	2	0	3	1	119	10.9	11	12	47.8	13:46
Mathias Johansson, Cal.	46	4	5	9	12	-15	1	0	0	0	54	7.4	202	174	53.7	12:39
Mathias Johansson, Pit.	12	1	5	6	4	1	1	0	0	0	16	6.3	73	101	42.0	17:04
Totals........................	58	5	10	15	16	-14	2	0	0	0	70	7.1	275	275	50.0	13:33
Ryan Johnson, Florida..	58	2	5	7	26	-13	0	0	0	0	54	3.7	331	358	48.0	10:39
Ryan Johnson, St.L.	17	0	0	0	12	0	0	0	0	0	13	0.0	93	87	51.7	10:33
Totals........................	75	2	5	7	38	-13	0	0	0	0	67	3.0	424	445	48.8	10:38

	Games	G	A	Pts.	PIM	+/-	PPG	SHG	GWG	GTG	Sht.	Sht. Pct.	Faceoffs Won	Lost	Pct.	TOI
Tomi Kallio, Atlanta.......	5	0	2	2	4	-2	0	0	0	0	3	0.0	0	0	_	12:46
Tomi Kallio, Columbus..	12	1	2	3	8	-7	0	0	0	0	20	5.0	1	1	50.0	14:52
Tomi Kallio, Phi............	7	1	0	1	2	-1	0	0	0	0	5	20.0	0	0	_	9:29
Totals......................	24	2	4	6	14	-10	0	0	0	0	28	7.1	1	1	50.0	12:51
Sami Kapanen, Car.	43	6	12	18	12	-17	3	0	1	1	108	5.6	5	11	31.3	18:36
Sami Kapanen, Phi.	28	4	9	13	6	-1	2	0	1	0	81	4.9	2	3	40.0	19:21
Totals......................	71	10	21	31	18	-18	5	0	2	1	189	5.3	7	14	33.3	18:54
Alexei Kovalev, Pit.	54	27	37	64	50	-11	8	0	1	0	212	12.7	6	13	31.6	24:03
Alexei Kovalev, N.Y.R.	24	10	3	13	20	2	3	0	2	1	59	16.9	8	11	42.1	20:09
Totals......................	78	37	40	77	70	-9	11	0	3	1	271	13.7	14	24	36.8	22:51
Maxim Kuznetsov, Det..	53	0	3	3	54	0	0	0	0	0	32	0.0	1	0	100.0	13:10
Maxim Kuznetsov, L.A..	3	0	0	0	0	1	0	0	0	0	1	0.0	0	0	_	16:37
Totals......................	56	0	3	3	54	1	0	0	0	0	33	0.0	1	0	100.0	13:21
J. Kwiatkowski, Ottawa ..	20	0	2	2	6	2	0	0	0	0	28	0.0	0	2	0.0	12:12
J. Kwiatkowski, Wash....	34	0	3	3	12	1	0	0	0	0	28	0.0	0	2	0.0	15:32
Totals......................	54	0	5	5	18	3	0	0	0	0	56	0.0	0	4	0.0	14:18
Dan LaCouture, Pit.	44	2	2	4	72	-8	0	0	0	0	30	6.7	4	1	80.0	9:12
Dan LaCouture, N.Y.R....	24	1	4	5	0	4	0	0	0	0	17	5.9	0	1	0.0	10:17
Totals......................	68	3	6	9	72	-4	0	0	0	0	47	6.4	4	2	66.7	9:35
Darren Langdon, Car....	9	0	0	0	16	0	0	0	0	0	4	0.0	0	0	_	2:45
Darren Langdon, Van....	45	0	1	1	143	-2	0	0	0	0	15	0.0	0	1	0.0	5:25
Totals......................	54	0	1	1	159	-2	0	0	0	0	19	0.0	0	1	0.0	4:58
Claude Lapointe, N.Y.I. ..	66	6	6	12	20	-3	0	0	1	0	67	9.0	377	309	55.0	12:15
Claude Lapointe, Phi.....	14	2	2	4	16	5	0	0	0	0	20	10.0	68	39	63.6	11:04
Totals......................	80	8	8	16	36	2	0	0	1	0	87	9.2	445	348	56.1	12:03
Janne Laukkanen, Pit....	17	1	6	7	8	-3	0	0	0	0	10	10.0	0	0	_	16:51
Janne Laukkanen, T.B....	2	1	0	1	0	1	0	0	0	0	2	50.0	0	0	_	18:14
Totals......................	19	2	6	8	8	-2	0	0	0	0	12	16.7	0	0	_	16:59
Guillaume Lefebvre, Phi.	14	0	0	0	4	1	0	0	0	0	5	0.0	0	0	_	7:26
Guillaume Lefebvre, Pit..	12	2	4	6	0	1	0	0	0	0	14	14.3	1	0	100.0	17:30
Totals......................	26	2	4	6	4	2	0	0	0	0	19	10.5	1	0	100.0	12:05
Claude Lemieux, Pho....	36	6	8	14	30	-3	1	1	0	1	74	8.1	138	157	46.8	14:01
Claude Lemieux, Dal.....	32	2	4	6	14	-9	0	0	0	0	45	4.4	17	18	48.6	13:13
Totals......................	68	8	12	20	44	-12	1	1	0	1	119	6.7	155	175	47.0	13:39
Andreas Lilja, L.A.	17	0	3	3	14	5	0	0	0	0	13	0.0	0	0	_	20:03
Andreas Lilja, Florida	56	4	8	12	56	8	0	0	0	0	59	6.8	0	0	_	19:10
Totals......................	73	4	11	15	70	13	0	0	0	0	72	5.6	0	0	_	19:22
Richard Lintner, N.Y.R. .	10	1	0	1	0	-5	1	0	0	1	9	11.1	0	0	_	14:19
Richard Lintner, Pit.......	19	3	2	5	10	-9	1	0	0	0	36	8.3	0	0	_	18:58
Totals......................	29	4	2	6	10	-14	2	0	0	1	45	8.9	0	0	_	17:22
Marek Malik, Carolina...	10	0	2	2	16	-3	0	0	0	0	9	0.0	0	0	_	17:01
Marek Malik, Van..........	69	7	11	18	52	23	1	1	2	1	68	10.3	0	1	0.0	18:05
Totals......................	79	7	13	20	68	20	1	1	2	1	77	9.1	0	1	0.0	17:57
Bryan Marchment, S.J..	67	2	9	11	108	-2	0	0	0	0	66	3.0	0	0	_	19:19
Bryan Marchment, Col...	14	0	3	3	33	4	0	0	0	0	18	0.0	0	0	_	16:41
Totals......................	81	2	12	14	141	2	0	0	0	0	84	2.4	0	0	_	18:51
Grant Marshall, C'bus	66	8	20	28	71	-8	3	0	2	0	96	8.3	12	14	46.2	13:56
Grant Marshall, N.J.......	10	1	3	4	7	-3	0	0	0	0	17	5.9	1	0	100.0	11:38
Totals......................	76	9	23	32	78	-11	3	0	2	0	113	8.0	13	14	48.1	13:38
Steve Martins, Ottawa ..	14	2	3	5	10	3	0	0	0	0	13	15.4	62	49	55.9	9:44
Steve Martins, St.L.......	28	3	3	6	18	-8	0	1	0	0	25	12.0	202	167	54.7	13:37
Totals......................	42	5	6	11	28	-5	0	1	0	0	38	13.2	264	216	55.0	12:19
Brad May, Phoenix........	20	3	4	7	32	3	0	0	0	0	24	12.5	0	0	_	9:56
Brad May, Vancouver....	3	0	0	0	10	1	0	0	0	0	1	0.0	0	0	_	7:47
Totals......................	23	3	4	7	42	4	0	0	0	0	25	12.0	0	0	_	9:39
Chris McAllister, Phi.....	19	0	0	0	21	-2	0	0	0	0	9	0.0	0	0	_	9:32
Chris McAllister, Colo. ..	14	0	1	1	26	6	0	0	0	0	4	0.0	0	0	_	8:02
Totals......................	33	0	1	1	47	4	0	0	0	0	13	0.0	0	0	_	8:53
Alyn McCauley, Tor.	64	6	9	15	16	3	0	0	0	0	79	7.6	229	286	44.5	12:53
Alyn McCauley, S.J.......	16	3	7	10	4	-2	3	0	0	0	29	10.3	41	40	50.6	17:29
Totals......................	80	9	16	25	20	1	3	0	0	0	108	8.3	270	326	45.3	13:48
Dan McGillis, Phi.........	24	0	3	3	20	7	0	0	0	0	41	0.0	0	0	_	18:13
Dan McGillis, S.J.........	37	3	13	16	30	-6	2	0	0	1	71	4.2	0	0	_	21:53
Dan McGillis, Boston	10	0	1	1	10	2	0	0	0	0	18	0.0	0	0	_	21:15
Totals......................	71	3	17	20	60	3	2	0	0	1	130	2.3	0	0	_	20:33
Boris Mironov, Chi........	20	3	1	4	22	-1	1	0	0	1	14	21.4	0	0	_	19:12
Boris Mironov, N.Y.R. ...	36	3	9	12	34	3	1	0	0	0	56	5.4	0	0	_	20:34
Totals......................	56	6	10	16	56	2	2	0	0	1	70	8.6	0	0	_	20:05
Ian Moran, Pittsburgh ..	70	0	7	7	46	-17	0	0	0	0	85	0.0	3	1	75.0	18:37
Ian Moran, Boston........	8	0	1	1	2	-1	0	0	0	0	11	0.0	1	0	100.0	16:22
Totals......................	78	0	8	8	48	-18	0	0	0	0	96	0.0	4	1	80.0	18:23

	Games	G	A	Pts.	PIM	+/-	PPG	SHG	GWG	GTG	Sht.	Sht. Pct.	Faceoffs Won	Lost	Pct.	TOI
Rem Murray, N.Y.R.	32	6	6	12	4	-3	1	1	1	0	62	9.7	63	55	53.4	15:39
Rem Murray, Nash.	53	6	13	19	18	1	1	0	0	0	81	7.4	354	366	49.2	17:16
Totals	85	12	19	31	22	-2	2	1	1	0	143	8.4	417	421	49.8	16:39
Rob Niedermayer, Cal.	54	8	10	18	42	-13	2	0	1	0	104	7.7	68	71	48.9	17:28
Rob Niedermayer, Ana.	12	2	2	4	15	3	1	0	0	0	21	9.5	6	8	42.9	15:20
Totals	66	10	12	22	57	-10	3	0	1	0	125	8.0	74	79	48.4	17:05
Janne Niinimaa, Edm.	63	4	24	28	66	-7	2	0	0	0	90	4.4	0	1	0.0	26:47
Janne Niinimaa, N.Y.I.	13	1	5	6	14	-2	1	0	0	0	11	9.1	0	0	–	23:02
Totals	76	5	29	34	80	-9	3	0	0	0	101	5.0	0	1	0.0	26:09
Owen Nolan, San Jose.	61	22	20	42	91	-5	8	3	4	0	192	11.5	114	112	50.4	18:08
Owen Nolan, Toronto.	14	7	5	12	16	2	5	0	1	0	29	24.1	27	29	48.2	16:59
Totals	75	29	25	54	107	-3	13	3	5	0	221	13.1	141	141	50.0	17:55
Michael Nylander, Chi.	9	0	4	4	4	0	0	0	0	0	20	0.0	42	44	48.8	15:19
Michael Nylander, Wash.	71	17	39	56	36	3	7	0	2	0	141	12.1	476	529	47.4	18:41
Totals	80	17	43	60	40	3	7	0	2	0	161	10.6	518	573	47.5	18:18
Lyle Odelein, Chicago	65	7	4	11	76	7	0	0	0	0	77	9.1	1	0	100.0	19:05
Lyle Odelein, Dallas	3	0	0	0	6	0	0	0	0	0	1	0.0	0	0	–	17:48
Totals	68	7	4	11	82	7	0	0	0	0	78	9.0	1	0	100.0	19:02
Krzysztof Oliwa, N.Y.R.	9	0	0	0	51	1	0	0	0	0	3	0.0	0	1	0.0	3:45
Krzysztof Oliwa, Bos.	33	0	0	0	110	-4	0	0	0	0	11	0.0	0	1	0.0	3:57
Totals	42	0	0	0	161	-3	0	0	0	0	14	0.0	0	2	0.0	3:55
Chris Osgood, N.Y.I.	37	0	0	0	12	0	0	0	0	0	0	–	0	0	–	–
Chris Osgood, St.L.	9	0	0	0	0	0	0	0	0	0	0	–	0	0	–	–
Totals	46	0	0	0	12	0	0	0	0	0	0	–	0	0	–	–
Sandis Ozolinsh, Fla.	51	7	19	26	40	-16	5	0	2	0	83	8.4	0	0	–	28:22
Sandis Ozolinsh, Ana.	31	5	13	18	16	10	1	0	1	0	54	9.3	0	0	–	22:08
Totals	82	12	32	44	56	-6	6	0	3	0	137	8.8	0	0	–	26:00
Justin Papineau, St.L.	11	2	1	3	0	-1	0	0	1	0	15	13.3	44	55	44.4	10:59
Justin Papineau, N.Y.I.	5	1	2	3	4	1	0	0	1	0	8	12.5	8	7	53.3	14:50
Totals	16	3	3	6	4	0	0	0	2	0	23	13.0	52	62	45.6	12:11
Scott Pellerin, Dallas	20	1	3	4	8	-3	1	0	0	0	20	5.0	1	4	20.0	10:42
Scott Pellerin, Pho.	23	0	1	1	8	-5	0	0	0	0	17	0.0	7	5	58.3	9:31
Totals	43	1	4	5	16	-8	1	0	0	0	37	2.7	8	9	47.1	10:04
Oleg Petrov, Montreal	53	7	16	23	16	-2	2	0	2	0	87	8.0	2	4	33.3	13:44
Oleg Petrov, Nashville	17	2	2	4	2	-4	0	0	0	0	37	5.4	1	0	100.0	16:19
Totals	70	9	18	27	18	-6	2	0	2	0	124	7.3	3	4	42.9	14:22
Ales Pisa, Edmonton	48	1	3	4	24	11	1	0	0	0	34	2.9	0	0	–	12:56
Ales Pisa, N.Y. Rangers	3	0	0	0	0	1	0	0	0	0	3	0.0	0	0	–	13:55
Totals	51	1	3	4	24	12	1	0	0	0	37	2.7	0	0	–	12:59
Wayne Primeau, Pit.	70	5	11	16	55	-30	1	0	0	0	101	5.0	625	615	50.4	16:16
Wayne Primeau, S.J.	7	1	1	2	0	2	0	0	0	0	13	7.7	45	53	45.9	15:58
Totals	77	6	12	18	55	-28	1	0	0	0	114	5.3	670	668	50.1	16:15
M. Ragnarsson, S.J.	25	1	7	8	30	2	0	0	0	0	27	3.7	2	0	100.0	24:56
M. Ragnarsson, Phi.	43	2	6	8	32	5	1	0	0	0	52	3.8	1	0	100.0	21:09
Totals	68	3	13	16	62	7	1	0	0	0	79	3.8	3	0	100.0	22:33
Paul Ranheim, Phi.	28	0	4	4	6	-4	0	0	0	0	37	0.0	8	6	57.1	11:56
Paul Ranheim, Pho.	40	3	4	7	10	-4	0	0	0	0	34	8.8	19	20	48.7	11:58
Totals	68	3	8	11	16	-8	0	0	0	0	71	4.2	27	26	50.9	11:57
Rob Ray, Buffalo	41	0	0	0	92	-5	0	0	0	0	14	0.0	1	2	33.3	4:23
Rob Ray, Ottawa	5	0	0	0	4	0	0	0	0	0	0	–	0	0	–	4:53
Totals	46	0	0	0	96	-5	0	0	0	0	14	0.0	1	2	33.3	4:26
Pascal Rheaume, Atl.	56	4	9	13	24	-8	0	2	1	0	70	5.7	282	320	46.8	12:16
Pascal Rheaume, N.J.	21	4	1	5	8	3	0	1	1	0	23	17.4	128	120	51.6	11:49
Totals	77	8	10	18	32	-5	0	3	2	0	93	8.6	410	440	48.2	12:09
Randy Robitaille, Pit.	41	5	12	17	8	5	1	0	2	0	61	8.2	240	189	55.9	13:57
Randy Robitaille, N.Y.I.	10	1	2	3	2	0	1	0	0	0	8	12.5	33	35	48.5	12:28
Totals	51	6	14	20	10	5	2	0	2	0	69	8.7	273	224	54.9	13:40
M. Samuelsson, N.Y.R.	58	8	14	22	32	0	1	1	2	1	118	6.8	15	20	42.9	15:32
M. Samuelsson, Pit.	22	2	0	2	8	-21	1	0	0	0	36	5.6	6	2	75.0	14:03
Totals	80	10	14	24	40	-21	2	1	2	1	154	6.5	21	22	48.8	15:07
Marc Savard, Calgary	10	1	2	3	8	-3	0	0	0	0	21	4.8	47	42	52.8	14:40
Marc Savard, Atlanta	57	16	31	47	77	-11	6	0	4	0	127	12.6	635	612	50.9	19:49
Totals	67	17	33	50	85	-14	6	0	4	0	148	11.5	682	654	51.0	19:03
M. Schneider, L.A.	65	14	29	43	57	0	10	0	1	0	162	8.6	0	0	–	22:20
M. Schneider, Det.	13	2	5	7	16	2	1	0	0	0	37	5.4	0	0	–	22:42
Totals	78	16	34	50	73	2	11	0	1	0	199	8.0	0	0	–	22:23
Jon Sim, Dallas	4	0	0	0	0	-1	0	0	0	0	7	0.0	1	1	50.0	9:10
Jon Sim, Nashville	4	1	0	1	0	0	0	0	0	0	3	33.3	5	9	35.7	9:18
Jon Sim, Los Angeles	14	0	2	2	19	-3	0	0	0	0	29	0.0	1	2	33.3	12:05
Totals	22	1	2	3	19	-4	0	0	0	0	39	2.6	7	12	36.8	11:03

	Games	G	A	Pts.	PIM	+/-	PPG	SHG	GWG	GTG	Sht.	Sht. Pct.	Faceoffs Won	Faceoffs Lost	Faceoffs Pct.	TOI
Chris Simon, Wash......	10	0	2	2	23	-3	0	0	0	0	16	0.0	0	0	_	8:52
Chris Simon, Chicago...	61	12	6	18	125	-4	2	0	2	1	72	16.7	1	4	20.0	11:05
Totals........................	71	12	8	20	148	-7	2	0	2	1	88	13.6	1	4	20.0	10:46
Richard Smehlik, Atl.	43	2	9	11	16	-4	0	0	0	0	38	5.3	0	0	_	19:42
Richard Smehlik, N.J. ...	12	0	2	2	0	-1	0	0	0	0	11	0.0	0	0	_	17:20
Totals........................	55	2	11	13	16	-5	0	0	0	0	49	4.1	0	0	_	19:11
Bryan Smolinski, L.A. ..	58	18	20	38	18	-1	6	1	8	0	150	12.0	385	446	46.3	19:02
Bryan Smolinski, Ott. ...	10	3	5	8	2	1	0	0	0	0	26	11.5	59	68	46.5	15:41
Totals........................	68	21	25	46	20	0	6	1	8	0	176	11.9	444	514	46.3	18:32
Bruno St. Jacques, Phi..	6	0	0	0	2	-1	0	0	0	0	5	0.0	0	0	_	14:34
Bruno St. Jacques, Car...	18	2	5	7	12	-3	0	0	0	0	14	14.3	0	0	_	18:14
Totals........................	24	2	5	7	14	-4	0	0	0	0	19	10.5	0	0	_	17:19
Niklas Sundstrom, S.J..	47	2	10	12	22	-4	0	0	0	0	36	5.6	0	1	0.0	14:09
Niklas Sundstrom, Mon.	33	5	9	14	8	3	0	0	1	0	35	14.3	4	6	40.0	14:25
Totals........................	80	7	19	26	30	-1	0	0	1	0	71	9.9	4	7	36.4	14:16
Joey Tetarenko, Florida.	2	0	0	0	4	-1	0	0	0	0	2	0.0	0	0	_	6:18
Joey Tetarenko, Ottawa.	2	0	0	0	5	0	0	0	0	0	1	0.0	0	0	_	6:29
Totals........................	4	0	0	0	9	-1	0	0	0	0	3	0.0	0	0	_	6:23
Steve Thomas, Chi.......	69	4	13	17	51	0	0	0	1	0	91	4.4	7	12	36.8	12:44
Steve Thomas, Ana.......	12	10	3	13	2	10	1	0	3	0	27	37.0	1	4	20.0	13:41
Totals........................	81	14	16	30	53	10	1	0	4	0	118	11.9	8	16	33.3	12:53
Pavel Trnka, Anaheim ...	24	3	6	9	6	2	1	0	0	0	33	9.1	0	0	_	15:59
Pavel Trnka, Florida	22	0	3	3	24	-1	0	0	0	0	25	0.0	0	0	_	17:24
Totals........................	46	3	9	12	30	1	1	0	0	0	58	5.2	0	0	_	16:40
Vaclav Varada, Buffalo..	44	7	4	11	23	-2	1	0	0	0	64	10.9	7	6	53.8	16:06
Vaclav Varada, Ottawa ..	11	2	6	8	8	3	1	0	0	0	17	11.8	0	8	0.0	14:57
Totals........................	55	9	10	19	31	1	2	0	0	0	81	11.1	7	14	33.3	15:52
Radim Vrbata, Colo......	66	11	19	30	16	0	3	0	4	1	171	6.4	7	7	50.0	13:54
Radim Vrbata, Car........	10	5	0	5	2	-7	3	0	0	0	44	11.4	7	8	46.7	19:00
Totals........................	76	16	19	35	18	-7	6	0	4	1	215	7.4	14	15	48.3	14:35
Lance Ward, Florida......	36	3	1	4	78	-4	0	0	1	0	34	8.8	0	0	_	9:07
Lance Ward, Anaheim...	29	0	1	1	43	-2	0	0	0	0	18	0.0	0	0	_	7:08
Totals........................	65	3	2	5	121	-6	0	0	1	0	52	5.8	0	0	_	8:14
Todd Warriner, Van.	30	4	6	10	22	0	0	0	0	0	53	7.5	12	17	41.4	11:41
Todd Warriner, Phi........	13	2	3	5	6	2	0	0	1	0	13	15.4	0	0	_	8:29
Todd Warriner, Nash.....	6	0	1	1	4	-1	0	0	0	0	6	0.0	3	2	60.0	11:15
Totals........................	49	6	10	16	32	1	0	0	1	0	72	8.3	15	19	44.1	10:47
Glen Wesley, Carolina ...	63	1	7	8	40	-5	1	0	0	0	72	1.4	0	0	_	21:24
Glen Wesley, Toronto.....	7	0	3	3	4	3	0	0	0	0	5	0.0	0	0	_	20:41
Totals........................	70	1	10	11	44	-2	1	0	0	0	77	1.3	0	0	_	21:20
Jason Woolley, Buf.......	14	0	3	3	29	-1	0	0	0	0	29	0.0	0	0	_	15:58
Jason Woolley, Detroit..	62	6	17	23	22	12	1	0	2	0	52	11.5	0	0	_	16:58
Totals........................	76	6	20	26	51	11	1	0	2	0	81	7.4	0	0	_	16:47
Jamie Wright, Calgary ..	19	2	2	4	12	1	0	0	0	0	16	12.5	6	8	42.9	11:43
Jamie Wright, Phi........	4	0	0	0	4	-1	0	0	0	0	2	0.0	0	0	_	9:26
Totals........................	23	2	2	4	16	0	0	0	0	0	18	11.1	6	8	42.9	11:19
D. Yushkevich, Fla	23	1	6	7	14	-12	0	0	0	0	23	4.3	1	2	33.3	23:40
D. Yushkevich, L.A........	42	0	3	3	24	-4	0	0	0	0	36	0.0	0	2	0.0	19:56
D. Yushkevich, Phi........	18	2	2	4	8	7	0	0	0	0	16	12.5	0	0	_	18:05
Totals........................	83	3	11	14	46	-9	0	0	0	0	75	4.0	1	4	20.0	20:34
Andrei Zyuzin, N.J.	1	0	1	1	2	-1	0	0	0	0	0	_	0	0	_	20:03
Andrei Zyuzin, Min........	66	4	12	16	34	-7	2	0	0	0	113	3.5	1	3	25.0	21:38
Totals........................	67	4	13	17	36	-8	2	0	0	0	113	3.5	1	3	25.0	21:36

GOALTENDING

	Games	GS	Min.	GA	SO	Avg.	W	L	T	EN	PPG Allow	SHG Allow	Shots	Save Pct.
Patrick DesRochers, Phoenix ...	4	3	175	11	0	3.77	0	3	0	0	4	0	88	.875
Patrick DesRochers, Carolina ...	2	2	122	7	0	3.44	1	1	0	0	2	0	71	.901
Totals..................................	6	5	297	18	0	3.64	1	4	0	0	6	0	159	.887
Mike Dunham, Nashville..........	15	13	819	43	0	3.15	2	9	2	0	16	2	397	.892
Mike Dunham, N.Y. Rangers.....	43	43	2467	94	5	2.29	19	17	5	3	35	5	1229	.924
Totals..................................	58	56	3286	137	5	2.50	21	26	7	3	51	7	1626	.916
John Grahame, Boston.............	23	23	1352	61	1	2.71	11	9	2	0	16	3	625	.902
John Grahame, Tampa Bay.......	17	15	914	34	2	2.23	6	5	4	1	8	0	424	.920
Totals..................................	40	38	2266	95	3	2.52	17	14	6	1	24	3	1049	.909
Jeff Hackett, Montreal	18	17	1063	45	0	2.54	7	8	2	1	13	2	606	.926
Jeff Hackett, Boston	18	17	991	53	1	3.21	8	9	0	1	10	3	500	.894
Totals..................................	36	34	2054	98	1	2.86	15	17	2	2	23	5	1106	.911
Chris Osgood, N.Y. Islanders....	37	36	1993	97	2	2.92	17	14	4	4	28	2	912	.894
Chris Osgood, St. Louis	9	9	532	27	2	3.05	4	3	2	1	6	0	241	.888
Totals..................................	46	45	2525	124	4	2.95	21	17	6	5	34	2	1153	.892

MISCELLANEOUS
HAT TRICKS

(Players scoring three or more goals in a game; numbers in parentheses denote multiple hat tricks)

Date	Player, Team	Opp.	Goals	Date	Player, Team	Opp.	Goals
10-12-02—	Mark Recchi, Philadelphia	Cal.	3	1-11-03—	Jaromir Jagr, Washington	Fla.	3
10-12-02—	Shawn McEachern, Atlanta	Fla.	3	1-13-03—	Petr Nedved, N.Y. Rangers	Tor.	3
10-15-02—	John LeClair, Philadelphia	Mon.	4	1-13-03—	Dany Heatley, Atlanta	Phil.	3
10-21-02—	Markus Naslund, Vancouver	S.J.	3	1-24-03—	Daymond Langkow, Phoenix	Edm.	3
10-25-02—	Sergei Fedorov, Detroit	Pit.	3	1-25-03—	Dany Heatley, Atlanta (2)	NYR	3
10-25-02—	Adam Deadmarsh, Los Angeles	NYR	3	1-25-03—	Alexei Kovalev, Pittsburgh	Chi.	3
10-27-02—	Tyler Wright, Columbus	L.A.	3	1-27-03—	Martin Havlat, Ottawa	Dal.	3
10-31-02—	Paul Kariya, Anaheim	Bos.	3	1-30-03—	Martin St. Louis, Tampa Bay	Car.	3
11-4-02—	Marian Gaborik, Minnesota	L.A.	3	2-4-03—	Jaromir Jagr, Washington (2)	T.B.	3
11-5-02—	Alexander Mogilny, Toronto	T.B.	3	2-5-03—	John Madden, New Jersey	Wash.	3
11-6-02—	Marian Hossa, Ottawa	Colo.	3	2-7-03—	Jarome Iginla, Calgary	Edm.	3
11-8-02—	Vincent Lecavalier, Tampa Bay	Pit.	3	2-7-03—	Bryan Smolinski, Los Angeles	Car.	3
11-18-02—	Saku Koivu, Montreal	Pit.	3	2-8-03—	Milan Hejduk, Colorado	Det.	3
11-23-02—	Erik Cole, Carolina	Mon.	3	2-9-03—	Peter Forsberg, Colorado (2)	Cal.	3
11-23-02—	Marian Hossa, Ottawa (2)	C'bus	3	2-11-03—	Dave Scatchard, N.Y. Islanders (2)	T.B.	3
11-23-02—	Marian Gaborik, Minnesota (2)	Nash.	3	2-20-03—	Brendan Shanahan, Detroit	Edm.	3
11-26-02—	Glen Murray, Boston	Cal.	3	2-23-03—	Jarome Iginla, Calgary (2)	Pho.	4
11-27-02—	Andreas Johansson, Nashville	S.J.	3	2-27-03—	Ray Whitney, Columbus	L.A.	3
11-29-02—	Jan Hlavac, Carolina	Det.	3	3-6-03—	Marty McInnis, Boston	NYI	3
11-29-02—	Pavol Demitra, St. Louis	Cal.	3	3-6-03—	Scott Mellanby, St. Louis	Pho.	4
12-3-02—	Pavel Bure, N.Y. Rangers	C'bus	3	3-7-03—	Sergei Fedorov, Detroit (2)	St.L.	3
12-4-02—	Curtis Brown, Buffalo	Ana.	3	3-9-03—	Steve Sullivan, Chicago	Bos.	3
12-4-02—	Jason Arnott, Dallas	Mon.	3	3-9-03—	Eric Daze, Chicago (2)	Bos.	3
12-6-02—	Miroslav Satan, Buffalo	NYR	3	3-13-03—	Martin Lapointe, Boston	N.J.	3
12-6-02—	Ilya Kovalchuk, Atlanta	Wash.	3	3-13-03—	Joe Sakic, Colorado	C'bus	3
12-7-02—	Marian Gaborik, Minnesota (3)	Van.	3	3-16-03—	Brett Hull, Detroit	Ott.	3
12-11-02—	Eric Daze, Chicago	NYR	3	3-17-03—	Todd Bertuzzi, Vancouver	Dal.	3
12-14-02—	Markus Naslund, Vancouver (2)	Edm.	4	3-20-03—	Tyler Wright, Columbus (2)	Tor.	3
12-17-02—	Eric Belanger, Los Angeles	St.L.	3	3-22-03—	Fernando Pisani, Edmonton	Wash.	3
12-23-02—	Alexander Mogilny, Toronto (2)	Atl.	3	3-22-03—	Alex Tanguay, Colorado	Chi.	3
12-27-02—	Tyler Arnason, Chicago	S.J.	3	3-22-03—	Vincent Lecavalier, Tampa Bay (2)	Pho.	3
12-29-02—	Peter Forsberg, Colorado	L.A.	3	3-25-03—	Alexei Yashin, N.Y. Islanders	Chi.	4
1-2-03—	Marian Hossa, Ottawa (3)	Atl.	4	3-28-03—	Taylor Pyatt, Buffalo	Mon.	3
1-3-03—	Mark Parrish, N.Y. Islanders	Bos.	3	3-29-03—	Geoff Sanderson, Columbus	Cal.	4
1-4-03—	Steve Reinprecht, Colorado	S.J.	3	3-29-03—	Brett Hull, Detroit (2)	St.L.	3
1-7-03—	Jere Lehtinen, Dallas	L.A.	3	3-30-03—	Patrik Elias, New Jersey	NYI	4
1-7-03—	Dave Scatchard, N.Y. Islanders	Pit.	3	4-6-03—	Kamil Piros, Atlanta	T.B.	3
1-11-03—	Jason Blake, N.Y. Islanders	Atl.	3				

OVERTIME GOALS

(Numbers in parentheses denote multiple overtime goals)

Date	Player, Team	Opponent	Time	Final score
10-10-02—	Vaclav Prospal, Tampa Bay	Florida	3:34	Tampa Bay 4, Florida 3
10-12-02—	Olli Jokinen, Florida	Atlanta	4:49	Florida 5, Atlanta 4
10-15-02—	Adrian Aucoin, N.Y. Islanders	Nashville	1:50	N.Y. Islanders 4, Nashville 3
10-15-02—	Tomas Koivisto, St. Louis	Carolina	3:49	St. Louis 2, Carolina 1
10-18-02—	Patrik Elias, New Jersey	Nashville	1:16	New Jersey 3, Nashville 2
10-20-02—	Andy McDonald, Anaheim	Colorado	4:49	Anaheim 3, Colorado 2
10-22-02—	Cliff Ronning, Minnesota	Calgary	1:58	Minnesota 4, Calgary 3
10-26-02—	Eric Boguniecki, St. Louis	Calgary	4:35	St. Louis 4, Calgary 3
10-28-02—	Mike Modano, Dallas	Edmonton	0:37	Dallas 4, Edmonton 3
10-28-02—	Petr Nedved, N.Y. Rangers	Phoenix	2:20	N.Y. Rangers 3, Phoenix 2
10-29-02—	Lubomir Sekeras, Minnesota	Colorado	3:43	Minnesota 3, Colorado 2
10-30-02—	Valeri Bure, Florida	Dallas	3:21	Florida 3, Dallas 2
10-31-02—	Phil Housley, Chicago	Los Angeles	1:35	Chicago 2, Los Angeles 1
10-31-02—	Sergei Zholtok, Minnesota	San Jose	4:50	Minnesota 2, San Jose 1
11-2-02—	Jaroslav Modry, Los Angeles	Nashville	1:45	Los Angeles 6, Nashville 5
11-3-02—	Daniel Briere, Phoenix	Nashville	4:20	Phoenix 2, Nashville 1
11-5-02—	John LeClair, Philadelphia	Carolina	1:56	Philadelphia 2, Carolina 1
11-5-02—	Peter Bondra, Washington	Columbus	4:56	Washington 4, Columbus 3
11-6-02—	Valeri Bure, Florida (2)	Pittsburgh	2:19	Florida 4, Pittsburgh 3
11-7-02—	Sergei Fedorov, Detroit	Boston	2:08	Detroit 2, Boston 1

Date	Player, Team	Opponent	Time	Final score
11-7-02—	Brian Leetch, N.Y. Rangers	Calgary	0:51	N.Y. Rangers 1, Calgary 0
11-7-02—	Jaromir Jagr, Washington	Florida	3:56	Washington 2, Florida 1
11-8-02—	Niclas Havelid, Anaheim	Colorado	0:20	Anaheim 3, Colorado 2
11-9-02—	Igor Korolev, Chicago	Tampa Bay	2:39	Chicago 3, Tampa Bay 2
11-12-02—	Jamie Langenbrunner, New Jersey	Anaheim	3:04	New Jersey 4, Anaheim 2
11-12-02—	Mats Sundin, Toronto	Los Angeles	3:20	Toronto 4, Los Angeles 3
11-13-02—	Slava Kozlov, Atlanta	San Jose	2:19	Atlanta 3, San Jose 2
11-14-02—	Todd White, Ottawa	Florida	3:00	Ottawa 3, Florida 2
11-15-02—	Sergei Fedorov, Detroit (2)	Anaheim	4:39	Detroit 2, Anaheim 1
11-17-02—	Cory Sarich, Tampa Bay	Carolina	3:45	Tampa Bay 2, Carolina 1
11-17-02—	Pierre Turgeon, Dallas	Columbus	3:19	Dallas 3, Columbus 2
11-18-02—	Donald Audette, Montreal	Pittsburgh	1:12	Montreal 5, Pittsburgh 4
11-19-02—	Scott Niedermayer, New Jersey	Buffalo	1:23	New Jersey 4, Buffalo 3
11-19-02—	Pavel Bure, N.Y. Rangers	Anaheim	0:57	N.Y. Rangers 3, Anaheim 2
11-19-02—	Shawn McEachern, Atlanta	Florida	3:23	Atlanta 4, Florida 3
11-20-02—	Andrei Markov, Montreal	Pittsburgh	2:25	Montreal 3, Pittsburgh 2
11-21-02—	Alexander Khavanov, St. Louis	Los Angeles	1:02	St. Louis 3, Los Angeles 2
11-25-02—	Jason Smith, Edmonton	Detroit	1:28	• Edmonton 5, Detroit 4
11-27-02—	Kris Draper, Detroit	New Jersey	1:55	Detroit 3, New Jersey 2
11-30-02—	Justin Williams, Philadelphia	Montreal	4:53	Philadelphia 2, Montreal 1
11-30-02—	Jeff Friesen, New Jersey	St. Louis	4:48	New Jersey 5, St. Louis 4
12-2-02—	Brian Gionta, New Jersey	Philadelphia	2:51	New Jersey 1, Philadelphia 0
12-3-02—	Mike York, Edmonton	Minnesota	1:29	Edmonton 2, Minnesota 1
12-3-02—	Karel Pilar, Toronto	Tampa Bay	3:48	Toronto 4, Tampa Bay 3
12-3-02—	Teemu Selanne, San Jose	Phoenix	4:17	San Jose 3, Phoenix 2
12-4-02—	Todd Bertuzzi, Vancouver	New Jersey	0:56	Vancouver 3, New Jersey 2
12-5-02—	Glen Murray, Boston	Atlanta	1:53	Boston 4, Atlanta 3
12-5-02—	Michal Handzus, Philadelphia	N.Y. Rangers	4:23	Philadelphia 3, N.Y. Rangers 2
12-6-02—	Radim Vrbata, Colorado	Montreal	1:52	Colorado 7, Montreal 6
12-6-02—	Michael Nylander, Washington	Atlanta	2:24	Washington 7, Atlanta 6
12-7-02—	Nick Boynton, Boston	Tampa Bay	3:11	Boston 3, Tampa Bay 2
12-8-02—	Henrik Zetterberg, Detroit	St. Louis	1:59	Detroit 4, St. Louis 3
12-13-02—	Jason Chimera, Edmonton	Colorado	3:21	Edmonton 4, Colorado 3
12-14-02—	Mathieu Schneider, Los Angeles	Pittsburgh	4:22	Los Angeles 3, Pittsburgh 2
12-14-02—	Mike Fisher, Ottawa	New Jersey	3:10	Ottawa 4, New Jersey 3
12-16-02—	Petr Nedved, N.Y. Rangers (2)	San Jose	2:25	N.Y. Rangers 2, San Jose 1
12-17-02—	Richard Park, Minnesota	Edmonton	4:43	Minnesota 4, Edmonton 3
12-20-02—	Aaron Ward, Carolina	Atlanta	3:52	Carolina 3, Atlanta 2
12-21-02—	Markus Naslund, Vancouver	Edmonton	2:20	Vancouver 4, Edmonton 3
12-23-02—	David Legwand, Nashville	Florida	0:48	Nashville 3, Florida 2
12-26-02—	Brad Chartrand, Los Angeles	Phoenix	3:14	Los Angeles 4, Phoenix 3
12-27-02—	Marian Hossa, Ottawa	Montreal	0:50	Ottawa 3, Montreal 2
12-27-02—	Eric Desjardins, Philadelphia	Colorado	1:38	Philadelphia 2, Colorado 1
12-28-02—	Todd Marchant, Edmonton	Toronto	4:35	Edmonton 3, Toronto 2
12-28-02—	Scott Niedermayer, New Jersey (2)	Washington	4:10	New Jersey 2, Washington 1
12-28-02—	Darius Kasparaitis, N.Y. Rangers	Florida	0:56	N.Y. Rangers 2, Florida 1
12-30-02—	Roman Hamrlik, N.Y. Islanders	Florida	4:03	N.Y. Islanders 2, Florida 1
12-30-02—	Ilya Kovalchuk, Atlanta	Pittsburgh	4:40	Atlanta 3, Pittsburgh 2
12-30-02—	Daymond Langkow, Phoenix	Edmonton	4:31	Phoenix 4, Edmonton 3
12-31-02—	Jason Blake, N.Y. Islanders	Buffalo	1:36	N.Y. Islanders 1, Buffalo 0
1-1-03—	Tony Amonte, Phoenix	Washington	1:20	Phoenix 2, Washington 1
1-2-03—	Jim Dowd, Minnesota	Edmonton	4:16	Minnesota 2, Edmonton 1
1-4-03—	Ryan Smyth, Edmonton	Montreal	4:00	Edmonton 5, Montreal 4
1-4-03—	Ales Kotalik, Buffalo	Ottawa	4:19	Buffalo 2, Ottawa 1
1-4-03—	Martin Straka, Pittsburgh	N.Y. Islanders	0:42	Pittsburgh 3, N.Y. Islanders 2
1-5-03—	Jason Woolley, Detroit	Chicago	1:11	Detroit 4, Chicago 3
1-7-03—	Andy Delmore, Nashville	St. Louis	4:44	Nashville 2, St. Louis 1
1-8-03—	Brett Hull, Detroit	Florida	1:34	Detroit 2, Florida 1
1-9-03—	Pierre Turgeon, Dallas (2)	Chicago	4:43	Dallas 4, Chicago 3
1-9-03—	Ilya Kovalchuk, Atlanta (2)	Tampa Bay	4:44	Atlanta 3, Tampa Bay 2
1-11-03—	Scott Walker, Nashville	Phoenix	0:37	Nashville 4, Phoenix 3
1-12-03—	Milan Hejduk, Colorado	Carolina	2:04	Colorado 3, Carolina 2
1-13-03—	Nicklas Lidstrom, Detroit	Chicago	0:47	Detroit 5, Chicago 4
1-13-03—	Jason Allison, Los Angeles	San Jose	3:50	Los Angeles 3, San Jose 2
1-13-03—	Jaromir Jagr, Washington (2)	N.Y. Islanders	4:23	Washington 4, N.Y. Islanders 3
1-15-03—	Joel Bouchard, N.Y. Rangers	Washington	1:58	N.Y. Rangers 2, Washington 1
1-16-03—	Oleg Kvasha, N.Y. Islanders	St. Louis	1:59	N.Y. Islanders 3, St. Louis 2
1-18-03—	Rob Niedermayer, Calgary	Los Angeles	2:42	Calgary 2, Los Angeles 1

Date	Player, Team	Opponent	Time	Final score
1-18-03—	Andy Delmore, Nashville (2)	Edmonton	3:35	Nashville 3, Edmonton 2
1-18-03—	Nik Antropov, Toronto	Montreal	0:56	Toronto 3, Montreal 2
1-20-03—	Antti Laaksonen, Minnesota	Anaheim	2:53	Minnesota 2, Anaheim 1
1-22-03—	Eric Brewer, Edmonton	Detroit	1:42	Edmonton 4, Detroit 3
1-22-03—	Joe Nieuwendyk, New Jersey	San Jose	4:32	New Jersey 5, San Jose 4
1-25-03—	Brian Rolston, Boston	Philadelphia	0:31	Boston 1, Philadelphia 0
1-25-03—	Zigmund Palffy, Los Angeles	New Jersey	3:50	Los Angeles 2, New Jersey 1
1-25-03—	Daniel Alfredsson, Ottawa	Buffalo	2:22	Ottawa 4, Buffalo 3
1-25-03—	Stephen Weiss, Florida	Carolina	3:40	Florida 3, Carolina 2
1-30-03—	Greg de Vries, Colorado	N.Y. Rangers	2:29	Colorado 4, N.Y. Rangers 3
1-30-03—	Keith Tkachuk, St. Louis	Buffalo	3:26	St. Louis 2, Buffalo 1
2-4-03—	Greg de Vries, Colorado (2)	Boston	4:17	Colorado 3, Boston 2
2-6-03—	Nik Antropov, Toronto (2)	Tampa Bay	3:49	Toronto 3, Tampa Bay 2
2-11-03—	Sergei Zubov, Dallas	Carolina	4:59	Dallas 2, Carolina 1
2-12-03—	Mike Leclerc, Anaheim	Calgary	0:10	Anaheim 4, Calgary 3
2-13-03—	Jaroslav Spacek, Columbus	Montreal	0:28	Columbus 2, Montreal 1
2-13-03—	Michal Handzus, Philadelphia (2)	St. Louis	2:02	Philadelphia 4, St. Louis 3
2-13-03—	Brendan Morrison, Vancouver	Colorado	1:58	Vancouver 2, Colorado 1
2-14-03—	Brian Rolston, Boston (2)	Florida	0:27	Boston 6, Florida 5
2-17-03—	Patrik Stefan, Atlanta	Buffalo	3:54	Atlanta 4, Buffalo 3
2-18-03—	Marek Malik, Vancouver	Detroit	3:02	Vancouver 4, Detroit 3
2-18-03—	Mario Lemieux, Pittsburgh	Edmonton	1:35	Pittsburgh 4, Edmonton 3
2-19-03—	Miroslav Satan, Buffalo	Montreal	3:49	Buffalo 2, Montreal 1
2-22-03—	Brendan Morrison, Vancouver (2)	Edmonton	1:22	Vancouver 3, Edmonton 2
2-22-03—	Shawn Heins, Pittsburgh	St. Louis	4:33	Pittsburgh 2, St. Louis 1
2-27-03—	Magnus Arvedson, Ottawa	Dallas	1:24	Ottawa 3, Dallas 2
2-27-03—	Marc Savard, Atlanta	Colorado	1:12	Atlanta 4, Colorado 3
3-1-03—	Jeremy Roenick, Philadelphia	Boston	1:00	Philadelphia 3, Boston 2
3-1-03—	Scott Stevens, New Jersey	Washington	2:54	New Jersey 2, Washington 1
3-1-03—	Jason Blake, N.Y. Islanders (2)	Buffalo	2:42	N.Y. Islanders 2, Buffalo 1
3-1-03—	Scott Walker, Nashville (2)	Chicago	2:49	Nashville 5, Chicago 4
3-2-03—	Alex Tanguay, Colorado	Chicago	3:38	Colorado 3, Chicago 2
3-4-03—	Justin Papineau, St. Louis	Nashville	1:45	St. Louis 2, Nashville 1
3-5-03—	Martin Gelinas, Calgary	New Jersey	1:54	Calgary 5, New Jersey 4
3-6-03—	Marco Sturm, San Jose	Montreal	3:58	San Jose 4, Montreal 3
3-6-03—	Rick Nash, Columbus	Vancouver	2:02	Columbus 5, Vancouver 4
3-8-03—	Sean O'Donnell, Boston	Washington	2:15	Boston 5, Washington 4
3-8-03—	Peter Forsberg, Colorado	Philadelphia	0:26	Colorado 2, Philadelphia 1
3-8-03—	Jarome Iginla, Calgary	Columbus	4:52	Calgary 3, Columbus 2
3-10-03—	Peter Bondra, Washington (2)	Philadelphia	0:21	Washington 2, Philadelphia 1
3-11-03—	Radek Bonk, Ottawa	Boston	0:28	Ottawa 4, Boston 3
3-12-03—	Craig Adams, Carolina	Buffalo	3:41	Carolina 3, Buffalo 2
3-13-03—	Chris Clark, Calgary	Toronto	4:30	Calgary 4, Toronto 3
3-13-03—	Wade Redden, Ottawa	N.Y. Rangers	1:34	Ottawa 3, N.Y. Rangers 2
3-13-03—	Steve Thomas, Anaheim	San Jose	2:04	Anaheim 3, San Jose 2
3-17-03—	Theo Fleury, Chicago	San Jose	1:26	Chicago 3, San Jose 2
3-19-03—	Mike Modano, Dallas (2)	Atlanta	2:24	Dallas 5, Atlanta 4
3-20-03—	Pavol Demitra, St. Louis	Anaheim	2:22	St. Louis 3, Anaheim 2
3-20-03—	Teppo Numminen, Phoenix	Edmonton	2:53	Phoenix 3, Edmonton 2
3-20-03—	Tyler Wright, Columbus	Toronto	4:16	Columbus 4, Toronto 3
3-21-03—	Wes Walz, Minnesota	Dallas	1:30	Minnesota 3, Dallas 2
3-22-03—	Glen Murray, Boston (2)	Los Angeles	2:05	Boston 4, Los Angeles 3
3-22-03—	Niclas Havelid, Anaheim (2)	San Jose	1:33	Anaheim 3, San Jose 2
3-22-03—	Bryan McCabe, Toronto	Buffalo	0:36	Toronto 3, Buffalo 2
3-23-03—	Cory Cross, Edmonton	Nashville	2:12	Edmonton 3, Nashville 2
3-24-03—	Jochen Hecht, Buffalo	Colorado	4:15	Buffalo 4, Colorado 3
3-25-03—	Andrew Cassels, Columbus	Los Angeles	4:12	Columbus 2, Los Angeles 1
3-25-03—	Josef Boumedienne, Washington	Montreal	3:09	Washington 4, Montreal 3
3-27-03—	Shean Donovan, Calgary	Dallas	2:51	Calgary 2, Dallas 1
3-28-03—	Richard Park, Minnesota (2)	Chicago	1:14	Minnesota 4, Chicago 3
3-29-03—	Mats Sundin, Toronto (2)	Washington	2:56	Toronto 4, Washington 3
3-31-03—	Yannick Tremblay, Atlanta	N.Y. Rangers	2:40	Atlanta 4, N.Y. Rangers 3
3-31-03—	Steve Kelly, Los Angeles	Phoenix	1:42	Los Angeles 5, Phoenix 4
4-1-03—	Tomas Kaberle, Toronto	New Jersey	2:44	Toronto 3, New Jersey 2
4-1-03—	Steve Thomas, Anaheim (2)	Nashville	4:07	Anaheim 2, Nashville 1
4-4-03—	Craig Conroy, Calgary	Los Angeles	2:13	Calgary 2, Los Angeles 1
4-4-03—	Milan Hejduk, Colorado (2)	Anaheim	4:50	Colorado 4, Anaheim 3
4-6-03—	Tyler Arnason, Chicago	Detroit	2:10	Chicago 4, Detroit 3

PENALTY-SHOT INFORMATION

(Numbers in parentheses denote multiple penalty shots)

Date	Shooter, Team	Goaltender, Team	Scored	Final score
10-15-02—	Brad Isbister, N.Y. Islanders	Tomas Vokoun, Nashville	No	N.Y. Islanders 4, Nashville 3
10-19-02—	Pavel Bure, N.Y. Rangers	Tomas Vokoun, Nashville (2)	Yes	Nashville 2, N.Y. Rangers 2
10-30-02—	Cory Stillman, St. Louis	Mike Dunham, Nashville	No	St. Louis 7, Nashville 0
11-6-02—	Brenden Morrow, Dallas	Dan Cloutier, Vancouver	Yes	Dallas 4, Vancouver 0
11-9-02—	Glen Murray, Boston	Martin Prusek, Ottawa	No	Boston 7, Ottawa 1
11-11-02—	Patrick Marleau, San Jose	Dan Blackburn, N.Y. Rangers	Yes	N.Y. Rangers 5, San Jose 4
11-12-02—	Dave Scatchard, N.Y. Islanders	Martin Prusek, Ottawa (2)	No	Ottawa 5, N.Y. Islanders 3
11-15-02—	Steve Sullivan, Chicago	Olaf Kolzig, Washington	No	Washington 2, Chicago 2
12-5-02—	Michal Handzus, Philadelphia	Dan Blackburn, N.Y. Rangers (2)	Yes	Philadelphia 3, N.Y. Rangers 2
12-6-02—	Mathieu Dandenault, Detroit	Marty Turco, Dallas	No	Detroit 3, Dallas 3
12-13-02—	Alexei Zhamnov, Chicago	Martin Biron, Buffalo	Yes	Chicago 1, Buffalo 1
12-21-02—	Michael Nylander, Washington	Rick DiPietro, N.Y. Islanders	No	Washington 3, N.Y. Islanders 1
12-28-02—	Mike Comrie, Edmonton	Ed Belfour, Toronto	No	Edmonton 3, Toronto 2
12-29-02—	Petr Sykora, Anaheim	Roman Turek, Calgary	No	Calgary 4, Anaheim 2
1-19-03—	Tomas Holmstrom, Detroit	Dan Cloutier, Vancouver (2)	No	Vancouver 4, Detroit 1
1-22-03—	Saku Koivu, Montreal	Nikolai Khabibulin, Tampa Bay	No	Montreal 2, Tampa Bay 2
1-22-03—	Magnus Arvedson, Ottawa	Jani Hurme, Florida	No	Ottawa 2, Florida 1
1-23-03—	Dean McAmmond, Colorado	Marc Denis, Columbus	No	Colorado 5, Columbus 0
1-23-03—	Rem Murray, Nashville	Mike Dunham, N.Y. Rangers (2)	No	N.Y. Rangers 4, Nashville 2
2-5-03—	Marian Gaborik, Minnesota	Jocelyn Thibault, Chicago	No	Minnesota 2, Chicago 1
2-15-03—	Miroslav Satan, Buffalo	Mike Dunham, N.Y. Rangers (3)	Yes	Buffalo 5, N.Y. Rangers 4
2-17-03—	Zigmund Palffy, Los Angeles	Evgeni Nabokov, San Jose	No	Los Angeles 3, San Jose 2
2-17-03—	Adam Hall, Nashville	Steve Shields, Boston	No	Nashville 5, Boston 1
2-19-03—	Vincent Lecavalier, Tampa Bay	Milan Hnilicka, Atlanta	No	Tampa Bay 2, Atlanta 0
2-23-03—	Robert Reichel, Toronto	Tomas Vokoun, Nashville (3)	No	Nashville 5, Toronto 2
2-25-03—	Steve Sullivan, Chicago (2)	Roman Cechmanek, Philadelphia	No	Philadelphia 2, Chicago 0
2-25-03—	Mats Sundin, Toronto	Garth Snow, N.Y. Islanders	No	Toronto 5, N.Y. Islanders 2
3-9-03—	Mike Knuble, Boston	Jocelyn Thibault, Chicago (2)	Yes	Chicago 8, Boston 5
3-13-03—	Pavel Bure, N.Y. Rangers (2)	Patrick Lalime, Ottawa	Yes	Ottawa 3, N.Y. Rangers 2
3-14-03—	Mike Johnson, Phoenix	Jocelyn Thibault, Chicago (3)	No	Chicago 4, Phoenix 0
3-15-03—	Jarome Iginla, Calgary	Vesa Toskala, San Jose	No	San Jose 3, Calgary 2
3-16-03—	Paul Kariya, Anaheim	Jamie McLennan, Calgary	No	Calgary 2, Anaheim 2
3-21-03—	Patrick Marleau, San Jose (2)	Steve Shields, Boston (2)	No	San Jose 3, Boston 2
3-24-03—	Martin St. Louis, Tampa Bay	Evgeni Nabokov, San Jose (2)	No	Tampa Bay 4, San Jose 1
3-25-03—	Andrej Nedorost, Columbus	Cristobal Huet, Los Angeles	No	Columbus 2, Los Angeles 1
3-25-03—	Andrei Markov, Montreal	Olaf Kolzig, Washington (2)	No	Washington 4, Montreal 3
3-29-03—	Dany Heatley, Atlanta	Tomas Vokoun, Nashville (4)	No	Atlanta 3, Nashville 2
4-1-03—	Steve Thomas, Anaheim	Tomas Vokoun, Nashville (5)	Yes	Anaheim 2, Nashville 1
4-3-03—	Mike Comrie, Edmonton (2)	Vesa Toskala, San Jose (2)	No	San Jose 3, Edmonton 3

TEAM STREAKS

Most consecutive games won

Vancouver, Nov. 9-30	10
St. Louis, Oct. 15-Nov. 5	9
Detroit, Feb. 20-Mar. 7	8
Philadelphia, Oct. 24-Nov. 5	6
Philadelphia, Jan. 2-11	6
New Jersey, Jan. 13-24	6
Colorado, Jan. 30-Feb. 11	6
Detroit, Mar. 10-22	6

Most consecutive home games won

Detroit, Feb. 20-Apr. 3	11
Boston, Nov. 2-29	8
Ottawa, Nov. 14-Dec. 14	8
Toronto, Nov. 19-Dec. 14	8
New Jersey, Jan. 3-Feb. 4	8

Most consecutive road games won

Toronto, Jan. 29-Feb. 22	7
Philadelphia, Jan. 2-21	6
Ottawa, Mar. 18-Apr. 5	6
St. Louis, Oct. 24-Nov. 5	5
Vancouver, Nov. 9-30	5
Ottawa, Dec. 10-26	5

Most consecutive games undefeated

Vancouver, Jan. 26-Feb. 25 (10 wins)	14
Tampa Bay, Mar. 7-Apr. 2 (7 wins)	13
Dallas, Dec. 27-Jan. 22 (9 wins)	12
St. Louis, Oct. 12-Nov. 5 (9 wins)	10
Vancouver, Nov. 9-30 (10 wins)	10
Ottawa, Nov. 12-30 (8 wins)	10
Colorado, Jan. 20-Feb. 11 (8 wins)	10

Most consecutive home games undefeated

Toronto, Nov. 19-Jan. 14 (12 wins)	13
Detroit, Feb. 20-Apr. 3 (11 wins)	11
Dallas, Nov. 6-Dec. 6 (7 wins)	9
Anaheim, Nov. 24-Dec. 22 (6 wins)	9
Tampa Bay, Feb. 25-Apr. 2 (5 wins)	9

Most consecutive road games undefeated

Dallas, Dec. 27-Feb. 25 (7 wins)	10
Vancouver, Feb. 4-Mar. 3 (6 wins)	9
Detroit, Dec. 5-Jan. 5 (4 wins)	7
Chicago, Dec. 10-Jan. 4 (4 wins)	7
Toronto, Jan. 29-Feb. 22 (7 wins)	7
New Jersey, Mar. 18-Apr. 6 (4 wins)	7

TEAM OVERTIME GAMES

Team	OVERALL					HOME					AWAY				
	G	W	L	T	Pct.	G	W	L	T	Pct.	G	W	L	T	Pct.
Ottawa	16	7	1	8	.688	11	7	1	3	.773	5	0	0	5	.500
Minnesota	19	8	1	10	.684	8	5	0	3	.813	11	3	1	7	.591
Toronto	17	7	3	7	.618	8	4	0	4	.750	9	3	3	3	.500
Vancouver	19	5	1	13	.605	8	2	0	6	.625	11	3	1	7	.591
N.Y. Islanders	18	5	2	11	.583	8	3	0	5	.688	10	2	2	6	.500
Detroit	21	7	4	10	.571	12	5	2	5	.625	9	2	2	5	.500
Atlanta	19	7	5	7	.553	10	3	3	4	.500	9	4	2	3	.611
N.Y. Rangers	20	6	4	10	.550	10	4	2	4	.600	10	2	2	6	.500
Boston	21	6	4	11	.548	11	4	2	5	.591	10	2	2	6	.500
Calgary	23	6	4	13	.543	16	5	1	10	.625	7	1	3	3	.357
Philadelphia	23	6	4	13	.543	11	1	2	8	.455	12	5	2	5	.625
New Jersey	24	8	6	10	.542	10	5	2	3	.650	14	3	4	7	.464
Columbus	15	4	3	8	.533	9	2	2	5	.500	6	2	1	3	.583
Dallas	24	5	4	15	.521	11	3	2	6	.545	13	2	2	9	.500
St. Louis	23	6	6	11	.500	12	5	3	4	.583	11	1	3	7	.409
Anaheim	21	6	6	9	.500	12	3	2	7	.542	9	3	4	2	.444
Washington	20	6	6	8	.500	8	4	2	2	.625	12	2	4	6	.417
Colorado	28	7	8	13	.482	12	1	3	8	.417	16	6	5	5	.531
Phoenix	20	4	5	11	.475	11	3	2	6	.545	9	1	3	5	.389
Los Angeles	19	6	7	6	.474	9	5	2	2	.667	10	1	5	4	.300
Edmonton	27	7	9	11	.463	15	6	4	5	.567	12	1	5	6	.333
Nashville	25	5	7	13	.460	9	3	1	5	.611	16	2	6	8	.375
Chicago	23	4	6	13	.457	11	2	2	7	.500	12	2	4	6	.417
Tampa Bay	23	2	5	16	.435	10	0	3	7	.350	13	2	2	9	.500
Pittsburgh	14	3	5	6	.429	7	3	2	2	.571	7	0	3	4	.286
Florida	26	4	9	13	.404	14	2	5	7	.393	12	2	4	6	.417
Carolina	19	2	6	11	.395	12	0	3	9	.375	7	2	3	2	.429
Buffalo	21	3	8	10	.381	9	2	2	5	.500	12	1	6	5	.292
San Jose	19	2	8	9	.342	9	1	3	5	.389	10	1	5	4	.300
Montreal	19	2	9	8	.316	10	1	4	5	.350	9	1	5	3	.278
Totals	313	156	156	157	.500	313	94	62	157	.551	313	62	94	157	.449

STANLEY CUP PLAYOFFS

CONFERENCE QUARTERFINALS

EASTERN CONFERENCE

	W	L	Pts.	GF	GA
Ottawa Senators	4	1	8	13	7
New York Islanders	1	4	2	7	13

(Ottawa wins Eastern Conference quarterfinals, 4-1)
Wed. April 9—N.Y. Islanders 3, at Ottawa 0
Sat. April 12—Ottawa 3, N.Y. Islanders 0
Mon. April 14—Ottawa 3, at N.Y. Islanders 2
Wed. April 16—Ottawa 3, at N.Y. Islanders 1
Thu. April 17—Ottawa 4, N.Y. Islanders 1

	W	L	Pts.	GF	GA
New Jersey Devils	4	1	8	13	8
Boston Bruins	1	4	2	8	13

(New Jersey wins Eastern Conference quarterfinals, 4-1)
Wed. April 9—New Jersey 2, Boston 1
Fri. April 11—New Jersey 4, Boston 2
Sun. April 13—New Jersey 3, at Boston 0
Tue. April 15—Boston 5, New Jersey 1
Thu. April 17—New Jersey 3, Boston 0

	W	L	Pts.	GF	GA
Tampa Bay Lightning	4	2	8	14	15
Washington Capitals	2	4	4	15	14

(Tampa Bay wins Eastern Conference quarterfinals, 4-2)
Thu. April 10—Washington 3, at Tampa Bay 0
Sat. April 12—Washington 6, at Tampa Bay 3
Tue. April 15—Tampa Bay 4, at Washington 3
Wed. April 16—Tampa Bay 3, at Washington 1
Fri. April 18—Tampa Bay 2, Washington 1
Sun. April 20—Tampa Bay 2, at Washington 1

	W	L	Pts.	GF	GA
Philadelphia Flyers	4	3	8	24	16
Toronto Maple Leafs	3	4	6	16	24

(Philadelphia wins Eastern Conference quarterfinals, 4-3)
Wed. April 9—Toronto 5, at Philadelphia 3
Fri. April 11—Philadelphia 4, Toronto 1
Mon. April 14—Toronto 4, Philadelphia 3
Wed. April 16—Philadelphia 3, at Toronto 2
Sat. April 19—Philadelphia 4, Toronto 1
Mon. April 21—Toronto 2, Philadelphia 1
Tue. April 22—Philadelphia 6, Toronto 1

WESTERN CONFERENCE

	W	L	Pts.	GF	GA
Dallas Stars	4	2	8	20	11
Edmonton Oilers	2	4	4	11	20

(Dallas wins Western Conference quarterfinals, 4-2)
Wed. April 9—Edmonton 2, at Dallas 1
Fri. April 11—Dallas 6, Edmonton 1
Sun. April 13—Edmonton 3, Dallas 2
Tue. April 15—Dallas 3, at Edmonton 1
Thu. April 17—Dallas 5, Edmonton 2
Sat. April 19—Dallas 3, at Edmonton 2

	W	L	Pts.	GF	GA
Detroit Red Wings	0	4	0	6	10
Anaheim Mighty Ducks	4	0	8	10	6

(Anaheim wins Western Conference quarterfinals, 4-0)
Thu. April 10—Anaheim 2, at Detroit 1
Sat. April 12—Anaheim 3, at Detroit 2
Mon. April 14—Anaheim 2, Detroit 1
Wed. April 16—Anaheim 3, Detroit 2

	W	L	Pts.	GF	GA
Colorado Avalanche	3	4	6	17	16
Minnesota Wild	4	3	8	16	17

(Minnesota wins Western Conference quarterfinals, 4-3)

Thu. April 10—Minnesota 4, at Colorado 2
Sat. April 12—Colorado 3, Minnesota 2
Mon. April 14—Colorado 3, at Minnesota 0
Wed. April 16—Colorado 3, at Minnesota 1
Sat. April 19—Minnesota 3, at Colorado 2
Mon. April 21—Minnesota 3, Colorado 2
Tue. April 22—Minnesota 3, at Colorado 2

	W	L	Pts.	GF	GA
Vancouver Canucks	4	3	8	17	21
St. Louis Blues	3	4	6	21	17

(Vancouver wins Western Conference quarterfinals, 4-3)
Thu. April 10—St. Louis 6, at Vancouver 0
Sat. April 12—Vancouver 2, St. Louis 1
Mon. April 14—St. Louis 3, Vancouver 1
Wed. April 16—St. Louis 4, Vancouver 1
Fri. April 18—Vancouver 5, St. Louis 3
Sun. April 20—Vancouver 4, at St. Louis 3
Tue. April 22—Vancouver 4, St. Louis 1

CONFERENCE SEMIFINALS

EASTERN CONFERENCE

	W	L	Pts.	GF	GA
Ottawa Senators	4	2	8	17	10
Philadelphia Flyers	2	4	4	10	17

(Ottawa wins Eastern Conference semifinals, 4-2)
Fri. April 25—Ottawa 4, Philadelphia 2
Sun. April 27—Philadelphia 2, at Ottawa 0
Tue. April 29—Ottawa 3, at Philadelphia 2
Thu. May 1—Philadelphia 1, Ottawa 0
Sat. May 3—Ottawa 5, Philadelphia 2
Mon. May 5—Ottawa 5, at Philadelphia 1

	W	L	Pts.	GF	GA
New Jersey Devils	4	1	8	14	8
Tampa Bay Lightning	1	4	2	8	14

(New Jersey wins Eastern Conference semifinals, 4-1)
Thu. April 24—New Jersey 3, Tampa Bay 0
Sat. April 26—New Jersey 3, Tampa Bay 2
Mon. April 28—Tampa Bay 4, New Jersey 3
Wed. April 30—New Jersey 3, at Tampa Bay 1
Fri. May 2—New Jersey 2, Tampa Bay 1

WESTERN CONFERENCE

	W	L	Pts.	GF	GA
Dallas Stars	2	4	4	14	14
Anaheim Mighty Ducks	4	2	8	14	14

(Anaheim wins Western Conference semifinals, 4-2)
Thu. April 24—Anaheim 4, at Dallas 3
Sat. April 26—Anaheim 3, at Dallas 2
Mon. April 28—Dallas 2, at Anaheim 1
Wed. April 30—Anaheim 1, Dallas 0
Sat. May 3—Dallas 4, Anaheim 1
Mon. May 5—Anaheim 4, Dallas 3

	W	L	Pts.	GF	GA
Vancouver Canucks	3	4	6	17	26
Minnesota Wild	4	3	8	26	17

(Minnesota wins Western Conference semifinals, 4-3)
Fri. April 25—Vancouver 4, Minnesota 3
Sun. April 27—Minnesota 3, at Vancouver 2
Tue. April 29—Vancouver 3, at Minnesota 2
Fri. May 2—Vancouver 3, at Minnesota 2
Mon. May 5—Minnesota 7, at Vancouver 2
Wed. May 7—Minnesota 5, Vancouver 1
Thu. May 8—Minnesota 4, at Vancouver 2

2002-03 NHL REVIEW *Stanley Cup playoffs*

CONFERENCE FINALS

EASTERN CONFERENCE

	W	L	Pts.	GF	GA
Ottawa Senators	3	4	6	13	17
New Jersey Devils	4	3	8	17	13

(New Jersey wins Eastern Conference Final, 4-3)

Sat. May 10—Ottawa 3, New Jersey 2
Tue. May 13—New Jersey 4, at Ottawa 1
Thu. May 15—New Jersey 1, Ottawa 0
Sat. May 17—New Jersey 5, Ottawa 2
Mon. May 19—Ottawa 3, New Jersey 1
Wed. May 21—Ottawa 2, at New Jersey 1
Fri. May 23—New Jersey 3, at Ottawa 2

WESTERN CONFERENCE

	W	L	Pts.	GF	GA
Minnesota Wild	0	4	0	1	9
Anaheim Mighty Ducks	4	0	8	9	1

(Anaheim wins Western Conference Final, 4-0)

Sat. May 10—Anaheim 1, at Minnesota 0
Mon. May 12—Anaheim 2, at Minnesota 0
Wed. May 14—Anaheim 4, Minnesota 0
Fri. May 16—Anaheim 2, Minnesota 1

STANLEY CUP FINALS

	W	L	Pts.	GF	GA
New Jersey Devils	4	3	8	19	12
Anaheim Mighty Ducks	3	4	6	12	19

(New Jersey wins Stanley Cup Final, 4-3)

Tue. May 27—New Jersey 3, Anaheim 0
Thu. May 29—New Jersey 3, Anaheim 0
Sat. May 31—Anaheim 3, New Jersey 2
Mon. June 2—Anaheim 1, New Jersey 0
Thu. June 5—New Jersey 6, Anaheim 3
Sat. June 7—Anaheim 5, New Jersey 2
Mon. June 9—New Jersey 3, Anaheim 0

GAME SUMMARIES, STANLEY CUP FINALS

GAME 1

AT NEW JERSEY, MAY 27
New Jersey 3, Anaheim 0

Anaheim	0	0	0	—	0
New Jersey	0	1	2	—	3

FIRST PERIOD—No Scoring. Penalties—McKenzie, New Jersey (charging), 9:17; White, New Jersey (cross-checking), 14:01; Carney, Anaheim (roughing), 18:10.

SECOND PERIOD—1. New Jersey, Friesen 6 (Brylin, Gionta), 1:45. Penalties—None.

THIRD PERIOD—2. New Jersey, Marshall 5 (Elias, Gomez), 5:34. 3. New Jersey, Friesen 7 (White, Brodeur), 19:38 (eng). Penalties—None.

Shots on goal—Anaheim 4-4-8—16; New Jersey 6-15-9—30. Power-play opportunities—Anaheim 0 of 2; New Jersey 0 of 1. Goalies—Anaheim, Giguere 12-3 (29 shots-27 saves) 58:53; New Jersey, Brodeur 13-5 (16 shots-16 saves) 60:00. A—19,040. Referees—Brad Watson, Dan Marouelli. Linesmen—Brian Murphy, Tim Nowak.

GAME 2

AT NEW JERSEY, MAY 29
New Jersey 3, Anaheim 0

Anaheim	0	0	0	—	0
New Jersey	0	2	1	—	3

FIRST PERIOD—No scoring. Penalties—Pahlsson, Anaheim (obstruction-interference), 6:10; Leclerc, Anaheim (hooking), 18:24.

SECOND PERIOD—1. New Jersey, Elias 3 (Tverdovsky, Gomez), 4:42 (pp). 2. New Jersey, Gomez 2 (Tverdovsky, Elias), 12:11. Penalties—Elias, New Jersey (stick holding), 2:23; Sykora, Anaheim (holding), 3:19.

THIRD PERIOD—3. New Jersey, Friesen 8 (Gionta, S.Niedermayer), 4:22. Penalties—Carney, Anaheim (high-sticking), 0:27; McKenzie, New Jersey (interference), 8:29; Stevens, New Jersey (holding), 19:19.

Shots on goal—Anaheim 7-2-7—16; New Jersey 7-6-12—25. Power-play opportunities—Anaheim 0 of 3; New Jersey 1 of 4. Goalies—Anaheim, Giguere 12-4 (25 shots, 22 saves) 60:00; New Jersey, Brodeur 14-5 (16 shots, 16 saves) 60:00. A—19,040. Referees—Paul Devorski, Bill McCreary. Linesmen—Brian Murphy, Tim Nowak.

GAME 3

AT ANAHEIM, MAY 31
Anaheim 3, New Jersey 2 (OT)

New Jersey	0	1	1	0	—	2
Anaheim	0	2	0	1	—	3

FIRST PERIOD—No Scoring. Penalties—Thomas, Anaheim (cross-checking), 0:15; Leclerc, Anaheim (slashing), 3:58; Brylin, New Jersey (stick holding), 8:04; Salei, Anaheim (obstruction-hooking), 8:04; Rafalski, New Jersey (hooking), 18:29.

SECOND PERIOD—1. Anaheim, Chouinard 1 (Ozolinsh), 3:39. 2. New Jersey, Elias 4 (Langenbrunner, Rafalski), 14:02. 3. Anaheim, Ozolinsh 2 (Giguere), 14:47. Penalties—Sykora, Anaheim (hooking), 19:31.

THIRD PERIOD—4. New Jersey, Gomez 3 (Marshall, Elias), 9:11. Penalties—Salei, Anaheim (hooking), 3:15; Gionta, New Jersey (slashing), 10:35.

OVERTIME—5. Anaheim, Salei 2 (Oates), 6:59. Penalties—None.

Shots on goal—New Jersey 8-12-8-3—31; Anaheim 9-9-10-5—33. Power-play opportunities—New Jersey 0 of 4; Anaheim 0 of 2. Goalies—New Jersey, Brodeur 14-6 (33 shots, 30 saves) 66:59; Anaheim, Giguere 13-4 (31 shots, 29 saves) 66:59. A—17,174. Referees—Dan Marouelli, Bill McCreary. Linesmen—Brad Lazarowich, Mark Wheler.

GAME 4

AT ANAHEIM, JUNE 2
Anaheim 1, New Jersey 0 (OT)

New Jersey	0	0	0	0	—	0
Anaheim	0	0	0	1	—	1

FIRST PERIOD— No Scoring. Penalties—Sauer, Anaheim (interference), 5:54; S.Niedermayer, New Jersey (holding), 7:15; Bylsma, Anaheim (goaltender interference), 16:46.

SECOND PERIOD— No Scoring. Penalties—R.Niedermayer, Anaheim (hooking), 8:50.

THIRD PERIOD— No Scoring. Penalties—None.

OVERTIME—1. Anaheim, Thomas 3 (Pahlsson, Ozolinsh), 0:39. Penalties—None.

Shots on goal—New Jersey 10-8-7-1—26; Anaheim 7-8-9-2—26. Power-play opportunities—New Jersey 0 of 3; Anaheim 0 of 1. Goalies—New Jersey, Brodeur 14-7 (26 shots, 25 saves) 60:39; Anaheim, Giguere 14-4 (26 shots, 26 saves) 60:39. A—17,174. Referees—Dan Marouelli, Brad Watson. Linesmen—Brad Lazarowich, Mark Wheler.

GAME 5

AT NEW JERSEY, JUNE 5
New Jersey 6, Anaheim 3

Anaheim	2	1	0	—	3
New Jersey	2	2	2	—	6

FIRST PERIOD—1. Anaheim, Sykora 3 (Oates), 0:42. 2. New Jersey, Rheaume 1 (Stevenson, Brylin), 3:35. 3. New Jersey,

Elias 5 (Rafalski, Gomez), 7:45 (pp). 4. Anaheim, Rucchin 5 (Sykora, Kariya), 12:50. Penalties—Oates, Anaheim (roughing), 4:34; S.Niedermayer, New Jersey (roughing), 4:34; Carney, Anaheim (tripping), 7:03; Stevenson, New Jersey (roughing), 14:34; Leclerc, Anaheim (roughing), 17:50.

SECOND PERIOD—5. New Jersey, Gionta 1 (Pandolfo, S.Niedermayer), 3:12. 6. Anaheim, Pahlsson 2 (R.Niedermayer, Carney), 6:35. 7. New Jersey, Pandolfo 5 (Gionta, Stevens), 9:02. Penalties—Oates, Anaheim (high-sticking), 0:18; Chistov, Anaheim (high-sticking), 6:39.

THIRD PERIOD—8. New Jersey, Langenbrunner 10 (Rupp, S.Niedermayer), 5:39. 9. New Jersey, Langenbrunner 11 (Gionta), 12:52. Penalties—Marshall, New Jersey (roughing), 11:52; Salei, Anaheim (roughing), 11:52.

Shots on goal—Anaheim 12-7-4—23; New Jersey 11-13-13—37. Power-play opportunities—Anaheim 0 of 1; New Jersey 1 of 4. Goalies—Anaheim, Giguere 14-5 (37 shots, 31 saves) 60:00; New Jersey, Brodeur 15-7 (23 shots, 20 saves) 60:00. A—19,040. Referees—Paul Devorski, Bill McCreary. Linesmen—Brian Murphy, Tim Nowak.

GAME 6

AT ANAHEIM, JUNE 7
Anaheim 5, New Jersey 2

New Jersey	0	1	1	—	2
Anaheim	3	1	1	—	5

FIRST PERIOD—1. Anaheim, Rucchin 6 (Kariya, Sykora); 4:26. 2. Anaheim, Rucchin 7 (Leclerc, R.Niedermayer), 13:42. 3. Anaheim, Thomas 4 (Kariya, Carney), 15:59 (pp). Penalties—Elias, New Jersey (obstruction-interference), 8:55; Langenbrunner, New Jersey (double roughing), 14:24; Salei, Anaheim (roughing), 14:24; Kariya, Anaheim (tripping), 18:39.

SECOND PERIOD—4. New Jersey, Pandolfo 6 (Madden, Gionta), 2:18. 5. Anaheim, Kariya 6 (Sykora, Oates), 17:15. Penalties—Langenbrunner, New Jersey (hooking), 6:26; Stevenson, New Jersey (slashing), 18:27.

THIRD PERIOD—6. Anaheim, Sykora 4 (Chistov, Havelid), 3:57 (pp). 7. New Jersey, Marshall 6 (Rafalski, Elias), 10:46 (pp). Penalties—Stevenson, New Jersey (double roughing), 1:15; Krog, Anaheim (high-sticking), 6:26; Pahlsson, Anaheim (tripping), 9:32; Rheaume, New Jersey (clipping), 14:45; Marshall, New Jersey (obstruction-tripping), 18:51; Thomas, Anaheim (slashing), 19:59; White, New Jersey (roughing), 19:59.

Shots on goal—New Jersey 9-10-9—28; Anaheim 9-10-5—24. Power-play opportunities—New Jersey 1 of 3; Anaheim 2 of 8. Goalies—New Jersey, Brodeur 15-8 (22 shots, 17 saves) 48:37; Schwab (2 shots, 2 saves) 11:23; Anaheim, Giguere 15-5 (28 shots, 26 saves) 59:58. A—17,174. Referees—Dan Marouelli, Brad Watson. Linesmen—Brad Lazarowich, Mark Wheler.

GAME 7

AT NEW JERSEY, JUNE 9
New Jersey 3, Anaheim 0

Anaheim	0	0	0	—	0
New Jersey	0	2	1	—	3

FIRST PERIOD—No scoring. Penalties—Stevenson, New Jersey (boarding), 17:31.

SECOND PERIOD—1. New Jersey, Rupp 1 (S.Niedermayer, White), 2:22. 2. New Jersey, Friesen 9 (Rupp, S.Niedermayer), 12:18. Penalties—R.Niedermayer, Anaheim (obstruction-interference), 3:58.

THIRD PERIOD—3. New Jersey, Friesen 10 (Rupp, Stevens), 16:16. Penalties—Leclerc, Anaheim (cross-checking), 16:45.

Shots on goal—Anaheim 5-9-10—24; New Jersey 7-12-6—25. Power-play opportunities—Anaheim 0 of 1; New Jersey 0 of 2. Goalies—Anaheim, Giguere 15-6 (25 shots, 22 saves) 60:00; New Jersey, Brodeur 16-8 (24 shots, 24 saves) 60:00.

A—19,040. Referees—Dan Marouelli, Bill McCreary. Linesmen—Brad Lazarowich, Brian Murphy.

INDIVIDUAL LEADERS

SCORING

LEADERS BY CATEGORY

Goals: Jamie Langenbrunner, New Jersey (11)
Assists: Scott Niedermayer, New Jersey (16)
Points: Scott Niedermayer, Jamie Langenbrunner, New Jersey (18)
Penalty Minutes: Todd Bertuzzi, Vancouver (60)
Best plus/minus: Scott Stevens, New Jersey (14)
Power play goals: Doug Weight, St. Louis (5)
Short-handed goals: Wes Walz, Minnesota, Rob Niedermayer, Anaheim, Martin St. Louis, Tampa Bay (2)
Game-winning goals: Jamie Langenbrunner, Jeff Friesen, New Jersey (4)
Shots: John Madden, New Jersey (77)

TOP SCORERS

	Games	G	A	Pts.	PIM
Jamie Langenbrunner, NJ	24	11	7	18	16
Scott Niedermayer, N.J.	24	2	16	18	16
Marian Gaborik, Minn.	18	9	8	17	6
Marian Hossa, Ottawa	18	5	11	16	6
John Madden, New Jersey	24	6	10	16	2
Mike Modano, Dallas	12	5	10	15	4
Sergei Zubov, Dallas	12	4	10	14	4
Jeff Friesen, New Jersey	24	10	4	14	6
Markus Naslund, Van.	14	5	9	14	18
Adam Oates, Anaheim	21	4	9	13	6
Wes Walz, Minnesota	18	7	6	13	14
Andrew Brunette, Minn.	18	7	6	13	4
Patrik Elias, New Jersey	24	5	8	13	26
Petr Sykora, Anaheim	21	4	9	13	12
Sergei Zholtok, Minnesota	18	2	11	13	0

	Games	G	A	Pts.	PIM
Doug Weight, St. Louis	7	5	8	13	2
Paul Kariya, Anaheim	21	6	6	12	6
Scott Gomez, New Jersey	24	3	9	12	2
Martin St. Louis, Tampa Bay	11	7	5	12	0
Jay Pandolfo, New Jersey	24	6	6	12	2

GOALTENDING

LEADERS BY CATEGORY

Goals allowed: Dan Cloutier, Vancouver (45)
Shutouts: Martin Brodeur, New Jersey (7)
Goals-against average: Jean-Sebastien Giguere, Anaheim (1.62)
Wins: Martin Brodeur, New Jersey (16)
Losses: Martin Brodeur, New Jersey (8)
Shots against: Jean-Sebastien Giguere, Anaheim (697)
Save percentage: Jean-Sebastien Giguere, Anaheim (.945)

TOP GOALTENDERS
(Based on goals-against average, minimum seven games)

	Gms.	W	L	T	Avg.	SO	GA
J. Giguere, Ana.	21	15	6	0	1.62	5	38
Martin Brodeur, N.J.	24	16	8	0	1.65	7	41
Patrick Lalime, Ott.	18	11	7	0	1.82	1	34
Marty Turco, Dallas	12	6	6	0	1.88	0	25
E. Fernandez, Min.	9	3	4	0	1.96	0	18
R. Cechmanek, Phil.	13	6	7	0	2.15	2	31
Patrick Roy, Colo.	7	3	4	0	2.27	1	16
N. Khabibulin, T.B.	10	5	5	0	2.42	0	26
Chris Osgood, St.L.	7	3	4	0	2.45	1	17
Dwayne Roloson, Min.	11	5	6	0	2.59	0	25

ANAHEIM MIGHTY DUCKS

(Lost Stanley Cup finals to New Jersey, 4-3)

SCORING

	Games	G	A	Pts.	PIM	+/-	PPG	SHG	GWG	GTG	Sht.	Sht. Pct.	Faceoffs Won	Lost	Pct.	TOI
Adam Oates...............	21	4	9	13	6	2	3	0	1	0	18	22.2	237	153	60.8	19:15
Petr Sykora	21	4	9	13	12	3	1	0	2	2	58	6.9	0	3	0.0	18:38
Paul Kariya	21	6	6	12	6	0	0	0	1	1	53	11.3	4	6	40.0	21:14
Mike Leclerc	21	2	9	11	12	3	1	0	2	1	55	3.6	0	2	0.0	19:01
Steve Rucchin	21	7	3	10	2	-2	1	0	2	1	46	15.2	246	223	52.5	23:34
Rob Niedermayer	21	3	7	10	18	-5	0	2	0	0	41	7.3	36	37	49.3	23:34
Steve Thomas	21	4	4	8	8	2	2	0	3	1	40	10.0	1	6	14.3	15:12
Sandis Ozolinsh	21	2	6	8	10	8	0	0	1	0	39	5.1	0	0	—	23:37
Stanislav Chistov.......	21	4	2	6	8	4	0	0	1	0	33	12.1	0	1	0.0	13:21
Samuel Pahlsson	21	2	4	6	12	1	0	0	0	0	24	8.3	134	115	53.8	16:40
Ruslan Salei	21	2	3	5	26	3	0	0	1	1	33	6.1	0	0	—	26:05
Jason Krog................	21	3	1	4	4	3	0	0	0	0	23	13.0	159	127	55.6	12:10
Keith Carney	21	0	4	4	16	3	0	0	0	0	26	0.0	0	0	—	26:39
Niclas Havelid...........	21	0	4	4	2	0	0	0	0	0	29	0.0	0	0	—	25:41
Kurt Sauer	21	1	1	2	6	3	0	1	1	0	8	12.5	0	1	0.0	20:44
Marc Chouinard.........	15	1	0	1	0	1	0	0	0	0	11	9.1	15	7	68.2	7:16
Dan Bylsma	11	0	1	1	2	3	0	0	0	0	12	0.0	0	2	0.0	9:44
J.S. Giguere (g).........	21	0	1	1	0	0	0	0	0	0	0	—	0	0	—	—
Vitaly Vishnevski	21	0	1	1	6	-3	0	0	0	0	8	0.0	0	0	—	10:01
Fredrik Olausson	1	0	0	0	0	0	0	0	0	0	0	—	0	0	—	3:19
Cam Severson	1	0	0	0	0	0	0	0	0	0	0	—	0	0	—	2:24
Martin Gerber (g)	2	0	0	0	0	0	0	0	0	0	0	—	0	0	—	—
Alexei Smirnov	4	0	0	0	2	0	0	0	0	0	3	0.0	0	0	—	4:21
Patric Kjellberg..........	10	0	0	0	0	-2	0	0	0	0	6	0.0	0	1	0.0	10:30

GOALTENDING

	Games	GS	Min.	GA	SO	Avg.	W	L	T	EN	PPG Allow	SHG Allow	Shots	Save Pct.
Jean-Sebastien Giguere............	21	21	1407	38	5	1.62	15	6	0	1	9	1	697	.945
Martin Gerber	2	0	20	1	0	3.00	0	0	0	0	0	0	6	.833

BOSTON BRUINS

(Lost Eastern Conference quarterfinals to New Jersey, 4-1)

SCORING

	Games	G	A	Pts.	PIM	+/-	PPG	SHG	GWG	GTG	Sht.	Sht. Pct.	Faceoffs Won	Lost	Pct.	TOI
Dan McGillis...............	5	3	0	3	2	-2	2	0	1	0	9	33.3	0	0	—	18:54
Joe Thornton..............	5	1	2	3	4	-5	1	0	0	0	12	8.3	54	49	52.4	20:13
Glen Murray	5	1	1	2	4	-5	0	0	0	0	12	8.3	0	0	—	19:36
Mike Knuble	5	0	2	2	2	-2	0	0	0	0	8	0.0	1	0	100.0	17:34
Brian Rolston	5	0	2	2	0	-1	0	0	0	0	6	0.0	44	35	55.7	18:39
Sergei Samsonov	5	0	2	2	0	-1	0	0	0	0	10	0.0	0	0	—	17:07
Jozef Stumpel	5	0	2	2	0	0	0	0	0	0	9	0.0	48	48	50.0	17:31
Bryan Berard	3	1	0	1	2	-1	0	0	0	0	5	20.0	0	0	—	21:50
Martin Lapointe.........	5	1	0	1	14	-2	0	0	0	0	6	16.7	1	2	33.3	14:39
Marty McInnis...........	5	1	0	1	2	1	0	0	0	0	6	16.7	3	7	30.0	14:29
Jonathan Girard	2	0	1	1	0	-1	0	0	0	0	4	0.0	0	0	—	16:39
Nick Boynton.............	5	0	1	1	4	-2	0	0	0	0	12	0.0	0	0	—	23:21
Ian Moran..................	5	0	1	1	4	-2	0	0	0	0	2	0.0	0	0	—	18:24
Don Sweeney	5	0	1	1	0	0	0	0	0	0	4	0.0	0	0	—	14:40
Steve Shields (g).......	2	0	0	0	0	0	0	0	0	0	0	—	0	0	—	—
Jeff Hackett (g)	3	0	0	0	0	0	0	0	0	0	0	—	0	0	—	—
P.J. Axelsson.............	5	0	0	0	6	-2	0	0	0	0	10	0.0	0	1	0.0	13:23
Hal Gill	5	0	0	0	4	-1	0	0	0	0	10	0.0	0	0	—	20:19
Lee Goren.................	5	0	0	0	5	-1	0	0	0	0	3	0.0	1	0	100.0	6:28
Michal Grosek	5	0	0	0	13	-1	0	0	0	0	3	0.0	14	15	48.3	6:12
Rob Zamuner	5	0	0	0	4	0	0	0	0	0	9	0.0	0	0	—	9:23

GOALTENDING

	Games	GS	Min.	GA	SO	Avg.	W	L	T	EN	PPG Allow	SHG Allow	Shots	Save Pct.
Jeff Hackett..............................	3	3	179	5	0	1.68	1	2	0	2	1	0	76	.934
Steve Shields...........................	2	2	119	6	0	3.03	0	2	0	0	2	0	58	.897

COLORADO AVALANCHE

(Lost Western Conference quarterfinals to Minnesota, 4-3)

SCORING

	Games	G	A	Pts.	PIM	+/-	PPG	SHG	GWG	GTG	Sht.	Sht. Pct.	Faceoffs Won	Lost	Pct.	TOI
Joe Sakic	7	6	3	9	2	1	2	0	1	0	26	23.1	106	69	60.6	22:28
Peter Forsberg	7	2	6	8	6	3	1	0	0	0	23	8.7	57	47	54.8	20:00
Milan Hejduk	7	2	2	4	2	4	1	0	0	0	21	9.5	0	1	0.0	20:42
Rob Blake	7	1	2	3	8	2	0	0	0	0	27	3.7	0	0	—	27:27
Dan Hinote	7	1	2	3	2	0	0	0	0	0	9	11.1	21	26	44.7	14:18
Steve Reinprecht	7	1	2	3	0	1	0	0	0	0	9	11.1	18	18	50.0	15:32
Alex Tanguay	7	1	2	3	4	-2	0	0	1	0	10	10.0	1	5	16.7	19:06
Derek Morris	7	0	3	3	6	2	0	0	0	0	12	0.0	0	0	—	22:44
Greg de Vries	7	2	0	2	0	2	0	0	0	0	12	16.7	0	0	—	22:10
Riku Hahl	6	0	2	2	2	2	0	0	0	0	11	0.0	3	3	50.0	13:48
Bates Battaglia	7	0	2	2	4	1	0	0	0	0	14	0.0	0	0	—	14:39
Brian Willsie	6	1	0	1	2	1	0	0	1	0	7	14.3	1	0	100.0	10:47
Adam Foote	6	0	1	1	8	2	0	0	0	0	3	0.0	0	0	—	24:12
Martin Skoula	7	0	1	1	4	-1	0	0	0	0	4	0.0	0	0	—	11:05
Chris McAllister	1	0	0	0	0	0	0	0	0	0	0	—	0	0	—	2:34
Scott Parker	1	0	0	0	2	0	0	0	0	0	0	—	0	0	—	1:44
Serge Aubin	5	0	0	0	4	1	0	0	0	0	4	0.0	2	7	22.2	5:25
Eric Messier	5	0	0	0	0	0	0	0	0	0	2	0.0	0	3	0.0	6:57
Mike Keane	6	0	0	0	2	0	0	0	0	0	1	0.0	0	0	—	7:56
Jeff Shantz	6	0	0	0	4	1	0	0	0	0	7	0.0	41	36	53.2	9:42
Bryan Marchment	7	0	0	0	4	1	0	0	0	0	3	0.0	0	0	—	16:01
Patrick Roy (g)	7	0	0	0	0	0	0	0	0	0	0	—	0	0	—	—

GOALTENDING

	Games	GS	Min.	GA	SO	Avg.	W	L	T	EN	PPG Allow	SHG Allow	Shots	Save Pct.
Patrick Roy	7	7	423	16	1	2.27	3	4	0	0	7	1	177	.910

DALLAS STARS

(Lost Western Conference semifinals to Anaheim, 4-2)

SCORING

	Games	G	A	Pts.	PIM	+/-	PPG	SHG	GWG	GTG	Sht.	Sht. Pct.	Faceoffs Won	Lost	Pct.	TOI
Mike Modano	12	5	10	15	4	2	1	0	2	0	30	16.7	134	123	52.1	23:52
Sergei Zubov	12	4	10	14	4	2	2	0	0	0	27	14.8	0	0	—	30:44
Brenden Morrow	12	3	5	8	16	3	2	0	0	0	28	10.7	1	3	25.0	21:02
Scott Young	10	4	3	7	6	5	2	0	1	0	32	12.5	0	0	—	19:12
Niko Kapanen	12	4	3	7	12	4	0	1	0	0	20	20.0	72	103	41.1	16:03
Darryl Sydor	12	0	6	6	6	-3	0	0	0	0	18	0.0	0	0	—	19:13
Jason Arnott	11	3	2	5	6	-2	1	0	0	0	18	16.7	90	85	51.4	15:35
Jere Lehtinen	12	3	2	5	0	1	1	0	1	0	42	7.1	0	1	0.0	21:12
Stu Barnes	12	2	3	5	0	0	0	0	2	0	22	9.1	70	76	47.9	19:06
Rob DiMaio	12	1	4	5	10	2	0	0	0	0	26	3.8	1	2	33.3	15:50
Ulf Dahlen	11	1	3	4	0	-3	1	0	0	0	19	5.3	0	1	0.0	12:54
Philippe Boucher	11	1	2	3	11	1	0	0	0	0	19	5.3	0	0	—	21:28
Derian Hatcher	11	1	2	3	33	8	0	0	0	0	22	4.5	0	0	—	30:01
Richard Matvichuk	12	0	3	3	8	1	0	0	0	0	12	0.0	0	0	—	19:54
Kirk Muller	12	1	1	2	8	0	0	0	0	0	14	7.1	2	7	22.2	10:45
Manny Malhotra	5	1	0	1	0	1	0	0	0	0	3	33.3	17	22	43.6	8:13
Pierre Turgeon	5	0	1	1	0	1	0	0	0	0	8	0.0	13	9	59.1	12:21
Claude Lemieux	7	0	1	1	10	-1	0	0	0	0	6	0.0	0	1	0.0	11:24
Stephane Robidas	12	0	1	1	20	1	0	0	0	0	10	0.0	0	0	—	13:53
Steve Ott	1	0	0	0	0	-1	0	0	0	0	0	—	0	0	—	6:57
Lyle Odelein	2	0	0	0	0	-1	0	0	0	0	2	0.0	0	0	—	12:52
Bill Guerin	4	0	0	0	4	-1	0	0	0	0	3	0.0	0	0	—	8:33
David Oliver	6	0	0	0	2	-2	0	0	0	0	1	0.0	0	0	—	6:32
Marty Turco (g)	12	0	0	0	8	0	0	0	0	0	—	—	0	0	—	—

GOALTENDING

	Games	GS	Min.	GA	SO	Avg.	W	L	T	EN	PPG Allow	SHG Allow	Shots	Save Pct.
Marty Turco	12	12	798	25	0	1.88	6	6	0	0	5	2	310	.919

DETROIT RED WINGS

(Lost Western Conference quarterfinals to Anaheim, 4-0)

SCORING

	Games	G	A	Pts.	PIM	+/-	PPG	SHG	GWG	GTG	Sht.	Sht. Pct.	Faceoffs Won	Lost	Pct.	TOI
Sergei Fedorov	4	1	2	3	0	-1	0	0	0	0	14	7.1	38	22	63.3	22:06
Tomas Holmstrom	4	1	1	2	4	1	1	0	0	0	7	14.3	0	0	—	14:36
Brendan Shanahan	4	1	1	2	4	-1	1	0	0	0	17	5.9	0	1	0.0	22:03
Nicklas Lidstrom	4	0	2	2	0	-1	0	0	0	0	15	0.0	0	0	—	33:35
Luc Robitaille	4	1	0	1	0	1	0	0	0	0	12	8.3	0	1	0.0	11:30
Jason Woolley	4	1	0	1	0	-2	0	0	0	0	3	33.3	0	0	—	15:25
Henrik Zetterberg	4	1	0	1	0	-4	0	0	0	0	10	10.0	1	3	25.0	18:18
Brett Hull	4	0	1	1	0	-4	0	0	0	0	15	0.0	0	0	—	20:16
Igor Larionov	4	0	1	1	0	1	0	0	0	0	6	0.0	15	17	46.9	15:10
Steve Yzerman	4	0	1	1	2	0	0	0	0	0	10	0.0	35	24	59.3	20:32
Dmitri Bykov	4	0	0	0	0	-2	0	0	0	0	4	0.0	0	0	—	11:13
Chris Chelios	4	0	0	0	2	-3	0	0	0	0	4	0.0	0	0	—	25:43
Mathieu Dandenault	4	0	0	0	2	-1	0	0	0	0	9	0.0	0	0	—	25:51
Pavel Datsyuk	4	0	0	0	0	-3	0	0	0	0	9	0.0	31	33	48.4	18:48
Kris Draper	4	0	0	0	4	-2	0	0	0	0	8	0.0	21	23	47.7	17:29
Curtis Joseph (g)	4	0	0	0	0	0	0	0	0	0	0	—	0	0	—	—
Kirk Maltby	4	0	0	0	4	-2	0	0	0	0	7	0.0	0	0	—	17:17
Darren McCarty	4	0	0	0	6	-3	0	0	0	0	9	0.0	19	11	63.3	15:44
Mathieu Schneider	4	0	0	0	6	-4	0	0	0	0	12	0.0	0	0	—	28:15

GOALTENDING

	Games	GS	Min.	GA	SO	Avg.	W	L	T	EN	PPG Allow	SHG Allow	Shots	Save Pct.
Curtis Joseph	4	4	289	10	0	2.08	0	4	0	0	0	0	120	.917

EDMONTON OILERS

(Lost Western Conference quarterfinals to Dallas, 4-2)

SCORING

	Games	G	A	Pts.	PIM	+/-	PPG	SHG	GWG	GTG	Sht.	Sht. Pct.	Faceoffs Won	Lost	Pct.	TOI
Shawn Horcoff	6	3	1	4	6	1	0	0	1	0	7	42.9	40	24	62.5	15:26
Eric Brewer	6	1	3	4	6	1	0	0	0	0	9	11.1	0	0	—	25:31
Georges Laraque	6	1	3	4	4	2	0	0	0	0	8	12.5	0	0	—	12:10
Ryan Smyth	6	2	0	2	16	-1	0	1	0	0	12	16.7	0	6	0.0	17:39
Jason Chimera	2	0	2	2	0	2	0	0	0	0	3	0.0	0	0	—	10:54
Todd Marchant	6	0	2	2	2	-1	0	0	0	0	5	0.0	62	55	53.0	20:03
Mike York	6	0	2	2	2	2	0	0	0	0	4	0.0	5	8	38.5	14:19
Radek Dvorak	4	1	0	1	0	0	0	0	1	0	10	10.0	0	2	0.0	15:04
Mike Comrie	6	1	0	1	10	-1	0	0	0	0	9	11.1	36	34	51.4	13:07
Fernando Pisani	6	1	0	1	2	-2	0	0	0	0	8	12.5	0	0	—	13:48
Marty Reasoner	6	1	0	1	2	-2	1	0	0	0	8	12.5	39	46	45.9	14:22
M.-Andre Bergeron	1	0	1	1	0	-1	0	0	0	0	3	0.0	0	0	—	19:20
Cory Cross	6	0	1	1	20	-3	0	0	0	0	10	0.0	0	0	—	20:36
Brad Isbister	6	0	1	1	12	-1	0	0	0	0	5	0.0	1	4	20.0	10:03
Ethan Moreau	6	0	1	1	16	-4	0	0	0	0	10	0.0	0	0	—	12:23
Tommy Salo (g)	6	0	1	1	0	0	0	0	0	0	0	—	0	0	—	—
J. Markkanen (g)	1	0	0	0	0	0	0	0	0	0	0	—	0	0	—	—
Scott Ferguson	5	0	0	0	8	0	0	0	0	0	1	0.0	0	0	—	11:44
Ales Hemsky	6	0	0	0	0	-5	0	0	0	0	7	0.0	0	0	—	12:45
Alexei Semenov	6	0	0	0	0	-1	0	0	0	0	2	0.0	0	0	—	13:04
Jason Smith	6	0	0	0	19	-2	0	0	0	0	6	0.0	0	0	—	21:16
Steve Staios	6	0	0	0	4	0	0	0	0	0	7	0.0	0	0	—	23:27

GOALTENDING

	Games	GS	Min.	GA	SO	Avg.	W	L	T	EN	PPG Allow	SHG Allow	Shots	Save Pct.
Tommy Salo	6	6	343	18	0	3.15	2	4	0	1	6	0	161	.888
Jussi Markkanen	1	0	14	1	0	4.29	0	0	0	0	1	0	12	.917

MINNESOTA WILD

(Lost Western Conference finals to Anaheim, 4-0)

SCORING

	Games	G	A	Pts.	PIM	+/-	PPG	SHG	GWG	GTG	Sht.	Sht. Pct.	Faceoffs Won	Lost	Pct.	TOI
Marian Gaborik	18	9	8	17	6	2	4	0	0	0	52	17.3	3	3	50.0	18:11
Andrew Brunette	18	7	6	13	4	-3	4	0	1	1	33	21.2	5	9	35.7	14:59
Wes Walz	18	7	6	13	14	5	0	2	2	0	29	24.1	161	200	44.6	17:24
Sergei Zholtok	18	2	11	13	0	-7	1	0	0	0	34	5.9	106	142	42.7	15:43
Cliff Ronning	17	2	7	9	4	-3	1	0	0	0	37	5.4	4	9	30.8	16:39
Pascal Dupuis	16	4	4	8	8	0	2	0	1	0	36	11.1	14	16	46.7	16:58
Filip Kuba	18	3	5	8	24	-8	3	0	0	0	21	14.3	0	0	—	26:45
Richard Park	18	3	3	6	4	-2	0	0	1	1	26	11.5	9	10	47.4	17:03
Darby Hendrickson	17	2	3	5	4	1	0	0	1	0	22	9.1	166	177	48.4	16:58
Jeremy Stevenson	14	0	5	5	12	0	0	0	0	0	17	0.0	0	0	—	12:32
Antti Laaksonen	16	1	3	4	4	-3	0	0	0	0	25	4.0	2	8	20.0	16:34
Willie Mitchell	18	1	3	4	14	5	0	0	0	0	18	5.6	0	0	—	24:48
Jason Marshall	15	1	1	2	16	-1	0	0	1	0	12	8.3	0	0	—	10:50
Lubomir Sekeras	15	1	1	2	6	-2	1	0	1	0	13	7.7	0	0	—	16:51
Jim Dowd	15	0	2	2	0	-1	0	0	0	0	24	0.0	93	107	46.5	12:58
P.-Marc Bouchard	5	0	1	1	2	-1	0	0	0	0	8	0.0	13	13	50.0	13:15
Nick Schultz	18	0	1	1	10	5	0	0	0	0	5	0.0	0	0	—	19:38
Andrei Zyuzin	18	0	1	1	14	-3	0	0	0	0	30	0.0	0	0	—	23:06
Brad Bombardir	4	0	0	0	0	-1	0	0	0	0	1	0.0	0	0	—	14:51
Bill Muckalt	5	0	0	0	0	-3	0	0	0	0	4	0.0	0	0	—	11:15
M. Fernandez (g)	9	0	0	0	0	0	0	0	0	0	0	—	0	0	—	—
Brad Brown	11	0	0	0	16	-1	0	0	0	0	0	—	0	0	—	8:22
D. Roloson (g)	11	0	0	0	4	0	0	0	0	0	0	—	0	0	—	—
Matt Johnson	12	0	0	0	25	0	0	0	0	0	2	0.0	0	1	0.0	6:38

GOALTENDING

	Games	GS	Min.	GA	SO	Avg.	W	L	T	EN	PPG Allow	SHG Allow	Shots	Save Pct.
Manny Fernandez	9	7	552	18	0	1.96	3	4	0	0	5	1	253	.929
Dwayne Roloson	11	11	579	25	0	2.59	5	6	0	0	7	2	257	.903

NEW JERSEY DEVILS

(Winner of 2003 Stanley Cup)

SCORING

	Games	G	A	Pts.	PIM	+/-	PPG	SHG	GWG	GTG	Sht.	Sht. Pct.	Faceoffs Won	Lost	Pct.	TOI
J. Langenbrunner	24	11	7	18	16	11	1	0	4	1	53	20.8	7	12	36.8	17:33
Scott Niedermayer	24	2	16	18	16	11	1	0	0	0	40	5.0	0	1	0.0	26:06
John Madden	24	6	10	16	2	10	2	1	1	0	77	7.8	250	283	46.9	19:38
Jeff Friesen	24	10	4	14	6	10	1	0	4	0	46	21.7	0	0	—	16:02
Patrik Elias	24	5	8	13	26	5	2	0	2	0	59	8.5	17	18	48.6	17:14
Jay Pandolfo	24	6	6	12	2	9	0	0	1	0	38	15.8	2	1	66.7	16:33
Scott Gomez	24	3	9	12	2	3	0	0	0	0	56	5.4	127	161	44.1	13:44
Brian Rafalski	23	2	9	11	8	7	2	0	0	0	36	5.6	0	0	—	25:46
Joe Nieuwendyk	17	3	6	9	4	-2	1	0	0	0	24	12.5	164	125	56.7	15:02
Scott Stevens	24	3	6	9	14	14	1	0	1	0	33	9.1	0	0	—	24:44
Brian Gionta	24	1	8	9	6	5	0	0	0	0	59	1.7	8	9	47.1	14:31
Grant Marshall	24	6	2	8	8	3	2	0	1	1	47	12.8	2	2	50.0	14:30
Colin White	24	0	5	5	29	3	0	0	0	0	21	0.0	0	0	—	22:01
Michael Rupp	4	1	3	4	0	4	0	0	1	0	2	50.0	16	27	37.2	11:28
Sergei Brylin	19	1	3	4	8	-4	0	0	0	0	25	4.0	26	49	34.7	17:02
Pascal Rheaume	24	1	2	3	13	-2	0	0	0	0	30	3.3	147	174	45.8	13:32
Oleg Tverdovsky	15	0	3	3	0	-4	0	0	0	0	5	0.0	0	0	—	15:06
Turner Stevenson	14	1	1	2	26	2	0	0	0	0	20	5.0	0	1	0.0	13:00
Tommy Albelin	16	1	0	1	2	3	0	0	0	0	6	16.7	0	0	—	14:17
Martin Brodeur (g)	24	0	1	1	6	0	0	0	0	0	0	—	0	0	—	—
Corey Schwab (g)	2	0	0	0	0	0	0	0	0	0	0	—	0	0	—	—
Jiri Bicek	5	0	0	0	0	-2	0	0	0	0	2	0.0	0	0	—	8:10
Richard Smehlik	5	0	0	0	2	-2	0	0	0	0	2	0.0	0	0	—	12:58
Ken Daneyko	13	0	0	0	2	2	0	0	0	0	2	0.0	0	0	—	13:43
Jim McKenzie	13	0	0	0	14	-2	0	0	0	0	3	0.0	0	0	—	7:59

GOALTENDING

	Games	GS	Min.	GA	SO	Avg.	W	L	T	EN	PPG Allow	SHG Allow	Shots	Save Pct.
Corey Schwab	2	0	28	0	0	0.00	0	0	0	0	0	0	8	1.000
Martin Brodeur	24	24	1491	41	7	1.65	16	8	0	0	8	2	622	.934

NEW YORK ISLANDERS

(Lost Eastern Conference quarterfinals to Ottawa, 4-1)

SCORING

	Games	G	A	Pts.	PIM	+/-	PPG	SHG	GWG	GTG	Sht.	Sht. Pct.	Faceoffs Won	Lost	Pct.	TOI
Alexei Yashin	5	2	2	4	2	-1	0	0	0	0	20	10.0	37	42	46.8	21:05
Adrian Aucoin	5	1	2	3	4	-1	0	0	0	0	19	5.3	0	0	—	31:43
Randy Robitaille	5	1	1	2	0	-1	1	0	0	0	8	12.5	27	19	58.7	13:02
Roman Hamrlik	5	0	2	2	2	-2	0	0	0	0	9	0.0	0	0	—	29:23
Shawn Bates	5	1	0	1	0	-2	1	0	0	0	7	14.3	9	14	39.1	18:35
Mark Parrish	5	1	0	1	4	-1	1	0	0	0	4	25.0	0	0	—	16:02
Dave Scatchard	5	1	0	1	6	-3	0	0	1	0	3	33.3	56	35	61.5	15:57
Eric Godard	2	0	1	1	4	1	0	0	0	0	0	—	0	0	—	1:09
Jason Blake	5	0	1	1	0	-2	0	0	0	0	12	0.0	1	1	50.0	19:39
Kenny Jonsson...........	5	0	1	1	0	-2	0	0	0	0	11	0.0	0	0	—	28:46
Oleg Kvasha	5	0	1	1	2	-1	0	0	0	0	11	0.0	7	10	41.2	16:25
Janne Niinimaa.........	5	0	1	1	12	-4	0	0	0	0	5	0.0	0	0	—	23:31
Rick DiPietro (g)	1	0	0	0	0	0	0	0	0	0	0	—	0	0	—	
Justin Papineau	1	0	0	0	0	0	0	0	0	0	0	—	0	3	0.0	5:12
Mattias Timander	1	0	0	0	0	1	0	0	0	0	0	—	0	0	—	4:08
Justin Mapletoft	2	0	0	0	0	0	0	0	0	0	1	0.0	5	4	55.6	7:23
Radek Martinek	4	0	0	0	4	-1	0	0	0	0	0	—	0	0	—	10:15
Arron Asham.............	5	0	0	0	16	-1	0	0	0	0	4	0.0	0	0	—	15:08
Eric Cairns................	5	0	0	0	13	-1	0	0	0	0	3	0.0	0	0	—	6:01
Michael Peca.............	5	0	0	0	4	-1	0	0	0	0	7	0.0	59	44	57.3	20:09
Garth Snow (g)	5	0	0	0	0	0	0	0	0	0	0	—	0	0	—	
Steve Webb...............	5	0	0	0	10	-2	0	0	0	0	3	0.0	0	0	—	6:46
Jason Wiemer	5	0	0	0	23	-3	0	0	0	0	9	0.0	16	17	48.5	13:36

GOALTENDING

	Games	GS	Min.	GA	SO	Avg.	W	L	T	EN	PPG Allow	SHG Allow	Shots	Save Pct.
Rick DiPietro...........................	1	0	15	0	0	0.00	0	0	0	0	0	0	3	1.000
Garth Snow...............................	5	5	305	12	1	2.36	1	4	0	1	4	0	134	.910

OTTAWA SENATORS

(Lost Eastern Conference finals to New Jersey, 4-3)

SCORING

	Games	G	A	Pts.	PIM	+/-	PPG	SHG	GWG	GTG	Sht.	Sht. Pct.	Faceoffs Won	Lost	Pct.	TOI
Marian Hossa	18	5	11	16	6	-1	3	0	1	0	54	9.3	1	2	33.3	18:41
Radek Bonk..............	18	6	5	11	10	2	2	0	0	0	28	21.4	173	178	49.3	17:43
Martin Havlat............	18	5	6	11	14	4	1	0	2	0	52	9.6	1	0	100.0	16:27
Bryan Smolinski........	18	2	7	9	6	4	0	0	0	0	32	6.3	118	140	45.7	15:20
Wade Redden............	18	1	8	9	10	1	0	0	1	1	32	3.1	0	0	—	25:28
Daniel Alfredsson	18	4	4	8	12	-3	4	0	1	0	41	9.8	5	1	83.3	17:59
Zdeno Chara.............	18	1	6	7	14	3	0	0	0	0	32	3.1	0	0	—	25:06
Todd White...............	18	5	1	6	6	-1	1	1	2	1	30	16.7	152	116	56.7	16:59
Chris Phillips............	18	2	4	6	12	3	0	0	1	1	22	9.1	0	0	—	21:36
Vaclav Varada............	18	2	4	6	18	4	0	0	0	0	23	8.7	1	1	50.0	13:57
Magnus Arvedson	18	1	5	6	16	-4	0	0	0	0	17	5.9	1	5	16.7	15:34
Peter Schaefer	16	2	3	5	6	3	0	1	0	0	15	13.3	2	6	25.0	11:51
Mike Fisher...............	18	2	2	4	16	-1	0	1	1	0	36	5.6	77	103	42.8	16:57
Karel Rachunek.........	17	1	3	4	14	-5	0	0	0	0	21	4.8	0	1	0.0	23:14
Jason Spezza	3	1	1	2	0	1	1	0	0	0	3	33.3	14	10	58.3	11:33
Anton Volchenkov	17	1	1	2	4	3	0	0	1	0	17	5.9	0	0	—	13:31
Shaun Van Allen........	18	1	1	2	12	-1	0	0	1	1	12	8.3	77	92	45.6	11:54
Chris Neil	15	1	0	1	24	1	0	0	0	0	16	6.3	0	0	—	7:57
Curtis Leschyshyn.....	18	0	1	1	10	0	0	0	0	0	8	0.0	0	0	—	14:11
Shane Hnidy	1	0	0	0	0	0	0	0	0	0	2	0.0	0	0	—	9:38
Brian Pothier	1	0	0	0	2	0	0	0	0	0	1	0.0	0	0	—	13:11
Jody Hull	2	0	0	0	0	0	0	0	0	0	0	—	0	0	—	8:16
Patrick Lalime (g)......	18	0	0	0	0	0	0	0	0	0	0	—	0	0	—	

GOALTENDING

	Games	GS	Min.	GA	SO	Avg.	W	L	T	EN	PPG Allow	SHG Allow	Shots	Save Pct.
Patrick Lalime........................	18	18	1122	34	1	1.82	11	7	0	0	6	1	449	.924

PHILADELPHIA FLYERS

(Lost Eastern Conference semifinals to Ottawa, 4-2)

SCORING

	Games	G	A	Pts.	PIM	+/-	PPG	SHG	GWG	GTG	Sht.	Sht. Pct.	Faceoffs Won	Lost	Pct.	TOI
Mark Recchi	13	7	3	10	2	4	1	0	1	1	29	24.1	11	10	52.4	18:00
Jeremy Roenick	13	3	5	8	8	1	0	0	1	0	37	8.1	94	128	42.3	21:06
Michal Handzus	13	2	6	8	6	3	0	0	1	0	20	10.0	120	103	53.8	18:22
Sami Kapanen	13	4	3	7	6	2	2	0	0	0	25	16.0	2	2	50.0	20:11
Tony Amonte	13	1	6	7	4	2	0	0	0	0	37	2.7	0	2	0.0	19:15
Justin Williams	12	1	5	6	8	2	0	0	1	0	21	4.8	0	2	0.0	14:11
Simon Gagne	13	4	1	5	6	1	0	1	1	0	31	12.9	0	3	0.0	18:13
Claude Lapointe	13	2	3	5	14	0	0	0	0	0	9	22.2	87	84	50.9	13:15
John LeClair	13	2	3	5	10	5	1	0	0	0	31	6.5	0	0	—	17:09
Eric Weinrich	13	2	3	5	12	-2	1	0	0	0	16	12.5	0	0	—	24:58
Dmitry Yushkevich	13	1	4	5	2	7	0	0	0	0	16	6.3	0	0	—	24:19
Eric Desjardins	5	2	1	3	0	2	0	0	0	0	16	12.5	0	1	0.0	27:37
Donald Brashear	13	1	2	3	21	-1	0	0	0	0	15	6.7	1	2	33.3	11:08
Kim Johnsson	13	0	3	3	8	-1	0	0	0	0	38	0.0	0	0	—	26:07
Radovan Somik	5	1	1	2	6	0	0	0	0	0	6	16.7	0	0	—	11:38
Keith Primeau	13	1	1	2	14	-2	0	0	0	0	28	3.6	164	126	56.6	20:21
Chris Therien	13	0	2	2	2	0	0	0	0	0	13	0.0	0	0	—	17:51
Jim Vandermeer	8	0	1	1	9	1	0	0	0	0	7	0.0	0	0	—	12:42
Marcus Ragnarsson	13	0	1	1	6	4	0	0	0	0	10	0.0	0	0	—	25:22
Robert Esche (g)	1	0	0	0	0	0	0	0	0	0	0	—	0	0	—	—
Todd Fedoruk	1	0	0	0	0	0	0	0	0	0	2	0.0	0	0	—	4:52
Marty Murray	4	0	0	0	4	-2	0	0	0	0	5	0.0	2	0	100.0	11:00
Joe Sacco	4	0	0	0	0	-2	0	0	0	0	4	0.0	0	2	0.0	7:56
R. Cechmanek (g)	13	0	0	0	0	0	0	0	0	0	0	—	0	0	—	—

GOALTENDING

	Games	GS	Min.	GA	SO	Avg.	W	L	T	EN	PPG Allow	SHG Allow	Shots	Save Pct.
Robert Esche	1	0	30	1	0	2.00	0	0	0	0	0	1	14	.929
Roman Cechmanek	13	13	867	31	2	2.15	6	7	0	1	9	3	339	.909

ST. LOUIS BLUES

(Lost Western Conference quarterfinals to Vancouver, 4-3)

SCORING

	Games	G	A	Pts.	PIM	+/-	PPG	SHG	GWG	GTG	Sht.	Sht. Pct.	Faceoffs Won	Lost	Pct.	TOI
Doug Weight	7	5	8	13	2	0	5	0	1	0	18	27.8	45	55	45.0	22:25
Martin Rucinsky	7	4	2	6	4	-3	0	0	0	0	16	25.0	3	5	37.5	16:51
Pavol Demitra	7	2	4	6	2	2	1	0	0	0	11	18.2	36	49	42.4	18:19
Alexander Khavanov	7	2	3	5	2	0	1	0	0	0	13	15.4	0	0	—	19:04
Dallas Drake	7	1	4	5	23	0	0	0	1	0	10	10.0	1	2	33.3	13:04
Cory Stillman	6	2	2	4	2	0	2	0	1	0	26	7.7	38	54	41.3	18:04
Chris Pronger	7	1	3	4	14	3	0	0	0	0	15	6.7	0	0	—	24:36
Keith Tkachuk	7	1	3	4	14	-1	0	0	0	0	19	5.3	27	33	45.0	19:21
Tyson Nash	7	2	1	3	6	3	0	0	0	0	6	33.3	1	5	16.7	9:05
Eric Boguniecki	7	1	2	3	2	-2	1	0	0	0	9	11.1	4	3	57.1	13:08
Valeri Bure	6	0	2	2	8	2	0	0	0	0	13	0.0	0	2	0.0	11:14
Ryan Johnson	6	0	2	2	6	3	0	0	0	0	1	0.0	27	30	47.4	8:13
Steve Martins	2	0	1	1	0	1	0	0	0	0	2	0.0	5	8	38.5	9:23
Al MacInnis	3	0	1	1	0	0	0	0	0	0	3	0.0	0	0	—	12:41
Scott Mellanby	6	0	1	1	10	0	0	0	0	0	13	0.0	0	0	—	16:18
Shjon Podein	7	0	1	1	6	1	0	0	0	0	4	0.0	19	24	44.2	10:30
Petr Cajanek	2	0	0	0	2	-1	0	0	0	0	2	0.0	9	15	37.5	11:07
Christian Laflamme	5	0	0	0	4	-1	0	0	0	0	4	0.0	0	0	—	12:28
Jeff Finley	6	0	0	0	6	1	0	0	0	0	3	0.0	0	0	—	15:11
Barret Jackman	7	0	0	0	14	-2	0	0	0	0	3	0.0	0	0	—	21:58
Chris Osgood (g)	7	0	0	0	4	0	0	0	0	0	0	—	0	0	—	—
Bryce Salvador	7	0	0	0	2	1	0	0	0	0	7	0.0	0	0	—	17:16

GOALTENDING

	Games	GS	Min.	GA	SO	Avg.	W	L	T	EN	PPG Allow	SHG Allow	Shots	Save Pct.
Chris Osgood	7	7	417	17	1	2.45	3	4	0	0	7	1	183	.907

TAMPA BAY LIGHTNING

(Lost Eastern Conference semifinals to New Jersey, 4-1)

SCORING

	Games	G	A	Pts.	PIM	+/-	PPG	SHG	GWG	GTG	Sht.	Sht. Pct.	Faceoffs Won	Lost	Pct.	TOI
Martin St. Louis	11	7	5	12	0	5	1	2	3	1	25	28.0	1	1	50.0	22:20
Dan Boyle	11	0	7	7	6	0	0	0	0	0	26	0.0	0	0	—	27:44
Vaclav Prospal	11	4	2	6	8	-3	2	0	0	0	23	17.4	8	6	57.1	21:15
Dave Andreychuk	11	3	3	6	10	-1	1	0	1	0	25	12.0	112	121	48.1	21:22
Vincent Lecavalier	11	3	3	6	22	-2	1	0	1	1	32	9.4	77	129	37.4	22:35
Brad Richards	11	0	5	5	12	-3	0	0	0	0	32	0.0	68	85	44.4	22:20
Fredrik Modin	11	2	0	2	18	2	0	0	0	0	27	7.4	3	2	60.0	19:17
Jassen Cullimore	11	1	1	2	4	-2	0	0	0	0	12	8.3	0	0	—	22:10
Stan Neckar	7	0	2	2	2	0	0	0	0	0	4	0.0	0	0	—	18:35
Ben Clymer	11	0	2	2	6	-2	0	0	0	0	11	0.0	1	3	25.0	13:29
Cory Sarich	11	0	2	2	6	2	0	0	0	0	16	0.0	0	0	—	21:17
Chris Dingman	10	1	0	1	4	1	0	0	0	0	18	5.6	0	0	—	12:44
Nikita Alexeev	11	1	0	1	0	-3	0	0	0	0	13	7.7	1	3	25.0	10:11
Nolan Pratt	4	0	1	1	0	-1	0	0	0	0	1	0.0	0	0	—	21:01
Andre Roy	5	0	1	1	2	0	0	0	0	0	11	0.0	1	1	50.0	12:30
Brad Lukowich	9	0	1	1	2	-2	0	0	0	0	4	0.0	0	0	—	17:47
Ruslan Fedotenko	11	0	1	1	2	-6	0	0	0	0	17	0.0	1	2	33.3	13:58
Tim Taylor	11	0	1	1	6	1	0	0	0	0	14	0.0	91	54	62.8	13:54
John Grahame (g)	1	0	0	0	0	0	0	0	0	0	0	—	0	0	—	—
Janne Laukkanen	2	0	0	0	2	1	0	0	0	0	1	0.0	0	0	—	22:27
Alexander Svitov	7	0	0	0	6	-2	0	0	0	0	3	0.0	11	22	33.3	7:19
N. Khabibulin (g)	10	0	0	0	0	0	0	0	0	0	0	—	0	0	—	—
Pavel Kubina	11	0	0	0	12	-4	0	0	0	0	14	0.0	0	0	—	24:51

GOALTENDING

	Games	GS	Min.	GA	SO	Avg.	W	L	T	EN	PPG Allow	SHG Allow	Shots	Save Pct.
John Grahame	1	1	111	2	0	1.08	0	1	0	0	1	0	48	.958
Nikolai Khabibulin	10	10	644	26	0	2.42	5	5	0	1	8	0	299	.913

TORONTO MAPLE LEAFS

(Lost Eastern Conference quarterfinals to Philadelphia, 4-3)

SCORING

	Games	G	A	Pts.	PIM	+/-	PPG	SHG	GWG	GTG	Sht.	Sht. Pct.	Faceoffs Won	Lost	Pct.	TOI
Alexander Mogilny	6	5	2	7	4	2	0	1	0	0	13	38.5	2	1	66.7	21:43
Mats Sundin	7	1	3	4	6	-1	1	0	0	0	16	6.3	120	84	58.8	24:17
Travis Green	4	2	1	3	4	3	0	1	1	1	6	33.3	36	34	51.4	18:08
Tomas Kaberle	7	2	1	3	0	-6	1	0	1	1	11	18.2	0	0	—	30:03
Robert Reichel	7	2	1	3	0	-4	0	0	0	0	16	12.5	45	60	42.9	20:54
Darcy Tucker	6	0	3	3	6	1	0	0	0	0	13	0.0	3	5	37.5	21:07
Bryan McCabe	7	0	3	3	10	-3	0	0	0	0	16	0.0	0	0	—	27:27
Robert Svehla	7	0	3	3	2	-5	0	0	0	0	14	0.0	0	0	—	28:54
Aki Berg	7	1	1	2	2	1	0	0	0	0	5	20.0	0	0	—	19:44
Gary Roberts	7	1	1	2	8	-4	0	0	0	0	13	7.7	1	3	25.0	21:04
Jyrki Lumme	7	0	2	2	4	4	0	0	0	0	7	0.0	0	0	—	20:40
Owen Nolan	7	0	2	2	2	-4	0	0	0	0	15	0.0	5	7	41.7	23:18
Tie Domi	7	1	0	1	13	0	0	0	0	0	11	9.1	0	0	—	14:47
Mikael Renberg	7	1	0	1	8	-4	1	0	1	0	3	33.3	0	1	0.0	14:39
Paul Healey	4	0	1	1	2	1	0	0	0	0	0	0.0	1	1	50.0	9:13
Glen Wesley	5	0	1	1	2	0	0	0	0	0	5	0.0	0	0	—	27:38
Tom Fitzgerald	7	0	1	1	4	-2	0	0	0	0	12	0.0	49	44	52.7	18:11
Jonas Hoglund	7	0	1	1	0	-1	0	0	0	0	4	0.0	0	0	—	14:14
Wade Belak	2	0	0	0	4	-2	0	0	0	0	0	—	0	0	—	8:21
Shayne Corson	2	0	0	0	2	-2	0	0	0	0	1	0.0	4	7	36.4	9:42
Nik Antropov	3	0	0	0	0	-3	0	0	0	0	5	0.0	17	21	44.7	19:17
Phil Housley	3	0	0	0	0	-3	0	0	0	0	0	—	0	0	—	13:35
Ed Belfour (g)	7	0	0	0	4	0	0	0	0	0	0	—	0	0	—	—

GOALTENDING

	Games	GS	Min.	GA	SO	Avg.	W	L	T	EN	PPG Allow	SHG Allow	Shots	Save Pct.
Ed Belfour	7	7	532	24	0	2.71	3	4	0	0	5	1	282	.915

VANCOUVER CANUCKS

(Lost Western Conference semifinals to Minnesota, 4-3)

SCORING

	Games	G	A	Pts.	PIM	+/-	PPG	SHG	GWG	GTG	Sht.	Sht. Pct.	Faceoffs Won	Faceoffs Lost	Faceoffs Pct.	TOI
Markus Naslund	14	5	9	14	18	-6	2	0	1	0	40	12.5	0	1	0.0	18:14
Brendan Morrison	14	4	7	11	18	-4	1	0	1	0	27	14.8	153	119	56.3	20:18
Ed Jovanovski	14	7	1	8	22	-5	4	1	2	0	37	18.9	1	0	100.0	23:40
Brent Sopel	14	2	6	8	4	-2	1	0	1	1	29	6.9	0	0	—	22:33
Mattias Ohlund	13	3	4	7	12	1	0	0	0	0	23	13.0	0	0	—	24:01
Todd Bertuzzi	14	2	4	6	60	-3	0	0	0	0	31	6.5	13	17	43.3	21:04
Trent Klatt	14	2	4	6	2	1	2	0	1	1	31	6.5	6	3	66.7	12:42
Daniel Sedin	14	1	5	6	8	-2	1	0	1	0	22	4.5	0	0	—	12:23
Henrik Sedin	14	3	2	5	8	-2	1	0	0	0	15	20.0	96	92	51.1	13:01
Sami Salo	12	1	3	4	0	-2	0	0	0	0	19	5.3	0	0	—	20:51
Murray Baron	14	0	4	4	10	0	0	0	0	0	8	0.0	0	0	—	17:34
Matt Cooke	14	2	1	3	12	3	0	0	0	0	15	13.3	2	7	22.2	14:06
Trevor Linden	14	1	2	3	10	-4	0	1	0	0	20	5.0	107	83	56.3	17:37
Marek Malik	14	1	1	2	10	-7	1	0	0	0	10	10.0	0	0	—	16:06
Jarkko Ruutu	13	0	2	2	14	1	0	0	0	0	10	0.0	1	0	100.0	11:58
Artem Chubarov	14	0	2	2	4	-2	0	0	0	0	18	0.0	127	94	57.5	14:56
Trevor Letowski	6	0	1	1	0	-1	0	0	0	0	6	0.0	3	3	50.0	9:39
Brandon Reid	9	0	1	1	0	0	0	0	0	0	8	0.0	46	44	51.1	9:36
Bryan Allen	1	0	0	0	2	-2	0	0	0	0	0	—	0	0	—	10:35
Alexander Auld (g)	1	0	0	0	0	0	0	0	0	0	0	—	0	0	—	—
Nolan Baumgartner	2	0	0	0	0	0	0	0	0	0	1	0.0	0	0	—	11:06
Dan Cloutier (g)	14	0	0	0	8	0	0	0	0	0	0	—	0	0	—	—
Brad May	14	0	0	0	15	-5	0	0	0	0	10	0.0	0	1	0.0	7:24

GOALTENDING

	Games	GS	Min.	GA	SO	Avg.	W	L	T	EN	PPG Allow	SHG Allow	Shots	Save Pct.
Alexander Auld	1	0	20	1	0	3.00	0	0	0	0	0	1	5	.800
Dan Cloutier	14	14	833	45	0	3.24	7	7	0	1	18	0	341	.868

WASHINGTON CAPITALS

(Lost Eastern Conference quarterfinals to Tampa Bay, 4-2)

SCORING

	Games	G	A	Pts.	PIM	+/-	PPG	SHG	GWG	GTG	Sht.	Sht. Pct.	Faceoffs Won	Faceoffs Lost	Faceoffs Pct.	TOI
Jaromir Jagr	6	2	5	7	2	2	1	0	0	0	22	9.1	0	0	—	25:13
Peter Bondra	6	4	2	6	8	2	2	0	0	0	29	13.8	1	1	50.0	22:38
Michael Nylander	6	3	2	5	8	0	1	0	1	0	15	20.0	32	44	42.1	16:44
Sergei Gonchar	6	0	5	5	4	2	0	0	0	0	15	0.0	0	0	—	29:00
Dainius Zubrus	6	2	2	4	4	-2	1	0	0	0	9	22.2	37	25	59.7	21:30
Robert Lang	6	2	1	3	2	3	0	0	1	0	9	22.2	30	37	44.8	21:54
Mike Grier	6	1	1	2	2	0	0	0	0	0	10	10.0	1	4	20.0	17:58
Kip Miller	5	0	2	2	2	0	0	0	0	0	1	0.0	0	0	—	10:36
Brendan Witt	6	1	0	1	0	-1	0	0	0	0	9	11.1	0	0	—	23:32
Ivan Ciernik	2	0	1	1	6	1	0	0	0	0	2	0.0	0	0	—	9:08
Sergei Berezin	6	0	1	1	0	-2	0	0	0	0	15	0.0	1	2	33.3	11:51
Jason Doig	6	0	1	1	6	1	0	0	0	0	5	0.0	0	0	—	16:52
Jeff Halpern	6	0	1	1	2	-2	0	0	0	0	9	0.0	69	51	57.5	19:58
Calle Johansson	6	0	1	1	0	-4	0	0	0	0	4	0.0	0	0	—	19:14
Brian Sutherby	5	0	0	0	10	0	0	0	0	0	3	0.0	0	1	0.0	4:09
Ken Klee	6	0	0	0	6	2	0	0	0	0	5	0.0	0	0	—	23:10
Olaf Kolzig (g)	6	0	0	0	4	0	0	0	0	0	0	—	0	0	—	—
Steve Konowalchuk	6	0	0	0	6	-3	0	0	0	0	5	0.0	10	2	83.3	16:06
Joel Kwiatkowski	6	0	0	0	2	1	0	0	0	0	9	0.0	0	0	—	17:48
Trent Whitfield	6	0	0	0	10	1	0	0	0	0	3	0.0	55	34	61.8	11:01

GOALTENDING

	Games	GS	Min.	GA	SO	Avg.	W	L	T	EN	PPG Allow	SHG Allow	Shots	Save Pct.
Olaf Kolzig	6	6	404	14	1	2.08	2	4	0	0	4	1	192	.927

2002-03 NHL REVIEW *Stanley Cup playoffs*

MISCELLANEOUS

HAT TRICKS

(Players scoring three or more goals in a game)

Date	Player, Team	Opp.	Goals
4-9-03—	Alexander Mogilny, Toronto	Phil.	3

OVERTIME GOALS

Date	Player, Team	Opponent	Time	Final score
4-10-03—	Paul Kariya, Anaheim	Detroit	3:18	Anaheim 2, Detroit 1
4-14-03—	Todd White, Ottawa	N.Y. Islanders	2:25	Ottawa 3, N.Y. Islanders 2
4-14-03—	Tomas Kaberle, Toronto	Philadelphia	7:20	Toronto 4, Philadelphia 3
4-15-03—	Vincent Lecavalier, Tampa Bay	Washington	2:29	Tampa Bay 4, Washington 3
4-16-03—	Mark Recchi, Philadelphia	Toronto	13:54	Philadelphia 3, Toronto 2
4-16-03—	Steve Rucchin, Anaheim	Detroit	6:53	Anaheim 3, Detroit 2
4-20-03—	Martin St. Louis, Tampa Bay	Washington	4:03	Tampa Bay 2, Washington 1
4-21-03—	Travis Green, Toronto	Philadelphia	10:51	Toronto 2, Philadelphia 1
4-21-03—	Richard Park, Minnesota	Colorado	4:22	Minnesota 3, Colorado 2
4-22-03—	Andrew Brunette, Minnesota	Colorado	3:25	Minnesota 3, Colorado 2
4-24-03—	Petr Sykora, Anaheim	Dallas	0:48	Anaheim 4, Dallas 3
4-25-03—	Trent Klatt, Vancouver	Minnesota	3:42	Vancouver 4, Minnesota 3
4-26-03—	Mike Leclerc, Anaheim	Dallas	1:44	Anaheim 3, Dallas 2
4-26-03—	Jamie Langenbrunner, New Jersey	Tampa Bay	2:09	New Jersey 3, Tampa Bay 2
4-29-03—	Wade Redden, Ottawa	Philadelphia	6:43	Ottawa 3, Philadelphia 2
5-2-03—	Grant Marshall, New Jersey	Tampa Bay	11:12	New Jersey 2, Tampa Bay 1
5-2-03—	Brent Sopel, Vancouver	Minnesota	15:52	Vancouver 3, Minnesota 2
5-10-03—	Shaun Van Allen, Ottawa	New Jersey	3:08	Ottawa 3, New Jersey 2
5-10-03—	Petr Sykora, Anaheim (2)	Minnesota	8:06	Anaheim 1, Minnesota 0
5-21-03—	Chris Phillips, Ottawa	New Jersey	15:51	Ottawa 2, New Jersey 1
5-31-03—	Ruslan Salei, Anaheim	New Jersey	6:59	Anaheim 3, New Jersey 2
6-2-03—	Steve Thomas, Anaheim	New Jersey	0:39	Anaheim 1, New Jersey 0

PENALTY-SHOT INFORMATION

Date	Shooter	Goaltender	Scored	Final score
4-15-03—	Dainius Zubrus, Washington	Nikolai Khabibulin, Tampa Bay	No	Tampa Bay 4, Washington 3
4-21-03—	Robert Reichel, Toronto	Roman Cechmanek, Philadelphia	No	Toronto 2, Philadelphia 1

ALL-STAR GAME

ROSTERS

EASTERN CONFERENCE
Coach: Jacques Martin, Ottawa Senators
Assistant coach: Ken Hitchcock, Philadelphia Flyers

Player (Pos.)	Club
Nikolai Khabibulin (G)	Tampa Bay Lightning
Patrick Lalime (G)	Ottawa Senators
Martin Brodeur (G)	New Jersey Devils
Tom Poti (D)	New York Rangers
Sandis Ozolinsh (D)	Florida Panthers
Zdeno Chara (D)	Ottawa Senators
Sergei Gonchar (D)	Washington Capitals
Roman Hamrlik (D)	New York Islanders
Scott Stevens (D)	New Jersey Devils
Vincent Lecavalier (F)	Tampa Bay Lightning
Jaromir Jagr (F)	Washington Capitals
Alexei Kovalev (F)	Pittsburgh Penguins
Dany Heatley (F)	Atlanta Thrashers
Marian Hossa (F)	Ottawa Senators
Olli Jokinen (F)	Florida Panthers
Glen Murray (F)	Boston Bruins
Jeff O'Neill (F)	Carolina Hurricanes
Jeremy Roenick (F)	Philadelphia Flyers
Martin St. Louis (F)	Tampa Bay Lightning
Miroslav Satan (F)	Buffalo Sabres
Joe Thornton (F)	Boston Bruins

WESTERN CONFERENCE
Coach: Marc Crawford, Vancouver Canucks
Assistant coach: Dave Lewis, Detroit Red Wings

Player (Pos.)	Club
Patrick Roy (G)	Colorado Avalanche
Jocelyn Thibault (G)	Chicago Blackhawks
Marty Turco (G)	Dallas Stars
Rob Blake (D)	Colorado Avalanche
Nicklas Lidstrom (D)	Detroit Red Wings
Eric Brewer (D)	Edmonton Oilers
Ed Jovanovski (D)	Vancouver Canucks
Al MacInnis (D)	St. Louis Blues
Mathieu Schneider (D)	Los Angeles Kings
Mike Modano (F)	Dallas Stars
Bill Guerin (F)	Dallas Stars
Teemu Selanne (F)	San Jose Sharks
Todd Bertuzzi (F)	Vancouver Canucks
Sergei Fedorov (F)	Detroit Red Wings
Peter Forsberg (F)	Colorado Avalanche
Marian Gaborik (F)	Minnesota Wild
Jarome Iginla (F)	Calgary Flames
Paul Kariya (F)	Anaheim Mighty Ducks
Markus Naslund (F)	Vancouver Canucks
Doug Weight (F)	St. Louis Blues
Ray Whitney (F)	Columbus Blue Jackets

GAME SUMMARY

Western Conf. 6, Eastern Conf. 5 (OT)

Western	3	1	1	0	1*	—	6
Eastern	2	2	1	0		—	5

FIRST PERIOD—1. East, Heatley 1 (Hamrlik), 5:39. 2. West, Forsberg 1 (Naslund, Lidstrom), 7:14. 3. West, Modano 1 (Whitney, Schneider), 8:58. 4. East, Heatley 2 (Jagr, Jokinen), 10:26. 5. West, Gaborik 1 (Schneider, Fedorov), 15:55. Penalties—None.

SECOND PERIOD—6. East, Heatley 3 (Jokinen), 2:47. 7. West, Jovanovski 1 (Iginla, Gaborik), 12:12. 8. East, Heatley 4 (Jokinen, Jagr), 13:58. Penalties—None.

THIRD PERIOD—9. West, MacInnis 1 (Fedorov, Gaborik), 1:26. 10. East, Jokinen 1 (Jagr, Heatley), 9:38. Penalties—None.

FIRST OVERTIME—No scoring. Penalties—None.

*Game decided by shootout after first overtime. Goal represents West victory in shootout. Results of shootout as follows: Fedorov (West), save; Kovalev (East), save; Naslund (West), scored; Heatley (East), scored; Guerin (West), scored; Satan (East), save; Kariya (West), scored; Jokinen (East), save. West wins shootout 3-1.

Shots on goal—West 14-9-14-4—41; East 11-12-8-3—34. Power-play opportunities—West 0 of 0; East 0 of 0. Goalies—West, Roy (11 shots, 9 saves), Thibault (0:00 second, 12-10), Turco W (0:00 third, 11-10); East, Khabibulin (14-11), Brodeur (0:00 second, 9-8), Lalime L (0:00 third, 18-17). A—19,250. Referees—Dan O'Halloran, Dennis Larue. Linesmen—Jean Morin, Tim Nowak.

AWARDS

THE SPORTING NEWS
ALL-STAR TEAM

First team	Position	Second team
Martin Brodeur, New Jersey	Goaltender	Marty Turco, Dallas
Nicklas Lidstrom, Detroit	Defense	Rob Blake, Colorado
Al MacInnis, St. Louis	Defense	Sergei Gonchar, Washington
Markus Naslund, Vancouver	Left wing	Marian Hossa, Ottawa
Peter Forsberg, Colorado	Center	Joe Thornton, Boston
Todd Bertuzzi, Vancouver	Right wing	Milan Hejduk, Colorado

Note: THE SPORTING NEWS All-Star Team is selected by the NHL players.

AWARD WINNERS

Player of the Year: Peter Forsberg, Colorado
Coach of the Year: Jacques Lemaire, Minnesota
Rookie of the Year: Henrik Zetterberg, Detroit
Executive of the Year: Doug Risebrough, Minnesota

Note: THE SPORTING NEWS player and rookie awards are selected by the NHL players, the coaches award by the NHL coaches and the executive award by NHL executives.

NATIONAL HOCKEY LEAGUE
ALL-STAR TEAMS

First team	Position	Second team
Martin Brodeur, New Jersey	Goaltender	Marty Turco, Dallas
Al MacInnis, St. Louis	Defense	Sergie Gonchar, Washington
Nicklas Lidstrom, Detroit	Defense	Derian Hatcher, Dallas
Markus Naslund, Vancouver	Left wing	Paul Kariya, Anaheim
Peter Forsberg, Colorado	Center	Joe Thornton, Boston
Todd Bertuzzi, Vancouver	Right wing	Milan Hejduk, Colorado

AWARD WINNERS

Art Ross Trophy: Peter Forsberg, Colorado
Maurice Richard Trophy: Milan Hejduk, Colorado
Hart Memorial Trophy: Peter Forsberg, Colorado
James Norris Memorial Trophy: Nicklas Lidstrom, Detroit
Vezina Trophy: Martin Brodeur, New Jersey
William M. Jennings Trophy: Roman Cechmanek, Robert Esche, Philadelphia; Martin Brodeur, New Jersey
Calder Memorial Trophy: Barret Jackman, St. Louis

Lady Byng Memorial Trophy: Alexander Mogilny, Toronto
Conn Smythe Trophy: Jean-Sebastien Giguere, Anaheim
Bill Masterson Memorial Trophy: Steve Yzerman, Detroit
Frank J. Selke Trophy: Jere Lehtinen, Dallas
Jack Adams Award: Jacques Lemaire, Minnesota
King Clancy Trophy: Brendan Shanahan, Detroit
Pearson Award: Markus Naslund, Vancouver

PLAYER DRAFT

ENTRY DRAFT—JUNE 20, 2003

FIRST ROUND

No.—Selecting club	Player	Pos.	Previous team (league)
1—Pittsburgh (from Florida)	Marc-Andre Fleury	G	Cape Breton (QMJHL)
2—Carolina	Eric Staal	C	Peterborough (OHL)
3—Florida (from Pittsburgh)	Nathan Horton	C	Oshawa (OHL)
4—Columbus	Nikolai Zherdev	RW	Russia
5—Buffalo	Thomas Vanek	LW	Minnesota (WCHA)
6—San Jose	Milan Michalek	RW	Czech Republic
7—Nashville	Ryan Suter	D	U.S. National under-18 (NTDP)
8—Atlanta	Braydon Coburn	D	Portland (WHL)
9—Calgary	Dion Phaneuf	D	Red Deer (WHL)
10—Montreal	Andrei Kastsitsyn	C-W	Belarus (Russia)
11—Philadelphia (from Phoenix)	Jeff Carter	C	Sault Ste. Marie (OHL)
12—N.Y. Rangers	Hugh Jessiman	RW	Dartmouth (ECAC)
13—Los Angeles	Dustin Brown	RW	Guelph (OHL)
14—Chicago	Brent Seabrook	D	Lethbridge (WHL)
15—N.Y. Islanders	Robert Nilsson	C	Sweden
16—San Jose (from Boston)	Steve Bernier	RW	Moncton (QMJHL)
17—New Jersey (from Edmonton)	Zach Parise	C	North Dakota (WCHA)
18—Washington	Eric Fehr	RW	Brandon (WHL)
19—Anaheim	Ryan Getzlaf	C	Calgary (WHL)
20—Minnesota	Brent Burns	RW	Brampton (OHL)
21—Boston (from San Jose via Toronto)	Mark Stuart	D	Colorado College (WCHA)
22—Edmonton (from N.J. via St. Louis)	Marc-Antoine Pouliot	C	Rimouski (QMJHL)
23—Vancouver	Ryan Kesler	C	Ohio State (CCHA)
24—Philadelphia	Mike Richards	C	Kitchener (OHL)
25—Florida (from Tampa Bay)	Anthony Stewart	C	Kingston (OHL)
26—Los Angeles (from Colorado)	Brian Boyle	C	St. Sebastian's (U.S. high school)
27—Los Angeles (from Detroit)	Jeff Tambellini	LW	Michigan (CCHA)
28—Anaheim (from Dallas)	Corey Perry	RW	London (OHL)
29—Ottawa	Patrick Eaves	RW	Boston College (H-East)
30—St. Louis (from New Jersey)	Shawn Belle	D	Tri-City (WHL)

SECOND ROUND

No.—Selecting club	Player	Pos.	Previous team (league)
31—Carolina	Danny Richmond	D	Michigan (CCHA)
32—Pittsburgh	Ryan Stone	C	Brandon (WHL)
33—Dallas (from Columbus)	Loui Eriksson	LW	Frolunda Jr. (Sweden)
34—Tampa Bay (from Florida)	Mike Egener	D	Calgary (WHL)
35—Nashville (from Buffalo)	Konstantin Glazachev	LW	Yaroslavl (Russia)
36—Dallas (from Anaheim via San Jose)	Vojtech Polak	W	Karlovy Vary (Czech Republic)
37—Nashville	Kevin Klein	D	Toronto-St. Michael's (OHL)
38—Florida (from Atlanta)	Kamil Kreps	C	Brampton (OHL)
39—Calgary	Tim Ramholt	D	Zurich (Switzerland)
40—Montreal	Cory Urquhart	C	Montreal (QMJHL)
41—Tampa Bay (from Florida via Phoenix)	Matt Smaby	D	Shattuck-St. Mary's (U.S. high schools)
42—New Jersey	Petr Vrana	LW	Halifax (QMJHL)
43—San Jose (from N.Y. Rangers)	Josh Hennessy	C	Quebec (QMJHL)
44—Los Angeles	Konstantin Pushkaryov	W	Ust-Kamenogorsk (Russia)
45—Boston	Patrice Bergeron-Cleary	C	Acadie-Bathurst (QMJHL)
46—Columbus (from Chicago)	Dan Fritsche	C	Sarnia (OHL)
47—San Jose (from Calgary)	Matthew Carle	D	River City (USHL)
48—N.Y. Islanders	Dimitri Chernykh	RW	Khimik (Russia)
49—Nashville	Shea Weber	D	Kelowna (WHL)
50—N.Y. Rangers (from Boston)	Ivan Baranka	D	Dubnica Jr. (Slovakia)
51—Edmonton	Colin McDonald	RW	New England (EJHL)
52—Chicago	Corey Crawford	G	Moncton (QMJHL)
53—N.Y. Islanders (from Wash. via Edm.)	Evgeni Tunik	C	Elektrostal (Russia)
54—Dallas (from Anaheim)	Brandon Crombeen	RW	Barrie (OHL)
55—Florida (from Pittsburgh)	Stefan Meyer	LW	Medicine Hat (WHL)
56—Minnesota	Patrick O'Sullivan	C	Mississauga (OHL)
57—Toronto	John Doherty	D	Andover (U.S. high schools)
58—N.Y. Islanders (from St. Louis)	Jeremy Colliton	C	Prince Albert (WHL)
59—Chicago	Michal Barinka	D	Budejovice (Czech Republic)

No.—Selecting club	Player	Pos.	Previous team (league)
60—Vancouver (conditional to Phoenix)	Marc-Andre Bernier	RW	Halifax (QMJHL)
61—Montreal (from Philadelphia)	Maxim Lapierre	C	Montreal (QMJHL)
62—St. Louis (from Tampa Bay)	David Backes	C-RW	Lincoln (USHL)
63—Colorado	David Liffiton	D	Plymouth (OHL)
64—Detroit	James Howard	G	Maine (Hockey East)
65—Buffalo (from Dallas)	Branislav Fabry	LW	Bratislava Jr. (Slovakia)
66—Boston (from San Jose)	Masi Marjamaki	LW	Red Deer (WHL)
67—Ottawa	Igor Mirnov	C-W	Dynamo (Russia)
68—Edmonton (from New Jersey)	Jean-Francois Jacques	LW	Baie Comeau (QMJHL)

THIRD ROUND

No.—Selecting club	Player	Pos.	Previous team (league)
69—Philadelphia (from Carolina)	Colin Fraser	C	Red Deer (WHL)
70—Pittsburgh	Jonathan Filewich	RW	Prince George (WHL)
71—Columbus	Dimitri Kosmachev	D	CSKA (Russia)
72—Edmonton	Mishail Joukov	LW	Arboga (Sweden)
73—Pittsburgh (from Florida)	Daniel Carcillo	LW	Sarnia (OHL)
74—Buffalo	Clarke MacArthur	LW	Medicine Hat (WHL)
75—N.Y. Rangers (from San Jose)	Ken Roche	C	St. Sebastian's (U.S. high school)
76—Nashville	Richard Stehlik	D	Sherbrooke (QMJHL)
77—Phoenix (from Atlanta via Philadelphia)	Tyler Redenbach	C/W	Swift Current (WHL)
78—Minnesota (from Calgary)	Danny Irmen	C	Lincoln (USHL)
79—Montreal	Ryan O'Byrne	D	Nanaimo (BCHL)
80—Phoenix	Dimitri Pestunov	C	Magnitogorsk (Russia)
81—Philadelphia (from N.Y. Rangers)	Stefan Ruzicka	RW	Nitra (Slovakia)
82—Los Angeles	Ryan Munce	G	Sarnia (OHL)
83—Washington (from Chicago)	Stephen Werner	RW	Massachusetts (Hockey East)
84—St. Louis (from N.Y. Islanders)	Konstantin Barulin	G	Tyumen (Russia)
85—Philadelphia	Alexandre Picard	D	Halifax (QMJHL)
86—Anaheim (from Boston)	Shane Hynes	RW	Cornell (ECAC)
87—Philadelphia (from Edmonton)	Ryan Potulny	C	Lincoln (USHL)
88—St. Louis	Zach Fitzgerald	D	Seattle (WHL)
89—Nashville (from Washington)	Paul Brown	RW	Kamloops (WHL)
90—Anaheim	Juha Alen	D	Northern Michigan (CCHA)
91—Toronto (from Minnesota)	Martin Sagat	LW	Trencin (Slovakia)
92—Nashville (from Toronto)	Alexander Sulzer	D	Hamburg (Germany)
93—New Jersey (from St. Louis)	Ivan Khomutov	C/W	Elektrostal (Russia)
94—Edmonton (from Vancouver via Wash.)	Zachery Stortini	RW	Sudbury (OHL)
95—Philadelphia	Rick Kozak	RW	Brandon (WHL)
96—Tampa Bay	Johnathan Boutin	G	Halifax (QMJHL)
97—Calgary (from Colorado)	Ryan Donally	LW	Windsor (OHL)
98—Nashville (from Detroit)	Grigory Shafigulin	C	Yaroslavl (Russia)
99—Dallas	Matt Nickerson	D	Texas (NAHL)
100—Ottawa	Philippe Seydoux	D	Kloten (Switzerland)
101—St. Louis (from New Jersey)	Konstantin Zakharov	F	Junost Minsk (Belarus)

FOURTH ROUND

No.—Selecting club	Player	Pos.	Previous team (league)
102—Carolina	Aaron Dawson	D	Peterborough (OHL)
103—Columbus (from Pittsburgh)	Kevin Jarman	LW	Stouffville (Ont. Prov. Jr. A)
104—Columbus	Philippe Dupuis	C	Hull (QMJHL)
105—Florida	Martin Lojek	D	Brampton (OHL)
106—Buffalo	Jan Hejda	D	Slavia (Czech Republic)
107—Boston (from San Jose)	Byron Bitz	RW	Nanaimo (BCHL)
108—Philadelphia	Kevin Romy	W	Geneve (Switzerland)
109—Washington (from Nash. via Montreal)	Andreas Valdix	LW	Malmo (Sweden)
110—Atlanta	James Sharrow	D	Halifax (QMJHL)
111—Vancouver	Brandon Nolan	C/LW	Oshawa (OHL)
112—Calgary	Jamie Tardif	RW	Peterborough (OHL)
113—Montreal	Corey Locke	C	Ottawa (OHL)
114—Buffalo	Denis Ezhov	D	Togliatti (Russia)
115—Phoenix	Liam Lindstrom	C	Mora (Sweden)
116—Atlanta (from N.Y. Rangers via Florida)	Guillaume Desbiens	RW	Rouyn Noranda (QMJHL)
117—Nashville (from Los Angeles)	Teemu Lassila	G	TPS (Finland)
118—Boston	Frank Rediker	D	Windsor (OHL)
119—Anaheim (from Chicago via Nashville)	Nathan Saunders	D	Moncton (QMJHL)
120—N.Y. Islanders	Stefan Blaho	RW	Trencin Jr. (Slovakia)
121—Pittsburgh (from Boston)	Paul Bissonnette	D	Saginaw (OHL)
122—N.Y. Rangers (from Edmonton)	Corey Potter	D	Michigan State (CCHA)

No.—Selecting club	Player	Pos.	Previous team (league)
123—Montreal (from Washington)	Danny Stewart	LW	Rimouski (QMJHL)
124—Florida (from Anaheim)	James Pemberton	D	Providence (Hockey East)
125—Toronto (from Minnesota)	Konstantin Volkov	RW	Dynamo Jr. (Russian Jr.)
126—Carolina (from Toronto)	Kevin Nastiuk	G	Medicine Hat (WHL)
127—St. Louis	Alexandre Bolduc	C	Rouyn Noranda (QMJHL)
128—Vancouver	Ty Morris	LW	St. Albert (AJHL)
129—Boston (from Philadelphia via L.A.)	Patrik Valcak	W	Ostrava Jr. (Czech Republic)
130—Carolina (from Tampa Bay)	Matej Trojovsky	D	Regina (WHL)
131—Colorado	David Svagrovsky	RW	Seattle (WHL)
132—Detroit	Kyle Quincey	D	London (OHL)
133—Nashville	Rustam Sidikov	G	CSKA (Russia)
134—Dallas	Alexander Naurov	W	Yaroslavl Jr. (Russia)
135—Ottawa	Mattias Karlsson	D	Brynas (Sweden)
136—Atlanta (from New Jersey)	Michael Vannelli	D	Sioux Falls (USHL)

FIFTH ROUND

No.—Selecting club	Player	Pos.	Previous team (league)
137—Carolina	Tyson Strachan	D	Vernon (BCHL)
138—Columbus (from Carolina)	Arsi Piispanen	RW	Jokerit Jr. (Finland)
139—San Jose (from Pittsburgh)	Patrick Ehelechner	G	Hannover (Germany)
140—Philadelphia (from Columbus)	David Tremblay	G	Hull (QMJHL)
141—Florida	Dan Travis	RW	Deerfield (U.S. high schools)
142—Ottawa (from Buffalo)	Tim Cook	D	River City (USHL)
143—Calgary (from San Jose)	Greg Moore	RW	Maine (Hockey East)
144—Dallas (from Nashville)	Eero Kilpelainen	G	Kalpa Jr. (Finland)
145—Atlanta	Brett Sterling	LW	Colorado Coll. (WCHA)
146—Colorado (from Calgary)	Mark McCutcheon	C	New England (EJHL)
147—Edmonton (from Montreal)	Kalle Olsson	W	Frolunda Jr. (Sweden Jr.)
148—St. Louis	Lee Stempniak	RW	Dartmouth (ECAC)
149—N.Y. Rangers	Nigel Dawes	LW	Kootenay (WHL)
150—Buffalo (from Los Angeles)	Thomas Morrow	D	Des Moines (USHL)
151—Chicago	Lasse Kukkonen	D	Karpat (Finland)
152—Los Angeles (from N.Y. Isl. via Fla.)	Brady Murray	C	Salmon Arm (BCHL)
153—Boston	Mike Brown	G	Saginaw (OHL)
154—Edmonton	David Rohlfs	RW	Compuware (NAHL)
155—Washington	Josh Robertson	C	Proctor (U.S. high schools)
156—Chicago (from Anaheim)	Alexei Ivanov	C	Yaroslavl Jr. (Russia Jr.)
157—Minnesota	Marcin Kolusz	F	Novy Targ (Poland)
158—Toronto	John Mitchell	C	Plymouth (OHL)
159—St. Louis	Chris Beckford-Tseu	G	Oshawa (OHL)
160—Vancouver	Nicklas Danielsson	RW	Brynas (Sweden)
161—Pittsburgh (from Phil. via N.Y. Isl.)	Evgeni Isakov	LW	Cherepovets (Russia)
162—Florida (from Tampa Bay)	Martin Tuma	D	Litvinov Jr. (Czech Republic Jr.)
163—Colorado (from San Jose via Colo.)	Brad Richardson	C	Owen Sound (OHL)
164—Detroit	Ryan Oulahen	C	Brampton (OHL)
165—Dallas	Gino Guyer	C	Minnesota (WCHA)
166—Ottawa	Sergei Gimayev	D	Cherepovets (Russia)
167—New Jersey	Zach Tarkir	D	Chilliwack (BCHL)

SIXTH ROUND

No.—Selecting club	Player	Pos.	Previous team (league)
168—Columbus (from Carolina)	Marc Methot	D	London (OHL)
169—Pittsburgh	Lukas Bolf	D	Sparta Jr. (Czech Republic Jr.)
170—Detroit (from Columbus)	Andreas Sundin	LW	Linkoping (Sweden)
171—Florida	Denis Stasyuk	C	Novokuznetsk (Russia)
172—Buffalo	Pavel Voroshnin	D	Mississauga (OHL)
173—Calgary (from San Jose)	Tyler Johnson	C	Moose Jaw (WHL)
174—Los Angeles (from Nashville)	Esa Pirnes	C	Tappara (Finland)
175—Atlanta	Mike Hamilton	F	Merritt (BCHL)
176—N.Y. Rangers (from Calgary)	Ivan Dornic	C	Bratislava Jr. (Slovakia Jr.)
177—Montreal	Christopher Heino-Lindberg	G	Hammarby (Sweden)
178—Phoenix	Ryan Gibbons	RW	Seattle (WHL)
179—N.Y. Rangers	Philippe Furrer	D	Bern (Switzerland)
180—N.Y. Rangers (from Los Angeles)	Chris Holt	G	U.S. National under-18
181—Chicago	Johan Andersson	C	Troja (Sweden)
182—N.Y. Islanders	Bruno Gervais	D	Acadie-Bathurst (QMJHL)
183—Boston	Nate Thompson	C	Seattle (WHL)
184—Edmonton	Dragan Umicevic	LW	Sodertalje (Sweden)
185—Dallas (from Washington)	Francis Wathier	LW	Hull (QMJHL)

No.— Selecting club	Player	Pos.	Previous team (league)
186—Anaheim	Andrew Miller	LW	River City (USHL)
187—Minnesota	Miroslav Kopriva	G	Kladno (Czech Republic)
188—Montreal (from Toronto)	Mark Flood	D	Peterborough (OHL)
189—St. Louis	Jonathan Lehun	C	St. Cloud State (WCHA)
190—Vancouver	Chad Brownlee	D	Vernon (BCHL)
191—Philadelphia	Rejean Beauchemin	G	Prince Albert (WHL)
192—Tampa Bay	Doug O'Brien	D	Hull (QMJHL)
193—Philadelphia (from Colorado)	Ville Hostikka	G	Saipa (Finland)
194—Detroit	Stefan Blom	D	Hammarby Jr. (Sweden Jr.)
195—Dallas	Drew Bagnall	D	Battlefords (SJHL)
196—Dallas (from Ottawa)	Elias Granath	D	Leksand Jr. (Sweden Jr.)
197—New Jersey	Jason Smith	G	Lennoxville (Quebec Jr.)

SEVENTH ROUND

No.— Selecting club	Player	Pos.	Previous team (league)
198—Carolina	Shay Stevenson	LW	Red Deer (WHL)
199—Pittsburgh	Andy Chiodo	G	Toronto-St. Michael's (OHL)
200—Columbus	Alexander Guskov	D	Yaroslavl (Russia)
201—San Jose (from Florida)	Jonathan Tremblay	RW	Acadie-Bathurst (QMJHL)
202—Buffalo	Nathan Paetsch	D	Moose Jaw (WHL)
203—Atlanta (from San Jose)	Denis Loginov	C	Kazan (Russia)
204—Colorado (from Nashville)	Linus Videll	LW	Sodertalje Jr. (Sweden Jr.)
205—San Jose (from Atlanta)	Joe Pavelski	C	Waterloo (USHL)
206—Calgary	Thomas Bellemare	D	Drummondville (QMJHL)
207—Minnesota (from Montreal)	Grigory Misharin	D	Yekaterinburg (Russia)
208—Phoenix	Randall Gelech	C/RW	Kelowna (WHL)
209—N.Y. Rangers	Dylan Reese	D	Pittsburgh (NAHL)
210—Nashville (from Los Angeles)	Andrei Mukhachev	D	CSKA (Russia)
211—Chicago	Mike Brodeur	G	Camrose (AJHL)
212—N.Y. Islanders	Denis Rehak	D	Trencin Jr. (Slovakia Jr.)
213—Nashville (from Boston)	Miroslav Hanuljak	G	Litvinov Jr. (Czech Republic Jr.)
214—Edmonton	Kyle Brodziak	C	Moose Jaw (WHL)
215—Edmonton	Mathieu Roy	D	Val D'Or (QMJHL)
216—San Jose	Kai Hospelt	F	Koln (Germany)
217—Montreal (from Washington)	Oskari Korpikari	D	Karpat (Finland)
218—Anaheim	Dirk Southern	C	Northern Michigan (CCHA)
219—Minnesota	Adam Courchaine	C	Vancouver (WHL)
220—Toronto	Jeremy Williams	C	Swift Current (WHL)
221—St. Louis	Evgeny Skachkov	LW	Kapitan Jr. (Russia)
222—Vancouver	Francois-Pierre Guenette	C/RW	Halifax (QMJHL)
223—Florida (from Philadelphia)	Dany Roussin	C	Rimouski (QMJHL)
224—Tampa Bay	Gerald Coleman	G	London (OHL)
225—Colorado	Brett Hemingway	W	Coquitlam (BCHL)
226—Detroit	Tomas Kollar	LW	Hammarby (Sweden)
227—Tampa Bay (from Dallas)	Jay Rosehill	D	Olds (AJHL)
228—Ottawa	William Colbert	D	Ottawa (OHL)
229—Pittsburgh (from New Jersey)	Stephen Dixon	C	Cape Breton (QMJHL)

EIGHTH ROUND

No.— Selecting club	Player	Pos.	Previous team (league)
230—Carolina	Jamie Hoffmann	C	Des Moines (USHL)
231—Los Angeles	Matt Zaba	G	Vernon (BCHL)
232—Pittsburgh	Joe Jensen	C	St. Cloud State (WCHA)
233—Columbus	Mathieu Gravel	LW	Shawinigan (QMJHL)
234—Florida	Petr Kadlec	D	Slavia (Czech Republic)
235—Buffalo	Jeff Weber	G	Plymouth (OHL)
236—San Jose	Alexander Hult	C	Tranas (Sweden)
237—Toronto (from Nashville)	Shaun Landolt	RW	Calgary (WHL)
238—N.Y. Islanders	Cody Blanshan	D	Nebraska-Omaha (CCHA)
239—Atlanta	Tobias Enstrom	D	MoDo (Sweden)
240—Calgary	Cam Cunning	LW	Kamloops (WHL)
241—Montreal	Jimmy Bonneau	LW	Montreal (QMJHL)
242—Phoenix	Eduard Lewandowski	F	Koln (Germany)
243—N.Y. Rangers	Jan Marek	F	Trinec (Czech Republic)
244—Los Angeles	Mike Sullivan	C	Stouffville (Ont. Prov. Jr. A)
245—Chicago	Dustin Byfuglien	D	Prince George (WHL)
246—N.Y. Islanders	Igor Volkov	RW	UFA (Russia)
247—Boston	Benoit Mondou	C	Shawinigan (QMJHL)
248—Edmonton	Josef Hrabal	D	Vsetin Jr. (Czech Republic Jr.)

No.—Selecting club	Player	Pos.	Previous team (league)
249—Washington	Andrew Joudrey	C	Notre Dame (SJHL)
250—Anaheim	Shane O'Brien	D	Toronto-St. Michael's (OHL)
251—Minnesota	Mathieu Melanson	LW	Chicoutimi (QMJHL)
252—Vancouver (from Toronto)	Sergei Topol	F	Omsk (Russia)
253—St. Louis	Andrei Pervyshin	D	Yaroslavl Jr. (Russia Jr.)
254—Vancouver	Nathan McIver	D	Toronto-St. Michael's (OHL)
255—Tampa Bay (from Philadelphia)	Raimonds Danilics	F	Stalkers (Latvia)
256—Tampa Bay	Brady Greco	D	Chicago (USHL)
257—Colorado	Darryl Yacboski	D	Regina (WHL)
258—Detroit	Vladimir Kutny	LW	Quebec (QMJHL)
259—Dallas (optional to Chicago)	Niko Vainio	D	Jokerit Jr. (Finland Jr.)
260—Ottawa	Ossi Louhivaara	F	Kookoo (Finland)
261—New Jersey	Joey Tenute	C	Sarnia (OHL)

NINTH ROUND

No.—Selecting club	Player	Pos.	Previous team (league)
262—Carolina	Ryan Rorabeck	C	Toronto-St. Michael's (OHL)
263—Pittsburgh	Matt Moulson	LW	Cornell (ECAC)
264—Florida (from Columbus)	John Hecimovic	RW	Sarnia (OHL)
265—Florida	Tanner Glass	F	Nanaimo (BCHL)
266—Buffalo	Louis-Philippe Martin	RW	Baie Comeau (QMJHL)
267—San Jose	Brian O'Hanley	D	Boston Coll. (Hockey East)
268—Nashville	Lauris Darzins	F	Lukko Jr. (Finland Jr.)
269—Atlanta	Rylan Kaip	C	Notre Dame (SJHL)
270—Calgary	Kevin Harvey	LW	Georgetown (Ont. Prov. Jr. A)
271—Montreal	Jaroslav Halak	G	Bratislava Jr. (Slovakia Jr.)
272—Phoenix	Sean Sullivan	D	St. Sebastian's (U.S. high schools)
273—Tampa Bay (from N.Y.R. via Pitt.)	Albert Vishnyakov	W	Kazan (Russia)
274—Los Angeles	Martin Guerin	RW	Des Moines (USHL)
275—Chicago	Michael Grenzy	D	Chicago (USHL)
276—San Jose (from N.Y. Islanders)	Carter Lee	F	Canterbury (U.S. high schools)
277—Boston	Kevin Regan	G	St. Sebastian's (U.S. high schools)
278—Edmonton	Troy Bodie	RW	Kelowna (WHL)
279—Washington (from Ottawa via Wash.)	Mark Olafson	RW	Kelowna (WHL)
280—Anaheim	Ville Mantymaa	D	Tappare (Finland)
281—Minnesota	Jean-Michel Bolduc	D	Quebec (QMJHL)
282—Chicago (from Toronto)	Chris Porter	C	Lincoln (USHL)
283—Columbus (from Los Angeles)	Trevor Hendrikx	D	Peterborough (OHL)
284—St. Louis	Juha-Matti Tapio Aaltonen	W	Karpat Jr. (Finland Jr.)
285—Vancouver	Matthew Hansen	D	Seattle (WHL)
286—Tampa Bay (from Philadephia)	Zbynek Hrdel	C	Rimouski (QMJHL)
287—Tampa Bay	Nick Tarnasky	C	Lethbridge (WHL)
288—Colorado	David Jones	RW	Coquitlam (BCHL)
289—Detroit	Mikael Johansson	C	Arvika (Sweden)
290—Phoenix (from Dallas)	Loic Burkhalter	F	Ambri (Switzerland)
291—Ottawa	Brian Elliott	G	Ajax (Ont. Prov. Jr. A)
292—New Jersey	Arseny Bonarev	LW	Yaroslavl (Russia)

NHL HISTORY

Stanley Cup champions

All-Star Games

Year-by-year standings

Records

Statistical leaders

Award winners

The Sporting News awards

Hall of Fame

Milestones

Team by team

STANLEY CUP CHAMPIONS

The Stanley Cup was donated in 1893 to be awarded to signify supremacy in Canadian amateur hockey. Eventually, other teams, including professional clubs and clubs outside of Canada, began vying for the trophy. Since 1926 only NHL clubs have competed for the Stanley Cup.

Season	Club	Coach
1892-93—Montreal Am. Ath. Assn.*		
1893-94—Montreal Am. Ath. Assn.*		
1894-95—Montreal Victorias*		Mike Grant†
1895-96—(Feb. '96) Winnipeg Victorias*		J. Armitage†
1895-96—(Dec. '96) Montreal Victorias*		Mike Grant†
1896-97—Montreal Victorias*		Mike Grant†
1897-98—Montreal Victorias*		F. Richardson†
1898-99—Montreal Shamrocks*		H.J. Trihey†
1899-1900—Montreal Shamrocks*		H.J. Trihey†
1900-01—Winnipeg Victorias*		D.H. Bain†
1901-02—Montreal Am. Ath. Assn.*		C. McKerrow
1902-03—Ottawa Silver Seven*		A.T. Smith
1903-04—Ottawa Silver Seven*		A.T. Smith
1904-05—Ottawa Silver Seven*		A.T. Smith
1905-06—Montreal Wanderers*		Cecil Blachford†
1906-07—(Jan. '07) Kenora Thistles*		Tommy Phillips†
1906-07—(Mar. '07) Montreal Wanderers*		Cecil Blachford†
1907-08—Montreal Wanderers*		Cecil Blachford†
1908-09—Ottawa Senators*		Bruce Stuart†
1909-10—Montreal Wanderers*		Pud Glass†
1910-11—Ottawa Senators*		Bruce Stuart†
1911-12—Quebec Bulldogs*		C. Nolan
1912-13—Quebec Bulldogs*		Joe Malone†
1913-14—Toronto Blueshirts*		Scotty Davidson†
1914-15—Vancouver Millionaires*		Frank Patrick
1915-16—Montreal Canadiens*		George Kennedy
1916-17—Seattle Metropolitans*		Pete Muldoon
1917-18—Toronto Arenas		Dick Carroll
1919-20—Ottawa Senators		Pete Green
1920-21—Ottawa Senators		Pete Green
1921-22—Toronto St. Pats		George O'Donoghue
1922-23—Ottawa Senators		Pete Green
1923-24—Montreal Canadiens		Leo Dandurand
1924-25—Victoria Cougars*		Lester Patrick
1925-26—Montreal Maroons		Eddie Gerard
1926-27—Ottawa Senators		Dave Gill
1927-28—New York Rangers		Lester Patrick
1928-29—Boston Bruins		Cy Denneny
1929-30—Montreal Canadiens		Cecil Hart
1930-31—Montreal Canadiens		Cecil Hart
1931-32—Toronto Maple Leafs		Dick Irvin
1932-33—New York Rangers		Lester Patrick
1933-34—Chicago Black Hawks		Tommy Gorman
1934-35—Montreal Maroons		Tommy Gorman
1935-36—Detroit Red Wings		Jack Adams
1936-37—Detroit Red Wings		Jack Adams
1937-38—Chicago Black Hawks		Bill Stewart
1938-39—Boston Bruins		Art Ross
1939-40—New York Rangers		Frank Boucher
1940-41—Boston Bruins		Cooney Weiland
1941-42—Toronto Maple Leafs		Hap Day
1942-43—Detroit Red Wings		Jack Adams
1943-44—Montreal Canadiens		Dick Irvin
1944-45—Toronto Maple Leafs		Hap Day
1945-46—Montreal Canadiens		Dick Irvin
1946-47—Toronto Maple Leafs		Hap Day
1947-48—Toronto Maple Leafs		Hap Day
1948-49—Toronto Maple Leafs		Hap Day
1949-50—Detroit Red Wings		Tommy Ivan
1950-51—Toronto Maple Leafs		Joe Primeau
1951-52—Detroit Red Wings		Tommy Ivan
1952-53—Montreal Canadiens		Dick Irvin
1953-54—Detroit Red Wings		Tommy Ivan
1954-55—Detroit Red Wings		Jimmy Skinner
1955-56—Montreal Canadiens		Toe Blake
1956-57—Montreal Canadiens		Toe Blake
1957-58—Montreal Canadiens		Toe Blake
1958-59—Montreal Canadiens		Toe Blake
1959-60—Montreal Canadiens		Toe Blake
1960-61—Chicago Black Hawks		Rudy Pilous
1961-62—Toronto Maple Leafs		Punch Imlach
1962-63—Toronto Maple Leafs		Punch Imlach
1963-64—Toronto Maple Leafs		Punch Imlach
1964-65—Montreal Canadiens		Toe Blake
1965-66—Montreal Canadiens		Toe Blake
1966-67—Toronto Maple Leafs		Punch Imlach
1967-68—Montreal Canadiens		Toe Blake
1968-69—Montreal Canadiens		Claude Ruel
1969-70—Boston Bruins		Harry Sinden
1970-71—Montreal Canadiens		Al MacNeil
1971-72—Boston Bruins		Tom Johnson
1972-73—Montreal Canadiens		Scotty Bowman
1973-74—Philadelphia Flyers		Fred Shero
1974-75—Philadelphia Flyers		Fred Shero
1975-76—Montreal Canadiens		Scotty Bowman
1976-77—Montreal Canadiens		Scotty Bowman
1977-78—Montreal Canadiens		Scotty Bowman
1978-79—Montreal Canadiens		Scotty Bowman
1979-80—New York Islanders		Al Arbour
1980-81—New York Islanders		Al Arbour
1981-82—New York Islanders		Al Arbour
1982-83—New York Islanders		Al Arbour
1983-84—Edmonton Oilers		Glen Sather
1984-85—Edmonton Oilers		Glen Sather
1985-86—Montreal Canadiens		Jean Perron
1986-87—Edmonton Oilers		Glen Sather
1987-88—Edmonton Oilers		Glen Sather
1988-89—Calgary Flames		Terry Crisp
1989-90—Edmonton Oilers		John Muckler
1990-91—Pittsburgh Penguins		Bob Johnson
1991-92—Pittsburgh Penguins		Scotty Bowman
1992-93—Montreal Canadiens		Jacques Demers
1993-94—New York Rangers		Mike Keenan
1994-95—New Jersey Devils		Jacques Lemaire
1995-96—Colorado Avalanche		Marc Crawford
1996-97—Detroit Red Wings		Scotty Bowman
1997-98—Detroit Red Wings		Scotty Bowman
1998-99—Dallas Stars		Ken Hitchcock
1999-00—New Jersey Devils		Larry Robinson
2000-01—Colorado Avalanche		Bob Hartley
2001-02—Detroit Red Wings		Scotty Bowman
2002-03—New Jersey Devils		Pat Burns

NOTE: 1918-19 series between Montreal and Seattle cancelled after five games because of influenza epidemic.

*Stanley Cups won by non-NHL clubs.

†Team captain.

ALL-STAR GAMES

RESULTS

Date	Site	Winning team, score	Losing team, score	Att.
2-14-34†	Maple Leaf Gardens, Toronto	Toronto Maple Leafs, 7	NHL All-Stars, 3	*14,000
11-3-37‡	Montreal Forum	NHL All-Stars, 6	Montreal All-Stars§, 5	8,683
10-29-39∞	Montreal Forum	NHL All-Stars, 5	Montreal Canadiens, 2	*6,000
10-13-47	Maple Leaf Gardens, Toronto	NHL All-Stars, 4	Toronto Maple Leafs, 3	14,169
11-3-48	Chicago Stadium	NHL All-Stars, 3	Toronto Maple Leafs, 1	12,794
10-10-49	Maple Leaf Gardens, Toronto	NHL All-Stars, 3	Toronto Maple Leafs, 1	13,541
10-8-50	Olympia Stadium, Detroit	Detroit Red Wings, 7	NHL All-Stars, 1	9,166
10-9-51	Maple Leaf Gardens, Toronto	First Team▲, 2	Second Team▲, 2	11,469
10-5-52	Olympia Stadium, Detroit	First Team▲, 1	Second Team▲, 1	10,680
10-3-53	Montreal Forum	NHL All-Stars, 3	Montreal Canadiens, 1	14,153
10-2-54	Olympia Stadium, Detroit	NHL All-Stars, 2	Detroit Red Wings, 2	10,689
10-2-55	Olympia Stadium, Detroit	Detroit Red Wings, 3	NHL All-Stars, 1	10,111
10-9-56	Montreal Forum	NHL All-Stars, 1	Montreal Canadiens, 1	13,095
10-5-57	Montreal Forum	NHL All-Stars, 5	Montreal Canadiens, 3	13,095
10-4-58	Montreal Forum	Montreal Canadiens, 6	NHL All-Stars, 3	13,989
10-3-59	Montreal Forum	Montreal Canadiens, 6	NHL All-Stars, 1	13,818
10-1-60	Montreal Forum	NHL All-Stars, 2	Montreal Canadiens, 1	13,949
10-7-61	Chicago Stadium	NHL All-Stars, 3	Chicago Blackhawks, 1	14,534
10-6-62	Maple Leaf Gardens, Toronto	Toronto Maple Leafs, 4	NHL All-Stars, 1	14,236
10-5-63	Maple Leaf Gardens, Toronto	NHL All-Stars, 3	Toronto Maple Leafs, 3	14,034
10-10-64	Maple Leaf Gardens, Toronto	NHL All-Stars, 3	Toronto Maple Leafs, 2	14,232
10-20-65	Montreal Forum	NHL All-Stars, 5	Montreal Canadiens, 2	14,284
1-18-67	Montreal Forum	Montreal Canadiens, 3	NHL All-Stars, 0	14,284
1-16-68	Maple Leaf Gardens, Toronto	Toronto Maple Leafs, 4	NHL All-Stars, 3	15,753
1-21-69	Montreal Forum	West Division, 3	East Division, 3	16,260
1-20-70	St. Louis Arena	East Division, 4	West Division, 1	16,587
1-19-71	Boston Garden	West Division, 2	East Division, 1	14,790
1-25-72	Met Sports Center, Bloomington, Minn.	East Division, 3	West Division, 2	15,423
1-30-73	Madison Square Garden, New York	East Division, 5	West Division, 4	16,986
1-29-74	Chicago Stadium	West Division, 6	East Division, 4	16,426
1-21-75	Montreal Forum	Wales Conference, 7	Campbell Conference, 1	16,080
1-20-76	The Spectrum, Philadelphia	Wales Conference, 7	Campbell Conference, 5	16,436
1-25-77	Pacific Coliseum, Vancouver	Wales Conference, 4	Campbell Conference, 3	15,607
1-24-78	Buffalo Memorial Auditorium	Wales Conference, 3	Campbell Conference, 2 (OT)	16,433
1979 All-Star Game replaced by Challenge Cup series between Team NHL and Soviet Union				
2-5-80	Joe Louis Arena, Detroit	Wales Conference, 6	Campbell Conference, 3	21,002
2-10-81	The Forum, Los Angeles	Campbell Conference, 4	Wales Conference, 1	15,761
2-9-82	Capital Centre, Landover, Md.	Wales Conference, 4	Campbell Conference, 2	18,130
2-8-83	Nassau Coliseum, Long Island, N.Y.	Campbell Conference, 9	Wales Conference, 3	15,230
1-31-84	Meadowlands Arena, East Rutherford, N.J.	Wales Conference, 7	Campbell Conference, 6	18,939
2-12-85	Olympic Saddledome, Calgary	Wales Conference, 6	Campbell Conference, 4	16,683
2-4-86	Hartford Civic Center	Wales Conference, 4	Campbell Conference, 3 (OT)	15,126
1987 All-Star Game replaced by Rendez-Vous '87 between Team NHL and Soviet Union				
2-9-88	St. Louis Arena	Wales Conference, 6	Campbell Conference, 5 (OT)	17,878
2-7-89	Northlands Coliseum, Edmonton	Campbell Conference, 9	Wales Conference, 5	17,503
1-21-90	Pittsburgh Civic Arena	Wales Conference, 12	Campbell Conference, 7	17,503
1-19-91	Chicago Stadium	Campbell Conference, 11	Wales Conference, 5	18,472
1-18-92	The Spectrum, Philadelphia	Campbell Conference, 10	Wales Conference, 6	17,380
2-6-93	Montreal Forum	Wales Conference, 16	Campbell Conference, 6	17,137
1-22-94	Madison Square Garden, New York	Eastern Conference, 9	Western Conference, 8	18,200
1995 All-Star Game canceled because of NHL lockout				
1-20-96	FleetCenter, Boston	Eastern Conference, 5	Western Conference, 4	17,565
1-18-97	San Jose Arena	Eastern Conference, 11	Western Conference, 7	17,442
1-18-98	General Motors Place, Vancouver	North America, 8	World, 7	18,422
1-24-99	Ice Palace, Tampa	North America, 8	World, 6	19,758
2-6-00	Air Canada Centre, Toronto	World, 9	North America, 4	19,300
2-4-01	Pepsi Center, Denver	North America, 14	World, 12	18,646
2-2-02	Staples Center, Los Angeles	World, 8	North America, 5	18,118
2-2-03	Office Depot Center, Sunrise, Florida	Western Conference, 6	Eastern Conference, 5 (2OT)	19,250

*Estimated figure.

†Benefit game for Toronto Maple Leafs left wing Ace Bailey, who suffered a career-ending skull injury earlier in the season.

‡Benefit game for the family of Montreal Canadiens center Howie Morenz, who died of a heart attack earlier in the year.

§Montreal All-Star roster made up of players from Montreal Canadiens and Maroons.

∞Benefit game for the family of Montreal Canadiens defenseman Babe Siebert, who drowned earlier in the year.

▲First Team roster supplemented by players from the four American clubs and Second Team roster supplemented by players from the two Canadian clubs.

NHL HISTORY *All-Star Games*

MOST VALUABLE PLAYERS

Date	Player, All-Star Game team (regular-season team)	Date	Player, All-Star Game team (regular-season team)
10-6-62	Eddie Shack, Toronto Maple Leafs	2-8-83	Wayne Gretzky, Campbell Conf. (Edmonton Oilers)
10-5-63	Frank Mahovlich, Toronto Maple Leafs	1-31-84	Don Maloney, Wales Conf. (New York Rangers)
10-10-64	Jean Beliveau, All-Stars (Montreal Canadiens)	2-12-85	Mario Lemieux, Wales Conf. (Pittsburgh Penguins)
10-20-65	Gordie Howe, All-Stars (Detroit Red Wings)	2-4-86	Grant Fuhr, Campbell Conf. (Edmonton Oilers)
1-18-67	Henri Richard, Montreal Canadiens	2-9-88	Mario Lemieux, Wales Conf. (Pittsburgh Penguins)
1-16-68	Bruce Gamble, Toronto Maple Leafs	2-7-89	Wayne Gretzky, Campbell Conf. (Los Angeles Kings)
1-21-69	Frank Mahovlich, East Div. (Detroit Red Wings)	1-21-90	Mario Lemieux, Wales Conf. (Pittsburgh Penguins)
1-20-70	Bobby Hull, East Div. (Chicago Blackhawks)	1-19-91	Vincent Damphousse, Camp. Conf. (Tor. Maple Leafs)
1-19-71	Bobby Hull, West Div. (Chicago Blackhawks)	1-18-92	Brett Hull, Campbell Conf. (St. Louis Blues)
1-25-72	Bobby Orr, East Division (Boston Bruins)	2-6-93	Mike Gartner, Wales Conf. (New York Rangers)
1-30-73	Greg Polis, West Division (Pittsburgh Penguins)	1-22-94	Mike Richter, Eastern Conf. (New York Rangers)
1-29-74	Garry Unger, West Division (St. Louis Blues)	1-20-96	Ray Bourque, Eastern Conf. (Boston Bruins)
1-21-75	Syl Apps Jr., Wales Conf. (Pittsburgh Penguins)	1-18-97	Mark Recchi, Eastern Conf. (Montreal Canadiens)
1-20-76	Peter Mahovlich, Wales Conf. (Montreal Canadiens)	1-18-98	Teemu Selanne, North America (Ana. Mighty Ducks)
1-25-77	Rick Martin, Wales Conference (Buffalo Sabres)	1-24-99	Wayne Gretzky, North America (New York Rangers)
1-24-78	Billy Smith, Campbell Conf. (New York Islanders)	2-6-00	Pavel Bure, World (Florida Panthers)
2-5-80	Reggie Leach, Campbell Conf. (Philadelphia Flyers)	2-4-01	Bill Guerin, North America (Boston Bruins)
2-10-81	Mike Liut, Campbell Conf. (St. Louis Blues)	2-2-02	Eric Daze, North America (Chicago Blackhawks)
2-9-82	Mike Bossy, Wales Conf. (New York Islanders)	2-2-03	Dany Heatley, Eastern Conference (Atlanta Thrashers)

YEAR-BY-YEAR STANDINGS

Note: Prior to 1926-27 season, clubs outside the NHL also competed for the Stanley Cup. Non-NHL clubs are denoted in parentheses. Sometimes playoff rounds were decided by total goals scored, rather than by games won.

1917-18

Team	W	L	T	Pts.	GF	GA
Montreal Canadiens	13	9	0	26	115	84
Toronto Arenas	13	9	0	26	108	109
Ottawa Senators	9	13	0	18	102	114
Montreal Wanderers	1	5	0	2	17	35

PLAYOFFS

Semifinals: Toronto 10 goals, Montreal Canadiens 7 goals (2-game series); Vancouver (PCHL) 3 goals, Seattle (PCHL) 2 goals (2-game series).
Stanley Cup finals: Toronto 3, Vancouver (PCHL) 2.

1918-19

Team	W	L	T	Pts.	GF	GA
Ottawa Senators	12	6	0	24	71	53
Montreal Canadiens	10	8	0	20	88	78
Toronto Arenas	5	13	0	10	64	92

PLAYOFFS

Semifinals: Seattle (PCHL) 7 goals, Vancouver 5 goals (2-game series); Montreal Canadiens 3, Ottawa 1.
Stanley Cup finals: Series between Montreal Canadiens and Seattle (PCHL) abandoned (with each team winning two games and one game tied) due to influenza epidemic.

1919-20

Team	W	L	T	Pts.	GF	GA
Ottawa Senators	19	5	0	38	121	64
Montreal Canadiens	13	11	0	26	129	113
Toronto St. Patricks	12	12	0	24	119	106
Quebec Bulldogs	4	20	0	8	91	177

PLAYOFFS

Semifinals: Seattle (PCHL) 7 goals, Vancouver (PCHL) 3 goals (2-game series).
Stanley Cup finals: Ottawa 3, Seattle (PCHL) 2.

1920-21

Team	W	L	T	Pts.	GF	GA
Toronto St. Patricks	15	9	0	30	105	100
Ottawa Senators	14	10	0	28	97	75
Montreal Canadiens	13	11	0	26	112	99
Hamilton Tigers	6	18	0	12	92	132

PLAYOFFS

Semifinals: Vancouver (PCHL) 2, Seattle (PCHL) 0; Ottawa 2, Toronto 0.
Stanley Cup finals: Ottawa 3, Vancouver (PCHL) 2.

1921-22

Team	W	L	T	Pts.	GF	GA
Ottawa Senators	14	8	2	30	106	84
Toronto St. Patricks	13	10	1	27	98	97
Montreal Canadiens	12	11	1	25	88	94
Hamilton Tigers	7	17	0	14	88	105

PLAYOFFS

Preliminaries: Regina (WCHL) 2 goals, Calgary (WCHL) 1 goal (2-game series); Regina (WCHL) 3, Edmonton (WCHL) 2; Vancouver (PCHL) 2, Seattle (PCHL) 0; Vancouver (PCHL) 5 goals, Regina (WCHL) 2 goals (2-game series); Toronto 5 goals, Ottawa 4 goals (2-game series).
Stanley Cup finals: Toronto 3, Vancouver (PCHL) 2.

1922-23

Team	W	L	T	Pts.	GF	GA
Ottawa Senators	14	9	1	29	77	54
Montreal Canadiens	13	9	2	28	73	61
Toronto St. Patricks	13	10	1	27	82	88
Hamilton Tigers	6	18	0	12	81	110

PLAYOFFS

Quarterfinals: Ottawa 3 goals, Montreal Canadiens 2 goals (2-game series); Vancouver (PCHL) 5 goals, Victoria (PCHL) 3 goals (2-game series). **Semifinals:** Ottawa 3, Vancouver (PCHL) 1; Edmonton (WCHL) 4 goals, Regina (WCHL) 3 goals (2-game series).
Stanley Cup finals: Ottawa 2, Edmonton (WCHL) 0.

1923-24

Team	W	L	T	Pts.	GF	GA
Ottawa Senators	16	8	0	32	74	54
Montreal Canadiens	13	11	0	26	59	48
Toronto St. Patricks	10	14	0	20	59	85
Hamilton Tigers	9	15	0	18	63	68

PLAYOFFS

First round: Vancouver (PCHL) 4 goals, Seattle (PCHL) 3 goals (2-game series); Calgary (WCHL) 4 goals, Regina (WCHL) 2 goals (2-game series). **Second round:** Montreal Canadiens 2, Ottawa 0; Calgary (WCHL) 2, Vancouver (PCHL) 1. **Third round:** Montreal Canadiens 2, Vancouver (PCHL) 0.
Stanley Cup finals: Montreal Canadiens 2, Calgary (WCHL) 0.

1924-25

Team	W	L	T	Pts.	GF	GA
Hamilton Tigers	19	10	1	39	90	60
Toronto St. Patricks	19	11	0	38	90	84
Montreal Canadiens	17	11	2	36	93	56
Ottawa Senators	17	12	1	35	83	66
Montreal Maroons	9	19	2	20	45	65
Boston Bruins	6	24	0	12	49	119

PLAYOFFS

Quarterfinals: Victoria (WCHL) 6 goals, Saskatoon (WCHL) 4 goals (2-game series). **Semifinals:** Montreal Canadiens 2, Toronto 0; Victoria (WCHL) 3 goals, Calgary (WCHL) 1 goal (2-game series).
Stanley Cup finals: Victoria (WCHL) 3, Montreal Canadiens 1.

1925-26

Team	W	L	T	Pts.	GF	GA
Ottawa Senators	24	8	4	52	77	42
Montreal Maroons	20	11	5	45	91	73
Pittsburgh Pirates	19	16	1	39	82	70
Boston Bruins	17	15	4	38	92	85
New York Americans	12	20	4	28	68	89
Toronto St. Patricks	12	21	3	27	92	114
Montreal Canadiens	11	24	1	23	79	108

PLAYOFFS

Quarterfinals: Victoria (WHL) 4 goals, Saskatoon (WHL) 3 goals (2-game series); Montreal Maroons 6 goals, Pittsburgh 4 goals (2-game series). **Semifinals:** Victoria (WHL) 5 goals, Edmonton (WHL) 3 goals (2-game series); Montreal Maroons 2 goals, Ottawa 1 goal (2-game series).
Stanley Cup finals: Montreal Maroons 3, Victoria (WHL) 1.

1926-27

AMERICAN DIVISION

Team	W	L	T	Pts.	GF	GA
New York Rangers	25	13	6	56	95	72
Boston Bruins	21	20	3	45	97	89
Chicago Blackhawks	19	22	3	41	115	116
Pittsburgh Pirates	15	26	3	33	79	108
Detroit Cougars	12	28	4	28	76	105

CANADIAN DIVISION

Team	W	L	T	Pts.	GF	GA
Ottawa Senators	30	10	4	64	89	69
Montreal Canadiens	28	14	2	58	99	67
Montreal Maroons	20	20	4	44	71	68
New York Americans	17	25	2	36	82	91
Toronto St. Patricks	15	24	5	35	79	94

PLAYOFFS

League quarterfinals: Montreal Canadiens 2 goals, Montreal Maroons 1 goal (2-game series); Boston 10 goals, Chicago 5 goals (2-game series). **Semifinals:** Ottawa 5 goals, Montreal Canadiens 1 goal (2-game series); Boston 3 goals, N.Y. Rangers 1 goal (2-game series).
Stanley Cup finals: Ottawa 2, Boston 0 (two ties).

1927-28

AMERICAN DIVISION

Team	W	L	T	Pts.	GF	GA
Boston Bruins	20	13	11	51	77	70
New York Rangers	19	16	9	47	94	79
Pittsburgh Pirates	19	17	8	46	67	76
Detroit Cougars	19	19	6	44	88	79
Chicago Blackhawks	7	34	3	17	68	134

CANADIAN DIVISION

Team	W	L	T	Pts.	GF	GA
Montreal Canadiens	26	11	7	59	116	48
Montreal Maroons	24	14	6	54	96	77
Ottawa Senators	20	14	10	50	78	57
Toronto Maple Leafs	18	18	8	44	89	88
New York Americans	11	27	6	28	63	128

PLAYOFFS

League quarterfinals: Montreal Maroons 3 goals, Ottawa 1 goal (2-game series); N.Y. Rangers 6 goals, Pittsburgh 4 goals (2-game series). **Semifinals:** Montreal Maroons 3 goals, Montreal Canadiens 2 goals (2-game series); N.Y. Rangers 5 goals, Boston 2 goals (2-game series).
Stanley Cup finals: N.Y. Rangers 3, Montreal Maroons 2.

1928-29

AMERICAN DIVISION

Team	W	L	T	Pts.	GF	GA
Boston Bruins	26	13	5	57	89	52
New York Rangers	21	13	10	52	72	65
Detroit Cougars	19	16	9	47	72	63
Pittsburgh Pirates	9	27	8	26	46	80
Chicago Blackhawks	7	29	8	22	33	85

CANADIAN DIVISION

Team	W	L	T	Pts.	GF	GA
Montreal Canadiens	22	7	15	59	71	43
New York Americans	19	13	12	50	53	53
Toronto Maple Leafs	21	18	5	47	85	69
Ottawa Senators	14	17	13	41	54	67
Montreal Maroons	15	20	9	39	67	65

PLAYOFFS

League quarterfinals: N.Y. Rangers 1 goal, N.Y. Americans 0 goals (2-game series); Toronto 7 goals, Detroit 2 goals (2-game series). **Semifinals:** Boston 3, Montreal Canadiens 0; N.Y. Rangers 2, Toronto 0.
Stanley Cup finals: Boston 2, N.Y. Rangers 0.

1929-30

AMERICAN DIVISION

Team	W	L	T	Pts.	GF	GA
Boston Bruins	38	5	1	77	179	98
Chicago Blackhawks	21	18	5	47	117	111
New York Rangers	17	17	10	44	136	143
Detroit Cougars	14	24	6	34	117	133
Pittsburgh Pirates	5	36	3	13	102	185

CANADIAN DIVISION

Team	W	L	T	Pts.	GF	GA
Montreal Maroons	23	16	5	51	141	114
Montreal Canadiens	21	14	9	51	142	114
Ottawa Senators	21	15	8	50	138	118
Toronto Maple Leafs	17	21	6	40	116	124
New York Americans	14	25	5	33	113	161

PLAYOFFS

League quarterfinals: Montreal Canadiens 3 goals, Chicago 2 goals (2-game series); N.Y. Rangers 6 goals, Ottawa 3 goals (2-game series). **Semifinals:** Boston 3, Montreal Maroons 1; Montreal Canadiens 2, N.Y. Rangers 0.
Stanley Cup finals: Montreal Canadiens 2, Boston 0.

1930-31

AMERICAN DIVISION

Team	W	L	T	Pts.	GF	GA
Boston Bruins	28	10	6	62	143	90
Chicago Blackhawks	24	17	3	51	108	78
New York Rangers	19	16	9	47	106	87
Detroit Falcons	16	21	7	39	102	105
Philadelphia Quakers	4	36	4	12	76	184

CANADIAN DIVISION

Team	W	L	T	Pts.	GF	GA
Montreal Canadiens	26	10	8	60	129	89
Toronto Maple Leafs	22	13	9	53	118	99
Montreal Maroons	20	18	6	46	105	106
New York Americans	18	16	10	46	76	74
Ottawa Senators	10	30	4	24	91	142

PLAYOFFS

League quarterfinals: Chicago 4 goals, Toronto 3 goals (2-game series); N.Y. Rangers 8 goals, Montreal Maroons 1 goal (2-game series). **Semifinals:** Montreal Canadiens 3, Boston 2; Chicago 3 goals, N.Y. Rangers 0 goals (2-game series).
Stanley Cup finals: Montreal Canadiens 3, Chicago 2.

1931-32

AMERICAN DIVISION

Team	W	L	T	Pts.	GF	GA
New York Rangers	23	17	8	54	134	112
Chicago Blackhawks	18	19	11	47	86	101
Detroit Falcons	18	20	10	46	95	108
Boston Bruins	15	21	12	42	122	117

CANADIAN DIVISION

Team	W	L	T	Pts.	GF	GA
Montreal Canadiens	25	16	7	57	128	111
Toronto Maple Leafs	23	18	7	53	155	127
Montreal Maroons	19	22	7	45	142	139
New York Americans	16	24	8	40	95	142

League quarterfinals: Toronto 6 goals, Chicago 2 goals (2-game series); Montreal Maroons 3 goals, Detroit 1 goal (2-game series). **Semifinals:** N.Y. Rangers 3, Montreal Canadiens 1; Toronto 4 goals, Montreal Maroons 3 (2-game series). **Stanley Cup finals:** Toronto 3, N.Y. Rangers 0.

1932-33

AMERICAN DIVISION

Team	W	L	T	Pts.	GF	GA
Boston Bruins	25	15	8	58	124	88
Detroit Red Wings	25	15	8	58	111	93
New York Rangers	23	17	8	54	135	107
Chicago Blackhawks	16	20	12	44	88	101

CANADIAN DIVISION

Team	W	L	T	Pts.	GF	GA
Toronto Maple Leafs	24	18	6	54	119	111
Montreal Maroons	22	20	6	50	135	119
Montreal Canadiens	18	25	—	41	92	115
New York Americans	15	22	11	41	91	118
Ottawa Senators	11	27	10	32	88	131

PLAYOFFS

League quarterfinals: Detroit 5 goals, Montreal Maroons 2 goals (2-game series); N.Y. Rangers 8 goals, Montreal Canadiens 5 goals (2-game series). **Semifinals:** Toronto 3, Boston 2; N.Y. Rangers 6 goals, Detroit 3 goals (2-game series). **Stanley Cup finals:** N.Y. Rangers 3, Toronto 1.

1933-34

AMERICAN DIVISION

Team	W	L	T	Pts.	GF	GA
Detroit Red Wings	24	14	10	58	113	98
Chicago Blackhawks	20	17	11	51	88	83
New York Rangers	21	19	8	50	120	113
Boston Bruins	18	25	5	41	111	130

CANADIAN DIVISION

Team	W	L	T	Pts.	GF	GA
Toronto Maple Leafs	26	13	9	61	174	119
Montreal Canadiens	22	20	6	50	99	101
Montreal Maroons	19	18	11	49	117	122
New York Americans	15	23	10	40	104	132
Ottawa Senators	13	29	6	32	115	143

PLAYOFFS

League quarterfinals: Chicago 4 goals, Montreal Canadiens 3 goals (2-game series); Montreal Maroons 2 goals, N.Y. Rangers 1 goal (2-game series). **Semifinals:** Detroit 3, Toronto 2; Chicago 6 goals, Montreal Maroons 2 goals (2-game series). **Stanley Cup finals:** Chicago 3, Detroit 1.

1934-35

AMERICAN DIVISION

Team	W	L	T	Pts.	GF	GA
Boston Bruins	26	16	6	58	129	112
Chicago Blackhawks	26	17	5	57	118	88
New York Rangers	22	20	6	50	137	139
Detroit Red Wings	19	22	7	45	127	114

CANADIAN DIVISION

Team	W	L	T	Pts.	GF	GA
Toronto Maple Leafs	30	14	4	64	157	111
Montreal Maroons	24	19	5	53	123	92
Montreal Canadiens	19	23	6	44	110	145
New York Americans	12	27	9	33	100	142
St. Louis Eagles	11	31	6	28	86	144

PLAYOFFS

League quarterfinals: Montreal Maroons 1 goal, Chicago 0 goals (2-game series); N.Y. Rangers 6 goals, Montreal Canadiens 5 goals (2-game series). **Semifinals:** Toronto 3, Boston 1; Montreal Maroons 5 goals, N.Y. Rangers 4 (2-game series). **Stanley Cup finals:** Montreal Maroons 3, Toronto 0.

1935-36

AMERICAN DIVISION

Team	W	L	T	Pts.	GF	GA
Detroit Red Wings	24	16	8	56	124	103
Boston Bruins	22	20	6	50	92	83
Chicago Blackhawks	21	19	8	50	93	92
New York Rangers	19	17	12	50	91	96

CANADIAN DIVISION

Team	W	L	T	Pts.	GF	GA
Montreal Maroons	22	16	10	54	114	106
Toronto Maple Leafs	23	19	6	52	126	106
New York Americans	16	25	7	39	109	122
Montreal Canadiens	11	26	11	33	82	123

PLAYOFFS

League quarterfinals: Toronto 8 goals, Boston 6 goals (2-game series); N.Y. Americans 7 goals, Chicago 5 goals (2-game series). **Semifinals:** Detroit 3, Montreal Maroons 0; Toronto 2, N.Y. Americans 1. **Stanley Cup finals:** Detroit 3, Toronto 1.

1936-37

AMERICAN DIVISION

Team	W	L	T	Pts.	GF	GA
Detroit Red Wings	25	14	9	59	128	102
Boston Bruins	23	18	7	53	120	110
New York Rangers	19	20	9	47	117	106
Chicago Blackhawks	14	27	7	35	99	131

CANADIAN DIVISION

Team	W	L	T	Pts.	GF	GA
Montreal Canadiens	24	18	6	54	115	111
Montreal Maroons	22	17	9	53	126	110
Toronto Maple Leafs	22	21	5	49	119	115
New York Americans	15	29	4	34	122	161

PLAYOFFS

League quarterfinals: Montreal Maroons 2, Boston 1; N.Y. Rangers 2, Toronto 0. **Semifinals:** Detroit 3, Montreal Canadiens 2; N.Y. Rangers 2, Montreal Maroons 0. **Stanley Cup finals:** Detroit 3, N.Y. Rangers 2.

1937-38

AMERICAN DIVISION

Team	W	L	T	Pts.	GF	GA
Boston Bruins	30	11	7	67	142	89
New York Rangers	27	15	6	60	149	96
Chicago Blackhawks	14	25	9	37	97	139
Detroit Red Wings	12	25	11	35	99	133

CANADIAN DIVISION

Team	W	L	T	Pts.	GF	GA
Toronto Maple Leafs	24	15	9	57	151	127
New York Americans	19	18	11	49	110	111
Montreal Canadiens	18	17	13	49	123	128
Montreal Maroons	12	30	6	30	101	149

PLAYOFFS

League quarterfinals: N.Y. Americans 2, N.Y. Rangers 1; Chicago 2, Montreal Canadiens 1. **Semifinals:** Toronto 3, Boston 0; Chicago 2, N.Y. Americans 1. **Stanley Cup finals:** Chicago 3, Toronto 1.

NHL HISTORY *Year-by-year standings*

1938-39

Team	W	L	T	Pts.	GF	GA
Boston Bruins	36	10	2	74	156	76
New York Rangers	26	16	6	58	149	105
Toronto Maple Leafs	19	20	9	47	114	107
New York Americans	17	21	10	44	119	157
Detroit Red Wings	18	24	6	42	107	128
Montreal Canadiens	15	24	9	39	115	146
Chicago Blackhawks	12	28	8	32	91	132

PLAYOFFS

League quarterfinals: Toronto 2, N.Y. Americans 0; Detroit 2, Montreal 1. **Semifinals:** Boston 4, N.Y. Rangers 3; Toronto 2, Detroit 1.
Stanley Cup finals: Boston 4, Toronto 1.

1939-40

Team	W	L	T	Pts.	GF	GA
Boston Bruins	31	12	5	67	170	98
New York Rangers	27	11	10	64	136	77
Toronto Maple Leafs	25	17	6	56	134	110
Chicago Blackhawks	23	19	6	52	112	120
Detroit Red Wings	16	26	6	38	90	126
New York Americans	15	29	4	34	106	140
Montreal Canadiens	10	33	5	25	90	168

PLAYOFFS

League quarterfinals: Toronto 2, Chicago 0; Detroit 2, N.Y. Americans 1. **Semifinals:** N.Y. Rangers 4, Boston 2; Toronto 2, Detroit 0.
Stanley Cup finals: N.Y. Rangers 4, Toronto 2.

1940-41

Team	W	L	T	Pts.	GF	GA
Boston Bruins	27	8	13	67	168	102
Toronto Maple Leafs	28	14	6	62	145	99
Detroit Red Wings	21	16	11	53	112	102
New York Rangers	21	19	8	50	143	125
Chicago Blackhawks	16	25	7	39	112	139
Montreal Canadiens	16	26	6	38	121	147
New York Americans	8	29	11	27	99	186

PLAYOFFS

League quarterfinals: Detroit 2, N.Y. Rangers 1; Chicago 2, Montreal 1. **Semifinals:** Boston 4, Toronto 3; Detroit 2, Chicago 0.
Stanley Cup finals: Boston 4, Detroit 0.

1941-42

Team	W	L	T	Pts.	GF	GA
New York Rangers	29	17	2	60	177	143
Toronto Maple Leafs	27	18	3	57	158	136
Boston Bruins	25	17	6	56	160	118
Chicago Blackhawks	22	23	3	47	145	155
Detroit Red Wings	19	25	4	42	140	147
Montreal Canadiens	18	27	3	39	134	173
Brooklyn Americans	16	29	3	35	133	175

PLAYOFFS

League quarterfinals: Boston 2, Chicago 1; Detroit 2, Montreal 1. **Semifinals:** Toronto 4, New York 2; Detroit 2, Boston 0.
Stanley Cup finals: Toronto 4, Detroit 3.

1942-43

Team	W	L	T	Pts.	GF	GA
Detroit Red Wings	25	14	11	61	169	124
Boston Bruins	24	17	9	57	195	176
Toronto Maple Leafs	22	19	9	53	198	159
Montreal Canadiens	19	19	12	50	181	191
Chicago Blackhawks	17	18	15	49	179	180
New York Rangers	11	31	8	30	161	253

PLAYOFFS

League semifinals: Detroit 4, Toronto 2; Boston 4, Montreal 1.
Stanley Cup finals: Detroit 4, Boston 0.

1943-44

Team	W	L	T	Pts.	GF	GA
Montreal Canadiens	38	5	7	83	234	109
Detroit Red Wings	26	18	6	58	214	177
Toronto Maple Leafs	23	23	4	50	214	174
Chicago Blackhawks	22	23	5	49	178	187
Boston Bruins	19	26	5	43	223	268
New York Rangers	6	39	5	17	162	310

PLAYOFFS

League semifinals: Montreal 4, Toronto 1; Chicago 4, Detroit 1.
Stanley Cup finals: Montreal 4, Chicago 0.

1944-45

Team	W	L	T	Pts.	GF	GA
Montreal Canadiens	38	8	4	80	228	121
Detroit Red Wings	31	14	5	67	218	161
Toronto Maple Leafs	24	22	4	52	183	161
Boston Bruins	16	30	4	36	179	219
Chicago Blackhawks	13	30	7	33	141	194
New York Rangers	11	29	10	32	154	247

PLAYOFFS

League semifinals: Toronto 4, Montreal 2; Detroit 4, Boston 3.
Stanley Cup finals: Toronto 4, Detroit 3.

1945-46

Team	W	L	T	Pts.	GF	GA
Montreal Canadiens	28	17	5	61	172	134
Boston Bruins	24	18	8	56	167	156
Chicago Blackhawks	23	20	7	53	200	178
Detroit Red Wings	20	20	10	50	146	159
Toronto Maple Leafs	19	24	7	45	174	185
New York Rangers	13	28	9	35	144	191

PLAYOFFS

League semifinals: Montreal 4, Chicago 0; Boston 4, Detroit 1.
Stanley Cup finals: Montreal 4, Boston 1.

1946-47

Team	W	L	T	Pts.	GF	GA
Montreal Canadiens	34	16	10	78	189	138
Toronto Maple Leafs	31	19	10	72	209	172
Boston Bruins	26	23	11	63	190	175
Detroit Red Wings	22	27	11	55	190	193
New York Rangers	22	32	6	50	167	186
Chicago Blackhawks	19	37	4	42	193	274

PLAYOFFS

League semifinals: Montreal 4, Boston 1; Toronto 4, Detroit 1.
Stanley Cup finals: Toronto 4, Montreal 2.

1947-48

Team	W	L	T	Pts.	GF	GA
Toronto Maple Leafs	32	15	13	77	182	143
Detroit Red Wings	30	18	12	72	187	148
Boston Bruins	23	24	13	59	167	168
New York Rangers	21	26	13	55	176	201
Montreal Canadiens	20	29	11	51	147	169
Chicago Blackhawks	20	34	6	46	195	225

PLAYOFFS

League semifinals: Toronto 4, Boston 1; Detroit 4, New York 2.
Stanley Cup finals: Toronto 4, Detroit 0.

1948-49

Team	W	L	T	Pts.	GF	GA
Detroit Red Wings	34	19	7	75	195	145
Boston Bruins	29	23	8	66	178	163
Montreal Canadiens	28	23	9	65	152	126
Toronto Maple Leafs	22	25	13	57	147	161
Chicago Blackhawks	21	31	8	50	173	211
New York Rangers	18	31	11	47	133	172

PLAYOFFS
League semifinals: Detroit 4, Montreal 3; Toronto 4, Boston 1.
Stanley Cup finals: Toronto 4, Detroit 0.

1949-50

Team	W	L	T	Pts.	GF	GA
Detroit Red Wings	37	19	14	88	229	164
Montreal Canadiens	29	22	19	77	172	150
Toronto Maple Leafs	31	27	12	74	176	173
New York Rangers	28	31	11	67	170	189
Boston Bruins	22	32	16	60	198	228
Chicago Blackhawks	22	38	10	54	203	244

PLAYOFFS
League semifinals: Detroit 4, Toronto 3; New York 4, Montreal 1.
Stanley Cup finals: Detroit 4, New York 3.

1950-51

Team	W	L	T	Pts.	GF	GA
Detroit Red Wings	44	13	13	101	236	139
Toronto Maple Leafs	41	16	13	95	212	138
Montreal Canadiens	25	30	15	65	173	184
Boston Bruins	22	30	18	62	178	197
New York Rangers	20	29	21	61	169	201
Chicago Blackhawks	13	47	10	36	171	280

PLAYOFFS
League semifinals: Montreal 4, Detroit 2; Toronto 4, Boston 1.
Stanley Cup finals: Toronto 4, Montreal 1.

1951-52

Team	W	L	T	Pts.	GF	GA
Detroit Red Wings	44	14	12	100	215	133
Montreal Canadiens	34	26	10	78	195	164
Toronto Maple Leafs	29	25	16	74	168	157
Boston Bruins	25	29	16	66	162	176
New York Rangers	23	34	13	59	192	219
Chicago Blackhawks	17	44	9	43	158	241

PLAYOFFS
League semifinals: Detroit 4, Toronto 0; Montreal 4, Boston 3.
Stanley Cup finals: Detroit 4, Montreal 0.

1952-53

Team	W	L	T	Pts.	GF	GA
Detroit Red Wings	36	16	18	90	222	133
Montreal Canadiens	28	23	19	75	155	148
Boston Bruins	28	29	13	69	152	172
Chicago Blackhawks	27	28	15	69	169	175
Toronto Maple Leafs	27	30	13	67	156	167
New York Rangers	17	37	16	50	152	211

PLAYOFFS
League semifinals: Boston 4, Detroit 2; Montreal 4, Chicago 3.
Stanley Cup finals: Montreal 4, Boston 1.

1953-54

Team	W	L	T	Pts.	GF	GA
Detroit Red Wings	37	19	14	88	191	132
Montreal Canadiens	35	24	11	81	195	141
Toronto Maple Leafs	32	24	14	78	152	131
Boston Bruins	32	28	10	74	177	181
New York Rangers	29	31	10	68	161	182
Chicago Blackhawks	12	51	7	31	133	242

PLAYOFFS
League semifinals: Detroit 4, Toronto 1; Montreal 4, Boston 0.
Stanley Cup finals: Detroit 4, Montreal 3.

1954-55

Team	W	L	T	Pts.	GF	GA
Detroit Red Wings	42	17	11	95	204	134
Montreal Canadiens	41	18	11	93	228	157
Toronto Maple Leafs	24	24	22	70	147	135
Boston Bruins	23	26	21	67	169	188
New York Rangers	17	35	18	52	150	210
Chicago Blackhawks	13	40	17	43	161	235

PLAYOFFS
League semifinals: Detroit 4, Toronto 0; Montreal 4, Boston 1.
Stanley Cup finals: Detroit 4, Montreal 3.

1955-56

Team	W	L	T	Pts.	GF	GA
Montreal Canadiens	45	15	10	100	222	131
Detroit Red Wings	30	24	16	76	183	148
New York Rangers	32	28	10	74	204	203
Toronto Maple Leafs	24	33	13	61	153	181
Boston Bruins	23	34	13	59	147	185
Chicago Blackhawks	19	39	12	50	155	216

PLAYOFFS
League semifinals: Montreal 4, New York 1; Detroit 4, Toronto 1.
Stanley Cup finals: Montreal 4, Detroit 1.

1956-57

Team	W	L	T	Pts.	GF	GA
Detroit Red Wings	38	20	12	88	198	157
Montreal Canadiens	35	23	12	82	210	155
Boston Bruins	34	24	12	80	195	174
New York Rangers	26	30	14	66	184	227
Toronto Maple Leafs	21	34	15	57	174	192
Chicago Blackhawks	16	39	15	47	169	225

PLAYOFFS
League semifinals: Boston 4, Detroit 1; Montreal 4, New York 1.
Stanley Cup finals: Montreal 4, Boston 1.

1957-58

Team	W	L	T	Pts.	GF	GA
Montreal Canadiens	43	17	10	96	250	158
New York Rangers	32	25	13	77	195	188
Detroit Red Wings	29	29	12	70	176	207
Boston Bruins	27	28	15	69	199	194
Chicago Blackhawks	24	39	7	55	163	202
Toronto Maple Leafs	21	38	11	53	192	226

PLAYOFFS
League semifinals: Montreal 4, Detroit 0; Boston 4, New York 2.
Stanley Cup finals: Montreal 4, Boston 2.

1958-59

Team	W	L	T	Pts.	GF	GA
Montreal Canadiens	39	18	13	91	258	158
Boston Bruins	32	29	9	73	205	215
Chicago Blackhawks	28	29	13	69	197	208
Toronto Maple Leafs	27	32	11	65	189	201
New York Rangers	26	32	12	64	201	217
Detroit Red Wings	25	37	8	58	167	218

PLAYOFFS

League semifinals: Montreal 4, Chicago 2; Toronto 4, Boston 3.
Stanley Cup finals: Montreal 4, Toronto 1.

1959-60

Team	W	L	T	Pts.	GF	GA
Montreal Canadiens	40	18	12	92	255	178
Toronto Maple Leafs	35	26	9	79	199	195
Chicago Blackhawks	28	29	13	69	191	180
Detroit Red Wings	26	29	15	67	186	197
Boston Bruins	28	34	8	64	220	241
New York Rangers	17	38	15	49	187	247

PLAYOFFS

League semifinals: Montreal 4, Chicago 0; Toronto 4, Detroit 2.
Stanley Cup finals: Montreal 4, Toronto 0.

1960-61

Team	W	L	T	Pts.	GF	GA
Montreal Canadiens	41	19	10	92	254	188
Toronto Maple Leafs	39	19	12	90	234	176
Chicago Blackhawks	29	24	17	75	198	180
Detroit Red Wings	25	29	16	66	195	215
New York Rangers	22	38	10	54	204	248
Boston Bruins	15	42	13	43	176	254

PLAYOFFS

League semifinals: Chicago 4, Montreal 2; Detroit 4, Toronto 1.
Stanley Cup finals: Chicago 4, Detroit 2.

1961-62

Team	W	L	T	Pts.	GF	GA
Montreal Canadiens	42	14	14	98	259	166
Toronto Maple Leafs	37	22	11	85	232	180
Chicago Blackhawks	31	26	13	75	217	186
New York Rangers	26	32	12	64	195	207
Detroit Red Wings	23	33	14	60	184	219
Boston Bruins	15	47	8	38	177	306

PLAYOFFS

League semifinals: Chicago 4, Montreal 2; Toronto 4, New York 2.
Stanley Cup finals: Toronto 4, Chicago 2.

1962-63

Team	W	L	T	Pts.	GF	GA
Toronto Maple Leafs	35	23	12	82	221	180
Chicago Blackhawks	32	21	17	81	194	178
Montreal Canadiens	28	19	23	79	225	183
Detroit Red Wings	32	25	13	77	200	194
New York Rangers	22	36	12	56	211	233
Boston Bruins	14	39	17	45	198	281

PLAYOFFS

League semifinals: Toronto 4, Montreal 1; Detroit 4, Chicago 2.
Stanley Cup finals: Toronto 4, Detroit 1.

1963-64

Team	W	L	T	Pts.	GF	GA
Montreal Canadiens	36	21	13	85	209	167
Chicago Blackhawks	36	22	12	84	218	169
Toronto Maple Leafs	33	25	12	78	192	172
Detroit Red Wings	30	29	11	71	191	204
New York Rangers	22	38	10	54	186	242
Boston Bruins	18	40	12	48	170	212

PLAYOFFS

League semifinals: Toronto 4, Montreal 3; Detroit 4, Chicago 3.
Stanley Cup finals: Toronto 4, Detroit 3.

1964-65

Team	W	L	T	Pts.	GF	GA
Detroit Red Wings	40	23	7	87	224	175
Montreal Canadiens	36	23	11	83	211	185
Chicago Blackhawks	34	28	8	76	224	176
Toronto Maple Leafs	30	26	14	74	204	173
New York Rangers	20	38	12	52	179	246
Boston Bruins	21	43	6	48	166	253

PLAYOFFS

League semifinals: Chicago 4, Detroit 3; Montreal 4, Toronto 2.
Stanley Cup finals: Montreal 4, Chicago 3.

1965-66

Team	W	L	T	Pts.	GF	GA
Montreal Canadiens	41	21	8	90	239	173
Chicago Blackhawks	37	25	8	82	240	187
Toronto Maple Leafs	34	25	11	79	208	187
Detroit Red Wings	31	27	12	74	221	194
Boston Bruins	21	43	6	48	174	275
New York Rangers	18	41	11	47	195	261

PLAYOFFS

League semifinals: Montreal 4, Toronto 0; Detroit 4, Chicago 2.
Stanley Cup finals: Montreal 4, Detroit 2.

1966-67

Team	W	L	T	Pts.	GF	GA
Chicago Blackhawks	41	17	12	94	264	170
Montreal Canadiens	32	25	13	77	202	188
Toronto Maple Leafs	32	27	11	75	204	211
New York Rangers	30	28	12	72	188	189
Detroit Red Wings	27	39	4	58	212	241
Boston Bruins	17	43	10	44	182	253

PLAYOFFS

League semifinals: Toronto 4, Chicago 2; Montreal 4, New York 0.
Stanley Cup finals: Toronto 4, Montreal 2.

1967-68

EAST DIVISION

Team	W	L	T	Pts.	GF	GA
Montreal Canadiens	42	22	10	94	236	167
New York Rangers	39	23	12	90	226	183
Boston Bruins	37	27	10	84	259	216
Chicago Blackhawks	32	26	16	80	212	222
Toronto Maple Leafs	33	31	10	76	209	176
Detroit Red Wings	27	35	12	66	245	257

WEST DIVISION

Team	W	L	T	Pts.	GF	GA
Philadelphia Flyers	31	32	11	73	173	179
Los Angeles Kings	31	33	10	72	200	224

NHL HISTORY *Year-by-year standings*

Team	W	L	T	Pts.	GF	GA
St. Louis Blues	27	31	16	70	177	191
Minnesota North Stars	27	32	15	69	191	226
Pittsburgh Penguins	27	34	13	67	195	216
Oakland Seals	15	42	17	47	153	219

PLAYOFFS

Division semifinals: Montreal 4, Boston 0; Chicago 4, New York 2; St. Louis 4, Philadelphia 3; Minnesota 4, Los Angeles 3. **Division finals:** Montreal 4, Chicago 1; St. Louis 4, Minnesota 3.
Stanley Cup finals: Montreal 4, St. Louis 0.

1968-69

EAST DIVISION

Team	W	L	T	Pts.	GF	GA
Montreal Canadiens	46	19	11	103	271	202
Boston Bruins	42	18	16	100	303	221
New York Rangers	41	26	9	91	231	196
Toronto Maple Leafs	35	26	15	85	234	217
Detroit Red Wings	33	31	12	78	239	221
Chicago Blackhawks	34	33	9	77	280	246

WEST DIVISION

Team	W	L	T	Pts.	GF	GA
St. Louis Blues	37	25	14	88	204	157
Oakland Seals	29	36	11	69	219	251
Philadelphia Flyers	20	35	21	61	174	225
Los Angeles Kings	24	42	10	58	185	260
Pittsburgh Penguins	20	45	11	51	189	252
Minnesota North Stars	18	43	15	51	189	270

PLAYOFFS

Division semifinals: Montreal 4, New York 0; Boston 4, Toronto 0; St. Louis 4, Philadelphia 0; Los Angeles 4, Oakland 3. **Division finals:** Montreal 4, Boston 2; St. Louis 4, Los Angeles 0.
Stanley Cup finals: Montreal 4, St. Louis 0.

1969-70

EAST DIVISION

Team	W	L	T	Pts.	GF	GA
Chicago Blackhawks	45	22	9	99	250	170
Boston Bruins	40	17	19	99	277	216
Detroit Red Wings	40	21	15	95	246	199
New York Rangers	38	22	16	92	246	189
Montreal Canadiens	38	22	16	92	244	201
Toronto Maple Leafs	29	34	13	71	222	242

WEST DIVISION

Team	W	L	T	Pts.	GF	GA
St. Louis Blues	37	27	12	86	224	179
Pittsburgh Penguins	26	38	12	64	182	238
Minnesota North Stars	19	35	22	60	224	257
Oakland Seals	22	40	14	58	169	243
Philadelphia Flyers	17	35	24	58	197	225
Los Angeles Kings	14	52	10	38	168	290

PLAYOFFS

Division semifinals: Chicago 4, Detroit 0; Boston 4, N.Y. Rangers 2; St. Louis 4, Minnesota 2; Pittsburgh 4, Oakland 0. **Division finals:** Boston 4, Chicago 0; St. Louis 4, Pittsburgh 2.
Stanley Cup finals: Boston 4, St. Louis 0.

1970-71

EAST DIVISION

Team	W	L	T	Pts.	GF	GA
Boston Bruins	57	14	7	121	399	207
New York Rangers	49	18	11	109	259	177

Team	W	L	T	Pts.	GF	GA
Montreal Canadiens	42	23	13	97	291	216
Toronto Maple Leafs	37	33	8	82	248	211
Buffalo Sabres	24	39	15	63	217	291
Vancouver Canucks	24	46	8	56	229	296
Detroit Red Wings	22	45	11	55	209	308

WEST DIVISION

Team	W	L	T	Pts.	GF	GA
Chicago Blackhawks	49	20	9	107	277	184
St. Louis Blues	34	25	19	87	223	208
Philadelphia Flyers	28	33	17	73	207	225
Minnesota North Stars	28	34	16	72	191	223
Los Angeles Kings	25	40	13	63	239	303
Pittsburgh Penguins	21	37	20	62	221	240
California Golden Seals	20	53	5	45	199	320

PLAYOFFS

Division semifinals: Montreal 4, Boston 3; N.Y. Rangers 4, Toronto 2; Chicago 4, Philadelphia 0; Minnesota 4, St. Louis 2. **Division finals:** Montreal 4, Minnesota 2; Chicago 4, N.Y. Rangers 3.
Stanley Cup finals: Montreal 4, Chicago 3.

1971-72

EAST DIVISION

Team	W	L	T	Pts.	GF	GA
Boston Bruins	54	13	11	119	330	204
New York Rangers	48	17	13	109	317	192
Montreal Canadiens	46	16	16	108	307	205
Toronto Maple Leafs	33	31	14	80	209	208
Detroit Red Wings	33	35	10	76	261	262
Buffalo Sabres	16	43	19	51	203	289
Vancouver Canucks	20	50	8	48	203	297

WEST DIVISION

Team	W	L	T	Pts.	GF	GA
Chicago Blackhawks	46	17	15	107	256	166
Minnesota North Stars	37	29	12	86	212	191
St. Louis Blues	28	39	11	67	208	247
Pittsburgh Penguins	26	38	14	66	220	258
Philadelphia Flyers	26	38	14	66	200	236
California Golden Seals	21	39	18	60	216	288
Los Angeles Kings	20	49	9	49	206	305

PLAYOFFS

Division semifinals: Boston 4, Toronto 1; N.Y. Rangers 4, Montreal 2; Chicago 4, Pittsburgh 0; St. Louis 4, Minnesota 3. **Division finals:** N.Y. Rangers 4, Chicago 0; Boston 4, St. Louis 0.
Stanley Cup finals: Boston 4, N.Y. Rangers 2.

1972-73

EAST DIVISION

Team	W	L	T	Pts.	GF	GA
Montreal Canadiens	52	10	16	120	329	184
Boston Bruins	51	22	5	107	330	235
New York Rangers	47	23	8	102	297	208
Buffalo Sabres	37	27	14	88	257	219
Detroit Red Wings	37	29	12	86	265	243
Toronto Maple Leafs	27	41	10	64	247	279
Vancouver Canucks	22	47	9	53	233	339
New York Islanders	12	60	6	30	170	347

WEST DIVISION

Team	W	L	T	Pts.	GF	GA
Chicago Blackhawks	42	27	9	93	284	225
Philadelphia Flyers	37	30	11	85	296	256
Minnesota North Stars	37	30	11	85	254	230
St. Louis Blues	32	34	12	76	233	251
Pittsburgh Penguins	32	37	9	73	257	265

Team	W	L	T	Pts.	GF	GA
Los Angeles Kings	31	36	11	73	232	245
Atlanta Flames	25	38	15	65	191	239
California Golden Seals	16	46	16	48	213	323

PLAYOFFS

Division semifinals: Montreal 4, Buffalo 2; N.Y. Rangers 4, Boston 1; Chicago 4, St. Louis 1; Philadelphia 4, Minnesota 2. **Division finals:** Montreal 4, Philadelphia 1; Chicago 4, N.Y. Rangers 1.
Stanley Cup finals: Montreal 4, Chicago 2.

1973-74

EAST DIVISION

Team	W	L	T	Pts.	GF	GA
Boston Bruins	52	17	9	113	349	221
Montreal Canadiens	45	24	9	99	293	240
New York Rangers	40	24	14	94	300	251
Toronto Maple Leafs	35	27	16	86	274	230
Buffalo Sabres	32	34	12	76	242	250
Detroit Red Wings	29	39	10	68	255	319
Vancouver Canucks	24	43	11	59	224	296
New York Islanders	19	41	18	56	182	247

WEST DIVISION

Team	W	L	T	Pts.	GF	GA
Philadelphia Flyers	50	16	12	112	273	164
Chicago Blackhawks	41	14	23	105	272	164
Los Angeles Kings	33	33	12	78	233	231
Atlanta Flames	30	34	14	74	214	238
Pittsburgh Penguins	28	41	9	65	242	273
St. Louis Blues	26	40	12	64	206	248
Minnesota North Stars	23	38	17	63	235	275
California Golden Seals	13	55	10	36	195	342

PLAYOFFS

Division semifinals: Boston 4, Toronto 0; N.Y. Rangers 4, Montreal 2; Philadelphia 4, Atlanta 0; Chicago 4, Los Angeles 1. **Division finals:** Boston 4, Chicago 2; Philadelphia 4, N.Y. Rangers 3.
Stanley Cup finals: Philadelphia 4, Boston 2.

1974-75

PRINCE OF WALES CONFERENCE

ADAMS DIVISION

Team	W	L	T	Pts.	GF	GA
Buffalo Sabres	49	16	15	113	354	240
Boston Bruins	40	26	14	94	345	245
Toronto Maple Leafs	31	33	16	78	280	309
California Golden Seals	19	48	13	51	212	316

NORRIS DIVISION

Team	W	L	T	Pts.	GF	GA
Montreal Canadiens	47	14	19	113	374	225
Los Angeles Kings	42	17	21	105	269	185
Pittsburgh Penguins	37	28	15	89	326	289
Detroit Red Wings	23	45	12	58	259	335
Washington Capitals	8	67	5	21	181	446

CLARENCE CAMPBELL CONFERENCE

PATRICK DIVISION

Team	W	L	T	Pts.	GF	GA
Philadelphia Flyers	51	18	11	113	293	181
New York Rangers	37	29	14	88	319	276
New York Islanders	33	25	22	88	264	221
Atlanta Flames	34	31	15	83	243	233

SMYTHE DIVISION

Team	W	L	T	Pts.	GF	GA
Vancouver Canucks	38	32	10	86	271	254
St. Louis Blues	35	31	14	84	269	267
Chicago Blackhawks	37	35	8	82	268	241
Minnesota North Stars	23	50	7	53	221	341
Kansas City Scouts	15	54	11	41	184	328

PLAYOFFS

Preliminaries: Toronto 2, Los Angeles 1; Chicago 2, Boston 1; Pittsburgh 2, St. Louis 0; N.Y. Islanders 2, N.Y. Rangers 1. **Quarterfinals:** Philadelphia 4, Toronto 0; Buffalo 4, Chicago 1; Montreal 4, Vancouver 1; N.Y. Islanders 4, Pittsburgh 3. **Semifinals:** Philadelphia 4, N.Y. Islanders 3; Buffalo 4, Montreal 2.
Stanley Cup finals: Philadelphia 4, Buffalo 2.

1975-76

PRINCE OF WALES CONFERENCE

ADAMS DIVISION

Team	W	L	T	Pts.	GF	GA
Boston Bruins	48	15	17	113	313	237
Buffalo Sabres	46	21	13	105	339	240
Toronto Maple Leafs	34	31	15	83	294	276
California Golden Seals	27	42	11	65	250	278

NORRIS DIVISION

Team	W	L	T	Pts.	GF	GA
Montreal Canadiens	58	11	11	127	337	174
Los Angeles Kings	38	33	9	85	263	265
Pittsburgh Penguins	35	33	12	82	339	303
Detroit Red Wings	26	44	10	62	226	300
Washington Capitals	11	59	10	32	224	394

CLARENCE CAMPBELL CONFERENCE

PATRICK DIVISION

Team	W	L	T	Pts.	GF	GA
Philadelphia Flyers	51	13	16	118	348	209
New York Islanders	42	21	17	101	297	190
Atlanta Flames	35	33	12	82	262	237
New York Rangers	29	42	9	67	262	333

SMYTHE DIVISION

Team	W	L	T	Pts.	GF	GA
Chicago Blackhawks	32	30	18	82	254	261
Vancouver Canucks	33	32	15	81	271	272
St. Louis Blues	29	37	14	72	249	290
Minnesota North Stars	20	53	7	47	195	303
Kansas City Scouts	12	56	12	36	190	351

PLAYOFFS

Preliminaries: Buffalo 2, St. Louis 1; N.Y. Islanders 2, Vancouver 0; Los Angeles 2, Atlanta 0; Toronto 2, Pittsburgh 1. **Quarterfinals:** Montreal 4, Chicago 0; Philadelphia 4, Toronto 3; Boston 4, Los Angeles 3; N.Y. Islanders 4, Buffalo 2. **Semifinals:** Montreal 4, N.Y. Islanders 1; Philadelphia 4, Boston 1.
Stanley Cup finals: Montreal 4, Philadelphia 0.

1976-77

PRINCE OF WALES CONFERENCE

ADAMS DIVISION

Team	W	L	T	Pts.	GF	GA
Boston Bruins	49	23	8	106	312	240
Buffalo Sabres	48	24	8	104	301	220
Toronto Maple Leafs	33	32	15	81	301	285
Cleveland Barons	25	42	13	63	240	292

NORRIS DIVISION

Team	W	L	T	Pts.	GF	GA
Montreal Canadiens	60	8	12	132	387	171
Los Angeles Kings	34	31	15	83	271	241
Pittsburgh Penguins	34	33	13	81	240	252
Washington Capitals	24	42	14	62	221	307
Detroit Red Wings	16	55	9	41	183	309

CLARENCE CAMPBELL CONFERENCE

PATRICK DIVISION

Team	W	L	T	Pts.	GF	GA
Philadelphia Flyers	48	16	16	112	323	213
New York Islanders	47	21	12	106	288	193
Atlanta Flames	34	34	12	80	264	265
New York Rangers	29	37	14	72	272	310

SMYTHE DIVISION

Team	W	L	T	Pts.	GF	GA
St. Louis Blues	32	39	9	73	239	276
Minnesota North Stars	23	39	18	64	240	310
Chicago Blackhawks	26	43	11	63	240	298
Vancouver Canucks	25	42	13	63	235	294
Colorado Rockies	20	46	14	54	226	307

PLAYOFFS

Preliminaries: N.Y. Islanders 2, Chicago 0; Buffalo 2, Minnesota 0; Los Angeles 2, Atlanta 1; Toronto 2, Pittsburgh 1. **Quarterfinals:** Montreal 4, St. Louis 0; Philadelphia 4, Toronto 2; Boston 4, Los Angeles 2; N.Y. Islanders 4, Buffalo 0. **Semifinals:** Montreal 4, N.Y. Islanders 2; Boston 4, Philadelphia 0.
Stanley Cup finals: Montreal 4, Boston 0.

1977-78

PRINCE OF WALES CONFERENCE

ADAMS DIVISION

Team	W	L	T	Pts.	GF	GA
Boston Bruins	51	18	11	113	333	218
Buffalo Sabres	44	19	17	105	288	215
Toronto Maple Leafs	41	29	10	92	271	237
Cleveland Barons	22	45	13	57	230	325

NORRIS DIVISION

Team	W	L	T	Pts.	GF	GA
Montreal Canadiens	59	10	11	129	359	183
Detroit Red Wings	32	34	14	78	252	266
Los Angeles Kings	31	34	15	77	243	245
Pittsburgh Penguins	25	37	18	68	254	321
Washington Capitals	17	49	14	48	195	321

CLARENCE CAMPBELL CONFERENCE

PATRICK DIVISION

Team	W	L	T	Pts.	GF	GA
New York Islanders	48	17	15	111	334	210
Philadelphia Flyers	45	20	15	105	296	200
Atlanta Flames	34	27	19	87	274	252
New York Rangers	30	37	13	73	279	280

SMYTHE DIVISION

Team	W	L	T	Pts.	GF	GA
Chicago Blackhawks	32	29	19	83	230	220
Colorado Rockies	19	40	21	59	257	305
Vancouver Canucks	20	43	17	57	239	320
St. Louis Blues	20	47	13	53	195	304
Minnesota North Stars	18	53	9	45	218	325

PLAYOFFS

Preliminaries: Philadelphia 2, Colorado 0; Buffalo 2, N.Y. Rangers 1; Toronto 2, Los Angeles 0; Detroit 2, Atlanta 0. **Quarterfinals:** Montreal 4, Detroit 1; Boston 4, Chicago 0; Toronto 4, N.Y.

Islanders 3; Philadelphia 4, Buffalo 1. **Semifinals:** Montreal 4, Toronto 0; Boston 4, Philadelphia 1.
Stanley Cup finals: Montreal 4, Boston 2.

1978-79

PRINCE OF WALES CONFERENCE

ADAMS DIVISION

Team	W	L	T	Pts.	GF	GA
Boston Bruins	43	23	14	100	316	270
Buffalo Sabres	36	28	16	88	280	263
Toronto Maple Leafs	34	33	13	81	267	252
Minnesota North Stars	28	40	12	68	257	289

NORRIS DIVISION

Team	W	L	T	Pts.	GF	GA
Montreal Canadiens	52	17	11	115	337	204
Pittsburgh Penguins	36	31	13	85	281	279
Los Angeles Kings	34	34	12	80	292	286
Washington Capitals	24	41	15	63	273	338
Detroit Red Wings	23	41	16	62	252	295

CLARENCE CAMPBELL CONFERENCE

PATRICK DIVISION

Team	W	L	T	Pts.	GF	GA
New York Islanders	51	15	14	116	358	214
Philadelphia Flyers	40	25	15	95	281	248
New York Rangers	40	29	11	91	316	292
Atlanta Flames	41	31	8	90	327	280

SMYTHE DIVISION

Team	W	L	T	Pts.	GF	GA
Chicago Blackhawks	29	36	15	73	244	277
Vancouver Canucks	25	42	13	63	217	291
St. Louis Blues	18	50	12	48	249	348
Colorado Rockies	15	53	12	42	210	331

PLAYOFFS

Preliminaries: Philadelphia 2, Vancouver 1; N.Y. Rangers 2, Los Angeles 0; Toronto 2, Atlanta 0; Pittsburgh 2, Buffalo 1. **Quarterfinals:** N.Y. Islanders 4, Chicago 0; Montreal 4, Toronto 0; Boston 4, Pittsburgh 0; N.Y. Rangers 4, Philadelphia 1. **Semifinals:** N.Y. Rangers 4, N.Y. Islanders 2; Montreal 4, Boston 3.
Stanley Cup finals: Montreal 4, N.Y. Rangers 1.

1979-80

PRINCE OF WALES CONFERENCE

ADAMS DIVISION

Team	W	L	T	Pts.	GF	GA
Buffalo Sabres	47	17	16	110	318	201
Boston Bruins	46	21	13	105	310	234
Minnesota North Stars	36	28	16	88	311	253
Toronto Maple Leafs	35	40	5	75	304	327
Quebec Nordiques	25	44	11	61	248	313

NORRIS DIVISION

Team	W	L	T	Pts.	GF	GA
Montreal Canadiens	47	20	13	107	328	240
Los Angeles Kings	30	36	14	74	290	313
Pittsburgh Penguins	30	37	13	73	251	303
Hartford Whalers	27	34	19	73	303	312
Detroit Red Wings	26	43	11	63	268	306

CLARENCE CAMPBELL CONFERENCE

PATRICK DIVISION

Team	W	L	T	Pts.	GF	GA
Philadelphia Flyers	48	12	20	116	327	254
New York Islanders	39	28	13	91	281	247

Team	W	L	T	Pts.	GF	GA
New York Rangers	38	32	10	86	308	284
Atlanta Flames	35	32	13	83	282	269
Washington Capitals	27	40	13	67	261	293

SMYTHE DIVISION

Team	W	L	T	Pts.	GF	GA
Chicago Blackhawks	34	27	19	87	241	250
St. Louis Blues	34	34	12	80	266	278
Vancouver Canucks	27	37	16	70	256	281
Edmonton Oilers	28	39	13	69	301	322
Winnipeg Jets	20	49	11	51	214	314
Colorado Rockies	19	48	13	51	234	308

PLAYOFFS

Preliminaries: Philadelphia 3, Edmonton 0; Buffalo 3, Vancouver 1; Montreal 3, Hartford 0; Boston 3, Pittsburgh 2; N.Y. Islanders 3, Los Angeles 1; Minnesota 3, Toronto 0; Chicago 3, St. Louis 0; N.Y. Rangers 3, Atlanta 1. **Quarterfinals:** Philadelphia 4, N.Y. Rangers 1; Buffalo 4, Chicago 0; Minnesota 4, Montreal 3; N.Y. Islanders 4, Boston 1. **Semifinals:** Philadelphia 4, Minnesota 1; N.Y. Islanders 4, Buffalo 2. **Stanley Cup finals:** N.Y. Islanders 4, Philadelphia 2.

1980-81

PRINCE OF WALES CONFERENCE

ADAMS DIVISION

Team	W	L	T	Pts.	GF	GA
Buffalo Sabres	39	20	21	99	327	250
Boston Bruins	37	30	13	87	316	272
Minnesota North Stars	35	28	17	87	291	263
Quebec Nordiques	30	32	18	78	314	318
Toronto Maple Leafs	28	37	15	71	322	367

NORRIS DIVISION

Team	W	L	T	Pts.	GF	GA
Montreal Canadiens	45	22	13	103	332	232
Los Angeles Kings	43	24	13	99	337	290
Pittsburgh Penguins	30	37	13	73	302	345
Hartford Whalers	21	41	18	60	292	372
Detroit Red Wings	19	43	18	56	252	339

CLARENCE CAMPBELL CONFERENCE

PATRICK DIVISION

Team	W	L	T	Pts.	GF	GA
New York Islanders	48	18	14	110	355	260
Philadelphia Flyers	41	24	15	97	313	249
Calgary Flames	39	27	14	92	329	298
New York Rangers	30	36	14	74	312	317
Washington Capitals	26	36	18	70	286	317

SMYTHE DIVISION

Team	W	L	T	Pts.	GF	GA
St. Louis Blues	45	18	17	107	352	281
Chicago Blackhawks	31	33	16	78	304	315
Vancouver Canucks	28	32	20	76	289	301
Edmonton Oilers	29	35	16	74	328	327
Colorado Rockies	22	45	13	57	258	344
Winnipeg Jets	9	57	14	32	246	400

PLAYOFFS

Preliminaries: N.Y. Islanders 3, Toronto 0; St. Louis 3, Pittsburgh 2; Edmonton 3, Montreal 0; N.Y. Rangers 3, Los Angeles 1; Buffalo 3, Vancouver 0; Philadelphia 3, Quebec 2; Calgary 3, Chicago 0; Minnesota 3, Boston 0. **Quarterfinals:** N.Y. Islanders 4, Edmonton 2; N.Y. Rangers 4, St. Louis 2; Minnesota 4, Buffalo 1; Calgary 4, Philadelphia 3. **Semifinals:** N.Y. Islanders 4, N.Y. Rangers 0; Minnesota 4, Calgary 2. **Stanley Cup finals:** N.Y. Islanders 4, Minnesota 1.

1981-82

PRINCE OF WALES CONFERENCE

ADAMS DIVISION

Team	W	L	T	Pts.	GF	GA
Montreal Canadiens	46	17	17	109	360	223
Boston Bruins	43	27	10	96	323	285
Buffalo Sabres	39	26	15	93	307	273
Quebec Nordiques	33	31	16	82	356	345
Hartford Whalers	21	41	18	60	264	351

PATRICK DIVISION

Team	W	L	T	Pts.	GF	GA
New York Islanders	54	16	10	118	385	250
New York Rangers	39	27	14	92	316	306
Philadelphia Flyers	38	31	11	87	325	313
Pittsburgh Penguins	31	36	13	75	310	337
Washington Capitals	26	41	13	65	319	338

CLARENCE CAMPBELL CONFERENCE

NORRIS DIVISION

Team	W	L	T	Pts.	GF	GA
Minnesota North Stars	37	23	20	94	346	288
Winnipeg Jets	33	33	14	80	319	332
St. Louis Blues	32	40	8	72	315	349
Chicago Blackhawks	30	38	12	72	332	363
Toronto Maple Leafs	20	44	16	56	298	380
Detroit Red Wings	21	47	12	54	270	351

SMYTHE DIVISION

Team	W	L	T	Pts.	GF	GA
Edmonton Oilers	48	17	15	111	417	295
Vancouver Canucks	30	33	17	77	290	286
Calgary Flames	29	34	17	75	334	345
Los Angeles Kings	24	41	15	63	314	369
Colorado Rockies	18	49	13	49	241	362

PLAYOFFS

Wales Conference division semifinals: Quebec 3, Montreal 2; Boston 3, Buffalo 1; N.Y. Islanders 3, Pittsburgh 2; N.Y. Rangers 3, Philadelphia 1. **Division finals:** Quebec 4, Boston 3; N.Y. Islanders 4, N.Y. Rangers 2. **Conference finals:** N.Y. Islanders 4, Quebec 0.
Campbell Conference division semifinals: Chicago 3, Minnesota 1; St. Louis 3, Winnipeg 1; Los Angeles 3, Edmonton 2; Vancouver 3, Calgary 0. **Division finals:** Chicago 4, St. Louis 2; Vancouver 4, Los Angeles 1. **Conference finals:** Vancouver 4, Chicago 1.
Stanley Cup finals: N.Y. Islanders 4, Vancouver 0.

1982-83

PRINCE OF WALES CONFERENCE

ADAMS DIVISION

Team	W	L	T	Pts.	GF	GA
Boston Bruins	50	20	10	110	327	228
Montreal Canadiens	42	24	14	98	350	286
Buffalo Sabres	38	29	13	89	318	285
Quebec Nordiques	34	34	12	80	343	336
Hartford Whalers	19	54	7	45	261	403

PATRICK DIVISION

Team	W	L	T	Pts.	GF	GA
Philadelphia Flyers	49	23	8	106	326	240
New York Islanders	42	26	12	96	302	226
Washington Capitals	39	25	16	94	306	283
New York Rangers	35	35	10	80	306	287
New Jersey Devils	17	49	14	48	230	338
Pittsburgh Penguins	18	53	9	45	257	394

CLARENCE CAMPBELL CONFERENCE

NORRIS DIVISION

Team	W	L	T	Pts	GF	GA
Chicago Blackhawks	47	23	10	104	338	268
Minnesota North Stars	40	24	16	96	321	290
Toronto Maple Leafs	28	40	12	68	293	330
St. Louis Blues	25	40	15	65	285	316
Detroit Red Wings	21	44	15	57	263	344

SMYTHE DIVISION

Team	W	L	T	Pts	GF	GA
Edmonton Oilers	47	21	12	106	424	315
Calgary Flames	32	34	14	78	321	317
Vancouver Canucks	30	35	15	75	303	309
Winnipeg Jets	33	39	8	74	311	333
Los Angeles Kings	27	41	12	66	308	365

PLAYOFFS

Wales Conference division semifinals: Boston 3, Quebec 1; Buffalo 3, Montreal 0; N.Y. Rangers 3, Philadelphia 0; N.Y. Islanders 3, Washington 1. **Division finals:** Boston 4, Buffalo 3; N.Y. Islanders 4, N.Y. Rangers 2. **Conference finals:** N.Y. Islanders 4, Boston 2.
Campbell Conference division semifinals: Chicago 3, St. Louis 1; Minnesota 3, Toronto 1; Edmonton 3, Winnipeg 0; Calgary 3, Vancouver 1. **Division finals:** Chicago 4, Minnesota 1; Edmonton 4, Calgary 1. **Conference finals:** Edmonton 4, Chicago 0.
Stanley Cup finals: N.Y. Islanders 4, Edmonton 0.

1983-84

PRINCE OF WALES CONFERENCE

ADAMS DIVISION

Team	W	L	T	Pts	GF	GA
Boston Bruins	49	25	6	104	336	261
Buffalo Sabres	48	25	7	103	315	257
Quebec Nordiques	42	28	10	94	360	278
Montreal Canadiens	35	40	5	75	286	295
Hartford Whalers	28	42	10	66	288	320

PATRICK DIVISION

Team	W	L	T	Pts	GF	GA
New York Islanders	50	26	4	104	357	269
Washington Capitals	48	27	5	101	308	226
Philadelphia Flyers	44	26	10	98	350	290
New York Rangers	42	29	9	93	314	304
New Jersey Devils	17	56	7	41	231	350
Pittsburgh Penguins	16	58	6	38	254	390

CLARENCE CAMPBELL CONFERENCE

NORRIS DIVISION

Team	W	L	T	Pts	GF	GA
Minnesota North Stars	39	31	10	88	345	344
St. Louis Blues	32	41	7	71	293	316
Detroit Red Wings	31	42	7	69	298	323
Chicago Blackhawks	30	42	8	68	277	311
Toronto Maple Leafs	26	45	9	61	303	387

SMYTHE DIVISION

Team	W	L	T	Pts	GF	GA
Edmonton Oilers	57	18	5	119	446	314
Calgary Flames	34	32	14	82	311	314
Vancouver Canucks	32	39	9	73	306	328
Winnipeg Jets	31	38	11	73	340	374
Los Angeles Kings	23	44	13	59	309	376

PLAYOFFS

Wales Conference division semifinals: Montreal 3, Boston 0; Quebec 3, Buffalo 0; N.Y. Islanders 3, N.Y. Rangers 2; Washington 3, Philadelphia 0. **Division finals:** Montreal 4,

Quebec 2; N.Y. Islanders 4, Washington 1. **Conference finals:** N.Y. Islanders 4, Montreal 2.
Campbell Conference division semifinals: Minnesota 3, Chicago 2; St. Louis 3, Detroit 1; Edmonton 3, Winnipeg 0; Calgary 3, Vancouver 1. **Division finals:** Minnesota 4, St. Louis 3; Edmonton 4, Calgary 3. **Conference finals:** Edmonton 4, Minnesota 0.
Stanley Cup finals: Edmonton 4, N.Y. Islanders 1.

1984-85

PRINCE OF WALES CONFERENCE

ADAMS DIVISION

Team	W	L	T	Pts.	GF	GA
Montreal Canadiens	41	27	12	94	309	262
Quebec Nordiques	41	30	9	91	323	275
Buffalo Sabres	38	28	14	90	290	237
Boston Bruins	36	34	10	82	303	287
Hartford Whalers	30	41	9	69	268	318

PATRICK DIVISION

Team	W	L	T	Pts.	GF	GA
Philadelphia Flyers	53	20	7	113	348	241
Washington Capitals	46	25	9	101	322	240
New York Islanders	40	34	6	86	345	312
New York Rangers	26	44	10	62	295	345
New Jersey Devils	22	48	10	54	264	346
Pittsburgh Penguins	24	51	5	53	276	385

CLARENCE CAMPBELL CONFERENCE

NORRIS DIVISION

Team	W	L	T	Pts.	GF	GA
St. Louis Blues	37	31	12	86	299	288
Chicago Blackhawks	38	35	7	83	309	299
Detroit Red Wings	27	41	12	66	313	357
Minnesota North Stars	25	43	12	62	268	321
Toronto Maple Leafs	20	52	8	48	253	358

SMYTHE DIVISION

Team	W	L	T	Pts.	GF	GA
Edmonton Oilers	49	20	11	109	401	298
Winnipeg Jets	43	27	10	96	358	332
Calgary Flames	41	27	12	94	363	302
Los Angeles Kings	34	32	14	82	339	326
Vancouver Canucks	25	46	9	59	284	401

PLAYOFFS

Wales Conference division semifinals: Montreal 3, Boston 2; Quebec 3, Buffalo 2; Philadelphia 3, N.Y. Rangers 0; N.Y. Islanders 3, Washington 2. **Division finals:** Quebec 4, Montreal 3; Philadelphia 4, N.Y. Islanders 1. **Conference finals:** Philadelphia 4, Quebec 2.
Campbell Conference division semifinals: Minnesota 3, St. Louis 0; Chicago 3, Detroit 0; Edmonton 3, Los Angeles 0; Winnipeg 3, Calgary 1. **Division finals:** Chicago 4, Minnesota 2; Edmonton 4, Winnipeg 0. **Conference finals:** Edmonton 4, Chicago 2.
Stanley Cup finals: Edmonton 4, Philadelphia 1.

1985-86

PRINCE OF WALES CONFERENCE

ADAMS DIVISION

Team	W	L	T	Pts.	GF	GA
Quebec Nordiques	43	31	6	92	330	289
Montreal Canadiens	40	33	7	87	330	280
Boston Bruins	37	31	12	86	311	288
Hartford Whalers	40	36	4	84	332	302
Buffalo Sabres	37	37	6	80	296	291

PATRICK DIVISION

Team	W	L	T	Pts.	GF	GA
Philadelphia Flyers	53	23	4	110	335	241
Washington Capitals	50	23	7	107	315	272
New York Islanders	39	29	12	90	327	284
New York Rangers	36	38	6	78	280	276
Pittsburgh Penguins	34	38	8	76	313	305
New Jersey Devils	28	49	3	59	300	374

CLARENCE CAMPBELL CONFERENCE

NORRIS DIVISION

Team	W	L	T	Pts.	GF	GA
Chicago Blackhawks	39	33	8	86	351	349
Minnesota North Stars	38	33	9	85	327	305
St. Louis Blues	37	34	9	83	302	291
Toronto Maple Leafs	25	48	7	57	311	386
Detroit Red Wings	17	57	6	40	266	415

SMYTHE DIVISION

Team	W	L	T	Pts.	GF	GA
Edmonton Oilers	56	17	7	119	426	310
Calgary Flames	40	31	9	89	354	315
Winnipeg Jets	26	47	7	59	295	372
Vancouver Canucks	23	44	13	59	282	333
Los Angeles Kings	23	49	8	54	284	389

PLAYOFFS

Wales Conference division semifinals: Hartford 3, Quebec 0; Montreal 3, Boston 0; N.Y. Rangers 3, Philadelphia 2; Washington 3, N.Y. Islanders 0. **Division finals:** Montreal 4, Hartford 3; N.Y. Rangers 4, Washington 2. **Conference finals:** Montreal 4, N.Y. Rangers 1.
Campbell Conference division semifinals: Toronto 3, Chicago 0; St. Louis 3, Minnesota 2; Edmonton 3, Vancouver 0; Calgary 3, Winnipeg 0. **Division finals:** St. Louis 4, Toronto 3; Calgary 4, Edmonton 3. **Conference finals:** Calgary 4, St. Louis 3.
Stanley Cup finals: Montreal 4, Calgary 1.

1986-87

PRINCE OF WALES CONFERENCE

ADAMS DIVISION

Team	W	L	T	Pts.	GF	GA
Hartford Whalers	43	30	7	93	287	270
Montreal Canadiens	41	29	10	92	277	241
Boston Bruins	39	34	7	85	301	276
Quebec Nordiques	31	39	10	72	267	276
Buffalo Sabres	28	44	8	64	280	308

PATRICK DIVISION

Team	W	L	T	Pts.	GF	GA
Philadelphia Flyers	46	26	8	100	310	245
Washington Capitals	38	32	10	86	285	278
New York Islanders	35	33	12	82	279	281
New York Rangers	34	38	8	76	307	323
Pittsburgh Penguins	30	38	12	72	297	290
New Jersey Devils	29	45	6	64	293	368

CLARENCE CAMPBELL CONFERENCE

NORRIS DIVISION

Team	W	L	T	Pts.	GF	GA
St. Louis Blues	32	33	15	79	281	293
Detroit Red Wings	34	36	10	78	260	274
Chicago Blackhawks	29	37	14	72	290	310
Toronto Maple Leafs	32	42	6	70	286	319
Minnesota North Stars	30	40	10	70	296	314

SMYTHE DIVISION

Team	W	L	T	Pts.	GF	GA
Edmonton Oilers	50	24	6	106	372	284
Calgary Flames	46	31	3	95	318	289

Team	W	L	T	Pts.	GF	GA
Winnipeg Jets	40	32	8	88	279	271
Los Angeles Kings	31	41	8	70	318	341
Vancouver Canucks	29	43	8	66	282	314

PLAYOFFS

Wales Conference division semifinals: Quebec 4, Hartford 2; Montreal 4, Boston 0; Philadelphia 4, N.Y. Rangers 2; N.Y. Islanders 4, Washington 3. **Division finals:** Montreal 4, Quebec 3; Philadelphia 4, N.Y. Islanders 3. **Conference finals:** Philadelphia 4, Montreal 2.
Campbell Conference division semifinals: Toronto 4, St. Louis 2; Detroit 4, Chicago 0; Edmonton 4, Los Angeles 1; Winnipeg 4, Calgary 2. **Division finals:** Detroit 4, Toronto 3; Edmonton 4, Winnipeg 0. **Conference finals:** Edmonton 4, Detroit 1.
Stanley Cup finals: Edmonton 4, Philadelphia 3.

1987-88

PRINCE OF WALES CONFERENCE

ADAMS DIVISION

Team	W	L	T	Pts.	GF	GA
Montreal Canadiens	45	22	13	103	298	238
Boston Bruins	44	30	6	94	300	251
Buffalo Sabres	37	32	11	85	283	305
Hartford Whalers	35	38	7	77	249	267
Quebec Nordiques	32	43	5	69	271	306

PATRICK DIVISION

Team	W	L	T	Pts.	GF	GA
New York Islanders	39	31	10	88	308	267
Philadelphia Flyers	38	33	9	85	292	292
Washington Capitals	38	33	9	85	281	249
New Jersey Devils	38	36	6	82	295	296
New York Rangers	36	34	10	82	300	283
Pittsburgh Penguins	36	35	9	81	319	316

CLARENCE CAMPBELL CONFERENCE

NORRIS DIVISION

Team	W	L	T	Pts.	GF	GA
Detroit Red Wings	41	28	11	93	322	269
St. Louis Blues	34	38	8	76	278	294
Chicago Blackhawks	30	41	9	69	284	328
Toronto Maple Leafs	21	49	10	52	273	345
Minnesota North Stars	19	48	13	51	242	349

SMYTHE DIVISION

Team	W	L	T	Pts.	GF	GA
Calgary Flames	48	23	9	105	397	305
Edmonton Oilers	44	25	11	99	363	288
Winnipeg Jets	33	36	11	77	292	310
Los Angeles Kings	30	42	8	68	318	359
Vancouver Canucks	25	46	9	59	272	320

PLAYOFFS

Wales Conference division semifinals: Montreal 4, Hartford 2; Boston 4, Buffalo 2; New Jersey 4, N.Y. Islanders 2; Washington 4, Philadelphia 3. **Division finals:** Boston 4, Montreal 1; New Jersey 4, Washington 3. **Conference finals:** Boston 4, New Jersey 3.
Campbell Conference division semifinals: Detroit 4, Toronto 2; St. Louis 4, Chicago 1; Calgary 4, Los Angeles 1; Edmonton 4, Winnipeg 1. **Division finals:** Detroit 4, St. Louis 1; Edmonton 4, Calgary 0. **Conference finals:** Edmonton 4, Detroit 1.
Stanley Cup finals: Edmonton 4, Boston 0.

PRINCE OF WALES CONFERENCE

ADAMS DIVISION

Team	W	L	T	Pts.	GF	GA
Montreal Canadiens	53	18	9	115	315	218
Boston Bruins	37	29	14	88	289	256
Buffalo Sabres	38	35	7	83	291	299
Hartford Whalers	37	38	5	79	299	290
Quebec Nordiques	27	46	7	61	269	342

PATRICK DIVISION

Team	W	L	T	Pts.	GF	GA
Washington Capitals	41	29	10	92	305	259
Pittsburgh Penguins	40	33	7	87	347	349
New York Rangers	37	35	8	82	310	307
Philadelphia Flyers	36	36	8	80	307	285
New Jersey Devils	27	41	12	66	281	325
New York Islanders	28	47	5	61	265	325

CLARENCE CAMPBELL CONFERENCE

NORRIS DIVISION

Team	W	L	T	Pts.	GF	GA
Detroit Red Wings	34	34	12	80	313	316
St. Louis Blues	33	35	12	78	275	285
Minnesota North Stars	27	37	16	70	258	278
Chicago Blackhawks	27	41	12	66	297	335
Toronto Maple Leafs	28	46	6	62	259	342

SMYTHE DIVISION

Team	W	L	T	Pts.	GF	GA
Calgary Flames	54	17	9	117	354	226
Los Angeles Kings	42	31	7	91	376	335
Edmonton Oilers	38	34	8	84	325	306
Vancouver Canucks	33	39	8	74	251	253
Winnipeg Jets	26	42	12	64	300	355

PLAYOFFS

Wales Conference division semifinals: Montreal 4, Hartford 0; Boston 4, Buffalo 1; Philadelphia 4, Washington 2; Pittsburgh 4, N.Y. Rangers 0. **Division finals:** Montreal 4, Boston 1; Philadelphia 4, Pittsburgh 3. **Conference finals:** Montreal 4, Philadelphia 2.

Campbell Conference division semifinals: Chicago 4, Detroit 2; St. Louis 4, Minnesota 1; Calgary 4, Vancouver 3; Los Angeles 4, Edmonton 3. **Division finals:** Chicago 4, St. Louis 1; Calgary 4, Los Angeles 0. **Conference finals:** Calgary 4, Chicago 1.

Stanley Cup finals: Calgary 4, Montreal 2.

PRINCE OF WALES CONFERENCE

ADAMS DIVISION

Team	W	L	T	Pts.	GF	GA
Boston Bruins	46	25	9	101	289	232
Buffalo Sabres	45	27	8	98	286	248
Montreal Canadiens	41	28	11	93	288	234
Hartford Whalers	38	33	9	85	275	268
Quebec Nordiques	12	61	7	31	240	407

PATRICK DIVISION

Team	W	L	T	Pts.	GF	GA
New York Rangers	36	31	13	85	279	267
New Jersey Devils	37	34	9	83	295	288
Washington Capitals	36	38	6	78	284	275
New York Islanders	31	38	11	73	281	288
Pittsburgh Penguins	32	40	8	72	318	359
Philadelphia Flyers	30	39	11	71	290	297

CLARENCE CAMPBELL CONFERENCE

NORRIS DIVISION

Team	W	L	T	Pts.	GF	GA
Chicago Blackhawks	41	33	6	88	316	294
St. Louis Blues	37	34	9	83	295	279
Toronto Maple Leafs	38	38	4	80	337	358
Minnesota North Stars	36	40	4	76	284	291
Detroit Red Wings	28	38	14	70	288	323

SMYTHE DIVISION

Team	W	L	T	Pts.	GF	GA
Calgary Flames	42	23	15	99	348	265
Edmonton Oilers	38	28	14	90	315	283
Winnipeg Jets	37	32	11	85	298	290
Los Angeles Kings	34	39	7	75	338	337
Vancouver Canucks	25	41	14	64	245	306

PLAYOFFS

Wales Conference division semifinals: Boston 4, Hartford 3; Montreal 4, Buffalo 2; N.Y. Rangers 4, N.Y. Islanders 1; Washington 4, New Jersey 2. **Division finals:** Boston 4, Montreal 1; Washington 4, N.Y. Rangers 1. **Conference finals:** Boston 4, Washington 0.

Campbell Conference division semifinals: Chicago 4, Minnesota 3; St. Louis 4, Toronto 1; Los Angeles 4, Calgary 2; Edmonton 4, Winnipeg 3. **Division finals:** Chicago 4, St. Louis 3; Edmonton 4, Los Angeles 0. **Conference finals:** Edmonton 4, Chicago 2.

Stanley Cup finals: Edmonton 4, Boston 1.

PRINCE OF WALES CONFERENCE

ADAMS DIVISION

Team	W	L	T	Pts.	GF	GA
Boston Bruins	44	24	12	100	299	264
Montreal Canadiens	39	30	11	89	273	249
Buffalo Sabres	31	30	19	81	292	278
Hartford Whalers	31	38	11	73	238	276
Quebec Nordiques	16	50	14	46	236	354

PATRICK DIVISION

Team	W	L	T	Pts.	GF	GA
Pittsburgh Penguins	41	33	6	88	342	305
New York Rangers	36	31	13	85	297	265
Washington Capitals	37	36	7	81	258	258
New Jersey Devils	32	33	15	79	272	264
Philadelphia Flyers	33	37	10	76	252	267
New York Islanders	25	45	10	60	223	290

CLARENCE CAMPBELL CONFERENCE

NORRIS DIVISION

Team	W	L	T	Pts.	GF	GA
Chicago Blackhawks	49	23	8	106	284	211
St. Louis Blues	47	22	11	105	310	250
Detroit Red Wings	34	38	8	76	273	298
Minnesota North Stars	27	39	14	68	256	266
Toronto Maple Leafs	23	46	11	57	241	318

SMYTHE DIVISION

Team	W	L	T	Pts.	GF	GA
Los Angeles Kings	46	24	10	102	340	254
Calgary Flames	46	26	8	100	344	263
Edmonton Oilers	37	37	6	80	272	272
Vancouver Canucks	28	43	9	65	243	315
Winnipeg Jets	26	43	11	63	260	288

PLAYOFFS

Wales Conference division semifinals: Boston 4, Hartford 2; Montreal 4, Buffalo 2; Pittsburgh 4, New Jersey 3; Washington

NHL HISTORY *Year-by-year standings*

4, N.Y. Rangers 2. **Division finals:** Boston 4, Montreal 3; Pittsburgh 4, Washington 1. **Conference finals:** Pittsburgh 4, Boston 2.
Campbell Conference division semifinals: Minnesota 4, Chicago 2; St. Louis 4, Detroit 3; Los Angeles 4, Vancouver 2; Edmonton 4, Calgary 3. **Division finals:** Minnesota 4, St. Louis 2; Edmonton 4, Los Angeles 2. **Conference finals:** Minnesota 4, Edmonton 1.
Stanley Cup finals: Pittsburgh 4, Minnesota 2.

1991-92

PRINCE OF WALES CONFERENCE

ADAMS DIVISION

Team	W	L	T	Pts.	GF	GA
Montreal Canadiens	41	28	11	93	267	207
Boston Bruins	36	32	12	84	270	275
Buffalo Sabres	31	37	12	74	289	299
Hartford Whalers	26	41	13	65	247	283
Quebec Nordiques	20	48	12	52	255	318

PATRICK DIVISION

Team	W	L	T	Pts.	GF	GA
New York Rangers	50	25	5	105	321	246
Washington Capitals	45	27	8	98	330	275
Pittsburgh Penguins	39	32	9	87	343	308
New Jersey Devils	38	31	11	87	289	259
New York Islanders	34	35	11	79	291	299
Philadelphia Flyers	32	37	11	75	252	273

CLARENCE CAMPBELL CONFERENCE

NORRIS DIVISION

Team	W	L	T	Pts.	GF	GA
Detroit Red Wings	43	25	12	98	320	256
Chicago Blackhawks	36	29	15	87	257	236
St. Louis Blues	36	33	11	83	279	266
Minnesota North Stars	32	42	6	70	246	278
Toronto Maple Leafs	30	43	7	67	234	294

SMYTHE DIVISION

Team	W	L	T	Pts.	GF	GA
Vancouver Canucks	42	26	12	96	285	250
Los Angeles Kings	35	31	14	84	287	296
Edmonton Oilers	36	34	10	82	295	297
Winnipeg Jets	33	32	15	81	251	244
Calgary Flames	31	37	12	74	296	305
San Jose Sharks	17	58	5	39	219	359

PLAYOFFS

Wales Conference division semifinals: Montreal 4, Hartford 3; Boston 4, Buffalo 3; N.Y. Rangers 4, New Jersey 3; Pittsburgh 4, Washington 3. **Division finals:** Boston 4, Montreal 0; Pittsburgh 4, N.Y. Rangers 2. **Conference finals:** Pittsburgh 4, Boston 0.
Campbell Conference division semifinals: Detroit 4, Minnesota 3; Chicago 4, St. Louis 2; Vancouver 4, Winnipeg 3; Edmonton 4, Los Angeles 2. **Division finals:** Chicago 4, Detroit 0; Edmonton 4, Vancouver 2. **Conference finals:** Chicago 4, Edmonton 0.
Stanley Cup finals: Pittsburgh 4, Chicago 0.

1992-93

PRINCE OF WALES CONFERENCE

ADAMS DIVISION

Team	W	L	T	Pts.	GF	GA
Boston Bruins	51	26	7	109	332	268
Quebec Nordiques	47	27	10	104	351	300
Montreal Canadiens	48	30	6	102	326	280

Team	W	L	T	Pts.	GF	GA
Buffalo Sabres	38	36	10	86	335	297
Hartford Whalers	26	52	6	58	284	369
Ottawa Senators	10	70	4	24	202	395

PATRICK DIVISION

Team	W	L	T	Pts.	GF	GA
Pittsburgh Penguins	56	21	7	119	367	268
Washington Capitals	43	34	7	93	325	286
New York Islanders	40	37	7	87	335	297
New Jersey Devils	40	37	7	87	308	299
Philadelphia Flyers	36	37	11	83	319	319
New York Rangers	34	39	11	79	304	308

CLARENCE CAMPBELL CONFERENCE

NORRIS DIVISION

Team	W	L	T	Pts.	GF	GA
Chicago Blackhawks	47	25	12	106	279	230
Detroit Red Wings	47	28	9	103	369	280
Toronto Maple Leafs	44	29	11	99	288	241
St. Louis Blues	37	36	11	85	282	278
Minnesota North Stars	36	38	10	82	272	293
Tampa Bay Lightning	23	54	7	53	245	332

SMYTHE DIVISION

Team	W	L	T	Pts.	GF	GA
Vancouver Canucks	46	29	9	101	346	278
Calgary Flames	43	30	11	97	322	282
Los Angeles Kings	39	35	10	88	338	340
Winnipeg Jets	40	37	7	87	322	320
Edmonton Oilers	26	50	8	60	242	337
San Jose Sharks	11	71	2	24	218	414

PLAYOFFS

Wales Conference division semifinals: Buffalo 4, Boston 0; Montreal 4, Quebec 2; Pittsburgh 4, New Jersey 1; N.Y. Islanders 4, Washington 2. **Division finals:** Montreal 4, Buffalo 0; N.Y. Islanders 4, Pittsburgh 3. **Conference finals:** Montreal 4, N.Y. Islanders 1.
Campbell Conference division semifinals: St. Louis 4, Chicago 0; Toronto 4, Detroit 3; Vancouver 4, Winnipeg 2; Los Angeles 4, Calgary 2. **Division finals:** Toronto 4, St. Louis 3; Los Angeles 4, Vancouver 2. **Conference finals:** Los Angeles 4, Toronto 3.
Stanley Cup finals: Montreal 4, Los Angeles 1.

1993-94

EASTERN CONFERENCE

ATLANTIC DIVISION

Team	W	L	T	Pts.	GF	GA
New York Rangers	52	24	8	112	299	231
New Jersey Devils	47	25	12	106	306	220
Washington Capitals	39	35	10	88	277	263
New York Islanders	36	36	12	84	282	264
Florida Panthers	33	34	17	83	233	233
Philadelphia Flyers	35	39	10	80	294	314
Tampa Bay Lightning	30	43	11	71	224	251

NORTHEAST DIVISION

Team	W	L	T	Pts.	GF	GA
Pittsburgh Penguins	44	27	13	101	299	285
Boston Bruins	42	29	13	97	289	252
Montreal Canadiens	41	29	14	96	283	248
Buffalo Sabres	43	32	9	95	282	218
Quebec Nordiques	34	42	8	76	277	292
Hartford Whalers	27	48	9	63	227	288
Ottawa Senators	14	61	9	37	201	397

WESTERN CONFERENCE

CENTRAL DIVISION

Team	W	L	T	Pts.	GF	GA
Detroit Red Wings	46	30	8	100	356	275
Toronto Maple Leafs	43	29	12	98	280	243
Dallas Stars	42	29	13	97	286	265
St. Louis Blues	40	33	11	91	270	283
Chicago Blackhawks	39	36	9	87	254	240
Winnipeg Jets	24	51	9	57	245	344

PACIFIC DIVISION

Team	W	L	T	Pts.	GF	GA
Calgary Flames	42	29	13	97	302	256
Vancouver Canucks	41	40	3	85	279	276
San Jose Sharks	33	35	16	82	252	265
Mighty Ducks of Anaheim ..	33	46	5	71	229	251
Los Angeles Kings	27	45	12	66	294	322
Edmonton Oilers	25	45	14	64	261	305

PLAYOFFS

Eastern Conference quarterfinals: N.Y. Rangers 4, N.Y. Islanders 0; Washington 4, Pittsburgh 2; New Jersey 4, Buffalo 3; Boston 4, Montreal 3. **Semifinals:** N.Y. Rangers 4, Washington 1; New Jersey 4, Boston 2. **Finals:** N.Y. Rangers 4, New Jersey 3.
Western Conference quarterfinals: San Jose 4, Detroit 3; Vancouver 4, Calgary 3; Toronto 4, Chicago 2; Dallas 4, St. Louis 0. **Semifinals:** Toronto 4, San Jose 3; Vancouver 4, Dallas 1. **Finals:** Vancouver 4, Toronto 1.
Stanley Cup finals: N.Y. Rangers 4, Vancouver 3.

1994-95

EASTERN CONFERENCE

ATLANTIC DIVISION

Team	W	L	T	Pts.	GF	GA
Philadelphia Flyers	28	16	4	60	150	132
New Jersey Devils	22	18	8	52	136	121
Washington Capitals	22	18	8	52	136	120
New York Rangers	22	23	3	47	139	134
Florida Panthers	20	22	6	46	115	127
Tampa Bay Lightning	17	28	3	37	120	144
New York Islanders	15	28	5	35	126	158

NORTHEAST DIVISION

Team	W	L	T	Pts.	GF	GA
Quebec Nordiques	30	13	5	65	185	134
Pittsburgh Penguins	29	16	3	61	181	158
Boston Bruins	27	18	3	57	150	127
Buffalo Sabres	22	19	7	51	130	119
Hartford Whalers	19	24	5	43	127	141
Montreal Canadiens	18	23	7	43	125	148
Ottawa Senators	9	34	5	23	117	174

WESTERN CONFERENCE

CENTRAL DIVISION

Team	W	L	T	Pts.	GF	GA
Detroit Red Wings	33	11	4	70	180	117
St. Louis Blues	28	15	5	61	178	135
Chicago Blackhawks	24	19	5	53	156	115
Toronto Maple Leafs	21	19	8	50	135	146
Dallas Stars	17	23	8	42	136	135
Winnipeg Jets	16	25	7	39	157	177

PACIFIC DIVISION

Team	W	L	T	Pts.	GF	GA
Calgary Flames	24	17	7	55	163	135
Vancouver Canucks	18	18	12	48	153	148
San Jose Sharks	19	25	4	42	129	161
Los Angeles Kings	16	23	9	41	142	174

Team	W	L	T	Pts.	GF	GA
Edmonton Oilers	17	27	4	38	136	183
Mighty Ducks of Anaheim ..	16	27	5	37	125	164

PLAYOFFS

Eastern Conference quarterfinals: N.Y. Rangers 4, Quebec 2; Pittsburgh 4, Washington 3; Philadelphia 4, Buffalo 1; New Jersey 4, Boston 1. **Semifinals:** New Jersey 4, Pittsburgh 1; Philadelphia 4, N.Y. Rangers 0. **Finals:** New Jersey 4, Philadelphia 2.
Western Conference quarterfinals: Detroit 4, Dallas 1; Vancouver 4, St. Louis 3; Chicago 4, Toronto 3; San Jose 4, Calgary 3. **Semifinals:** Detroit 4, San Jose 0; Chicago 4, Vancouver 0. **Finals:** Detroit 4, Chicago 1.
Stanley Cup finals: New Jersey 4, Detroit 0.

1995-96

EASTERN CONFERENCE

ATLANTIC DIVISION

Team	W	L	T	Pts.	GF	GA
Philadelphia Flyers	45	24	13	103	282	208
New York Rangers	41	27	14	96	272	237
Florida Panthers	41	31	10	92	254	234
Washington Capitals	39	32	11	89	234	204
Tampa Bay Lightning	38	32	12	88	238	248
New Jersey Devils	37	33	12	86	215	202
New York Islanders	22	50	10	54	229	315

NORTHEAST DIVISION

Team	W	L	T	Pts.	GF	GA
Pittsburgh Penguins	49	29	4	102	362	284
Boston Bruins	40	31	11	91	282	269
Montreal Canadiens	40	32	10	90	265	248
Hartford Whalers	34	39	9	77	237	259
Buffalo Sabres	33	42	7	73	247	262
Ottawa Senators	18	59	5	41	191	291

WESTERN CONFERENCE

CENTRAL DIVISION

Team	W	L	T	Pts.	GF	GA
Detroit Red Wings	62	13	7	131	325	181
Chicago Blackhawks	40	28	14	94	273	220
Toronto Maple Leafs	34	36	12	80	247	252
St. Louis Blues	32	34	16	80	219	248
Winnipeg Jets	36	40	6	78	275	291
Dallas Stars	26	42	14	66	227	280

PACIFIC DIVISION

Team	W	L	T	Pts.	GF	GA
Colorado Avalanche	47	25	10	104	326	240
Calgary Flames	34	37	11	79	241	240
Vancouver Canucks	32	35	15	79	278	278
Mighty Ducks of Anaheim ..	35	39	8	78	234	247
Edmonton Oilers	30	44	8	68	240	304
Los Angeles Kings	24	40	18	66	256	302
San Jose Sharks	20	55	7	47	252	357

PLAYOFFS

Eastern Conference quarterfinals: Philadelphia 4, Tampa Bay 2; Pittsburgh 4, Washington 2; N.Y. Rangers 4, Montreal 2; Florida 4, Boston 1. **Semifinals:** Florida 4, Philadelphia 2; Pittsburgh 4, N.Y. Rangers 1. **Finals:** Florida 4, Pittsburgh 3.
Western Conference quarterfinals: Detroit 4, Winnipeg 2; Colorado 4, Vancouver 2; Chicago 4, Calgary 0; St. Louis 4, Toronto 2. **Semifinals:** Detroit 4, St. Louis 3; Colorado 4, Chicago 2. **Finals:** Colorado 4, Detroit 2.
Stanley Cup finals: Colorado 4, Florida 0.

1996-97

EASTERN CONFERENCE

ATLANTIC DIVISION

Team	W	L	T	Pts.	GF	GA
New Jersey Devils	45	23	14	104	231	182
Philadelphia Flyers	45	24	13	103	274	217
Florida Panthers	35	28	19	89	221	201
New York Rangers	38	34	10	86	258	231
Washington Capitals	33	40	9	75	214	231
Tampa Bay Lightning	32	40	10	74	217	247
New York Islanders	29	41	12	70	240	250

NORTHEAST DIVISION

Team	W	L	T	Pts.	GF	GA
Buffalo Sabres	40	30	12	92	237	208
Pittsburgh Penguins	38	36	8	84	285	280
Ottawa Senators	31	36	15	77	226	234
Montreal Canadiens	31	36	15	77	249	276
Hartford Whalers	32	39	11	75	226	256
Boston Bruins	26	47	9	61	234	300

WESTERN CONFERENCE

CENTRAL DIVISION

Team	W	L	T	Pts.	GF	GA
Dallas Stars	48	26	8	104	252	198
Detroit Red Wings	38	26	18	94	253	197
Phoenix Coyotes	38	37	7	83	240	243
St. Louis Blues	36	35	11	83	236	239
Chicago Blackhawks	34	35	13	81	223	210
Toronto Maple Leafs	30	44	8	68	230	273

PACIFIC DIVISION

Team	W	L	T	Pts.	GF	GA
Colorado Avalanche	49	24	9	107	277	205
Mighty Ducks of Anaheim	36	33	13	85	245	233
Edmonton Oilers	36	37	9	81	252	247
Vancouver Canucks	35	40	7	77	257	273
Calgary Flames	32	41	9	73	214	239
Los Angeles Kings	28	43	11	67	214	268
San Jose Sharks	27	47	8	62	211	278

PLAYOFFS

Eastern Conference quarterfinals: New Jersey 4, Montreal 1; Buffalo 4, Ottawa 3; Philadelphia 4, Pittsburgh 1; N.Y. Rangers 4, Florida 1. **Semifinals:** N.Y. Rangers 4, New Jersey 1; Philadelphia 4, Buffalo 1. **Finals:** Philadelphia 4, N.Y. Rangers 1. **Western Conference quarterfinals:** Colorado 4, Chicago 2; Edmonton 4, Dallas 3; Detroit 4, St. Louis 2; Anaheim 4, Phoenix 3. **Semifinals:** Colorado 4, Edmonton 1; Detroit 4, Anaheim 0. **Finals:** Detroit 4, Colorado 2. **Stanley Cup finals:** Detroit 4, Philadelphia 0.

1997-98

EASTERN CONFERENCE

ATLANTIC DIVISION

Team	W	L	T	Pts.	GF	GA
New Jersey Devils	48	23	11	107	225	166
Philadelphia Flyers	42	29	11	95	242	193
Washington Capitals	40	30	12	92	219	202
New York Islanders	30	41	11	71	212	225
New York Rangers	25	39	18	68	197	231
Florida Panthers	24	43	15	63	203	256
Tampa Bay Lightning	17	55	10	44	151	269

NORTHEAST DIVISION

Team	W	L	T	Pts.	GF	GA
Pittsburgh Penguins	40	24	18	98	228	188
Boston Bruins	39	30	13	91	221	194
Buffalo Sabres	36	29	17	89	211	187
Montreal Canadiens	37	32	13	87	235	208
Ottawa Senators	34	33	15	83	193	200
Carolina Hurricanes	33	41	8	74	200	219

WESTERN CONFERENCE

CENTRAL DIVISION

Team	W	L	T	Pts.	GF	GA
Dallas Stars	49	22	11	109	242	167
Detroit Red Wings	44	23	15	103	250	196
St. Louis Blues	45	29	8	98	256	204
Phoenix Coyotes	35	35	12	82	224	227
Chicago Blackhawks	30	39	13	73	192	199
Toronto Maple Leafs	30	43	9	69	194	237

PACIFIC DIVISION

Team	W	L	T	Pts.	GF	GA
Colorado Avalanche	39	26	17	95	231	205
Los Angeles Kings	38	33	11	87	227	225
Edmonton Oilers	35	37	10	80	215	224
San Jose Sharks	34	38	10	78	210	216
Calgary Flames	26	41	15	67	217	252
Mighty Ducks of Anaheim	26	43	13	65	205	261
Vancouver Canucks	25	43	14	64	224	273

PLAYOFFS

Eastern Conference quarterfinals: Ottawa 4, New Jersey 2; Washington 4, Boston 2; Buffalo 4, Philadelphia 1; Montreal 4, Pittsburgh 2. **Semifinals:** Washington 4, Ottawa 1; Buffalo 4, Montreal 0. **Finals:** Washington 4, Buffalo 2. **Western Conference quarterfinals:** Edmonton 4, Colorado 3; Dallas 4, San Jose 2; Detroit 4, Phoenix 2; St. Louis 4, Los Angeles 0. **Semifinals:** Dallas 4, Edmonton 1; Detroit 4, St. Louis 2. **Finals:** Detroit 4, Dallas 2. **Stanley Cup finals:** Detroit 4, Washington 0.

1998-99

EASTERN CONFERENCE

ATLANTIC DIVISION

Team	W	L	T	Pts.	GF	GA
New Jersey Devils	47	24	11	105	248	196
Philadelphia Flyers	37	26	19	93	231	196
Pittsburgh Penguins	38	30	14	90	242	225
New York Rangers	33	38	11	77	217	227
New York Islanders	24	48	10	58	194	244

NORTHEAST DIVISION

Team	W	L	T	Pts.	GF	GA
Ottawa Senators	44	23	15	103	239	179
Toronto Maple Leafs	45	30	7	97	268	231
Boston Bruins	39	30	13	91	214	181
Buffalo Sabres	37	28	17	91	207	175
Montreal Canadiens	32	39	11	75	184	209

SOUTHEAST DIVISION

Team	W	L	T	Pts.	GF	GA
Carolina Hurricanes	34	30	18	86	210	202
Florida Panthers	30	34	18	78	210	228
Washington Capitals	31	45	6	68	200	218
Tampa Bay Lightning	19	54	9	47	179	292

WESTERN CONFERENCE

CENTRAL DIVISION

Team	W	L	T	Pts.	GF	GA
Detroit Red Wings	43	32	7	93	245	202
St. Louis Blues	37	32	13	87	237	209
Chicago Blackhawks	29	41	12	70	202	248
Nashville Predators	28	47	7	63	190	261

PACIFIC DIVISION

Team	W	L	T	Pts.	GF	GA
Dallas Stars	51	19	12	114	236	168
Phoenix Coyotes	39	31	12	90	205	197
Anaheim Mighty Ducks	35	34	13	83	215	206
San Jose Sharks	31	33	18	80	196	191
Los Angeles Kings	32	45	5	69	189	222

NORTHWEST DIVISION

Team	W	L	T	Pts.	GF	GA
Colorado Avalanche	44	28	10	98	239	205
Edmonton Oilers	33	37	12	78	230	226
Calgary Flames	30	40	12	72	211	234
Vancouver Canucks	23	47	12	58	192	258

PLAYOFFS

Eastern Conference quarterfinals: Pittsburgh 4, New Jersey 3; Buffalo 4, Ottawa 0; Boston 4, Carolina 2; Toronto 4, Philadelphia 2. **Semifinals:** Toronto 4, Pittsburgh 2; Buffalo 4, Boston 2. **Finals:** Buffalo 4, Toronto 1.
Western Conference quarterfinals: Dallas 4, Edmonton 0; Colorado 4, San Jose 2; Detroit 4, Anaheim 0; St. Louis 4, Phoenix 3. **Semifinals:** Dallas 4, St. Louis 2; Colorado 4, Detroit 2. **Finals:** Dallas 4, Colorado 3.
Stanley Cup finals: Dallas 4, Buffalo 2.

1999-2000

EASTERN CONFERENCE

ATLANTIC DIVISION

Team	W	L	T	OTL	Pts.	GF	GA
Philadelphia Flyers	45	22	12	3	105	237	179
New Jersey Devils	45	24	8	5	103	251	203
Pittsburgh Penguins	37	31	8	6	88	241	236
New York Rangers	29	38	12	3	73	218	246
New York Islanders	24	48	9	1	58	194	275

NORTHEAST DIVISION

Team	W	L	T	OTL	Pts.	GF	GA
Toronto Maple Leafs	45	27	7	3	100	246	222
Ottawa Senators	41	28	11	2	95	244	210
Buffalo Sabres	35	32	11	4	85	213	204
Montreal Canadiens	35	34	9	4	83	196	194
Boston Bruins	24	33	19	6	73	210	248

SOUTHEAST DIVISION

Team	W	L	T	OTL	Pts.	GF	GA
Washington Capitals	44	24	12	2	102	227	194
Florida Panthers	43	27	6	6	98	244	209
Carolina Hurricanes	37	35	10	0	84	217	216
Tampa Bay Lightning	19	47	9	7	54	204	310
Atlanta Thrashers	14	57	7	4	39	170	313

WESTERN CONFERENCE

CENTRAL DIVISION

Team	W	L	T	OTL	Pts.	GF	GA
St. Louis Blues	51	19	11	1	114	248	165
Detroit Red Wings	48	22	10	2	108	278	210
Chicago Blackhawks	33	37	10	2	78	242	245
Nashville Predators	28	40	7	7	70	199	240

PACIFIC DIVISION

Team	W	L	T	OTL	Pts.	GF	GA
Dallas Stars	43	23	10	6	102	211	184
Los Angeles Kings	39	27	12	4	94	245	228
Phoenix Coyotes	39	31	8	4	90	232	228
San Jose Sharks	35	30	10	7	87	225	214
Mighty Ducks of Anaheim	34	33	12	3	83	217	227

NORTHWEST DIVISION

Team	W	L	T	OTL	Pts.	GF	GA
Colorado Avalanche	42	28	11	1	96	233	201
Edmonton Oilers	32	26	16	8	88	226	212
Vancouver Canucks	30	29	15	8	83	227	237
Calgary Flames	31	36	10	5	77	211	256

PLAYOFFS

Eastern Conference quarterfinals: Philadelphia 4, Buffalo 1; Pittsburgh 4, Washington 1; Toronto 4, Ottawa 2; New Jersey 4, Florida 0. **Semifinals:** Philadelphia 4, Pittsburgh 2; New Jersey 4, Toronto 2. **Finals:** New Jersey 4, Philadelphia 3.
Western Conference quarterfinals: San Jose 4, St. Louis 3; Dallas 4, Edmonton 1; Colorado 4, Phoenix 1; Detroit 4, Los Angeles 0. **Semifinals:** Dallas 4, San Jose 1; Colorado 4, Detroit 1. **Finals:** Dallas 4, Colorado 3.
Stanley Cup finals: New Jersey 4, Dallas 2.

2000-01

EASTERN CONFERENCE

ATLANTIC DIVISION

Team	W	L	T	OTL	Pts.	GF	GA
New Jersey Devils	48	19	12	3	111	295	195
Philadelphia Flyers	43	25	11	3	100	240	207
Pittsburgh Penguins	42	28	9	3	96	281	256
New York Rangers	33	43	5	1	72	250	290
New York Islanders	21	51	7	3	52	185	268

NORTHEAST DIVISION

Team	W	L	T	OTL	Pts.	GF	GA
Ottawa Senators	48	21	9	4	109	274	205
Buffalo Sabres	46	30	5	1	98	218	184
Toronto Maple Leafs	37	29	11	5	90	232	207
Boston Bruins	36	30	8	8	88	227	249
Montreal Canadiens	28	40	8	6	70	206	232

SOUTHEAST DIVISION

Team	W	L	T	OTL	Pts.	GF	GA
Washington Capitals	41	27	10	4	96	233	211
Carolina Hurricanes	38	32	9	3	88	212	225
Florida Panthers	22	38	13	9	66	200	246
Atlanta Thrashers	23	45	12	2	60	211	289
Tampa Bay Lightning	24	47	6	5	59	201	280

WESTERN CONFERENCE

CENTRAL DIVISION

Team	W	L	T	OTL	Pts.	GF	GA
Detroit Red Wings	49	20	9	4	111	253	202
St. Louis Blues	43	22	12	5	103	249	195
Nashville Predators	34	36	9	3	80	186	200
Chicago Blackhawks	29	40	8	5	71	210	246
Columbus Blue Jackets	28	39	9	6	71	190	233

PACIFIC DIVISION

Team	W	L	T	OTL	Pts.	GF	GA
Dallas Stars	48	24	8	2	106	241	187
San Jose Sharks	40	27	12	3	95	217	192
Los Angeles Kings	38	28	13	3	92	252	228
Phoenix Coyotes	35	27	17	3	90	214	212
Mighty Ducks of Anaheim	25	41	11	5	66	188	245

NHL HISTORY Year-by-year standings

– 159 –

NORTHWEST DIVISION

Team	W	L	T	OTL	Pts.	GF	GA
Colorado Rockies	52	16	10	4	118	270	192
Edmonton Oilers	39	28	12	3	93	243	222
Vancouver Canucks	36	28	11	7	90	239	238
Calgary Flames	27	36	15	4	73	197	236
Minnesota Wild	25	39	13	5	68	168	210

PLAYOFFS

Eastern Conference quarterfinals: New Jersey 4, Carolina 2; Toronto 4, Ottawa 0; Pittsburgh 4, Washington 2; Buffalo 4, Philadelphia 2. **Semifinals:** New Jersey 4, Toronto 3; Pittsburgh 4, Buffalo 3. **Finals:** New Jersey 4, Pittsburgh 1.
Western Conference quarterfinals: Colorado 4, Vancouver 0; Los Angeles 4, Detroit 2; Dallas 4, Edmonton 2; St. Louis 4, San Jose 2. **Semifinals:** Colorado 4, Los Angeles 3; St. Louis 4, Dallas 0. **Finals:** Colorado 4, St. Louis 1.
Stanley Cup finals: Colorado 4, New Jersey 3.

2001-02

EASTERN CONFERENCE

NORTHEAST DIVISION

Team	W	L	T	OTL	Pts.	GF	GA
Boston Bruins	43	24	6	9	101	236	201
Toronto Maple Leafs	43	25	10	4	100	249	207
Ottawa Senators	39	27	9	7	94	243	208
Montreal Canadiens	36	31	12	3	87	207	209
Buffalo Sabres	35	35	11	1	82	213	200

ATLANTIC DIVISION

Team	W	L	T	OTL	Pts.	GF	GA
Philadelphia Flyers	42	27	10	3	97	234	192
New York Islanders	42	28	8	4	96	239	220
New Jersey Devils	41	28	9	4	95	205	187
New York Rangers	36	38	4	4	80	227	258
Pittsburgh Penguins	28	41	8	5	69	198	249

SOUTHEAST DIVISION

Team	W	L	T	OTL	Pts.	GF	GA
Carolina Hurricanes	35	26	16	5	91	217	217
Washington Capitals	36	33	11	2	85	228	240
Tampa Bay Lightning	27	40	11	4	69	178	219
Florida Panthers	22	44	10	6	60	180	250
Atlanta Thrashers	19	47	11	5	54	187	288

WESTERN CONFERENCE

CENTRAL DIVISION

Team	W	L	T	OTL	Pts.	GF	GA
Detroit Red Wings	51	17	10	4	116	251	187
St. Louis Blues	43	27	8	4	98	227	188
Chicago Blackhawks	41	27	13	1	96	216	207
Nashville Predators	28	41	13	0	69	196	230
Columbus Blue Jackets	22	47	8	5	57	164	255

PACIFIC DIVISION

Team	W	L	T	OTL	Pts.	GF	GA
San Jose Sharks	44	27	8	3	99	248	199
Phoenix Coyotes	40	27	9	6	95	228	210
Los Angeles Kings	40	27	11	4	95	214	190
Dallas Stars	36	28	13	5	90	215	213
Mighty Ducks of Anaheim	29	42	8	3	69	175	198

NORTHWEST DIVISION

Team	W	L	T	OTL	Pts.	GF	GA
Colorado Avalanche	45	28	8	1	99	212	169
Vancouver Canucks	42	30	7	3	94	254	211
Edmonton Oilers	38	28	12	4	92	205	182
Calgary Flames	32	35	12	3	79	201	220
Minnesota Wild	26	35	12	9	73	195	238

PLAYOFFS

Eastern Conference quarterfinals: Ottawa 4, Philadelphia 1; Montreal 4, Boston 2; Carolina 4, New Jersey 2; Toronto 4, N.Y. Islanders 3. **Semifinals:** Toronto 4, Ottawa 3; Carolina 4, Montreal 2. **Finals:** Carolina 4, Toronto 2.
Western Conference quarterfinals: San Jose 4, Phoenix 1; St. Louis 4, Chicago 1; Colorado 4, Los Angeles 3; Detroit 4, Vancouver 2. **Semifinals:** Colorado 4, San Jose 3; Detroit 4, St. Louis 1. **Finals:** Detroit 4, Colorado 3.
Stanley Cup finals: Detroit 4, Carolina 1.

RECORDS

Most seasons
   NHL: 26—Gordie Howe, Detroit Red Wings and Hartford Whalers, 1946-47 through 1970-71 and 1979-80.
   CHL: 9—Richie Hansen, Fort Worth Texans, Salt Lake Golden Eagles, Wichita Wind, 1975-76 through 1983-84.
   AHL: 20—Fred Glover, Indianapolis Caps, St. Louis Flyers, Cleveland Barons.
         Willie Marshall, Pittsburgh Hornets, Rochester Americans, Hershey Bears, Providence Reds, Baltimore Clippers.
   IHL: 18—Glenn Ramsay, Cincinnati Mohawks, Fort Wayne Komets, Troy Bruins, Toledo Blades, St. Paul Saints, Omaha Knights, Des Moines Oak Leafs, Toledo Hornets, Port Huron Flags, 1956-57 through 1973-74.

Most games played
   NHL: 1,767—Gordie Howe, Detroit Red Wings and Hartford Whalers (26 seasons).
   AHL: 1,205—Willie Marshall, Pittsburgh Hornets, Rochester Americans, Hershey Bears, Providence Reds, Baltimore Clippers (20 seasons).
   IHL: 1,054—Jock Callander, Toledo Goaldiggers, Muskegon Lumberjacks, Atlanta Knights and Cleveland Lumberjacks (17 seasons).
   CHL: 575—Richie Hansen, Fort Worth Texans, Salt Lake Golden Eagles, Wichita Wind (9 seasons).
   WHA: 551—Andre Lacroix, Philadelphia Blazers, New York Golden Blades, Jersey Knights, San Diego Mariners, Houston Aeros and New England Whalers (7 seasons).

Most goals
   NHL: 894—Wayne Gretzky, Edmonton Oilers, Los Angeles Kings, St. Louis Blues, New York Rangers (20 seasons).
   IHL: 547—Dave Michayluk, Kalamazoo Wings, Muskegon Lumberjacks, Cleveland Lumberjacks (13 seasons).
   AHL: 523—Willie Marshall, Pittsburgh Hornets, Rochester Americans, Hershey Bears, Providence Reds, Baltimore Clippers (20 seasons).
   WHA: 316—Marc Tardif, Quebec Nordiques (6 seasons).
   CHL: 204—Richie Hansen, Fort Worth Texans, Salt Lake Golden Eagles, Wichita Wind (9 seasons).

Most assists
   NHL: 1,963—Wayne Gretzky, Edmonton Oilers, Los Angeles Kings, St. Louis Blues, New York Rangers (20 seasons).
   AHL: 852—Willie Marshall, Pittsburgh Hornets, Hershey Bears, Rochester Americans, Providence Reds, Baltimore Clippers (20 seasons).
   IHL: 826—Len Thornson, Huntington Hornets, Indianapolis Chiefs, Fort Wayne Komets (13 seasons).
   WHA: 547—Andre Lacroix, Philadelphia Blazers, Jersey Knights, San Diego Mariners, Houston Aeros, New England Whalers (7 seasons).
   CHL: 374—Richie Hansen, Fort Worth Texans, Salt Lake Golden Eagles, Wichita Wind (9 seasons).

Most points
   NHL: 2,857—Wayne Gretzky, Edmonton Oilers, Los Angeles Kings, St. Louis Blues, New York Rangers (20 seasons).
   AHL: 1,375—Willie Marshall, Pittsburgh Hornets, Hershey Bears, Rochester Americans, Providence Reds, Baltimore Clippers (20 seasons).
   IHL: 1,252—Len Thornson, Huntington Hornets, Indianapolis Chiefs, Fort Wayne Komets (13 seasons).
   WHA: 798—Andre Lacroix, Philadelphia Blazers, Jersey Knights, San Diego Mariners, Houston Aeros, New England Whalers (7 seasons).
   CHL: 578—Richie Hansen, Fort Worth Texans, Salt Lake Golden Eagles, Wichita Wind (9 seasons).

Most penalty minutes
   NHL: 3,966—Dave "Tiger" Williams, Toronto Maple Leafs, Vancouver Canucks, Detroit Red Wings, Los Angeles Kings, Hartford Whalers (13 seasons).
   AHL: 2,402—Fred Glover, Indianapolis Caps, St. Louis Flyers, Cleveland Barons (20 seasons).
   IHL: 3,085—Kevin Evans, Kalamazoo Wings, Kansas City Blades, Peoria Rivermen (10 seasons).
   WHA: 962—Paul Baxter, Cleveland Crusaders, Quebec Nordiques (5 seasons).
   CHL: 899—Brad Gassoff, Tulsa Oilers, Dallas Black Hawks (5 seasons).

Most shutouts
   NHL: 103—Terry Sawchuk, Detroit Red Wings, Boston Bruins, Los Angeles Kings, New York Rangers, Toronto Maple Leafs (21 seasons).
   AHL: 45—Johnny Bower, Cleveland Barons, Providence Reds (11 seasons).
   IHL: 45—Glenn Ramsay, Cincinnati Mohawks, Fort Wayne Komets, Troy Bruins, Toledo Blades, St. Paul Saints, Omaha Knights, Des Moines Oak Leafs, Toledo Hornets, Port Huron Flags (18 seasons).
   WHA: 16—Ernie Wakely, Winnipeg Jets, San Diego Mariners, Houston Aeros (6 seasons).
   CHL: 12—Michel Dumas, Dallas Black Hawks (4 seasons).
         Mike Veisor, Dallas Black Hawks (5 seasons).

Most goals
   NHL: 92—Wayne Gretzky, Edmonton Oilers, 1981-82 season.
   WHA: 77—Bobby Hull, Winnipeg Jets, 1974-75 season.
   CHL: 77—Alain Caron, St. Louis Braves, 1963-64 season.
   IHL: 75—Daniel Lecours, Milwaukee Admirals, 1982-83 season.
   AHL: 70—Stephan Lebeau, Sherbrooke Canadiens, 1988-89 season.

Most goals by a defenseman
   NHL: 48—Paul Coffey, Edmonton Oilers, 1985-86 season.
   IHL: 34—Roly McLenahan, Cincinnati Mohawks, 1955-56 season.

CHL: 29—Dan Poulin, Nashville South Stars, 1981-82 season.
AHL: 28—Greg Tebbutt, Baltimore Skipjacks, 1982-83 season.
WHA: 24—Kevin Morrison, Jersey Knights, 1973-74 season.

Most assists
NHL: 163—Wayne Gretzky, Edmonton Oilers, 1985-86 season.
IHL: 113—Rob Brown, Kalamazoo Wings, 1993-94 season.
WHA: 106—Andre Lacroix, San Diego Mariners, 1974-75 season.
AHL: 89—George "Red" Sullivan, Hershey Bears, 1953-54 season.
CHL: 81—Richie Hansen, Salt Lake Golden Eagles, 1981-82 season.

Most assists by a defenseman
NHL: 102—Bobby Orr, Boston Bruins, 1970-71 season.
IHL: 86—Gerry Glaude, Muskegon Zephyrs, 1962-63 season.
WHA: 77—J. C. Tremblay, Quebec Nordiques, 1975-76 season.
AHL: 62—Craig Levie, Nova Scotia Voyageurs, 1980-81 season.
        Shawn Evans, Nova Scotia Oilers, 1987-88 season.
CHL: 61—Barclay Plager, Omaha Knights, 1963-64 season.

Most points
NHL: 215—Wayne Gretzky, Edmonton Oilers, 1985-86 season.
IHL: 157—John Cullen, Flint Spirits, 1987-88 season.
WHA: 154—Marc Tardif, Quebec Nordiques, 1977-78 season.
AHL: 138—Don Biggs, Binghamton Rangers, 1992-93 season.
CHL: 125—Alain Caron, St. Louis Braves, 1963-64 season.

Most points by a defenseman
NHL: 139—Bobby Orr, Boston Bruins, 1970-71 season.
IHL: 101—Gerry Glaude, Muskegon Zephyrs, 1962-63 season.
WHA: 89—J. C. Tremblay, Quebec Nordiques, 1972-73 and 1975-76 seasons.
CHL: 85—Dan Poulin, Nashville South Stars, 1981-82 season.
AHL: 84—Greg Tebbutt, Baltimore Skipjacks, 1982-83 season.

Most penalty minutes
IHL: 648—Kevin Evans, Kalamazoo, 1986-87 season.
NHL: 472—Dave Schultz, Philadelphia Flyers, 1974-75 season.
AHL: 446—Robert Ray, Rochester Americans, 1988-89 season.
CHL: 411—Randy Holt, Dallas Black Hawks, 1974-75 season.
WHA: 365—Curt Brackenbury, Minnesota Fighting Saints and Quebec Nordiques, 1975-76 season.

Most shutouts
NHL: 22—George Hainsworth, Montreal Canadiens, 1928-29 season.
NHL: 15—(modern era) Tony Esposito, Chicago Black Hawks, 1969-70 season.
IHL: 10—Charlie Hodge, Cincinnati Mohawks, 1953-54 season.
CHL: 9—Marcel Pelletier, St. Paul Rangers, 1963-64 season.
AHL: 9—Gordie Bell, Buffalo Bisons, 1942-43 season.
WHA: 5—Gerry Cheevers, Cleveland Crusaders, 1972-73 season.
        Joe Daley, Winnipeg Jets, 1975-76 season.

Lowest goals against average
NHL: 0.92—George Hainsworth, Montreal Canadiens, 1928-29 season.
AHL: 1.79—Frank Brimsek, Providence Reds, 1937-38 season.
IHL: 1.83—Nikolai Khabibulin, Long Beach Ice Dogs, 1999-2000 season.
CHL: 2.16—Russ Gillow, Oklahoma City Blazers, 1967-68 season.
WHA: 2.57—Don McLeod, Houston Aeros, 1973-74 season.

INDIVIDUAL—GAME

Most goals
NHL: 7—Joe Malone, Quebec Bulldogs vs. Toronto St. Pats, January 31, 1920.
NHL: 6—(modern era) Syd Howe, Detroit Red Wings vs. N.Y. Rangers, Feb. 3, 1944.
        Gordon "Red" Berenson, St. Louis Blues vs. Philadelphia, Nov. 7, 1968.
        Darryl Sittler, Toronto Maple Leafs vs. Boston, Feb. 7, 1976.
CHL: 6—Jim Mayer, Dallas Black Hawks, February 23, 1979.
AHL: 6—Bob Heron, Pittsburgh Hornets, 1941-42.
        Harry Pidhirny, Springfield Indians, 1953-54.
        Camille Henry, Providence Reds, 1955-56.
        Patrick Lebeau, Fredericton Canadiens, Feb. 1, 1991.
IHL: 6—Pierre Brillant, Indianapolis Chiefs, Feb. 18, 1959.
        Bryan McLay, Muskegon Zephyrs, Mar. 8, 1961.
        Elliott Chorley, St. Paul Saints, Jan. 17, 1962.
        Joe Kastelic, Muskegon Zephyrs, Mar. 1, 1962.
        Tom St. James, Flint Generals, Mar. 15, 1985.
WHA: 5—Ron Ward, New York Raiders vs. Ottawa, January 4, 1973.
        Ron Climie, Edmonton Oilers vs. N.Y. Golden Blades, November 6, 1973.
        Andre Hinse, Houston Aeros vs. Edmonton, Jan. 16, 1975.
        Vaclav Nedomansky, Toronto Toros vs. Denver Spurs, Nov. 13, 1975.
        Wayne Connelly, Minnesota Fighting Saints vs. Cincinnati Stingers, Nov. 27, 1975.
        Ron Ward, Cleveland Crusaders vs. Toronto Toros, Nov. 30, 1975.
        Real Cloutier, Quebec Nordiques fs. Phoenix Roadrunners, Oct. 26, 1976.

Most assists

AHL: 9—Art Stratton, Buffalo Bisons vs. Pittsburgh, Mar. 17, 1963.
IHL: 9—Jean-Paul Denis, St. Paul Saints, Jan. 17, 1962.
NHL: 7—Billy Taylor, Detroit Red Wings vs. Chicago, Mar. 16, 1947.
　　　　Wayne Gretzky, Edmonton Oilers vs. Washington, Feb. 15, 1980.
　　　　Wayne Gretzky, Edmonton Oilers vs. Chicago, Dec. 11, 1985.
　　　　Wayne Gretzky, Edmonton Oilers vs. Quebec, Feb. 14, 1986.
WHA: 7—Jim Harrison, Alberta Oilers vs. New York, January 30, 1973.
　　　　Jim Harrison, Cleveland Crusaders vs. Toronto, Nov. 30, 1975.
CHL: 6—Art Stratton, St. Louis Braves, 1966-67.
　　　　Ron Ward, Tulsa Oilers, 1967-68.
　　　　Bill Hogaboam, Omaha Knights, January 15, 1972.
　　　　Jim Wiley, Tulsa Oilers, 1974-75.
Most points
IHL: 11—Elliott Chorley, St. Paul Saints, Jan. 17, 1962.
　　　　Jean-Paul Denis, St. Paul Saints, Jan. 17, 1962.
NHL: 10—Darryl Sittler, Toronto Maple Leafs vs. Boston, Feb. 7, 1976.
WHA: 10—Jim Harrison, Alberta Oilers vs. New York, January 30, 1973.
AHL: 9—Art Stratton, Buffalo Bisons vs Pittsburgh, Mar. 17, 1963.
CHL: 8—Steve Vickers, Omaha Knights vs. Kansas City, Jan. 15, 1972.
Most penalty minutes
NHL: 67—Randy Holt, Los Angeles Kings vs. Philadelphia, March 11, 1979.
IHL: 66—Tim Molle, Milwaukee Admirals vs. Kalamazoo, Dec. 28, 1988.
AHL: 54—Wally Weir, Rochester Americans vs. New Brunswick, Jan. 16, 1981.
CHL: 49—Gary Rissling, Birmingham Bulls vs. Salt Lake, Dec. 5, 1980.
WHA: 46—Dave Hanson, Birmingham Bulls vs. Indianapolis, Feb. 5, 1978.

STANLEY CUP PLAYOFFS

INDIVIDUAL—CAREER

Most years in playoffs: 21—Ray Bourque, Boston, Colorado.
Most consecutive years in playoffs: 20—Larry Robinson, Montreal, Los Angeles.
Most games: 236—Mark Messier, Edmonton, New York Rangers.
Most games by goaltender: 247—Patrick Roy, Montreal, Colorado.
Most goals: 122—Wayne Gretzky, Edmonton, Los Angeles, St. Louis, New York Rangers.
Most assists: 260—Wayne Gretzky, Edmonton, Los Angeles, St. Louis, New York Rangers.
Most points: 382—Wayne Gretzky, Edmonton, Los Angeles, St. Louis, New York Rangers.
Most penalty minutes: 729—Dale Hunter, Quebec, Washington, Colorado.
Most shutouts: 23—Patrick Roy, Montreal, Colorado.

INDIVIDUAL—SEASON

Most goals: 19—Reggie Leach, Philadelphia (1975-76).
　　　　　Jari Kurri, Edmonton (1984-85).
Most goals by a defenseman: 12—Paul Coffey, Edmonton (1984-85).
Most assists: 31—Wayne Gretzky, Edmonton (1987-88).
Most assists by a defenseman: 25—Paul Coffey, Edmonton (1984-85).
Most points: 47—Wayne Gretzky, Edmonton (1984-85).
Most points by a defenseman: 37—Paul Coffey, Edmonton (1984-85).
Most penalty minutes: 141—Chris Nilan, Montreal (1985-86).
Most shutouts: 7—Martin Brodeur, New Jersey (2002-03).
Most consecutive shutouts: 3—Frank McCool, Toronto (1944-45); Brent Johnson, St. Louis (2001-02); Patrick Lalime, Ottawa (2001-02); Jean-Sebastien Giguere (2002-03).

INDIVIDUAL—GAME

Most goals: 5—Maurice Richard, Montreal vs. Toronto, March 23, 1944.
　　　　　Darryl Sittler, Toronto vs. Philadelphia, April 22, 1976.
　　　　　Reggie Leach, Philadelphia vs. Boston, May 6, 1976.
　　　　　Mario Lemieux, Pittsburgh vs. Philadelphia, April 25, 1989.
Most assists: 6—Mikko Leinonen, N.Y. Rangers vs. Philadelphia, April 8, 1982.
　　　　　Wayne Gretzky, Edmonton vs. Los Angeles, April 9, 1987.
Most points: 8—Patrik Sundstrom, New Jersey vs. Washington, April 22, 1988.
　　　　　Mario Lemieux, Pittsburgh vs. Philadelphia, April 25, 1989.

CLUB

Most Stanley Cup championships: 24—Montreal Canadiens.
Most consecutive Stanley Cup championships: 5—Montreal Canadiens.
Most final series apperances: 32—Montreal Canadiens.
Most years in playoffs: 73—Montreal Canadiens.
Most consecutive playoff appearances: 29—Boston Bruins.
Most consecutive playoff game victories: 14—Pittsburgh Penguins.
Most goals, one team, one game: 13—Edmonton vs. Los Angeles, April 9, 1987.
Most goals, one team, one period: 7—Montreal Canadiens vs. Toronto, March 30, 1944, 3rd period.

NHL HISTORY *Records*

STATISTICAL LEADERS

1917-18

Goals
Joe Malone, Mon. Canadiens	44
Cy Denneny, Ottawa	36
Reg Noble, Toronto	28
Newsy Lalonde, Mon. Canadiens	23
Corbett Denneny, Toronto	20

Lowest goals-against average
(Min. 15 games)
Georges Vezina, Mon. Canadiens	3.82
Hap Holmes, Toronto	4.75
Clint Benedict, Ottawa	5.18

Shutouts
Clint Benedict, Ottawa	1
Georges Vezina, Mon. Canadiens	1

1918-19

Goals
Odie Cleghorn, Montreal	24
Newsy Lalonde, Montreal	21
Cy Denneny, Ottawa	18
Frank Nighbor, Ottawa	17
Didier Pitre, Montreal	15

Lowest goals-against average
(Min. 15 games)
Clint Benedict, Ottawa	2.94
Georges Vezina, Montreal	4.33
Bert Lindsay, Toronto	5.19

Shutouts
Clint Benedict, Ottawa	2
Georges Vezina, Montreal	1

1919-20

Goals
Joe Malone, Quebec	39
Newsy Lalonde, Montreal	36
Frank Nighbor, Ottawa	26
Corbett Denneny, Toronto	23
Reg Noble, Toronto	24

Lowest goals-against average
(Min. 15 games)
Clint Benedict, Ottawa	2.67
Georges Vezina, Montreal	4.71
Frank Brophy, Quebec	7.05

Shutouts
Clint Benedict, Ottawa	5

1920-21

Goals
Babe Dye, Tor.-Ham.	35
Cy Denneny, Ottawa	34
Newsy Lalonde, Montreal	33
Joe Malone, Hamilton	28
Three players tied with	19

Lowest goals-against average
(Min. 15 games)
Clint Benedict, Ottawa	3.13
Jake Forbes, Toronto	3.90

Georges Vezina, Montreal	4.13
Howard Lockhart, Hamilton	5.50

Shutouts
Clint Benedict, Ottawa	2
Howard Lockhart, Hamilton	1
Georges Vezina, Montreal	1

1921-22

Goals
Harry Broadbent, Ottawa	30
Babe Dye, Toronto	30
Cy Denneny, Ottawa	28
Joe Malone, Hamilton	23
Odie Cleghorn, Montreal	21

Lowest goals-against average
(Min. 15 games)
Clint Benedict, Ottawa	3.50
Georges Vezina, Montreal	3.92
John Roach, Toronto	4.14
Howard Lockhart, Hamilton	4.29

Shutouts
Clint Benedict, Ottawa	2

1922-23

Goals
Babe Dye, Toronto	26
Billy Boucher, Montreal	25
Cy Denneny, Ottawa	23
Odie Cleghorn, Montreal	18
Jack Adams, Toronto	18

Lowest goals-against average
(Min. 15 games)
Clint Benedict, Ottawa	2.25
Georges Vezina, Montreal	2.54
John Roach, Toronto	3.67
Jake Forbes, Hamilton	4.58

Shutouts
Clint Benedict, Ottawa	4
Georges Vezina, Montreal	2
John Roach, Toronto	1

1923-24

Goals
Cy Denneny, Ottawa	22
Billy Burch, Hamilton	16
Billy Boucher, Montreal	16
Babe Dye, Toronto	16
Aurel Joliat, Montreal	15

Lowest goals-against average
(Min. 15 games)
Georges Vezina, Montreal	2.00
Clint Benedict, Ottawa	2.05
Jake Forbes, Hamilton	2.83
John Roach, Toronto	3.48

Shutouts
Clint Benedict, Ottawa	3
Georges Vezina, Montreal	3
Jake Forbes, Hamilton	1
John Roach, Toronto	1

1924-25

Goals
Babe Dye, Toronto	38
Howie Morenz, Mon. Canadiens	30
Aurel Joliat, Mon. Canadiens	29
Cy Denneny, Ottawa	28
Jack Adams, Toronto	21
Billy Burch, Hamilton	21

Points
Babe Dye, Toronto	44
Cy Denneny, Ottawa	42
Aurel Joliat, Mon. Canadiens	40
Howie Morenz, Mon. Canadiens	34
Billy Boucher, Mon. Canadiens	31

Lowest goals-against average
(Min. 15 games)
Georges Vezina, Mon. Canadiens	1.87
Jake Forbes, Hamilton	2.00
Clint Benedict, Mon. Maroons	2.17
Alex Connell, Ottawa	2.20
John Roach, Toronto	2.80

Shutouts
Alex Connell, Ottawa	7
Jake Forbes, Hamilton	6
Georges Vezina, Mon. Canadiens	5
Clint Benedict, Mon. Maroons	2
Charles Stewart, Boston	2

1925-26

Goals
Nels Stewart, Mon. Maroons	34
Carson Cooper, Boston	28
Jimmy Herberts, Boston	26
Cy Denneny, Ottawa	24
Howie Morenz, Mon. Canadiens	23

Points
Nels Stewart, Mon. Maroons	42
Cy Denneny, Ottawa	36
Carson Cooper, Boston	31
Jimmy Herberts, Boston	31
Three players tied with	26

Lowest goals-against average
(Min. 15 games)
Alex Connell, Ottawa	1.17
Roy Worters, Pittsburgh	1.94
Clint Benedict, Mon. Maroons	2.03
Charles Stewart, Boston	2.29
Jake Forbes, New York	2.39

Shutouts
Alex Connell, Ottawa	15
Roy Worters, Pittsburgh	7
Clint Benedict, Mon. Maroons	6
Charles Stewart, Boston	6
Jake Forbes, New York	2
John Roach, Toronto	2

1926-27

Goals
Bill Cook, N.Y. Rangers	33
Babe Dye, Chicago	25

Howie Morenz, Mon. Canadiens...........25
Billy Burch, N.Y. Americans.................19
Three players tied with.......................18

Assists
Dick Irvin, Chicago..............................18
Frank Boucher, N.Y. Rangers.............15
Irvine Bailey, Toronto 13
Frank Fredrickson, Bos.-Det...............13
Frank Clancy, Ottawa 10

Points
Bill Cook, N.Y. Rangers 37
Dick Irvin, Chicago.............................36
Howie Morenz, Mon. Canadiens..........32
Frank Fredrickson, Det.-Bos...............31
Babe Dye, Chicago.............................30

Penalty minutes
Nels Stewart, Mon. Maroons..............133
Eddie Shore, Boston..........................130
Reginald Smith, Ottawa.....................125
Albert Siebert, Mon. Maroons............116
George Boucher, Ottawa....................115

Lowest goals-against average
(Min. 25 games)
Clint Benedict, Mon. Maroons...........1.51
George Hainsworth, Mon. Canadiens..1.52
Lorne Chabot, N.Y. Rangers 1.56
Alex Connell, Ottawa 1.57
Hal Winkler, NYR-Bos. 1.81

Shutouts
George Hainsworth, Mon. Canadiens...14
Clint Benedict, Mon. Maroons............13
Alex Connell, Ottawa 13
Lorne Chabot, N.Y. Rangers 10
Jake Forbes, N.Y. Americans 8

1927-28

Goals
Howie Morenz, Mon. Canadiens..........33
Aurel Joliat, Mon. Canadiens..............28
Nels Stewart, Mon. Maroons...............27
Frank Boucher, N.Y. Rangers.............23
George Hay, Detroit............................22

Assists
Howie Morenz, Mon. Canadiens..........18
Fred Cook, N.Y. Rangers 14
George Hay, Detroit............................13
Frank Boucher, N.Y. Rangers.............12
Aurel Joliat, Mon. Canadiens..............11
Sylvio Mantha, Mon. Canadiens..........11

Points
Howie Morenz, Mon. Canadiens..........51
Aurel Joliat, Mon. Canadiens..............39
Frank Boucher, N.Y. Rangers.............35
George Hay, Detroit............................35
Nels Stewart, Mon. Maroons...............34

Penalty minutes
Eddie Shore, Boston..........................165
Ivan Johnson, N.Y. Rangers 146
Clarence Boucher, N.Y. Americans 129
Albert Siebert, Mon. Maroons............109
Aurel Joliat, Mon. Canadiens.............105

Lowest goals-against average
(Min. 25 games)
George Hainsworth, Mon. Canadiens...1.09
Alex Connell, Ottawa 1.29
Hal Winkler, Boston............................1.59
Roy Worters, Pittsburgh 1.73
Clint Benedict, Mon. Maroons...........1.75

Shutouts
Alex Connell, Ottawa 15
Hal Winkler, Boston............................15
George Hainsworth, Mon. Canadiens...13
Lorne Chabot, N.Y. Rangers 11
Harry Holmes, Detroit 11

1928-29

Goals
Irvine Bailey, Toronto 22
Nels Stewart, Mon. Maroons...............21
Carson Cooper, Detroit.......................18
Howie Morenz, Mon. Canadiens..........17
Harry Oliver, Boston...........................17

Assists
Frank Boucher, N.Y. Rangers.............16
Andy Blair, Toronto.............................15
Gerald Lowrey, Pit.-Tor......................12
Irvine Bailey, Toronto 10
Howie Morenz, Mon. Canadiens..........10

Points
Ace Bailey, Toronto.............................32
Nels Stewart, Mon. Maroons...............29
Carson Cooper, Detroit.......................27
Howie Morenz, Mon. Canadiens..........27
Andy Blair, Toronto.............................27

Penalty minutes
Mervyn Dutton, Mon. Maroons..........139
Lionel Conacher, N.Y. Americans.......132
Reginald Smith, Mon. Maroons 120
Eddie Shore, Boston............................96
Alex Smith, Ottawa..............................96

Lowest goals-against average
(Min. 25 games)
George Hainsworth, Mon. Canadiens..0.92
Tiny Thompson, Boston.......................1.18
Roy Worters, N.Y. Americans 1.21
Clarence Dolson, Detroit 1.43
John Roach, N.Y. Rangers 1.48

Shutouts
George Hainsworth, Mon. Canadiens.....22
John Roach, N.Y. Rangers 13
Roy Worters, N.Y. Americans 13
Lorne Chabot, Toronto 12
Tiny Thompson, Boston 12

1929-30

Goals
Ralph Weiland, Boston........................43
Aubrey Clapper, Boston......................41
Howie Morenz, Mon. Canadiens..........40
Nels Stewart, Mon. Maroons...............39
Hec Kilrea, Ottawa..............................36

Assists
Frank Boucher, N.Y. Rangers.............36
Norman Gainor, Boston.......................31
Bill Cook, N.Y. Rangers 30
Ralph Weiland, Boston........................30
Frank Clancy, Ottawa..........................23

Points
Ralph Weiland, Boston........................73
Frank Boucher, N.Y. Rangers.............62
Aubrey Clapper, Boston......................61
Bill Cook, N.Y. Rangers 59
Hec Kilrea, Ottawa..............................58

Penalty minutes
Joe Lamb, Ottawa 119
Sylvio Mantha, Mon. Canadiens.........108

Eddie Shore, Boston..........................105
Mervyn Dutton, Mon. Maroons............98
Harvey Rockburn, Detroit....................97

Lowest goals-against average
(Min. 25 games)
Tiny Thompson, Boston 2.23
Charles Gardiner, Chicago 2.52
James Walsh, Mon. Maroons..............2.55
George Hainsworth, Mon. Canadiens..2.57
Alex Connell, Ottawa 2.68

Shutouts
Lorne Chabot, Toronto 6
George Hainsworth, Mon. Canadiens.....4
Alex Connell, Ottawa 3
Charles Gardiner, Chicago 3
Tiny Thompson, Boston 3

1930-31

Goals
Charlie Conacher, Toronto 31
Bill Cook, N.Y. Rangers 30
Howie Morenz, Mon. Canadiens..........28
Ebbie Goodfellow, Detroit...................25
Nels Stewart, Mon. Maroons...............25
Ralph Weiland, Boston........................25

Assists
Joe Primeau, Toronto..........................32
Frank Boucher, N.Y. Rangers.............27
Ebbie Goodfellow, Detroit...................23
Howie Morenz, Mon. Canadiens..........23
Aurel Joliat, Mon. Canadiens..............22

Points
Howie Morenz, Mon. Canadiens..........51
Ebbie Goodfellow, Detroit...................48
Charlie Conacher, Toronto 43
Bill Cook, N.Y. Rangers 42
Ace Bailey, Toronto.............................42

Penalty minutes
Harvey Rockburn, Detroit..................118
Eddie Shore, Boston..........................105
D'Arcy Coulson, Philadelphia 103
Allan Shields, Philadelphia 98
Marty Burke, Mon. Canadiens 91
Joe Lamb, Ottawa 91

Lowest goals-against average
(Min. 25 games)
Roy Worters, N.Y. Americans 1.68
Charles Gardiner, Chicago 1.77
John Roach, N.Y. Rangers 1.98
George Hainsworth, Mon. Canadiens..2.02
Tiny Thompson, Boston 2.05

Shutouts
Charles Gardiner, Chicago 12
George Hainsworth, Mon. Canadiens.....8
Roy Worters, N.Y. Americans 8
John Roach, N.Y. Rangers 7
Lorne Chabot, Toronto 6
Clarence Dolson, Detroit 6

1931-32

Goals
Charlie Conacher, Toronto 34
Bill Cook, N.Y. Rangers 34
Harvey Jackson, Toronto....................28
Dave Trottier, Mon. Maroons...............26
Howie Morenz, Mon. Canadiens..........24

Assists
Joe Primeau, Toronto..........................37
Hooley Smith, Mon. Maroons 33

Harvey Jackson, Toronto......................25
Howie Morenz, Mon. Canadiens..........25
Aurel Joliat, Mon. Canadiens..............24

Points
Harvey Jackson, Toronto......................53
Joe Primeau, Toronto...........................50
Howie Morenz, Mon. Canadiens..........49
Charlie Conacher, Toronto 48
Bill Cook, N.Y. Rangers 48

Penalty minutes
Red Dutton, N.Y. Americans...............107
Ivan Johnson, N.Y. Rangers 106
Reginald Horner, Toronto 97
Dave Trottier, Mon. Maroons................94
Earl Seibert, N.Y. Rangers 88

Lowest goals-against average
(Min. 25 games)
Charles Gardiner, Chicago.................2.10
Alex Connell, Detroit...........................2.25
George Hainsworth, Mon. Canadiens..2.32
John Roach, N.Y. Rangers 2.34
Tiny Thompson, Boston 2.42

Shutouts
John Roach, N.Y. Rangers 9
Tiny Thompson, Boston 9
Alex Connell, Detroit................................6
George Hainsworth, Mon. Canadiens.....6
Roy Worters, N.Y. Americans..................5

1932-33

Goals
Bill Cook, N.Y. Rangers 28
Harvey Jackson, Toronto........................27
Martin Barry, Boston 24
Fred Cook, N.Y. Rangers 22
Lawrence Northcott, Mon. Maroons 22

Assists
Frank Boucher, N.Y. Rangers 28
Eddie Shore, Boston...............................27
Paul Haynes, Mon. Maroons 25
Norman Himes, N.Y. Americans 25
Johnny Gagnon, Mon. Canadiens 23

Points
Bill Cook, N.Y. Rangers 50
Harvey Jackson, Toronto........................44
Lawrence Northcott, Mon. Maroons 43
Hooley Smith, Mon. Maroons 41
Paul Haynes, Mon. Maroons 41

Penalty minutes
Reginald Horner, Toronto 144
Ivan Johnson, N.Y. Rangers 127
Allan Shields, Ottawa 119
Eddie Shore, Boston...........................102
Vern Ayres, N.Y. Americans..................97

Lowest goals-against average
(Min. 25 games)
Tiny Thompson, Boston 1.83
John Roach, Detroit 1.93
Charles Gardiner, Chicago.................2.10
Dave Kerr, Mon. Maroons 2.20
Andy Aitkenhead, N.Y. Rangers.........2.23

Shutouts
Tiny Thompson, Boston 11
John Roach, Detroit 10
George Hainsworth, Mon. Canadiens.....8
Bill Beveridge, Ottawa 5
Lorne Chabot, Toronto 5
Charles Gardiner, Chicago 5
Roy Worters, N.Y. Americans..................5

1933-34

Goals
Charlie Conacher, Toronto 32
Marty Barry, Boston 27
Aurel Joliat, Mon. Canadiens...............22
Nels Stewart, Boston..............................22
Johnny Sorrell, Detroit...........................21

Assists
Joe Primeau, Toronto.............................32
Frank Boucher, N.Y. Rangers................30
Cecil Dillon, N.Y. Rangers.....................26
Elwyn Romnes, Chicago.........................21
Charlie Conacher, Toronto 20

Points
Charlie Conacher, Toronto 52
Joe Primeau, Toronto.............................46
Frank Boucher, N.Y. Rangers................44
Marty Barry, Boston 39
Cecil Dillon, N.Y. Rangers.....................39

Penalty minutes
Reginald Horner, Toronto 146
Lionel Conacher, Chicago......................87
Ivan Johnson, N.Y. Rangers 86
Nels Stewart, Boston..............................68
Earl Seibert, N.Y. Rangers 66

Lowest goals-against average
(Min. 25 games)
Charles Gardiner, Chicago.................1.73
Wilfred Cude, Det.-Mon. C..................1.57
Roy Worters, N.Y. Americans.............2.14
Lorne Chabot, Mon. Canadiens.........2.15
Andy Aitkenhead, N.Y. Rangers.........2.35

Shutouts
Charles Gardiner, Chicago 10
Lorne Chabot, Mtl Canadiens..................8
Andy Aitkenhead, N.Y. Rangers.............7
Dave Kerr, Mon. Maroons 6
Wilfred Cude, Det.-Mon. C. 5
Tiny Thompson, Boston 5

1934-35

Goals
Charlie Conacher, Toronto 36
Cecil Dillon, N.Y. Rangers.....................25
Syd Howe, St.L.-Det...............................22
Harvey Jackson, Toronto........................22
Three players tied with...........................21

Assists
Art Chapman, N.Y. Americans 34
Frank Boucher, N.Y. Rangers................32
Larry Aurie, Detroit 29
Herb Lewis, Detroit 27
Howie Morenz, Chicago.........................26
Eddie Shore, Boston..............................26

Points
Charlie Conacher, Toronto 57
Syd Howe, St. Louis-Detroit..................47
Larry Aurie, Detroit 46
Frank Boucher, N.Y. Rangers................45
Harvey Jackson, Toronto........................44

Penalty minutes
Reginald Horner, Toronto 125
Irvine Frew, St. Louis 89
Earl Seibert, N.Y. Rangers 86
Albert Siebert, Boston 80
Ralph Bowman, St.L.-Det.......................72

Lowest goals-against average
(Min. 25 games)
Lorne Chabot, Chicago.......................1.83
Alex Connell, Mon. Maroons 1.92
Norman Smith, Detroit........................2.08
George Hainsworth, Toronto 2.28
Tiny Thompson, Boston 2.33

Shutouts
Alex Connell, Mon. Maroons 9
Lorne Chabot, Chicago............................8
George Hainsworth, Toronto 8
Tiny Thompson, Boston 8
Dave Kerr, N.Y. Rangers 4
John Roach, Det.-Tor. 4

1935-36

Goals
Charlie Conacher, Toronto 23
Bill Thoms, Toronto...............................23
Marty Barry, Detroit...............................21
David Schriner, N.Y. Americans...........19
Hooley Smith, Mon. Maroons 19

Assists
Art Chapman, N.Y. Americans 28
David Schriner, N.Y. Americans...........26
Elwyn Romnes, Chicago.........................25
Herb Lewis, Detroit 23
Paul Thompson, Chicago 23

Points
David Schriner, N.Y. Americans...........45
Marty Barry, Detroit...............................40
Paul Thompson, Chicago 40
Five players tied with.............................38

Penalty minutes
Reginald Horner, Toronto 167
Allan Shields, Mon. Maroons 81
Hooley Smith, Mon. Maroons 75
Charlie Conacher, Toronto 74
Three players tied with...........................69

Lowest goals-against average
(Min. 25 games)
Tiny Thompson, Boston 1.73
Mike Karakas, Chicago 1.92
Dave Kerr, N.Y. Rangers 2.02
Norman Smith, Detroit........................2.14
Bill Beveridge, Mon. Maroons 2.22

Shutouts
Tiny Thompson, Boston 10
Mike Karakas, Chicago 9
George Hainsworth, Toronto 8
Dave Kerr, N.Y. Rangers 8
Wilfred Cude, Mon. Canadiens...............6
Norman Smith, Detroit.............................6

1936-37

Goals
Larry Aurie, Detroit 23
Nels Stewart, Bos.-NYA.........................23
Mehlville Keeling, N.Y. Rangers............22
Harvey Jackson, Toronto........................21
David Schriner, N.Y. Americans...........21

Assists
Syl Apps, Toronto...................................29
Marty Barry, Detroit...............................27
Bob Gracie, Mon. Maroons 25
David Schriner, N.Y. Americans...........25
Art Chapman, N.Y. Americans 23

Points

David Schriner, N.Y. Americans............46
Syl Apps, Toronto................................45
Marty Barry, Detroit..............................44
Larry Aurie, Detroit...............................43
Harvey Jackson, Toronto......................40

Penalty minutes

Reginald Horner, Toronto 124
Allan Shields, NYA-Bos. 94
Lionel Conacher, Mon. Maroons 64
Jack Portland, Boston............................58
Joe Jerwa, Bos.-NYA.............................57

Lowest goals-against average
(Min. 25 games)

Norman Smith, Detroit......................2.13
Dave Kerr, N.Y. Rangers 2.21
Wilfred Cude, Mon. Canadiens 2.24
Tiny Thompson, Boston.....................2.29
Turk Broda, Toronto 2.32

Shutouts

Norman Smith, Detroit............................6
Tiny Thompson, Boston...........................6
Wilfred Cude, Mon. Canadiens...............5
Mike Karakas, Chicago 5
Dave Kerr, N.Y. Rangers 4

1937-38

Goals

Gord Drillon, Toronto 26
Georges Mantha, Mon. Canadiens 23
Paul Thompson, Chicago 22
Syl Apps, Toronto.................................21
Cecil Dillon, N.Y. Rangers....................21
David Schriner, N.Y. Americans............21

Assists

Syl Apps, Toronto.................................29
Art Chapman, N.Y. Americans 27
Gord Drillon, Toronto 26
Phil Watson, N.Y. Rangers 25
Bill Thoms, Toronto..............................24

Points

Gord Drillon, Toronto 52
Syl Apps, Toronto.................................50
Paul Thompson, Chicago 44
Georges Mantha, Mon. Canadiens 42
Cecil Dillon, N.Y. Rangers....................39
Bill Cowley, Boston...............................39

Penalty minutes

Reginald Horner, Toronto 82
Art Coulter, N.Y. Rangers.....................80
Ott Heller, N.Y. Rangers.......................68
Al Shields, Mon. Maroons.....................67
Stew Evans, Mon. Maroons 59

Lowest goals-against average
(Min. 25 games)

Tiny Thompson, Boston......................1.85
Dave Kerr, N.Y. Rangers 2.00
Earl Robertson, N.Y. Americans 2.31
Turk Broda, Toronto 2.64
Wilfred, Cude, Mon. Canadiens 2.68

Shutouts

Dave Kerr, N.Y. Rangers 8
Tiny Thompson, Boston...........................7
Turk Broda, Toronto 6
Earl Robertson, N.Y. Americans 6
Wilfred Cude, Mon. Canadiens...............3
Norman Smith, Detroit............................3

1938-39

Goals

Roy Conacher, Boston..........................26
Toe Blake, Montreal..............................24
Alex Shibicky, N.Y. Rangers 24
Clint Smith, N.Y. Rangers.....................21
Bryan Hextall, N.Y. Rangers.................20

Assists

Bill Cowley, Boston...............................34
Paul Haynes, Montreal 33
David Schriner, N.Y. Americans............31
Marty Barry, Detroit..............................28
Tom Anderson, N.Y. Americans............27

Points

Toe Blake, Montreal..............................47
David Schriner, N.Y. Americans............44
Bill Cowley, Boston...............................42
Clint Smith, N.Y. Rangers.....................41
Marty Barry, Detroit..............................41

Penalty minutes

Reginald Horner, Toronto 85
Murray Patrick, N.Y. Rangers...............64
Art Coulter, N.Y. Rangers.....................58
Stew Evans, Montreal...........................58
Earl Seibert, Chicago 57

Lowest goals-against average
(Min. 25 games)

Frank Brimsek, Boston 1.59
Dave Kerr, N.Y. Rangers 2.18
Turk Broda, Toronto 2.23
Tiny Thompson, Bos.-Det. 2.49
Mike Karakas, Chicago 2.75

Shutouts

Frank Brimsek, Boston..........................10
Turk Broda, Toronto 8
Dave Kerr, N.Y. Rangers 6
Mike Karakas, Chicago 5
Tiny Thompson, Bos.-Det. 4

1939-40

Goals

Bryan Hextall, N.Y. Rangers 24
Woody Dumart, Boston.........................22
Milt Schmidt, Boston 22
Herb Cain, Boston 21
Gord Drillon, Toronto 21

Assists

Milt Schmidt, Boston 30
Phil Watson, N.Y. Rangers 28
Bill Cowley, Boston...............................27
Bob Bauer, Boston 26
Syd Howe, Detroit.................................23

Points

Milt Schmidt, Boston 52
Woody Dumart, Boston.........................43
Bob Bauer, Boston 43
Gord Drillon, Toronto 40
Bill Cowley, Boston...............................40

Penalty minutes

Reginald Horner, Toronto 87
Art Coulter, N.Y. Rangers.....................68
Erwin Chamberlain, Toronto.................63
Jack Church, Toronto............................62
Walter Pratt, N.Y. Rangers....................61

Lowest goals-against average
(Min. 25 games)

Dave Kerr, N.Y. Rangers 1.60
Paul Goodman, Chicago....................2.00

Frank Brimsek, Boston 2.04
Turk Broda, Toronto 2.30
Tiny Thompson, Detroit 2.61

Shutouts

Dave Kerr, N.Y. Rangers 8
Frank Brimsek, Boston............................6
Earl Robertson, N.Y. Americans 6
Turk Broda, Toronto 4
Paul Goodman, Chicago.........................4

1940-41

Goals

Bryan Hextall, N.Y. Rangers 26
Roy Conacher, Boston..........................24
David Schriner, Toronto........................24
Gord Drillon, Toronto 23
Three players tied with.........................20

Assists

Bill Cowley, Boston...............................45
Neil Colville, N.Y. Rangers 28
Bill Taylor, Toronto...............................26
Milton Schmidt, Boston 25
Phil Watson, N.Y. Rangers 25

Points

Bill Cowley, Boston...............................62
Bryan Hextall, N.Y. Rangers 44
Gord Drillon, Toronto 44
Syl Apps, Toronto.................................44
Lynn Patrick, N.Y. Rangers...................44
Syd Howe, Detroit.................................44

Penalty minutes

Jimmy Orlando, Detroit.........................99
Clifford Goupille, Montreal 81
Erwin Chamberlain, Montreal...............75
Joe Cooper, Chicago 66
Des Smith, Boston 61

Lowest goals-against average
(Min. 25 games)

Turk Broda, Toronto 2.06
Frank Brimsek, Boston 2.12
John Mowers, Detroit.........................2.12
Dave Kerr, N.Y. Rangers 2.60
Bert Gardiner, Montreal.....................2.84

Shutouts

Frank Brimsek, Boston............................6
Turk Broda, Toronto 5
John Mowers, Detroit..............................4
Bert Gardiner, Montreal..........................2
Paul Goodman, Chicago.........................2
Dave Kerr, N.Y. Rangers 2

1941-42

Goals

Lynn Patrick, New York.........................32
Roy Conacher, Boston..........................24
Robert Hamill, Bos.-Chi........................24
Bryan Hextall, New York.......................24
Gord Drillon, Toronto 23
Don Grosso, Detroit 23

Assists

Phil Watson, New York..........................37
Bryan Hextall, New York.......................32
Sid Abel, Detroit...................................31
Don Grosso, Detroit 30
Bill Thoms, Chicago 30

Points

Bryan Hextall, New York.......................56
Lynn Patrick, New York.........................54
Don Grosso, Detroit 53

Phil Watson, New York.........................52
Sid Abel, Detroit.................................49

Penalty minutes

Pat Egan, Brooklyn.............................124
Jimmy Orlando, Detroit.......................111
Jack Stewart, Detroit...........................93
Ken Reardon, Montreal 93
Des Smith, Boston 70

Lowest goals-against average
(Min. 25 games)

Frank Brimsek, Boston 2.44
Turk Broda, Toronto 2.83
Jim Henry, New York..........................2.98
John Mowers, Detroit.........................3.06
Sam LoPresti, Chicago.......................3.23

Shutouts

Turk Broda, Toronto 6
John Mowers, Detroit..............................5
Frank Brimsek, Boston 3
Sam LoPresti, Chicago.............................3
Three players tied with 1

1942-43

Goals

Doug Bentley, Chicago 33
Joseph Benoit, Montreal 30
Gord Drillon, Montreal 28
Lorne Carr, Toronto 27
Bill Cowley, Boston 27
Bryan Hextall, New York.......................27

Assists

Bill Cowley, Boston..............................45
Max Bentley, Chicago..........................44
Herbert O'Connor, Montreal 43
Billy Taylor, Toronto.............................42
Doug Bentley, Chicago 40
Elmer Lach, Montreal 40

Points

Doug Bentley, Chicago 73
Bill Cowley, Boston 72
Max Bentley, Chicago...........................70
Lynn Patrick, New York.........................61
Lorne Carr, Toronto 60
Billy Taylor, Toronto..............................60

Penalty minutes

Jimmy Orlando, Detroit.........................99
Reginald Hamilton, Toronto 68
Jack Stewart, Detroit............................68
Erwin Chamberlain, Boston.................67
Victor Myles, New York.........................57

Lowest goals-against average
(Min. 25 games)

John Mowers, Detroit.........................2.48
Turk Broda, Toronto 3.18
Frank Brimsek, Boston 3.52
Bert Gardiner, Chicago 3.60
Paul Bibeault, Montreal 3.82

Shutouts

John Mowers, Detroit..............................6
Bill Beveridge, New York 1
Paul Bibeault, Montreal 1
Frank Brimsek, Boston 1
Turk Broda, Toronto 1
Bert Gardiner, Chicago 1

1943-44

Goals

Doug Bentley, Chicago 38
Herb Cain, Boston 36

Lorne Carr, Toronto 36
Carl Liscombe, Detroit 36
Moderre Bruneteau, Detroit.................35

Assists

Clint Smith, Chicago.............................49
Elmer Lach, Montreal...........................48
Herb Cain, Boston................................46
Herbert O'Connor, Montreal 42
Bill Cowley, Boston...............................41
Art Jackson, Boston 41

Points

Herb Cain, Boston................................82
Doug Bentley, Chicago 77
Lorne Carr, Toronto 74
Carl Liscombe, Detroit 73
Elmer Lach, Montreal...........................72
Clint Smith, Chicago.............................72

Penalty minutes

Mike McMahon, Montreal 98
Pat Egan, Det.-Bos..............................95
Erwin Chamberlain, Montreal..............85
Hal Jackson, Detroit.............................76
Bob Dill, New York 66

Lowest goals-against average
(Min. 25 games)

Bill Durnan, Montreal 2.18
Paul Bibeault, Toronto 3.00
Connie Dion, Detroit 3.08
Mike Karakas, Chicago 3.04
Bert Gardiner, Boston........................5.17

Shutouts

Paul Bibeault, Toronto 5
Mike Karakas, Chicago 3
Bill Durnan, Montreal 2
Connie Dion, Detroit 1
Jim Franks, Bos.-Det...............................1
Bert Gardiner, Boston..............................1

1944-45

Goals

Maurice Richard, Montreal...................50
Herb Cain, Boston 32
Toe Blake, Montreal.............................29
Ted Kennedy, Toronto..........................29
Bill Mosienko, Chicago.........................28

Assists

Elmer Lach, Montreal 54
Bill Cowley, Boston...............................40
Toe Blake, Montreal.............................38
Gus Bodnar, Toronto 36
Syd Howe, Detroit 36

Points

Elmer Lach, Montreal 80
Maurice Richard, Montreal...................73
Toe Blake, Montreal.............................67
Bill Cowley, Boston...............................65
Five players tied with...........................54

Penalty minutes

Pat Egan, Boston..................................86
Bob Dill, New York 69
Leo Lamovreux, Montreal 58
Joe Cooper, Chicago 50
Bob Davidson, Toronto.........................49

Lowest goals-against average
(Min. 25 games)

Bill Durnan, Montreal 2.42
Harry Lumley, Detroit.........................3.22
Frank McCool, Toronto.......................3.22

Mike Karakas, Chicago 3.90
Paul Bibeault, Boston 4.46

Shutouts

Mike Karakas, Chicago 4
Frank McCool, Toronto 4
Bill Durnan, Montreal 1
Harry Lumley, Detroit..............................1
Ken McAuley, New York 1

1945-46

Goals

Gaye Stewart, Toronto..........................37
Max Bentley, Chicago...........................31
Toe Blake, Montreal.............................29
Maurice Richard, Montreal...................27
Clint Smith, Chicago.............................26

Assists

Elmer Lach, Montreal 34
Max Bentley, Chicago...........................30
Bill Mosienko, Chicago.........................30
Albert DeMarco, New York 27
Alex Kaleta, Chicago............................27

Points

Max Bentley, Chicago...........................61
Gaye Stewart, Toronto..........................52
Toe Blake, Montreal.............................50
Clint Smith, Chicago.............................50
Maurice Richard, Montreal...................48
Bill Mosienko, Chicago.........................48

Penalty minutes

Jack Stewart, Detroit............................73
Armand Guidolin, Boston 62
John Mariucci, Chicago........................58
Emile Bouchard, Montreal 52
Maurice Richard, Montreal...................48

Lowest goals-against average
(Min. 25 games)

Bill Durnan, Montreal 2.60
Paul Bibeault, Bos.-Mon....................2.88
Harry Lumley, Detroit.........................3.18
Frank Brimsek, Boston 3.26
Mike Karakas, Chicago 3.46

Shutouts

Bill Durnan, Montreal 4
Paul Bibeault, Bos.-Mon.........................2
Frank Brimsek, Boston 2
Harry Lumley, Detroit..............................2
Three players tied with 1

1946-47

Goals

Maurice Richard, Montreal...................45
Bobby Bauer, Boston............................30
Roy Conacher, Detroit..........................30
Max Bentley, Chicago...........................29
Ted Kennedy, Toronto..........................28

Assists

Billy Taylor, Detroit 46
Max Bentley, Chicago...........................43
Milt Schmidt, Boston 35
Doug Bentley, Chicago 34
Ted Kennedy, Toronto..........................32

Points

Max Bentley, Chicago 72
Maurice Richard, Montreal...................71
Billy Taylor, Detroit 63
Milt Schmidt, Boston 62
Ted Kennedy, Toronto..........................60

Penalty minutes

Gus Mortson, Toronto 133
Johnny Mariucci, Chicago 110
Murph Chamberlain, Montreal 97
Jimmy Thomson, Toronto 97
Bill Ezinicki, Toronto 93

Lowest goals-against average
(Min. 25 games)

Bill Durnan, Montreal 2.30
Turk Broda, Toronto 2.86
Frank Brimsek, Boston 2.91
Charlie Rayner, New York 3.05
Harry Lumley, Detroit 3.05

Shutouts

Charlie Rayner, New York 5
Turk Broda, Toronto 4
Bill Durnan, Montreal 4
Frank Brimsek, Boston 3
Harry Lumley, Detroit 3

1947-48

Goals

Ted Lindsay, Detroit 33
Elmer Lach, Montreal 30
Maurice Richard, Montreal 28
Gaye Stewart, Tor.-Chi. 27
Syl Apps, Toronto 26
Max Bentley, Chi.-Tor. 26

Assists

Doug Bentley, Chicago 37
Buddy O'Connor, New York 36
Edgar Laprade, New York 34
Elmer Lach, Montreal 31
Sid Abel, Detroit 30

Points

Elmer Lach, Montreal 61
Buddy O'Connor, New York 60
Doug Bentley, Chicago 57
Gaye Stewart, Tor.-Chi. 56
Max Bentley, Chi.-Tor. 54
Bud Poile, Tor.-Chi. 54

Penalty minutes

Bill Barilko, Toronto 147
Ken Reardon, Montreal 129
Gus Mortson, Toronto 118
Bill Ezinicki, Toronto 97
Ted Lindsay, Detroit 95

Lowest goals-against average
(Min. 25 games)

Turk Broda, Toronto 2.38
Harry Lumley, Detroit 2.45
Bill Durnan, Montreal 2.74
Frank Brimsek, Boston 2.82
Jim Henry, New York 3.19

Shutouts

Harry Lumley, Detroit 7
Turk Broda, Toronto 5
Bill Durnan, Montreal 5
Frank Brimsek, Boston 3
Jim Henry, New York 2

1948-49

Goals

Sid Abel, Detroit 28
Jim Conacher, Det.-Chi. 26
Roy Conacher, Chicago 26
Ted Lindsay, Detroit 26
Harry Watson, Toronto 26

Assists

Doug Bentley, Chicago 43
Roy Conacher, Chicago 42
Paul Ronty, Boston 29
Ted Lindsay, Detroit 28
Sid Abel, Detroit 26
Gus Bodnar, Chicago 26

Points

Roy Conacher, Chicago 68
Doug Bentley, Chicago 66
Sid Abel, Detroit 54
Ted Lindsay, Detroit 54
Jim Conacher, Det.-Chi. 49
Paul Ronty, Boston 49

Penalty minutes

Bill Ezinicki, Toronto 145
Bep Guidolin, Det.-Chi. 116
Erwin Chamberlain, Montreal 111
Maurice Richard, Montreal 110
Ken Reardon, Montreal 103

Lowest goals-against average
(Min. 25 games)

Bill Durnan, Montreal 2.10
Harry Lumley, Detroit 2.42
Turk Broda, Toronto 2.68
Frank Brimsek, Boston 2.72
Claude Rayner, New York 2.90

Shutouts

Bill Durnan, Montreal 10
Claude Rayner, New York 7
Harry Lumley, Detroit 6
Turk Broda, Toronto 5
Frank Brimsek, Boston 1
Gordon Henry, Boston 1

1949-50

Goals

Maurice Richard, Montreal 43
Gordie Howe, Detroit 35
Sid Abel, Detroit 34
Metro Prystai, Chicago 29
John Peirson, Boston 27

Assists

Ted Lindsay, Detroit 55
Paul Ronty, Boston 36
Sid Abel, Detroit 35
Bep Guidolin, Chicago 34
Doug Bentley, Chicago 33
Gordie Howe, Detroit 33
Elmer Lach, Montreal 33

Points

Ted Lindsay, Detroit 78
Sid Abel, Detroit 69
Gordie Howe, Detroit 68
Maurice Richard, Montreal 65
Paul Ronty, Boston 59

Penalty minutes

Bill Ezinicki, Toronto 144
Gus Kyle, New York 143
Ted Lindsay, Detroit 141
Bill Gadsby, Chicago 138
Gus Mortson, Toronto 125

Lowest goals-against average
(Min. 25 games)

Bill Durnan, Montreal 2.20
Harry Lumley, Detroit 2.35
Turk Broda, Toronto 2.45
Chuck Rayner, New York 2.62
Jack Gelineau, Boston 3.28

Shutouts

Turk Broda, Toronto 9
Bill Durnan, Montreal 8
Harry Lumley, Detroit 7
Chuck Rayner, New York 6
Frank Brimsek, Chicago 5

1950-51

Goals

Gordie Howe, Detroit 43
Maurice Richard, Montreal 42
Tod Sloan, Toronto 31
Sid Smith, Toronto 30
Roy Conacher, Chicago 26

Assists

Gordie Howe, Detroit 43
Ted Kennedy Toronto 43
Max Bentley, Toronto 41
Milt Schmidt, Boston 39
Sid Abel, Detroit 38

Points

Gordie Howe, Detroit 86
Maurice Richard, Montreal 66
Max Bentley, Toronto 62
Sid Abel, Detroit 61
Milt Schmidt, Boston 61
Ted Kennedy, Toronto 61

Penalty minutes

Gus Mortson, Toronto 142
Tom Johnson, Montreal 128
Bill Ezinicki, Boston 119
Tony Leswick, New York 112
Ted Lindsay, Detroit 110

Lowest goals-against average
(Min. 25 games)

Al Rollins, Toronto 1.75
Terry Sawchuk, Detroit 1.98
Turk Broda, Toronto 2.19
Gerry McNeil, Montreal 2.63
Jack Gelineau, Boston 2.81

Shutouts

Terry Sawchuk, Detroit 11
Turk Broda, Toronto 6
Gerry McNeil, Montreal 6
Al Rollins, Toronto 5
Jack Gelineau, Boston 4

1951-52

Goals

Gordie Howe, Detroit 47
Bill Mosienko, Chicago 31
Bernie Geoffrion, Montreal 30
Ted Lindsay, Detroit 30
Maurice Richard, Montreal 27
Sid Smith, Toronto 27

Assists

Elmer Lach, Montreal 50
Don Raleigh, New York 42
Gordie Howe, Detroit 39
Ted Lindsay, Detroit 39
Sid Abel, Detroit 36

Points

Gordie Howe, Detroit 86
Ted Lindsay, Detroit 69
Elmer Lach, Montreal 65
Don Raleigh, New York 61
Sid Smith, Toronto 57

NHL HISTORY Statistical leaders

– 169 –

Penalty minutes

Gus Kyle, Boston	127
Ted Lindsay, Detroit	123
Fern Flaman, Toronto	110
Gus Mortson, Toronto	106
Al Dewsbury, Chicago	99

Lowest goals-against average
(Min. 25 games)

Terry Sawchuk, Detroit	1.90
Al Rollins, Toronto	2.20
Gerry McNeil, Montreal	2.34
Jim Henry, Boston	2.51
Claude Rayner, New York	3.00

Shutouts

Terry Sawchuk, Detroit	12
Jim Henry, Boston	7
Gerry McNeil, Montreal	5
Al Rollins, Toronto	5
Harry Lumley, Chicago	2
Claude Rayner, New York	2

1952-53

Goals

Gordie Howe, Detroit	49
Ted Lindsay, Detroit	32
Wally Hergesheimer, New York	30
Maurice Richard, Montreal	28
Fleming Mackell, Boston	27

Assists

Gordie Howe, Detroit	46
Alex Delvecchio, Detroit	43
Ted Lindsay, Detroit	39
Paul Ronty, New York	38
Metro Prystai, Detroit	34

Points

Gordie Howe, Detroit	95
Ted Lindsay, Detroit	71
Maurice Richard, Montreal	61
Wally Hergesheimer, New York	59
Alex Delvecchio, Detroit	59

Penalty minutes

Maurice Richard, Montreal	112
Ted Lindsay, Detroit	111
Fern Flaman, Toronto	110
George Gee, Chicago	99
Leo Boivin, Toronto	97
Al Dewsbury, Chicago	97

Lowest goals-against average
(Min. 25 games)

Terry Sawchuk, Detroit	1.90
Gerry McNeil, Montreal	2.12
Harry Lumley, Toronto	2.38
Jim Henry, Boston	2.46
Al Rollins, Chicago	2.50

Shutouts

Harry Lumley, Toronto	10
Gerry McNeil, Montreal	10
Terry Sawchuk, Detroit	9
Jim Henry, Boston	7
Al Rollins, Chicago	6

1953-54

Goals

Maurice Richard, Montreal	37
Gordie Howe, Detroit	33
Bernie Geoffrion, Montreal	29
Wally Hergesheimer, New York	27
Ted Lindsay, Detroit	26

Assists

Gordie Howe, Detroit	48
Bert Olmstead, Montreal	37
Ted Lindsay, Detroit	36
Four players tied with	33

Points

Gordie Howe, Detroit	81
Maurice Richard, Montreal	67
Ted Lindsay, Detroit	62
Bernie Geoffrion, Montreal	54
Bert Olmstead, Montreal	52

Penalty minutes

Gus Mortson, Chicago	132
Maurice Richard, Montreal	112
Doug Harvey, Montreal	110
Ted Lindsay, Detroit	110
Gordie Howe, Detroit	109
Ivan Irwin, New York	109

Lowest goals-against average
(Min. 25 games)

Harry Lumley, Toronto	1.85
Terry Sawchuk, Detroit	1.92
Gerry McNeil, Montreal	2.15
Jim Henry, Boston	2.58
John Bower, New York	2.60

Shutouts

Harry Lumley, Toronto	13
Terry Sawchuk, Detroit	12
Jim Henry, Boston	8
Gerry McNeil, Montreal	6
John Bower, New York	5
Jacques Plante, Montreal	5
Al Rollins, Chicago	5

1954-55

Goals

Bernie Geoffrion, Montreal	38
Maurice Richard, Montreal	38
Jean Beliveau, Montreal	37
Sid Smith, Toronto	33
Gordie Howe, Detroit	29
Danny Lewicki, New York	29

Assists

Bert Olmstead, Montreal	48
Doug Harvey, Montreal	43
Ted Kennedy, Toronto	42
George Sullivan, Chicago	42
Earl Reibel, Detroit	41

Points

Bernie Geoffrion, Montreal	75
Maurice Richard, Montreal	74
Jean Beliveau, Montreal	73
Earl Reibel, Detroit	66
Gordie Howe, Detroit	62

Penalty minutes

Fern Flaman, Boston	150
Tony Leswick, Detroit	137
Bucky Hollingworth, Chicago	135
Gus Mortson, Chicago	133
Maurice Richard, Montreal	125

Lowest goals-against average
(Min. 25 games)

Terry Sawchuk, Detroit	1.94
Harry Lumley, Toronto	1.94
Jacques Plante, Montreal	2.11
John Henderson, Boston	2.40
Jim Henry, Boston	3.00

Shutouts

Terry Sawchuk, Detroit	12
Harry Lumley, Toronto	8

John Henderson, Boston ... 5
Jacques Plante, Montreal ... 5
Gump Worsley, New York ... 4

1955-56

Goals

Jean Beliveau, Montreal	47
Gordie Howe, Detroit	38
Maurice Richard, Montreal	38
Tod Sloan, Toronto	37
Bernie Geoffrion, Montreal	29

Assists

Bert Olmstead, Montreal	56
Andy Bathgate, New York	47
Bill Gadsby, New York	42
Jean Beliveau, Montreal	41
Gordie Howe, Detroit	41

Points

Jean Beliveau, Montreal	88
Gordie Howe, Detroit	79
Maurice Richard, Montreal	71
Bert Olmstead, Montreal	70
Tod Sloan, Toronto	66
Andy Bathgate, New York	66

Penalty minutes

Lou Fontinato, New York	202
Ted Lindsay, Detroit	161
Jean Beliveau, Montreal	143
Bob Armstrong, Boston	122
Vic Stasiuk, Boston	118

Lowest goals-against average
(Min. 25 games)

Jacques Plante, Montreal	1.86
Glenn Hall, Detroit	2.11
Terry Sawchuk, Boston	2.66
Harry Lumley, Toronto	2.69
Gump Worsley, New York	2.90

Shutouts

Glenn Hall, Detroit	12
Terry Sawchuk, Boston	9
Jacques Plante, Montreal	7
Gump Worsley, New York	4
Harry Lumley, Toronto	3
Al Rollins, Chicago	3

1956-57

Goals

Gordie Howe, Detroit	44
Jean Beliveau, Montreal	33
Maurice Richard, Montreal	33
Ed Litzenberger, Chicago	32
Real Chevrefils, Boston	31

Assists

Ted Lindsay, Detroit	55
Jean Beliveau, Montreal	51
Andy Bathgate, New York	50
Gordie Howe, Detroit	45
Doug Harvey, Montreal	44

Points

Gordie Howe, Detroit	89
Ted Lindsay, Detroit	85
Jean Beliveau, Montreal	84
Andy Bathgate, New York	77
Ed Litzenberger, Chicago	64

Penalty minutes

Gus Mortson, Chicago	147
Lou Fontinato, New York	139

Leo LaBine, Boston 128
Pierre Pilote, Chicago.......................117
Jack Evans, New York 110

Lowest goals-against average
(Min. 25 games)
Jacques Plante, Montreal 2.02
Glenn Hall, Detroit............................2.24
Terry Sawchuk, Boston 2.38
Don Simmons, Boston 2.42
Ed Chadwick, Toronto 2.74

Shutouts
Jacques Plante, Montreal 9
Eddie Chadwick, Toronto 5
Glenn Hall, Detroit...................................4
Don Simmons, Boston 4
Al Rollins, Chicago 3
Gump Worsley, New York 3

1957-58

Goals
Dickie Moore, Montreal 36
Gordie Howe, Detroit............................33
Camille Henry, New York......................32
Ed Litzenberger, Chicago.....................32
Andy Bathgate, New York.....................30
Bronco Horvath, Boston........................30

Assists
Henri Richard, Montreal 52
Andy Bathgate, New York......................48
Dickie Moore, Montreal 48
Gordie Howe, Detroit.............................44
Fleming Mackell, Boston 40

Points
Dickie Moore, Montreal 84
Henri Richard, Montreal 80
Andy Bathgate, New York.......................78
Gordie Howe, Detroit..............................77
Bronco Horvath, Boston..........................66

Penalty minutes
Lou Fontinato, New York.....................152
Forbes Kennedy, Detroit.....................135
Doug Harvey, Montreal 131
Ted Lindsay, Chicago 110
Jack Evans, New York 108

Lowest goals-against average
(Min. 25 games)
Jacques Plante, Montreal 2.09
Gump Worsley, New York 2.32
Don Simmons, Boston 2.45
Harry Lumley, Boston 2.84
Glenn Hall, Chicago 2.88

Shutouts
Jacques Plante, Montreal 9
Glenn Hall, Chicago 7
Don Simmons, Boston 5
Gump Worsley, New York 4
Ed Chadwick, Toronto 4

1958-59

Goals
Jean Beliveau, Montreal 45
Dickie Moore, Montreal 41
Andy Bathgate, N.Y Rangers 40
Ed Litzenberger, Chicago......................33
Andy Hebenton, New York 33

Assists
Dickie Moore, Montreal 55
Andy Bathgate, New York......................48

Jean Beliveau, Montreal 46
Bill Gadsby, New York 46
Gordie Howe, Detroit.............................46

Points
Dickie Moore, Montreal 96
Jean Beliveau, Montreal 91
Andy Bathgate, New York......................88
Gordie Howe, Detroit..............................78
Ed Litzenberger, Chicago......................77

Penalty minutes
Ted Lindsay, Chicago 184
Lou Fontinato, New York.....................149
Forbes Kennedy, Detroit.....................149
Carl Brewer, Toronto 125
Jim Bartlett, New York 118

Lowest goals-against average
(Min. 25 games)
Jacques Plante, Montreal 2.15
Johnny Bower, Toronto 2.74
Glenn Hall, Chicago 2.97
Eddie Chadwick, Toronto 3.00
Gump Worsley, New York 3.06

Shutouts
Jacques Plante, Montreal 9
Terry Sawchuk, Detroit.............................5
Johnny Bower, Toronto 3
Eddie Chadwick, Toronto 3
Don Simmons, Boston 3

1959-60

Goals
Bobby Hull, Chicago..............................39
Bronco Horvath, Boston........................39
Jean Beliveau, Montreal 34
Dean Prentice, New York......................32
Bernie Geoffrion, Montreal 30
Henri Richard, Montreal 30

Assists
Don McKenney, Boston 49
Andy Bathgate, New York......................48
Gordie Howe, Detroit.............................45
Henri Richard, Montreal 43
Bobby Hull, Chicago..............................42

Points
Bobby Hull, Chicago..............................81
Bronco Horvath, Boston........................80
Jean Beliveau, Montreal 74
Andy Bathgate, New York......................74
Henri Richard, Montreal 73
Gordie Howe, Detroit.............................73

Penalty minutes
Carl Brewer, Toronto 150
Lou Fontinato, New York.....................137
Vic Stasiuk, Boston 121
Stan Mikita, Chicago 119
Fern Flaman, Boston 112

Lowest goals-against average
(Min. 25 games)
Jacques Plante, Montreal 2.54
Glenn Hall, Chicago 2.57
Terry Sawchuk, Detroit.......................2.69
Johnny Bower, Toronto 2.73
Don Simmons, Boston 3.36

Shutouts
Glenn Hall, Chicago 6
Johnny Bower, Toronto 5
Terry Sawchuk, Detroit.............................5
Jacques Plante, Montreal 3

Harry Lumley, Boston 2
Don Simmons, Boston 2

1960-61

Goals
Bernie Geoffrion, Montreal 50
Frank Mahovlich, Toronto......................48
Dickie Moore, Montreal 35
Jean Beliveau, Montreal 32
Bobby Hull, Chicago..............................31

Assists
Jean Beliveau, Montreal 58
Red Kelly, Toronto.................................50
Gordie Howe, Detroit.............................49
Andy Bathgate, New York......................48
Bill Hay, Chicago...................................48

Points
Bernie Geoffrion, Montreal 95
Jean Beliveau, Montreal 90
Frank Mahovlich, Toronto......................84
Andy Bathgate, New York......................77
Gordie Howe, Detroit.............................72

Penalty minutes
Pierre Pilote, Chicago..........................165
Reg Fleming, Chicago 145
Jean Guy Talbot, Montreal...................143
Frank Mahovlich, Toronto.....................131
Eric Nesterenko, Chicago 125

Lowest goals-against average
(Min. 25 games)
Johnny Bower, Toronto 2.50
Charlie Hodge, Montreal......................2.53
Jacques Plante, Montreal 2.80
Hank Bassen, Detroit...........................2.97
Terry Sawchuk, Detroit.......................3.17

Shutouts
Glenn Hall, Chicago 6
Charlie Hodge, Montreal..........................4
Johnny Bower, Toronto 2
Jacques Plante, Montreal 2
Terry Sawchuk, Detroit.............................2

1961-62

Goals
Bobby Hull, Chicago..............................50
Gordie Howe, Detroit.............................33
Frank Mahovlich, Toronto......................33
Claude Provost, Montreal......................33
Gilles Tremblay, Montreal 32

Assists
Andy Bathgate, New York......................56
Bill Hay, Chicago 52
Stan Mikita, Chicago 52
Gordie Howe, Detroit.............................44
Alex Delvecchio, Detroit 43

Points
Bobby Hull, Chicago..............................84
Andy Bathgate, New York......................84
Gordie Howe, Detroit.............................77
Stan Mikita, Chicago 77
Frank Mahovlich, Toronto......................71

Penalty minutes
Lou Fontinato, Montreal 167
Ted Green, Boston...............................116
Bob Pulford, Toronto 98
Stan Mikita, Chicago 97
Eric Nesterenko, Chicago 97
Pierre Pilote, Chicago.............................97

Lowest goals-against average
(Min. 25 games)
Jacques Plante, Montreal 2.37
John Bower, Toronto 2.58
Glenn Hall, Chicago 2.66
Henry Bassen, Detroit 2.81
Gump Worsley, New York 2.90
Shutouts
Glenn Hall, Chicago 9
Terry Sawchuk, Detroit 5
Jacques Plante, Montreal 4
Henry Bassen, Detroit 3
Three players tied with 2

1962-63

Goals
Gordie Howe, Detroit 38
Camille Henry, New York 37
Frank Mahovlich, Toronto 36
Andy Bathgate, New York 35
Parker MacDonald, Detroit 33
Assists
Henri Richard, Montreal 50
Jean Beliveau, Montreal 49
Gordie Howe, Detroit 48
Andy Bathgate, New York 46
Stan Mikita, Chicago 45
Points
Gordie Howe, Detroit 86
Andy Bathgate, New York 81
Stan Mikita, Chicago 76
Frank Mahovlich, Toronto 73
Henri Richard, Montreal 73
Penalty minutes
Howie Young, Detroit 273
Carl Brewer, Toronto 168
Lou Fontinato, Montreal 141
Ted Green, Boston 117
Bill Gladsby, Detroit 116
Lowest goals-against average
(Min. 25 games)
Jacques Plante, Montreal 2.46
Terry Sawchuk, Detroit 2.48
Don Simmons, Toronto 2.50
Glenn Hall, Chicago 2.51
Johnny Bower, Toronto 2.62
Shutouts
Glenn Hall, Chicago 5
Jacques Plante, Montreal 5
Terry Sawchuk, Detroit 3
Gump Worsley, New York 2
Four players tied with 1

1963-64

Goals
Bobby Hull, Chicago 43
Stan Mikita, Chicago 39
Ken Wharram, Chicago 39
Camille Henry, New York 29
Jean Beliveau, Montreal 28
Assists
Andy Bathgate, N.Y.-Tor. 58
Jean Beliveau, Montreal 50
Stan Mikita, Chicago 50
Gordie Howe, Detroit 47
Pierre Pilote, Chicago 46
Points
Stan Mikita, Chicago 89
Bobby Hull, Chicago 87
Jean Beliveau, Montreal 78

Andy Bathgate, N.Y.-Tor. 77
Gordie Howe, Detroit 73
Penalty minutes
Vic Hadfield, New York 151
Terry Harper, Montreal 149
Stan Mikita, Chicago 146
Ted Green, Boston 145
Reg Fleming, Chicago 140
Lowest goals-against average
(Min. 25 games)
Johnny Bower, Toronto 2.11
Charlie Hodge, Montreal....................2.26
Glenn Hall, Chicago 2.30
Terry Sawchuk, Detroit 2.70
Eddie Johnston, Boston 3.01
Shutouts
Charlie Hodge, Montreal........................8
Glenn Hall, Chicago 7
Eddie Johnston, Boston 6
Johnny Bower, Toronto 5
Terry Sawchuk, Detroit 5

1964-65

Goals
Norm Ullman, Detroit 42
Bobby Hull, Chicago 39
Gordie Howe, Detroit 29
Stan Mikita, Chicago 28
Claude Provost, Montreal.....................27
Assists
Stan Mikita, Chicago 59
Gordie Howe, Detroit 47
Pierre Pilote, Chicago 45
Alex Delvecchio, Detroit 42
Norm Ullman, Detroit 41
Points
Stan Mikita, Chicago 87
Norm Ullman, Detroit 83
Gordie Howe, Detroit 76
Bobby Hull, Chicago 71
Alex Delvecchio, Detroit 67
Penalty minutes
Carl Brewer, Toronto 177
Ted Lindsay, Detroit 173
Pierre Pilote, Chicago 162
Bob Baun, Toronto 160
John Ferguson, Montreal 156
Ted Green, Boston 156
Lowest goals-against average
(Min. 25 games)
Johnny Bower, Toronto 2.38
Roger Crozier, Detroit........................2.42
Glenn Hall, Chicago 2.43
Denis DeJordy, Chicago 2.52
Terry Sawchuk, Toronto 2.56
Shutouts
Roger Crozier, Detroit...........................6
Glenn Hall, Chicago 4
Johnny Bower, Toronto 3
Denis DeJordy, Chicago 3
Charlie Hodge, Montreal........................3
Ed Johnston, Boston 3

1965-66

Goals
Bobby Hull, Chicago 54
Frank Mahovlich, Toronto....................32
Alex Delvecchio, Detroit 31
Norm Ullman, Detroit 31

Stan Mikita, Chicago 30
Bobby Rousseau, Montreal 30
Assists
Jean Beliveau, Montreal 48
Stan Mikita, Chicago 48
Bobby Rousseau, Montreal 48
Gordie Howe, Detroit 46
Bobby Hull, Chicago 43
Points
Bobby Hull, Chicago 97
Stan Mikita, Chicago 78
Bobby Rousseau, Montreal 78
Jean Beliveau, Montreal 77
Gordie Howe, Detroit 75
Penalty minutes
Reg Fleming, Bos.-N.Y. 166
John Ferguson, Montreal 153
Bryan Watson, Detroit 133
Ted Green, Boston 113
Vic Hadfield, New York 112
Lowest goals-against average
(Min. 25 games)
Johnny Bower, Toronto 2.25
Gump Worsley, Montreal 2.36
Charlie Hodge, Montreal....................2.58
Glenn Hall, Chicago 2.63
Roger Crozier, Detroit........................2.78
Shutouts
Roger Crozier, Detroit...........................7
Bruce Gamble, Toronto 4
Glenn Hall, Chicago 4
Johnny Bower, Toronto 3
Cesare Maniago, New York 2
Gump Worsley, Montreal 2

1966-67

Goals
Bobby Hull, Chicago 52
Stan Mikita, Chicago 35
Ken Wharram, Chicago 31
Rod Gilbert, New York 28
Bruce MacGregor, Detroit...................28
Assists
Stan Mikita, Chicago 62
Phil Goyette, New York 49
Pierre Pilote, Chicago 46
Bobby Rousseau, Montreal 44
Norm Ullman, Detroit 44
Points
Stan Mikita, Chicago 97
Bobby Hull, Chicago 80
Norm Ullman, Detroit 70
Ken Wharram, Chicago 65
Gordie Howe, Detroit 65
Penalty minutes
John Ferguson, Montreal 177
Reg Fleming, New York 146
Gary Bergman, Detroit 129
Gilles Marotte, Boston 112
Ed Van Impe, Chicago 111
Lowest goals-against average
(Min. 25 games)
Glenn Hall, Chicago 2.38
Denis DeJordy, Chicago 2.46
Charlie Hodge, Montreal....................2.60
Ed Giacomin, New York 2.61
Johnny Bower, Toronto 2.64
Shutouts
Ed Giacomin, New York.........................9
Roger Crozier, Detroit...........................4

Denis DeJordy, Chicago 4
Charlie Hodge, Montreal.......................3
Three players tied with 2

1967-68

Goals
Bobby Hull, Chicago.............................44
Stan Mikita, Chicago 40
Gordie Howe, Detroit............................39
Phil Esposito, Boston 35
Wayne Connelly, Minnesota 35
Norm Ullman, Det.-Tor. 35

Assists
Phil Esposito, Boston 49
Alex Delvecchio, Detroit 48
Rod Gilbert, New York..........................48
Stan Mikita, Chicago 47
Jean Ratelle, New York.........................46

Points
Stan Mikita, Chicago 87
Phil Esposito, Boston 84
Gordie Howe, Detroit............................82
Jean Ratelle, New York.........................78
Rod Gilbert, New York..........................77

Penalty minutes
Barclay Plager, St. Louis 153
Don Awrey, Boston.............................150
Noel Picard, St. Louis 142
Ed Van Impe, Philadelphia.................141
Gary Dornhoefer, Philadelphia...........134

Lowest goals-against average
(Min. 25 games)
Gump Worsley, Montreal 1.98
Johnny Bower, Toronto 2.25
Boug Favell, Philadelphia 2.27
Bruce Gamble, Toronto.....................2.31
Ed Giacomin, New York.....................2.44

Shutouts
Ed Giacomin, New York...........................8
Les Binkley, Pittburgh 6
Cesare Maniago, Minnesota 6
Gump Worsley, Montreal 6
Bruce Gamble, Toronto 5
Glenn Hall, St. Louis 5

1968-69

Goals
Bobby Hull, Chicago.............................58
Phil Esposito, Boston 49
Frank Mahovlich, Detroit 49
Ken Hodge, Boston 45
Gordie Howe, Detroit............................44

Assists
Phil Esposito, Boston 77
Stan Mikita, Chicago 67
Gordie Howe, Detroit............................59
Alex Delvecchio, Detroit 58
Four players tied with...........................49

Points
Phil Esposito, Boston 126
Bobby Hull, Chicago............................107
Gordie Howe, Detroit..........................103
Stan Mikita, Chicago 97
Ken Hodge, Boston 90

Penalty minutes
Forbes Kennedy, Phi.-Tor. 219
Jim Dorey, Toronto.............................200
John Ferguson, Montreal 185
Carol Vadnais, Oakland 151
Don Awrey, Boston.............................149

Lowest goals-against average
(Min. 25 games)
Jacques Plante, St. Louis 1.96
Glenn Hall, St. Louis 2.17
Gump Worsley, Montreal 2.26
Ron Edwards, Detroit........................2.54
Ed Giacomin, New York.....................2.55

Shutouts
Glenn Hall, St. Louis 8
Ed Giacomin, New York...........................7
Jacques Plante, St. Louis 5
Gump Worsley, Montreal 5
Roy Edwards, Detroit 4
Gary Smith, Oakland 4
Gerry Desjardins, Los Angeles..............4

1969-70

Goals
Phil Esposito, Boston 43
Garry Unger, Detroit 42
Stan Mikita, Chicago 39
Bobby Hull, Chicago.............................38
Frank Mahovlich, Detroit 38

Assists
Bobby Orr, Boston................................87
Phil Esposito, Boston 56
Tommy Williams, Minnesota 52
Walt Tkaczuk, New York.......................50
Phil Goyette, St. Louis..........................49

Points
Bobby Orr, Boston..............................120
Phil Esposito, Boston 99
Stan Mikita, Chicago 86
Phil Goyette, St. Louis..........................78
Walt Tkaczuk, New York.......................77

Penalty minutes
Keith Magnuson, Chicago 213
Carol Vadnais, Oakland 212
Bryan Watson, Pittsburgh 189
Barry Gibbs, Minnesota......................182
Earl Heiskala, Philadelphia 171

Lowest goals-against average
(Min. 25 games)
Ernie Wakely, St. Louis.......................2.11
Tony Esposito, Chicago 2.17
Jacques Plante St. Louis 2.19
Ed Giacomin, New York......................2.36
Roy Edwards, Detroit 2.59

Shutouts
Tony Esposito, Chicago 15
Ed Giacomin, New York...........................6
Bruce Gamble, Toronto 5
Jacques Plante, St. Louis 5
Gerry Cheevers, Boston 4
Rogie Vachon, Montreal 4
Ernie Wakely, St. Louis..........................4

Wins by goaltenders
Tony Esposito, Chicago 38
Ed Giacomin, New York..........................35
Rogie Vachon, Montreal 31
Gerry Cheevers, Boston 24
Roy Edwards, Detroit 24

1970-71

Goals
Phil Esposito, Boston 76
John Bucyk, Boston 51
Bobby Hull, Chicago.............................44
Ken Hodge, Boston 43
Dennis Hull, Chicago............................40

Assists
Bobby Orr, Boston..............................102
Phil Esposito, Boston 76
John Bucyk, Boston 65
Ken Hodge, Boston 62
Wayne Cashman, Boston 58

Points
Phil Esposito, Boston 152
Bobby Orr, Boston..............................139
John Bucyk, Boston 116
Ken Hodge, Boston 105
Bobby Hull, Chicago..............................96

Penalty minutes
Keith Magnuson, Chicago 291
Dennis Hextall, California 217
Jim Dorey, Toronto.............................198
Pete Mahovlich, Montreal...................181
Tracy Pratt, Buffalo.............................179

Lowest goals-against average
(Min. 25 games)
Jacques Plante, Toronto......................1.88
Ed Giacomin, New York.....................2.16
Tony Esposito, Chicago 2.27
Gilles Villemure, New York 2.30
Glenn Hall, St. Louis 2.41

Shutouts
Ed Giacomin, New York...........................8
Tony Esposito, Chicago 6
Cesare Maniago, Minnesota 5
Jacques Plante, Toronto.........................4
Ed Johnston, Boston 4
Gilles Villemure, New York 4

Wins by goaltenders
Tony Esposito, Chicago 35
Ed Johnston, Boston 30
Gerry Cheevers, Boston 27
Ed Giacomin, New York..........................27
Jacques Plante, Toronto.........................24

1971-72

Goals
Phil Esposito, Boston 66
Vic Hadfield, New York.........................50
Bobby Hull, Chicago.............................50
Yvan Cournoyer, Montreal...................47
Jean Ratelle, New York.........................46

Assists
Bobby Orr, Boston................................80
Phil Esposito, Boston 67
Jean Ratelle, New York.........................63
Vic Hadfield, New York.........................56
Fred Stanfield, Boston..........................56

Points
Phil Esposito, Boston 133
Bobby Orr, Boston..............................117
Jean Ratelle, New York.......................109
Vic Hadfield, New York.......................106
Rod Gilbert, New York..........................97

Penalty minutes
Bryan Watson, Pittsburgh 212
Keith Magnuson, Chicago 201
Gary Dornhoefer, Philadelphia...........183
Barclay Plager, St. Louis 176
Rick Foley, Philadelphia.....................168

Lowest goals-against average
(Min. 25 games)
Tony Esposito, Chicago 1.77
Gilles Villemure, New York 2.08

Gump Worsley, Minnesota 2.12
Ken Dryden, Montreal 2.34
Gary Smith, Chicago 2.42

Shutouts
Tony Esposito, Chicago 9
Ken Dryden, Montreal 8
Gary Smith, Chicago 5
Doug Favell, Philadelphia 5
Al Smith, Detroit...................................4
Gilles Meloche, California 4

Wins by goaltenders
Ken Dryden, Montreal 39
Tony Esposito, Chicago 31
Gerry Cheevers, Boston 27
Ed Johnston, Boston 27
Ed Giacomin, New York........................24
Gilles Villemure, New York 24

1972-73

Goals
Phil Esposito, Boston 55
Mickey Redmond, Detroit.....................52
Rick MacLeish, Philadelphia................50
Jacques Lemaire, Montreal 44
Three players tied with........................41

Assists
Phil Esposito, Boston 75
Bobby Orr, Boston................................72
Bobby Clarke, Philadelphia..................67
Pit Martin, Chicago...............................61
Gilbert Perreault, Buffalo 60

Points
Phil Esposito, Boston 130
Bobby Clarke, Philadelphia................104
Bobby Orr, Boston..............................101
Rick MacLeish, Philadelphia..............100
Jacques Lemaire, Montreal 95

Penalty minutes
Dave Schultz, Philadelphia 259
Bob Kelly, Philadelphia 238
Steve Durbano, St. Louis 231
Andre Dupont, St.L.-Phi......................215
Don Saleski, Philadelphia 205

Lowest goals-against average
(Min. 25 games)
Ken Dryden, Montreal 2.26
Gilles Villemure, N.Y. Rangers...........2.29
Tony Esposito, Chicago 2.51
Roy Edwards, Detroit 2.63
Dave Dryden, Buffalo 2.68

Shutouts
Ken Dryden, Montreal 6
Roy Edwards, Detroit 6
Eddie Johnston, Boston 5
Cesare Maniago, Minnesota 5
Three tied with 4

Wins by goaltenders
Ken Dryden, Montreal 33
Tony Esposito, Chicago 32
Roy Edwards, Detroit 27
Ed Giacomin, N.Y. Rangers 26
Ed Johnston, Boston 24

1973-74

Goals
Phil Esposito, Boston 68
Richard Martin, Buffalo 52

Mickey Redmond, Detroit.....................51
Ken Hodge, Boston 50
Bill Goldsworthy, Minnesota.................48

Assists
Bobby Orr, Boston................................90
Phil Esposito, Boston 77
Dennis Hextall, Minnesota....................62
Syl Apps, Pittsburgh 61
Andre Boudrias, Vancouver...................59
Wayne Cashman, Boston 59

Points
Phil Esposito, Boston 145
Bobby Orr, Boston..............................122
Ken Hodge, Boston 105
Wayne Cashman, Boston 89
Bobby Clarke, Philadelphia..................87

Penalty minutes
Dave Schultz, Philadelphia 348
Steve Durbano, St.L.-Pit.....................284
Bryan Watson, Pit.-St.L.-Det. 255
Andre Dupont, Philadelphia.................216
Garry Howatt, N.Y. Islanders 204

Lowest goals-against average
(Min. 25 games)
Bernie Parent, Philadelphia 1.89
Tony Esposito, Chicago 2.04
Doug Favell, Toronto 2.71
Wayne Thomas, Montreal 2.76
Dan Bouchard, Atlanta 2.77

Shutouts
Bernie Parent, Philadelphia 12
Tony Esposito, Chicago 10
Gilles Gilbert, Boston 6
Dan Bouchard, Atlanta 5
Ed Giacomin, N.Y. Rangers 5
Rogie Vachon, Los Angeles...................5

Wins by goaltenders
Bernie Parent, Philadelphia 47
Tony Esposito, Chicago 34
Gilles Gilbert, Boston 34
Ed Giacomin, N.Y. Rangers 30
Rogie Vachon, Los Angeles.................28

1974-75

Goals
Phil Esposito, Boston 61
Guy Lafleur, Montreal 53
Rick Martin, Buffalo 52
Danny Grant, Detroit 50
Marcel Dionne, Detroit 47

Assists
Bobby Clarke, Philadelphia..................89
Bobby Orr, Boston................................89
Pete Mahovlich, Montreal.....................82
Marcel Dionne, Detroit 74
Phil Esposito, Boston 66
Guy Lafleur, Montreal 66

Points
Bobby Orr, Boston..............................135
Phil Esposito, Boston 127
Marcel Dionne, Detroit 121
Guy Lafleur, Montreal 119
Pete Mahovlich, Montreal...................117

Penalty minutes
Dave Schultz, Philadelphia 472
Andre Dupont, Philadelphia.................276
Phil Russell, Chicago 260
Bryan Watson, Detroit 238
Bob Gassoff, St. Louis 222

Lowest goals-against average
(Min. 25 games)
Bernie Parent, Philadelphia 2.03
Rogie Vachon, Los Angeles.................2.24
Gary Edwards, Los Angeles 2.34
Chico Resch, N.Y. Islanders 2.47
Ken Dryden, Montreal 2.69

Shutouts
Bernie Parent, Philadelphia 12
Tony Esposito, Chicago 6
Gary Smith, Vancouver 6
Rogie Vachon, Los Angeles...................6
Phil Myre, Atlanta 5

Wins by goaltenders
Bernie Parent, Philadelphia 44
Tony Esposito, Chicago 34
Gary Smith, Vancouver 32
Ken Dryden, Montreal 30
Rogie Vachon, Los Angeles.................27

1975-76

Goals
Reggie Leach, Philadelphia 61
Guy Lafleur, Montreal 56
Pierre Larouche, Pittsburgh 53
Jean Pronovost, Pittsburgh..................52
Bill Barber, Philadelphia.......................50
Danny Gare, Buffalo 50

Assists
Bobby Clarke, Philadelphia..................89
Pete Mahovlich, Montreal.....................71
Guy Lafleur, Montreal 69
Gilbert Perreault, Buffalo 69
Jean Ratelle, NYR-Bos..........................69

Points
Guy Lafleur, Montreal 125
Bobby Clarke, Philadelphia................119
Gilbert Perreault, Buffalo 113
Bill Barber, Philadelphia.....................112
Pierre Larouche, Pittsburgh 111

Penalty minutes
Steve Durbano, Pit.-K.C. 370
Bryan Watson, Detroit 322
Dave Schultz, Philadelphia 307
Bob Gassoff, St. Louis 306
Dennis Polonich, Detroit 302

Lowest goals-against average
(Min. 25 games)
Ken Dryden, Montreal 2.03
Chico Resch, N.Y. Islanders 2.07
Dan Bouchard, Atlanta 2.54
Wayne Stephenson, Philadelphia 2.58
Billy Smith, N.Y. Islanders..................2.61

Shutouts
Ken Dryden, Montreal 8
Chico Resch, N.Y. Islanders 7
Rogie Vachon, Los Angeles...................5
Tony Esposito, Chicago 4
Jim Rutherford, Detroit 4

Wins by goaltenders
Ken Dryden, Montreal 42
Wayne Stephenson, Philadelphia 40
Gilles Gilbert, Boston 33
Tony Esposito, Chicago 30
Gerry Desjardins, Buffalo 29

1976-77

Goals
Steve Shutt, Montreal...........................60
Guy Lafleur, Montreal 56

Marcel Dionne, Los Angeles..................53
Rick MacLeish, Philadelphia.................49
Lanny McDonald, Toronto.....................46

Assists

Guy Lafleur, Montreal............................80
Marcel Dionne, Los Angeles..................69
Larry Robinson, Montreal 66
Borje Salming, Toronto 66
Tim Young, Minnesota 66

Points

Guy Lafleur, Montreal..........................136
Marcel Dionne, Los Angeles................122
Steve Shutt, Montreal..........................105
Rick MacLeish, Philadelphia.................97
Gilbert Perreault, Buffalo......................95
Tim Young, Minnesota 95

Penalty minutes

Dave Williams, Toronto.......................338
Dennis Polonich, Detroit 274
Bob Gassoff, St. Louis 254
Phil Russell, Chicago 233
Dave Schultz, Los Angeles 232

Lowest goals-against average
(Min. 25 games)

Michel Larocque, Montreal................2.09
Ken Dryden, Montreal 2.14
Chico Resch, N.Y. Islanders 2.28
Billy Smith, N.Y. Islanders.................2.50
Don Edwards, Buffalo..........................2.51

Shutouts

Ken Dryden, Montreal 10
Rogie Vachon, Los Angeles....................8
Bernie Parent, Philadelphia 5
Dunc Wilson, Pittsburgh 5
Michel Larocque, Montreal......................4
Mike Palmateer, Toronto 4
Chico Resch, N.Y. Islanders 4

Wins by goaltenders

Ken Dryden, Montreal 41
Bernie Parent, Philadelphia 35
Rogie Vachon, Los Angeles..................33
Gerry Desjardins, Buffalo......................31
Gerry Cheevers, Boston 30

1977-78

Goals

Guy Lafleur, Montreal............................60
Mike Bossy, N.Y. Islanders 53
Steve Shutt, Montreal............................49
Lanny McDonald, Toronto.....................47
Bryan Trottier, N.Y. Islanders...............46

Assists

Bryan Trottier, N.Y. Islanders...............77
Guy Lafleur, Montreal............................72
Darryl Sittler, Toronto............................72
Bobby Clarke, Philadelphia...................68
Denis Potvin, N.Y. Islanders 64

Points

Guy Lafleur, Montreal..........................132
Bryan Trottier, N.Y. Islanders.............123
Darryl Sittler, Toronto..........................117
Jacques Lemaire, Montreal 97
Denis Potvin, N.Y. Islanders 94

Penalty minutes

Dave Schultz, L.A.-Pit.........................405
Dave Williams, Toronto 351
Dennis Polonich, Detroit 254
Randy Holt, Chi.-Cle............................249
Andre Dupont, Philadelphia.................225

Lowest goals-against average
(Min. 25 games)

Ken Dryden, Montreal..........................2.05
Bernie Parent, Philadelphia 2.22
Gilles Gilbert, Boston 2.53
Chico Resch, N.Y. Islanders 2.55
Tony Esposito, Chicago.......................2.63

Shutouts

Bernie Parent, Philadelphia 7
Ken Dryden, Montreal 5
Don Edwards, Buffalo..............................5
Tony Esposito, Chicago 5
Mike Palmateer, Toronto 5

Wins by goaltenders

Don Edwards, Buffalo..............................38
Ken Dryden, Montreal 37
Mike Palmateer, Toronto 34
Bernie Parent, Philadelphia 29
Rogie Vachon, Los Angeles...................29

1978-79

Goals

Mike Bossy, N.Y. Islanders 69
Marcel Dionne, Los Angeles..................59
Guy Lafleur, Montreal............................52
Guy Chouinard, Atlanta 50
Bryan Trottier, N.Y. Islanders...............47

Assists

Bryan Trottier, N.Y. Islanders...............87
Guy Lafleur, Montreal............................77
Marcel Dionne, Los Angeles..................71
Bob MacMillan, Atlanta 71
Denis Potvin, N.Y. Islanders 70

Points

Bryan Trottier, N.Y. Islanders.............134
Marcel Dionne, Los Angeles................130
Guy Lafleur, Montreal..........................129
Mike Bossy, N.Y. Islanders 126
Bob MacMillan, Atlanta 108

Penalty minutes

Dave Williams, Toronto 298
Randy Holt, Van.-L.A...........................282
Dave Schultz, Pit.-Buf.........................243
Dave Hutchison, Toronto.....................235
Willi Plett, Atlanta................................213

Lowest goals-against average
(Min. 25 games)

Ken Dryden, Montreal..........................2.30
Chico Resch, N.Y. Islanders 2.50
Bernie Parent, Philadelphia 2.70
Michel Larocque, Montreal.................2.84
Billy Smith, N.Y. Islanders.................2.87

Shutouts

Ken Dryden, Montreal 5
Tony Esposito, Chicago 4
Mario Lessard, Los Angeles....................4
Mike Palmateer, Toronto 4
Bernie Parent, Philadelphia 4

Wins by goaltenders

Dan Bouchard, Atlanta 32
Ken Dryden, Montreal 30
Don Edwards, Buffalo.............................26
Mike Palmateer, Toronto 26
Chico Resch, N.Y. Islanders 26

1979-80

Goals

Charlie Simmer, Los Angeles 56
Blaine Stoughton, Hartford...................56

Danny Gare, Buffalo 56
Marcel Dionne, Los Angeles..................53
Mike Bossy, N.Y. Islanders 51
Wayne Gretzky, Edmonton 51

Assists

Wayne Gretzky, Edmonton 86
Marcel Dionne, Los Angeles..................84
Guy Lafleur, Montreal............................75
Gil Perreault, Buffalo.............................66
Bryan Trottier, N.Y. Islanders...............62

Points

Marcel Dionne, Los Angeles................137
Wayne Gretzky, Edmonton 137
Guy Lafleur, Montreal..........................125
Gil Perreault, Buffalo...........................106
Mike Rogers, Hartford.........................105

Penalty minutes

Jimmy Mann, Winnipeg 287
Dave Williams, Tor.-Van. 278
Paul Holmgren, Philadelphia 267
Terry O'Reilly, Boston.........................265
Terry Ruskowski, Chicago...................252

Lowest goals-against average
(Min. 25 games)

Bob Sauve, Buffalo.............................2.36
Denis Herron, Montreal.......................2.51
Don Edwards, Buffalo..........................2.57
Gilles Gilbert, Boston 2.73
Pete Peeters, Philadelphia 2.73

Shutouts

Tony Esposito, Chicago 6
Gerry Cheevers, Boston 4
Bob Sauve, Buffalo..................................4
Rogie Vachon, Detroit 4
Michel Larocque, Montreal.......................3
Chico Resch, N.Y. Islanders 3

Wins by goaltenders

Mike Liut, St. Louis 32
Tony Esposito, Chicago 31
Pete Peeters, Philadelphia 29
Don Edwards, Buffalo.............................27
Gilles Meloche, Minnesota 27

1980-81

Goals

Mike Bossy, N.Y. Islanders 68
Marcel Dionne, Los Angeles..................58
Charlie Simmer, Los Angeles 56
Wayne Gretzky, Edmonton 55
Rick Kehoe, Pittsburgh..........................55

Assists

Wayne Gretzky, Edmonton 109
Kent Nilsson, Calgary............................82
Marcel Dionne, Los Angeles..................77
Bernie Federko, St. Louis 73
Bryan Trottier, N.Y. Islanders...............72

Points

Wayne Gretzky, Edmonton 164
Marcel Dionne, Los Angeles................135
Kent Nilsson, Calgary..........................131
Mike Bossy, N.Y. Islanders 119
Dave Taylor, Los Angeles 112

Penalty minutes

Dave Williams, Vancouver...................343
Paul Holmgren, Philadelphia 306
Chris Nilan, Montreal 262
Jim Korn, Detroit.................................246
Willi Plett, Calgary...............................239

Lowest goals-against average
(Min. 25 games)
Richard Sevigny, Montreal 2.40
Rick St. Croix, Philadelphia 2.49
Don Edwards, Buffalo......................2.96
Pete Peeters, Philadelphia.................2.96
Michel Larocque, Montreal...............3.03

Shutouts
Don Edwards, Buffalo.........................3
Chico Resch, N.Y.I.-Colo. 3
11 goalies tied with 2

Wins by goaltenders
Mario Lessard, Los Angeles.................35
Mike Liut, St. Louis 33
Tony Esposito, Chicago 29
Greg Millen, Pittsburgh 25
Rogie Vachon, Boston.........................25

1981-82

Goals
Wayne Gretzky, Edmonton 92
Mike Bossy, N.Y. Islanders.................64
Dennis Maruk, Washington 60
Dino Ciccarelli, Minnesota..................55
Rick Vaive, Toronto 54

Assists
Wayne Gretzky, Edmonton 120
Peter Stastny, Quebec 93
Denis Savard, Chicago 87
Mike Bossy, N.Y. Islanders.................83
Bryan Trottier, N.Y. Islanders...........79

Points
Wayne Gretzky, Edmonton 212
Mike Bossy, N.Y. Islanders...............147
Peter Stastny, Quebec 139
Dennis Maruk, Washington 136
Bryan Trottier, N.Y. Islanders...........129

Penalty minutes
Paul Baxter, Pittsburgh......................409
Dave Williams, Toronto 341
Glen Cochrane, Philadelphia..............329
Pat Price, Pittsburgh 322
Al Secord, Chicago.............................303

Lowest goals-against average
(Min. 25 games)
Denis Herron, Montreal......................2.64
Rick Wamsley, Montreal....................2.75
Bill Smith, N.Y. Islanders..................2.97
Roland Melanson, N.Y. Islanders 3.23
Grant Fuhr, Edmonton........................3.31

Shutouts
Denis Herron, Montreal..........................3
Richard Brodeur, Vancouver 2
Gary Edwards, St.L.-Pit.........................2
Mario Lessard, Los Angeles 2
Mike Liut, St. Louis 2
Pat Riggin, Calgary 2
Doug Soetaert, Winnipeg 2
Rick Wamsley, Montreal........................2

Wins by goaltenders
Billy Smith, N.Y. Islanders.................32
Grant Fuhr, Edmonton.........................28
Mike Liut, St. Louis 28
Dan Bouchard, Quebec.........................27
Don Edwards, Buffalo..........................26
Gilles Meloche, Minnesota 26

1982-83

Goals
Wayne Gretzky, Edmonton 71
Lanny McDonald, Calgary 66

Mike Bossy, N.Y. Islanders..................60
Michel Goulet, Quebec.........................57
Marcel Dionne, Los Angeles.................56

Assists
Wayne Gretzky, Edmonton 125
Denis Savard, Chicago 86
Peter Stastny, Quebec 77
Paul Coffey, Edmonton.........................67
Bobby Clarke, Philadelphia..................62

Points
Wayne Gretzky, Edmonton 196
Peter Stastny, Quebec 124
Denis Savard, Chicago 121
Mike Bossy, N.Y. Islanders...............118
Marcel Dionne, Los Angeles...............107
Barry Pederson, Boston 107

Penalty minutes
Randy Holt, Washington 275
Dave Williams, Vancouver.................265
Brian Sutter, St. Louis 254
Paul Baxter, Pittsburgh......................238
Glen Cochrane, Philadelphia..............237

Lowest goals-against average
(Min. 25 games)
Pete Peeters, Boston...........................2.36
Roland Melanson, N.Y. Islanders 2.66
Billy Smith, N.Y. Islanders................2.87
Pelle Lindbergh, Philadelphia 2.98
Murray Bannerman, Chicago..............3.10

Shutouts
Pete Peeters, Boston...............................8
Murray Bannerman, Chicago..................4
Bob Froese, Philadelphia 4
Pelle Lindbergh, Philadelphia 3
Corrado Micalef, Detroit 2
Markus Mattsson, Min.-L.A..................2
Ed Mio, N.Y. Rangers 2

Wins by goaltenders
Pete Peeters, Boston.............................40
Andy Moog, Edmonton 33
Rick Wamsley, Montreal.....................27
Bob Sauve, Buffalo 25
Murray Bannerman, Chicago..............24
Roland Melanson, N.Y. Islanders 24

1983-84

Goals
Wayne Gretzky, Edmonton 87
Michel Goulet, Quebec.........................56
Glenn Anderson, Edmonton 54
Tim Kerr, Philadelphia 54
Jari Kurri, Edmonton 52
Rick Vaive, Toronto 52

Assists
Wayne Gretzky, Edmonton 118
Paul Coffey, Edmonton.........................86
Barry Pederson, Boston 77
Peter Stastny, Quebec 73
Bryan Trottier, N.Y. Islanders...........71

Points
Wayne Gretzky, Edmonton 205
Paul Coffey, Edmonton.......................126
Michel Goulet, Quebec.......................121
Peter Stastny, Quebec 119
Mike Bossy, N.Y. Islanders...............118

Penalty minutes
Chris Nilan, Montreal 338
Willie Plett, Minnesota 316
Gary Rissling, Pittsburgh 297

Dave Williams, Vancouver.................294
Jim Korn, Toronto 257

Lowest goals-against average
(Min. 25 games)
Pat Riggin, Washington 2.66
Tom Barrasso, Buffalo.........................2.84
Al Jensen, Washington 2.91
Doug Keans, Boston.............................3.10
Bob Froese, Philadelphia 3.14

Shutouts
Pat Riggin, Washington 4
Al Jensen, Washington 4
Mike Liut, St. Louis 3
Nine goalies tied with 2

Wins by goaltenders
Grant Fuhr, Edmonton.........................30
Peter Peeters, Boston...........................29
Dan Bouchard, Quebec.........................29
Bob Froese, Philadelphia 28
Glen Hanlon, N.Y. Rangers 28

1984-85

Goals
Wayne Gretzky, Edmonton 73
Jari Kurri, Edmonton 71
Mike Bossy, N.Y. Islanders.................58
Michel Goulet, Quebec.........................55
John Ogrodnick, Detroit........................55

Assists
Wayne Gretzky, Edmonton 135
Paul Coffey, Edmonton.........................84
Marcel Dionne, Los Angeles.................80
Dale Hawerchuk, Winnipeg 77
Bernie Federko, St. Louis 73

Points
Wayne Gretzky, Edmonton 208
Jari Kurri, Edmonton 135
Dale Hawerchuk, Winnipeg 130
Marcel Dionne, Los Angeles...............126
Paul Coffey, Edmonton.......................121

Penalty minutes
Chris Nilan, Montreal 358
Torrie Robertson, Hartford 337
John Blum, Boston...............................263
Tim Hunter, Calgary 259
Bob McGill, Toronto 250

Lowest goals-against average
(Min. 25 games)
Tom Barrasso, Buffalo.........................2.66
Pat Riggin, Washington 2.98
Pelle Lindbergh, Philadelphia............3.02
Steve Penney, Montreal 3.08
Bob Sauve, Buffalo 3.22
Warren Skorodenski, Chicago...........3.22

Shutouts
Tom Barrasso, Buffalo.............................5
Kelly Hrudey, N.Y. Islanders 2
Bob Janecyk, Los Angeles 2
Mike Liut, St. Louis-Hartford................2
Pelle Lindbergh, Philadelphia 2
Pat Riggin, Washington 2
Warren Skorodenski, Chicago...............2
Steve Weeks, Hartford............................2

Wins by goaltenders
Pelle Lindbergh, Philadelphia..............40
Brian Hayward, Winnipeg 33
Reggie Lemelin, Calgary 30
Pat Riggin, Washington 28
Murray Bannerman, Chicago...............27

1985-86

Goals
Jari Kurri, Edmonton 68
Mike Bossy, N.Y. Islanders 61
Tim Kerr, Philadelphia 58
Glenn Anderson, Edmonton 54
Michel Goulet, Quebec 53

Assists
Wayne Gretzky, Edmonton 163
Mario Lemieux, Pittsburgh 93
Paul Coffey, Edmonton........................90
Peter Stastny, Quebec 81
Neal Broten, Minnesota 76

Points
Wayne Gretzky, Edmonton 215
Mario Lemieux, Pittsburgh..................141
Paul Coffey, Edmonton......................138
Jari Kurri, Edmonton..........................131
Mike Bossy, N.Y. Islanders 123

Penalty minutes
Joey Kocur, Detroit..............................377
Torrie Robertson, Hartford 358
Dave Williams, Los Angeles 320
Tim Hunter, Calgary 291
Rick Tocchet, Philadelphia..................284

Lowest goals-against average
(Min. 25 games)
Bob Froese, Philadelphia..................2.55
Al Jensen, Washington......................3.18
Kelly Hrudey, N.Y. Islanders 3.21
Clint Malarchuk, Quebec 3.21
John Vanbiesbrouck, N.Y. Rangers ...3.32

Shutouts
Bob Froese, Philadelphia......................5
Clint Malarchuk, Quebec 4
Doug Soetaert, Montreal 3
John Vanbiesbrouck, N.Y. Rangers 3

Wins by goaltenders
Bob Froese, Philadelphia......................31
John Vanbiesbrouck, N.Y. Rangers ...31
Tom Barrasso, Buffalo..........................29
Reggie Lemelin, Calgary 29
Grant Fuhr, Edmonton 29

1986-87

Goals
Wayne Gretzky, Edmonton 62
Tim Kerr, Philadelphia 58
Mario Lemieux, Pittsburgh..................54
Jari Kurri, Edmonton............................54
Dino Ciccarelli, Minnesota..................52

Assists
Wayne Gretzky, Edmonton 121
Ray Bourque, Boston............................72
Mark Messier, Edmonton 70
Bryan Trottier, N.Y. Islanders..............64
Ron Francis, Hartford............................63
Doug Gilmour, St. Louis......................63

Points
Wayne Gretzky, Edmonton 183
Jari Kurri, Edmonton..........................108
Mario Lemieux, Pittsburgh..................107
Mark Messier, Edmonton 107
Doug Gilmour, St. Louis....................105

Penalty minutes
Tim Hunter, Calgary 361
Dave Williams, Los Angeles 358

Brian Curran, N.Y. Islanders 356
Basil McRae, Det.-Que. 342
Rick Tocchet, Philadelphia..................288

Lowest goals-against average
(Min. 25 games)
Brian Hayward, Montreal..................2.81
Patrick Roy, Montreal........................2.93
Ron Hextall, Philadelphia..................3.00
Daniel Berthiaume, Winnipeg............3.17
Mario Gosselin, Quebec 3.18
Glen Hanlon, Detroit..........................3.18

Shutouts
Mike Liut, Hartford 4
Bill Ranford, Boston..............................3
Rejean Lemelin, Calgary 2
Allan Bester, Toronto 2
Tom Barrasso, Buffalo 2

Wins by goaltenders
Ron Hextall, Philadelphia 37
Mike Liut, Hartford 31
Mike Vernon, Calgary 30
Andy Moog, Edmonton 28
Alain Chevrier, New Jersey................24

1987-88

Goals
Mario Lemieux, Pittsburgh..................70
Craig Simpson, Pit.-Edm.....................56
Jimmy Carson, Los Angeles................55
Luc Robitaille, Los Angeles................53
Joe Nieuwendyk, Calgary 51

Assists
Wayne Gretzky, Edmonton 109
Mario Lemieux, Pittsburgh..................98
Denis Savard, Chicago 87
Dale Hawerchuk, Winnipeg..................77
Mark Messier, Edmonton 74

Points
Mario Lemieux, Pittsburgh..................168
Wayne Gretzky, Edmonton 149
Denis Savard, Chicago 131
Dale Hawerchuk, Winnipeg................121
Luc Robitaille, Los Angeles................111
Peter Stastny, Quebec 111
Mark Messier, Edmonton 111

Penalty minutes
Bob Probert, Detroit............................398
Basil McRae, Minnesota....................382
Tim Hunter, Calgary 337
Richard Zemlak, Minnesota..............307
Chris Nilan, Mon.-N.Y.R. 305

Lowest goals-against average
(Min. 25 games)
Pete Peeters, Washington 2.78
Brian Hayward, Montreal..................2.86
Patrick Roy, Montreal........................2.90
Reggie Lemelin, Boston....................2.93
Greg Stefan, Detroit 3.11

Shutouts
Grant Fuhr, Edmonton 4
Glen Hanlon, Detroit..............................4
Clint Malarchuk, Washington 4
Kelly Hrudey, N.Y. Islanders 3
Reggie Lemelin, Boston 3
Patrick Roy, Montreal 3

Wins by goaltenders
Grant Fuhr, Edmonton 40
Mike Vernon, Calgary 39
Ron Hextall, Philadelphia 30

John Vanbiesbrouck, N.Y. Rangers 27
Tom Barrasso, Buffalo..........................25
Mike Liut, Hartford 25

1988-89

Goals
Mario Lemieux, Pittsburgh..................85
Bernie Nicholls, Los Angeles..............70
Steve Yzerman, Detroit........................65
Wayne Gretzky, Los Angeles..............54
Joe Nieuwendyk, Calgary 51
Joe Mullen, Calgary............................51

Assists
Mario Lemieux, Pittsburgh..................114
Wayne Gretzky, Los Angeles..............114
Steve Yzerman, Detroit........................90
Paul Coffey, Pittsburgh........................83
Bernie Nicholls, Los Angeles..............80

Points
Mario Lemieux, Pittsburgh..................199
Wayne Gretzky, Los Angeles 168
Steve Yzerman, Detroit......................155
Bernie Nicholls, Los Angeles............150
Rob Brown, Pittsburgh........................115

Penalty minutes
Tim Hunter, Calgary 375
Basil McRae, Minnesota....................365
Dave Manson, Chicago......................352
Marty McSorley, Los Angeles............350
Mike Hartman, Buffalo 316

Lowest goals-against average
(Min. 25 games)
Patrick Roy, Montreal........................2.47
Mike Vernon, Calgary........................2.65
Pete Peeters, Washington 2.85
Brian Hayward, Montreal....................2.90
Rick Wamsley, Calgary......................2.96

Shutouts
Greg Millen, St. Louis 6
Pete Peeters, Washington 4
Kirk McLean, Vancouver 4
Peter Sidorkiewicz, Hartford................4
Patrick Roy, Montreal............................4

Wins by goaltenders
Mike Vernon, Calgary 37
Patrick Roy, Montreal 33
Ron Hextall, Philadelphia 30
John Vanbiesbrouck, N.Y. Rangers 28
Kelly Hrudey, NYI-L.A..........................28

1989-90

Goals
Brett Hull, St. Louis..............................72
Steve Yzerman, Detroit........................62
Cam Neely, Boston..............................55
Brian Bellows, Minnesota....................55
Pat LaFontaine, N.Y. Islanders............54

Assists
Wayne Gretzky, Los Angeles 102
Mark Messier, Edmonton 84
Adam Oates, St. Louis........................79
Mario Lemieux, Pittsburgh..................78
Paul Coffey, Pittsburgh........................74

Points
Wayne Gretzky, Los Angeles 142
Mark Messier, Edmonton 129
Steve Yzerman, Detroit......................127
Mario Lemieux, Pittsburgh................123
Brett Hull, St. Louis............................113

Penalty minutes

Basil McRae, Minnesota 351
Alan May, Washington 339
Marty McSorley, Los Angeles 322
Troy Mallette, N.Y. Rangers 305
Wayne Van Dorp, Chicago 303

Lowest goals-against average
(Min. 25 games)

Mike Liut, Har.-Was. 2.527
Patrick Roy, Montreal 2.534
Rejean Lemelin, Boston 2.81
Andy Moog, Boston 2.886
Daren Puppa, Buffalo 2.888

Shutouts

Mike Liut, Har.-Was. 4
Andy Moog, Boston 3
Mike Fitzpatrick, N.Y. Islanders 3
Patrick Roy, Montreal 3
Jon Casey, Minnesota 3

Wins by goaltenders

Patrick Roy, Montreal 31
Daren Puppa, Buffalo 31
Jon Casey, Minnesota 31
Andy Moog, Boston 24
Bill Ranford, Edmonton 24

1990-91

Goals

Brett Hull, St. Louis 86
Cam Neely, Boston 51
Theo Fleury, Calgary 51
Steve Yzerman, Detroit 51
Mike Gartner, N.Y. Rangers 49

Assists

Wayne Gretzky, Los Angeles 122
Adam Oates, St. Louis 90
Al MacInnis, Calgary 75
Ray Bourque, Boston 73
Mark Recchi, Pittsburgh 73

Points

Wayne Gretzky, Los Angeles 163
Brett Hull, St. Louis 131
Adam Oates, St. Louis 115
Mark Recchi, Pittsburgh 113
John Cullen, Pit.-Har. 110

Penalty minutes

Rob Ray, Buffalo 350
Mike Peluso, Chicago 320
Bob Probert, Detroit 315
Gino Odjick, Vancouver 296
Craig Berube, Philadelphia 293

Lowest goals-against average
(Min. 25 games)

Ed Belfour, Chicago 2.47
Don Beaupre, Washington 2.64
Patrick Roy, Montreal 2.71
Andy Moog, Boston 2.87
Pete Peeters, Philadelphia 2.88

Shutouts

Don Beaupre, Washington 5
Andy Moog, Boston 4
Bob Essensa, Winnipeg 4
Ed Belfour, Chicago 4
John Vanbiesbrouck, N.Y. Rangers 3
Jon Casey, Minnesota 3
Kelly Hrudey, Los Angeles 3
Vincent Riendeau, St. Louis 3

Wins by goaltenders

Ed Belfour, Chicago 43
Mike Vernon, Calgary 31
Tim Cheveldae, Detroit 30
Vincent Riendeau, St. Louis 29
Tom Barrasso, Pittsburgh 27
Bill Ranford, Edmonton 27

1991-92

Goals

Brett Hull, St. Louis 70
Kevin Stevens, Pittsburgh 54
Gary Roberts, Calgary 53
Jeremy Roenick, Chicago 53
Pat LaFontaine, Buffalo 46

Assists

Wayne Gretzky, Los Angeles 90
Mario Lemieux, Pittsburgh 87
Brian Leetch, N.Y. Rangers 80
Adam Oates, St.L.-Bos. 79
Dale Hawerchuk, Buffalo 75

Points

Mario Lemieux, Pittsburgh 131
Kevin Stevens, Pittsburgh 123
Wayne Gretzky, Los Angeles 121
Brett Hull, St. Louis 109
Luc Robitaille, Los Angeles 107
Mark Messier, N.Y. Rangers 107

Penalty minutes

Mike Peluso, Chicago 408
Rob Ray, Buffalo 354
Gino Odjick, Vancouver 348
Ronnie Stern, Calgary 338
Link Gaetz, San Jose 326

Lowest goals-against average
(Min. 25 games)

Patrick Roy, Montreal 2.36
Ed Belfour, Chicago 2.70
Kirk McLean, Vancouver 2.74
John Vanbiesbrouck, N.Y Rangers 2.85
Bob Essensa, Winnipeg 2.88

Shutouts

Ed Belfour, Chicago 5
Bob Essensa, Winnipeg 5
Kirk McLean, Vancouver 5
Patrick Roy, Montreal 5
Ron Hextall, Philadelphia 3
Mike Richter, N.Y Rangers 3
Kay Whitmore, Hartford 3

Wins by goaltenders

Tim Cheveldae, Detroit 38
Kirk McLean, Vancouver 38
Patrick Roy, Montreal 36
Don Beaupre, Washington 29
Andy Moog, Boston 28

1992-93

Goals

Alexander Mogilny, Buffalo 76
Teemu Selanne, Winnipeg 76
Mario Lemieux, Pittsburgh 69
Luc Robitaille, Los Angeles 63
Pavel Bure, Vancouver 60

Assists

Adam Oates, Boston 97
Doug Gilmour, Toronto 95
Pat LaFontaine, Buffalo 95
Mario Lemieux, Pittsburgh 91
Craig Janney, St. Louis 82

Points

Mario Lemieux, Pittsburgh 160
Pat LaFontaine, Buffalo 148
Adam Oates, Boston 142
Steve Yzerman, Detroit 137
Teemu Selanne, Winnipeg 132

Penalty minutes

Marty McSorley, Los Angeles 399
Gino Odjick, Vancouver 370
Tie Domi, NYR-Win. 344
Nick Kypreos, Hartford 325
Mike Peluso, Ottawa 318

Lowest goals-against average
(Min. 25 games)

Felix Potvin, Toronto 2.50
Ed Belfour, Chicago 2.59
Tom Barrasso, Pittsburgh 3.01
Curtis Joseph, St. Louis 3.02
Kay Whitmore, Vancouver 3.10

Shutouts

Ed Belfour, Chicago 7
Tommy Soderstrom, Philadelphia 5
Tom Barrasso, Pittsburgh 4
Tim Cheveldae, Detroit 4
John Vanbiesbrouck, N.Y. Rangers 4

Wins by goaltenders

Tom Barrasso, Pittsburgh 43
Ed Belfour, Chicago 41
Andy Moog, Boston 37
Tim Cheveldae, Detroit 34
Bob Essensa, Winnipeg 33

1993-94

Goals

Pavel Bure, Vancouver 60
Brett Hull, St. Louis 57
Sergei Fedorov, Detroit 56
Dave Andreychuk, Toronto 53
Adam Graves, N.Y. Rangers 52
Brendan Shanahan, St. Louis 52
Ray Sheppard, Detroit 52

Assists

Wayne Gretzky, Los Angeles 92
Doug Gilmour, Toronto 84
Adam Oates, Boston 80
Sergei Zubov, N.Y. Rangers 77
Ray Bourque, Boston 71

Points

Wayne Gretzky, Los Angeles 130
Sergei Fedorov, Detroit 120
Adam Oates, Boston 112
Doug Gilmour, Toronto 111
Pavel Bure, Vancouver 107
Mike Recchi, Philadelphia 107
Jeremy Roenick, Chicago 107

Penalty minutes

Tie Domi, Winnipeg 347
Shane Churla, Dallas 333
Warren Rychel, Los Angeles 322
Craig Berube, Washington 305
Kelly Chase, St. Louis 278

Lowest goals-against average
(Min. 27 games)

Dominik Hasek, Buffalo 1.95
Martin Brodeur, New Jersey 2.40
Patrick Roy, Montreal 2.50
John Vanbiesbrouck, Florida 2.53
Mike Richter, N.Y. Rangers 2.57

Shutouts

Ed Belfour, Chicago 7
Dominik Hasek, Buffalo 7
Patrick Roy, Montreal 7
Ron Hextall, N.Y. Islanders 5
Mike Richter, N.Y. Rangers 5

Wins by goaltenders

Mike Richter, N.Y. Rangers 42
Ed Belfour, Chicago 37
Curtis Joseph, St. Louis 36
Patrick Roy, Montreal 35
Felix Potvin, Toronto 34

1994-95

Goals

Peter Bondra, Washington 34
Jaromir Jagr, Pittsburgh 32
Owen Nolan, Quebec 30
Ray Sheppard, Detroit 30
Alexei Zhamnov, Winnipeg 30

Assists

Ron Francis, Pittsburgh 48
Paul Coffey, Detroit 44
Joe Sakic, Quebec 43
Eric Lindros, Philadelphia 41
Adam Oates, Boston 41

Points

Jaromir Jagr, Pittsburgh 70
Eric Lindros, Philadelphia 70
Alexei Zhamnov, Winnipeg 65
Joe Sakic, Quebec 62
Ron Francis, Pittsburgh 59

Penalty minutes

Enrico Ciccone, Tampa Bay 225
Shane Churla, Dallas 186
Bryan Marchment, Edmonton 184
Craig Berube, Washington 173
Rob Ray, Buffalo 173

Lowest goals-against average
(Min. 13 games)

Dominik Hasek, Buffalo 2.111
Rick Tabaracci, Was.-Cal. 2.114
Jim Carey, Washington 2.13
Chris Osgood, Detroit 2.26
Ed Belfour, Chicago 2.28

Shutouts

Ed Belfour, Chicago 5
Dominik Hasek, Buffalo 5
Jim Carey, Washington 4
Arturs Irbe, San Jose 4
Blaine Lacher, Boston 4
John Vanbiesbrouck, Florida 4

Wins by goaltenders

Ken Wregget, Pittsburgh 25
Ed Belfour, Chicago 22
Trevor Kidd, Calgary 22
Curtis Joseph, St. Louis 20
Martin Brodeur, New Jersey 19
Dominik Hasek, Buffalo 19
Blaine Lacher, Boston 19
Mike Vernon, Detroit 19

1995-96

Goals

Mario Lemieux, Pittsburgh 69
Jaromir Jagr, Pittsburgh 62
Alexander Mogilny, Vancouver 55
Peter Bondra, Washington 52
John LeClair, Philadelphia 51
Joe Sakic, Colorado 51

Assists

Ron Francis, Pittsburgh 92
Mario Lemieux, Pittsburgh 92
Jaromir Jagr, Pittsburgh 87
Peter Forsberg, Colorado 86
Wayne Gretzky, L.A.-St.L 79
Doug Weight, Edmonton 79

Points

Mario Lemieux, Pittsburgh 161
Jaromir Jagr, Pittsburgh 149
Joe Sakic, Colorado 120
Ron Francis, Pittsburgh 119
Peter Forsberg, Colorado 116

Penalty minutes

Matthew Barnaby, Buffalo 335
Enrico Ciccone, T.B.-Chi. 306
Tie Domi, Toronto 297
Brad May, Buffalo 295
Rob Ray, Buffalo 287

Lowest goals-against average
(Min. 25 games)

Ron Hextall, Philadelphia 2.176
Chris Osgood, Detroit 2.178
Jim Carey, Washington 2.256
Mike Vernon, Detroit 2.264
Martin Brodeur, New Jersey 2.34

Shutouts

Jim Carey, Washington 9
Martin Brodeur, New Jersey 6
Chris Osgood, Detroit 5
Daren Puppa, Tampa Bay 5
Sean Burke, Hartford 4
Jeff Hackett, Chicago 4
Guy Hebert, Anaheim 4
Ron Hextall, Philadelphia 4

Wins by goaltenders

Chris Osgood, Detroit 39
Jim Carey, Washington 35
Martin Brodeur, New Jersey 34
Bill Ranford, Edm.-Bos. 34
Patrick Roy, Mon.-Col. 34

1996-97

Goals

Keith Tkachuk, Phoenix 52
Teemu Selanne, Anaheim 51
John LeClair, Philadelphia 50
Mario Lemieux, Pittsburgh 50
Zigmund Palffy, N.Y. Islanders 48

Assists

Wayne Gretzky, N.Y. Rangers 72
Mario Lemieux, Pittsburgh 72
Ron Francis, Pittsburgh 63
Steve Yzerman, Detroit 63
Doug Weight, Edmonton 61

Points

Mario Lemieux, Pittsburgh 122
Teemu Selanne, Anaheim 109
Paul Kariya, Anaheim 99
Wayne Gretzky, N.Y. Rangers 97
John LeClair, Philadelphia 97

Penalty minutes

Gino Odjick, Vancouver 371
Bob Probert, Chicago 326
Paul Laus, Florida 313
Rob Ray, Buffalo 286
Tie Domi, Toronto 275

Lowest goals-against average
(Min. 25 games)

Martin Brodeur, New Jersey 1.88
Andy Moog, Dallas 2.15

Goals

Jeff Hackett, Chicago 2.16
Dominik Hasek, Buffalo 2.27
John Vanbiesbrouck, Florida 2.29

Shutouts

Martin Brodeur, New Jersey 10
Nikolai Khabibulin, Phoenix 7
Patrick Roy, Colorado 7
Curtis Joseph, Edmonton 6
Chris Osgood, Detroit 6

Wins by goaltenders

Patrick Roy, Colorado 38
Martin Brodeur, New Jersey 37
Dominik Hasek, Buffalo 37
Grant Fuhr, St. Louis 33
Mike Richter, N.Y. Rangers 33

1997-98

Goals

Peter Bondra, Washington 52
Teemu Selanne, Anaheim 52
Pavel Bure, Vancouver 51
John LeClair, Philadelphia 51
Zigmund Palffy, N.Y. Islanders 45

Assists

Wayne Gretzky, N.Y. Rangers 67
Jaromir Jagr, Pittsburgh 67
Peter Forsberg, Colorado 66
Ron Francis, Pittsburgh 62
Adam Oates, Washington 58
Jozef Stumpel, Los Angeles 58

Points

Jaromir Jagr, Pittsburgh 102
Peter Forsberg, Colorado 91
Pavel Bure, Vancouver 90
Wayne Gretzky, N.Y. Rangers 90
John LeClair, Philadelphia 87
Zigmund Palffy, N.Y. Islanders 87
Ron Francis, Pittsburgh 87

Penalty minutes

Donald Brashear, Vancouver 372
Tie Domi, Toronto 365
Krzysztof Oliwa, New Jersey 295
Paul Laus, Florida 293
Richard Pilon, N.Y. Islanders 291

Lowest goals-against average
(Min. 25 games)

Ed Belfour, Dallas 1.88
Martin Brodeur, New Jersey 1.89
Tom Barrasso, Pittsburgh 2.07
Dominik Hasek, Buffalo 2.09
Ron Hextall, Philadelphia 2.165
Trevor Kidd, Carolina 2.168
Jamie McLennan, St. Louis 2.171

Shutouts

Dominik Hasek, Buffalo 13
Martin Brodeur, New Jersey 10
Ed Belfour, Dallas 9
Jeff Hackett, Chicago 8
Curtis Joseph, Edmonton 8

Wins by goaltenders

Martin Brodeur, New Jersey 43
Ed Belfour, Dallas 37
Dominik Hasek, Buffalo 33
Olaf Kolzig, Washington 33
Chris Osgood, Detroit 33

1998-99

Goals

Teemu Selanne, Anaheim 47
Tony Amonte, Chicago 44

Jaromir Jagr, Pittsburgh 44
Alexei Yashin, Ottawa 44
John LeClair, Philadelphia 43

Assists

Jaromir Jagr, Pittsburgh 83
Peter Forsberg, Colorado 67
Paul Kariya, Anaheim 62
Teemu Selanne, Anaheim 60
Joe Sakic, Colorado 55

Points

Jaromir Jagr, Pittsburgh 127
Teemu Selanne, Anaheim 107
Paul Kariya, Anaheim 101
Peter Forsberg, Colorado 97
Joe Sakic, Colorado 96

Penalty minutes

Rob Ray, Buffalo 261
Jeff Odgers, Colorado 259
Peter Worrell, Florida 258
Patrick Cote, Nashville 242
Krzysztof Oliwa, New Jersey 240

Lowest goals-against average
(Min. 25 games)

Ron Tugnutt, Ottawa 1.79
Dominik Hasek, Buffalo 1.87
Byron Dafoe, Boston 1.9845
Ed Belfour, Dallas 1.9953
Roman Turek, Dallas 2.08

Shutouts

Byron Dafoe, Boston 10
Dominik Hasek, Buffalo 9
Nikolai Khabibulin, Phoenix 8
Guy Hebert, Anaheim 6
Arturs Irbe, Carolina 6
Garth Snow, Vancouver 6
John Vanbiesbrouck, Philadelphia 6

Wins by goaltenders

Martin Brodeur, New Jersey 39
Ed Belfour, Dallas 35
Curtis Joseph, Toronto 35
Chris Osgood, Detroit 34
Byron Dafoe, Boston 32
Nikolai Khabibulin, Phoenix 32
Patrick Roy, Colorado 32

1999-2000

Goals

Pavel Bure, Florida 58
Owen Nolan, San Jose 44
Tony Amonte, Chicago 43
Jaromir Jagr, Pittsburgh 42
Paul Kariya, Anaheim 42

Assists

Mark Recchi, Philadelphia 63
Adam Oates, Washington 56
Jaromir Jagr, Pittsburgh 54
Viktor Kozlov, Florida 53
Nicklas Lidstrom, Detroit 53

Points

Jaromir Jagr, Pittsburgh 96
Pavel Bure, Florida 94
Mark Recchi, Philadelphia 91
Paul Kariya, Anaheim 86
Teemu Selanne, Anaheim 85

Penalty minutes

Denny Lambert, Atlanta......................219
Todd Simpson, Florida 202
Tie Domi, Toronto 198
Matthew Barnaby, Pittsburgh 197
Eric Cairns, N.Y. Islanders 196

Lowest goals-against average
(Min. 25 games)

Brian Boucher, Philadelphia...............1.91
Roman Turek, St. Louis......................1.95
Ed Belfour, Dallas 2.10
Jose Theodore, Montreal 2.10
John Vanbiesbrouck, Philadelphia.....2.20

Shutouts

Roman Turek, St. Louis..........................7
Martin Brodeur, New Jersey 6
Chris Osgood, Detroit.............................6
Martin Biron, Buffalo 5
Fred Brathwaite, Calgary 5
Arturs Irbe, Carolina...............................5
Olaf Kolzig, Washington 5
Jose Theodore, Montreal 5

Wins by goaltenders

Martin Brodeur, New Jersey 43
Roman Turek, St. Louis 42
Olaf Kolzig, Washington 41
Curtis Joseph, Toronto 36
Arturs Irbe, Carolina............................34

2000-01

Goals

Pavel Bure, Florida 59
Joe Sakic, Colorado 54
Jaromir Jagr, Pittsburgh 52
Peter Bondra, Washington 45
Alexei Kovalev, Pittsburgh 44

Assists

Jaromir Jagr, Pittsburgh 69
Adam Oates, Washington 69
Martin Straka, Pittsburgh 68
Doug Weight, Edmonton 65
Joe Sakic, Colorado 64

Points

Jaromir Jagr, Pittsburgh 121
Joe Sakic, Colorado 118
Patrik Elias, New Jersey 96
Jason Allison, Boston...........................95
Alexei Kovalev, Pittsburgh 95
Martin Straka, Pittsburgh 95

Penalty minutes

Matthew Barnaby, Pit.-T.B. 265
Peter Worrell, Florida 248
Stu Grimson, Los Angeles 235
Andrei Nazarov, Ana.-Bos. 229
Jeff Odgers, Atlanta............................226

Lowest goals-against average
(Min. 25 games)

Marty Turco, Dallas 1.90
Roman Cechmanek, Philadelphia 2.01
Manny Legace, Detroit 2.05
Dominik Hasek, Buffalo......................2.11
Brent Johnson, St. Louis...................2.17

Shutouts

Dominik Hasek, Buffalo 11
Roman Cechmanek, Philadelphia 10
Martin Brodeur, New Jersey 9
Tommy Salo, Edmonton 8
Ed Belfour, Dallas 8

Wins by goaltenders

Martin Brodeur, New Jersey 42
Patrick Roy, Colorado 40
Dominik Hasek, Buffalo 37
Arturs Irbe, Carolina 37
Olaf Kolzig, Washington 37

2001-02

Goals

Jarome Iginla, Calgary 52
Bill Guerin, Boston 41
Glen Murray, L.A.-Bos. 41
Mats Sundin, Toronto 41
Markus Naslund, Vancouver 40

Assists

Adam Oates, Wash.-Phi. 64
Jason Allison, Los Angeles 55
Joe Sakic, Colorado 53
Ron Francis, Carolina 50
Nicklas Lidstrom, Detroit 50
Markus Naslund, Vancouver 50
Jozef Stumpel, L.A.-Bos. 50

Points

Jarome Iginla, Calgary 96
Markus Naslund, Vancouver 90
Todd Bertuzzi, Vancouver 85
Mats Sundin, Toronto...........................80
Jaromir Jagr, Pittsburgh 79
Joe Sakic, Colorado 79

Penalty minutes

Peter Worrell, Florida 354
Brad Ference, Florida 254
Chris Neil, Ottawa 231
Kevin Sawyer, Anaheim......................221
Theo Fleury, N.Y. Rangers..................216

Lowest goals-against average
(Min. 25 games)

Patrick Roy, Colorado.........................1.94
Roman Cechmanek, Philadelphia 2.05
Marty Turco, Dallas 2.09
Jose Theodore, Montreal 2.11
Jean-Sebastien Giguere, Anaheim.....2.13

Shutouts

Patrick Roy, Colorado 9
Dan Cloutier, Vancouver 7
Nikolai Khabibulin, Tampa Bay 7
Patrick Lalime, Ottawa 7
Evgeni Nabokov, San Jose 7
Jose Theodore, Montreal 7

Wins by goaltenders

Dominik Hasek, Detroit 41
Martin Brodeur, New Jersey 38
Evgeni Nabokov, San Jose 37
Byron Dafoe, Boston...........................35
Brent Johnson, St. Louis 34

AWARD WINNERS

LEAGUE AWARDS

ART ROSS TROPHY

(Leading scorer)

Season	Player, Team	Pts.
1917-18	Joe Malone, Montreal	48
1918-19	Newsy Lalonde, Montreal	32
1919-20	Joe Malone, Quebec Bulldogs	49
1920-21	Newsy Lalonde, Montreal	43
1921-22	Punch Broadbent, Ottawa	46
1922-23	Babe Dye, Toronto	37
1923-24	Cy Denneny, Ottawa	24
1924-25	Babe Dye, Toronto	46
1925-26	Nels Stewart, Montreal Maroons	42
1926-27	Bill Cook, N.Y. Rangers	37
1927-28	Howie Morenz, Montreal	51
1928-29	Ace Bailey, Toronto	32
1929-30	Cooney Weiland, Boston	73
1930-31	Howie Morenz, Montreal	51
1931-32	Harvey Jackson, Toronto	53
1932-33	Bill Cook, N.Y. Rangers	50
1933-34	Charlie Conacher, Toronto	52
1934-35	Charlie Conacher, Toronto	57
1935-36	Dave Schriner, N.Y. Americans	45
1936-37	Dave Schriner, N.Y. Americans	46
1937-38	Gordie Drillion, Toronto	52
1938-39	Toe Blake, Montreal	47
1939-40	Milt Schmidt, Boston	52
1940-41	Bill Cowley, Boston	62
1941-42	Bryan Hextall, N.Y. Rangers	56
1942-43	Doug Bentley, Chicago	73
1943-44	Herbie Cain, Boston	82
1944-45	Elmer Lach, Montreal	80
1945-46	Max Bentley, Chicago	61
1946-47	Max Bentley, Chicago	72
1947-48	Elmer Lach, Montreal	61
1948-49	Roy Conacher, Chicago	68
1949-50	Ted Lindsay, Detroit	78
1950-51	Gordie Howe, Detroit	86
1951-52	Gordie Howe, Detroit	86
1952-53	Gordie Howe, Detroit	95
1953-54	Gordie Howe, Detroit	81
1954-55	Bernie Geoffrion, Montreal	75
1955-56	Jean Beliveau, Montreal	88
1956-57	Gordie Howe, Detroit	89
1957-58	Dickie Moore, Montreal	84
1958-59	Dickie Moore, Montreal	96
1959-60	Bobby Hull, Chicago	81
1960-61	Bernie Geoffrion, Montreal	95
1961-62	Bobby Hull, Chicago	84
1962-63	Gordie Howe, Detroit	86
1963-64	Stan Mikita, Chicago	89
1964-65	Stan Mikita, Chicago	87
1965-66	Bobby Hull, Chicago	97
1966-67	Stan Mikita, Chicago	97
1967-68	Stan Mikita, Chicago	87
1968-69	Phil Esposito, Boston	126
1969-70	Bobby Orr, Boston	120
1970-71	Phil Esposito, Boston	152
1971-72	Phil Esposito, Boston	133
1972-73	Phil Esposito, Boston	130
1973-74	Phil Esposito, Boston	145
1974-75	Bobby Orr, Boston	135
1975-76	Guy Lafleur, Montreal	125
1976-77	Guy Lafleur, Montreal	136
1977-78	Guy Lafleur, Montreal	132
1978-79	Bryan Trottier, N.Y. Islanders	134

Season	Player, Team	Pts.
1979-80	Marcel Dionne, Los Angeles	137
1980-81	Wayne Gretzky, Edmonton	164
1981-82	Wayne Gretzky, Edmonton	212
1982-83	Wayne Gretzky, Edmonton	196
1983-84	Wayne Gretzky, Edmonton	205
1984-85	Wayne Gretzky, Edmonton	208
1985-86	Wayne Gretzky, Edmonton	215
1986-87	Wayne Gretzky, Edmonton	183
1987-88	Mario Lemieux, Pittsburgh	168
1988-89	Mario Lemieux, Pittsburgh	199
1989-90	Wayne Gretzky, Los Angeles	142
1990-91	Wayne Gretzky, Los Angeles	163
1991-92	Mario Lemieux, Pittsburgh	131
1992-93	Mario Lemieux, Pittsburgh	160
1993-94	Wayne Gretzky, Los Angeles	130
1994-95	Jaromir Jagr, Pittsburgh	70
1995-96	Mario Lemieux, Pittsburgh	161
1996-97	Mario Lemieux, Pittsburgh	122
1997-98	Jaromir Jagr, Pittsburgh	102
1998-99	Jaromir Jagr, Pittsburgh	127
1999-00	Jaromir Jagr, Pittsburgh	96
2000-01	Jaromir Jagr, Pittsburgh	121
2001-02	Jarome Iginla, Calgary	96
2002-03	Peter Forsberg, Colorado	106

The award was originally known as the Leading Scorer Trophy. The present trophy, first given in 1947, was presented to the NHL by Art Ross, former manager-coach of the Boston Bruins. In event of a tie, the player with the most goals receives the award.

MAURICE RICHARD TROPHY

(Leading goal scorer)

Season	Player, Team	Goals
1998-99	Teemu Selanne, Anaheim	47
1999-00	Pavel Bure, Florida	58
2000-01	Pavel Bure, Florida	59
2001-02	Jarome Iginla, Calgary	52
2002-03	Milan Hejduk, Colorado	50

HART MEMORIAL TROPHY

(Most Valuable Player)

Season	Player, Team
1923-24	Frank Nighbor, Ottawa
1924-25	Billy Burch, Hamilton
1925-26	Nels Stewart, Montreal Maroons
1926-27	Herb Gardiner, Montreal
1927-28	Howie Morenz, Montreal
1928-29	Roy Worters, N.Y. Americans
1929-30	Nels Stewart, Montreal Maroons
1930-31	Howie Morenz, Montreal
1931-32	Howie Morenz, Montreal
1932-33	Eddie Shore, Boston
1933-34	Aurel Joliat, Montreal
1934-35	Eddie Shore, Boston
1935-36	Eddie Shore, Boston
1936-37	Babe Siebert, Montreal
1937-38	Eddie Shore, Boston
1938-39	Toe Blake, Montreal
1939-40	Ebbie Goodfellow, Detroit
1940-41	Bill Cowley, Boston
1941-42	Tom Anderson, Brooklyn
1942-43	Bill Cowley, Boston
1943-44	Babe Pratt, Toronto
1944-45	Elmer Lach, Montreal
1945-46	Max Bentley, Chicago

Season	Player, Team
1946-47	Maurice Richard, Montreal
1947-48	Buddy O'Connor, N.Y. Rangers
1948-49	Sid Abel, Detroit
1949-50	Chuck Rayner, N.Y. Rangers
1950-51	Milt Schmidt, Boston
1951-52	Gordie Howe, Detroit
1952-53	Gordie Howe, Detroit
1953-54	Al Rollins, Chicago
1954-55	Ted Kennedy, Toronto
1955-56	Jean Beliveau, Montreal
1956-57	Gordie Howe, Detroit
1957-58	Gordie Howe, Detroit
1958-59	Andy Bathgate, N.Y. Rangers
1959-60	Gordie Howe, Detroit
1960-61	Bernie Geoffrion, Montreal
1961-62	Jacques Plante, Montreal
1962-63	Gordie Howe, Detroit
1963-64	Jean Beliveau, Montreal
1964-65	Bobby Hull, Chicago
1965-66	Bobby Hull, Chicago
1966-67	Stan Mikita, Chicago
1967-68	Stan Mikita, Chicago
1968-69	Phil Esposito, Boston
1969-70	Bobby Orr, Boston
1970-71	Bobby Orr, Boston
1971-72	Bobby Orr, Boston
1972-73	Bobby Clarke, Philadelphia
1973-74	Phil Esposito, Boston
1974-75	Bobby Clarke, Philadelphia
1975-76	Bobby Clarke, Philadelphia
1976-77	Guy Lafleur, Montreal
1977-78	Guy Lafleur, Montreal
1978-79	Bryan Trottier, N.Y. Islanders
1979-80	Wayne Gretzky, Edmonton
1980-81	Wayne Gretzky, Edmonton
1981-82	Wayne Gretzky, Edmonton
1982-83	Wayne Gretzky, Edmonton
1983-84	Wayne Gretzky, Edmonton
1984-85	Wayne Gretzky, Edmonton
1985-86	Wayne Gretzky, Edmonton
1986-87	Wayne Gretzky, Edmonton
1987-88	Mario Lemieux, Pittsburgh
1988-89	Wayne Gretzky, Los Angeles
1989-90	Mark Messier, Edmonton
1990-91	Brett Hull, St. Louis
1991-92	Mark Messier, N.Y. Rangers
1992-93	Mario Lemieux, Pittsburgh
1993-94	Sergei Fedorov, Detroit
1994-95	Eric Lindros, Philadelphia
1995-96	Mario Lemieux, Pittsburgh
1996-97	Dominik Hasek, Buffalo
1997-98	Dominik Hasek, Buffalo
1998-99	Jaromir Jagr, Pittsburgh
1999-00	Chris Pronger, St. Louis
2000-01	Joe Sakic, Colorado
2001-02	Jose Theodore, Montreal
2002-03	Peter Forsberg, Colorado

LESTER B. PEARSON AWARD

(Most Outstanding Player as selected by NHL Players' Association members)

Season	Player, Team
1970-71	Phil Esposito, Boston
1971-72	Jean Ratelle, N.Y. Rangers
1972-73	Bobby Clarke, Philadelphia
1973-74	Phil Esposito, Boston
1974-75	Bobby Orr, Boston
1975-76	Guy Lafleur, Montreal
1976-77	Guy Lafleur, Montreal
1977-78	Guy Lafleur, Montreal
1978-79	Marcel Dionne, Los Angeles
1979-80	Marcel Dionne, Los Angeles

Season	Player, Team
1980-81	Mike Liut, St. Louis
1981-82	Wayne Gretzky, Edmonton
1982-83	Wayne Gretzky, Edmonton
1983-84	Wayne Gretzky, Edmonton
1984-85	Wayne Gretzky, Edmonton
1985-86	Mario Lemieux, Pittsburgh
1986-87	Wayne Gretzky, Edmonton
1987-88	Mario Lemieux, Pittsburgh
1988-89	Steve Yzerman, Detroit
1989-90	Mark Messier, Edmonton
1990-91	Brett Hull, St. Louis
1991-92	Mark Messier, N.Y. Rangers
1992-93	Mario Lemieux, Pittsburgh
1993-94	Sergei Fedorov, Detroit
1994-95	Eric Lindros, Philadelphia
1995-96	Mario Lemieux, Pittsburgh
1996-97	Dominik Hasek, Buffalo
1997-98	Dominik Hasek, Buffalo
1998-99	Jaromir Jagr, Pittsburgh
1999-00	Jaromir Jagr, Pittsburgh
2000-01	Joe Sakic, Colorado
2001-02	Jarome Iginla, Calgary
2002-03	Markus Naslund, Vancouver

JAMES NORRIS MEMORIAL TROPHY

(Outstanding defenseman)

Season	Player, Team
1953-54	Red Kelly, Detroit
1954-55	Doug Harvey, Montreal
1955-56	Doug Harvey, Montreal
1956-57	Doug Harvey, Montreal
1957-58	Doug Harvey, Montreal
1958-59	Tom Johnson, Montreal
1959-60	Doug Harvey, Montreal
1960-61	Doug Harvey, Montreal
1961-62	Doug Harvey, N.Y. Rangers
1962-63	Pierre Pilote, Chicago
1963-64	Pierre Pilote, Chicago
1964-65	Pierre Pilote, Chicago
1965-66	Jacques Laperriere, Montreal
1966-67	Harry Howell, N.Y. Rangers
1967-68	Bobby Orr, Boston
1968-69	Bobby Orr, Boston
1969-70	Bobby Orr, Boston
1970-71	Bobby Orr, Boston
1971-72	Bobby Orr, Boston
1972-73	Bobby Orr, Boston
1973-74	Bobby Orr, Boston
1974-75	Bobby Orr, Boston
1975-76	Denis Potvin, N.Y. Islanders
1976-77	Larry Robinson, Montreal
1977-78	Denis Potvin, N.Y. Islanders
1978-79	Denis Potvin, N.Y. Islanders
1979-80	Larry Robinson, Montreal
1980-81	Randy Carlyle, Pittsburgh
1981-82	Doug Wilson, Chicago
1982-83	Rod Langway, Washington
1983-84	Rod Langway, Washington
1984-85	Paul Coffey, Edmonton
1985-86	Paul Coffey, Edmonton
1986-87	Ray Bourque, Boston
1987-88	Ray Bourque, Boston
1988-89	Chris Chelios, Montreal
1989-90	Ray Bourque, Boston
1990-91	Ray Bourque, Boston
1991-92	Brian Leetch, N.Y. Rangers
1992-93	Chris Chelios, Chicago
1993-94	Ray Bourque, Boston
1994-95	Paul Coffey, Detroit
1995-96	Chris Chelios, Chicago
1996-97	Brian Leetch, N.Y. Rangers
1997-98	Rob Blake, Los Angeles

Season	Player, Team
1998-99	Al MacInnis, St. Louis
1999-00	Chris Pronger, St. Louis
2000-01	Nicklas Lidstrom, Detroit
2001-02	Nicklas Lidstrom, Detroit
2002-03	Nicklas Lidstrom, Detroit

VEZINA TROPHY

(Outstanding goaltender)

Season	Player, Team	GAA
1926-27	George Hainsworth, Montreal	1.52
1927-28	George Hainsworth, Montreal	1.09
1928-29	George Hainsworth, Montreal	0.98
1929-30	Tiny Thompson, Boston	2.23
1930-31	Roy Worters, N.Y. Americans	1.68
1931-32	Charlie Gardiner, Chicago	2.10
1932-33	Tiny Thompson, Boston	1.83
1933-34	Charlie Gardiner, Chicago	1.73
1934-35	Lorne Chabot, Chicago	1.83
1935-36	Tiny Thompson, Boston	1.71
1936-37	Normie Smith, Detroit	2.13
1937-38	Tiny Thompson, Boston	1.85
1938-39	Frank Brimsek, Boston	1.60
1939-40	Dave Kerr, N.Y. Rangers	1.60
1940-41	Turk Broda, Toronto	2.60
1941-42	Frank Brimsek, Boston	2.38
1942-43	Johnny Mowers, Detroit	2.48
1943-44	Bill Durnan, Montreal	2.18
1944-45	Bill Durnan, Montreal	2.42
1945-46	Bill Durnan, Montreal	2.60
1946-47	Bill Durnan, Montreal	2.30
1947-48	Turk Broda, Toronto	2.38
1948-49	Bill Durnan, Montreal	2.10
1949-50	Bill Durnan, Montreal	2.20
1950-51	Al Rollins, Toronto	1.75
1951-52	Terry Sawchuk, Detroit	1.98
1952-53	Terry Sawchuk, Detroit	1.94
1953-54	Harry Lumley, Toronto	1.85
1954-55	Terry Sawchuk, Detroit	1.94
1955-56	Jacques Plante, Montreal	1.86
1956-57	Jacques Plante, Montreal	2.02
1957-58	Jacques Plante, Montreal	2.09
1958-59	Jacques Plante, Montreal	2.15
1959-60	Jacques Plante, Montreal	2.54
1960-61	Johnny Bower, Toronto	2.50
1961-62	Jacques Plante, Montreal	2.37
1962-63	Glenn Hall, Chicago	2.51
1963-64	Charlie Hodge, Montreal	2.26
1964-65	Terry Sawchuk, Toronto	2.56
	Johnny Bower, Toronto	2.38
1965-66	Lorne Worsley, Montreal	2.36
	Charlie Hodge, Montreal	2.58
1966-67	Glenn Hall, Chicago	2.38
	Denis DeJordy, Chicago	2.46
1967-68	Lorne Worsley, Montreal	1.98
	Rogatien Vachon, Montreal	2.48
1968-69	Glenn Hall, St. Louis	2.17
	Jacques Plante, St. Louis	1.96
1969-70	Tony Esposito, Chicago	2.17
1970-71	Ed Giacomin, N.Y. Rangers	2.16
	Gilles Villemure, N.Y. Rangers	2.30
1971-72	Tony Esposito, Chicago	1.77
	Gary Smith, Chicago	2.42
1972-73	Ken Dryden, Montreal	2.26
1973-74	Bernie Parent, Philadelphia	1.89
	Tony Esposito, Chicago	2.04
1974-75	Bernie Parent, Philadelphia	2.03
1975-76	Ken Dryden, Montreal	2.03
1976-77	Ken Dryden, Montreal	2.14
	Michel Larocque, Montreal	2.09

Season	Player, Team	GAA
1977-78	Ken Dryden, Montreal	2.05
	Michel Larocque, Montreal	2.67
1978-79	Ken Dryden, Montreal	2.30
	Michel Larocque, Montreal	2.84
1979-80	Bob Sauve, Buffalo	2.36
	Don Edwards, Buffalo	2.57
1980-81	Richard Sevigny, Montreal	2.40
	Michel Larocque, Montreal	3.03
	Denis Herron, Montreal	3.50
1981-82	Billy Smith, N.Y. Islanders	2.97
1982-83	Pete Peeters, Boston	2.36
1983-84	Tom Barrasso, Buffalo	2.84
1984-85	Pelle Lindbergh, Philadelphia	3.02
1985-86	John Vanbiesbrouck, N.Y. Rangers	3.32
1986-87	Ron Hextall, Philadelphia	3.00
1987-88	Grant Fuhr, Edmonton	3.43
1988-89	Patrick Roy, Montreal	2.47
1989-90	Patrick Roy, Montreal	2.53
1990-91	Ed Belfour, Chicago	2.47
1991-92	Patrick Roy, Montreal	2.36
1992-93	Ed Belfour, Chicago	2.59
1993-94	Dominik Hasek, Buffalo	1.95
1994-95	Dominik Hasek, Buffalo	2.11
1995-96	Jim Carey, Washington	2.26
1996-97	Dominik Hasek, Buffalo	2.27
1997-98	Dominik Hasek, Buffalo	2.09
1998-99	Dominik Hasek, Buffalo	1.87
1999-00	Olaf Kolzig, Washington	2.24
2000-01	Dominik Hasek, Buffalo	2.11
2001-02	Jose Theodore, Montreal	2.11
2002-03	Martin Brodeur, New Jersey	2.02

The award was formerly presented to the goaltender(s) having played a minimum of 25 games for the team with the fewest goals scored against. Beginning with the 1981-82 season, it was awarded to the outstanding goaltender.

WILLIAM M. JENNINGS TROPHY

(Leading goaltender)

Season	Player, Team	GAA
1981-82	Denis Herron, Montreal	2.64
	Rick Wamsley, Montreal	2.75
1982-83	Roland Melanson, N.Y. Islanders	2.66
	Billy Smith, N.Y. Islanders	2.87
1983-84	Pat Riggin, Washington	2.66
	Al Jensen, Washington	2.91
1984-85	Tom Barrasso, Buffalo	2.66
	Bob Sauve, Buffalo	3.22
1985-86	Bob Froese, Philadelphia	2.55
	Darren Jensen, Philadelphia	3.68
1986-87	Brian Hayward, Montreal	2.81
	Patrick Roy, Montreal	2.93
1987-88	Brian Hayward, Montreal	2.86
	Patrick Roy, Montreal	2.90
1988-89	Patrick Roy, Montreal	2.47
	Brian Hayward, Montreal	2.90
1989-90	Rejean Lemelin, Boston	2.81
	Andy Moog, Boston	2.89
1990-91	Ed Belfour, Chicago	2.47
1991-92	Patrick Roy, Montreal	2.36
1992-93	Ed Belfour, Chicago	2.59
1993-94	Dominik Hasek, Buffalo	1.95
	Grant Fuhr, Buffalo	3.68
1994-95	Ed Belfour, Chicago	2.28
1995-96	Chris Osgood, Detroit	2.17
	Mike Vernon, Detroit	2.26
1996-97	Martin Brodeur, New Jersey	1.88
	Mike Dunham, New Jersey	2.55

Season	Player, Team	GAA
1997-98	Martin Brodeur, New Jersey	1.89
1998-99	Ed Belfour, Dallas	1.99
	Roman Turek, Dallas	2.08
1999-00	Roman Turek, St. Louis	1.95
2000-01	Dominik Hasek, Buffalo	2.11
2001-02	Patrick Roy, Colorado	1.94
2002-03	Roman Cechmanek, Philadelphia	1.83
	Robert Esche, Philadelphia	2.20
	Martin Brodeur, New Jersey	2.02

The award is presented to the goaltender(s) having played a minimum of 25 games for the team with the fewest goals scored against.

CALDER MEMORIAL TROPHY

(Rookie of the year)

Season   Player, Team
1932-33—Carl Voss, Detroit
1933-34—Russ Blinco, Montreal Maroons
1934-35—Dave Schriner, N.Y. Americans
1935-36—Mike Karakas, Chicago
1936-37—Syl Apps, Toronto
1937-38—Cully Dahlstrom, Chicago
1938-39—Frank Brimsek, Boston
1939-40—Kilby Macdonald, N.Y. Rangers
1940-41—John Quilty, Montreal
1941-42—Grant Warwick, N.Y. Rangers
1942-43—Gaye Stewart, Toronto
1943-44—Gus Bodnar, Toronto
1944-45—Frank McCool, Toronto
1945-46—Edgar Laprade, N.Y. Rangers
1946-47—Howie Meeker, Toronto
1947-48—Jim McFadden, Detroit
1948-49—Pentti Lund, N.Y. Rangers
1949-50—Jack Gelineau, Boston
1950-51—Terry Sawchuk, Detroit
1951-52—Bernie Geoffrion, Montreal
1952-53—Lorne Worsley, N.Y. Rangers
1953-54—Camille Henry, N.Y. Rangers
1954-55—Ed Litzenberger, Chicago
1955-56—Glenn Hall, Detroit
1956-57—Larry Regan, Boston
1957-58—Frank Mahovlich, Toronto
1958-59—Ralph Backstrom, Montreal
1959-60—Bill Hay, Chicago
1960-61—Dave Keon, Toronto
1961-62—Bobby Rousseau, Montreal
1962-63—Kent Douglas, Toronto
1963-64—Jacques Laperriere, Montreal
1964-65—Roger Crozier, Detroit
1965-66—Brit Selby, Toronto
1966-67—Bobby Orr, Boston
1967-68—Derek Sanderson, Boston
1968-69—Danny Grant, Minnesota
1969-70—Tony Esposito, Chicago
1970-71—Gilbert Perreault, Buffalo
1971-72—Ken Dryden, Montreal
1972-73—Steve Vickers, N.Y. Rangers
1973-74—Denis Potvin, N.Y. Islanders
1974-75—Eric Vail, Atlanta
1975-76—Bryan Trottier, N.Y. Islanders
1976-77—Willi Plett, Atlanta
1977-78—Mike Bossy, N.Y. Islanders
1978-79—Bobby Smith, Minnesota
1979-80—Ray Bourque, Boston
1980-81—Peter Stastny, Quebec
1981-82—Dale Hawerchuk, Winnipeg
1982-83—Steve Larmer, Chicago
1983-84—Tom Barrasso, Buffalo
1984-85—Mario Lemieux, Pittsburgh
1985-86—Gary Suter, Calgary
1986-87—Luc Robitaille, Los Angeles

Season   Player, Team
1987-88—Joe Nieuwendyk, Calgary
1988-89—Brian Leetch, N.Y. Rangers
1989-90—Sergei Makarov, Calgary
1990-91—Ed Belfour, Chicago
1991-92—Pavel Bure, Vancouver
1992-93—Teemu Selanne, Winnipeg
1993-94—Martin Brodeur, New Jersey
1994-95—Peter Forsberg, Quebec
1995-96—Daniel Alfredsson, Ottawa
1996-97—Bryan Berard, N.Y. Islanders
1997-98—Sergei Samsonov, Boston
1998-99—Chris Drury, Colorado
1999-00—Scott Gomez, New Jersey
2000-01—Evgeni Nabokov, San Jose
2001-02—Dany Heatley, Atlanta
2002-03—Barret Jackman, St. Louis

The award was originally known as the Leading Rookie Award. It was renamed the Calder Trophy in 1936-37 and became the Calder Memorial Trophy in 1942-43, following the death of NHL President Frank Calder.

LADY BYNG MEMORIAL TROPHY

(Most gentlemanly player)

Season   Player, Team
1924-25—Frank Nighbor, Ottawa
1925-26—Frank Nighbor, Ottawa
1926-27—Billy Burch, N.Y. Americans
1927-28—Frank Boucher, N.Y. Rangers
1928-29—Frank Boucher, N.Y. Rangers
1929-30—Frank Boucher, N.Y. Rangers
1930-31—Frank Boucher, N.Y. Rangers
1931-32—Joe Primeau, Toronto
1932-33—Frank Boucher, N.Y. Rangers
1933-34—Frank Boucher, N.Y. Rangers
1934-35—Frank Boucher, N.Y. Rangers
1935-36—Doc Romnes, Chicago
1936-37—Marty Barry, Detroit
1937-38—Gordie Drillon, Toronto
1938-39—Clint Smith, N.Y. Rangers
1939-40—Bobby Bauer, Boston
1940-41—Bobby Bauer, Boston
1941-42—Syl Apps, Toronto
1942-43—Max Bentley, Chicago
1943-44—Clint Smith, Chicago
1944-45—Bill Mosienko, Chicago
1945-46—Toe Blake, Montreal
1946-47—Bobby Bauer, Boston
1947-48—Buddy O'Connor, N.Y. Rangers
1948-49—Bill Quackenbush, Detroit
1949-50—Edgar Laprade, N.Y. Rangers
1950-51—Red Kelly, Detroit
1951-52—Sid Smith, Toronto
1952-53—Red Kelly, Detroit
1953-54—Red Kelly, Detroit
1954-55—Sid Smith, Toronto
1955-56—Earl Reibel, Detroit
1956-57—Andy Hebenton, N.Y. Rangers
1957-58—Camille Henry, N.Y. Rangers
1958-59—Alex Delvecchio, Detroit
1959-60—Don McKenney, Boston
1960-61—Red Kelly, Toronto
1961-62—Dave Keon, Toronto
1962-63—Dave Keon, Toronto
1963-64—Ken Wharram, Chicago
1964-65—Bobby Hull, Chicago
1965-66—Alex Delvecchio, Detroit
1966-67—Stan Mikita, Chicago
1967-68—Stan Mikita, Chicago
1968-69—Alex Delvecchio, Detroit
1969-70—Phil Goyette, St. Louis

Season Player, Team
1970-71—John Bucyk, Boston
1971-72—Jean Ratelle, N.Y. Rangers
1972-73—Gilbert Perreault, Buffalo
1973-74—John Bucyk, Boston
1974-75—Marcel Dionne, Detroit
1975-76—Jean Ratelle, N.Y. R.-Boston
1976-77—Marcel Dionne, Los Angeles
1977-78—Butch Goring, Los Angeles
1978-79—Bob MacMillan, Atlanta
1979-80—Wayne Gretzky, Edmonton
1980-81—Rick Kehoe, Pittsburgh
1981-82—Rick Middleton, Boston
1982-83—Mike Bossy, N.Y. Islanders
1983-84—Mike Bossy, N.Y. Islanders
1984-85—Jari Kurri, Edmonton
1985-86—Mike Bossy, N.Y. Islanders
1986-87—Joe Mullen, Calgary
1987-88—Mats Naslund, Montreal
1988-89—Joe Mullen, Calgary
1989-90—Brett Hull, St. Louis
1990-91—Wayne Gretzky, Los Angeles
1991-92—Wayne Gretzky, Los Angeles
1992-93—Pierre Turgeon, N.Y. Islanders
1993-94—Wayne Gretzky, Los Angeles
1994-95—Ron Francis, Pittsburgh
1995-96—Paul Kariya, Anaheim
1996-97—Paul Kariya, Anaheim
1997-98—Ron Francis, Pittsburgh
1998-99—Wayne Gretzky, N.Y. Rangers
1999-00—Pavol Demitra, St. Louis
2000-01—Joe Sakic, Colorado
2001-02—Ron Francis, Carolina
2002-03—Alexander Mogilny, Toronto

The award was originally known as the Lady Byng Trophy. After winning the award seven times, Frank Boucher received permanent possession and a new trophy was donated to the NHL in 1936. After Lady Byng's death in 1949, the NHL changed the name to Lady Byng Memorial Trophy.

CONN SMYTHE TROPHY

(Playoff MVP)

Season Player, Team
1964-65—Jean Beliveau, Montreal
1965-66—Roger Crozier, Detroit
1966-67—Dave Keon, Toronto
1967-68—Glenn Hall, St. Louis
1968-69—Serge Savard, Montreal
1969-70—Bobby Orr, Boston
1970-71—Ken Dryden, Montreal
1971-72—Bobby Orr, Boston
1972-73—Yvan Cournoyer, Montreal
1973-74—Bernie Parent, Philadelphia
1974-75—Bernie Parent, Philadelphia
1975-76—Reggie Leach, Philadelphia
1976-77—Guy Lafleur, Montreal
1977-78—Larry Robinson, Montreal
1978-79—Bob Gainey, Montreal
1979-80—Bryan Trottier, N.Y. Islanders
1980-81—Butch Goring, N.Y. Islanders
1981-82—Mike Bossy, N.Y. Islanders
1982-83—Billy Smith, N.Y. Islanders
1983-84—Mark Messier, Edmonton
1984-85—Wayne Gretzky, Edmonton
1985-86—Patrick Roy, Montreal
1986-87—Ron Hextall, Philadelphia
1987-88—Wayne Gretzky, Edmonton
1988-89—Al MacInnis, Calgary
1989-90—Bill Ranford, Edmonton
1990-91—Mario Lemieux, Pittsburgh

Season Player, Team
1991-92—Mario Lemieux, Pittsburgh
1992-93—Patrick Roy, Montreal
1993-94—Brian Leetch, N.Y. Rangers
1994-95—Claude Lemieux, New Jersey
1995-96—Joe Sakic, Colorado
1996-97—Mike Vernon, Detroit
1997-98—Steve Yzerman, Detroit
1998-99—Joe Nieuwendyk, Dallas
1999-00—Scott Stevens, New Jersey
2000-01—Patrick Roy, Colorado
2001-02—Niklas Lidstrom, Detroit
2002-03—Jean-Sebastien Giguere, Anaheim

BILL MASTERTON MEMORIAL TROPHY

(Sportsmanship—dedication to hockey)

Season Player, Team
1967-68—Claude Provost, Montreal
1968-69—Ted Hampson, Oakland
1969-70—Pit Martin, Chicago
1970-71—Jean Ratelle, N.Y. Rangers
1971-72—Bobby Clarke, Philadelphia
1972-73—Lowell MacDonald, Pittsburgh
1973-74—Henri Richard, Montreal
1974-75—Don Luce, Buffalo
1975-76—Rod Gilbert, N.Y. Rangers
1976-77—Ed Westfall, N.Y. Islanders
1977-78—Butch Goring, Los Angeles
1978-79—Serge Savard, Montreal
1979-80—Al MacAdam, Minnesota
1980-81—Blake Dunlop, St. Louis
1981-82—Glenn Resch, Colorado
1982-83—Lanny McDonald, Calgary
1983-84—Brad Park, Detroit
1984-85—Anders Hedberg, N.Y. Rangers
1985-86—Charlie Simmer, Boston
1986-87—Doug Jarvis, Hartford
1987-88—Bob Bourne, Los Angeles
1988-89—Tim Kerr, Philadelphia
1989-90—Gord Kluzak, Boston
1990-91—Dave Taylor, Los Angeles
1991-92—Mark Fitzpatrick, N.Y. Islanders
1992-93—Mario Lemieux, Pittsburgh
1993-94—Cam Neely, Boston
1994-95—Pat LaFontaine, Buffalo
1995-96—Gary Roberts, Calgary
1996-97—Tony Granato, San Jose
1997-98—Jamie McLennan, St. Louis
1998-99—John Cullen, Tampa Bay
1999-00—Ken Daneyko, New Jersey
2000-01—Adam Graves, N.Y. Rangers
2001-02—Saku Koivu, Montreal
2002-03—Steve Yzerman, Detroit

Presented by the Professional Hockey Writers' Association to the player who best exemplifies the qualities of perseverance, sportsmanship and dedication to hockey.

FRANK J. SELKE TROPHY

(Best defensive forward)

Season Player, Team
1977-78—Bob Gainey, Montreal
1978-79—Bob Gainey, Montreal
1979-80—Bob Gainey, Montreal
1980-81—Bob Gainey, Montreal
1981-82—Steve Kasper, Boston
1982-83—Bobby Clarke, Philadelphia
1983-84—Doug Jarvis, Washington
1984-85—Craig Ramsay, Buffalo
1985-86—Troy Murray, Chicago

Season	Player, Team
1986-87	Dave Poulin, Philadelphia
1987-88	Guy Carbonneau, Montreal
1988-89	Guy Carbonneau, Montreal
1989-90	Rick Meagher, St. Louis
1990-91	Dirk Graham, Chicago
1991-92	Guy Carbonneau, Montreal
1992-93	Doug Gilmour, Toronto
1993-94	Sergei Fedorov, Detroit
1994-95	Ron Francis, Pittsburgh
1995-96	Sergei Fedorov, Detroit
1996-97	Michael Peca, Buffalo
1997-98	Jere Lehtinen, Dallas
1998-99	Jere Lehtinen, Dallas
1999-00	Steve Yzerman, Detroit
2000-01	John Madden, New Jersey
2001-02	Michael Peca, N.Y. Islanders
2002-03	Jere Lehtinen, Dallas

JACK ADAMS AWARD

(Coach of the year)

Season	Coach, Team
1973-74	Fred Shero, Philadelphia
1974-75	Bob Pulford, Los Angeles
1975-76	Don Cherry, Boston
1976-77	Scotty Bowman, Montreal
1977-78	Bobby Kromm, Detroit
1978-79	Al Arbour, N.Y. Islanders
1979-80	Pat Quinn, Philadelphia
1980-81	Red Berenson, St. Louis
1981-82	Tom Watt, Winnipeg
1982-83	Orval Tessier, Chicago
1983-84	Bryan Murray, Washington
1984-85	Mike Keenan, Philadelphia
1985-86	Glen Sather, Edmonton
1986-87	Jacques Demers, Detroit
1987-88	Jacques Demers, Detroit
1988-89	Pat Burns, Montreal
1989-90	Bob Murdoch, Winnipeg
1990-91	Brian Sutter, St. Louis
1991-92	Pat Quinn, Vancouver
1992-93	Pat Burns, Toronto
1993-94	Jacques Lemaire, New Jersey
1994-95	Marc Crawford, Quebec
1995-96	Scotty Bowman, Detroit
1996-97	Ted Nolan, Buffalo
1997-98	Pat Burns, Boston
1998-99	Jacques Martin, Ottawa
1999-00	Joel Quenneville, St. Louis
2000-01	Bill Barber, Philadelphia
2001-02	Bob Francis, Phoenix
2002-03	Jacques Lemaire, Minnesota

KING CLANCY TROPHY

(Humanitarian contributions)

Season	Player, Team
1987-88	Lanny McDonald, Calgary
1988-89	Bryan Trottier, N.Y. Islanders
1989-90	Kevin Lowe, Edmonton
1990-91	Dave Taylor, Los Angeles
1991-92	Ray Bourque, Boston
1992-93	Dave Poulin, Boston
1993-94	Adam Graves, N.Y. Rangers
1994-95	Joe Nieuwendyk, Calgary
1995-96	Kris King, Winnipeg
1996-97	Trevor Linden, Vancouver
1997-98	Kelly Chase, St. Louis
1998-99	Rob Ray, Buffalo
1999-00	Curtis Joseph, Toronto

Season	Player, Team
2000-01	Shjon Podein, Colorado
2001-02	Ron Francis, Carolina
2002-03	Brendan Shanahan, Detroit

ALL-STAR TEAMS

(As selected by members of the Professional
Hockey Writers' Association at the end of each season)

1930-31

First team		Second team
Aurel Joliat, Mon. C.	LW	Bun Cook, N.Y.R.
Howie Morenz, Mon. C.	C	Frank Boucher, N.Y.R.
Bill Cook, N.Y.R.	RW	Dit Clapper, Bos.
Eddie Shore, Bos.	D	Sylvio Mantha, Mon. C.
King Clancy, Tor.	D	Ching Johnson, N.Y.R.
Charlie Gardiner, Chi.	G	Tiny Thompson, Bos.

1931-32

First team		Second team
Harvey Jackson, Tor.	LW	Aurel Joliat, Mon. C.
Howie Morenz, Mon. C.	C	Hooley Smith, Mon. M.
Bill Cook, N.Y.R.	RW	Charlie Conacher, Tor.
Eddie Shore, Bos.	D	Sylvio Mantha, Mon. C.
Ching Johnson, N.Y.R.	D	King Clancy, Tor.
Charlie Gardiner, Chi.	G	Roy Worters, N.Y.A.

1932-33

First team		Second team
Baldy Northcott, Mon. M.	LW	Harvey Jackson, Tor.
Frank Boucher, N.Y.R.	C	Howie Morenz, Mon. C.
Bill Cook, N.Y.R.	RW	Charlie Conacher, Tor.
Eddie Shore, Bos.	D	King Clancy, Tor.
Ching Johnson, N.Y.R.	D	Lionel Conacher, Mon. M.
John Ross Roach, Det.	G	Charlie Gardiner, Chi.

1933-34

First team		Second team
Harvey Jackson, Tor.	LW	Aurel Joliat, Mon. C.
Frank Boucher, N.Y.R.	C	Joe Primeau, Tor.
Charlie Conacher, Tor.	RW	Bill Cook, N.Y.R.
King Clancy, Tor.	D	Eddie Shore, Bos.
Lionel Conacher, Chi.	D	Ching Johnson, N.Y.R.
Charlie Gardiner, Chi.	G	Roy Worters, N.Y.A.

1934-35

First team		Second team
Harvey Jackson, Tor.	LW	Aurel Joliat, Mon. C.
Frank Boucher, N.Y.R.	C	Cooney Weiland, Det.
Charlie Conacher, Tor.	RW	Dit Clapper, Bos.
Eddie Shore, Bos.	D	Cy Wentworth, Mon. M.
Earl Seibert, N.Y.R.	D	Art Coulter, Chi.
Lorne Chabot, Chi.	G	Tiny Thompson, Bos.

1935-36

First team		Second team
Dave Schriner, N.Y.A.	LW	Paul Thompson, Chi.
Hooley Smith, Mon. M.	C	Bill Thoms, Tor.
Charlie Conacher, Tor.	RW	Cecil Dillon, N.Y.R.
Eddie Shore, Bos.	D	Earl Seibert, Chi.
Babe Siebert, Bos.	D	Ebbie Goodfellow, Det.
Tiny Thompson, Bos.	G	Wilf Cude, Mon. C.

1936-37

First team		Second team
Harvey Jackson, Tor.	LW	Dave Schriner, N.Y.A.
Marty Barry, Det.	C	Art Chapman, N.Y.A.
Larry Aurie, Det.	RW	Cecil Dillon, N.Y.R.
Babe Siebert, Mon. C.	D	Earl Seibert, Chi.
Ebbie Goodfellow, Det.	D	Lionel Conacher, Mon. M.
Norm Smith, Det.	G	Wilf Cude, Mon. C.

1937-38

First team		Second team
Paul Thompson, Chi.	LW	Toe Blake, Mon. C.
Bill Cowley, Bos.	C	Syl Apps, Tor.
Cecil Dillon, N.Y.R.	RW	Cecil Dillon, N.Y.R.
Gord Drillon, Tor.	(tied)	Gord Drillon, Tor.
Eddie Shore, Bos.	D	Art Coulter, N.Y.R.
Babe Siebert, Mon. C.	D	Earl Seibert, Chi.
Tiny Thompson, Bos.	G	Dave Kerr, N.Y.R.

1938-39

First team		Second team
Toe Blake, Mon.	LW	Johnny Gottselig, Chi.
Syl Apps, Tor.	C	Neil Colville, N.Y.R.
Gord Drillon, Tor.	RW	Bobby Bauer, Bos.
Eddie Shore, Bos.	D	Earl Seibert, Chi.
Dit Clapper, Bos.	D	Art Coulter, N.Y.R.
Frank Brimsek, Bos.	G	Earl Robertson, N.Y.A.

1939-40

First team		Second team
Toe Blake, Mon.	LW	Woody Dumart, Bos.
Milt Schmidt, Bos.	C	Neil Colville, N.Y.R.
Bryan Hextall, N.Y.R.	RW	Bobby Bauer, Bos.
Dit Clapper, Bos.	D	Art Coulter, N.Y.R.
Ebbie Goodfellow, Det.	D	Earl Seibert, Chi.
Dave Kerr, N.Y.R.	G	Frank Brimsek, Bos.

1940-41

First team		Second team
Dave Schriner, Tor.	LW	Woody Dumart, Bos.
Bill Cowley, Bos.	C	Syl Apps, Tor.
Bryan Hextall, N.Y.R.	RW	Bobby Bauer, Bos.
Dit Clapper, Bos.	D	Earl Seibert, Chi.
Wally Stanowski, Tor.	D	Ott Heller, N.Y.R.
Turk Broda, Tor.	G	Frank Brimsek, Bos.

1941-42

First team		Second team
Lynn Patrick, N.Y.R.	LW	Sid Abel, Det.
Syl Apps, Tor.	C	Phil Watson, N.Y.R.
Bryan Hextall, N.Y.R.	RW	Gord Drillon, Tor.
Earl Seibert, Chi.	D	Pat Egan, Bkl.
Tommy Anderson, Bkl.	D	Bucko McDonald, Tor.
Frank Brimsek, Bos.	G	Turk Broda, Tor.

1942-43

First team		Second team
Doug Bentley, Chi.	LW	Lynn Patrick, N.Y.R.
Bill Cowley, Bos.	C	Syl Apps, Tor.
Lorne Carr, Tor.	RW	Bryan Hextall, N.Y.R.
Earl Seibert, Chi.	D	Jack Crawford, Bos.
Jack Stewart, Det.	D	Bill Hollett, Bos.
Johnny Mowers, Det.	G	Frank Brimsek, Bos.

1943-44

First team		Second team
Doug Bentley, Chi.	LW	Herb Cain, Bos.
Bill Cowley, Bos.	C	Elmer Lach, Mon.
Lorne Carr, Tor.	RW	Maurice Richard, Mon.
Earl Seibert, Chi.	D	Emile Bouchard, Mon.
Babe Pratt, Tor.	D	Dit Clapper, Bos.
Bill Durnan, Mon.	G	Paul Bibeault, Tor.

1944-45

First team		Second team
Toe Blake, Mon.	LW	Syd Howe, Det.
Elmer Lach, Mon.	C	Bill Cowley, Bos.
Maurice Richard, Mon.	RW	Bill Mosienko, Chi.
Emile Bouchard, Mon.	D	Glen Harmon, Mon.
Bill Hollett, Det.	D	Babe Pratt, Tor.
Bill Durnan, Mon.	G	Mike Karakas, Chi.

1945-46

First team		Second team
Gaye Stewart, Tor.	LW	Toe Blake, Mon.
Max Bentley, Chi.	C	Elmer Lach, Mon.
Maurice Richard, Mon.	RW	Bill Mosienko, Chi.
Jack Crawford, Bos.	D	Kenny Reardon, Mon.
Emile Bouchard, Mon.	D	Jack Stewart, Det.
Bill Durnan, Mon.	G	Frank Brimsek, Bos.

1946-47

First team		Second team
Doug Bentley, Chi.	LW	Woody Dumart, Bos.
Milt Schmidt, Bos.	C	Max Bentley, Chi.
Maurice Richard, Mon.	RW	Bobby Bauer, Bos.
Kenny Reardon, Mon.	D	Jack Stewart, Det.
Emile Bouchard, Mon.	D	Bill Quackenbush, Det.
Bill Durnan, Mon.	G	Frank Brimsek, Bos.

1947-48

First team		Second team
Ted Lindsay, Det.	LW	Gaye Stewart, Chi.
Elmer Lach, Mon.	C	Buddy O'Connor, N.Y.R.
Maurice Richard, Mon.	RW	Bud Poile, Chi.
Bill Quackenbush, Det.	D	Kenny Reardon, Mon.
Jack Stewart, Det.	D	Neil Colville, N.Y.R.
Turk Broda, Tor.	G	Frank Brimsek, Bos.

1948-49

First team		Second team
Roy Conacher, Chi.	LW	Ted Lindsay, Det.
Sid Abel, Det.	C	Doug Bentley, Chi.
Maurice Richard, Mon.	RW	Gordie Howe, Det.
Bill Quackenbush, Det.	D	Glen Harmon, Mon.
Jack Stewart, Det.	D	Kenny Reardon, Mon.
Bill Durnan, Mon.	G	Chuck Rayner, N.Y.R.

1949-50

First team		Second team
Ted Lindsay, Det.	LW	Tony Leswick, N.Y.R.
Sid Abel, Det.	C	Ted Kennedy, Tor.
Maurice Richard, Mon.	RW	Gordie Howe, Det.
Gus Mortson, Tor.	D	Leo Reise, Det.
Kenny Reardon, Mon.	D	Red Kelly, Det.
Bill Durnan, Mon.	G	Chuck Rayner, N.Y.R.

1950-51

First team		Second team
Ted Lindsay, Det.	LW	Sid Smith, Tor.
Milt Schmidt, Bos.	C	Sid Abel, Det.
	(tied)	Ted Kennedy, Tor.
Gordie Howe, Det.	RW	Maurice Richard, Mon.
Red Kelly, Det.	D	Jim Thomson, Tor.
Bill Quackenbush, Bos.	D	Leo Reise, Det.
Terry Sawchuk, Det.	G	Chuck Rayner, N.Y.R.

1951-52

First team		Second team
Ted Lindsay, Det.	LW	Sid Smith, Tor.
Elmer Lach, Mon.	C	Milt Schmidt, Bos.
Gordie Howe, Det.	RW	Maurice Richard, Mon.
Red Kelly, Det.	D	Hy Buller, N.Y.R.
Doug Harvey, Mon.	D	Jim Thomson, Tor.
Terry Sawchuk, Det.	G	Jim Henry, Bos.

1952-53

First team		Second team
Ted Lindsay, Det.	LW	Bert Olmstead, Mon.
Fleming Mackell, Bos.	C	Alex Delvecchio, Det.
Gordie Howe, Det.	RW	Maurice Richard, Mon.
Red Kelly, Det.	D	Bill Quackenbush, Bos.
Doug Harvey, Mon.	D	Bill Gadsby, Chi.
Terry Sawchuk, Det.	G	Gerry McNeil, Mon.

1953-54

First team		Second team
Ted Lindsay, Det.	LW	Ed Sandford, Bos.
Ken Mosdell, Mon.	C	Ted Kennedy, Tor.
Gordie Howe, Det.	RW	Maurice Richard, Mon.
Red Kelly, Det.	D	Bill Gadsby, Chi.
Doug Harvey, Mon.	D	Tim Horton, Tor.
Harry Lumley, Tor.	G	Terry Sawchuk, Det.

1954-55

First team		Second team
Sid Smith, Tor.	LW	Danny Lewicki, N.Y.R.
Jean Beliveau, Mon.	C	Ken Mosdell, Mon.
Maurice Richard, Mon.	RW	Bernie Geoffrion, Mon.
Doug Harvey, Mon.	D	Bob Goldham, Det.
Red Kelly, Det.	D	Fern Flaman, Bos.
Harry Lumley, Tor.	G	Terry Sawchuk, Det.

1955-56

First team		Second team
Ted Lindsay, Det.	LW	Bert Olmstead, Mon.
Jean Beliveau, Mon.	C	Tod Sloan, Tor.
Maurice Richard, Mon.	RW	Gordie Howe, Det.
Doug Harvey, Mon.	D	Red Kelly, Det.
Bill Gadsby, N.Y.R.	D	Tom Johnson, Mon.
Jacques Plante, Mon.	G	Glenn Hall, Det.

1956-57

First team		Second team
Ted Lindsay, Det.	LW	Real Chevrefils, Bos.
Jean Beliveau, Mon.	C	Eddie Litzenberger, Chi.
Gordie Howe, Det.	RW	Maurice Richard, Mon.
Doug Harvey, Mon.	D	Fern Flaman, Bos.
Red Kelly, Det.	D	Bill Gadsby, N.Y.R.
Glenn Hall, Det.	G	Jacques Plante, Mon.

1957-58

First team		Second team
Dickie Moore, Mon.	LW	Camille Henry, N.Y.R.
Henri Richard, Mon.	C	Jean Beliveau, Mon.
Gordie Howe, Det.	RW	Andy Bathgate, N.Y.R.
Doug Harvey, Mon.	D	Fern Flaman, Bos.
Bill Gadsby, N.Y.R.	D	Marcel Pronovost, Det.
Glenn Hall, Chi.	G	Jacques Plante, Mon.

1958-59

First team		Second team
Dickie Moore, Mon.	LW	Alex Delvecchio, Det.
Jean Beliveau, Mon.	C	Henri Richard, Mon.
Andy Bathgate, N.Y.R.	RW	Gordie Howe, Det.
Tom Johnson, Mon.	D	Marcel Pronovost, Det.
Bill Gadsby, N.Y.R.	D	Doug Harvey, Mon.
Jacques Plante, Mon.	G	Terry Sawchuk, Det.

1959-60

First team		Second team
Bobby Hull, Chi.	LW	Dean Prentice, N.Y.R.
Jean Beliveau, Mon.	C	Bronco Horvath, Bos.
Gordie Howe, Det.	RW	Bernie Geoffrion, Mon.
Doug Harvey, Mon.	D	Allan Stanley, Tor.
Marcel Pronovost, Det.	D	Pierre Pilote, Chi.
Glenn Hall, Chi.	G	Jacques Plante, Mon.

1960-61

First team		Second team
Frank Mahovlich, Tor.	LW	Dickie Moore, Mon.
Jean Beliveau, Mon.	C	Henri Richard, Mon.
Bernie Geoffrion, Mon.	RW	Gordie Howe, Det.
Doug Harvey, Mon.	D	Allan Stanley, Tor.
Marcel Pronovost, Det.	D	Pierre Pilote, Chi.
Johnny Bower, Tor.	G	Glenn Hall, Chi.

1961-62

First team		Second team
Bobby Hull, Chi.	LW	Frank Mahovlich, Tor.
Stan Mikita, Chi.	C	Dave Keon, Tor.
Andy Bathgate, N.Y.R.	RW	Gordie Howe, Det.
Doug Harvey, N.Y.R.	D	Carl Brewer, Tor.
Jean-Guy Talbot, Mon.	D	Pierre Pilote, Chi.
Jacques Plante, Mon.	G	Glenn Hall, Chi.

1962-63

First team		Second team
Frank Mahovlich, Tor.	LW	Bobby Hull, Chi.
Stan Mikita, Chi.	C	Henri Richard, Mon.
Gordie Howe, Det.	RW	Andy Bathgate, N.Y.R.
Pierre Pilote, Chi.	D	Tim Horton, Tor.
Carl Brewer, Tor.	D	Elmer Vasko, Chi.
Glenn Hall, Chi.	G	Terry Sawchuk, Det.

1963-64

First team		Second team
Bobby Hull, Chi.	LW	Frank Mahovlich, Tor.
Stan Mikita, Chi.	C	Jean Beliveau, Mon.
Ken Wharram, Chi.	RW	Gordie Howe, Det.
Pierre Pilote, Chi.	D	Elmer Vasko, Chi.
Tim Horton, Tor.	D	Jacques Laperriere, Mon.
Glenn Hall, Chi.	G	Charlie Hodge, Mon.

1964-65

First team		Second team
Bobby Hull, Chi.	LW	Frank Mahovlich, Tor.
Norm Ullman, Det.	C	Stan Mikita, Chi.
Claude Provost, Mon.	RW	Gordie Howe, Det.
Pierre Pilote, Chi.	D	Bill Gadsby, Det.
Jacques Laperriere, Mon.	D	Carl Brewer, Tor.
Roger Crozier, Det.	G	Charlie Hodge, Mon.

1965-66

First team		Second team
Bobby Hull, Chi.	LW	Frank Mahovlich, Tor.
Stan Mikita, Chi.	C	Jean Beliveau, Mon.
Gordie Howe, Det.	RW	Bobby Rousseau, Mon.
Jacques Laperriere, Mon.	D	Allan Stanley, Tor.
Pierre Pilote, Chi.	D	Pat Stapleton, Chi.
Glenn Hall, Chi.	G	Gump Worsley, Mon.

1966-67

First team		Second team
Bobby Hull, Chi.	LW	Don Marshall, N.Y.R.
Stan Mikita, Chi.	C	Norm Ullman, Det.
Ken Wharram, Chi.	RW	Gordie Howe, Det.
Pierre Pilote, Chi.	D	Tim Horton, Tor.
Harry Howell, N.Y.R.	D	Bobby Orr, Bos.
Ed Giacomin, N.Y.R.	G	Glenn Hall, Chi.

1967-68

First team		Second team
Bobby Hull, Chi.	LW	Johnny Bucyk, Bos.
Stan Mikita, Chi.	C	Phil Esposito, Bos.
Gordie Howe, Det.	RW	Rod Gilbert, N.Y.R.
Bobby Orr, Bos.	D	J.C. Tremblay, Mon.
Tim Horton, Tor.	D	Jim Neilson, N.Y.R.
Gump Worsley, Mon.	G	Ed Giacomin, N.Y.R.

1968-69

First team		Second team
Bobby Hull, Chi.	LW	Frank Mahovlich, Det.
Phil Esposito, Bos.	C	Jean Beliveau, Mon.
Gordie Howe, Det.	RW	Yvan Cournoyer, Mon.
Bobby Orr, Bos.	D	Ted Green, Bos.
Tim Horton, Tor.	D	Ted Harris, Mon.
Glenn Hall, St.L.	G	Ed Giacomin, N.Y.R.

1969-70

First team		Second team
Bobby Hull, Chi.	LW	Frank Mahovlich, Det.
Phil Esposito, Bos.	C	Stan Mikita, Chi.
Gordie Howe, Det.	RW	John McKenzie, Bos.
Bobby Orr, Bos.	D	Carl Brewer, Det.
Brad Park, N.Y.R.	D	Jacques Laperriere, Mon.
Tony Esposito, Chi.	G	Ed Giacomin, N.Y.R.

1970-71

First team		Second team
Johnny Bucyk, Bos.	LW	Bobby Hull, Chi.
Phil Esposito, Bos.	C	Dave Keon, Tor.
Ken Hodge, Bos.	RW	Yvan Cournoyer, Mon.
Bobby Orr, Bos.	D	Brad Park, N.Y.R.
J.C. Tremblay, Mon.	D	Pat Stapleton, Chi.
Ed Giacomin, N.Y.R.	G	Jacques Plante, Tor.

1971-72

First team		Second team
Bobby Hull, Chi.	LW	Vic Hadfield, N.Y.R.
Phil Esposito, Bos.	C	Jean Ratelle, N.Y.R.
Rod Gilbert, N.Y.R.	RW	Yvan Cournoyer, Mon.
Bobby Orr, Bos.	D	Bill White, Chi.
Brad Park, N.Y.R.	D	Pat Stapleton, Chi.
Tony Esposito, Chi.	G	Ken Dryden, Mon.

1972-73

First team		Second team
Frank Mahovlich, Mon.	LW	Dennis Hull, Chi.
Phil Esposito, Bos.	C	Bobby Clarke, Phi.
Mickey Redmond, Det.	RW	Yvan Cournoyer, Mon.
Bobby Orr, Bos.	D	Brad Park, N.Y.R.
Guy Lapointe, Mon.	D	Bill White, Chi.
Ken Dryden, Mon.	G	Tony Esposito, Chi.

1973-74

First team		Second team
Richard Martin, Buf.	LW	Wayne Cashman, Bos.
Phil Esposito, Bos.	C	Bobby Clarke, Phi.
Ken Hodge, Bos.	RW	Mickey Redmond, Det.
Bobby Orr, Bos.	D	Bill White, Chi.
Brad Park, N.Y.R.	D	Barry Ashbee, Phi.
Bernie Parent, Phi.	G	Tony Esposito, Chi.

1974-75

First team		Second team
Richard Martin, Buf.	LW	Steve Vickers, N.Y.R.
Bobby Clarke, Phi.	C	Phil Esposito, Bos.
Guy Lafleur, Mon.	RW	Rene Robert, Buf.
Bobby Orr, Bos.	D	Guy Lapointe, Mon.
Denis Potvin, N.Y.I.	D	Borje Salming, Tor.
Bernie Parent, Phi.	G	Rogie Vachon, L.A.

1975-76

First team		Second team
Bill Barber, Phi.	LW	Richard Martin, Buf.
Bobby Clarke, Phi.	C	Gilbert Perreault, Buf.
Guy Lafleur, Mon.	RW	Reggie Leach, Phi.
Denis Potvin, N.Y.I.	D	Borje Salming, Tor.
Brad Park, Bos.	D	Guy Lapointe, Mon.
Ken Dryden, Mon.	G	Glenn Resch, N.Y.I.

1976-77

First team		Second team
Steve Shutt, Mon.	LW	Richard Martin, Buf.
Marcel Dionne, L.A.	C	Gilbert Perreault, Buf.
Guy Lafleur, Mon.	RW	Lanny McDonald, Tor.
Larry Robinson, Mon.	D	Denis Potvin, N.Y.I.
Borje Salming, Tor.	D	Guy Lapointe, Mon.
Ken Dryden, Mon.	G	Rogie Vachon, L.A.

1977-78

First team		Second team
Clark Gillies, N.Y.I.	LW	Steve Shutt, Mon.
Bryan Trottier, N.Y.I.	C	Darryl Sittler, Tor.
Guy Lafleur, Mon.	RW	Mike Bossy, N.Y.I.
Denis Potvin, N.Y.I.	D	Larry Robinson, Mon.
Brad Park, Bos.	D	Borje Salming, Tor.
Ken Dryden, Mon.	G	Don Edwards, Buf.

1978-79

First team		Second team
Clark Gillies, N.Y.I.	LW	Bill Barber, Phi.
Bryan Trottier, N.Y.I.	C	Marcel Dionne, L.A.
Guy Lafleur, Mon.	RW	Mike Bossy, N.Y.I.
Denis Potvin, N.Y.I.	D	Borje Salming, Tor.
Larry Robinson, Mon.	D	Serge Savard, Mon.
Ken Dryden, Mon.	G	Glenn Resch, N.Y.I.

1979-80

First team		Second team
Charlie Simmer, L.A.	LW	Steve Shutt, Mon.
Marcel Dionne, L.A.	C	Wayne Gretzky, Edm.
Guy Lafleur, Mon.	RW	Danny Gare, Buf.
Larry Robinson, Mon.	D	Borje Salming, Tor.
Ray Bourque, Bos.	D	Jim Schoenfeld, Buf.
Tony Esposito, Chi.	G	Don Edwards, Buf.

1980-81

First team		Second team
Charlie Simmer, L.A.	LW	Bill Barber, Phi.
Wayne Gretzky, Edm.	C	Marcel Dionne, L.A.
Mike Bossy, N.Y.I.	RW	Dave Taylor, L.A.
Denis Potvin, N.Y.I.	D	Larry Robinson, Mon.
Randy Carlyle, Pit.	D	Ray Bourque, Bos.
Mike Liut, St.L.	G	Mario Lessard, L.A.

1981-82

First team		Second team
Mark Messier, Edm.	LW	John Tonelli, N.Y.I.
Wayne Gretzky, Edm.	C	Bryan Trottier, N.Y.I.
Mike Bossy, N.Y.I.	RW	Rick Middleton, Bos.
Doug Wilson, Chi.	D	Paul Coffey, Edm.
Ray Bourque, Bos.	D	Brian Engblom, Mon.
Bill Smith, N.Y.I.	G	Grant Fuhr, Edm.

1982-83

First team		Second team
Mark Messier, Edm.	LW	Michel Goulet, Que.
Wayne Gretzky, Edm.	C	Denis Savard, Chi.
Mike Bossy, N.Y.I.	RW	Lanny McDonald, Cal.
Mark Howe, Phi.	D	Ray Bourque, Bos.
Rod Langway, Was.	D	Paul Coffey, Edm.
Pete Peeters, Bos.	G	Roland Melanson, N.Y.I.

1983-84

First team		Second team
Michel Goulet, Que.	LW	Mark Messier, Edm.
Wayne Gretzky, Edm.	C	Bryan Trottier, N.Y.I.
Mike Bossy, N.Y.I.	RW	Jari Kurri, Edm.
Rod Langway, Was.	D	Paul Coffey, Edm.
Ray Bourque, Bos.	D	Denis Potvin, N.Y.I.
Tom Barrasso, Buf.	G	Pat Riggin, Was.

1984-85

First team		Second team
John Ogrodnick, Det.	LW	John Tonelli, N.Y.I.
Wayne Gretzky, Edm.	C	Dale Hawerchuk, Win.
Jari Kurri, Edm.	RW	Mike Bossy, N.Y.I.
Paul Coffey, Edm.	D	Rod Langway, Was.
Ray Bourque, Bos.	D	Doug Wilson, Chi.
Pelle Lindbergh, Phi.	G	Tom Barrasso, Buf.

1985-86

First team		Second team
Michel Goulet, Que.	LW	Mats Naslund, Mon.
Wayne Gretzky, Edm.	C	Mario Lemieux, Pit.
Mike Bossy, N.Y.I.	RW	Jari Kurri, Edm.
Paul Coffey, Edm.	D	Larry Robinson, Mon.
Mark Howe, Phi.	D	Ray Bourque, Bos.
John Vanbiesbrouck, N.Y.R.	G	Bob Froese, Phi.

1986-87

First team		Second team
Michel Goulet, Que.	LW	Luc Robitaille, L.A.
Wayne Gretzky, Edm.	C	Mario Lemieux, Pit.
Jari Kurri, Edm.	RW	Tim Kerr, Phi.
Ray Bourque, Bos.	D	Larry Murphy, Was.
Mark Howe, Phi.	D	Al MacInnis, Cal.
Ron Hextall, Phi.	G	Mike Liut, Har.

1987-88

First team		Second team
Luc Robitaille, L.A.	LW	Michel Goulet, Que.
Mario Lemieux, Pit.	C	Wayne Gretzky, Edm.
Hakan Loob, Cal.	RW	Cam Neely, Bos.
Ray Bourque, Bos.	D	Gary Suter, Cal.
Scott Stevens, Was.	D	Brad McCrimmon, Cal.
Grant Fuhr, Edm.	G	Patrick Roy, Mon.

1988-89

First team		Second team
Luc Robitaille, L.A.	LW	Gerard Gallant, Det.
Mario Lemieux, Pit.	C	Wayne Gretzky, L.A.
Joe Mullen, Cal.	RW	Jari Kurri, Edm.
Chris Chelios, Mon.	D	Al MacInnis, Cal.
Paul Coffey, Pit.	D	Ray Bourque, Bos.
Patrick Roy, Mon.	G	Mike Vernon, Cal.

1989-90

First team		Second team
Luc Robitaille, L.A.	LW	Brian Bellows, Min.
Mark Messier, Edm.	C	Wayne Gretzky, L.A.
Brett Hull, St.L.	RW	Cam Neely, Bos.
Ray Bourque, Bos.	D	Paul Coffey, Pit.
Al MacInnis, Cal.	D	Doug Wilson, Chi.
Patrick Roy, Mon.	G	Daren Puppa, Buf.

1990-91

First team		Second team
Luc Robitaille, L.A.	LW	Kevin Stevens, Pit.
Wayne Gretzky, L.A.	C	Adam Oates, St.L.
Brett Hull, St.L.	RW	Cam Neely, Bos.
Ray Bourque, Bos.	D	Chris Chelios, Chi.
Al MacInnis, Cal.	D	Brian Leetch, N.Y.R.
Ed Belfour, Chi.	G	Patrick Roy, Mon.

1991-92

First team		Second team
Kevin Stevens, Pit.	LW	Luc Robitaille, L.A.
Mark Messier, N.Y.R.	C	Mario Lemieux, Pit.
Brett Hull, St.L.	RW	Mark Recchi, Pit., Phi.
Brian Leetch, N.Y.R.	D	Phil Housley, Win.
Ray Bourque, Bos.	D	Scott Stevens, N.J.
Patrick Roy, Mon.	G	Kirk McLean, Van.

1992-93

First team		Second team
Luc Robitaille, L.A.	LW	Kevin Stevens, Pit.
Mario Lemieux, Pit.	C	Pat LaFontaine, Buf.
Teemu Selanne, Win.	RW	Alexander Mogilny, Buf.
Chris Chelios, Chi.	D	Larry Murphy, Pit.
Ray Bourque, Bos.	D	Al Iafrate, Was.
Ed Belfour, Chi.	G	Tom Barrasso, Pit.

1993-94

First team		Second team
Brendan Shanahan, St.L.	LW	Adam Graves, N.Y.R.
Sergei Fedorov, Det.	C	Wayne Gretzky, L.A.

First team		Second team
Pavel Bure, Van.	RW	Cam Neely, Bos.
Ray Bourque, Bos.	D	Al MacInnis, Cal.
Scott Stevens, N.J.	D	Brian Leetch, N.Y.R.
Dominik Hasek, Buf.	G	John Vanbiesbrouck, Fla.

1994-95

First team		Second team
John LeClair, Mon., Phi.	LW	Keith Tkachuk, Win.
Eric Lindros, Phi.	C	Alexei Zhamnov, Win.
Jaromir Jagr, Pit.	RW	Theo Fleury, Cal.
Paul Coffey, Det.	D	Ray Bourque, Bos.
Chris Chelios, Chi.	D	Larry Murphy, Pit.
Dominik Hasek, Buf.	G	Ed Belfour, Chi.

1995-96

First team		Second team
Paul Kariya, Ana.	LW	John LeClair, Phi.
Mario Lemieux, Pit.	C	Eric Lindros, Phi.
Jaromir Jagr, Pit.	RW	Alexander Mogilny, Van.
Chris Chelios, Chi.	D	Vladimir Konstantinov, Det.
Ray Bourque, Bos.	D	Brian Leetch, N.Y.R.
Jim Carey, Was.	G	Chris Osgood, Det.

1996-97

First team		Second team
Paul Kariya, Ana.	LW	John LeClair, Phi.
Mario Lemieux, Pit.	C	Wayne Gretzky, N.Y.R.
Teemu Selanne, Ana.	RW	Jaromir Jagr, Pit.
Brian Leetch, N.Y.R.	D	Chris Chelios, Chi.
Sandis Ozolinsh, Col.	D	Scott Stevens, N.J.
Dominik Hasek, Buf.	G	Martin Brodeur, N.J.

1997-98

First team		Second team
John LeClair, Phi.	LW	Keith Tkachuk, Pho.
Peter Forsberg, Col.	C	Wayne Gretzky, N.Y.R.
Jaromir Jagr, Pit.	RW	Teemu Selanne, Ana.
Nicklas Lidstrom, Det.	D	Chris Pronger, St.L.
Rob Blake, L.A.	D	Scott Niedermayer, N.J.
Dominik Hasek, Buf.	G	Martin Brodeur, N.J.

1998-99

First team		Second team
Paul Kariya, Ana.	LW	John LeClair, Phi.
Peter Forsberg, Col.	C	Alexei Yashin, Ott.
Jaromir Jagr, Pit.	RW	Teemu Selanne, Ana.
Nicklas Lidstrom, Det.	D	Ray Bourque, Bos.
Al MacInnis, St.L.	D	Eric Desjardins, Phi.
Dominik Hasek, Buf.	G	Byron Dafoe, Bos.

1999-2000

First team		Second team
Brendan Shanahan, Det.	LW	Paul Kariya, Ana.
Steve Yzerman, Det.	C	Mike Modano, Dal.
Jaromir Jagr, Pit.	RW	Pavel Bure, Florida
Nicklas Lidstrom, Det.	D	Rob Blake, L.A.-Colo.
Chris Pronger, St.L.	D	Eric Desjardins, Phi.
Olaf Kolzig, Was.	G	Roman Turek, St.L.

2000-01

First team		Second team
Patrik Elias, N.J.	LW	Luc Robitaille, L.A.
Joe Sakic, Col.	C	Mario Lemieux, Pit.
Jaromir Jagr, Pit.	RW	Pavel Bure, Fla.
Ray Bourque, Colorado	D	Rob Blake, L.A.
Nicklas Lidstrom, Det.	D	Scott Stevens, N.J.
Dominik Hasek, Buf.	G	Roman Cechmanek, Phi.

2001-02

First team		Second team
Markus Naslund, Van.	LW	Brendan Shanahan, Det.
Joe Sakic, Col.	C	Mats Sundin, Tor.
Jarome Iginla, Cal.	RW	Bill Guerin, Bos.
Chris Chelios, Det.	D	Rob Blake, Colo.
Nicklas Lidstrom, Det.	D	Sergei Gonchar, Was.
Patrick Roy, Colo.	G	Jose Theodore, Mon.

2002-03

First team		Second team	
Martin Brodeur, N.J.	G	Marty Turco, Dallas	
Al MacInnis, St. Louis	D	Sergie Gonchar, Was.	
Nicklas Lidstrom, Detroit	D	Derian Hatcher, Dallas	
Markus Naslund, Van.	LW	Paul Kariya, Anaheim	
Peter Forsberg, Colo.	C	Joe Thornton, Boston	
Todd Bertuzzi, Van.	RW	Milan Hejduk, Colo.	

NHL ALL-ROOKIE TEAMS

(As selected by members of the Professional
Hockey Writers' Association at the end of each season)

1982-83

Rookie team			
Mats Naslund, Mon.	LW	Phil Housley, Buf.	D
Dan Daoust, Mon.-Tor.	C	Scott Stevens, Was.	D
Steve Larmer, Chi.	RW	Pelle Lindbergh, Phi.	G

1983-84

Rookie team			
Sylvain Turgeon, Hart.	LW	Thomas Eriksson, Phi.	D
Steve Yzerman, Det.	C	Jamie Macoun, Cal.	D
Hakan Loob, Cal.	RW	Tom Barrasso, Buf.	G

1984-85

Rookie team			
Warren Young, Pit.	LW	Bruce Bell, Que.	D
Mario Lemieux, Pit.	C	Chris Chelios, Mon.	D
Tomas Sandstrom, N.Y.R.	RW	Steve Penney, Mon.	G

1985-86

Rookie team			
Wendel Clark, Tor.	LW	Dana Murzin, Hart.	D
Mike Ridley, N.Y.R.	C	Gary Suter, Cal.	D
Kjell Dahlin, Mon.	RW	Patrick Roy, Col.	G

1986-87

Rookie team			
Luc Robitaille, L.A.	LW	Brian Benning, St.L.	D
Jimmy Carson, L.A.	C	Steve Duchesne, L.A.	D
Jim Sandlak, Van.	RW	Ron Hextall, Phi.	G

1987-88

Rookie team			
Iain Duncan, Win.	LW	Calle Johansson, Buf.	D
Joe Nieuwendyk, Cal.	C	Glen Wesley, Bos.	D
Ray Sheppard, Buf.	RW	Darren Pang, Chi.	G

1988-89

Rookie team			
David Volek, N.Y.I.	LW	Brian Leetch, N.Y.R.	D
Trevor Linden, Van.	C	Zarley Zalapski, Pit.	D
Tony Granato, N.Y.R.	RW	Peter Sidorkiewicz, Hart.	G

1989-90

Rookie team			
Rod Brind'Amour, St.L.	LW	Brad Shaw, Hart.	D
Mike Modano, Min.	C	Geoff Smith, Edm.	D
Sergei Makarov, Cal.	RW	Bob Essensa, Win.	G

1990-91

Rookie team			
Jaromir Jagr, Pit.	LW	Rob Blake, L.A.	D
Sergei Fedorov, Det.	C	Eric Weinrich, N.J.	D
Ken Hodge, Bos.	RW	Ed Belfour, Chi.	G

1991-92

Rookie team			
Gilbert Dionne, Mon.	LW	Vlad. Konstantinov, Det.	D
Kevin Todd, N.J.	C	Niklas Lidstrom, Det.	D
Tony Amonte, N.Y.R.	RW	Dominik Hasek, Chi.	G

1992-93

Rookie team			
Eric Lindros, Phi.	C	Vlad. Malakhov, N.Y.I.	D
Joe Juneau, Bos.	W	Scott Niedermayer, N.J.	D
Teemu Selanne, Win.	W	Felix Potvin, Tor.	G

1993-94

Rookie team			
Jason Arnott, Edm.	C	Boris Mironov, Win.-Edm.	D
Oleg Petrov, Mon.	W	Chris Pronger, Hart.	D
Mikael Renberg, Phi.	W	Martin Brodeur, N.J.	G

1994-95

Rookie team			
Peter Forsberg, Que.	F	Kenny Jonsson, Tor.	D
Jeff Friesen, S.J.	F	Chris Therien, Phi.	D
Paul Kariya, Ana.	F	Jim Carey, Was.	G

1995-96

Rookie team			
Daniel Alfredsson, Ott.	F	Ed Jovanovski, Fla.	D
Eric Daze, Chi.	F	Kyle McLaren, Bos.	D
Petr Sykora, N.J.	F	Corey Hirsch, Van.	G

1996-97

Rookie team			
Sergei Berezin, Tor.	F	Bryan Berard, N.Y.I.	D
Jim Campbell, St.L.	F	Janne Niinimaa, Phi.	D
Jarome Iginla, Cal.	F	Patrick Lalime, Pit.	G

1997-98

Rookie team			
Patrick Elias, N.J.	F	Derek Morris, Cal.	D
Mike Johnson, Tor.	F	Mattias, Ohlund, Van.	D
Sergei Samsonov, Bos.	F	Jamie Storr, L.A.	G

1998-99

Rookie team			
Chris Drury, Col.	F	Tom Poti, Edm.	D
Milan Hejduk, Col.	F	Sami Salo, Ott.	D
Marian Hossa, Ott.	F	Jamie Storr, L.A.	G

1999-2000

Rookie team			
Simon Gagne, Phi.	F	Brian Rafalski, N.J.	D
Scott Gomez, N.J.	F	Brad Stuart, S.J.	D
Michael York, N.Y.R.	F	Brian Boucher, Phi.	G

2000-01

Rookie team			
Martin Havlat, Ott.	F	Lubomir Visnovsky, L.A.	D
Brad Richards, T.B.	F	Colin White, N.J.	D
Shane Willis, Car.	F	Evgeni Nabokov, S.J.	G

2001-02

Rookie team			
Dany Heatley, Atl.	F	Nick Boynton, Bos.	D
Kristian Huselius, Fla.	F	Rostislav Klesla, C'bus.	D
Ilya Kovalchuk, Atl.	F	Dan Blackburn, N.Y.R.	G

2002-03

Rookie team			
Henrik Zetterberg, Det.	F	Barret Jackman, St.L.	D
Rick Nash, C'bus.	F	Jay Bouwmeester, Fla.	D
Tyler Arnason, Chi.	F	Sebastien Caron, Pit.	G

THE SPORTING NEWS AWARDS

PLAYER OF THE YEAR

1967-68—E. Div.: Stan Mikita, Chicago
W. Div.: Red Berenson, St. Louis
1968-69—E. Div.: Phil Esposito, Boston
W. Div.: Red Berenson, St. Louis
1969-70—E. Div.: Bobby Orr, Boston
W. Div.: Red Berenson, St. Louis
1970-71—E. Div.: Phil Esposito, Boston
W. Div.: Bobby Hull, Chicago
1971-72—E. Div.: Jean Ratelle, N.Y. Rangers
W. Div.: Bobby Hull, Chicago
1972-73—E. Div.: Phil Esposito, Boston
W. Div.: Bobby Clarke, Philadelphia
1973-74—E. Div.: Phil Esposito, Boston
W. Div.: Bernie Parent, Philadelphia
1974-75—Camp. Conf.: Bobby Clarke, Philadelphia
Wales Conf.: Guy Lafleur, Montreal
1975-76—Bobby Clarke, Philadelphia
1976-77—Guy Lafleur, Montreal
1977-78—Guy Lafleur, Montreal
1978-79—Bryan Trottier, N.Y. Islanders
1979-80—Marcel Dionne, Los Angeles
1980-81—Wayne Gretzky, Edmonton
1981-82—Wayne Gretzky, Edmonton
1982-83—Wayne Gretzky, Edmonton
1983-84—Wayne Gretzky, Edmonton
1984-85—Wayne Gretzky, Edmonton
1985-86—Wayne Gretzky, Edmonton
1986-87—Wayne Gretzky, Edmonton
1987-88—Mario Lemieux, Pittsburgh
1988-89—Mario Lemieux, Pittsburgh
1989-90—Mark Messier, Edmonton
1990-91—Brett Hull, St. Louis
1991-92—Mark Messier, N.Y. Rangers
1992-93—Mario Lemieux, Pittsburgh
1993-94—Sergei Fedorov, Detroit
1994-95—Eric Lindros, Philadelphia
1995-96—Mario Lemieux, Pittsburgh
1996-97—Dominik Hasek, Buffalo
1997-98—Dominik Hasek, Buffalo
1998-99—Jaromir Jagr, Pittsburgh
1999-00—Jaromir Jagr, Pittsburgh
2000-01—Joe Sakic, Colorado
2001-02—Jarome Iginla, Calgary
2002-03—Peter Forsberg, Colorado

ROOKIE OF THE YEAR

1967-68—E. Div.: Derek Sanderson, Boston
W. Div.: Bill Flett, Los Angeles
1968-69—E. Div.: Brad Park, N.Y. Rangers
W. Div.: Norm Ferguson, Oakland
1969-70—E. Div.: Tony Esposito, Chicago
W. Div.: Bobby Clarke, Philadelphia
1970-71—E. Div.: Gil Perreault, Buffalo
W. Div.: Jude Drouin, Minnesota
1971-72—E. Div.: Richard Martin, Buffalo
W. Div.: Gilles Meloche, California
1972-73—E. Div.: Steve Vickers, N.Y. Rangers
W. Div.: Bill Barber, Philadelphia
1973-74—E. Div.: Denis Potvin, N.Y. Islanders
W. Div.: Tom Lysiak, Atlanta
1974-75—Camp. Conf.: Eric Vail, Atlanta
Wales Conf.: Pierre Larouche, Pittsburgh
1975-76—Bryan Trottier, N.Y. Islanders
1976-77—Willi Plett, Atlanta
1977-78—Mike Bossy, N.Y. Islanders
1978-79—Bobby Smith, Minnesota
1979-80—Ray Bourque, Boston

1980-81—Peter Stastny, Quebec
1981-82—Dale Hawerchuk, Winnipeg
1982-83—Steve Larmer, Chicago
1983-84—Steve Yzerman, Detroit
1984-85—Mario Lemieux, Pittsburgh
1985-86—Wendel Clark, Toronto
1986-87—Ron Hextall, Philadelphia
1987-88—Joe Nieuwendyk, Calgary
1988-89—Brian Leetch, N.Y. Rangers
1989-90—Jeremy Roenick, Chicago
1990-91—Ed Belfour, Chicago
1991-92—Tony Amonte, N.Y. Rangers
1992-93—Teemu Selanne, Winnipeg
1993-94—Jason Arnott, Edmonton
1994-95—Peter Forsberg, Quebec
1995-96—Eric Daze, Chicago
1996-97—Bryan Berard, N.Y. Islanders
1997-98—Sergei Samsonov, Boston
1998-99—Chris Drury, Colorado
1999-00—Scott Gomez, New Jersey
2000-01—Evgeni Nabokov, San Jose
2001-02—Dany Heatley, Atlanta
2002-03—Henrik Zetterberg, Detroit

NHL COACH OF THE YEAR

1944-45—Dick Irvin, Montreal
1945-46—Johnny Gottselig, Chicago
1979-80—Pat Quinn, Philadelphia
1980-81—Red Berenson, St. Louis
1981-82—Herb Brooks, N.Y. Rangers
1982-83—Gerry Cheevers, Boston
1983-84—Bryan Murray, Washington
1984-85—Mike Keenan, Philadelphia
1985-86—Jacques Demers, St. Louis
1986-87—Jacques Demers, Detroit
1987-88—Terry Crisp, Calgary
1988-89—Pat Burns, Montreal
1989-90—Mike Milbury, Boston
1990-91—Tom Webster, Los Angeles
1991-92—Pat Quinn, Vancouver
1992-93—Pat Burns, Toronto
1993-94—Jacques Lemaire, New Jersey
1994-95—Marc Crawford, Quebec
1995-96—Scotty Bowman, Detroit
1996-97—Ken Hitchcock, Dallas
1997-98—Pat Burns, Boston
1998-99—Jacques Martin, Ottawa
1999-00—Joel Quenneville, St. Louis
2000-01—Scotty Bowman, Detroit
2001-02—Brian Sutter, Chicago
2002-03—Jacques Lemaire, Minnesota
NOTE: The Coach of the Year Award was not given from 1946-47 through 1978-79 seasons.

NHL EXECUTIVE OF THE YEAR

1972-73—Sam Pollock, Montreal
1973-74—Keith Allen, Philadelphia
1974-75—Bill Torrey, N.Y. Islanders
1975-76—Sam Pollock, Montreal
1976-77—Harry Sinden, Boston
1977-78—Ted Lindsay, Detroit
1978-79—Bill Torrey, N.Y. Islanders
1979-80—Scotty Bowman, Buffalo
1980-81—Emile Francis, St. Louis
1981-82—John Ferguson, Winnipeg
1982-83—David Poile, Washington
1983-84—David Poile, Washington
1984-85—John Ferguson, Winnipeg

NHL HISTORY *Award winners*

1985-86—Emile Francis, Hartford
1986-87—John Ferguson, Winnipeg
1987-88—Cliff Fletcher, Calgary
1988-89—Bruce McNall, Los Angeles
1989-90—Harry Sinden, Boston
1990-91—Craig Patrick, Pittsburgh
1991-92—Neil Smith, N.Y. Rangers
1992-93—Cliff Fletcher, Toronto
1993-94—Bobby Clarke, Florida
1994-95—Bobby Clarke, Philadelphia
1995-96—Bryan Murray, Florida
1996-97—John Muckler, Buffalo
1997-98—Craig Patrick, Pittsburgh
1998-99—Craig Patrick, Pittsburgh
1999-00—Larry Pleau, St. Louis
2000-01—Brian Burke, Vancouver
2001-02—Mike Smith, Chicago
2002-03—Doug Risebrough, Minnesota

THE SPORTING NEWS ALL-STAR TEAMS

(As selected by six hockey writers in 1944-45 and 1945-46
and by a vote of league players since 1967-68;
no teams selected from 1946-47 through 1966-67)

1944-45

First team		Second team
Maurice Richard, Mon.	W	Bill Mosienko, Chi.
Toe Blake, Mon.	W	Sweeney Schriner, Tor.
Elmer Lach, Mon.	C	Bill Cowley, Bos.
Emile Bouchard, Mon.	D	Earl Seibert, Det.
Bill Hollett, Det.	D	Babe Pratt, Tor.
Bill Durnan, Mon.	G	Frank McCool, Tor.

1945-46

First team		Second team
Gaye Stewart, Tor.	LW	Doug Bentley, Chi.
Max Bentley, Chi.	C	Elmer Lach, Mon.
Bill Mosienko, Chi.	RW	Maurice Richard, Mon.
Emile Bouchard, Mon.	D	Jack Crawford, Bos.
Jack Stewart, Det.	D	Babe Pratt, Tor.
Bill Durnan, Mon.	G	Harry Lumley, Det.

1967-68

EAST DIVISION First team		WEST DIVISION First team
Bobby Hull, Chi.	LW	Ab McDonald, Pit.
Stan Mikita, Chi.	C	Red Berenson, St.L.
Gordie Howe, Det.	RW	Wayne Connelly, Min.
Bobby Orr, Bos.	D	Bill White, L.A.
Tim Horton, Tor.	D	Mike McMahon, Min.
Ed Giacomin, N.Y.R.	G	Glenn Hall, St.L.

Second team		Second team
Johnny Bucyk, Bos.	LW	Bill Sutherland, Phi.
Phil Esposito, Bos.	C	Ray Cullen, Min.
Rod Gilbert, N.Y.R.	RW	Bill Flett, L.A.
J.C. Tremblay, Mon.	D	Al Arbour, St.L.
Gary Bergman, Det.	D	Ed Van Impe, Phi.
Gump Worsley, Mon.	G	Doug Favell, Phi.

1968-69

EAST DIVISION First team		WEST DIVISION First team
Bobby Hull, Chi.	LW	Danny Grant, Min.
Phil Esposito, Bos.	C	Red Berenson, St.L.
Gordie Howe, Det.	RW	Norm Ferguson, Oak.
Bobby Orr, Bos.	D	Bill White, L.A.
Tim Horton, Tor.	D	Al Arbour, St.L.
Ed Giacomin, N.Y.R.	G	Glenn Hall, St.L.

Second team		Second team
Frank Mahovlich, Det.	LW	Ab McDonald, St.L.
Stan Mikita, Chi.	C	Ted Hampson, Oak.
Yvan Cournoyer, Mon.	RW	Claude LaRose, Min.
J.C. Tremblay, Mon.	D	Carol Vadnais, Oak.
Jim Neilson, N.Y.R.	D	Ed Van Impe, Phi.
Bruce Gamble, Tor.	G	Bernie Parent, Phi.

1969-70

EAST DIVISION		WEST DIVISION
Bobby Hull, Chi.	LW	Dean Prentice, Pit.
Stan Mikita, Chi.	C	Red Berenson, St.L.
Ron Ellis, Tor.	RW	Bill Goldsworthy, Min.
Bobby Orr, Bos.	D	Al Arbour, St.L.
Brad Park, N.Y.R.	D	Bob Woytowich, Pit.
Tony Esposito, Chi.	G	Bernie Parent, Phi.

1970-71

EAST DIVISION		WEST DIVISION
Johnny Bucyk, Bos.	LW	Bobby Hull, Chi.
Phil Esposito, Bos.	C	Stan Mikita, Chi.
Ken Hodge, Bos.	RW	Bill Goldsworthy, Min.
Bobby Orr, Bos.	D	Pat Stapleton, Chi.
J.C. Tremblay, Mon.	D	Bill White, Chi.
Ed Giacomin, N.Y.R.	G	Tony Esposito, Chi.

1971-72

EAST DIVISION		WEST DIVISION
Vic Hadfield, N.Y.R.	LW	Bobby Hull, Chi.
Phil Esposito, Bos.	C	Bobby Clarke, Phi.
Rod Gilbert, N.Y.R.	RW	Bill Goldsworthy, Min.
Bobby Orr, Bos.	D	Pat Stapleton, Chi.
Brad Park, N.Y.R.	D	Bill White, Chi.
Ken Dryden, Mon.	G	Tony Esposito, Chi.

1972-73

EAST DIVISION		WEST DIVISION
Frank Mahovlich, Mon.	LW	Dennis Hull, Chi.
Phil Esposito, Bos.	C	Bobby Clarke, Phi.
Mickey Redmond, Det.	RW	Bill Flett, Phi.
Bobby Orr, Bos.	D	Bill White, Chi.
Guy Lapointe, Mon.	D	Barry Gibbs, Min.
Ken Dryden, Mon.	G	Tony Esposito, Chi.

1973-74

EAST DIVISION First team		WEST DIVISION First team
Richard Martin, Buf.	LW	Lowell MacDonald, Pit.
Phil Esposito, Bos.	C	Bobby Clarke, Phi.
Ken Hodge, Bos.	RW	Bill Goldsworthy, Min.
Bobby Orr, Bos.	D	Bill White, Chi.
Brad Park, N.Y.R.	D	Barry Ashbee, Phi.
Gilles Gilbert, Bos.	G	Bernie Parent, Phi.

Second team		Second team
Frank Mahovlich, Mon.	LW	Dennis Hull, Chi.
Darryl Sittler, Tor.	C	Stan Mikita, Chi.
Mickey Redmond, Det.	RW	Jean Pronovost, Pit.
Guy Lapointe, Mon.	D	Don Awrey, St.L.
Borje Salming, Tor.	D	Dave Burrows, Pit.
Ed Giacomin, N.Y.R.	D	Tony Esposito, Chi.

1974-75

CAMPBELL CONFERENCE First team		WALES CONFERENCE First team
Steve Vickers, N.Y.R.	LW	Richard Martin, Buf.
Bobby Clarke, Phi.	C	Phil Esposito, Bos.
Rod Gilbert, N.Y.R.	RW	Guy Lafleur, Mon.
Denis Potvin, N.Y.I.	D	Bobby Orr, Bos.
Brad Park, N.Y.R.	D	Guy Lapointe, Mon.
Bernie Parent, Phi.	G	Rogie Vachon, L.A.

NHL HISTORY *Award winners*

Second team	Pos	Second team
Eric Vail, Atl.	LW	Danny Grant, Det.
Stan Mikita, Chi.	C	Gilbert Perreault, Buf.
Reggie Leach, Phi.	RW	Rene Robert, Buf.
Jim Watson, Phi.	D	Borje Salming, Tor.
Phil Russell, Chi.	D	Terry Harper, L.A.
Gary Smith, Van.	G	Ken Dryden, Mon.

1975-76

First team	Pos	Second team
Bill Barber, Phi.	LW	Richard Martin, Buf.
Bobby Clarke, Phi.	C	Pete Mahovlich, Mon.
Guy Lafleur, Mon.	RW	Reggie Leach, Phi.
Denis Potvin, N.Y.I.	D	Guy Lapointe, Mon.
Brad Park, Bos.	D	Borje Salming, Tor.
Ken Dryden, Mon.	G	Glenn Resch, N.Y.I.

1976-77

First team	Pos	Second team
Steve Shutt, Mon.	LW	Clark Gillies, N.Y.I.
Marcel Dionne, L.A.	C	Gilbert Perreault, Buf.
Guy Lafleur, Mon.	RW	Lanny McDonald, Tor.
Larry Robinson, Mon.	D	Guy Lapointe, Mon.
Borje Salming, Tor.	D	Serge Savard, Mon.
	(tied)	Denis Potvin, N.Y.I.
Rogie Vachon, L.A.	G	Ken Dryden, Mon.

1977-78

First team	Pos	Second team
Clark Gillies, N.Y.I.	LW	Steve Shutt, Mon.
Bryan Trottier, N.Y.I.	C	Darryl Sittler, Tor.
Guy Lafleur, Mon.	RW	Terry O'Reilly, Bos.
Borje Salming, Tor.	D	Denis Potvin, N.Y.I.
Larry Robinson, Mon.	D	Serge Savard, Mon.
Ken Dryden, Mon.	G	Don Edwards, Buf.

1978-79

First team	Pos	Second team
Clark Gillies, N.Y.I.	LW	Bob Gainey, Mon.
Bryan Trottier, N.Y.I.	C	Marcel Dionne, L.A.
Guy Lafleur, Mon.	RW	Mike Bossy, N.Y.I.
Denis Potvin, N.Y.I.	D	Borje Salming, Tor.
Larry Robinson, Mon.	D	Serge Savard, Mon.
Ken Dryden, Mon.	G	Glenn Resch, N.Y.I.

1979-80

First team	Pos	Second team
Charlie Simmer, L.A.	LW	Steve Shutt, Mon.
Marcel Dionne, L.A.	C	Wayne Gretzky, Edm.
Guy Lafleur, Mon.	RW	Danny Gare, Buf.
Larry Robinson, Mon.	D	Barry Beck, Col., N.Y.R.
Borje Salming, Tor.	D	Mark Howe, Har.
Tony Esposito, Chi.	G	Don Edwards, Buf.

1980-81

First team	Pos	Second team
Charlie Simmer, L.A.	LW	Bill Barber, Phi.
Wayne Gretzky, Edm.	C	Marcel Dionne, L.A.
Mike Bossy, N.Y.I.	RW	Dave Taylor, L.A.
Randy Carlyle, Pit.	D	Larry Robinson, Mon.
Denis Potvin, N.Y.I.	D	Ray Bourque, Bos.
Mike Liut, St.L.	G	Don Beaupre, Min.

1981-82

First team	Pos	Second team
Mark Messier, Edm.	LW	John Tonelli, N.Y.I.
Wayne Gretzky, Edm.	C	Bryan Trottier, N.Y.I.
Mike Bossy, N.Y.I.	RW	Rick Middleton, Bos.
Doug Wilson, Chi.	D	Paul Coffey, Edm.
Ray Bourque, Bos.	D	Larry Robinson, Mon.
Bill Smith, N.Y.I.	G	Grant Fuhr, Edm.

1982-83

First team	Pos	Second team
Mark Messier, Edm.	LW	Michel Goulet, Que.
Wayne Gretzky, Edm.	C	Denis Savard, Chi.
Lanny McDonald, Cal.	RW	Mike Bossy, N.Y.I.
Mark Howe, Phi.	D	Ray Bourque, Bos.
Rod Langway, Was.	D	Paul Coffey, Edm.
Pete Peeters, Bos.	G	Andy Moog, Edm.

1983-84

First team	Pos	Second team
Michel Goulet, Que.	LW	John Ogrodnick, Det.
Wayne Gretzky, Edm.	C	Bryan Trottier, N.Y.I.
Rick Middleton, Bos.	RW	Mike Bossy, N.Y.I.
Ray Bourque, Bos.	D	Paul Coffey, Edm.
Rod Langway, Was.	D	Denis Potvin, N.Y.I.
Pat Riggin, Was.	G	Tom Barrasso, Buf.

1984-85

First team	Pos	Second team
Michel Goulet, Que.	LW	John Ogrodnick, Det.
Wayne Gretzky, Edm.	C	Dale Hawerchuk, Win.
Jari Kurri, Edm.	RW	Mike Bossy, N.Y.I.
Ray Bourque, Bos.	D	Rod Langway, Was.
Paul Coffey, Edm.	D	Doug Wilson, Chi.
Pelle Lindbergh, Phi.	G	Tom Barrasso, Buf.

1985-86

First team	Pos	Second team
Michel Goulet, Que.	LW	Mats Naslund, Mon.
Wayne Gretzky, Edm.	C	Mario Lemieux, Pit.
Mike Bossy, N.Y.I.	RW	Jari Kurri, Edm.
Paul Coffey, Edm.	D	Ray Bourque, Bos.
Mark Howe, Phi.	D	Larry Robinson, Mon.
John Vanbiesbrouck, N.Y.R.	G	Grant Fuhr, Edm.

1986-87

First team	Pos	Second team
Michel Goulet, Que.	LW	Luc Robitaille, L.A.
Wayne Gretzky, Edm.	C	Mark Messier, Edm.
Tim Kerr, Phi.	RW	Kevin Dineen, Har.
Ray Bourque, Bos.	D	Larry Murphy, Was.
Mark Howe, Phi.	D	Paul Coffey, Edm.
Mike Liut, Har.	G	Ron Hextall, Phi.

1987-88

First team	Pos	Second team
Luc Robitaille, L.A.	LW	Michel Goulet, Que.
Mario Lemieux, Pit.	C	Wayne Gretzky, Edm.
Cam Neely, Bos.	RW	Hakan Loob, Cal.
Ray Bourque, Bos.	D	Scott Stevens, Was.
Gary Suter, Cal.	D	Brad McCrimmon, Cal.
Grant Fuhr, Edm.	G	Tom Barrasso, Buf.

1988-89

First team	Pos	Second team
Luc Robitaille, L.A.	LW	Mats Naslund, Mon.
Mario Lemieux, Pit.	C	Wayne Gretzky, L.A.
Joe Mullen, Cal.	RW	Jari Kurri, Edm.
Paul Coffey, Pit.	D	Ray Bourque, Bos.
Chris Chelios, Mon.	D	Gary Suter, Cal.
Patrick Roy, Mon.	G	Mike Vernon, Cal.

1989-90

First team	Pos	Second team
Luc Robitaille, L.A.	LW	Brian Bellows, Min.
Mark Messier, Edm.	C	Pat LaFontaine, N.Y.I.
Brett Hull, St.L.	RW	Cam Neely, Bos.
Ray Bourque, Bos.	D	Doug Wilson, Chi.
Al MacInnis, Cal.	D	Paul Coffey, Pit.
Patrick Roy, Mon.	G	Daren Puppa, Buf.

1990-91

First team		Second team
Luc Robitaille, L.A.	LW	Kevin Stevens, Pit.
Wayne Gretzky, L.A.	C	Adam Oates, St.L.
Brett Hull, St.L.	RW	Cam Neely, Bos.
Ray Bourque, Bos.	D	Brian Leetch, N.Y.R.
Al MacInnis, Cal.	D	Chris Chelios, Chi.
Ed Belfour, Chi.	G	Patrick Roy, Mon.

1991-92

First team		Second team
Kevin Stevens, Pit.	LW	Luc Robitaille, L.A.
Mark Messier, N.Y.R.	C	Wayne Gretzky, L.A.
Brett Hull, St.L.	RW	Joe Mullen, Pit.
Brian Leetch, N.Y.R.	D	Phil Housley, Win.
Ray Bourque, Bos.	D	Chris Chelios, Chi.
Patrick Roy, Mon.	G	Kirk McLean, Van.

1992-93

First team		Second team
Luc Robitaille, L.A.	LW	Kevin Stevens, Pit.
Mario Lemieux, Pit.	C	Doug Gilmour, Tor.
Teemu Selanne, Win.	RW	Alexander Mogilny, Buf.
Chris Chelios, Chi.	D	Larry Murphy, Pit.
Ray Bourque, Bos.	D	Al Iafrate, Was.
Tom Barrasso, Pit.	G	Ed Belfour, Chi.

1993-94

First team		Second team
Adam Graves, N.Y.R.	LW	Dave Andreychuk, Tor.
Sergei Fedorov, Det.	C	Wayne Gretzky, L.A.
Cam Neely, Bos.	RW	Pavel Bure, Van.
Ray Bourque, Bos.	D	Brian Leetch, N.Y.R.
Scott Stevens, N.J.	D	Al MacInnis, Cal.
John Vanbiesbrouck, Fla.	G	Dominik Hasek, Buf.

1994-95

LW	John LeClair, Mon.-Phi.
C	Eric Lindros, Philadelphia
RW	Jaromir Jagr, Pittsburgh
D	Paul Coffey, Detroit
D	Ray Bourque, Boston
G	Dominik Hasek, Buffalo

1995-96

LW	Keith Tkachuk, Winnipeg
C	Mario Lemieux, Pittsburgh
RW	Jaromir Jagr, Pittsburgh
D	Chris Chelios, Chicago
D	Ray Bourque, Boston
G	Chris Osgood, Detroit

1996-97

LW	John LeClair, Philadelphia
C	Mario Lemieux, Pittsburgh
RW	Teemu Selanne, Anaheim
D	Chris Chelios, Chicago
D	Brian Leetch, N.Y. Rangers
G	Dominik Hasek, Buffalo

1997-98

LW	John LeClair, Philadelphia
C	Peter Forsberg, Colorado
RW	Teemu Selanne, Anaheim
D	Rob Blake, Los Angeles
D	Nicklas Lidstrom, Detroit
G	Dominik Hasek, Buffalo

1998-99

LW	Paul Kariya, Anaheim
C	Alexei Yashin, Ottawa
RW	Jaromir Jagr, Pittsburgh
D	Al MacInnis, St. Louis
D	Nicklas Lidstrom, Detroit
G	Dominik Hasek, Buffalo

1999-2000

LW	Paul Kariya, Anaheim
C	Steve Yzerman, Detroit
RW	Jaromir Jagr, Pittsburgh
D	Nicklas Lidstrom, Detroit
D	Chris Pronger, St. Louis
G	Roman Turek, St. Louis

2000-01

First team		Second team
Alexei Kovalev, Pit.	LW	Patrik Elias, N.J.
Joe Sakic, Col.	C	Mario Lemieux, Pit.
Jaromir Jagr, Pit.	RW	Pavel Bure, Fla.
Rob Blake, L.A.-Col.	D	Brian Leetch, N.Y.R.
Nicklas Lidstrom, Det.	D	Chris Pronger, St.L.
Martin Brodeur, N.J.	G	Sean Burke, Pho.

2001-02

LW	Markus Naslund, Vancouver
C	Joe Sakic, Colorado
RW	Jarome Iginla, Calgary
D	Rob Blake, Colorado
D	Nicklas Lidstrom, Detroit
G	Patrick Roy, Colorado

2002-03

First team		Second team
Martin Brodeur, N.J.	G	Marty Turco, Dallas
Nicklas Lidstrom, Detroit	D	Rob Blake, Colorado
Al MacInnis, St. Louis	D	Sergei Gonchar, Was.
Markus Naslund, Van.	LW	Marian Hossa, Ottawa
Peter Forsberg, Colo.	C	Joe Thornton, Boston
Todd Bertuzzi, Van.	RW	Milan Hejduk, Colo.

HALL OF FAME

NOTE: Leagues other than the NHL with which Hall of Fame members are associated are denoted in parentheses. Abbreviations:
AAHA: Alberta Amateur Hockey Association. **AHA:** Amateur Hockey Association of Canada. **CAHL:** Canadian Amateur Hockey League. **EAA:** Eaton Athletic Association. **ECAHA:** Eastern Canada Amateur Hockey Association. **ECHA:** Eastern Canada Hockey Association. **FAHL:** Federal Amateur Hockey League. **IHL:** International Professional Hockey League. **MHL:** Manitoba Hockey League. **MNSHL:** Manitoba and Northwestern Senior Hockey League. **MPHL:** Maritime Pro Hockey League. **MSHL:** Manitoba Senior Hockey League. **NHA:** National Hockey Association. **NOHA:** Northern Ontario Hockey Association. **OHA:** Ontario Hockey Association. **OPHL:** Ontario Professional Hockey League. **PCHA:** Pacific Coast Hockey Association. **WCHL:** Western Canada Hockey League. **WHA:** World Hockey Association. **WHL:** Western Hockey League. **WinHL:** Winnipeg Hockey League. **WOHA:** Western Ontario Hockey Association.

PLAYERS

Player	Elec. year/ how elected*	Pos.†	First season	Last season	Stanley Cup wins‡	Teams as player
Abel, Sid	1969/P	C	1938-39	1953-54	3	Detroit Red Wings, Chicago Blackhawks
Adams, Jack	1959/P	C	1917-18	1926-27	2	Toronto Arenas, Vancouver Millionaires (PCHA), Toronto St. Pats, Ottawa Senators
Apps, Syl	1961/P	C	1936-37	1947-48	3	Toronto Maple Leafs
Armstrong, George	1975/P	RW	1949-50	1970-71	4	Toronto Maple Leafs
Bailey, Ace	1975/P	RW	1926-27	1933-34	1	Toronto Maple Leafs
Bain, Dan	1945/P	C	1895-96	1901-02	3	Winnipeg Victorias (MHL)
Baker, Hobey	1945/P	Ro.	1910	1915	0	Princeton University, St. Nicholas
Barber, Bill	1990/P	LW	1972-73	1983-84	2	Philadelphia Flyers
Barry, Marty	1965/P	C	1927-28	1939-40	2	New York Americans, Boston Bruins, Detroit Red Wings, Montreal Canadiens
Bathgate, Andy	1978/P	RW	1952-53	1974-75	1	New York Rangers, Toronto Maple Leafs, Detroit Red Wings, Pittsburgh Penguins, Vancouver Blazers (WHA)
Bauer, Bobby	1996/V	LW	1936-37	1951-52	2	Boston Bruins
Beliveau, Jean	1972/P	C	1950-51	1970-71	10	Montreal Canadiens
Benedict, Clint	1965/P	G	1917-18	1929-30	4	Ottawa Senators, Montreal Maroons
Bentley, Doug	1964/P	LW	1939-40	1953-54	0	Chicago Blackhawks, New York Rangers
Bentley, Max	1966/P	C	1940-41	1953-54	3	Chicago Blackhawks, Toronto Maple Leafs, New York Rangers
Blake, Toe	1966/P	LW	1934-35	1947-48	3	Montreal Maroons, Montreal Canadiens
Boivin, Leo	1986/P	D	1951-52	1969-70	0	Toronto Maple Leafs, Boston Bruins, Detroit Red Wings, Pittsburgh Penguins, Minnesota North Stars
Boon, Dickie	1952/P	D	1897	1905	2	Montreal Monarchs, Montreal AAA (CAHL), Montreal Wanderers (FAHL)
Bossy, Mike	1991/P	RW	1977-78	1986-87	4	New York Islanders
Bouchard, Butch	1966/P	D	1941-42	1955-56	4	Montreal Canadiens
Boucher, Frank	1958/P	C	1921-22	1943-44	2	Ottawa Senators, Vancouver Maroons, New York Rangers
Boucher, Georges	1960/P	F/D	1917-18	1931-32	4	Ottawa Senators, Montreal Maroons, Chicago Blackhawks
Bower, Johnny	1976/P	G	1953-54	1969-70	0	New York Rangers, Toronto Maple Leafs
Bowie, Russell	1945/P	C	1898-99	1907-08	1	Montreal Victorias
Brimsek, Frank	1966/P	G	1938-39	1949-50	2	Boston Bruins, Chicago Blackhawks
Broadbent, Punch	1962/P	RW	1912-13	1928-29	4	Ottawa Senators, Montreal Maroons, New York Americans
Broda, Turk	1967/P	G	1936-37	1951-52	0	Toronto Maple Leafs
Bucyk, John	1981/P	LW	1955-56	1977-78	2	Detroit Red Wings, Boston Bruins
Burch, Billy	1974/P	C	1922-23	1932-33	0	Hamilton Tigers, New York Americans, Boston Bruins, Chicago Blackhawks
Cameron, Harry	1962/P	D	1912-13	1925-26	3	Toronto Blueshirts, Toronto Arenas, Montreal Wanderers, Ottawa Senators, Toronto St. Pats, Montreal Canadiens, Saskatoon (WCHL)
Cheevers, Gerry	1985/P	G	1961-62	1979-80	2	Toronto Maple Leafs, Boston Bruins, Cleveland Crusaders (WHA)
Clancy, King	1958/P	D	1921-22	1936-37	3	Ottawa Senators, Toronto Maple Leafs
Clapper, Dit	1947/P	RW	1927-28	1946-47	3	Boston Bruins
Clarke, Bobby	1987/P	C	1969-70	1983-84	2	Philadelphia Flyers
Cleghorn, Sprague	1958/P	D	1909-10	1927-28	3	New York Crescents, Renfrew Creamery Kings (NHA), Montreal Wanderers, Ottawa Senators, Toronto St. Pats, Montreal Canadiens, Boston Bruins
Colville, Neil	1967/P	C/D	1935-36	1948-49	1	New York Rangers
Conacher, Charlie	1961/P	RW	1929-30	1940-41	1	Toronto Maple Leafs, Detroit Red Wings, New York Americans
Conacher, Lionel	1994/V	D	1925-26	1936-37	2	Pittsburgh Pirates, New York Americans, Montreal Maroons, Chicago Blackhawks
Conacher, Roy	1998/V	LW	1938-39	1951-52	2	Boston Bruins, Detroit Red Wings, Chicago Blackhawks
Connell, Alex	1958/P	G	1924-25	1936-37	2	Ottawa Senators, Detroit Falcons, New York Americans, Montreal Maroons

NHL HISTORY *Hall of Fame*

Player	Elec. year/ how elected*	Pos.†	First season	Last season	Stanley Cup wins‡	Teams as player
Cook, Bill	1952/P	RW	1921-22	1936-37	2	Saskatoon (WCHL/WHL), New York Rangers
Cook, Bun	1995/V	LW	1926-27	1936-37	2	New York Rangers, Boston Bruins
Coulter, Art	1974/P	D	1931-32	1941-42	2	Chicago Blackhawks, New York Rangers
Cournoyer, Yvan	1982/P	RW	1963-64	1978-79	10	Montreal Canadiens
Cowley, Bill	1968/P	C	1934-35	1946-47	2	St. Louis Eagles, Boston Bruins
Crawford, Rusty	1962/P	LW	1912-13	1925-26	1	Quebec Bulldogs, Ottawa Senators, Toronto Arenas, Saskatoon (WCHL), Calgary (WCHL), Vancouver (WHL)
Darragh, Jack	1962/P	RW	1910-11	1923-24	4	Ottawa Senators
Davidson, Scotty	1950/P	RW	1912-13	1913-14	0	Toronto (NHA)
Day, Hap	1961/P	D	1924-25	1937-38	1	Toronto St. Pats, Toronto Maple Leafs, New York Americans
Delvecchio, Alex	1977/P	C	1950-51	1973-74	3	Detroit Red Wings
Denneny, Cy	1959/P	LW	1914-15	1928-29	5	Toronto Shamrocks (NHA), Toronto Blueshirts (NHA), Ottawa Senators, Boston Bruins
Dionne, Marcel	1992/P	C	1971-72	1988-89	0	Detroit Red Wings, Los Angeles Kings, New York Rangers
Drillon, Gord	1975/P	RW	1936-37	1942-43	1	Toronto Maple Leafs, Montreal Canadiens
Drinkwater, Graham	1950/P	F/D	1892-93	1898-99	5	Montreal Victorias
Dryden, Ken	1983/P	G	1970-71	1978-79	6	Montreal Canadiens
Dumart, Woody	1992/V	LW	1935-36	1953-54	2	Boston Bruins
Dunderdale, Tommy	1974/P	C	1906-07	1923-24	0	Winnipeg Maple Leafs (MHL), Montreal Shamrocks (NHA), Quebec Bulldogs (NHA), Victoria (PCHA), Portland (PCHA), Saskatoon (WCHL), Edmonton (WCHL)
Durnan, Bill	1964/P	G	1943-44	1949-50	2	Montreal Canadiens
Dutton, Red	1958/P	D	1921-22	1935-36	0	Calgary Tigers (WCHL), Montreal Maroons, New York Americans
Dye, Babe	1970/P	RW	1919-20	1930-31	1	Toronto St. Pats, Hamilton Tigers, Chicago Blackhawks, New York Americans, Toronto Maple Leafs
Esposito, Phil	1984/P	C	1963-64	1980-81	2	Chicago Blackhawks, Boston Bruins, New York Rangers
Esposito, Tony	1988/P	G	1968-69	1983-84	1	Montreal Canadiens, Chicago Blackhawks
Farrell, Arthur	1965/P	F	1896-97	1900-01	2	Montreal Shamrocks (AHA/CAHL)
Federko, Bernie	2002/P	C	1976-77	1989-90	0	St. Louis Blues, Detroit Red Wings
Fetisov, Viacheslav	2001/P	D	1974-75	1997-98	2	CSKA Moscow, New Jersey Devils, Detroit Red Wings
Flaman, Fern	1990/V	D	1944-45	1960-61	1	Boston Bruins, Toronto Maple Leafs
Foyston, Frank	1958/P	C	1912-13	1927-28	3	Toronto Blueshirts (NHA), Seattle Metropolitans (PCHA), Victoria Cougars (WCHL/WHL), Detroit Cougars
Fredrickson, Frank	1958/P	C	1920-21	1930-31	1	Victoria Aristocrats (PCHA), Victoria Cougars (PCHA/WCHL/WHL), Detroit Cougars, Boston Bruins, Pittsburgh Pirates, Detroit Falcons
Fuhr, Grant	2003/P	G	1979-80	1999-00	5	Victoria Cougars (WHL), Edmonton Oilers, Toronto Maple Leafs, Buffalo Sabres, St. Louis Blues, Calgary Flames
Gadsby, Bill	1970/P	D	1946-47	1965-66	0	Chicago Blackhawks, New York Rangers, Detroit Red Wings
Gainey, Bob	1992/P	LW	1973-74	1988-89	5	Montreal Canadiens
Gardiner, Chuck	1945/P	G	1927-28	1933-34	1	Chicago Blackhawks
Gardiner, Herb	1958/P	D	1921-22	1928-29	0	Calgary Tigers (WCHL), Montreal Canadiens, Chicago Blackhawks
Gardner, Jimmy	1962/P	LW	1900-01	1914-15	3	Montreal Hockey Club (CAHL), Montreal Wanderers (FAHL/ECHA/NHA), Calumet (IHL), Pittsburgh (IHL), Montreal Shamrocks (ECAHA),New Westminster Royals (PCHA), Montreal Canadiens (NHA)
Gartner, Mike	2001/P	RW	1978-79	1997-98	0	Cincinnati Stingers (WHA), Washington Capitals, Minnesota North Stars, New York Rangers, Toronto Maple Leafs, Phoenix Coyotes
Geoffrion, Boom Boom	1972/P	RW	1950-51	1967-68	6	Montreal Canadiens, New York Rangers
Gerard, Eddie	1945/P	F/D	1913-14	1922-23	4	Ottawa Senators (NHA/NHL), Toronto St. Pats
Giacomin, Eddie	1987/P	G	1965-66	1977-78	0	New York Rangers, Detroit Red Wings
Gilbert, Rod	1982/P	RW	1960-61	1977-78	0	New York Rangers
Gillies, Clark	2002/P	LW	1974-75	1987-88	4	New York Islanders, Buffalo Sabres
Gilmour, Billy	1962/P	RW	1902-03	1915-16	5	Ottawa Silver Seven (CAHL/FAHL/ECAHA), Montreal Victorias (ECAHA), Ottawa Senators (ECHA/NHA)
Goheen, Moose	1952/P	D	1914	1918	0	St. Paul Athletic Club, 1920 U.S. Olympic Team
Goodfellow, Ebbie	1963/P	C	1929-30	1942-43	3	Detroit Cougars, Detroit Falcons, Detroit Red Wings
Goulet, Michel	1998/P	LW	1978-79	1993-94	0	Birmingham Bulls (WHA), Quebec Nordiques, Chicago Blackhawks
Grant, Mike	1950/P	D	1893-94	1901-02	5	Montreal Victorias (AHA/CAHL), Montreal Shamrocks (CAHL)
Green, Shorty	1962/P	RW	1923-24	1926-27	0	Hamilton Tigers, New York Americans
Gretzky, Wayne	1999/P	C	1978-79	1998-99	4	Indianapolis Racers (WHA), Edmonton (WHA/NHL), Los Angeles Kings, St. Louis Blues, New York Rangers
Griffis, Si	1950/P	Ro./D	1902-03	1918-19	2	Rat Portage Thistles (MNSHL), Kenora Thistles (MSHL), Vancouver Millionaires (PCHA)
Hainsworth, George	1961/P	G	1923-24	1936-37	2	Saskatoon Crescents (WCHL/WHL), Montreal Canadiens, Toronto Maple Leafs

Player	Elec. year/ how elected*	Pos.†	First season	Last season	Stanley Cup wins‡	Teams as player
Hall, Glenn	1975/P	G	1952-53	1970-71	1	Detroit Red Wings, Chicago Blackhawks, St. Louis Blues
Hall, Joe	1961/P	F/D	1903-04	1918-19	2	Winnipeg (MSHL), Quebec Bulldogs (ECAHA/NHA), Brandon (MHL), Montreal (ECAHA), Montreal Shamrocks (ECAHA/NHA), Montreal Wanderers (ECHA), Montreal Canadiens
Harvey, Doug	1973/P	D	1947-48	1968-69	6	Montreal Canadiens, New York Rangers, Detroit Red Wings, St. Louis Blues
Hawerchuk, Dale	2001/P	C	1981-82	1996-97	0	Winnipeg Jets, Buffalo Sabres, St. Louis Blues, Philadelphia Flyers
Hay, George	1958/P	LW	1921-22	1933-34	0	Regina Capitals (WCHL), Portland Rosebuds (WHL), Chicago Blackhawks, Detroit Cougars, Detroit Falcons, Detroit Red Wings
Hern, Riley	1962/P	G	1906-07	1910-11	3	Montreal Wanderers (ECAHA/ECHA/NHA)
Hextall, Bryan	1969/P	RW	1936-37	1947-48	1	New York Rangers
Holmes, Hap	1972/P	G	1912-13	1927-28	0	Toronto Blueshirts (NHA), Seattle Metropolitans (PCHA), Toronto Arenas, Victoria Cougars (WCHL/WHL), Detroit Cougars
Hooper, Tom	1962/P	F	1904-05	1907-08	2	Rat Portage Thistles (MNSHL), Kenora Thistles (SHL), Montreal Wanderers (ECAHA), Montreal (ECAHA)
Horner, Red	1965/P	D	1928-29	1939-40	1	Toronto Maple Leafs
Horton, Tim	1977/P	D	1949-50	1973-74	4	Toronto Maple Leafs, New York Rangers, Pittsburgh Penguins, Buffalo Sabres
Howe, Gordie	1972/P	RW	1946-47	1979-80	4	Detroit Red Wings, Houston Aeros (WHA), New England Whalers (WHA), Hartford Whalers
Howe, Syd	1965/P	F/D	1929-30	1945-46	3	Ottawa Senators, Philadelphia Quakers, Toronto Maple Leafs, St. Louis Eagles, Detroit Red Wings
Howell, Harry	1979/P	D	1952-53	1975-76	0	New York Rangers, Oakland Seals, California Golden Seals, Los Angeles Kings, New York Golden Blades/Jersey Knights (WHA), San Diego Mariners (WHA), Calgary Cowboys (WHA)
Hull, Bobby	1983/P	LW	1957-58	1979-80	1	Chicago Blackhawks, Winnipeg Jets (WHA/NHL), Hartford Whalers
Hutton, Bouse	1962/P	G	1898-99	1903-04	1	Ottawa Silver Seven (CAHL)
Hyland, Harry	1962/P	RW	1908-09	1917-18	1	Montreal Shamrocks (ECHA), Montreal Wanderers (NHA), New Westminster Royals (PCHA), Ottawa Senators
Irvin, Dick	1958/P	C	1916-17	1928-29	0	Portland Rosebuds (PCHA), Regina Capitals (WCHL), Chicago Blackhawks
Jackson, Busher	1971/P	LW	1929-30	1943-44	1	Toronto Maple Leafs, New York Americans, Boston Bruins
Johnson, Ching	1958/P	D	1926-27	1937-38	2	New York Rangers, New York Americans
Johnson, Moose	1952/P	LW/D	1903-04	1921-22	4	Montreal AAA (CAHL), Montreal Wanderers (ECAHA/ECHA/NHA), New Westminster Royals (PCHA), Portland Rosebuds (PCHA), Victoria Aristocrats (PCHA)
Johnson, Tom	1970/P	D	1947-48	1964-65	6	Montreal Canadiens, Boston Bruins
Joliat, Aurel	1947/P	LW	1922-23	1937-38	3	Montreal Canadiens
Keats, Duke	1958/P	C	1915-16	1928-29	0	Toronto Blueshirts (NHA), Edmonton Eskimos (WCHL/WHL), Boston Bruins, Detroit Cougars, Chicago Blackhawks
Kelly, Red	1969/P	C	1947-48	1966-67	8	Detroit Red Wings, Toronto Maple Leafs
Kennedy, Ted	1966/P	C	1942-43	1956-57	5	Toronto Maple Leafs
Keon, Dave	1986/P	C	1960-61	1981-82	4	Toronto Maple Leafs, Minnesota Fighting Saints (WHA), Indianapolis Racers (WHA), New England Whalers (WHA), Hartford Whalers
Kurri, Jari	2001/P	C/RW	1980-81	1997-98	5	Edmonton Oilers, Los Angeles Kings, New York Rangers, Mighty Ducks of Anaheim, Colorado Avalanche
Lach, Elmer	1966/P	C	1940-41	1953-54	3	Montreal Canadiens
Lafleur, Guy	1988/P	RW	1971-72	1990-91	5	Montreal Canadiens, New York Rangers, Quebec Nordiques
LaFontaine, Pat	2003/P	C	1983-84	1997-98	0	New York Islanders, Buffalo Sabres, New York Rangers
Lalonde, Newsy	1950/P	C/Ro.	1904-05	1926-27	1	Cornwall (FAHL), Portage La Prairie (MHL), Toronto (OPHL), Montreal Canadiens (NHA/NHL), Renfrew Creamery Kings (NHA), Vancouver Millionaires (PCHA), Saskatoon Sheiks (WCHL), Saskatoon Crescents (WCHL/WHL), New York Americans
Langway, Rod	2002/P	D	1978-79	1992-93	1	Montreal Canadiens, Washington Capitals
Laperriere, Jacques	1987/P	D	1962-63	1973-74	6	Montreal Canadiens
Lapointe, Guy	1993/P	D	1968-69	1983-84	6	Montreal Canadiens, St. Louis Blues, Boston Bruins
Laprade, Edgar	1993/V	C	1945-46	1954-55	0	New York Rangers
Laviolette, Jack	1962/P	D/LW	1903-04	1917-18	1	Montreal Nationals (FAHL), Montreal Shamrocks (ECAHA/ECHA), Montreal Canadiens (NHA/NHL)
Lehman, Hugh	1958/P	G	1908-09	1927-28	1	Berlin Dutchmen (OPHL), Galt (OPHL), New Westminster Royals (PCHA), Vancouver Millionaires (PCHA), Vancouver Maroons (PCHA), Chicago Blackhawks
Lemaire, Jacques	1984/P	C	1967-68	1978-79	8	Montreal Canadiens

Player	Elec. year/ how elected*	Pos.†	First season	Last season	Stanley Cup wins‡	Teams as player
Lemieux, Mario	1997/P	C	1984-85	2002-03	2	Pittsburgh Penguins
LeSueur, Percy	1961/P	G	1905-06	1915-16	3	Smith Falls (FAHL), Ottawa Senators (ECAHA/ECHA/NHA), Toronto Shamrocks (NHA), Toronto Blueshirts (NHA)
Lewis, Herbie	1989/V	LW	1928-29	1938-39	2	Detroit Cougars, Detroit Falcons, Detroit Red Wings
Lindsay, Ted	1966/P	LW	1944-45	1964-65	4	Detroit Red Wings, Chicago Blackhawks
Lumley, Harry	1980/P	G	1943-44	1959-60	1	Detroit Red Wings, New York Rangers, Chicago Blackhawks, Toronto Maple Leafs, Boston Bruins
MacKay, Mickey	1952/P	C/Ro.	1914-15	1929-30	1	Vancouver Millionaires (PCHA), Vancouver Maroons (PCHA/WCHL/WHL), Chicago Blackhawks, Pittsburgh Pirates, Boston Bruins
Mahovlich, Frank	1981/P	LW	1956-57	1977-78	6	Toronto Maple Leafs, Detroit Red Wings, Montreal Canadiens, Toronto Toros (WHA), Birmingham Bulls (WHA)
Malone, Joe	1950/P	C/LW	1908-09	1923-24	3	Quebec (ECHA), Waterloo (OPHL), Quebec Bulldogs (NHA/NHL), Montreal Canadiens, Hamilton Tigers
Mantha, Sylvio	1960/P	D	1923-24	1936-37	3	Montreal Canadiens, Boston Bruins
Marshall, Jack	1965/P	C/D	1900-01	1916-17	6	Winnipeg Victorias, Montreal AAA (CAHL), Montreal Wanderers (FAHL/ECAHA/NHA), Ottawa Montagnards (FAHL), Montreal Shamrocks (ECAHA/ECHA), Toronto Blueshirts (NHA)
Maxwell, Fred	1962/P	Ro.	1914	1925	0	Winnipeg Monarchs (MSHL), Winnipeg Falcons (MSHL)
McDonald, Lanny	1992/P	RW	1973-74	1988-89	1	Toronto Maple Leafs, Colorado Rockies, Calgary Flames
McGee, Frank	1945/P	C/Ro.	1902-03	1905-06	4	Ottawa Silver Seven
McGimsie, Billy	1962/P	F	1902-03	1906-07	1	Rat Portage Thistles (MNSHL/MSHL), Kenora Thistles (MSHL)
McNamara, George	1958/P	D	1907-08	1916-17	1	Montreal Shamrocks (ECAHA/ECHA), Waterloo (OPHL), Toronto Tecumsehs (NHA), Toronto Ontarios (NHA), Toronto Blueshirts (NHA), Toronto Shamrocks (NHA), 228th Battalion (NHA)
Mikita, Stan	1983/P	C	1958-59	1979-80	1	Chicago Blackhawks
Moore, Dickie	1974/P	LW	1951-52	1967-68	6	Montreal Canadiens, Toronto Maple Leafs, St. Louis Blues
Moran, Paddy	1958/P	G	1901-02	1916-17	2	Quebec Bulldogs (CAHL/ECAHA/ECHA/NHA), Haileybury (NHA)
Morenz, Howie	1945/P	C	1923-24	1936-37	3	Montreal Canadiens, Chicago Blackhawks, New York Rangers
Mosienko, Bill	1965/P	RW	1941-42	1954-55	0	Chicago Blackhawks
Mullen, Joe	2000/P	RW	1979-80	1996-97	3	St. Louis Blues, Calgary Flames, Pittsburgh Penguins, Boston Bruins
Nighbor, Frank	1947/P	LW/C	1912-13	1929-30	5	Toronto Blueshirts (NHA), Vancouver Millionaires, (PCHA), Ottawa Senators, Toronto Maple Leafs
Noble, Reg	1962/P	LW/C/D	1916-17	1932-33	3	Toronto Blueshirts (NHA), Montreal Canadiens (NHA), Toronto Arenas, Toronto St. Pats, Montreal Maroons, Detroit Cougars, Detroit Falcons, Detroit Red Wings
O'Connor, Buddy	1988/V	C	1941-42	1950-51	2	Montreal Canadiens, New York Rangers
Oliver, Harry	1967/P	RW	1921-22	1936-37	1	Calgary Tigers (WCHL/WHL), Boston Bruins, New York Americans
Olmstead, Bert	1985/P	LW	1948-49	1961-62	5	Chicago Blackhawks, Montreal Canadiens, Toronto Maple Leafs
Orr, Bobby	1979/P	D	1966-67	1978-79	2	Boston Bruins, Chicago Blackhawks
Parent, Bernie	1984/P	G	1965-66	1978-79	2	Boston Bruins, Philadelphia Flyers, Toronto Maple Leafs, Philadelphia Blazers (WHA)
Park, Brad	1988/P	D	1968-69	1984-85	0	New York Rangers, Boston Bruins, Detroit Red Wings
Patrick, Lester	1947/P	D	1903-04	1926-27	3	Brandon, Westmount (CAHL), Montreal Wanderers (ECAHA), Edmonton Eskimos (AAHA), Renfrew Creamery Kings (NHA), Victoria Aristocrats (PCHA), Spokane Canaries (PCHA), Seattle Metropolitans (PCHA), Seattle Metropolitans(PCHA), Victoria Cougars (WHL), New York Rangers
Patrick, Lynn	1980/P	LW	1934-35	1945-46	1	New York Rangers
Perreault, Gilbert	1990/P	C	1970-71	1986-87	0	Buffalo Sabres
Phillips, Tommy	1945/P	LW	1902-03	1911-12	1	Montreal AAA (CAHL), Toronto Marlboros (OHA), Rat Portage Thistles, Kenora Thistles (MHL), Ottawa Ottawa Senators (ECAHA), Edmonton Eskimos (AAHA), Vancouver Millionaires (PCHA)
Pilote, Pierre	1975/P	D	1955-56	1968-69	1	Chicago Blackhawks, Toronto Maple Leafs
Pitre, Didier	1962/P	D/RW	1903-04	1922-23	0	Montreal Nationals (FAHL/CAHL), Montreal Shamrocks (ECAHA), Edmonton Eskimos (AAHA), Montreal Canadiens (NHA/NHL), Vancouver Millionaires (PCHA)
Plante, Jacques	1978/P	G	1952-53	1974-75	6	Montreal Canadiens, New York Rangers, St. Louis Blues, Toronto Maple Leafs, Boston Bruins, Edmonton Oilers (WHA)
Potvin, Denis	1991/P	D	1973-74	1987-88	4	New York Islanders

Player	Elec. year/ how elected*	Pos.†	First season	Last season	Stanley Cup wins‡	Teams as player
Pratt, Babe	1966/P	D	1935-36	1946-47	2	New York Rangers, Toronto Maple Leafs, Boston Bruins
Primeau, Joe	1963/P	C	1927-28	1935-36	1	Toronto Maple Leafs
Pronovost, Marcel	1978/P	D	1949-50	1969-70	5	Detroit Red Wings, Toronto Maple Leafs
Pulford, Bob	1991/P	LW	1956-57	1971-72	4	Toronto Maple Leafs, Los Angeles Kings
Pulford, Harvey	1945/P	D	1893-94	1907-08	4	Ottawa Silver Seven/Senators (AHA/CAHL/FAHL/ECAHA)
Quackenbush, Bill	1976/P	D	1942-43	1955-56	0	Detroit Red Wings, Boston Bruins
Rankin, Frank	1961/P	Ro.	1906	1914	0	Stratford (OHA), Eatons (EAA), Toronto St. Michaels (OHA)
Ratelle, Jean	1985/P	C	1960-61	1980-81	0	New York Rangers, Boston Bruins
Rayner, Chuck	1973/P	G	1940-41	1952-53	0	New York Americans, New York Rangers
Reardon, Ken	1966/P	D	1940-41	1949-50	1	Montreal Canadiens
Richard, Henri	1979/P	C	1955-56	1974-75	11	Montreal Canadiens
Richard, Rocket	1961/P	RW	1942-43	1959-60	8	Montreal Canadiens
Richardson, George	1950/P		1906	1912	0	14th Regiment, Queen's University
Roberts, Gordon	1971/P	LW	1909-10	1919-20	0	Ottawa Senators (NHA), Montreal Wanderers (NHA), Vancouver Millionaires (PCHA), Seattle Metropolitans (PCHA)
Robinson, Larry	1995/P	D	1972-73	1991-92	6	Montreal Canadiens, Los Angeles Kings
Ross, Art	1945/P	D	1904-05	1917-18	2	Westmount (CAHL), Brandon (MHL), Kenora Thistles (MHL), Montreal Wanderers (ECAHA/ECHA/NHA/NHL), Haileybury (NHA), Ottawa Senators (NHA)
Russell, Blair	1965/P	RW/C	1899-00	1907-08	0	Montreal Victorias (CAHL/ECAHA)
Russell, Ernie	1965/P	Ro./C	1904-05	1913-14	4	Montreal Winged Wheelers (CAHL), Montreal Wanderers (ECAHA/NHA)
Ruttan, Jack	1962/P		1905	1913	0	Armstrong's Point, Rustler, St. John's College, Manitoba Varsity (WSHL), Winnipeg (WinHL)
Salming, Borje	1996/P	D	1973-74	1989-90	0	Toronto Maple Leafs, Detroit Red Wings
Savard, Dennis	2000/P	C	1980-81	1996-97	1	Chicago Blackhawks, Montreal Canadiens, Tampa Bay Lightning
Savard, Serge	1986/P	D	1966-67	1982-83	7	Montreal Canadiens, Winnipeg Jets
Sawchuk, Terry	1971/P	G	1949-50	1969-70	4	Detroit Red Wings, Boston Bruins, Toronto Maple Leafs, Los Angeles Kings, New York Rangers
Scanlan, Fred	1965/P	F	1897-98	1902-03	3	Montreal Shamrocks (AHA/CAHL), Winnipeg Victorias (MSHL)
Schmidt, Milt	1961/P	C	1936-37	1954-55	2	Boston Bruins
Schriner, Sweeney	1962/P	LW	1934-35	1945-46	2	New York Americans, Toronto Maple Leafs
Seibert, Earl	1963/P	D	1931-32	1945-46	2	New York Rangers, Chicago Blackhawks, Detroit Red Wings
Seibert, Oliver	1961/P	D	1900	1906	0	Berlin Rangers (WOHA), Houghton (IHL), Guelph (OPHL), London (OPHL)
Shore, Eddie	1947/P	D	1924-25	1939-40	2	Regina Capitals (WCHL), Edmonton Eskimos (WHL), Boston Bruins, New York Americans
Shutt, Steve	1993/P	LW	1972-73	1984-85	5	Montreal Canadiens, Los Angeles Kings
Siebert, Babe	1964/P	LW/D	1925-26	1938-39	2	Montreal Maroons, New York Rangers, Boston Bruins, Montreal Canadiens
Simpson, Joe	1962/P	D	1921-22	1930-31	0	Edmonton Eskimos (WCHL), New York Americans
Sittler, Darryl	1989/P	C	1970-71	1984-85	0	Toronto Maple Leafs, Philadelphia Flyers, Detroit Red Wings
Smith, Alf	1962/P	RW	1894-95	1907-08	4	Ottawa Silver Seven/Senators (AHA/CAHL/FAHL/ECAHA), Kenora Thistles (MHL)
Smith, Billy	1993/P	G	1971-72	1988-89	4	Los Angeles Kings, New York Islanders
Smith, Clint	1991/V	C	1936-37	1946-47	1	New York Rangers, Chicago Blackhawks
Smith, Hooley	1972/P	RW	1924-25	1940-41	2	1924 Canadian Olympic Team, Ottawa Senators, Montreal Maroons, Boston Bruins, New York Americans
Smith, Tommy	1973/P	LW/C	1905-06	1919-20	1	Ottawa Vics (FAHL), Ottawa Senators (ECAHA), Brantford (OPHL), Moncton (MPHL), Quebec Bulldogs (NHA/NHL), Toronto Shamrocks (NHA), Montreal Canadiens (NHA)
Stanley, Allan	1981/P	D	1948-49	1968-69	4	New York Rangers, Chicago Blackhawks, Boston Bruins, Toronto Maple Leafs, Philadelphia Flyers
Stanley, Barney	1962/P	RW/D	1914-15	1927-28	1	Vancouver Millionaires (PCHA), Calgary Tigers (WCHL), Regina Capitals (WCHL), Edmonton Eskimos (WCHL/WHL), Chicago Blackhawks
Stastny, Peter	1998/P	C	1980-81	1994-95	0	Quebec Nordiques, New Jersey Devils, St. Louis Blues
Stewart, Black Jack	1964/P	D	1938-39	1951-52	2	Detroit Red Wings, Chicago Blackhawks
Stewart, Nels	1962/P	C	1925-26	1939-40	1	Montreal Maroons, Boston Bruins, New York Americans
Stuart, Bruce	1961/P	F	1989-99	1910-11	3	Ottawa Senators (CAHL/ECHA/NHA), Quebec Bulldogs (CAHL), Pittsburgh (IHL), Houghton (IHL), Portage Lake (IHL), Montreal Wanderers (ECAHA)
Stuart, Hod	1945/P	D	1898-99	1906-07	1	Ottawa Senators, Quebec Bulldogs, Calumet (IHL), Pittsburgh (IHL), Montreal Wanderers

Player	Elec. year/ how elected*	Pos.†	First season	Last season	Stanley Cup wins‡	Teams as player
Taylor, Cyclone	1947/P	D/Ro./C	1907-08	1922-23	2	Ottawa Senators (ECAHA/ECHA), Renfrew Creamery Kings (NHA), Vancouver Maroons (PCHA)
Thompson, Tiny	1959/P	G	1928-29	1939-40	1	Boston Bruins, Detroit Red Wings
Tretiak, Vladislav	1989/P	G	1969	1984	0	CSKA Moscow
Trihey, Harry	1950/P	C	1896-97	1900-01	2	Montreal Shamrocks (AHA/CAHL)
Trottier, Bryan	1997/P	C	1975-76	1993-94	6	New York Islanders, Pittsburgh Penguins
Ullman, Norm	1982/P	C	1955-56	1976-77	0	Detroit Red Wings, Toronto Maple Leafs, Edmonton Oilers (WHA)
Vezina, Georges	1945/P	G	1910-11	1925-26	2	Montreal Canadiens (NHA/NHL)
Walker, Jack	1960/P	LW/Ro.	1912-13	1927-28	3	Port Arthur, Toronto Blueshirts (NHA), Seattle Metropolitans (PCHA), Victoria Cougars (WCHL/WHL), Detroit Cougars
Walsh, Marty	1962/P	C	1905-06	1911-12	2	Queens University (OHA), Ottawa Senators (ECAHA/ECHA/NHA)
Watson, Harry E.	1962/P	C	1915	1931	0	St. Andrews (OHA), Aura Lee Juniors (OHA), Toronto Dentals (OHA), Toronto Granites (OHA), 1924 Canadian Olympic Team, Toronto National Sea Fleas (OHA)
Watson, Harry P.	1994/V	LW	1941-42	1956-57	5	Brooklyn Americans, Detroit Red Wings, Toronto Maple Leafs, Chicago Blackhawks
Weiland, Cooney	1971/P	C	1928-29	1938-39	2	Boston Bruins, Ottawa Senators, Detroit Red Wings
Westwick, Harry	1962/P	Ro.	1894-95	1907-08	4	Ottawa Senators/Silver Seven (AHA/CAHL/FAHL/ECAHA), Kenora Thistles
Whitcroft, Frederick	1962/P	Ro.	1906-07	1909-10	0	Kenora Thistles (MSHL), Edmonton Eskimos (AAHA), Renfrew Creamery Kings (NHA)
Wilson, Gord	1962/P	D	1918	1933	0	Port Arthur War Veterans (OHA), Iroquois Falls (NOHA), Port Arthur Bearcats (OHA)
Worsley, Gump	1980/P	G	1952-53	1973-74	4	New York Rangers, Montreal Canadiens, Minnesota North Stars
Worters, Roy	1969/P	G	1925-26	1936-37	0	Pittsburgh Pirates, New York Americans, Montreal Canadiens

*Denotes whether enshrinee was elected by regular election (P) or veterans committee (V).
†Primary positions played during career: C—center; D—defense; G—goaltender; LW—left wing; Ro.—rover; RW—right wing.
‡Stanley Cup wins column refers to wins as a player in the players section and as a coach in the coaches section.

BUILDERS

Builder	Election year	Stanley Cup wins‡	Designation for induction
Adams, Charles F.	1960		Founder, Boston Bruins (1924)
Adams, Weston W.	1972		President and chairman, Boston Bruins(1936-69)
Ahearn, Frank	1962		Owner, Ottawa Senators (1924-34)
Ahearne, Bunny	1977		President, International Hockey Federation (1957-75)
Allan, Sir Montagu	1945		Donator of Allan Cup, awarded anually to senior amateur champion of Canada (1908)
Allen, Keith	1992	0	Coach, Philadelphia Flyers (1967-68 and 1968-69); general manager and executive, Philadelphia Flyers (1966-present)
Arbour, Al	1996	4	Coach, St. Louis Blues, New York Islanders, 1970-71, 1971-72 to 1972-73, 1973-74 through 1985-86 and 1988-89 to 1993-94; vice president of hockey operations and consultant, New York Islanders (1994 to 1998)
Ballard, Harold	1977		Owner and chief executive, Toronto Maple Leafs (1961-90)
Bauer, Father David	1989		Developer and coach of first Canadian National Hockey Team
Bickell, J.P.	1978		First president and chairman of the board, Toronto Maple Leafs (1927-51)
Bowman, Scotty	1991	9	Coach, St. Louis Blues, Montreal Canadiens, Buffalo Sabres, Pittsburgh Penguins, Detroit Red Wings (1967-68 through 1979-80, 1981-82 through 1986-87 and 1991-92 through 2001-02); general manager, St. Louis Blues, Buffalo Sabres (1969-70, 1970-71 and 1979-80 through 1986-87)
Brown, George V.	1961		U.S. hockey pioneer; organizer, Boston Athletic Association hockey team (1910); general manager, Boston Arena and Boston Garden (1934-37)
Brown, Walter A.	1962		Co-owner and president, Boston Bruins (1951-64); general manager, Boston Gardens
Buckland, Frank	1975		Amateur hockey coach and manager; president and treasurer, Ontario Hockey Association
Bush, Walter L.	2000		President, Minnesota North Stars (1967-1978); president, USA Hockey; vice president, International Ice Hockey Federation
Butterfield, Jack	1980		President, American Hockey League
Calder, Frank	1947		First president, National Hockey League (1917-43)
Campbell, Angus	1964		First president, Northern Ontario Hockey Association (1919); executive, Ontario Hockey Association
Campbell, Clarence	1966		Referee (1929-40); president, National Hockey League (1946-77)
Cattarinich, Joseph	1977		General manager, Montreal Canadiens (1909-10); co-owner, Montreal Canadiens (1921-35)

Builder	Election year	Stanley Cup wins‡	Designation for induction
Dandurand, Leo	1963	1	Co-owner, Montreal Canadiens (1921-35); coach, Montreal Canadiens (1920-21 through 1925-26 and 1934-35); general manager, Montreal Canadiens (1920-21 through 1934-35)
Dilio, Frank	1964		Secretary and president, Junior Amateur Hockey Association; registrar and secretary, Quebec Amateur Hockey League (1943-62)
Dudley, George	1958		President, Canadian Amateur Hockey Association (1940-42); treasurer, Ontario Hockey Association; president, International Ice Hockey Federation
Dunn, Jimmy	1968		President, Manitoba Amateur Hockey Association (1945-51); president, Canadian Amateur Hockey Association
Francis, Emile	1982	0	General manager, New York Rangers,St. Louis Blues, Hartford Whalers (1964-65 through 1988-89); coach, New York Rangers, St. Louis Blues (1965-66 through 1974-75, 1976-77, 1981-82 and 1982-83); president, Hartford Whalers (1983-1993)
Gibson, Jack	1976		Organizer, International League (1903-07), world's first professional hockey league
Gorman, Tommy	1963	2	Co-founder, National Hockey League (1917); coach, Ottawa Senators, New York Americans, Chicago Blackhawks, Montreal Maroons (1917-1938); general manager, Montreal Canadiens (1941-42 through 1945-46)
Griffiths, Frank	1993		Chairman, Vancouver Canucks (1974 through 1994)
Hanley, Bill	1986		Secretary-manager, Ontario Hockey Association
Hay, Charles	1974		Coordinator, 1972 series between Canada and Soviet Union; president, Hockey Canada
Hendy, Jim	1968		President, United States Hockey League; general manager, Cleveland Barons (AHL); publisher, Hockey Guide (1933-51)
Hewitt, Foster	1965		Hockey broadcaster
Hewitt, William	1947		Sports editor, Toronto Star; secretary, Ontario Hockey Association (1903-61); registrar and treasurer, Canadian Amateur Hockey Association
Hume, Fred	1962		Co-developer, Western Hockey League, New Westminster Royals
Ilitch, Mike	2003	3	Owner, Detroit Red Wings (1982-83 through 2002-03)
Imlach, Punch	1984	4	Coach, Toronto Maple Leafs, Buffalo Sabres (1958-59 through 1968-69, 1970-71, 1971-72 and 1979-80); general manager, Toronto Maple Leafs, Buffalo Sabres (1958-59 through 1968-69, 1970-71 through 1977-78 and 1979-80 through 1981-82)
Ivan, Tommy	1974	3	Coach, Detroit Red Wings, Chicago Blackhawks (1947-48 through 1953-54, 1956-57 and 1957-58); general manager, Chicago Blackhawks (1954-55 through 1976-77)
Jennings, Bill	1975		President, New York Rangers
Johnson, Bob	1992	1	Coach, Calgary Flames, Pittsburgh Penguins (1982-83 through 1986-87, 1990-91 and 1991-92)
Juckes, Gordon	1979		President, Saskatchewan Amateur Hockey Association; director, Canadian Amateur Hockey Association (1960-78)
Kilpatrick,General J.R.	1960		President, New York Rangers, Madison Square Garden; director, NHL Players' Pension Society; NHL Governor
Kilrea, Brian	2003		Player, Detroit Red Wings (1957-58) and Los Angeles Kings (1967-68); general manager and head coach, Ottawa 67's of the Ontario Hockey League (1974-75 through 1983-84, 1986-87 through 1993-94 and 1995-96 through 2002-03); assistant coach, New York Islanders (1984-85 through 1985-86)
Knox III, Seymour	1993		Chairman and president, Buffalo Sabres (1970-71 through 1995-96)
Leader, Al	1969		President, Western Hockey League (1944-69)
LeBel, Bob	1970		Founder and president, Interprovincial Senior League (1944-47); president, Quebec Amateur Hockey League, Canadian Amateur Hockey Association, International Ice Hockey Federation (1955-63)
Lockhart, Tommy	1965		Organizer and president, Eastern Amateur Hockey League, Amateur Hockey Association of the United States; business manager, New York Rangers
Loicq, Paul	1961		President and referee, International Ice Hockey Federation (1922-47)
Mariucci, John	1985		Minnesota hockey pioneer; coach, 1956 U.S. Olympic Team
Mathers, Frank	1992		Coach, president and general manager, Hershey Bears (AHL)
McLaughlin, Major Frederic	1963		Owner and first president, Chicago Blackhawks; general manager, Chicago Blackhawks (1926-27 through 1941-42)
Milford, Jake	1984		Coach, New York Rangers organization; general manager, Los Angeles Kings, Vancouver Canucks (1973-74 through 1981-82)
Molson, Senator Hartland De Montarville	1973		President and chairman, Montreal Canadiens (1957-68)
Morrison, Scotty	1999		Referee-in-chief; chairman, Hall of Fame
Murray, Monsignor Athol	1998		Founded hockey programs in Saskatchewan; founded Notre Dame College in Wilcox
Neilson, Roger	2002		Coach, Toronto Maple Leafs, Buffalo Sabres, Vancouver Canucks, Los Angeles Kings, New York Rangers, Florida Panthers, Philadelphia Flyers, Ottawa Senators (1977-78 through 1983-84, 1989-90 through 1994-95, 1997-98 through 1999-2000 and 2001-02
Nelson, Francis	1947		Sports editor, Toronto Globe; vice president, Ontario Hockey Association (1903-05); Governor, Amateur Athletic Union of Canada
Norris, Bruce	1969		Owner, Detroit Red Wings, Olympic Stadium (1955-82)
Norris, James Sr.	1958		Co-owner, Detroit Red Wings (1933-43)
Norris, James Dougan	1962		Co-owner, Detroit Red Wings (1933-43), Chicago Blackhawks (1946-66)
Northey, William	1947		President, Montreal Amateur Athletic Association; managing director, Montreal Forum; first trustee, Allan Cup (1908)
O'Brien, J. Ambrose	1962		Organizer, National Hockey Association (1909); co-founder, Montreal Canadiens
O'Neil, Brian	1994		Director of administration, NHL (1966); executive director, NHL (1971); executive vice-president, NHL (1977)

Builder	Election year	Stanley Cup wins‡	Designation for induction
Page, Fred	1993		President, Canadian Amateur Hockey Association (1966-68); chairman of the board, British Columbia Junior Hockey League (1983 through 1997)
Patrick, Craig	2001		Builder of U.S. National & Olympic programs; general manager, New York Rangers (1981 through 1986), general manager, Pittsburgh Penguins (1989 to present), coach, Pittsburgh Penguins (1989-90 and1996-97)
Patrick, Frank	1958		Co-organizer and president, Pacific Coast Hockey Association (1911); owner, manager, player/coach, Vancouver Millionaires (PCHA), managing director, National Hockey League (1933-34); coach, Boston Bruins (1934-35 and 1935-36); business manager, Montreal Canadiens (1941-42)
Pickard, Allan	1958		President, Saskatchewan Amateur Hockey Association, Saskatchewan Senior League (1933-34), Western Canada Senior League;governor, Saskatchewan Junior League, Western Canada Junior League; president, Canadian Amateur Hockey Association (1947-50)
Pilous, Rudy	1985	1	Coach, Chicago Blackhawks, Winnipeg Jets (1957-58 through 1962-63 and 1974-75); manager, Winnipeg Jets (WHA); scout, Detroit Red Wings, Los Angeles Kings
Poile, Bud	1990		General manager, Philadelphia Flyers, Vancouver Canucks (1967-68 through 1972-73); vice president, World Hockey Association; commissioner, Central Hockey League, International Hockey League
Pollock, Sam	1978		Director of personnel, Montreal Canadiens (1950-64); general manager, Montreal Canadiens (1964-65 through 1977-78)
Raymond, Sen. Donat	1958		President, Canadian Arena Company (Montreal Maroons, Montreal Canadiens) (1924-25 through 1955); chairman, Canadian Arena Company (1955-63)
Robertson, John Ross	1947		President, Ontario Hockey Association (1901-05)
Robinson, Claude	1947		First secretary, Canadian Amateur Hockey Association (1914); manager, 1932 Canadian Olympic Team
Ross, Philip	1976		Trustee, Stanley Cup (1893-1949)
Sabetzki, Gunther	1995		President, International Ice Hockey Federation (1975-1994)
Sather, Glen	1997	4	Coach, Edmonton Oilers (1976-89 and 1993-94); general manager, Edmonton Oilers (1979 to 2000); general manager, New York Rangers (2000 to present)
Selke, Frank	1960		Assistant general manager, Toronto Maple Leafs; general manager, Montreal Canadiens (1946-47 through 1963-64)
Sinden, Harry	1983	1	Coach, Boston Bruins (1966-67 through 1969-70, 1979-80 and 1984-85); coach, 1972 Team Canada; general manager, Boston Bruins (1972-73 through 1988-89); President, Boston bruins (1989-90 through present)
Smith, Frank	1962		Co-founder and secretary, Beaches Hockey League (later Metropolitan Toronto Hockey League (1911-62)
Smythe, Conn	1958	0	President, Toronto Maple Leafs, Maple Leaf Gardens, general manager, Toronto Maple Leafs (1927-28 through 1956-57); coach, Toronto Maple Leafs (1927-28 through 1930-31)
Snider, Ed	1988		Owner, Philadelphia Flyers (1967-68 through present)
Stanley of Preston, Lord	1945		Donator, Stanley Cup (1893)
Sutherland, Capt. James	1947		President, Ontario Hockey Association (1915-17); president, Canadian Amateur Hockey Association (1919-21)
Tarasov, Anatoli	1974		Coach, Soviet National Team
Torrey, Bill	1995		Executive vice president, California Seals; general manager, New York Islanders; president, Florida Panthers (1967-present)
Turner, Lloyd	1958		Co-organizer, Western Canadian Hockey League (1918); organizer, Calgary Tigers
Tutt, Thayer	1978		President, International Ice Hockey Federation (1966-69), Amateur Hockey Association of the United States
Voss, Carl	1974		President, U.S. Hockey League; first NHL referee-in-chief
Waghorne, Fred	1961		Pioneer and hockey official, Toronto Hockey League
Wirtz, Arthur	1971		Co-owner, Detroit Red Wings, Olympia Stadium, Chicago Stadium, St. Louis Arena, Madison Square Garden, Chicago Blackhawks
Wirtz, Bill	1976		President, Chicago Blackhawks (1966 through present); chairman, NHL Board of Governors
Ziegler, John	1987		President, National Hockey League (1977-92)

‡Stanley Cup wins column refers to wins as a player in the players section and as a coach in the builders section.

REFEREES/LINESMEN

Referee/linesman	Election year	First season	Last season	Position
Armstrong, Neil	1991	1957	1977	Linesman and referee
Ashley, John	1981	1959	1972	Referee
Chadwick, Bill	1964	1940	1955	Linesman and referee
D'Amico, John	1993	1964-65	1987-88	Linesman
Elliott, Chaucer	1961	1903	1913	Referee (OHA)
Hayes, George	1988	1946-47	1964-65	Linesman
Hewitson, Bobby	1963	1924	1934	Referee
Ion, Mickey	1961	1913	1943	Referee (PCHL/NHL)
Pavelich, Matt	1987	1956-57	1978-79	Linesman
Rodden, Mike	1962			Referee
Smeaton, Cooper	1961			Referee (NHA/NHL); referee-in-chief (NHL) (1931-37); trustee, Stanley Cup (1946-78)
Storey, Red	1967	1951	1959	Referee
Udvari, Frank	1973	1951-52	1965-66	Referee; supervisor of NHL officials
Van Hellemond, Andy	1999	1972-73	1995-96	Referee

MILESTONES

(Players and coaches active in the NHL in the 2002-03 season are in boldface)

CAREER

FORWARDS/DEFENSEMEN

20 SEASONS

Rk. Player	No.
1. Gordie Howe	26
2. Alex Delvecchio	24
Tim Horton	24
Mark Messier	**24**
5. John Bucyk	23
6. Ray Bourque	22
Ron Francis	**22**
Al MacInnis	**22**
Stan Mikita	22
Doug Mohns	22
Dean Prentice	22
12. **Dave Andreychuk**	**21**
George Armstrong	21
Paul Coffey	21
Phil Housley	**21**
Harry Howell	21
Larry Murphy	21
Eric Nesterenko	21
Marcel Pronovost	21
Jean Ratelle	21
Allan Stanley	21
Scott Stevens	**21**
Ron Stewart	21
24. Jean Beliveau	20
Chris Chelios	**20**
Bill Gadsby	20
Doug Gilmour	**20**
Wayne Gretzky	20
Red Kelly	20
Claude Lemieux	**20**
James Patrick	**20**
Henri Richard	20
Larry Robinson	20
Norm Ullman	20
Pat Verbeek	20
Steve Yzerman	**20**

Total number of players: (36)

1,200 GAMES

Rk. Player	No.
1. Gordie Howe	1,767
2. **Mark Messier**	**1,680**
3. **Ron Francis**	**1,651**
4. Larry Murphy	1,615
5. Ray Bourque	1,612
6. **Scott Stevens**	**1,597**
7. Alex Delvecchio	1,549
8. John Bucyk	1,540
9. **Dave Andreychuk**	**1,515**
10. **Phil Housley**	**1,495**
11. Wayne Gretzky	1,487
12. **Doug Gilmour**	**1,474**
13. Tim Horton	1,446
14. Mike Gartner	1,432
15. Pat Verbeek	1,424
16. **Al MacInnis**	**1,413**
17. Harry Howell	1,411
18. Norm Ullman	1,410
19. Paul Coffey	1,409
20. Dale Hunter	1,407

Rk. Player	No.
21. Stan Mikita	1,394
22. Doug Mohns	1,390
23. Larry Robinson	1,384
24. Dean Prentice	1,378
Steve Yzerman	**1,378**
26. Ron Stewart	1,353
27. **Kirk Muller**	**1,349**
28. Marcel Dionne	1,348
29. **Chris Chelios**	**1,326**
30. Guy Carbonneau	1,318
31. Red Kelly	1,316
32. Dave Keon	1,296
Vincent Damphousse	**1,296**
34. **Luc Robitaille**	**1,286**
35. **Ken Daneyko**	**1,283**
36. Phil Esposito	1,282
37. Jean Ratelle	1,281
38. Bryan Trottier	1,279
39. **Adam Oates**	**1,277**
40. Ray Ferraro	1,258
41. Craig Ludwig	1,256
Henri Richard	1,256
43. Kevin Lowe	1,254
44. Jari Kurri	1,251
45. Bill Gadsby	1,248
46. Allan Stanley	1,244
47. Dino Ciccarelli	1,232
48. Eddie Westfall	1,227
49. **James Patrick**	**1,225**
50. **Scott Mellanby**	**1,223**
51. Brad McCrimmon	1,222
52. Eric Nesterenko	1,219
53. Marcel Pronovost	1,206

Total number of players: (53)

500 GOALS

Rk. Player	No.
1. Wayne Gretzky	894
2. Gordie Howe	801
3. Marcel Dionne	731
4. Phil Esposito	717
5. **Brett Hull**	**716**
6. Mike Gartner	708
7. **Mario Lemieux**	**682**
8. **Mark Messier**	**676**
9. **Steve Yzerman**	**660**
10. **Luc Robitaille**	**631**
11. **Dave Andreychuk**	**613**
12. Bobby Hull	610
13. Dino Ciccarelli	608
14. Jari Kurri	601
15. Mike Bossy	573
16. Guy Lafleur	560
17. John Bucyk	556
18. Michel Goulet	548
19. Maurice Richard	544
20. Stan Mikita	541
21. **Ron Francis**	**536**
22. Frank Mahovlich	533
Brendan Shanahan	**533**
24. Bryan Trottier	524

Rk. Player	No.
25. Pat Verbeek	522
26. Dale Hawerchuk	518
27. Gilbert Perreault	512
28. **Joe Nieuwendyk**	**511**
29. **Joe Sakic**	**509**
30. Jean Beliveau	507
31. **Jaromir Jagr**	**506**
32. Joe Mullen	502
33. Lanny McDonald	500

Total number of players: (33)

700 ASSISTS

Rk. Player	No.
1. Wayne Gretzky	1,963
2. **Ron Francis**	**1,222**
3. Ray Bourque	1,169
4. **Mark Messier**	**1,168**
5. Paul Coffey	1,135
6. **Adam Oates**	**1,063**
7. Gordie Howe	1,049
8. Marcel Dionne	1,040
9. **Steve Yzerman**	**1,010**
Mario Lemieux	**1,010**
11. **Doug Gilmour**	**964**
12. **Al MacInnis**	**932**
13. Larry Murphy	929
14. Stan Mikita	926
15. Bryan Trottier	901
16. **Phil Housley**	**894**
17. Dale Hawerchuk	891
18. Phil Esposito	873
19. Denis Savard	865
20. Bobby Clarke	852
21. Alex Delvecchio	825
22. Gilbert Perreault	814
23. John Bucyk	813
24. **Joe Sakic**	**806**
25. Jari Kurri	797
26. Guy Lafleur	793
27. Peter Stastny	789
28. Jean Ratelle	776
29. Bernie Federko	761
30. **Pierre Turgeon**	**754**
31. Larry Robinson	750
32. **Vincent Damphousse**	**744**
33. Denis Potvin	742
34. Norm Ullman	739
35. Bernie Nicholls	734
36. **Jaromir Jagr**	**729**
37. **Brian Leetch**	**718**
38. **Chris Chelios**	**717**
39. Jean Beliveau	712
40. **Scott Stevens**	**703**

Total number of players: (40)

1,000 POINTS

Rk. Player	No.
1. Wayne Gretzky	2,857
2. Gordie Howe	1,850

Rk.	Player	No.
3.	**Mark Messier**	**1,844**
4.	Marcel Dionne	1,771
5.	**Ron Francis**	**1,758**
6.	**Mario Lemieux**	**1,692**
7.	**Steve Yzerman**	**1,670**
8.	Phil Esposito	1,590
9.	Ray Bourque	1,579
10.	Paul Coffey	1,531
11.	Stan Mikita	1,467
12.	Bryan Trottier	1,425
13.	**Doug Gilmour**	**1,414**
14.	Dale Hawerchuk	1,409
15.	**Adam Oates**	**1,402**
16.	Jari Kurri	1,398
17.	John Bucyk	1,369
18.	Guy Lafleur	1,353
19.	Denis Savard	1,338
20.	Mike Gartner	1,335
21.	Gilbert Perreault	1,326
22.	**Brett Hull**	**1,322**
23.	**Luc Robitaille**	**1,319**
24.	**Joe Sakic**	**1,315**
25.	**Dave Andreychuk**	**1,281**
	Alex Delvecchio	1,281
27.	**Al MacInnis**	**1,272**
28.	Jean Ratelle	1,267
29.	Peter Stastny	1,239
30.	**Jaromir Jagr**	**1,235**
31.	**Pierre Turgeon**	**1,234**
32.	**Phil Housley**	**1,232**
33.	Norm Ullman	1,229
34.	Jean Beliveau	1,219
35.	Larry Murphy	1,216
36.	Bobby Clarke	1,210
37.	Bernie Nicholls	1,209
38.	Dino Ciccarelli	1,200
39.	Bobby Hull	1,170
40.	**Vincent Damphousse**	**1,164**
41.	Michel Goulet	1,152
42.	Bernie Federko	1,130
43.	Mike Bossy	1,126
	Mark Recchi	**1,126**
45.	Darryl Sittler	1,121
46.	Frank Mahovlich	1,103
47.	Glenn Anderson	1,099
48.	**Brendan Shanahan**	**1,098**
49.	**Theo Fleury**	**1,088**
50.	**Jeremy Roenick**	**1,073**
51.	Dave Taylor	1,069
52.	Joe Mullen	1,063
	Pat Verbeek	1,063
54.	**Mike Modano**	**1,062**
55.	Denis Potvin	1,052
56.	Henri Richard	1,046
57.	Bobby Smith	1,036
58.	Brian Bellows	1,022
59.	Rod Gilbert	1,021
60.	Dale Hunter	1,020
61.	**Mats Sundin**	**1,014**
62.	Pat LaFontaine	1,013
63.	Steve Larmer	1,012
	Joe Nieuwendyk	**1,012**
65.	Lanny McDonald	1,006
66.	Brian Propp	1,004

Total number of players: (66)

2,000 PENALTY MINUTES

Rk.	Player	No.
1.	Tiger Williams	3,966
2.	Dale Hunter	3,565
3.	Marty McSorley	3,381
4.	Bob Probert	3,300
5.	**Tie Domi**	**3,198**
6.	**Rob Ray**	**3,193**
7.	**Craig Berube**	**3,149**
8.	Tim Hunter	3,146
9.	Chris Nilan	3,043
10.	Rick Tocchet	2,974
11.	Pat Verbeek	2,905
12.	Dave Manson	2,792
13.	**Scott Stevens**	**2,763**
14.	**Chris Chelios**	**2,634**
15.	Willi Plett	2,572
16.	Gino Odjick	2,567
17.	**Ken Daneyko**	**2,519**
	Joey Kocur	2,519
19.	Basil McRae	2,457
20.	Ulf Samuelsson	2,453
21.	**Jeff Odgers**	**2,364**
22.	Jay Wells	2,359
23.	**Shayne Corson**	**2,328**
24.	Garth Butcher	2,302
25.	Shane Churla	2,301
26.	Dave Schultz	2,294
27.	**Scott Mellanby**	**2,285**
28.	Laurie Boschman	2,265
29.	**Gary Roberts**	**2,261**
30.	Ken Baumgartner	2,244
31.	**Kevin Dineen**	**2,229**
32.	Rob Ramage	2,226
33.	Bryan Watson	2,212
34.	**Kelly Buchberger**	**2,188**
35.	**Lyle Odelein**	**2,178**
36.	**Brendan Shanahan**	**2,156**
37.	Steve Smith	2,139
38.	Bryan Marchment	2,126
39.	Stu Grimson	2,113
40.	Matthew Barnaby	2,100
41.	Terry O'Reilly	2,095
42.	Al Secord	2,093
43.	Ronnie Stern	2,077
44.	Mick Vukota	2,071
45.	Gord Donnelly	2,069
46.	Mike Foligno	2,049
47.	Phil Russell	2,038
48.	Kris King	2,030
49.	Kelly Chase	2,017
50.	Harold Snepsts	2,009

Total number of players: (50)

GOALTENDERS

15 SEASONS

Rk.	Goaltender	No.
1.	Terry Sawchuk	21
	Gump Worsley	21
3.	John Vanbiesbrouck	20
4.	**Tom Barrasso**	**19**
	Grant Fuhr	19
	Patrick Roy	**19**
	Mike Vernon	19

Rk.	Player	No.
8.	Glenn Hall	18
	Gilles Meloche	18
	Andy Moog	18
	Jacques Plante	18
	Billy Smith	18
13.	Don Beaupre	17
	Ken Wregget	17
15.	Tony Esposito	16
	Eddie Johnston	16
	Harry Lumley	16
	Kirk McLean	16
	Rogie Vachon	16
20.	**Craig Billington**	**15**
	Johnny Bower	15
	Sean Burke	**15**
	Kelly Hrudey	15
	Reggie Lemelin	15
	Cesare Maniago	15
	Darren Puppa	15
	Bill Ranford	15

Total number of goaltenders: (27)

600 GAMES

Rk.	Goaltender	No.
1.	**Patrick Roy**	**1,029**
2.	Terry Sawchuk	971
3.	Glenn Hall	906
4.	Tony Esposito	886
5.	John Vanbiesbrouck	882
6.	Grant Fuhr	868
7.	Gump Worsley	861
8.	Jacques Plante	837
9.	Harry Lumley	803
10.	**Ed Belfour**	**797**
11.	Rogie Vachon	795
12.	Gilles Meloche	788
13.	Mike Vernon	781
14.	**Tom Barrasso**	**777**
15.	**Curtis Joseph**	**767**
16.	**Sean Burke**	**715**
17.	Andy Moog	713
18.	Billy Smith	680
19.	Kelly Hrudey	677
20.	Don Beaupre	667
21.	**Mike Richter**	**666**
22.	**Martin Brodeur**	**665**
23.	Mike Liut	664
24.	Dan Bouchard	655
25.	Bill Ranford	647
26.	Turk Broda	629
27.	Kirk McLean	612
28.	Ed Giacomin	610
29.	Ron Hextall	608
	Bernie Parent	608
31.	**Felix Potvin**	**607**
32.	Greg Millen	604

Total number of goaltenders: (32)

30,000 MINUTES

Rk.	Goaltender	No.
1.	**Patrick Roy**	**60,235**
2.	Terry Sawchuk	57,194
3.	Glenn Hall	53,484
4.	Tony Esposito	52,585
5.	John Vanbiesbrouck	50,475

Rk.	Goaltender	No.
6.	Gump Worsley	50,183
7.	Jacques Plante	49,493
8.	Grant Fuhr	48,945
9.	Harry Lumley	48,044
10.	Rogie Vachon	46,298
11.	**Ed Belfour**	**46,065**
12.	Gilles Meloche	45,401
13.	**Curtis Joseph**	**44,688**
14.	Mike Vernon	44,449
15.	**Tom Barrasso**	**44,180**
16.	**Sean Burke**	**40,799**
17.	Andy Moog	40,151
18.	**Martin Brodeur**	**38,956**
19.	Billy Smith	38,431
20.	Mike Liut	38,215
21.	**Mike Richter**	**38,183**
22.	Turk Broda	38,167
23.	Kelly Hrudey	38,084
24.	Dan Bouchard	37,919
25.	Don Beaupre	37,396
26.	Bill Ranford	35,936
27.	Ed Giacomin	35,693
28.	Greg Millen	35,377
29.	**Felix Potvin**	**35,160**
30.	Bernie Parent	35,136
31.	Kirk McLean	35,090
32.	Ron Hextall	34,750
33.	Eddie Johnston	34,216
34.	Tiny Thompson	34,175
35.	Dominik Hasek	33,745
36.	Cesare Maniago	32,570
37.	Glenn Resch	32,279
38.	Johnny Bower	32,016
39.	Ken Wregget	31,663
40.	**Arturs Irbe**	**31,502**
41.	Frank Brimsek	31,210
42.	John Roach	30,444
43.	Roy Worters	30,175

Total number of goaltenders: (43)

2.50 OR UNDER GOALS-AGAINST AVERAGE

(Goaltenders with 10,000 or more minutes)

Rk.	Goaltender	Min.	GAA
1.	Alex Connell	26,050	1.91
2.	George Hainsworth	29,087	1.93
3.	Chuck Gardiner	19,687	2.02
4.	Lorne Chabot	25,307	2.04
5.	Tiny Thompson	34,175	2.08
6.	Dave Kerr	26,639	2.15
7.	**Martin Brodeur**	**38,956**	**2.19**
8.	Dominik Hasek	33,745	2.23
9.	Ken Dryden	23,352	2.24
10.	Roy Worters	30,175	2.27
11.	**Roman Turek**	**18,064**	**2.31**
12.	Clint Benedict	22,367	2.32
13.	Norman Smith	12,357	2.33
14.	Bill Durnan	22,945	2.36
	Gerry McNeil	16,535	2.36
16.	**Evgeni Nabokov**	**11,242**	**2.38**
17.	Jacques Plante	49,493	2.38
18.	**Patrick Lalime**	**15,229**	**2.41**
19.	**Martin Biron**	**10,802**	**2.42**
20.	**J.S. Giguere**	**10,517**	**2.44**
21.	**Ed Belfour**	**46,065**	**2.45**
22.	**Chris Osgood**	**28,743**	**2.46**
	John Roach	30,444	2.46
24.	Glenn Hall	53,484	2.49

Total number of goaltenders: (24)

200 GAMES WON

Rk.	Goaltender	No.
1.	**Patrick Roy**	**551**
2.	Terry Sawchuk	447
3.	Jacques Plante	435
4.	Tony Esposito	423
5.	Glenn Hall	407
6.	Grant Fuhr	403
7.	**Ed Belfour**	**401**
8.	Mike Vernon	385
9.	**Curtis Joseph**	**380**
10.	John Vanbiesbrouck	374
11.	Andy Moog	372
12.	**Tom Barrasso**	**369**
13.	**Martin Brodeur**	**365**
14.	Rogie Vachon	355
15.	Gump Worsley	335
16.	Harry Lumley	330
17.	Billy Smith	305
18.	Turk Broda	302
19.	**Mike Richter**	**301**
20.	Ron Hextall	296
21.	Mike Liut	294
22.	Ed Giacomin	289
23.	**Sean Burke**	**288**
	Dominik Hasek	288
25.	Dan Bouchard	286
26.	Tiny Thompson	284
27.	**Chris Osgood**	**274**
28.	Kelly Hrudey	271
	Bernie Parent	271
30.	Gilles Meloche	270
31.	Don Beaupre	268
32.	Ken Dryden	258
33.	**Felix Potvin**	**254**
34.	Frank Brimsek	252
35.	Johnny Bower	250
36.	George Hainsworth	246
	Pete Peeters	246
38.	Kirk McLean	245
39.	Bill Ranford	240
40.	Reggie Lemelin	236
41.	Eddie Johnston	234
42.	Glenn Resch	231
43.	Gerry Cheevers	230
44.	Ken Wregget	225
45.	**Jocelyn Thibault**	**222**
46.	John Roach	219
47.	Greg Millen	215
	Olaf Kolzig	215
49.	**Arturs Irbe**	**213**
50.	Bill Durnan	208
	Don Edwards	208
52.	Lorne Chabot	206
	Roger Crozier	206
54.	Rick Wamsley	204
55.	Dave Kerr	203

Total number of goaltenders: (55)

200 GAMES LOST

Rk.	Goaltender	No.
1.	Gump Worsley	352
2.	Gilles Meloche	351
3.	John Vanbiesbrouck	346
4.	Terry Sawchuk	330
5.	Harry Lumley	329

Rk.	Goaltender	No.
6.	Glenn Hall	326
7.	**Patrick Roy**	**315**
8.	Tony Esposito	306
9.	**Sean Burke**	**301**
10.	Grant Fuhr	295
11.	Rogie Vachon	291
12.	Greg Millen	284
13.	**Curtis Joseph**	**279**
	Bill Ranford	279
15.	**Tom Barrasso**	**277**
	Don Beaupre	277
17.	Mike Vernon	273
18.	Mike Liut	271
19.	Kelly Hrudey	265
20.	**Ed Belfour**	**262**
	Kirk McLean	262
22.	Gary Smith	261
23.	Cesare Maniago	259
24.	**Mike Richter**	**258**
25.	Eddie Johnston	257
26.	**Felix Potvin**	**252**
27.	Ken Wregget	248
28.	Jacques Plante	247
29.	**Jeff Hackett**	**234**
	Arturs Irbe	**234**
31.	Billy Smith	233
32.	Dan Bouchard	232
	Ron Tugnutt	**232**
34.	Roy Worters	229
35.	Jim Rutherford	227
36.	Turk Broda	224
	Glenn Resch	224
38.	Guy Hebert	222
39.	Ron Hextall	214
40.	**Jocelyn Thibault**	**210**
41.	Andy Moog	209
42.	Ed Giacomin	208
	Chuck Rayner	208
44.	Al Rollins	205
45.	John Roach	204
	Tommy Salo	**204**
47.	Denis Herron	203
	Ron Low	203
49.	Glen Hanlon	202

Total number of goaltenders: (49)

75 GAMES TIED

Rk.	Goaltender	No.
1.	Terry Sawchuk	172
2.	Glenn Hall	163
3.	Tony Esposito	151
4.	Gump Worsley	150
5.	Jacques Plante	145
6.	Harry Lumley	142
7.	Gilles Meloche	131
	Patrick Roy	**131**
9.	Rogie Vachon	127
10.	Bernie Parent	121
11.	John Vanbiesbrouck	119
12.	Grant Fuhr	114
13.	Dan Bouchard	113
14.	**Ed Belfour**	**105**
	Billy Smith	105
16.	Turk Broda	101
17.	Ed Giacomin	97
18.	Cesare Maniago	96
19.	**Martin Brodeur**	**94**
	Sean Burke	**94**

Rk.	Goaltender	No.
21.	Mike Vernon	92
22.	Johnny Bower	90
23.	Greg Millen	89
24.	Kelly Hrudey	88
	Andy Moog	88
26.	**Curtis Joseph**	**87**
27.	**Tom Barrasso**	**86**
28.	Al Rollins	83
29.	Glenn Resch	82
30.	Frank Brimsek	80
	Dominik Hasek	80
	Eddie Johnston	80
33.	**Felix Potvin**	**79**
34.	**Arturs Irbe**	**78**
35.	Chuck Rayner	77
36.	Denis Herron	76
	Phil Myre	76
	Bill Ranford	76
39.	Don Beaupre	75
	Dave Kerr	75
	Tiny Thompson	75

Total number of goaltenders: (41)

30 SHUTOUTS

Rk.	Goaltender	No.
1.	Terry Sawchuk	103
2.	George Hainsworth	94
3.	Glenn Hall	84
4.	Jacques Plante	82
5.	Alex Connell	81
	Tiny Thompson	81
7.	Tony Esposito	76
8.	Lorne Chabot	73
9.	Harry Lumley	71
10.	Roy Worters	67
11.	**Patrick Roy**	**66**
12.	**Ed Belfour**	**65**
13.	**Martin Brodeur**	**64**
14.	Turk Broda	62
15.	Dominik Hasek	61
16.	John Roach	58
17.	Clint Benedict	57
18.	Ed Giacomin	54
	Bernie Parent	54
20.	Dave Kerr	51
	Rogie Vachon	51
22.	Ken Dryden	46
23.	Gump Worsley	43
24.	Charlie Gardiner	42
25.	**Curtis Joseph**	**41**
26.	Frank Brimsek	40
	John Vanbiesbrouck	40
28.	**Tom Barrasso**	**38**
	Chris Osgood	**38**
30.	Johnny Bower	37
31.	**Jocelyn Thibault**	**35**
32.	Bill Durnan	34
	Tommy Salo	**34**
34.	**Sean Burke**	**33**
	Arturs Irbe	**33**
36.	Eddie Johnston	32
	Nikolai Khabibulin	**32**
38.	**Olaf Kolzig**	**31**
39.	Roger Crozier	30
	Cesare Maniago	30

Total number of goaltenders: (40)

COACHES

500 GAMES

Rk.	Coach	No.
1.	Scotty Bowman	2,141
2.	Al Arbour	1,606
3.	Dick Irvin	1,449
4.	**Mike Keenan**	**1,207**
5.	Billy Reay	1,102
6.	**Pat Quinn**	**1,154**
7.	Bryan Murray	1,057
8.	Jacques Demers	1,006
9.	Roger Neilson	1,000
10.	Sid Abel	964
	Jack Adams	964
12.	**Brian Sutter**	**946**
13.	**Pat Burns**	**937**
14.	Toe Blake	914
15.	Punch Imlach	889
16.	Bob Berry	860
17.	Glen Sather	842
18.	Bob Pulford	829
19.	Michel Bergeron	792
20.	Emile Francis	778
21.	**Jacques Martin**	**770**
	Milt Schmidt	770
23.	**Ron Wilson**	**763**
24.	Art Ross	758
25.	Red Kelly	742
26.	Terry Murray	737
27.	Fred Shero	734
28.	**Jacques Lemaire**	**721**
29.	**Darryl Sutter**	**696**
30.	**Marc Crawford**	**659**
31.	John Muckler	648
32.	**Paul Maurice**	**644**
33.	Pierre Page	636
34.	Terry Crisp	631
35.	Jack Evans	614
36.	Lester Patrick	604
37.	Eddie Johnston	596
38.	**Ken Hitchcock**	**585**
39.	Jim Schoenfeld	580
40.	Tommy Ivan	573
41.	Hap Day	546
42.	**Joel Quenneville**	**532**
43.	Frank Boucher	527
44.	Johnny Wilson	517
45.	Bob McCammon	512
46.	Herb Brooks	507
47.	Ron Low	505

Total number of coaches: (47)

250 GAMES WON

Rk.	Coach	No.
1.	Scotty Bowman	1,244
2.	Al Arbour	781
3.	Dick Irvin	692
4.	**Mike Keenan**	**579**
5.	**Pat Quinn**	**571**
6.	Billy Reay	542
7.	Bryan Murray	513
8.	Toe Blake	500

Rk.	Coach	No.
9.	Glen Sather	464
10.	Roger Neilson	460
11.	**Pat Burns**	**458**
12.	**Brian Sutter**	**431**
13.	Jack Adams	413
14.	Jacques Demers	409
15.	Punch Imlach	402
16.	Fred Shero	390
17.	Emile Francis	388
18.	Bob Berry	384
19.	Sid Abel	382
20.	Art Ross	368
21.	**Jacques Martin**	**364**
22.	Bob Pulford	363
23.	Terry Murray	360
24.	**Jacques Lemaire**	**340**
25.	Michel Bergeron	338
26.	**Ron Wilson**	**331**
27.	**Marc Crawford**	**326**
28.	**Ken Hitchcock**	**322**
29.	**Darryl Sutter**	**321**
30.	Tommy Ivan	288
31.	Terry Crisp	286
32.	Lester Patrick	281
33.	Red Kelly	278
	Joel Quenneville	**278**
35.	John Muckler	276
36.	Eddie Johnston	266
37.	**Paul Maurice**	**260**
38.	Hap Day	259
39.	Jim Schoenfeld	256
40.	Pierre Page	253
41.	Don Cherry	250
	Milt Schmidt	250

Total number of coaches: (42)

250 GAMES LOST

Rk.	Coach	No.
1.	Scotty Bowman	584
2.	Al Arbour	577
3.	Dick Irvin	527
4.	**Mike Keenan**	**483**
5.	Jacques Demers	467
6.	**Pat Quinn**	**439**
7.	Sid Abel	427
8.	Bryan Murray	413
9.	Milt Schmidt	394
10.	Jack Adams	390
11.	**Brian Sutter**	**386**
12.	Billy Reay	385
13.	Roger Neilson	381
14.	Bob Berry	355
15.	Michel Bergeron	350
16.	**Ron Wilson**	**343**
17.	**Pat Burns**	**340**
18.	Punch Imlach	337
19.	Red Kelly	330
	Bob Pulford	330
21.	Jack Evans	303
22.	Pierre Page	301
23.	Art Ross	300
24.	**Jacques Martin**	**297**
25.	**Paul Maurice**	**293**

Rk.	Coach	No.
26.	John Muckler	288
	Terry Murray	288
28.	**Darryl Sutter**	**281**
29.	Rick Bowness	277
	Jacques Lemaire	**277**
31.	Emile Francis	273
32.	Glen Sather	268
33.	Terry Crisp	267
34.	Frank Boucher	263
	Tom McVie	263
36.	Toe Blake	255
37.	Tom Watt	252
38.	Eddie Johnston	251

Total number of coaches: (38)

100 GAMES TIED

Rk.	Coach	No.
1.	Scotty Bowman	313
2.	Al Arbour	248
3.	Dick Irvin	230
4.	Billy Reay	175
5.	Jack Adams	161
6.	Toe Blake	159
	Roger Neilson	159
8.	Sid Abel	155
9.	Punch Imlach	150
10.	**Mike Keenan**	**145**
11.	**Pat Quinn**	**144**
12.	**Pat Burns**	**139**
13.	Bob Pulford	136

Rk.	Coach	No.
14.	Red Kelly	134
15.	Bryan Murray	131
16.	Jacques Demers	130
17.	**Brian Sutter**	**129**
18.	Milt Schmidt	126
19.	Bob Berry	121
20.	Fred Shero	119
21.	Emile Francis	117
22.	Tommy Ivan	111
23.	Glen Sather	110
24.	**Jacques Martin**	**109**
25.	Lester Patrick	107
26.	Michel Bergeron	104
	Jacques Lemaire	**104**

Total number of coaches: (27)

.550 WINNING PERCENTAGE
(Coaches with 500 or more games)

Rk.	Coach	Games	Pct.
1.	Scotty Bowman	2,141	.654
2.	Toe Blake	914	.634
3.	Glen Sather	842	.616
4.	**Ken Hitchcock**	**585**	**.613**
5.	Fred Shero	734	.612
6.	Tommy Ivan	573	.599
7.	**Joel Quenneville**	**532**	**.588**
8.	Emile Francis	778	.574
9.	Billy Reay	1,102	.571
10.	**Marc Crawford**	**659**	**.565**
11.	Al Arbour	1,606	.564

Rk.	Coach	Games	Pct.
12.	**Pat Burns**	**937**	**.563**
13.	**Pat Quinn**	**1,154**	**.557**
14.	Dick Irvin	1,449	.557
15.	Lester Patrick	604	.554

Total number of coaches: (15)

STANLEY CUP CHAMPIONSHIPS
(Includes Stanley Cup championships as NHL coach only)

Rk.	Coach	No.
1.	Scotty Bowman	9
2.	Toe Blake	8
3.	Hap Day	5
4.	Al Arbour	4
	Dick Irvin	4
	Punch Imlach	4
	Glen Sather	4
8.	Jack Adams	3
	Pete Green	3
	Tommy Ivan	3
11.	Tommy Gorman	2
	Cecil Hart	2
	Lester Patrick	2
	Claude Ruel	2
	Fred Shero	2

Total number of coaches with 2 or more: (15)

SEASON

FORWARDS/DEFENSEMEN

60 GOALS

Season	Player, Team	No.
1981-82	Wayne Gretzky, Edm.	92
1983-84	Wayne Gretzky, Edm.	87
1990-91	**Brett Hull, St.L.**	**86**
1988-89	**Mario Lemieux, Pit.**	**85**
1970-71	Phil Esposito, Bos.	76
1992-93	**Alexander Mogilny, Buf.**	**76**
1992-93	**Teemu Selanne, Win.**	**76**
1984-85	Wayne Gretzky, Edm.	73
1989-90	**Brett Hull, St.L.**	**72**
1982-83	Wayne Gretzky, Edm.	71
1984-85	Jari Kurri, Edm.	71
1991-92	**Brett Hull, St.L.**	**70**
1987-88	**Mario Lemieux, Pit.**	**70**
1988-89	Bernie Nicholls, L.A.	70
1978-79	Mike Bossy, NYI	69
1992-93	**Mario Lemieux, Pit.**	**69**
1995-96	**Mario Lemieux, Pit.**	**69**
1980-81	Mike Bossy, NYI	68
1973-74	Phil Esposito, Bos.	68
1985-86	Jari Kurri, Edm.	68
1972-73	Phil Esposito, Bos.	66
1982-83	Lanny McDonald, Cal.	66
1988-89	**Steve Yzerman, Det.**	**65**
1981-82	Mike Bossy, NYI	64
1992-93	**Luc Robitaille, L.A.**	**63**
1986-87	Wayne Gretzky, Edm.	62
1995-96	**Jaromir Jagr, Pit.**	**62**

Season	Player, Team	No.
1989-90	**Steve Yzerman, Det.**	**62**
1985-86	Mike Bossy, NYI	61
1974-75	Phil Esposito, Bos.	61
1975-76	Reggie Leach, Phi.	61
1982-83	Mike Bossy, NYI	60
1992-93	**Pavel Bure, Van.**	**60**
1993-94	**Pavel Bure, Van.**	**60**
1977-78	Guy Lafleur, Mon.	60
1981-82	Dennis Maruk, Was.	60
1976-77	Steve Shutt, Mon.	60

Total number of occurrences: (37)

50-GOAL SEASONS

Rk.	Player	No.	Cons.
1.	Mike Bossy	9	9
	Wayne Gretzky	9	8
3.	Guy Lafleur	6	6
	Marcel Dionne	6	5
	Mario Lemieux	**6**	**3**
6.	Phil Esposito	5	5
	Brett Hull	**5**	**5**
	Steve Yzerman	**5**	**4**
	Bobby Hull	5	2
	Pavel Bure	**5**	**2**
11.	Michel Goulet	4	4
	Tim Kerr	4	4
	Jari Kurri	4	4
14.	**John LeClair**	**3**	**3**
	Rick Vaive	3	3
	Cam Neely	3	2
	Teemu Selanne	**3**	**2**

Rk.	Player	No.	Cons.
	Luc Robitaille	3	1
19.	**Dave Andreychuk**	**2**	**2**
	Rick Martin	2	2
	Dennis Maruk	2	2
	Joe Nieuwendyk	**2**	**2**
	Mickey Redmond	2	2
	Jeremy Roenick	**2**	**2**
	Brendan Shanahan	**2**	**2**
	Charlie Simmer	2	2
	Kevin Stevens	**2**	**2**
	Keith Tkachuk	**2**	**2**
	Glenn Anderson	2	1
	Peter Bondra	**2**	**1**
	Dino Ciccarelli	2	1
	Danny Gare	2	1
	Jaromir Jagr	**2**	**1**
	Pat LaFontaine	2	1
	Pierre Larouche	2	1
	Reggie Leach	2	1
	Alexander Mogilny	**2**	**1**
	Stephane Richer	2	1
	Joe Sakic	**2**	**1**
	Blaine Stoughton	2	1
41.	Wayne Babych	1	1
	Bill Barber	1	1
	Brian Bellows	1	1
	John Bucyk	1	1
	Mike Bullard	1	1
	Bob Carpenter	1	1
	Jimmy Carson	1	1
	Guy Chouinard	1	1

Rk.	Player	No.	Cons.
	Sergei Fedorov	1	1
	Theo Fleury	1	1
	Mike Gartner	1	1
	Bernie Geoffrion	1	1
	Danny Grant	1	1
	Adam Graves	1	1
	Vic Hadfield	1	1
	Dale Hawerchuk	1	1
	Milan Hejduk	1	1
	Ken Hodge	1	1
	Jarome Iginla	1	1
	Paul Kariya	1	1
	Rick Kehoe	1	1
	Gary Leeman	1	1
	Hakan Loob	1	1
	Rick MacLeish	1	1
	Lanny McDonald	1	1
	Mark Messier	1	1
	Rick Middleton	1	1
	Mike Modano	1	1
	Joe Mullen	1	1
	Bernie Nicholls	1	1
	John Ogrodnick	1	1
	Jean Pronovost	1	1
	Mark Recchi	1	1
	Jacques Richard	1	1
	Maurice Richard	1	1
	Gary Roberts	1	1
	Al Secord	1	1
	Ray Sheppard	1	1
	Steve Shutt	1	1
	Craig Simpson	1	1
	Bryan Trottier	1	1
	Pierre Turgeon	1	1

Total number of players: (82)

40 GOALS BY ROOKIES

Season	Player, Team	No.
1992-93	**Teemu Selanne, Win.**	76
1977-78	Mike Bossy, NYI	53
1987-88	**Joe Nieuwendyk, Cal.**	51
1981-82	Dale Hawerchuk, Win.	45
1986-87	**Luc Robitaille, L.A.**	45
1971-72	Rick Martin, Buf.	44
1981-82	Barry Pederson, Bos.	44
1982-83	Steve Larmer, Chi.	43
1984-85	**Mario Lemieux, Pit.**	43
1992-93	Eric Lindros, Phi.	41
1980-81	Darryl Sutter, Chi.	40
1983-84	Sylvain Turgeon, Har.	40
1984-85	Warren Young, Pit.	40

Total number of players: (13)

125 POINTS

Season	Player	No.
1985-86	Wayne Gretzky, Edm.	215
1981-82	Wayne Gretzky, Edm.	212
1984-85	Wayne Gretzky, Edm.	208
1983-84	Wayne Gretzky, Edm.	205
1988-89	**Mario Lemieux, Pit.**	199
1982-83	Wayne Gretzky, Edm.	196
1986-87	Wayne Gretzky, Edm.	183
1988-89	Wayne Gretzky, L.A.	168
1987-88	**Mario Lemieux, Pit.**	168

Season	Player	No.
1980-81	Wayne Gretzky, Edm.	164
1990-91	Wayne Gretzky, L.A.	163
1995-96	**Mario Lemieux, Pit.**	161
1992-93	**Mario Lemieux, Pit.**	160
1988-89	**Steve Yzerman, Det.**	155
1970-71	Phil Esposito, Bos.	152
1988-89	Bernie Nicholls, L.A.	150
1987-88	Wayne Gretzky, Edm.	149
1995-96	**Jaromir Jagr, Pit.**	149
1992-93	Pat LaFontaine, Buf.	148
1981-82	Mike Bossy, NYI	147
1973-74	Phil Esposito, Bos.	145
1989-90	Wayne Gretzky, L.A.	142
1992-93	**Adam Oates, Bos.**	142
1985-86	**Mario Lemieux, Pit.**	141
1970-71	Bobby Orr, Bos.	139
1981-82	Peter Stastny, Que.	139
1985-86	Paul Coffey, Edm.	138
1979-80	Wayne Gretzky, Edm.	137
1979-80	Marcel Dionne, L.A.	137
1992-93	**Steve Yzerman, Det.**	137
1976-77	Guy Lafleur, Mon.	136
1981-82	Dennis Maruk, Was.	136
1980-81	Marcel Dionne, L.A.	135
1984-85	Jari Kurri, Edm.	135
1974-75	Bobby Orr, Bos.	135
1978-79	Bryan Trottier, NYI	134
1971-72	Phil Esposito, Bos.	133
1977-78	Guy Lafleur, Mon.	132
1992-93	**Pierre Turgeon, NYI**	132
1992-93	**Teemu Selanne, Win.**	132
1990-91	**Brett Hull, St.L.**	131
1991-92	**Mario Lemieux, Pit.**	131
1985-86	Jari Kurri, Edm.	131
1980-81	Kent Nilsson, Cal.	131
1987-88	Denis Savard, Chi.	131
1972-73	Phil Esposito, Bos.	130
1978-79	Marcel Dionne, L.A.	130
1984-85	Dale Hawerchuk, Win.	130
1993-94	Wayne Gretzky, L.A.	130
1989-90	**Mark Messier, Edm.**	129
1978-79	Guy Lafleur, Mon.	129
1981-82	Bryan Trottier, NYI	129
1974-75	Phil Esposito, Bos.	127
1992-93	**Doug Gilmour, Tor.**	127
1992-93	**Alexander Mogilny, Buf.**	127
1989-90	Steve Yzerman, Det.	127
1998-99	**Jaromir Jagr, Pit.**	127
1968-69	Phil Esposito, Bos.	126
1978-79	Mike Bossy, NYI	126
1983-84	Paul Coffey, Edm.	126
1984-85	Marcel Dionne, L.A.	126
1975-76	Guy Lafleur, Mon.	125
1979-80	Guy Lafleur, Mon.	125

Total number of occurrences: (63)

100-POINT SEASONS

Rk.	Player	No.	Cons.
1.	Wayne Gretzky	15	13
2.	**Mario Lemieux**	10	6
3.	Marcel Dionne	8	5
4.	Mike Bossy	7	6
	Peter Stastny	7	6
6.	Guy Lafleur	6	6

Rk.	Player	No.	Cons.
	Bobby Orr	6	6
	Steve Yzerman	6	6
	Phil Esposito	6	5
	Dale Hawerchuk	6	5
	Jari Kurri	6	5
	Bryan Trottier	6	5
	Mark Messier	6	2
14.	**Joe Sakic**	5	2
	Denis Savard	5	2
16.	**Brett Hull**	4	4
	Paul Coffey	4	3
	Bernie Federko	4	3
	Michel Goulet	4	2
	Adam Oates	4	2
	Luc Robitaille	4	2
	Jaromir Jagr	4	1
23.	Mike Rogers	3	3
	Glenn Anderson	3	2
	Bobby Clarke	3	2
	Doug Gilmour	3	2
	Bernie Nicholls	3	2
	Mark Recchi	3	2
	Ron Francis	3	1
30.	**Pavel Bure**	2	2
	Jimmy Carson	2	2
	Pete Mahovlich	2	2
	Barry Pederson	2	2
	Jeremy Roenick	2	2
	Charlie Simmer	2	2
	Kevin Stevens	2	2
	Dave Taylor	2	2
	Dino Ciccarelli	2	1
	Sergei Fedorov	2	1
	Theo Fleury	2	1
	Peter Forsberg	2	1
	Pat LaFontaine	2	1
	Rick Middleton	2	1
	Alexander Mogilny	2	1
	Kent Nilsson	2	1
	Gilbert Perreault	2	1
	Jean Ratelle	2	1
	Darryl Sittler	2	1
	Teemu Selanne	2	1
	Pierre Turgeon	2	1

Total number of players with 2 or more: (50)

75 POINTS BY ROOKIES

Season	Player, Team	No.
1992-93	**Teemu Selanne, Win.**	132
1980-81	Peter Stastny, Que.	109
1981-82	Dale Hawerchuk, Win.	103
1992-93	**Joe Juneau, Bos.**	102
1984-85	**Mario Lemieux, Pit.**	100
1981-82	Neal Broten, Min.	98
1975-76	Bryan Trottier, NYI	95
1987-88	**Joe Nieuwendyk, Cal.**	92
1981-82	Barry Pederson, Bos.	92
1977-78	Mike Bossy, NYI	91
1982-83	Steve Larmer, Chi.	90
1981-82	Marian Stastny, Que.	89
1983-84	**Steve Yzerman, Det.**	87
1989-90	Sergei Makarov, Cal.	86
1980-81	Anton Stastny, Que.	85
1986-87	**Luc Robitaille, L.A.**	84
1993-94	Mikael Renberg, Phi.	82

Season	Player, Team	No.
1986-87	Jimmy Carson, L.A.	79
1990-91	**Sergei Fedorov, Det.**	**79**
1993-94	**Alexei Yashin, Ott.**	**79**
1971-72	Marcel Dionne, L.A.	77
1980-81	Larry Murphy, L.A.	76
1981-82	Mark Pavelich, NYR	76
1983-84	Dave Poulin, Phi.	76
1992-93	Eric Lindros, Phi.	75
1980-81	Jari Kurri, Edm.	75
1989-90	**Mike Modano, Min.**	**75**
1979-80	Brian Propp, Phi.	75
1980-81	Denis Savard, Chi.	75

Total number of players: (29)

350 PENALTY MINUTES

Season	Player, Team	No.
1974-75	Dave Schultz, Phi.	472
1981-82	Paul Baxter, Pit.	409
1991-92	Mike Peluso, Chi.	408
1977-78	Dave Schultz, L.A.-Pit.	405
1992-93	Marty McSorley, L.A.	399
1987-88	Bob Probert, Det.	398
1987-88	Basil McRae, Min.	382
1985-86	Joey Kocur, Det.	377
1988-89	Tim Hunter, Cal.	375
1997-98	**Donald Brashear, Van.**	**372**
1996-97	Gino Odjick, Van.	371
1975-76	Steve Durbano, Pit.-K.C.	370
1992-93	Gino Odjick, Van.	370
1988-89	Basil McRae, Min.	365
1997-98	**Tie Domi, Tor.**	**365**
1986-87	Tim Hunter, Cal.	361

Season	Player, Team	No.
1984-85	Chris Nilan, Mon.	358
1985-86	Torrie Robertson, Har.	358
1986-87	Tiger Williams, L.A.	358
1986-87	Brian Curran, NYI	356
1991-92	**Rob Ray, Buf.**	**354**
2001-02	**Peter Worrell, Fla.**	**354**
1988-89	Dave Manson, Chi.	352
1977-78	Tiger Williams, Tor.	351
1989-90	Basil McRae, Min.	351
1988-89	Marty McSorley, L.A.	350
1990-91	**Rob Ray, Buf.**	**350**

Total number of occurrences: (27)

GOALTENDERS

10 SHUTOUTS

Season	Goaltender, Team	No.
1928-29	George Hainsworth, Mon. C.	22
1925-26	Alex Connell, Ott.	15
1927-28	Alex Connell, Ott.	15
1927-28	Hal Winkler, Bos.	15
1969-70	Tony Esposito, Chi.	15
1926-27	George Hainsworth, Mon. C.	14
1926-27	Clint Benedict, Mon. M.	13
1926-27	Alex Connell, Ott.	13
1927-28	George Hainsworth, Mon. C.	13
1928-29	John Roach, NYR	13
1928-29	Roy Worters, NYA	13
1953-54	Harry Lumley, Tor.	13
1997-98	Dominik Hasek, Buf.	13
1928-29	Lorne Chabot, Tor.	12

Season	Player, Team	No.
1928-29	Tiny Thompson, Bos.	12
1930-31	Chuck Gardiner, Chi.	12
1951-52	Terry Sawchuk, Det.	12
1953-54	Terry Sawchuk, Det.	12
1954-55	Terry Sawchuk, Det.	12
1955-56	Glenn Hall, Det.	12
1973-74	Bernie Parent, Phi.	12
1974-75	Bernie Parent, Phi.	12
1927-28	Lorne Chabot, NYR	11
1927-28	Harry Holmes, Det.	11
1928-29	Clint Benedict, Mon. M.	11
1928-29	Joe Miller, Pit.	11
1932-33	Tiny Thompson, Bos.	11
1950-51	Terry Sawchuk, Det.	11
2000-01	Dominik Hasek, Buf.	11
1926-27	Lorne Chabot, NYR	10
1927-28	Roy Worters, Pit.	10
1928-29	Clarence Dolson, Det.	10
1932-33	John Roach, Det.	10
1933-34	Chuck Gardiner, Chi.	10
1935-36	Tiny Thompson, Bos.	10
1938-39	Frank Brimsek, Bos.	10
1948-49	Bill Durnan, Mon.	10
1952-53	Harry Lumley, Tor.	10
1952-53	Gerry McNeil, Mon.	10
1973-74	Tony Esposito, Chi.	10
1976-77	Ken Dryden, Mon.	10
1996-97	**Martin Brodeur, N.J.**	**10**
1997-98	**Martin Brodeur, N.J.**	**10**
1998-99	**Byron Dafoe, Bos.**	**10**
2000-01	**Roman Cechmanek, Phi.**	**10**

Total number of occurrences: (45)

GAME

FORWARDS/DEFENSEMEN

FIVE GOALS

Date	Player	Team	Opponents	Goals
December 19, 1917	Joe Malone	Montreal	at Ottawa	5
December 19, 1917	Harry Hyland	Montreal Wanderers	vs. Toronto	5
January 12, 1918	Joe Malone	Montreal	vs. Ottawa	5
February 2, 1918	Joe Malone	Montreal	vs. Toronto	5
January 10, 1920	Newsy Lalonde	Montreal	vs Toronto	6
January 31, 1920	Joe Malone	Quebec Bulldogs	vs. Toronto	7
March 6, 1920	Mickey Roach	Toronto St. Pats	vs. Quebec	5
March 10, 1920	Joe Malone	Quebec Bulldogs	vs. Ottawa	6
January 26, 1921	Corb Denneny	Toronto St. Pats	vs. Hamilton	6
February 16, 1921	Newsy Lalonde	Montreal	vs. Hamilton	6
March 7, 1921	Cy Denneny	Ottawa Senators	vs. Hamilton	6
December 16, 1922	Babe Dye	Toronto St. Pats	vs. Montreal	5
December 5, 1924	Redvers Green	Hamilton Tigers	at Toronto	5
December 22, 1924	Babe Dye	Toronto St. Pats	at Boston	5
January 7, 1925	Harry Broadbent	Montreal Maroons	at Hamilton	5
December 14, 1929	Pit Lepine	Montreal	vs. Ottawa	5
March 18, 1930	Howie Morenz	Montreal	vs. New York Americans	5
January 19, 1932	Charlie Conacher	Toronto	vs. New York Americans	5
February 6, 1943	Ray Getliffe	Montreal	vs. Boston	5
February 3, 1944	Syd Howe	Detroit	vs. New York Rangers	6
December 28, 1944	Maurice Richard	Montreal	vs. Detroit	5
January 8, 1947	Howie Meeker	Toronto	vs. Chicago	5
February 19, 1955	Bernie Geoffrion	Montreal	vs. New York Rangers	5
February 1, 1964	Bobby Rousseau	Montreal	vs. Detroit	5
November 7, 1968	Red Berenson	St. Louis	at Philadelphia	6
February 15, 1975	Yvan Cournoyer	Montreal	vs. Chicago	5

Date	Player	Team	Opponents		Goals
February 7, 1976	Darryl Sittler	Toronto	vs. Boston		6
October 12, 1976	Don Murdoch	New York Rangers	at Minnesota		5
February 2, 1977	Ian Turnbull	Toronto	vs. Detroit		5
December 23, 1978	Bryan Trottier	New York Islanders	vs. New York Rangers		5
January 15, 1979	Tim Young	Minnesota	at New York Rangers		5
January 6, 1981	John Tonelli	New York Islanders	vs. Toronto		5
February 18, 1981	Wayne Gretzky	Edmonton	vs. St. Louis		5
December 30, 1981	Wayne Gretzky	Edmonton	vs. Philadelphia		5
February 3, 1982	Grant Mulvey	Chicago	vs. St. Louis		5
February 13, 1982	Bryan Trottier	New York Islanders	vs. Philadelphia		5
March 2, 1982	Willie Lindstrom	Winnipeg	at Philadelphia		5
February 23, 1983	Mark Pavelich	New York Rangers	vs. Hartford		5
November 19, 1983	Jari Kurri	Edmonton	vs. New Jersey		5
January 8, 1984	Bengt Gustafsson	Washington	at Philadelphia		5
February 3, 1984	Pat Hughes	Edmonton	vs. Calgary		5
December 15, 1984	Wayne Gretzky	Edmonton	at St. Louis		5
February 6, 1986	**Dave Andreychuk**	**Buffalo**	**at Boston**		**5**
December 6, 1987	Wayne Gretzky	Edmonton	vs. Minnesota		5
December 31, 1988	**Mario Lemieux**	**Pittsburgh**	**vs. New Jersey**		**5**
January 11, 1989	**Joe Nieuwendyk**	**Calgary**	**vs. Winnipeg**		**5**
March 5, 1992	**Mats Sundin**	**Quebec**	**at Hartford**		**5**
April 9, 1993	**Mario Lemieux**	**Pittsburgh**	**at New York Rangers**		**5**
February 5, 1994	**Peter Bondra**	**Washington**	**vs. Tampa Bay**		**5**
February 17, 1994	**Mike Ricci**	**Quebec**	**at San Jose**		**5**
April 1, 1995	**Alexei Zhamnov**	**Winnipeg**	**at Los Angeles**		**5**
March 26, 1996	**Mario Lemieux**	**Pittsburgh**	**vs. St. Louis**		**5**
December 26, 1996	**Sergei Fedorov**	**Detroit**	**vs. Washington**		**5**

Total number of occurrences: (53)

TEAM BY TEAM

MIGHTY DUCKS OF ANAHEIM
YEAR-BY-YEAR RECORDS

	REGULAR SEASON						PLAYOFFS			
Season	W	L	T	OTL	Pts.	Finish	W	L	Highest round	Coach
1993-94	33	46	5	—	71	4th/Pacific	—	—		Ron Wilson
1994-95	16	27	5	—	37	6th/Pacific	—	—		Ron Wilson
1995-96	35	39	8	—	78	4th/Pacific	—	—		Ron Wilson
1996-97	36	33	13	—	85	2nd/Pacific	4	7	Conference semifinals	Ron Wilson
1997-98	26	43	13	—	65	6th/Pacific	—	—		Pierre Page
1998-99	35	34	13	—	83	3rd/Pacific	0	4	Conference quarterfinals	Craig Hartsburg
1999-00	34	33	12	3	83	5th/Pacific	—	—		Craig Hartsburg
2000-01	25	41	11	5	66	5th/Pacific	—	—		Craig Hartsburg, Guy Charron
2001-02	29	42	8	3	69	5th/Pacific	—	—		Bryan Murray
2002-03	40	27	9	6	95	2nd/Pacific	15	6	Stanley Cup finals	Mike Babcock

FIRST-ROUND ENTRY DRAFT CHOICES

Year   Player, Overall, Last amateur team (league)
1993—Paul Kariya, 4, University of Maine
1994—Oleg Tverdovsky, 2, Krylja Sovetov, CIS
1995—Chad Kilger, 4, Kingston (OHL)
1996—Ruslan Salei, 9, Las Vegas (IHL)
1997—Mikael Holmqvist, 18, Djurgarden Stockholm, Sweden
1998—Vitali Vishnevsky, 5, Torpedo Yaroslavl, Russia

Year   Player, Overall, Last amateur team (league)
1999—No first-round selection
2000—Alexei Smirnov, 12, Dynamo, Russia
2001—Stanislav Chistov, 5, OMDK, Russia
2002—Joffrey Lupul, 7, Medicine Hat (WHL)
2003—Ryan Getzlaf, 19, Calgary (WHL)
         Corey Perry, 28, London (OHL)

SINGLE-SEASON INDIVIDUAL RECORDS

FORWARDS/DEFENSEMEN

Most goals
52—Teemu Selanne, 1997-98

Most assists
62—Paul Kariya, 1998-99

Most points
109—Teemu Selanne, 1996-97

Most penalty minutes
285—Todd Ewen, 1995-96

Most power play goals
25—Teemu Selanne, 1998-99

Most shorthanded goals
3—Bob Corkum, 1993-94
     Paul Kariya, 1995-96

Paul Kariya, 1996-97
Paul Kariya, 1999-00
Paul Kariya, 2000-01

Most games with three or more goals
3—Teemu Selanne, 1997-98

Most shots
429—Paul Kariya, 1998-99

GOALTENDERS

Most games
69—Guy Hebert, 1998-99

Most minutes
4,083—Guy Hebert, 1998-99

Most shots against
2,133—Guy Hebert, 1996-97

Most goals allowed
172—Guy Hebert, 1996-97

Lowest goals-against average
2.13—Jean-Sebastien Giguere, 2001-02

Most shutouts
8—Jean-Sebastien Giguere, 2002-03

Most wins
34—Jean-Sebastien Giguere, 2002-03

Most losses
31—Guy Hebert, 1999-2000

Most ties
12—Guy Hebert, 1996-97

FRANCHISE LEADERS

Players in boldface played for club in 2002-03

FORWARDS/DEFENSEMEN

Games
Paul Kariya 606
Steve Rucchin.........................534
Ruslan Salei 434
Matt Cullen 427
Teemu Selanne.......................394

Goals
Paul Kariya 300
Teemu Selanne.......................225
Steve Rucchin.........................133
Matt Cullen 65
Joe Sacco................................62

Assists
Paul Kariya 369
Teemu Selanne.......................257
Steve Rucchin.........................256
Matt Cullen 135
Oleg Tverdovsky.....................125

Points
Paul Kariya 669
Teemu Selanne.......................482
Steve Rucchin.........................389
Matt Cullen 200
Oleg Tverdovsky.....................170

Penalty minutes
David Karpa............................788
Jason Marshall.......................706
Todd Ewen.............................647
Stu Grimson...........................583
Ruslan Salei 511

GOALTENDERS

Games
Guy Hebert.............................441
Jean-Sebastien Giguere.............152
Mikhail Shtalenkov 122
Dominic Roussel 51
Steve Shields...........................33

Shutouts
Guy Hebert................................27
Jean-Sebastien Giguere 16
Mikhail Shtalenkov 3
Dominic Roussel 2
Martin Gerber 1
Ron Tugnutt 1

Goals-against average
(2400 minutes minimum)
Jean-Sebastien Giguere..............2.30
Guy Hebert.............................2.75
Dominic Roussel 2.85
Mikhail Shtalenkov 3.14

Wins
Guy Hebert.............................173
Jean-Sebastien Giguere 65
Mikhail Shtalenkov 34
Dominic Roussel 12
Ron Tugnutt 10

ATLANTA THRASHERS
YEAR-BY-YEAR RECORDS

Season	W	L	T	OTL	Pts.	Finish	W	L	Highest round	Coach
			REGULAR SEASON						PLAYOFFS	
1999-00	14	57	7	4	39	5th/Southeast	—	—		Curt Fraser
2000-01	23	45	12	2	60	4th/Southeast	—	—		Curt Fraser
2001-02	19	47	11	5	54	5th/Southeast	—	—		Curt Fraser
2002-03	31	39	7	5	74	3rd/Southeast	—	—		C. Fraser, Don Waddell, Bob Hartley

FIRST-ROUND ENTRY DRAFT CHOICES

Year   Player, Overall, Last amateur team (league)
1999—Patrik Stefan, 1, Long Beach (IHL)*
2000—Dany Heatley, 2, Wisconsin (WCHA)
2001—Ilja Kovalchuk, 1, Spartak Jr., Russia*

Year   Player, Overall, Last amateur team (league)
2002—Kari Lehtonen, 2, Jokerit, Finland
    Jim Slater, 30, Michigan State (CCHA)
2003—Braydon Coburn, 8, Portland (WHL)
*Designates first player chosen in draft.

SINGLE-SEASON INDIVIDUAL RECORDS

FORWARDS/DEFENSEMEN

Most goals
41—Dany Heatley, 2002-03

Most assists
49—Vyacheslav Kozlov, 2002-03

Most points
89—Dany Heatley, 2002-03

Most penalty minutes
226—Jeff Odgers, 2000-01

Most power play goals
19—Dany Heatley, 2002-03

Most shorthanded goals
3—Shean Donovan, 2000-01

Most games with three or more goals
2—Donald Audette, 2000-01
    Ray Ferraro, 2000-01

Most shots
257—Ilya Kovalchuk, 2002-03

GOALTENDERS

Most games
60—Milan Hnilicka, 2001-02

Most minutes
3,367—Milan Hnilicka, 2001-02

Most shots against
1,956—Milan Hnilicka, 2001-02

Most goals allowed
179—Milan Hnilicka, 2001-02

Lowest goals-against average
2.88—Pasi Nurminen, 2002-03

Most shutouts
3—Milan Hnilicka, 2001-02

Most wins
21—Pasi Nurminen, 2002-03

Most losses
33—Milan Hnilicka, 2001-02

Most ties
10—Milan Hnilicka, 2001-02

FRANCHISE LEADERS

Players in boldface played for club in 2002-03

FORWARDS/DEFENSEMEN

Games
Chris Tamer 301
Patrik Stefan 268
Yannick Tremblay 262
Per Svartvadet 247
Ray Ferraro 223

Goals
Dany Heatley 67
Ilya Kovalchuk 67
Ray Ferraro 56
Donald Audette 39
Andrew Brunette 38

Assists
Ray Ferraro 91
Dany Heatley 89
Andrew Brunette 71
Patrik Stefan 78
Yannick Tremblay 66

Points
Dany Heatley 156
Ray Ferraro 147
Ilya Kovalchuk 118
Patrik Stefan 113
Andrew Brunette 109

Penalty minutes
Jeff Odgers 532
Chris Tamer 448
Denny Lambert 434
Ray Ferraro 245
Steve Staios 203

GOALTENDERS
Games
Milan Hnilicka 117
Damian Rhodes 81
Pasi Nurminen 61
Norm Maracle 46
Scott Fankhouser 23

Shutouts
Milan Hnilicka 5
Pasi Nurminen 2
Norm Maracle 1
Damian Rhodes 1

Goals-against average
(1200 minutes minimum)
Pasi Nurminen 2.98
Milan Hnilicka 3.30
Norm Maracle 3.46

Wins
Milan Hnilicka 29
Pasi Nurminen 23
Damian Rhodes 14
Norm Maracle 6
Byron Dafoe 5

BOSTON BRUINS
YEAR-BY-YEAR RECORDS

Season	W	L	T	OTL	Pts.	Finish	W	L	Highest round	Coach
			REGULAR SEASON						PLAYOFFS	
1924-25	6	24	0	—	12	6th	—	—		Art Ross
1925-26	17	15	4	—	38	4th	—	—		Art Ross
1926-27	21	20	3	—	45	2nd/American	*2	2	Stanley Cup finals	Art Ross
1927-28	20	13	11	—	51	1st/American	*0	1	Semifinals	Art Ross
1928-29	26	13	5	—	57	1st/American	5	0	Stanley Cup champ	Cy Denneny

				REGULAR SEASON				PLAYOFFS		
Season	W	L	T	OTL	Pts.	Finish	W	L	Highest round	Coach
1929-30	38	5	1	—	77	1st/American	3	3	Stanley Cup finals	Art Ross
1930-31	28	10	6	—	62	1st/American	2	3	Semifinals	Art Ross
1931-32	15	21	12	—	42	4th/American	—	—		Art Ross
1932-33	25	15	8	—	58	1st/American	2	3	Semifinals	Art Ross
1933-34	18	25	5	—	41	4th/American	—	—		Art Ross
1934-35	26	16	6	—	58	1st/American	1	3	Semifinals	Frank Patrick
1935-36	22	20	6	—	50	2nd/American	1	1	Quarterfinals	Frank Patrick
1936-37	23	18	7	—	53	2nd/American	1	2	Quarterfinals	Art Ross
1937-38	30	11	7	—	67	1st/American	0	3	Semifinals	Art Ross
1938-39	36	10	2	—	74	1st	8	4	Stanley Cup champ	Art Ross
1939-40	31	12	5	—	67	1st	2	4	Semifinals	Ralph (Cooney) Weiland
1940-41	27	8	13	—	67	1st	8	3	Stanley Cup champ	Ralph (Cooney) Weiland
1941-42	25	17	6	—	56	3rd	2	3	Semifinals	Art Ross
1942-43	24	17	9	—	57	2nd	4	5	Stanley Cup finals	Art Ross
1943-44	19	26	5	—	43	5th	—	—		Art Ross
1944-45	16	30	4	—	36	4th	3	4	League semifinals	Art Ross
1945-46	24	18	8	—	56	2nd	5	5	Stanley Cup finals	Dit Clapper
1946-47	26	23	11	—	63	3rd	1	4	League semifinals	Dit Clapper
1947-48	23	24	13	—	59	3rd	1	4	League semifinals	Dit Clapper
1948-49	29	23	8	—	66	2nd	1	4	League semifinals	Dit Clapper
1949-50	22	32	16	—	60	5th	—	—		George Boucher
1950-51	22	30	18	—	62	4th	†1	4	League semifinals	Lynn Patrick
1951-52	25	29	16	—	66	4th	3	4	League semifinals	Lynn Patrick
1952-53	28	29	13	—	69	3rd	5	6	Stanley Cup finals	Lynn Patrick
1953-54	32	28	10	—	74	4th	0	4	League semifinals	Lynn Patrick
1954-55	23	26	21	—	67	4th	1	4	League semifinals	Lynn Patrick, Milt Schmidt
1955-56	23	34	13	—	59	5th	—	—		Milt Schmidt
1956-57	34	24	12	—	80	3rd	5	5	Stanley Cup finals	Milt Schmidt
1957-58	27	28	15	—	69	4th	6	6	Stanley Cup finals	Milt Schmidt
1958-59	32	29	9	—	73	2nd	3	4	League semifinals	Milt Schmidt
1959-60	28	34	8	—	64	5th	—	—		Milt Schmidt
1960-61	15	42	13	—	43	6th	—	—		Milt Schmidt
1961-62	15	47	8	—	38	6th	—	—		Phil Watson
1962-63	14	39	17	—	45	6th	—	—		Phil Watson, Milt Schmidt
1963-64	18	40	12	—	48	6th	—	—		Milt Schmidt
1964-65	21	43	6	—	48	6th	—	—		Milt Schmidt
1965-66	21	43	6	—	48	5th	—	—		Milt Schmidt
1966-67	17	43	10	—	44	6th	—	—		Harry Sinden
1967-68	37	27	10	—	84	3rd/East	0	4	Division semifinals	Harry Sinden
1968-69	42	18	16	—	100	2nd/East	6	4	Division finals	Harry Sinden
1969-70	40	17	19	—	99	2nd/East	12	2	Stanley Cup champ	Harry Sinden
1970-71	57	14	7	—	121	1st/East	3	4	Division semifinals	Tom Johnson
1971-72	54	13	11	—	119	1st/East	12	3	Stanley Cup champ	Tom Johnson
1972-73	51	22	5	—	107	2nd/East	1	4	Division semifinals	Tom Johnson, Bep Guidolin
1973-74	52	17	9	—	113	1st/East	10	6	Stanley Cup finals	Bep Guidolin
1974-75	40	26	14	—	94	2nd/Adams	1	2	Preliminaries	Don Cherry
1975-76	48	15	17	—	113	1st/Adams	5	7	Semifinals	Don Cherry
1976-77	49	23	8	—	106	1st/Adams	8	6	Stanley Cup finals	Don Cherry
1977-78	51	18	11	—	113	1st/Adams	10	5	Stanley Cup finals	Don Cherry
1978-79	43	23	14	—	100	1st/Adams	7	4	Semifinals	Don Cherry
1979-80	46	21	13	—	105	2nd/Adams	4	6	Quarterfinals	Fred Creighton, Harry Sinden
1980-81	37	30	13	—	87	2nd/Adams	0	3	Preliminaries	Gerry Cheevers
1981-82	43	27	10	—	96	2nd/Adams	6	5	Division finals	Gerry Cheevers
1982-83	50	20	10	—	110	1st/Adams	9	8	Conference finals	Gerry Cheevers
1983-84	49	25	6	—	104	1st/Adams	0	3	Division semifinals	Gerry Cheevers
1984-85	36	34	10	—	82	4th/Adams	2	3	Division semifinals	Gerry Cheevers, Harry Sinden
1985-86	37	31	12	—	86	3rd/Adams	0	3	Division semifinals	Butch Goring
1986-87	39	34	7	—	85	3rd/Adams	0	4	Division semifinals	Butch Goring, Terry O'Reilly
1987-88	44	30	6	—	94	2nd/Adams	12	10	Stanley Cup finals	Terry O'Reilly
1988-89	37	29	14	—	88	2nd/Adams	5	5	Division finals	Terry O'Reilly
1989-90	46	25	9	—	101	1st/Adams	13	8	Stanley Cup finals	Mike Milbury
1990-91	44	24	12	—	100	1st/Adams	10	9	Conference finals	Mike Milbury
1991-92	36	32	12	—	84	2nd/Adams	8	7	Conference finals	Rick Bowness
1992-93	51	26	7	—	109	1st/Adams	0	4	Division semifinals	Brian Sutter
1993-94	42	29	13	—	97	2nd/Northeast	6	7	Conference semifinals	Brian Sutter
1994-95	27	18	3	—	57	3rd/Northeast	1	4	Conference quarterfinals	Brian Sutter
1995-96	40	31	11	—	91	3rd/Northeast	1	4	Conference quarterfinals	Steve Kasper
1996-97	26	47	9	—	61	6th/Northeast	—	—		Steve Kasper
1997-98	39	30	13	—	91	2nd/Northeast	2	4	Conference quarterfinals	Pat Burns
1998-99	39	30	13	—	91	2nd/Northeast	6	6	Conference semifinals	Pat Burns
1999-00	24	33	19	6	73	5th/Northeast	—	—		Pat Burns
2000-01	36	30	8	8	88	4th/Northeast	—	—		Pat Burns, Mike Keenan
2001-02	43	24	6	9	101	1st/Northeast	2	4	Conference quarterfinals	Robbie Ftorek
2002-03	36	31	11	4	87	3rd/Northeast	1	4	Conference quarterfinals	Robbie Ftorek, Mike O'Connell

*Won-lost record does not indicate tie(s) resulting from two-game, total-goals series that year (two-game, total-goals series were played from 1917-18 through 1935-36).
†Tied after one overtime (curfew law).

FIRST-ROUND ENTRY DRAFT CHOICES

Year	Player, Overall, Last amateur team (league)
1969	Don Tannahill, 3, Niagara Falls (OHL)
	Frank Spring, 4, Edmonton (WCHL)
	Ivan Boldirev, 11, Oshawa (OHL)
1970	Reggie Leach, 3, Flin Flon (WCHL)
	Rick MacLeish, 4, Peterborough (OHL)
	Ron Plumb, 9, Peterborough (OHL)
	Bob Stewart, 13, Oshawa (OHL)
1971	Ron Jones, 6, Edmonton (WCHL)
	Terry O'Reilly, 14, Oshawa (OHL)
1972	Mike Bloom, 16, St. Catharines (OHL)
1973	Andre Savard, 6, Quebec (QMJHL)
1974	Don Laraway, 18, Swift Current (WCHL)
1975	Doug Halward, 14, Peterborough (OHL)
1976	Clayton Pachal, 16, New Westminster (WCHL)
1977	Dwight Foster, 16, Kitchener (OHL)
1978	Al Secord, 16, Hamilton (OHL)
1979	Ray Bourque, 8, Verdun (QMJHL)
	Brad McCrimmon, 15, Brandon (WHL)
1980	Barry Pederson, 18, Victoria (WHL)
1981	Norm Leveille, 14, Chicoutimi (QMJHL)
1982	Gord Kluzak, 1, Billings (WHL)*
1983	Nevin Markwart, 21, Regina (WHL)
1984	Dave Pasin, 19, Prince Albert (WHL)
1985	No first-round selection

Year	Player, Overall, Last amateur team (league)
1986	Craig Janney, 13, Boston College
1987	Glen Wesley, 3, Portland (WHL)
	Stephane Quintal, 14, Granby (QMJHL)
1988	Robert Cimetta, 18, Toronto (OHL)
1989	Shayne Stevenson, 17, Kitchener (OHL)
1990	Bryan Smolinski, 21, Michigan State University
1991	Glen Murray, 18, Sudbury (OHL)
1992	Dmitri Kvartalnov, 16, San Diego (IHL)
1993	Kevyn Adams, 25, Miami of Ohio
1994	Evgeni Riabchikov, 21, Molot-Perm (Russia)
1995	Kyle McLaren, 9, Tacoma (WHL)
	Sean Brown, 21, Belleville (OHL)
1996	Johnathan Aitken, 8, Medicine Hat (WHL)
1997	Joe Thornton, 1, Sault Ste. Marie (OHL)*
	Sergei Samsonov, 8, Detroit (IHL)
1998	No first-round selection
1999	Nicholas Boynton, 21, Ottawa (OHL)
2000	Lars Jonsson, 7, Leksand, Sweden
	Martin Samuelsson, 27, MoDo, Sweden
2001	Shaone Morrisonn, 19, Kamloops (WHL)
2002	Hannu Toivonen, 29, HPK, Finland
2003	Mark Stuart, 21, Colorado College (WCHA)

*Designates first player chosen in draft.

SINGLE-SEASON INDIVIDUAL RECORDS

FORWARDS/DEFENSEMEN

Most goals
76—Phil Esposito, 1970-71

Most assists
102—Bobby Orr, 1970-71

Most points
152—Phil Esposito, 1970-71

Most penalty minutes
302—Jay Miller, 1987-88

Most power play goals
28—Phil Esposito, 1971-72

Most shorthanded goals
9—Brian Rolston, 2001-02

Most games with three or more goals
7—Phil Esposito, 1970-71

Most shots
550—Phil Esposito, 1970-71

GOALTENDERS

Most games
70—Frank Brimsek, 1949-50
Jack Gelineau, 1950-51
Eddie Johnston, 1964-64

Most minutes
4,200—Frank Brimsek, 1949-50
Jack Gelineau, 1950-51
Eddie Johnston, 1964-64

Most goals allowed
244—Frank Brimsek, 1949-50

Lowest goals-against average
1.18—Tiny Thompson, 1928-29

Most shutouts
15—Hal Winkler, 1927-28

Most wins
40—Pete Peeters, 1982-83

FRANCHISE LEADERS

Players in boldface played for club in 2002-03

FORWARDS/DEFENSEMEN

Games
Ray Bourque	1518
John Bucyk	1436
Don Sweeney	**1052**
Wayne Cashman	1027
Terry O'Reilly	891

Goals
John Bucyk	545
Phil Esposito	459
Rick Middleton	402
Ray Bourque	395
Cam Neely	344

Assists
Ray Bourque	1111
John Bucyk	794
Bobby Orr	624
Phil Esposito	553
Wayne Cashman	516

Points
Ray Bourque	1506
John Bucyk	1339
Phil Esposito	1012
Rick Middleton	898
Bobby Orr	888

Penalty minutes
Terry O'Reilly	2095
Mike Milbury	1552
Keith Crowder	1261
Ray Bourque	1087
Wayne Cashman	1041

GOALTENDERS

Games
Cecil Thompson	468
Frankie Brimsek	444
Eddie Johnston	444
Gerry Cheevers	416
Byron Dafoe	283

Shutouts
Cecil Thompson	74
Frankie Brimsek	35
Eddie Johnston	27
Gerry Cheevers	26
Byron Dafoe	25

Goals-against average (2400 minutes minimum)
Hal Winkler	1.56
Cecil Thompson	1.99
Byron Dafoe	2.30
Charles Stewart	2.46
John Henderson	2.52

Wins
Tiny Thompson	252
Frankie Brimsek	230
Gerry Cheevers	229
Eddie Johnston	180
Gilles Gilbert	155

NHL HISTORY Team by team

BUFFALO SABRES
YEAR-BY-YEAR RECORDS

	REGULAR SEASON						PLAYOFFS			
Season	W	L	T	OTL	Pts.	Finish	W	L	Highest round	Coach
1970-71	24	39	15	—	63	5th/East	—	—		Punch Imlach
1971-72	16	43	19	—	51	6th/East	—	—		Punch Imlach, Joe Crozier
1972-73	37	27	14	—	88	4th/East	2	4	Division semifinals	Joe Crozier
1973-74	32	34	12	—	76	5th/East	—	—		Joe Crozier
1974-75	49	16	15	—	113	1st/Adams	10	7	Stanley Cup finals	Floyd Smith
1975-76	46	21	13	—	105	2nd/Adams	4	5	Quarterfinals	Floyd Smith
1976-77	48	24	8	—	104	2nd/Adams	2	4	Quarterfinals	Floyd Smith
1977-78	44	19	17	—	105	2nd/Adams	3	5	Quarterfinals	Marcel Pronovost
1978-79	36	28	16	—	88	2nd/Adams	1	2	Preliminaries	Marcel Pronovost, Bill Inglis
1979-80	47	17	16	—	110	1st/Adams	9	5	Semifinals	Scotty Bowman
1980-81	39	20	21	—	99	1st/Adams	4	4	Quarterfinals	Roger Neilson
1981-82	39	26	15	—	93	3rd/Adams	1	3	Division semifinals	Jim Roberts, Scotty Bowman
1982-83	38	29	13	—	89	3rd/Adams	6	4	Division finals	Scotty Bowman
1983-84	48	25	7	—	103	2nd/Adams	0	3	Division semifinals	Scotty Bowman
1984-85	38	28	14	—	90	3rd/Adams	2	3	Divison semifinals	Scotty Bowman
1985-86	37	37	6	—	80	5th/Adams	—	—		Jim Schoenfeld, Scotty Bowman
1986-87	28	44	8	—	64	5th/Adams	—	—		Scotty Bowman, Craig Ramsay
1987-88	37	32	11	—	85	3rd/Adams	2	4	Division semifinals	Ted Sator
1988-89	38	35	7	—	83	3rd/Adams	1	4	Division semifinals	Ted Sator
1989-90	45	27	8	—	98	2nd/Adams	2	4	Division semifinals	Rick Dudley
1990-91	31	30	19	—	81	3rd/Adams	2	4	Division semifinals	Rick Dudley, Ted Sator
1991-92	31	37	12	—	74	3rd/Adams	3	4	Division semifinals	Rick Dudley, John Muckler
1992-93	38	36	10	—	86	4th/Adams	4	4	Division finals	John Muckler
1993-94	43	32	9	—	95	4th/Northeast	3	4	Conference quarterfinals	John Muckler
1994-95	22	19	7	—	51	4th/Northeast	1	4	Conference quarterfinals	John Muckler
1995-96	33	42	7	—	73	5th/Northeast	—	—		Ted Nolan
1996-97	40	30	12	—	92	1st/Northeast	5	7	Conference semifinals	Ted Nolan
1997-98	36	29	17	—	89	3rd/Northeast	10	5	Conference finals	Lindy Ruff
1998-99	37	28	17	—	91	4rd/Northeast	14	7	Stanley Cup finals	Lindy Ruff
1999-00	35	32	11	4	85	3rd/Northeast	1	4	Conference quarterfinals	Lindy Ruff
2000-01	46	30	5	1	98	2nd/Northeast	7	6	Conference semifinals	Lindy Ruff
2001-02	35	35	11	1	82	5th/Northeast	—	—		Lindy Ruff
2002-03	27	37	10	8	72	5th/Northeast	—	—		Lindy Ruff

FIRST-ROUND ENTRY DRAFT CHOICES

Year   Player, Overall, Last amateur team (league)
1970—Gilbert Perreault, 1, Montreal (OHL)*
1971—Rick Martin, 5, Montreal (OHL)
1972—Jim Schoenfeld, 5, Niagara Falls (OHL)
1973—Morris Titanic, 12, Sudbury (OHL)
1974—Lee Fogolin, 11, Oshawa (OHL)
1975—Robert Sauve, 17, Laval (QMJHL)
1976—No first-round selection
1977—Ric Seiling, 14, St. Catharines (OHL)
1978—Larry Playfair, 13, Portland (WHL)
1979—Mike Ramsey, 11, University of Minnesota
1980—Steve Patrick, 20, Brandon (WHL)
1981—Jiri Dudacek, 17, Kladno (Czechoslovakia)
1982—Phil Housley, 6, South St. Paul H.S. (Minn.)
        Paul Cyr, 9, Victoria (WHL)
        Dave Andreychuk, 16, Oshawa (OHL)
1983—Tom Barrasso, 5, Acton Boxboro H.S. (Mass.)
        Norm Lacombe, 10, Univ. of New Hampshire
        Adam Creighton, 11, Ottawa (OHL)
1984—Bo Andersson, 18, Vastra Frolunda, Sweden
1985—Carl Johansson, 14, Vastra Frolunda, Sweden
1986—Shawn Anderson, 5, Team Canada

Year   Player, Overall, Last amateur team (league)
1987—Pierre Turgeon, 1, Granby (QMJHL)*
1988—Joel Savage, 13, Victoria (WHL)
1989—Kevin Haller, 14, Regina (WHL)
1990—Brad May, 14, Niagara Falls (OHL)
1991—Philippe Boucher, 13, Granby (QMJHL)
1992—David Cooper, 11, Medicine Hat (WHL)
1993—No first-round selection
1994—Wayne Primeau, 17, Owen Sound (OHL)
1995—Jay McKee, 14, Niagara Falls (OHL)
        Martin Biron, 16, Beauport (QMJHL)
1996—Erik Rasmussen, 7, University of Minnesota
1997—Mika Noronen, 21, Tappara Tampere, Finland
1998—Dimitri Kalinin, 18, Traktor Chelyabinsk, Russia
1999—Barrett Heisten, 20, Maine (H. East)
2000—Artem Kriukov, 15, Yaroslavl, Russia
2001—Jiri Novotny, 22, Budejovice, Czech Republic
2002—Keith Ballard, 11, University of Minnesota (WCHA)
        Daniel Paille, 20, Guelph (OHL)
2003—Thomas Vanek, 5, Minnesota (WCHA)
*Designates first player chosen in draft.

SINGLE-SEASON INDIVIDUAL RECORDS

FORWARDS/DEFENSEMEN

Most goals
76—Alexander Mogilny, 1992-93

Most assists
95—Pat LaFontaine, 1992-93

Most points
148—Pat LaFontaine, 1992-93

Most penalty minutes
354—Rob Ray, 1991-92

Most power play goals
28—Dave Andreychuk, 1991-92

Most shorthanded goals
8—Don Luce, 1974-75

Most games with three or more goals
7—Rick Martin, 1975-76
    Alexander Mogilny, 1992-93

NHL HISTORY   Team by team

Most shots
360—Alexander Mogilny, 1992-93

GOALTENDERS

Most games
72—Don Edwards, 1977-78
Dominik Hasek, 1997-98
Martin Biron, 2001-02

Most minutes
4,220—Dominik Hasek, 1997-98

Most shots against
2,190—Roger Crozier, 1971-72

Most goals allowed
214—Roger Crozier, 1971-72
Tom Barrasso, 1985-86

Lowest goals-against average
1.87—Dominik Hasek, 1998-99

Most shutouts
13—Dominik Hasek, 1997-98

Most wins
38—Don Edwards, 1977-78

Most losses
34—Roger Crozier, 1971-72

Most ties
17—Don Edwards, 1977-78

FRANCHISE LEADERS

Players in boldface played for club in 2002-03

FORWARDS/DEFENSEMEN

Games
Gilbert Perreault 1191
Craig Ramsay.................................1070
Mike Ramsey.....................................911
Rob Ray.......................................889
Bill Hajt..854

Goals
Gilbert Perreault 512
Rick Martin...382
Dave Andreychuk 368
Danny Gare..267
Craig Ramsay.....................................252

Assists
Gilbert Perreault 814
Dave Andreychuk 436
Craig Ramsay.....................................420
Phil Housley.......................................380
Rene Robert.......................................330

Points
Gilbert Perreault 1326
Dave Andreychuk 804
Rick Martin...695
Craig Ramsay.....................................672
Phil Housley.......................................558

Penalty minutes
Rob Ray 3189
Mike Foligno.....................................1450
Larry Playfair....................................1392
Brad May..1323
Matthew Barnaby 1248

GOALTENDERS

Games
Dominik Hasek 491
Don Edwards......................................307
Tom Barrasso.....................................266
Bob Sauve..246
Daren Puppa 215

Shutouts
Dominik Hasek 55
Martin Biron 15
Don Edwards..14
Tom Barrasso.......................................13
Roger Crozier.......................................10

Goals-against average
(2400 minutes minimum)
Dominik Hasek 2.22
Martin Biron 2.42
Gerry Desjardins 2.81
Don Edwards......................................2.90
Dave Dryden......................................3.06

Wins
Dominik Hasek 234
Don Edwards......................................156
Tom Barrasso.....................................124
Bob Sauve..119
Daren Puppa 96

CALGARY FLAMES
YEAR-BY-YEAR RECORDS

		REGULAR SEASON					PLAYOFFS			
Season	W	L	T	OTL	Pts.	Finish	W	L	Highest round	Coach
1972-73*	25	38	15	—	65	7th/West	—	—		Bernie Geoffrion
1973-74*	30	34	14	—	74	4th/West	0	4	Division semifinals	Bernie Geoffrion
1974-75*	34	31	15	—	83	4th/Patrick	—	—		Bernie Geoffrion, Fred Creighton
1975-76*	35	33	12	—	82	3rd/Patrick	0	2	Preliminaries	Fred Creighton
1976-77*	34	34	12	—	80	3rd/Patrick	1	2	Preliminaries	Fred Creighton
1977-78*	34	27	19	—	87	3rd/Patrick	0	2	Preliminaries	Fred Creighton
1978-79*	41	31	8	—	90	4th/Patrick	0	2	Preliminaries	Fred Creighton
1979-80*	35	32	13	—	83	4th/Patrick	1	3	Preliminaries	Al MacNeil
1980-81	39	27	14	—	92	3rd/Patrick	9	7	Semifinals	Al MacNeil
1981-82	29	34	17	—	75	3rd/Smythe	0	3	Division semifinals	Al MacNeil
1982-83	32	34	14	—	78	2nd/Smythe	4	5	Division finals	Bob Johnson
1983-84	34	32	14	—	82	2nd/Smythe	6	5	Division finals	Bob Johnson
1984-85	41	27	12	—	94	3rd/Smythe	1	3	Division semifinals	Bob Johnson
1985-86	40	31	9	—	89	2nd/Smythe	12	10	Stanley Cup finals	Bob Johnson
1986-87	46	31	3	—	95	2nd/Smythe	2	4	Division semifinals	Bob Johnson
1987-88	48	23	9	—	105	1st/Smythe	4	5	Division finals	Terry Crisp
1988-89	54	17	9	—	117	1st/Smythe	16	6	Stanley Cup champ	Terry Crisp
1989-90	42	23	15	—	99	1st/Smythe	2	4	Division semifinals	Terry Crisp
1990-91	46	26	8	—	100	2nd/Smythe	3	4	Division semifinals	Doug Risebrough
1991-92	31	37	12	—	74	5th/Smythe	—	—		Doug Risebrough, Guy Charron
1992-93	43	30	11	—	97	2nd/Smythe	2	4	Division semifinals	Dave King
1993-94	42	29	13	—	97	1st/Pacific	3	4	Conference quarterfinals	Dave King
1994-95	24	17	7	—	55	1st/Pacific	3	4	Conference quarterfinals	Dave King
1995-96	34	37	11	—	79	2nd/Pacific	0	4	Conference quarterfinals	Pierre Page
1996-97	32	41	9	—	73	5th/Pacific	—	—		Pierre Page
1997-98	26	41	15	—	67	5th/Pacific	—	—		Brian Sutter
1998-99	30	40	12	—	72	3rd/Northwest	—	—		Brian Sutter
1999-00	31	36	10	5	77	4th/Northwest	—	—		Brian Sutter
2000-01	27	36	15	4	73	4th/Northwest	—	—		Don Hay, Greg Gilbert
2001-02	32	35	12	3	79	4th/Northwest	—	—		Greg Gilbert
2002-03	29	36	13	4	75	5th/Northwest	—	—		G. Gilbert, Al MacNeil, Daryl Sutter

*Atlanta Flames.

FIRST-ROUND ENTRY DRAFT CHOICES

Year	Player, Overall, Last amateur team (league)
1972	Jacques Richard, 2, Quebec (QMJHL)
1973	Tom Lysiak, 2, Medicine Hat (WCHL)
	Vic Mercredi, 16, New Westminster (WCHL)
1974	No first-round selection
1975	Richcard Mulhern, 8, Sherbrooke (QMJHL)
1976	Dave Shand, 8, Peterborough (OHL)
	Harold Phillipoff, 10, New Westminster (WCHL)
1977	No first-round selection
1978	Brad Marsh, 11, London (OHL)
1979	Paul Reinhart, 12, Kitchener (OHL)
1980	Denis Cyr, 13, Montreal (OHL)
1981	Al MacInnis, 15, Kitchener (OHL)
1982	No first-round selection
1983	Dan Quinn, 13, Belleville (OHL)
1984	Gary Roberts, 12, Ottawa (OHL)
1985	Chris Biotti, 17, Belmont Hill H.S. (Mass.)
1986	George Pelawa, 16, Bemidji H.S. (Minn.)
1987	Bryan Deasley, 19, University of Michigan

Year	Player, Overall, Last amateur team (league)
1988	Jason Muzzatti, 21, Michigan State University
1989	No first-round selection
1990	Trevor Kidd, 11, Brandon (WHL)
1991	Niklas Sundblad, 19, AIK, Sweden
1992	Cory Stillman, 6, Windsor (OHL)
1993	Jesper Mattsson, 18, Malmo, Sweden
1994	Chris Dingman, 19, Brandon (WHL)
1995	Denis Gauthier, 20, Drummondville (QMJHL)
1996	Derek Morris, 13, Regina (WHL)
1997	Daniel Tkaczuk, 6, Barrie (OHL)
1998	Rico Fata, 6, London (OHL)
1999	Oleg Saprykin, 11, Seattle (WHL)
2000	Brent Krahn, 9, Calgary (WHL)
2001	Chuck Kobasew, 14, Boston College
2002	Eric Nystrom, 10, University of Michigan (CCHA)
2003	Dion Phaneuf, 9, Red Deer (WHL)

SINGLE-SEASON INDIVIDUAL RECORDS

FORWARDS/DEFENSEMEN

Most goals
66—Lanny McDonald, 1982-83

Most assists
82—Kent Nilsson, 1980-81

Most points
131—Kent Nilsson, 1980-81

Most penalty minutes
375—Tim Hunter, 1988-89

Most power play goals
31—Joe Nieuwendyk, 1987-88

Most shorthanded goals
9—Kent Nilsson, 1984-85

Most games with three or more goals
5—Hakan Loob, 1987-88
    Theo Fleury, 1990-91

Most shots
353—Theo Fleury, 1995-96

GOALTENDERS

Most games
69—Roman Turek, 2001-02

Most minutes
4,081—Roman Turek, 2001-02

Most shots against
1,853—Mike Vernon, 1991-92

Most goals allowed
229—Rejean Lemelin, 1985-86

Lowest goals-against average
2.32—Fred Brathwaite, 2000-01

Most shutouts
5—Dan Bouchard, 1973-74
    Phil Myre, 1974-75
    Fred Brathwaite, 1999-2000
    Fred Brathwaite, 2000-01
    Roman Turek, 2001-02

Most wins
39—Mike Vernon, 1987-88

Most losses
30—Mike Vernon, 1991-92

Most ties
19—Dan Bouchard, 1977-78

FRANCHISE LEADERS

Players in boldface played for club in 2002-03

FORWARDS/DEFENSEMEN

Games
Al MacInnis	803
Theo Fleury	791
Joel Otto	730
Jim Peplinski	711
Gary Suter	617

Goals
Theo Fleury	364
Joe Nieuwendyk	314
Gary Roberts	257
Kent Nilsson	229
Lanny McDonald	215

Assists
Al MacInnis	609
Theo Fleury	466
Gary Suter	437
Guy Chouinard	336
Paul Reinhart	336

Points
Theo Fleury	830
Al MacInnis	822
Joe Nieuwendyk	616
Gary Suter	565
Kent Nilsson	562

Penalty minutes
Tim Hunter	2405
Gary Roberts	1736
Joel Otto	1642
Jim Peplinski	1467
Ronnie Stern	1288

GOALTENDERS

Games
Mike Vernon	526
Dan Bouchard	398
Reggie Lemelin	324
Phil Myre	211
Trevor Kidd	178

Shutouts
Dan Bouchard	20
Mike Vernon	13
Fred Brathwaite	11
Phil Myre	11
Trevor Kidd	10

Goals-against average
(2400 minutes minimum)
Fred Brathwaite	2.54
Roman Turek	**2.55**
Rick Tabaracci	2.81
Trevor Kidd	2.83
Dwayne Roloson	2.95

Wins
Mike Vernon	262
Dan Bouchard	168
Reggie Lemelin	144
Phil Myre	76
Trevor Kidd	72

NHL HISTORY — Team by team

CAROLINA HURRICANES
YEAR-BY-YEAR RECORDS

Season	W	L	T	OTL	Pts.	Finish	W	L	Highest round	Coach
				REGULAR SEASON			PLAYOFFS			
1972-73*	46	30	2	—	94	1st	12	3	Avco World Cup champ	Jack Kelley
1973-74*	43	31	4	—	90	1st	3	4	League quarterfinals	Ron Ryan
1974-75*	43	30	5	—	91	1st	2	4	League quarterfinals	Ron Ryan, Jack Kelley
1975-76*	33	40	7	—	73	3rd	10	7	League semifinals	Jack Kelley, Don Blackburn,
										Harry Neale
1976-77*	35	40	6	—	76	4th	1	4	League quarterfinals	Harry Neale
1977-78*	44	31	5	—	93	2nd	8	6	Avco World Cup finals	Harry Neale
1978-79*	37	34	9	—	83	4th	5	5	League semifinals	Bill Dineen, Don Blackburn
1979-80†	27	34	19	—	73	4th/Norris	0	3	Preliminaries	Don Blackburn
1980-81†	21	41	18	—	60	4th/Norris	—	—		Don Blackburn, Larry Pleau
1981-82†	21	41	18	—	60	5th/Adams	—	—		Larry Pleau
1982-83†	19	54	7	—	45	5th/Adams	—	—		Larry Kish, Larry Pleau, John Cunniff
1983-84†	28	42	10	—	66	5th/Adams	—	—		Jack Evans
1984-85†	30	41	9	—	69	5th/Adams	—	—		Jack Evans
1985-86†	40	36	4	—	84	4th/Adams	6	4	Division finals	Jack Evans
1986-87†	43	30	7	—	93	1st/Adams	2	4	Division semifinals	Jack Evans
1987-88†	35	38	7	—	77	4th/Adams	2	4	Division semifinals	Jack Evans, Larry Pleau
1988-89†	37	38	5	—	79	4th/Adams	0	4	Division semifinals	Larry Pleau
1989-90†	38	33	9	—	85	4th/Adams	3	4	Division semifinals	Rick Ley
1990-91†	31	38	11	—	73	4th/Adams	2	4	Division semifinals	Rick Ley
1991-92†	26	41	13	—	65	4th/Adams	3	4	Division semifinals	Jim Roberts
1992-93†	26	52	6	—	58	5th/Adams	—	—		Paul Holmgren
1993-94†	27	48	9	—	63	6th/Northeast	—	—		Paul Holmgren, Pierre McGuire
1994-95†	19	24	5	—	43	5th/Northeast	—	—		Paul Holmgren
1995-96†	34	39	9	—	77	4th/Northeast	—	—		Paul Holmgren, Paul Maurice
1996-97†	32	39	11	—	75	5th/Northeast	—	—		Paul Maurice
1997-98	33	41	8	—	74	6th/Northeast	—	—		Paul Maurice
1998-99	34	30	18	—	86	1st/Southeast	2	4	Conference quarterfinals	Paul Maurice
1999-00	37	35	10	0	84	3rd/Southeast	—	—		Paul Maurice
2000-01	38	32	9	3	88	2nd/Southeast	2	4	Conference quarterfinals	Paul Maurice
2001-02	35	26	16	5	91	1st/Southeast	13	10	Stanley Cup finals	Paul Maurice
2002-03	22	43	11	6	61	5th/Southeast	—	—		Paul Maurice

*New England Whalers, members of World Hockey Association.
†Hartford Whalers.

FIRST-ROUND ENTRY DRAFT CHOICES

Year   Player, Overall, Last amateur team (league)
1979—Ray Allison, 18, Brandon (WHL)
1980—Fred Arthur, 8, Cornwall (QMJHL)
1981—Ron Francis, 4, Sault Ste. Marie (OHL)
1982—Paul Lawless, 14, Windsor (OHL)
1983—Sylvain Turgeon, 2, Hull (QMJHL)
        David A. Jensen, 20, Lawrence Academy (Mass.)
1984—Sylvain Cote, 11, Quebec (QMJHL)
1985—Dana Murzyn, 5, Calgary (WHL)
1986—Scott Young, 11, Boston University
1987—Jody Hull, 18, Peterborough (OHL)
1988—Chris Govedaris, 11, Toronto (OHL)
1989—Robert Holik, 10, Jihlava, Czechoslovakia
1990—Mark Greig, 15, Lethbridge (WHL)
1991—Patrick Poulin, 9, St. Hyacinthe (QMJHL)
1992—Robert Petrovicky, 9, Dukla Trencin, Czech Republic

Year   Player, Overall, Last amateur team (league)
1993—Chris Pronger, 2, Peterborough (OHL)
1994—Jeff O'Neill, 5, Guelph (OHL)
1995—Jean-Sebastien Giguere, 13, Halifax (QMJHL)
1996—No first-round selection
1997—Nikos Tselios, 22, Belleville (OHL)
1998—Jeff Heerema, 11, Sarnia (OHL)
1999—David Tanabe, 16, Wisconsin (WCHA)
2000—No first-round selection
2001—Igor Knyazev, 15, Spartak Jr., Russia
2002—Cam Ward, 25, Red Deer (WHL)
2003—Eric Staal, 2, Peterborough (OHL)
NOTE: Hartford chose Jordy Douglas, John Garrett and Mark Howe as priority selections before the 1979 expansion draft.

SINGLE-SEASON INDIVIDUAL RECORDS

FORWARDS/DEFENSEMEN

Most goals
56—Blaine Stoughton, 1979-80

Most assists
69—Ron Francis, 1989-90

Most points
105—Mike Rogers, 1979-80
        Mike Rogers, 1980-81

Most penalty minutes
358—Torrie Robertson, 1985-86

Most power play goals
21—Geoff Sanderson, 1992-93

Most shorthanded goals
4—Mike Rogers, 1980-81
      Kevin Dineen, 1984-85

Most games with three or more goals
3—Mike Rogers, 1980-81
      Blaine Stoughton, 1981-82

Most shots
316—Jeff O'Neill, 2002-03

GOALTENDERS

Most games
77—Arturs Irbe, 2000-01

Most minutes
4,406—Arturs Irbe, 2000-01

Most shots against
1,947—Arturs Irbe, 2000-01

Most goals allowed
282—Greg Millen, 1982-83

Lowest goals-against average
2.17—Trevor Kidd, 1997-98

Most shutouts
6—Arturs Irbe, 1998-99
　Arturs Irbe, 2000-01

Most wins
37—Arturs Irbe, 2000-01

Most losses
38—Greg Millen, 1982-83

Most ties
12—John Garrett, 1980-81
　Greg Millen, 1982-83
　Arturs Irbe, 1998-99

FRANCHISE LEADERS

Players in boldface played for club in 2002-03

FORWARDS/DEFENSEMEN

Games

Ron Francis	1118
Kevin Dineen	708
Glen Wesley	**629**
Adam Burt	626
Jeff O'Neill	**606**

Goals

Ron Francis	372
Kevin Dineen	250
Blaine Stoughton	219
Geoff Sanderson	196
Pat Verbeek	192

Assists

Ron Francis	773
Kevin Dineen	294
Andrew Cassels	253
Pat Verbeek	211
Sami Kapanen	**203**

Points

Ron Francis	1145
Kevin Dineen	544
Pat Verbeek	403
Jeff O'Neill	**382**
Blaine Stoughton	377

Penalty Minutes

Kevin Dineen	1439
Torrie Robertson	1368
Pat Verbeek	1144
Ulf Samuelsson	1110
Adam Burt	875

GOALTENDERS

Games

Arturs Irbe	**299**
Sean Burke	281
Mike Liut	252
Greg Millen	219
Peter Sidorkiewicz	178

Shutouts

Arturs Irbe	**20**
Mike Liut	13
Sean Burke	11
Peter Sidorkiewicz	8
Trevor Kidd	5
Kevin Weekes	**5**

Goals-against average
(2400 minutes minimum)

Trevor Kidd	2.35
Arturs Irbe	**2.49**
Kevin Weekes	**2.51**
Sean Burke	3.09
Jason Muzzatti	3.23

Wins

Arturs Irbe	**125**
Mike Liut	115
Sean Burke	107
Peter Sidorkiewicz	71
Greg Millen	62

CHICAGO BLACKHAWKS
YEAR-BY-YEAR RECORDS

		REGULAR SEASON					PLAYOFFS		
Season	W	L	T	OTL	Pts.	Finish	W	L	Highest round	Coach
1926-27	19	22	3	—	41	3rd/American	*0	1	Quarterfinals	Pete Muldoon
1927-28	7	34	3	—	17	5th/American	—	—		Barney Stanley, Hugh Lehman
1928-29	7	29	8	—	22	5th/American	—	—		Herb Gardiner
1929-30	21	18	5	—	47	2nd/American	*0	1	Quarterfinals	Tom Schaughnessy, Bill Tobin
1930-31	24	17	3	—	51	2nd/American	*5	3	Stanley Cup finals	Dick Irvin
1931-32	18	19	11	—	47	2nd/American	1	1	Quarterfinals	Dick Irvin, Bill Tobin
1932-33	16	20	12	—	44	4th/American	—	—		Godfrey Matheson, Emil Iverson
1933-34	20	17	11	—	51	2nd/American	*6	1	Stanley Cup champ	Tom Gorman
1934-35	26	17	5	—	57	2nd/American	*0	1	Quarterfinals	Clem Loughlin
1935-36	21	19	8	—	50	3rd/American	1	1	Quarterfinals	Clem Loughlin
1936-37	14	27	7	—	35	4th/American	—	—		Clem Loughlin
1937-38	14	25	9	—	37	3rd/American	7	3	Stanley Cup champ	Bill Stewart
1938-39	12	28	8	—	32	7th	—	—		Bill Stewart, Paul Thompson
1939-40	23	19	6	—	52	4th	0	2	Quarterfinals	Paul Thompson
1940-41	16	25	7	—	39	5th	2	3	Semifinals	Paul Thompson
1941-42	22	23	3	—	47	4th	1	2	Quarterfinals	Paul Thompson
1942-43	17	18	15	—	49	5th	—	—		Paul Thompson
1943-44	22	23	5	—	49	4th	4	5	Stanley Cup finals	Paul Thompson
1944-45	13	30	7	—	33	5th	—	—		Paul Thompson, John Gottselig
1945-46	23	20	7	—	53	3rd	0	4	League semifinals	John Gottselig
1946-47	19	37	4	—	42	6th	—	—		John Gottselig
1947-48	20	34	6	—	46	6th	—	—		John Gottselig, Charlie Conacher
1948-49	21	31	8	—	50	5th	—	—		Charlie Conacher
1949-50	22	38	10	—	54	6th	—	—		Charlie Conacher
1950-51	13	47	10	—	36	6th	—	—		Ebbie Goodfellow
1951-52	17	44	9	—	43	6th	—	—		Ebbie Goodfellow
1952-53	27	28	15	—	69	4th	3	4	League semifinals	Sid Abel
1953-54	12	51	7	—	31	6th	—	—		Sid Abel
1954-55	13	40	17	—	43	6th	—	—		Frank Eddolls
1955-56	19	39	12	—	50	6th	—	—		Dick Irvin
1956-57	16	39	15	—	47	6th	—	—		Tommy Ivan

Season	W	L	T	OTL	Pts.	Finish	W	L	Highest round	Coach
				REGULAR SEASON			PLAYOFFS			
1957-58	24	39	7	—	55	5th	—	—		Tommy Ivan, Rudy Pilous
1958-59	28	29	13	—	69	3rd	2	4	League semifinals	Rudy Pilous
1959-60	28	29	13	—	69	3rd	0	4	League semifinals	Rudy Pilous
1960-61	29	24	17	—	75	3rd	8	4	Stanley Cup champ	Rudy Pilous
1961-62	31	26	13	—	75	3rd	6	6	Stanley Cup finals	Rudy Pilous
1962-63	32	21	17	—	81	2nd	2	4	League semifinals	Rudy Pilous
1963-64	36	22	12	—	84	2nd	3	4	League semifinals	Billy Reay
1964-65	34	28	8	—	76	3rd	7	7	Stanley Cup finals	Billy Reay
1965-66	37	25	8	—	82	2nd	2	4	League semifinals	Billy Reay
1966-67	41	17	12	—	94	1st	2	4	League semifinals	Billy Reay
1967-68	32	26	16	—	80	4th/East	5	6	Division finals	Billy Reay
1968-69	34	33	9	—	77	6th/East	—	—		Billy Reay
1969-70	45	22	9	—	99	1st/East	4	4	Division finals	Billy Reay
1970-71	49	20	9	—	107	1st/West	11	7	Stanley Cup finals	Billy Reay
1971-72	46	17	15	—	107	1st/West	4	4	Division finals	Billy Reay
1972-73	42	27	9	—	93	1st/West	10	6	Stanley Cup finals	Billy Reay
1973-74	41	14	23	—	105	2nd/West	6	5	Division finals	Billy Reay
1974-75	37	35	8	—	82	3rd/Smythe	3	5	Quarterfinals	Billy Reay
1975-76	32	30	18	—	82	1st/Smythe	0	4	Quarterfinals	Billy Reay
1976-77	26	43	11	—	63	3rd/Smythe	0	2	Preliminaries	Billy Reay, Bill White
1977-78	32	29	19	—	83	1st/Smythe	0	4	Quarterfinals	Bob Pulford
1978-79	29	36	15	—	73	1st/Smythe	0	4	Quarterfinals	Bob Pulford
1979-80	34	27	19	—	87	1st/Smythe	3	4	Quarterfinals	Eddie Johnston
1980-81	31	33	16	—	78	2nd/Smythe	0	3	Preliminaries	Keith Magnuson
1981-82	30	38	12	—	72	4th/Norris	8	7	Conference finals	Keith Magnuson, Bob Pulford
1982-83	47	23	10	—	104	1st/Norris	7	6	Conference finals	Orval Tessier
1983-84	30	42	8	—	68	4th/Norris	2	3	Division semifinals	Orval Tessier
1984-85	38	35	7	—	83	2nd/Norris	9	6	Conference finals	Orval Tessier, Bob Pulford
1985-86	39	33	8	—	86	1st/Norris	0	3	Division semifinals	Bob Pulford
1986-87	29	37	14	—	72	3rd/Norris	0	4	Division semifinals	Bob Pulford
1987-88	30	41	9	—	69	3rd/Norris	1	4	Division semifinals	Bob Murdoch
1988-89	27	41	12	—	66	4th/Norris	9	7	Conference finals	Mike Keenan
1989-90	41	33	6	—	88	1st/Norris	10	10	Conference finals	Mike Keenan
1990-91	49	23	8	—	106	1st/Norris	2	4	Division semifinals	Mike Keenan
1991-92	36	29	15	—	87	2nd/Norris	12	6	Stanley Cup finals	Mike Keenan
1992-93	47	25	12	—	106	1st/Norris	0	4	Division semifinals	Darryl Sutter
1993-94	39	36	9	—	87	5th/Central	2	4	Conference quarterfinals	Darryl Sutter
1994-95	24	19	5	—	53	3rd/Central	9	7	Conference finals	Darryl Sutter
1995-96	40	28	14	—	94	2nd/Central	6	4	Conference semifinals	Craig Hartsburg
1996-97	34	35	13	—	81	5th/Central	2	4	Conference quarterfinals	Craig Hartsburg
1997-98	30	39	13	—	73	5th/Central	—	—		Craig Hartsburg
1998-99	29	41	12	—	70	3rd/Central	—	—		Dirk Graham, Lorne Molleken
1999-00	33	37	10	2	78	3rd/Central	—	—		Lorne Molleken, Bob Pulford
2000-01	29	40	8	5	71	4th/Central	—	—		Alpo Suhonen, Denis Savard, Al MacAdam
2001-02	41	27	13	1	96	3rd/Central	1	4	Conference quarterfinals	Brian Sutter
2002-03	30	33	13	6	79	3rd/Central	—	—		Brian Sutter

*Won-lost record does not indicate tie(s) resulting from two-game, total-goals series that year (two-game, total-goals series were played from 1917-18 through 1935-36).

FIRST-ROUND ENTRY DRAFT CHOICES

Year Player, Overall, Last amateur team (league)

1969—J.P. Bordeleau, 13, Montreal (OHL)
1970—Dan Maloney, 14, London (OHL)
1971—Dan Spring, 12, Edmonton (WCHL)
1972—Phil Russell, 13, Edmonton (WCHL)
1973—Darcy Rota, 13, Edmonton (WCHL)
1974—Grant Mulvey, 16, Calgary (WCHL)
1975—Greg Vaydik, 7, Medicine Hat (WCHL)
1976—Real Cloutier, 9, Quebec (WHA)
1977—Doug Wilson, 6, Ottawa (OHL)
1978—Tim Higgins, 10, Ottawa (OHL)
1979—Keith Brown, 7, Portland (WHL)
1980—Denis Savard, 3, Montreal (QMJHL)
          Jerome Dupont, 15, Toronto (OHL)
1981—Tony Tanti, 12, Oshawa (OHL)
1982—Ken Yaremchuk, 7, Portland (WHL)
1983—Bruce Cassidy, 18, Ottawa (OHL)
1984—Ed Olczyk, 3, U.S. Olympic Team

Year Player, Overall, Last amateur team (league)

1985—Dave Manson, 11, Prince Albert (WHL)
1986—Everett Sanipass, 14, Verdun (QMJHL)
1987—Jimmy Waite, 8, Chicoutimi (QMJHL)
1988—Jeremy Roenick, 8, Thayer Academy (Mass.)
1989—Adam Bennett, 6, Sudbury (OHL)
1990—Karl Dykhuis, 16, Hull (QMJHL)
1991—Dean McAmmond, 22, Prince Albert (WHL)
1992—Sergei Krivokrasov, 12, Central Red Army, CIS
1993—Eric Lecompte, 24, Hull (QMJHL)
1994—Ethan Moreau, 14, Niagara Falls (OHL)
1995—Dimitri Nabokov, 19, Krylja Sovetov, CIS
1996—No first-round selection
1997—Daniel Cleary, 13, Belleville (OHL)
          Ty Jones, 16, Spokane (WHL)
1998—Mark Bell, 8, Ottawa (OHL)
1999—Steve McCarthy, 23, Kootenay (WHL)

Year	Player, Overall, Last amateur team (league)
2000—	Mikhail Yakubov, 10, Togliatta, Russia
	Pavel Vorobiev, 11, Yaroslavl, Russia
2001—	Tuomo Ruutu, 9, Jokerit, Finland
	Adam Munro, 29, Erie (OHL)

Year	Player, Overall, Last amateur team (league)
2002—	Anton Babchuk, 21, Elektrostal Jr., Russia
2003—	Brent Seabrook, 14, Lethbridge (WHL)

SINGLE-SEASON INDIVIDUAL RECORDS

FORWARDS/DEFENSEMEN

Most goals
58—Bobby Hull, 1968-69

Most assists
87—Denis Savard, 1981-82
Denis Savard, 1987-88

Most points
131—Denis Savard, 1987-88

Most penalty minutes
408—Mike Peluso, 1991-92

Most power play goals
24—Jeremy Roenick, 1993-94

Most shorthanded goals
10—Dirk Graham, 1988-89

Most games with three or more goals
4—Bobby Hull, 1959-60
Bobby Hull, 1965-66

Most shots
414—Bobby Hull, 1968-69

GOALTENDERS

Most games
74—Ed Belfour, 1990-91

Most minutes
4,219—Tony Esposito, 1974-75

Most goals allowed
246—Harry Lumley, 1950-51
Tony Esposito, 1980-81

Lowest goals-against average
1.73—Charles Gardiner, 1933-34

Most shutouts
15—Tony Esposito, 1969-70

Most wins
43—Ed Belfour, 1990-91

Most losses
47—Al Rollins, 1953-54

Most ties
21—Tony Esposito, 1973-74

FRANCHISE LEADERS

Players in boldface played for club in 2002-03

FORWARDS/DEFENSEMEN

Games
Stan Mikita 1394
Bobby Hull....................................1036
Eric Nesterenko 1013
Bob Murray 1008
Doug Wilson...................................938

Goals
Bobby Hull.......................................604
Stan Mikita 541
Steve Larmer 406
Denis Savard 377
Dennis Hull......................................298

Assists
Stan Mikita 926
Denis Savard 719
Doug Wilson 554
Bobby Hull.......................................549
Steve Larmer..................................517

Points
Stan Mikita 1467
Bobby Hull.....................................1153
Denis Savard 1096
Steve Larmer 923
Doug Wilson.....................................779

Penalty minutes
Chris Chelios................................1495
Keith Magnuson 1442
Al Secord 1426
Dave Manson 1322
Phil Russell.....................................1288

GOALTENDERS

Games
Tony Esposito..................................873
Glenn Hall..618
Ed Belfour 415
Mike Karakas 331
Charlie Gardiner 316

Shutouts
Tony Esposito....................................74
Glenn Hall..51
Chuck Gardiner 42
Ed Belfour 30
Mike Karakas 28

Goals-against average
(2400 minutes minimum)
Lorne Chabot 1.80
Charlie Gardiner 2.02
Paul Goodman...............................2.17
Jeff Hackett...................................2.45
Glenn Hall......................................2.60

Wins
Tony Esposito..................................418
Glenn Hall..275
Ed Belfour 201
Jocelyn Thibault.........................132
Murray Bannerman..........................116

CLEVELAND BARONS (DEFUNCT)
YEAR-BY-YEAR RECORDS

		REGULAR SEASON				PLAYOFFS			
Season	W	L	T	Pts.	Finish	W	L	Highest round	Coach
1967-68*	15	42	17	47	6th/West	—	—		Bert Olmstead, Gordie Fashoway
1968-69*	29	36	11	69	2nd/West	3	4	Division semifinals	Fred Glover
1969-70*	22	40	14	58	4th/West	0	4	Division semifinals	Fred Glover
1970-71†	20	53	5	45	7th/West	—	—		Fred Glover
1971-72†	21	39	18	60	6th/West	—	—		Fred Glover, Vic Stasiuk
1972-73†	16	46	16	48	8th/West	—	—		Garry Young, Fred Glover
1973-74†	13	55	10	36	8th/West	—	—		Fred Glover, Marsh Johnston
1974-75†	19	48	13	51	4th/Adams	—	—		Marsh Johnston
1975-76†	27	42	11	65	4th/Adams	—	—		Jack Evans
1976-77	25	42	13	63	4th/Adams	—	—		Jack Evans
1977-78	22	45	13	57	4th/Adams	—	—		Jack Evans

*Oakland Seals.
†California Golden Seals.
  Barons disbanded after 1977-78 season. Owners merged with Minnesota franchise and a number of Cleveland players were awarded to North Stars; remaining players were dispersed to other clubs in draft.

NHL HISTORY *Team by team*

YEAR-BY-YEAR RECORDS

Season		REGULAR SEASON					PLAYOFFS			
	W	L	T	OTL	Pts.	Finish	W	L	Highest round	Coach
1972-73*	33	40	5	—	71	5th	—	—		Maurice Richard, Maurice Filion
1973-74*	38	36	4	—	80	5th	—	—		Jacques Plante
1974-75*	46	32	0	—	92	1st	8	7	Avco World Cup finals	Jean-Guy Gendron
1975-76*	50	27	4	—	104	2nd	1	4	League quarterfinals	Jean-Guy Gendron
1976-77*	47	31	3	—	97	1st	12	5	Avco World Cup champ	Marc Boileau
1977-78*	40	37	3	—	83	4th	5	6	League semifinals	Marc Boileau
1978-79*	41	34	5	—	87	2nd	0	4	League semifinals	Jacques Demers
1979-80†	25	44	11	—	61	5th/Adams	—	—		Jacques Demers
1980-81†	30	32	18	—	78	4th/Adams	2	3	Preliminaries	Maurice Richard, Michel Bergeron
1981-82†	33	31	16	—	82	4th/Adams	7	9	Conference finals	Michel Bergeron
1982-83†	34	34	12	—	80	4th/Adams	1	3	Division semifinals	Michel Bergeron
1983-84†	42	28	10	—	94	3rd/Adams	5	4	Division finals	Michel Bergeron
1984-85†	41	30	9	—	91	2nd/Adams	9	9	Conference finals	Michel Bergeron
1985-86†	43	31	6	—	92	1st/Adams	0	3	Division semifinals	Michel Bergeron
1986-87†	31	39	10	—	72	4th/Adams	7	6	Division finals	Michel Bergeron
1987-88†	32	43	5	—	69	5th/Adams	—	—		Andre Savard, Ron Lapointe
1988-89†	27	46	7	—	61	5th/Adams	—	—		Ron Lapointe, Jean Perron
1989-90†	12	61	7	—	31	5th/Adams	—	—		Michel Bergeron
1990-91†	16	50	14	—	46	5th/Adams	—	—		Dave Chambers
1991-92†	20	48	12	—	52	5th/Adams	—	—		Dave Chambers, Pierre Page
1992-93†	47	27	10	—	104	2nd/Adams	2	4	Division semifinals	Pierre Page
1993-94†	34	42	8	—	76	5th/Northeast	—	—		Pierre Page
1994-95†	30	13	5	—	65	1st/Northeast	2	4	Conference quarterfinals	Marc Crawford
1995-96	47	25	10	—	104	1st/Pacific	16	6	Stanley Cup champ	Marc Crawford
1996-97	49	24	9	—	107	1st/Pacific	10	7	Conference finals	Marc Crawford
1997-98	39	26	17	—	95	1st/Pacific	3	4	Conference quarterfinals	Marc Crawford
1998-99	44	28	10	—	98	1st/Northwest	11	8	Conference finals	Bob Hartley
1999-00	42	28	11	1	96	1st/Northwest	11	6	Conference finals	Bob Hartley
2000-01	52	16	10	4	118	1st/Northwest	16	7	Stanley Cup champ	Bob Hartley
2001-02	45	28	8	1	99	1st/Northwest	11	10	Conference finals	Bob Hartley
2002-03	42	19	13	8	105	1st/Northwest	3	4	Conference quarterfinals	Bob Hartley, Tony Granato

*Quebec Nordiques, members of World Hockey Association.
†Quebec Nordiques.

FIRST-ROUND ENTRY DRAFT CHOICES

Year   Player, Overall, Last amateur team (league)
1979—Michel Goulet, 20, Birmingham (WHA)
1980—No first-round selection
1981—Randy Moller, 11, Lethbridge (WHL)
1982—David Shaw, 13, Kitchener (OHL)
1983—No first-round selection
1984—Trevor Steinburg, 15, Guelph (OHL)
1985—Dave Latta, 15, Kitchener (OHL)
1986—Ken McRae, 18, Sudbury (OHL)
1987—Bryan Fogarty, 9, Kingston (OHL)
         Joe Sakic, 15, Swift Current (WHL)
1988—Curtis Leschyshyn, 3, Saskatoon (WHL)
         Daniel Dore, 5, Drummondville (QMJHL)
1989—Mats Sundin, 1, Nacka (Sweden)*
1990—Owen Nolan, 1, Cornwall (OHL)*
1991—Eric Lindros, 1, Oshawa (OHL)*
1992—Todd Warriner, 4, Windsor (OHL)
1993—Jocelyn Thibault, 10, Sherbrooke (QMJHL)
         Adam Deadmarsh, 14, Portland (WHL)

Year   Player, Overall, Last amateur team (league)
1994—Wade Belak, 12, Saskatoon (WHL)
         Jeffrey Kealty, 22, Catholic Memorial H.S.
1995—Marc Denis, 25, Chicoutimi (QMJHL)
1996—Peter Ratchuk, 25, Shattuck-St. Mary's H.S. (Min.)
1997—Kevin Grimes, 26, Kingston (OHL)
1998—Alex Tanguay, 12, Halifax (QMJHL)
         Martin Skoula, 17, Barrie (OHL)
         Robyn Regehr, 19, Kamloops (WHL)
         Scott Parker, 20, Kelowna (WHL)
1999—Mihail Kuleshov, 25, Cherepovec, Russia
2000—Vaclav Nedorost, 14, Budejovice, Czech Republic
2001—No first-round selection
2002—Jonas Johansson, 28, HV 71, Sweden
2003—No first-round selection.
*Designates first player chosen in draft.
NOTE: Quebec chose Paul Baxter, Richard Brodeur and Garry Larivierre as priority selections before the 1979 expansion draft.

SINGLE-SEASON INDIVIDUAL RECORDS

FORWARDS/DEFENSEMEN

Most goals
57—Michel Goulet, 1982-83

Most assists
93—Peter Stastny, 1981-82

Most points
139—Peter Stastny, 1981-82

Most penalty minutes
301—Gord Donnelly, 1987-88

Most power play goals
29—Michel Goulet, 1987-88

Most shorthanded goals
6—Michel Goulet, 1981-82
    Scott Young, 1992-93
    Joe Sakic, 1995-96

Most games with three or more goals
4—Miroslav Frycer, 1981-82
    Peter Stastny, 1982-83

Most shots
332—Joe Sakic, 2000-01

GOALTENDERS

Most games
65—Patrick Roy, 1997-98

Most minutes
3,835—Patrick Roy, 1997-98

Most shots against
1,861—Patrick Roy, 1996-97

Most goals allowed
230—Dan Bouchard, 1981-82

Lowest goals-against average
1.94—Patrick Roy, 2001-02

Most shutouts
9—Patrick Roy, 2001-02

Most wins
40—Patrick Roy, 2000-01

Most losses
29—Ron Tugnutt, 1990-91

Most ties
13—Patrick Roy, 1997-98

FRANCHISE LEADERS

Players in boldface played for club in 2002-03

FORWARDS/DEFENSEMEN

Games

Joe Sakic	**1074**
Michel Goulet	813
Peter Stastny	737
Adam Foote	**726**
Alain Cote	696

Goals

Joe Sakic	**509**
Michel Goulet	456
Peter Stastny	380
Anton Stastny	252
Peter Forsberg	**198**

Assists

Joe Sakic	**806**
Peter Stastny	668
Michel Goulet	489
Peter Forsberg	**488**
Anton Stastny	384

Points

Joe Sakic	**1315**
Peter Stastny	1048
Michel Goulet	945
Peter Forsberg	**686**
Anton Stastny	636

Penalty minutes

Dale Hunter	1562
Steven Finn	1514
Paul Gillis	1351
Adam Foote	**1053**
Randy Moller	1002

GOALTENDERS

Games

Patrick Roy	**478**
Dan Bouchard	225
Mario Gosselin	192
Stephane Fiset	188
Ron Tugnutt	153

Shutouts

Patrick Roy	37
David Aebischer	**6**
Stephane Fiset	6
Mario Gosselin	6
Dan Bouchard	5
Clint Malarchuk	5

Goals-against average
(2400 minutes minimum)

David Aebischer	**2.19**
Patrick Roy	**2.27**
Craig Billington	2.61
Jocelyn Thibault	2.96
Stephane Fiset	3.32

Wins

Patrick Roy	**262**
Dan Bouchard	107
Stephane Fiset	84
Mario Gosselin	79
Clint Malarchuk	62

COLUMBUS BLUE JACKETS
YEAR-BY-YEAR RECORDS

		REGULAR SEASON					PLAYOFFS			
Season	W	L	T	OTL	Pts.	Finish	W	L	Highest round	Coach
2000-01	28	39	9	6	71	5th/Central	—	—		Dave King
2001-02	22	47	8	5	57	5th/Central	—	—		Dave King
2002-03	29	42	8	3	69	5th/Central	—	—		Dave King, Doug MacLean

FIRST-ROUND ENTRY DRAFT CHOICES

Year   Player, Overall, Last amateur team (league)
2000—Rostislav Klesla, 4, Brampton (OHL)
2001—Pascal LeClaire, 8, Halifax (QMJHL)
2002—Rick Nash, 1, London (OHL)*

Year   Player, Overall, Last amateur team (league)
2003—Nikolai Zherdev, 4, Russia
*Designates first player chosen in draft.

SINGLE-SEASON INDIVIDUAL RECORDS

FORWARDS/DEFENSEMEN

Most goals
34—Geoff Sanderson, 2002-03

Most assists
52—Ray Whitney, 2002-03

Most points
76—Ray Whitney, 2002-03

Most penalty minutes
249—Jody Shelley, 2001-02

Most power play goals
15—Geoff Sanderson, 2002-03

Most shorthanded goals
3—Mike Sillinger, 2002-03

Most games with three or more goals
1—Deron Quint, 2000-01
Geoff Sanderson, 2000-01
Tyler Wright, 2000-01
Espen Knutsen, 2001-02

Most shots
286—Geoff Sanderson, 2002-03

GOALTENDERS

Most games
77—Marc Denis, 2002-03

Most minutes
3,129—Ron Tugnutt, 2000-01

Most shots against
2,404—Marc Denis, 2002-03

Most goals allowed
232—Marc Denis, 2002-03

Lowest goals-against average
2.44—Ron Tugnutt, 2000-01

Most shutouts
5—Marc Denis, 2002-03

Most wins
27—Marc Denis, 2002-03

Most losses
41—Marc Denis, 2002-03

Most ties
8—Marc Denis, 2002-03

FRANCHISE LEADERS

Players in boldface played for club in 2002-03

FORWARDS/DEFENSEMEN

Games
David Vyborny 233
Tyler Wright 223
Geoff Sanderson.......................192
Jean-Luc Grand-Pierre 186
Espen Knutsen 174

Goals
Geoff Sanderson 75
Tyler Wright.................................48
David Vyborny 46
Ray Whitney 45
Mike Sillinger 38

Assists
Ray Whitney 95
Espen Knutsen............................77

Geoff Sanderson 64
David Vyborny 63
Andrew Cassels 48
Mike Sillinger 48

Points
Ray Whitney...............................140
Geoff Sanderson.......................139
David Vyborny 109
Espen Knutsen 104
Mike Sillinger 86
Tyler Wright................................86

Penalty minutes
Jody Shelley 465
Tyler Wright 353
Jean-Luc Grand-Pierre 227
Lyle Odelein..................................207
Kevin Dineen............................200

GOALTENDERS

Games
Marc Denis 151
Ron Tugnutt 97
Jean Labbe 14

Shutouts
Marc Denis 6
Ron Tugnutt 6

Goals-against average
(1200 minutes minimum)
Ron Tugnutt 2.62
Marc Denis 3.13

Wins
Marc Denis....................................42
Ron Tugnutt 34
Jean-Francois Labbe 3

DALLAS STARS
YEAR-BY-YEAR RECORDS

Season	W	L	T	OTL	Pts.	Finish	W	L	Highest round	Coach
1967-68*	27	32	15	—	69	4th/West	7	7	Division finals	Wren Blair
1968-69*	18	43	15	—	51	6th/West	—	—		Wren Blair, John Muckler
1969-70*	19	35	22	—	60	3rd/West	2	4	Division semifinals	Wren Blair, Charlie Burns
1970-71*	28	34	16	—	72	4th/West	6	6	Division finals	Jack Gordon
1971-72*	37	29	12	—	86	2nd/West	3	4	Division semifinals	Jack Gordon
1972-73*	37	30	11	—	85	3rd/West	2	4	Division semifinals	Jack Gordon
1973-74*	23	38	17	—	63	7th/West	—	—		Jack Gordon, Parker MacDonald
1974-75*	23	50	7	—	53	4th/Smythe	—	—		Jack Gordon, Charlie Burns
1975-76*	20	53	7	—	47	4th/Smythe	—	—		Ted Harris
1976-77*	23	39	18	—	64	2nd/Smythe	0	2	Preliminaries	Ted Harris
1977-78*	18	53	9	—	45	5th/Smythe	—	—		Ted Harris, Andre Beaulieu, Lou Nanne
1978-79*	28	40	12	—	68	4th/Adams	—	—		Harry Howell, Glen Sonmor
1979-80*	36	28	16	—	88	3rd/Adams	8	7	Semifinals	Glen Sonmor
1980-81*	35	28	17	—	87	3rd/Adams	12	7	Stanley Cup finals	Glen Sonmor
1981-82*	37	23	20	—	94	1st/Norris	1	3	Division semifinals	Glen Sonmor, Murray Oliver
1982-83*	40	24	16	—	96	2nd/Norris	4	5	Division finals	Glen Sonmor, Murray Oliver
1983-84*	39	31	10	—	88	1st/Norris	7	9	Conference finals	Bill Maloney
1984-85*	25	43	12	—	62	4th/Norris	5	4	Division finals	Bill Maloney, Glen Sonmor
1985-86*	38	33	9	—	85	2nd/Norris	2	3	Division semifinals	Lorne Henning
1986-87*	30	40	10	—	70	5th/Norris	—	—		Lorne Henning, Glen Sonmor
1987-88*	19	48	13	—	51	5th/Norris	—	—		Herb Brooks
1988-89*	27	37	16	—	70	3rd/Norris	1	4	Division semifinals	Pierre Page
1989-90*	36	40	4	—	76	4th/Norris	3	4	Division semifinals	Pierre Page
1990-91*	27	39	14	—	68	4th/Norris	14	9	Stanley Cup finals	Bob Gainey
1991-92*	32	42	6	—	70	4th/Norris	3	4	Division semifinals	Bob Gainey
1992-93*	36	38	10	—	82	5th/Norris	—	—		Bob Gainey
1993-94	42	29	13	—	97	3rd/Central	5	4	Conference semifinals	Bob Gainey
1994-95	17	23	8	—	42	5th/Central	1	4	Conference quarterfinals	Bob Gainey
1995-96	26	42	14	—	66	6th/Central	—	—		Bob Gainey, Ken Hitchcock
1996-97	48	26	8	—	104	1st/Central	3	4	Conference quarterfinals	Ken Hitchcock
1997-98	49	22	11	—	109	1st/Central	10	7	Conference finals	Ken Hitchcock
1998-99	51	19	12	—	114	1st/Pacific	16	7	Stanley Cup champ	Ken Hitchcock
1999-00	43	23	10	6	102	1st/Pacific	14	9	Stanley Cup finals	Ken Hitchcock
2000-01	48	24	8	2	106	1st/Pacific	4	6	Conference semifinals	Ken Hitchcock
2001-02	36	28	13	5	90	4th/Pacific	—	—		Ken Hitchcock, Rick Wilson
2002-03	46	17	15	4	111	1st/Pacific	6	6	Conference semifinals	Dave Tippett

*Minnesota North Stars.

NHL HISTORY *Team by team*

FIRST-ROUND ENTRY DRAFT CHOICES

Year Player, Overall, Last amateur team (league)
1969—Dick Redmond, 5, St. Catharines (OHL)
      Dennis O'Brien, 14, St. Catharines (OHL)
1970—No first-round selection
1971—No first-round selection
1972—Jerry Byers, 12, Kitchener (OHL)
1973—No first-round selection
1974—Doug Hicks, 6, Flin Flon (WCHL)
1975—Brian Maxwell, 4, Medicine Hat (WCHL)
1976—Glen Sharpley, 3, Hull (QMJHL)
1977—Brad Maxwell, 7, New Westminster (WCHL)
1978—Bobby Smith, 1, Ottawa (OHL)*
1979—Craig Hartsburg, 6, Birmingham (WHA)
      Tom McCarthy, 10, Oshawa (OHL)
1980—Brad Palmer, 16, Victoria (WHL)
1981—Ron Meighan, 13, Niagara Falls (OHL)
1982—Brian Bellows, 2, Kitchener (OHL)
1983—Brian Lawton, 1, Mount St. Charles H.S. (R.I.)*
1984—David Quinn, 13, Kent H.S. (Ct.)
1985—No first-round selection

Year Player, Overall, Last amateur team (league)
1986—Warren Babe, 12, Lethbridge (WHL)
1987—Dave Archibald, 6, Portland (WHL)
1988—Mike Modano, 1, Prince Albert (WHL)*
1989—Doug Zmolek, 7, John Marshall H.S. (Minn.)
1990—Derian Hatcher, 8, North Bay (OHL)
1991—Richard Matvichuk, 8, Saskatoon (WHL)
1992—No first-round selection
1993—Todd Harvey, 9, Detroit (OHL)
1994—Jason Botterill, 20, Michigan (CCHA)
1995—Jarome Iginla, 11, Kamloops (WHL)
1996—Richard Jackman, 5, Sault Ste. Marie (OHL)
1997—Brenden Morrow, 25, Portland (WHL)
1998—No first-round selection
1999—No first-round selection
2000—Steve Ott, 25, Windsor (OHL)
2001—Jason Bacashihua, 26, Chicago (NAHL)
2002—Martin Vagner, 26, Hull (QMJHL)
2003—No first-round selection
*Designates first player chosen in draft.

SINGLE-SEASON INDIVIDUAL RECORDS

FORWARDS/DEFENSEMEN

Most goals
55—Dino Ciccarelli, 1981-82
    Brian Bellows, 1989-90

Most assists
76—Neal Broten, 1985-86

Most points
114—Bobby Smith, 1981-82

Most penalty minutes
382—Basil McRae, 1987-88

Most power play goals
22—Dino Ciccarelli, 1986-87

Most shorthanded goals
6—Bill Collins, 1969-70

Most games with three or more goals
3—Bill Goldsworthy, 1973-74
   Dino Ciccarelli, 1981-82
   Dino Ciccarelli, 1983-84
   Tom McCarthy, 1984-85
   Scott Bjugstad, 1985-86
   Dino Ciccarelli, 1985-86
   Mike Modano, 1998-99

Most shots
321—Bill Goldsworthy, 1973-74

GOALTENDERS

Most games
64—Cesare Maniago, 1968-69

Most minutes
3,687—Ed Belfour, 2000-01

Most shots against
1,604—Andy Moog, 1993-94

Most goals allowed
216—Pete LoPresti, 1977-78

Lowest goals-against average
1.88—Ed Belfour, 1997-98

Most shutouts
9—Ed Belfour, 1997-98

Most wins
37—Ed Belfour, 1997-98

Most losses
35—Pete LoPresti, 1977-78

Most ties
16—Cesare Maniago, 1969-70

FRANCHISE LEADERS

Players in boldface played for club in 2002-03

FORWARDS/DEFENSEMEN

Games
Mike Modano 1025
Neal Broten 992
Derian Hatcher 827
Curt Giles 760
Brian Bellows 753

Goals
Mike Modano 444
Brian Bellows 342
Dino Ciccarelli 332
Neal Broten 274
Bill Goldsworthy 267

Assists
Mike Modano 618
Neal Broten 593
Brian Bellows 380
Bobby Smith 369
Dino Ciccarelli 319

Points
Mike Modano 1062
Neal Broten 867
Brian Bellows 722
Dino Ciccarelli 651
Bobby Smith 554

Penalty minutes
Shane Churla 1883
Basil McRae 1567
Derian Hatcher 1380
Willi Plett 1137
Brad Maxwell 1031

GOALTENDERS

Games
Cesare Maniago 420
Gilles Meloche 327
Jon Casey 325
Don Beaupre 316
Ed Belfour 307

Shutouts
Ed Belfour 27
Cesare Maniago 26
Jon Casey 12
Marty Turco 12
Gilles Meloche 9

Goals-against average
(2400 minutes minimum)
Marty Turco 1.85
Roman Turek 2.14
Ed Belfour 2.19
Gump Worsley 2.62
Andy Moog 2.75

Wins
Ed Belfour 160
Cesare Maniago 144
Gilles Meloche 141
Jon Casey 128
Don Beaupre 126

Season	W	L	T	OTL	Pts.	Finish	W	L	Highest round	Coach
			REGULAR SEASON				PLAYOFFS			
1926-27†	12	28	4	—	28	5th/American	—	—		Art Duncan, Duke Keats
1927-28†	19	19	6	—	44	4th/American	—	—		Jack Adams
1928-29†	19	16	9	—	47	3rd/American	0	2	Quarterfinals	Jack Adams
1929-30†	14	24	6	—	34	4th/American	—	—		Jack Adams
1930-31‡	16	21	7	—	39	4th/American	—	—		Jack Adams
1931-32‡	18	20	10	—	46	3rd/American	*0	1	Quarterfinals	Jack Adams
1932-33	25	15	8	—	58	2nd/American	2	2	Semifinals	Jack Adams
1933-34	24	14	10	—	58	1st/American	4	5	Stanley Cup finals	Jack Adams
1934-35	19	22	7	—	45	4th/American	—	—		Jack Adams
1935-36	24	16	8	—	56	1st/American	6	1	Stanley Cup champ	Jack Adams
1936-37	25	14	9	—	59	1st/American	6	4	Stanley Cup champ	Jack Adams
1937-38	12	25	11	—	35	4th/American	—	—		Jack Adams
1938-39	18	24	6	—	42	5th	3	3	Semifinals	Jack Adams
1939-40	16	26	6	—	38	5th	2	3	Semifinals	Jack Adams
1940-41	21	16	11	—	53	3rd	4	5	Stanley Cup finals	Jack Adams
1941-42	19	25	4	—	42	5th	7	5	Stanley Cup finals	Jack Adams
1942-43	25	14	11	—	61	1st	8	2	Stanley Cup champ	Jack Adams
1943-44	26	18	6	—	58	2nd	1	4	League semifinals	Jack Adams
1944-45	31	14	5	—	67	2nd	7	7	Stanley Cup finals	Jack Adams
1945-46	20	20	10	—	50	4th	1	4	League semifinals	Jack Adams
1946-47	22	27	11	—	55	4th	1	4	League semifinals	Jack Adams
1947-48	30	18	12	—	72	2nd	4	6	Stanley Cup finals	Tommy Ivan
1948-49	34	19	7	—	75	1st	4	7	Stanley Cup finals	Tommy Ivan
1949-50	37	19	14	—	88	1st	8	6	Stanley Cup champ	Tommy Ivan
1950-51	44	13	13	—	101	1st	2	4	League semifinals	Tommy Ivan
1951-52	44	14	12	—	100	1st	8	0	Stanley Cup champ	Tommy Ivan
1952-53	36	16	18	—	90	1st	2	4	League semifinals	Tommy Ivan
1953-54	37	19	14	—	88	1st	8	4	Stanley Cup champ	Tommy Ivan
1954-55	42	17	11	—	95	1st	8	3	Stanley Cup champ	Jimmy Skinner
1955-56	30	24	16	—	76	2nd	5	5	Stanley Cup finals	Jimmy Skinner
1956-57	38	20	12	—	88	1st	1	4	League semifinals	Jimmy Skinner
1957-58	29	29	12	—	70	3rd	0	4	League semifinals	Jimmy Skinner, Sid Abel
1958-59	25	37	8	—	58	6th	—	—		Sid Abel
1959-60	26	29	15	—	67	4th	2	4	League semifinals	Sid Abel
1960-61	25	29	16	—	66	4th	6	5	Stanley Cup finals	Sid Abel
1961-62	23	33	14	—	60	5th	—	—		Sid Abel
1962-63	32	25	13	—	77	4th	5	6	Stanley Cup finals	Sid Abel
1963-64	30	29	11	—	71	4th	7	7	Stanley Cup finals	Sid Abel
1964-65	40	23	7	—	87	1st	3	4	League semifinals	Sid Abel
1965-66	31	27	12	—	74	4th	6	6	Stanley Cup finals	Sid Abel
1966-67	27	39	4	—	58	5th	—	—		Sid Abel
1967-68	27	35	12	—	66	6th/East	—	—		Sid Abel
1968-69	33	31	12	—	78	5th/East	—	—		Bill Gadsby
1969-70	40	21	15	—	95	3rd/East	0	4	Division semifinals	Bill Gadsby, Sid Abel
1970-71	22	45	11	—	55	7th/East	—	—		Ned Harkness, Doug Barkley
1971-72	33	35	10	—	76	5th/East	—	—		Doug Barkley, Johnny Wilson
1972-73	37	29	12	—	86	5th/East	—	—		Johnny Wilson
1973-74	29	39	10	—	68	6th/East	—	—		Ted Garvin, Alex Delvecchio
1974-75	23	45	12	—	58	4th/Norris	—	—		Alex Delvecchio
1975-76	26	44	10	—	62	4th/Norris	—	—		Ted Garvin, Alex Delvecchio
1976-77	16	55	9	—	41	5th/Norris	—	—		Alex Delvecchio, Larry Wilson
1977-78	32	34	14	—	78	2nd/Norris	3	4	Quarterfinals	Bobby Kromm
1978-79	23	41	16	—	62	5th/Norris	—	—		Bobby Kromm
1979-80	26	43	11	—	63	5th/Norris	—	—		Bobby Kromm, Ted Lindsay
1980-81	19	43	18	—	56	5th/Norris	—	—		Ted Lindsay, Wayne Maxner
1981-82	21	47	12	—	54	6th/Norris	—	—		Wayne Maxner, Billy Dea
1982-83	21	44	15	—	57	5th/Norris	—	—		Nick Polano
1983-84	31	42	7	—	69	3rd/Norris	1	3	Division semifinals	Nick Polano
1984-85	27	41	12	—	66	3rd/Norris	0	3	Division semifinals	Nick Polano
1985-86	17	57	6	—	40	5th/Norris	—	—		Harry Neale, Brad Park, Dan Belisle
1986-87	34	36	10	—	78	2nd/Norris	9	7	Conference finals	Jacques Demers
1987-88	41	28	11	—	93	1st/Norris	9	7	Conference finals	Jacques Demers
1988-89	34	34	12	—	80	1st/Norris	2	4	Division semifinals	Jacques Demers
1989-90	28	38	14	—	70	5th/Norris	—	—		Jacques Demers
1990-91	34	38	8	—	76	3rd/Norris	3	4	Division semifinals	Bryan Murray
1991-92	43	25	12	—	98	1st/Norris	4	7	Division finals	Bryan Murray
1992-93	47	28	9	—	103	2nd/Norris	3	4	Division semifinals	Bryan Murray

			REGULAR SEASON					PLAYOFFS			
Season	W	L	T	OTL	Pts.	Finish	W	L	Highest round	Coach
1993-94	46	30	8	—	100	1st/Central	3	4	Division semifinals	Scotty Bowman
1994-95	33	11	4	—	70	1st/Central	12	6	Stanley Cup finals	Scotty Bowman
1995-96	62	13	7	—	131	1st/Central	10	9	Conference finals	Scotty Bowman
1996-97	38	26	18	—	94	2nd/Central	16	4	Stanley Cup champ	Scotty Bowman
1997-98	44	23	15	—	103	2nd/Central	16	6	Stanley Cup champ	Scotty Bowman
1998-99	43	32	7	—	93	1st/Central	6	4	Conference semifinals	Dave Lewis, Barry Smith, Scotty Bowman
1999-00	48	22	10	2	108	2nd/Central	5	4	Conference semifinals	Scotty Bowman
2000-01	49	20	9	4	111	1st/Central	2	4	Conference quarterfinals	Scotty Bowman
2001-02	51	17	10	4	116	1st/Central	16	7	Stanley Cup champ	Scotty Bowman
2002-03	48	20	10	4	110	1st/Central	0	4	Conference quarterfinals	Dave Lewis

*Won-lost record does not indicate tie(s) resulting from two-game, total goals series that year (two-game, total-goals series were played from 1917-18 through 1935-36).
†Detroit Cougars.
‡Detroit Falcons.

FIRST-ROUND ENTRY DRAFT CHOICES

Year   Player, Overall, Last amateur team (league)
1969—Jim Rutherford, 10, Hamilton (OHL)
1970—Serge Lajeunesse, 12, Montreal (OHL)
1971—Marcel Dionne, 2, St. Catharines (OHL)
1972—No first-round selection
1973—Terry Richardson, 11, New Westminster (WCHL)
1974—Bill Lochead, 9, Oshawa (OHL)
1975—Rick Lapointe, 5, Victoria (WCHL)
1976—Fred Williams, 4, Saskatoon (WCHL)
1977—Dale McCourt, 1, St. Catharines (OHL)*
1978—Willie Huber, 9, Hamilton (OHL)
    Brent Peterson, 12, Portland (WCHL)
1979—Mike Foligno, 3, Sudbury (OHL)
1980—Mike Blaisdell, 11, Regina (WHL)
1981—No first-round selection
1982—Murray Craven, 17, Medicine Hat (WHL)
1983—Steve Yzerman, 4, Peterborough (OHL)
1984—Shawn Burr, 7, Kitchener (OHL)
1985—Brent Fedyk, 8, Regina (WHL)
1986—Joe Murphy, 1, Michigan State University*

Year   Player, Overall, Last amateur team (league)
1987—Yves Racine, 11, Longueuil (QMJHL)
1988—Kory Kocur, 17, Saskatoon (WHL)
1989—Mike Sillinger, 11, Regina (WHL)
1990—Keith Primeau, 3, Niagara Falls (OHL)
1991—Martin Lapointe, 10, Laval (QMJHL)
1992—Curtis Bowen, 22, Ottawa (OHL)
1993—Anders Eriksson, 22, MoDo, Sweden
1994—Yan Golvbovsky, 23, Dynamo Moscow, CIS
1995—Maxim Kuznetsov, 26, Dynamo Moscow, CIS
1996—Jesse Wallin, 26, Red Deer (WHL)
1997—No first-round selection
1998—Jiri Fischer, 25, Hull (QMJHL)
1999—No first-round selection
2000—Niklas Kronvall, 29, Djurgarden, Sweden
2001—No first-round selection
2002—No first-round selection
2003—No first-round selection
*Designates first player chosen in draft.

SINGLE-SEASON INDIVIDUAL RECORDS

FORWARDS/DEFENSEMEN

Most goals
65—Steve Yzerman, 1988-89

Most assists
90—Steve Yzerman, 1988-89

Most points
155—Steve Yzerman, 1988-89

Most penalty minutes
398—Bob Probert, 1987-88

Most power play goals
21—Mickey Redmond, 1973-74
    Dino Ciccarelli, 1992-93

Most shorthanded goals
10—Marcel Dionne, 1974-75

Most games with three or more goals
4—Frank Mahovlich, 1968-69

Most shots
388—Steve Yzerman, 1988-89

GOALTENDERS

Most games
72—Tim Cheveldae, 1991-92

Most minutes
4,236—Tim Cheveldae, 1991-92

Most goals allowed
226—Tim Cheveldae, 1991-92

Lowest goals-against average
1.43—Dolly Dodson, 1928-29

Most shutouts
12—Terry Sawchuk, 1951-52
    Terry Sawchuk, 1953-54
    Terry Sawchuk, 1954-55
    Glenn Hall, 1955-56

Most wins
44—Terry Sawchuk, 1950-51
    Terry Sawchuk, 1951-52

FRANCHISE LEADERS

Players in boldface played for club in 2002-03

FORWARDS/DEFENSEMEN

Games
Gordie Howe 1687
Alex Delvecchio 1549
Steve Yzerman 1378
Marcel Pronovost.....................983
Niklas Lidstrom.......................935

Goals
Gordie Howe 786
Steve Yzerman.........................660

Alex Delvecchio 456
Sergei Fedorov 400
Ted Lindsay 335

Assists
Gordie Howe 1023
Steve Yzerman 1010
Alex Delvecchio 825
Sergei Fedorov 554
Niklas Lidstrom........................525

Points
Gordie Howe 1809
Steve Yzerman 1670
Alex Delvecchio 1281
Sergei Fedorov 954
Norm Ullman.....................................758

Penalty minutes
Bob Probert..............................2090
Joey Kocur 1963
Gordie Howe 1543

| Gerard Gallant | 1600 |
| Ted Lindsay | 1423 |

GOALTENDERS

Games

Terry Sawchuk	734
Chris Osgood	389
Harry Lumley	324
Jim Rutherford	314
Roger Crozier	313

Shutouts

Terry Sawchuk	85
Chris Osgood	30
Harry Lumley	26
Roger Crozier	20
Glenn Hall	17
Hap Holmes	17
Norm Smith	17

Goals-against average
(2400 minutes minimum)

Dolly Dolson	1.98
Hap Holmes	1.98
Glenn Hall	2.12
Alex Connell	2.12
Dominik Hasek	2.17

Wins

Terry Sawchuk	351
Chris Osgood	221
Harry Lumley	163
Roger Crozier	131
Tim Cheveldae	128

EDMONTON OILERS
YEAR-BY-YEAR RECORDS

| Season | REGULAR SEASON | | | | | | PLAYOFFS | | |
	W	L	T	OTL	Pts.	Finish	W	L	Highest round	Coach
1972-73*	38	37	3	—	79	5th	—	—		Ray Kinasewich
1973-74†	38	37	3	—	79	3rd	1	4	League quarterfinals	Brian Shaw
1974-75†	36	38	4	—	76	5th	—	—		Brian Shaw, Bill Hunter
1975-76†	27	49	5	—	59	4th	0	4	League quarterfinals	Clare Drake, Bill Hunter
1976-77†	34	43	4	—	72	4th	1	4	League quarterfinals	Bep Guidolin, Glen Sather
1977-78†	38	39	3	—	79	5th	1	4	League quarterfinals	Glen Sather
1978-79†	48	30	2	—	98	1st	6	7	Avco World Cup finals	Glen Sather
1979-80	28	39	13	—	69	4th/Smythe	0	3	Preliminaries	Glen Sather
1980-81	29	35	16	—	74	4th/Smythe	5	4	Quarterfinals	Glen Sather
1981-82	48	17	15	—	111	1st/Smythe	2	3	Division semifinals	Glen Sather
1982-83	47	21	12	—	106	1st/Smythe	11	5	Stanley Cup finals	Glen Sather
1983-84	57	18	5	—	119	1st/Smythe	15	4	Stanley Cup champ	Glen Sather
1984-85	49	20	11	—	109	1st/Smythe	15	3	Stanley Cup champ	Glen Sather
1985-86	56	17	7	—	119	1st/Smythe	6	4	Division finals	Glen Sather
1986-87	50	24	6	—	106	1st/Smythe	16	5	Stanley Cup champ	Glen Sather
1987-88	44	25	11	—	99	2nd/Smythe	16	2	Stanley Cup champ	Glen Sather
1988-89	38	34	8	—	84	3rd/Smythe	3	4	Division semifinals	Glen Sather
1989-90	38	28	14	—	90	2nd/Smythe	16	6	Stanley Cup champ	John Muckler
1990-91	37	37	6	—	80	3rd/Smythe	9	9	Conference finals	John Muckler
1991-92	36	34	10	—	82	3rd/Smythe	8	8	Conference finals	Ted Green
1992-93	26	50	8	—	60	5th/Smythe	—	—		Ted Green
1993-94	25	45	14	—	64	6th/Pacific	—	—		Ted Green, Glen Sather
1994-95	17	27	4	—	38	5th/Pacific	—	—		George Burnett, Ron Low
1995-96	30	44	8	—	68	5th/Pacific	—	—		Ron Low
1996-97	36	37	9	—	81	3rd/Pacific	5	7	Conference semifinals	Ron Low
1997-98	35	37	10	—	80	3rd/Pacific	5	7	Conference semifinals	Ron Low
1998-99	33	37	12	—	78	2nd/Northwest	0	4	Conference quarterfinals	Ron Low
1999-00	32	26	16	8	88	2nd/Northwest	1	4	Conference quarterfinals	Kevin Lowe
2000-01	39	28	12	3	93	2nd/Northwest	2	4	Conference quarterfinals	Craig MacTavish
2001-02	38	28	12	4	92	3rd/Northwest	—	—		Craig MacTavish
2002-03	36	26	11	9	92	4th/Northwest	2	4	Conference quarterfinals	Craig MacTavish

*Alberta Oilers, members of World Hockey Association.
†Members of World Hockey Association.

FIRST-ROUND ENTRY DRAFT CHOICES

Year   Player, Overall, Last amateur team (league)

1979—Kevin Lowe, 21, Quebec (QMJHL)
1980—Paul Coffey, 6, Kitchener (OHL)
1981—Grant Fuhr, 8, Victoria (WHL)
1982—Jim Playfair, 20, Portland (WHL)
1983—Jeff Beukeboom, 19, Sault Ste. Marie (OHL)
1984—Selmar Odelein, 21, Regina (WHL)
1985—Scott Metcalfe, 20, Kingston (OHL)
1986—Kim Issel, 21, Prince Albert (WHL)
1987—Peter Soberlak, 21, Swift Current (WHL)
1988—Francois Leroux, 19, St. Jean (QMJHL)
1989—Jason Soules, 15, Niagara Falls (OHL)
1990—Scott Allison, 17, Prince Albert (WHL)
1991—Tyler Wright, 12, Swift Current (WHL)
      Martin Rucinsky, 20, Litvinov, Czechoslovakia
1992—Joe Hulbig, 13, St. Sebastian H.S. (Mass.)
1993—Jason Arnott, 7, Oshawa (OHL)
      Nick Stajduhar, 16, London (OHL)

Year   Player, Overall, Last amateur team (league)

1994—Jason Bonsignore, 4, Niagara Falls (OHL)
      Ryan Smyth, 6, Moose Jaw (WHL)
1995—Steve Kelly, 6, Prince Albert (WHL)
1996—Boyd Devereaux, 6, Kitchener (OHL)
      Matthieu Descoteaux, 19, Shawinigan (QMJHL)
1997—Michel Riessen, 14, HC Biel, Switzerland
1998—Michael Henrich, 13, Barrie (OHL)
1999—Jani Rita, 13, Jokerit Helsinki, Finland
2000—Alexei Mikhnov, 17, Yaroslavl, Russia
2001—Ales Hemsky, 13, Hull (QMJHL)
2002—Jesse Niinimaki, 15, Ilves, Finland
2003—Marc-Antoine Pouliot, 22, Rimouski (QMJHL)
NOTE: Edmonton chose Dave Dryden, Bengt Gustafsson and Ed Mio
as priority selections before the 1979 expansion draft.

SINGLE-SEASON INDIVIDUAL RECORDS

FORWARDS/DEFENSEMEN

Most goals
92—Wayne Gretzky, 1981-82

Most assists
163—Wayne Gretzky, 1985-86

Most points
215—Wayne Gretzky, 1985-86

Most penalty minutes
286—Steve Smith, 1987-88

Most power play goals
20—Wayne Gretzky, 1983-84
Ryan Smyth, 1996-97

Most shorthanded goals
12—Wayne Gretzky, 1983-84

Most games with three or more goals
10—Wayne Gretzky, 1981-82
Wayne Gretzky, 1983-84

Most shots
369—Wayne Gretzky, 1981-82

GOALTENDERS

Most games
75—Grant Fuhr, 1987-88

Most minutes
4,364—Tommy Salo, 2000-01

Most goals allowed
246—Grant Fuhr, 1987-88

Lowest goals-against average
2.22—Tommy Salo, 2001-02

Most shutouts
8—Curtis Joseph, 1997-98
Tommy Salo, 2000-01

Most wins
40—Grant Fuhr, 1987-88

Most losses
38—Bill Ranford, 1992-93

Most ties
14—Grant Fuhr, 1981-82

FRANCHISE LEADERS

Players in boldface played for club in 2002-03

FORWARDS/DEFENSEMEN

Games

Kevin Lowe	1037
Mark Messier	851
Glenn Anderson	845
Kelly Buchberger	795
Jari Kurri	754

Goals

Wayne Gretzky	583
Jari Kurri	474
Glenn Anderson	417
Mark Messier	392
Paul Coffey	209

Assists

Wayne Gretzky	1086
Mark Messier	642
Jari Kurri	569
Glenn Anderson	489
Paul Coffey	460

Points

Wayne Gretzky	1669
Jari Kurri	1043
Mark Messier	1034
Glenn Anderson	906
Paul Coffey	669

Penalty minutes

Kelly Buchberger	1747
Kevin McClelland	1291
Kevin Lowe	1236
Mark Messier	1122
Steve Smith	1080

GOALTENDERS

Games

Bill Ranford	449
Grant Fuhr	423
Tommy Salo	**290**
Andy Moog	235
Curtis Joseph	177

Shutouts

Tommy Salo	**20**
Curtis Joseph	14
Grant Fuhr	9
Bill Ranford	8
Jussi Markkanen	**5**

Goals-against average
(2400 minutes minimum)

Tommy Salo	**2.42**
Bob Essensa	2.73
Curtis Joseph	2.90
Bill Ranford	3.51
Andy Moog	3.61

Wins

Grant Fuhr	226
Bill Ranford	167
Andy Moog	143
Tommy Salo	**130**
Curtis Joseph	76

FLORIDA PANTHERS
YEAR-BY-YEAR RECORDS

	REGULAR SEASON						PLAYOFFS			
Season	W	L	T	OTL	Pts.	Finish	W	L	Highest round	Coach
1993-94	33	34	17	—	83	5th/Atlantic	—	—		Roger Neilson
1994-95	20	22	6	—	46	5th/Atlantic	—	—		Roger Neilson
1995-96	41	31	10	—	92	3rd/Atlantic	12	10	Stanley Cup finals	Doug MacLean
1996-97	35	28	19	—	89	3rd/Atlantic	1	4	Conference quarterfinals	Doug MacLean
1997-98	24	43	15	—	63	6th/Atlantic	—	—		Doug MacLean, Bryan Murray
1998-99	30	34	18	—	78	2nd/Southeast	—	—		Terry Murray
1999-00	43	27	6	6	98	2nd/Southeast	0	4	Conference quarterfinals	Terry Murray
2000-01	22	38	13	9	66	3rd/Southeast	—	—		Terry Murray, Duane Sutter
2001-02	22	44	10	6	60	4th/Southeast	—	—		Duane Sutter, Mike Keenan
2002-03	24	36	13	9	70	4th/Southeast	—	—		Mike Keenan

FIRST-ROUND ENTRY DRAFT CHOICES

Year   Player, Overall, Last amateur team (league)
1993—Rob Niedermayer, 5, Medicine Hat (WHL)
1994—Ed Jovanovski, 1, Windsor (OHL)*
1995—Radek Dvorak, 10, Budejovice, Czech Republic
1996—Marcus Nilson, 20, Djurgarden-Stockholm, Sweden
1997—Mike Brown, 20, Red Deer (WHL)
1998—No first-round selection
1999—Denis Shvidki, 12, Barrie (OHL)
2000—No first-round selection

Year   Player, Overall, Last amateur team (league)
2001—Stephen Weiss, 4, Plymouth (OHL)
        Lukas Krajicek, 24, Peterborough (OHL)
2002—Jay Bouwmeester, 3, Medicine Hat (WHL)
        Petr Taticek, 9, Sault Ste. Marie (OHL)
2003—Nathan Horton, 3, Oshawa (OHL)
        Anthony Stewart, 25, Kingston (OHL)
*Designates first player chosen in draft.

NHL HISTORY *Team by team*

FORWARDS/DEFENSEMEN

Most goals
59—Pavel Bure, 2000-01

Most assists
53—Viktor Kozlov, 1999-2000

Most points
94—Pavel Bure, 1999-2000

Most penalty minutes
354—Peter Worrell, 2001-02

Most power play goals
19—Scott Mellanby, 1995-96
    Pavel Bure, 2000-01

Most shorthanded goals
6—Tom Fitzgerald, 1995-96

Most games with three or more goals
4—Pavel Bure, 1999-2000
    Pavel Bure, 2000-01

Most shots
384—Pavel Bure, 2000-01

GOALTENDERS

Most games
65—Roberto Longo, 2002-03

Most minutes
3,451—John Vanbiesbrouck, 1997-98

Most shots against
2,011—John Vanbiesbrouck, 1993-94

Most goals allowed
165—John Vanbiesbrouck, 1997-98

Lowest goals-against average
2.29—John Vanbiesbrouck, 1996-97

Most shutouts
5—Robert Luongo, 2000-01

Most wins
27—John Vanbiesbrouck, 1996-97

Most losses
33—Robert Luongo, 2001-02

Most ties
14—Sean Burke, 1998-99

FRANCHISE LEADERS

Players in boldface played for club in 2002-03

FORWARDS/DEFENSEMEN

Games

Robert Svehla	573
Scott Mellanby	552
Paul Laus	530
Rob Niedermayer	518
Bill Lindsay	506

Goals

Scott Mellanby	157
Pavel Bure	152
Rob Niedermayer	101
Ray Whitney	97
Viktor Kozlov	**90**

Assists

Robert Svehla	229
Scott Mellanby	197
Viktor Kozlov	**174**
Rob Niedermayer	165
Ray Whitney	130

Points

Scott Mellanby	354
Robert Svehla	290
Rob Niedermayer	266
Viktor Kozlov	**264**
Pavel Bure	251

Penalty minutes

Paul Laus	1702
Peter Worrell	**1375**
Scott Mellanby	953
Bill Lindsay	609
Robert Svehla	603

GOALTENDERS

Games

John Vanbiesbrouck	268
Robert Luongo	**170**
Mark Fitzpatrick	119
Trevor Kidd	103
Sean Burke	66

Shutouts

Robert Luongo	**15**
John Vanbiesbrouck	13
Mark Fitzpatrick	4
Sean Burke	3
Trevor Kidd	3

**Goals-against average
(2400 minutes minimum)**

John Vanbiesbrouck	2.58
Robert Luongo	**2.66**
Sean Burke	2.65
Mark Fitzpatrick	2.71
Trevor Kidd	3.09

Wins

John Vanbiesbrouck	106
Robert Luongo	**48**
Mark Fitzpatrick	43
Trevor Kidd	28
Sean Burke	23

LOS ANGELES KINGS
YEAR-BY-YEAR RECORDS

	REGULAR SEASON						PLAYOFFS			
Season	W	L	T	OTL	Pts.	Finish	W	L	Highest round	Coach
1967-68	31	33	10	—	72	2nd/West	3	4	Division semifinals	Red Kelly
1968-69	24	42	10	—	58	4th/West	4	7	Division finals	Red Kelly
1969-70	14	52	10	—	38	6th/West	—	—		Hal Laycoe, Johnny Wilson
1970-71	25	40	13	—	63	5th/West	—	—		Larry Regan
1971-72	20	49	9	—	49	7th/West	—	—		Larry Regan, Fred Glover
1972-73	31	36	11	—	73	6th/West	—	—		Bob Pulford
1973-74	33	33	12	—	78	3rd/West	1	4	Division semifinals	Bob Pulford
1974-75	42	17	21	—	105	2nd/Norris	1	2	Preliminaries	Bob Pulford
1975-76	38	33	9	—	85	2nd/Norris	5	4	Quarterfinals	Bob Pulford
1976-77	34	31	15	—	83	2nd/Norris	4	5	Quarterfinals	Bob Pulford
1977-78	31	34	15	—	77	3rd/Norris	0	2	Preliminaries	Ron Stewart
1978-79	34	34	12	—	80	3rd/Norris	0	2	Preliminaries	Bob Berry
1979-80	30	36	14	—	74	2nd/Norris	1	3	Preliminaries	Bob Berry
1980-81	43	24	13	—	99	2nd/Norris	1	3	Preliminaries	Bob Berry
1981-82	24	41	15	—	63	4th/Smythe	4	6	Division finals	Parker MacDonald, Don Perry,
1982-83	27	41	12	—	66	5th/Smythe	—	—		Don Perry
1983-84	23	44	13	—	59	5th/Smythe	—	—		Don Perry, Rogie Vachon, Roger Neilson
1984-85	34	32	14	—	82	4th/Smythe	0	3	Division semifinals	Pat Quinn
1985-86	23	49	8	—	54	5th/Smythe	—	—		Pat Quinn
1986-87	31	41	8	—	70	4th/Smythe	1	4	Division semifinals	Pat Quinn, Mike Murphy
1987-88	30	42	8	—	68	4th/Smythe	1	4	Division semifinals	Mike Murphy, Rogie Vachon, Robbie Ftorek

NHL HISTORY *Team by team*

			REGULAR SEASON						PLAYOFFS		
Season	W	L	T	OTL	Pts.	Finish	W	L	Highest round	Coach
1988-89	42	31	7	—	91	2nd/Smythe	4	7	Division finals	Robbie Ftorek
1989-90	34	39	7	—	75	4th/Smythe	4	6	Division finals	Tom Webster
1990-91	46	24	10	—	102	1st/Smythe	6	6	Division finals	Tom Webster
1991-92	35	31	14	—	84	2nd/Smythe	2	4	Division semifinals	Tom Webster
1992-93	39	35	10	—	88	3rd/Smythe	13	11	Stanley Cup finals	Barry Melrose
1993-94	27	45	12	—	66	5th/Pacific	—	—		Barry Melrose
1994-95	16	23	9	—	41	4th/Pacific	—	—		Barry Melrose, Rogie Vachon
1995-96	24	40	18	—	66	6th/Pacific	—	—		Larry Robinson
1996-97	28	43	11	—	67	6th/Pacific	—	—		Larry Robinson
1997-98	38	33	11	—	87	2nd/Pacific	0	4	Conference quarterfinals	Larry Robinson
1998-99	32	45	5	—	69	5th/Pacific	—	—		Larry Robinson
1999-00	39	27	12	4	94	2nd/Pacific	0	4	Conference quarterfinals	Andy Murray
2000-01	38	28	13	3	92	3rd/Pacific	7	6	Conference semifinals	Andy Murray
2001-02	40	27	11	4	95	3rd/Pacific	3	4	Conference quarterfinals	Andy Murray
2002-03	33	37	6	6	78	3rd/Pacific	—	—		Andy Murray, Dave Tippett

FIRST-ROUND ENTRY DRAFT CHOICES

Year   Player, Overall, Last amateur team (league)

1969—No first-round selection
1970—No first-round selection
1971—No first-round selection
1972—No first-round selection
1973—No first-round selection
1974—No first-round selection
1975—Tim Young, 16, Ottawa (OHL)
1976—No first-round selection
1977—No first-round selection
1978—No first-round selection
1979—Jay Wells, 16, Kingston (OHL)
1980—Larry Murphy, 4, Peterborough (OHL)
     Jim Fox, 10, Ottawa (OHL)
1981—Doug Smith, 2, Ottawa (OHL)
1982—No first-round selection
1983—No first-round selection
1984—Craig Redmond, 6, Canadian Olympic Team
1985—Craig Duncanson, 9, Sudbury (OHL)
     Dan Gratton, 10, Oshawa (OHL)
1986—Jimmy Carson, 2, Verdun (QMJHL)
1987—Wayne McBean, 4, Medicine Hat (WHL)

Year   Player, Overall, Last amateur team (league)

1988—Martin Gelinas, 7, Hull (QMJHL)
1989—No first-round selection
1990—Darryl Sydor, 7, Kamloops (WHL)
1991—No first-round selection
1992—No first-round selection
1993—No first-round selection
1994—Jamie Storr, 7, Owen Sound (OHL)
1995—Aki-Petteri Berg, 3, TPS Jrs., Finland
1996—No first-round selection
1997—Olli Jokinen, 3, IFK Helsinki, Finland
     Matt Zultek, 15, Ottawa (OHL)
1998—Mathieu Biron, 21, Shawinigan (QMJHL)
1999—No first-round selection
2000—Alexander Frolov, 20, Yaroslavl, Russia
2001—Jens Karlsson, 18, Frolunda, Sweden
     David Steckel, 30, Ohio State
2002—Denis Grebeshkov, 18, Yaroslavl, Russia
2003—Dustin Brown, 13, Guelph (OHL)
     Brian Boyle, 26, St. Sebastian's (U.S. high school)
     Jeff Tambellini, 27, Michigan (CCHA)

SINGLE-SEASON INDIVIDUAL RECORDS

FORWARDS/DEFENSEMEN

Most goals
70—Bernie Nicholls, 1988-89

Most assists
122—Wayne Gretzky, 1990-91

Most points
168—Wayne Gretzky, 1988-89

Most penalty minutes
399—Marty McSorley, 1992-93

Most power play goals
26—Luc Robitaille, 1991-92

Most shorthanded goals
8—Bernie Nicholls, 1988-89

Most games with three or more goals
5—Jimmy Carson, 1987-88

Most shots
385—Bernie Nicholls, 1988-89

GOALTENDERS

Most games
71—Felix Potvin, 2001-02

Most minutes
4,107—Rogie Vachon, 1977-78

Most shots against
2,219—Kelly Hrudey, 1993-94

Most goals allowed
228—Kelly Hrudey, 1993-94

Lowest goals-against average
2.24—Rogie Vachon, 1974-75

Most shutouts
8—Rogie Vachon, 1976-77

Most wins
35—Mario Lessard, 1980-81

Most losses
31—Kelly Hrudey, 1993-94

Most ties
13—Rogie Vachon, 1974-75
    Rogie Vachon, 1977-78
    Kelly Hrudey, 1991-92

FRANCHISE LEADERS

Players in boldface played for club in 2002-03

FORWARDS/DEFENSEMEN

Games
Dave Taylor 1111
Luc Robitaille 932
Marcel Dionne 921

Butch Goring 736
Mike Murphy 673

Goals
Marcel Dionne 550
Luc Robitaille 520

Dave Taylor 431
Bernie Nicholls 327
Butch Goring 275

Assists
Marcel Dionne 757

Wayne Gretzky 672	Rob Blake 1051	**Goals-against average**
Dave Taylor 638	**Ian Laperriere**.........................**959**	**(2400 minutes minimum)**
Luc Robitaille 559		Felix Potvin............................**2.35**
Bernie Nicholls 431	**GOALTENDERS**	**Jamie Storr**............................**2.52**
	Games	Stephane Fiset........................2.83
Points	Rogie Vachon............................389	Rogie Vachon 2.86
Marcel Dionne 1307	Kelly Hrudey............................360	Wayne Rutledge 3.34
Luc Robitaille 1079	Mario Lessard............................240	
Dave Taylor 1069	**Jamie Storr**.............................**205**	**Wins**
Wayne Gretzky 918	Stephane Fiset............................200	Rogie Vachon............................171
Bernie Nicholls 758		Kelly Hrudey............................145
	Shutouts	Mario Lessard............................92
Penalty minutes	Rogie Vachon............................32	**Jamie Storr** **85**
Marty McSorley................1846	**Jamie Storr** **16**	Stephane Fiset............................80
Dave Taylor 1589	**Felix Potvin** **14**	
Jay Wells.......................1446	Stephane Fiset............................10	
	Kelly Hrudey............................10	

MINNESOTA WILD
YEAR-BY-YEAR RECORDS

	REGULAR SEASON					PLAYOFFS			
Season	W	L	T	OTL	Pts.	Finish	W	L	Highest round	Coach
2000-01	25	39	13	5	68	5th/Northwest	—	—		Jacques Lemaire
2001-02	26	35	12	9	73	5th/Northwest	—	—		Jacques Lemaire
2002-03	42	29	10	1	95	3rd/Northwest	8	10	Conference finals	Jacques Lemaire

FIRST-ROUND ENTRY DRAFT CHOICES

Year Player, Overall, Last amateur team (league)
2000—Marian Gaborik, 3, Trencin, Slovakia
2001—Mikko Koivu, 6, TPS, Finland

Year Player, Overall, Last amateur team (league)
2002—Pierre-Marc Bouchard, 8, Chicoutimi
2003—Brent Burns, 20, Brampton (OHL)

SINGLE-SEASON INDIVIDUAL RECORDS

FORWARDS/DEFENSEMEN

Most goals
30—Marian Gaborik, 2002-03

Most assists
48—Andrew Brunette, 2001-02

Most points
69—Andrew Brunette, 2001-02

Most penalty minutes
201—Matt Johnson, 2002-03

Most power play goals
10—Andrew Brunette, 2001-02
     Marian Gaborik, 2001-02
     Sergei Zholtok, 2001-02

Most shorthanded goals
7—Wes Walz, 2000-01

Most games with three or more goals
2—Marian Gaborik, 2001-02

Most shots
280—Marian Gaborik, 2002-03

GOALTENDERS

Most games
45—Dwayne Roloson, 2001-02

Most minutes
2,506—Dwayne Roloson, 2001-02

Most shots against
1,334—Dwayne Roloson, 2001-02

Most goals allowed
125—Manny Fernandez, 2001-02

Lowest goals-against average
2.24—Manny Fernandez, 2002-03

Most shutouts
5—Dwayne Roloson, 2001-02

Most wins
23—Dwayne Roloson, 2002-03

Most losses
24—Manny Fernandez, 2001-02

Most ties
9—Jamie McLennan, 2000-01

FRANCHISE LEADERS

Players in boldface played for club in 2002-03

FORWARDS/DEFENSEMEN

Games
Antti Laaksonen 246
Marian Gaborik 230
Jim Dowd 228
Wes Walz 226
Filip Kuba...............................215

Goals
Marian Gaborik............................78
Antti Laaksonen 43
Wes Walz 41
Andrew Brunette 39
Pascal Dupuis 36

Assists
Marian Gaborik............................90
Andrew Brunette 76
Jim Dowd 69
Filip Kuba...............................61
Lubomir Sekeras 52

Points
Marian Gaborik............................168
Andrew Brunette.........................115
Jim Dowd 97
Antti Laaksonen 92
Wes Walz...............................92

Penalty minutes
Matt Johnson............................521
Sylvain Blouin 251

Jason Marshall 217
Brad Brown 213
Andy Sutton 166

GOALTENDERS
Games
Manny Fernandez 121
Dwayne Roloson 95
Jamie McLennan......................38
Derek Gustafson........................5
Zac Bierk 1
Dieter Kochan 1

Shutouts
Dwayne Roloson 9
Manny Fernandez 7
Jamie McLennan........................2

Goals-against average (1200 minutes minimum)		Wins	
Dwayne Roloson	2.31	Manny Fernandez	50
Manny Fernandez	2.53	Dwayne Roloson	37
Jamie McLennan	2.64	Jamie McLennan	5
		Derek Gustafson	1

MONTREAL CANADIENS
YEAR-BY-YEAR RECORDS

	REGULAR SEASON						PLAYOFFS		
Season	W	L	T	OTL	Pts.	Finish	W	L	Highest round	Coach
1917-18	13	9	0	—	26	1st/3rd	1	1	Semifinals	George Kennedy
1918-19	10	8	0	—	20	1st/2nd	†*6	3	Stanley Cup finals	George Kennedy
1919-20	13	11	0	—	26	2nd/3rd	—	—		George Kennedy
1920-21	13	11	0	—	26	3rd/2nd	—	—		George Kennedy
1921-22	12	11	1	—	25	3rd	—	—		Leo Dandurand
1922-23	13	9	2	—	28	2nd	1	1	Quarterfinals	Leo Dandurand
1923-24	13	11	0	—	26	2nd	6	0	Stanley Cup champ	Leo Dandurand
1924-25	17	11	2	—	36	3rd	3	3	Stanley Cup finals	Leo Dandurand
1925-26	11	24	1	—	23	7th	—	—		Cecil Hart
1926-27	28	14	2	—	58	2nd/Canadian	*1	1	Semifinals	Cecil Hart
1927-28	26	11	7	—	59	1st/Canadian	*0	1	Semifinals	Cecil Hart
1928-29	22	7	15	—	59	1st/Canadian	0	3	Semifinals	Cecil Hart
1929-30	21	14	9	—	51	2nd/Canadian	*5	0	Stanley Cup champ	Cecil Hart
1930-31	26	10	8	—	60	1st/Canadian	6	4	Stanley Cup champ	Cecil Hart
1931-32	25	16	7	—	57	1st/Canadian	1	3	Semifinals	Cecil Hart
1932-33	18	25	5	—	41	3rd/Canadian	*0	1	Quarterfinals	Newsy Lalonde
1933-34	22	20	6	—	50	2nd/Canadian	*0	1	Quarterfinals	Newsy Lalonde
1934-35	19	23	6	—	44	3rd/Canadian	*0	1	Quarterfinals	Newsy Lalonde, Leo Dandurand
1935-36	11	26	11	—	33	4th/Canadian	—	—		Sylvio Mantha
1936-37	24	18	6	—	54	1st/Canadian	2	3	Semifinals	Cecil Hart
1937-38	18	17	13	—	49	3rd/Canadian	1	2	Quarterfinals	Cecil Hart
1938-39	15	24	9	—	39	6th	1	2	Quarterfinals	Cecil Hart, Jules Dugal
1939-40	10	33	5	—	25	7th	—	—		Pit Lepine
1940-41	16	26	6	—	38	6th	1	2	Quarterfinals	Dick Irvin
1941-42	18	27	3	—	39	6th	1	2	Quarterfinals	Dick Irvin
1942-43	19	19	12	—	50	4th	1	4	League semifinals	Dick Irvin
1943-44	38	5	7	—	83	1st	8	1	Stanley Cup champ	Dick Irvin
1944-45	38	8	4	—	80	1st	2	4	League semifinals	Dick Irvin
1945-46	28	17	5	—	61	1st	8	1	Stanley Cup champ	Dick Irvin
1946-47	34	16	10	—	78	1st	6	5	Stanley Cup finals	Dick Irvin
1947-48	20	29	11	—	51	5th	—	—		Dick Irvin
1948-49	28	23	9	—	65	3rd	3	4	League semifinals	Dick Irvin
1949-50	29	22	19	—	77	2nd	1	4	League semifinals	Dick Irvin
1950-51	25	30	15	—	65	3rd	5	6	Stanley Cup finals	Dick Irvin
1951-52	34	26	10	—	78	2nd	4	7	Stanley Cup finals	Dick Irvin
1952-53	28	23	19	—	75	2nd	8	4	Stanley Cup champ	Dick Irvin
1953-54	35	24	11	—	81	2nd	7	4	Stanley Cup finals	Dick Irvin
1954-55	41	18	11	—	93	2nd	7	5	Stanley Cup finals	Dick Irvin
1955-56	45	15	10	—	100	1st	8	2	Stanley Cup champ	Toe Blake
1956-57	35	23	12	—	82	2nd	8	2	Stanley Cup champ	Toe Blake
1957-58	43	17	10	—	96	1st	8	2	Stanley Cup champ	Toe Blake
1958-59	39	18	13	—	91	1st	8	3	Stanley Cup champ	Toe Blake
1959-60	40	18	12	—	92	1st	8	0	Stanley Cup champ	Toe Blake
1960-61	41	19	10	—	92	1st	2	4	League semifinals	Toe Blake
1961-62	42	14	14	—	98	1st	2	4	League semifinals	Toe Blake
1962-63	28	19	23	—	79	3rd	1	4	League semifinals	Toe Blake
1963-64	36	21	13	—	85	1st	3	4	League semifinals	Toe Blake
1964-65	36	23	11	—	83	2nd	8	5	Stanley Cup champ	Toe Blake
1965-66	41	21	8	—	90	1st	8	2	Stanley Cup champ	Toe Blake
1966-67	32	25	13	—	77	2nd	6	4	Stanley Cup finals	Toe Blake
1967-68	42	22	10	—	94	1st/East	12	1	Stanley Cup champ	Toe Blake
1968-69	46	19	11	—	103	1st/East	12	2	Stanley Cup champ	Claude Ruel
1969-70	38	22	16	—	92	5th/East	—	—		Claude Ruel
1970-71	42	23	13	—	97	3rd/East	12	8	Stanley Cup champ	Claude Ruel, Al MacNeil
1971-72	46	16	16	—	108	3rd/East	2	4	Division semifinals	Scotty Bowman
1972-73	52	10	16	—	120	1st/East	12	5	Stanley Cup champ	Scotty Bowman
1973-74	45	24	9	—	99	2nd/East	2	4	Division semifinals	Scotty Bowman
1974-75	47	14	19	—	113	1st/Norris	6	5	Semifinals	Scotty Bowman
1975-76	58	11	11	—	127	1st/Norris	12	1	Stanley Cup champ	Scotty Bowman
1976-77	60	8	12	—	132	1st/Norris	12	2	Stanley Cup champ	Scotty Bowman
1977-78	59	10	11	—	129	1st/Norris	12	3	Stanley Cup champ	Scotty Bowman

		REGULAR SEASON						PLAYOFFS			
Season	W	L	T	OTL	Pts.	Finish	W	L	Highest round	Coach
1978-79	52	17	11	—	115	1st/Norris	12	4	Stanley Cup champ	Scotty Bowman
1979-80	47	20	13	—	107	1st/Norris	6	4	Quarterfinals	Bernie Geoffrion, Claude Ruel
1980-81	45	22	13	—	103	1st/Norris	0	3	Preliminaries	Claude Ruel
1981-82	46	17	17	—	109	1st/Adams	2	3	Division semifinals	Bob Berry
1982-83	42	24	14	—	98	2nd/Adams	0	3	Division semifinals	Bob Berry
1983-84	35	40	5	—	75	4th/Adams	9	6	Conference finals	Bob Berry, Jacques Lemaire
1984-85	41	27	12	—	94	1st/Adams	6	6	Division finals	Jacques Lemaire
1985-86	40	33	7	—	87	2nd/Adams	15	5	Stanley Cup champ	Jean Perron
1986-87	41	29	10	—	92	2nd/Adams	10	7	Conference finals	Jean Perron
1987-88	45	22	13	—	103	1st/Adams	5	6	Division finals	Jean Perron
1988-89	53	18	9	—	115	1st/Adams	14	7	Stanley Cup finals	Pat Burns
1989-90	41	28	11	—	93	3rd/Adams	5	6	Division finals	Pat Burns
1990-91	39	30	11	—	89	2nd/Adams	7	6	Division finals	Pat Burns
1991-92	41	28	11	—	93	1st/Adams	4	7	Division finals	Pat Burns
1992-93	48	30	6	—	102	3rd/Adams	16	4	Stanley Cup champ	Jacques Demers
1993-94	41	29	14	—	96	3rd/Northeast	3	4	Conference quarterfinals	Jacques Demers
1994-95	18	23	7	—	43	6th/Northeast	—	—		Jacques Demers
1995-96	40	32	10	—	90	3rd/Northeast	2	4	Conference quarterfinals	Jacques Demers, Mario Tremblay
1996-97	31	36	15	—	77	4th/Northeast	1	4	Conference quarterfinals	Mario Tremblay
1997-98	37	32	13	—	87	4th/Northeast	4	6	Conference semifinals	Alain Vigneault
1998-99	32	39	11	—	75	5th/Northeast	—	—		Alain Vigneault
1999-00	35	34	9	4	83	4th/Northeast	—	—		Alain Vigneault
2000-01	28	40	8	6	70	5th/Northeast	—	—		Alain Vigneault, Michel Therrien
2001-02	36	31	12	3	87	4th/Northeast	6	6	Conference semifinals	Michel Therrien
2002-03	30	35	8	9	77	4th/Northeast	—	—		Michael Therrien, Claude Julien

*Won-lost record does not indicate tie(s) resulting from two-game, total-goals series that year (two-game, total-goals series were played from 1917-18 through 1935-36).

†1918-19 series abandoned with no Cup holder due to influenza epidemic.

FIRST-ROUND ENTRY DRAFT CHOICES

Year   Player, Overall, Last amateur team (league)
1969—Rejean Houle, 1, Montreal (OHL)*
     Marc Tardif, 2, Montreal (OHL)
1970—Ray Martiniuk, 5, Flin Flon (WCHL)
     Chuck Lefley, 6, Canadian Nationals
1971—Guy Lafleur, 1, Quebec (QMJHL)*
     Chuck Arnason, 7, Flin Flon (WCHL)
     Murray Wilson, 11, Ottawa (OHL)
1972—Steve Shutt, 4, Toronto (OHL)
     Michel Larocque, 6, Ottawa (OHL)
     Dave Gardner, 8, Toronto (OHL)
     John Van Boxmeer, 14, Guelph (SOJHL)
1973—Bob Gainey, 8, Peterborough (OHL)
1974—Cam Connor, 5, Flin Flon (WCHL)
     Doug Risebrough, 7, Kitchener (OHL)
     Rick Chartraw, 10, Kitchener (OHL)
     Mario Tremblay, 12, Montreal (OHL)
     Gord McTavish, 15, Sudbury (OHL)
1975—Robin Sadler, 9, Edmonton (WCHL)
     Pierre Mondou, 15, Montreal (QMJHL)
1976—Peter Lee, 12, Ottawa (OHL)
     Rod Schutt, 13, Sudbury (OHL)
     Bruce Baker, 18, Ottawa (OHL)
1977—Mark Napier, 10, Birmingham (WHA)
     Normand Dupont, 18, Montreal (QMJHL)
1978—Danny Geoffrion, 8, Cornwall (QMJHL)
     Dave Hunter, 17, Sudbury (OHL)
1979—No first-round selection
1980—Doug Wickenheiser, 1, Regina (WHL)*
1981—Mark Hunter, 7, Brantford (OHL)
     Gilbert Delorme, 18, Chicoutimi (QMJHL)
     Jan Ingman, 19, Farjestads (Sweden)

Year   Player, Overall, Last amateur team (league)
1982—Alain Heroux, 19, Chicoutimi (QMJHL)
1983—Alfie Turcotte, 17, Portland (WHL)
1984—Petr Svoboda, 5, Czechoslovakia
     Shayne Corson, 8, Brantford (OHL)
1985—Jose Charbonneau, 12, Drummondville (QMJHL)
     Tom Chorske, 16, Minneapolis SW H.S. (Minn.)
1986—Mark Pederson, 15, Medicine Hat (WHL)
1987—Andrew Cassels, 17, Ottawa (OHL)
1988—Eric Charron, 20, Trois-Rivieres (QMJHL)
1989—Lindsay Vallis, 13, Seattle (WHL)
1990—Turner Stevenson, 12, Seattle (WHL)
1991—Brent Bilodeau, 17, Seattle (WHL)
1992—David Wilkie, 20, Kamloops (WHL)
1993—Saku Koivu, 21, TPS Turku (Finland)
1994—Brad Brown, 18, North Bay (OHL)
1995—Terry Ryan, 8, Tri-City (WHL)
1996—Matt Higgins, 18, Moose Jaw (WHL)
1997—Jason Ward, 11, Erie (OHL)
1998—Eric Chouinard, 16, Quebec (QMJHL)
1999—No first-round selection
2000—Ron Hainsey, 13, Univ. of Mass.-Lowell
     Marcel Hossa, 16, Portland (WHL)
2001—Michael Komisarek, 7, Univ. of Michigan
     Alexander Perezhogin, 25, OMSK, Russia
2002—Christopher Higgins, 14, Yale (ECAC)
2003—Andrei Kastsitsyn, 10, Belarus
*Designates first player chosen in draft.

SINGLE-SEASON INDIVIDUAL RECORDS

FORWARDS/DEFENSEMEN

Most goals
60—Steve Shutt, 1976-77
     Guy Lafleur, 1977-78

Most assists
82—Pete Mahovlich, 1974-75

Most points
136—Guy Lafleur, 1976-77

Most penalty minutes
358—Chris Nilan, 1984-85

Most power play goals
20—Yvan Cournoyer, 1966-67

Most shorthanded goals
8—Guy Carbonneau, 1983-84

Most games with three or more goals
7—Joe Malone, 1917-18

GOALTENDERS

Most games
70—Gerry McNeil, 1950-51
　　Gerry McNeil, 1951-52
　　Jacques Plante, 1961-62

Most minutes
4,200—Gerry McNeil, 1950-51
　　　　Gerry McNeil, 1951-52
　　　　Jacques Plante, 1961-62

Most goals allowed
192—Patrick Roy, 1992-93

Lowest goals-against average
0.92—George Hainsworth, 1928-29

Most shutouts
22—George Hainsworth, 1928-29

Most wins
42—Jacques Plante, 1955-56
　　Jacques Plante, 1961-62
　　Ken Dryden, 1975-76

Most losses
31—Jose Theodore, 2002-03

Most ties
19—Jacques Plante, 1962-63

FRANCHISE LEADERS

Players in boldface played for club in 2002-03

FORWARDS/DEFENSEMEN

Games
Henri Richard 1256
Larry Robinson 1202
Bob Gainey 1160
Jean Beliveau 1125
Claude Provost..............................1005

Goals
Maurice Richard 544
Guy Lafleur......................................518
Jean Beliveau 507
Yvan Cournoyer...............................428
Steve Shutt......................................408

Assists
Guy Lafleur.......................................728
Jean Beliveau 712
Henri Richard 688
Larry Robinson 686
Jacques Lemaire 469

Points
Guy Lafleur....................................1246
Jean Beliveau 1219
Henri Richard 1046
Maurice Richard 965
Larry Robinson 883

Penalty minutes
Chris Nilan.......................................2248
Lyle Odelein.....................................1367
Shayne Corson.................................1341
Maurice Richard 1285
John Ferguson 1214

GOALTENDERS

Games
Jacques Plante 556
Patrick Roy..551
Ken Dryden 397
Bill Durnan 383
George Hainsworth 318

Shutouts
George Hainsworth 75
Jacques Plante 58
Ken Dryden 46
Bill Durnan 34
Patrick Roy..29

**Goals-against average
(2400 minutes minimum)**
George Hainsworth 1.78
Lorne Chabot 2.07
Jacques Plante 2.23
Ken Dryden 2.24
Jerry McNeal.....................................2.36

Wins
Jacques Plante 312
Patrick Roy..289
Ken Dryden 258
Bill Durnan 208
George Hainsworth 167

MONTREAL MAROONS (DEFUNCT)
YEAR-BY-YEAR RECORDS

| | REGULAR SEASON | | | | | PLAYOFFS | | | |
Season	W	L	T	Pts.	Finish	W	L	Highest round	Coach
1924-25	9	19	2	20	5th	—	—		Eddie Gerard
1925-26	20	11	5	45	2nd	3	1	Stanley Cup champ	Eddie Gerard
1926-27	20	20	4	44	3rd/Canadian	*0	1	Quarterfinals	Eddie Gerard
1927-28	24	14	6	54	2nd/Canadian	*5	3	Stanley Cup finals	Eddie Gerard
1928-29	15	20	9	39	5th/Canadian	—	—		Eddie Gerard
1929-30	23	16	5	51	1st/Canadian	1	3	Semifinals	Dunc Munro
1930-31	20	18	6	46	3rd/Canadian	*0	2	Quarterfinals	Dunc Munro, George Boucher
1931-32	19	22	7	45	3rd/Canadian	*1	1	Semifinals	Sprague Cleghorn
1932-33	22	20	6	50	2nd/Canadian	0	2	Quarterfinals	Eddie Gerard
1933-34	19	18	11	49	3rd/Canadian	*1	2	Semifinals	Eddie Gerard
1934-35	24	19	5	53	2nd/Canadian	*5	0	Stanley Cup champ	Tommy Gorman
1935-36	22	16	10	54	1st/Canadian	0	3	Semifinals	Tommy Gorman
1936-37	22	17	9	53	2nd/Canadian	2	3	Semifinals	Tommy Gorman
1937-38	12	30	6	30	4th/Canadian	—	—		King Clancy, Tommy Gorman

*Won-lost record does not indicate tie(s) resulting from two-game, total goals series that year (two-game, total-goals series were played from 1917-18 through 1935-36).

MONTREAL WANDERERS (DEFUNCT)
YEAR-BY-YEAR RECORDS

| | REGULAR SEASON | | | | | PLAYOFFS | | | |
Season	W	L	T	Pts.	Finish	W	L	Highest round	Coach
1917-18*	1	5	0	2	4th	—	—		Art Ross

*Franchise disbanded after Montreal Arena burned down. Montreal Canadiens and Toronto each counted one win for defaulted games with Wanderers.

NASHVILLE PREDATORS
YEAR-BY-YEAR RECORDS

	REGULAR SEASON						PLAYOFFS			
Season	W	L	T	OTL	Pts.	Finish	W	L	Highest round	Coach
1998-99	28	47	7	—	63	4th/Central	—	—		Barry Trotz
1999-00	28	40	7	7	70	4th/Central	—	—		Barry Trotz
2000-01	34	36	9	3	80	3rd/Central	—	—		Barry Trotz
2001-02	28	41	13	0	69	4th/Central	—	—		Barry Trotz
2002-03	27	35	13	7	74	4th/Central	—	—		Barry Trotz

FIRST-ROUND ENTRY DRAFT CHOICES

Year   Player, Overall, Last amateur team (league)
1998—David Legwand, 2, Plymouth (OHL)
1999—Brian Finley, 6, Barrie (OHL)
2000—Scott Hartnell, 6, Prince Albert (WHL)

Year   Player, Overall, Last amateur team (league)
2001—Dan Hamhuis, 12, Prince George (WHL)
2002—Scottie Upshall, 6, Kamloops (WHL)
2003—Ryan Suter, 7, U.S. National under-18 (NTDP)

SINGLE-SEASON INDIVIDUAL RECORDS

FORWARDS/DEFENSEMEN

Most goals
26—Cliff Ronning, 1999-2000

Most assists
43—Cliff Ronning, 2000-01

Most points
62—Cliff Ronning, 1999-2000
Cliff Ronning, 2000-01

Most penalty minutes
242—Patrick Cote, 1998-99

Most power play goals
14—Andy Delmore, 2002-03

Most shorthanded goals
3—Greg Johnson, 1998-99

Tom Fitzgerald, 1999-2000
Scott Walker, 2000-01

Most games with three or more goals
1—Robert Valicevic, 1999-2000
Scott Walker, 2000-01
Petr Tenkrat, 2001-02

Most shots
248—Cliff Ronning, 1999-2000

GOALTENDERS

Most games
69—Tomas Vokoun, 2002-03

Most minutes
3,316—Mike Dunham, 2001-02

Most shots against
1,771—Tomas Vokoun, 2002-03

Most goals allowed
146—Mike Dunham, 1999-2000
Tomas Vokoun, 2002-03

Lowest goals-against average
2.20—Tomas Vokoun, 2002-03

Most shutouts
4—Mike Dunham, 2000-01

Most wins
25—Tomas Vokoun, 2002-03

Most losses
31—Tomas Vokoun, 2002-03

Most ties
11—Tomas Vokoun, 2002-03

FRANCHISE LEADERS

Players in boldface played for club in 2002-03

FORWARDS/DEFENSEMEN

Games
Greg Johnson 352
Vitali Yachmenev.....................338
Kimmo Timonen 337
Tom Fitzgerald...............................307
Karlis Skrastins.......................307

Goals
Cliff Ronning 81
Greg Johnson..............................68
Scott Walker 66
Vitali Yachmenev 54
David Legwand............................54

Assists
Cliff Ronning 145
Greg Johnson 119
Kimmo Timonen 109

Scott Walker 98
David Legwand..........................93

Points
Cliff Ronning 226
Greg Johnson 187
Scott Walker 164
Kimmo Timonen 152
David Legwand 147

Penalty minutes
Cale Hulse.......................................370
Scott Walker 335
Drake Berehowsky............................327
Patrick Cote.....................................312
Scott Hartnell 260

GOALTENDERS

Games
Mike Dunham 217

Tomas Vokoun 205
Eric Fichaud...9
Chris Mason...4
Jan Lasak..6

Shutouts
Tomas Vokoun 9
Mike Dunham.......................................8

Goals-against average
(2400 minutes minimum)
Tomas Vokoun 2.53
Mike Dunham 2.72

Wins
Mike Dunham..................................81
Tomas Vokoun 64

NEW JERSEY DEVILS
YEAR-BY-YEAR RECORDS

	REGULAR SEASON						PLAYOFFS			
Season	W	L	T	OTL	Pts.	Finish	W	L	Highest round	Coach
1974-75*	15	54	11	—	41	5th/Smythe	—	—		Bep Guidolin
1975-76*	12	56	12	—	36	5th/Smythe	—	—		Bep Guidolin, Sid Abel, Eddie Bush
1976-77†	20	46	14	—	54	5th/Smythe	—	—		John Wilson
1977-78†	19	40	21	—	59	2nd/Smythe	0	2	Preliminaries	Pat Kelly

			REGULAR SEASON					PLAYOFFS		
Season	W	L	T	OTL	Pts.	Finish	W	L	Highest round	Coach
1978-79†	15	53	12	—	42	4th/Smythe	—	—		Pat Kelly, Bep Guidolin
1979-80†	19	48	13	—	51	6th/Smythe	—	—		Don Cherry
1980-81†	22	45	13	—	57	5th/Smythe	—	—		Billy MacMillan
1981-82†	18	49	13	—	49	5th/Smythe	—	—		Bert Marshall, Marshall Johnston
1982-83	17	49	14	—	48	5th/Patrick	—	—		Billy MacMillan
1983-84	17	56	7	—	41	5th/Patrick	—	—		Billy MacMillan, Tom McVie
1984-85	22	48	10	—	54	5th/Patrick	—	—		Doug Carpenter
1985-86	28	49	3	—	59	6th/Patrick	—	—		Doug Carpenter
1986-87	29	45	6	—	64	6th/Patrick	—	—		Doug Carpenter
1987-88	38	36	6	—	82	4th/Patrick	11	9	Conference finals	Doug Carpenter, Jim Schoenfeld
1988-89	27	41	12	—	66	5th/Patrick	—	—		Jim Schoenfeld
1989-90	37	34	9	—	83	2nd/Patrick	2	4	Division semifinals	Jim Schoenfeld, John Cunniff
1990-91	32	33	15	—	79	4th/Patrick	3	4	Division semifinals	John Cunniff, Tom McVie
1991-92	38	31	11	—	87	4th/Patrick	3	4	Division semifinals	Tom McVie
1992-93	40	37	7	—	87	4th/Patrick	1	4	Division semifinals	Herb Brooks
1993-94	47	25	12	—	106	2nd/Atlantic	11	9	Conference finals	Jacques Lemaire
1994-95	22	18	8	—	52	2nd/Atlantic	16	4	Stanley Cup champ	Jacques Lemaire
1995-96	37	33	12	—	86	6th/Atlantic	—	—		Jacques Lemaire
1996-97	45	23	14	—	104	1st/Atlantic	5	5	Conference semifinals	Jacques Lemaire
1997-98	48	23	11	—	107	1st/Atlantic	2	4	Conference quarterfinals	Jacques Lemaire
1998-99	47	24	11	—	105	1st/Atlantic	3	4	Conference quarterfinals	Robbie Ftorek
1999-00	45	24	8	5	103	2nd/Atlantic	16	7	Stanley Cup champ	Robbie Ftorek, Larry Robinson
2000-01	48	19	12	3	111	1st/Atlantic	15	10	Stanley Cup finals	Larry Robinson
2001-02	41	28	9	4	95	3rd/Atlantic	2	4	Conference quarterfinals	Larry Robinson, Kevin Constantine
2002-03	46	20	10	6	108	1st/Atlantic	16	8	Stanley Cup finals	Pat Burns

*Kansas City Scouts.
†Colorado Rockies.

FIRST-ROUND ENTRY DRAFT CHOICES

Year Player, Overall, Last amateur team (league)

1974—Wilf Paiement, 2, St. Catharines (OHL)
1975—Barry Dean, 2, Medicine Hat (WCHL)
1976—Paul Gardner, 11, Oshawa (OHL)
1977—Barry Beck, 2, New Westminster (WCHL)
1978—Mike Gillis, 5, Kingston (OHL)
1979—Rob Ramage, 1, Birmingham (WHA)*
1980—Paul Gagne, 19, Windsor (OHL)
1981—Joe Cirella, 5, Oshawa (OHL)
1982—Rocky Trottier, 8, Billings (WHL)
      Ken Daneyko, 18, Seattle (WHL)
1983—John MacLean, 6, Oshawa (OHL)
1984—Kirk Muller, 2, Guelph (OHL)
1985—Craig Wolanin, 3, Kitchener (OHL)
1986—Neil Brady, 3, Medicine Hat (WHL)
1987—Brendan Shanahan, 2, London (OHL)
1988—Corey Foster, 12, Peterborough (OHL)
1989—Bill Guerin, 5, Springfield (Mass.) Jr.
      Jason Miller, 18, Medicine Hat (WHL)

Year Player, Overall, Last amateur team (league)

1990—Martin Brodeur, 20, St. Hyacinthe (QMJHL)
1991—Scott Niedermayer, 3, Kamloops (WHL)
      Brian Rolston, 11, Detroit Compuware Jr.
1992—Jason Smith, 18, Regina (WHL)
1993—Denis Pederson, 13, Prince Albert (WHL)
1994—Vadim Sharifjanov, 25, Salavat (Russia)
1995—Petr Sykora, 18, Detroit (IHL)
1996—Lance Ward, 10, Red Deer (WHL)
1997—Jean-Francois Damphousse, 24, Moncton (QMJHL)
1998—Mike Van Ryn, 26, Michigan
      Scott Gomez, 27, Tri-City (WHL)
1999—Ari Ahonen, 27, Jyvaskyla, Finland
2000—David Hale, 22, Sioux City (USHL)
2001—Adrian Foster, 28, Saskatoon (WHL)
2002—No first-round selection
2003—Zach Parise, 17, North Dakota (WCHA)

*Designates first player chosen in draft.

SINGLE-SEASON INDIVIDUAL RECORDS

FORWARDS/DEFENSEMEN

Most goals
46—Pat Verbeek, 1987-88

Most assists
60—Scott Stevens, 1993-94

Most points
96—Patrik Elias, 2000-01

Most penalty minutes
295—Krzysztof Oliwa, 1997-98

Most power play goals
19—John MacLean, 1990-91

Most shorthanded goals
6—John Madden, 1999-2000

Most games with three or more goals
3—Kirk Muller, 1987-88
   John MacLean, 1988-89
   Patrik Elias, 2000-01

Most shots
322—John MacLean, 1989-90

GOALTENDERS

Most games
77—Martin Brodeur, 1995-96

Most minutes
4,433—Martin Brodeur, 1995-96

Most shots against
1,954—Martin Brodeur, 1995-96

Most goals allowed
243—Denis Herron, 1975-76

Lowest goals-against average
1.88—Martin Brodeur, 1996-97

Most shutouts
10—Martin Brodeur, 1996-97
    Martin Brodeur, 1997-98

Most wins
43—Martin Brodeur, 1997-98
    Martin Brodeur, 1999-2000

Most losses
39—Denis Herron, 1975-76

Most ties
13—Martin Brodeur, 1996-97

FRANCHISE LEADERS

Players in boldface played for club in 2002-03

FORWARDS/DEFENSEMEN

Games
Ken Daneyko...................................**1283**
John MacLean......................................934
Scott Stevens **918**
Scott Niedermayer **811**
Randy McKay 760

Goals
John MacLean.....................................347
Bobby Holik..198
Kirk Muller...185
Pat Verbeek.......................................170
Patrick Elias.............................**169**

Assists
John MacLean.....................................354
Kirk Muller...335
Scott Stevens **328**
Scott Niedermayer **324**
Bruce Driver 316

Points
John MacLean......................................701
Kirk Muller...520
Aaron Broten......................................469
Bobby Holik..463
Scott Niedermayer **422**

Penalty minutes
Ken Daneyko...........................**2519**
Randy McKay 1418
John MacLean......................................1168
Scott Stevens **985**
Pat Verbeek.......................................943

GOALTENDERS

Games
Martin Brodeur...........................**665**
Chris Terreri 302
Chico Resch 267
Sean Burke 162
Michel Plasse 150

Shutouts
Martin Brodeur **64**
Chris Terreri 7
Craig Billington 4
Sean Burke...4
Mike Dunham.......................................3

Goals-against average
(2400 minutes minimum)
Martin Brodeur.........................**2.19**
Chris Terreri 3.07
Sean Burke 3.65
Hardy Astrom 3.76
Doug Favell 3.84

Wins
Martin Brodeur...........................**365**
Chris Terreri 118
Chico Resch 67
Sean Burke 62
Alain Chevrier......................................53

NEW YORK AMERICANS (DEFUNCT)
YEAR-BY-YEAR RECORDS

	REGULAR SEASON					**PLAYOFFS**			
Season	W	L	T	Pts.	Finish	W	L	Highest round	Coach
1919-20*	4	20	0	8	4th/4th	—	—		Mike Quinn
1920-21†	6	18	0	12	4th/4th	—	—		Percy Thompson
1921-22†	7	17	0	14	4th	—	—		Percy Thompson
1922-23†	6	18	0	12	4th	—	—		Art Ross
1923-24†	9	15	0	18	4th	—	—		Percy Lesueur
1924-25†	19	10	1	39	1st	‡—	—		Jimmy Gardner
1925-26	12	20	4	28	5th	—	—		Tommy Gorman
1926-27	17	25	2	36	4th/Canadian	—	—		Newsy Lalonde
1927-28	11	27	6	28	5th/Canadian	—	—		Wilf Green
1928-29	19	13	12	50	2nd/Canadian	§0	1	Semifinals	Tommy Gorman
1929-30	14	25	5	33	5th/Canadian	—	—		Lionel Conacher
1930-31	18	16	10	46	4th/Canadian	—	—		Eddie Gerard
1931-32	16	24	8	40	4th/Canadian	—	—		Eddie Gerard
1932-33	15	22	11	41	4th/Canadian	—	—		Joe Simpson
1933-34	15	23	10	40	4th/Canadian	—	—		Joe Simpson
1934-35	12	27	9	33	4th/Canadian	—	—		Joe Simpson
1935-36	16	25	7	39	3rd/Canadian	2	3	Semifinals	Red Dutton
1936-37	15	29	4	34	4th/Canadian	—	—		Red Dutton
1937-38	19	18	11	49	2nd/Canadian	3	3	Semifinals	Red Dutton
1938-39	17	21	10	44	4th	0	2	Quarterfinals	Red Dutton
1939-40	15	29	4	34	6th	1	2	Quarterfinals	Red Dutton
1940-41	8	29	11	27	7th	—	—		Red Dutton
1941-42∞	16	29	3	35	7th	—	—		Red Dutton

*Quebec Bulldogs.

†Hamilton Tigers.

∞Brooklyn Americans.

‡Refused to participate in playoffs—held out for more compensation.

§Won-lost record does not indicate tie(s) resulting from two-game, total goals series that year (two-game, total-goals series were played from 1917-18 through 1935-36).

NEW YORK ISLANDERS
YEAR-BY-YEAR RECORDS

			REGULAR SEASON				PLAYOFFS		
Season	W	L	T	OTL	Pts.	Finish	W	L	Highest round	Coach
1972-73	12	60	6	—	30	8th/East	—	—		Phil Goyette, Earl Ingarfield
1973-74	19	41	18	—	56	8th/East	—	—		Al Arbour
1974-75	33	25	22	—	88	3rd/Patrick	9	8	Semifinals	Al Arbour
1975-76	42	21	17	—	101	2nd/Patrick	7	6	Semifinals	Al Arbour
1976-77	47	21	12	—	106	2nd/Patrick	8	4	Semifinals	Al Arbour
1977-78	48	17	15	—	111	1st/Patrick	3	4	Quarterfinals	Al Arbour
1978-79	51	15	14	—	116	1st/Patrick	6	4	Semifinals	Al Arbour
1979-80	39	28	13	—	91	2nd/Patrick	15	6	Stanley Cup champ	Al Arbour
1980-81	48	18	14	—	110	1st/Patrick	15	3	Stanley Cup champ	Al Arbour
1981-82	54	16	10	—	118	1st/Patrick	15	4	Stanley Cup champ	Al Arbour
1982-83	42	26	12	—	96	2nd/Patrick	15	5	Stanley Cup champ	Al Arbour
1983-84	50	26	4	—	104	1st/Patrick	12	9	Stanley Cup finals	Al Arbour
1984-85	40	34	6	—	86	3rd/Patrick	4	6	Division finals	Al Arbour
1985-86	39	29	12	—	90	3rd/Patrick	0	3	Division semifinals	Al Arbour
1986-87	35	33	12	—	82	3rd/Patrick	7	7	Division finals	Terry Simpson
1987-88	39	31	10	—	88	1st/Patrick	2	4	Division semifinals	Terry Simpson
1988-89	28	47	5	—	61	6th/Patrick	—	—		Terry Simpson, Al Arbour
1989-90	31	38	11	—	73	4th/Patrick	1	4	Division semifinals	Al Arbour
1990-91	25	45	10	—	60	6th/Patrick	—	—		Al Arbour
1991-92	34	35	11	—	79	5th/Patrick	—	—		Al Arbour
1992-93	40	37	7	—	87	3rd/Patrick	9	9	Conference finals	Al Arbour
1993-94	36	36	12	—	84	4th/Atlantic	0	4	Conference quarterfinals	Al Arbour, Lorne Henning
1994-95	15	28	5	—	35	7th/Atlantic	—	—		Lorne Henning
1995-96	22	50	10	—	54	7th/Atlantic	—	—		Mike Milbury
1996-97	29	41	12	—	70	7th/Atlantic	—	—		Mike Milbury, Rick Bowness
1997-98	30	41	11	—	71	4th/Atlantic	—	—		Rick Bowness, Mike Milbury
1998-99	24	48	10	—	58	5th/Atlantic	—	—		Mike Milbury, Bill Stewart
1999-00	24	48	9	1	58	5th/Atlantic	—	—		Butch Goring
2000-01	21	51	7	3	52	5th/Atlantic	—	—		Butch Goring, Lorne Henning
2001-02	42	28	8	4	96	2nd/Atlantic	3	4	Conference quarterfinals	Peter Laviolette
2002-03	35	34	11	2	83	3rd/Atlantic	1	4	Conference quarterfinals	Peter Laviolette

FIRST-ROUND ENTRY DRAFT CHOICES

Year   Player, Overall, Last amateur team (league)

1972—Billy Harris, 1, Toronto (OHL)*
1973—Denis Potvin, 1, Ottawa (OHL)*
1974—Clark Gillies, 4, Regina (WCHL)
1975—Pat Price, 11, Vancouver (WHA)
1976—Alex McKendry, 14, Sudbury (OHL)
1977—Mike Bossy, 15, Laval (QMJHL)
1978—Steve Tambellini, 15, Lethbridge (WCHL)
1979—Duane Sutter, 17, Lethbridge (WHL)
1980—Brent Sutter, 17, Red Deer (AJHL)
1981—Paul Boutilier, 21, Sherbrooke (QMJHL)
1982—Pat Flatley, 21, University of Wisconsin
1983—Pat LaFontaine, 3, Verdun (QMJHL)
            Gerald Diduck, 16, Lethbridge (WHL)
1984—Duncan MacPherson, 20, Saskatoon (WHL)
1985—Brad Dalgarno, 6, Hamilton (OHL)
            Derek King, 13, Sault Ste. Marie (OHL)
1986—Tom Fitzgerald, 17, Austin Prep (Mass.)
1987—Dean Chynoweth, 13, Medicine Hat (WHL)
1988—Kevin Cheveldayoff, 16, Brandon (WHL)
1989—Dave Chyzowski, 2, Kamloops (WHL)

Year   Player, Overall, Last amateur team (league)

1990—Scott Scissons, 6, Saskatoon (WHL)
1991—Scott Lachance, 4, Boston University
1992—Darius Kasparaitis, 5, Dynamo Moscow (CIS)
1993—Todd Bertuzzi, 23, Guelph (OHL)
1994—Brett Lindros, 9, Kingston (OHL)
1995—Wade Redden, 2, Brandon (WHL)
1996—Jean-Pierre Dumont, 3, Val-d'Or (QMJHL)
1997—Roberto Luongo, 4, Val d'Or (QMJHL)
            Eric Brewer, 5, Prince George (WHL)
1998—Michael Rupp, 9, Erie (OHL)
1999—Tim Connolly, 5, Erie (OHL)
            Taylor Pyatt, 8, Sudbury (OHL)
            Branislav Mezei, 10, Belleville (OHL)
            Kristian Kudroc, 28, Michalovce, Slovakia
2000—Rick DiPietro, 1, Boston University*
            Raffi Torres, 5, Brampton (OHL)
2001—No first-round selection
2002—Sean Bergenheim, 22, Jokerit, Finland
2003—Robert Nilsson, 15, Sweden
*Designates first player chosen in draft.

SINGLE-SEASON INDIVIDUAL RECORDS

FORWARDS/DEFENSEMEN

Most goals
69—Mike Bossy, 1978-79

Most assists
87—Bryan Trottier, 1978-79

Most points
147—Mike Bossy, 1981-82

Most penalty minutes
356—Brian Curran, 1986-87

Most power play goals
28—Mike Bossy, 1980-81

Most shorthanded goals
7—Bob Bourne, 1980-81

Most games with three or more goals
9—Mike Bossy, 1980-81

Most shots
315—Mike Bossy, 1980-81

NHL HISTORY   Team by team

GOALTENDERS

Most games
66—Chris Osgood, 2001-02

Most minutes
3,743—Chris Osgood, 2001-02

Most shots against
1,801—Ron Hextall, 1993-94

Most goals allowed
195—Gerry Desjardins, 1972-73

Lowest goals-against average
2.07—Chico Resch, 1975-76

Most shutouts
7—Chico Resch, 1975-76

Most wins
32—Billy Smith, 1981-82
Chris Osgood, 2001-02

Most losses
35—Gerry Desjardins, 1972-73

Most ties
17—Billy Smith, 1974-75

FRANCHISE LEADERS

Players in boldface played for club in 2002-03

FORWARDS/DEFENSEMEN

Games
Bryan Trottier	1123
Denis Potvin	1060
Bob Nystrom	900
Clark Gillies	872
Bob Bourne	814

Goals
Mike Bossy	573
Bryan Trottier	500
Denis Potvin	310
Clark Gillies	304
Pat LaFontaine	287
Brent Sutter	287

Assists
Bryan Trottier	853
Denis Potvin	742
Mike Bossy	553
Clark Gillies	359
John Tonelli	338

Points
Bryan Trottier	1353
Mike Bossy	1126
Denis Potvin	1052
Clark Gillies	663
Brent Sutter	610

Penalty minutes
Mick Vukota	1879
Rich Pilon	1525
Garry Howatt	1466
Denis Potvin	1354
Bob Nystrom	1248

GOALTENDERS

Games
Billy Smith	675
Chico Resch	282
Kelly Hrudey	241
Tommy Salo	187
Glenn Healy	176

Shutouts
Chico Resch	25
Billy Smith	22
Tommy Salo	14
Kelly Hrudey	6
Chris Osgood	**6**

**Goals-against average
(2400 minutes minimum)**
Garth Snow	**2.45**
Chico Resch	2.56
Chris Osgood	**2.65**
Tommy Salo	2.77
Wade Flaherty	2.84

Wins
Billy Smith	304
Chico Resch	157
Kelly Hrudey	106
Roland Melanson	77
Glenn Healy	66

NEW YORK RANGERS
YEAR-BY-YEAR RECORDS

		REGULAR SEASON						PLAYOFFS		
Season	W	L	T	OTL	Pts.	Finish	W	L	Highest round	Coach
1926-27	25	13	6	—	56	1st/American	*0	1	Semifinals	Lester Patrick
1927-28	19	16	9	—	47	2nd/American	*5	3	Stanley Cup champ	Lester Patrick
1928-29	21	13	10	—	52	2nd/American	*3	2	Stanley Cup finals	Lester Patrick
1929-30	17	17	10	—	44	3rd/American	*1	2	Semifinals	Lester Patrick
1930-31	19	16	9	—	47	3rd/American	2	2	Semifinals	Lester Patrick
1931-32	23	17	8	—	54	1st/American	3	4	Stanley Cup finals	Lester Patrick
1932-33	23	17	8	—	54	3rd/American	*6	1	Stanley Cup champ	Lester Patrick
1933-34	21	19	8	—	50	3rd/American	*0	1	Quarterfinals	Lester Patrick
1934-35	22	20	6	—	50	3rd/American	*1	1	Semifinals	Lester Patrick
1935-36	19	17	12	—	50	4th/American	—	—		Lester Patrick
1936-37	19	20	9	—	47	3rd/American	6	3	Stanley Cup finals	Lester Patrick
1937-38	27	15	6	—	60	2nd/American	1	2	Quarterfinals	Lester Patrick
1938-39	26	16	6	—	58	2nd	3	4	Semifinals	Lester Patrick
1939-40	27	11	10	—	64	2nd	8	4	Stanley Cup champ	Frank Boucher
1940-41	21	19	8	—	50	4th	1	2	Quarterfinals	Frank Boucher
1941-42	29	17	2	—	60	1st	2	4	Semifinals	Frank Boucher
1942-43	11	31	8	—	30	6th	—	—		Frank Boucher
1943-44	6	39	5	—	17	6th	—	—		Frank Boucher
1944-45	11	29	10	—	32	6th	—	—		Frank Boucher
1945-46	13	28	9	—	35	6th	—	—		Frank Boucher
1946-47	22	32	6	—	50	5th	—	—		Frank Boucher
1947-48	21	26	13	—	55	4th	2	4	League semifinals	Frank Boucher
1948-49	18	31	11	—	47	6th	—	—		Frank Boucher, Lynn Patrick
1949-50	28	31	11	—	67	4th	7	5	Stanley Cup finals	Lynn Patrick
1950-51	20	29	21	—	61	5th	—	—		Neil Colville
1951-52	23	34	13	—	59	5th	—	—		Neil Colville, Bill Cook
1952-53	17	37	16	—	50	6th	—	—		Bill Cook
1953-54	29	31	10	—	68	5th	—	—		Frank Boucher, Muzz Patrick
1954-55	17	35	18	—	52	5th	—	—		Muzz Patrick

Season	W	L	T	OTL	Pts.	Finish	W	L	Highest round	Coach
					REGULAR SEASON				**PLAYOFFS**	
1955-56	32	28	10	—	74	3rd	1	4	League semifinals	Phil Watson
1956-57	26	30	14	—	66	4th	1	4	League semifinals	Phil Watson
1957-58	32	25	13	—	77	2nd	2	4	League semifinals	Phil Watson
1958-59	26	32	12	—	64	5th	—	—		Phil Watson
1959-60	17	38	15	—	49	6th	—	—		Phil Watson, Alf Pike
1960-61	22	38	10	—	54	5th	—	—		Alf Pike
1961-62	26	32	12	—	64	4th	2	4	League semifinals	Doug Harvey
1962-63	22	36	12	—	56	5th	—	—		Muzz Patrick, Red Sullivan
1963-64	22	38	10	—	54	5th	—	—		Red Sullivan
1964-65	20	38	12	—	52	5th	—	—		Red Sullivan
1965-66	18	41	11	—	47	6th	—	—		Red Sullivan, Emile Francis
1966-67	30	28	12	—	72	4th	0	4	League semifinals	Emile Francis
1967-68	39	23	12	—	90	2nd/East	2	4	Division semifinals	Emile Francis
1968-69	41	26	9	—	91	3rd/East	0	4	Division semifinals	Bernie Geoffrion, Emile Francis
1969-70	38	22	16	—	92	4th/East	2	4	Division semifinals	Emile Francis
1970-71	49	18	11	—	109	2nd/East	7	6	Division finals	Emile Francis
1971-72	48	17	13	—	109	2nd/East	10	6	Stanley Cup finals	Emile Francis
1972-73	47	23	8	—	102	3rd/East	5	5	Division finals	Emile Francis
1973-74	40	24	14	—	94	3rd/East	7	6	Division finals	Larry Popein, Emile Francis
1974-75	37	29	14	—	88	2nd/Patrick	1	2	Preliminaries	Emile Francis
1975-76	29	42	9	—	67	4th/Patrick	—	—		Ron Stewart, John Ferguson
1976-77	29	37	14	—	72	4th/Patrick	—	—		John Ferguson
1977-78	30	37	13	—	73	4th/Patrick	1	2	Preliminaries	Jean-Guy Talbot
1978-79	40	29	11	—	91	3rd/Patrick	11	7	Stanley Cup finals	Fred Shero
1979-80	38	32	10	—	86	3rd/Patrick	4	5	Quarterfinals	Fred Shero
1980-81	30	36	14	—	74	4th/Patrick	7	7	Semifinals	Fred Shero, Craig Patrick
1981-82	39	27	14	—	92	2nd/Patrick	5	5	Division finals	Herb Brooks
1982-83	35	35	10	—	80	4th/Patrick	5	4	Division finals	Herb Brooks
1983-84	42	29	9	—	93	4th/Patrick	2	3	Division semifinals	Herb Brooks
1984-85	26	44	10	—	62	4th/Patrick	0	3	Division semifinals	Herb Brooks, Craig Patrick
1985-86	36	38	6	—	78	4th/Patrick	8	8	Conference finals	Ted Sator
1986-87	34	38	8	—	76	4th/Patrick	2	4	Division semifinals	Ted Sator, Tom Webster, Phil Esposito
1987-88	36	34	10	—	82	5th/Patrick	—	—		Michel Bergeron
1988-89	37	35	8	—	82	3rd/Patrick	0	4	Division semifinals	Michel Bergeron, Phil Esposito
1989-90	36	31	13	—	85	1st/Patrick	5	5	Division finals	Roger Neilson
1990-91	36	31	13	—	85	2nd/Patrick	2	4	Division semifinals	Roger Neilson
1991-92	50	25	5	—	105	1st/Patrick	6	7	Division finals	Roger Neilson
1992-93	34	39	11	—	79	6th/Patrick	—	—		Roger Neilson, Ron Smith
1993-94	52	24	8	—	112	1st/Atlantic	16	7	Stanley Cup champ	Mike Keenan
1994-95	22	23	3	—	47	4th/Atlantic	4	6	Conference semifinals	Colin Campbell
1995-96	41	27	14	—	96	2nd/Atlantic	5	6	Conference semifinals	Colin Campbell
1996-97	38	34	10	—	86	4th/Atlantic	9	6	Conference finals	Colin Campbell
1997-98	25	39	18	—	68	5th/Atlantic	—	—		Colin Campbell, John Muckler
1998-99	33	38	11	—	77	4th/Atlantic	—	—		John Muckler
1999-00	29	38	12	3	73	4th/Atlantic	—	—		John Muckler, John Tortorella
2000-01	33	43	5	1	72	4th/Atlantic	—	—		Ron Low
2001-02	36	38	4	4	80	4th/Atlantic	—	—		Ron Low
2002-03	32	36	10	4	78	4th/Atlantic	—	—		Bryan Trottier, Glen Sather

*Won-lost record does not indicate tie(s) resulting from two-game, total goals series that year (two-game, total-goals series were played from 1917-18 through 1935-36).

FIRST-ROUND ENTRY DRAFT CHOICES

Year Player, Overall, Last amateur team (league)

1969—Andre Dupont, 8, Montreal (OHL)
Pierre Jarry, 12, Ottawa (OHL)
1970—Normand Gratton, 11, Montreal (OHL)
1971—Steve Vickers, 10, Toronto (OHL)
Steve Durbano, 13, Toronto (OHL)
1972—Albert Blanchard, 10, Kitchener (OHL)
Bobby MacMillan, 15, St. Catharines (OHL)
1973—Rick Middleton, 14, Oshawa (OHL)
1974—Dave Maloney, 14, Kitchener (OHL)
1975—Wayne Dillon, 12, Toronto (WHA)
1976—Don Murdoch, 6, Medicine Hat (WCHL)
1977—Lucien DeBlois, 8, Sorel (QMJHL)
Ron Duguay, 13, Sudbury (OHL)
1978—No first-round selection
1979—Doug Sulliman, 13, Kitchener (OHL)
1980—Jim Malone, 14, Toronto (OHL)
1981—James Patrick, 9, Prince Albert (AJHL)

Year Player, Overall, Last amateur team (league)

1982—Chris Kontos, 15, Toronto (OHL)
1983—Dave Gagner, 12, Brantford (OHL)
1984—Terry Carkner, 14, Peterborough (OHL)
1985—Ulf Dahlen, 7, Ostersund (Sweden)
1986—Brian Leetch, 9, Avon Old Farms Prep (Ct.)
1987—Jayson More, 10, New Westminster (WCHL)
1988—No first-round selection
1989—Steven Rice, 20, Kitchener (OHL)
1990—Michael Stewart, 13, Michigan State University
1991—Alexei Kovalev, 15, Dynamo Moscow, USSR
1992—Peter Ferraro, 24, Waterloo (USHL)
1993—Niklas Sundstrom, 8, Ornskoldsvik, Sweden
1994—Dan Cloutier, 26, Sault Ste. Marie (OHL)
1995—No first-round selection
1996—Jeff Brown, 22, Sarnia (OHL)
1997—Stefan Cherneski, 19, Brandon (WHL)
1998—Manny Malhotra, 7, Guelph (OHL)

Year	Player, Overall, Last amateur team (league)	Year	Player, Overall, Last amateur team (league)
1999—Pavel Brendl, 4, Calgary (WHL)		2001—Daniel Blackburn, 10, Kootenay (WHL)	
Jamie Lundmark, 9, Moose Jaw (WHL)		2002—No first-round selection	
2000—No first-round selection		2003—Hugh Jessiman, 12, Dartmouth (ECAC)	

SINGLE-SEASON INDIVIDUAL RECORDS

FORWARDS/DEFENSEMEN

Most goals
52—Adam Graves, 1993-94

Most assists
80—Brian Leetch, 1991-92

Most points
109—Jean Ratelle, 1971-72

Most penalty minutes
305—Troy Mallette, 1989-90

Most power play goals
23—Vic Hadfield, 1971-72

Most shorthanded goals
7—Theo Fleury, 2000-01

Most games with three or more goals
4—Tomas Sandstrom, 1986-87

Most shots
344—Phil Esposito, 1976-77

GOALTENDERS

Most games
72—Mike Richter, 1997-98

Most minutes
4,200—Johnny Bower, 1953-54
Gump Worsley, 1955-56

Most goals allowed
310—Ken McAuley, 1943-44

Lowest goals-against average
1.48—John Ross Roach, 1928-29

Most shutouts
13—John Ross Roach, 1928-29

Most wins
42—Mike Richter, 1993-94

Most losses
39—Ken McAuley, 1943-44

Most ties
20—Chuck Rayner, 1950-51

FRANCHISE LEADERS

Players in boldface played for club in 2002-03

FORWARDS/DEFENSEMEN

Games

Harry Howell	1160
Brian Leetch	**1072**
Rod Gilbert	1065
Ron Greschner	982
Walt Tkaczuk	945

Goals

Rod Gilbert	406
Jean Ratelle	336
Adam Graves	280
Andy Bathgate	272
Vic Hadfield	262

Assists

Brian Leetch	**718**
Rod Gilbert	615
Jean Ratelle	481
Andy Bathgate	457
Walt Tkaczuk	451

Points

Rod Gilbert	1021
Brian Leetch	**945**
Jean Ratelle	817
Andy Bathgate	729
Walt Tkaczuk	678

Penalty minutes

Ron Greschner	1226
Jeff Beukeboom	1157
Harry Howell	1147
Don Maloney	1113
Vic Hadfield	1036

GOALTENDERS

Games

Mike Richter	**666**
Gump Worsley	582
Ed Giacomin	539
John Vanbiesbrouck	449
Chuck Rayner	376

Shutouts

Ed Giacomin	49
Dave Kerr	40
John Ross Roach	30
Chuck Rayner	24
Mike Richter	**24**
Gump Worsley	24

Goals-against average
(2400 minutes minimum)

Lorne Chabot	1.61
Dave Kerr	2.07
John Ross Roach	2.16
Mike Dunham	**2.29**
Andy Aitkenhead	2.35

Wins

Mike Richter	**301**
Ed Giacomin	266
Gump Worsley	204
John Vanbiesbrouck	200
Dave Kerr	157

OTTAWA SENATORS (SECOND CLUB)

YEAR-BY-YEAR RECORDS

	REGULAR SEASON					PLAYOFFS			
Season	W	L	T	OTL	Pts.	Finish	W	L	Highest round	Coach
1992-93	10	70	4	—	24	6th/Adams	—	—		Rick Bowness
1993-94	14	61	9	—	37	7th/Northeast	—	—		Rick Bowness
1994-95	9	34	5	—	23	7th/Northeast	—	—		Rick Bowness
1995-96	18	59	5	—	41	6th/Northeast	—	—		Rick Bowness, Dave Allison, Jacques Martin
1996-97	31	36	15	—	77	3rd/Northeast	3	4	Conference quarterfinals	Jacques Martin
1997-98	34	33	15	—	83	5th/Northeast	5	6	Conference semifinals	Jacques Martin
1998-99	44	23	15	—	103	1st/Northeast	0	4	Conference quarterfinals	Jacques Martin
1999-00	41	28	11	2	95	2nd/Northeast	2	4	Conference quarterfinals	Jacques Martin
2000-01	48	21	9	4	109	1st/Northeast	0	4	Conference quarterfinals	Jacques Martin
2001-02	39	27	9	7	94	3rd/Northeast	7	5	Conference semifinals	Jacques Martin, Roger Neilson
2002-03	52	21	8	1	113	1st/Northeast	11	7	Conference finals	Jacques Martin

NHL HISTORY Team by team

FIRST-ROUND ENTRY DRAFT CHOICES

Year	Player, Overall, Last amateur team (league)
1992	Alexei Yashin, 2, Dynamo Moscow (CIS)
1993	Alexandre Daigle, 1, Victoriaville (QMJHL)*
1994	Radek Bonk, 3, Las Vegas (IHL)
1995	Bryan Berard, 1, Detroit (OHL)*
1996	Chris Phillips, 1, Prince Albert (WHL)*
1997	Marian Hossa, 12, Dukla Trencin, Czechoslovakia
1998	Mathieu Chouinard, 15, Shawinigan (QMJHL)

Year	Player, Overall, Last amateur team (league)
1999	Martin Havlat, 26, Trinec, Czech Republic
2000	Anton Volchenkov, 21, CSKA, Russia
2001	Jason Spezza, 2, Windsor (OHL)
	Tim Gleason, 23, Windsor (OHL)
2002	Jakub Klepis, 16, Portland (WHL)
2003	Patrick Eaves, 29, Boston College (H-East)
	*Designates first player chosen in draft.

SINGLE-SEASON INDIVIDUAL RECORDS

FORWARDS/DEFENSEMEN

Most goals
45—Marian Hosson, 2002-03

Most assists
51—Daniel Alfredsson, 2002-03

Most points
94—Alexei Yashin, 1998-99

Most penalty minutes
318—Mike Peluso, 1992-93

Most power play goals
19—Alexei Yashin, 1998-99

Most shorthanded goals
4—Magnus Arvedson, 1998-99

Most games with three or more goals
2—Daniel Alfredsson, 2001-02

Most shots
337—Alexei Yashin, 1998-99

GOALTENDERS

Most games
67—Patrick Lalime, 2002-03

Most minutes
3,943—Patrick Lalime, 2002-03

Most shots against
1,801—Craig Billington, 1993-94

Most goals allowed
254—Craig Billington, 1993-94

Lowest goals-against average
1.79—Ron Tugnutt, 1998-99

Most shutouts
8—Patrick Lalime, 2002-03

Most wins
39—Patrick Lalime, 2002-03

Most losses
46—Peter Sidorkiewicz, 1992-93

Most ties
14—Damian Rhodes, 1996-97

FRANCHISE LEADERS

Players in boldface played for club in 2002-03

FORWARDS/DEFENSEMEN

Games
Radek Bonk	**623**
Daniel Alfredsson	**552**
Wade Redden	**548**
Alexei Yashin	504
Shawn McEachern	454

Goals
Alexei Yashin	218
Daniel Alfredsson	**187**
Marian Hossa	**152**
Shawn McEachern	142
Radek Bonk	**140**

Assists
Daniel Alfredsson	**301**
Alexei Yashin	273
Radek Bonk	**215**
Wade Redden	**182**
Shawn McEachern	162

Points
Alexei Yashin	491
Daniel Alfredsson	**488**
Radek Bonk	**355**
Marian Hossa	**308**
Shawn McEachern	304

Penalty minutes
Dennis Vial	625
Denny Lambert	467
Andre Roy	462
Chris Neil	**378**
Troy Mallette	372

GOALTENDERS

Games
Patrick Lalime	**226**
Damian Rhodes	181
Ron Tugnutt	166
Craig Billington	72
Don Beaupre	71

Shutouts
Patrick Lalime	**25**
Ron Tugnutt	13
Damian Rhodes	11
Jani Hurme	5
Don Beaupre	2

Goals-against average (2400 minutes minimum)
Ron Tugnutt	2.32
Patrick Lalime	**2.32**
Jani Hurme	2.48
Damian Rhodes	2.56
Don Beaupre	3.53

Wins
Patrick Lalime	**121**
Ron Tugnutt	72
Damian Rhodes	65
Jani Hurme	25
Don Beaupre	14

PHILADELPHIA FLYERS
YEAR-BY-YEAR RECORDS

		REGULAR SEASON						PLAYOFFS		
Season	W	L	T	OTL	Pts.	Finish	W	L	Highest round	Coach
1967-68	31	32	11	—	73	1st/West	3	4	Division semifinals	Keith Allen
1968-69	20	35	21	—	61	3rd/West	0	4	Division semifinals	Keith Allen
1969-70	17	35	24	—	58	5th/West	—	—		Vic Stasiuk
1970-71	28	33	17	—	73	3rd/West	0	4	Division semifinals	Vic Stasiuk
1971-72	26	38	14	—	66	5th/West	—	—		Fred Shero
1972-73	37	30	11	—	85	2nd/West	5	6	Division finals	Fred Shero
1973-74	50	16	12	—	112	1st/West	12	5	Stanley Cup champ	Fred Shero
1974-75	51	18	11	—	113	1st/Patrick	12	5	Stanley Cup champ	Fred Shero

NHL HISTORY *Team by team*

			REGULAR SEASON				PLAYOFFS		
Season	W	L	T	OTL	Pts.	Finish	W	L	Highest round	Coach
1975-76	51	13	16	—	118	1st/Patrick	8	8	Stanley Cup finals	Fred Shero
1976-77	48	16	16	—	112	1st/Patrick	4	6	Semifinals	Fred Shero
1977-78	45	20	15	—	105	2nd/Patrick	7	5	Semifinals	Fred Shero
1978-79	40	25	15	—	95	2nd/Patrick	3	5	Quarterfinals	Bob McCammon, Pat Quinn
1979-80	48	12	20	—	116	1st/Patrick	13	6	Stanley Cup finals	Pat Quinn
1980-81	41	24	15	—	97	2nd/Patrick	6	6	Quarterfinals	Pat Quinn
1981-82	38	31	11	—	87	3rd/Patrick	1	3	Division semifinals	Pat Quinn, Bob McCammon
1982-83	49	23	8	—	106	1st/Patrick	0	3	Division semifinals	Bob McCammon
1983-84	44	26	10	—	98	3rd/Patrick	0	3	Division semifinals	Bob McCammon
1984-85	53	20	7	—	113	1st/Patrick	12	7	Stanley Cup finals	Mike Keenan
1985-86	53	23	4	—	110	1st/Patrick	2	3	Division semifinals	Mike Keenan
1986-87	46	26	8	—	100	1st/Patrick	15	11	Stanley Cup finals	Mike Keenan
1987-88	38	33	9	—	85	3rd/Patrick	3	4	Division semifinals	Mike Keenan
1988-89	36	36	8	—	80	4th/Patrick	10	9	Conference finals	Paul Holmgren
1989-90	30	39	11	—	71	6th/Patrick	—	—		Paul Holmgren
1990-91	33	37	10	—	76	5th/Patrick	—	—		Paul Holmgren
1991-92	32	37	11	—	75	6th/Patrick	—	—		Paul Holmgren, Bill Dineen
1992-93	36	37	11	—	83	5th/Patrick	—	—		Bill Dineen
1993-94	35	39	10	—	80	6th/Atlantic	—	—		Terry Simpson
1994-95	28	16	4	—	60	1st/Atlantic	10	5	Conference finals	Terry Murray
1995-96	45	24	13	—	103	1st/Atlantic	6	6	Conference semifinals	Terry Murray
1996-97	45	24	13	—	103	2nd/Atlantic	12	7	Stanley Cup finals	Terry Murray
1997-98	42	29	11	—	95	2nd/Atlantic	1	4	Conference quarterfinals	Wayne Cashman, Roger Neilson
1998-99	37	26	19	—	93	2nd/Atlantic	2	4	Conference quarterfinals	Roger Neilson
1999-00	45	22	12	3	105	1st/Atlantic	11	7	Conference finals	Roger Neilson, Craig Ramsay
2000-01	43	25	11	3	100	2nd/Atlantic	2	4	Conference quarterfinals	Craig Ramsay, Bill Barber
2001-02	42	27	10	3	97	1st/Atlantic	1	4	Conference quarterfinals	Bill Barber
2002-03	45	20	13	4	107	2nd/Atlantic	6	7	Conference semifinals	Ken Hitchcock

FIRST-ROUND ENTRY DRAFT CHOICES

Year   Player, Overall, Last amateur team (league)
1969—Bob Currier, 6, Cornwall (QMJHL)
1970—No first-round selection
1971—Larry Wright, 8, Regina (WCHL)
 Pierre Plante, 9, Drummondville (QMJHL)
1972—Bill Barber, 7, Kitchener (OHL)
1973—No first-round selection
1974—No first-round selection
1975—Mel Bridgeman, 1, Victoria (WCHL)*
1976—Mark Suzor, 17, Kingston (OHL)
1977—Kevin McCarthy, 17, Winnipeg (WCHL)
1978—Behn Wilson, 6, Kingston (OHL)
 Ken Linseman, 7, Birmingham (WHA)
 Dan Lucas, 14, Sault Ste. Marie (OHL)
1979—Brian Propp, 14, Brandon (WHL)
1980—Mike Stothers, 21, Kingston (OHL)
1981—Steve Smith, 16, Sault Ste. Marie (OHL)
1982—Ron Sutter, 4, Lethbridge (WHL)
1983—No first-round selection
1984—No first-round selection
1985—Glen Seabrooke, 21, Peterborough (OHL)

Year   Player, Overall, Last amateur team (league)
1986—Kerry Huffman, 20, Guelph (OHL)
1987—Darren Rumble, 20, Kitchener (OHL)
1988—Claude Boivin, 14, Drummondville (QMJHL)
1989—No first-round selection
1990—Mike Ricci, 4, Peterborough (OHL)
1991—Peter Forsberg, 6, Modo, Sweden
1992—Ryan Sittler, 7, Nichols H.S. (N.Y.)
 Jason Bowen, 15, Tri-City (WHL)
1993—No first-round selection
1994—No first-round selection
1995—Brian Boucher, 22, Tri-City (WHL)
1996—Dainius Zubrus, 15, Pembroke, Tier II
1997—No first-round selection
1998—Simon Gagne, 22, Quebec (QMJHL)
1999—Maxime Ouellet, 22, Quebec (QMJHL)
2000—Justin Williams, 28, Plymouth (OHL)
2001—Jeff Woywitka, 27, Red Deer (WHL)
2002—Joni Pitkanen, 4, Karpat, Finland
2003—Jeff Carter, 11, Sault Ste. Marie (OHL)
 Mike Richards, 24, Kitchener (OHL)
*Designates first player chosen in draft.

SINGLE-SEASON INDIVIDUAL RECORDS

FORWARDS/DEFENSEMEN

Most goals
61—Reggie Leach, 1975-76

Most assists
89—Bobby Clarke, 1974-75
 Bobby Clarke, 1975-76

Most points
123—Mark Recchi, 1992-93

Most penalty minutes
472—Dave Schultz, 1974-75

Most power play goals
34—Tim Kerr, 1985-86

Most shorthanded goals
7—Brian Propp, 1984-85
 Mark Howe, 1985-86

Most games with three or more goals
5—Tim Kerr, 1984-85

Most shots
380—Bill Barber, 1975-76

GOALTENDERS

Most games
73—Bernie Parent, 1973-74

Most minutes
4,314—Bernie Parent, 1973-74

Most goals allowed
208—Ron Hextall, 1987-88

Lowest goals-against average
1.83—Roman Cechmanek, 2002-03

Most shutouts
12—Bernie Parent, 1973-74
 Bernie Parent, 1974-75

Most wins
47—Bernie Parent, 1973-74

Most losses
29—Bernie Parent, 1969-70

Most ties
20—Bernie Parent, 1969-70

NHL HISTORY *Team by team*

FRANCHISE LEADERS

Players in boldface played for club in 2002-03

FORWARDS/DEFENSEMEN

Games
Bobby Clarke	1144
Bill Barber	903
Brian Propp	790
Joe Watson	746
Bob Kelly	741
Rick MacLeish	741

Goals
Bill Barber	420
Brian Propp	369
Tim Kerr	363
Bobby Clarke	358
Rick MacLeish	328

Assists
Bobby Clarke	852
Brian Propp	480
Bill Barber	463
Rick MacLeish	369

Eric Lindros 369

Points
Bobby Clarke	1210
Bill Barber	883
Brian Propp	849
Rick MacLeish	697
Eric Lindros	659

Penalty minutes
Rick Tocchet	1817
Paul Holmgren	1600
Andre Dupont	1505
Bobby Clarke	1453
Dave Schultz	1386

GOALTENDERS
Games
Ron Hextall	489
Bernie Parent	486
Doug Favell	215
Pete Peeters	179
Wayne Stephenson	165

Shutouts
Bernie Parent	50
Roman Cechmanek	**20**
Ron Hextall	18
Doug Favell	16
Bob Froese	12

Goals-against average (2400 minutes minimum)
Roman Cechmanek	**1.96**
John Vanbiesbrouck	2.19
Bernie Parent	2.42
Brian Boucher	2.45
Garth Snow	2.59

Wins
Ron Hextall	240
Bernie Parent	232
Wayne Stephenson	93
Roman Cechmanek	**92**
Bob Froese	92

PHOENIX COYOTES
YEAR-BY-YEAR RECORDS

	REGULAR SEASON						PLAYOFFS			
Season	W	L	T	OTL	Pts.	Finish	W	L	Highest round	Coach
1972-73*	43	31	4	—	90	1st	9	5	Avco World Cup finals	Nick Mickoski, Bobby Hull
1973-74*	34	39	5	—	73	4th	0	4	League quarterfinals	Nick Mickoski, Bobby Hull
1974-75*	38	35	5	—	81	3rd	—	—		Rudy Pilous
1975-76*	52	27	2	—	106	1st	12	1	Avco World Cup champ	Bobby Kromm
1976-77*	46	32	2	—	94	2nd	11	9	Avco World Cup finals	Bobby Kromm
1977-78*	50	28	2	—	102	1st	8	1	Avco World Cup champ	Larry Hillman
1978-79*	39	35	6	—	84	3rd	8	2	Avco World Cup champ	Larry Hillman, Tom McVie
1979-80†	20	49	11	—	51	5th/Smythe	—	—		Tom McVie
1980-81†	9	57	14	—	32	6th/Smythe	—	—		Tom McVie, Bill Sutherland, Mike Smith
1981-82†	33	33	14	—	80	2nd/Norris	1	3	Division semifinals	Tom Watt
1982-83†	33	39	8	—	74	4th/Smythe	0	3	Division semifinals	Tom Watt
1983-84†	31	38	11	—	73	4th/Smythe	0	3	Division semifinals	Tom Watt, Barry Long
1984-85†	43	27	10	—	96	2nd/Smythe	3	5	Division finals	Barry Long
1985-86†	26	47	7	—	59	3rd/Smythe	0	3	Division semifinals	Barry Long, John Ferguson
1986-87†	40	32	8	—	88	3rd/Smythe	4	6	Division finals	Dan Maloney
1987-88†	33	36	11	—	77	3rd/Smythe	1	4	Division semifinals	Dan Maloney
1988-89†	26	42	12	—	64	5th/Smythe	—	—		Dan Maloney, Rick Bowness
1989-90†	37	32	11	—	85	3rd/Smythe	3	4	Division semifinals	Bob Murdoch
1990-91†	26	43	11	—	63	5th/Smythe	—	—		Bob Murdoch
1991-92†	33	32	15	—	81	4th/Smythe	3	4	Division semifinals	John Paddock
1992-93†	40	37	7	—	87	4th/Smythe	2	4	Division semifinals	John Paddock
1993-94†	24	51	9	—	57	6th/Central	—	—		John Paddock
1994-95†	16	25	7	—	39	6th/Central	—	—		John Paddock, Terry Simpson
1995-96†	36	40	6	—	78	5th/Central	—	—		Terry Simpson
1996-97	38	37	7	—	83	3rd/Central	3	4	Conference quarterfinals	Don Hay
1997-98	35	35	12	—	82	4th/Central	2	4	Conference quarterfinals	Jim Schoenfeld
1998-99	39	31	12	—	90	2nd/Pacific	3	4	Conference quarterfinals	Jim Schoenfeld
1999-00	39	31	8	4	90	3rd/Pacific	1	4	Conference quarterfinals	Bob Francis
2000-01	35	27	17	3	90	4th/Pacific	—	—		Bob Francis
2001-02	40	27	9	6	95	2nd/Pacific	1	4	Conference quarterfinals	Bob Francis
2002-03	31	35	11	5	78	4th/Pacific	—	—		Bob Francis

*Winnipeg Jets, members of World Hockey Association.
†Winnipeg Jets.

FIRST-ROUND ENTRY DRAFT CHOICES

Year	Player, Overall, Last amateur team (league)
1979	Jimmy Mann, 19, Sherbrooke (QMJHL)
1980	David Babych, 2, Portland (WHL)
1981	Dale Hawerchuk, 1, Cornwall (QMJHL)*
1982	Jim Kyte, 12, Cornwall (OHL)
1983	Andrew McBain, 8, North Bay (OHL)
	Bobby Dollas, 14, Laval (QMJHL)
1984	No first-round selection
1985	Ryan Stewart, 18, Kamloops (WHL)
1986	Pat Elynuik, 8, Prince Albert (WHL)
1987	Bryan Marchment, 16, Belleville (OHL)
1988	Teemu Selanne, 10, Jokerit, Finland
1989	Stu Barnes, 4, Tri-City (WHL)
1990	Keith Tkachuk, 19, Malden Cath. H.S. (Mass.)
1991	Aaron Ward, 5, University of Michigan
1992	Sergei Bautin, 17, Dynamo Moscow (CIS)
1993	Mats Lindgren, 15, Skelleftea, Sweden

Year	Player, Overall, Last amateur team (league)
1994	No first-round selection
1995	Shane Doan, 7, Kamloops (WHL)
1996	Dan Focht, 11, Tri-City (WHL)
	Daniel Briere, 24, Drummondville (QMJHL)
1997	No first-round selection
1998	Patrick DesRochers, 14, Sarnia (OHL)
1999	Scott Kelman, 15, Seattle (WHL)
	Kirill Safronov, 19, SKA St. Petersburg, Russia
2000	Krystofer Kolanos, 19, Boston College
2001	Fredrik Sjostrom, 11, Frolunda, Sweden
2002	Jakub Koreis, 19, Plzen, Czechoslovakia
	Ben Eager, 23, Oshawa (OHL)
2003	No first-round selection

*Designates first player chosen in draft.
NOTE: Winnipeg chose Scott Campbell, Morris Lukowich and Markus Mattsson as priority selections before the 1979 expansion draft.

SINGLE-SEASON INDIVIDUAL RECORDS

FORWARDS/DEFENSEMEN

Most goals
76—Teemu Selanne, 1992-93

Most assists
79—Phil Housley, 1992-93

Most points
132—Teemu Selanne, 1992-93

Most penalty minutes
347—Tie Domi, 1993-94

Most power play goals
24—Teemu Selanne, 1992-93

Most shorthanded goals
7—Dave McLlwain, 1989-90

Most games with three or more goals
5—Teemu Selanne, 1992-93

Most shots
387—Teemu Selanne, 1992-93

GOALTENDERS

Most games
72—Nikolai Khabibulin, 1996-97

Most minutes
4,091—Nikolai Khabibulin, 1996-97

Most shots against
2,119—Bob Essensa, 1992-93

Most goals allowed
227—Bob Essensa, 1992-93

Lowest goals-against average
2.13—Nikolai Khabibulin, 1998-99

Most shutouts
8—Nikolai Khabibulin, 1998-99

Most wins
33—Brian Hayward, 1984-85
   Bob Essensa, 1992-93
   Sean Burke, 2001-02

Most losses
33—Nikolai Khabibulin, 1996-97

Most ties
13—Sean Burke, 2000-01

FRANCHISE LEADERS

Players in boldface played for club in 2001-2

FORWARDS/DEFENSEMEN

Games
Teppo Numminen	**1098**
Thomas Steen	950
Dale Hawerchuk	713
Doug Smail	691
Keith Tkachuk	640

Goals
Dale Hawerchuk	379
Keith Tkachuk	323
Thomas Steen	264
Paul MacLean	248
Doug Smail	189

Assists
Thomas Steen	553
Dale Hawerchuk	550
Teppo Numminen	**426**
Keith Tkachuk	300
Paul MacLean	270

Points
Dale Hawerchuk	929
Thomas Steen	817
Keith Tkachuk	623
Teppo Numminen	**534**
Paul MacLean	518

Penalty minutes
Keith Tkachuk	1508
Laurie Boschman	1338
Jim Kyte	772
Kris King	762
Tim Watters	760

GOALTENDERS

Games
Bob Essensa	311
Nikolai Khabibulin	284
Sean Burke	**179**
Brian Hayward	165
Doug Soetaert	130

Shutouts
Nikolai Khabibulin	21
Bob Essensa	15
Sean Burke	**14**
Daniel Berthiaume	4
Robert Esche	3
Markus Mattsson	3

Goals-against average (2400 minutes minimum)
Sean Burke	**2.31**
Nikolai Khabibulin	2.75
Robert Esche	2.97
Brian Boucher	**3.02**
Bob Essensa	3.32

Wins
Bob Essensa	129
Nikolai Khabibulin	126
Sean Burke	**87**
Brian Hayward	63
Daniel Berthiaume	50
Doug Soetaert	50

NHL HISTORY *Team by team*

PITTSBURGH PENGUINS
YEAR-BY-YEAR RECORDS

		REGULAR SEASON					PLAYOFFS		
Season	W	L	T	OTL	Pts.	Finish	W	L	Highest round	Coach

Season	W	L	T	OTL	Pts.	Finish	W	L	Highest round	Coach
1967-68	27	34	13	—	67	5th/West	—	—		Red Sullivan
1968-69	20	45	11	—	51	5th/West	—	—		Red Sullivan
1969-70	26	38	12	—	64	2nd/West	6	4	Division finals	Red Kelly
1970-71	21	37	20	—	62	6th/West	—	—		Red Kelly
1971-72	26	38	14	—	66	4th/West	0	4	Division semifinals	Red Kelly
1972-73	32	37	9	—	73	5th/West	—	—		Red Kelly, Ken Schinkel
1973-74	28	41	9	—	65	5th/West	—	—		Ken Schinkel, Marc Boileau
1974-75	37	28	15	—	89	3rd/Norris	5	4	Quarterfinals	Marc Boileau
1975-76	35	33	12	—	82	3rd/Norris	1	2	Preliminaries	Marc Boileau, Ken Schinkel
1976-77	34	33	13	—	81	3rd/Norris	1	2	Preliminaries	Ken Schinkel
1977-78	25	37	18	—	68	4th/Norris	—	—		Johnny Wilson
1978-79	36	31	13	—	85	2nd/Norris	2	5	Quarterfinals	Johnny Wilson
1979-80	30	37	13	—	73	3rd/Norris	2	3	Preliminaries	Johnny Wilson
1980-81	30	37	13	—	73	4th/Norris	2	3	Preliminaries	Eddie Johnston
1981-82	31	36	13	—	75	4th/Patrick	2	3	Division semifinals	Eddie Johnston
1982-83	18	53	9	—	45	6th/Patrick	—	—		Eddie Johnston
1983-84	16	58	6	—	38	6th/Patrick	—	—		Lou Angotti
1984-85	24	51	5	—	53	6th/Patrick	—	—		Bob Berry
1985-86	34	38	8	—	76	5th/Patrick	—	—		Bob Berry
1986-87	30	38	12	—	72	5th/Patrick	—	—		Bob Berry
1987-88	36	35	9	—	81	6th/Patrick	—	—		Pierre Creamer
1988-89	40	33	7	—	87	2nd/Patrick	7	4	Division finals	Gene Ubriaco
1989-90	32	40	8	—	72	5th/Patrick	—	—		Gene Ubriaco, Craig Patrick
1990-91	41	33	6	—	88	1st/Patrick	16	8	Stanley Cup champ	Bob Johnson
1991-92	39	32	9	—	87	3rd/Patrick	16	5	Stanley Cup champ	Scotty Bowman
1992-93	56	21	7	—	119	1st/Patrick	7	5	Division finals	Scotty Bowman
1993-94	44	27	13	—	101	1st/Northeast	2	4	Conference quarterfinals	Eddie Johnston
1994-95	29	16	3	—	61	2nd/Northeast	5	7	Conference semifinals	Eddie Johnston
1995-96	49	29	4	—	102	1st/Northeast	11	7	Conference finals	Eddie Johnston
1996-97	38	36	8	—	84	2nd/Northeast	1	4	Conference quarterfinals	Eddie Johnston, Craig Patrick
1997-98	40	24	18	—	98	1st/Northeast	2	4	Conference quarterfinals	Kevin Constantine
1998-99	38	30	14	—	90	3rd/Atlantic	6	7	Conference semifinals	Kevin Constantine
1999-00	37	31	8	6	88	3rd/Atlantic	6	5	Conference semifinals	Kevin Constantine, Herb Brooks
2000-01	42	28	9	3	96	3rd/Atlantic	9	9	Conference finals	Ivan Hlinka
2001-02	28	41	8	5	69	5th/Atlantic	—	—		Ivan Hlinka, Rick Kehoe
2002-03	27	44	6	5	65	5th/Atlantic	—	—		Rick Kehoe

FIRST-ROUND ENTRY DRAFT CHOICES

Year   Player, Overall, Last amateur team (league)

1969—No first-round selection
1970—Greg Polis, 7, Estevan (WCHL)
1971—No first-round selection
1972—No first-round selection
1973—Blaine Stoughton, 7, Flin Flon (WCHL)
1974—Pierre Larouche, 8, Sorel (QMJHL)
1975—Gord Laxton, 13, New Westminster (WCHL)
1976—Blair Chapman, 2, Saskatoon (WCHL)
1977—No first-round selection
1978—No first-round selection
1979—No first-round selection
1980—MIke Bullard, 9, Brantford (OHL)
1981—No first-round selection
1982—Rich Sutter, 10, Lethbridge (WHL)
1983—Bob Errey, 15, Peterborough (OHL)
1984—Mario Lemieux, 1, Laval (QMJHL)*
   Doug Bodger, 9, Kamloops (WHL)
   Roger Belanger, 16, Kingston (OHL)
1985—Craig Simpson, 2, Michigan State University

1986—Zarley Zalapski, 4, Team Canada
1987—Chris Joseph, 5, Seattle (WHL)
1988—Darrin Shannon, 4, Windsor (OHL)
1989—Jamie Heward, 16, Regina (WHL)
1990—Jaromir Jagr, 5, Poldi Kladno, Czech. Republic
1991—Markus Naslund, 16, MoDo, Sweden
1992—Martin Straka, 19, Skoda Plzen, Czech. Republic
1993—Stefan Bergqvist, 26, Leksand, Sweden
1994—Chris Wells, 24, Seattle (WHL)
1995—Alexei Morozov, 24, Krylja Sovetov, CIS
1996—Craig Hillier, 23, Ottawa (OHL)
1997—Robert Dome, 17, Las Vegas (IHL)
1998—Milan Kraft, 23, Plzen (Czech.)
1999—Konstantin Koltsov, 18, Cherepovec, Russia
2000—Brooks Orpik, 18, Boston College
2001—Colby Armstrong, 21, Red Deer (WHL)
2002—Ryan Whitney, Boston University (H. East)
2003—Marc-Andre Fleury, 1, Cape Breton (QMJHL)*
*Designates first player chosen in draft.

SINGLE-SEASON INDIVIDUAL RECORDS

FORWARDS/DEFENSEMEN

Most goals
85—Mario Lemieux, 1988-89

Most assists
114—Mario Lemieux, 1988-89

Most points
199—Mario Lemieux, 1988-89

409—Paul Baxter, 1981-82

Most power play goals
31—Mario Lemieux, 1988-89
   Mario Lemieux, 1995-96

Most shorthanded goals
13—Mario Lemieux, 1988-89

Most games with three or more goals
9—Mario Lemieux, 1988-89

Most shots
403—Jaromir Jagr, 1995-96

GOALTENDERS

Most games
66—Johan Hedberg, 2001-02

Most minutes
3,877—Johan Hedberg, 2001-02

Most shots against
1,885—Tom Barrasso, 1992-93

Most goals allowed
258—Greg Millen, 1980-81

Lowest goals-against average
2.07—Tom Barrasso, 1997-98

Most shutouts
7—Tom Barrasso, 1997-98

Most wins
43—Tom Barrasso, 1992-93

Most losses
34—Johan Hedberg, 2001-02

Most ties
15—Denis Herron, 1977-78

FRANCHISE LEADERS

Players in boldface played for club in 2002-03

FORWARDS/DEFENSEMEN

Games

Mario Lemieux	**879**
Jaromir Jagr	806
Jean Pronovost	753
Rick Kehoe	722
Ron Stackhouse	621

Goals

Mario Lemieux	**682**
Jaromir Jagr	439
Jean Pronovost	316
Rick Kehoe	312
Kevin Stevens	260

Assists

Mario Lemieux	**1110**
Jaromir Jagr	640
Ron Francis	449
Syl Apps	349
Paul Coffey	332

Points

Mario Lemieux	**1692**
Jaromir Jagr	1079
Rick Kehoe	636
Ron Francis	613
Jean Pronovost	603

Penalty minutes

Kevin Stevens	1048
Troy Loney	980
Rod Buskas	959
Bryan Watson	871
Paul Baxter	851

GOALTENDERS

Games

Tom Barrasso	460
Denis Herron	290
Ken Wregget	212
Les Binkley	196
Michel Dion	151

Shutouts

Tom Barrasso	22
Les Binkley	11
Johan Hedberg	**7**
Denis Herron	6
Ken Wregget	6

**Goals-against average
(2400 minutes minimum)**

Peter Skudra	2.65
Johan Hedberg	**2.88**
Jean-Sebastien Aubin	**2.91**
Al Smith	3.07
Les Binkley	3.12

Wins

Tom Barrasso	226
Ken Wregget	104
Denis Herron	88
Les Binkley	58
Greg Millen	57

PITTSBURGH PIRATES (DEFUNCT)
YEAR-BY-YEAR RECORDS

	REGULAR SEASON					PLAYOFFS			
Season	W	L	T	Pts.	Finish	W	L	Highest round	Coach
1925-26	19	16	1	39	3rd	—	—		Odie Cleghorn
1926-27	15	26	3	33	4th/American	—	—		Odie Cleghorn
1927-28	19	17	8	46	3rd/American	1	1	Quarterfinals	Odie Cleghorn
1928-29	9	27	8	26	4th/American	—	—		Odie Cleghorn
1929-30	5	36	3	13	5th/American	—	—		Frank Frederickson
1930-31*	4	36	4	12	5th/American	—	—		Cooper Smeaton

*Philadelphia Quakers.

ST. LOUIS BLUES
YEAR-BY-YEAR RECORDS

	REGULAR SEASON						PLAYOFFS			
Season	W	L	T	OTL	Pts.	Finish	W	L	Highest round	Coach
1967-68	27	31	16	—	70	3rd/West	8	10	Stanley Cup finals	Lynn Patrick, Scotty Bowman
1968-69	37	25	14	—	88	1st/West	8	4	Stanley Cup finals	Scotty Bowman
1969-70	37	27	12	—	86	1st/West	8	8	Stanley Cup finals	Scotty Bowman
1970-71	34	25	19	—	87	2nd/West	2	4	Division semifinals	Al Arbour, Scotty Bowman
1971-72	28	39	11	—	67	3rd/West	4	7	Division finals	Sid Abel, Bill McCreary, Al Arbour
1972-73	32	34	12	—	76	4th/West	1	4	Division semifinals	Al Arbour, Jean-Guy Talbot
1973-74	26	40	12	—	64	6th/West	—	—		Jean-Guy Talbot, Lou Angotti
1974-75	35	31	14	—	84	2nd/Smythe	0	2	Preliminaries	Lou Angotti, Lynn Patrick, Garry Young
1975-76	29	37	14	—	72	3rd/Smythe	1	2	Preliminaries	Garry Young, Lynn Patrick, Leo Boivin
1976-77	32	39	9	—	73	1st/Smythe	0	4	Quarterfinals	Emile Francis

		REGULAR SEASON					PLAYOFFS			
Season	W	L	T	OTL	Pts.	Finish	W	L	Highest round	Coach
1977-78	20	47	13	—	53	4th/Smythe	—	—		Leo Boivin, Barclay Plager
1978-79	18	50	12	—	48	3rd/Smythe	—	—		Barclay Plager
1979-80	34	34	12	—	80	2nd/Smythe	0	3	Preliminaries	Barclay Plager, Red Berenson
1980-81	45	18	17	—	107	1st/Smythe	5	6	Quarterfinals	Red Berenson
1981-82	32	40	8	—	72	3rd/Norris	5	5	Division finals	Red Berenson, Emile Francis
1982-83	25	40	15	—	65	4th/Norris	1	3	Division semifinals	Emile Francis, Barclay Plager
1983-84	32	41	7	—	71	2nd/Norris	6	5	Division finals	Jacques Demers
1984-85	37	31	12	—	86	1st/Norris	0	3	Division semifinals	Jacques Demers
1985-86	37	34	9	—	83	3rd/Norris	10	9	Conference finals	Jacques Demers
1986-87	32	33	15	—	79	1st/Norris	2	4	Division semifinals	Jacques Martin
1987-88	34	38	8	—	76	2nd/Norris	5	5	Division finals	Jacques Martin
1988-89	33	35	12	—	78	2nd/Norris	5	5	Division finals	Brian Sutter
1989-90	37	34	9	—	83	2nd/Norris	7	5	Division finals	Brian Sutter
1990-91	47	22	11	—	105	2nd/Norris	6	7	Division finals	Brian Sutter
1991-92	36	33	11	—	83	3rd/Norris	2	4	Division semifinals	Brian Sutter
1992-93	37	36	11	—	85	4th/Norris	7	4	Division finals	Bob Plager, Bob Berry
1993-94	40	33	11	—	91	4th/Central	0	4	Conference quarterfinals	Bob Berry
1994-95	28	15	5	—	61	2nd/Central	3	4	Conference quarterfinals	Mike Keenan
1995-96	32	34	16	—	80	4th/Central	7	6	Conference semifinals	Mike Keenan
1996-97	36	35	11	—	83	4th/Central	2	4	Conference quarterfinals	Mike Keenan, Jimmy Roberts, Joel Quenneville
1997-98	45	29	8	—	98	3rd/Central	6	4	Conference semifinals	Joel Quenneville
1998-99	37	32	13	—	87	2nd/Central	6	7	Conference semifinals	Joel Quenneville
1999-00	51	19	11	1	114	1st/Central	3	4	Conference quarterfinals	Joel Quenneville
2000-01	43	22	12	5	103	2nd/Central	9	6	Conference finals	Joel Quenneville
2001-02	43	27	8	4	98	2nd/Central	5	5	Conference semifinals	Joel Quenneville
2002-03	41	24	11	6	99	2nd/Central	3	4	Conference quarterfials	Joel Quenneville

FIRST-ROUND ENTRY DRAFT CHOICES

Year Player, Overall, Last amateur team (league)

1969—No first-round selection
1970—No first-round selection
1971—Gene Carr, 4, Flin Flon (WCHL)
1972—Wayne Merrick, 9, Ottawa (OHL)
1973—John Davidson, 5, Calgary (WCHL)
1974—No first-round selection
1975—No first-round selection
1976—Bernie Federko, 7, Saskatoon (WCHL)
1977—Scott Campbell, 9, London (OHL)
1978—Wayne Babych, 3, Portland (WCHL)
1979—Perry Turnbull, 2, Portland (WHL)
1980—Rik Wilson, 12, Kingston (OHL)
1981—Marty Ruff, 20, Lethbridge (WHL)
1982—No first-round selection
1983—No first-round selection
1984—No first-round selection
1985—No first-round selection
1986—Jocelyn Lemieux, 10, Laval (QMJHL)

Year Player, Overall, Last amateur team (league)

1987—Keith Osborne, 12, North Bay (OHL)
1988—Rod Brind'Amour, 9, Notre Dame Academy (Sask.)
1989—Jason Marshall, 9, Vernon (B.C.) Tier II
1990—No first-round selection
1991—No first-round selection
1992—No first-round selection
1993—No first-round selection
1994—No first-round selection
1995—No first-round selection
1996—Marty Reasoner, 14, Boston College
1997—No first-round selection
1998—Christian Backman, 24, Frolunda HC Goteborg, Sweden
1999—Barret Jackman, 17, Regina (WHL)
2000—Jeff Taffe, 30, University of Minnesota
2001—No first-round selection
2002—No first-round selection
2003—Shawn Belle, 30, Tri-City (WHL)

SINGLE-SEASON INDIVIDUAL RECORDS

FORWARDS/DEFENSEMEN

Most goals
86—Brett Hull, 1990-91

Most assists
90—Adam Oates, 1990-91

Most points
131—Brett Hull, 1990-91

Most penalty minutes
306—Bob Gassoff, 1975-76

Most power play goals
29—Brett Hull, 1990-91
Brett Hull, 1992-93

Most shorthanded goals
8—Chuck Lefley, 1975-76
Larry Patey, 1980-81

Most games with three or more goals
8—Brett Hull, 1991-92

Most shots
408—Brett Hull, 1991-92

GOALTENDERS

Most games
79—Grant Fuhr, 1995-96

Most minutes
4,365—Grant Fuhr, 1995-96

Most shots against
2,382—Curtis Joseph, 1993-94

Most goals allowed
250—Mike Liut, 1991-92

Lowest goals-against average
1.95—Roman Turek, 1999-2000

Most shutouts
8—Glenn Hall, 1968-69

Most wins
42—Roman Turek, 1999-2000

Most losses
29—Mike Liut, 1983-84

Most ties
16—Grant Fuhr, 1995-96

Players in boldface played for club in 2002-03

FORWARDS/DEFENSEMEN

Games

Bernie Federko	927
Brian Sutter	779
Brett Hull	744
Garry Unger	662
Bob Plager	615

Goals

Brett Hull	527
Bernie Federko	352
Brian Sutter	303
Garry Unger	292
Pavel Demitra	**181**

Assists

Bernie Federko	721
Brett Hull	409
Brian Sutter	333
Al MacInnis	**323**
Garry Unger	283

Points

Bernie Federko	1073
Brett Hull	936
Brian Sutter	636
Garry Unger	575
Al MacInnis	**450**

Penalty minutes

Brian Sutter	1786
Kelly Chase	1497
Barclay Plager	1115
Rob Ramage	898
Bob Gassoff	866

GOALTENDERS

Games

Mike Liut	347
Curtis Joseph	280
Grant Fuhr	249
Greg Millen	209
Rick Wamsley	154

Shutouts

Glenn Hall	16
Roman Turek	13
Grant Fuhr	11
Brent Johnson	**11**
Mike Liut	10
Jacques Plante	10

Goals-against average (2400 minutes minimum)

Jacques Plante	2.07
Roman Turek	2.10
Jamie McLennan	2.21
Brent Johnson	**2.25**
Glenn Hall	2.43

Wins

Mike Liut	151
Curtis Joseph	137
Grant Fuhr	108
Greg Millen	85
Rick Wamsley	75

ST. LOUIS EAGLES (DEFUNCT)
YEAR-BY-YEAR RECORDS

	REGULAR SEASON					PLAYOFFS			
Season	W	L	T	Pts.	Finish	W	L	Highest round	Coach
1917-18*	9	13	0	18	3rd/2nd	—	—		Eddie Gerard
1918-19*	12	6	0	24	2nd/1st	1	4	Semifinals	Alf Smith
1919-20*	19	5	0	38	1st/1st	3	2	Stanley Cup champ	Pete Green
1920-21*	14	10	0	28	1st/3rd	†4	2	Stanley Cup champ	Pete Green
1921-22*	14	8	2	30	1st	†0	1	Semifinals	Pete Green
1922-23*	14	9	1	29	1st	6	2	Stanley Cup champ	Pete Green
1923-24*	16	8	0	32	1st	0	2	Semifinals	Pete Green
1924-25*	17	12	1	35	4th	—	—		Pete Green
1925-26*	24	8	4	52	1st	†0	1	Semifinals	Pete Green
1926-27*	30	10	4	64	1st/Canadian	†3	0	Stanley Cup champ	Dave Gill
1927-28*	20	14	10	50	3rd/Canadian	0	2	Quarterfinals	Dave Gill
1928-29*	14	17	13	41	4th/Canadian	—	—		Dave Gill
1929-30*	21	15	8	50	3rd/Canadian	†0	1	Semifinals	Newsy Lalonde
1930-31*	10	30	4	24	5th/Canadian	—	—		Newsy Lalonde
1931-32*					Club suspended operations for one season.				
1932-33*	11	27	10	32	5th/Canadian	—	—		Cy Denneny
1933-34*	13	29	6	32	5th/Canadian	—	—		George Boucher
1934-35*	11	31	6	28	5th/Canadian	—	—		Eddie Gerard, George Boucher

*Ottawa Senators (first club).

†Won-lost record does not indicate tie(s) resulting from two-game, total goals series that year (two-game, total-goals series were played from 1917-18 through 1935-36).

SAN JOSE SHARKS
YEAR-BY-YEAR RECORDS

	REGULAR SEASON						PLAYOFFS			
Season	W	L	T	OTL	Pts.	Finish	W	L	Highest round	Coach
1991-92	17	58	5	—	39	6th/Smythe	—	—		George Kingston
1992-93	11	71	2	—	24	6th/Smythe	—	—		George Kingston
1993-94	33	35	16	—	82	3rd/Pacific	7	7	Conference semifinals	Kevin Constantine
1994-95	19	25	4	—	42	3rd/Pacific	4	7	Conference semifinals	Kevin Constantine
1995-96	20	55	7	—	47	7th/Pacific	—	—		Kevin Constantine, Jim Wiley
1996-97	27	47	8	—	62	7th/Pacific	—	—		Al Sims
1997-98	34	38	10	—	78	4th/Pacific	2	4	Conference quarterfinals	Darryl Sutter
1998-99	31	33	18	—	80	4th/Pacific	2	4	Conference quarterfinals	Darryl Sutter
1999-00	35	30	10	7	87	4th/Pacific	5	7	Conference semifinals	Darryl Sutter
2000-01	40	27	12	3	95	2nd/Pacific	2	4	Conference quarterfinals	Darryl Sutter

NHL HISTORY — Team by team

Season	W	L	T	OTL	Pts.	Finish	W	L	Highest round	Coach
						REGULAR SEASON			**PLAYOFFS**	
2001-02	44	27	8	3	99	1st/Pacific	7	5	Conference semifinals	Darryl Sutter
2002-03	28	37	9	8	73	5th/Pacific	—	—		Darryl Sutter, Ron Wilson

FIRST-ROUND ENTRY DRAFT CHOICES

Year   Player, Overall, Last amateur team (league)
1991—Pat Falloon, 2, Spokane (WHL)
1992—Mike Rathje, 3, Medicine Hat (WHL)
        Andrei Nazarov, 10, Dynamo Moscow, CIS
1993—Viktor Kozlov, 6, Moscow, CIS
1994—Jeff Friesen, 11, Regina (WHL)
1995—Teemu Riihijarvi, 12, Espoo Jrs., Finland
1996—Andrei Zyuzin, 2, Salavat Yulayev UFA, CIS
        Marco Sturm, 21, Landshut, Germany
1997—Patrick Marleau, 2, Seattle (WHL)
        Scott Hannan, 23, Kelowna (WHL)

Year   Player, Overall, Last amateur team (league)
1998—Brad Stuart, 3, Regina (WHL)
1999—Jeff Jillson, 14, University of Michigan
2000—No first-round selection
2001—Marcel Goc, 20, Schwennigen, Germany
2002—Mike Morris, 27, St. Sebastian's (USHSE)
2003—Milan Michalek, 6, Czech Republic
        Steve Bernier, 16, Moncton (QMJHL)

SINGLE-SEASON INDIVIDUAL RECORDS

FORWARDS/DEFENSEMEN

Most goals
44—Owen Nolan, 1999-2000

Most assists
52—Kelly Kisio, 1992-93

Most points
84—Owen Nolan, 1999-2000

Most penalty minutes
326—Link Gaetz, 1991-92

Most power play goals
18—Owen Nolan, 1999-2000

Most shorthanded goals
6—Jamie Baker, 1995-96
    Jeff Friesen, 1997-98

Most games with three or more goals
2—Rob Gaudreau, 1992-93
    Igor Larionov, 1993-94
    Tony Granato, 1996-97

Most shots
261—Owen Nolan, 1999-2000

GOALTENDERS

Most games
74—Arturs Irbe, 1993-94

Most minutes
4,412—Arturs Irbe, 1993-94

Most shots against
2,064—Arturs Irbe, 1993-94

Most goals allowed
209—Arturs Irbe, 1993-94

Lowest goals-against average
2.19—Evgeni Nabokov, 2000-01

Most shutouts
7—Evgeni Nabokov, 2001-02

Most wins
37—Evgeni Nabokov, 2001-02

Most losses
30—Jeff Hackett, 1992-93
    Steve Shields, 1999-2000

Most ties
16—Arturs Irbe, 1993-94

FRANCHISE LEADERS

Players in boldface played for club in 2002-03

FORWARDS/DEFENSEMEN

Games
Mike Rathje 591
Owen Nolan 568
Marcus Ragnarsson 519
Jeff Friesen.............................512
Patrick Marleau.......................478

Goals
Owen Nolan 206
Jeff Friesen.............................149
Patrick Marleau.......................125
Marco Sturm 101
Mike Ricci...............................94

Assists
Owen Nolan 245
Jeff Friesen.............................201
Vincent Damphousse 168
Patrick Marleau.......................145
Mike Ricci 143

Points
Owen Nolan 451
Jeff Friesen.............................350
Patrick Marleau.......................270
Vincent Damphousse 248
Mike Ricci 237

Penalty minutes
Jeff Odgers.........................1001
Owen Nolan 934
Bryan Marchment 706
Jay More 545
Andrei Nazarov 490

GOALTENDERS

Games
Evgeni Nabokov.......................199
Arturs Irbe.............................183
Mike Vernon 126
Steve Shields...........................125
Jeff Hackett 78

Shutouts
Evgeni Nabokov 17
Steve Shields...........................10
Mike Vernon 9
Arturs Irbe..................................8
Miikka Kiprusoff 3

Goals-against average
(2400 minutes minimum)
Evgeni Nabokov.......................2.38
Mike Vernon 2.39
Steve Shields...........................2.44
Kelly Hrudey...........................3.04
Chris Terreri 3.39

Wins
Evgeni Nabokov 90
Arturs Irbe................................57
Mike Vernon 52
Steve Shields.............................48
Kelly Hrudey 20

TAMPA BAY LIGHTNING
YEAR-BY-YEAR RECORDS

		REGULAR SEASON						PLAYOFFS			
Season	W	L	T	OTL	Pts.	Finish	W	L	Highest round		Coach
1992-93	23	54	7	—	53	6th/Norris	—	—			Terry Crisp
1993-94	30	43	11	—	71	7th/Atlantic	—	—			Terry Crisp
1994-95	17	28	3	—	37	6th/Atlantic	—	—			Terry Crisp
1995-96	38	32	12	—	88	5th/Atlantic	2	4	Conference quarterfinals		Terry Crisp
1996-97	32	40	10	—	74	6th/Atlantic	—	—			Terry Crisp
1997-98	17	55	10	—	44	7th/Atlantic	—	—			Terry Crisp, Rick Paterson, Jacques Demers
1998-99	19	54	9	—	47	4th/Southeast	—	—			Jacques Demers
1999-00	19	47	9	7	54	4th/Southeast	—	—			Steve Ludzik
2000-01	24	47	6	5	59	5th/Southeast	—	—			Steve Ludzik, John Tortorella
2001-02	27	40	11	4	69	3rd/Southeast	—	—			John Tortorella
2002-03	36	25	16	5	93	1st/Southeast	5	6	Conference semifinals		John Tortorella

FIRST-ROUND ENTRY DRAFT CHOICES

Year Player, Overall, Last amateur team (league)
1992—Roman Hamrlik, 1, Zlin, Czechoslovakia*
1993—Chris Gratton, 3, Kingston (OHL)
1994—Jason Weimer, 8, Portland (WHL)
1995—Daymond Langkow, 5, Tri-City (WHL)
1996—Mario Larocque, 16, Hull (QMJHL)
1997—Paul Mara, 7, Sudbury (OHL)
1998—Vincent Lecavalier, 1, Rimouski (QMJHL)*

Year Player, Overall, Last amateur team (league)
1999—No first-round selection
2000—Nikita Alexeev, 8, Erie (OHL)
2001—Alexander Svitov, 3, OMSK, Russia
2002—No first-round selection
2003—No first-round selection
*Designates first player chosen in draft.

SINGLE-SEASON INDIVIDUAL RECORDS

FORWARDS/DEFENSEMEN

Most goals
42—Brian Bradley, 1992-93

Most assists
57—Vaclav Prospal, 2002-03

Most points
86—Brian Bradley, 1992-93

Most penalty minutes
258—Enrico Ciccone, 1995-96

Most power play goals
16—Brian Bradley, 1992-93

Most shorthanded goals
4—Rob Zamuner, 1996-97

Most games with three or more goals
3—Wendel Clark, 1998-99

Most shots
281—Roman Hamrlik, 1995-96

GOALTENDERS

Most games
70—Nikolai Khabibulin, 2001-02

Most minutes
3,896—Nikolai Khabibulin, 2001-02

Most shots against
1,914—Nikolai Khabibulin, 2001-02

Most goals allowed
177—Kevin Weekes, 2000-01

Lowest goals-against average
2.36—Nikolai Khabibulin, 2001-02

Most shutouts
7—Nikolai Khabibulin, 2001-02

Most wins
30—Nikolai Khabibulin, 2002-03

Most losses
33—Daren Puppa, 1993-94
      Kevin Weekes, 2000-01

Most ties
11—Nikolai Khabibulin, 2002-03

FRANCHISE LEADERS

Players in boldface played for club in 2002-03

FORWARDS/DEFENSEMEN

Games
Rob Zamuner 475
Mikael Andersson...............................435
Chris Gratton......................................404
Vincent Lecavalier 386
Roman Hamrlik 377

Goals
Vincent Lecavalier 114
Brian Bradley......................................111
Chris Gratton...88
Fredrik Modin 85
Rob Zamuner...84

Assists
Brian Bradley......................................189

Chris Gratton......................................148
Vincent Lecavalier 147
Brad Richards........................140
Roman Hamrlik 133

Points
Brian Bradley......................................300
Vincent Lecavalier 261
Chris Gratton......................................236
Rob Zamuner......................................200
Brad Richards........................198

Penalty minutes
Chris Gratton......................................741
Enrico Ciccone 604
Pavel Kubina 482
Roman Hamrlik 474
Rudy Poeschek 418

GOALTENDERS

Games
Daren Puppa 206
Nikolai Khabibulin 137
Corey Schwab.......................................87
Kevin Weekes.......................................80
Dan Cloutier 76

Shutouts
Daren Puppa 12
Nikolai Khabibulin 11
Kevin Weekes...6
Rick Tabaracci 4
Corey Schwab...3

**Goals-against average
(2400 minutes minimum)**
Nikolai Khabibulin 2.42

Daren Puppa 2.68	
Rick Tabaracci 2.75	
Kevin Weekes 3.09	
Corey Schwab 3.25	

Wins

Daren Puppa 77
Nikolai Khabibulin **55**
Kevin Weekes 23
Corey Schwab 21
Rick Tabaracci 20

TORONTO MAPLE LEAFS
YEAR-BY-YEAR RECORDS

	REGULAR SEASON						PLAYOFFS			
Season	W	L	T	OTL	Pts.	Finish	W	L	Highest round	Coach
1917-18‡	13	9	0	—	26	2nd/1st	4	3	Stanley Cup champ	Dick Carroll
1918-19‡	5	13	0	—	10	3rd/3rd	—	—		Dick Carroll
1919-20§	12	12	0	—	24	3rd/2nd	—	—		Frank Heffernan, Harry Sproule
1920-21§	15	9	0	—	30	2nd/1st	0	2	Semifinals	Dick Carroll
1921-22§	13	10	1	—	27	2nd	*4	2	Stanley Cup champ	Eddie Powers
1922-23§	13	10	1	—	27	3rd	—	—		Charlie Querrie, Jack Adams
1923-24§	10	14	0	—	20	3rd	—	—		Eddie Powers
1924-25§	19	11	0	—	38	2nd	0	2	Semifinals	Eddie Powers
1925-26§	12	21	3	—	27	6th	—	—		Eddie Powers
1926-27§	15	24	5	—	35	5th/Canadian	—	—		Conn Smythe
1927-28	18	18	8	—	44	4th/Canadian	—	—		Alex Roveril, Conn Smythe
1928-29	21	18	5	—	47	3rd/Canadian	2	2	Semifinals	Alex Roveril, Conn Smythe
1929-30	17	21	6	—	40	4th/Canadian	—	—		Alex Roveril, Conn Smythe
1930-31	22	13	9	—	53	2nd/Canadian	*0	1	Quarterfinals	Conn Smythe, Art Duncan
1931-32	23	18	7	—	53	2nd/Canadian	*5	1	Stanley Cup champ	Art Duncan, Dick Irvin
1932-33	24	18	6	—	54	1st/Canadian	4	5	Stanley Cup finals	Dick Irvin
1933-34	26	13	9	—	61	1st/Canadian	2	3	Semifinals	Dick Irvin
1934-35	30	14	4	—	64	1st/Canadian	3	4	Stanley Cup finals	Dick Irvin
1935-36	23	19	6	—	52	2nd/Canadian	4	5	Stanley Cup finals	Dick Irvin
1936-37	22	21	5	—	49	3rd/Canadian	0	2	Quarterfinals	Dick Irvin
1937-38	24	15	9	—	57	1st/Canadian			Stanley Cup finals	Dick Irvin
1938-39	19	20	9	—	47	3rd	5	5	Stanley Cup finals	Dick Irvin
1939-40	25	17	6	—	56	3rd	6	4	Stanley Cup finals	Dick Irvin
1940-41	28	14	6	—	62	2nd	3	4	Semifinals	Hap Day
1941-42	27	18	3	—	57	2nd	8	5	Stanley Cup champ	Hap Day
1942-43	22	19	9	—	53	3rd	2	4	League semifinals	Hap Day
1943-44	23	23	4	—	50	3rd	1	4	League semifinals	Hap Day
1944-45	24	22	4	—	52	3rd	8	5	Stanley Cup champ	Hap Day
1945-46	19	24	7	—	45	5th	—	—		Hap Day
1946-47	31	19	10	—	72	2nd	8	3	Stanley Cup champ	Hap Day
1947-48	32	15	13	—	77	1st	8	1	Stanley Cup champ	Hap Day
1948-49	22	25	13	—	57	4th	8	1	Stanley Cup champ	Hap Day
1949-50	31	27	12	—	74	3rd	3	4	League semifinals	Hap Day
1950-51	41	16	13	—	95	2nd	†8	2	Stanley Cup champ	Joe Primeau
1951-52	29	25	16	—	74	3rd	0	4	League semifinals	Joe Primeau
1952-53	27	30	13	—	67	5th	—	—		Joe Primeau
1953-54	32	24	14	—	78	3rd	1	4	League semifinals	King Clancy
1954-55	24	24	22	—	70	3rd	0	4	League semifinals	King Clancy
1955-56	24	33	13	—	61	4th	1	4	League semifinals	King Clancy
1956-57	21	34	15	—	57	5th	—	—		Howie Meeker
1957-58	21	38	11	—	53	6th	—	—		Billy Reay
1958-59	27	32	11	—	65	4th	5	7	Stanley Cup finals	Billy Reay, Punch Imlach
1959-60	35	26	9	—	79	2nd	4	6	Stanley Cup finals	Punch Imlach
1960-61	39	19	12	—	90	2nd	1	4	League semifinals	Punch Imlach
1961-62	37	22	11	—	85	2nd	8	4	Stanley Cup champ	Punch Imlach
1962-63	35	23	12	—	82	1st	8	2	Stanley Cup champ	Punch Imlach
1963-64	33	25	12	—	78	3rd	8	6	Stanley Cup champ	Punch Imlach
1964-65	30	26	14	—	74	4th	2	4	League semifinals	Punch Imlach
1965-66	34	25	11	—	79	3rd	0	4	League semifinals	Punch Imlach
1966-67	32	27	11	—	75	3rd	8	4	Stanley Cup champ	Punch Imlach
1967-68	33	31	10	—	76	5th/East	—	—		Punch Imlach
1968-69	35	26	15	—	85	4th/East	0	4	Division semifinals	Punch Imlach
1969-70	29	34	13	—	71	6th/East	—	—		John McLellan
1970-71	37	33	8	—	82	4th/East	2	4	Division semifinals	John McLellan
1971-72	33	31	14	—	80	4th/East	1	4	Division semifinals	John McLellan
1972-73	27	41	10	—	64	6th/East	—	—		John McLellan
1973-74	35	27	16	—	86	4th/East	0	4	Division semifinals	Red Kelly
1974-75	31	33	16	—	78	3rd/Adams	2	5	Quarterfinals	Red Kelly
1975-76	34	31	15	—	83	3rd/Adams	5	5	Quarterfinals	Red Kelly

NHL HISTORY *Team by team*

	REGULAR SEASON						PLAYOFFS			
Season	W	L	T	OTL	Pts.	Finish	W	L	Highest round	Coach
1976-77	33	32	15	—	81	3rd/Adams	4	5	Quarterfinals	Red Kelly
1977-78	41	29	10	—	92	3rd/Adams	6	7	Semifinals	Roger Neilson
1978-79	34	33	13	—	81	3rd/Adams	2	4	Quarterfinals	Roger Neilson
1979-80	35	40	5	—	75	4th/Adams	0	3	Preliminaries	Floyd Smith
1980-81	28	37	15	—	71	5th/Adams	0	3	Preliminaries	Punch Imlach, Joe Crozier
1981-82	20	44	16	—	56	5th/Norris	—	—		Mike Nykoluk
1982-83	28	40	12	—	68	3rd/Norris	1	3	Division semifinals	Mike Nykoluk
1983-84	26	45	9	—	61	5th/Norris	—	—		Mike Nykoluk
1984-85	20	52	8	—	48	5th/Norris	—	—		Dan Maloney
1985-86	25	48	7	—	57	4th/Norris	6	4	Division finals	Dan Maloney
1986-87	32	42	6	—	70	4th/Norris	7	6	Division finals	John Brophy
1987-88	21	49	10	—	52	4th/Norris	2	4	Division semifinals	John Brophy
1988-89	28	46	6	—	62	5th/Norris	—	—		John Brophy, George Armstrong
1989-90	38	38	4	—	80	3rd/Norris	1	4	Division semifinals	Doug Carpenter
1990-91	23	46	11	—	57	5th/Norris	—	—		Doug Carpenter, Tom Watt
1991-92	30	43	7	—	67	5th/Norris	—	—		Tom Watt
1992-93	44	29	11	—	99	3rd/Norris	11	10	Conference finals	Pat Burns
1993-94	43	29	12	—	98	2nd/Central	9	9	Conference finals	Pat Burns
1994-95	21	19	8	—	50	4th/Central	3	4	Conference quarterfinals	Pat Burns
1995-96	34	36	12	—	80	3rd/Central	2	4	Conference quarterfinals	Pat Burns, Nick Beverley
1996-97	30	44	8	—	68	6th/Central	—	—		Mike Murphy
1997-98	30	43	9	—	69	6th/Central	—	—		Mike Murphy
1998-99	45	30	7	—	97	2nd/Northeast	9	8	Conference finals	Pat Quinn
1999-00	45	27	7	3	100	1st/Northeast	6	6	Conference semifinals	Pat Quinn
2000-01	37	29	11	5	90	3rd/Northeast	7	4	Conference semifinals	Pat Quinn
2001-02	43	25	10	4	100	2nd/Northeast	10	10	Conference finals	Pat Quinn
2002-03	44	28	7	3	98	2nd/Northeast	3	4	Conference quarterfinals	Pat Quinn

*Won-lost record does not indicate tie(s) resulting from two-game, total-goals series that year (two-game, total-goals series were played from 1917-18 through 1935-36).
†Game 2 semifinals vs. Boston tied 1-1 after one overtime (curfew law).
‡Toronto Arenas.
§Toronto St. Patricks (until April 14, 1927).

FIRST-ROUND ENTRY DRAFT CHOICES

Year Player, Overall, Last amateur team (league)
1969—Ernie Moser, 9, Esteven (WCHL)
1970—Darryl Sittler, 8, London (OHL)
1971—No first-round selection
1972—George Ferguson, 11, Toronto (OHL)
1973—Lanny McDonald, 4, Medicine Hat (WCHL)
    Bob Neely, 10, Peterborough (OHL)
    Ian Turnbull, 15, Ottawa (OHL)
1974—Jack Valiquette, 13, Sault Ste. Marie (OHL)
1975—Don Ashby, 6, Calgary (WCHL)
1976—No first-round selection
1977—John Anderson, 11, Toronto (OHA)
    Trevor Johansen, 12, Toronto (OHA)
1978—No first-round selection
1979—Laurie Boschman, 9, Brandon (WHL)
1980—No first-round selection
1981—Jim Benning, 6, Portland (WHL)
1982—Gary Nylund, 3, Portland (WHL)
1983—Russ Courtnall, 7, Victoria (WHL)
1984—Al Iafrate, 4, U.S. Olympics/Belleville (OHL)
1985—*Wendel Clark, 1, Saskatoon (WHL)
1986—Vincent Damphousse, 6, Laval (QMJHL)
1987—Luke Richardson, 7, Peterborough (OHL)

Year Player, Overall, Last amateur team (league)
1988—Scott Pearson, 6, Kingston (OHL)
1989—Scott Thornton, 3, Belleville (OHL)
    Rob Pearson, 12, Belleville (OHL)
    Steve Bancroft, 21, Belleville (OHL)
1990—Drake Berehowsky, 10, Kingston (OHL)
1991—No first-round selection
1992—Brandon Convery, 8, Sudbury (OHL)
    Grant Marshall, 23, Ottawa (OHL)
1993—Kenny Jonsson, 12, Rogle, Sweden
    Landon Wilson, 19, Dubuque (USHL)
1994—Eric Fichaud, 16, Chicoutimi (QMJHL)
1995—Jeff Ware, 15, Oshawa (OHL)
1996—No first-round selection
1997—No first-round selection
1998—Nikolai Antropov, 10, Torpedo, Russia
1999—Luca Cereda, 24, Ambri, Switzerland
2000—Brad Boyes, 24, Erie (OHL)
2001—Carlo Colaiacovo, 17, Erie (OHL)
2002—Alexander Steen, 24, Frolunda, Sweden
2003—No first-round selection
*Designates first player chosen in draft.

SINGLE-SEASON INDIVIDUAL RECORDS

FORWARDS/DEFENSEMEN

Most goals
54—Rick Vaive, 1981-82

Most assists
95—Doug Gilmour, 1992-93

Most points
127—Doug Gilmour, 1992-93

Most penalty minutes
365—Tie Domi, 1997-98

Most power play goals
21—Dave Andreychuk, 1993-94
    Wendell Clark, 1993-94

Most shorthanded goals
8—Dave Keon, 1970-71
    Dave Reid, 1990-91

Most games with three or more goals
5—Darryl Sittler, 1980-81

Most shots
346—Darryl Sittler, 1975-76

GOALTENDERS

Most games
74—Felix Potvin, 1996-97

Most minutes
4,271—Felix Potvin, 1996-97

Most goals allowed
230—Grant Fuhr, 1991-92

Lowest goals-against average
1.61—Lorne Chabot, 1928-29

Most shutouts
13—Harry Lumley, 1953-54

Most wins
37—Ed Belfour, 2002-03

Most losses
38—Ed Chadwick, 1957-58

Most ties
22—Harry Lumley, 1954-55

FRANCHISE LEADERS

Players in boldface played for club in 2002-03

FORWARDS/DEFENSEMEN

Games

George Armstrong	1187
Tim Horton	1185
Borje Salming	1099
Dave Keon	1062
Ron Ellis	1034

Goals

Darryl Sittler	389
Dave Keon	365
Ron Ellis	332
Mats Sundin	**299**
Rick Vaive	299

Assists

Borje Salming	620
Darryl Sittler	527
Dave Keon	493
George Armstrong	417
Mats Sundin	**381**

Points

Darryl Sittler	916
Dave Keon	858
Borje Salming	768
George Armstrong	713
Mats Sundin	**680**

Penalty minutes

Tie Domi	**1948**
Dave Williams	1670
Wendel Clark	1535
Tim Horton	1389
Borje Salming	1292

GOALTENDERS

Games

Turk Broda	629
Johnny Bower	475
Felix Potvin	369
Mike Palmateer	296
Harry Lumley	267

Shutouts

Turk Broda	62
Harry Lumley	34
Lorne Chabot	33
Johnny Bower	32
Bruce Gamble	19
George Hainsworth	19

Goals-against average
(2400 minutes minimum)

Al Rollins	2.06
Lorne Chabot	2.20
Harry Lumley	2.20
George Hainsworth	2.26
Ed Belfour	2.26

Wins

Turk Broda	302
Johnny Bower	219
Felix Potvin	160
Curtis Joseph	133
Mike Palmateer	129

VANCOUVER CANUCKS
YEAR-BY-YEAR RECORDS

	REGULAR SEASON					PLAYOFFS			
Season	W	L	T	OTL	Pts.	Finish	W	L	Highest round	Coach
1970-71	24	46	8	—	56	6th/East	—	—		Hal Laycoe
1971-72	20	50	8	—	48	7th/East	—	—		Hal Laycoe
1972-73	22	47	9	—	53	7th/East	—	—		Vic Stasiuk
1973-74	24	43	11	—	59	7th/East	—	—		Bill McCreary, Phil Maloney
1974-75	38	32	10	—	86	1st/Smythe	1	4	Quarterfinals	Phil Maloney
1975-76	33	32	15	—	81	2nd/Smythe	0	2	Preliminaries	Phil Maloney
1976-77	25	42	13	—	63	4th/Smythe	—	—		Phil Maloney, Orland Kurtenbach
1977-78	20	43	17	—	57	3rd/Smythe	—	—		Orland Kurtenbach
1978-79	25	42	13	—	63	2nd/Smythe	1	2	Preliminaries	Harry Neale
1979-80	27	37	16	—	70	3rd/Smythe	1	3	Preliminaries	Harry Neale
1980-81	28	32	20	—	76	3rd/Smythe	0	3	Preliminaries	Harry Neale
1981-82	30	33	17	—	77	2nd/Smythe	11	6	Stanley Cup finals	Harry Neale, Roger Neilson
1982-83	30	35	15	—	75	3rd/Smythe	1	3	Division semifinals	Roger Neilson
1983-84	32	39	9	—	73	3rd/Smythe	1	3	Division semifinals	Roger Neilson, Harry Neale
1984-85	25	46	9	—	59	5th/Smythe	—	—		Bill Laforge, Harry Neale
1985-86	23	44	13	—	59	4th/Smythe	0	3	Division semifinals	Tom Watt
1986-87	29	43	8	—	66	5th/Smythe	—	—		Tom Watt
1987-88	25	46	9	—	59	5th/Smythe	—	—		Bob McCammon
1988-89	33	39	8	—	74	4th/Smythe	3	4	Division semifinals	Bob McCammon
1989-90	25	41	14	—	64	5th/Smythe	—	—		Bob McCammon
1990-91	28	43	9	—	65	4th/Smythe	2	4	Division semifinals	Bob McCammon, Pat Quinn
1991-92	42	26	12	—	96	1st/Smythe	6	7	Division finals	Pat Quinn
1992-93	46	29	9	—	101	1st/Smythe	6	6	Division finals	Pat Quinn
1993-94	41	40	3	—	85	2nd/Pacific	15	9	Stanley Cup finals	Pat Quinn
1994-95	18	18	12	—	48	2nd/Pacific	4	7	Conference semifinals	Rick Ley
1995-96	32	35	15	—	79	3rd/Pacific	2	4	Conference quarterfinals	Rick Ley, Pat Quinn
1996-97	35	40	7	—	77	4th/Pacific	—	—		Tom Renney
1997-98	25	43	14	—	64	7th/Pacific	—	—		Tom Renney, Mike Keenan
1998-99	23	47	12	—	58	4th/Northwest	—	—		Mike Keenan, Marc Crawford
1999-00	30	29	15	8	83	3rd/Northwest	—	—		Marc Crawford
2000-01	36	28	11	7	90	3rd/Northwest	0	4	Conference quarterfinals	Marc Crawford
2001-02	42	30	7	3	94	2nd/Northwest	2	4	Conference quarterfinals	Marc Crawford
2002-03	45	23	13	1	104	2nd/Northwest	7	7	Conference semifinals	Marc Crawford

FIRST-ROUND ENTRY DRAFT CHOICES

Year	Player, Overall, Last amateur team (league)
1970	Dale Tallon, 2, Toronto (OHL)
1971	Jocelyn Guevremont, 3, Montreal (OHL)
1972	Don Lever, 3, Niagara Falls (OHL)
1973	Dennis Ververgaert, 3, London (OHL)
	Bob Dailey, 9, Toronto (OHL)
1974	No first-round selection
1975	Rick Blight, 10, Brandon (WCHL)
1976	No first-round selection
1977	Jere Gillis, 4, Sherbrooke (QMJHL)
1978	Bill Derlago, 4, Brandon (WCHL)
1979	Rick Vaive, 5, Birmingham (WHA)
1980	Rick Lanz, 7, Oshawa (OHL)
1981	Garth Butcher, 10, Regina (WHL)
1982	Michel Petit, 11, Sherbrooke (QMJHL)
1983	Cam Neely, 9, Portland (WHL)
1984	J.J. Daigneault, 10, Can. Ol./Longueuil (QMJHL)
1985	Jim Sandlak, 4, London (OHL)
1986	Dan Woodley, 7, Portland (WHL)
1987	No first-round selection

Year	Player, Overall, Last amateur team (league)
1988	Trevor Linden, 2, Medicine Hat (WHL)
1989	Jason Herter, 8, University of North Dakota
1990	Petr Nedved, 2, Seattle (WHL)
	Shawn Antoski, 18, North Bay (OHL)
1991	Alex Stojanov, 7, Hamilton (OHL)
1992	Libor Polasek, 21, TJ Vikovice (Czech.)
1993	Mike Wilson, 20, Sudbury (OHL)
1994	Mattias Ohlund, 13, Pitea Div. I (Sweden)
1995	No first-round selection
1996	Josh Holden, 12, Regina (WHL)
1997	Brad Ference, 10, Spokane (WHL)
1998	Bryan Allen, 4, Oshawa (OHL)
1999	Daniel Sedin, 2, Modo Ornskoldsvik, Sweden
	Henrik Sedin, 3, Modo Ornskoldsvik, Sweden
2000	Nathan Smith, 23, Swift Current (WHL)
2001	R.J. Umberger, 16, Ohio State
2002	No first-round selection
2003	Ryan Kesler, 23, Ohio State (CCHA)

SINGLE-SEASON INDIVIDUAL RECORDS

FORWARDS/DEFENSEMEN

Most goals
60—Pavel Bure, 1992-93
    Pavel Bure, 1993-94

Most assists
62—Andre Boudrias, 1974-75

Most points
110—Pavel Bure, 1992-93

Most penalty minutes
372—Donald Brashear, 1997-98

Most power play goals
25—Pavel Bure, 1993-94
    Todd Bertuzzi, 2002-03

Most shorthanded goals
7—Pavel Bure, 1992-93

Most games with three or more goals
4—Petri Skriko, 1986-87

Most shots
407—Pavel Bure, 1992-93

GOALTENDERS

Most games
72—Gary Smith, 1974-75

Most minutes
3,852—Kirk McLean, 1991-92

Most shots against
1,804—Kirk McLean, 1989-90

Most goals allowed
240—Richard Brodeur, 1985-86

Lowest goals-against average
2.42—Dan Cloutier, 2001-02

Most shutouts
7—Dan Cloutier, 2002-03

Most wins
38—Kirk McLean, 1991-92

Most losses
33—Gary Smith, 1973-74

Most ties
16—Richard Brodeur, 1980-81

FRANCHISE LEADERS

Players in boldface played for club in 2002-03

FORWARDS/DEFENSEMEN

Games
Stan Smyl	896
Trevor Linden	**837**
Harold Snepsts	781
Dennis Kearns	677
Doug Lidster	666

Goals
Trevor Linden	**278**
Stan Smyl	262
Pavel Bure	254
Tony Tanti	250
Markus Naslund	**230**

Assists
Stan Smyl	411
Trevor Linden	**366**
Thomas Gradin	353
Dennis Kearns	290
Andre Boudrias	267

Points
Stan Smyl	673
Trevor Linden	**644**
Thomas Gradin	550
Pavel Bure	478
Markus Naslund	**478**

Penalty minutes
Gino Odjick	2127
Garth Butcher	1668
Stan Smyl	1556
Harold Snepsts	1446
Tiger Williams	1324

GOALTENDERS

Games
Kirk McLean	516
Richard Brodeur	377
Gary Smith	189
Dunc Wilson	148
Glen Hanlon	137

Shutouts
Kirk McLean	20
Gary Smith	11
Dan Cloutier	**9**
Richard Brodeur	6
Garth Snow	6

Goals-against average
(2400 minutes minimum)
Dan Cloutier	**2.43**
Felix Potvin	2.84
Garth Snow	2.87
Corey Hirsch	3.12
Kirk McLean	3.28

Wins
Kirk McLean	211
Richard Brodeur	126
Gary Smith	72
Dan Cloutier	**68**
Glen Hanlon	43

NHL HISTORY   *Team by team*

YEAR-BY-YEAR RECORDS

		REGULAR SEASON					PLAYOFFS			
Season	W	L	T	OTL	Pts.	Finish	W	L	Highest round	Coach
1974-75	8	67	5	—	21	5th/Norris	—	—		Jim Anderson, Red Sullivan, Milt Schmidt
1975-76	11	59	10	—	32	5th/Norris	—	—		Milt Schmidt, Tom McVie
1976-77	24	42	14	—	62	4th/Norris	—	—		Tom McVie
1977-78	17	49	14	—	48	5th/Norris	—	—		Tom McVie
1978-79	24	41	15	—	63	4th/Norris	—	—		Dan Belisle
1979-80	27	40	13	—	67	5th/Patrick	—	—		Dan Belisle, Gary Green
1980-81	26	36	18	—	70	5th/Patrick	—	—		Gary Green
1981-82	26	41	13	—	65	5th/Patrick	—	—		Gary Green, Roger Crozier, Bryan Murray
1982-83	39	25	16	—	94	3rd/Patrick	1	3	Division semifinals	Bryan Murray
1983-84	48	27	5	—	101	2nd/Patrick	4	4	Division finals	Bryan Murray
1984-85	46	25	9	—	101	2nd/Patrick	2	3	Division semifinals	Bryan Murray
1985-86	50	23	7	—	107	2nd/Patrick	5	4	Division finals	Bryan Murray
1986-87	38	32	10	—	86	2nd/Patrick	3	4	Division semifinals	Bryan Murray
1987-88	38	33	9	—	85	2nd/Patrick	7	7	Division finals	Bryan Murray
1988-89	41	29	10	—	92	1st/Patrick	2	4	Division semifinals	Bryan Murray
1989-90	36	38	6	—	78	3rd/Patrick	8	7	Conference finals	Bryan Murray, Terry Murray
1990-91	37	36	7	—	81	3rd/Patrick	5	6	Division finals	Terry Murray
1991-92	45	27	8	—	98	2nd/Patrick	3	4	Division semifinals	Terry Murray
1992-93	43	34	7	—	93	2nd/Patrick	2	4	Division semifinals	Terry Murray
1993-94	39	35	10	—	88	3rd/Atlantic	5	6	Conference semifinals	Terry Murray, Jim Schoenfeld
1994-95	22	18	8	—	52	3rd/Atlantic	3	4	Conference quarterfinals	Jim Schoenfeld
1995-96	39	32	11	—	89	4th/Atlantic	2	4	Conference quarterfinals	Jim Schoenfeld
1996-97	33	40	9	—	75	5th/Atlantic	—	—		Jim Schoenfeld
1997-98	40	30	12	—	92	3rd/Atlantic	12	9	Stanley Cup finals	Ron Wilson
1998-99	31	45	6	—	68	3rd/Southeast	—	—		Ron Wilson
1999-00	44	24	12	2	102	1st/Southeast	1	4	Conference quarterfinals	Ron Wilson
2000-01	41	27	10	4	96	1st/Southeast	2	4	Conference quarterfinals	Ron Wilson
2001-02	36	33	11	2	85	2nd/Southeast	—	—		Ron Wilson
2002-03	39	29	8	6	92	2nd/Southeast	2	4	Conference quarterfinals	Bruce Cassidy

FIRST-ROUND ENTRY DRAFT CHOICES

Year Player, Overall, Last amateur team (league)
1974—Greg Joly, 1, Regina (WCHL)*
1975—Alex Forsyth, 18, Kingston (OHA)
1976—Rick Green, 1, London (OHL)*
       Greg Carroll, 15, Medicine Hat (WCHL)
1977—Robert Picard, 3, Montreal (QMJHL)
1978—Ryan Walter, 2, Seattle (WCHL)
       Tim Coulis, 18, Hamilton (OHL)
1979—Mike Gartner, 4, Cincinnati (WHA)
1980—Darren Veitch, 5, Regina (WHL)
1981—Bobby Carpenter, 3, St. John's H.S. (Mass.)
1982—Scott Stevens, 5, Kitchener (OHL)
1983—No first-round selection
1984—Kevin Hatcher, 17, North Bay (OHL)
1985—Yvon Corriveau, 19, Toronto (OHL)
1986—Jeff Greenlaw, 19, Team Canada
1987—No first-round selection
1988—Reggie Savage, 15, Victoriaville (QMJHL)
1989—Olaf Kolzig, 19, Tri-City (WHL)
1990—John Slaney, 9, Cornwall (OHL)
1991—Pat Peake, 14, Detroit (OHL)

Year Player, Overall, Last amateur team (league)
       Trevor Halverson, 21, North Bay (OHL)
1992—Sergei Gonchar, 14, Dynamo Moscow, CIS
1993—Brendan Witt, 11, Seattle (WHL)
       Jason Allison, 17, London (OHL)
1994—Nolan Baumgartner, 10, Kamloops (WHL)
       Alexander Kharlamov, 15, CSKA Moscow, CIS
1995—Brad Church, 17, Prince Albert (WHL)
       Miikka Elomo, 23, Kiekko-67, Finland
1996—Alexander Volchkov, 4, Barrie (OHL)
       Jaroslav Svejkovsky, 17, Tri-City (WHL)
1997—Nick Boynton, 9, Ottawa (OHL)
1998—No first-round selection
1999—Kris Breech, 7, Calgary (WHL)
2000—Brian Sutherby, 26, Moose Jaw (WHL)
2001—No first-round selection
2002—Steve Eminger, 12, Kitchener (OHL)
       Alexander Syemin, 13, Chelyabinsk, Russia
       Boyd Gordon, 17, Red Deer (WHL)
2003—Eric Fehr, 18, Brandon (WHL)
*Designates first player chosen in draft.

SINGLE-SEASON INDIVIDUAL RECORDS

FORWARDS/DEFENSEMEN

Most goals
60—Dennis Maruk, 1981-82

Most assists
76—Dennis Maruk, 1981-82

Most points
136—Dennis Maruk, 1981-82

Most penalty minutes
339—Alan May, 1989-90

Most power play goals
22—Peter Bondra, 2000-01

Most shorthanded goals
6—Mike Gartner, 1986-87
    Peter Bondra, 1994-95

Most games with three or more goals
4—Dennis Maruk, 1980-81
   Dennis Maruk, 1981-82
   Peter Bondra, 1995-96

Most shots
333—Peter Bondra, 2001-02

NHL HISTORY *Team by team*

GOALTENDERS

Most games
73—Olaf Kolzig, 1999-2000

Most minutes
4,371—Olaf Kolzig, 1999-2000

Most shots against
1,977—Olaf Kolzig, 2001-02

Most goals allowed
235—Ron Low, 1974-75

Lowest goals-against average
2.13—Jim Carey, 1994-95

Most shutouts
9—Jim Carey, 1995-96

Most wins
41—Olaf Kolzig, 1999-2000

Most losses
36—Ron Low, 1974-75

Most ties
11—Olaf Kolzig, 1999-2000

FRANCHISE LEADERS

Players in boldface played for club in 2002-03

FORWARDS/DEFENSEMEN

Games
Calle Johansson **983**
Kelly Miller 940
Peter Bondra **907**
Dale Hunter 872
Michal Pivonka 825

Goals
Peter Bondra **451**
Mike Gartner 397
Mike Ridley 218
Bengt Gustafsson 196
Dave Christian 193

Assists
Michal Pivonka 418
Mike Gartner 392
Dale Hunter 375
Calle Johansson **361**
Bengt Gustafsson 359

Points
Peter Bondra **790**
Mike Gartner 789
Michal Pivonka 599
Dale Hunter 556
Bengt Gustafsson 555

Penalty minutes
Dale Hunter 2003
Scott Stevens 1628
Craig Berube 1220
Alan May 1189
Kevin Hatcher 999

GOALTENDERS

Games
Olaf Kolzig **481**
Don Beaupre 269
Al Jensen..173
Ron Low..145
Pat Riggin 143

Goals-against average
(2400 minutes minimum)
Jim Carey 2.37
Olaf Kolzig.............................**2.52**
Rick Tabaracci 2.71
Pat Riggin 3.02
Don Beaupre 3.05

Wins
Olaf Kolzig...............................**215**
Don Beaupre 128
Al Jensen..94
Jim Carey 70
Pete Peeters 70

Shutouts
Olaf Kolzig **31**
Jim Carey 14
Don Beaupre 12
Al Jensen..8
Pete Peeters 7

MINOR LEAGUES

American Hockey League

East Coast Hockey League

Central Hockey League

United Hockey League

AMERICAN HOCKEY LEAGUE

2002-03 REGULAR SEASON
FINAL STANDINGS

MINOR LEAGUES *AHL*

EASTERN CONFERENCE

EAST DIVISION

Team	G	W	L	T	OTL	Pts.	GF	GA
Binghamton	80	43	26	9	2	97	239	207
Bridgeport...........	80	40	26	11	3	94	219	198
Hartford	80	33	27	12	8	86	255	236
Springfield	80	34	38	7	1	76	202	243
Albany.................	80	25	37	11	7	68	197	235

NORTH DIVISION

Team	G	W	L	T	OTL	Pts.	GF	GA
Providence..........	80	44	20	11	5	104	268	227
Manchester.........	80	40	23	11	6	97	254	209
Worcester	80	35	27	15	3	88	235	220
Portland..............	80	33	28	13	6	85	221	195
Lowell	80	19	51	7	3	48	175	275

CANADIAN DIVISION

Team	G	W	L	T	OTL	Pts.	GF	GA
Hamilton	80	49	19	8	4	110	279	191
Manitoba.............	80	37	33	8	2	84	229	228
St. John's	80	32	40	6	2	72	236	285
Saint John	80	32	41	6	1	71	203	223

WESTERN CONFERENCE

WEST DIVISION

Team	G	W	L	T	OTL	Pts.	GF	GA
Houston	80	47	23	7	3	104	266	222
Chicago...............	80	43	25	8	4	98	276	237
San Antonio........	80	36	29	11	4	87	235	226
Milwaukee...........	80	32	27	14	7	85	247	251
Utah...................	80	37	34	4	5	83	227	243

CENTRAL DIVISION

Team	G	W	L	T	OTL	Pts.	GF	GA
Grand Rapids.......	80	48	22	8	2	106	240	177
Rochester	80	31	30	14	5	81	219	221
Cincinnati............	80	26	35	13	6	71	202	242
Syracuse.............	80	27	41	8	4	66	201	256
Cleveland	80	22	48	5	5	54	203	286

SOUTH DIVISION

Team	G	W	L	T	OTL	Pts.	GF	GA
Norfolk................	80	37	26	12	5	91	201	187
Hershey	80	36	27	14	3	89	217	209
Wilkes-Barre	80	36	32	7	5	84	245	248
Philadelphia	80	33	33	6	8	80	198	212

INDIVIDUAL LEADERS

Points: Steve Maltais, Chicago (86)
Goals: Eric Healey, Manchester (42)
Assists: Steve Maltais, Chicago (56)
Goaltending average: Craig Andersson, Norfolk (1.94)
Shutouts: Maxime Ouellet, Portland (7)
  Ray Emery, Binghamton (7)

TOP SCORERS

	Games	G	A	Pts.
Steve Maltais, Chicago....................	79	30	56	86
Jean-Guy Trudel, Houston................	79	31	54	85
Michel Picard, Grand Rapids............	78	32	52	84
Mark Mowers, Grand Rapids	78	34	47	81
Simon Gamache, Chicago	76	35	42	77
Keith Aucoin, Providence	78	25	51	76

	Games	G	A	Pts.
Darren Haydar, Milwaukee................	75	29	46	75
Cory Larose, Hartford	82	27	48	75
Mark Greig, Philadelphia	73	30	44	74
Craig Darby, Albany	76	23	51	74
Eric Healey, Manchester	75	42	31	73
Matt Herr, Providence.....................	77	34	38	72
Jason Ward, Hamilton	69	31	41	72
Stacy Roest, Grand Rapids	70	24	48	72
Trent Hunter, Bridgeport.................	70	30	41	71
Andy Hilbert, Providence.................	64	35	35	70
Lee Goren, Providence	65	32	37	69
Jim Montgomery, Utah.....................	72	22	46	68
Michael Ryder, Hamilton..................	69	34	33	67
Chris Taylor, Rochester...................	61	12	55	67

INDIVIDUAL STATISTICS

ALBANY RIVER RATS
SCORING

	Games	G	A	Pts.	PIM
Darby, Craig	76	23	51	74	42
Giroux, Ray	67	11	38	49	49
Crozier, Greg..............................	56	19	19	38	46
Roche, Dave...............................	76	21	16	37	89
Sutton, Ken.................................	74	6	26	32	70
Kariya, Steve..............................	31	12	19	31	20
Guolla, Stephen	22	11	17	28	4
Cameron, Scott...........................	80	9	19	28	17
Lehoux, Jason	64	10	11	21	175
Hulbig, Joe.................................	35	11	9	20	20
Berglund, Christian	26	6	14	20	57
Jokela, Mikko..............................	44	8	11	19	35
Rupp, Mike	47	8	11	19	74

	Games	G	A	Pts.	PIM
Johansson, Eric	66	7	9	16	24
Bicek, Jiri	24	4	10	14	28
Clouthier, Brett...........................	74	6	7	13	220
Birbraer, Max	57	6	6	12	42
Hartsburg, Chris	40	7	3	10	22
Redlihs, Krisjanis	61	1	9	10	20
Andrews, Daryl	75	3	6	9	52
Brooks, Alex...............................	66	0	7	7	56
Skrlac, Rob	42	2	3	5	165
Matteucci, Mike	68	1	3	4	133
Foster, Adrian	9	3	0	3	4
Albelin, Tommy............................	5	0	2	2	2
Ruid, J.C.	6	2	0	2	2
Uchevatov, Victor	55	0	2	2	27
Cole, Phil...................................	4	0	0	0	6
Clemmensen, Scott	47	0	0	0	0
Ahonen, Ari................................	38	0	0	0	8

GOALTENDING

	Gms.	Min.	W	L	T	G	SO	Avg.
Clemmensen, Scott.	47	2694	12	24	8	119	1	2.65
Ahonen, Ari	38	2171	13	20	3	110	1	3.04

BINGHAMTON SENATORS

SCORING

	Games	G	A	Pts.	PIM
Vermette, Antoine	80	34	28	62	57
Smyth, Brad	69	24	32	56	77
Spezza, Jason	43	22	32	54	71
Pothier, Brian	68	7	40	47	58
Murphy, Joe	73	22	24	46	27
Giroux, Alexandre	67	19	16	35	101
Langfeld, Josh	59	14	21	35	38
Hymovitz, David	76	15	19	34	46
Kelly, Chris	77	17	14	31	73
Bala, Chris	51	6	18	24	20
Dahlman, Toni	59	6	18	24	14
Vauclair, Julien	67	6	16	22	30
Ulmer, Jeff	57	8	12	20	40
McGrattan, Brian	59	9	10	19	173
Boumedienne, Josef	26	2	15	17	62
Martins, Steve	26	5	11	16	31
Wren, Bob	14	2	12	14	23
Bicanek, Radim	21	3	10	13	42
Bancroft, Steve	29	1	11	12	40
Schubert, Christoph	70	2	8	10	102
Bonvie, Dennis	51	7	3	10	311
Hedlund, Andy	59	1	7	8	48
Melanson, Dean	35	4	3	7	93
Ricci, Scott	50	0	6	6	23
Tetarenko, Joey	14	2	2	4	33
Emery, Ray	50	0	3	3	52
Rachunek, Karel	6	0	2	2	10
Connolly, Sean	14	0	1	1	6
Szwez, Jeff	9	1	0	1	5
Lynch, Chris	1	0	0	0	0
Ruid, J.C.	1	0	0	0	0
Johnstone, Alex	1	0	0	0	7
Pepperall, Colin	3	0	0	0	0
DiLauro, Ray	4	0	0	0	2
Brookbank, Wade	8	0	0	0	28
Kwiatkowski, Joel	1	0	0	0	2
Plamondon, Justin	8	0	0	0	11
Prusek, Martin	4	0	0	0	5
Chouinard, Mathieu	4	0	0	0	0
Lajeunesse, Simon	19	0	0	0	0
Allen, Andrew	5	0	0	0	0
Symington, Jeremy	5	0	0	0	0
Thompson, Billy	1	0	0	0	0

GOALTENDING

	Gms.	Min.	W	L	T	G	SO	Avg.
Prusek, Martin	4	242	1	2	1	7	1	1.73
Allen, Andrew	5	218	2	1	0	7	0	1.92
Chouinard, Mathieu	4	151	2	0	0	5	0	1.98
Symington, Jeremy	5	284	3	1	1	11	0	2.32
Emery, Ray	50	2923	27	17	6	118	7	2.42
Lajeunesse, Simon	19	966	7	7	1	47	1	2.92
Thompson, Billy	1	60	1	0	0	5	0	5.00

BRIDGEPORT SOUND TIGERS

SCORING

	Games	G	A	Pts.	PIM
Hunter, Trent	70	30	41	71	39
Manlow, Eric	62	19	40	59	58
Smith, Brandon	63	9	32	41	37
Mapletoft, Justin	63	13	26	39	47
Hamilton, Jeff	67	22	16	38	35
Torres, Raffi	49	17	15	32	54
Chabada, Martin	66	17	13	30	50
Tkaczuk, Daniel	69	9	18	27	44

	Games	G	A	Pts.	PIM
Adduono, Jeremy	54	13	13	26	14
Letang, Alan	70	3	21	24	21
Higgins, Matt	45	11	12	23	30
Souza, Mike	59	7	15	22	89
Weinhandl, Mattias	23	9	12	21	14
Down, Blaine	54	8	13	21	30
Kalmikov, Konstantin	60	10	9	19	12
Butenschon, Sven	36	3	13	16	58
Nasreddine, Alain	67	3	9	12	114
Schultz, Ray	51	2	8	10	105
Pettinen, Tomi	75	1	8	9	56
Papineau, Justin	5	7	1	8	4
Mitchell, Kevin	18	1	4	5	16
DiPietro, Rick	34	0	4	4	12
Godard, Eric	46	2	2	4	199
Martinek, Radek	3	0	3	3	2
Tetrault, Daniel	28	0	3	3	47
Robinson, Jody	28	0	3	3	24
Charpentier, Marco	16	1	1	2	6
Caudron, J.F.	2	1	0	1	0
Bilotto, Nic	4	1	0	1	2
Stirling, Scott	10	0	1	1	2
McKay, Konrad	3	0	1	1	11
Belak, Graham	30	0	1	1	60
David, J.F.	6	0	0	0	0
Schmidt, Doug	1	0	0	0	2
Emond, Marco	1	0	0	0	0
St. Germain, David	5	0	0	0	0
Gaffney, Mike	3	0	0	0	4
Bolibruck, Kevin	20	0	0	0	22
Wood, Dustin	6	0	0	0	2
Valiquette, Stephen	34	0	0	0	0

GOALTENDING

	Gms.	Min.	W	L	T	G	SO	Avg.
DiPietro, Rick	34	2044	16	10	8	73	3	2.14
St. Germain, David	5	270	1	3	0	10	0	2.22
Stirling, Scott	10	571	8	2	0	23	0	2.41
Valiquette, Stephen	34	1962	15	14	3	86	2	2.63
Emond, Marco	1	5	0	0	0	1	0	11.25

CHICAGO WOLVES

SCORING

	Games	G	A	Pts.	PIM
Maltais, Steve	79	30	56	86	86
Gamache, Simon	76	35	42	77	37
Brown, Rob	59	15	48	63	83
Vigier, J.P.	63	29	27	56	54
Hartigan, Mark	55	15	31	46	43
Foster, Kurtis	75	15	27	42	159
Simon, Ben	69	15	17	32	78
MacKenzie, Derek	80	14	18	32	97
Karlsson, Andreas	41	12	20	32	16
Tobler, Ryan	58	13	18	31	143
Snyder, Dan	35	11	12	23	39
Tapper, Brad	28	9	14	23	42
Blatny, Zdenek	72	12	9	21	62
Safronov, Kirill	44	4	15	19	29
DiPenta, Joe	76	2	17	19	107
Piros, Kamil	51	10	9	19	16
Farkas, Jeff	24	5	12	17	14
Eakins, Dallas	72	4	11	15	84
Sellars, Luke	42	4	11	15	117
Nardella, Bob	15	1	9	10	18
Butsayev, Yuri	7	6	3	9	0
Exelby, Garnet	53	3	6	9	140
Nielsen, Chris	18	3	4	7	4
Lessard, Francis	50	2	5	7	194
Medak, Judd	9	2	2	4	6
Weaver, Mike	33	2	2	4	32
Maracle, Norm	49	0	3	3	2
Herperger, Chris	7	1	1	2	14

	Games	G	A	Pts.	PIM
Ustrnul, Libor	40	1	1	2	94
Levokari, Pauli	6	0	1	1	12
Maloney, Brian	4	0	1	1	11
Nielsen, Evan	5	1	0	1	4
Svartvadet, Per	3	0	0	0	2
Hnilicka, Milan	15	0	0	0	0
Garnett, Michael	2	0	0	0	0
Fermoyle, Andy	1	0	0	0	2
Mills, Dylan	2	0	0	0	0
Rebek, Jeremy	2	0	0	0	0
Cassivi, Frederic	21	0	0	0	4
Aquino, Anthony	5	0	0	0	4

GOALTENDING

	Gms.	Min.	W	L	T	G	SO	Avg.
Hnilicka, Milan	15	838	11	2	1	33	1	2.36
Maracle, Norm	49	2794	22	18	6	134	2	2.88
Cassivi, Frederic	21	1170	10	8	1	62	0	3.18
Garnett, Michael	2	33	0	1	0	2	0	3.64

CINCINNATI MIGHTY DUCKS

SCORING

	Games	G	A	Pts.	PIM
Martensson, Tony	79	17	36	53	20
Brigley, Travis	64	18	27	45	58
Valicevic, Rob	69	17	26	43	38
Smith, Nick	79	12	26	38	28
Hedstrom, Jonathan	50	14	21	35	62
Yarema, Brendan	59	19	16	35	111
Pecker, Cory	77	20	13	33	66
Guite, Ben	80	13	16	29	44
Popovic, Mark	73	3	21	24	46
Severson, Cam	71	12	9	21	156
Reirden, Todd	58	7	13	20	97
DeWolf, Josh	67	1	17	18	105
Podhradsky, Peter	78	9	8	17	85
O'Sullivan, Chris	27	2	13	15	8
Belanger, Francis	40	4	10	14	50
Commodore, Mike	61	2	9	11	210
Smirnov, Alexei	19	7	3	10	12
Pratt, Harlan	43	4	6	10	34
Pahlsson, Samuel	13	1	7	8	24
Riva, Dan	33	2	6	8	11
Krog, Jason	9	3	4	7	6
Clarke, Dale	13	1	6	7	6
Gornick, Brian	54	2	4	6	14
Brown, Mike	27	3	3	6	85
York, Jason	4	3	2	5	8
Zion, Jonathan	12	2	1	3	20
Damphousse, Jean-Fra	31	0	3	3	0
Reierson, Andy	14	2	1	3	4
Brown, Bobby	6	0	2	2	4
Cass, Bill	2	0	2	2	0
Kos, Kyle	9	0	1	1	8
Gobert, Chris	3	1	0	1	2
Esdale, Paul	5	0	1	1	0
Lee, Brian	9	1	0	1	4
Smith, Jarrett	6	0	0	0	2
Gerber, Martin	1	0	0	0	0
Ellis-Tdingtn, Kerry	1	0	0	0	0
Parillo, Nick	3	0	0	0	0
Keyes, Richard	2	0	0	0	6
Yablonski, Jeremy	9	0	0	0	42
Gaffney, Mike	2	0	0	0	2
Tabacek, Jan	12	0	0	0	8
Vandermeer, Dan	1	0	0	0	0
Cummings, Brian	1	0	0	0	0
Naumenko, Gregg	2	0	0	0	2
Thompson, Chris B	10	0	0	0	28
Ferhi, Eddy	1	0	0	0	0
Bryzgalov, Ilja	54	0	0	0	24

GOALTENDING

	Gms.	Min.	W	L	T	G	SO	Avg.
Gerber, Martin	1	60	1	0	0	2	0	2.00
Ferhi, Eddy	1	60	1	0	0	2	0	2.00
Bryzgalov, Ilja	54	3019	12	26	9	142	1	2.82
Damphousse, J-F	31	1668	12	14	4	87	0	3.13
Naumenko, Gregg	2	65	0	1	0	6	0	5.50

CLEVELAND BARONS

SCORING

	Games	G	A	Pts.	PIM
Nelson, Jeff	80	12	48	60	26
Wiseman, Chad	77	17	35	52	44
Zalesak, Miroslav	50	27	22	49	35
Dimitrakos, Niko	55	15	29	44	30
Hansen, Tavis	80	23	21	44	81
Kraft, Ryan	53	14	27	41	12
Rissmiller, Pat	72	14	26	40	24
Cloutier, David	80	10	·17	27	90
Mischler, Graig	67	12	12	24	64
LaPlante, Eric	76	8	10	18	240
Fahey, Jim	25	3	14	17	42
Loyns, Lynn	36	7	8	15	39
Fibiger, Jesse	59	3	11	14	63
Boyes, Brad	15	7	6	13	21
Thomas, Scott	23	7	3	10	6
Levesque, Willie	64	4	5	9	32
Jillson, Jeff	19	3	5	8	12
Cheechoo, Jonathan	9	3	4	7	16
Matzka, Scott	14	1	6	7	10
Mitchell, Kevin	24	2	5	7	22
Watson, Dan	17	2	4	6	12
Carkner, Matt	39	1	4	5	104
Lutz, Nathan	11	1	3	4	14
Davison, Rob	42	1	3	4	82
Jakopin, John	18	0	4	4	27
Ling, Jamie	4	1	3	4	0
Gaucher, Ryan	2	0	3	3	0
McCambridge, Keith	38	0	3	3	106
Moscevsky, Yuri	65	1	2	3	172
Longo, Chris	9	1	1	2	4
Toskala, Vesa	49	0	2	2	12
Prosofsky, Garrett	3	1	0	1	0
Knox, Ryan	9	0	1	1	4
Church, Brad	8	1	0	1	4
Drevitch, Scott	2	1	0	1	2
Wells, Jeff	4	0	1	1	2
Jackson, Mark	7	0	1	1	6
Naumenko, Gregg	2	0	0	0	0
Glumac, Mike	2	0	0	0	0
Roy, Philippe	1	0	0	0	0
Eldred, Matt	1	0	0	0	2
Mulick, Robert	24	0	0	0	14
Moore, Grady	5	0	0	0	2
Henkel, Jimmy	2	0	0	0	0
Bootland, Nick	1	0	0	0	2
Torney, Mike	14	0	0	0	23
Wood, Derek	1	0	0	0	0
Fleenor, Brandon	1	0	0	0	17
Labenski, Greg	10	0	0	0	15
Concannon, Mark	3	0	0	0	0
Magliarditi, Marc	1	0	0	0	0
Hogan, Peter	2	0	0	0	2
Martin, P.J.	2	0	0	0	2
Forget, Dominic	2	0	0	0	2
Gillis, Ryan	15	0	0	0	12
Miller, Kelly	2	0	0	0	8
Crain, Jason	6	0	0	0	0
Kotyk, Seamus	34	0	0	0	12

GOALTENDING

	Gms.	Min.	W	L	T	G	SO	Avg.
Magliarditi, Marc.....	1	22	0	0	0	0	0	0.00
Toskala, Vesa	49	2824	15	30	2	151	1	3.21
Naumenko, Gregg ...	2	124	0	1	1	8	0	3.85
Kotyk, Seamus	34	1837	7	22	2	118	2	3.85

GRAND RAPIDS GRIFFINS

SCORING

	Games	G	A	Pts.	PIM
Picard, Michel	78	32	52	84	34
Mowers, Mark	78	34	47	81	47
Roest, Stacy	70	24	48	72	28
Williams, Jason	45	23	22	45	18
King, Derek	59	13	28	41	20
Kopecky, Tomas	70	17	21	38	32
Boisvert, Hugo	78	18	13	31	68
Collins, Rob	73	11	20	31	16
Skarperud, Tim	68	12	17	29	23
Richards, Travis	73	6	21	27	52
Adams, Bryan	74	8	17	25	37
Plante, Philippe	57	11	13	24	36
Robinson, Nathan	53	3	14	17	24
Boileau, Patrick	23	2	11	13	39
Brookbank, Sheldon	69	2	11	13	136
Van Drunen, David	80	3	10	13	106
Avery, Sean	15	6	6	12	82
Campbell, Ed	80	0	12	12	140
Barnes, Ryan	73	5	6	11	151
Groulx, Danny	71	3	7	10	52
Bootland, Darryl	16	1	4	5	41
Greenough, Nick	18	2	1	3	51
Knox, Ryan	9	2	1	3	4
Luciuk, Andrew	2	1	0	1	4
Parillo, Nick	1	1	0	1	0
McCarthy, Jeremiah	11	0	1	1	2
MacDonald, Joey	25	0	1	1	2
Lamothe, Marc	60	0	1	1	6
Dolyny, Rustyn	1	0	0	0	2
Eldred, Matt	2	0	0	0	0
Ballantyne, Paul	7	0	0	0	8
Whitecotton, Dustin	2	0	0	0	2
Alban, Chad	2	0	0	0	0
Schneekloth, Aaron	2	0	0	0	0

GOALTENDING

	Gms.	Min.	W	L	T	G	SO	Avg.
Lamothe, Marc	60	3438	33	18	8	122	6	2.13
MacDonald, Joey	25	1336	14	6	0	49	3	2.20
Alban, Chad	2	77	1	0	0	3	0	2.34

HAMILTON BULLDOGS

SCORING

	Games	G	A	Pts.	PIM
Ward, Jason	69	31	41	72	78
Ryder, Michael	69	34	33	67	43
Gratton, Benoit	43	21	39	60	78
Stoll, Jarret	76	21	33	54	86
Rita, Jani	64	21	27	48	18
Plekanec, Tomas	77	19	27	46	74
Bergeron, Marc-Andre	66	8	31	39	73
Salmelainen, Tony	67	14	19	33	14
Hossa, Marcel	37	19	13	32	18
Pisani, Fernando	41	17	15	32	24
Komisarek, Mike	56	5	25	30	79
Beauchemin, Francois	75	7	21	28	92
Hinz, Chad	65	12	12	24	36
Czerkawski, Mariusz	20	8	12	20	12
Balej, Jozef	56	5	15	20	29
Lindsay, Bill	28	6	12	18	89
DiCasmirro, Nate	49	5	12	17	22
Bouillon, Francis	29	1	12	13	31

	Games	G	A	Pts.	PIM
Allen, Bobby	56	1	12	13	24
Hainsey, Ron	33	2	11	13	26
Bishai, Mike	27	7	5	12	11
Audette, Donald	11	5	5	10	8
Torres, Raffi	11	1	7	8	14
Semenov, Alexei	37	4	3	7	45
Blouin, Sylvain	19	2	4	6	39
Haakana, Kari	12	0	4	4	12
Carpentier, Benjamin	52	3	1	4	140
Reasoner, Marty	2	0	2	2	2
Rennette, Tyler	4	0	2	2	4
Dufresne, Sylvain	7	0	2	2	6
Hogan, Peter	4	0	2	2	2
Ribeiro, Mike	3	0	1	1	0
Pisa, Ales	7	0	1	1	14
Roach, Gary	3	0	1	1	0
Dewan, Adam	4	0	1	1	11
Periard, Dominic	4	0	1	1	4
Conklin, Ty	38	0	1	1	4
Vellinga, Mike	2	0	0	0	0
O'Dette, Matt	8	0	0	0	8
Antila, Kristian	2	0	0	0	0
Garon, Mathieu	20	0	0	0	0
Henrich, Michael	12	0	0	0	2
Nolan, Doug	2	0	0	0	0
Vancik, Jay	21	0	0	0	15
Vince, Ryan	1	0	0	0	0
McKie, Ryan	3	0	0	0	0
Risidore, Ryan	6	0	0	0	2
Power, Aaron	1	0	0	0	0
McAslan, Sean	1	0	0	0	0
Hunter, J.J.	2	0	0	0	2
Fichaud, Eric	27	0	0	0	2

GOALTENDING

	Gms.	Min.	W	L	T	G	SO	Avg.
Garon, Mathieu	20	1150	15	2	2	34	4	1.77
Fichaud, Eric	27	1446	14	7	3	55	4	2.28
Conklin, Ty	38	2140	19	13	3	91	4	2.55
Antila, Kristian	2	96	1	1	0	6	0	3.71

HARTFORD WOLF PACK

SCORING

	Games	G	A	Pts.	PIM
Ekman, Nils	57	30	36	66	73
Ward, Dixon	67	23	41	64	108
Lyashenko, Roman	71	23	35	58	44
Tripp, John	57	29	21	50	68
Gernander, Ken	72	17	19	36	22
Ulmer, Layne	68	12	20	32	16
Kinch, Matt	66	7	22	29	28
Murray, Garth	64	10	14	24	121
Dusablon, Benoit	50	8	16	24	41
Lintner, Richard	26	6	15	21	30
Bouchard, Joel	22	6	14	20	22
Donato, Ted	18	8	12	20	14
Larose, Cory	24	9	10	19	20
Mottau, Mike	29	1	18	19	24
Lundmark, Jamie	22	9	9	18	18
Tibbetts, Billy	35	7	10	17	172
Fata, Rico	9	8	6	14	6
Andrews, Bobby	58	6	7	13	33
Yetman, Patrick	28	5	6	11	6
Nycholat, Lawrence	15	2	9	11	6
Pittman, Chris	19	5	5	10	13
Henderson, Jay	14	3	4	7	27
Aufiero, Pat	32	1	6	7	29
Karpa, Dave	34	0	7	7	70
Chebaturkin, Vladimi	53	4	3	7	88
Inman, David	17	1	6	7	8
Kloucek, Tomas	20	3	4	7	102
Burnett, Garrett	62	6	1	7	346
Lampman, Bryce	45	0	6	6	32

	Games	G	A	Pts.	PIM
Scott, Richard	32	0	5	5	150
Dwyer, Gordie	15	3	2	5	117
Arsene, Dean	50	1	3	4	94
State, Jeff	39	1	3	4	103
Wilson, Mike	5	1	2	3	5
Laukkanen, Janne	5	0	3	3	2
Caulfield, Kevin	4	0	3	3	2
Bast, Ryan	18	0	3	3	18
LaBarbera, Jason	46	0	2	2	6
Oliwa, Krzysztof	15	0	1	1	30
Stals, Juris	2	0	1	1	0
Cross, Cory	2	0	0	0	2
Bilotto, Nic	2	0	0	0	2
Meyer, Scott	9	0	0	0	0
Sundberg, Niklas	1	0	0	0	0
Holmqvist, Johan	35	0	0	0	4
Weller, Craig	11	0	0	0	8

GOALTENDING

	Gms.	Min.	W	L	T	G	SO	Avg.
LaBarbera, Jason	46	2451	18	17	6	105	2	2.57
Holmqvist, Johan	35	1904	14	13	5	84	2	2.65
Meyer, Scott	9	498	1	5	1	36	0	4.34
Sundberg, Niklas	1	3	0	0	0	1	0	18.75

HERSHEY BEARS

SCORING

	Games	G	A	Pts.	PIM
Bertrand, Eric	67	19	40	59	87
Willsie, Brian	59	29	28	57	49
Freer, Mark	70	21	32	53	34
Stephens, Charlie	74	17	33	50	38
Brule, Steve	49	18	19	37	30
Clark, Brett	80	8	27	35	26
Krestanovich, Jordan	70	13	21	34	24
MacLean, Cail	74	16	13	29	14
Moore, Steve	58	10	13	23	41
Muir, Bryan	36	9	12	21	75
Kuleshov, Mikhail	77	7	13	20	76
Thompson, Brent	61	2	17	19	134
Riazantsev, Alex	57	5	10	15	65
Hahl, Riku	28	7	7	14	17
Svatos, Marek	30	9	4	13	10
Busenburg, Marc	44	5	6	11	10
Larsen, Brad	25	3	6	9	25
Richardson, Bruce	33	4	4	8	60
Brigley, Travis	13	3	5	8	4
Wedderburn, Tim	67	1	6	7	22
Clarke, Dale	33	1	5	6	12
Davyduke, Kent	12	2	3	5	0
Nedorost, Vaclav	5	3	2	5	0
Paul, Jeff	50	2	3	5	123
Voltera, Rob	54	1	4	5	180
Saviels, Agris	43	0	3	3	33
Sauve, Philippe	60	0	3	3	8
Deschatelets, Sylvai	4	0	2	2	13
Goodenow, Joe	23	0	2	2	18
Emond, Pierre-Luc	4	1	0	1	2
Goneau, Daniel	3	0	1	1	0
Edinger, Adam	5	0	1	1	0
Bootland, Nick	16	1	0	1	10
Liles, John-Michael	5	0	1	1	4
Henrich, Michael	9	0	1	1	4
Tremblay, Simon	1	0	0	0	2
Gyori, Dylan	1	0	0	0	4
Bogas, Chris	1	0	0	0	2
Timmons, K.C.	2	0	0	0	0
Rymsha, Steve	2	0	0	0	0
Sbrocca, Sandro	1	0	0	0	5
Klyazmin, Sergei	8	0	0	0	2
Varhaug, Mike	2	0	0	0	12
Smith, D.J.	2	0	0	0	4
Wingfield, Brad	2	0	0	0	0
Budaj, Peter	28	0	0	0	0

GOALTENDING

	Gms.	Min.	W	L	T	G	SO	Avg.
Sauve, Philippe	60	3394	26	20	12	134	5	2.37
Budaj, Peter	28	1467	10	10	2	65	2	2.66

HOUSTON AEROS

SCORING

	Games	G	A	Pts.	PIM
Trudel, Jean-Guy	79	31	54	85	85
Domenichelli, Hnat	62	29	34	63	58
Larose, Cory	58	18	38	56	57
Murphy, Curtis	80	23	31	54	63
Roche, Travis	65	14	34	48	42
Cullen, Mark	72	22	25	47	20
Nycholat, Lawrence	66	11	28	39	155
Wallin, Rickard	52	13	22	35	70
Cullen, David	72	2	27	29	42
Wanvig, Kyle	57	13	16	29	137
Pavlikovsky, Rastisl	44	14	13	27	47
Cavanaugh, Dan	77	13	13	26	126
Reitz, Erik	62	6	13	19	112
Cavosie, Marc	54	5	14	19	24
Virta, Tony	39	6	12	18	14
Cloutier, Sylvain	69	4	11	15	129
Tuzzolino, Tony	50	9	6	15	92
Michalek, Zbynek	62	4	10	14	26
Stevenson, Jeremy	18	6	7	13	77
Veilleux, Stephane	29	8	4	12	43
Henderson, Jay	22	7	4	11	65
Hoggan, Jeff	65	6	5	11	45
Dyment, Chris	40	2	3	5	64
Benysek, Ladislav	39	0	4	4	23
Crozier, Greg	7	0	1	1	6
Hradecky, Tomas	1	0	1	1	0
Gustafson, Derek	41	0	1	1	0
Royer, Remi	3	0	0	0	15
Shiryaev, Dennis	2	0	0	0	5
McArthur, Darryl	2	0	0	0	2
Legault, Shawn	1	0	0	0	20
McCambridge, Keith	11	0	0	0	22
Kochan, Dieter	25	0	0	0	2
Brady, Peter-Emmanue	1	0	0	0	0
Cloutier, Frederic	12	0	0	0	2
Holmqvist, Johan	8	0	0	0	0

GOALTENDING

	Gms.	Min.	W	L	T	G	SO	Avg.
Cloutier, Frederic	12	586	4	3	2	24	0	2.46
Kochan, Dieter	25	1446	15	6	3	61	1	2.53
Gustafson, Derek	41	2300	23	14	2	108	2	2.82
Holmqvist, Johan	8	479	5	3	0	23	1	2.88
Brady, Peter	1	33	0	0	0	2	0	3.62

LOWELL LOCK MONSTERS

SCORING

	Games	G	A	Pts.	PIM
Bayda, Ryan	53	11	32	43	32
Heerema, Jeff	36	15	17	32	25
Zigomanis, Mike	38	13	18	31	19
Daw, Jeff	51	14	16	30	18
Kurka, Tomas	61	17	12	29	10
MacDonald, Craig	27	7	20	27	38
Halko, Steve	71	4	22	26	34
Watt, Mike	61	9	14	23	35
DeFauw, Brad	61	11	12	23	48
Surma, Damian	68	11	11	22	46
Druken, Harold	24	8	10	18	8
McCarthy, Jeremiah	44	1	16	17	44
Astashenko, Kaspars	47	6	11	17	60

	Games	G	A	Pts.	PIM
McDonald, Brent	52	7	8	15	29
Lysak, Brett	49	6	9	15	59
Tselios, Nikos	61	4	8	12	65
Dolyny, Rustyn	12	3	6	9	6
McNamara, Chris	28	2	6	8	54
Knyazev, Igor	68	2	5	7	68
Schutte, Michael	13	2	5	7	8
Bonsignore, Jason	12	1	4	5	8
Kuznik, Greg	61	2	3	5	74
Westlund, Tommy	22	1	3	4	12
Johnston, Marty	17	2	2	4	20
Rooney, Brad	7	2	2	4	0
Hill, Ed	29	1	3	4	30
Malec, Tomas	30	0	4	4	50
Murphy, Ryan	12	1	2	3	4
Smith, Don	21	2	1	3	10
Whitecotton, Dustin	7	2	1	3	2
Goneau, Daniel	13	2	1	3	8
Svoboda, Jaroslav	9	1	1	2	10
St. Jacques, Bruno	8	1	1	2	8
Cummings, Brian	3	2	0	2	2
Curry, Sean	35	0	2	2	62
Bast, Ryan	45	1	0	1	68
DesRochers, Patrick	17	0	1	1	6
Petruk, Randy	30	0	1	1	6
Sullivan, Dan	5	0	1	1	9
Ferguson, Troy	6	1	0	1	2
Gillies, Trevor	25	0	1	1	132
Greenough, Nick	20	0	1	1	67
Fast, Brad	7	0	1	1	12
Varhaug, Mike	1	0	0	0	0
Henley, Brent	3	0	0	0	11
Rhodes, Damian	7	0	0	0	0
Irbe, Arturs	7	0	0	0	2
Cheredaryk, Steve	2	0	0	0	0
Slonina, Steve	2	0	0	0	0
Campbell, John	2	0	0	0	0
Zepp, Rob	5	0	0	0	0
Kaiman, Tom	10	0	0	0	19
Battaglia, Anthony	9	0	0	0	0
Leger, Jim	3	0	0	0	0
Platt, Jayme	3	0	0	0	0
Mole, Michael	1	0	0	0	0
Pelletier, Jean-Marc	17	0	0	0	0

GOALTENDING

	Gms.	Min.	W	L	T	G	SO	Avg.
DesRochers, P.	17	1029	4	12	1	48	0	2.80
Irbe, Arturs	7	426	3	3	1	21	0	2.95
Petruk, Randy	30	1641	4	20	3	84	1	3.07
Zepp, Rob	5	303	1	3	1	16	1	3.16
Pelletier, Jean-Marc	17	861	6	10	0	51	1	3.55
Platt, Jayme	3	164	0	2	1	11	0	4.01
Rhodes, Damian	7	379	1	4	0	26	0	4.12
Mole, Michael	1	20	0	0	0	4	0	12.00

MANCHESTER MONARCHS
SCORING

	Games	G	A	Pts.	PIM
Healey, Eric	75	42	31	73	47
Kelly, Steve	54	19	44	63	144
Rosa, Pavel	61	28	35	63	20
Aulin, Jared	44	12	32	44	21
Zizka, Tomas	61	13	30	43	50
Bekar, Derek	51	19	19	38	49
Lehoux, Yanick	78	16	21	37	26
Holland, Jason	67	4	27	31	53
Corvo, Joe	26	8	18	26	8
Smithson, Jerred	38	4	21	25	60
Schmidt, Chris	53	12	13	25	58
Pudlick, Mike	68	7	17	24	52

	Games	G	A	Pts.	PIM
Cammalleri, Mike	13	5	15	20	12
Jackson, Dane	63	6	14	20	80
Seeley, Richard	69	4	14	18	127
Barney, Scott	57	13	5	18	74
Heinze, Steve	18	8	9	17	12
Giuliano, Jeff	47	4	11	15	8
Koehler, Greg	13	1	13	14	26
Aldous, Chris	61	5	9	14	16
Welch, Dan	42	3	9	12	22
Dietrich, Brandon	28	3	8	11	15
Rullier, Joe	62	3	6	9	166
Brennan, Kip	35	3	2	5	195
Flinn, Ryan	27	2	2	4	95
Bogas, Chris	12	1	2	3	13
Riva, Dan	19	2	1	3	10
Hayward, Leon	7	1	2	3	15
Snesrud, Mat	29	0	3	3	12
Armstrong, Derek	2	3	0	3	4
Nolan, Doug	10	1	1	2	6
Clarke, Noah	3	1	1	2	0
Scott, Travis	50	0	2	2	15
Huet, Cristobal	30	0	1	1	4
Loach, Lonnie	3	0	1	1	0
Davyduke, Kent	13	1	0	1	9
Parros, George	9	0	1	1	7
Belza, Anthony	3	0	0	0	4
DiLauro, Ray	1	0	0	0	0
McAlpine, Chris	3	0	0	0	0
Boxma, B.J.	1	0	0	0	0
McCullough, Brian	6	0	0	0	2
Schueller, Doug	3	0	0	0	0
Goulet, Louis	5	0	0	0	0
Insana, Jon	2	0	0	0	2
Sanger, Jeff	4	0	0	0	0

GOALTENDING

	Gms.	Min.	W	L	T	G	SO	Avg.
Huet, Cristobal	30	1783	16	8	5	68	1	2.29
Scott, Travis	50	2829	23	19	5	116	4	2.46
Sanger, Jeff	4	241	1	1	1	14	0	3.48
Boxma, B.J.	1	24	0	1	0	4	0	9.79

MANITOBA MOOSE
SCORING

	Games	G	A	Pts.	PIM
Reid, Brandon	73	18	36	54	18
Ready, Ryan	68	24	26	50	52
Kurtz, Justin	71	11	29	40	65
King, Jason	67	20	20	40	15
Baumgartner, Nolan	59	8	31	39	82
Vasiljevs, Herbert	69	10	29	39	30
Bouck, Tyler	76	10	28	38	103
Helmer, Bryan	60	7	24	31	82
Kavanagh, Pat	63	15	15	30	96
Kariya, Steve	38	14	14	28	18
Farkas, Jeff	39	11	14	25	28
Fedorov, Fedor	50	10	13	23	61
Komarniski, Zenith	53	15	8	23	94
Obsut, Jaroslav	60	6	13	19	59
Smith, Nathan	53	9	8	17	30
Chapman, Brian	60	3	14	17	65
Morrison, Justin	30	10	6	16	13
Roy, Jimmy	50	5	10	15	95
Craighead, John	47	5	10	15	109
Hay, Darrell	43	3	10	13	29
Nielsen, Chris	33	3	10	13	13
Herperger, Chris	15	6	6	12	12
Jokela, Mikko	32	3	7	10	17
Vydareny, Rene	71	2	8	10	46
Goulet, Jason	23	1	2	3	2
Lindgren, Mats	4	0	1	1	6
Allen, Bryan	7	0	1	1	4
Moss, Tyler	42	0	1	1	20
Payette, Andre	8	0	0	0	67
Shmyr, Jason	4	0	0	0	2

MINOR LEAGUES *AHL*

	Games	G	A	Pts.	PIM
Darby, Regan	10	0	0	0	30
St. Croix, Chris	10	0	0	0	12
Skudra, Peter	1	0	0	0	0
Smith, Tim	3	0	0	0	0
Auld, Alex	37	0	0	0	4
Martynyuk, Denis	8	0	0	0	4
Minard, Mike	1	0	0	0	0
Teskey, Doug	0	0	0	0	0

GOALTENDING

	Gms.	Min.	W	L	T	G	SO	Avg.
Auld, Alex	37	2208	15	19	3	97	3	2.64
Moss, Tyler	42	2502	21	15	5	117	3	2.81
Skudra, Peter	1	60	1	0	0	3	0	3.00
Minard, Mike	1	59	0	1	0	5	0	5.06

MILWAUKEE ADMIRALS
SCORING

	Games	G	A	Pts.	PIM
Haydar, Darren	75	29	46	75	36
Mann, Cameron	59	26	31	57	75
Smith, Wyatt	56	24	27	51	89
Classen, Greg	72	20	28	48	61
Erat, Martin	45	10	22	32	41
Pittis, Domenic	30	11	21	32	65
Panov, Konstantin	67	11	20	31	30
Hamhuis, Dan	68	6	21	27	81
Koehler, Greg	43	16	10	26	51
Hutchinson, Andrew	63	9	17	26	40
Lundbohm, Bryan	80	9	17	26	63
Trepanier, Pascal	52	9	15	24	33
Fiddler, Vern	54	8	16	24	70
Lambert, Denny	39	12	12	24	132
Smrek, Peter	68	3	20	23	70
Berenzweig, Andy	48	6	11	17	26
Simpson, Reid	17	6	6	12	40
Anderson, Erik	34	4	8	12	10
Beckett, Jason	64	2	10	12	130
Andersson, Jonas	49	7	4	11	12
Schnabel, Robert	62	3	6	9	178
Wren, Bob	16	1	6	7	17
Riazantsev, Alex	14	3	4	7	9
Kloucek, Tomas	34	0	6	6	80
Ricci, Scott	16	1	4	5	6
Mason, Wes	21	3	1	4	16
Richardson, Bruce	4	3	0	3	2
Fritz, Mitch	13	1	2	3	33
Perrott, Nathan	27	1	2	3	106
Rebek, Jeremy	2	1	1	2	0
Lasak, Jan	40	0	2	2	8
Eaton, Mark	3	1	0	1	2
Helbling, Timo	23	0	1	1	37
Upshall, Scottie	2	1	0	1	2
Hall, Adam	1	0	0	0	2
Durak, Miroslav	1	0	0	0	0
Nicklin, Brant	1	0	0	0	0
Murphy, Dan	1	0	0	0	0
Peters, Geoff	8	0	0	0	7
Parillo, Nick	3	0	0	0	7
Angell, Nick	2	0	0	0	2
Finley, Brian	22	0	0	0	2
Madden, Chris	22	0	0	0	2
Ivanans, Raitis	17	0	0	0	38
Bathe, Landon	3	0	0	0	6

GOALTENDING

	Gms.	Min.	W	L	T	G	SO	Avg.
Lasak, Jan	40	2377	18	14	7	113	1	2.85
Finley, Brian	22	1207	7	11	2	59	2	2.93
Madden, Chris	22	1170	7	7	5	64	0	3.28
Murphy, Dan	1	60	0	1	0	4	0	4.00
Nicklin, Brant	1	58	0	1	0	4	0	4.08

NORFOLK ADMIRALS
SCORING

	Games	G	A	Pts.	PIM
McLean, Brett	77	23	38	61	60
Peluso, Mike	74	24	31	55	35
Hankinson, Casey	78	27	28	55	59
Wilford, Marty	80	13	35	48	87
Henderson, Matt	77	18	29	47	95
Henry, Burke	60	6	22	28	121
Radulov, Igor	62	18	9	27	26
Huskins, Kent	80	5	22	27	48
White, Peter	31	6	17	23	21
Baines, Ajay	74	8	14	22	108
Tolkunov, Dmitri	47	1	17	18	39
Laing, Quintin	69	5	12	17	33
Helperl, Jeff	74	3	12	15	124
Cote, Brandin	65	2	12	14	46
Thornton, Shawn	50	11	2	13	213
Valk, Garry	22	6	5	11	16
Yakubov, Mikhail	62	6	5	11	36
Aitken, Johnathan	80	1	7	8	207
McCarthy, Steve	19	1	6	7	14
Korolev, Igor	14	4	3	7	0
Treille, Yorick	27	3	2	5	25
Souza, Mike	5	2	2	4	7
Bristow, Cam	22	3	1	4	43
Gaucher, Ryan	19	3	1	4	12
Gill, Todd	9	0	3	3	10
Moen, Travis	42	1	2	3	62
Vandenbussche, Ryan	4	0	1	1	5
DeBrusk, Louie	20	1	0	1	10
Jaffray, Jason	2	0	0	0	0
Passmore, Steve	14	0	0	0	2
Balan, Scott	15	0	0	0	27
Leighton, Michael	36	0	0	0	4
LaPlante, Sebastien	2	0	0	0	0
Andersson, Craig	32	0	0	0	2

GOALTENDING

	Gms.	Min.	W	L	T	G	SO	Avg.
Andersson, Craig	32	1794	15	11	5	58	4	1.94
Passmore, Steve	14	831	4	7	2	33	2	2.38
Leighton, Michael	36	2183	18	13	5	91	4	2.50
LaPlante, Sebastien	2	58	0	0	0	3	0	3.06

PHILADELPHIA PHANTOMS
SCORING

	Games	G	A	Pts.	PIM
Greig, Mark	73	30	44	74	127
White, Peter	47	17	26	43	16
Slaney, John	55	9	33	42	36
Savage, Andre	64	11	31	42	66
Law, Kirby	74	22	19	41	166
Tiley, Brad	79	8	28	36	28
Sharp, Patrick	53	14	19	33	39
Stafford, Ben	80	12	15	27	38
Wright, Jamie	33	10	14	24	31
MacNeil, Ian	71	10	13	23	132
Harlock, David	59	2	18	20	83
Lephart, Mike	75	6	8	14	23
Lefebvre, Guillaume	47	7	6	13	113
Vandermeer, Peter	77	5	8	13	335
Siklenka, Mike	64	6	6	12	169
Vandermeer, Jim	48	4	8	12	122
Seidenberg, Dennis	19	5	6	11	17
Kohn, Ladislav	15	4	7	11	2
Skolney, Wade	68	2	7	9	102
Baker, Jack	30	4	4	8	35
Sacco, Joe	6	4	3	7	4
St. Jacques, Bruno	30	0	7	7	46
Furey, Kirk	31	0	7	7	17
Peters, Dan	41	1	4	5	48
Betournay, Eric	34	2	0	2	41
Forbes, Ian	20	1	1	2	38
Bogas, Chris	15	0	2	2	11

	Games	G	A	Pts.	PIM
Brunel, Craig	7	1	0	1	7
Harrold, Josh	3	0	1	1	2
Smith, Jeff	11	1	0	1	22
Bast, Ryan	11	0	1	1	21
Yeats, Matthew	2	0	0	0	2
White, Kam	2	0	0	0	6
Corrinet, Chris	1	0	0	0	0
McAllister, Chris	4	0	0	0	12
Zultek, Matt	13	0	0	0	2
Niittymaki, Antero	40	0	0	0	0
Little, Neil	42	0	0	0	2

GOALTENDING

	Gms.	Min.	W	L	T	G	SO	Avg.
Little, Neil	42	2478	18	19	4	103	4	2.49
Niittymaki, Antero	40	2283	14	21	2	98	0	2.58
Yeats, Matthew	2	89	1	1	0	4	0	2.67

PORTLAND PIRATES
SCORING

	Games	G	A	Pts.	PIM
Ferraro, Peter	59	22	41	63	123
Whitfield, Trent	64	27	34	61	42
Forbes, Colin	69	22	38	60	73
Ferraro, Chris	57	19	32	51	121
Murphy, Mark	55	18	24	42	84
Mink, Graham	71	22	15	37	115
Boumedienne, Josef	44	8	22	30	77
Metropolit, Glen	33	7	23	30	23
Pettinger, Matt	69	14	13	27	72
Hajt, Chris	71	11	15	26	61
Salomonsson, Andreas	31	7	17	24	23
Farrell, Mike	68	12	12	24	107
Parsons, Brad	75	4	14	18	17
Cutta, Jakub	66	3	12	15	106
Libby, Matt	44	0	12	12	27
Rohloff, Todd	64	2	10	12	65
Ciernik, Ivan	13	4	6	10	6
Tvrdon, Roman	35	5	4	9	17
Barch, Krys	36	1	7	8	49
Zinger, Dwayne	65	1	7	8	67
Angelstad, Mel	57	5	2	7	139
Sutherby, Brian	5	0	5	5	11
Doig, Jason	21	1	4	5	66
Melanson, Dean	23	1	4	5	40
Yonkman, Nolan	24	1	4	5	40
Forster, Nate	14	1	2	3	9
Corrinet, Chris	33	0	3	3	23
Fortin, J.F.	10	2	1	3	17
Spiewak, Kevin	3	1	1	2	4
Henry, Alex	3	0	1	1	0
Williams, Jeff	9	0	1	1	4
Stroshein, Garret	28	0	1	1	86
Stana, Rastislav	24	0	1	1	8
Ouellet, Maxime	48	0	1	1	2
Reid, Matt	2	0	0	0	0
Lent, Nick	3	0	0	0	0
Charpentier, Sebasti	12	0	0	0	2
Peat, Stephen	18	0	0	0	52
Van Buskirk, Ryan	1	0	0	0	0
Peters, Warren	1	0	0	0	0
Zion, Jonathan	6	0	0	0	4

GOALTENDING

	Gms.	Min.	W	L	T	G	SO	Avg.
Stana, Rastislav	24	1354	8	11	4	49	2	2.17
Charpentier, Sebasti	12	727	3	7	2	28	2	2.31
Ouellet, Maxime	48	2773	22	16	7	111	7	2.40

PROVIDENCE BRUINS
SCORING

	Games	G	A	Pts.	PIM
Aucoin, Keith	78	25	49	74	71
Herr, Matt	77	34	38	72	146
Hilbert, Andy	64	35	35	70	119
Goren, Lee	65	32	37	69	106
Leahy, Pat	66	20	23	43	63
Samuelsson, Martin	64	24	15	39	34
Kelleher, Chris	72	8	27	35	50
Kultanen, Jarno	59	9	25	34	35
Brennan, Rich	41	3	29	32	51
VanOene, Darren	78	11	17	28	109
Vernarsky, Kris	65	12	15	27	49
Huml, Ivan	30	10	16	26	42
Dallman, Kevin	72	2	19	21	53
Morrisonn, Shaone	60	5	16	21	103
Henderson, Jay	39	7	13	20	152
Kutlak, Zdenek	68	4	12	16	52
Gellard, Mike	63	5	11	16	24
Jillson, Jeff	30	4	11	15	26
Myhres, Brantt	63	3	10	13	185
Corazzini, Carl	33	7	6	13	4
Paradise, Chris	46	4	7	11	53
White, Brian	51	2	5	7	34
Metcalf, Peter	40	0	6	6	24
Beechey, Tyler	3	2	1	3	2
Hamerlik, Peter	1	0	0	0	0
Raycroft, Andrew	39	0	0	0	4
Thomas, Tim	35	0	0	0	0
Orr, Colton	1	0	0	0	7
Hauser, Adam	1	0	0	0	0
Parsons, Steve	25	0	0	0	82
Underhill, Matt	7	0	0	0	0

GOALTENDING

	Gms.	Min.	W	L	T	G	SO	Avg.
Raycroft, Andrew	39	2255	23	10	3	94	1	2.5
Hauser, Adam	1	64	0	0	1	3	0	2.799
Thomas, Tim	35	2048	18	12	5	98	1	2.87
Underhill, Matt	7	428	3	3	1	22	0	3.077
Hamerlik, Peter	1	65	0	0	1	4	0	3.692

ROCHESTER AMERICANS
SCORING

	Games	G	A	Pts.	PIM
Taylor, Chris	61	12	55	67	44
Botterill, Jason	64	37	22	59	105
Gaustad, Paul	80	14	39	53	137
Methot, Francois	58	19	34	53	22
Milley, Norm	67	16	32	48	39
Hamel, Denis	48	27	20	47	64
Pominville, Jason	73	13	21	34	16
Kristek, Jaroslav	47	15	17	32	24
Ratchuk, Peter	70	11	21	32	64
Bartovic, Milan	74	18	10	28	84
Houda, Doug	77	3	22	25	191
Hecl, Radoslav	58	6	14	20	41
Fitzpatrick, Rory	41	5	11	16	65
Janik, Doug	75	3	13	16	120
Bolibruck, Kevin	43	3	11	14	31
Novotny, Jiri	43	2	9	11	14
Nelson, Riley	28	4	7	11	4
Mosovsky, Karel	62	5	4	9	75
O'Connell, Tim	24	1	3	4	17
Jelenic, Lee	17	1	2	3	11
Peters, Andrew	57	3	0	3	223
Kotalik, Ales	8	0	2	2	4
Ritson, Joe	17	1	1	2	29
Jorde, Ryan	70	0	2	2	136
Robinson, Jody	9	0	1	1	8
Schmidt, Doug	3	0	1	1	2
McMorrow, Sean	64	0	1	1	315
Kalinin, Dmitri	1	0	0	0	0
Henley, Brent	1	0	0	0	0
Askey, Tom	16	0	0	0	10
Noronen, Mika	19	0	0	0	6
Bilotto, Nic	10	0	0	0	10
Miller, Ryan	47	0	0	0	6

GOALTENDING

	Gms.	Min.	W	L	T	G	SO	Avg.
Miller, Ryan	47	2816	23	18	5	110	2	2.34
Noronen, Mika	19	1168	5	9	5	55	2	2.82
Askey, Tom	16	895	3	8	4	49	0	3.28

SAINT JOHN FLAMES

SCORING

	Games	G	A	Pts.	PIM
Dome, Robert	56	27	29	56	41
Morgan, Jason	80	13	40	53	63
Lombardi, Matthew	76	25	21	46	41
DuPont, Micki	44	12	21	33	73
Kobasew, Chuck	48	21	12	33	61
Kohn, Ladislav	35	8	19	27	30
Christie, Ryan	67	10	14	24	84
Saprykin, Oleg	21	12	9	21	22
Sonnenberg, Martin	54	11	10	21	63
Martin, Mike	71	2	18	20	73
Bembridge, Garett	64	9	10	19	33
Kelly, Brent	67	6	11	17	28
Mottau, Mike	32	5	12	17	14
Verot, Darcy	73	5	11	16	299
Filipowicz, Jayme	63	2	13	15	106
Boutin, J.F.	27	3	11	14	25
Betts, Blair	19	6	7	13	6
Mrozik, Rick	68	2	10	12	46
Sutter, Shaun	25	7	4	11	14
Branham, Tim	30	1	8	9	24
Lowry, Dave	22	3	6	9	16
Montador, Steve	11	1	7	8	20
Manzano, Ian	26	1	5	6	25
Mather, Shawn	40	2	3	5	12
Vodrazka, Jan	80	1	4	5	169
Spence, Jason	35	2	2	4	104
Leopold, Jordan	3	1	2	3	0
Wright, Jamie	3	2	1	3	0
Commodore, Mike	7	0	3	3	18
Shmyr, Ryan	21	1	1	2	41
Courchesne, Pierre-L	3	0	2	2	8
Doman, Matt	17	1	0	1	15
Payne, Jason	29	1	0	1	72
Szuper, Levente	35	0	1	1	0
Sabourin, Dany	41	0	1	1	0
Huntzicker, Dave	4	0	0	0	6
Sullivan, Jeff	6	0	0	0	8
Jacques, Alexandre	8	0	0	0	5
Underhill, Jason	1	0	0	0	0
Lovell, Tim	2	0	0	0	2
St. Pierre, Samuel	2	0	0	0	2
Aubry, Peter	3	0	0	0	0
Geris, David	2	0	0	0	5
Langager, Jay	9	0	0	0	2
Damphousse, Jean-Fra	10	0	0	0	0

GOALTENDING

	Gms.	Min.	W	L	T	G	SO	Avg.
Damphousse, J-F.	10	591	5	5	0	23	0	2.33
Szuper, Levente	35	1903	12	18	2	82	1	2.58
Sabourin, Dany	41	2219	15	17	4	100	4	2.70
Aubry, Peter	3	109	0	2	0	6	0	3.29

ST. JOHN'S MAPLE LEAFS

SCORING

	Games	G	A	Pts.	PIM
Leeb, Brad	79	35	26	61	78
Holden, Josh	65	24	29	53	123
Boyes, Brad	65	23	28	51	45
Ponikarovsky, Alexei	63	24	22	46	68
Gavey, Aaron	70	14	29	43	83
Eriksson, Anders	72	5	34	39	133
Barrett, Nathan	69	9	22	31	35
Rourke, Allan	65	12	19	31	49
Hay, Dwayne	51	10	19	29	31

	Games	G	A	Pts.	PIM
Chartier, Chris	67	4	22	26	48
Mills, Craig	65	10	16	26	121
Cereda, Luca	68	7	18	25	26
Doull, Doug	70	15	10	25	257
Wren, Bob	27	8	11	19	25
Kelly, Regan	71	3	15	18	36
Healey, Paul	17	6	10	16	12
Warren, Morgan	58	8	8	16	16
Perrott, Nathan	36	7	8	15	97
Moro, Marc	68	3	8	11	128
Harrison, Jay	72	2	8	10	72
Trepanier, Pascal	12	4	6	10	10
Bonni, Ryan	61	1	8	9	86
Jackman, Richard	8	2	6	8	24
Pilar, Karel	7	2	5	7	28
Druken, Harold	6	0	3	3	2
Van Ryn, Mike	11	0	3	3	20
Yakushin, Dmitri	29	1	2	3	23
Svoboda, Petr	3	0	1	1	4
Chapdelaine, Rene	6	0	1	1	0
Chaplin, Mark	7	1	0	1	2
Vellinga, Mike	3	0	1	1	0
Stajan, Matt	1	0	1	1	0
Palahnuk, Robb	2	0	0	0	0
Centomo, Sebastien	19	0	0	0	4
Cote, Riley	6	0	0	0	5
Hodson, Jamie	22	0	0	0	4
Tellqvist, Mikael	47	0	0	0	4

GOALTENDING

	Gms.	Min.	W	L	T	G	SO	Avg.
Tellqvist, Mikael	47	2651	17	25	3	148	1	3.349
Hodson, Jamie	22	1136	8	7	2	64	1	3.379
Centomo, S.	19	1045	7	10	1	68	0	3.903

SAN ANTONIO RAMPAGE

SCORING

	Games	G	A	Pts.	PIM
Toms, Jeff	64	30	33	63	28
Green, Mike	80	26	34	60	25
Campbell, Jim	64	16	37	53	55
Payer, Serge	78	10	31	41	30
Kolnik, Juraj	65	25	15	40	36
Beaudoin, Eric	41	14	23	37	36
Dagenais, Pierre	49	21	14	35	28
Gove, Dave	72	15	20	35	30
Jardine, Ryan	64	14	17	31	37
Novak, Filip	57	10	17	27	79
Shvidki, Denis	54	8	18	26	28
Rivers, Jamie	50	6	19	25	68
Ritchie, Byron	26	3	14	17	68
Tetarenko, Joey	50	4	12	16	123
Elliott, Paul	63	4	11	15	44
Van Ryn, Mike	44	2	11	13	36
Thompson, Rocky	79	1	11	12	275
Biron, Mathieu	43	3	8	11	58
Reierson, Andy	48	1	10	11	18
Schneider, Eric	24	7	4	11	27
Trepanier, Pascal	12	4	6	10	10
Gagnon, Sean	42	3	6	9	157
Periard, Michel	10	3	5	8	6
Walsh, Brendan	48	2	5	7	202
Rossiter, Kyle	67	0	7	7	107
Morisset, Dave	30	3	3	6	13
Van Ryn, Mike	11	0	3	3	20
Lundbohm, Andy	13	1	1	2	17
Ulanov, Igor	5	1	0	1	4
Vellinga, Mike	3	0	1	1	0
Olson, Josh	23	0	1	1	14
Krajicek, Lukas	3	0	1	1	0
Smith, Matt	2	0	0	0	0
Garner, Tyrone	1	0	0	0	0
Matteau, Stephane	3	0	0	0	4
Sapozhnikov, Vladimi	4	0	0	0	4

	Games	G	A	Pts.	PIM
O'Connor, Sean	8	0	0	0	4
Kelman, Scott	1	0	0	0	0
Flaherty, Wade	30	0	0	0	0
Lajeunesse, Simon	2	0	0	0	0
Mezei, Branislav	1	0	0	0	0
Mason, Chris	50	0	0	0	8

GOALTENDING

	Gms.	Min.	W	L	T	G	SO	Avg.
Mason, Chris	50	2914	25	18	6	122	1	2.51
Flaherty, Wade	30	1791	11	13	5	86	1	2.88
Lajeunesse, Simon	2	78	0	1	0	6	0	4.60
Garner, Tyrone	1	60	0	1	0	5	0	5.00

SPRINGFIELD FALCONS

SCORING

	Games	G	A	Pts.	PIM
Taffe, Jeff	57	23	26	49	44
Banham, Frank	62	23	17	40	36
Kane, Boyd	72	15	22	37	121
Foster, Corey	54	8	26	34	48
Westrum, Erik	70	10	22	32	65
Willis, Shane	56	16	16	32	26
Keefe, Sheldon	33	16	15	31	28
Holzinger, Brian	28	6	20	26	16
Abid, Ramzi	27	15	10	25	50
Rumble, Darren	33	5	17	22	18
Bonsignore, Jason	37	9	12	21	39
Cibak, Martin	62	5	15	20	78
Jaspers, Jason	63	4	15	19	57
Schutte, Michael	48	5	11	16	27
Smith, Dan	69	1	14	15	53
Afanasenkov, Dmitry	41	4	9	13	25
Alexeev, Nikita	36	7	5	12	8
Murray, Rob	71	2	10	12	94
Fabus, Peter	33	5	7	12	25
Grenier, Martin	73	2	10	12	232
Svitov, Alexander	11	4	5	9	17
Focht, Dan	37	2	7	9	80
Royer, Gaetan	33	2	5	7	50
Ralph, Brad	16	2	5	7	6
Bezina, Goran	64	3	4	7	27
Gill, Todd	15	1	5	6	20
Daw, Jeff	12	2	4	6	4
Kudroc, Kristian	35	0	4	4	58
Hordichuk, Darcy	22	1	3	4	38
Quint, Deron	4	1	2	3	4
Sarault, Yves	4	1	1	2	10
Tobler, Ryan	11	0	2	2	44
Tselios, Nikos	13	0	2	2	12
Pratt, Harlan	13	1	0	1	2
Olvestad, Jimmie	6	0	1	1	13
DiLauro, Ray	4	0	1	1	2
Sjostrom, Fredrik	2	1	0	1	0
Harder, Mike	1	0	0	0	0
Zulianello, Colin	1	0	0	0	0
Podlesak, Martin	3	0	0	0	4
DesRochers, Patrick	8	0	0	0	0
Bierk, Zac	13	0	0	0	6
Van Hoof, Jeremy	4	0	0	0	6
Berehowsky, Drake	2	0	0	0	0
Leroux, Francois	6	0	0	0	0
Konstantinov, Evgeny	39	0	0	0	0
Pelletier, Jean-Marc	24	0	0	0	2
Eklund, Brian	1	0	0	0	0
Lauzon, Ryan	5	0	0	0	2
Leach, Jay	9	0	0	0	0

GOALTENDING

	Gms.	Min.	W	L	T	G	SO	Avg.
Eklund, Brian	1	60	1	0	0	1	0	1.00
Pelletier, Jean-Marc	24	1390	12	7	4	55	2	2.37
DesRochers, P.	8	454	2	4	1	20	0	2.64
Bierk, Zac	13	685	6	4	1	33	0	2.89
Konstantinov, E.	39	2188	13	23	1	118	1	3.24
Zulianello, Colin	1	59	0	1	0	5	0	5.07

SYRACUSE CRUNCH

SCORING

	Games	G	A	Pts.	PIM
Darche, Mathieu	76	32	32	64	38
Ling, David	46	7	34	41	129
McDonell, Kent	72	14	24	38	93
Davidson, Matt	48	18	16	34	26
Nedorost, Andrej	63	14	19	33	85
Bellefeuille, Blake	63	12	19	31	44
Moran, Brad	47	12	19	31	22
Reich, Jeremy	78	14	13	27	195
Bicanek, Radim	56	6	17	23	111
Dzieduszycki, Matt	66	12	10	22	38
Walser, Derrick	28	7	14	21	30
MacLean, Donald	17	9	9	18	6
Pandolfo, Mike	74	9	9	18	31
Jackman, Tim	77	9	7	16	48
Scoville, Darrel	24	4	9	13	26
Westcott, Duvie	22	1	10	11	54
Traynor, Paul	42	3	8	11	44
Levokari, Pauli	45	4	6	10	88
Borzecki, Adam	65	1	9	10	77
Watson, Dan	50	2	7	9	36
Cull, Trent	40	0	8	8	115
Manning, Paul	52	2	5	7	37
Van Impe, Darren	6	1	4	5	8
Colley, Kevin	16	2	3	5	6
Nielsen, Chris	19	1	3	4	8
Ettinger, Trevor	38	1	2	3	145
Sloan, Tyler	39	2	1	3	46
Tremblay, Alexandre	5	0	2	2	2
Knopp, Ben	12	1	1	2	2
Goehring, Karl	49	0	2	2	4
DiRoberto, Torrey	4	0	1	1	6
Paroulek, Martin	9	0	1	1	6
Schill, Jonathan	31	0	1	1	22
Grand-Pierre, Jean-L	2	1	0	1	6
Smith, Scooter	3	0	1	1	0
Seher, Kurt	3	0	1	1	2
Galbraith, Lance	5	0	1	1	10
Wingfield, Brad	1	0	0	0	2
Neilson, Corey	4	0	0	0	2
Crain, Jason	1	0	0	0	0
Labbe, J.F.	4	0	0	0	2
Leclaire, Pascal	36	0	0	0	0
Hanchuck, Tyler	1	0	0	0	7
Walsh, Mike	2	0	0	0	0
Motzko, Joe	2	0	0	0	0
Leinweber, Chris	2	0	0	0	0

GOALTENDING

	Gms.	Min.	W	L	T	G	SO	Avg.
Goehring, Karl	49	2608	18	21	4	116	4	2.67
Labbe, J.F.	4	246	1	2	1	11	0	2.68
Leclaire, Pascal	36	1886	8	21	3	112	0	3.56
Walsh, Mike	2	96	0	1	0	6	0	3.74

UTAH GRIZZLIES

SCORING

	Games	G	A	Pts.	PIM
Montgomery, Jim	72	22	46	68	109
Landry, Eric	73	26	36	62	119
Hawgood, Greg	70	15	42	57	76
Sim, Jon	42	16	31	47	85
Morgan, Gavin	73	15	24	39	244
Wotton, Mark	69	8	26	34	68
Gosselin, David	80	12	22	34	141
Gainey, Steve	68	9	17	26	106
Oliver, David	37	11	14	25	14
Chouinard, Eric	32	12	12	24	16
Ott, Steve	40	9	11	20	98
Heisten, Barrett	58	10	10	20	47
Thinel, Marc-Andre	44	5	15	20	10

	Games	G	A	Pts.	PIM
Kristoffersson, Marc	62	10	9	19	58
Berenzweig, Andy	26	6	11	17	4
Komarov, Alexei	55	5	12	17	44
Bateman, Jeff	60	8	8	16	60
MacMillan, Jeff	78	8	7	15	132
Cox, Justin	53	3	12	15	22
Jancevski, Dan	76	1	10	11	172
Gyori, Dylan	19	8	2	10	4
Erskine, John	52	2	8	10	274
Descoteaux, Matthieu	48	3	3	6	47
Garrow, Mike	12	1	2	3	8
Draney, Brett	11	1	1	2	7
Hirsch, Corey	35	0	2	2	6
Sgroi, Mike	26	1	0	1	59
Clair, Fraser	15	0	1	1	12
Bacashihua, Jason	39	0	1	1	2
Hogan, Peter	1	0	0	0	0
Banach, Jay	1	0	0	0	2
Helenius, Sami	4	0	0	0	14
Smith, Mike	11	0	0	0	12
Murphy, Cory	1	0	0	0	0

GOALTENDING

	Gms.	Min.	W	L	T	G	SO	Avg.
Hirsch, Corey	35	1953	14	16	2	86	0	2.64
Bacashihua, Jason	39	2244	18	18	2	118	3	3.15
Smith, Mike	11	613	5	5	0	33	0	3.23

WILKES-BARRE/SCRANTON PENGUINS

SCORING

	Games	G	A	Pts.	PIM
Petersen, Toby	80	31	35	66	24
Kostopoulos, Tom	71	21	42	63	131
Murley, Matt	73	21	37	58	45
Beech, Kris	50	19	24	43	76
Endicott, Shane	74	13	26	39	68
Surovy, Tomas	39	19	20	39	18
Daigle, Alexandre	40	9	29	38	18
Kraft, Milan	40	13	24	37	28
Lupaschuk, Ross	74	18	18	36	101
Koltsov, Konstantin	65	9	21	30	41
Meloche, Eric	59	12	17	29	95
Sivek, Michal	40	10	17	27	33
Hussey, Matt	69	12	11	23	28
Scuderi, Rob	74	4	17	21	44
Armstrong, Colby	73	7	11	18	76
Orpik, Brooks	71	4	14	18	105
MacDonald, Jason	56	4	7	11	137
Wilson, Mike	45	4	5	9	89
Robinson, Darcy	48	1	7	8	89
Buckley, Brendan	80	2	6	8	99
Russell, Bobby	26	4	3	7	14
Zevakhin, Alexander	13	4	2	6	2
Lintner, Richard	6	1	4	5	2
DuPont, Micki	14	1	4	5	16
Leroux, Francois	57	1	3	4	124
Ouellet, Michel	4	0	2	2	0
Konopka, Zenon	4	0	1	1	9
Tallas, Robbie	33	0	1	1	4
Malone, Ryan	3	0	1	1	2
Lefebvre, Guillaume	1	1	0	1	0
Caron, Sebastien	27	0	1	1	2
Ference, Andrew	1	0	0	0	2
Valley, Mike	10	0	0	0	2
Koci, David	9	0	0	0	4
Aubin, Jean-Sebastien	16	0	0	0	2

GOALTENDING

	Gms.	Min.	W	L	T	G	SO	Avg.
Aubin, Jean-Seb.	16	919	8	6	1	29	3	1.89
Valley, Mike	10	578	2	6	2	29	1	3.01
Caron, Sebastien	27	1560	12	14	1	81	1	3.11
Tallas, Robbie	33	1762	14	11	3	99	0	3.37

WORCESTER ICECATS

SCORING

	Games	G	A	Pts.	PIM
Varlamov, Sergei	72	23	38	61	79
Pohl, John	58	26	32	58	34
Panzer, Jeff	80	22	32	54	36
Dawe, Jason	71	17	28	45	47
Papineau, Justin	44	21	17	38	42
Virtue, Terry	78	5	30	35	144
Evans, Blake	78	13	21	34	79
Nickulas, Eric	39	17	16	33	40
Brown, Marc	58	13	15	28	24
Backman, Christian	72	8	19	27	66
Rycroft, Mark	45	8	18	26	35
Pollock, Jame	44	5	17	22	50
Brimanis, Aris	38	8	13	21	51
Davis, Greg	54	8	10	18	18
Corrinet, Chris	28	6	12	18	27
Valeev, Igor	72	6	12	18	153
Koivisto, Tom	47	4	13	17	32
Hartlieb, Ernie	24	7	8	15	12
Day, Greg	25	6	7	13	18
Bancroft, Steve	21	4	6	10	32
Van Ryn, Mike	33	2	8	10	16
Walker, Matt	40	1	8	9	58
Colley, Kevin	22	3	4	7	33
Dubinsky, Steve	6	1	5	6	4
Stuart, Mike	41	1	5	6	19
Laflamme, Christian	8	0	4	4	6
Colley, Kevin	6	1	1	2	27
Scheffelmaier, Brett	54	0	2	2	143
Starling, Chad	34	0	1	1	36
Osaer, Phil	24	0	1	1	4
Sanford, Curtis	41	0	1	1	2
Tremblay, Simon	4	1	0	1	2
Yablonski, Jeremy	20	1	0	1	50
Corso, Daniel	1	0	0	0	0
Stirling, Scott	1	0	0	0	0
Johnson, Brent	2	0	0	0	0
Voth, Brad	10	0	0	0	27
Baker, Trevor	13	0	0	0	10
Divis, Reinhard	9	0	0	0	0
Rudkowsky, Cody	10	0	0	0	0
McLaren, Steve	40	0	0	0	80

GOALTENDING

	Gms.	Min.	W	L	T	G	SO	Avg.
Divis, Reinhard	9	452	6	1	0	17	0	2.25
Sanford, Curtis	41	2316	18	14	8	93	3	2.41
Osaer, Phil	24	1328	9	9	3	64	1	2.89
Rudkowsky, Cody	10	577	1	5	3	28	0	2.91
Johnson, Brent	2	125	0	1	1	8	0	3.84
Stirling, Scott	1	60	1	0	0	4	0	4.00

PLAYERS WITH TWO OR MORE TEAMS

SCORING

	Games	G	A	Pts.	PIM
Bancroft, Steve, WOR	21	4	6	10	32
Bancroft, Steve, BNG	29	1	11	12	40
Totals	50	5	17	22	72
Bast, Ryan, LOW	45	1	0	1	68
Bast, Ryan, PHI	11	0	1	1	21
Bast, Ryan, HFD	18	0	3	3	18
Totals	74	1	4	5	107
Berenzweig, Andy, MIL	48	6	11	17	30
Berenzweig, Andy, UTA	26	6	11	17	4
Totals	74	12	22	34	30
Bicanek, Radim, SYR	56	6	17	23	111
Bicanek, Radim, BNG	21	3	10	13	42
Totals	77	9	27	36	153
Bilotto, Nic, HFD	2	0	0	0	2
Bilotto, Nic, BRI	4	1	0	1	2
Bilotto, Nic, ROC	10	0	0	0	10
Totals	16	1	0	1	14

	Games	G	A	Pts.	PIM
Bogas, Chris, HER	1	0	0	0	2
Bogas, Chris, MCH	12	1	2	3	13
Bogas, Chris, PHI	15	0	2	2	11
Totals	28	1	4	5	26
Bolibruck, Kevin, BRI	20	0	0	0	22
Bolibruck, Kevin, ROC	43	3	11	14	31
Totals	63	3	11	14	53
Bonsignore, Jason, SPR	37	9	12	21	39
Bonsignore, Jason, LOW	12	1	4	5	8
Totals	49	10	16	26	47
Bootland, Nick, CLE	1	0	0	0	2
Bootland, Nick, HER	16	1	0	1	10
Totals	17	1	0	1	12
Boumedienne, Josef, BNG	26	2	15	17	62
Boumedienne, Josef, POR	44	8	22	30	77
Totals	70	10	37	47	139
Boyes, Brad, SJS	65	23	28	51	45
Boyes, Brad, CLE	15	7	6	13	21
Totals	80	30	34	64	66
Brigley, Travis, CIN	64	18	27	45	58
Brigley, Travis, HER	13	3	5	8	4
Totals	77	21	32	53	62
Clarke, Dale, HER	33	1	5	6	12
Clarke, Dale, CIN	13	1	6	7	6
Totals	46	2	11	13	18
Colley, Kevin, SYR	16	2	3	5	6
Colley, Kevin, WOR	6	1	1	2	27
Totals	22	3	4	7	33
Commodore, Mike, CIN	61	2	9	11	210
Commodore, Mike, SJN	7	0	3	3	18
Totals	68	2	12	14	228
Corrinet, Chris, POR	33	0	3	3	23
Corrinet, Chris, PHI	1	0	0	0	0
Corrinet, Chris, WOR	28	6	12	18	27
Totals	62	6	15	21	50
Crain, Jason, SYR	1	0	0	0	0
Crain, Jason, CLE	6	0	0	0	0
Totals	7	0	0	0	0
Crozier, Greg, HOU	7	0	1	1	6
Crozier, Greg, ALB	56	19	19	38	46
Totals	63	19	20	39	52
Cummings, Brian, CIN	1	0	0	0	0
Cummings, Brian, LOW	3	2	0	2	2
Totals	4	2	0	2	2
Damphousse, Jean-Fra, CIN	31	0	3	3	0
Damphousse, Jean-Fra, SJN	10	0	0	0	0
Totals	41	0	3	3	0
Davyduke, Kent, HER	12	2	3	5	0
Davyduke, Kent, MCH	13	1	0	1	9
Totals	25	3	3	6	9
Daw, Jeff, LOW	51	14	16	30	18
Daw, Jeff, SPR	12	2	4	6	2
Totals	63	16	20	36	20
DesRochers, Patrick, SPR	8	0	0	0	0
DesRochers, Patrick, LOW	17	0	1	1	6
Totals	25	0	1	1	6
DiLauro, Ray, BNG	4	0	0	0	2
DiLauro, Ray, MCH	1	0	0	0	0
DiLauro, Ray, SPR	4	0	1	1	2
Totals	9	0	1	1	4
Dolyny, Rustyn, GRA	1	0	0	0	2
Dolyny, Rustyn, LOW	12	3	6	9	6
Totals	13	3	6	9	8
Druken, Harold, SJS	6	0	3	3	2
Druken, Harold, LOW	24	8	10	18	8
Totals	30	8	13	21	10
DuPont, Micki, SJN	44	12	21	33	73
DuPont, Micki, WIL	14	1	4	5	16
Totals	58	13	25	38	89
Eldred, Matt, CLE	1	0	0	0	2
Eldred, Matt, GRA	2	0	0	0	0
Totals	3	0	0	0	2

	Games	G	A	Pts.	PIM
Farkas, Jeff, MTB	39	11	14	25	28
Farkas, Jeff, CHI	24	5	12	17	14
Totals	63	16	26	42	42
Gaffney, Mike, BRI	3	0	0	0	4
Gaffney, Mike, CIN	2	0	0	0	2
Totals	5	0	0	0	6
Gaucher, Ryan, CLE	2	0	3	3	0
Gaucher, Ryan, NOR	19	3	1	4	12
Totals	21	3	4	7	12
Gill, Todd, SPR	15	1	5	6	20
Gill, Todd, NOR	9	0	3	3	10
Totals	24	1	8	9	30
Goneau, Daniel, HER	3	0	1	1	0
Goneau, Daniel, LOW	13	2	1	3	8
Totals	16	2	2	4	8
Greenough, Nick, GRA	18	2	1	3	51
Greenough, Nick, LOW	20	0	1	1	67
Totals	38	2	2	4	118
Gyori, Dylan, HER	1	0	0	0	4
Gyori, Dylan, UTA	19	8	2	10	4
Totals	20	8	2	10	8
Henderson, Jay, PRO	39	7	13	20	152
Henderson, Jay, HFD	14	3	4	7	27
Henderson, Jay, HOU	22	7	4	11	65
Totals	75	17	21	38	244
Henley, Brent, LOW	3	0	0	0	11
Henley, Brent, ROC	1	0	0	0	0
Totals	4	0	0	0	11
Henrich, Michael, HAM	12	0	0	0	2
Henrich, Michael, HER	9	0	1	1	4
Totals	21	0	1	1	6
Herperger, Chris, CHI	7	1	1	2	14
Herperger, Chris, MTB	15	6	6	12	12
Totals	22	7	7	14	26
Hogan, Peter, UTA	1	0	0	0	0
Hogan, Peter, CLE	2	0	0	0	2
Hogan, Peter, HAM	4	0	2	2	4
Totals	7	0	2	2	6
Holmqvist, Johan, HFD	35	0	0	0	4
Holmqvist, Johan, HOU	8	0	0	0	0
Totals	43	0	0	0	4
Jillson, Jeff, CLE	19	3	5	8	12
Jillson, Jeff, PRO	30	4	11	15	26
Totals	49	7	16	23	38
Jokela, Mikko, ALB	44	8	11	19	35
Jokela, Mikko, MTB	32	3	7	10	17
Totals	76	11	18	29	52
Kariya, Steve, MTB	38	14	14	28	18
Kariya, Steve, ALB	31	12	19	31	20
Totals	69	26	33	59	38
Kloucek, Tomas ,HFD	20	3	4	7	102
Kloucek, Tomas, MIL	34	0	6	6	80
Totals	54	3	10	13	182
Knox, Ryan, CLE	9	0	1	1	4
Knox, Ryan, GRA	9	2	1	3	4
Totals	18	2	2	4	8
Koehler, Greg, MIL	43	16	10	26	51
Koehler, Greg, MCH	13	1	13	14	26
Totals	56	17	23	40	77
Kohn, Ladislav, SJN	35	8	19	27	30
Kohn, Ladislav, PHI	15	4	7	11	2
Totals	50	12	26	38	32
Lajeunesse, Simon, BNG	19	0	0	0	0
Lajeunesse, Simon, SAN	2	0	0	0	0
Totals	21	0	0	0	0
Larose, Cory, HOU	58	18	38	56	57
Larose, Cory, HFD	24	9	10	19	20
Totals	82	27	48	75	77
Lefebvre, Guillaume, PHI	47	7	6	13	113
Lefebvre, Guillaume, WIL	1	1	0	1	0
Totals	48	8	6	14	113

	Games	G	A	Pts.	PIM
Leroux, Francois, WIL	57	1	3	4	124
Leroux, Francois, SPR	6	0	0	0	0
Totals	63	1	3	4	124
Levokari, Pauli, CHI	6	0	1	1	12
Levokari, Pauli, SYR	45	4	6	10	88
Totals	51	4	7	11	100
Lintner, Richard, HFD	26	6	15	21	30
Lintner, Richard, WIL	6	1	4	5	2
Totals	32	7	19	26	32
McCambridge, Keith, HOU	11	0	0	0	22
McCambridge, Keith, CLE	38	0	3	3	106
Totals	49	0	3	3	128
McCarthy, Jeremiah, LOW	44	1	16	17	44
McCarthy, Jeremiah, GRA	11	0	1	1	2
Totals	55	1	17	18	46
Melanson, Dean, POR	23	1	4	5	40
Melanson, Dean, BNG	35	4	3	7	93
Totals	58	5	7	12	133
Mitchell, Kevin, BRI	18	1	4	5	16
Mitchell, Kevin, CLE	24	2	5	7	22
Totals	42	3	9	12	38
Mottau, Mike, HFD	29	1	18	19	24
Mottau, Mike, SJN	32	5	12	17	14
Totals	61	6	30	36	38
Naumenko, Gregg, CLE	2	0	0	0	0
Naumenko, Gregg, CIN	2	0	0	0	2
Totals	4	0	0	0	2
Nielsen, Chris, SYR	19	1	3	4	8
Nielsen, Chris, CHI	18	3	4	7	4
Nielsen, Chris, MTB	33	3	10	13	13
Totals	70	7	17	24	25
Nolan, Doug, HAM	2	0	0	0	0
Nolan, Doug, MCH	10	1	1	2	6
Totals	12	1	1	2	6
Nycholat, Lawrence, HOU	66	11	28	39	155
Nycholat, Lawrence, HFD	15	2	9	11	6
Totals	81	13	37	50	161
Papineau, Justin, WOR	44	21	17	38	42
Papineau, Justin, BRI	5	7	1	8	4
Totals	49	28	18	46	46
Parillo, Nick, MIL	3	0	0	0	7
Parillo, Nick, GRA	1	1	0	1	0
Parillo, Nick, CIN	3	0	0	0	0
Totals	7	1	0	1	7
Pelletier, Jean-Marc, LOW	17	0	0	0	0
Pelletier, Jean-Marc, SPR	24	0	0	0	2
Totals	41	0	0	0	2
Perrott, Nathan, MIL	27	1	2	3	106
Perrott, Nathan, SJS	36	7	8	15	97
Totals	63	8	10	18	203
Pratt, Harlan, SPR	13	1	0	1	2
Pratt, Harlan, CIN	43	4	6	10	34
Totals	56	5	6	11	36
Rebek, Jeremy, MIL	2	1	1	2	0
Rebek, Jeremy, CHI	2	0	0	0	0
Totals	4	1	1	2	0
Reierson, Andy, SAN	48	1	10	11	18
Reierson, Andy, CIN	14	2	1	3	4
Totals	62	3	11	14	22
Riazantsev, Alex, HER	57	5	10	15	65
Riazantsev, Alex, MIL	14	3	4	7	9
Totals	71	8	14	22	74
Ricci, Scott, BNG	50	0	6	6	23
Ricci, Scott, MIL	16	1	4	5	6
Totals	66	1	10	11	29
Richardson, Bruce, MIL	4	3	0	3	2
Richardson, Bruce, HER	33	4	4	8	60
Totals	37	7	4	11	62
Riva, Dan, MCH	19	2	1	3	10
Riva, Dan, CIN	33	2	6	8	11
Totals	52	4	7	11	21
Robinson, Jody, ROC	9	0	1	1	8
Robinson, Jody, BRI	28	0	3	3	24
Totals	37	0	4	4	32
Ruid, J.C., BNG	1	0	0	0	0
Ruid, J.C., ALB	6	2	0	2	2
Totals	7	2	0	2	2
Schmidt, Doug, BRI	1	0	0	0	2
Schmidt, Doug, ROC	3	0	1	1	2
Totals	4	0	1	1	4
Schutte, Michael, SPR	48	5	11	16	27
Schutte, Michael, LOW	13	2	5	7	8
Totals	61	7	16	23	35
Souza, Mike, NOR	5	2	2	4	7
Souza, Mike, BRI	59	7	15	22	89
Totals	64	9	17	26	96
St. Jacques, Bruno, PHI	30	0	7	7	46
St. Jacques, Bruno, LOW	8	1	1	2	8
Totals	38	1	8	9	54
Stirling, Scott, WOR	1	0	0	0	0
Stirling, Scott, BRI	10	0	1	1	2
Totals	11	0	1	1	2
Tetarenko, Joey, SAN	50	4	12	16	123
Tetarenko, Joey, BNG	14	2	2	4	33
Totals	64	6	14	20	156
Tobler, Ryan, SPR	11	0	2	2	44
Tobler, Ryan, CHI	58	13	18	31	143
Totals	69	13	20	33	187
Torres, Raffi, BRI	49	17	15	32	54
Torres, Raffi, HAM	11	1	7	8	14
Totals	60	18	22	40	68
Tremblay, Simon, HER	1	0	0	0	2
Tremblay, Simon, WOR	4	1	0	1	2
Totals	5	1	0	1	4
Trepanier, Pascal, MIL	52	9	15	24	33
Trepanier, Pascal, SAN	12	4	6	10	10
Totals	64	13	21	34	43
Tselios, Nikos, LOW	61	4	8	12	65
Tselios, Nikos, SPR	13	0	2	2	12
Totals	74	4	10	14	77
Van Ryn, Mike, WOR	33	2	8	10	16
Van Ryn, Mike, SAN	11	0	3	3	20
Totals	44	2	11	13	36
Varhaug, Mike, HER	2	0	0	0	12
Varhaug, Mike, LOW	1	0	0	0	0
Totals	3	0	0	0	12
Vellinga, Mike, HAM	2	0	0	0	0
Vellinga, Mike, SAN	3	0	1	1	0
Totals	5	0	1	1	0
Watson, Dan, SYR	50	2	7	9	36
Watson, Dan, CLE	17	2	4	6	12
Totals	67	4	11	15	48
White, Peter, PHI	47	17	26	43	16
White, Peter, NOR	31	6	17	23	21
Totals	78	23	43	66	37
Whitecotton, Dustin, GRA	2	0	0	0	2
Whitecotton, Dustin, LOW	7	2	1	3	2
Totals	9	2	1	3	4
Wilson, Mike, WIL	45	4	5	9	89
Wilson, Mike, HFD	5	1	2	3	5
Totals	50	5	7	12	94
Wingfield, Brad, SYR	1	0	0	0	2
Wingfield, Brad, HER	2	0	0	0	0
Totals	3	0	0	0	2
Wren, Bob, SJS	27	8	11	19	25
Wren, Bob, MIL	16	1	6	7	17
Wren, Bob, BNG	14	2	12	14	23
Totals	57	11	29	40	65
Wright, Jamie, SJN	3	2	1	3	0
Wright, Jamie, PHI	33	10	14	24	31
Totals	36	12	15	27	31
Yablonski, Jeremy, CIN	9	0	0	0	42
Yablonski, Jeremy, WOR	20	1	0	1	50
Totals	29	1	0	1	92
Zion, Jonathan, CIN	12	2	1	3	20
Zion, Jonathan, POR	6	0	0	0	4
Totals	18	2	1	3	24

GOALTENDING

	Gms.	Min.	W	L	T	G	SO	Avg.
Damphousse, J., CIN	31	1668	12	14	4	87	0	3.13
Damphousse, J., SJN	10	591	5	5	0	23	0	2.33
Totals	41	2259	17	19	4	110	0	2.92
DesRochers, P, SPR	8	454	2	4	1	20	0	2.64
DesRochers, P, LOW	17	1029	4	12	1	48	0	2.80
Totals	25	1484	6	16	2	68	0	2.75
Holmqvist, J., HFD...	35	1904	14	13	5	84	2	2.65
Holmqvist, J., HOU...	8	479	5	3	0	23	1	2.88
Totals	43	2383	19	16	5	107	3	2.69
Lajeunesse, S., BNG	19	966	7	7	1	47	1	2.92
Lajeunesse, S., SAN	2	78	0	1	0	6	0	4.60
Totals	21	1044	7	8	1	53	1	3.04
Naumenko, G., CLE..	2	124	0	1	1	8	0	3.85
Naumenko, G., CIN..	2	65	0	1	0	6	0	5.50
Totals	4	190	0	2	1	14	0	4.42
Pelletier, J-M, LOW..	17	861	6	10	0	51	1	3.55
Pelletier, J-M, SPR...	24	1390	12	7	4	55	2	2.37
Totals	41	2251	18	17	4	106	3	2.82
Stirling, S., WOR	1	60	1	0	0	4	0	4.00
Stirling, S., BRI........	10	571	8	2	0	23	0	2.41
Totals.................	11	631	9	2	0	27	0	2.57

2003 CALDER CUP PLAYOFFS

RESULTS

CALDER CUP FINAL

Hamilton Bulldogs vs. Houston Aeros
Game 1 - May 28, Houston 2, Hamilton 1
Game 2 - May 30 Hamilton 2, Houston 1, 4OT
Game 3 - June 4 Hamilton 4, Houston 2
Game 4 - June 6 Houston 3, Hamilton 2, OT
Game 5 - June 7 Houston 6, Hamilton 4
Game 6 - June 9 Hamilton 2, Houston 1
Game 7 - June 12 Houston 3, Hamilton 0

CONFERENCE FINALS

Western Conference
Grand Rapids Griffins vs. Houston Aeros
Game 1 - May 12 Houston 3, Grand Rapids 2
Game 2 - May 14 Grand Rapids 3, Houston 1
Game 3 - May 16 Houston 2, Grand Rapids 1
Game 4 - May 17 Houston 2, Grand Rapids 1
Game 5 - May 19 Grand Rapids 5, Houston 4
Game 6 - May 21 Grand Rapids 2, Houston 1
Game 7 - May 22 Houston 2, Grand Rapids 1

Eastern Conference
Hamilton Bulldogs vs. Binghamton Senators
Game 1 - May 13 Hamilton 5, Binghamton 1
Game 2 - May 15 Hamilton 2, Binghamton 1
Game 3 - May 19 Binghamton 6, Hamilton 4
Game 4 - May 20 Hamilton 6, Binghamton 3
Game 5 - May 22 Hamilton 8, Binghamton 3

CONFERENCE SEMIFINALS

Western Conference
Grand Rapids Griffins vs. Chicago Wolves
Game 1 - April 28 Grand Rapids 4, Chicago 3
Game 2 - April 29 Grand Rapids 3, Chicago 1
Game 3 - May 1 Grand Rapids 2, Chicago 1
Game 4 - May 2 Grand Rapids 2, Chicago 0

Houston Aeros vs. Norfolk Admirals
Game 1 - April 26 Houston 5, Norfolk 4
Game 2 - April 27 Norfolk 4, Houston 0
Game 3 - April 30 Norfolk 3, Houston 2
Game 4 - May 2 Houston 3, Norfolk 2
Game 5 - May 4 Houston 4, Norfolk 1
Game 6 - May 7 Houston 3, Norfolk 1

Eastern Conference
Hamilton Bulldogs vs. Manitoba Moose
Game 1 - April 27 Manitoba 2, Hamilton 1
Game 2 - April 29 Hamilton 5, Manitoba 2
Game 3 - May 2 Hamilton 2, Manitoba 1
Game 4 - May 4 Hamilton 6, Manitoba 2
Game 5 - May 5 Manitoba 3, Hamilton 1
Game 6 - May 8 Manitoba 4, Hamilton 3
Game 7 - May 11 Hamilton 3, Manitoba 2

Binghamton Senators vs. Bridgeport Sound Tigers
Game 1 - April 26 Binghamton 2, Bridgeport 1
Game 2 - April 27 Binghamton 3, Bridgeport 2
Game 3 - April 30 Bridgeport 5, Binghamton 0
Game 4 - May 2 Bridgeport 3, Binghamton 2
Game 5 - May 3 Binghamton 3, Bridgeport 0
Game 6 - May 5 Binghamton 2, Bridgeport 1

CONFERENCE QUARTERFINALS

Western Conference
Grand Rapids Griffins vs. Wilkes-Barre/Scranton Penguins
Game 1 - April 16 Grand Rapids 3, Wilkes-Barre/Scranton 1
Game 2 - April 18 Grand Rapids 2, Wilkes-Barre/Scranton 1
Game 3 - April 19 Wilkes-Barre/Scranton 6, Grand Rapids 2
Game 4 - April 21 Grand Rapids 3, Wilkes-Barre/Scranton 2

Houston Aeros vs. Milwaukee Admirals
Game 1 - April 16 Houston 3, Milwaukee 2
Game 2 - April 18 Houston 4, Milwaukee 2
Game 3 - April 19 Houston 3, Milwaukee 2

Norfolk Admirals vs. San Antonio Rampage
Game 1 - April 10 Norfolk 4, San Antonio 3
Game 2 - April 11 Norfolk 2, San Antonio 1
Game 3 - April 13 Norfolk 3, San Antonio 1

Chicago Wolves vs. Hershey Bears
Game 1 - April 13 Chicago 3, Hershey 2
Game 2 - April 16 Hershey 5, Chicago 3
Game 3 - April 19 Hershey 3, Chicago 1
Game 4 - April 20 Chicago 6, Hershey 0
Game 5 - April 22 Chicago 3, Hershey 2

Eastern Conference
Hamilton Bulldogs vs. Springfield Falcons
Game 1 -- April 15 Hamilton 4, Springfield 0
Game 2 -- April 17 Hamilton 7, Springfield 6
Game 3 -- April 18 Springfield 3, Hamilton 0
Game 4 -- April 21 Hamilton 2, Springfield 1

Providence Bruins vs. Manitoba Moose
Game 1 - April 16 Manitoba 2, Providence 1
Game 2 - April 18 Manitoba 1, Providence 0
Game 3 - April 20 Providence 1, Manitoba 0
Game 4 - April 22 Manitoba 3, Providence 2

Binghamton Senators vs. Worcester IceCats
Game 1 - April 10 Binghamton 3, Worcester 2
Game 2 - April 11 Binghamton 4, Worcester 2
Game 3 - April 18 Binghamton 1, Worcester 0

Manchester Monarchs vs. Bridgeport Sound Tigers
Game 1 - April 12 Bridgeport 2, Manchester 1
Game 2 - April 13 Bridgeport 6, Manchester 3
Game 3 - April 18 Bridgeport 6, Manchester 3

CONFERENCE QUALIFYING SERIES
Western Conference
Milwaukee Admirals vs. Rochester Americans
Game 1 - April 10 Milwaukee 4, Rochester 3
Game 2 - April 12 Rochester 6, Milwaukee 1
Game 3 - April 13 Milwaukee 6, Rochester 1

Wilkes-Barre/Scranton Penguins vs. Utah Grizzlies
Game 1 - April 10 Wilkes-Barre/Scranton 5, Utah 2
Game 2 - April 12 Wilkes-Barre/Scranton 2, Utah 1

Eastern Conference
Hartford Wolf Pack vs. Springfield Falcons
Game 1 - April 9 Springfield 3, Hartford 1
Game 2 - April 11 Springfield 3, Hartford 2

Portland Pirates vs. Manitoba Moose
Game 1 - April 10 Manitoba 4, Portland 1
Game 2 - April 11 Portland 4, Manitoba 2
Game 3 - April 13 Manitoba 6, Portland 3

INDIVIDUAL LEADERS

Goals: Jason Ward, Hamilton (12)
Assists: Benoit Gratton, Hamilton (15)
Points: Jason Ward, Hamilton (21)
Penalty minutes: Dennis Bonvie, Binghamton (85)
Goaltending average: Andrew Raycroft, Providence (1.36)
Shutouts: Ray Emery, Binghamton (2)

	Games	G	A	Pts.
Ryder, Michael, HAM	23	11	6	17
Gratton, Benoit, HAM	22	2	15	17
Roest, Stacy, GRA	15	10	6	16
Trudel, Jean-Guy, HOU	23	7	9	16
Wallin, Rickard, HOU	23	4	11	15
Domenichelli, Hnat, HOU	23	6	8	14
Salmelainen, Tony, HAM	17	6	8	14
King, Derek, GRA	15	4	10	14

TOP SCORERS

	Games	G	A	Pts.
Ward, Jason, HAM	23	12	9	21
Veilleux, Stephane, HOU	23	7	11	18

INDIVIDUAL STATISTICS

BINGHAMTON SENATORS
(Lost conference finals to Hamilton Bulldogs)

SCORING

	Games	G	A	Pts.	PIM
Smyth, Brad	14	7	6	13	12
Vermette, Antoine	14	2	9	11	10
Pothier, Brian	8	2	8	10	4
Murphy, Joe	14	5	5	10	2
Wren, Bob	14	2	8	10	31
Langfeld, Josh	13	5	3	8	8
Bala, Chris	14	2	5	7	4
Bonvie, Dennis	14	2	4	6	85
Bicanek, Radim	14	2	4	6	26
Kelly, Chris	14	2	3	5	8
Spezza, Jason	2	1	2	3	4
Melanson, Dean	13	0	1	1	48
Vauclair, Julien	14	0	1	1	8
Giroux, Alexandre	10	1	0	1	10
Schubert, Christoph	8	0	1	1	2
Hymovitz, David	14	1	0	1	11
Ulmer, Jeff	13	0	1	1	30
Chouinard, Mathieu	1	0	0	0	0
McGrattan, Brian	1	0	0	0	0
Hedlund, Andy	10	0	0	0	0
Bancroft, Steve	14	0	0	0	12
Tetarenko, Joey	14	0	0	0	36
Dahlman, Toni	5	0	0	0	14
Emery, Ray	14	0	0	0	0

GOALTENDING

	Gms.	Min.	W	L	T	G	SO	Avg.
Chouinard, Mathieu	1	2	0	0	0	0	0	0.00
Emery, Ray	14	848	8	6	0	40	2	2.83

BRIDGEPORT SOUND TIGERS
(Lost conference semifinals to Binghamton Senators)

SCORING

	Games	G	A	Pts.	PIM
Hunter, Trent	9	7	4	11	10
Tkaczuk, Daniel	9	3	7	10	18

	Games	G	A	Pts.	PIM
Butenschon, Sven	9	3	6	9	6
Chabada, Martin	9	3	4	7	4
Adduono, Jeremy	9	2	5	7	2
Manlow, Eric	9	0	6	6	2
Hamilton, Jeff	9	3	3	6	0
Smith, Brandon	9	1	3	4	5
Papineau, Justin	7	1	3	4	7
Mapletoft, Justin	7	1	2	3	6
Schultz, Ray	9	1	0	1	14
Souza, Mike	9	0	1	1	12
Letang, Alan	8	1	0	1	0
DiPietro, Rick	5	0	1	1	4
Rennette, Tyler	2	0	0	0	0
Edinger, Adam	2	0	0	0	0
Belak, Graham	2	0	0	0	0
Valiquette, Stephen	4	0	0	0	0
Higgins, Matt	2	0	0	0	2
Robinson, Jody	1	0	0	0	10
Pettinen, Tomi	9	0	0	0	17
Down, Blaine	9	0	0	0	21
Kalmikov, Konstantin	5	0	0	0	5
Nasreddine, Alain	9	0	0	0	27
Godard, Eric	6	0	0	0	16

GOALTENDING

	Gms.	Min.	W	L	T	G	SO	Avg.
DiPietro, Rick	5	298	2	3	0	10	1	2.01
Valiquette, Stephen	4	253	3	1	0	9	0	2.13

CHICAGO WOLVES
(Lost conference semifinals to Grand Rapids Griffins)

SCORING

	Games	G	A	Pts.	PIM
Gamache, Simon	9	7	2	9	4
Maltais, Steve	9	3	5	8	12
Brown, Rob	9	1	6	7	6
Foster, Kurtis	9	1	3	4	14
Tapper, Brad	9	1	3	4	10
Vigier, J.P.	9	3	1	4	4
Karlsson, Andreas	9	1	3	4	4

	Games	G	A	Pts.	PIM
Hartigan, Mark	9	1	2	3	10
Weaver, Mike	9	0	3	3	4
Safronov, Kirill	9	1	2	3	4
Blatny, Zdenek	9	0	2	2	20
Exelby, Garnet	9	0	1	1	27
DiPenta, Joe	9	0	1	1	7
Eakins, Dallas	9	1	0	1	31
Piros, Kamil	9	1	0	1	4
Lessard, Francis	1	0	0	0	0
Ustrnul, Libor	6	0	0	0	0
Maracle, Norm	8	0	0	0	0
Simon, Ben	9	0	0	0	6
Tobler, Ryan	2	0	0	0	0
MacKenzie, Derek	9	0	0	0	4
Cassivi, Frederic	2	0	0	0	2

GOALTENDING

	Gms.	Min.	W	L	T	G	SO	Avg.
Cassivi, Frederic	2	90	0	2	0	3	0	2.00
Maracle, Norm	8	462	3	4	0	17	1	2.21

GRAND RAPIDS GRIFFINS
(Lost conference finals to Houston Aeros)

SCORING

	Games	G	A	Pts.	PIM
Roest, Stacy	15	10	6	16	8
King, Derek	15	4	10	14	6
Collins, Rob	15	3	8	11	10
Williams, Jason	15	1	7	8	16
Mowers, Mark	15	3	4	7	4
Boisvert, Hugo	15	5	1	6	10
Bootland, Darryl	15	3	2	5	46
Picard, Michel	15	3	1	4	8
Brookbank, Sheldon	15	1	3	4	28
Richards, Travis	15	0	4	4	6
Robinson, Nathan	8	0	3	3	0
Adams, Bryan	13	2	0	2	4
Plante, Philippe	15	0	2	2	10
Barnes, Ryan	15	1	1	2	17
Skarperud, Tim	6	0	1	1	0
Campbell, Ed	15	0	1	1	22
Van Drunen, David	15	0	1	1	12
McCarthy, Jeremiah	12	0	1	1	6
Groulx, Danny	7	0	1	1	7
MacDonald, Joey	1	0	0	0	0
Kopecky, Tomas	14	0	0	0	6
Lamothe, Marc	15	0	0	0	2

GOALTENDING

	Gms.	Min.	W	L	T	G	SO	Avg.
Lamothe, Marc	15	944	10	5	0	29	1	1.84
MacDonald, Joey	1	7	0	0	0	1	0	7.95

HAMILTON BULLDOGS
(Won 2003 Calder Cup)

SCORING

	Games	G	A	Pts.	PIM
Ward, Jason	23	12	9	21	20
Ryder, Michael	23	11	6	17	8
Gratton, Benoit	22	2	15	17	73
Salmelainen, Tony	17	6	8	14	0
Lindsay, Bill	23	10	3	13	31
Stoll, Jarret	23	5	8	13	25
Hainsey, Ron	23	1	10	11	20
Hossa, Marcel	21	4	7	11	12
Beauchemin, Francois	23	1	9	10	16
Bergeron, Marc-Andre	20	0	7	7	25
Rita, Jani	23	3	4	7	2
Torres, Raffi	23	6	1	7	29
Hinz, Chad	22	1	5	6	17
Komisarek, Mike	23	1	5	6	60

	Games	G	A	Pts.	PIM
Allen, Bobby	23	0	5	5	10
Plekanec, Tomas	13	3	2	5	8
Czerkawski, Mariusz	6	1	3	4	6
DiCasmirro, Nate	16	2	1	3	8
Bishai, Mike	6	2	1	3	2
Haakana, Kari	14	1	2	3	6
Blouin, Sylvain	11	1	1	2	28
Balej, Jozef	3	1	0	1	2
Conklin, Ty	17	0	1	1	2
Fichaud, Eric	8	0	0	0	2
Carpentier, Benjamin	6	0	0	0	12
Hogan, Peter	7	0	0	0	0

GOALTENDING

	Gms.	Min.	W	L	T	G	SO	Avg.
Fichaud, Eric	8	472	5	3	0	17	0	2.16
Conklin, Ty	17	1023	9	6	0	38	1	2.23

HERSHEY BEARS
(Lost conference quarterfinals to Chicago Wolves)

SCORING

	Games	G	A	Pts.	PIM
Muir, Bryan	5	2	6	8	6
Clark, Brett	5	0	4	4	4
Nedorost, Vaclav	5	2	2	4	0
Brule, Steve	5	4	0	4	8
Brigley, Travis	5	1	2	3	2
Bertrand, Eric	3	0	2	2	4
Stephens, Charlie	5	1	1	2	2
Larsen, Brad	4	1	1	2	8
Krestanovich, Jordan	4	0	1	1	2
Busenburg, Marc	5	0	1	1	0
Moore, Steve	5	0	1	1	4
Richardson, Bruce	5	1	0	1	4
Henrich, Michael	1	0	0	0	0
Budaj, Peter	1	0	0	0	0
Liles, John-Michael	5	0	0	0	2
Freer, Mark	3	0	0	0	2
MacLean, Cail	5	0	0	0	0
Kuleshov, Mikhail	5	0	0	0	6
Voltera, Rob	4	0	0	0	5
Saviels, Agris	3	0	0	0	0
Wedderburn, Tim	5	0	0	0	0
Thompson, Brent	3	0	0	0	7
Sauve, Philippe	5	0	0	0	0

GOALTENDING

	Gms.	Min.	W	L	T	G	SO	Avg.
Sauve, Philippe	5	294	2	3	0	14	0	2.85
Budaj, Peter	1	5	0	0	0	2	0	20.81

HARTFORD WOLF PACK
(Lost conference qualifying series to Springfield Falcons)

SCORING

	Games	G	A	Pts.	PIM
Ekman, Nils	2	0	2	2	4
Lyashenko, Roman	2	1	1	2	0
Nycholat, Lawrence	2	2	0	2	0
Larose, Cory	2	0	1	1	0
Lampman, Bryce	2	0	1	1	0
Dusablon, Benoit	1	0	0	0	0
Kinch, Matt	2	0	0	0	0
Tripp, John	2	0	0	0	2
Gernander, Ken	2	0	0	0	0
Andrews, Bobby	2	0	0	0	0
Murray, Garth	2	0	0	0	6
Lundmark, Jamie	2	0	0	0	0
Ulmer, Layne	2	0	0	0	0
Scott, Richard	2	0	0	0	16
Burnett, Garrett	1	0	0	0	2
Karpa, Dave	2	0	0	0	0

	Games	G	A	Pts.	PIM
Bast, Ryan	2	0	0	0	2
Weller, Craig	2	0	0	0	0
Lawson, Lucas	2	0	0	0	0
LaBarbera, Jason	2	0	0	0	0

GOALTENDING

	Gms.	Min.	W	L	T	G	SO	Avg.
LaBarbera, Jason	2	117	0	2	0	6	0	3.07

HOUSTON AEROS
(Lost Calder Cup finals to Hamilton Bulldogs)
SCORING

	Games	G	A	Pts.	PIM
Veilleux, Stephane	23	7	11	18	12
Trudel, Jean-Guy	23	7	9	16	22
Wallin, Rickard	23	4	11	15	22
Domenichelli, Hnat	23	6	8	14	8
Pavlikovsky, Rastisl	23	3	10	13	18
Cullen, Mark	15	3	7	10	4
Wanvig, Kyle	21	6	4	10	27
Murphy, Curtis	23	2	7	9	22
Roche, Travis	23	3	5	8	26
Tuzzolino, Tony	23	4	4	8	43
Cavosie, Marc	19	3	5	8	12
Cullen, David	23	3	4	7	14
Cloutier, Sylvain	23	3	3	6	28
Cavanaugh, Dan	23	2	2	4	20
Henderson, Jay	23	2	2	4	25
Reitz, Erik	11	0	3	3	31
Hoggan, Jeff	14	1	2	3	23
Benysek, Ladislav	18	0	3	3	6
Michalek, Zbynek	23	1	1	2	6
Dyment, Chris	17	0	1	1	8
Kochan, Dieter	2	0	0	0	0
Holmqvist, Johan	23	0	0	0	2

GOALTENDING

	Gms.	Min.	W	L	T	G	SO	Avg.
Kochan, Dieter	2	20	0	0	0	0	0	0.00
Holmqvist, Johan	23	1498	15	8	0	50	1	2.00

MANCHESTER MONARCHS
(Lost conference quarterfinals to Bridgeport Sound Tigers)
SCORING

	Games	G	A	Pts.	PIM
Aulin, Jared	3	0	4	4	0
Rosa, Pavel	3	3	1	4	4
Avery, Sean	3	2	1	3	8
Zizka, Tomas	3	0	2	2	2
Seeley, Richard	3	0	1	1	0
Kelly, Steve	3	0	1	1	0
Giuliano, Jeff	3	1	0	1	0
Schmidt, Chris	2	0	1	1	4
Healey, Eric	3	1	0	1	2
Jackson, Dane	3	0	1	1	0
Huet, Cristobal	1	0	0	0	0
Lehoux, Yanick	1	0	0	0	0
Aldous, Chris	2	0	0	0	2
Holland, Jason	3	0	0	0	0
Corvo, Joe	3	0	0	0	0
Rullier, Joe	3	0	0	0	2
Pudlick, Mike	1	0	0	0	0
Bekar, Derek	3	0	0	0	2
Smithson, Jerred	3	0	0	0	4
Welch, Dan	3	0	0	0	0
Brennan, Kip	3	0	0	0	0
Scott, Travis	3	0	0	0	0

GOALTENDING

	Gms.	Min.	W	L	T	G	SO	Avg.
Scott, Travis	3	147	0	2	0	9	0	3.65
Huet, Cristobal	1	29	0	1	0	4	0	8.08

MANITOBA MOOSE
(Lost conference semifinals to Hamilton Bulldogs)
SCORING

	Games	G	A	Pts.	PIM
Kavanagh, Pat	14	7	4	11	20
Roy, Jimmy	14	4	4	8	27
Vasiljevs, Herbert	14	3	5	8	8
Ready, Ryan	14	2	5	7	2
Kurtz, Justin	14	3	4	7	17
King, Jason	14	4	3	7	14
Jokela, Mikko	14	1	4	5	2
Morrison, Justin	14	2	3	5	4
Komarniski, Zenith	13	2	2	4	30
Bouck, Tyler	14	2	2	4	10
Smith, Nathan	14	1	3	4	25
Helmer, Bryan	14	0	4	4	20
Obsut, Jaroslav	14	0	4	4	8
Fedorov, Fedor	3	1	2	3	0
Nielsen, Chris	14	1	2	3	16
Goulet, Jason	10	0	2	2	4
Vydareny, Rene	14	0	2	2	16
Chapman, Brian	14	0	2	2	20
Craighead, John	14	0	2	2	32
Reid, Brandon	1	1	1	2	0
Minard, Mike	5	0	0	0	0
Baumgartner, Nolan	1	0	0	0	4
Moss, Tyler	10	0	0	0	2

GOALTENDING

	Gms.	Min.	W	L	T	G	SO	Avg.
Minard, Mike	5	282	2	2	0	9	0	1.91
Moss, Tyler	10	617	6	4	0	23	0	2.23

MILWAUKEE ADMIRALS
(Lost conference quarterfinals to Houston Aeros)
SCORING

	Games	G	A	Pts.	PIM
Erat, Martin	6	5	4	9	4
Mann, Cameron	6	3	3	6	0
Lundbohm, Bryan	6	1	5	6	0
Pittis, Domenic	6	2	4	6	8
Haydar, Darren	6	1	4	5	2
Riazantsev, Alex	5	0	4	4	2
Lambert, Denny	6	2	2	4	42
Hamhuis, Dan	6	0	3	3	2
Fiddler, Vern	6	1	2	3	14
Classen, Greg	6	1	1	2	4
Beckett, Jason	6	0	1	1	12
Ricci, Scott	6	1	0	1	0
Hutchinson, Andrew	3	1	0	1	0
Smith, Wyatt	4	1	0	1	2
Andersson, Jonas	5	0	1	1	4
Panov, Konstantin	2	0	0	0	0
Ivanans, Raitis	1	0	0	0	15
Smrek, Peter	5	0	0	0	0
Upshall, Scottie	6	0	0	0	0
Schnabel, Robert	6	0	0	0	34
Bathe, Landon	5	0	0	0	21
Lasak, Jan	6	0	0	0	0

GOALTENDING

	Gms.	Min.	W	L	T	G	SO	Avg.
Lasak, Jan	6	365	2	4	0	19	0	3.12

NORFOLK ADMIRALS
(Lost conference semifinals to Houston Aeros)
SCORING

	Games	G	A	Pts.	PIM
McLean, Brett	9	2	6	8	9
Gill, Todd	9	2	5	7	10
Hankinson, Casey	9	4	3	7	10
White, Peter	9	2	4	6	5

	Games	G	A	Pts.	PIM
Korolev, Igor	9	2	4	6	4
Laing, Quintin	8	2	2	4	0
Huskins, Kent	9	2	2	4	4
McCarthy, Steve	9	0	4	4	0
Radulov, Igor	9	2	2	4	8
Wilford, Marty	9	0	3	3	16
Aitken, Johnathan	9	2	1	3	18
Peluso, Mike	9	1	2	3	4
Henry, Burke	9	1	2	3	9
Baines, Ajay	9	2	1	3	18
Thornton, Shawn	9	0	2	2	28
Henderson, Matt	1	0	0	0	0
Leighton, Michael	4	0	0	0	2
Cote, Brandin	1	0	0	0	0
Moen, Travis	9	0	0	0	20
Helperl, Jeff	8	0	0	0	11
Yakubov, Mikhail	9	0	0	0	8
Andersson, Craig	5	0	0	0	4

GOALTENDING

	Gms.	Min.	W	L	T	G	SO	Avg.
Leighton, Michael	4	240	3	1	0	7	1	1.75
Andersson, Craig	5	344	2	3	0	15	0	2.61

PORTLAND PIRATES
(Lost conference qualifying series to Manitoba Moose)
SCORING

	Games	G	A	Pts.	PIM
Salomonsson, Andreas	3	4	0	4	0
Forbes, Colin	3	2	2	4	4
Pettinger, Matt	3	0	2	2	2
Ferraro, Peter	3	0	2	2	16
Metropolit, Glen	3	1	1	2	0
Farrell, Mike	3	0	1	1	0
Ferraro, Chris	3	0	1	1	6
Spiewak, Kevin	3	1	0	1	0
Murphy, Mark	3	0	1	1	2
Parsons, Brad	3	0	1	1	2
Yonkman, Nolan	3	0	1	1	2
Ouellet, Maxime	2	0	0	0	0
Stroshein, Garret	2	0	0	0	6
Stana, Rastislav	1	0	0	0	0
Zinger, Dwayne	3	0	0	0	2
Hajt, Chris	1	0	0	0	2
Rohloff, Todd	3	0	0	0	2
Kariya, Martin	3	0	0	0	0
Angelstad, Mel	3	0	0	0	6
Cutta, Jakub	3	0	0	0	2
Libby, Matt	3	0	0	0	0

GOALTENDING

	Gms.	Min.	W	L	T	G	SO	Avg.
Stana, Rastislav	1	58	0	1	0	3	0	3.08
Ouellet, Maxime	2	120	1	1	0	8	0	4.00

PROVIDENCE BRUINS
(Lost conference quarterfinals to Manitoba Moose)
SCORING

	Games	G	A	Pts.	PIM
Huml, Ivan	4	2	0	2	0
Jillson, Jeff	4	0	2	2	8
Kelleher, Chris	4	0	1	1	0
Aucoin, Keith	4	0	1	1	6
Kutlak, Zdenek	4	1	0	1	2
Herr, Matt	4	0	1	1	12
Leahy, Pat	4	1	0	1	18
Hilbert, Andy	4	0	1	1	4
White, Brian	4	0	1	1	8
Goren, Lee	3	0	1	1	0
Liscak, Robert	1	0	0	0	0
Samuelsson, Martin	4	0	0	0	0
Corazzini, Carl	4	0	0	0	0
Vernarsky, Kris	4	0	0	0	20
Kultanen, Jarno	4	0	0	0	6

	Games	G	A	Pts.	PIM
Morrisonn, Shaone	4	0	0	0	6
VanOene, Darren	4	0	0	0	21
Raycroft, Andrew	4	0	0	0	0
Gellard, Mike	4	0	0	0	2
Myhres, Brantt	4	0	0	0	2

GOALTENDING

	Gms.	Min.	W	L	T	G	SO	Avg.
Raycroft, Andrew	4	264	1	3	0	6	1	1.36

ROCHESTER AMERICANS
(Lost conference qualifying series to Milwaukee Admirals)
SCORING

	Games	G	A	Pts.	PIM
Hamel, Denis	3	3	2	5	4
Taylor, Chris	3	3	1	4	2
Methot, Francois	3	0	4	4	0
Pominville, Jason	3	1	1	2	0
Botterill, Jason	3	1	1	2	21
Milley, Norm	3	2	0	2	2
Houda, Doug	3	0	2	2	22
Ratchuk, Peter	3	0	1	1	6
Novotny, Jiri	3	0	1	1	10
Hecl, Radoslav	3	0	0	0	2
Janik, Doug	3	0	0	0	6
Bartovic, Milan	3	0	0	0	0
Gaustad, Paul	3	0	0	0	4
Bolibruck, Kevin	3	0	0	0	10
McMorrow, Sean	3	0	0	0	17
Nelson, Riley	3	0	0	0	2
Miller, Ryan	3	0	0	0	0
O'Connell, Tim	3	0	0	0	4
Peters, Andrew	3	0	0	0	24

GOALTENDING

	Gms.	Min.	W	L	T	G	SO	Avg.
Miller, Ryan	3	189	1	2	0	13	0	4.11

SAN ANTONIO RAMPAGE
(Lost conference quarterfinals to Norfolk Admirals)
SCORING

	Games	G	A	Pts.	PIM
Dagenais, Pierre	3	2	0	2	2
Green, Mike	3	0	2	2	0
Walsh, Brendan	3	0	1	1	0
Beaudoin, Eric	3	1	0	1	0
Ritchie, Byron	3	1	0	1	0
Jardine, Ryan	3	1	0	1	0
Gove, Dave	3	0	1	1	0
Kolnik, Juraj	3	0	1	1	4
Rivers, Jamie	3	0	1	1	10
Toms, Jeff	1	0	0	0	0
Novak, Filip	1	0	0	0	0
Payer, Serge	1	0	0	0	2
Trepanier, Pascal	2	0	0	0	2
Krajicek, Lukas	3	0	0	0	0
Gagnon, Sean	3	0	0	0	4
Van Ryn, Mike	3	0	0	0	0
Elliott, Paul	2	0	0	0	0
Campbell, Jim	1	0	0	0	0
O'Connor, Sean	1	0	0	0	0
Mezei, Branislav	3	0	0	0	0
Thompson, Rocky	3	0	0	0	4
Rossiter, Kyle	3	0	0	0	0
Mason, Chris	3	0	0	0	0

GOALTENDING

	Gms.	Min.	W	L	T	G	SO	Avg.
Mason, Chris	3	194	0	3	0	9	0	2.77

SPRINGFIELD FALCONS
(Lost conference quarterfinals to Hamilton Bulldogs)

SCORING

	Games	G	A	Pts.	PIM
Willis, Shane	6	4	2	6	4
Foster, Corey	6	2	3	5	8
Westrum, Erik	6	0	4	4	6
Kane, Boyd	6	3	1	4	8
Taffe, Jeff	5	0	3	3	8
Banham, Frank	6	2	1	3	2
Cibak, Martin	6	1	2	3	4
Smith, Dan	6	0	2	2	0
Daw, Jeff	6	0	2	2	2
Royer, Gaetan	6	2	0	2	15
Sjostrom, Frederik	6	2	0	2	12
Murray, Rob	6	0	2	2	4
Grenier, Martin	6	0	1	1	12
Leroux, Francois	6	0	1	1	2
Bezina, Goran	6	0	1	1	0
Pelletier, Jean-Marc	6	0	1	1	2
Fabus, Peter	1	0	0	0	0
Jaspers, Jason	6	0	0	0	4
Keefe, Sheldon	6	0	0	0	4
Tselios, Nikos	6	0	0	0	4

GOALTENDING

	Gms.	Min.	W	L	T	G	SO	Avg.
Pelletier, Jean-Marc	6	368	3	3	0	16	1	2.61

UTAH GRIZZLIES
(Lost conference qualifying series to Wilkes-Barre/Scranton Penguins)

SCORING

	Games	G	A	Pts.	PIM
Hawgood, Greg	2	1	0	1	14
Landry, Eric	2	0	1	1	2
Morgan, Gavin	2	0	1	1	17
Gosselin, David	2	0	1	1	6
Kristoffersson, Marc	2	1	0	1	2
Gyori, Dylan	2	1	0	1	0
Jancevski, Dan	2	0	1	1	12
Erskine, John	1	0	1	1	15
Storey, Ben	1	0	0	0	6
Komarov, Alexei	1	0	0	0	2
Bacashihua, Jason	1	0	0	0	0
Berenzweig, Andy	1	0	0	0	0
Heisten, Barrett	2	0	0	0	4
Clair, Fraser	2	0	0	0	12
Bateman, Jeff	2	0	0	0	0
Gainey, Steve	2	0	0	0	11
Thinel, Marc-Andre	2	0	0	0	0
Montgomery, Jim	2	0	0	0	2
MacMillan, Jeff	2	0	0	0	6
Cox, Justin	2	0	0	0	2
Wotton, Mark	2	0	0	0	2
Hirsch, Corey	1	0	0	0	0

GOALTENDING

	Gms.	Min.	W	L	T	G	SO	Avg.
Bacashihua, Jason	1	58	0	1	0	2	0	2.05
Hirsch, Corey	1	60	0	1	0	5	0	5.00

WILKES-BARRE/SCRANTON PENGUINS
(Lost conference quarterfinals to Grand Rapids Griffins)

SCORING

	Games	G	A	Pts.	PIM
Kraft, Milan	6	2	4	6	4
Koltsov, Konstantin	6	2	4	6	4
Sivek, Michal	6	3	2	5	20
Surovy, Tomas	6	2	3	5	2
Petersen, Toby	6	1	3	4	4
DuPont, Micki	6	3	0	3	21
Kostopoulos, Tom	6	1	2	3	7
Lupaschuk, Ross	4	0	2	2	20
Beech, Kris	5	1	1	2	0
Endicott, Shane	6	0	2	2	4
Murley, Matt	6	0	2	2	15
Daigle, Alexandre	4	0	1	1	0
Scuderi, Rob	6	0	1	1	4
Robinson, Darcy	6	1	0	1	5
Meloche, Eric	6	1	0	1	20
Aubin, Jean-Sebastie	6	0	1	1	0
MacDonald, Jason	1	0	0	0	0
Orpik, Brooks	6	0	0	0	14
Hussey, Matt	2	0	0	0	0
Armstrong, Colby	3	0	0	0	4
Buckley, Brendan	6	0	0	0	2
Lefebvre, Guillaume	5	0	0	0	6

GOALTENDING

	Gms.	Min.	W	L	T	G	SO	Avg.
Aubin, J.-Sebastien.	6	355	3	3	0	12	0	2.02

WORCESTER ICECATS
(Lost conference quarterfinals to Binghamton Senators)

SCORING

	Games	G	A	Pts.	PIM
Corrinet, Chris	3	0	2	2	2
Panzer, Jeff	3	1	1	2	0
Varlamov, Sergei	3	2	0	2	0
Pohl, John	3	0	1	1	6
Pollock, Jame	3	1	0	1	2
Backman, Christian	3	0	1	1	5
Yablonski, Jeremy	1	0	0	0	0
Rycroft, Mark	1	0	0	0	0
Day, Greg	2	0	0	0	0
Sanford, Curtis	3	0	0	0	0
Brimanis, Aris	3	0	0	0	2
Koivisto, Tom	3	0	0	0	0
Dawe, Jason	3	0	0	0	5
Nickulas, Eric	3	0	0	0	2
McClement, Jay	1	0	0	0	0
Evans, Blake	3	0	0	0	0
Davis, Greg	1	0	0	0	0
McLaren, Steve	3	0	0	0	4
Scheffelmaier, Brett	3	0	0	0	7
Hartlieb, Ernie	3	0	0	0	0
Stuart, Mike	3	0	0	0	2
Valeev, Igor	3	0	0	0	2

GOALTENDING

	Gms.	Min.	W	L	T	G	SO	Avg.
Sanford, Curtis	3	179	0	3	0	8	0	2.68

2002-03 AWARD WINNERS

ALL-STAR TEAMS

Planet USA	Pos.	Canadian
Philippe Sauve, HER	G	Maxime Ouellet, POR
Mike Komisarek, HAM	D	Ray Giroux, ALB
Brian Pothier, BNG	D	John Slaney, PHI
Matt Herr, PRO	F	Jason Spezza, BNG
Chris Ferraro, POR	F	Jason Ward, HAM
Niko Dimitrakos, CLE	F	Darren Haydar, MIL

TROPHY WINNERS

John B. Sollenberger Trophy: Steve Maltais, Chicago
Les Cunningham Award: Jason Ward, Hamilton
Harry (Hap) Holmes Memorial Trophy: Marc Lemotha, G.R.
Joey MacDonald, Grand Rapids
Dudley Garrett Trophy: Darren Haydar, Milwaukee
Eddie Shore Award: Curtis Murphy, Houston

Fred T. Hunt Memorial Award: Eric Healey, Manchester
Chris Ferraro, Portland
Louis A.R. Pieri Memorial Award: Claude Julien, Hamilton
Jason Ward, Hamilton
Aldege Bastien Award: Marc Lemothe, Grand Rapids
Jack Butterfield Trophy: Johan Holmqvist, Houston

ALL-TIME AWARD WINNERS

JOHN B. SOLLENBERGER TROPHY
(Leading scorer)

Season	Player, Team
1936-37	Jack Markle, Syracuse
1937-38	Jack Markle, Syracuse
1938-39	Don Deacon, Pittsburgh
1939-40	Norm Locking, Syracuse
1940-41	Les Cunningham, Cleveland
1941-42	Pete Kelly, Springfield
1942-43	Wally Kilrea, Hershy
1943-44	Tommy Burlington, Cleveland
1944-45	Bob Gracie, Pittsburgh
	Bob Walton, Pittsburgh
1945-46	Les Douglas, Indianapolis
1946-47	Phil Hergesheimer, Philadelphia
1947-48	Carl Liscombe, Providence
1948-49	Sid Smith, Pittsburgh
1949-50	Les Douglas, Cleveland
1950-51	Ab DeMarco, Buffalo
1951-52	Ray Powell, Providence
1952-53	Eddie Olson, Cleveland
1953-54	George Sullivan, Hershey
1954-55	Eddie Olson, Cleveland
1955-56	Zellio Toppazzini, Providence
1956-57	Fred Glover, Cleveland
1957-58	Willie Marshall, Hershey
1958-59	Bill Hicke, Rochester
1959-60	Fred Glover, Cleveland
1960-61	Bill Sweeney, Springfield
1961-62	Bill Sweeney, Springfield
1962-63	Bill Sweeney, Springfield
1963-64	Gerry Ehman, Rochester
1964-65	Art Stratton, Buffalo
1965-66	Dick Gamble, Rochester
1966-67	Gordon Labossiere, Quebec
1967-68	Simon Nolet, Quebec
1968-69	Jeannot Gilbert, Hershey
1969-70	Jude Drouin, Montreal
1970-71	Fred Speck, Baltimore
1971-72	Don Blackburn, Providence
1972-73	Yvon Lambert, Nova Scotia
1973-74	Steve West, New Haven
1974-75	Doug Gibson, Rochester
1975-76	Jean-Guy Gratton, Hershey
1976-77	Andre Peloffy, Springfield
1977-78	Gord Brooks, Philadelphia
	Rick Adduono, Rochester
1978-79	Bernie Johnston, Maine
1979-80	Norm Dube, Nova Scotia
1980-81	Mark Lofthouse, Hershey
1981-82	Mike Kasczyki, New Brunswick
1982-83	Ross Yates, Binghamton
1983-84	Claude Larose, Sherbrooke
1984-85	Paul Gardner, Binghamton
1985-86	Paul Gardner, Rochester
1986-87	Tim Tookey, Hershey
1987-88	Bruce Boudreau, Springfield
1988-89	Stephan Lebeau, Sherbrooke
1989-90	Paul Ysebaert, Utica
1990-91	Kevin Todd, Utica
1991-92	Shaun Van Allen, Cape Breton
1992-93	Don Biggs, Binghamton
1993-94	Tim Taylor, Adirondack
1994-95	Peter White, Cape Breton
1995-96	Brad Smyth, Carolina

Season	Player, Team
1996-97	Peter White, Philadelphia
1997-98	Peter White, Philadelphia
1998-99	Domenic Pittis, Rochester
1999-00	Christian Matte, Hershey
2000-01	Derek Armstrong, Hartford
2001-02	Donald MacLean, St. John's
2002-03	Steve Maltais, Chicago

LES CUNNINGHAM AWARD
(Most Valuable Player)

Season	Player, Team
1947-48	Carl Liscombe, Providence
1948-49	Carl Liscombe, Providence
1949-50	Les Douglas, Cleveland
1950-51	Ab DeMarco, Buffalo
1951-52	Ray Powell, Providence
1952-53	Eddie Olson, Cleveland
1953-54	George "Red" Sullivan, Hershey
1954-55	Ross Lowe, Springfield
1955-56	Johnny Bower, Providence
1956-57	Johnny Bower, Providence
1957-58	Johnny Bower, Cleveland
1958-59	Bill Hicke, Rochester
	Rudy Migay, Rochester
1959-60	Fred Glover, Cleveland
1960-61	Phil Maloney, Buffalo
1961-62	Fred Glover, Cleveland
1962-63	Denis DeJordy, Buffalo
1963-64	Fred Glover, Cleveland
1964-65	Art Stratton, Buffalo
1965-66	Dick Gamble, Rochester
1966-67	Mike Nykoluk, Hershey
1967-68	Dave Creighton, Providence
1968-69	Gilles Villemure, Buffalo
1969-70	Gilles Villemure, Buffalo
1970-71	Fred Speck, Baltimore
1971-72	Garry Peters, Boston
1972-73	Billy Inglis, Cincinnati
1973-74	Art Stratton, Rochester
1974-75	Doug Gibson, Rochester
1975-76	Ron Andruff, Nova Scotia
1976-77	Doug Gibson, Rochester
1977-78	Blake Dunlop, Maine
1978-79	Rocky Saganiuk, New Brunswick
1979-80	Norm Dube, Nova Scotia
1980-81	Pelle Lindbergh, Maine
1981-82	Mike Kasczyki, New Brunswick
1982-83	Ross Yates, Binghamton
1983-84	Mal Davis, Rochester
	Garry Lariviere, St. Catharines
1984-85	Paul Gardner, Binghamton
1985-86	Paul Gardner, Rochester
1986-87	Tim Tookey, Hershey
1987-88	Jody Gage, Rochester
1988-89	Stephan Lebeau, Sherbrooke
1989-90	Paul Ysebaert, Utica
1990-91	Kevin Todd, Utica
1991-92	John Anderson, Hew Haven
1992-93	Don Biggs, Binghamton
1993-94	Rich Chernomaz, St. John's
1994-95	Steve Larouche, Prince Edward Island
1995-96	Brad Smyth, Carolina
1996-97	Jean-Francois Labbe, Hershey
1997-98	Steve Guolla, Kentucky

Season	Player, Team
1998-99	Randy Robitaille, Providence
1999-00	Martin Brochu, Portland
2000-01	Derek Armstrong, Hartford
2001-02	Eric Boguniecki, Worcester
2002-03	Jason Ward, Hamilton

HARRY (HAP) HOLMES MEMORIAL TROPHY
(Outstanding goaltender)

Season	Player, Team
1936-37	Bert Gardiner, Philadelphia
1937-38	Frank Brimsek, Providence
1938-39	Alfie Moore, Hershey
1939-40	Moe Roberts, Cleveland
1940-41	Chuck Rayner, Springfield
1941-42	Bill Beveridge, Cleveland
1942-43	Gordie Bell, Buffalo
1943-44	Nick Damore, Hershey
1944-45	Yves Nadon, Buffalo
1945-46	Connie Dion, St. Louis-Buffalo
1946-47	Baz Bastien, Pittsburgh
1947-48	Baz Bastien, Pittsburgh
1948-49	Baz Bastien, Pittsburgh
1949-50	Gil Mayer, Pittsburgh
1950-51	Gil Mayer, Pittsburgh
1951-52	Johnny Bower, Cleveland
1952-53	Gil Mayer, Pittsburgh
1953-54	Jacques Plante, Buffalo
1954-55	Gil Mayer, Pittsburgh
1955-56	Gil Mayer, Pittsburgh
1956-57	Johnny Bower, Providence
1957-58	Johnny Bower, Cleveland
1958-59	Bob Perreault, Hershey
1959-60	Ed Chadwick, Rochester
1960-61	Marcel Paille, Springfield
1961-62	Marcel Paille, Springfield
1962-63	Denis DeJordy, Buffalo
1963-64	Roger Crozier, Pittsburgh
1964-65	Gerry Cheevers, Rochester
1965-66	Les Binkley, Cleveland
1966-67	Andre Gill, Hershey
1967-68	Bob Perreault, Rochester
1968-69	Gilles Villemure, Buffalo
1969-70	Gilles Villemure, Buffalo
1970-71	Gary Kurt, Cleveland
1971-72	Dan Bouchard, Boston
	Ross Brooks, Boston
1972-73	Michel Larocque, Nova Scotia
1973-74	Jim Shaw, Nova Scotia
	Dave Elenbaas, Nova Scotia
1974-75	Ed Walsh, Nova Scotia
	Dave Elenbaas, Nova Scotia
1975-76	Dave Elenbaas, Nova Scotia
	Ed Walsh, Nova Scotia
1976-77	Ed Walsh, Nova Scotia
	Dave Elenbaas, Nova Scotia
1977-78	Bob Holland, Nova Scotia
	Maurice Barrette, Nova Scotia
1978-79	Pete Peeters, Maine
	Robbie Moore, Maine
1979-80	Rick St. Croix, Maine
	Robbie Moore, Maine
1980-81	Pelle Lindbergh, Maine
	Robbie Moore, Maine
1981-82	Bob Janecyk, New Brunswick
	Warren Skorodenski, New Brunswick
1982-83	Brian Ford, Fredericton
	Clint Malarchuk, Fredericton
1983-84	Brian Ford, Fredericton
1984-85	Jon Casey, Baltimore
1985-86	Sam St. Laurent, Maine
	Karl Friesen, Maine
1986-87	Vincent Riendeau, Sherbrooke
1987-88	Vincent Riendeau, Sherbrooke
	Jocelyn Perreault, Sherbrooke
1988-89	Randy Exelby, Sherbrooke
	Francois Gravel, Sherbrooke

Season	Player, Team
1989-90	Jean Claude Bergeron, Sherbrooke
	Andre Racicot, Sherbrooke
1990-91	David Littman, Rochester
	Darcy Wakaluk, Rochester
1991-92	David Littman, Rochester
1992-93	Corey Hirsch, Binghamton
	Boris Rousson, Binghamton
1993-94	Byron Dafoe, Portland
	Olaf Kolzig, Portland
1994-95	Mike Dunham, Albany
	Corey Schwab, Albany
1995-96	Scott Langkow, Springfield
	Manny Legace, Springfield
1996-97	Jean-Francois Labbe, Hershey
1997-98	Jean-Sebastien Giguere, Saint John
	Tyler Moss, Saint John
1998-99	Martin Biron, Rochester
	Tom Draper, Rochester
1999-00	Milan Hnilicka, Hartford
	Jean-Francois Labbe, Hartford
2000-01	Mika Noronen, Rochester
2001-02	Mathieu Chouinard, Grand Rapids
	Simon Lajeunesse, Grand Rapids
	Martin Prusek, Grand Rapids
2002-03	Marc Lemothe, Grand Rapids
	Joey MacDonald, Grand Rapids

Beginning with the 1983-84 season, the award goes to the top goaltending team with each goaltender having played a minimum of 25 games for the team with the fewest goals against.

DUDLEY (RED) GARRETT MEMORIAL TROPHY
(Top rookie)

Season	Player, Team
1947-48	Bob Solinger, Cleveland
1948-49	Terry Sawchuk, Indianapolis
1949-50	Paul Meger, Buffalo
1950-51	Wally Hergesheimer, Cleveland
1951-52	Earl "Dutch" Reibel, Indianapolis
1952-53	Guyle Fielder, St. Louis
1953-54	Don Marshall, Buffalo
1954-55	Jimmy Anderson, Springfield
1955-56	Bruce Cline, Providence
1956-57	Boris "Bo" Elik, Cleveland
1957-58	Bill Sweeney, Providence
1958-59	Bill Hicke, Rochester
1959-60	Stan Baluik, Providence
1960-61	Ronald "Chico" Maki, Buffalo
1961-62	Les Binkley, Cleveland
1962-63	Doug Robinson, Buffalo
1963-64	Roger Crozier, Pittsburgh
1964-65	Ray Cullen, Buffalo
1965-66	Mike Walton, Rochester
1966-67	Bob Rivard, Quebec
1967-68	Gerry Desjardins, Cleveland
1968-69	Ron Ward, Rochester
1969-70	Jude Drouin, Montreal
1970-71	Fred Speck, Baltimore
1971-72	Terry Caffery, Cleveland
1972-73	Ron Anderson, Boston
1973-74	Rick Middleton, Providence
1974-75	Jerry Holland, Providence
1975-76	Greg Holst, Providence
	Pierre Mondou, Nova Scotia
1976-77	Rod Schutt, Nova Scotia
1977-78	Norm Dupont, Nova Scotia
1978-79	Mike Meeker, Binghamton
1979-80	Darryl Sutter, New Brunswick
1980-81	Pelle Lindbergh, Maine
1981-82	Bob Sullivan, Binghamton
1982-83	Mitch Lamoureux, Baltimore
1983-84	Claude Verret, Rochester
1984-85	Steve Thomas, St. Catharines
1985-86	Ron Hextall, Hershey
1986-87	Brett Hull, Moncton
1987-88	Mike Richard, Binghamton

Season	Player, Team
1988-89	Stephan Lebeau, Sherbrooke
1989-90	Donald Audette, Rochester
1990-91	Patrick Lebeau, Fredericton
1991-92	Felix Potvin, St. John's
1992-93	Corey Hirsch, Binghamton
1993-94	Rene Corbet, Cornwall
1994-95	Jim Carey, Portland
1995-96	Darcy Tucker, Fredericton
1996-97	Jaroslav Svejkovsky, Portland
1997-98	Daniel Briere, Springfield
1998-99	Shane Willis, New Haven
1999-00	Mika Noronen, Rochester
2000-01	Ryan Kraft, Kentucky
2001-02	Tyler Arnason, Norfolk
2002-03	Darren Haydar, Milwaukee

EDDIE SHORE AWARD
(Outstanding defenseman)

Season	Player, Team
1958-59	Steve Kraftcheck, Rochester
1959-60	Larry Hillman, Providence
1960-61	Bob McCord, Springfield
1961-62	Kent Douglas, Springfield
1962-63	Marc Reaume, Hershey
1963-64	Ted Harris, Cleveland
1964-65	Al Arbour, Rochester
1965-66	Jim Morrison, Quebec
1966-67	Bob McCord, Pittsburgh
1967-68	Bill Needham, Cleveland
1968-69	Bob Blackburn, Buffalo
1969-70	Noel Price, Springfield
1970-71	Marshall Johnston, Cleveland
1971-72	Noel Price, Nova Scotia
1972-73	Ray McKay, Cincinnati
1973-74	Gordon Smith, Springfield
1974-75	Joe Zanussi, Providence
1975-76	Noel Price, Nova Scotia
1976-77	Brian Engblom, Nova Scotia
1977-78	Terry Murray, Maine
1978-79	Terry Murray, Maine
1979-80	Rick Vasko, Adirondack
1980-81	Craig Levie, Nova Scotia
1981-82	Dave Farrish, New Brunswick
1982-83	Greg Tebbutt, Baltimore
1983-84	Garry Lariviere, St. Catharines
1984-85	Richie Dunn, Binghamton
1985-86	Jim Wiemer, New Haven
1986-87	Brad Shaw, Binghamton
1987-88	Dave Fenyves, Hershey
1988-89	Dave Fenyves, Hershey
1989-90	Eric Weinrich, Utica
1990-91	Norm Maciver, Cape Breton
1991-92	Greg Hawgood, Cape Breton
1992-93	Bobby Dollas, Adirondack
1993-94	Chris Snell, St. John's
1994-95	Jeff Serowik, Providence
1995-96	Barry Richter, Binghamton
1996-97	Darren Rumble, Philadelphia
1997-98	Jamie Heward, Philadelphia
1998-99	Ken Sutton, Albany
1999-00	Brad Tiley, Springfield
2000-01	John Slaney, Philadelphia
2001-02	John Slaney, Philadelphia
2002-03	Curtis Murphy, Houston

FRED T. HUNT MEMORIAL AWARD
(Sportsmanship, determination and dedication)

Season	Player, Team
1977-78	Blake Dunlop, Maine
1978-79	Bernie Johnston, Maine
1979-80	Norm Dube, Nova Scotia
1980-81	Tony Cassolato, Hershey
1981-82	Mike Kasczyki, New Brunswick
1982-83	Ross Yates, Binghamton
1983-84	Claude Larose, Sherbrooke

Season	Player, Team
1984-85	Paul Gardner, Binghamton
1985-86	Steve Tsujiura, Maine
1986-87	Glenn Merkosky, Adirondack
1987-88	Bruce Boudreau, Springfield
1988-89	Murray Eaves, Adirondack
1989-90	Murray Eaves, Adirondack
1990-91	Glenn Merkosky, Adirondack
1991-92	John Anderson, New Haven
1992-93	Tim Tookey, Hershey
1993-94	Jim Nesich, Cape Breton
1994-95	Steve Larouche, Prince Edward Island
1995-96	Ken Gernander, Binghamton
1996-97	Steve Passmore, Hamilton
1997-98	Craig Charron, Rochester
1998-99	Mitch Lamoureux, Hershey
1999-00	Randy Cunneyworth, Rochester
2000-01	Kent Hulst, Providence
2001-02	Nathan Dempsey, St. John's
2002-03	Eric Healey, Manchester
	Chris Ferraro, Portland

LOUIS A.R. PIERI MEMORIAL AWARD
(Top coach)

Season	Coach, Team
1967-68	Vic Stasiuk, Quebec
1968-69	Frank Mathers, Hershey
1969-70	Fred Shero, Buffalo
1970-71	Terry Reardon, Baltimore
1971-72	Al MacNeil, Nova Scotia
1972-73	Floyd Smith, Cincinnati
1973-74	Don Cherry, Rochester
1974-75	John Muckler, Providence
1975-76	Chuck Hamilton, Hershey
1976-77	Al MacNeil, Nova Scotia
1977-78	Bob McCammon, Maine
1978-79	Parker MacDonald, New Haven
1979-80	Doug Gibson, Hershey
1980-81	Bob McCammon, Maine
1981-82	Orval Tessier, New Brunswick
1982-83	Jacques Demers, Fredericton
1983-84	Gene Ubriaco, Baltimore
1984-85	Bill Dineen, Adirondack
1985-86	Bill Dineen, Adirondack
1986-87	Larry Pleau, Binghamton
1987-88	John Paddock, Hershey
	Mike Milbury, Maine
1988-89	Tom McVie, Utica
1989-90	Jimmy Roberts, Springfield
1990-91	Don Lever, Rochester
1991-92	Doug Carpenter, New Haven
1992-93	Marc Crawford, St. John's
1993-94	Barry Trotz, Portland
1994-95	Robbie Ftorek, Albany
1995-96	Robbie Ftorek, Albany
1996-97	Greg Gilbert, Worcester
1997-98	Bill Stewart, Saint John
1998-99	Peter Laviolette, Providence
1999-00	Glen Hanlon, Portland
2000-01	Don Granato, Worcester
2001-02	Bruce Cassidy, Grand Rapids
2002-03	Claude Julien, Hamilton
	Jason Ward, Hamilton

ALDEGE (BAZ) BASTIEN TROPHY
(Coaches pick as top goaltender)

Season	Player, Team
1983-84	Brian Ford, Fredericton
1984-85	Jon Casey, Baltimore
1985-86	Sam St. Laurent, Maine
1986-87	Mark Laforest, Adirondack
1987-88	Wendell Young, Hershey
1988-89	Randy Exelby, Sherbrooke
1989-90	Jean Claude Bergeron, Sherbrooke
1990-91	Mark Laforest, Binghamton
1991-92	Felix Potvin, St. John's

Season	Player, Team
1992-93	Corey Hirsch, Binghamton
1993-94	Frederic Chabot, Hershey
1994-95	Jim Carey, Portland
1995-96	Manny Legace, Springfield
1996-97	Jean-Francois Labbe, Hershey
1997-98	Scott Langkow, Springfield
1998-99	Martin Biron, Rochester
1999-00	Martin Brochu, Portland
2000-01	Dwayne Roloson, Worcester
2001-02	Martin Prusek, Grand Rapids
2002-03	Marc Lemothe, Grand Rapids

JACK BUTTERFIELD TROPHY
(Calder Cup playoff MVP)

Season	Player, Team
1983-84	Bud Stefanski, Maine
1984-85	Brian Skrudland, Sherbrooke
1985-86	Tim Tookey, Hershey

Season	Player, Team
1986-87	Dave Fenyves, Rochester
1987-88	Wendell Young, Hershey
1988-89	Sam St. Laurent, Adirondack
1989-90	Jeff Hackett, Springfield
1990-91	Kay Whitmore, Springfield
1991-92	Allan Bester, Adirondack
1992-93	Bill McDougall, Cape Breton
1993-94	Olaf Kolzig, Portland
1994-95	Mike Dunham, Albany
	Corey Schwab, Albany
1995-96	Dixon Ward, Rochester
1996-97	Mike McHugh, Hershey
1997-98	Mike Maneluk, Philadelphia
1998-99	Peter Ferraro, Providence
1999-00	Derek Armstrong, Hartford
2000-01	Steve Begin, Saint John
2001-02	Pasi Nurminen, Chicago
2002-03	Johan Holmqvist, Houston

ALL-TIME LEAGUE CHAMPIONS

REGULAR-SEASON CHAMPION   PLAYOFF CHAMPION

Season	Team	Coach	Team	Coach
1936-37	Philadelphia (E)	Herb Gardiner	Syracuse	Eddie Powers
	Syracuse (W)	Eddie Powers		
1937-38	Providence (E)	Bun Cook	Providence	Bun Cook
	Cleveland (W)	Bill Cook		
1938-39	Philadelphia (E)	Herb Gardiner	Cleveland	Bill Cook
	Hershey (W)	Herb Mitchell		
1939-40	Providence (E)	Bun Cook	Providence	Bun Cook
	Indianapolis (W)	Herb Lewis		
1940-41	Providence (E)	Bun Cook	Cleveland	Bill Cook
	Cleveland (W)	Bill Cook		
1941-42	Springfield (E)	Johnny Mitchell	Indianapolis	Herb Lewis
	Indianapolis (W)	Herb Lewis		
1942-43	Hershey	Cooney Weiland	Buffalo	Art Chapman
1943-44	Hershey (E)	Cooney Weiland	Buffalo	Art Chapman
	Cleveland (W)	Bun Cook		
1944-45	Buffalo (E)	Art Chapman	Cleveland	Bun Cook
	Cleveland (W)	Bun Cook		
1945-46	Buffalo (E)	Frank Beisler	Buffalo	Frank Beisler
	Indianapolis (W)	Earl Seibert		
1946-47	Hershey (E)	Don Penniston	Hershey	Don Penniston
	Cleveland (W)	Bun Cook		
1947-48	Providence (E)	Terry Reardon	Cleveland	Bun Cook
	Cleveland (W)	Bun Cook		
1948-49	Providence (E)	Terry Reardon	Providence	Terry Reardon
	St. Louis (W)	Ebbie Goodfellow		
1949-50	Buffalo (E)	Roy Goldsworthy	Indianapolis	Ott Heller
	Cleveland (W)	Bun Cook		
1950-51	Buffalo (E)	Roy Goldsworthy	Cleveland	Bun Cook
	Cleveland (W)	Bun Cook		
1951-52	Hershey (E)	John Crawford	Pittsburgh	King Clancy
	Pittsburgh (W)	King Clancy		
1952-53	Cleveland	Bun Cook	Cleveland	Bun Cook
1953-54	Buffalo	Frank Eddolls	Cleveland	Bun Cook
1954-55	Pittsburgh	Howie Meeker	Pittsburgh	Howie Meeker
1955-56	Providence	John Crawford	Providence	John Crawford
1956-57	Providence	John Crawford	Cleveland	Jack Gordon
1957-58	Hershey	Frank Mathers	Hershey	Frank Mathers
1958-59	Buffalo	Bobby Kirk	Hershey	Frank Mathers
1959-60	Springfield	Pat Egan	Springfield	Pat Egan
1960-61	Springfield	Pat Egan	Springfield	Pat Egan
1961-62	Springfield (E)	Pat Egan	Springfield	Pat Egan
	Cleveland (W)	Jack Gordon		
1962-63	Providence (E)	Fern Flaman	Buffalo	Billy Reay
	Buffalo (W)	Billy Reay		
1963-64	Quebec (E)	Floyd Curry	Cleveland	Fred Glover
	Pittsburgh (W)	Vic Stasiuk		
1964-65	Quebec (E)	Bernie Geoffrion	Rochester	Joe Crozier
	Rochester (W)	Joe Crozier		
1965-66	Quebec (E)	Bernie Geoffrion	Rochester	Joe Crozie
	Rochester (W)	Joe Crozier		

REGULAR-SEASON CHAMPION   PLAYOFF CHAMPION

Season	Team	Coach	Team	Coach
1966-67—	Hershey (E)	Frank Mathers	Pittsburgh	Baz Bastien
	Pittsburgh (W)	Baz Bastien		
1967-68—	Hershey (E)	Frank Mathers	Rochester	Joe Crozier
	Rochester (W)	Joe Crozier		
1968-69—	Hershey (E)	Frank Mathers	Hershey	Frank Mathers
	Buffalo (W)	Fred Shero		
1969-70—	Montreal (E)	Al MacNeil	Buffalo	Fred Shero
	Buffalo (W)	Fred Shero		
1970-71—	Providence (E)	Larry Wilson	Springfield	John Wilson
	Baltimore (W)	Terry Reardon		
1971-72—	Boston (E)	Bep Guidolin	Nova Scotia	Al MacNeil
	Baltimore (W)	Terry Reardon		
1972-73—	Nova Scotia (E)	Al MacNeil	Cincinnati	Floyd Smith
	Cincinnati (W)	Floyd Smith		
1973-74—	Rochester (N)	Don Cherry	Hershey	Chuck Hamilton
	Baltimore (S)	Terry Reardon		
1974-75—	Providence (N)	John Muckler	Springfield	Ron Stewart
	Virginia (S)	Doug Barkley		
1975-76—	Nova Scotia (N)	Al MacNeil	Nova Scotia	Al MacNeil
	Hershey (S)	Chuck Hamilton		
1976-77—	Nova Scotia	Al MacNeil	Nova Scotia	Al MacNeil
1977-78—	Maine (N)	Bob McCammon	Maine	Bob McCammon
	Rochester (S)	Duane Rupp		
1978-79—	Maine (N)	Bob McCammon	Maine	Bob McCammon
	New Haven (S)	Parker MacDonald		
1979-80—	New Brunswick (N)	Joe Crozier-Lou Angotti	Hershey	Doug Gibson
	New Haven (S)	Parker MacDonald		
1980-81—	Maine (N)	Bob McCammon	Adirondack	Tom Webster-J.P. LeBlanc
	Hershey (S)	Bryan Murray		
1981-82—	New Brunswick (N)	Orval Tessier	New Brunswick	Orval Tessier
	Binghamton (S)	Larry Kish		
1982-83—	Fredericton (N)	Jacques Demers	Rochester	Mike Keenan
	Rochester (S)	Mike Keenan		
1983-84—	Fredericton (N)	Earl Jessiman	Maine	John Paddock
	Baltimore (S)	Gene Ubriaco		
1984-85—	Maine (N)	Tom McVie-John Paddock	Sherbrooke	Pierre Creamer
	Binghamton (S)	Larry Pleau		
1985-86—	Adirondack (N)	Bill Dineen	Adirondack	Bill Dineen
	Hershey (S)	John Paddock		
1986-87—	Sherbrooke (N)	Pierre Creamer	Rochester	John Van Boxmeer
	Rochester (S)	John Van Boxmeer*		
1987-88—	Maine (N)	Mike Milbury	Hershey	John Paddock
	Hershey (S)	John Paddock		
1988-89—	Sherbrooke (N)	Jean Hamel	Adirondack	Bill Dineen
	Adirondack (S)	Bill Dineen		
1989-90—	Sherbrooke (N)	Jean Hamel	Springfield	Jimmy Roberts
	Rochester (S)	John Van Boxmeer		
1990-91—	Springfield (N)	Jimmy Roberts	Springfield	Jimmy Roberts
	Rochester (S)	Don Lever		
1991-92—	Springfield (N)	Jay Leach	Adirondack	Barry Melrose
	Binghamton (S)	Ron Smith		
	Fredericton (A)	Paulin Bordeleau		
1992-93—	Providence (N)	Mike O'Connell	Cape Breton	George Burnett
	Binghamton (S)	Ron Smith-Colin Campbell		
	St. John's (A)	Marc Crawford		
1993-94—	Adirondack (N)	Newell Brown	Portland	Barry Trotz
	Hershey (S)	Jay Leach		
	St. John's (A)	Marc Crawford		
1994-95—	Albany (N)	Robbie Ftorek	Albany	Robbie Ftorek
	Binghamton (S)	Al Hill		
	Prince Edward Island (A)	Dave Allison		
1995-96—	Albany (N)	Robbie Ftorek	Rochester	John Tortorella
1996-97—	Philadelphia (MA)	Bill Barber	Hershey	Bob Hartley
1997-98—	Philadelphia (MA)	Bill Barber	Philadelphia	Bill Barber
1998-99—	Providence (NE)	Peter Laviolette	Providence	Peter Laviolette
1999-00—	Hartford (NE)	John Paddock	Hartford	John Paddock
2000-01—	Worcester (NE)	Don Granato	Saint John	Jim Playfair
2001-02—	Bridgeport (E)	Steve Stirling	Chicago	John Anderson
2002-03—	Hamilton (C)	Claude Julien/Geoff Ward	Houston	Todd McLellan

*Rochester awarded division championship based on season-series record.

EAST COAST HOCKEY LEAGUE

2002-03 REGULAR SEASON
FINAL STANDINGS

NORTHERN CONFERENCE

NORTHEAST DIVISION

Team	G	W	L	OTL	Pts.	GF	GA
Atlantic City	72	41	19	12	94	268	224
Greensboro	72	42	21	9	93	235	211
Roanoke	72	42	24	6	90	265	239
Trenton	72	38	24	10	86	229	207
Charlotte	72	41	28	3	85	262	234
Richmond	72	35	31	6	76	240	239
Reading	72	32	35	5	69	261	303

NORTHWEST DIVISION

Team	G	W	L	OTL	Pts.	GF	GA
Toledo	72	47	15	10	104	247	196
Peoria	72	48	17	7	103	241	181
Cincinnati	72	36	29	7	79	257	236
Lexington	72	34	31	7	75	188	212
Johnstown	72	28	33	11	67	214	243
Wheeling	72	28	41	3	59	193	261
Dayton	72	24	38	10	58	191	247

SOUTHERN CONFERENCE

SOUTHEAST DIVISION

Team	G	W	L	OTL	Pts.	GF	GA
Columbia	72	47	23	2	96	265	202
South Carolina	72	42	22	8	92	248	225
Pee Dee	72	40	26	6	86	244	213
Florida	72	35	23	14	84	239	243
Greenville	72	28	36	8	64	217	262
Augusta	72	27	39	6	60	203	256
Columbus	72	25	39	8	58	197	270

SOUTHWEST DIVISION

Team	G	W	L	OTL	Pts.	GF	GA
Mississippi	72	44	24	4	92	250	211
Louisiana	72	40	20	12	92	249	210
Arkansas	72	37	24	11	85	238	236
Jackson	72	38	26	8	84	210	195
Pensacola	72	33	30	9	75	228	241
Baton Rouge	72	20	43	9	49	184	266

INDIVIDUAL LEADERS

Goals: Greg Pankewicz, PEN (46)
Assists: Buddy Smith, ARK (74)
Points: Buddy Smith, ARK (104)
Penalty minutes: T.J. Reynolds, WHL (371)
Goaltending average: Alfie Michaud, PEO (2.10)
Shutouts: Adam Hauser, JCK (5)

	Games	G	A	Pts.
Walby, Steffon, MIS	59	42	47	89
Pankewicz, Greg, PEN	67	46	41	87
Rooney, Brad, REA	63	27	60	87
Caudron, J.F., ATC	70	39	46	85
Jaffray, Jason, RNK	64	34	51	85
Williamson, Andrew, AUG	69	31	54	85
Seitz, Dave, SC	70	23	60	83
Kowalsky, Rick, RNK	68	27	55	82
Pettersen, Lars, RMD	65	26	54	80
Brown, Bobby, LA	65	37	42	79
Gyori, Dylan, RNK	61	26	53	79
Carlson, Dan, RNK	72	35	43	78
Rymsha, Steve, REA	70	38	39	77
Paradise, Dave, MIS	65	39	36	75
Noga, Matt, CIN	72	24	51	75

TOP SCORERS

	Games	G	A	Pts.
Smith, Buddy, ARK	72	30	74	104
Stringer, Rejean, CBA	72	37	59	96
McCullough, Brian, REA	69	39	56	95
McNeil, Shawn, LA	72	40	51	91

INDIVIDUAL STATISTICS

ARKANSAS RIVERBLADES

SCORING

	Games	G	A	Pts.	PIM
Smith, Buddy	72	30	74	104	28
Bermingham, Jason	72	38	35	73	100
Marchant, Terry	72	21	47	68	66
Pagnutti, Matthew	66	15	43	58	58
Hartlieb, Ernie	47	21	34	55	43
Long, Eric	60	14	32	46	102
Whitten, Damon	67	12	27	39	127
Cirillo, Mike	63	20	14	34	216
Stork, Dean	68	15	13	28	84
Sandbeck, Mike	72	12	16	28	82
Stock, Dean	55	8	17	25	76
Toor, Garry	49	3	15	18	16
Kos, Kyle	23	3	9	12	83
Coole, Ryan	70	2	8	10	164
Renzi, Mike	26	5	4	9	28
Poapst, Matt	13	2	6	8	14
Deskins, Jason	13	3	4	7	14
Scott, Mark	69	1	6	7	142

	Games	G	A	Pts.	PIM
Davis, Aaron	23	2	3	5	11
Korol, Kevin	6	3	0	3	4
Lakos, Phillippe	22	0	3	3	22
Mamane, Shawn	10	2	0	2	34
St. John, Jimi	21	0	2	2	6
Paquet, Samuel	5	1	1	2	2
Linnik, Maxim	23	0	2	2	28
Gibbons, Jarret	1	0	1	1	2
Kaiman, Tom	23	0	1	1	73
Saal, Jason	38	0	1	1	0
Bachusz, Jeremy	7	0	1	1	0
Fankhouser, Scott	19	0	1	1	0
Baker, Korey	7	0	0	0	2
Harvey, Paul	3	0	0	0	2
O'Brien, Jack	4	0	0	0	0

GOALTENDING

	Gms.	Min.	W	L	T	G	SO	Avg.
Fankhouser, Scott	19	1110	11	5	2	49	1	2.69
Saal, Jason	38	2158	20	10	7	109	2	3.03
St. John, Jimi	21	1123	6	9	2	67	1	3.58

ATLANTIC CITY BOARDWALK BULLIES
SCORING

	Games	G	A	Pts.	PIM
Caudron, J.F.	70	39	46	85	93
Galbraith, Jade	69	27	47	74	70
Colley, Kevin	50	33	38	71	190
Henkel, Jimmy	68	32	36	68	25
Matzka, Scott	45	20	31	51	89
Rivard, Stefan	55	20	30	50	174
Curtin, Luke	40	11	34	45	32
Spadafora, Paul	71	9	34	43	157
Maltby, Shawn	51	14	23	37	162
Mougenel, Ryan	53	15	20	35	95
Furey, Kirk	44	4	25	29	70
Walterson, Ian	65	4	19	23	45
Corazzini, Carl	27	13	8	21	14
Metcalf, Peter	18	2	11	13	48
Munn, Steve	72	2	9	11	170
Vickers, Jim	48	2	7	9	64
Nicholishen, Mike	60	0	9	9	71
Galway, Jerry	49	1	7	8	12
Paradise, Chris	14	5	2	7	12
Martinello, Mike	30	4	3	7	39
Mallett, Kurt	2	3	0	3	0
Loeding, Mark	50	0	3	3	73
Walsh, Brendan	6	0	2	2	40
Palmer, Chris	2	1	1	2	4
Talbot, Joe	8	2	0	2	0
Hahn, Derek	3	0	1	1	0
Reid, Dave	5	1	0	1	0
Yeats, Matthew	48	0	1	1	0
Cheredaryk, Steve	19	0	1	1	51
Demone, James	4	0	1	1	2
Scott, Mike	2	0	0	0	0
Marlin, Dave	1	0	0	0	0
Gojdycz, Andy	1	0	0	0	2
Gargiles, Michael	1	0	0	0	0
Noack, Erik	2	0	0	0	0
James, Erik	2	0	0	0	2
Conschafter, Shawn	1	0	0	0	0
Stirling, Scott	25	0	0	0	10

GOALTENDING

	Gms.	Min.	W	L	T	G	SO	Avg.
Marlin, Dave	1	60	1	0	0	1	0	1.00
Stirling, Scott	25	1494	17	3	4	73	2	2.93
Yeats, Matthew	48	2811	23	16	8	141	4	3.01
Conschafter, Shawn	1	9	0	0	0	1	0	6.08

AUGUSTA LYNX
SCORING

	Games	G	A	Pts.	PIM
Williamson, Andrew	50	27	47	74	36
Shepherd, Jim	66	15	33	48	138
Lauzon, Ryan	65	20	20	40	10
Lapointe, Martin	44	9	29	38	42
Legg, Mike	41	11	25	36	16
St. Louis, Josh	57	18	12	30	24
Ralph, Brad	44	11	15	26	80
Yetman, Patrick	39	11	14	25	26
Szwez, Jeff	48	10	15	25	30
Crane, Ryan	68	8	16	24	82
Holly, Tyson	56	8	16	24	28
Galbraith, Lance	48	9	14	23	240
Leach, Jay	65	8	11	19	162
Kuznetsov, Sergei	27	3	12	15	30
Thompson, Chris M.	14	4	9	13	18
Shmyr, Jason	32	6	5	11	161
Ianiero, Andrew	16	0	10	10	16
Christiansen, Doug	39	0	8	8	25
Gauvreau, Brent	18	4	3	7	25
Toor, Garry	16	2	4	6	12
Laplante, Darryl	19	2	4	6	16
Roy, Philippe	8	3	3	6	13
Thompson, Mark	51	1	5	6	127

	Games	G	A	Pts.	PIM
Brown, Kevin	14	1	4	5	16
Campbell, John	11	2	3	5	14
Gauthier, Jonathon	31	2	3	5	24
Oliveira, Mike	9	1	3	4	2
Malts, Vince	10	0	3	3	26
Gustafson, Chris	25	1	2	3	13
Andersson, Likit	10	0	2	2	8
Lakos, Andre	5	0	2	2	8
Lakos, Phillippe	20	0	2	2	44
Moore, Mark	15	0	2	2	22
Murphy, Luke	4	1	1	2	2
Cruickshank, Curtis	17	0	2	2	4
Cirillo, Mike	3	1	0	1	10
Perna, Mike	11	1	0	1	23
Blackburn, Josh	6	0	0	0	0
Bowen, Eric	1	0	0	0	2
Faulkner, Geoffrey	13	0	0	0	0
Patafie, Brian	1	0	0	0	10
Van Laar, Grant	1	0	0	0	0
Murray, Ryan	7	0	0	0	0
Brumby, David	12	0	0	0	4
Zulianello, Colin	19	0	0	0	2
Draper, Tom	17	0	0	0	4

GOALTENDING

	Gms.	Min.	W	L	T	G	SO	Avg.
Draper, Tom	17	863	6	5	2	43	1	2.99
Cruickshank, Curtis.	17	941	8	8	1	48	0	3.06
Faulkner, Geoffrey ...	13	607	4	5	1	33	0	3.26
Brumby, David	12	692	3	7	1	39	1	3.38
Zulianello, Colin	19	1012	6	10	1	59	1	3.50
Blackburn, Josh	6	209	0	4	0	21	0	6.01
Van Laar, Grant	1	19	0	0	0	3	0	9.47

BATON ROUGE KINGFISH
SCORING

	Games	G	A	Pts.	PIM
Richardson, Bryan	50	24	28	52	60
Demmans, Trevor	48	7	33	40	59
Guenther, Joe	51	17	22	39	22
Norrie, Jason	58	20	16	36	153
Mathieu, Marquis	44	13	17	30	104
Jones, Clarke	58	8	19	27	23
Paquet, Samuel	56	12	11	23	109
Cheredaryk, Steve	31	6	13	19	93
Crawford, Glenn	27	4	14	18	30
Kiesman, Michael	56	6	11	17	65
Peach, Sean	38	3	13	16	67
Blais, Dwayne	31	5	10	15	32
Trsek, Ryan	30	5	8	13	4
Gernander, Jerry	47	7	6	13	26
Scanzano, Wesley	16	5	5	10	6
Oliveira, Mike	17	4	6	10	0
Wasyluk, Trevor	16	3	6	9	34
Ferguson, Jesse	25	1	8	9	22
Kaiman, Tom	45	1	8	9	151
Bell, Chris	17	2	7	9	20
Jacobson, Garnet	66	3	6	9	220
Gore, Forrest	19	4	3	7	35
Sullivan, Dan	21	4	3	7	49
Vickers, Jim	17	2	5	7	28
Renzi, Mike	14	3	4	7	17
Fraser, Brad	17	0	6	6	13
Burrows, Alexandre	13	4	2	6	64
Tucker, Kevin	58	1	5	6	66
Hewson, Scott	14	2	3	5	6
Perna, Mike	6	1	3	4	10
Adams, Erik	18	1	2	3	10
Sundberg, Niklas	22	0	2	2	8
Schafer, Paxton	6	0	1	1	0
Bader, Toni	14	0	1	1	24
Silverman, Eric	3	0	0	0	0
Scanzano, Shawn	22	0	0	0	71
Leitza, Brian	8	0	0	0	0
Joseph, Yann	3	0	0	0	0
Menzul, Curtis	10	0	0	0	6
Blair, Jeff	37	0	0	0	0
Martinello, Mike	15	0	0	0	18
Saltarelli, Jon	1	0	0	0	0

GOALTENDING

	Gms.	Min.	W	L	T	G	SO	Avg.
Saltarelli, Jon	1	0	0	0	0	0	0	0.00
Sundberg, Niklas	22	1307	10	10	2	68	0	3.12
Blair, Jeff	37	2211	5	26	5	133	0	3.61
Leitza, Brian	8	498	3	3	2	30	0	3.61
Schafer, Paxton	6	356	2	4	0	25	0	4.21

CHARLOTTE CHECKERS

SCORING

	Games	G	A	Pts.	PIM
Pershin, Eduard	70	17	48	65	91
Egeland, Allan	72	20	41	61	191
Caulfield, Kevin	70	27	28	55	138
Suzuki, Takahito	72	24	25	49	44
Jamieson, Dusty	50	27	18	45	23
Bilotto, Nic	50	13	30	43	116
Seher, Kurt	71	9	33	42	56
Inman, David	45	19	22	41	26
Evans, David	67	19	21	40	22
McKay, Konrad	51	13	24	37	209
Cullen, Brandon	58	13	16	29	202
Malts, Vince	49	11	17	28	134
Wilchynski, Chad	42	8	19	27	68
Preston, Dan	48	3	22	25	33
Smith, Kenton	48	2	20	22	28
MacDonald, Walker	38	8	8	16	37
Christiansen, Doug	17	7	7	14	15
Weller, Craig	48	3	11	14	84
Aufiero, Pat	8	2	4	6	6
Murray, Ryan	37	0	6	6	15
Yarema, Brendan	5	5	0	5	20
Valentine, Curtis	9	2	2	4	2
Hartman, Mike	4	1	3	4	7
State, Jeff	29	1	3	4	65
Jarvis, Wes	12	0	2	2	61
Kopischke, Jay	5	0	1	1	0
Scott, Richard	3	0	1	1	4
Sundberg, Niklas	16	0	1	1	2
McPherson, Andrew	4	1	0	1	0
Meyer, Scott	27	0	1	1	0
Traynor, Paul	1	0	0	0	0
Holmqvist, Johan	1	0	0	0	0
Powell, Danny	6	0	0	0	4
Copley, Randy	7	0	0	0	0
Wandler, Bryce	8	0	0	0	2
McIver, Chad	16	0	0	0	14
Derouin, Geoff	5	0	0	0	0
Burgess, Steve	6	0	0	0	2
Zulianello, Colin	12	0	0	0	0
Salajko, Jeff	18	0	0	0	23

GOALTENDING

	Gms.	Min.	W	L	T	G	SO	Avg.
Derouin, Geoff	5	1	0	0	0	0	0	0.00
Holmqvist, Johan	1	60	1	0	0	2	0	2.00
Meyer, Scott	27	1494	20	5	0	65	2	2.61
Zulianello, Colin	12	674	7	4	1	30	2	2.67
Sundberg, Niklas	16	789	8	6	0	43	0	3.27
Salajko, Jeff	18	932	6	8	1	57	0	3.67
Wandler, Bryce	8	392	0	4	1	31	0	4.74

CINCINNATI CYCLONES

SCORING

	Games	G	A	Pts.	PIM
Noga, Matt	72	24	51	75	97
Cardarelli, Joe	57	36	34	70	8
Brand, Aaron	72	23	42	65	70
Gaucher, Ryan	54	19	46	65	100
Casselman, Mike	61	16	37	53	64
Cheverie, Evan	56	18	31	49	26
Bootland, Nick	54	19	24	43	114
Twordik, Brent	72	13	30	43	84
Labenski, Greg	69	14	21	35	173
Gallace, Steve	70	14	20	34	109

	Games	G	A	Pts.	PIM
Crummer, Bob	52	10	8	18	119
Prosofsky, Garrett	23	8	8	16	22
Jozefowicz, Mike	22	4	11	15	22
Henderson, Mike	19	4	9	13	6
Norrie, Jason	20	4	9	13	41
Ryan, Terry	12	1	8	9	58
Campbell, John	33	3	6	9	16
Strand, Paul	12	3	6	9	6
Cannon, Jason	14	1	6	7	35
Bergin, Kevin	18	0	6	6	16
Thornton, Bob	16	3	2	5	22
McIver, Chad	43	2	3	5	42
Rissmiller, Pat	2	2	2	4	0
Rodberg, Steve	11	3	1	4	8
Blevins, Wes	51	2	2	4	52
Maser, Josh	28	2	2	4	86
Wismer, Chris	11	2	1	3	10
Scantlebury, Thomas	16	0	2	2	44
Mercer, Jeff	5	1	1	2	15
Turner, Tim	3	0	2	2	0
Kielkucki, Mark	23	0	1	1	0
Naumenko, Gregg	17	0	1	1	23
Hewitt, Greg	28	0	1	1	2
Belak, Graham	40	1	0	1	157
Thinel, Sebastien	2	0	0	0	0
Miller, Kelly	1	0	0	0	0
DeLacoure, Robin	3	0	0	0	0
Strand, Ryan	1	0	0	0	17
Meduecz, Matt	3	0	0	0	0
Hamerlik, Peter	5	0	0	0	2
Baker, Korey	9	0	0	0	0
Fukufuji, Yutama	9	0	0	0	0

GOALTENDING

	Gms.	Min.	W	L	T	G	SO	Avg.
Hewitt, Greg	28	1538	15	10	1	76	2	2.96
Naumenko, Gregg	17	913	6	6	3	47	1	3.09
Fukufuji, Yutama	9	403	4	3	0	21	0	3.13
Kielkucki, Mark	23	1256	9	9	2	69	0	3.30
Hamerlik, Peter	5	250	2	1	1	14	0	3.35

COLUMBIA INFERNO

SCORING

	Games	G	A	Pts.	PIM
Stringer, Rejean	72	37	59	96	16
Smith, Tim	68	22	37	59	44
Moore, Barrie	72	23	33	56	52
Morrison, Justin	40	20	35	55	39
Ulwelling, Matt	72	17	36	53	121
St. Croix, Chris	56	13	36	49	101
Pittman, Chris	59	22	26	48	89
Wansborough, Shawn	55	21	25	46	135
Carruthers, Robin	62	23	18	41	53
Hessler, Corey	69	17	23	40	64
Owens, Sean	70	8	23	31	90
Adams, Erik	54	3	21	24	14
Martynyuk, Denis	56	10	10	20	84
Vial, Dennis	69	3	15	18	158
Labelle, Eric	58	5	9	14	281
Legg, Mike	20	5	7	12	10
Demmans, Trevor	15	2	10	12	4
Way, Clint	64	4	5	9	39
Darby, Regan	48	1	7	8	170
Cabana, Paul	17	2	6	8	20
Hay, Darrell	12	2	3	5	13
Crimin, Derek	12	3	1	4	2
Blackburn, Josh	33	0	1	1	2
Swanson, Kevin	5	0	0	0	0
Christiansen, Doug	6	0	0	0	2
Brown, Jason	1	0	0	0	0
Couture, Patrick	39	0	0	0	13

GOALTENDING

	Gms.	Min.	W	L	T	G	SO	Avg.
Brown, Jason	1	4	0	0	0	0	0	0.00
Couture, Patrick	39	2235	27	11	0	90	4	2.42
Blackburn, Josh	33	1927	19	11	2	96	2	2.99
Swanson, Kevin	5	164	1	1	0	13	0	4.74

COLUMBUS COTTONMOUTHS

SCORING

	Games	G	A	Pts.	PIM
Cullaton, Brent	72	18	44	62	110
Zehr, Jeff	58	23	35	58	229
Hunter, J.J.	70	17	36	53	82
Long, Andrew	66	18	30	48	36
Morlang, John	69	18	19	37	56
Lewis, Carlyle	59	15	20	35	275
McAslan, Sean	53	15	17	32	132
Bishai, Mike	25	12	17	29	24
McAusland, Darren	71	10	18	28	34
Tiemstra, Darren	70	5	22	27	90
Risidore, Ryan	62	5	15	20	139
Bechard, Jerome	69	11	5	16	199
Vancik, Jay	36	5	10	15	46
Copley, Randy	16	7	5	12	6
Lee, Mike	63	2	7	9	281
Cole, Phil	51	4	5	9	135
Marois, Jerome	20	0	6	6	6
Fritz, Mitch	33	2	4	6	144
Hamilton, Chad	57	1	5	6	51
Rushmer, Bart	61	2	3	5	95
Nelson, Mike	14	2	2	4	16
Dolinar, Ales	23	0	4	4	4
Zinevych, Alexander	16	0	2	2	6
Morrison, Mike	38	0	1	1	6
Palmer, Tyler	2	0	0	0	4
Kostur, Matus	44	0	0	0	49

GOALTENDING

	Gms.	Min.	W	L	T	G	SO	Avg.
Morrison, Mike	38	1948	9	18	6	113	1	3.48
Kostur, Matus	44	2422	16	21	2	150	1	3.72

DAYTON BOMBERS

SCORING

	Games	G	A	Pts.	PIM
Vince, Ryan	66	27	26	53	98
Ling, Jamie	69	19	31	50	73
Thompson, Chris M.	48	15	28	43	215
Slukynsky, Fred	72	17	24	41	107
Nemeth, Tom	65	9	30	39	57
Crain, Jason	50	5	27	32	22
DiRoberto, Torrey	58	17	12	29	79
Ianiero, Andrew	44	11	13	24	35
Vellinga, Mike	57	3	20	23	140
Knopp, Ben	53	7	13	20	83
Deskins, Jason	34	8	12	20	22
Cummings, Brian	54	6	13	19	80
Nolan, Doug	49	4	13	17	85
Leger, Jim	15	7	6	13	12
Williamson, Andrew	19	4	7	11	26
Dzieduszycki, Matt	10	6	3	9	19
Joseph, Yann	22	2	7	9	12
Galbraith, Lance	8	5	4	9	47
Poapst, Matt	27	3	5	8	34
Renzi, Mike	16	2	5	7	69
Gauthier, Jonathon	16	2	3	5	24
Thompson, Chris B.	41	1	3	4	153
Schill, Jonathan	9	2	2	4	23
Stayzer, Blair	23	2	2	4	61
Sloan, Tyler	14	1	2	3	22
Ettinger, Trevor	18	0	2	2	126
Yetman, Patrick	4	0	2	2	0
Naumann, Richard	7	0	2	2	0
Heffernan, Scott	6	1	0	1	7
Jerant, Mark	12	0	1	1	47
McCauley, Bill	1	0	1	1	4
Tabacek, Jan	2	0	1	1	16
Paul, Richard	20	0	1	1	34
Kos, Kyle	9	0	1	1	18
Bendera, Shane	39	0	1	1	6
Platt, Jayme	11	0	1	1	0
Ridolfi, Brian	7	1	0	1	0
Aceti, T.J.	5	0	1	1	0
Nutcher, Nick	7	1	0	1	18
Brosseau, David	4	0	0	0	8
McIver, Chad	5	0	0	0	6
Lariviere, Jacques	1	0	0	0	29
Wismer, Chris	16	0	0	0	20
Allen, Andrew	19	0	0	0	2
Linnik, Maxim	2	0	0	0	0
Fail, Robert	6	0	0	0	4
McCaffrey, Joe	1	0	0	0	0
Carlson, Kris	1	0	0	0	0
Fraser, Brad	12	0	0	0	16
Stewart, Patrick	2	0	0	0	0
Ruff, Lee	12	0	0	0	4
Wiegand, Jake	4	0	0	0	0
Roe, Chris	2	0	0	0	2
Zasowski, Tony	3	0	0	0	0

GOALTENDING

	Gms.	Min.	W	L	T	G	SO	Avg.
Bendera, Shane	39	2242	13	19	5	106	1	2.84
Aceti, T.J.	5	293	1	4	0	16	0	3.27
Allen, Andrew	19	1033	5	9	3	60	1	3.48
Platt, Jayme	11	665	3	6	2	39	1	3.52
Zasowski, Tony	3	135	2	0	0	8	0	3.54

FLORIDA EVERBLADES

SCORING

	Games	G	A	Pts.	PIM
Blaznek, Joe	71	34	32	66	26
Johnston, Marty	55	22	41	63	52
Brown, Kevin	52	23	37	60	72
Buckley, Tom	57	10	41	51	93
Meunier, Laurent	68	20	31	51	106
Awada, George	72	21	29	50	67
Murphy, Ryan	58	28	17	45	47
Anderson, Keith	72	16	22	38	56
Smith, Don	53	14	23	37	57
Nelson, Tom	56	7	22	29	90
Goudie, Brian	63	6	19	25	171
Harmer, Duane	39	6	13	19	40
Verdule, Jimmy	48	0	17	17	233
McDonald, Brent	18	10	4	14	14
Battaglia, Anthony	48	6	7	13	26
Ruff, Lee	34	3	8	11	31
Reynolds, Peter	66	1	9	10	111
Curry, Sean	32	1	6	7	77
Hill, Ed	16	1	5	6	10
Insana, Jon	23	1	4	5	12
Stewart, Ryan	27	2	2	4	31
Kos, Kyle	10	1	3	4	60
Fisher, Shaun	10	1	1	2	8
Newman, Jared	29	1	1	2	82
St. Louis, Jonathan	2	1	0	1	7
Williams, Vince	12	1	0	1	22
Kerestes, Jaroslav	3	0	1	1	6
Campbell, John	14	0	1	1	12
Royer, Remi	2	0	1	1	18
Boisclair, Daniel	4	0	0	0	0
McMeekin, Brian	4	0	0	0	2
Wismer, Chris	5	0	0	0	22
Zinevych, Alexander	6	0	0	0	4
McCormick, Cam	17	0	0	0	0
Zepp, Rob	41	0	0	0	0
Petruk, Randy	6	0	0	0	0
Leitza, Brian	10	0	0	0	2

GOALTENDING

	Gms.	Min.	W	L	T	G	SO	Avg.
Zepp, Rob	41	2371	20	13	7	112	3	2.83
Leitza, Brian	10	544	3	4	3	27	0	2.98
McCormick, Cam	17	870	9	2	2	53	0	3.65
Petruk, Randy	6	365	3	2	1	23	0	3.78
Boisclair, Daniel	4	223	0	2	1	15	0	4.03

GREENSBORO GENERALS

SCORING

	Games	G	A	Pts.	PIM
Turner, Mark	70	20	43	63	80
Ftorek, Sam	72	33	28	61	135
Gardiner, Pete	66	25	30	55	69

	Games	G	A	Pts.	PIM
Turek, Matt	69	20	30	50	34
Murphy, Jay	43	21	26	47	107
Whitworth, David	72	12	34	46	76
Parrish, Geno	72	5	38	43	85
Bell, Chris	51	15	20	35	79
Aldoff, Rod	54	9	23	32	36
Drummond, Kurtis	41	7	20	27	46
Campbell, Shane	67	9	17	26	200
Kjenstad, Olaf	31	10	15	25	41
Serov, Vlad	26	11	11	22	38
Chandler, Matt	62	10	11	21	26
Richardson, Bryan	20	7	11	18	14
Allen, Chris	51	6	8	14	58
Bayrack, Mike	12	4	5	9	10
Grimes, Kevin	54	1	7	8	141
Marakhovski, Roman	58	2	5	7	80
Del Monte, David	13	0	6	6	14
Oliveira, Mike	18	1	4	5	2
Andreyev, Alex	43	0	5	5	132
Berthiaume, Daniel	53	0	3	3	6
Lupandin, Andrei	14	0	1	1	20
Crimin, Derek	2	0	1	1	0
Byfuglien, Derrick	14	0	1	1	10
Hrooshkin, Dalen	2	0	0	0	0
Smith, Travis	1	0	0	0	0
Tkatch, Stas	2	0	0	0	2
Hodson, Jamie	14	0	0	0	2
Fingerhut, Tim	2	0	0	0	2
Fournel, Dan	2	0	0	0	20
Slovak, Juraj	33	0	0	0	30
Centomo, Sebastien	10	0	0	0	26

GOALTENDING

	Gms.	Min.	W	L	T	G	SO	Avg.
Hodson, Jamie	14	816	9	4	1	33	0	2.43
Centomo, Sebastien	10	564	3	3	3	24	1	2.55
Berthiaume, Daniel	53	2998	30	14	5	145	2	2.90

GREENVILLE GRRROWL

SCORING

	Games	G	A	Pts.	PIM
Demarski, Matt	72	25	38	63	59
Deis, Tyler	72	24	38	62	158
Medak, Judd	62	17	26	43	104
Henderson, Mike	38	13	26	39	12
Masa, Martin	69	20	17	37	57
Roy, Jonathan	31	16	17	33	22
Sivonen, Mikko	39	16	17	33	14
Lynch, Chris	31	14	15	29	47
Wieckowski, Krzyszto	58	11	17	28	49
Hurley, Mike	40	8	18	26	18
Burrows, Alexandre	53	9	17	26	201
Gouett, Mark	63	5	11	16	42
Lind, Eric	63	2	13	15	85
Nail, John	31	7	7	14	30
Theuer, Chad	15	2	10	12	12
Fatticci, Rico	58	2	10	12	46
Gustafson, Chris	40	2	9	11	22
Kaczowka, David	59	3	7	10	242
Flache, Paul	46	1	9	10	64
Legge, Josh	59	2	6	8	91
Gauthier, Jonathon	21	3	5	8	22
Emmett, Rick	11	2	5	7	14
Gross, Gable	11	1	4	5	16
Sellars, Luke	4	2	2	4	6
Van Acker, Eric	50	0	4	4	127
Blevins, Wes	15	2	2	4	18
Fisher, Shaun	12	1	2	3	20
Wismer, Chris	13	1	2	3	4
Flache, Paul	3	2	1	3	9
Muswagon, Jamie	2	0	1	1	4
Morin, Etienne	4	0	1	1	4
Garnett, Michael	38	0	1	1	0
Menzul, Curtis	1	0	0	0	0
Levokari, Pauli	4	0	0	0	8
Platt, Jayme	26	0	0	0	4
McIntyre, Dan	3	0	0	0	2
Rhodes, Damian	12	0	0	0	8

GOALTENDING

	Gms.	Min.	W	L	T	G	SO	Avg.
Platt, Jayme	26	1472	9	12	3	77	3	3.14
Garnett, Michael	38	2092	16	15	3	119	0	3.41
Rhodes, Damian	12	686	2	8	2	43	1	3.76
McIntyre, Dan	3	112	0	2	0	13	0	6.96

JACKSON BANDITS

SCORING

	Games	G	A	Pts.	PIM
McNabb, John	72	35	35	70	131
Bes, Jeff	63	23	39	62	115
Gauvreau, Brent	49	14	28	42	61
Fortier, Eric	72	19	18	37	50
Kelman, Scott	51	14	18	32	93
Forslund, Bryan	72	13	19	32	116
Gillam, Sean	66	4	23	27	74
Olson, Josh	39	10	17	27	13
O'Connor, Sean	49	12	11	23	149
Stewart, Dave	64	6	16	22	353
Lupandin, Andrei	45	5	17	22	10
Laplante, Darryl	49	6	14	20	42
Vigilante, Mike	55	9	11	20	12
Rome, Reagan	64	6	12	18	94
Newson, Bill	56	7	11	18	33
Theriault, Nick	62	7	11	18	144
Oliveira, Mike	22	6	5	11	16
Royer, Gaetan	11	3	6	9	58
Mackie, Kevin	60	1	8	9	68
Grimes, Kevin	20	1	5	6	64
Thompson, Mark	22	1	5	6	59
Copley, Randy	10	0	4	4	19
MacIver, Doug	27	1	3	4	103
Palmer, Tyler	19	0	2	2	26
Garner, Tyrone	39	0	2	2	21
Tropper, Marc	1	1	0	1	0
O'Keefe, Ryan	6	0	1	1	8
Rice, Mike	1	0	1	1	0
Crawford, Scott	1	0	0	0	0
Spiller, Rich	3	0	0	0	2
Hauser, Adam	34	0	0	0	8

GOALTENDING

	Gms.	Min.	W	L	T	G	SO	Avg.
Hauser, Adam	34	2021	20	9	4	83	5	2.46
Garner, Tyrone	39	2350	18	17	4	106	4	2.71

JOHNSTOWN CHIEFS

SCORING

	Games	G	A	Pts.	PIM
Forget, Dominic	70	23	39	62	47
Boutin, J.F.	47	20	38	58	144
St. Pierre, Samuel	59	23	35	58	38
Tarabrin, Dmitri	71	17	25	42	101
Hildenbrand, Steve	72	11	30	41	120
Smital, Lukas	52	18	16	34	52
Roy, Philippe	56	11	19	30	68
Nemec, Vladamir	70	12	17	29	38
Courchesne, Pierre	67	14	14	28	68
Bilodeau, Brent	71	10	17	27	62
Leger, Jim	30	12	9	21	20
Langager, Jay	61	1	15	16	57
Sullivan, Jeff	58	5	11	16	196
Manzano, Ian	43	3	12	15	34
Doktorchik, Andy	62	4	7	11	74
Sutter, Shaun	9	7	3	10	4
Rodrigues, Mike	40	1	8	9	32
Mather, Shawn	16	3	5	8	12
Branham, Tim	30	1	7	8	32
Doman, Matt	16	2	4	6	20
Shmyr, Jason	12	3	2	5	53
Shmyr, Ryan	45	2	3	5	129
Spence, Jason	23	2	2	4	91

	Games	G	A	Pts.	PIM
Varhaug, Mike	24	1	3	4	157
Townsend, Ryan	32	1	2	3	27
Aubry, Peter	48	0	3	3	4
Dallaire, Dany	8	0	1	1	0
Hodgson, Gavin	10	1	0	1	10
Clifford, Shane	1	0	0	0	0
Piro, Josh	1	0	0	0	0
Scally, Mark	20	0	0	0	0

GOALTENDING

	Gms.	Min.	W	L	T	G	SO	Avg.
Clifford, Shane	1	1	0	0	0	0	0	0.00
Aubry, Peter	48	2870	21	18	8	140	3	2.93
Dallaire, Dany	8	402	2	5	0	23	0	3.43
Scally, Mark	20	1116	5	10	3	69	0	3.71

LEXINGTON MEN O'WAR

SCORING

	Games	G	A	Pts.	PIM
Burgess, Van	71	21	34	55	34
Smith, Mark	65	22	33	54	38
Vandermeer, Joe	67	9	42	51	54
Storey, Ben	62	18	27	45	105
Mathieu, Alexandre	61	14	31	45	50
Draney, Brett	50	13	19	32	64
Thinel, Marc-Andre	27	14	14	28	6
Clair, Fraser	52	13	14	27	92
Fultz, Ryan	45	9	15	24	40
Smyth, Jared	67	9	13	22	55
Sgroi, Mike	41	10	10	20	179
Banach, Jay	59	4	9	13	191
Knopp, Kevin	65	6	7	13	78
Periard, Dominic	62	2	10	12	88
Mizerek, Josh	67	2	8	10	38
Van Parys, Justin	59	2	7	9	63
Fiacconi, Adriano	17	2	2	4	0
Cook, Jesse	54	1	3	4	48
Moor, Daryl	52	1	3	4	100
Del Monte, David	17	2	1	3	12
Bateman, Jeff	2	1	1	2	8
Dirkes, Chris	34	0	2	2	24
Murphy, Dan	43	0	1	1	0
Smith, Mike	27	1	0	1	20
Miskovich, Aaron	14	1	0	1	2
Otis, Jessi	4	0	0	0	0
Annetts, Brett	9	0	0	0	15
Rice, Brad	4	0	0	0	24
Wandler, Bryce	4	0	0	0	0
Craven, Terry	1	0	0	0	0

GOALTENDING

	Gms.	Min.	W	L	T	G	SO	Avg.
Craven, Terry	1	1	0	0	0	0	0	0.00
Smith, Mike	27	1552	11	10	4	66	1	2.55
Murphy, Dan	43	2591	21	19	3	123	2	2.85
Wandler, Bryce	4	244	2	2	0	14	0	3.43

LOUISIANA ICEGATORS

SCORING

	Games	G	A	Pts.	PIM
McNeil, Shawn	72	40	51	91	58
Brown, Bobby	65	37	42	79	49
Goneau, Daniel	48	21	43	64	102
Richardson, Bruce	40	19	42	61	131
Rempel, Nathan	67	25	28	53	150
Benazic, Cal	61	12	32	44	151
Corupe, Kenny	71	20	22	42	56
Mitchell, Kevin	30	5	29	34	93
Sarich, Rod	72	6	26	32	69
Taliercio, Chris	52	10	14	24	48
Morin, J.P.	72	2	18	20	119
DePourcq, John	15	3	13	16	4
Skiehar, Shawn	65	8	8	16	149
Ben-Amor, Semir	61	3	13	16	113
Tuzzolino, Tony	12	8	7	15	47
Shiryaev, Dennis	34	4	8	12	106

	Games	G	A	Pts.	PIM
Kesselring, Casey	21	4	8	12	8
Bartek, Martin	8	4	7	11	6
Kvetan, Branislav	53	2	7	9	55
Mass, Louis	61	2	6	8	80
Proskurnicki, Andrew	10	5	2	7	24
Mastad, Milt	18	3	2	5	20
Kalmikov, Konstantin	3	1	3	4	0
Boogaard, Derek	33	1	2	3	240
Mamane, Shawn	7	1	1	2	33
Worlton, Jeff	58	0	1	1	302
Cammarata, Nick	9	0	1	1	4
Kerestes, Jaroslav	9	0	0	0	21
Valentine, Curtis	1	0	0	0	0
Cloutier, Frederic	26	0	0	0	14
Gustafson, Derek	2	0	0	0	0
Kettles, Kyle	41	0	0	0	12
Osaer, Phil	4	0	0	0	0

GOALTENDING

	Gms.	Min.	W	L	T	G	SO	Avg.
Osaer, Phil	4	243	2	1	1	9	0	2.21
Kettles, Kyle	41	2438	21	12	7	106	5	2.61
Cloutier, Frederic	26	1577	16	6	4	80	1	3.04
Gustafson, Derek	2	118	1	1	0	8	0	4.07

MISSISSIPPI SEA WOLVES

SCORING

	Games	G	A	Pts.	PIM
Walby, Steffon	59	42	47	89	51
Paradise, Dave	65	39	36	75	143
Baxter, Jim	68	16	58	74	45
Scott, Mike	64	26	41	67	100
Bowtell, Cody	56	25	33	58	46
Davyduke, Kent	25	12	24	36	26
Lisabeth, Travis	70	18	17	35	140
Campbell, Darryl	66	15	17	32	54
Hutchins, Jeff	68	10	19	29	216
Kuznetsov, Sergei	31	9	18	27	36
Rochon, Patrick	72	1	24	25	126
Evangelista, John	66	9	12	21	96
Byfuglien, Derrick	49	2	12	14	58
Miller, Austin	51	6	7	13	75
Blais, Dwayne	40	6	6	12	37
Pietersma, Stu	55	5	6	11	275
Allen, Chris	11	2	8	10	6
Cava, Chris	57	1	9	10	223
Cornacchia, David	8	0	7	7	18
Clark, Ryan	66	0	5	5	93
Bennett, Josh	35	1	3	4	155
Stayzer, Blair	12	1	2	3	19
Crain, Jason	16	0	3	3	8
Renzi, Mike	5	1	2	3	4
Peach, Sean	17	0	3	3	36
Menzul, Curtis	10	0	2	2	14
Gardner, Greg	55	0	1	1	29
Matile, Sean	24	0	1	1	6
Buckley, Mike	1	0	0	0	0
Hyacinthe, Seneque	3	0	0	0	6
Christiansen, Doug	4	0	0	0	12

GOALTENDING

	Gms.	Min.	W	L	T	G	SO	Avg.
Gardner, Greg	55	3140	32	17	4	145	0	2.77
Buckley, Mike	1	21	0	0	0	1	0	2.81
Matile, Sean	24	1182	12	7	0	60	1	3.04

PEE DEE PRIDE

SCORING

	Games	G	A	Pts.	PIM
Reid, Matt	62	28	44	72	51
Schmidt, Greg	70	20	52	72	136
Glumac, Mike	69	37	32	69	49
Mizzi, Preston	67	22	35	57	84
Goldie, Wes	72	27	24	51	54
Sirois, Allan	71	20	29	49	127
Carriere, Daniel	72	9	27	36	33
Naud, Eric	54	10	21	31	157
Halldorson, Derek	70	9	21	30	84
Krajnc, Gregor	44	14	15	29	62

	Games	G	A	Pts.	PIM
Kidney, Kyle	71	9	19	28	50
Knox, Ryan	48	6	17	23	24
Torney, Mike	46	12	9	21	122
Gates, Aaron	66	3	15	18	134
Adams, B.J.	63	5	12	17	122
Robinson, Jason	72	2	13	15	126
Metcalfe, Jason	66	0	6	6	126
Petz, Ryan	9	2	1	3	14
Fregoe, Peter	4	1	2	3	4
Vogel, Ron	41	0	2	2	32
Mass, Louis	9	0	1	1	8
Underhill, Matt	33	0	1	1	0
Anderson, Rob	1	0	0	0	0

GOALTENDING

	Gms.	Min.	W	L	T	G	SO	Avg.
Vogel, Ron	41	2434	24	13	3	109	4	2.69
Underhill, Matt	33	1877	16	13	2	88	0	2.81
Anderson, Rob	1	64	0	0	1	4	0	3.74

PENSACOLA ICE PILOTS

SCORING

	Games	G	A	Pts.	PIM
Pankewicz, Greg	67	46	41	87	340
Dumont, Louis	68	20	51	71	97
Baumgartner, Gregor	58	28	24	52	29
Dexter, Brad	72	8	44	52	54
Cloutier, Kevin	69	14	31	45	78
Allman, Trevor	72	16	24	40	51
Theuer, Chad	52	8	25	33	20
Minard, Chris	72	15	17	32	71
Harrold, Josh	45	8	18	26	36
Royer, Gaetan	31	6	16	22	118
Bartek, Martin	19	11	10	21	26
Jones, Mike	24	5	12	17	57
O'Keefe, Ryan	64	1	16	17	216
Hewson, Scott	52	6	10	16	56
Royer, Gaetan	20	3	10	13	60
Ellis-Tdingtn, Kerry	27	6	7	13	25
Mathieu, Marquis	15	3	10	13	74
Van Hoof, Jeremy	66	4	5	9	51
Elich, Matt	12	4	4	8	6
Herrington, Jamie	5	3	4	7	4
Cruikshank, Brad	53	3	4	7	221
Poapst, Matt	26	3	4	7	24
Vigilante, Mike	11	0	4	4	6
Foremsky, Taras	6	3	1	4	4
Gignac, Chris	4	1	2	3	2
Oliver, David	16	1	2	3	70
Priechodsky, Marek	35	0	3	3	28
Rome, Reagan	6	0	2	2	11
Bergin, Kevin	30	0	2	2	78
Spiller, Rich	44	1	1	2	53
Van Acker, Eric	15	0	2	2	20
Pratt, Harlan	2	0	1	1	2
Mackie, Kevin	5	1	0	1	2
Mortier, Darren	6	1	0	1	17
Currie, Kris	1	0	0	0	0
Holeczy, Roger	1	0	0	0	2
Eklund, Brian	19	0	0	0	2
Gingras, Maxime	57	0	0	0	4

GOALTENDING

	Gms.	Min.	W	L	T	G	SO	Avg.
Gingras, Maxime	57	3381	23	24	9	169	3	3.00
Eklund, Brian	19	998	10	6	0	61	0	3.66

PEORIA RIVERMEN

SCORING

	Games	G	A	Pts.	PIM
Rennette, Tyler	65	42	32	74	98
Rowe, Randy	69	28	40	68	38
Brooks, Brendan	55	23	29	52	79
Clark, Darren	71	6	39	45	54
Lawmaster, Jason	64	12	30	42	252
Baker, Trevor	55	23	17	40	187
Finnerty, Ryan	66	11	27	38	193

	Games	G	A	Pts.	PIM
DeCecco, Bret	59	15	19	34	62
Copley, Randy	34	15	13	28	36
Day, Greg	31	12	15	27	4
Rekis, Arvid	57	4	19	23	56
Booth, Derek	55	5	17	22	80
Crawford, Scott	50	3	14	17	22
Kern, Josh	52	7	5	12	94
Kinos, Lauri	33	2	9	11	34
Nelson, Mike	16	7	4	11	24
Granato, Kevin	30	3	7	10	22
Davis, Greg	10	5	5	10	4
Stuart, Mike	19	2	7	9	12
Belza, Anthony	68	2	7	9	262
Wells, Chris	9	3	4	7	24
Starling, Chad	10	3	4	7	6
Voth, Brad	54	1	4	5	283
Yablonski, Jeremy	24	1	2	3	154
Zinevych, Alexander	15	0	3	3	4
Tucker, Kevin	8	1	1	2	10
Derksen, Duane	29	0	2	2	4
Kiesman, Michael	3	0	1	1	9
Beaudoin, Nic	5	0	1	1	0
Crawford, Glenn	2	0	1	1	2
Taylor, Rod	2	0	1	1	0
Gillies, Trevor	24	0	1	1	180
Malcolm, Kevin	1	0	0	0	2
Chouinard, Mathieu	15	0	0	0	2
Lajeunesse, Simon	4	0	0	0	0
Gore, Forrest	7	0	0	0	2
Michaud, Alfie	30	0	0	0	0

GOALTENDING

	Gms.	Min.	W	L	T	G	SO	Avg.
Lajeunesse, Simon	4	238	2	2	0	8	0	2.01
Michaud, Alfie	30	1685	20	4	4	59	1	2.10
Chouinard, Mathieu	15	820	12	2	0	29	3	2.12
Derksen, Duane	29	1629	14	9	3	74	3	2.72

READING ROYALS

SCORING

	Games	G	A	Pts.	PIM
McCullough, Brian	69	39	56	95	84
Rooney, Brad	63	27	60	87	130
Rymsha, Steve	70	38	39	77	86
Dietrich, Brandon	49	17	32	49	54
Kim, Alex	61	22	24	46	71
Tremblay, Simon	55	9	35	44	127
Pepperall, Colin	52	13	24	37	116
Snesrud, Mat	48	10	23	33	54
Giuliano, Jeff	38	7	23	30	6
Rouleau, Tom	70	11	19	30	30
Peters, Geoff	40	15	13	28	40
Grande, Duilio	54	11	13	24	112
DiLauro, Ray	53	7	14	21	47
Riva, Dan	14	8	8	16	8
Royer, Remi	29	7	7	14	186
Dube, James	68	6	8	14	90
Bogas, Chris	27	4	5	9	44
Bergeron, Antoine	37	1	6	7	49
Lahache, Hunter	49	0	4	4	128
Goodenow, Joe	12	1	3	4	10
Verdule, Jimmy	22	1	2	3	85
Brunel, Craig	9	0	3	3	25
Rodrigues, Mike	18	2	1	3	23
Waltze, Kris	20	1	1	2	77
McAvoy, Keegan	20	0	2	2	34
Sanger, Jeff	40	0	1	1	8
Saviels, Agris	8	1	0	1	4
Magnuson, Will	9	0	1	1	15
Lutz, Nathan	1	0	0	0	2
Minard, Mike	2	0	0	0	0
Fankhouser, Scott	26	0	0	0	10
Herhal, Matt	1	0	0	0	0
Altschul, Doug	5	0	0	0	2
Boxma, B.J.	2	0	0	0	0
Herhal, Matt	2	0	0	0	0
Schmidt, Jeff	13	0	0	0	0
Snee, Brandon	11	0	0	0	4
Kohansky, Matt	3	0	0	0	0

GOALTENDING

	Gms.	Min.	W	L	T	G	SO	Avg.
Sanger, Jeff	40	2132	20	12	4	129	1	3.63
Fankhouser, Scott	26	1462	11	12	1	94	0	3.86
Snee, Brandon	11	540	1	8	0	39	0	4.33
Boxma, B.J.	2	88	0	1	0	10	0	6.77
Minard, Mike	2	119	0	2	0	17	0	8.55

RICHMOND RENEGADES

SCORING

	Games	G	A	Pts.	PIM
Pettersen, Lars	65	26	54	80	42
Church, Brad	64	29	45	74	121
Pitirri, Richard	66	18	38	56	77
Zion, Jonathan	58	14	38	52	46
Brosseau, David	60	24	27	51	64
Lent, Nick	54	24	18	42	74
Hogan, Peter	67	8	32	40	64
Herrington, Jamie	45	13	23	36	32
Vandermeer, Dan	72	11	20	31	130
Matieroukine, Alex	69	13	13	26	70
Hayward, Leon	67	12	13	25	107
Bartlett, Russ	62	7	17	24	53
Ellis-Tdingtn, Kerry	47	2	15	17	20
Turner, Ian	59	6	9	15	58
Van Buskirk, Ryan	60	4	9	13	125
Harrold, Josh	17	1	9	10	14
Flipowicz, Jayme	20	1	8	9	36
Mastad, Milt	39	3	5	8	66
Plamondon, Justin	12	3	4	7	4
St. Louis, Jonathan	25	5	2	7	46
Goneau, Daniel	8	3	4	7	8
Lamarre, Sandy	6	4	2	6	2
Bartek, Martin	5	3	1	4	4
Palmer, Tyler	34	1	2	3	26
Mamane, Shawn	6	2	0	2	13
McKinney, Bryan	4	0	2	2	4
Goudie, Brian	5	1	0	1	6
Magliarditi, Marc	49	0	1	1	8
Spiller, Rich	2	0	0	0	2
Van Parys, Justin	2	0	0	0	2
Gillies, Trevor	6	0	0	0	20
Selix, Kelly	2	0	0	0	0
Seremak, Don	2	0	0	0	0
Stroshein, Garret	2	0	0	0	7
Lombard, Dan	29	0	0	0	2

GOALTENDING

	Gms.	Min.	W	L	T	G	SO	Avg.
Magliarditi, Marc	49	2804	23	19	5	142	3	3.04
Lombard, Dan	29	1546	12	12	1	85	1	3.30

ROANOKE EXPRESS

SCORING

	Games	G	A	Pts.	PIM
Jaffray, Jason	64	34	51	85	89
Kowalsky, Rick	68	27	55	82	132
Gyori, Dylan	61	26	53	79	140
Carlson, Dan	72	35	43	78	76
Dusbabek, Joe	62	27	34	61	143
Peron, Mike	52	13	33	46	113
Novock, Frank	67	21	20	41	34
Dalmao, Duncan	68	11	29	40	60
Bristow, Cam	40	17	20	37	55
Limpright, Shawn	63	14	19	33	154
O'Connell, Tim	49	7	22	29	80
Mazurak, Chad	66	7	22	29	90
Silverstone, David	52	1	12	13	189
Sullivan, Dan	25	4	7	11	64
Fischer, Cole	69	3	7	10	119
Schueller, Doug	66	2	8	10	61
Barker, Josh	65	4	6	10	45
Balan, Scott	44	1	9	10	63
Essex, Brad	36	2	5	7	102
Stayzer, Blair	15	2	3	5	42
Colagiacomo, Adam	15	1	3	4	16
Lindsay, Evan	38	0	3	3	2
LaPlante, Sebastien	39	0	2	2	4
Weasler, Dean	1	0	0	0	0

GOALTENDING

	Gms.	Min.	W	L	T	G	SO	Avg.
Weasler, Dean	1	65	1	0	0	3	0	2.77
Lindsay, Evan	38	2102	21	12	3	107	0	3.05
LaPlante, Sebastien	39	2203	20	12	3	119	1	3.24

SOUTH CAROLINA STINGRAYS

SCORING

	Games	G	A	Pts.	PIM
Seitz, Dave	70	23	60	83	65
Calder, Adam	70	29	42	71	123
Jickling, Mike	67	26	35	61	44
Huppe, Curtis	72	23	36	59	64
Clapton, Marty	68	14	42	56	110
Desrosiers, Matt	69	18	25	43	81
Williamson, Brad	71	9	32	41	105
Irving, Joel	57	17	23	40	105
Schneekloth, Aaron	41	8	22	30	36
Brindley, Ryan	62	13	17	30	119
Gomez, Robin	69	11	16	27	208
Powers, Andy	65	12	13	25	61
Marietti, Brett	44	7	16	23	142
Johnson, Trevor	66	7	12	19	200
Taylor, Rod	31	8	10	18	22
Boulanger, Jeff	55	7	9	16	80
Armbrust, Peter	72	6	10	16	30
Henley, Brent	50	2	10	12	306
Kesselring, Casey	2	0	3	3	2
Daubenspeck, Kirk	58	0	2	2	17
Snell, Chris	2	0	0	0	0
Concannon, Rob	3	0	0	0	2
Duke, Steve	2	0	0	0	2
Rucinski, Jeff	1	0	0	0	0
Weasler, Dean	7	0	0	0	2
Spiller, Rich	2	0	0	0	0
Brumby, David	9	0	0	0	0

GOALTENDING

	Gms.	Min.	W	L	T	G	SO	Avg.
Brumby, David	9	558	5	2	2	26	0	2.79
Daubenspeck, Kirk	58	3454	36	16	6	167	0	2.90
Weasler, Dean	7	374	1	4	0	25	0	4.00

TOLEDO STORM

SCORING

	Games	G	A	Pts.	PIM
Parillo, Nick	66	23	38	61	193
Ellis, Matt	71	27	32	59	34
Moore, Grady	65	7	40	47	73
Junkin, Dale	64	14	31	45	22
Johnstone, Jeff	43	15	25	40	30
Verbeek, Tim	70	17	22	39	217
Jacques, Alexandre	37	21	15	36	20
Bootland, Darryl	54	17	19	36	322
Mason, Wes	48	17	19	36	40
Read, Trevor	60	6	23	29	39
Mitchell, Jeff	57	10	19	29	184
Bayrack, Mike	47	11	16	27	47
Ballantyne, Paul	56	10	16	26	41
Lutz, Nathan	54	5	20	25	122
Anderson, Erik	36	9	15	24	10
Brown, Jim	21	12	7	19	18
Durak, Miroslav	51	3	13	16	72
Robinson, Nathan	9	5	9	14	29
Helbling, Timo	35	3	8	11	75
Fleenor, Brandon	71	2	9	11	200
Eldred, Matt	20	2	5	7	70
Hutchinson, Andrew	10	2	5	7	4
Payette, Andre	11	3	2	5	83
Wilchynski, Chad	8	0	4	4	30
Guenther, Joe	4	0	4	4	0
Waltze, Kris	30	1	3	4	169
Menzul, Curtis	12	0	2	2	32
Del Monte, David	6	1	0	1	0
Panov, Konstantin	2	1	0	1	0
Minard, Mike	19	0	1	1	8

	Games	G	A	Pts.	PIM
Teskey, Doug	47	0	1	1	12
Fillion, Martin	2	0	0	0	0
McMahon, Mark	2	0	0	0	2
Karunakar, Avi	1	0	0	0	0
Maser, Josh	2	0	0	0	2
Carney, Dan	7	0	0	0	8
Fraser, Brad	1	0	0	0	0
Draper, Tom	4	0	0	0	0
Hartje, Tod	1	0	0	0	0
Wells, Jeff	1	0	0	0	0
Longo, Chris	3	0	0	0	2
Finley, Brian	7	0	0	0	0
Marlin, Dave	1	0	0	0	0
Taylor, Rod	2	0	0	0	2

GOALTENDING

	Gms.	Min.	W	L	T	G	SO	Avg.
Fillion, Martin	2	43	1	0	0	0	0	0.00
Karunakar, Avi	1	0	0	0	0	0	0	0.00
Marlin, Dave	1	4	0	0	0	0	0	0.00
Draper, Tom	4	243	3	1	0	7	1	1.72
Minard, Mike	19	1093	8	4	5	42	1	2.31
Finley, Brian	7	305	4	2	0	12	0	2.36
Teskey, Doug	47	2677	31	8	5	129	1	2.89

TRENTON TITANS
SCORING

	Games	G	A	Pts.	PIM
Edinger, Adam	63	33	37	70	67
Bertoli, Scott	47	21	39	60	46
Zultek, Matt	58	25	27	52	205
Beechey, Tyler	51	8	38	46	33
Kilbourne, B.J.	72	16	20	36	81
Charpentier, Marco	43	14	20	34	14
Apps, Syl	55	11	21	32	119
Hurley, Mike	32	19	12	31	38
Wood, Dustin	63	4	23	27	28
Davyduke, Kent	20	7	13	20	21
Lynch, Chris	36	7	13	20	99
Tetrault, Daniel	39	6	12	18	38
O'Brien, Steve	26	2	16	18	26
Schneider, David	26	5	11	16	22
Betournay, Eric	33	9	7	16	35
Fisher, Shaun	32	3	10	13	30
Joseph, Yann	28	5	7	12	45
White, Kam	62	2	9	11	241
Traynor, Paul	22	4	6	10	26
Nail, John	35	4	5	9	24
Smith, Jeff	39	1	7	8	122
Williams, Vince	16	1	6	7	20
Connolly, Sean	32	3	4	7	34
Davis, Aaron	15	2	4	6	10
David, J.F.	11	0	5	5	16
Baker, Jack	22	4	1	5	16
Insana, Jon	20	2	2	4	22
Hedlund, Andy	13	1	2	3	14
Mehalko, Brad	6	2	0	2	12
Henderson, Mike	13	2	0	2	0
Forbes, Ian	32	0	2	2	122
Brunel, Craig	39	1	1	2	157
Bergin, Kevin	3	1	0	1	11
Ortmeyer, Jake	3	1	0	1	0
Deskins, Jason	10	1	0	1	6
St. Germain, David	33	0	1	1	2
Herneisen, Matt	2	0	1	1	4
Rudkowsky, Cody	31	0	1	1	6
Wilson, Jeff	2	0	0	0	0
McMeekin, Brian	13	0	0	0	9
Belak, Graham	2	0	0	0	15
Schmidt, Jeff	1	0	0	0	0
Marlin, Dave	1	0	0	0	0
Snee, Brandon	2	0	0	0	0
Osaer, Phil	2	0	0	0	0
Allen, Andrew	4	0	0	0	0

GOALTENDING

	Gms.	Min.	W	L	T	G	SO	Avg.
Allen, Andrew	4	243	3	0	1	4	3	0.99
Snee, Brandon	2	125	2	0	0	5	2	2.40
Rudkowsky, Cody	31	1866	17	9	5	85	2	2.73
St. Germain, David	33	1947	15	13	4	90	2	2.77
Osaer, Phil	2	117	0	2	0	7	0	3.57
Marlin, Dave	1	60	1	0	0	4	0	4.00

WHEELING NAILERS
SCORING

	Games	G	A	Pts.	PIM
Konopka, Zenon	68	22	48	70	231
Ouellet, Michel	55	20	26	46	40
Larocque, Mario	66	18	26	44	194
Russell, Bobby	37	26	13	39	38
Major, Mark	68	17	22	39	135
Crampton, Steve	69	13	26	39	79
Soucy, Jean-Philippe	66	7	26	33	128
McNamara, Chris	47	12	20	32	42
Doulebenets, Dmitri	52	13	18	31	26
Mihaly, Arpad	69	8	22	30	38
Gillis, Ryan	61	5	16	21	62
Smith, Matt	53	6	13	19	132
Reynolds, T.J.	71	2	8	10	371
Elich, Matt	25	3	6	9	32
Cummings, Brian	19	2	6	8	23
Preston, Tim	22	4	4	8	6
Nelson, Mike	36	3	3	6	20
Ernest, Derek	64	2	3	5	240
Moore, Mark	7	2	0	2	6
Robinson, Darcy	1	0	1	1	0
Burgess, Steve	5	0	1	1	2
Cameron, Jeff	14	1	0	1	12
McPherson, Andrew	19	0	1	1	21
Valley, Mike	44	0	1	1	4
Lariviere, Jacques	21	0	1	1	77
Koci, David	48	0	1	1	103
MacKay, Tyler	27	0	1	1	8
Vychodil, David	1	0	0	0	4
Pietersma, Stu	3	0	0	0	19
Chant, David	9	0	0	0	0
Del Monte, David	2	0	0	0	0
Thornton, Bob	8	0	0	0	2

GOALTENDING

	Gms.	Min.	W	L	T	G	SO	Avg.
Valley, Mike	44	2439	16	23	3	131	4	3.22
MacKay, Tyler	27	1521	11	12	0	87	2	3.43
Chant, David	9	391	1	6	0	38	0	5.82

PLAYERS WITH TWO OR MORE TEAMS
SCORING

	Games	G	A	Pts.	PIM
Adams, Erik, CBA	54	3	21	24	14
Adams, Erik, BR	18	1	2	3	10
Totals	72	4	23	27	24
Allen, Andrew, DAY	19	0	0	0	2
Allen, Andrew, TRE	4	0	0	0	0
Totals	23	0	0	0	2
Allen, Chris, GBO	51	6	8	14	58
Allen, Chris, MIS	11	2	8	10	6
Totals	62	8	16	24	64
Baker, Korey, ARK	7	0	0	0	2
Baker, Korey, CIN	9	0	0	0	0
Totals	16	0	0	0	2
Bartek, Martin, PEN	19	11	10	21	26
Bartek, Martin, RMD	5	3	1	4	4
Bartek, Martin, LA	8	4	7	11	6
Totals	32	18	18	36	36
Bayrack, Mike, TOL	47	11	16	27	47
Bayrack, Mike, GBO	12	4	5	9	10
Totals	59	15	21	36	57
Belak, Graham, TRE	2	0	0	0	15
Belak, Graham, CIN	40	1	0	1	157
Totals	42	1	0	1	172
Bell, Chris, GBO	51	15	20	35	79
Bell, Chris, BR	17	2	7	9	20
Totals	68	17	27	44	99
Bergin, Kevin, TRE	3	1	0	1	11
Bergin, Kevin, PEN	30	0	2	2	78
Bergin, Kevin, CIN	18	0	6	6	16
Totals	51	1	8	9	105
Blackburn, Josh, AUG	6	0	0	0	0
Blackburn, Josh, CBA	33	0	1	1	2
Totals	39	0	1	1	2

	Games	G	A	Pts.	PIM
Blais, Dwayne, MIS	40	6	6	12	37
Blais, Dwayne, BR	31	5	10	15	32
Totals	71	11	16	27	69
Blevins, Wes, CIN	51	2	2	4	52
Blevins, Wes, GRV	15	2	2	4	18
Totals	66	4	4	8	70
Brosseau, David, DAY	4	0	0	0	8
Brosseau, David, RMD	60	24	27	51	64
Totals	64	24	27	51	72
Brown, Kevin, AUG	14	1	4	5	16
Brown, Kevin, FLA	52	23	37	60	72
Totals	66	24	41	65	88
Brumby, David, AUG	12	0	0	0	4
Brumby, David, SC	9	0	0	0	0
Totals	21	0	0	0	4
Brunel, Craig, TRE	39	1	1	2	157
Brunel, Craig, REA	9	0	3	3	25
Totals	48	1	4	5	182
Burgess, Steve, WHL	5	0	1	1	2
Burgess, Steve, CHR	6	0	0	0	2
Totals	11	0	1	1	4
Burrows, Alexandre, GRV	53	9	17	26	201
Burrows, Alexandre, BR	13	4	2	6	64
Totals	66	13	19	32	265
Byfuglien, Derrick, MIS	49	2	12	14	58
Byfuglien, Derrick, GBO	14	0	1	1	10
Totals	63	2	13	15	68
Campbell, John, FLA	14	0	1	1	12
Campbell, John, AUG	11	2	3	5	14
Campbell, John, CIN	33	3	6	9	16
Totals	58	5	10	15	42
Cheredaryk, Steve, BR	31	6	13	19	93
Cheredaryk, Steve, ATC	19	0	1	1	51
Totals	50	6	14	20	144
Christiansen, Doug, MIS	4	0	0	0	12
Christiansen, Doug, CBA	6	0	0	0	2
Christiansen, Doug, AUG	39	0	8	8	25
Christiansen, Doug, CHR	17	7	7	14	15
Totals	66	7	15	22	54
Cirillo, Mike, AUG	3	1	0	1	10
Cirillo, Mike, ARK	63	20	14	34	216
Totals	66	21	14	35	226
Copley, Randy, JCK	10	0	4	4	19
Copley, Randy, CHR	7	0	0	0	0
Copley, Randy, PEO	34	15	13	28	36
Copley, Randy, CBS	16	7	5	12	6
Totals	67	22	22	44	61
Crain, Jason, MIS	16	0	3	3	8
Crain, Jason, DAY	50	5	27	32	22
Totals	66	5	30	35	30
Crawford, Glenn, BR	27	4	14	18	30
Crawford, Glenn, PEO	2	0	1	1	2
Totals	29	4	15	19	32
Crawford, Scott, JCK	1	0	0	0	0
Crawford, Scott, PEO	50	3	14	17	22
Totals	51	3	14	17	22
Crimin, Derek, GBO	2	0	1	1	0
Crimin, Derek, CBA	12	3	1	4	2
Totals	14	3	2	5	2
Cummings, Brian, WHL	19	2	6	8	23
Cummings, Brian, DAY	54	6	13	19	80
Totals	73	8	19	27	103
Davis, Aaron, TRE	15	2	4	6	10
Davis, Aaron, ARK	23	2	3	5	11
Totals	38	4	7	11	21
Davyduke, Kent, TRE	20	7	13	20	21
Davyduke, Kent, MIS	25	12	24	36	26
Totals	45	19	37	56	47
Del Monte, David, LEX	17	2	1	3	12
Del Monte, David, TOL	6	1	0	1	0
Del Monte, David, WHL	2	0	0	0	0
Del Monte, David, GBO	13	0	6	6	14
Totals	38	3	7	10	26
Demmans, Trevor, BR	48	7	33	40	59
Demmans, Trevor, CBA	15	2	10	12	4
Totals	63	9	43	52	63

	Games	G	A	Pts.	PIM
Deskins, Jason, TRE	10	1	0	1	6
Deskins, Jason, ARK	13	3	4	7	14
Deskins, Jason, DAY	34	8	12	20	22
Totals	57	12	16	28	42
Draper, Tom, TOL	4	0	0	0	0
Draper, Tom, AUG	17	0	0	0	4
Totals	21	0	0	0	4
Elich, Matt, PEN	12	4	4	8	6
Elich, Matt, WHL	25	3	6	9	32
Totals	37	7	10	17	38
Ellis-Tdingtn, Kerry, RMD	47	2	15	17	20
Ellis-Tdingtn, Kerry, PEN	27	6	7	13	25
Totals	74	8	22	30	45
Fankhouser, Scott, REA	26	0	0	0	10
Fankhouser, Scott, ARK	19	0	1	1	0
Totals	45	0	1	1	10
Fisher, Shaun, FLA	10	1	1	2	8
Fisher, Shaun, GRV	12	1	2	3	20
Fisher, Shaun, TRE	32	3	10	13	30
Totals	54	5	13	18	58
Flache, Paul, GRV	46	1	9	10	64
Flache, Paul, GRV	3	2	1	3	9
Totals	49	3	10	13	73
Fraser, Brad, TOL	1	0	0	0	0
Fraser, Brad, DAY	12	0	0	0	16
Fraser, Brad, BR	17	0	6	6	13
Totals	30	0	6	6	29
Galbraith, Lance, AUG	48	9	14	23	240
Galbraith, Lance, DAY	8	5	4	9	47
Totals	56	14	18	32	287
Gauthier, Jonathon, DAY	16	2	3	5	24
Gauthier, Jonathon, AUG	31	2	3	5	24
Gauthier, Jonathon, GRV	21	3	5	8	22
Totals	68	7	11	18	70
Gauvreau, Brent, AUG	18	4	3	7	25
Gauvreau, Brent, JCK	49	14	28	42	61
Totals	67	18	31	49	86
Gillies, Trevor, RMD	6	0	0	0	20
Gillies, Trevor, PEO	24	0	1	1	180
Totals	30	0	1	1	200
Goneau, Daniel, LA	48	21	43	64	102
Goneau, Daniel, RMD	8	3	4	7	8
Totals	56	24	47	71	110
Gore, Forrest, BR	19	4	3	7	35
Gore, Forrest, PEO	7	0	0	0	2
Totals	26	4	3	7	37
Goudie, Brian, RMD	5	1	0	1	6
Goudie, Brian, FLA	63	6	19	25	171
Totals	68	7	19	26	177
Grimes, Kevin, JCK	20	1	5	6	64
Grimes, Kevin, GBO	54	1	7	8	141
Totals	74	2	12	14	205
Guenther, Joe, TOL	4	0	4	4	0
Guenther, Joe, BR	51	17	22	39	22
Totals	55	17	26	43	22
Gustafson, Chris, GRV	40	2	9	11	22
Gustafson, Chris, AUG	25	1	2	3	13
Totals	65	3	11	14	35
Harrold, Josh, PEN	45	8	18	26	36
Harrold, Josh, RMD	17	1	9	10	14
Totals	62	9	27	36	50
Henderson, Mike, CIN	19	4	9	13	6
Henderson, Mike, TRE	13	2	0	2	0
Henderson, Mike, GRV	38	13	26	39	12
Totals	70	19	35	54	18
Herhal, Matt, REA	2	0	0	0	0
Herhal, Matt, REA	1	0	0	0	0
Totals	3	0	0	0	0
Herrington, Jamie, RMD	45	13	23	36	32
Herrington, Jamie, PEN	5	3	4	7	4
Totals	50	16	27	43	36
Hewson, Scott, PEN	52	6	10	16	56
Hewson, Scott, BR	14	2	3	5	6
Totals	66	8	13	21	62
Hurley, Mike, GRV	40	8	18	26	18
Hurley, Mike, TRE	32	19	12	31	38
Totals	72	27	30	57	56
Ianiero, Andrew, DAY	44	11	13	24	35
Ianiero, Andrew, AUG	16	0	10	10	16
Totals	60	11	23	34	51

	Games	G	A	Pts.	PIM
Insana, Jon, TRE	20	2	2	4	22
Insana, Jon, FLA	23	1	4	5	12
Totals	43	3	6	9	34
Joseph, Yann, TRE	28	5	7	12	45
Joseph, Yann, BR	3	0	0	0	0
Joseph, Yann, DAY	22	2	7	9	12
Totals	53	7	14	21	57
Kaiman, Tom, ARK	23	0	1	1	73
Kaiman, Tom, BR	45	1	8	9	151
Totals	68	1	9	10	224
Kerestes, Jaroslav, LA	9	0	0	0	21
Kerestes, Jaroslav, FLA	3	0	1	1	6
Totals	12	0	1	1	27
Kesselring, Casey, SC	2	0	3	3	2
Kesselring, Casey, LA	21	4	8	12	8
Totals	23	4	11	15	10
Kiesman, Michael, PEO	3	0	1	1	9
Kiesman, Michael, BR	56	6	11	17	65
Totals	59	6	12	18	74
Kos, Kyle, ARK	23	3	9	12	83
Kos, Kyle, DAY	9	0	1	1	18
Kos, Kyle, FLA	10	1	3	4	60
Totals	42	4	13	17	161
Kuznetsov, Sergei, AUG	27	3	12	15	30
Kuznetsov, Sergei, MIS	31	9	18	27	36
Totals	58	12	30	42	66
Lakos, Phillippe, AUG	20	0	2	2	44
Lakos, Phillippe, ARK	22	0	3	3	22
Totals	42	0	5	5	66
Laplante, Darryl, AUG	19	2	4	6	16
Laplante, Darryl, JCK	49	6	14	20	42
Totals	68	8	18	26	58
Lariviere, Jacques, DAY	1	0	0	0	29
Lariviere, Jacques, WHL	21	0	1	1	77
Totals	22	0	1	1	106
Leger, Jim, JHN	30	12	9	21	20
Leger, Jim, DAY	15	7	6	13	12
Totals	45	19	15	34	32
Legg, Mike, CBA	20	5	7	12	10
Legg, Mike, AUG	41	11	25	36	16
Totals	61	16	32	48	26
Leitza, Brian, BR	8	0	0	0	0
Leitza, Brian, FLA	10	0	0	0	2
Totals	18	0	0	0	2
Linnik, Maxim, DAY	2	0	0	0	0
Linnik, Maxim, ARK	23	0	2	2	28
Totals	25	0	2	2	28
Lupandin, Andrei, GBO	14	0	1	1	20
Lupandin, Andrei, JCK	45	5	17	22	10
Totals	59	5	18	23	30
Lutz, Nathan, REA	1	0	0	0	2
Lutz, Nathan, TOL	54	5	20	25	122
Totals	55	5	20	25	124
Lynch, Chris, TRE	36	7	13	20	99
Lynch, Chris, GRV	31	14	15	29	47
Totals	67	21	28	49	146
Mackie, Kevin, PEN	5	1	0	1	2
Mackie, Kevin, JCK	60	1	8	9	68
Totals	65	2	8	10	70
Malts, Vince, CHR	49	11	17	28	134
Malts, Vince, AUG	10	0	3	3	26
Totals	59	11	20	31	160
Mamane, Shawn, RMD	6	2	0	2	13
Mamane, Shawn, ARK	10	2	0	2	34
Mamane, Shawn, LA	7	1	1	2	33
Totals	23	5	1	6	80
Marlin, Dave, ATC	1	0	0	0	0
Marlin, Dave, TRE	1	0	0	0	0
Marlin, Dave, TOL	1	0	0	0	0
Totals	3	0	0	0	0
Martinello, Mike, ATC	30	4	3	7	39
Martinello, Mike, BR	15	0	0	0	18
Totals	45	4	3	7	57
Maser, Josh, CIN	28	2	2	4	86
Maser, Josh, TOL	2	0	0	0	2
Totals	30	2	2	4	88
Mass, Louis, PD	9	0	1	1	8
Mass, Louis, LA	61	2	6	8	80
Totals	70	2	7	9	88

	Games	G	A	Pts.	PIM
Mastad, Milt, RMD	39	3	5	8	66
Mastad, Milt, LA	18	3	2	5	20
Totals	57	6	7	13	86
Mathieu, Marquis, BR	44	13	17	30	104
Mathieu, Marquis, PEN	15	3	10	13	74
Totals	59	16	27	43	178
McIver, Chad, DAY	5	0	0	0	6
McIver, Chad, CHR	16	0	0	0	14
McIver, Chad, CIN	43	2	3	5	42
Totals	64	2	3	5	62
McMeekin, Brian, TRE	13	0	0	0	9
McMeekin, Brian, FLA	4	0	0	0	2
Totals	17	0	0	0	11
McPherson, Andrew, WHL	19	0	1	1	21
McPherson, Andrew, CHR	4	1	0	1	0
Totals	23	1	1	2	21
Menzul, Curtis, GRV	1	0	0	0	0
Menzul, Curtis, TOL	12	0	2	2	32
Menzul, Curtis, MIS	10	0	2	2	14
Menzul, Curtis, BR	10	0	0	0	6
Totals	33	0	4	4	52
Minard, Mike, REA	2	0	0	0	0
Minard, Mike, TOL	19	0	1	1	8
Totals	21	0	1	1	8
Moore, Mark, AUG	15	0	2	2	22
Moore, Mark, WHL	7	2	0	2	6
Totals	22	2	2	4	28
Murray, Ryan, CHR	37	0	6	6	15
Murray, Ryan, AUG	7	0	0	0	0
Totals	44	0	6	6	15
Nail, John, TRE	35	4	5	9	24
Nail, John, GRV	31	7	7	14	30
Totals	66	11	12	23	54
Nelson, Mike, WHL	36	3	3	6	20
Nelson, Mike, CBS	14	2	2	4	16
Nelson, Mike, PEO	16	7	4	11	24
Totals	66	12	9	21	60
Norrie, Jason, BR	58	20	16	36	153
Norrie, Jason, CIN	20	4	9	13	41
Totals	78	24	25	49	194
O'Keefe, Ryan, JCK	6	0	1	1	8
O'Keefe, Ryan, PEN	64	1	16	17	216
Totals	70	1	17	18	224
Oliveira, Mike, JCK	22	6	5	11	16
Oliveira, Mike, AUG	9	1	3	4	2
Oliveira, Mike, BR	17	4	6	10	0
Oliveira, Mike, GBO	18	1	4	5	2
Totals	66	12	18	30	20
Osaer, Phil, TRE	2	0	0	0	0
Osaer, Phil, LA	4	0	0	0	0
Totals	6	0	0	0	0
Palmer, Tyler, CBS	2	0	0	0	4
Palmer, Tyler, JCK	19	0	2	2	26
Palmer, Tyler, RMD	34	1	2	3	26
Totals	55	1	4	5	56
Paquet, Samuel, BR	56	12	11	23	109
Paquet, Samuel, ARK	5	1	1	2	2
Totals	61	13	12	25	111
Peach, Sean, BR	38	3	13	16	67
Peach, Sean, MIS	17	0	3	3	36
Totals	55	3	16	19	103
Perna, Mike, AUG	11	1	0	1	23
Perna, Mike, BR	6	1	3	4	10
Totals	17	2	3	5	33
Pietersma, Stu, WHL	3	0	0	0	19
Pietersma, Stu, MIS	55	5	6	11	275
Totals	58	5	6	11	294
Platt, Jayme, GRV	26	0	0	0	4
Platt, Jayme, DAY	11	0	1	1	0
Totals	37	0	1	1	4
Poapst, Matt, ARK	13	2	6	8	14
Poapst, Matt, DAY	27	3	5	8	34
Poapst, Matt, PEN	26	3	4	7	24
Totals	66	8	15	23	72
Renzi, Mike, DAY	16	2	5	7	69
Renzi, Mike, MIS	5	1	2	3	4
Renzi, Mike, ARK	26	5	4	9	28
Renzi, Mike, BR	14	3	4	7	17
Totals	61	11	15	26	118

	Games	G	A	Pts.	PIM
Richardson, Bryan, BR	50	24	28	52	60
Richardson, Bryan, GBO	20	7	11	18	14
Totals	70	31	39	70	74
Rodrigues, Mike, JHN	40	1	8	9	32
Rodrigues, Mike, REA	18	2	1	3	23
Totals	58	3	9	12	55
Rome, Reagan, PEN	6	0	2	2	11
Rome, Reagan, JCK	64	6	12	18	94
Totals	70	6	14	20	105
Roy, Philippe, JHN	56	11	19	30	68
Roy, Philippe, AUG	8	3	3	6	13
Totals	64	14	22	36	81
Royer, Gaetan, JCK	11	3	6	9	58
Royer, Gaetan, PEN	20	3	10	13	60
Totals	31	6	16	22	118
Royer, Remi, FLA	2	0	1	1	18
Royer, Remi, REA	29	7	7	14	186
Totals	31	7	8	15	204
Ruff, Lee, FLA	34	3	8	11	31
Ruff, Lee, DAY	12	0	0	0	4
Totals	46	3	8	11	35
Schmidt, Jeff, TRE	1	0	0	0	0
Schmidt, Jeff, REA	13	0	0	0	2
Totals	14	0	0	0	2
Scott, Mike, ATC	2	0	0	0	0
Scott, Mike, MIS	64	26	41	67	100
Totals	66	26	41	67	100
Shmyr, Jason, AUG	32	6	5	11	161
Shmyr, Jason, JHN	12	3	2	5	53
Totals	44	9	7	16	214
Snee, Brandon, TRE	2	0	0	0	0
Snee, Brandon, REA	11	0	0	0	4
Totals	13	0	0	0	4
Spiller, Rich, RMD	2	0	0	0	2
Spiller, Rich, JCK	3	0	0	0	2
Spiller, Rich, PEN	44	1	1	2	53
Spiller, Rich, SC	2	0	0	0	0
Totals	51	1	1	2	57
St. Louis, Jonathan, FLA	2	1	0	1	7
St. Louis, Jonathan, RMD	25	5	2	7	46
Totals	27	6	2	8	53
Stayzer, Blair, MIS	12	1	2	3	19
Stayzer, Blair, RNK	15	2	3	5	42
Stayzer, Blair, DAY	23	2	2	4	61
Totals	50	5	7	12	122
Sullivan, Dan, RNK	25	4	7	11	64
Sullivan, Dan, BR	21	4	3	7	49
Totals	46	8	10	18	113
Sundberg, Niklas, CHR	16	0	1	1	2
Sundberg, Niklas, BR	22	0	2	2	8
Totals	38	0	3	3	10
Taylor, Rod, SC	31	8	10	18	22
Taylor, Rod, PEO	2	0	1	1	0
Taylor, Rod, TOL	2	0	0	0	2
Totals	35	8	11	19	24
Theuer, Chad, PEN	52	8	25	33	20
Theuer, Chad, GRV	15	2	10	12	12
Totals	67	10	35	45	32
Thompson, Chris M., DAY	48	15	28	43	215
Thompson, Chris M., AUG	14	4	9	13	18
Totals	62	19	37	56	233
Thompson, Mark, JCK	22	1	5	6	59
Thompson, Mark, AUG	51	1	5	6	127
Totals	73	2	10	12	186
Thornton, Bob, WHL	8	0	0	0	2
Thornton, Bob, CIN	16	3	2	5	22
Totals	24	3	2	5	24
Toor, Garry, AUG	16	2	4	6	12
Toor, Garry, ARK	49	3	15	18	16
Totals	65	5	19	24	28
Traynor, Paul, CHR	1	0	0	0	0
Traynor, Paul, TRE	22	4	6	10	26
Totals	23	4	6	10	26
Tucker, Kevin, PEO	8	1	1	2	10
Tucker, Kevin, BR	58	1	5	6	66
Totals	66	2	6	8	76
Valentine, Curtis, LA	1	0	0	0	0
Valentine, Curtis, CHR	9	2	2	4	2
Totals	10	2	2	4	2

	Games	G	A	Pts.	PIM
Van Acker, Eric, GRV	50	0	4	4	127
Van Acker, Eric, PEN	15	0	2	2	20
Totals	65	0	6	6	147
Van Parys, Justin, RMD	2	0	0	0	2
Van Parys, Justin, LEX	59	2	7	9	63
Totals	61	2	7	9	65
Verdule, Jimmy, REA	22	1	2	3	85
Verdule, Jimmy, FLA	48	0	17	17	233
Totals	70	1	19	20	318
Vickers, Jim, ATC	48	2	7	9	64
Vickers, Jim, BR	17	2	5	7	28
Totals	65	4	12	16	92
Vigilante, Mike, PEN	11	0	4	4	6
Vigilante, Mike, JCK	55	9	11	20	12
Totals	66	9	15	24	18
Waltze, Kris, REA	20	1	1	2	77
Waltze, Kris, TOL	30	1	3	4	169
Totals	50	2	4	6	246
Wandler, Bryce, CHR	8	0	0	0	0
Wandler, Bryce, LEX	4	0	0	0	0
Totals	12	0	0	0	2
Weasler, Dean, SC	7	0	0	0	2
Weasler, Dean, RNK	1	0	0	0	0
Totals	8	0	0	0	2
Wilchynski, Chad, TOL	8	0	4	4	30
Wilchynski, Chad, CHR	42	8	19	27	68
Totals	50	8	23	31	98
Williams, Vince, FLA	12	1	0	1	22
Williams, Vince, TRE	16	1	6	7	20
Totals	28	2	6	8	42
Williamson, Andrew, DAY	19	4	7	11	26
Williamson, Andrew, AUG	50	27	47	74	36
Totals	69	31	54	85	62
Wismer, Chris, DAY	16	0	0	0	20
Wismer, Chris, FLA	5	0	0	0	22
Wismer, Chris, CIN	11	2	1	3	10
Wismer, Chris, GRV	13	1	2	3	4
Totals	45	3	3	6	56
Yetman, Patrick, AUG	39	11	14	25	26
Yetman, Patrick, DAY	4	0	2	2	0
Totals	43	11	16	27	26
Zinevych, Alexander, FLA	6	0	0	0	4
Zinevych, Alexander, CBS	16	0	2	2	6
Zinevych, Alexander, PEO	15	0	3	3	4
Totals	37	0	5	5	14
Zulianello, Colin, AUG	19	0	0	0	2
Zulianello, Colin, CHR	12	0	0	0	0
Totals	31	0	0	0	2

GOALTENDING

	Gms.	Min.	W	L	T	G	SO	Avg.
Allen, Andrew, DAY	19	1033	5	9	3	60	1	3.48
Allen, Andrew, TRE	4	243	3	0	1	4	3	0.99
Totals	23	1276	8	9	4	64	4	3.01
Blackburn, J., AUG	6	209	0	4	0	21	0	6.01
Blackburn, J., CBA	33	1927	19	11	2	96	2	2.99
Totals	39	2137	19	15	2	117	2	3.28
Brumby, D., AUG	12	692	3	7	1	39	1	3.38
Brumby, D., SC	9	558	5	2	2	26	0	2.79
Totals	21	1251	8	9	3	65	1	3.12
Draper, Tom, TOL	4	243	3	1	0	7	1	1.72
Draper, Tom, AUG	17	863	6	5	2	43	1	2.99
Totals	21	1107	9	6	2	50	2	2.71
Fankhouser, S., REA	26	1462	11	12	1	94	0	3.86
Fankhouser, S., ARK	19	1110	11	5	2	49	1	2.65
Totals	45	2572	22	17	3	143	1	3.33
Leitza, Brian, BR	8	498	3	3	2	30	0	3.61
Leitza, Brian, FLA	10	544	3	4	3	27	0	2.98
Totals	18	1042	6	7	5	57	0	3.28
Marlin, Dave, ATC	1	60	1	0	0	1	0	1.00
Marlin, Dave, TRE	1	60	1	0	0	4	0	4.00
Marlin, Dave, TOL	1	4	0	0	0	0	0	0.00
Totals	3	124	2	0	0	5	0	2.41
Minard, Mike, REA	2	119	0	2	0	17	0	8.55
Minard, Mike, TOL	19	1093	8	4	5	42	1	2.31
Totals	21	1212	8	6	5	59	1	3.18
Osaer, Phil, TRE	2	117	0	2	0	7	0	3.57
Osaer, Phil, LA	4	243	2	1	1	9	0	2.21
Totals	6	361	2	3	1	16	0	2.66

	Gms.	Min.	W	L	T	G	SO	Avg.
Platt, Jayme, GRV	26	1472	9	12	3	77	3	3.14
Platt, Jayme, DAY.....	11	665	3	6	2	39	1	3.52
Totals	37	2138	12	18	5	116	4	3.26
Snee, Brandon, TRE.	2	125	2	0	0	5	0	2.40
Snee, Brandon, REA.	11	540	1	8	0	39	0	4.33
Totals	13	665	3	8	0	44	0	3.96
Sundberg, N., CHR...	16	789	8	6	0	43	0	3.27
Sundberg, N., BR	22	1307	10	10	2	68	0	3.12
Totals	38	2096	18	16	2	111	0	3.18

	Gms.	Min.	W	L	T	G	SO	Avg.
Wandler, Bryce, CHR	8	392	0	4	1	31	0	4.74
Wandler, Bryce, LEX.	4	244	2	2	0	14	0	3.43
Totals	12	636	2	6	1	45	0	4.24
Weasler, Dean, SC....	7	374	1	4	0	25	0	4.00
Weasler, Dean, RNK .	1	65	1	0	0	3	0	2.77
Totals	8	439	2	4	0	28	0	3.82
Zulianello, C., AUG ...	19	1012	6	10	1	59	1	3.50
Zulianello, C., CHR ...	12	674	7	4	1	30	2	2.67
Totals	31	1686	13	14	2	89	3	3.17

2003 KELLY CUP PLAYOFFS

RESULTS

KELLY CUP FINALS
Atlantic City vs. Columbia
Game 1 - May 7, Atlantic City 1, Columbia 0
Game 2 - May 9, Atlantic City 3, Columbia 0
Game 3 - May 10, Columbia 5, Atlantic City 3
Game 4 - May 12, Atlantic City 3, Columbia 1
Game 5 - May 14, Atlantic City 3, Columbia 1
Atlantic City wins series 4-1

CONFERENCE FINALS
NORTHERN CONFERENCE
Atlantic City vs. Cincinnati
Game 1 - April 23, Atlantic City 5, Cincinnati 4
Game 2 - April 25, Atlantic City 5, Cincinnati 0
Game 3 - April 26, Atlantic City 3, Cincinnati 1
Game 4 - April 28, Cincinnati 3, Atlantic City 1
Game 5 - April 29, Cincinnati 6, Atlantic City 3
Game 6 - May 2, Cincinnati 4, Atlantic City 3
Game 7 - May 3, Atlantic City 3, Cincinnati 2
Atlantic City wins series 4-3

SOUTHERN CONFERENCE
Columbia vs. Mississippi
Game 1 - April 23, Columbia 5, Mississippi 2
Game 2 - April 25, Columbia 3, Mississippi 2, OT
Game 3 - April 27, Columbia 4, Mississippi 3
Game 4 - April 28, Mississippi 3, Columbia 1
Game 5 - April 30, Mississippi 2, Columbia 1, OT
Game 6 - May 2, Columbia 4, Mississippi 2
Columbia wins series 4-2

DIVISION FINALS
NORTHEAST DIVISION
Atlantic City vs. Greensboro
Game 1 - April 11, Atlantic City 3, Greensboro 2, OT
Game 2 - April 12, Greensboro 3, Atlantic City 2, OT
Game 3 - April 16, Atlantic City 6, Greensboro 3
Game 4 - April 18, Atlantic City 3, Greensboro 2
Atlantic City wins series 3-1

NORTHWEST DIVISION
Toledo vs. Cincinnati
Game 1 - April 11, Cincinnati 2, Toledo 1
Game 2 - April 12, Cincinnati 4, Toledo 2
Game 3 - April 15, Toledo 1, Cincinnati 0
Game 4 - April 16, Cincinnati 4, Toledo 1
Cincinnati wins series 3-1

SOUTHEAST DIVISION
Pee Dee vs. Columbia
Game 1 - April 11, Columbia 5, Pee Dee 2
Game 2 - April 12, Columbia 2, Pee Dee 1
Game 3 - April 16, Columbia 5, Pee Dee 1
Columbia wins series 3-0

SOUTHWEST DIVISION
Louisiana vs. Mississippi
Game 1 - April 9, Mississippi 5, Louisiana 2
Game 2 - April 12, Mississippi 4, Louisiana 0
Game 3 - April 14, Mississippi 3, Louisiana 2
Mississippi wins series 3-0

DIVISION SEMIFINALS
NORTHEAST DIVISION
Atlantic City vs. Trenton
Game 1 - April 2, Atlantic City 4, Trenton 3
Game 2 - April 4, Atlantic City 4, Trenton 0
Game 3 - April 7, Atlantic City 7, Trenton 3
Atlantic City wins series 3-0

Roanoke vs. Greensboro
Game 1 - April 3, Greensboro 7, Roanoke 2
Game 2 - April 4, Roanoke 3, Greensboro 1
Game 3 - April 5, Greensboro 3, Roanoke 2
Game 4 - April 8, Greensboro 5, Roanoke 3
Greensboro wins series 3-1

NORTHWEST DIVISION
Peoria vs. Cincinnati
Game 1 - April 1, Cincinnati 4, Peoria 3
Game 2 - April 2, Peoria 2, Cincinnati 1, OT
Game 3 - April 5, Cincinnati 1, Peoria 0, OT
Game 4 - April 6, Cincinnati 4, Peoria 3, OT
Cincinnati wins series 3-1

Toledo vs. Lexington
Game 1 - April 2, Toledo 9, Lexington 1
Game 2 - April 4, Toledo 3, Lexington 0
Game 3 - April 5, Toledo 5, Lexington 1
Toledo wins series 3-0

SOUTHEAST DIVISION
South Carolina vs. Pee Dee
Game 1 - April 2, Pee Dee 3, South Carolina 0
Game 2 - April 4, South Carolina 7, Pee Dee 1
Game 3 - April 5, Pee Dee 4, South Carolina 3
Game 4 - April 7, Pee Dee 4, South Carolina 3, OT
Pee Dee wins series 3-1

Columbia vs. Greenville
Game 1 - April 2, Columbia 6, Greenville 2
Game 2 - April 4, Columbia 6, Greenville 4
Game 3 - April 7, Columbia 6, Greenville 4
Columbia wins series 3-0

SOUTHWEST DIVISION
Pensacola vs. Mississippi
Game 1 - April 2, Mississippi 5, Pensacola 1
Game 2 - April 4, Mississippi 5, Pensacola 1
Game 3 - April 5, Mississippi 5, Pensacola 1
Mississippi wins series 3-0

Arkansas vs. Louisiana
Game 1 - April 2, Louisiana 2, Arkansas 0
Game 2 - April 3, Louisiana 3, Arkansas 1
Game 3 - April 5, Louisiana 3, Arkansas 1
Louisiana wins series 3-0

WILD CARD
April 1
Southwest Division
Pensacola 3, Jackson 2, OT

April 1
Southeast Division
Greenville 3, Florida 2

INDIVIDUAL LEADERS

Goals: Kevin Colley, ATC (13)
J.F. Caudron, ATC (13)
Assists: Luke Curtin, ATC (18)
Points: J.F. Caudron, ATC (22)
Penalty minutes: Shawn Wansborough, CBA (56)
Goaltending average: Duane Derksen, PEO (0.91)
Shutouts: Scott Stirling, ATC (3)

TOP SCORERS

	Games	G	A	Pts.
Caudron, J.F., ATC	19	13	9	22
Colley, Kevin, ATC	17	13	7	20
Curtin, Luke, ATC	19	2	18	20
Bootland, Nick, CIN	15	10	7	17
Stringer, Rejean, CBA	17	3	14	17

	Games	G	A	Pts.
Kuznetsov, Sergei, MIS	12	7	9	16
Smith, Tim, CBA	17	5	11	16
Henkel, Jimmy, ATC	19	3	12	15
Carruthers, Robin, CBA	17	9	5	14
Moore, Barrie, CBA	14	8	6	14
Walby, Steffon, MIS	12	5	9	14
Casselman, Mike, CIN	15	3	11	14
Paradise, Dave, MIS	11	5	8	13
Demmans, Trevor, CBA	17	3	10	13
Ulwelling, Matt, CBA	17	3	10	13
Scott, Mike, MIS	12	6	6	12
Murphy, Jay, GBO	8	5	7	12
Spadafora, Paul, ATC	19	5	7	12
Davyduke, Kent, MIS	12	3	9	12

INDIVIDUAL STATISTICS

ARKANSAS RIVERBLADES

(Lost division semifinals to Louisiana Icegators)

SCORING

	Games	G	A	Pts.	PIM
Marchant, Terry	3	1	1	2	0
Cirillo, Mike	3	0	2	2	10
Toor, Garry	3	1	0	1	2
Stork, Dean	3	0	0	0	2
Linnik, Maxim	3	0	0	0	0
Pagnutti, Matthew	3	0	0	0	4
Smith, Buddy	3	0	0	0	2
Davis, Aaron	3	0	0	0	0
Bermingham, Jason	3	0	0	0	4
Bachusz, Jeremy	3	0	0	0	0
Coole, Ryan	3	0	0	0	2
Paquet, Samuel	3	0	0	0	2
Whitten, Damon	3	0	0	0	2
Stock, Dean	3	0	0	0	2
Sandbeck, Mike	3	0	0	0	2
Fankhouser, Scott	3	0	0	0	2

GOALTENDING

	Gms.	Min.	W	L	T	G	SO	Avg.
Fankhouser, Scott	3	176	0	3	0	7	0	2.38

ATLANTIC CITY BOARDWALK BULLIES

(Won 2003 Kelly Cup)

SCORING

	Games	G	A	Pts.	PIM
Caudron, J.F.	19	13	9	22	14
Colley, Kevin	17	13	7	20	27
Curtin, Luke	19	2	18	20	20
Henkel, Jimmy	19	3	12	15	8
Spadafora, Paul	19	5	7	12	38
Rivard, Stefan	19	5	6	11	40
Furey, Kirk	17	1	10	11	8
Metcalf, Peter	19	4	6	10	25
Walterson, Ian	19	3	6	9	4
Maltby, Shawn	19	7	2	9	15
Mougenel, Ryan	17	1	8	9	16
Galbraith, Jade	15	2	5	7	8
Cheredaryk, Steve	19	1	5	6	20
Nicholishen, Mike	19	0	6	6	6
Matzka, Scott	19	5	1	6	27
Munn, Steve	19	0	1	1	18
Demone, James	1	0	0	0	2
Reid, Dave	2	0	0	0	2
Moreland, Jake	2	0	0	0	0
Stanfield, Rob	1	0	0	0	0
Yeats, Matthew	8	0	0	0	0
Talbot, Joe	7	0	0	0	16
Stirling, Scott	12	0	0	0	4

GOALTENDING

	Gms.	Min.	W	L	T	G	SO	Avg.
Moreland, Jake	2	106	2	0	0	3	0	1.69
Stirling, Scott	12	638	8	4	0	22	3	2.07
Yeats, Matthew	8	396	4	0	1	16	1	2.42

CINCINNATI CYCLONES

(Lost conference finals to Atlantic City Boardwalk Bullies)

SCORING

	Games	G	A	Pts.	PIM
Bootland, Nick	15	10	7	17	10
Casselman, Mike	15	3	11	14	12
Cardarelli, Joe	15	3	8	11	4
Noga, Matt	15	2	8	10	6
Brand, Aaron	15	4	5	9	12
Gaucher, Ryan	11	2	7	9	12
Norrie, Jason	15	5	3	8	13
Strand, Paul	15	2	4	6	28
Gallace, Steve	15	2	3	5	18
Twordik, Brent	14	3	2	5	23
Rodberg, Steve	15	1	4	5	10
Baker, Korey	15	1	2	3	4
Cannon, Jason	15	1	2	3	18
Turner, Tim	15	1	1	2	10
Bergin, Kevin	4	0	0	0	0
Hewitt, Greg	11	0	0	0	0
McIver, Chad	15	0	0	0	12
Labenski, Greg	15	0	0	0	32
Hamerlik, Peter	6	0	0	0	0

GOALTENDING

	Gms.	Min.	W	L	T	G	SO	Avg.
Hewitt, Greg	11	622	6	4	1	24	1	2.31
Hamerlik, Peter	6	307	3	1	0	12	0	2.34

COLUMBIA INFERNO

(Lost Kelly Cup finals to Atlantic City Boardwalk Bullies)

SCORING

	Games	G	A	Pts.	PIM
Stringer, Rejean	17	3	14	17	12
Smith, Tim	17	5	11	16	16
Carruthers, Robin	17	9	5	14	8
Moore, Barrie	14	8	6	14	12
Demmans, Trevor	17	3	10	13	4
Ulwelling, Matt	17	3	10	13	18
Wansborough, Shawn	17	6	5	11	56
Hay, Darrell	17	2	9	11	23
St. Croix, Chris	17	1	7	8	24
Pittman, Chris	14	4	4	8	20

	Games	G	A	Pts.	PIM
Hessler, Corey	14	2	5	7	4
Owens, Sean	16	3	3	6	13
Labelle, Eric	16	1	5	6	52
Cabana, Paul	11	2	1	3	16
Martynyuk, Denis	12	2	0	2	8
Darby, Regan	17	0	1	1	20
Vial, Dennis	17	0	1	1	27
Way, Clint	3	0	0	0	0
Blackburn, Josh	3	0	0	0	0
Morrison, Justin	2	0	0	0	4
Couture, Patrick	16	0	0	0	0

GOALTENDING

	Gms.	Min.	W	L	T	G	SO	Avg.
Couture, Patrick	16	893	9	4	1	31	0	2.08
Blackburn, Josh	3	146	2	1	0	7	0	2.87

FLORIDA EVERBLADES

(Lost wild card to Greenville Grrrowl)

SCORING

	Games	G	A	Pts.	PIM
Meunier, Laurent	1	1	1	2	0
Goudie, Brian	1	0	1	1	0
McDonald, Brent	1	1	0	1	2
Buckley, Tom	1	0	1	1	0
Curry, Sean	1	0	0	0	0
Awada, George	1	0	0	0	0
Harmer, Duane	1	0	0	0	0
Johnston, Marty	1	0	0	0	0
Smith, Don	1	0	0	0	2
Blaznek, Joe	1	0	0	0	0
Insana, Jon	1	0	0	0	0
Hill, Ed	1	0	0	0	0
Reynolds, Peter	1	0	0	0	0
Anderson, Keith	1	0	0	0	0
Leitza, Brian	1	0	0	0	0
Murphy, Ryan	1	0	0	0	0
Brown, Kevin	1	0	0	0	2

GOALTENDING

	Gms.	Min.	W	L	T	G	SO	Avg.
Leitza, Brian	1	58	0	1	0	3	0	3.08

GREENSBORO GENERALS

(Lost division finals to Atlantic City Boardwalk Bullies)

SCORING

	Games	G	A	Pts.	PIM
Murphy, Jay	8	5	7	12	10
Bayrack, Mike	8	2	8	10	4
Richardson, Bryan	8	3	4	7	20
Turner, Mark	8	3	4	7	8
Ftorek, Sam	8	2	4	6	26
Drummond, Kurtis	8	2	3	5	14
Aldoff, Rod	8	2	2	4	4
Gardiner, Pete	8	1	3	4	10
Turek, Matt	8	2	2	4	4
Parrish, Geno	8	0	3	3	8
Whitworth, David	8	2	1	3	8
Campbell, Shane	8	0	3	3	10
Grimes, Kevin	8	2	0	2	27
Marakhovski, Roman	8	0	1	1	6
Oliveira, Mike	1	0	0	0	0
Andreyev, Alex	7	0	0	0	5
Chandler, Matt	7	0	0	0	2
Berthiaume, Daniel	8	0	0	0	0

GOALTENDING

	Gms.	Min.	W	L	T	G	SO	Avg.
Berthiaume, Daniel	8	482	4	3	1	24	0	2.98

GREENVILLE GRRROWL

(Lost division semifinals to Columbia Inferno)

SCORING

	Games	G	A	Pts.	PIM
Flache, Paul	4	0	4	4	6
Lynch, Chris	4	1	3	4	18
Henderson, Mike	4	2	2	4	2
Demarski, Matt	4	2	2	4	2
Masa, Martin	4	1	2	3	6
Medak, Judd	4	0	3	3	6
Flache, Peter	4	3	0	3	2
Nail, John	4	0	2	2	0
Deis, Tyler	4	1	1	2	12
Wismer, Chris	4	1	1	2	2
Fatticci, Rico	4	1	1	2	2
Legge, Josh	4	0	1	1	4
Lind, Eric	4	1	0	1	4
Theuer, Chad	4	0	1	1	2
Rhodes, Damian	1	0	0	0	0
Kaczowka, David	4	0	0	0	18
Gouett, Mark	4	0	0	0	4
Garnett, Michael	3	0	0	0	0

GOALTENDING

	Gms.	Min.	W	L	T	G	SO	Avg.
Garnett, Michael	3	178	1	2	0	13	0	4.38
Rhodes, Damian	1	60	0	1	0	6	0	6.00

JACKSON BANDITS

(Lost wild card to Pensacola Ice Pilots)

SCORING

	Games	G	A	Pts.	PIM
Gauvreau, Brent	1	1	1	2	0
Gillam, Sean	1	1	0	1	0
Lupandin, Andrei	1	0	1	1	0
Fortier, Eric	1	0	1	1	0
Olson, Josh	1	0	1	1	0
Rome, Reagan	1	0	0	0	0
Laplante, Darryl	1	0	0	0	0
Bes, Jeff	1	0	0	0	4
Stewart, Dave	1	0	0	0	10
Kelman, Scott	1	0	0	0	4
O'Connor, Sean	1	0	0	0	0
Vigilante, Mike	1	0	0	0	0
MacIver, Doug	1	0	0	0	0
Theriault, Nick	1	0	0	0	2
Forslund, Bryan	1	0	0	0	0
Mackie, Kevin	1	0	0	0	0
Garner, Tyrone	1	0	0	0	0

GOALTENDING

	Gms.	Min.	W	L	T	G	SO	Avg.
Garner, Tyrone	1	76	0	0	1	3	0	2.35

LEXINGTON MEN O'WAR

(Lost division semifinals to Toledo Storm)

SCORING

	Games	G	A	Pts.	PIM
Burgess, Van	3	1	1	2	2
Sgroi, Mike	3	0	1	1	14
Draney, Brett	3	1	0	1	10
Storey, Ben	3	0	1	1	4
Periard, Dominic	3	0	1	1	5
Murphy, Dan	2	0	0	0	0
Dirkes, Chris	2	0	0	0	0
Mathieu, Alexandre	3	0	0	0	6
Cook, Jesse	3	0	0	0	5
Smith, Mark	3	0	0	0	0
Smyth, Jared	3	0	0	0	0

	Games	G	A	Pts.	PIM
Fultz, Ryan	3	0	0	0	2
Banach, Jay	3	0	0	0	4
Van Parys, Justin	3	0	0	0	8
Mizerek, Josh	3	0	0	0	0
Knopp, Kevin	3	0	0	0	11
Smith, Mike	2	0	0	0	0
Vandermeer, Joe	3	0	0	0	0

GOALTENDING

	Gms.	Min.	W	L	T	G	SO	Avg.
Smith, Mike	2	93	0	1	0	8	0	5.14
Murphy, Dan	2	85	0	2	0	8	0	5.64

LOUISIANA ICEGATORS

(Lost division finals to Mississippi Sea Wolves)

SCORING

	Games	G	A	Pts.	PIM
Bartek, Martin	6	1	3	4	4
Rempel, Nathan	5	4	0	4	2
Proskurnicki, Andrew	6	3	1	4	0
McNeil, Shawn	6	1	2	3	8
Brown, Bobby	6	1	2	3	6
Mitchell, Kevin	6	0	2	2	10
Kesselring, Casey	6	0	2	2	4
Ben-Amor, Semir	6	1	1	2	6
Benazic, Cal	6	0	2	2	14
DePourcq, John	2	0	1	1	2
Sarich, Rod	6	0	1	1	6
Corupe, Kenny	6	0	1	1	0
Skiehar, Shawn	6	0	1	1	7
Kettles, Kyle	6	0	1	1	0
Boogaard, Derek	2	0	0	0	0
Morin, J.P.	6	0	0	0	0
Mass, Louis	3	0	0	0	0
Taliercio, Chris	1	0	0	0	0
Mastad, Milt	6	0	0	0	6

GOALTENDING

	Gms.	Min.	W	L	T	G	SO	Avg.
Kettles, Kyle	6	359	3	3	0	13	1	2.17

MISSISSIPPI SEA WOLVES

(Lost conference finals to Columbia Inferno)

SCORING

	Games	G	A	Pts.	PIM
Kuznetsov, Sergei	12	7	9	16	6
Walby, Steffon	12	5	9	14	2
Paradise, Dave	11	5	8	13	10
Scott, Mike	12	6	6	12	8
Davyduke, Kent	12	3	9	12	8
Bowtell, Cody	12	4	7	11	6
Baxter, Jim	5	2	6	8	0
Lisabeth, Travis	12	1	5	6	33
Cornacchia, David	11	2	3	5	20
Evangelista, John	12	2	3	5	21
Miller, Austin	11	0	4	4	12
Campbell, Darryl	12	3	0	3	14
Hutchins, Jeff	10	0	3	3	36
Peach, Sean	12	0	1	1	8
Clark, Ryan	12	1	0	1	12
Cava, Chris	3	0	1	1	0
Allen, Chris	5	0	0	0	4
Pietersma, Stu	2	0	0	0	4
Rochon, Patrick	12	0	0	0	18
Bennett, Josh	2	0	0	0	0
Gardner, Greg	12	0	0	0	2

GOALTENDING

	Gms.	Min.	W	L	T	G	SO	Avg.
Gardner, Greg	12	740	8	3	1	25	1	2.03

PEE DEE PRIDE

(Lost division finals to Columbia Inferno)

SCORING

	Games	G	A	Pts.	PIM
Fregoe, Peter	7	1	4	5	4
Kidney, Kyle	7	2	2	4	6
Goldie, Wes	7	3	1	4	2
Schmidt, Greg	7	1	3	4	4
Carriere, Daniel	7	1	2	3	4
Naud, Eric	7	1	2	3	34
Reid, Matt	7	1	1	2	14
Sirois, Allan	7	2	0	2	12
Adams, B.J.	7	2	0	2	12
Mizzi, Preston	7	1	1	2	18
Metcalfe, Jason	7	0	2	2	8
Knox, Ryan	3	0	1	1	2
Torney, Mike	6	0	1	1	21
Gates, Aaron	7	0	1	1	17
Robinson, Jason	1	0	0	0	0
Anderson, Rob	1	0	0	0	0
Halldorson, Derek	7	0	0	0	2
Vogel, Ron	7	0	0	0	4

GOALTENDING

	Gms.	Min.	W	L	T	G	SO	Avg.
Vogel, Ron	7	413	3	4	0	22	1	3.19
Anderson, Rob	1	20	0	0	0	2	0	6.00

PENSACOLA ICE PILOTS

(Lost division semifinals to Mississippi Sea Wolves)

SCORING

	Games	G	A	Pts.	PIM
Pankewicz, Greg	4	3	1	4	0
Dexter, Brad	4	1	1	2	2
Ellis-Tdingtn, Kerry	4	2	0	2	2
Dumont, Louis	4	0	2	2	6
Allman, Trevor	4	0	2	2	4
Van Acker, Eric	4	0	2	2	2
Cloutier, Kevin	4	0	2	2	6
Van Hoof, Jeremy	4	0	1	1	4
Foremsky, Taras	4	0	0	0	4
Mathieu, Marquis	4	0	0	0	4
Jones, Mike	4	0	0	0	6
Mortier, Darren	4	0	0	0	0
Minard, Chris	4	0	0	0	6
O'Keefe, Ryan	4	0	0	0	0
Cruikshank, Brad	4	0	0	0	22
Gingras, Maxime	4	0	0	0	0
Poapst, Matt	4	0	0	0	4

GOALTENDING

	Gms.	Min.	W	L	T	G	SO	Avg.
Gingras, Maxime	4	256	1	3	0	17	0	3.98

PEORIA RIVERMEN

(Lost division semifinals to Cincinnati Cyclones)

SCORING

	Games	G	A	Pts.	PIM
Clark, Darren	3	2	1	3	4
Baker, Trevor	4	0	3	3	14
Rennette, Tyler	4	1	2	3	6
Davis, Greg	4	1	1	2	2
Kinos, Lauri	4	1	1	2	2

	Games	G	A	Pts.	PIM
Granato, Kevin	4	0	2	2	0
Finnerty, Ryan	4	2	0	2	8
Crawford, Scott	4	1	1	2	0
Rekis, Arvid	4	0	2	2	2
Nelson, Mike	3	0	1	1	0
Belza, Anthony	1	0	0	0	0
Voth, Brad	2	0	0	0	0
Kern, Josh	1	0	0	0	0
Michaud, Alfie	2	0	0	0	0
Starling, Chad	4	0	0	0	4
DeCecco, Bret	4	0	0	0	2
Rowe, Randy	4	0	0	0	2
Derksen, Duane	2	0	0	0	0
Booth, Derek	4	0	0	0	0
Lawmaster, Jason	4	0	0	0	4

GOALTENDING

	Gms.	Min.	W	L	T	G	SO	Avg.
Derksen, Duane	2	132	1	0	1	2	0	0.91
Michaud, Alfie	2	141	0	1	1	8	0	3.40

ROANOKE EXPRESS

(Lost division semifinals to Greensboro Generals)

SCORING

	Games	G	A	Pts.	PIM
Dusbabek, Joe	4	2	3	5	8
Limpright, Shawn	4	1	2	3	0
Bristow, Cam	4	1	2	3	10
Mazurak, Chad	4	2	1	3	2
Jaffray, Jason	4	0	3	3	4
Carlson, Dan	4	1	2	3	8
Novock, Frank	4	1	1	2	6
Barker, Josh	4	0	2	2	2
Schueller, Doug	4	1	0	1	4
Dalmao, Duncan	4	0	1	1	0
Peron, Mike	4	1	0	1	4
Kowalsky, Rick	4	0	1	1	6
Fischer, Cole	4	0	0	0	7
Silverstone, David	4	0	0	0	9
Essex, Brad	4	0	0	0	9
Lindsay, Evan	4	0	0	0	0
Balan, Scott	4	0	0	0	2

GOALTENDING

	Gms.	Min.	W	L	T	G	SO	Avg.
Lindsay, Evan	4	237	1	3	0	16	0	4.03

SOUTH CAROLINA STINGRAYS

(Lost division semifinals to Pee Dee Pride)

SCORING

	Games	G	A	Pts.	PIM
Irving, Joel	4	3	2	5	14
Seitz, Dave	4	1	4	5	4
Johnson, Trevor	4	3	1	4	10
Brindley, Ryan	4	2	2	4	0
Calder, Adam	4	0	2	2	17
Gomez, Robin	4	1	1	2	14
Schneekloth, Aaron	4	1	1	2	6
Powers, Andy	4	0	1	1	2
Huppe, Curtis	4	0	1	1	2
Williamson, Brad	4	0	1	1	6
Henley, Brent	4	0	1	1	4
Marietti, Brett	4	1	0	1	4
Boulanger, Jeff	4	1	0	1	4
Daubenspeck, Kirk	4	0	1	1	2
Spiller, Richard	1	0	0	0	2
Clapton, Marty	4	0	0	0	4
Desrosiers, Matt	4	0	0	0	2
Armbrust, Peter	4	0	0	0	0

GOALTENDING

	Gms.	Min.	W	L	T	G	SO	Avg.
Daubenspeck, Kirk	4	253	1	2	1	12	0	2.84

TOLEDO STORM

(Lost division finals to Cincinnati Cyclones)

SCORING

	Games	G	A	Pts.	PIM
Mason, Wes	7	2	6	8	12
Ellis, Matt	7	3	5	8	0
Anderson, Erik	7	3	4	7	6
Brown, Jim	7	2	4	6	12
Verbeek, Tim	7	4	2	6	15
Moore, Grady	7	0	5	5	6
Mitchell, Jeff	7	3	1	4	37
Waltze, Kris	4	1	2	3	4
Lutz, Nathan	7	1	1	2	9
Read, Trevor	7	0	2	2	4
Johnstone, Jeff	7	1	1	2	0
Parillo, Nick	7	0	2	2	0
Junkin, Dale	6	2	0	2	2
Fleenor, Brandon	6	0	1	1	4
Helbling, Timo	7	0	1	1	2
Ballantyne, Paul	7	0	1	1	2
Durak, Miroslav	1	0	0	0	2
Teskey, Doug	6	0	0	0	0
Payette, Andre	3	0	0	0	0
Finley, Brian	1	0	0	0	0

GOALTENDING

	Gms.	Min.	W	L	T	G	SO	Avg.
Teskey, Doug	6	357	4	2	0	7	2	1.17
Finley, Brian	1	60	0	1	0	4	0	4.00

TRENTON TITANS

(Lost division semifinals to Atlantic City Boardwalk Bullies)

SCORING

	Games	G	A	Pts.	PIM
Bertoli, Scott	3	0	3	3	2
Beechey, Tyler	3	2	0	2	0
Edinger, Adam	3	0	2	2	0
Charpentier, Marco	3	1	1	2	0
Williams, Vince	3	0	1	1	8
Betournay, Eric	3	1	0	1	2
O'Brien, Steve	3	0	1	1	0
Kilbourne, B.J.	2	1	0	1	0
Connolly, Sean	3	0	1	1	0
Wood, Dustin	3	0	1	1	2
Zultek, Matt	3	1	0	1	2
Smith, Jeff	2	0	1	1	2
Tetrault, Daniel	1	0	0	0	0
Apps, Syl	1	0	0	0	4
Smith, Jeff	1	0	0	0	4
Rudkowsky, Cody	3	0	0	0	0
White, Kam	3	0	0	0	18
Forbes, Ian	3	0	0	0	2
Hurley, Mike	3	0	0	0	6
Herneisen, Matt	2	0	0	0	2

GOALTENDING

	Gms.	Min.	W	L	T	G	SO	Avg.
Rudkowsky, Cody	3	178	0	3	0	14	0	4.72

2002-03 AWARD WINNERS

ALL-STAR TEAMS

Southern	Pos.	Northern
Rob Zepp, Florida	G	Scott Stirling, Atlantic City
Kevin Mitchell, Louisiana	D	Simon Tremblay, Reading
Jim Baxter, Mississippi	D	Ryan Gaucher, Cincinnati
Rejean Stringer, Columbia	F	Jason Jaffray, Roanoke
Buddy Smith, Arkansas	F	Tyler Rennette, Peoria
Steffon Walby, Mississippi	F	Kevin Colley, Atlantic City

TROPHY WINNERS

Most Valuable Player: Dennis Vial, Columbia
Mike Blumac, Pee Dee
Scoring leader: Buddy Smith, Arkansas
Outstanding defenseman: Jim Baxter, Mississippi
Outstanding goaltender: Alfie Michaud, Peoria
Rookie of the Year: Jason Jaffray, Roanoke
Playoff MVP: Kevin Colley, Atlantic City
Coach of the Year: Claude Noel, Toledo

ALL-TIME AWARD WINNERS

MOST VALUABLE PLAYER

Season	Player, Team
1988-89	Daryl Harpe, Erie
1989-90	Bill McDougall, Erie
1990-91	Stan Drulia, Knoxville
1991-92	Phil Berger, Greensboro
1992-93	Trevor Jobe, Nashville
1993-94	Joe Flanagan, Birmingham
1994-95	Vadim Slivchenko, Wheeling
1995-96	Hugo Belanger, Nashville
1996-97	Mike Ross, South Carolina
1997-98	Jamey Hicks, Birmingham
1998-99	Chris Valicevic, Louisiana
1999-00	Andrew Williamson, Toledo
2000-01	Scott King, Charlotte
2001-02	Frederic Cloutier, Louisiana
2002-03	Dennis Vial, Columbia
	Mike Blumac, Pee Dee

TOP SCORER

Season	Player, Team
1988-89	Daryl Harpe, Erie
1989-90	Bill McDougall, Erie
1990-91	Stan Drulia, Knoxville
1991-92	Phil Berger, Greensboro
1992-93	Trevor Jobe, Nashville
1993-94	Phil Berger, Greensboro
1994-95	Scott Burfoot, Erie
1995-96	Hugo Belanger, Nashville
1996-97	Ed Courtenay, South Carolina
	Mike Ross, South Carolina
1997-98	Jamey Hicks, Birmingham
1998-99	John Spoltore, Louisiana
1999-00	John Spoltore, Louisiana
2000-01	Scott King, Charlotte
2001-02	Louis Dumont, Pensacola
2002-03	Buddy Smith, Arkansas

ROOKIE OF THE YEAR

Season	Player, Team
1988-89	Tom Sasso, Johnstown
1989-90	Bill McDougall, Erie
1990-91	Dan Gauthier, Knoxville
1991-92	Darren Colbourne, Dayton
1992-93	Joe Flanagan, Birmingham
1993-94	Dan Gravelle, Greensboro
1994-95	Kevin McKinnon, Erie
1995-96	Keli Corpse, Wheeling
1996-97	Dany Bousquet, Birmingham
1997-98	Sean Venedam, Toledo
1998-99	Maxime Gingras, Richmond
1999-00	Jan Lasak, Hampton Roads
2000-01	Scott Stirling, Trenton
2001-02	Frederic Cloutier, Louisiana
2002-03	Jason Jaffray, Roanoke

TOP GOALTENDER

Season	Player, Team
1988-89	Scott Gordon, Johnstown
1989-90	Alain Raymond, Hampton Roads
1990-91	Dean Anderson, Knoxville
1991-92	Frederic Chabot, Winston-Salem
1992-93	Nick Vitucci, Hampton Roads
1993-94	Cory Cadden, Knoxville
1994-95	Chris Gordon, Huntington
1995-96	Alain Morissette, Louisville
1996-97	Marc Delorme, Louisiana
1997-98	Nick Vitucci, Toledo
1998-99	Maxime Gingras, Richmond
1999-00	Jan Lasak, Hampton Roads
2000-01	Scott Stirling, Trenton
2001-02	Frederic Cloutier, Louisiana
2002-03	Alfie Michaud, Peoria

PLAYOFF MVP

Season	Player, Team
1988-89	Nick Vitucci, Carolina
1989-90	Wade Flaherty, Greensboro
1990-91	Dave Gagnon, Hampton Rds.
	Flanagan, Hampton Roads
1991-92	Mark Bernard, Hampton Roads
1992-93	Rick Judson, Toledo
1993-94	Dave Gagnon, Toledo
1994-95	Blaine Moore, Richmond
1995-96	Nick Vitucci, Charlotte
1996-97	Jason Fitzsimmons, South Carolina
1997-98	Sebastian Charpentier, Hampton Roads
1998-99	Travis Scott, Mississippi
1999-00	J.F. Boutin, Peoria
	Jason Christie, Peoria
2000-01	Dave Seitz, South Carolina
2001-02	Simon Gamache, Greenville
	Tyrone Garner, Greenville
2002-03	Kevin Colley, Atlantic City

COACH OF THE YEAR

Season	Coach, Team
1988-89	Ron Hansis, Erie
1989-90	Dave Allison, Virginia
1990-91	Don Jackson, Knoxville
1991-92	Doug Sauter, Winston-Salem
1992-93	Kurt Kleinendorst, Raleigh
1993-94	Barry Smith, Knoxville
1994-95	Jim Playfair, Dayton
1995-96	Roy Sommer, Richmond
1996-97	Brian McCutcheon, Columbus
1997-98	Chris Nilan, Chesapeake
1998-99	Bob Ferguson, Florida
1999-00	Bob Ferguson, Florida

MINOR LEAGUES ECHL

Season	Player, Team
2000-01	Troy Ward, Trenton
2001-02	Dave Farrish, Louisiana
2002-03	Claude Noel, Toledo

TOP DEFENSEMAN

Season	Player, Team
1988-89	Kelly Szautner, Erie
1989-90	Bill Whitfield, Virginia
1990-91	Brett McDonald, Nashville
1991-92	Scott White, Greensboro
1992-93	Derek Booth, Toledo

Season	Player, Team
1993-94	Tom Nemeth, Dayton
1994-95	Brandon Smith, Dayton
1995-96	Chris Valicevic, Louisiana
1996-97	Chris Valicevic, Louisiana
1997-98	Chris Valicevic, Louisiana
1998-99	Chris Valicevic, Louisiana
1999-00	Tom Nemeth, Dayton
2000-01	Tom Nemeth, Dayton
2001-02	Duncan Dalmao, Roanoke
2002-03	Jim Baxter, Mississippi

ALL-TIME LEAGUE CHAMPIONS

	REGULAR-SEASON CHAMPION		PLAYOFF CHAMPION	
Season	Team	Coach	Team	Coach
1988-89	Erie Panthers	Ron Hansis	Carolina Thunderbirds	Brendon Watson
1989-90	Winston-Salem Thunderbirds	C. McSorley, J. Fraser	Greensboro Monarchs	Jeff Brubaker
1990-91	Knoxville Cherokees	Don Jackson	Hampton Roads Admirals	John Brophy
1991-92	Toledo Storm	Chris McSorley	Hampton Roads Admirals	John Brophy
1992-93	Wheeling Thunderbirds	Doug Sauter	Toledo Storm	Chris McSorley
1993-94	Knoxville Cherokees	Barry Smith	Toledo Storm	Chris McSorley
1994-95	Wheeling Thunderbirds	Doug Sauter	Richmond Renegades	Roy Sommer
1995-96	Richmond Renegades	Roy Sommer	Charlotte Checkers	John Marks
1996-97	South Carolina Stingrays	Rick Vaive	South Carolina Stingrays	Rick Vaive
1997-98	Louisiana Icegators	Doug Shedden	Hampton Roads Admirals	John Brophy
1998-99	Pee Dee Pride	Jack Capuano	Mississippi Sea Wolves	Bruce Boudreau
1999-00	Florida Everblades	Bob Ferguson	Peoria Rivermen	Don Granato
2000-01	Trenton Titans	Troy Ward	South Carolina Stingrays	Rick Adduono
2001-02	Louisiana Icegators	Dave Farrish	Greenville Grrrowl	John Marks
2002-03	Toledo Storm	Claude Noel	Atl. City Boardwalk Bullies	Mike Haviland

The ECHL regular season champion is awarded the Brabham Cup. The playoff champion was awarded the Riley Cup through the 1995-96 season. Playoff champions are now awarded the Patrick J. Kelly Cup.

CENTRAL HOCKEY LEAGUE

2002-03 REGULAR SEASON
FINAL STANDINGS

NORTHERN CONFERENCE

NORTHEAST DIVISION

Team	G	W	L	SOL	Pts.	GF	GA
Indianapolis	64	39	16	9	87	206	173
Memphis	64	39	21	4	82	235	190
Bossier-Shreveport	64	33	22	9	75	206	176
Fort Worth	64	16	41	7	39	146	251

NORTHWEST DIVISION

Team	G	W	L	SOL	Pts.	GF	GA
Oklahoma City	64	37	20	7	81	225	196
Amarillo	64	39	23	2	80	205	176
Tulsa	64	37	22	5	79	218	195
Wichita	64	21	35	8	50	216	261

SOUTHERN CONFERENCE

SOUTHEAST DIVISION

Team	G	W	L	SOL	Pts.	GF	GA
Austin	64	46	14	4	96	198	139
Laredo	64	41	17	6	88	253	184
Corpus Christi	64	31	30	3	65	197	204
San Angelo	64	20	36	8	48	196	272

SOUTHWEST DIVISION

Team	G	W	L	SOL	Pts.	GF	GA
Odessa	64	35	22	7	77	195	185
New Mexico	64	31	28	5	67	185	195
Lubbock	64	29	28	7	65	212	215
El Paso	64	18	40	6	42	184	265

INDIVIDUAL LEADERS

Goals: Don Parsons, Memphis (57)
Assists: Blair Manning, Oklahoma City (59)
Points: Don Parsons, Memphis (106)
Penalty minutes: Kori Davison, San Angelo (380)
Goaltending average: Matt Barnes, Austin (1.96)
Shutouts: Matt Barnes, Austin (8)
Rod Branch, Tulsa (8)

TOP SCORERS

	Games	G	A	Pts.
Parsons, Don, MEM	64	57	49	106
Marcellus, Todd, TUL	64	40	53	93
Clayton, Travis, WIC	63	35	57	92
Grenville, Chris, LAR	64	40	50	90
Burton, Joe, OKC	64	46	38	84
Duda, Jason, WIC	64	31	52	83
Manning, Blair, OKC	64	23	59	82
Schneider, Eric, LAR	44	38	43	81

	Games	G	A	Pts.
St. Jacques, Kevin, IND	64	22	56	78
Richards, Chris, NMX	62	30	46	76
Emersic, Blaz, LUB	63	33	40	73
Smart, Kelly, AUS	64	29	42	71
Dupaul, Cosmo, CRP	62	29	42	71
Gilmore, Dave, LAR	56	27	44	71
Baird, Jason, IND	64	26	44	70
Rutter, Mike, ODE	64	22	48	70
Kuster, Henry, AMA	64	36	33	69
Peach, Chris, SNG	64	23	44	67
Thomas, Kahlil, MEM	63	23	44	67
Sauter, Hardy, OKC	59	10	57	67
Gomes, Tom, WIC	64	28	38	66
Wildfong, Dan, BOS	61	27	39	66
Baines, Tyler, NMX	63	25	41	66
John, Bernie, IND	64	14	52	66
Sicinski, John, CRP	64	30	35	65

INDIVIDUAL STATISTICS

AMARILLO GORILLAS
SCORING

	Games	G	A	Pts.	PIM
Kuster, Henry	64	36	33	69	49
Anneck, Dorian	64	25	38	63	34
Hahn, Derek	46	25	27	52	14
Carper, Brandon	64	18	32	50	36
DeSantis, Mark	64	7	41	48	106
Maidment, Ben	58	15	30	45	61
Gustavson, Ben	63	12	30	42	98
Wray, Scott	56	17	16	33	108
Dean, John	64	12	19	31	56
Pellerin, Brian	59	11	18	29	110
Curry, Darren	59	12	15	27	30
Rattray, David	63	9	13	22	163
Shannon, Ryan	63	2	7	9	77
Robertson, Chris	16	1	6	7	18
Andersen, Eric	62	2	4	6	159
Posillico, Neil	59	1	3	4	228
Brown, Matt	62	0	2	2	75
Debus, Steve	38	0	1	1	6
Cholak, Justin	2	0	0	0	0
Degagne, Shawn	32	0	0	0	21
Schabes, Justin	6	0	0	0	4

	Games	G	A	Pts.	PIM
St. Louis, Todd	7	0	0	0	34
Wright, Jason	1	0	0	0	0

GOALTENDING

	Games	Min.	W	L	OTL	G	SO	Avg.
Degagne, Shawn	32	1737	19	10	0	73	3	2.52
Debus, Steve	38	2124	20	13	2	95	3	2.68
Wright, Jason	1	28	0	0	0	3	0	6.21

AUSTIN ICE BATS
SCORING

	Games	G	A	Pts.	PIM
Smart, Kelly	64	29	42	71	49
Price, Dan	62	27	37	64	85
Tallaire, Gerald	64	25	37	62	58
Seguin, Brett	53	16	38	54	36
Lardner, Tab	64	21	28	49	64
Gaffney, Mike	61	14	28	42	58
McArthur, Darryl	61	14	24	38	134
Brownlee, Pat	64	12	20	32	34
Legault, Shawn	40	13	14	27	251
Sharuga, Matt	56	8	19	27	48
Rees, Mike	64	5	18	23	149

	Games	G	A	Pts.	PIM
Olynyk, Mike	60	4	11	15	135
Greenlaw, Jeff	49	4	6	10	88
McCallum, Scott	60	1	9	10	124
Rivard, Ryan	37	4	4	8	142
Johnson, Doug	64	1	3	4	51
Larocque, Ian	5	0	2	2	12
Ponte, Randy	25	0	2	2	98
Kresac, Jaroslav	6	0	1	1	2
Barnes, Matt	47	0	0	0	2
Brady, Peter	17	0	0	0	0
Fournier, Kevin	4	0	0	0	0
O'Brien, Keith	5	0	0	0	8

GOALTENDING

	Games	Min.	W	L	OTL	G	SO	Avg.
Barnes, Matt	47	2848	33	10	4	93	8	1.96
Brady, Peter	17	1023	13	4	0	39	0	2.29

BOSSIER-SHREVEPORT MUDBUGS

SCORING

	Games	G	A	Pts.	PIM
Wildfong, Dan	61	27	39	66	250
MacPherson, Forbes	58	28	33	61	57
Campbell, Jason	59	25	26	51	27
Buchanan, Trevor	64	17	30	47	102
Brassard, Chris	45	11	26	37	98
Oliver, David	42	14	21	35	61
Spurr, Chad	47	13	15	28	44
Bergin, Tony	61	9	16	25	71
Minard, Craig	63	6	19	25	42
Burgess, Dru	64	8	15	23	16
Glowa, Jeff	64	7	15	22	36
Sprott, Jim	63	13	9	22	142
Basile, Jason	64	5	12	17	56
Hubloo, Willie	56	4	9	13	23
Rupnow, Mark	16	7	4	11	17
Chelios, Chris	39	2	6	8	63
McGee, Jay	26	4	4	8	20
Theoret, Luc	23	1	7	8	43
Dougan, Darren	8	3	1	4	4
Hodgson, Gavin	33	2	2	4	22
Maruk, Jon	6	0	2	2	6
Carroll, Ken	44	0	1	1	6
Forest, Jonathan	23	0	0	0	0
Kern, Derek	2	0	0	0	2
Mills, David	19	0	0	0	28

GOALTENDING

	Games	Min.	W	L	OTL	G	SO	Avg.
Carroll, Ken	44	2605	25	14	4	96	4	2.21
Forest, Jonathan	23	1288	8	8	5	66	0	3.07

CORPUS CHRISTI ICERAYS

SCORING

	Games	G	A	Pts.	PIM
Dupaul, Cosmo	62	29	42	71	36
Sicinski, John	64	30	35	65	30
Richardson, Ken	52	23	23	46	239
Tilson, Mike	40	15	22	37	98
Roland, Layne	32	15	20	35	20
Hogue, Russell	53	5	29	34	16
Fairweather, Shaun	53	11	21	32	18
Prentice, Ryan	43	9	20	29	53
Jabrocky, Jaroslav	40	12	15	27	10
Brandvold, Trent	64	7	18	25	88
Giffin, Rob	20	7	17	24	12
Colborne, Brett	27	4	16	20	47
Carriere, Jason	64	3	11	14	89
Bourque, David	26	1	12	13	28
Beck, Martin	38	4	6	10	32
Goetz, Ken	61	6	4	10	374
Bumstead, Geoff	10	3	4	7	11
Fail, Robert	14	2	5	7	10
Cilladi, John	39	1	5	6	46
Munro, Matt	24	3	3	6	14
Nelson, Chad	9	1	5	6	33
Marks, Lloyd	12	2	3	5	15
Belecki, Brent	58	0	2	2	0

	Games	G	A	Pts.	PIM
Kholomeyev, Alex	6	2	0	2	6
Bina, Jerod	3	0	1	1	2
Lewis, Roger	13	0	1	1	14
Renard, Jason	10	1	0	1	65
Savioli, Joe	9	0	1	1	6
Sharuga, Matt	8	1	0	1	21
Hollens, Chris	2	0	0	0	0
Miller, Aren	2	0	0	0	0
Skazyk, Eddy	7	0	0	0	0
Werfelman, Cam	4	0	0	0	0

GOALTENDING

	Games	Min.	W	L	OTL	G	SO	Avg.
Belecki, Brent	58	3417	29	26	3	158	2	2.77
Skazyk, Eddy	7	352	2	3	0	30	0	5.11
Miller, Aren	2	91	0	1	0	9	0	5.90

EL PASO BUZZARDS

SCORING

	Games	G	A	Pts.	PIM
Upton, Derrell	64	23	38	61	20
Scharf, Jeff	52	22	37	59	21
Guzior, Russ	55	29	24	53	54
Linna, Troy	56	23	23	46	79
Gray, Joe	53	16	26	42	98
Tessier, Jason	64	9	29	38	87
Dudley, Rhett	46	6	29	35	103
Vokes, Jeremy	64	17	13	30	40
Tymchak, Josh	47	9	14	23	228
Rapoza, Bob	41	9	13	22	14
Forsberg, Markus	43	9	8	17	61
Zeibaq, Mike	64	2	15	17	158
Paul, Mathieu	39	1	15	16	80
Mahar, Scott	63	2	12	14	142
Potter, Jeff	34	2	7	9	27
Reynolds, Derek	15	4	4	8	51
Grasso, Joey	7	1	1	2	2
McKinlay, Derek	12	0	2	2	11
Carmichael, Matt	23	0	1	1	0
Sawyer, Mike	3	0	1	1	0
Baier, Josh	4	0	0	0	0
Bolduc, Tommy	15	0	0	0	69
Glenday, Pat	17	0	0	0	24
Lewis, Roger	1	0	0	0	0
Moore, Kenny	3	0	0	0	2
Ronayne, James	19	0	0	0	4
Russell, Blaine	27	0	0	0	0
Sawyer, Curtis	8	0	0	0	14
Weil, Tony	3	0	0	0	0

GOALTENDING

	Games	Min.	W	L	OTL	G	SO	Avg.
Carmichael, Matt	23	1268	6	14	2	67	0	3.17
Ronayne, James	19	975	4	12	0	69	1	4.25
Russell, Blaine	27	1419	8	12	4	102	1	4.31
Baier, Josh	4	184	0	2	0	15	0	4.89

FORT WORTH BRAHMAS

SCORING

	Games	G	A	Pts.	PIM
Woollard, Chad	60	35	24	59	182
Van Volsen, Joe	63	19	37	56	82
Reesor, Jason	60	8	22	30	20
Davis, Adam	64	8	15	23	54
Giffin, Rob	38	6	16	22	18
Midgley, Jim	44	6	16	22	10
Hughes, Sean	50	9	12	21	35
Williams, Justin	58	10	8	18	42
Marks, Lloyd	40	6	11	17	10
Warkus, T.J.	46	6	9	15	14
Grills, Chad	32	7	6	13	53
Tilson, Mike	23	3	10	13	38
Jacobson, Lee	64	1	8	9	273
Foddrill, Craig	10	5	3	8	0
Reeves, Kyle	7	3	5	8	10
Brandimore, Chad	9	0	7	7	2
Michalchuk, Chad	14	2	5	7	20
Murphy, John	50	0	7	7	365

	Games	G	A	Pts.	PIM
Rusk, Mike	33	2	5	7	26
Washbrook, Jeff	37	2	3	5	109
McKinnon, Mike	41	0	4	4	44
Cameron, Jeff	9	2	1	3	8
Rivard, Ryan	23	0	3	3	65
Somerville, Brant	12	1	2	3	4
Fry, David	11	1	1	2	6
Johnson, Craig	11	2	0	2	52
Curry, Darren	1	1	0	1	2
Fricker, Jason	32	0	1	1	0
Leibel, Cody	3	1	0	1	4
Munro, Matt	10	0	1	1	2
Batten, Cory	2	0	0	0	0
Droscher, Dustin	16	0	0	0	0
MacDonald, Cameron	3	0	0	0	0
Mullin, Matt	26	0	0	0	0
Saltarelli, Erasmo	15	0	0	0	0

GOALTENDING

	Games	Min.	W	L	OTL	G	SO	Avg.
Mullin, Matt	26	1401	5	13	4	73	0	3.12
Saltarelli, Erasmo	15	806	5	7	2	51	0	3.80
Fricker, Jason	32	1477	5	19	1	95	0	3.86
MacDonald, C.	3	161	1	2	0	13	0	4.84
Batten, Cory	2	21	0	0	0	5	0	13.73

INDIANAPOLIS ICE
SCORING

	Games	G	A	Pts.	PIM
St. Jacques, Kevin	64	22	56	78	86
Baird, Jason	64	26	44	70	98
John, Bernie	64	14	52	66	30
Dumba, Jared	47	27	20	47	33
Holmes, Randy	64	13	31	44	59
Morin, Etienne	59	25	15	40	12
Taylor, Andrew	59	13	24	37	63
Lewis, Scott	64	11	17	28	54
Olsen, Greg	63	11	16	27	149
Carter, Ryan	61	9	14	23	46
Classen, Bryce	64	12	10	22	30
Kearns, Justin	64	9	12	21	59
Aikia, Ryan	63	2	17	19	88
Elliott, Nate	64	8	8	16	37
Pool, Byron	46	0	7	7	118
Popp, Kevin	40	3	0	3	119
Morris, Jamie	22	0	2	2	18
Duplessis, Simon	15	1	0	1	25
Silver, Shawn	46	0	1	1	6
Suderman, Marc	5	0	1	1	2
Carroll, Jamie	2	0	0	0	2
Connell, Jerry	15	0	0	0	22
Sejna, Milan	9	0	0	0	4

GOALTENDING

	Games	Min.	W	L	OTL	G	SO	Avg.
Silver, Shawn	46	2719	29	12	4	100	6	2.21
Morris, Jamie	22	1184	10	4	5	62	1	3.14

LAREDO BUCKS
SCORING

	Games	G	A	Pts.	PIM
Grenville, Chris	64	40	50	90	48
Schneider, Eric	44	38	43	81	20
Gilmore, Dave	56	27	44	71	39
Periard, Michel	50	18	35	53	26
Ask, Morten	48	21	30	51	57
Dube, Serge	64	10	36	46	70
Kotsopoulos, Tom	51	13	31	44	69
Sewell, Joe	64	26	17	43	94
Lundbohm, Andy	37	10	24	34	54
Myson, David	64	12	18	30	270
Petruic, Jeff	26	13	15	28	8
Gove, David	8	4	12	16	15
Hyman, Dion	53	5	11	16	204
Stanfield, Rob	57	1	11	12	75
Weidlich, Steve	44	1	11	12	82
Jabrocky, Jaroslav	24	4	6	10	22
Cornish, Jeremy	40	2	7	9	159
Breen, Neil	19	2	4	6	29
Oke, Andrew	19	1	4	5	37

	Games	G	A	Pts.	PIM
Picard, Jean-Francoi	19	0	5	5	26
Smith, Matt	7	3	2	5	54
Ahearn, Mitch	19	0	0	4	6
Van Horlick, Matt	42	1	0	4	112
Keski-Kungas,Stefan	8	0	0	3	4
Leslie, Lance	48	0	0	3	0
Girvitch, Sandis	2	0	0	2	2
Leclerc, Marc-Andre	24	0	0	1	0
Varteressian, Marc	8	1	0	1	36
Duplain, Samuel	3	0	0	0	2
Duplessis, Simon	4	0	0	0	11
Ronnelow, Benny	7	0	0	0	2

GOALTENDING

	Games	Min.	W	L	OTL	G	SO	Avg.
Leclerc, Marc-Andre	24	1172	13	4	3	48	1	2.46
Leslie, Lance	48	2710	28	13	3	127	1	2.81

LUBBOCK COTTON KINGS
SCORING

	Games	G	A	Pts.	PIM
Emersic, Blaz	63	33	40	73	4
MacIntyre, Dave	62	26	38	64	92
Fioroni, Paul	63	20	36	56	118
Melichercik, Jan	54	20	35	55	34
Dawson, Mike	64	12	31	43	62
Kralj, Matic	64	17	24	41	58
Holland, Derek	49	7	30	37	107
McKinlay, Barry	55	15	20	35	55
Sheehan, James	60	6	26	32	78
Dewar, Jeff	55	8	20	28	85
Gauthier, Derek	31	10	17	27	74
Donskov, Anthony	55	15	9	24	40
Halfkenny, Julius	63	8	10	18	42
Hiebert, Mike	64	4	10	14	148
Ambler, Dave	58	7	4	11	156
Binns, Craig	35	3	5	8	33
Volk, Luke	40	1	5	6	24
Brusseau, Mike	53	0	4	4	19
Penko, Jure	17	0	0	0	2
Reigstad, Jared	9	0	0	0	10

GOALTENDING

	Games	Min.	W	L	OTL	G	SO	Avg.
Brusseau, Mike	53	3037	23	22	6	154	4	3.04
Penko, Jure	17	839	6	6	1	53	0	3.79

MEMPHIS RIVERKINGS
SCORING

	Games	G	A	Pts.	PIM
Parsons, Don	64	57	49	106	71
Thomas, Kahlil	63	23	44	67	74
Neal, Jay	57	20	41	61	53
Landmesser, Derek	63	13	44	57	151
Gagnon, Jonathan	44	26	22	48	55
Stastny, Michal	47	23	24	47	30
Mueller, Brad	58	14	17	31	118
Tucker, Brian	62	10	20	30	206
Nasato, Luch	53	4	25	29	133
Palahnuk, Robb	48	10	14	24	54
Gorewich, Ben	32	7	15	22	33
Aitken, A.J.	57	6	9	15	76
Cote, Riley	51	8	6	14	241
Visegorodcevs, Serge	48	7	7	14	28
Margeson, Stephen	27	0	8	8	42
Cunningham, Jerry	12	3	2	5	2
DiPalma, Anthony	39	1	4	5	52
Racine, Jean-Francoi	35	0	4	4	25
Zavoral, Vaclav	53	2	2	4	143
Currie, Kris	32	0	3	3	121
Johnson, Matt	12	1	2	3	0
Alcombrack, Jeff	18	0	2	2	8
Paul, Mathieu	10	0	2	2	15
Lakovic, Greg	7	0	1	1	21
Fricke, Kevin	2	0	0	0	0
Goetzinger, Jeremy	7	0	0	0	4
Richards, Mark	32	0	0	0	8

GOALTENDING

	Games	Min.	W	L	OTL	G	SO	Avg.
Racine, J-F	35	2050	22	9	3	94	0	2.75
Richards, Mark	32	1821	17	12	1	89	2	2.93

NEW MEXICO SCORPIONS

SCORING

	Games	G	A	Pts.	PIM
Richards, Chris	62	30	46	76	104
Baines, Tyler	63	25	41	66	56
Kupaks, Arturs	62	15	41	56	103
Brearley, Pete	55	25	29	54	18
Ambroziak, Peter	52	20	32	52	44
Gorewich, Ben	31	11	16	27	32
Dumoulin, Mario	32	8	12	20	47
Stahl, Craig	62	9	9	18	209
Mattersdorfer, Fred	30	5	12	17	16
Cameron, Jeff	31	2	14	16	42
Roy, Jasmin	21	7	7	14	29
O'Malley, Mike	44	5	6	11	27
Mauer, Nate	22	4	6	10	34
Margeson, Stephen	24	0	9	9	24
Peet, Shaun	62	1	8	9	240
Praznik, Tobin	11	3	6	9	2
Dean, Leigh	41	0	8	8	40
Hartinger, Vladimir	13	3	5	8	4
Rech, Neal	20	3	4	7	14
Robbins, Adam	20	3	3	6	49
Bourque, David	27	2	3	5	10
McPherson, Andrew	10	1	3	4	30
Alcombrack, Jeff	31	1	1	2	14
Beck, Martin	11	0	2	2	12
Caravaggio, Luciano	45	0	2	2	2
Currie, Kris	31	1	1	2	118
Plenzich, Dominic	20	1	1	2	13
Boucher, Tyler	8	0	1	1	17
Deitsch, Marc	6	0	1	1	2
Myers, Scott	23	0	1	1	6
Breen, Neil	4	0	0	0	0
Osipenko, Billy	1	0	0	0	2
Payne, Mike	25	0	0	0	65
Schulz, Jason	3	0	0	0	6
Sedlacek, Lukas	16	0	0	0	13

GOALTENDING

	Games	Min.	W	L	OTL	G	SO	Avg.
Caravaggio, L.	45	2574	25	16	2	107	2	2.49
Myers, Scott	23	1294	6	12	3	78	0	3.62

ODESSA JACKALOPES

SCORING

	Games	G	A	Pts.	PIM
Rutter, Mike	64	22	48	70	20
Hillman, Scott	62	16	45	61	38
Thinel, Sebastien	57	20	27	47	22
Bossio, John	57	26	20	46	61
Willers, Greg	63	12	28	40	58
Gatto, Greg	64	19	18	37	143
Green, Scott	44	14	17	31	23
Cressman, Matt	62	9	20	29	54
Margettie, Donnie	64	10	18	28	229
Francis, Dave	64	12	14	26	25
Hansen, Kevin	61	10	13	23	94
Kennedy, Travis	26	10	8	18	15
Yoder, Jami	55	1	16	17	52
Frid, Robert	61	8	7	15	225
Marois, Jerome	29	3	5	8	11
Desmarais, Denis	61	0	6	6	96
Stachniak, Pat	28	2	3	5	40
Cunningham, Jerry	14	1	3	4	0
Gorman, Mike	53	0	4	4	8
Doyle, Adam	24	0	3	3	39
Carney, Matt	8	0	2	2	0
Daniels, Charlie	5	0	0	0	0
Edwards, Ryan	11	0	0	0	19
Galatiuk, Rob	5	0	0	0	8
Kane, Andrew	4	0	0	0	2

GOALTENDING

	Games	Min.	W	L	OTL	G	SO	Avg.
Carney, Matt	8	459	6	2	0	18	0	2.35
Gorman, Mike	53	3183	28	18	6	142	4	2.68
Galatiuk, Rob	5	244	1	2	1	18	0	4.43

OKLAHOMA CITY BLAZERS

SCORING

	Games	G	A	Pts.	PIM
Burton, Joe	64	46	38	84	17
Manning, Blair	64	23	59	82	69
Sauter, Hardy	59	10	57	67	30
DuBois, Jonathan	64	18	43	61	170
Standish, Marty	64	24	29	53	174
Robertson, Peter	63	10	29	39	42
Arvanitis, Peter	57	23	11	34	123
Shields, Dave	63	17	17	34	190
Watson, Ryan	54	15	15	30	42
Campbell, Ryan	64	12	16	28	67
Fleck, Tyler	64	5	13	18	223
Roy, Jasmin	35	6	4	10	76
Borsheim, Les	62	1	8	9	250
Laurila, Tim	46	1	8	9	45
Stone, Derek	46	2	7	9	79
Dumba, Jared	15	5	2	7	18
Mamane, Shawn	8	2	3	5	6
Cefalo, Marco	14	1	3	4	46
Quilty, Jim	17	0	4	4	19
Weisgerber, Trevor	11	2	2	4	10
Kot, Justin	14	2	1	3	11
Payne, Mike	18	0	3	3	59
Ballard, Boyd	47	0	2	2	6
Migdal, Thomas	14	0	2	2	13
Miller, Aren	12	0	1	1	0
Unser, Cory	9	0	1	1	16
Fricker, Jason	1	0	0	0	0
Rousseau, Ghyslain	8	0	0	0	0
Thurston, Cale	4	0	0	0	4

GOALTENDING

	Games	Min.	W	L	OTL	G	SO	Avg.
Ballard, Boyd	47	2784	29	12	5	121	2	2.61
Rousseau, Ghyslain	8	385	1	4	1	18	0	2.80
Fricker, Jason	1	60	1	0	0	4	0	4.00
Miller, Aren	12	646	6	4	1	44	0	4.09

SAN ANGELO SAINTS

SCORING

	Games	G	A	Pts.	PIM
Peach, Chris	64	23	44	67	82
Mann, Troy	64	20	44	64	46
Cook, Brad	63	11	36	47	67
Roberts, Steve	34	27	15	42	18
Weisgerber, Trevor	39	17	22	39	29
Davison, Kori	60	22	12	34	380
Moffat, Corri	51	7	27	34	20
Pecush, Cory	54	10	20	30	32
Frick, Matt	61	5	24	29	56
Metz, Jarett	54	14	15	29	39
Abel, Jason	36	6	20	26	76
Jas, Jan	34	7	14	21	13
Miller, Kelly	33	9	10	19	42
Cheeseman, Jeff	27	4	13	17	16
Currie, Brent	64	2	15	17	189
Reid, Ryan	51	4	7	11	223
Brand, Konrad	39	2	6	8	36
Sheane, Graeme	13	2	4	6	18
Fournier, Kevin	16	1	3	4	5
Thompson, Jamie	6	3	1	4	18
McKay, Mike	7	0	3	3	18
Kent, Corbie	21	0	2	2	23
Wandler, Bryce	15	0	1	1	4
Beattie, Graeme	6	0	0	0	5
Forsberg, Markus	3	0	0	0	10
Grasso, Joey	6	0	0	0	0
Reid, Scott	41	0	0	0	0
Ronayne, James	21	0	0	0	0

GOALTENDING

	Games	Min.	W	L	OTL	G	SO	Avg.
Reid, Scott	41	2165	12	22	4	143	1	3.96
Wandler, Bryce	15	700	3	5	2	47	0	4.03
Ronayne, James	21	1026	5	10	1	74	0	4.33

TULSA OILERS

SCORING

	Games	G	A	Pts.	PIM
Marcellus, Todd	64	40	53	93	57
Steer, Jamie	45	23	31	54	14
Hallett, Pat	62	20	22	42	122
Millar, Aaron	64	11	30	41	56
Kaebel, Klage	59	15	22	37	54
Ossachuk, Justin	55	26	11	37	214
Welsh, Jorin	64	8	23	31	90
Steenbergen, Lyle	58	11	19	30	59
Johnson, Mike	57	6	23	29	66
Toninato, Derek	49	9	18	27	61
Mohr, Mike	58	9	14	23	109
Johnston, Chris	37	7	15	22	40
Anderson, Dallas	48	13	8	21	365
Reigstad, Jared	54	4	13	17	79
Flodell, Jordan	64	6	7	13	128
MacKellar, Peter	18	5	8	13	6
Harper, Regan	20	1	8	9	10
Livingston, Kevin	44	1	8	9	68
Wilkinson, Neil	13	1	6	7	8
Oke, Andrew	18	1	2	3	45
Branch, Rod	57	0	2	2	16
Carmichael, Matt	6	0	1	1	0
Pirnak, Doug	5	1	0	1	19
Ernewein, Carey	6	0	0	0	2
Stone, Jason	6	0	0	0	0

GOALTENDING

	Games	Min.	W	L	OTL	G	SO	Avg.
Branch, Rod	57	3314	32	18	5	159	8	2.88
Carmichael, Matt	6	279	3	1	0	14	0	3.01
Stone, Jason	6	274	2	3	0	17	0	3.71

WICHITA THUNDER

SCORING

	Games	G	A	Pts.	PIM
Clayton, Travis	63	35	57	92	109
Duda, Jason	64	31	52	83	60
Gomes, Tom	64	28	38	66	61
Petruic, Jeff	37	19	16	35	30
MacKellar, Peter	43	18	14	32	25
Johnson, Todd	49	12	17	29	14
Reynolds, Derek	38	11	14	25	65
Dumoulin, Mario	21	1	21	22	57
Hartinger, Vladimir	41	10	12	22	111
McLean, Ryan	63	12	10	22	212
Stachniak, Pat	35	4	15	19	106
Cunningham, Jerry	24	9	6	15	15
Nelson, Chad	32	5	10	15	112
Picard, Jean-Francoi	27	3	12	15	28
Rapoza, Bob	20	1	12	13	16
Johnson, Paul	31	3	9	12	58
Leiter, Jeff	49	2	10	12	289
Plumb, Aaron	45	5	7	12	161
Stay, Tim	19	0	6	6	4
Bina, Jerod	25	1	4	5	32
Livingston, Kevin	20	0	4	4	38
Marble, Evan	5	0	4	4	6
Payne, Mike	7	2	2	4	55
Oke, Andrew	23	0	3	3	54
Pappas, Colen	16	1	2	3	2
Grasso, Joey	14	1	1	2	6
Perry, Sean	5	1	1	2	8
Sereno, Dominic	11	0	2	2	8
Lovisek, Patrik	24	0	1	1	10
Lucas, Corey	6	0	1	1	2
Merrell, Doug	13	1	0	1	10
Penny, Andy	5	0	1	1	4
Antila, Kristian	21	0	0	0	2
Cardwell, Matt	12	0	0	0	12
Greenway, Jason	5	0	0	0	0
Plenzich, Dominic	1	0	0	0	0
Raisanen, Tomi	3	0	0	0	0
Sjerven, Grant	18	0	0	0	0
Wagner, Stephen	8	0	0	0	0
Werfelman, Cam	6	0	0	0	23

GOALTENDING

	Games	Min.	W	L	OTL	G	SO	Avg.
Antila, Kristian	21	1147	10	7	2	70	0	3.66
Raisanen, Tomi	3	144	1	0	1	9	0	3.74
Sjerven, Grant	18	936	3	13	0	61	0	3.91
Lovisek, Patrik	24	1188	6	11	3	81	0	4.09
Wagner, Stephen	8	441	1	5	1	34	0	4.62

PLAYERS WITH TWO OR MORE TEAMS

SCORING

	Games	G	A	Pts.	PIM
Alcombrack, Jeff, MEM	18	0	2	2	8
Alcombrack, Jeff, NMX	31	1	1	2	14
Totals	49	1	3	4	22
Beck, Martin, CRP	38	4	6	10	32
Beck, Martin, NMX	11	0	2	2	12
Totals	49	4	8	12	44
Bina, Jerod, CRP	3	0	1	1	2
Bina, Jerod, WIC	25	1	4	5	32
Totals	28	1	5	6	34
Bourque, David, CRP	26	1	12	13	28
Bourque, David, NMX	27	2	3	5	10
Totals	53	3	15	18	38
Breen, Neil, LAR	19	2	4	6	29
Breen, Neil, NMX	4	0	0	0	0
Totals	23	2	4	6	29
Cameron, Jeff, FTW	9	2	1	3	8
Cameron, Jeff, NMX	31	2	14	16	42
Totals	40	4	15	19	50
Carmichael, Matt, ELP	23	0	1	1	0
Carmichael, Matt, TUL	6	0	1	1	0
Totals	29	0	2	2	0
Cunningham, Jerry, MEM	12	3	2	5	2
Cunningham, Jerry, ODE	14	1	3	4	0
Cunningham, Jerry, WIC	24	9	6	15	15
Totals	50	13	11	24	17
Currie, Kris, MEM	32	0	3	3	121
Currie, Kris, NMX	31	1	1	2	118
Totals	63	1	4	5	239
Curry, Darren, AMA	59	12	15	27	30
Curry, Darren, FTW	1	1	0	1	2
Totals	60	13	15	28	32
Dumba, Jared, IND	47	27	20	47	33
Dumba, Jared, OKC	15	5	2	7	18
Totals	62	32	22	54	51
Dumoulin, Mario, NMX	32	8	12	20	47
Dumoulin, Mario, WIC	21	1	21	22	57
Totals	53	9	33	42	104
Duplessis, Simon, IND	15	1	0	1	25
Duplessis, Simon, LAR	4	0	0	0	11
Totals	19	1	0	1	36
Forsberg, Markus, ELP	43	9	8	17	61
Forsberg, Markus, SNG	3	0	0	0	10
Totals	46	9	8	17	71
Fournier, Kevin, AUS	4	0	0	0	0
Fournier, Kevin, SNG	16	1	3	4	5
Totals	20	1	3	4	5
Fricker, Jason, FTW	32	0	1	1	0
Fricker, Jason, OKC	1	0	0	0	0
Totals	33	0	1	1	0
Giffin, Rob, CRP	20	7	17	24	12
Giffin, Rob, FTW	38	6	16	22	18
Totals	58	13	33	46	30
Gorewich, Ben, MEM	32	7	15	22	33
Gorewich, Ben, NMX	31	11	16	27	32
Totals	63	18	31	49	65
Grasso, Joey, ELP	7	1	1	2	2
Grasso, Joey, SNG	6	0	0	0	0
Grasso, Joey, WIC	27	2	2	4	8
Totals	14	1	1	2	6
Hartinger, Vladimir, NMX	13	3	5	8	4
Hartinger, Vladimir, WIC	41	10	12	22	111
Totals	54	13	17	30	115
Jabrocky, Jaroslav, CRP	40	12	15	27	10
Jabrocky, Jaroslav, LAR	24	4	6	10	22
Totals	64	16	21	37	32
Lewis, Roger, CRP	13	0	1	1	14
Lewis, Roger, ELP	1	0	0	0	0
Totals	14	0	1	1	14

	Games	G	A	Pts.	PIM
Livingston, Kevin, TUL	44	1	8	9	68
Livingston, Kevin, WIC	20	0	4	4	38
Totals	64	1	12	13	106
MacKellar, Peter, TUL	18	5	8	13	6
MacKellar, Peter, WIC	43	18	14	32	25
Totals	61	23	22	45	31
Margeson, Stephen, MEM	27	0	8	8	42
Margeson, Stephen, NMX	24	0	9	9	24
Totals	51	0	17	17	66
Marks, Lloyd, CRP	12	2	3	5	15
Marks, Lloyd, FTW	40	6	11	17	10
Totals	52	8	14	22	25
Miller, Aren, CRP	2	0	0	0	0
Miller, Aren, OKC	12	0	1	1	0
Totals	14	0	1	1	0
Munro, Matt, CRP	24	3	3	6	14
Munro, Matt, FTW	10	0	1	1	2
Totals	34	3	4	7	16
Nelson, Chad, CRP	9	1	5	6	33
Nelson, Chad, WIC	32	5	10	15	112
Totals	41	6	15	21	145
Oke, Andrew, LAR	19	1	4	5	37
Oke, Andrew, TUL	18	1	2	3	45
Oke, Andrew, WIC	23	0	3	3	54
Totals	60	2	9	11	136
Paul, Mathieu, ELP	39	1	15	16	80
Paul, Mathieu, MEM	10	0	2	2	15
Totals	49	1	17	18	95
Payne, Mike, NMX	25	0	0	0	65
Payne, Mike, OKC	18	0	3	3	59
Payne, Mike, WIC	7	2	2	4	55
Totals	50	2	5	7	179
Petruic, Jeff, LAR	26	13	15	28	8
Petruic, Jeff, WIC	37	19	16	35	30
Totals	63	32	31	63	38
Picard, Jean-Francoi, LAR	19	0	5	5	26
Picard, Jean-Francoi, WIC	27	3	12	15	28
Totals	46	3	17	20	54
Plenzich, Dominic, NMX	20	1	1	2	13
Plenzich, Dominic, WIC	1	0	0	0	0
Totals	21	1	1	2	13
Rapoza, Bob, ELP	41	9	13	22	14
Rapoza, Bob, WIC	20	1	12	13	16
Totals	61	10	25	35	30

	Games	G	A	Pts.	PIM
Reigstad, Jared, LUB	9	0	0	0	10
Reigstad, Jared, TUL	54	4	13	17	79
Totals	63	4	13	17	89
Reynolds, Derek, ELP	15	4	4	8	51
Reynolds, Derek, WIC	38	11	14	25	65
Totals	53	15	18	33	116
Rivard, Ryan, AUS	37	4	4	8	142
Rivard, Ryan, FTW	23	0	3	3	65
Totals	60	4	7	11	207
Ronayne, James, ELP	19	0	0	0	4
Ronayne, James, SNG	21	0	0	0	0
Totals	40	0	0	0	4
Roy, Jasmin, NMX	21	7	7	14	29
Roy, Jasmin, OKC	35	6	4	10	76
Totals	56	13	11	24	105
Sharuga, Matt, AUS	56	8	19	27	48
Sharuga, Matt, CRP	8	1	0	1	21
Totals	64	9	19	28	69
Stachniak, Pat, ODE	28	2	3	5	40
Stachniak, Pat, WIC	35	4	15	19	106
Totals	63	6	18	24	146
Tilson, Mike, CRP	40	15	22	37	98
Tilson, Mike, FTW	23	3	10	13	38
Totals	63	18	32	50	136
Weisgerber, Trevor, OKC	11	2	2	4	10
Weisgerber, Trevor, SNG	39	17	22	39	29
Totals	50	19	24	43	39
Werfelman, Cam, CRP	4	0	0	0	0
Werfelman, Cam, WIC	6	0	0	0	23
Totals	10	0	0	0	23

GOALTENDING

	Gms.	Min.	W	L	OTL	G	SO	Avg.
Carmichael, M., ELP	23	1268	6	14	2	67	0	3.17
Carmichael, M., TUL	6	279	3	1	0	14	0	3.01
Totals	29	1547	9	15	2	81	0	3.14
Fricker, Jason, FTW	32	1477	5	19	1	95	0	3.86
Fricker, Jason, OKC.	1	60	1	0	0	4	0	4.00
Totals	33	1537	6	19	1	99	0	3.86
Miller, Aren, CRP	2	91	0	1	0	9	0	5.90
Miller, Aren, OKC	12	646	6	4	1	44	0	4.09
Totals	14	737	6	5	1	53	0	4.31
Ronayne, J., ELP	19	975	4	12	0	69	1	4.25
Ronayne, J., SNG	21	1026	5	10	1	74	0	4.33
Totals	40	2001	9	22	1	143	1	4.29

2003 PLAYOFFS
RESULTS

PRESIDENTS CUP FINAL
Game 1 - April 17, Memphis 3, Austin 0
Game 2 - April 18, Memphis, 1, Austin, 2 (OT)
Game 3 - April 21, Austin, 1, Memphis, 6
Game 4 - April 23, Austin, 2, Memphis, 7
Game 5 - April 25, Austin, 3, Memphis, 4 (2 OT)
Memphis wins series 4-1

NORTHERN FINAL
Game 1 - April 4, Indianapolis, 4, Memphis, 5
Game 2 - April 8, Indianapolis, 1, Memphis, 3
Game 3 - April 10, Memphis, 2, Indianapolis, 1 (2 OT)
Game 4 - April 12, Memphis, 6, Indianapolis, 3
Memphis wins series 4-0

SOUTHERN FINAL
Game 1 - April 3, Laredo, 1, Austin, 0 (OT)
Game 2 - April 6, Laredo, 1, Austin, 4
Game 3 - April 8, Austin, 3, Laredo, 4
Game 4 - April 10, Austin, 4, Laredo, 3
Game 5 - April 11, Laredo, 3, Austin, 4
Game 6 - April 12, Austin, 3, Laredo, 2
Austin wins series 4-2

NORTHERN CONFERENCE SEMIFINALS
Game 1 - March 21, Amarillo, 2, Indianapolis, 4
Game 2 - March 22, Amarillo, 2, Indianapolis, 3

Game 3 - March 28, Indianapolis, 2, Amarillo, 6
Game 4 - March 29, Indianapolis, 8, Amarillo, 4
Indianapolis wins series 3-1

Game 1 - March 22, Oklahoma City, 5, Memphis, 7
Game 2 - March 27, Memphis, 3, Oklahoma City, 5
Game 3 - March 28, Memphis, 3, Oklahoma City, 4 (OT)
Game 4 - April 1, Oklahoma City, 3, Memphis, 5
Game 5 - April 2, Memphis, 5, Oklahoma City, 2
Memphis wins series 3-2

SOUTHERN CONFERENCE SEMIFINALS
Game 1 - March 21, New Mexico, 4, Austin, 3
Game 2 - March 22, New Mexico, 0, Austin, 2
Game 3 - March 28, Austin, 2, New Mexico, 1
Game 4 - March 29, Austin, 3, New Mexico, 2
Austin wins series 3-1

Game 1 - March 21, Laredo, 3, Odessa, 2 (2 OT)
Game 2 - March 22, Laredo, 2, Odessa, 3
Game 3 - March 28, Odessa, 2, Laredo, 1
Game 4 - March 29, Odessa, 2, Laredo, 4
Game 5 - April 1, Laredo, 3, Odessa, 2
Laredo wins series 3-2

Goals: Don Parsons, Memphis (14)
Assists: Kahlil Thomas, Memphis (18)
Points: Don Parsons, Memphis (23)
       Kahlil Thomas, Memphis (23)
Penalty minutes: Shaun Legault, Austin (56)
Goaltending average: Lance Leslie, Laredo (2.16)
Shutouts: Mark Richareds, Memphis (1)
       Matt Barnes, Austin (1)
       Lance Leslie, Laredo (1)

TOP SCORERS

	Games	G	A	Pts.
Parsons, Don, Memphis	14	14	9	23
Thomas, Kahlil, Memphis	14	5	18	23
Gagnon, Jonathan, Memphis	14	11	9	20
Seguin, Brett, Austin	15	7	13	20
Tallaire, Gerald, Austin	13	6	10	16
Price, Dan, Austin	15	4	12	16
Stastny, Michal, Memphis	14	6	8	14
Nasato, Luch, Memphis	14	5	8	13
Gaffney, Mike, Austin	15	2	10	12
Neal, Jay, Memphis	14	2	10	12

AMARILLO GORILLAS
(Lost conference semifinals to Indianapolis Ice)

SCORING

	Games	G	A	Pts.	PIM
Anneck, Dorian	4	3	2	5	0
Carper, Brandon	4	2	3	5	8
Dean, John	4	2	3	5	6
Hahn, Derek	4	1	4	5	0
DeSantis, Mark	4	0	5	5	10
Rattray, Dave	4	2	1	3	6
Curry, Darren	4	2	0	2	0
Butler, Tyler	4	1	1	2	0
Wray, Scott	4	0	2	2	4
Pellerin, Brian	4	0	2	2	8
Kuster, Henry	4	1	0	1	6
Andersen, Eric	4	0	1	1	4
Gustavson, Ben	4	0	1	1	2
Brown, Matt	4	0	0	0	4
Maidment, Ben	4	0	0	0	6
Degagne, Shawn	3	0	0	0	0
Posillico, Neil	2	0	0	0	0
Debus, Steve	2	0	0	0	0
Zirnis, Karlis	2	0	0	0	0

GOALTENDING

	Games	Min.	W	L	T	G	SO	Avg.
Degagne, Shawn	3	139	0	2	0	9	0	3.86

AUSTIN ICE BATS
(Lost Presidents Cup finals to Memphis Riverkings)

SCORING

	Games	G	A	Pts.	PIM
Seguin, Brett	15	7	13	20	8
Tallaire, Gerald	13	6	10	16	8
Price, Dan	15	4	12	16	26
Gaffney, Mike	15	2	10	12	10
Lardner, Tab	15	5	2	7	15
Brownlee, Pat	14	3	3	6	6
Smart, Kelly	15	0	5	5	6
Rees, Mike	15	2	2	4	12
Legault, Shawn	15	2	2	4	56
McArthur, Darryl	15	2	2	4	25
Sharuga, Matt	15	2	1	3	33
Hughes, Brent	10	1	1	2	2
Greenlaw, Jeff	15	0	2	2	26
Olynyk, Mike	15	0	0	0	48
McCallum, Scott	15	0	0	0	11
Johnson, Doug	15	0	0	0	23
Barnes, Matt	15	0	0	0	0
Rivard, Ryan	8	0	0	0	19
Brady, Peter	1	0	0	0	0

GOALTENDING

	Games	Min.	W	L	T	G	SO	Avg.
Brady, Peter	1	14	0	0	0	0	0	0.00
Barnes, Matt	15	979	8	7	0	42	1	2.57

INDIANAPOLIS ICE
(Lost conference finals to Memphis Riverkings)

SCORING

	Games	G	A	Pts.	PIM
St. Jacques, Kevin	8	6	4	10	8
John, Bernie	8	2	8	10	2
Baird, Jason	8	4	4	8	10
Dumba, Jared	8	4	4	8	6
Holmes, Randy	8	2	6	8	6
Morin, Etienne	8	1	5	6	4
Taylor, Andrew	8	2	3	5	4
Carter, Ryan	7	2	3	5	4
Lewis, Scott	8	0	4	4	18
Olsen, Greg	8	2	1	3	10
Classen, Bryce	8	1	0	1	6
Popp, Kevin	8	0	1	1	4
Elliott, Nate	8	0	1	1	10
Aikia, Ryan	8	0	1	1	8
Morris, Jamie	5	0	1	1	0
Kearns, Justin	8	0	0	0	14
Leasa, Ryan	4	0	0	0	0
Silver, Shawn	4	0	0	0	2
Pool, Byron	3	0	0	0	4
Chapman, Adam	1	0	0	0	0

GOALTENDING

	Games	Min.	W	L	T	G	SO	Avg.
Morris, Jamie	5	294	2	2	0	13	0	2.65
Silver, Shawn	4	206	1	3	0	15	0	4.37

LAREDO BUCKS
(Lost conference finals to Austin Ice Bats)

SCORING

	Games	G	A	Pts.	PIM
Lundbohm, Andy	10	4	4	8	8
Periard, Michel	9	3	5	8	4
Schneider, Eric	9	3	5	8	8
Grenville, Chris	11	2	6	8	6
Dube, Serge	11	2	4	6	8
Ask, Morten	11	3	2	5	22
Gilmore, Dave	11	2	3	5	2
Leroux, Jonah	11	2	3	5	8
Petruic, Jeff	11	1	4	5	6
Stanfield, Rob	11	1	3	4	8
Weidlich, Steve	11	1	3	4	30
Sewell, Joe	11	1	2	3	21
Keski-Kungas, Stefan	11	1	1	2	6
Myson, David	11	1	1	2	22
Van Horlick, Matt	11	0	1	1	8
Leclerc, Marc-Andre	5	0	1	1	0
Cornish, Jeremy	9	0	0	0	7
Leslie, Lance	7	0	0	0	0
Hyman, Dion	7	0	0	0	16

GOALTENDING

	Games	Min.	W	L	T	G	SO	Avg.
Leslie, Lance	7	472	2	5	0	17	1	2.16
Leclerc, Marc-Andre	5	254	3	1	0	11	0	2.59

MEMPHIS RIVERKINGS
(Won 2003 Presidents Cup)
SCORING

	Games	G	A	Pts.	PIM
Parsons, Don	14	14	9	23	12
Thomas, Kahlil	14	5	18	23	11
Gagnon, Jonathan....................	14	11	9	20	16
Stastny, Michal	14	6	8	14	16
Nasato, Luch	14	5	8	13	36
Neal, Jay	14	2	10	12	17
Tucker, Brian	14	5	6	11	36
Landmesser, Derek	14	1	9	10	28
Palahnuk, Robb	14	2	6	8	8
DiPalma, Anthony	12	2	4	6	16
Lakovic, Greg..........................	14	5	0	5	24
Aitken, A.J.	14	1	2	3	18
Cote, Riley..............................	14	1	0	1	54
Mueller, Brad..........................	14	0	1	1	24
Goetzinger, Jeremy	2	0	1	1	0
Amadio, Greg..........................	14	0	0	0	24
Richards, Mark	14	0	0	0	2
Schneider, Tim........................	7	0	0	0	5
Margeson, Stephen	7	0	0	0	0
Racine, Jean-Francoi	1	0	0	0	17

GOALTENDING

	Games	Min.	W	L	T	G	SO	Avg.
Richards, Mark	14	848	11	2	0	31	1	2.19
Racine, J-F.............	1	58	0	1	0	5	0	5.14

NEW MEXICO SCORPIONS
(Lost conference semifinals to Austin Ice Bats)
SCORING

	Games	G	A	Pts.	PIM
Baines, Tyler	4	1	2	3	6
Ambroziak, Peter	4	2	0	2	4
Roy, Jasmin	4	1	1	2	4
Kupaks, Arturs	4	1	1	2	8
Richards, Chris	4	0	2	2	8
Hartinger, Vladimir..................	4	0	2	2	4
Robbins, Adam	4	1	0	1	10
Gorewich, Ben	4	1	0	1	6
Brearley, Peter........................	4	0	1	1	2
McPherson, Andrew	4	0	1	1	6
Currie, Kris.............................	4	0	0	0	4
Cameron, Jeff	4	0	0	0	6
Rech, Neal..............................	4	0	0	0	4
Peet, Shaun............................	4	0	0	0	2
Stahl, Craig	4	0	0	0	2
Caravaggio, Luciano	4	0	0	0	0
Alcombrack, Jeff......................	4	0	0	0	2

GOALTENDING

	Games	Min.	W	L	T	G	SO	Avg.
Caravaggio, L..........	4	248	1	3	0	10	0	2.41

ODESSA JACKALOPES
(Lost conference semifinals to Laredo Bucks)
SCORING

	Games	G	A	Pts.	PIM
Green, Scott............................	5	3	3	6	0
Rutter, Mike	5	1	3	4	14
Bossio, John............................	5	1	3	4	4
Thinel, Sebastien	5	2	1	3	4
Hillman, Scott..........................	5	1	2	3	4
Willers, Greg............................	5	1	2	3	2
Margettie, Donnie	5	1	0	1	12
Hansen, Kevin	5	1	0	1	8
Francis, Dave	5	0	1	1	2
Stachniak, Pat	5	0	1	1	4
Doyle, Adam	5	0	0	0	2
Yoder, Jami	5	0	0	0	6
Desmarais, Denis	5	0	0	0	0
Gatto, Greg	5	0	0	0	20
Cressman, Matt	5	0	0	0	6
Gorman, Mike	5	0	0	0	2
Frid, Robert..............................	5	0	0	0	11

GOALTENDING

	Games	Min.	W	L	T	G	SO	Avg.
Gorman, Mike	5	318	2	3	0	12	0	2.26

OKLAHOMA CITY BLAZERS
(Lost conference semifinals to Memphis Riverkings)
SCORING

	Games	G	A	Pts.	PIM
Sauter, Hardy	5	2	6	8	5
Manning, Blair	5	2	5	7	0
Burton, Joe..............................	5	3	3	6	0
DuBois, Jonathan	5	3	1	4	8
Standish, Marty	5	2	2	4	10
Arvanitis, Peter	5	2	2	4	10
Watson, Ryan	5	1	2	3	2
Campbell, Ryan........................	5	2	0	2	4
Robertson, Peter......................	5	1	1	2	4
Fleck, Tyler..............................	5	0	2	2	21
Borsheim, Les..........................	5	1	0	1	16
Mamane, Shawn	5	0	1	1	2
Weiman, Shawn	4	0	1	1	2
Stone, Derek	5	0	0	0	8
Shields, Dave	5	0	0	0	15
Ballard, Boyd..........................	5	0	0	0	7
Willmott, Dan	3	0	0	0	15
Kot, Justin	2	0	0	0	9
Laurila, Tim	1	0	0	0	2
Rousseau, Ghyslain	1	0	0	0	0

GOALTENDING

	Games	Min.	W	L	T	G	SO	Avg.
Rousseau, Ghyslain	1	1	0	0	0	0	0	0.00
Ballard, Boyd..........	5	304	2	3	0	21	0	4.14

2002-03 AWARD WINNERS

ALL-STAR TEAMS

Northern	Pos.	Southern
Joe Burton, OKC	F	Cosmo Dupaul, COR
Travis Clayton, WIC	F	Blaz Emersic, LUB
Henry Kuster, AMA	F	Chris Grenville, LAR
Mark DeSantis, AMA	D	Mike Gaffney, AUS
Vladimir Hartinger, WIC	D	Scott Hillman, ODE
Rod Branch, TUL	G	Matt Barnes, AUS

TROPHY WINNERS

Most Valuable Player: Don Parsons, Memphis
Scoring Champion: Don Parsons, Memphis
Most Outstanding Goaltender: Matt Barnes, Austin
Most Outstanding Defenseman: Michel Periard, Laredo
Rookie of the Year: Derek Hahn, Amarillo
Playoff Most Valuable Player: Kahlil Thomas, Memphis
Coach of the Year: Ken McRae, Indianapolis

MOST VALUABLE PLAYER

Season	Player, Team
1992-93	Sylvain Fleury, Oklahoma City
1993-94	Robert Desjardins, Wichita
1994-95	Paul Jackson, San Antonio
1995-96	Brian Shantz, San Antonio
1996-97	Trevor Jobe, Columbus-Wichita
1997-98	Joe Burton, Oklahoma City
1998-99	Derek Puppa, Huntsville
1999-00	Yvan Corbin, Indianapolis
	Chris MacKenzie, Indianapolis
2000-01	Joe Burton, Oklahoma City
2001-02	Don Parsons, Memphis
2002-03	Don Parsons, Memphis

SCORING CHAMPION

Season	Player, Team
1992-93	Sylvain Fleury, Oklahoma City
1993-94	Paul Jackson, Wichita
1994-95	Brian Shantz, San Antonio
1995-96	Brian Shantz, San Antonio
1996-97	Trevor Jobe, Columbus-Wichita
1997-98	Luc Beausoleil, Tulsa
1998-99	Derek Grant, Memphis
1999-00	Yvan Corbin, Indianapolis
	Chris MacKenzie, Indianapolis
2000-01	Yvan Corbin, Indianapolis
2001-02	Dan Price, Austin
2002-03	Don Parsons, Memphis

MOST OUTSTANDING GOALTENDER

Season	Player, Team
1992-93	Tony Martino, Tulsa
1993-94	Alan Perry, Oklahoma City
1994-95	Alan Perry, Oklahoma City
1995-96	Jean-Ian Filiatrault, Oklahoma City
1996-97	Jean-Ian Filiatrault, Oklahoma City
1997-98	Brian Elder, Oklahoma City
1998-99	Jean-Ian Filiatrault, Oklahoma City
1999-00	Frankie Ouellette, Columbus
2000-01	Brant Nicklin, Oklahoma City
2001-02	Mike Gorman, Odessa
2002-03	Matt Barnes, Austin

MOST OUTSTANDING DEFENSEMAN

Season	Player, Team
1992-93	Dave Doucette, Dallas
1993-94	Guy Girouard, Oklahoma City
1994-95	Eric Ricard, Fort Worth
1995-96	Dan Brown, Memphis
1996-97	Hardy Sauter, Oklahoma City

Season	Player, Team
1997-98	Hardy Sauter, Oklahoma City
1998-99	Igor Bondarev, Huntsville
1999-00	Brett Colborne, Fayetteville
2000-01	Derek Landmesser, Memphis
2001-02	Daniel Tetrault, Austin
2002-03	Michel Periard, Laredo

ROOKIE OF THE YEAR

Season	Player, Team
1992-93	Robert Desjardins, Wichita
1993-94	Chad Seibel, Memphis
1994-95	Michel St. Jacques, Oklahoma City
1995-96	Derek Grant, Memphis
1996-97	Cory Dosdall, Wichita
1997-98	David Beauregard, Wichita
1998-99	Johnny Brdarovic, San Antonio
1999-00	James Patterson, Huntsville
2000-01	Derek Reynolds, Huntsville
2001-02	Sebastien Centomo, Memphis
2002-03	Derek Hahn, Amarillo

PLAYOFF MOST VALUABLE PLAYER

Season	Player, Team
1992-93	Tony Fiore, Tulsa
1993-94	Ron Handy, Wichita
1994-95	Ron Handy, Wichita
1995-96	Jean-Ian Filiatrault, Oklahoma City
1996-97	Steve Plouffe, Fort Worth
1997-98	Mike Martens, Columbus
1998-99	Derek Puppa, Huntsville
1999-00	Jamie Morris, Indianapolis
2000-01	Rod Branch, Oklahoma City
2001-02	Don Parsons, Memphis
2002-03	Kahlil Thomas, Memphis

COACH OF THE YEAR
(Commissioner's Trophy)

Season	Coach, Team
1992-93	Garry Unger, Tulsa
1993-94	Doug Shedden, Wichita
1994-95	John Torchetti, San Antonio
1995-96	Doug Sauter, Oklahoma City
1996-97	Bill McDonald, Fort Worth
1997-98	David Lohrei, Nashville
1998-99	Chris Stewart, Huntsville
1999-00	David Lohrie, Fayetteville
2000-01	Paul Kelly, Topeka
2001-02	Don McKee, Odessa
2002-03	Ken McRae, Indianapolis

ALL-TIME LEAGUE CHAMPIONS

	REGULAR-SEASON CHAMPION		PLAYOFF CHAMPION	
Season	Team	Coach	Team	Coach
1992-93	Oklahoma City Blazers	Michael McEwen	Tulsa Oilers	Garry Unger
1993-94	Wichita Thunder	Doug Shedden	Wichita Thunder	Doug Shedden
1994-95	Wichita Thunder	Doug Shedden	Wichita Thunder	Doug Shedden
1995-96	Oklahoma City Blazers	Doug Sauter	Oklahoma City Blazers	Doug Sauter
1996-97	Oklahoma City Blazers	Doug Sauter	Fort Worth Fire	Bill McDonald
1997-98	Columbus Cottonmouths	Bruce Garber	Columbus Cottonmouths	Bruce Garber
1998-99	Oklahoma City Blazers	Doug Sauter	Huntsville Channel Cats	Chris Stewart
1999-00	Fayetteville Force	David Lohrie	Indianapolis Ice	Rod Davidson
2000-01	Oklahoma City Blazers	Doug Sauter	Oklahoma City Blazers	Doug Sauter
2001-02	Odessa Jackalopes	Don McKee	Memphis Riverkings	Doug Shedden
2002-03	Austin Ice Bats	Brent Hughes	Memphis Riverkings	Doug Shedden

The Central League regular season champion is awarded the Governors' Cup. The playoff champion is awarded the President's Cup.

UNITED HOCKEY LEAGUE

(NOTE: The United Hockey League operated under the name Colonial Hockey League through the 1996-97 season.)

2002-03 REGULAR SEASON
FINAL STANDINGS

EASTERN CONFERENCE

Team	G	W	L	SOP	Pts.	GF	GA
Fort Wayne	76	44	21	11	99	249	191
Adirondack	76	44	28	4	92	300	245
Elmira	76	41	28	7	89	257	254
Port Huron	76	38	30	8	84	248	268
Flint	76	32	36	8	72	257	298

WESTERN CONFERENCE

Team	G	W	L	SOP	Pts.	GF	GA
Quad City	76	41	25	10	92	281	240
Missouri	76	38	28	10	86	262	236
Muskegon	76	38	29	9	85	245	257
Rockford	76	35	34	7	77	233	271
Kalamazoo	76	29	39	8	66	210	282

INDIVIDUAL LEADERS

Goals: Dominic Chiasson, Adirondack (53)
Assists: Hugo Belanger, Adirondack (101)
Points: Hugo Belanger, Adirondack (143)
Penalty minutes: Brad Wingfield, Elmira (576)
Goaltending average: Tom Lawson, Fort Wayne (2.00)
Shutouts: Tom Lawson, Fort Wayne (7)

	Games	G	A	Pts.
Duhart, Jim, FLT	74	49	40	89
Whitecotton, Dustin, MIS	66	35	54	89
Chiasson, Dominic, ADI	76	53	35	88
Stewart, Bobby, FW	72	48	34	82
Blackned, Brant, MUS	76	40	42	82
Chaulk, Colin, FW	70	23	59	82
Stewart, Glenn, ELM	70	36	43	79
Loach, Lonnie, MIS	68	29	48	77
MacKenzie, Chris, PH	52	30	46	76
Phillips, Aaron, ELM	76	33	42	75
Luciuk, Andrew, MUS	74	32	42	74
Loen, Matt, RCK	76	22	52	74
Cygan, Steve, RCK	76	27	45	72
Virag, Dustin, FW	72	25	43	68

TOP SCORERS

	Games	G	A	Pts.
Belanger, Hugo P., ADI	76	42	101	143
Bouchard, Robin, MUS	73	43	55	98
Firth, Jason, PH	74	26	72	98
Reynolds, Bobby, FLT	73	35	62	97
Ruid, J.C., ADI	71	40	56	96
Murphy, Randy, ELM	76	26	67	93

INDIVIDUAL STATISTICS

ADIRONDACK ICEHAWKS
SCORING

	Games	G	A	Pts.	PIM
Belanger, Hugo P.	76	42	101	143	16
Ruid, J.C.	71	40	56	96	68
Chiasson, Dominic	76	53	35	88	8
Rudenko, Bogdan	74	34	31	65	99
Patterson, James	61	19	45	64	46
Littlejohn, Frank	75	30	26	56	306
Senn, Trevor	60	12	30	42	466
Batten, John	48	11	26	37	81
Dumas, Alex	73	6	26	32	50
Sjolund, Andreas	75	15	14	29	143
Kuriplach, Kamil	76	4	23	27	155
Blais, Benjamin	76	5	16	21	64
Rooney, Jesse	27	6	9	15	6
Schmidt, Doug	50	7	7	14	137
Johnstone, Alex	69	2	12	14	307
Bennefield, Blue	30	4	3	7	147
Wolfe, Jason	49	0	5	5	6
Galligan, Seamus	64	1	3	4	6
Bone, Jason	43	0	4	4	287
Low, Steven	6	1	3	4	12
Villeneuve, Martin	18	0	3	3	0
Dartsch, David	5	0	1	1	0
Hallee, Yan	13	0	1	1	21
Vessio, Rob	13	1	0	1	7
Ferraris, Bob	10	1	0	1	6
Rapoza, Bob	6	0	1	1	2
Ricci, Scott	2	0	0	0	0
MacKay, Tyler	15	0	0	0	10
Chant, David	2	0	0	0	0
Draper, Tom	5	0	0	0	0
Carr, Greg	9	0	0	0	2

GOALTENDING

	Gms.	Min.	W	L	SOL	G	SO	Avg.
Chant, David	2	8	0	0	0	0	0	0.00
Wolfe, Jason	49	2589	25	13	4	127	2	2.94
Draper, Tom	5	249	3	1	0	13	0	3.13
Villeneuve, Martin	18	924	11	5	0	49	0	3.18
MacKay, Tyler	15	778	5	9	0	47	0	3.62

ELMIRA JACKALS
SCORING

	Games	G	A	Pts.	PIM
Murphy, Randy	76	26	67	93	38
Stewart, Glenn	70	36	43	79	62
Phillips, Aaron	76	33	42	75	67
Lessard, David	75	21	36	57	90
Neilson, Corey	72	10	44	54	136
Hofstrand, Mike	68	15	33	48	30
Thompson, Mike	76	22	26	48	98
Wingfield, Brad	63	29	16	45	576
Lowe, Ed	76	18	22	40	90
Guinn, Rob	73	4	19	23	67
Esselmont, Ryan	73	2	20	22	40
Kerr, Kevin	33	11	9	20	51
Clayton, Tom	72	10	8	18	160
Burgess, Trevor	20	1	15	16	20
Lyke, R.C.	68	2	10	12	70
Robinson, Jody	43	2	9	11	56
Mallette, Kris	70	2	7	9	310
Hickey, Gerry	56	1	3	4	235
Garvey, Liam	5	1	2	3	4
Borzecki, Adam	8	0	2	2	20
Jackson, Dean	7	1	1	2	0
Emond, Marco	56	0	2	2	4
Plamondon, Justin	4	1	0	1	2

	Games	G	A	Pts.	PIM
Frost, Rob	5	0	1	1	4
Symington, Jeremy	26	0	1	1	2
Gagnon, Jonathan	1	0	0	0	0
Forsberg, Marcus	2	0	0	0	0
Makikyro, Antti	5	0	0	0	0
McCormick, Cam	1	0	0	0	0
Hill, Sam	4	0	0	0	0

GOALTENDING

	Gms.	Min.	W	L	SOL	G	SO	Avg.
McCormick, Cam	1	59	0	1	0	3	0	3.02
Emond, Marco	56	3119	33	15	3	160	2	3.08
Symington, Jeremy	26	1375	8	12	4	79	2	3.45

FLINT GENERALS

SCORING

	Games	G	A	Pts.	PIM
Reynolds, Bobby	73	35	62	97	88
Duhart, Jim	74	49	40	89	172
Woods, Martin	68	19	43	62	105
Perry, Tom	74	26	36	62	57
Greenwood, Dale	68	23	37	60	91
Dufresne, Sylvain	74	16	34	50	61
Roach, Gary	42	10	28	38	46
Woodcroft, Jay	63	17	18	35	81
Labarre, Jean-Franco	52	8	25	33	42
Sullivan, Brent	69	10	22	32	95
Jelenic, Lee	39	13	12	25	109
Lindin, Anders	61	9	9	18	57
Betik, Karel	56	5	11	16	51
Nault, Frankie	72	5	10	15	41
Gates, R.J.	68	5	9	14	80
Disher, Jason	32	3	4	7	137
Sullivan, Brent	17	0	7	7	14
Laniuk, Corey	70	0	7	7	292
Sangiuliano, Jason	23	1	5	6	2
Schafer, Paxton	27	0	4	4	0
Kutchma, Greg	39	2	0	2	18
Langdone, Ashlee	6	0	1	1	67
Alexeev, Kirill	7	0	1	1	10
Machuta, Pavel	29	1	0	1	37
Beland, Dan	7	0	1	1	10
Bray, Mike	5	0	1	1	0
Doucette, Adam	8	0	1	1	7
Weaver, Sean	32	0	1	1	2
Legault, Jean Luc	1	0	0	0	0
Braaten, Paul	7	0	0	0	21
Cornish, Jeremy	18	0	0	0	153
McCormick, Cam	2	0	0	0	7
Ross, Nick	1	0	0	0	0
Villeneuve, Martin	28	0	0	0	6
Varhaug, Mike	6	0	0	0	17
Statkus, Joe	13	0	0	0	22
Werfelman, Cam	15	0	0	0	9

GOALTENDING

	Gms.	Min.	W	L	SOL	G	SO	Avg.
Schafer, Paxton	27	1524	9	12	3	89	1	3.50
Weaver, Sean	32	1455	10	14	2	90	1	3.71
Villeneuve, Martin	28	1490	13	9	3	95	1	3.83
McCormick, Cam	2	80	0	1	0	9	0	6.75

FORT WAYNE KOMETS

SCORING

	Games	G	A	Pts.	PIM
Stewart, Bobby	72	48	34	82	70
Chaulk, Colin	70	23	59	82	116
Virag, Dustin	72	25	43	68	104
Perrault, Kelly	73	12	52	64	138
Venedam, Sean	74	13	40	53	58
Massie, Michel	69	24	28	52	162
Beauregard, David	75	30	17	47	46
Kotyluk, Kevin	70	17	14	31	251
Severson, Ryan	71	13	17	30	32
Barlow, Marc	74	3	22	25	17

	Games	G	A	Pts.	PIM
Ortmeyer, Jake	71	6	18	24	65
Selleke, Jason	45	10	10	20	114
Neumeier, Troy	76	5	11	16	56
Lewis, Adam	67	5	9	14	100
Bertram, Kevin	42	5	6	11	131
Schmidt, Kevin	76	1	8	9	78
Tataryn, Josh	8	3	5	8	0
Baker, Ron	33	1	4	5	17
Cabana, Chad	7	1	3	4	56
Stevens, Bart	22	0	3	3	22
Eade, Chris	7	0	3	3	2
Lawson, Tom	56	0	2	2	8
Lanthier, Michael	8	0	1	1	16
Franke, Joe	1	0	1	1	0
Reddick, Eldon	9	0	1	1	0
Forte, Joey	5	1	0	1	0
Campbell, Cory	8	0	1	1	0
Johnson, Darcy	3	0	0	0	0
Boone, Ken	4	0	0	0	26
Miller, Kelly	5	0	0	0	19
Fletcher, Steve	1	0	0	0	7
Rideout, Scott	7	0	0	0	0
Duffus, Parris	5	0	0	0	0

GOALTENDING

	Gms.	Min.	W	L	SOL	G	SO	Avg.
Lawson, Tom	56	3177	29	15	10	106	7	2.00
Campbell, Cory	8	425	6	1	0	16	0	2.26
Reddick, Eldon	9	401	3	2	1	21	0	3.14
Duffus, Parris	5	241	3	1	0	14	0	3.47
Rideout, Scott	7	291	2	2	0	18	0	3.71
Franke, Joe	1	11	1	0	0	2	0	10.86

KALAMAZOO WINGS

SCORING

	Games	G	A	Pts.	PIM
Roed, Peter	72	21	36	57	84
Lawrence, Mark	69	10	41	51	89
Keyes, Richard	56	27	23	50	35
Miller, Kurt	58	22	24	46	40
Brown, Jim	35	18	11	29	40
O'Leary, Pat	68	16	13	29	80
Bilick, Craig	53	12	10	22	214
Turgeon, Tyson	59	4	18	22	53
Vilneff, Mark	51	2	18	20	24
Cardwell, Justin	26	11	7	18	16
Carpentier, Yannick	23	9	9	18	22
Ford, Michael	46	6	9	15	24
Roed, Shawn	30	8	7	15	65
Hodge, Dan	37	3	11	14	14
Lightbody, Quade	73	2	10	12	110
Trew, Jordan	56	3	7	10	128
Cominetti, Glendon	14	4	4	8	2
Brooks, Chris	11	3	5	8	10
Lawson, Eric	44	2	5	7	22
Pierman, Pepper	27	2	4	6	6
Elezi, Charlie	63	4	2	6	216
Farquhar, Bryan	17	1	4	5	8
Phenow, Mark	46	1	4	5	32
Dameworth, Chad	37	1	4	5	48
Machuta, Pavel	12	0	4	4	31
Pecoraro, Joe	22	2	2	4	6
Hultgren, Herman	37	2	2	4	37
Kruzich, Matt	16	3	1	4	20
Whidden, Jarret	8	1	3	4	0
Velebny, Lubos	8	2	1	3	10
Alexeev, Kirill	9	1	1	2	6
Foddrill, Craig	5	0	1	1	0
Vessio, Rob	6	0	1	1	9
Alban, Chad	54	0	1	1	20
Akright, Josh	6	0	1	1	6
Rogers, Brian	4	0	0	0	0
Disch, Andy	7	0	0	0	0
McCarthy, Liam	1	0	0	0	0
Dunn, Stu	3	0	0	0	0
Reynaert, Jeff	18	0	0	0	0
Brown, Jason	6	0	0	0	0

MINOR LEAGUES UHL

GOALTENDING

	Gms.	Min.	W	L	SOL	G	SO	Avg.
Reynaert, Jeff	18	950	7	6	3	42	1	2.65
Alban, Chad	54	3083	21	25	5	175	1	3.40
Brown, Jason	6	246	1	3	0	17	0	4.14
Dunn, Stu	3	49	0	1	0	5	0	6.05
Rogers, Brian	4	209	0	4	0	23	0	6.59

MISSOURI RIVER OTTERS
SCORING

	Games	G	A	Pts.	PIM
Whitecotton, Dustin	66	35	54	89	30
Loach, Lonnie	68	29	48	77	48
Gudmundson, Jason	58	17	45	62	58
Bastien, Joey	61	21	39	60	38
Nelson, Riley	51	27	27	54	22
Ritson, Joe	38	25	25	50	52
Blyth, Charlie	76	24	20	44	72
Chabbert, Kevin	76	10	16	26	63
Sullivan, Brent	52	10	15	25	81
Hughes, Jason	71	3	21	24	73
Cappelletti, Anthony	73	4	16	20	92
Searle, Doug	66	3	13	16	42
Burnham, Andy	38	5	10	15	225
Beilsten, J.P	47	6	7	13	88
Newans, Chris	19	4	8	12	35
Stinson, Ryan	35	6	5	11	29
Amstutz, Claude	66	1	10	11	61
Antonovich, Jeff	14	9	1	10	12
Karrer, Guillaume	49	3	7	10	90
White, Tony	35	2	7	9	12
Jacobs, Ian	20	1	7	8	10
Hill, Kiley	9	2	4	6	8
Wendell, Erik	13	1	5	6	12
Vincent, Paul	6	0	5	5	0
Melnychuk, Marty	24	1	4	5	169
White, Ben	16	0	3	3	14
Hebert, Jay	6	0	3	3	4
Page, Chris	10	1	2	3	2
Melinder, Henrik	13	0	3	3	24
Antonelli, Marty	2	0	2	2	2
Brown, Jason	1	0	1	1	0
Budaj, Jozef	6	1	0	1	2
Regan, Brian	53	0	1	1	6
Campbell, Cory	4	0	0	0	0
Labarre, Jean-Franco	2	0	0	0	0
McIntosh, Ryan	1	0	0	0	0
Schuster, Brian	1	0	0	0	0
Taylor, Chris	21	0	0	0	8
Blyth, Brian	2	0	0	0	4
Pazourek, Vaclav	2	0	0	0	4

GOALTENDING

	Gms.	Min.	W	L	SOL	G	SO	Avg.
Regan, Brian	53	3076	29	15	7	133	2	2.59
McIntosh, Ryan	1	18	0	0	0	1	0	3.22
Campbell, Cory	4	238	2	2	0	13	0	3.28
Taylor, Chris	21	1149	6	11	3	65	0	3.39
Brown, Jason	1	60	1	0	0	4	0	4.00

MUSKEGON FURY
SCORING

	Games	G	A	Pts.	PIM
Bouchard, Robin	73	43	55	98	131
Blackned, Brant	76	40	42	82	110
Luciuk, Andrew	74	32	42	74	80
Robinson, Todd	56	16	43	59	40
Hollis, Scott	64	33	25	58	112
Dolyny, Rustyn	61	17	34	51	65
Thiessen, Travis	63	8	26	34	60
Glover, Shane	71	10	20	30	6
Kozakowski, Jeff	47	6	21	27	58

	Games	G	A	Pts.	PIM
Lukasak, Jeff	71	6	13	19	82
Feasby, Scott	53	2	16	18	123
Burk, Josh	59	3	11	14	30
Pugliese, Billy	39	3	11	14	13
Pecoraro, Joe	49	2	5	7	8
Glavota, John	63	1	6	7	32
Daigle, Sylvain	62	0	7	7	8
Plante, Philippe	13	1	5	6	6
Johnson, Trevor	7	0	6	6	2
Burgess, David	7	4	2	6	6
Ricciardi, Gary	62	2	3	5	159
Jaworski, Jason	7	1	3	4	6
Busniuk, Bryson	6	3	1	4	2
MacIntyre, Steve	54	2	1	3	279
Lizotte, David	7	0	3	3	0
Berry, Justin	38	0	2	2	10
McCabe, John	8	1	0	1	12
Morrison, Justin	1	0	1	1	0
Hutson, Rob	3	1	0	1	2
Boersema, Dan	1	0	0	0	0
Wilkins, Matt	2	0	0	0	0
Otis, Jessi	8	0	0	0	0
Farquhar, Bryan	3	0	0	0	0
Williams, Jack	2	0	0	0	0
Busniuk, Jake	4	0	0	0	0
Makikyro, Antti	4	0	0	0	0
Snee, Brandon	12	0	0	0	0
Reale, Scott	1	0	0	0	0
Ruchty, Matt	4	0	0	0	4
Bresciani, Joel	6	0	0	0	21
Rochefort, Normand	7	0	0	0	16
Lanicek, Michal	10	0	0	0	0
Graupner, Max	13	0	0	0	4

GOALTENDING

	Gms.	Min.	W	L	SOL	G	SO	Avg.
Daigle, Sylvain	62	3472	31	19	9	166	1	2.87
Lanicek, Michal	10	503	3	4	0	33	0	3.93
Snee, Brandon	12	569	4	6	0	43	0	4.53

PORT HURON BEACONS
SCORING

	Games	G	A	Pts.	PIM
Firth, Jason	74	26	72	98	26
MacKenzie, Chris	52	30	46	76	108
Drevitch, Scott	75	13	50	63	46
Gretzky, Brent	45	31	29	60	12
Bournazakis, Peter	61	22	31	53	92
Beausoleil, Michel	76	22	29	51	100
Vary, John	76	12	33	45	44
Harris, Casey	72	12	29	41	237
McKillop, Bobby	55	20	15	35	41
Carpentier, Yannick	51	10	18	28	34
Wood, Derek	33	11	11	22	17
Poirier, Simon	75	3	11	14	113
Powers, Pat	48	4	9	13	115
Muswagon, Jamie	52	9	4	13	32
Milburn, Marc	67	5	3	8	30
Simon, Jason	27	4	2	6	79
Shannon, Matt	66	3	3	6	91
Jacobs, Ian	25	3	2	5	6
Lawson, Eric	23	0	4	4	8
Cooper, Kory	54	0	3	3	4
Bowen, Eric	29	1	2	3	13
McMonagle, Tom	14	0	2	2	4
Shrieves, Aaron	8	0	2	2	26
Eddy, Ken	14	0	1	1	10
Hellegards, Justin	8	0	1	1	7
Skaleski, Ryan	2	0	0	0	0
Elezi, Charlie	10	0	0	0	44
Bartley, Joey	17	0	0	0	0
Martin, Shawn	14	0	0	0	6
Montgomery, Rob	11	0	0	0	34
Dunn, Stu	3	0	0	0	0
Amidovski, Bujar	28	0	0	0	4

GOALTENDING

	Gms.	Min.	W	L	SOL	G	SO	Avg.
Dunn, Stu	3	125	1	0	1	4	0	1.91
Cooper, Kory	54	2938	26	17	7	156	3	3.19
Amidovski, Bujar	28	1482	11	13	0	94	1	3.80

QUAD CITY MALLARDS

SCORING

	Games	G	A	Pts.	PIM
Meyers, Bret	74	31	36	67	136
Williams, Jeff	41	29	28	57	26
Menicci, Tom	75	17	39	56	64
Dufour, Jean-Francoi	57	17	34	51	35
Gibson, Steve	59	24	22	46	77
Possin, Mike	64	15	28	43	73
Lawrence, Tony	71	14	29	43	82
Nadeau, Patrick	54	22	19	41	47
Goulet, Jason	35	12	23	35	16
Mills, Dylan	74	10	25	35	126
Rooney, Jesse	45	10	18	28	25
Proulx, Hugo	29	6	20	26	70
Timmons, K.C.	63	10	16	26	81
Ganga, Nick	54	5	20	25	138
Bolf, Brian	50	10	15	25	16
Fermoyle, Andy	71	5	14	19	92
Jobin, Frederick	43	5	11	16	83
Quinnell, Bob	43	5	10	15	29
Roed, Shawn	16	8	3	11	28
Hanson, Mike	10	4	4	8	15
Batten, John	24	2	6	8	28
Toporowski, Kerry	38	1	7	8	244
Hodge, Dan	21	1	6	7	13
Ford, Michael	10	5	2	7	2
Nardella, Bob	2	2	1	3	2
Nittel, Adam	3	1	2	3	26
McMahon, Mark	6	1	1	2	41
Cabana, Clint	11	0	2	2	60
Velebny, Lubos	39	0	2	2	40
O'Leary, Pat	3	0	1	1	0
Bader, Toni	14	1	0	1	0
Kollar, Andy	7	0	1	1	0
McCarthy, Liam	3	0	1	1	7
Reynaert, Jeff	21	0	1	1	2
Dimaline, Joe	35	0	1	1	2
Latour, Yannick	3	0	0	0	2
Goodenow, Joe	4	0	0	0	0
Budaj, Jozef	2	0	0	0	0
Schafer, Paxton	9	0	0	0	0
Fillion, Martin	9	0	0	0	0
Francisco, Jon	1	0	0	0	0
Kragthorpe, Adam	2	0	0	0	2

GOALTENDING

	Gms.	Min.	W	L	SOL	G	SO	Avg.
Reynaert, Jeff	21	1257	15	4	2	50	0	2.39
Fillion, Martin	9	462	3	4	1	19	0	2.47
Schafer, Paxton	9	453	4	1	2	21	0	2.78
Dimaline, Joe	35	2023	19	12	3	106	1	3.14
Kollar, Andy	7	342	0	4	2	27	0	4.73

ROCKFORD ICEHOGS

SCORING

	Games	G	A	Pts.	PIM
Loen, Matt	76	22	52	74	48
Cygan, Steve	76	27	45	72	62
Rebek, Jeremy	69	20	39	59	100
Antonovich, Jeff	59	22	27	49	61
DaCosta, Jeff	48	7	38	45	26
Dumonski, Steve	62	17	21	38	118
Wensley, Clint	48	11	23	34	33
Wendell, Erik	60	17	13	30	36
Homer, Kenzie	76	16	12	28	173
Alexeev, Alex	73	2	24	26	77
Kerr, Kevin	18	14	12	26	12

	Games	G	A	Pts.	PIM
Hebert, Jay	40	7	13	20	35
Davies, Dan	73	8	12	20	108
Hewer, Oak	53	8	9	17	38
Angell, Nick	73	6	10	16	92
Olsen, Brad	64	3	10	13	113
Bastien, Joey	14	3	4	7	6
Fiacconi, Adriano	15	2	4	6	4
Ivanans, Raitis	50	4	2	6	208
Statkus, Joe	50	0	4	4	134
Van Horlick, Quinten	34	2	1	3	79
Betik, Karel	10	1	2	3	8
Murray, Darwin	11	0	2	2	4
Lindin, Anders	11	0	2	2	20
Fillion, Martin	9	0	1	1	6
Nicklin, Brant	50	0	1	1	4
Ziedins, Maris	4	1	0	1	2
Wenkus, Eric	2	0	0	0	0
McIntosh, Ryan	8	0	0	0	2
Saurdiff, Corwin	12	0	0	0	0
Burfoot, Scott	3	0	0	0	0
Rivard, J.F.	6	0	0	0	0
Disher, Jason	13	0	0	0	63
Kersey, Brant	4	0	0	0	0

GOALTENDING

	Gms.	Min.	W	L	SOL	G	SO	Avg.
Rivard, J.F.	6	358	3	3	0	15	0	2.51
Nicklin, Brant	50	2722	21	20	5	150	4	3.31
Fillion, Martin	9	469	3	4	1	27	0	3.45
McIntosh, Ryan	8	345	2	3	0	21	0	3.64
Saurdiff, Corwin	12	648	6	4	1	41	0	3.79

PLAYERS WITH TWO OR MORE TEAMS

SCORING

	Games	G	A	Pts.	PIM
Alexeev, Kirill, KAL	9	1	1	2	6
Alexeev, Kirill, FLT	7	0	1	1	10
Totals	16	1	2	3	16
Antonovich, Jeff, RCK	59	22	27	49	61
Antonovich, Jeff, MIS	14	9	1	10	12
Totals	73	31	28	59	73
Bastien, Joey, MIS	61	21	39	60	38
Bastien, Joey, RCK	14	3	4	7	6
Totals	75	24	43	67	44
Batten, John, ADI	48	11	26	37	81
Batten, John, QCY	24	2	6	8	28
Totals	72	13	32	45	109
Betik, Karel, FLT	56	5	11	16	51
Betik, Karel, RCK	10	1	2	3	8
Totals	66	6	13	19	59
Brown, Jason, MIS	1	0	1	1	0
Brown, Jason, KAL	6	0	0	0	0
Totals	7	0	1	1	0
Budaj, Jozef, QCY	2	0	0	0	0
Budaj, Jozef, MIS	6	1	0	1	2
Totals	8	1	0	1	2
Campbell, Cory, MIS	4	0	0	0	0
Campbell, Cory, FW	8	0	1	1	0
Totals	12	0	1	1	0
Carpenter, Yannick, PH	51	10	18	28	34
Carpenter, Yannick, KAL	23	9	9	18	22
Totals	74	19	27	46	56
Disher, Jason, FLT	32	3	4	7	137
Disher, Jason, RCK	13	0	0	0	63
Totals	45	3	4	7	200
Dunn, Stu, KAL	3	0	0	0	0
Dunn, Stu, PH	3	0	0	0	0
Totals	6	0	0	0	0
Elezi, Charlie, PH	10	0	0	0	44
Elezi, Charlie, KAL	63	4	2	6	216
Totals	73	4	2	6	260

	Games	G	A	Pts.	PIM
Farquhar, Bryan, KAL	17	1	4	5	8
Farquhar, Bryan, MUS	3	0	0	0	0
Totals	20	1	4	5	8
Fillion, Martin, QCY	9	0	0	0	0
Fillion, Martin, RCK	9	0	1	1	6
Totals	18	0	1	1	6
Ford, Michael, KAL	46	6	9	15	24
Ford, Michael, QCY	10	5	2	7	2
Totals	56	11	11	22	26
Hebert, Jay, RCK	40	7	13	20	35
Hebert, Jay, MIS	6	0	3	3	4
Totals	46	7	16	23	39
Hodge, Dan, QCY	21	1	6	7	13
Hodge, Dan, KAL	37	3	11	14	14
Totals	58	4	17	21	27
Jacobs, Ian, MIS	20	1	7	8	10
Jacobs, Ian, PH	25	3	2	5	6
Totals	45	4	9	13	16
Kerr, Kevin, ELM	33	11	9	20	51
Kerr, Kevin, RCK	18	14	12	26	12
Totals	51	25	21	46	63
Labarre, Jean-Franco, FLT	52	8	25	33	42
Labarre, Jean-Franco, MIS	2	0	0	0	0
Totals	54	8	25	33	42
Lawson, Eric, KAL	44	2	5	7	22
Lawson, Eric, PH	23	0	4	4	8
Totals	67	2	9	11	30
Lindin, Anders, FLT	61	9	9	18	57
Lindin, Anders, RCK	11	0	2	2	20
Totals	72	9	11	20	77
Machuta, Pavel, FLT	29	1	0	1	37
Machuta, Pavel, KAL	12	0	4	4	31
Totals	41	1	4	5	68
Makikyro, Antti, ELM	5	0	0	0	0
Makikyro, Antti, MUS	4	0	0	0	0
Totals	9	0	0	0	0
McCarthy, Liam, QCY	3	0	1	1	7
McCarthy, Liam, KAL	1	0	0	0	0
Totals	4	0	1	1	7
McCormick, Cam, FLT	2	0	0	0	7
McCormick, Cam, ELM	1	0	0	0	0
Totals	3	0	0	0	7
McIntosh, Ryan, RCK	8	0	0	0	2
McIntosh, Ryan, MIS	1	0	0	0	0
Totals	9	0	0	0	2
O'Leary, Pat, QCY	3	0	1	1	0
O'Leary, Pat, KAL	68	16	13	29	80
Totals	71	16	14	30	80
Pecoraro, Joe, KAL	22	2	2	4	6
Pecoraro, Joe, MUS	49	2	5	7	8
Totals	71	4	7	11	14
Reynaert, Jeff, KAL	18	0	0	0	0
Reynaert, Jeff, QCY	21	0	1	1	2
Totals	39	0	1	1	2

	Games	G	A	Pts.	PIM
Roed, Shawn, QCY	16	8	3	11	28
Roed, Shawn, KAL	30	8	7	15	65
Totals	46	16	10	26	93
Rooney, Jesse, QCY	45	10	18	28	25
Rooney, Jesse, ADI	27	6	9	15	6
Totals	72	16	27	43	31
Schafer, Paxton, QCY	9	0	0	0	0
Schafer, Paxton, FLT	27	0	4	4	0
Totals	36	0	4	4	0
Statkus, Joe, RCK	50	0	4	4	134
Statkus, Joe, FLT	13	0	0	0	22
Totals	63	0	4	4	156
Sullivan, Brent, MIS	52	10	15	25	81
Sullivan, Brent, FLT	17	0	7	7	14
Totals	69	10	22	32	95
Velebny, Lubos, QCY	39	0	2	2	40
Velebny, Lubos, KAL	8	2	1	3	10
Totals	47	2	3	5	50
Vessio, Rob, KAL	6	0	1	1	9
Vessio, Rob, ADI	13	1	0	1	7
Totals	19	1	1	2	16
Villeneuve, Martin, FLT	28	0	0	0	6
Villeneuve, Martin, ADI	18	0	3	3	0
Totals	46	0	3	3	6
Wendell, Erik, RCK	60	17	13	30	36
Wendell, Erik, MIS	13	1	5	6	12
Totals	73	18	18	36	48

GOALTENDING

	Gms.	Min.	W	L	SOL	G	SO	Avg.
Brown, Jason, MIS..	1	60	1	0	0	4	0	4.00
Brown, Jason, KAL..	6	246	1	3	0	17	0	4.14
Totals	7	306	2	3	0	21	0	4.11
Campbell, Cory, MIS	4	238	2	2	0	13	0	3.28
Campbell, Cory, FW..	8	425	6	1	0	16	0	2.26
Totals	12	663	8	3	0	29	0	2.62
Dunn, Stu, KAL	3	49	0	1	0	5	0	6.05
Dunn, Stu, PH	3	125	1	0	1	4	0	1.91
Totals	6	174	1	1	1	9	0	3.09
Fillion, Martin, QCY..	9	462	3	4	1	19	0	2.47
Fillion, Martin, RCK..	9	469	3	4	1	27	0	3.45
Totals	18	931	6	8	2	46	0	2.96
McCormick, C., FLT .	2	80	0	1	0	9	0	6.75
McCormick, C., ELM	1	59	0	1	0	3	0	3.02
Totals	3	139	0	2	0	12	0	5.16
McIntosh, R., RCK..	8	345	2	3	0	21	0	3.64
McIntosh, R., MIS ...	1	18	0	0	0	1	0	3.22
Totals	9	364	2	3	0	22	0	3.62
Reynaert, Jeff, KAL..	18	950	7	6	3	42	1	2.65
Reynaert, Jeff, QCY .	21	1257	15	4	2	50	0	2.39
Totals	39	2208	22	10	5	92	1	2.50
Schafer, P., QCY	9	453	4	1	2	21	0	2.78
Schafer, P., FLT	27	1524	9	12	3	89	1	3.50
Totals	36	1978	13	13	5	110	1	3.34
Villeneuve, M., FLT..	28	1490	13	9	3	95	1	3.83
Villeneuve, M., ADI..	18	924	11	5	0	49	0	3.18
Totals	46	2415	24	14	3	144	1	3.58

2003 COLONIAL CUP PLAYOFFS
RESULTS

COLONIAL CUP FINALS

Fort Wayne vs. Quad City
Game 1 - April 25, Quad City 2, Fort Wayne 4
Game 2 - April 26, Quad City 4, Fort Wayne 3 (2 OT)
Game 3 - May 1, Fort Wayne 4, Quad City 3
Game 4 - May 3, Fort Wayne 7, Quad City 0
Game 5 - May 4, Quad City 1, Fort Wayne 2 (OT)
Fort Wayne wins series 4-1

CONFERENCE SEMIFINALS

Fort Wayne vs. Elmira
Game 1 - April 11, Elmira 2, Fort Wayne 3
Game 2 - April 13, Elmira 0, Fort Wayne 6

Game 3 - April 16, Fort Wayne 3, Elmira 1
Game 4 - April 18, Fort Wayne 4, Elmira 3
Fort Wayne wins series 4-0

Quad City vs. Muskegon
Game 1 - April 11, Muskegon 3, Quad City 5
Game 2 - April 12, Muskegon 1, Quad City 4
Game 3 - April 15, Quad City 2, Muskegon 6
Game 4 - April 16, Quad City 7, Muskegon 3
Game 5 - April 17, Muskegon 2, Quad City 0
Game 6 - April 19, Quad City 4, Muskegon 3 (OT)
Quad City wins series 4-2

CONFERENCE QUARTERFINALS

Fort Wayne vs. Port Huron
Game 1 - April 2, Port Huron 2, Fort Wayne 4
Game 2 - April 4, Port Huron 1, Fort Wayne 2
Game 3 - April 6, Fort Wayne 6, Port Huron 2
Fort Wayne wins series 3-0

Quad City vs. Rockford
Game 1 - April 3, Rockford 0, Quad City 4
Game 2 - April 5, Rockford 4, Quad City 8
Game 3 - April 6, Quad City 3, Rockford 2 (2 OT)
Quad City wins series 3-0

Adirondack vs. Elmira
Game 1 - April 1, Elmira 2, Adirondack 6
Game 2 - April 4, Elmira 3, Adirondack 2
Game 3 - April 5, Adirondack 1, Elmira 5
Game 4 - April 6, Adirondack 2, Elmira 4
Elmira wins series 3-1

Missouri vs. Muskegon
Game 1 - April 2, Muskegon 6, Missouri 1
Game 2 - April 4, Muskegon 6, Missouri 3
Game 3 - April 5, Missouri 1, Muskegon 2 (2 OT)
Muskegon wins series 3-0

INDIVIDUAL LEADERS

Goals: Bobby Stewart, FW (10)
Assists: Colin Chaulk, FW (12)
Points: Jeff Williams, QCY (18)
Penalty minutes: Trevor Senn, ADI (55)
Goaltending average: Tom Lawson, FW (1.68)
Shutouts: Tom Lawson, FW (2)

TOP SCORERS

	Games	G	A	Pts.
Williams, Jeff, QCY	14	7	11	18
Virag, Dustin, FW	12	6	12	18
Chaulk, Colin, FW	11	4	12	16
Stewart, Bobby, FW	12	10	5	15
Blackned, Brant, MUS	9	7	8	15
Bouchard, Robin, MUS	9	8	5	13

	Games	G	A	Pts.
Venedam, Sean, FW	12	6	5	11
Nadeau, Patrick, QCY	14	5	6	11
Luciuk, Andrew, MUS	9	4	7	11
Menicci, Tom, QCY	14	4	7	111
Dufour, Jean-Francoi, QCY	14	5	5	10
Johnson, Trevor, MUS	9	4	6	10
Perrault, Kelly, FW	12	3	7	10
Burgess, David, MUS	9	2	8	10
Mills, Dylan, QCY	14	2	8	10
Robinson, Todd, MUS	9	0	10	107
Beauregard, David, FW	12	4	5	9
Gibson, Steve, QCY	14	3	6	9
Meyers, Bret, QCY	11	4	4	8
Severson, Ryan, FW	12	3	5	8

INDIVIDUAL STATISTICS

ADIRONDACK ICEHAWKS
(Lost conference quarterfinals to Elmira Jackals)
SCORING

	Games	G	A	Pts.	PIM
Chiasson, Dominic	4	2	3	5	2
Patterson, James	4	1	4	5	2
Ruid, J.C.	4	1	3	4	2
Belanger, Hugo P.	4	3	1	4	2
Rudenko, Bogdan	4	2	1	3	0
Senn, Trevor	4	1	1	2	55
Low, Steven	4	0	2	2	2
Littlejohn, Frank	3	1	0	1	0
Dumas, Alex	4	0	1	1	2
Kuriplach, Kamil	4	0	1	1	2
Blais, Benjamin	4	0	1	1	4
Rapoza, Bob	4	0	0	0	0
Galligan, Seamus	4	0	0	0	2
Sjolund, Andreas	4	0	0	0	38
Ferraris, Bob	1	0	0	0	0
Johnstone, Alex	4	0	0	0	11
Rooney, Jesse	4	0	0	0	2
Villeneuve, Martin	2	0	0	0	2
Wolfe, Jason	3	0	0	0	0

GOALTENDING

	Gms.	Min.	W	L	T	G	SO	Avg.
Wolfe, Jason	3	169	1	2	0	9	0	3.18
Villeneuve, Martin	2	66	0	1	0	4	0	3.60

ELMIRA JACKALS
(Lost conference semifinals to For Wayne Komets)
SCORING

	Games	G	A	Pts.	PIM
Stewart, Glenn	8	3	4	7	2
Murphy, Randy	8	4	3	7	2
Guinn, Rob	8	2	4	6	12
Clayton, Tom	8	3	2	5	8
Lessard, David	8	0	5	5	35
Neilson, Corey	8	1	4	5	26
Lowe, Ed	8	2	2	4	4
Burgess, Trevor	8	1	2	3	4
Thompson, Mike	8	1	2	3	4
Mallette, Kris	8	0	3	3	40
Phillips, Aaron	8	1	2	3	4
Hofstrand, Mike	8	1	1	2	4
Wingfield, Brad	8	1	1	2	40
Symington, Jeremy	5	0	0	0	0
Esselmont, Ryan	7	0	0	0	0
St. Jean, Marc	3	0	0	0	0
Jackson, Dean	8	0	0	0	0
Lyke, R.C.	5	0	0	0	2
Emond, Marco	4	0	0	0	0

GOALTENDING

	Gms.	Min.	W	L	T	G	SO	Avg.
Symington, Jeremy	5	285	3	2	0	12	0	2.52
Emond, Marco	4	192	0	3	0	15	0	4.68

FORT WAYNE KOMETS
(Won 2003 Colonial Cup)
SCORING

	Games	G	A	Pts.	PIM
Virag, Dustin	12	6	12	18	17
Chaulk, Colin	11	4	12	16	10
Stewart, Bobby	12	10	5	15	14
Venedam, Sean	12	6	5	11	18
Perrault, Kelly	12	3	7	10	22
Beauregard, David	12	4	5	9	2
Severson, Ryan	12	3	5	8	6
Cabana, Chad	12	1	6	7	47
Massie, Michel	12	2	5	7	25
Lewis, Adam	12	3	3	6	6
Barlow, Marc	12	3	2	5	8

	Games	G	A	Pts.	PIM
Neumeier, Troy	10	0	4	4	6
Schmidt, Kevin	12	1	1	2	8
Bertram, Kevin	8	0	2	2	35
Ortmeyer, Jake	12	0	2	2	10
Tataryn, Josh	8	1	1	2	4
Lawson, Tom	12	0	2	2	0
Kotyluk, Kevin	5	1	0	1	15
Eade, Chris	4	0	0	0	4
Stevens, Bart	2	0	0	0	0

GOALTENDING

	Gms.	Min.	W	L	T	G	SO	Avg.
Lawson, Tom	12	749	11	0	1	21	2	1.68

MISSOURI RIVER OTTERS
(Lost conference quarterfinals to Muskegon Fury)

SCORING

	Games	G	A	Pts.	PIM
Newans, Chris	3	3	0	3	8
Whitecotton, Dustin	3	0	2	2	0
Hill, Kiley	3	1	1	2	17
Cappelletti, Anthony	3	1	0	1	17
Hughes, Jason	3	0	1	1	2
Antonovich, Jeff	3	0	1	1	0
Ritson, Joe	3	0	1	1	4
Wendell, Erik	3	0	1	1	0
Blyth, Charlie	3	0	1	1	12
Loach, Lonnie	3	0	1	1	0
Chambers, Craig	1	0	0	0	0
Page, Chris	2	0	0	0	0
White, Tony	1	0	0	0	2
Searle, Doug	2	0	0	0	2
Karrer, Guillaume	3	0	0	0	14
Chabbert, Kevin	3	0	0	0	6
Elzinga, Adam	2	0	0	0	0
Vincent, Paul	2	0	0	0	2
Melnychuk, Marty	2	0	0	0	17
Schafer, Paxton	3	0	0	0	0

GOALTENDING

	Gms.	Min.	W	L	T	G	SO	Avg.
Schafer, Paxton	3	205	0	2	1	13	0	3.80

MUSKEGON FURY
(Lost conference semifinals to Quad City Mallards)

SCORING

	Games	G	A	Pts.	PIM
Blackned, Brant	9	7	8	15	4
Bouchard, Robin	9	8	5	13	21
Luciuk, Andrew	9	4	7	11	13
Johnson, Trevor	9	4	6	10	10
Burgess, David	9	2	8	10	6
Robinson, Todd	9	0	10	10	4
Feasby, Scott	9	2	3	5	29
Pugliese, Billy	9	0	4	4	25
Glover, Shane	9	2	1	3	2
Dolyny, Rustyn	4	2	1	3	4
Lizotte, David	9	1	2	3	15
Jaworski, Jason	9	0	1	1	16
Ricciardi, Gary	8	0	1	1	26
Busniuk, Bryson	3	0	1	1	0
McIntyre, Steve	5	0	0	0	24
Bresciani, Joel	4	0	0	0	4
Berry, Justin	2	0	0	0	0
Rochefort, Normand	8	0	0	0	2
Lukasak, Jeff	7	0	0	0	6
Hollis, Scott	4	0	0	0	4
Daigle, Sylvain	9	0	0	0	4

GOALTENDING

	Gms.	Min.	W	L	T	G	SO	Avg.
Daigle, Sylvain	9	581	5	3	1	27	1	2.79

PORT HURON BEACONS
(Lost conference quarterfinals to Fort Wayne Komets)

SCORING

	Games	G	A	Pts.	PIM
Firth, Jason	3	0	4	4	18
Gretzky, Brent	3	3	0	3	2
Drevitch, Scott	3	0	1	1	0
Bournazakis, Peter	3	0	1	1	2
Harris, Casey	3	1	0	1	14
MacKenzie, Chris	3	0	1	1	0
Wood, Derek	3	1	0	1	4
Vary, John	3	0	1	1	4
Hellegards, Justin	3	0	0	0	0
Muswagon, Jamie	3	0	0	0	0
Jacobs, Ian	3	0	0	0	0
Beausoleil, Michel	3	0	0	0	8
Lawson, Eric	3	0	0	0	0
McMonagle, Tom	3	0	0	0	2
Shrieves, Aaron	3	0	0	0	0
Poirier, Simon	3	0	0	0	2
Cooper, Kory	3	0	0	0	0

GOALTENDING

	Gms.	Min.	W	L	T	G	SO	Avg.
Cooper, Kory	3	178	0	3	0	12	0	4.03

QUAD CITY MALLARDS
(Lost Colonial Cup finals to Fort Wayne Komets)

SCORING

	Games	G	A	Pts.	PIM
Williams, Jeff	14	7	11	18	6
Nadeau, Patrick	14	5	6	11	18
Menicci, Tom	14	4	7	11	14
Mills, Dylan	14	2	8	10	32
Dufour, Jean-Francoi	14	5	5	10	13
Gibson, Steve	14	3	6	9	18
Meyers, Bret	11	4	4	8	10
Proulx, Hugo	11	4	3	7	31
Hanson, Mike	12	4	2	6	31
Timmons, K.C.	14	1	5	6	19
Francisco, Jon	8	4	2	6	4
Lawrence, Tony	14	2	4	6	40
Toporowski, Kerry	12	0	5	5	28
Fermoyle, Andy	14	0	3	3	12
Batten, John	10	1	2	3	22
Cabana, Clint	13	0	1	1	41
Ganga, Nick	4	1	0	1	4
Goulet, Jason	2	0	0	0	0
Dimaline, Joe	1	0	0	0	0
Possin, Mike	7	0	0	0	6
Quinnell, Bob	6	0	0	0	4
Reynaert, Jeff	14	0	0	0	2

GOALTENDING

	Gms.	Min.	W	L	T	G	SO	Avg.
Reynaert, Jeff	14	870	8	5	1	41	1	2.83
Dimaline, Joe	1	34	0	0	0	3	0	5.25

ROCKFORD ICEHOGS
(Lost conference quarterfinals to Quad City Mallards)

SCORING

	Games	G	A	Pts.	PIM
Ford, Michael	2	1	2	3	0
Rebek, Jeremy	3	1	1	2	6
Kerr, Kevin	3	2	0	2	8
Kersey, Brant	3	0	2	2	0
Dumonski, Steve	2	0	1	1	8
Homer, Kenzie	3	0	1	1	6
Hewer, Oak	3	0	1	1	2
Loen, Matt	3	0	1	1	6
Angell, Nick	3	0	1	1	8
Davies, Dan	2	1	0	1	0
Bastien, Joey	3	1	0	1	0

	Games	G	A	Pts.	PIM
Wensley, Clint	2	0	0	0	0
Nicklin, Brant	2	0	0	0	0
Fillion, Martin	1	0	0	0	0
Disher, Jason	3	0	0	0	12
Alexeev, Alex	3	0	0	0	8
Lindin, Anders	1	0	0	0	0
Cygan, Steve	3	0	0	0	4
Betik, Karel	3	0	0	0	4

	Games	G	A	Pts.	PIM
Olsen, Brad	3	0	0	0	19
Rivard, J.F.	1	0	0	0	0

GOALTENDING

	Gms.	Min.	W	L	T	G	SO	Avg.
Rivard, J.F.	1	85	0	0	1	3	0	2.12
Fillion, Martin	1	30	0	0	0	3	0	5.95
Nicklin, Brant	2	89	0	2	0	9	0	6.02

2002-03 AWARD WINNERS

ALL-STAR TEAMS

First team	Pos.	Second team
Robin Bouchard, Musk.	RW	Bobby Stewart, Fort Wayne
Dustin Whitecotton, Miss.	C	J.C. Ruid, Adirondack
Hugo Belanger, Adirondack	LW	Dominic Chiasson, Adi.
Tom Menicci, Quad City	D	Jeremy Rebek, Rockford
Kelly Perrault, Fort Wayne	D	Scott Drevitch, Port Huron
Tom Lawson, Fort Wayne	G	Sylvain Daigle, Muskegon

TROPHY WINNERS

Most Valuable Player: Hugo Belanger, Adirondack
Scoring leader: Hugo Belanger, Adirondack
Outstanding defenseman: Kelly Perrault, Fort Wayne
Outstanding defensive forward: Colin Chaulk, Fort Wayne
Outstanding goaltender: Tom Lawson, Fort Wayne
Rookie of the Year: Steve Cygan, Rockford
Most sportsmanlike player: Lonnie Loach, Missouri
Playoff MVP: Tom Lawson, Fort Wayne
Coach of the Year: Greg Puhalski, Fort Wayne

ALL-TIME AWARD WINNERS

MOST VALUABLE PLAYER

Season	Player, Team
1991-92	Terry McCutcheon, Brantford
1992-93	Jason Firth, Thunder Bay
1993-94	Kevin Kerr, Flint
1994-95	Mark Green, Utica
	Paul Polillo, Brantford
1995-96	Paul Polillo, Brantford
1996-97	Paul Polillo, Brantford
1997-98	Jason Firth, Thunder Bay
1998-99	Jason Firth, Thunder Bay
1999-00	Brian Regan, Missouri
2000-01	Hugo Belanger, Adirondack
2001-02	Hugo Belanger, Adirondack
2002-03	Hugo Belanger, Adirondack

SCORING LEADER

Season	Player, Team
1991-92	Tom Sasso, Flint
1992-93	Len Soccio, St. Thomas
1993-94	Paul Polillo, Brantford
1994-95	Paul Polillo, Brantford
1995-96	Paul Polillo, Brantford
1996-97	Paul Polillo, Brantford
1997-98	Paul Polillo, Brantford
1998-99	Jason Firth, Thunder Bay
1999-00	Brent Gretzky, Asheville
2000-01	Hugo Belanger, Adirondack
2001-02	Jeff Petruic, Asheville
2002-03	Hugo Belanger, Adirondack

ROOKIE OF THE YEAR

Season	Player, Team
1991-92	Kevin Butt, St. Thomas
1992-93	Jason Firth, Thunder Bay
1993-94	Jean-Francois Labbe, Thunder Bay
1994-95	Lance Leslie, Thunder Bay
1995-96	Matt Loen, Madison
1996-97	Forbes MacPherson, Thunder Bay
1997-98	Jason Weaver, Muskegon
1998-99	Mike Melas, Quad City
1999-00	Jason Goulet, Fort Wayne
2000-01	Jason Ulmer, Quad City
2001-02	Jean-Francois Dufour, Asheville
2002-03	Steve Cygan, Rockford

DEFENSEMAN OF THE YEAR

Season	Player, Team
1991-92	Tom Searle, Brantford
1992-93	Tom Searle, Brantford
1993-94	Barry McKinlay, Thunder Bay
1994-95	Barry McKinlay, Thunder Bay
1995-96	Chris Hynnes, Thunder Bay
1996-97	Barry McKinlay, Thunder Bay
1997-98	John Vary, Muskegon
1998-99	Stephan Brochu, Flint
1999-00	Gary Roach, Flint
2000-01	Jeremy Rebek, Missouri
2001-02	Martin Woods, Flint
2002-03	Kelly Perrault, Fort Wayne

BEST DEFENSIVE FORWARD

Season	Player, Team
1991-92	Tim Bean, St. Thomas
1992-93	Todd Howarth, Thunder Bay
1993-94	Jamie Hicks, Brantford
1994-95	Terry Menard, Thunder Bay
1995-96	Brian Downey, Madison
1996-97	Brian Downey, Madison
1997-98	Brad Jones, B.C.
1998-99	Paul Willett, Muskegon
1999-00	Jay Neal, Port Huron
2000-01	Jason Ulmer, Quad City
2001-02	Steve Gibson, Quad City
2002-03	Colin Chaulk, Fort Wayne

BEST GOALTENDER

Season	Player, Team
1991-92	Jamie Stewart, Detroit
1992-93	Jamie Stewart, Detroit
1993-94	J.F. Labbe, Thunder Bay
1994-95	Maxim Machialovsky, Detroit
1995-96	Rich Parent, Muskegon
1996-97	Sergei Zvyagin, Quad City
1997-98	Darryl Gilmour, Madison
1998-99	Joe Dimaline, Muskegon
1999-00	Brian Regan, Missouri
2000-01	Blair Allison, Quad City
2001-02	Sylvain Daigle, Muskegon
2002-03	Tom Lawson, Fort Wayne

MOST SPORTSMANLIKE PLAYER

Season	Player, Team
1991-92	Tom Sasso, Flint
1992-93	Paul Polillo, Brantford
1993-94	Paul Polillo, Brantford
1994-95	Paul Polillo, Brantford
1995-96	Scott Burfoot, Flint
1996-97	Kent Hawley, Madison
1997-98	Brian Sakic, Flint
1998-99	Brian Sakic, Flint
1999-00	Keli Corpse, Fort Wayne
2000-01	Brent Gretzky, Fort Wayne
2001-02	Dustin Whitecotton, Missouri
2002-03	Lonnie Loach, Missouri

PLAYOFF MVP

Season	Player, Team
1991-92	Gary Callaghan, Thunder Bay
1992-93	Roland Melanson, Brantford
1993-94	Jean-Francois Labbe, Thunder Bay
1994-95	Lance Leslie, Thunder Bay
1995-96	Scott Burfoot, Flint

Season	Player, Team
1996-97	Sergei Zvyagin, Quad City
1997-98	Jim Brown, Quad City
1998-99	Sergei Kharin, Muskegon
1999-00	Nick Stajduhar, Flint
2000-01	Jason Ulmer, Quad City
2001-02	Todd Robinson, Muskegon
2002-03	Tom Lawson, Fort Wayne

COACH OF THE YEAR

Season	Coach, Team
1991-92	Peter Horachek, St. Thomas
1992-93	Bill McDonald, Thunder Bay
1993-94	Tom Barrett, Chatham
1994-95	Steve Ludzik, Muskegon
1995-96	Mark Johnson, Madison
1996-97	Robbie Nichols, Flint
1997-98	Robert Dirk, Winston-Salem
1998-99	Rich Kromm, Muskegon
1999-00	Brad Jones, B.C.
2000-01	Terry Ruskowski, Knoxville
2001-02	Mark Reeds, Missouri
2002-03	Greg Puhalski, Fort Wayne

ALL-TIME LEAGUE CHAMPIONS

REGULAR-SEASON CHAMPION

Season	Team	Coach
1991-92	Michigan Falcons	Terry Christensen
1992-93	Brantford Smoke	Ken Mann & Ken Gratton
1993-94	Thunder Bay Senators	Bill MacDonald
1994-95	Thunder Bay Senators	Bill MacDonald
1995-96	Flint Generals	Robbie Nichols
1996-97	Flint Generals	Robbie Nichols
1997-98	Quad City Mallards	Paul Gillis
1998-99	Muskegon Fury	Rich Kromm
1999-00	Flint Generals	Doug Shedden
2000-01	Quad City Mallards	Paul MacLean
2001-02	Quad City Mallards	Paul MacLean
2002-03	Fort Wayne Komets	Greg Puhalski

PLAYOFF CHAMPION

Team	Coach
Thunder Bay Thunder Hawks	Bill MacDonald
Brantford Smoke	Ken Gratton
Thunder Bay Senators	Bill MacDonald
Thunder Bay Senators	Bill MacDonald
Flint Generals	Robbie Nichols
Quad City Mallards	John Anderson
Quad City Mallards	Paul Gillis
Muskegon Fury	Rich Kromm
Flint Generals	Doug Shedden
Quad City Mallards	Paul MacLean
Muskegon Fury	Rich Kromm
Fort Wayne Komets	Greg Puhalski

OTHER LEAGUES

Canadian Hockey League

Ontario Hockey League

Quebec Major Junior Hockey League

Western Hockey League

NCAA Division I

Central Collegiate Hockey Association

Eastern College Athletic Conference

Hockey East

Western Collegiate Hockey Association

Canadian Interuniversity Sport

Canadian colleges

CANADIAN HOCKEY LEAGUE

FINAL STANDINGS

Team	G	W	L	T	GF	GA	Pts.
Kitchener	4	4	0	0	18	9	8
Hull	5	3	2	0	15	15	6
Kelowna	4	1	3	0	7	12	2
Québec	3	0	3	0	8	12	0

ONTARIO HOCKEY LEAGUE

2002-03 REGULAR SEASON
FINAL STANDINGS

EAST DIVISION

Team	G	W	L	T	OTL	GF	GA	Pts.
Ottawa	68	44	14	7	3	318	210	98
Peterborough	68	32	22	11	3	222	215	78
Belleville	68	33	27	6	2	195	200	74
Oshawa	68	34	30	2	2	243	225	72
Kingston	68	25	37	2	4	222	287	56

MIDWEST DIVISION

Team	G	W	L	T	OTL	GF	GA	Pts.
Kitchener	68	46	14	5	3	275	188	100
London	68	31	27	7	3	220	205	72
Guelph	68	29	28	9	2	217	208	69
Owen Sound	68	27	30	7	4	206	243	65
Erie	68	24	35	6	3	181	248	57

CENTRAL DIVISION

Team	G	W	L	T	OTL	GF	GA	Pts.
Brampton	68	34	24	6	4	239	202	78
St. Michael's	68	32	24	7	5	207	214	76
Barrie	68	29	26	4	9	228	223	71
Mississauga	68	23	31	11	3	212	231	60
Sudbury	68	16	46	4	2	175	273	38

WEST DIVISION

Team	G	W	L	T	OTL	GF	GA	Pts.
Plymouth	68	43	14	9	2	259	174	97
Sarnia	68	41	19	7	1	251	193	90
Windsor	68	37	25	5	1	259	221	80
Sault Ste. Marie	68	26	33	6	3	232	284	61
Saginaw	68	11	45	5	7	158	275	34

QUEBEC LEAGUE

2002-03 REGULAR SEASON
FINAL STANDINGS

ROBERT LE BEL CONFERENCE

West Division

Team	G	W	L	T	OTL	GF	GA	Pts.
Val-d'Or	71	38	23	6	4	238	219	86
Hull	71	39	26	4	2	265	216	84
Montreal	71	32	26	5	8	254	258	77
Rouyn-Noranda	71	30	33	0	8	262	272	68

Central Division

Team	G	W	L	T	OTL	GF	GA	Pts.
Sherbrooke	71	37	24	7	3	234	209	84
Victoriaville	71	37	26	6	2	260	234	82
Shawinigan	71	25	35	7	4	205	245	61
Drummondville	71	15	49	3	4	172	309	37

FRANK DILIO CONFERENCE

East Division

Team	G	W	L	T	OTL	GF	GA	Pts.
Baie-Comeau	71	49	14	6	2	314	210	106
Quebec	71	41	24	3	3	272	202	88
Chicoutimi	71	28	39	1	3	236	287	60
Rimouski	71	11	57	3	0	187	379	25

Maritime Division

Team	G	W	L	T	OTL	GF	GA	Pts.
Halifax	71	44	15	9	3	287	204	100
Acadie-Bathurst	71	43	21	4	3	272	187	93
Moncton	71	37	19	10	5	253	212	89
Cape Breton	71	21	37	8	5	198	266	55

OTHER LEAGUES

WESTERN HOCKEY LEAGUE

2002-03 REGULAR SEASON
FINAL STANDINGS

EAST DIVISION

Team	G	W	L	T	OTL	GF	GA	Pts.
Brandon	72	43	17	9	3	258	187	98
Moose Jaw	72	36	22	11	3	266	208	86
Saskatoon	72	40	27	5	0	234	205	85
Regina	72	25	28	14	5	171	217	69
Prince Albert	72	27	37	3	5	185	258	62

B.C. DIVISION

Team	G	W	L	T	OTL	GF	GA	Pts.
Kelowna	72	51	14	6	1	311	164	109
Kamloops	72	39	27	5	1	261	222	84
Kootenay	72	36	25	6	5	234	202	83
Vancouver	72	26	37	5	4	217	292	61
Prince George	72	26	41	3	2	257	317	57

CENTRAL DIVISION

Team	G	W	L	T	OTL	GF	GA	Pts.
Red Deer	72	50	17	3	2	271	160	105
Swift Current	72	38	24	7	3	240	215	86
Medicine Hat	72	29	34	2	7	278	314	67
Calgary	72	27	36	7	2	240	260	63
Lethbridge	72	28	40	2	2	236	303	60

U.S. DIVISION

Team	G	W	L	T	OTL	GF	GA	Pts.
Seattle	72	44	22	3	3	280	224	94
Spokane	72	26	36	6	4	216	261	62
Portland	72	19	40	8	5	192	243	51
Tri-City	72	20	44	3	5	240	335	48

NCAA DIVISION I

2002-03 SEASON
NCAA TOURNAMENT

EAST REGIONAL
(Providence, R.I.)
SEMIFINALS
Cornell 5, Minnesota State-Mankato 2
Boston College 1, Ohio State 0
FINALS
Cornell 2, Boston College 1 (2OT)

NORTHEAST REGIONAL
(Worcester, Mass.)
SEMIFINALS
New Hampshire 5, St. Cloud State 2
Boston University 6, Harvard 4
FINALS
New Hampshire 3, Boston University 0

MIDWEST REGIONAL
(Ann Arbor, Mich.)
SEMIFINALS
Colorado College 4, Wayne State 2
Michigan 2, Maine 1
FINALS
Michigan 5, Colorado College 3

WEST REGIONAL
(Minneapolis, Minn.)
SEMIFINALS
Minnesota 9, Mercyhurst 2
Ferris State 5, North Dakota 2
FINALS
Minnesota 7, Ferris State 4

FROZEN FOUR
(Buffalo, N.Y.)
SEMIFINALS
New Hampshire 3, Cornell 2
Minnesota 3, Michigan 2 (OT)
CHAMPIONSHIP GAME
Minnesota 5, New Hampshire 1

ALL-TOURNAMENT TEAM

Player	Pos.	College
Travis Weber	G	Minnesota
Paul Martin	D	Minnesota
Matt DeMarchi	D	Minnesota
Nathan Martz	F	New Hampshire
Steve Saviano	F	New Hampshire
Thomas Vanek	F	Minnesota

OTHER LEAGUES

CENTRAL COLLEGIATE HOCKEY ASSOCIATION

2002-03 SEASON
FINAL STANDINGS

Team	G	W	L	T	Pts.	GF	GA
Ferris State (31-10-1)	28	22	5	1	45	121	64
Michigan (30-10-3)	28	18	7	3	39	111	72
Ohio State (25-13-5)	28	16	8	4	36	90	63
Michigan St. (23-14-2)	28	17	10	1	35	113	83
N. Michigan (22-17-2)	28	14	13	1	29	91	83
Miami (21-17-3)	28	13	12	3	29	86	66
Notre Dame (17-17-6)	28	13	12	3	29	90	90
W. Michigan (15-21-2)	28	13	14	1	27	92	101
A. Fairbanks (15-14-7)	28	10	11	7	27	78	104
Neb.-Omaha (13-22-5)	28	9	17	2	20	64	97
Bowl. Green (8-25-3)	28	5	20	3	13	71	116
Lake Sup. St. (6-28-4)	28	3	24	1	7	40	108

Overall record in parentheses.

EASTERN COLLEGE ATHLETIC CONFERENCE

2002-03 SEASON
FINAL STANDINGS

Team	G	W	L	T	Pts.	GF	GA
Cornell (30-5-1)	22	19	2	1	39	89	29
Harvard (22-10-2)	22	17	4	1	35	94	47
Dartmouth (20-13-1)	22	13	9	0	26	77	71
Yale (18-14-0)	22	13	9	0	26	94	73
Brown (16-14-5)	22	10	8	4	24	65	54
Union (14-18-4)	22	10	10	2	22	62	68
Clarkson (12-20-3)	22	9	10	3	21	69	56
Colgate (17-19-4)	22	9	10	3	21	49	71
St. Lawrence (11-21-5)	22	7	12	3	17	65	80
Vermont (13-20-3)	22	8	14	0	16	58	85
Rensselaer (12-25-3)	22	4	15	3	11	49	84
Princeton (3-26-2)	22	2	18	2	6	46	99

Overall record in parentheses.

HOCKEY EAST

2002-03 SEASON
FINAL STANDINGS

Team	G	W	L	T	Pts.	GF	GA
New Hamp. (28-8-6)	24	15	5	4	34	84	55
Boston Col. (24-11-4)	24	16	6	2	34	97	55
Maine (24-10-5)	24	14	6	4	32	81	61
Providence (19-14-3)	24	12	9	3	27	76	71
Boston U. (25-14-3)	24	13	10	1	27	78	66
Mass. (19-17-1)	24	10	14	0	20	60	80
Merrimack (12-18-6)	24	7	13	4	18	59	80
Lowell (11-20-5)	24	4	16	4	12	63	95
Northeastern (10-21-3)	24	5	17	2	12	54	89

Overall record in parentheses.

WESTERN COLLEGIATE HOCKEY ASSOCIATION

2002-03 SEASON
FINAL STANDINGS

Team	G	W	L	T	Pts.	GF	GA
Colorado C. (30-7-5)	28	19	4	5	43	125	70
Minnesota (28-8-9)	28	15	6	7	37	106	81
M., Mankato (20-11-10)	28	15	6	7	37	116	104
N. Dakota (26-12-5)	28	14	9	5	33	103	82
M.-Duluth (22-15-5)	28	14	10	4	32	95	80
St. Cloud St. (17-16-5)	28	12	11	5	29	96	85
Denver (21-14-6)	28	11	11	6	28	95	85
Wisconsin (13-23-4)	28	7	17	4	18	61	101
Mich. Tech (10-24-4)	28	7	18	3	17	77	116
A'ka-Anch. (1-28-7)	28	0	22	6	6	41	111

Overall record in parentheses.

CANADIAN INTERUNIVERSITY SPORT

2003 NATIONAL CHAMPIONSHIPS
PLAYOFF STANDINGS

POOL A

Team (League)	W	L	Pts.	GF	GA
StFX	2	0	4	8	6
Alberta	1	1	2	6	3
York	0	2	0	4	9

POOL B

Team (League)	W	L	Pts.	GF	GA
UQTR	2	0	4	6	4
UNB	1	1	2	7	7
Lakehead	0	2	0	4	6

CANADIAN COLLEGES

ATLANTIC UNIVERSITY SPORT, 2002-03 SEASON
FINAL STANDINGS

Team	G	W	L	T	GF	GA	Pts.
St. Thomas	28	16	7	5	119	104	37
Dalhousie	28	16	9	3	102	88	35
UNB	28	15	12	1	107	88	31
StFX	28	14	12	2	98	90	30
Saint Mary's	28	14	13	1	102	92	29
UPEI	28	10	15	3	87	110	23
Acadia	28	10	17	1	88	108	21
Moncton	28	9	19	0	82	105	18

CANADA WEST UNIVERSITIES ATHLETIC ASSOCIATION, 2002-03 SEASON
FINAL STANDINGS

EAST DIVISION

Team (Overall)	G	W	L	T	GF	GA	Pts.
Saskatchewan	28	16	10	2	128	94	34
Manitoba	28	12	13	3	93	102	27
Regina	28	11	16	1	74	103	23

WEST DIVISION

Team	G	W	L	T	GF	GA	Pts.
Alberta	28	24	2	2	129	54	50
Calgary	28	14	12	2	90	79	30
Lethbridge	28	10	16	2	104	120	22
UBC	28	5	23	0	59	125	10

OTHER LEAGUES

FINAL STANDINGS

FAR EAST DIVISION

Team (Overall)	G	W	L	T	GF	GA	Pts.
UQTR	24	20	2	2	132	61	42
McGill	24	16	6	2	92	62	34
Ottawa	24	13	9	2	105	77	28
Concordia	24	9	13	2	84	94	20

MID WEST DIVISION

Team (Overall)	G	W	L	T	GF	GA	Pts.
York	24	17	6	1	128	61	35
Laurier	24	12	11	1	89	99	25
Brock	24	8	16	0	78	113	16
Guelph	24	6	17	1	82	116	13

MID EAST DIVISION

Team (Overall)	G	W	L	T	GF	GA	Pts.
Toronto	24	16	5	3	109	67	35
Queens	24	7	17	0	73	124	14
RMC	24	6	17	1	61	121	13
Ryerson	24	2	21	1	53	133	5

FAR WEST DIVISION

Team (Overall)	G	W	L	T	GF	GA	Pts.
Western	24	24	0	0	135	39	48
Lakehead	24	18	6	0	125	64	36
Windsor	24	8	15	1	80	107	17
Waterloo	24	1	22	1	56	144	3

OTHER LEAGUES